Frommer's®

POSTCARDS

FRANCE

The Provence countryside takes on a purplish hue just before the midsummer harvest. Lavender fields blossom straight out to the horizon. See chapter 19. ©Uwe Schmid/ The Stock Market

The views of Paris are spectacular from the Tour Eiffel, which stretches 1,056 feet into the air. See chapter 4. ©Bob Krist Photography

Visitors can't help but enjoy the art at the Louvre in Paris, one of the world's largest museums. See chapter 4. ©Dave Bartruff Photography

To enter the Louvre, you have to pass through this controversial 71-foot glass pyramid, designed by I.M. Pei. See chapter 4. ©Kevin Galvin Photography

The facade of the Cathédrale Notre-Dame is one of the most beautiful sights in Paris. See chapter 4. © Kevin Galvin Photography

The Pont du Gard outside of Nimes dates back to 19 B.C. Built without mortar, the bridge evokes the ancient glory and technical competence of the Romans. See chapter 18. © Tom Kirkman Photography

A typical street in Alsace, the "least French of French provinces." See chapter 10. © Markham Johnson/Robert Holmes photography

In Giverney, you can stroll through Monet's gardens and see the water lilies that inspired this great painter. See chapter 5. ©Dave G. Houser Photography

The Château de Chambord, built during the height of the French Renaissance, is the largest château in the Loire Valley. See chapter 6. © Kevin Galvin Photography

Visitors are welcome at wineries throughout La Route du Vin in Alsace-Lorraine (see chapter 10), Burgundy (see chapter 12), and the Beaujolais Country (see chapter 13). © Tom Kirkman Photography

Vineyards unfold as you drive through the rolling landscape of the Rhone Valley. See chapter 13. © *Brigitte Merle/Tony Stone Images*

Half-timbered houses from the 17th century line the streets of Rouen. See chapter 7. © Dave G. Houser Photography

Residents of St-Paul-de-Vence on the Côte d'Azur enjoy a game of pétanque. See chapter 20. © Nik Wheeler Photography

The abbey of Mont-St-Michel is one of Europe's most important Gothic monuments. See chapter 7. ©Kindra Clineff Photography

The remains of 9,386 American soldiers are buried at the Normandy American Cemetery at Omaha Beach. It commemorates those who died here during the D-Day invasion. See chapter 7. ©Yannick Le Gal/Image Bank

In Rocamadour in the Dordogne Valley, towers, old buildings, and oratories rise in stages up the side of a cliff. See chapter 15. © Markham Johnson/Robert Holmes Photography

The landscape in Burgundy seems almost surreal. See chapter 12 for a full description of how to explore this area by car. ©Kindra Clineff Photography

The produce is fresh on market day in Dijon. See chapter 12. ©Len Kaufman Photography

During the Great Schism from 1378 to 1417, a succession of popes ruled here at the Palais des Papes in Avignon, while others held on to power in Rome. See chapter 19. © Nik Wheeler Photography

No trip to France would be complete without wine, cheese, pastries, and a French chef. See the "Regional Cuisine" section at the beginning of each chapter. ©*Harvey Lloyd/The Stock Market*

The fun is just beginning when the sun sets on the Côte d'Azur. See chapter 20.
© Kelly/Mooney Photography

The views of the Provençal coast are breathtaking from Eze and other hilltop villages that dot the Côte d'Azur. See chapter 20. © Derek Croucher/The Stock Market

Sunflower fields like this one in Burgundy have inspired van Gogh and countless other artists.
©*Bob Krist Photgraphy*

When should I travel to get the best airfare?
Where do I go for answers to my travel questions?
What's the best and easiest way to plan and book my trip?

frommers.travelocity.com

Frommer's, the travel guide leader, has teamed up with **Travelocity.com**, the leader in online travel, to bring you an in-depth, easy-to-use resource designed to help you plan and book your trip online.

At **frommers.travelocity.com**, you'll find free online updates about your destination from the experts at Frommer's plus the outstanding travel planning and purchasing features of Travelocity.com. Travelocity.com provides reservations capabilities for 95 percent of all airline seats sold, more than 47,000 hotels, and over 50 car rental companies. In addition, Travelocity.com offers more than 2,000 exciting vacation and cruise packages. Travelocity.com puts you in complete control of your travel planning with these and other great features:

Expert travel guidance from Frommer's - over 150 writers reporting from around the world!

Best Fare Finder - an interactive calendar tells you when to travel to get the best airfare

Fare Watcher - we'll track airfare changes to your favorite destinations

Dream Maps - a mapping feature that suggests travel opportunities based on your budget

Shop Safe Guarantee - 24 hours a day / 7 days a week live customer service, and more!

Whether you're traveling on a tight budget, looking for a quick weekend getaway, or planning the trip of a lifetime, Frommer's guides and Travelocity.com will make your travel dreams a reality. You've bought the book, now book the trip!

Here's what the critics say about Frommer's:

"Amazingly easy to use. Very portable, very complete."
—Booklist

♦

"The only mainstream guide to list specific prices. The Walter Cronkite of guidebooks—with all that implies."
—Travel & Leisure

♦

"Complete, concise, and filled with useful information."
—New York Daily News

♦

"Hotel information is close to encyclopedic."
—Des Moines Sunday Register

♦

"Detailed, accurate and easy-to-read information for all price ranges."
—Glamour Magazine

Other Great Guides for Your Trip:

Frommer's Paris

Frommer's Provence & the Riviera

Frommer's Paris from $80 a Day

Frommer's Memorable Walks in Paris

Frommer's Irreverent Guide to Manhattan

Frommer's Portable Paris

The Unofficial Guide to Paris

Frommer's®

France
2001

by Darwin Porter & Danforth Prince

IDG Books Worldwide, Inc.
An International Data Group Company
Foster City, CA • Chicago, IL • Indianapolis, IN • New York, NY

ABOUT THE AUTHORS

France is a second home to **Darwin Porter,** a native of North Carolina, and **Danforth Prince,** who lived in France for many years. Darwin, who worked in television advertising and as a bureau chief for the *Miami Herald,* wrote the original edition of this guide back in 1971. Danforth, who began his association with Darwin in 1982, worked for the Paris bureau of the *New York Times* between renovations of a 14th-century château in the Loire Valley. Both these writers know their destination well, for they have made countless annual trips through the countryside and have lived and worked from Brittany to Provence.

IDG BOOKS WORLDWIDE, INC.

An International Data Group Company
919 E. Hillsdale Blvd.
Suite 400
Foster City, CA 94404

Find us online at **www.frommers.com**

ISBN 0-7645-6137-5
ISSN 0899-3351

Editor: John Rosenthal/Dog-Eared Pages
Production Editor: Stephanie Lucas
Photo Editor: Richard Fox
Design by Michele Laseau
Staff Cartographers: John Decamillis, Roberta Stockwell, and Elizabeth Puhl
Production by IDG Books Indianapolis Production Department

SPECIAL SALES

For general information on IDG Books Worldwide's books in the U.S., please call our Consumer Customer Service department at 1-800-762-2974. For reseller information, including discounts, bulk sales, customized editions, and premium sales, please call our Reseller Customer Service department at 1-800-434-3422.

Manufactured in the United States of America

5 4 3 2 1

Contents

4   Exploring Paris   127

5   Side Trips from Paris: Versailles, Chartres & the Best of Île de France   181

viii **Contents**

List of Maps

An Invitation to the Reader

In researching this book, we discovered many wonderful places—hotels, restaurants, shops, and more. We're sure you'll find others. Please tell us about them, so we can share the information with your fellow travelers in upcoming editions. If you were disappointed with a recommendation, we'd love to know that, too. Please write to:

Frommer's France, 2001
IDG Travel
909 Third Avenue
New York, NY 10022

An Additional Note

Please be advised that travel information is subject to change at any time—and this is especially true of prices. We therefore suggest that you write or call ahead for confirmation when making your travel plans. The authors, editors, and publisher cannot be held responsible for the experiences of readers while traveling. Your safety is important to us, however, so we encourage you to stay alert and be aware of your surroundings. Keep a close eye on cameras, purses, and wallets, all favorite targets of thieves and pickpockets.

What the Symbols Mean

✪ **Frommer's Favorites**

Our favorite places and experiences—outstanding for quality, value, or both.

The following abbreviations are used for credit cards:

AE	American Express	EURO	Eurocard
CB	Carte Blanche	JCB	Japan Credit Bank
DC	Diners Club	MC	MasterCard
DISC	Discover	V	Visa

Find Frommer's Online

www.frommers.com offers of up-to-the-minute listings for almost 200 cities around the globe—including the latest bargains and candid, personal articles updated daily by Arthur Frommer himself. No other Web site offers such comprehensive and timely coverage of the world of travel.

The Best of France

1

France presents visitors with an embarrassment of riches—you may find yourself bewildered at all the choices you'll have to make when planning your trip. We've tried to make the task easier for you by compiling a list of our favorite experiences and discoveries. In the following pages, you'll find the kind of candid advice we'd give our closest friends.

1 The Best Travel Experiences

- **Hunting Antiques:** The 18th- and 19th-century French aesthetic was gloriously different from those of England and North America, and many worthwhile objects bear designs with mythological references to the French experience. It's estimated that there are more than 13,000 antiques shops throughout the country. Stop wherever the sign ANTIQUAIRE or BROCANTE is displayed.
- **Dining Out:** The art of fine dining is still serious business in France. Even casual bistros with affordable menus are likely to offer fresh (seasonal) ingredients used in time-tested recipes that may add up to one of the most memorable meals of your life. Food here is as cerebral as it is sensual. For our favorite restaurants in all of France, see "The Best Upscale Restaurants" and "The Best Affordable Restaurants," later in this chapter.
- **Biking in the Countryside:** The country that invented La Tour de France, the world's most impassioned bicycle race, offers thousands of options for leisurely bike trips. For a modest charge, trains throughout France will carry your bicycle to any point you specify, allowing you to avoid the urban congestion of Paris and other large cities. Some of the best excursions are offered by **Euro-Bike Tours** in DeKalb, Illinois (☎ **800/321-6060**), which features tours of some of the most desirable hiking regions in France, including Provence, Burgundy, and the Loire Valley. See also "Special-Interest Vacations" in chapter 2.
- **Cruising on a Luxury Barge:** Take a leisurely cruise on the canals and waterways of Burgundy, Brittany, Alsace, Languedoc, the Dordogne, or Provence. Many barges have been upgraded into luxury craft with superb dining facilities and comfortable accommodations. You can sit back and enjoy the lovely scenery,

perhaps stopping here and there to sightsee or to visit local wineries. Contact **Première Selections,** a division of the Kemwel Company (☎ **800/234-4000**). Inclusive fares begin at $1,495 for 3 nights and $2,615 for 6 nights. See also "Special-Interest Vacations" in chapter 2.

- **Shopping in Parisian Boutiques:** The French ferociously guard their image as Europe's most stylish people. The citadels of Right Bank chic are found along rue du Faubourg St-Honoré and its extension, rue St-Honoré. The most glamorous shops sprawl for about a mile along these interconnected narrow streets, which stretch between the Palais Royal (to the east) and Palais de l'Elysée (to the west). Follow in the footsteps of Coco Chanel, Yves Saint Laurent, and Karl Lagerfeld for a shopper's tour of a lifetime. See chapter 4.

- **Strolling Along the Seine in Paris:** Lovers still walk hand in hand along the river, while on its banks the *bouquinistes* still peddle their postcards, perhaps some 100-year-old pornography, or a tattered history of Indochina. Some visitors walk the full 7-mile stretch of the river through the city, but you may want to confine your stroll to central Paris, passing the Tuileries, the Louvre, and Notre-Dame and crossing one or more of the historic bridges, like pont Neuf, over the Seine and onto Île de la Cité or Île St-Louis and back again. See chapter 4.

- **Exploring the Loire Valley:** Exploring the châteaux scattered among the valley's rich fields and forests will familiarize you with the French Renaissance's architectural aesthetics and with the intrigues, dalliances, and scandals of the French kings and their courts. Nothing conjures up the aristocratic ancien régime better than a leisurely tour of these legendary châteaux. See chapter 6.

- **Climbing to the Heights of Mont-St-Michel:** Straddling the tidal flats between Normandy and Brittany, this is the most spectacular fortress in northern Europe. Believed to be protected by the archangel Michael himself, most of this Gothic marvel stands just as it did during the 1200s. See chapter 7.

- **Paying Tribute to Fallen Heroes on Normandy's D-Day Beaches:** On June 6, 1944, the largest armada ever assembled departed under cover of rough seas and dense fog from the English coast. Its success was anything but guaranteed, and for about a week the future of the civilized world hung in a bloody and brutal balance between the Nazi and Allied armies. Today you'll see only the sticky sands and wind-torn, gray-green seas of a rather chilly beach. But even if you haven't seen *Saving Private Ryan* or *The Longest Day,* you can picture the struggles of the frightened yet determined young soldiers who established a bulkhead on the Nazi-occupied continent of Europe at a terrible price. See chapter 7.

- **Touring Burgundy During the Grape Gathering:** Medieval lore and legend permeate the harvests in Burgundy, when thousands of workers (armed with vintner's shears and baskets) head over the rolling hills to gather the ripened grapes that have made the classified wines of Burgundy so famous. You can sample the local wines in any of the area restaurants, which always stock impressive collections. See chapter 11.

- **Schussing Down the Alps:** France is noted for its world-class skiing and its luxurious resorts. Our favorites are Morzine and Avoriaz, Chamonix, Courchevel, and Megève. Here you'll find vertical cliffs only the experts should brave as well as challenging runs for intermediates and beginners; off the slopes, the après-ski scene roars into the wee hours. See chapter 13.

- **Marveling at the Riviera's Modern-Art Museums:** Since the 1890s, when Signac, Bonnard, and Matisse discovered St-Tropez, artists and their patrons have been drawn to the French Riviera. You can experience an unforgettable trip by driving across southern Provence, interspersing museum visits with wonderful meals, people-watching, lounging on the beach, and stops at the area's architectural and artistic marvels. Highlights are Aix-en-Provence (Cézanne's studio and the Vasarély Museum), Biot (the Léger museum), Cagnes-sur-Mer (the Museum of Modern Mediterranean Art), Cap d'Antibes (the Grimaldi Château's Picasso collection), La Napoule (the Henry Clews Museum), and Menton (the Cocteau Museum). If that's not enough, Nice, St-Paul-de-Vence, and St-Tropez all have impressive modern-art collections. See chapter 15.

• **Partying on the Côte d'Azur:** Until Edwardian escapists "discovered" it about a century ago, the coastline of Provence was dotted with sleepy fishing villages; today this region is famous for its glamorous sense of hedonism, despite its desperate overcrowding (and impossible traffic jams). Our vote for best beach goes to the Plage de Tahiti, just outside St-Tropez, where there's lots of topless (and bottomless) action going on. If you bother to wear a bikini, it should be only the most daring. See chapter 15.

2 The Best Romantic Escapes

• **Deauville** (Normandy): Using the resort of Deauville to propel herself to stardom, Coco Chanel added greatly to its sense of glamour and romance. Try your hand at the casinos, ride horses, stroll along the world's most discreetly elegant boardwalk, or simply revel in the resort's wonderful sense of style and nostalgia. See chapter 7.

• **La Baule** (Brittany): Consider an escape with your significant other to La Baule, a coastal resort in southern Brittany. The salt air; the moody, windswept Atlantic; and the lovely belle époque architecture help justify the name of its 5-mile beach, La Côte d'Amour. See chapter 8.

• **Talloires** (The French Alps): The bracing climate, the history that goes back to the early Middle Ages, and the Gallic flair of the local innkeepers make for a memorable stay in Talloires. Accommodations range from a converted medieval monastery to an intimate B&B. The cuisine is world-class, as is the opportunity for quiet, relaxed romance. See chapter 13.

• **Les Baux** (Provence): During the Middle Ages, troubadours in southern Europe were encouraged to present their courtly love ballads to audiences at the craggy fortress of Les Baux. The romantic tradition continues today, with escapists from all over congregating in the weirdly eroded, rocky, arid Les Baux landscapes. The town contains an abundance of hideaways where you can concentrate on romance. See chapter 14.

• **St-Tropez** (Côte d'Azur): Somehow, any blonde manages to feel like Brigitte Bardot in sunny St-Tropez, and the sheer number of scantily clad satyrs and nymphs who slink through town in midsummer could perk up the most sluggish libido. The real miracle here is that the charm of the place actually manages to survive both its own hype and the hordes of visitors. See chapter 15.

3 The Best Driving Tours

• **La Route des Crêtes** (Alsace-Lorraine): The Vosges are one of the oldest mountain ranges in France and for many years formed one of the country's boundaries with Germany. Richly forested with tall hardwood trees and firs, they skirt the western edge of the Rhine and resemble Germany's Black Forest. Some parts of it are the closest thing in France to a wilderness. La Route des Crêtes, originally chiseled out of the mountains as a supply line, begins just west of Colmar, at the Col du Bonhomme. High points are Münster (home of the famous cheese), Col de la Schlucht (a resort with sweeping panoramas as far as the Jura and the Black Forest), and Markstein. At any point along the way, you can stop and strike out on some of the well-marked hiking trails. See chapter 10.

- **La Côte d'Or** (Burgundy): Stretching only 37 miles from Santenay to Dijon, this route is for wine lovers. Rows of carefully terraced vines rise in tiers above the D122/N74/D1138 highways (La Route des Grands Crus), passing through the timeless towns of Puligny-Montrachet, Volnay, Beaune, Nuits-St-Georges, Vosne-Romanée, Gevrey-Chambertin, and Marsannay-la-Côte. Travel at your leisure, stopping wherever you like to sample and purchase the noble vintages whose growers are identified by signs sprouting from the sides of the highway. See chapter 11.

- **The Gorges of the Ardèche** (The Rhône Valley): The river that carved these canyons (the Ardèche, a tributary of the Rhône) is the most temperamental of any French waterway: Its ebbs and flows have created the Grand Canyon of France. Riddled with alluvial deposits, canyons sometimes more than 950 feet deep, grottoes, and caves, the valley is one of the country's most unusual geological spectacles. A panoramic road (D290) runs along one rim of these canyons, providing views over a striking, arid landscape. Plan to park at many of the belvederes scattered along the route and walk for a few minutes on some of the well-marked footpaths. The drive, which you can do in a day even if you stop frequently for sightseeing, stretches in a southeast-to-northwest trajectory between the towns of Vallon-Pont-d'Arc and Pont St-Esprit. See chapter 12.

- **La Route des Grandes Alpes** (The French Alps): One of the most panoramic drives in Western Europe stretches southward from the lakefront town of Evian to the coastal resort of Nice. En route, you'll see alpine uplands, larch forests, glaciers, and the foothills of Mont Blanc sheathed in mountain scenery. Plan on spending anywhere from 2 to 6 days for the drive, stopping for R and R along the way in such towns as Morzine, Avoriaz, Chamonix, and Megève. The route covers some 460 miles and crosses about 20 of France's dramatic mountain passes. Some sections are passable only in midsummer. See chapter 13.

4 The Best Châteaux & Palaces

- **Château de Chantilly** (Île de France): This palace was begun in 1528 by Anne de Montmorency, a constable of France who advised six monarchs. To save costs, she ordered that her new building be placed atop the foundations of a derelict castle completed in 1386. Her descendants enlarged and embellished the premises, added the massive stables for which the palace is admired today, and hired Le Nôtre to design gardens that later inspired Louis XVI to create similar (though larger) ones at Versailles. See chapter 5.

- **Château de Vaux-le-Vicomte** (Île de France): Vaux-le-Vicomte symbolizes the dangers of conspicuous consumption. It was built in 1661 for Nicolas Fouquet, Louis XIV's finance minister, and its lavishness made many wonder if some of the money for its construction had been pilfered from the treasury—it had. This act did not amuse the Sun King, who had Fouquet jailed and his château confiscated. As a backhanded compliment to Fouquet, Louis swiftly hired the complex's designers (Mansard, Le Nôtre, Le Brun, Girardon, and de Legendre) to design his own palace and gardens at Versailles. See chapter 5.

- **Château de Versailles** (Île de France): This is the most spectacular palace in the world. Its construction was riddled with ironies and tragedies, and its hyper-inflated costs can be partly blamed for the bloodbath of the French Revolution. Ringed with world-class gardens and a network of canals whose excavations required an army of laborers, the site also contains the Grand and Petit Trianons as well as miles of ornate corridors lined with the spoils of a vanished era. See chapter 5.
- **Palais de Fontainebleau** (Île de France): Since the time of the earliest Frankish kings, the forest here has served as a royal hunting ground. Various dwellings had been erected for medieval kings in the heart of the forest, but in 1528, François I commissioned the core of the building that would be enlarged, expanded, and embellished by subsequent monarchs, including Henri II, Henri III, Catherine de Médici, Charles IX, and Louis XIII. Napoléon declared it his favorite château, delivering an emotional farewell to his troops from its horseshoe-shaped staircase just after his 1814 abdication. See chapter 5.
- **Château d'Azay-le-Rideau** (The Loire Valley): Many visitors consider this château among their three or four favorites, thrilling to its fairy-tale proportions and innate sense of beauty. Poised above the waters of the Indre (a tributary of the Loire), it boasts purely decorative remnants of medieval fortifications and an allure that prefigured the Renaissance embellishments of subsequent Loire Valley châteaux. See chapter 6.
- **Château de Chambord** (The Loire Valley): Despite the incorporation (probably by Michelangelo) of feudal trappings in its layout, this château was designed exclusively for pleasure—a manifestation of the political and military successes of the 21-year-old François I. Begun in 1519 as the Loire Valley's most opulent status symbol, Chambord heralded the end of the feudal age and the debut of the Renaissance. Ironically, after military defeats in Italy, a much-chastened François rarely visited here, opting instead to live in châteaux closer to Paris. See chapter 6.
- **Château de Chenonceau** (The Loire Valley): Its builders daringly placed this palace on arched stone vaults above the rushing river Cher, a tributary of the Loire. Built between 1513 and 1521, Chenonceau was later fought over by two of France's most influential women, each of whom imposed her will on Renaissance politics and the château's design. Henri II gave the palace to his mistress, Diane de Poitiers, whose allure, it was rumored, was kept alive by milk baths, morning horseback rides, and witchcraft. After the king's death, his scheming widow, Catherine de Médici, forced Diane to a less prestigious château nearby (Chaumont), thoroughly humiliating her in the process. See chapter 6.
- **Château de Villandry** (The Loire Valley): Built in 1538, Villandry is a truly dignified palace, but the real attraction is its spectacular 17 acres of formal gardens. Brought to their full magnificence after 1906 by the noted French scholar Dr. Carvallo, they're a mandatory stop for anyone who wants to tour the great gardens of Europe. See chapter 6.

5 The Best Museums

- **Centre Pompidou** (Paris): Back in business after a long restoration, "the most avant-garde building in the world" is a citadel of 20th-century art, with a constantly rotating exhibition drawn from more than 40,000 works. Everything is here, from Calder's 1928 *Josephine Baker* (one of his earliest versions of the mobile) to the re-created jazz age studio of Brancusi. See chapter 4.

- **Musée d'Orsay** (Paris): The spidery glass-and-iron canopies of an abandoned railway station were adapted into one of Europe's most thrilling museums. Devoted exclusively to 19th-century art, it contains paintings by most of the French impressionists, as well as thousands of sculptures and decorative objects whose design changed forever the way Europe interpreted line, movement, and color. See chapter 4.
- **Musée du Louvre** (Paris): The Louvre's exterior is a triumph of grandiloquent French architecture, while its interior contains an embarrassment of artistic riches, with more paintings (around 300,000) than can be displayed at any one time. The collection somehow manages to retain its dignity despite the thousands of visitors who traipse through the corridors every day, particularly looking for the *Mona Lisa* and the *Venus de Milo*. In the 1980s the grandeur of its Cour Carrée was neatly offset by I. M. Pei's controversial Great Pyramid. See chapter 4.
- **Musée de la Tapisserie de Bayeux** (Bayeux, Normandy): This museum's star exhibit is a 900-year-old tapestry named in honor of medieval Queen Mathilda. Housed in a glass case, the Bayeaux tapestry is a long, narrow band of linen embroidered with depictions of the war machine that sailed from Normandy to conquer England in 1066. See chapter 7.
- **Musée Historique Lorrain** (Nancy, Alsace-Lorraine): Few other French museums reflect a specific province as pointedly as this one. Its eclectic collections include 16th-century engravings, 17th-century masterpieces by local painters, exhibits devoted to Jewish history in eastern France, antique furniture, wrought iron, and domestic accessories. See chapter 10.
- **Fondation Maeght** (St-Paul-de-Vence, Côte d'Azur): Established as a showcase for modern art by the 20th-century collectors Aimé and Marguerite Maeght, this museum is an avant-garde compendium of works by Giacometti, Chagall, Braque, Miró, Matisse, and Barbara Hepworth. Built on many levels in a design by the fabled architect José Luís Sert, it boasts glass walls that allow views over the surrounding ancient arid landscapes of Provence. See chapter 15.
- **Musée Île-de-France** (St-Jean-Cap-Ferrat, Côte d'Azur): This breathtaking villa is loaded with paintings and furniture that have remained more or less in their original positions since the donor's death in 1934. The source of the museum's grand ostentation was the baronne Ephrussi, scion of the Rothschilds, who scoured Europe in pursuit of her treasures. See chapter 15.
- **Musée Fabre** (Montpellier, Languedoc): This museum occupies a historic villa where Molière once presented some of his plays. Today it boasts one of the worthiest collections of French, Italian, and Spanish paintings in the south of France. See chapter 16.
- **Musée Toulouse-Lautrec** (Albi, Languedoc): The artist Toulouse-Lautrec was born in Albi in 1864. Much to his family's horror, he opted to move to a scandalous neighborhood in Paris, where his affectionate and amused depictions of the belle époque scene are priceless treasures today. Also on view here are works by Degas, Bonnard, and Matisse. See chapter 16.
- **Musée Ingres** (Montauban, the Dordogne): This museum, housed in a 17th-century archbishop's palace, was created in 1867 when Jean-Auguste-Dominique Ingres (one of the most admired classicists since the Revolution) bequeathed the city more than 4,000 drawings and paintings. See chapter 19.

6 The Best Cathedrals

- **Notre-Dame de Paris** (Paris): A triumph of medieval French architecture, this structure's gray stone walls symbolize the power of Paris in the Middle Ages. Begun in 1163, Notre-Dame is the cathedral of the nation. It's especially dazzling in the early morning and at sunset, when its image is reflected in the Seine. See chapter 4.
- **Notre-Dame de Chartres** (Chartres, Île de France): No less a talent than Rodin declared this cathedral a French acropolis. The site it occupies was holy for both the prehistoric Druids and the ancient Romans. One of the first High Gothic cathedrals, the first to use flying buttresses, Chartres is one of the largest cathedrals in the world. It also contains what might be the finest stained-glass windows in history, more than 3,000 square yards of glass whose vivid hues and patterns of light are truly mystical. See chapter 5.
- **Notre-Dame de Rouen** (Rouen, Normandy): Consecrated in 1063 and rebuilt after a fire in 1200, this cathedral was immortalized in the late 19th century, when Monet spent hours painting a series of moody impressions of the facade at various times of day. Some sections of the cathedral are masterpieces of the Flamboyant Gothic style; others are plainer, though equally dignified. See chapter 7.
- **Notre-Dame d'Amiens** (Amiens, the Ardennes): A lavishly decorated example of High Gothic architecture, this cathedral boasts a soaring nave whose roof is supported by 126 breathtakingly slender pillars. It was begun in 1220 to house the head of St. John the Baptist, brought back from the Crusades in 1206, and at 469 feet long is the largest church in France. Amazingly, it escaped destruction during the bombings of the world wars, despite the fierce fighting that took place nearby. See chapter 9.
- **Notre-Dame de Reims** (Reims, Champagne): One of France's first Christian bishops, St. Rémi, baptized the pagan king of the Franks, Clovis, on this site in 496, thereby elevating Reims to one of the holiest sites in northern Europe. The cathedral commemorating that event was conceived as a religious sanctuary where the French kings would be anointed; it was suitably large, spectacular, and (in our eyes) rather cold. The coronation of every king between 1137 and 1825 was celebrated here. Damaged by World War I bombings, the cathedral was largely restored by American donations during the 1920s and 1930s. See chapter 9.
- **Notre-Dame de Strasbourg** (Strasbourg, Alsace-Lorraine): One of the largest buildings in the Christian world, this is also one of the most architecturally harmonious Gothic cathedrals of the Middle Ages. Built of russet-colored stone between 1176 and 1439, it's a perfect symbol of Alsatian pride and one of our favorite cathedrals. The monument's 16th-century astrological clock is a showstopper, gathering crowds daily for its 12:30pm exhibition of allegorical figures from myth and fable. See chapter 10.

7 The Best Vineyards & Wineries

A terrific source for information about French wines is the **Centre d'Information, de Documentation, et de Dégustation Sur le Vin (CIDD),** 30 rue de la Sablière, 75014 Paris (☎ **01-45-45-44-20;** fax 01-45-42-78-20). Throughout the year, this self-funded school presents about a dozen courses addressing all aspects of wine tasting, producing, buying, and merchandising. Conducted in French and English, they're tailored to wine merchants, wine growers, and restaurant-industry professionals. The organization is a gold mine of information for anyone anticipating a vineyard tour.

And if your primary interest lies with the wines of Bordeaux, an organization that will document virtually any aspect of the wine trade as it relates to that particular region is the **Maison des Vins de Bordeaux,** 1 cours de 30 Juillet, 33000 Bordeaux (☎ **05-56-00-22-88**).

- **Couly-Dutheil** (Chinon; ☎ 02-47-97-20-20): The cellars here are suitably medieval, many carved into the rock undulating through the area's forests. Most of this company's production involves Chinon wines (mostly reds), though two that they're justifiably proud of are Borgeuil and St-Nicolas de Borgeuil, whose popularity in the North American market has grown in recent years. See chapter 6.

- **Champagne Taittinger** (Reims; ☎ 03-26-85-84-33): Taittinger is a grand *marque* of French champagne, one of the few whose ownership is still controlled by members of the family who founded it in 1930. It's one of the most visitor-friendly of the champagne houses. See chapter 9.

- **Domaines Schlumberger** (Guebwiller, near Colmar; ☎ 03-89-74-27-00): Established by Schlumberger beginning in 1810, these cellars are an unusual combination of early 19th-century brickwork and modern stainless steel; a visit will go far in enhancing your understanding of the subtle differences among wines produced by the seven varieties of grape cultivated in Alsace. See chapter 10.

- **Domaine Protheau** (Château d'Etroyes, Mercurey; ☎ 03-85-98-99-10): The 150 acres of grapevines straddle at least two appellations contrôlées, so you'll have a chance to immerse yourself in the subtle differences among reds (both pinot noirs and burgundies), whites, and rosés produced under the auspices of both Rully and Mercurey. The headquarters of the organization, founded in the 1740s, is a château built in the late 1700s and early 1800s. See chapter 11.

  Two miles away, you can visit the **Château de Rully,** site of the **Domaine de la Bressande** (☎ 03-85-87-01-99), a well-respected producer of white and, to a lesser extent, red burgundies. Originally built in the 12th century as a stronghold of the comtes de Ternay, it offers tours of its cellars, winemaking facilities, and vineyards. See chapter 11.

- **The Wine-Growing Region Around Bordeaux:** This region is among the most glamorous in France, with a strong English influence, thanks to centuries of wine buying by London- and Bristol-based dealers. One of the area's prestigious growers is the **Société Duboscq,** Château Haut-Marbuzet, 33180 St-Estephe (☎ 05-56-59-30-54), which welcomes visitors daily. Free visits to the cellars are followed by a complimentary *dégustation des vins* of whichever of the company's products a visitor requests. See chapter 18.

8 The Best Luxury Hotels

- **Le Ritz** (Paris; ☎ 800/223-6800 in the U.S. and Canada, or 01-43-16-30-30): This hotel occupies a palace overlooking the octagonal borders of one of the most aesthetically perfect plazas in France: place Vendôme. The decor is pure opulence. Marcel Proust wrote parts of *Remembrance of Things Past* in an apartment here, and Georges-Auguste Escoffier perfected many of his legendary recipes in its kitchens. See chapter 3.

- **Hôtel de Crillon** (Paris; ☎ **800/241-3333** in the U.S. and Canada, or 01-44-71-15-00): This hotel's majestic exterior was designed by the 18th-century architect Jacques-Ange Gabriel and forms part of the symmetrical backdrop for place de la Concorde. The decor encompasses the reigns of Cardinal Richelieu and Marie Antoinette, and nearly every surface is polished weekly by a battalion of well-trained attendants. See chapter 3.
- **Château d'Artigny** (Montbazon, Loire Valley; ☎ **02-47-34-30-30**): The perfume king François Coty once lived and entertained lavishly at this mansion outside Tours—and you can do the same today, as it's been converted into one of the poshest hotels in the Loire Valley. You can live in the grandeur and total comfort once enjoyed by Elizabeth Taylor and other celebs, taking in the popular weekend soirées and musical evenings. See chapter 6.
- **L'Oustau de Beaumanière** (Les Baux, outside Marseille, Provence; ☎ **04-90-54-33-07**): This Relais & Châteaux stands in the valley at the foot of Les Baux de Provence. The cuisine is superb, as are the luxurious accommodations, some of which are in buildings dating from the 16th and 17th centuries. See chapter 14.
- **Grand Hôtel du Cap-Ferrat** (St-Jean-Cap-Ferrat, Côte d'Azur; ☎ **04-93-76-50-50**): A destination in its own right, the Grand Hôtel occupies 14 prime acres on one of the world's most exclusive peninsulas. It's housed in a belle époque palace and since the turn of the century has been the temporary home for royals, aristocrats, and wealthy wanna-bes. See chapter 15.
- **Hôtel du Cap-Eden Roc** (Cap d'Antibes, Côte d'Azur; ☎ **04-93-61-39-01**): Built during the grand Second Empire and set on 22 acres of splendidly landscaped gardens, this hotel is one of Europe's most legendary, evoking shades of the F. Scott Fitzgerald classic *Tender Is the Night*. Swimmers will revel in a pool blasted from the dark rock of the glamorous coastline of Cap d'Antibes. See chapter 15.
- **Hôtel Négresco** (Nice, Côte d'Azur; ☎ **04-93-16-64-00**): Built in 1913 as a layered wedding cake in the château style, the Négresco was a lavish holiday escape for the Edwardian era's most respected and most notorious figures. Among them was the actress Lillie Langtry, the long-term mistress of Britain's Edward VII. After her fall from grace, she sat in the Négresco's lobby, swathed in veils, refusing to utter a word. Following tasteful renovations, the hotel is better now than it was even during its Jazz Age heyday. See chapter 15.
- **Hôtel du Palais** (Biarritz, Basque Country; ☎ **800/223-6800** in the U.S. and Canada, or 05-59-41-64-00): Delectably beautiful, this place was built in 1845 as a pink-walled summer palace for Napoléon III and his empress, Eugénie. Adept at housing such guests as Edward VII of England, Alfonso XIII of Spain, and the duke of Windsor, the hotel is a belle époque fantasy. See chapter 17.

9 The Best Affordable Hotels

- **Hôtel de Lutèce** (Paris; ☎ **01-43-26-23-52**): It slumbers on Paris's "other island," the Île St-Louis, which usually avoids the crush of visitors that swarm onto the more popular Île de la Cité, just across the bridge. You'll still be right in the city, but you can imagine yourself in a country inn at this tasteful retreat on the Seine. See chapter 3.
- **Hostellerie Lechat** (Honfleur, Normandy; ☎ **02-31-14-49-49**): Views from its windows overlook a Norman 18th-century port favored by the French novelist

Flaubert. The amenities here aren't particularly grand, but you'll get the feeling that Madame Bovary herself may be about to roll into view in her notorious carriage. The setting, which includes a rustically appealing restaurant, is charming and—even more surprising—the price tag is reasonable. See chapter 7.

- **Hôtel d'Avaugour** (Dinan, Brittany; ☎ 02-96-39-07-49): Its exterior is as antique looking as the fortifications that ring the medieval harbor of Dinan, but a radical restoration transformed the interior into a cozy getaway on the Norman coast. Add to that its aesthetic appeal and the old-time flavor of Dinan's winding alleys and views out over the Channel, and you've got all the ingredients you'll need for an affordable escape. See chapter 8.
- **Hostellerie du Vieux-Pérouges** (Pérouges, Rhône Valley; ☎ 04-74-61-00-88): This hotel, often described as a museum of the 13th century, is one of the most significant in central France. Composed of a group of much-restored 13th-century buildings with low ceilings and thick walls, it vividly evokes the France of another day and doesn't overcharge for the privilege. See chapter 12.
- **Hôtel Clair Logis** (St-Jean-Cap-Ferrat, Côte d'Azur; ☎ 04-93-76-04-57): The real estate that surrounds this converted 19th-century villa is among the most expensive in Europe, but despite that, this hotel manages to keep its prices beneath levels that really hurt. If you check into a room here (each named after a flower that thrives in the 2-acre garden surrounding the place), you'll be in good company: Even General de Gaulle, who knew the value of a centime, stayed here. See chapter 15.
- **Hôtel du Donjon** (Carcassonne, Languedoc; ☎ 800/528-1234 in the U.S. and Canada, or 04-68-11-23-00): Built into the solid bulwarks of Carcassonne, one of France's most perfectly preserved medieval fortresses, is this small-scale hotel whose well-appointed furnishings provide a vivid contrast to the crude stone shell that contains them. A stay here truly allows you personal contact with a site that often provoked bloody battles between medieval armies. See chapter 16.
- **La Réserve** (Albi, Languedoc; ☎ 05-63-60-80-80): This dignified farmhouse is surrounded by scrublands, vineyards, groves of olives, and cypresses. It's less expensive than many of the ultraluxurious hideaways along the nearby Côte d'Azur and has the added benefit of a location just outside the center of one of our favorite fortified sites in Europe, the medieval town of Albi. See chapter 16.
- **Tulip Inn Le Bayonne Etche-Ona** (Bordeaux, Atlantic Coast; ☎ 05-56-48-00-88): Like much of the rest of the neighborhood that surrounds it, this hotel was conceived during the 18th century as a showcase for French neoclassicism. Today, after a recent interior renovation, it offers modern comforts in an antique setting—and it's a great value. See chapter 18.

10 The Best Historic Places to Stay

- **Hôtel Trianon Palace** (Versailles, Île de France; ☎ 01-30-84-38-00): Louis XIV nearly bankrupted the treasury of France during the construction of his nearby palace, but this hotel overlooking its gardens might have been even more influential. In 1919 the Versailles Peace Treaty was ratified by delegates who retired, after the momentous but ill-conceived event, to the same rooms housing guests today. In addition to all the history you'll get, you'll be pampered at this plush and elegant hotel, which boasts its own spa. See chapter 5.
- **Château de Locguénolé** (Hennebont, Brittany; ☎ 02-97-76-76-76): No professional decorator could ever have accumulated the wide array of furnishings

and artifacts that 500 years' occupancy by successive generations of the same family have managed to cram into this Breton manor house. Some visitors think it's the most charming hotel in southern Brittany, a fact that's very easy to believe once you experience its style and charm. See chapter 8.

- **Manoir du Stang** (La Forêt-Fouesnant, Brittany; ☎ 02-98-56-97-37): Even the ivy that twines across the facade of this 16th-century Breton manor house looks as though it had been planted by someone very important, very long ago. Formal gardens segue into forested parkland, modern amenities are juxtaposed with enviable antiques—overall, the place is a gem that also happens to be a glamorous hotel. Some of the staff wear traditional Breton costumes, adding to the allure. See chapter 8.

- **Château de Rochegude** (Rochegude, Provence; ☎ 04-75-97-21-10): During the thousand years of this château's existence, its owners have included popes, dauphins, and dozens of less prominent aristocrats who have showered it with taste and money. Today each guest room is outfitted in a different antique style inspired by a specific emperor or king. The setting is 20 acres of parkland adjacent to the Rhône, outside Orange. See chapter 14.

- **Château de Roussan** (St-Rémy-de-Provence, Provence; ☎ 04-90-92-11-63): One of its outbuildings was the home of the Renaissance psychic Nostradamus, and its main building, sheltered by a stone neoclassical facade erected in 1701, is among the most beautiful in Provence. Wandering around the place will evoke another time and another place, with absolutely none of the artificiality that dominates the nearby Côte d'Azur. See chapter 14.

- **Château de Brindos** (Anglet, Basque Country; ☎ 05-59-23-17-68): Built between 1923 and 1926 by the heiress to an American railway fortune (Virginia Gould) with her English husband (Reginald Wright), this château has an Art Deco facade, 14th-century Gothic ruins in its garden, and fireplaces and ceilings imported from other Renaissance palaces of Europe. Today it offers an alluring combination of the Gilded Age as interpreted by the Jazz Age, superb food, and some of the most spectacular architectural adornments in France's southwest. See chapter 17.

- **Château de la Vallée Bleue** (La Châtre, Massif Central; ☎ 02-54-31-01-91): If you happen to stay in a room named for Liszt, Chopin, Flaubert, or Delacroix, it's probably because they slept in the same spot. The place was built by a doctor firmly committed to the well-being of his nearby patient, George Sand, famous author and feminist trendsetter whose masquerades as a man still provoke curiosity in this part of France. See chapter 20.

11 The Best Upscale Restaurants

- **Alain Ducasse** (Paris; ☎ 01-47-27-12-27): Achieving a coveted three-star rating from Michelin seemed hardly a daunting challenge to this brash chef who's taken Paris and Monaco by storm. Ducasse is the world's first six-star chef (three for Paris and three for his Louis XV in Monte Carlo). He's the darling of today's foodies and the spiritual heir of the legendary Escoffier. Who can outdo his homemade pasta bathed in cream, sweetbreads, truffles, and (get this) the combs and kidneys of a proud, strutting cock? See chapter 3.

- **Le Grand Véfour** (Paris; ☎ 01-42-96-56-27): Amid the arcades of the Palais Royal, this has been a dining spot since the reign of Louis XV, attracting over the years such notables as Colette, Victor Hugo, and the forever-loyal Jean Cocteau.

Jean Taittinger of the champagne family runs it today, and his kitchen brings originality to the French classics—everything from pigeon in the style of Rainier of Monaco to French-roasted sole and sea scallops in a velvety pumpkin sauce. See chapter 3.

- **Taillevent** (Paris; ☎ **01-44-95-15-01**): Dining here is still the social and gastronomic high point of a Paris visit. Its premises (an antique house near the Arc de Triomphe, laden with flowers) are suitably grand and its cuisine appropriately stylish to the Jackie Onassis look-alikes who sometimes dine here. See chapter 3.

- **Boyer-les-Crayères** (Reims, Champagne; ☎ **03-26-82-80-80**): This restaurant's setting is a lavish but dignified château with soaring ceilings and a flawless French Empire decor. Built in 1904 as the home of the Pommery family (of champagne fortune) and surrounded by a 14-acre park, it's maintained by an impeccably trained staff who appreciate the nuances of elaborate service rituals. You can retire directly to your accommodations after consuming a bottle or two of the region's famous bubbly. See chapter 9.

- **Auberge de l'Ill** (near Colmar, Alsace-Lorraine; ☎ **03-89-71-89-00**): After a meal here, you'll understand why France and Germany fought so bitterly for control of Alsace. Set amid well-tended farmland on the edge of the river Ill, this half-timbered manor house presents an almost idyllic setting. The food and wine served are rich, lush, and firmly rooted in the vineyards surrounding the place. See chapter 10.

- **À la Côte St-Jacques** (Joigny, Burgundy; ☎ **03-86-62-09-70**): Set on the edge of Burgundy, beside the river Yonne, this is the quintessential *restaurant avec chambres*. Indulge your taste for supremely well-prepared food and wine, then totter off to one of about a dozen carefully furnished guest rooms scattered among several buildings in this historic compound. One of our favorite dishes is cassolette of morels and frogs' legs, especially sublime when accompanied by a half bottle of fine red burgundy. See chapter 11.

- **L'Espérance** (Vézelay, Burgundy; ☎ **03-86-33-39-10**): Housed in an antique farmhouse at the base of a hill (La Colline de Vézelay) that has been a holy site for thousands of years, L'Espérance is run by one of Europe's most famous chefs, Marc Meneau, and his wife, Françoise. The place combines country comforts with world-class sophistication. See chapter 11.

- **Paul Bocuse** (Collonges-au-Mont-d'Or, near Lyon, Rhône Valley; ☎ **04-72-42-90-90**): Bocuse was the *enfant terrible* of French gastronomy throughout most of his youth. Today he's the world's most famous living chef, catering to Europe's hardest-to-please customers. The cuisine is ostensibly Lyonnais, but Bocuse has never allowed himself to be hemmed in by such provincialism, and his mind wanders the world for culinary inspiration. He creates his own signature dishes to delight the palates of his international fans—ranging from roast pigeon in puff pastry with foie gras to his celebrated black truffle soup. See chapter 12.

- **Hôtel/Restaurant des Troisgros** (Roanne, Rhône Valley; ☎ **04-77-71-66-97**): The setting is the dining room of a once-nondescript hotel near a railway station. The cuisine, however, is a joyfully lush celebration of the agrarian bounty of France. Mingling specialties from all the regions, it attracts diners from as far away as Paris and Brussels. Years after they dine here, many people still speak reverently of their meal. See chapter 12.

- **Auberge du Père-Bise** (Talloires, French Alps; ☎ **04-50-60-72-01**): A mysterious alchemy transformed what was a simple lakeside chalet into an illustrious restaurant. Set beside Lac d'Annecy in eastern France, it's outfitted like the

Impressions

Who can help loving the land that has taught us six hundred and eighty-five ways to dress eggs?

—Thomas Moore, *The Fudge Family in Paris* (1818)

prosperous provincial home of local gentry, yet it serves sublimely elegant food favored by many generations of people like the Rothschilds. See chapter 13.

- **Le Moulin de Mougins** (Mougins, Côte d'Azur; ☎ 04-93-75-78-24): Occupying a 16th-century olive mill in a Provence pine forest, this restaurant is the creation of chef Roger Vergé, the most sophisticated media genius in the French culinary world. See chapter 15.

12 The Best Affordable Restaurants

- **Crémerie-Restaurant Polidor** (Paris; ☎ 01-43-26-95-34): For many Parisians, the cuisine here evokes memories of what their grandmothers might have concocted for a family supper in the days after World War II. The unpretentious setting, where lace curtains filter the sunlight, was a favorite even of such iconoclasts as André Gide. See chapter 3.
- **Les Vapeurs** (Trouville, Normandy; ☎ 02-31-88-15-24): An anomaly among the Norman coast's steeply priced brasseries, this restaurant overlooking the port is no-frills all the way, from its Art Deco decor to its fresh, well-priced seafood. People really seem to enjoy the festive ambience. See chapter 7.
- **Chez La Mère Pourcel** (Dinan, Brittany; ☎ 02-96-39-03-80): The references this place makes to someone's grandmother (Mère Pourcel) are completely justified, since the cuisine hasn't changed very much in decades. That's just fine with its guests, many of whom drive from Paris for a day in the countryside and a well-priced dinner. See chapter 8.
- **Brasserie de l'Ancienne Douane** (Strasbourg, Alsace-Lorraine; ☎ 03-88-15-78-78): In a city known for its celebrated Alsatian cuisine, this large, colorful restaurant is a frontrunner in the moderate category. In a medieval building, you can feast on the famous sauerkraut and foie gras of the region, as well as on a particularly succulent specialty, chicken in Riesling wine. See chapter 10.
- **Au Chalet de Brou** (Bourg-en-Bresse, Rhône Valley; ☎ 04-74-22-26-28): Located in a town famous for the quality of its poultry, this restaurant sits just across from the village church. It offers amazingly low prices on the wonderful local birds, and many food critics travel here from all over France for the hearty roast chicken. See chapter 12.
- **Le Bistro Latin** (Aix-en-Provence, Provence; ☎ 04-42-38-22-88): The great deal here lies in the fixed-price menus, which are as carefully composed as a symphony. Prices are low, flavors are sensational, and hints of Italian zest pop up frequently in such dishes as risotto with scampi. See chapter 14.
- **Le Safari** (Nice, Côte d'Azur; ☎ 04-93-80-18-44): This ever-popular, ever-crowded brasserie overlooking the cours Saleya market soaks up the Riviera sun. Dressed in jeans, waiters hurry back and forth, serving the regulars and the visitors alike on the sprawling terrace. This place makes one of the best salade Niçoise concoctions in town, as well as a drop-dead spring lamb roasted in a wood-fired oven. See chapter 15.

2 Planning Your Trip: The Basics

In the pages that follow, we've compiled everything you need to know to handle the practical details of planning your trip: what documents you'll need, how to use French currency, how to find the best airfare, when to go, and more.

1 The Regions in Brief

Though France covers only 212,741 square miles (making it slightly smaller than Texas), no other country concentrates such a fabulous diversity of sights and scenery into so compact an area. It encompasses each of the characteristics that make up Europe: the north's flat, fertile lands; the central Loire Valley's rolling green hills; the east's snowcapped alpine ranges; the southwest's towering Pyrénées; the Massif Central's plateaus and rock outcroppings; and the southeast's lushly semitropical Mediterranean coast. Even more noteworthy are the strong cultural and historic differences defining each region.

And all these contrasts beckon within easy traveling range of Paris (conveniently located in the center of the country) and each other. The train trip from the capital is just 4 hours to Alsace, 5 to the Alps, 7 to the Pyrénées, and 8 to the Côte d'Azur. **France's National Railroads (SNCF)** operate one of the finest lines in the world, with impressively fast service to and from Paris (though trains tend to crawl on routes unconnected with the capital).

You'll find some 44,000 miles of roadway at your disposal, most in good condition for fast long-distance driving. (But try not to stick to the Route Nationale network all the time. Nearly all of France's scenic splendors lie along secondary roads, and what you'll lose in mileage you'll more than make up for in enjoyment.)

A "grand tour" of France is nearly impossible for the average visitor, who doesn't have a lifetime to explore the country. If you want to get to know a province in depth, it's good to devote a week to a specific region if you can; you may have a more rewarding trip if you concentrate on getting to know two or three areas in greater depth and at a leisurely pace rather than racing around, trying to cram in too much. You're going to be faced with hard choices about where to go in your limited time, so with this in mind, we've summarized the highlights of each region for you.

ÎLE DE FRANCE (INCLUDING PARIS) The Île de France is an island only in the sense that its boundaries (following about a 50-mile

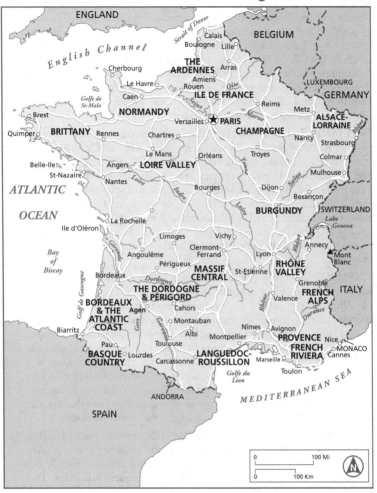

ENGLAND

Strait of Dover

BELGIUM

Calais
Boulogne Lille

English Channel

Cherbourg

THE
ARDENNES Arras

Le Havre Amiens
Rouen *Oise* LUXEMBOURG

*Golfe de
St-Malo* Caen ILE DE FRANCE GERMANY

Brest NORMANDY Reims Metz

Quimper Versailles ○ ★ PARIS ALSACE-
LORRAINE

BRITTANY Rennes Chartres ○ CHAMPAGNE Nancy Strasbourg

Belle-Ile Le Mans Orléans Troyes Colmar

St-Nazaire Angers LOIRE VALLEY Mulhouse

Nantes *Loire* Bourges Dijon *Saône* Besançon

ATLANTIC

OCEAN La Rochelle BURGUNDY SWITZERLAND

Ile d'Oléron Limoges Vichy *Lake
Geneva*

*Bay
of
Biscay* Angoulême Clermont-
Ferrand Lyon Annecy
Mont
Blanc

Périgueux MASSIF
CENTRAL St-Étienne RHÔNE
VALLEY

Bordeaux *Dordogne* Grenoble

THE DORDOGNE
& PÉRIGORD Valence FRENCH ITALY
ALPS

BORDEAUX
& THE
ATLANTIC
COAST Agen Cahors *Rhône* *Durance*

Biarritz Montauban Nîmes Avignon

Albi Montpellier PROVENCE Nice

Pau Lourdes Toulouse FRENCH
RIVIERA MONACO
Cannes

BASQUE
COUNTRY Carcassonne LANGUEDOC-
ROUSSILLON Marseille Toulon

*Golfe du
Lion*

ANDORRA *MEDITERRANEAN SEA*

SPAIN

0 ——— 100 Mi
0 ——— 100 Km

N

radius from the center of Paris) are delineated by rivers with odd-sounding names like Essonne, Epte, Aisne, Eure, and Ourcq, plus a handful of canals. It was in this temperate basin that France was born. This region's spectacular attractions include **Paris, Versailles, Fontainebleau, Notre-Dame de Chartres,** and **Giverny,** yet it also incorporates endless dreary suburbs and even Disneyland Paris. Despite creeping industrialization, pockets of verdant charm remain, including the forests of Rambouillet and Fontainebleau and the artists' hamlet of Barbizon. See chapters 3, 4, and 5.

THE LOIRE VALLEY   This area includes two ancient provinces, Touraine (centered on Tours) and Anjou (centered on Angers). It was beloved by royalty and nobility until Henry IV moved his court to Paris. Head here to see the most magnificent castles in France. Irrigated by the Loire River and its many tributaries, this valley produces many superb and reasonably priced wines. See chapter 6.

NORMANDY This region will forever be linked to the 1944 D-Day invasion. Some readers consider their visit to the D-Day beaches the most emotionally worthwhile part of their trip to France. Normandy boasts 372 miles of coastline and a long-standing maritime tradition. It's a popular weekend getaway from Paris, and many glamorous hotels and restaurants thrive here, especially around the casino town of **Deauville.** This area has hundreds of half-timbered houses reminiscent of medieval England, charming seaports like **Trouville,** and mighty ports like **Le Havre,** where the Seine flows into the English Channel. Normandy's great attractions include **Rouen** cathedral, the abbey of **Jumièges,** and medieval **Bayeux.** See chapter 7.

BRITTANY Jutting out into the Atlantic, the westernmost (and one of the poorest) region of France is known for its rocky coastlines, Celtic roots, frequent rains, and ancient dialect, which is akin to the Gaelic tongues of Wales and Ireland. Many French vacationers love the seacoast (rivaled only by the Côte d'Azur) for its sandy beaches, high cliffs, and relatively modest prices (by French standards, anyway). Highlights of the region are **Carnac** (home to ancient Celtic dolmens and burial mounds) and atmospheric fishing ports like Quimper, Quiberon, Quimperlé, and Concarneau. The region's most sophisticated resort, **La Baule,** lies near some of southern Brittany's best beaches. See chapter 8.

CHAMPAGNE Every French monarch since A.D. 496 was crowned at Reims, and much of French history revolved around this holy site and the fertile hills ringing it. Joan of Arc was burned at the stake thanks partly to her efforts to lead her dauphin through enemy lines to **Reims.** Directly in the path of any invader wishing to occupy Paris, both Reims and the fertile Champagne district have been awash in more blood throughout the centuries, including the terrible World War I battles of Somme and Marne. There are industrial sites concentrated among patches of verdant forest, and the steep sides of valleys are sheathed in vineyards. The 78-mile road from Reims to Vertus, one of the three **Routes du Champagne,** takes in a trio of wine-growing regions that produce 80% of the bubbly used for celebrations around the world. See chapter 9.

THE ARDENNES & NORTHERN BEACHES France's northern region is often ignored by North Americans (which is why we feature it only as a side trip from Reims in Champagne). In summer, French families arrive by the thousands to visit Channel beach resorts like **Le Touquet-Paris-Plage.** This district is heavily industrialized and (like neighboring Champagne) has always been horribly war-torn. The region's best-known port, **Calais,** was a bitterly contested English stronghold on the French mainland for hundreds of years. Ironically, Calais functions today as the port of disembarkation for the ferries, hydrofoils, and Channel Tunnel arrivals from Britain. **Notre-Dame Cathedral in Amiens,** the medieval capital of Picardy, is a treasure, with a 140-foot-high nave—the highest in France. Other than Amiens, the town holding the most interest is **Laon,** 74 miles southeast; it's still surrounded by medieval ramparts, which are the northeast's most rewarding attraction. See chapter 9.

ALSACE-LORRAINE Between Germany and the forests of the Vosges is the most Teutonic of France's provinces: Alsace, with cosmopolitan **Strasbourg** as its capital. Celebrated for its cuisine, particularly its foie gras and *choucroute* (sauerkraut), this area is home to villages whose half-timbered designs will make you think of the Black Forest. If you travel the **Route de Vin (Wine Road),** you can visit historic towns like Colmar, Riquewihr, and Illhaeusern, all famous to those who love great food and wine. **Lorraine,** birthplace of Joan of Arc and site of the industrial center of Mulhouse, witnessed countless bloody battles during the world wars. Its capital, **Nancy,** is the proud guardian of a grand 18th-century plaza: Place Stanislaus. The much-eroded peaks of the Vosges forest, the closest thing to a wilderness left in France, offer rewarding hiking. See chapter 10.

BURGUNDY   Few trips will prove as rewarding as several leisurely days spent exploring Burgundy, with its splendid old cities like **Dijon.** Besides being famous for its cuisine (*boeuf* and *escargots à la bourguignonne,* for example), the district contains, along its Côte d'Or, hamlets whose names (Mercurey, Beaune, Puligny-Montrachet, Vougeot, and Nuits-St-Georges, among others) are synonymous with great wines. See chapter 11.

THE RHÔNE VALLEY   A fertile area of alpine foothills and sloping valleys in eastern and southeastern France, the upper Rhône Valley ranges from the cosmopolitan French suburbs of the Swiss city of Geneva to the northern borders of Provence. The district is thoroughly French, unflinchingly bourgeois, and dedicated to preserving the gastronomic and cultural traditions that have produced some of the most celebrated chefs in French history.

Only 2 hours by train from Paris, the region's cultural centerpiece, **Lyon,** is France's "second city." North of here, you can travel the Beaujolais trail or head for Bresse's ancient capital, **Bourg-en-Bresse,** which produces the world's finest poultry. You can explore the Rhône Valley en route from northern climes to Provence and the south. Try to visit the medieval villages of **Pérouges** and **Vienne,** 17 miles south of Lyon, the latter known for its Roman ruins. See chapter 12.

THE FRENCH ALPS   This area's resorts rival those of neighboring Switzerland and contain some incredible scenery: snowcapped peaks, glaciers, and alpine lakes. **Chamonix** is a world-famous ski resort facing **Mont Blanc,** Western Europe's highest mountain. However, **Courchevel** and **Megève** are more chic. During summer in the Alps you can enjoy such spa resorts as **Evian** and the calm and restful 19th-century resorts ringing **Lake Geneva.** See chapter 13.

PROVENCE   One of France's most fabled regions flanks the Alps and the Italian border along its eastern end and incorporates a host of sites the rich and famous have long frequented. Premier destinations are **Aix-en-Provence,** associated with Cézanne; **Arles,** "the soul of Provence," captured so brilliantly by van Gogh; **Avignon,** the 14th-century capital of Christendom during the papal schism; and **Marseille,** a port city established by the ancient Phoenicians (in some ways more North African than French). Special Provence gems are the small villages, like **Les Baux, Gordes,** and **St-Rémy-de-Provence,** birthplace of Nostradamus. The strip of glittering coastal towns along Provence's southern edge is known as the **Côte d'Azur** (the French Riviera; see below). See chapter 14.

THE FRENCH RIVIERA (CÔTE D'AZUR)   The fabled gold-plated Côte d'Azur (Blue Coast) has become hideously overbuilt and spoiled by tourism. Even so, the names of its resorts still evoke glamour and excitement: **Cannes, St-Tropez, Cap d'Antibes, St-Jean-Cap-Ferrat.** July and August are the most crowded, but spring and fall can be a delight. **Nice** (pronounced niece) is the biggest city along this coast, and the most convenient base for exploring the area. The independent principality of **Monaco,** the most fabled piece of real estate along the Côte d'Azur, occupies less than a square mile. Along the coast are some sandy beaches, but many are rocky or pebbly. Topless bathing is common, especially in St-Tropez, and some of the restaurants here are fabled citadels of conspicuous consumption. This is not just a place for sun and fun, however. Dozens of artists and their patrons have littered the landscape with world-class galleries and art museums. See chapter 15.

LANGUEDOC-ROUSSILLON Languedoc may not be as chic as Provence, but it's also less frenetic and more affordable. **Roussillon** is the rock-strewn arid French answer to ancient Catalonia, just across the Spanish border. **The Camargue** is the name given to the steaming marshy delta formed by two arms of the Rhône River. Rich in bird life, it's famous for its flat expanses of tough grasses and for such fortified medieval sites as **Aigues-Mortes.** Also appealing are **Auch,** the capital of Gascony; **Toulouse,** the bustling pink capital of Languedoc; and the "red city" of **Albi,** birthplace of Toulouse-Lautrec. **Carcassonne,** a marvelously preserved walled city with fortifications begun around A.D. 500, is the region's highlight. See chapter 16.

THE BASQUE COUNTRY Since prehistoric times the rugged Pyrénées have formed a natural boundary between France and Spain. Sheltered within the mountain valleys flourished one of Europe's most unusual cultures: the Basques. In the 19th century, resorts like **Biarritz** and **St-Jean-de-Luz** attracted the French aristocracy—the empress Eugénie's palace at Biarritz is now a celebrated hotel. The **Parc National des Pyrénées** is crisscrossed with gorgeous hiking trails, and four million Catholics annually visit the pilgrimage city of Lourdes. In the isolated villages and towns of the Pyrénées, the old folkloric traditions, strongly permeated with Spanish influences, continue to thrive. See chapter 17.

THE ATLANTIC COAST Flat, fertile, and frequently ignored by North Americans, this region incorporates towns pivotal in French history (**Saintes, Poitiers, Angoulême,** and **La Rochelle**) and wine- and liquor-producing villages (**Cognac, Margaux, St-Emilion,** and **Sauternes**) whose names are celebrated around the world. **Bordeaux,** the district's largest city, has an economy firmly based on wine merchandising and boasts truly grand 18th-century architecture. See chapter 18.

THE DORDOGNE & PÉRIGORD The land of foie gras and truffles is the site of some of Europe's oldest prehistoric settlements. For biking or just indulging in decadent gourmet meals, the region is among the top vacation spots in France. In the Périgord, traces of Cro-Magnon settlements are evidenced by the cave paintings at **Les Eyzies.** The Dordogne is the second-largest *département* (French equivalent of an American state). Some of France's most unusual châteaux were built in the valley of the Dordogne during the early Middle Ages, and many of the towns that grew here are spectacularly beautiful. The region is, unfortunately, no longer undiscovered, as retirees from abroad have moved into the elegant stone manor houses dotting the banks of the many rivers. Highlights are the ancient towns of **Périgueux, Les Eyzies-de-Tayac, Sarlat-le-Canéda, Beynac-et-Cazenac,** and **Souillac.** See chapter 19.

THE MASSIF CENTRAL The rugged heartland of south-central France, this underpopulated district contains ancient cities, unspoiled scenery, and an abundance of black lava, from which many area buildings were created. According to Parisians, the Massif Central is provincial with a vengeance—and the locals work hard to keep it that way. The largest cities are historic **Clermont-Ferrand** and **Limoges**—the medieval capitals of the provinces of the Auvergne and the Limousin, respectively. **Bourges,** a gateway to the region and once capital of Aquitaine, has a beautiful Gothic cathedral. See chapter 20.

2 Visitor Information

Your best source of information before you go is the **French Government Tourist Office (www.fgtousa.org),** which can be also reached at the following addresses:

In the United States, at 444 Madison Ave., 16th floor, New York, NY 10022 (☎ 212/838-7800); 676 N. Michigan Ave., Suite 3360, Chicago, IL 60611-2819 (☎ 312/751-7800); or 9454 Wilshire Blvd., Suite 715, Beverly Hills, CA 90212-2967 (☎ 310/271-6665). To request information, you can also try **France on Call** at ☎ 410/286-8310.

In Canada, contact the **Maison de la France/French Government Tourist Office,** 1981 av. McGill College, Suite 490, Montreal, H3A 2W9 (☎ 514/288-4264).

In the United Kingdom, contact the Maison de la France/French Government Tourist Office, 178 Piccadilly, London, W1V 0AL (☎ 020/7399-3540; fax 020/7493-6594).

In Ireland, call the Maison de la France/French Government Tourist Office, 10 Suffolk St., Dublin 2, Ireland (☎ 01/679-0813).

In Australia, contact the **French Tourist Bureau,** 6 Perth Ave., Xarralumia, NSW 2000, Australia (☎ 02/6216-0100; fax 02/9221-8682).

In New Zealand, there's no representative, so you can contact the Australia phone or fax listed above.

3 Entry Requirements & Customs Regulations

DOCUMENTS

All foreign (non-French) nationals need a valid passport to enter France.

The French government no longer requires visas for **U.S. citizens,** providing they're staying in France for less than 90 days. For longer stays, U.S. visitors must apply for a long-term visa, residence card, or temporary-stay visa. Each requires proof of income or a viable means of support in France and a legitimate purpose for remaining in the country. Applications are available from the **Consulate Section of the French Embassy,** 4101 Reservoir Rd. NW, Washington, DC 20007 (☎ 202/944-6000), or from the visa section of the French Consulate at 10 E. 74th St., New York, NY 10021 (☎ 212/606-3689). Visas are required for students planning to study in France even if the stay is for less than 90 days.

At the moment, citizens of **Britain, Canada, New Zealand, Switzerland, Japan,** and **European Union** countries do not need visas.

Australians need visas to enter France. They're available from the French Consulate, Consulate General, 31 Market St., 26th Floor, Sydney, NSW 2000 (☎ 02/9261-5931).

South Africans also need visas to enter France. They're available from the French Consulate, 2 Dean St. (next to Queen Victoria St.), Cape Town 8001 (☎ 0421/23-15-75; fax 021/24-84-70).

CUSTOMS

WHAT YOU CAN BRING INTO FRANCE   Customs restrictions for visitors entering France differ for citizens of the European Union and for citizens of non-EU countries. Non-EU nationals can bring in duty-free 200 cigarettes, 100 cigarillos, 50 cigars, or 250 grams of smoking tobacco. This amount is doubled if you live outside Europe. You can also bring in 2 liters of wine and

Planning Basics

Teeny tiny Monaco (1.21 square miles in all) is technically an independent nation, but you'd hardly know it. Document requirements for travel to Monaco are exactly the same as those for travel to France, and there are virtually no border patrols or passport formalities at the Monégasque frontier. (You will, however, need a coat and tie if you want to wager at the upscale casinos in Monte Carlo.)

If you'd like information specifically about the principality of Monaco, contact the **Monaco Government Tourist and Convention Bureau,** 565 Fifth Ave., 23rd Floor, New York, NY 10017 (☎ **212/286-3330;** fax 212/286-9890). Most of its facilities (along with its consulate) are in New York at the above address.

In London, the office is at 3/18 Chelsea Garden Market, The Chambers, Chelsea Harbour, London SW10 OXF (☎ **029/7352-9962;** fax 020/ 7352-2103).

---

1 liter of alcohol over 22 proof and 2 liters of wine 22 proof or under. In addition, you can bring in 50 grams of perfume, a quarter liter of eau de toilette, 500 grams of coffee, and 200 grams of tea. Visitors ages 15 and over can bring in other goods totaling 300 F ($48); for those 14 and under the limit is 600 F ($96). (Customs officials tend to be lenient about general merchandise, realizing that the limits are unrealistically low.)

Citizens of European Union countries can bring in any amount of goods as long as these goods are intended for their personal use and not for resale.

WHAT YOU CAN BRING HOME   Returning **U.S. citizens** who have been away for 48 hours or more are allowed to bring back, once every 30 days, $400 worth of merchandise duty-free. You'll be charged a flat rate of 10% duty on the next $1,000 worth of purchases. Be sure to have your receipts handy. On gifts, the duty-free limit is $100. You cannot bring fresh foodstuffs into the United States; canned foods, however, are allowed. For more information, contact the **U.S. Customs Service,** 1301 Constitution Ave. (P.O. Box 7407), Washington, DC 20044 (☎ **202/927-6724;** www.customs.ustreas.gov.) and request the free pamphlet *Know Before You Go.* It's also available on the Web at www.customs.ustreas.gov.

Citizens of the U.K. who are **returning from a European Community (EC) country** will go through a separate Customs Exit (called the "Blue Exit") especially for EC travelers. In essence, there is no limit on what you can bring back from an EC country, as long as the items are for personal use (this includes gifts), and you have already paid the necessary duty and tax. However, customs law sets out guidance levels. If you bring in more than these levels, you may be asked to prove that the goods are for your own use. Guidance levels on goods bought in the EC for your own use are 800 cigarettes, 200 cigars, 1kg smoking tobacco, 10 liters of spirits, 90 liters of wine (of this not more than 60 liters can be sparkling wine), and 110 liters of beer. For more information, contact **HM Customs & Excise,** Passenger Enquiry Point, 2nd Floor Wayfarer House, Great South West Road, Feltham, Middlesex, TW14 8NP (☎ **020/8910-3744,** or 44/181-910-3744 from outside the U.K.), or consult their Web site at www.hmce.gov.uk.

For a clear summary of **Canadian** rules, visit the comprehensive Web site of the Canada Customs and Revenue Agency at www.ccra-adrc.gc.ca. You can also write for the booklet *I Declare,* issued by **Revenue Canada,** 2265 St. Laurent Blvd., Ottawa K1G 4KE (☎ **613/993-0534**). Canada allows its citizens a $750 exemption, and you're allowed to bring back duty-free 200 cigarettes, 2.2 pounds of tobacco, 1.5 liters of liquor, and 50 cigars. In addition, you're allowed to mail gifts to Canada from abroad at the rate of Can$60 a day, provided they're unsolicited and don't contain alcohol or tobacco (write on the package "Unsolicited gift, under $60 value").

Citizens of Australia should request the helpful **Australian Customs** brochure *Know Before You Go,* available by calling ☎ **1-300/363-263** from within Australia, or 61-2/6275-6666 from abroad. For additional information, go online to www.dfat.gov.au and click on Hints for Australian Travellers. The duty-free allowance in Australia is A$400 or, for those under 18, A$200. In addition, Australian citizens can bring back 250 cigarettes or 250 grams of loose tobacco, and 1.125 liters of alcohol.

For New Zealand customs information, contact the **New Zealand Customs Service** 50 Anzac Ave., P.O. Box 29, Auckland; ☎ **09/359-6655,** or go online to www.customs.govt.nz. The duty-free allowance for **New Zealand** is NZ$700. Citizens over 17 can bring in 200 cigarettes, or 50 cigars, or 250 grams of tobacco (or a mixture of all three if their combined weight doesn't exceed 250 grams); plus 4.5 liters of wine and beer, or 1.125 liters of liquor.

4 Money

France is one of the world's most expensive destinations. But, to compensate, it often offers top-value food and lodging. Part of the problem is the value-added tax (VAT in English, or TVA in French), which tacks between 6% and 33% on top of everything.

It's expensive to rent and drive a car in France (gasoline is costly, too), and flying within France costs more than flying within the United States. Train travel is relatively inexpensive, however, especially if you purchase a railpass.

Remember that prices in Paris and on the Riviera will be higher than those in the provinces. Three of the most touristed areas—Brittany, Normandy, and the Loire Valley—have reasonably priced hotels and scads of restaurants offering superb food at moderate prices.

THE FRENCH FRANC

The basic unit of French currency is the franc (F), which consists of 100 centimes. Coins are issued in units of 5, 10, 20, and 50 centimes, plus 1, 2, 5, and 10 francs. Notes are denominated in 20, 50, 100, 200, 500, and 1,000 francs.

All banks are equipped for foreign exchange, and you'll find exchange offices at the airports and airline terminals. Banks are open Monday through Friday from 9am to noon and 2 to 4pm. Major bank branches also open their exchange departments on Saturday from 9am to noon.

When converting your home currency into francs, be aware that rates may vary. Your hotel will offer the worst rate. In general, banks offer the best, but even they charge a commission, depending on the transaction. Whenever you can, stick to the big banks of France, like Crédit Lyonnais, which usually offer the best rates and charge the least commission. Always make sure you have enough francs for *le week-end.*

If you need a check denominated in French francs before your trip (for example, to pay a deposit on a hotel room), contact **Ruesch International** (☎ **800/424-2923**). Ruesch performs a wide variety of conversion-related services, usually for $5 to $15 per transaction. You can also inquire at a local bank.

THE EURO

The euro, the new single European currency, became the official currency of France and 10 other countries on January 1, 1999, but not in the form of cash. (There are still no euro banknotes or coins in circulation—payment in euros can only be made by check, credit card, or some other bank-related system.)

The French franc will remain the only currency in France for cash transactions until December 21, 2001, when more and more businesses will start posting their prices in euros alongside those in French francs, which will continue to exist for a while longer. Over a maximum 6-month transition period, French franc banknotes and coins will be withdrawn from circulation.

The symbol of the euro is a stylized **E,** which actually looks like an uppercase C with a horizontal double bar through the middle (€); its official abbreviation is EUR.

Although at this time, very few, if any, French hotel and restaurant bills are actually paid in euros, there will be an increasing emphasis on the new pan-European currency.

ATMS

ATMs are linked to a national network that most likely includes your bank at home. **Cirrus/MasterCard** (☎ **800/424-7787;** www.mastercard.com/atm/) and **PLUS/Visa** (☎ **800/843-7587;** www.visa.com/atms) are the two most popular networks; check the back of your ATM card to see which network your bank belongs to. Use the 800 numbers to locate ATMs in your destination. Cirrus is linked to **Credit Lyonnais, Banque Nationale de Paris, Ceile de France,** and **Société Generale.** PLUS is linked to **Société Generale, Banque National de Paris, Carte Bleue Group,** and **Credit Lyonnais.** You can also ask your bank for a list of overseas ATMs. Be sure to check the daily withdrawal limit. Also, make sure you have a PIN number that you can use in Europe. Depending on the number of digits in your PIN, you may not be able to use your ATM abroad.

TRAVELER'S CHECKS

Traveler's checks are something of an anachronism from the days before the ATM made cash accessible at any time. These days, traveler's checks seem less necessary because most cities have 24-hour ATMs that allow travelers to withdraw small amounts of cash as needed right from their own bank accounts, although you might be subject to a small fee for doing so. But some travelers still prefer the security offered by traveler's checks, since you can get a refund if they're lost or stolen, if you've kept a record of their serial numbers.

You can get traveler's checks at almost any bank. **American Express** offers checks in denominations of $10, $20, $50, $100, $500, and $1,000. You'll pay a service charge ranging from 1% to 4%. You can also get American Express traveler's checks over the phone by calling ☎ **800/221-7282** or 800/721-9768; you can also purchase checks online at **www.americanexpress. com**. AmEx gold or platinum cardholders can avoid paying the fee by ordering over the telephone; platinum cardholders can also purchase checks fee-free in person at AmEx Travel Service locations (check the Web site for the office nearest you). American Automobile Association members can obtain checks fee-free at most AAA offices.

The French Franc, U.S. Dollar, the British Pound & the Euro

For American Readers At this writing, $1 = approximately 6.30 F (or 1 F= 16¢). This was the rate of exchange used to calculate the dollar values given in this book

For British Readers At this writing, £1= approximately 10.10 F (or 1 F = 10 pence), the rate of exchange used to calculate the pound values in the table below.

The Euro As a rough guideline, subject to multiple revisions as the currency increases in viability and visibility, one euro equals approximately 6.6 F, US$1, or 63 pence.

FF	U.S.$	U.K.£	Euro	FF	U.S.$	U.K.£	Euro
1	0.16	0.10	0.15	75.00	12.00	7.5	11.25
2	0.32	0.20	0.30	100.00	16.00	10.00	15.00
3	0.48	0.30	0.45	125.00	20.00	12.50	18.75
4	0.64	0.40	0.60	150.00	24.00	15.00	22.50
5	0.80	0.50	0.75	175.00	28.00	17.50	26.25
6	0.96	0.60	0.90	200.00	32.00	20.00	30.00
7	1.12	0.70	1.05	225.00	36.00	22.50	33.75
8	1.28	0.80	1.20	250.00	40.00	25.00	37.50
9	1.44	0.90	1.35	275.00	44.00	27.50	41.25
10	1.60	1.00	1.50	300.00	48.00	30.00	45.00
15	2.40	1.50	2.25	350.00	56.00	35.00	52.50
20	3.20	2.00	3.00	400.00	64.00	40.00	60.00
25	4.00	2.50	3.75	500.00	80.00	50.00	75.00
50	8.00	5.00	7.50	1000.00	160.00	100.00	150.00

Visa offers traveler's checks at Citibank branches and other financial institutions nationwide; call ☎ **800/227-6811** to locate the purchase location near you. **MasterCard** also offers traveler's checks through **Thomas Cook Currency Services;** call ☎ **800/223-9920** for a location near you.

If you carry traveler's checks, be sure to keep a record of their serial numbers (separately from the checks, of course), so you're ensured a refund in case they're lost or stolen.

CREDIT CARDS

Credit cards are invaluable when traveling. They are a safe way to carry money and provide a convenient record of all your expenses. You can also withdraw cash advances from your credit cards at any bank (though you'll start paying hefty interest on the advance the moment you receive the cash, and you won't receive frequent-flyer miles on an airline credit card). At most banks, you don't even need to go to a teller; you can get a cash advance at the ATM if you know your PIN number. (If you've forgotten your PIN number or didn't even know you had one, call the phone number on the back of your credit card and ask the bank to send it to you. It usually takes 5 to 7 business days, though some banks will provide the number over the phone if you tell them your mother's maiden name or pass some other security clearance.)

Almost every credit card company has an emergency 800-number that you can call if your wallet or purse is stolen. They may be able to wire you a cash advance off your credit card immediately, and in many places, they can deliver an emergency credit card in a day or two. Citicorp Visa's U.S. emergency number is ☎ **800/336-8472.** American Express cardholders and traveler's check holders should call ☎ **800/221-7282** for all money emergencies. MasterCard holders should call ☎ **800/307-7309.**

5 When to Go

July and August are the worst months. Parisians desert their city, leaving it to the crowds of tourists and the businesses that cater to them.

The best time to come to Paris is off-season, either in the uncommonly long spring (April through June) or the equally extensive autumn (September through November), when the tourist trade has trickled to a manageable flow and everything is easier to come by—from Métro seats to good-tempered waiters. The weather, however, is temperate throughout the year.

Hotels used to charge off-season rates during the cold, rainy period from November through February, when tourism slowed; now, however, they're often packed with business clients, trade fairs, and winter tour groups in those months, and there's less incentive for hoteliers to offer big reductions. Airfares, however, are still cheaper in these months, and more promotions are available. They rise in the spring and fall, peaking in the heavily trafficked summer months when tickets will cost the most.

Don't come to Paris in the first 2 weeks of October without a confirmed hotel reservation. The weather's fine, but the city is jammed for the annual motor show, when the French indulge their passion for cars.

WEATHER

France's weather varies considerably from region to region and sometimes from town to town as little as 12 miles apart. Despite its north latitude, Paris never gets very cold—snow is a rarity. The hands-down winner for wetness is Brittany, where Brest (known for the mold that adds flavor to its bleu cheeses—probably caused by the constant rainfall) receives a staggering amount of rain between October and December. The rain usually falls in a kind of steady, foggy drizzle and rarely lasts more than a day. May is the driest month.

The Mediterranean coast in the south has the driest climate. When it does rain, it's usually heaviest in spring and autumn. (Cannes sometimes receives more rainfall than Paris.) Summers are comfortably dry—beneficial to humans but deadly to much of the vegetation, which (unless it's irrigated) often dries and burns up in the parched months.

Provence dreads *le mistral* (an unrelenting, hot, dry, dusty wind), which most often blows in winter for a few days but can last for up to 2 weeks.

For up-to-the-minute weather forecasts, you can get updates from the **Weather Channel** by calling ☎ **900/WEATHER** in the United States (95¢ per minute). The 24-hour service reports on conditions in Paris and several other large cities throughout France.

HOLIDAYS

In France, holidays are known as *jours feriés*. Shops and many businesses (banks and some museums and restaurants) close on holidays, but hotels and emergency services remain open.

The main holidays—a mix of both secular and religious ones—include New Year's Day (January 1), Easter Sunday and Monday (April 15 to 16 in 2001; March 31 to April 2 in 2002), Labor Day (May 1), V-E Day in Europe (May 8), Whit Monday (May 19), Ascension Thursday (40 days after Easter: May 25 in 2001; May 10 in 2002), Bastille Day (July 14), Assumption of the Blessed Virgin (August 15), All Saints' Day (November 1), Armistice Day (November 11), and Christmas (December 25).

France Calendar of Events

January

- **Monte Carlo Motor Rally.** The world's most venerable car race. For more information, call ☎ **92-16-61-66.** Usually mid-January.
- **International Ready-to-Wear Fashion Shows (Le Salon International de Prêt-à-porter),** Parc des Expositions, Porte de Versailles, Paris 15e (☎ **01-44-94-70-00**). Here you'll see what the public will be wearing in 6 months. Mid-January to mid-February.

February

- ✪ **Carnival of Nice.** Float processions, parades, confetti battles, boat races, street music and food, masked balls, and fireworks are all part of this ancient celebration. The climax follows the 113-year-old tradition of burning King Carnival in effigy, an event preceded by Les Batailles des Fleurs (Battles of the Flowers), during which members of opposing teams pelt one another with flowers. Make your hotel reservation well in advance. For information or reservations, contact the **Nice Convention and Visitors Bureau,** 1 esplanade Kennedy (BP 4079), 06302 Nice CEDEX 4 (☎ **04-92-14-48-00;** fax 04-92-14-48-03). Mid-February to early March.

March

- **Foire du Trône,** on the Neuilly Lawn of the Bois de Vincennes, Paris. This mammoth amusement park operates daily from 2pm to midnight. Call ☎ **01-46-27-52-29.** End of March to late May.

April

- **The 24-hour Le Mans Motorcycle Race.** For information, contact Automobile Club de l'ouest (☎ **02-43-40-24-24**).
- **International Marathon of Paris.** Runners from around the world compete. Call ☎ **01-41-33-15-68.** First weekend in April.
- **Son-et-Lumière (Sound-and-Light) Shows,** Loire Valley. April to September.

May

- **Anniversary of the End of World War II,** Paris and Reims. Though the capitulation of the Nazis was signed on May 7, 1945, the celebration lasts several days in Paris, and with even more festivity in Reims. May 5 to 8.
- ✪ **Cannes Film Festival.** Movie madness transforms this city into a media circus, with daily melodramas acted out in cafes, on sidewalks, and in hotel lobbies. Great for people-watching. Reserve early and make a deposit. Getting a table on the Carlton terrace is even more difficult than procuring a room. Admission to some of the prestigious films is by invitation only. There are box-office tickets for the less important films,

which play 24 hours. For information, contact the **Festival Internation-al du Film (FIF),** at 99 bd. Des Malesherbes, 75008 Paris (☎ **01-45-61-66-00;** fax 01-45-61-87-60). Two weeks before the festival, the event's administration moves en masse to the **Palais des Festivals,** esplanade Georges-Pompidou, 06400 Cannes (☎ **04-93-39-01-01**). May 10 to 21.

- **French Open Tennis Championship,** Stade Roland-Garros, 16e (Métro: Porte d'Auteuil). The Open features 10 days of Grand Slam men's and women's tennis. European and South American players tradi-tionally dominate on the hot, red, slow, dusty courts. To get tickets call ☎ **01-97-43-48-60.** Late May to early June.

June

- **Monaco Grand Prix.** Hundreds of cars race through the narrow streets and winding corniche roads in a surreal blend of high-tech machinery and medieval architecture. For more information, call ☎ **01-42-96-12-23.** June 1 to 4.
- **Le Prix du Jockey Club** (June 1 at 2pm) and the **Prix Diane-Hermès** (June 8 at 2pm), Hippodrome de Chantilly. Thoroughbreds from as far away as Kentucky and Brunei, as well as mounts owned by European aristocrats, compete in a very genteel race that's broadcast around France and talked about in horsey circles around the world. On race days, as many as 30 trains depart from Paris's Gare du Nord for Chantilly, where they are met with free shuttle buses to the track. Alternatively, buses depart on race days from Place de la République and Porte de St-Cloud, on a schedule that coincides with the beginning and end of the races. Call ☎ **01-49-10-20-30** for information on this and on all other equine events in this calendar.
- **Cinéscénie de Puy du Fou,** son-et-lumière at the Château du Puy du Fou, Les Epesses (Poitou-Charentes). With a cast of 650 actors, dozens of horses, laser shows, and a soundtrack by famous actors, it celebrates the achievements of the Middle Ages. For information, call ☎ **02-51-64-11-11.** Early June to early September.
- **Les Nocturnes du Mont-St-Michel.** This is a sound-and-light tour through the maze of stairways and corridors of one of Europe's most impressive medieval monuments. Performances are Monday to Saturday evenings from June to mid-September. In the off-season, performances are on Saturday and Sunday only. For more information, call **02-33-89-80-00.**
- **Festival de St-Denis.** This series presents 4 days of music in the burial place of the French kings, a grim early Gothic monument in Paris's industrialized northern suburb of St-Denis. Call ☎ **01-48-13-06-07** for information; Métro: St-Denis-Basilique. June 13 to 16.
- **Paris Air Show.** This is where the military-industrial complex of France shows off enough high-tech hardware to make anyone think twice about invading La Patrie. Fans, competitors, and industrial spies mob the exhi-bition halls of Le Bourget Airport for a taste of what Gallic technocrats have wrought. For information, call ☎ **01-53-23-33-33.** Mid-June in alternate years only. The 2001 dates are June 15 to June 19.
- **The 24-Hour Le Mans Car Race.** For information, contact Automobile Club de l'ouest (☎ **02-43-40-24-24**). June 17 to 18.
- **Festival Chopin,** Paris. Everything you've ever wanted to hear from the Polish exile who lived most of his life in Paris. Piano recitals are held in

the Orangerie du Parc de Bagatelle. For information, call ☎ **01-45-00-22-19.** June 17 to July 14.

- **Gay Pride Parade,** Paris. A week of expositions and parties climaxes in a massive parade patterned after those in New York and San Francisco. It begins at place de l'Odéon and proceeds to place de la Bastille, then is followed by the Grand Bal de Gay Pride at the Palais de Bercy, a major convention hall/sports arena. For information, contact Centre Gai et Lesbien, 3 rue Keller, 75011 Paris (☎ **01-43-57-21-47**). June 24, 2001.
- **La Villette Jazz Festival.** Some 50 concerts are held in churches, auditoriums, and concert halls in all neighborhoods of the Paris suburb of La Villette. Past festivals have included Herbie Hancock, Shirley Horn, Michel Portal, and other artists from around Europe and the world. For information, call ☎ **08-03-30-63-06.** Late June to early July.

July

- **Colmar International Music Festival,** Colmar. Different classical musical concerts are held in various public buildings of one of the most folkloric towns in Alsace. For more information, call ☎ **03-89-20-68-92.** July 1 to July 15.
- **Le Grand Tour de France.** Europe's most prominent, most highly contested, and most overabundantly televised bicycle race pits crews of wind-tunnel-tested athletes along an itinerary that detours deep into the Massif Central and ranges across the Alps. The race is decided at a finish line drawn across the Champs-Elysées. For information, call ☎ **01-41-33-15-00.** July 3 to 21.
- ✪ **Festival d'Avignon.** One of France's most prestigious theater events, this world-class festival has a reputation for exposing new talent to critical acclaim. The focus is usually on avant-garde works in theater, dance, and music by groups from around the world. Make hotel reservations early. For information, call ☎ **04-32-74-32-74** or fax 04-90-82-95-03. July 5 to July 30.
- ✪ **Festival d'Aix-en-Provence.** A musical event par excellence, featuring everything from Gregorian chant to melodies composed on computer synthesizers. The audience sits on the sloping lawns of the 14th-century papal palace for operas and concerti. Local recitals are performed in the medieval cloister of the Cathédrale St-Sauveur. Make advance hotel reservations and bring written confirmation with you. Expect heat, crowds, and traffic. For information, contact the Festival International d'Art Lyrique et Academie Europeénne de Musique, Palais de l'Ancien Archevêche, 13100 Aix-en-Provence (☎ **04-42-17-34-34;** fax 04-42-66-13-74). July 7 to 28.
- **Les Chorégies d'Orange,** Orange. One of southern France's most important lyric festivals presents oratorios and choral works by master performers whose voices are amplified by the ancient acoustics of France's best-preserved Roman amphitheater. For information, call ☎ **04-90-34-24-24.** July 12 to August 1.
- ✪ **Bastille Day.** Celebrating the birth of modern-day France, the nation's festivities reach their peak in Paris with street fairs, pageants, fireworks, and feasts. In Paris, the day begins with a parade down the Champs-Elysées and ends with fireworks at Montmartre. No matter where you are, by the end of the day you'll hear Edith Piaf warbling "La Foule" (The Crowd), the song that celebrated her passion for the stranger she met and later lost in a crowd on Bastille Day. July 14.

- **Paris Quartier d'Eté.** These 4 weeks of music evoke the style of the pop orchestral music of an English village green. The setting is either the Arènes de Lutèce or the Cour d'Honneur at the Sorbonne, both in the Latin Quarter. The dozen or so concerts are usually grander than the outdoorsy setting would imply and include performances by the Orchestre de Paris, the Orchestre National de France, and the Baroque Orchestra of the European Union. Spin-offs of this include plays and jazz concerts. For information, call ☎ **01-44-94-98-00** or fax 01-44-94-98-01. July 15 to August 15.

- ✪ **Nice Jazz Festival.** This is the biggest, flashiest, and most prestigious jazz festival in Europe, with world-class entertainers. Concerts begin in early afternoon and go on until late at night (sometimes all night in the clubs) on the Arènes de Cimiez, a hill above the city. Reserve hotel rooms way in advance. For information, contact the Grand Parade du Jazz, Cultural Affairs Department of the city of Nice (☎ **04-93-92-82-82**; fax 04-93-92-82-85). July 22 to 29.

- **St-Guilhem Music Season,** St-Guilhem le Désert (Languedoc). This festival of baroque organ and choral music is held in a medieval monastery. For information, call ☎ **04-67-63-14-99.** July 25 to August 19.

August

- **Festival Interceltique de Lorient,** Brittany. Traditional Celtic verse and lore are celebrated in the Celtic heart of France. The 150 concerts include 3,500 classical and folkloric musicians, dancers, singers, and painters from all over. Traditional Breton pardons (religious processions) take place in this once-independent maritime duchy. For information, call ☎ **02-97-21-24-29.** First week of August.

- ✪ **Festival International de Folklore et Fête de la Vigne (Les Folkloriades),** Dijon, Beaune, and about 20 villages of the Côte d'Or. At the International Festival of Folklore and Wine in Dijon, dance troupes from around the world perform, parade, and participate in folkloric events in celebration of the famous wines of Burgundy. For information, contact the Festival de Musique et Danse Populares, 27 bd. de la Tremouille, 21025 Dijon (☎ **03-80-30-37-95**; fax 03-80-30-23-44). Late August and early September.

September

- **Festival Musique en l'Île.** A series of concerts, mostly dignified masses composed between the 17th and late 19th centuries, are given within medieval churches in the 4th, 5th, and 6th arrondissements. Sites include St-Louis-en-l'Île, St-Severin, and St-Germain-des-Prés. Call ☎ **01-43-55-47-09** for more information. September 5 to October 17.

- **Festival d'Automne,** Paris. One of France's most famous festivals in France is also one of its most eclectic, concentrating mainly on modern music, ballet, theater, and modern art. Tickets cost 100 F to 300 F ($18 to $54), depending on the venue. For details, call or write to the Festival d'Automne, 156 rue de Rivoli, 75001 Paris (☎ **01-53-45-17-01**; fax 01-53-45-17-01). During the festival itself, call ☎ **01-53-45-17-17** to reserve tickets for any of the events. Mid-September to mid-December.

- **International Ready-to-Wear Fashion Shows** (Le Salon International de Prêt-à-porter), Parc des Expositions, Porte de Versailles, Paris. Late September.

Getting Tickets

Edwards and Edwards can order tickets to many of the musical or theatrical events at the Avignon festival, as well as at other cultural events throughout France. You'll pay an extremely hefty fee (as much as 20%) for the convenience. Contact them at 1270 Ave. of the Americas, Suite 2414, New York, NY 10020 (☎ **800/223-6108**).

October
- **Perpignan Jazz Festival.** Musicians from everywhere jam in what many visitors consider Languedoc's most appealing season. For information, call ☎ **04-68-66-30-30.** Throughout October and November.
- **Festival d'Automne,** Paris. Ballet performances, both classical and modern, are presented, along with theatrical performances, contemporary music performances, and exhibitions of modern art. The venues occur all over town. Throughout October.
- ✪ **Paris Auto Show,** Parc des Expositions, near the Porte de Versailles in western Paris. This is the showcase for European car design, complete with glistening metal, glitzy attendees, lots of hype, and the latest models from world automakers. Check *Pariscope* for details or contact the French Government Tourist Office (see "Visitor Information" earlier in this chapter), or call ☎ **01-56-88-22-40.** Fifteen days in early October.
- **Prix de l'Arc de Triomphe.** France's answer to England's Ascot is the country's most prestigious horse race, culminating the equine season in Europe. Hippodrome de Longchamp, 16e (☎ **01-49-10-20-30**). Early October.

November
- **Festival d'Automne,** Paris. Throughout November.
- **Armistice Day,** nationwide. In Paris, the signing of the controversial document that ended World War I is celebrated with a military parade from the Arc de Triomphe to the Hôtel des Invalides. November 11.
- **Les Trois Glorieuses,** Clos-de-Vougeot, Beaune, and Meursault. The country's most important wine festival is celebrated in three Burgundian towns. Though you may not gain access to many of the gatherings, there are enough wine tastings and other amusements to keep you occupied. Festivities include wine auctions from some of the district's most historic cellars. Reserve early or visit as part of day trips from any of several nearby villages. Confirm information by contacting the Office de Tourisme de Beaune, rue de l'Hôtel-Dieu, 21200 Beaune (☎ **03-80-26-21-30**). Third week in November.
- **City of Paris's Festival of Sacred Art.** This dignified series of concerts is held in five of the oldest and most recognizable Paris churches. For information, call ☎ **01-44-70-64-10.** Mid-November to mid-December.

December
- **Festival d'Automne,** Paris. Through late December.
- **The Boat Fair** (Le Salon International de la Navigation de Plaisance). Europe's most visible exposition of what's afloat and of interest to wholesalers, retailers, individual boat owners (or wanna-bes), and anyone involved in the business of waterborne holiday-making. Parc des Expositions, Porte de Versailles, Paris, 15e (☎ **01-41-90-47-10;** fax

01-41-90-47-00; Métro: Porte de Versailles). The fair lasts for 8 days in early December.

- **Fête des Lumières,** Lyon. In honor of the Virgin, lights are placed in thousands of windows throughout the city. December 8 until sometime after Christmas.
- **Foire de Noël,** Mougins. Hundreds of merchants, selling all manner of Christmas ornaments and gifts, descend on Mougins, a small but choice village in Provence, to herald the Christmas spirit. December 11 and 12.
- **Christmas Fairs,** Alsace (especially Strasbourg). More than 60 Alsatian villages celebrate a traditional Christmas. The events in Strasbourg have continued for some 430 years. Other towns with noteworthy celebrations are Münster, Selestat, Riquewihr, Kaysersberg, Saverne, Wissembourg, and Than. Late November to December 24.
- **Fête de St-Sylvestre (New Year's Eve),** nationwide. In Paris, it's most boisterously celebrated in the Quartier Latin around the Sorbonne. At midnight, the city explodes. Strangers kiss strangers and boulevard St-Michel and the Champs-Elysées become virtual pedestrian malls. December 31.

6 Special-Interest Vacations

BALLOONING The world's largest hot-air-balloon operator is **Bombard Society,** 333 Pershing Way, West Palm Beach, FL 33401 (☎ **800/862-8537** or 561/837-6610; fax 561/837-6623). It maintains about three dozen hot-air balloons, some stationed in the Loire Valley and Burgundy. The 5-day/4-night tours, costing $5,988 per person (double occupancy), incorporate food and wine tasting and include all meals, lodging in Relais & Châteaux hotels, sightseeing, rail transfers to and from Paris, and a daily balloon ride over vineyards and fields. Lunches are served in the best restaurants in the district; dinners are elegant picnics offered hunt-board style after a daily late-afternoon balloon ride.

Bonaventura Balloon Co., 133 Wall Rd., Napa, CA 94558 (☎ **800/ 359-6272**), meets you in Paris and takes you via high-speed TGV train to Burgundy, where your balloon tour begins, carrying you over the most scenic parts of the region. Guests stay in a 14th-century mill converted into an inn and owned by a three-star chef. An 8-night/9-day trip is $2,595 per person, including a full day sightseeing in Paris, two balloon excursions, lodging, cooking classes, wine tasting, and at least one meal per day.

BARGE CRUISES Before the advent of the railways, many of the crops, building supplies, raw materials, and finished products of France were barged through a series of rivers, canals, and estuaries. Many of these waterways are still graced with their old-fashioned locks and pumps, allowing shallow-draft barges easy access through the idyllic countryside. Many companies offer wonderful barging tours.

French Country Waterways, P.O. Box 2195, Duxbury, MA 02331 (☎ **800/222-1236** or 781/934-2454), leads 1-week tours focusing on Burgundy and Champagne. For double occupancy, the price ranges from $2,995 to $4,595.

Le Boat, 105 Franklin Turnpike, Suite 204-B, Ramsey, NJ 07446 (☎ **800/ 992-0291** or 201/236-2333), focuses on regions of France not covered by many other barge operators. The company's pair of barges are luxury craft of a size and shape that fit through the relatively narrow canals and locks of the

Camarque, Languedoc, and Provence. Each 6-night tour involves no more than 10 passengers in five cabins outfitted with mahogany and brass, plus meals prepared by a Cordon Bleu chef. Prices depend on many factors and are highly variable. However, 6 nights in Upper Burgundy will cost $1,990 per person, double occupancy. Six nights in the Upper Loire begin at $1,690 per person, rising to $4,000 per person in the peak summer season.

European Waterways, 140 E. 56th St., Suite 4C, New York, NY 10022 (☎ **800/456-4777** or 212/688-9489; fax 800/296-4554 or 212/688-3778), operates Great Island Voyages, a program featuring river cruise ships that ply Europe's historic rivers. The *Lafayette, Litote,* and *Escargot* traverse France's Burgundy region. Fares range from $1,990 to $3,500 per person (double occupancy) for a 1-week cruise. Bicycles are carried on board for sightseeing trips. This company also offers cruises in the Loire Valley and the south of France.

The Crown Blue Line, c/o Maupintour, 1515 St. Andrews Dr., Lawrence, KS 66407 (☎ **800/243-6244**), acts as a clearinghouse for the chartering of at least 400 cruise craft, each with a shallow draft, that can slowly navigate the locks and channels of France's waterways. You choose from among 27 kinds of boats, each suitable for between two and about a dozen passengers. Charters last for a week and can be arranged with a staff. Plan on cruising no more than 5 hours a day, then devoting the rest of your holiday to exploring the countryside, perhaps via bicycle. A 7-day rental of any of the vessels costs from $12,000 and up, depending on its capacity and the season.

With **Premier Selections,** 106 Calvert St., Harrison, NY 10528 (☎ **800/234-4000** or 914/835-5555; fax 914/835-8756), discover the secret corners of France as you wend your way along waterways on board a luxury hotel barge. Enjoy fine wines and cuisine, bicycling, walking, and exploring. Visit châteaux, old towns, and timeless villages. Its fleet can accommodate individuals as well as groups and offers a wide array of cruising areas, including Burgundy, Champagne, the Upper Loire, Alsace-Lorraine, and the south of France. Inclusive fares per person for 3 nights (double occupancy) begin at $1,495, with 6 nights beginning at $2,615.

BIKING TOURS   Holland Bicycling Tours, P.O. Box 6086, Huntington Beach, CA 92615 (☎ **800/852-3258;** fax 714/593-1710), leads 10-day bicycle tours through Brittany and Normandy, incorporating visits to medieval monasteries, to Romanesque and early Gothic cathedrals, and past the jagged granite coastlines that painters and poets always found so intriguing. The price of the land portion (without airfare) is $1,750 per person. An equivalent 10-day tour through Provence, incorporating views of van Gogh's sunflowers, ancient Roman ruins, and fields pungent with lavender, thyme, and basil is $1,850 per person. Both prices include double occupancy hotel accommodations, all breakfasts and dinners, bike rentals, the services of a tour leader, and rides whenever it's necessary in a touring van.

Châteaux Bike Tours, P.O. Box 5706, Denver, CO 80217 (☎ **800/678-2453**), promotes luxury tours of France with small groups, van supports, two guides, and stays in châteaux. Tours (usually for 5 to 16 people) range from 5 to 9 days and cost $2,500 to $3,700 per person, double occupancy.

Classic Adventures, P.O. Box 143, Hamlin, NY 14464 (☎ **800/777-8090**), sponsors 7- to 11-day spring and fall tours of the Loire Valley, Burgundy, and the Dordogne. Accommodations are upscale, and all tours are van supported and escorted. The 7-day/6-night tours are $1,889 per person for the Loire Valley and $1,889 per person for Burgundy; an 11-day/10-night tour of the Dordogne is $2,489 per person.

Euro-Bike Tours, P.O. Box 990, DeKalb, IL 60115 (☎ **800/321-6060**), offers 10-day tours in the Dordogne ($2,495 per person), 11-day tours in Provence ($2,845 per person), 6-day tours of Burgundy ($1,645 per person), and 8-day tours of the Loire Valley ($2,195). All are supported and escorted. Finally, **Uniquely Europe** (a subsidiary of Europe Express), 1805 N. Creek Parkway, Suite 100, Bothell, WA 98011 (☎ **800/426-3615**), has biking and walking tours of Alsace, Burgundy, the Dordogne, the Loire Valley, and Provence. A 7-day guided bike tour is $2,149 to $2,227 per person, double occupancy; a 7- or 8-day self-guided bike tour is $988 to $1,891 per person, double occupancy. Each of this company's tours include overnight accommodations and most meals, but whereas guided tours include van support and a guide, non-guided tours don't offer van support or a constant guide, but you'll always have the name of an English-speaking local contact to guide self-starters through any rough spots in the cultural adjustments to the French countryside.

COOKING SCHOOLS If you've always wanted to learn to cook *à la française,* you can take those all-important lessons from Maxime and Eliane Rochereau at their hotel/restaurant, **Le Castel de Bray-et-Monts,** Brehemont, 37130 Langeais (☎ **02-47-96-70-47;** fax 02-47-96-57-36; www.cooking-class-infrance.com). Before settling on the banks of the Loire, in the heart of châteaux country, the Rochereaux spent 15 years living and working in the United States—Maxime as chef de cuisine at Chicago's Ritz-Carlton and Palm Beach's Breakers, Eliane as a caterer for the Palm Beach jet set. In the charming vineyard village of Brehemont, Maxime now offers classes in classic French cooking at an 18th-century manor surrounded by a magnificent garden and stream. Classes are in English; the price, including a week's accommodation and full board, is 9,800 F ($1,568) per person, double occupancy. No classes are conducted during December and January.

The famous/infamous Georges-Auguste Escoffier (1846–1935) taught the Edwardians how to eat. Today Le Ritz, once the site of many of Escoffier's meals, maintains the **Ritz-Escoffier École de Gastronomie Française,** 15 place Vendôme, 75001 Paris (☎ **888/801-1126** in the U.S., or 01-43-16-30-50), offering demonstration classes of the master's techniques on Monday, Tuesday, and Thursday afternoons. These demonstrations cost 275 F ($44) each. Courses, taught in French and English, start at 6,000 F ($960) for 1 week, going up to 72,000 F ($11,520) for 12 weeks.

Le Cordon Bleu, 8 rue Léon-Delhomme, 75015 Paris (☎ **800/457-CHEF** in the U.S., or 01-53-68-22-50), established in 1895, is the most famous French cooking school—this is where Julia Child learned to perfect her *pâté brisée* and *mousse au chocolat.* Bon appétit! Its best-known courses last 10 weeks, at the end of which certificates are issued. Many gourmet enthusiasts prefer a less intense immersion and opt for either a 4-day workshop or a 3-hour demonstration class. Enrollment in either of these is on a first-come, first-served basis; costs are 220 F ($35.20) for a demonstration and around 4,000 F ($640) for the 4-day workshop. Classes are in English.

LANGUAGE SCHOOLS The **Alliance Française,** 101 bd. Raspail, 75270 Paris, CEDEX 06 (☎ **01-45-44-38-28;** fax 01-45-44-25-95), is a state-approved nonprofit organization with a network of 1,100 establishments in 138 countries, offering French-language courses to some 350,000 students. The international school in Paris is open all year; month-long courses range from 1,600 F to 3,200 F ($256 to $512). Write for information and application forms at least 1 month before your departure. In North America, the largest branch is the **Alliance Française,** 2819 Ordway St. NW, Washington, DC 20008 (☎ **800/6-FRANCE;** fax 202/362-1587).

A clearinghouse for information on French-language schools is **Lingua Service Worldwide,** 75 Prospect St., Suite 4, Huntington, NY 10743 (☎ **800/394-LEARN** or 212/867-1225; fax 212/983-2590; www.linguaserviceworldwide. com). Its programs cover not only Paris but also Aix-en-Provence, Antibes, Avignon, Bordeaux, Cannes, Nice, St. Malo, Tours, and others. They range from $425 to $993 for 2 weeks, depending on the city, the school, and the accommodations.

7 Health & Insurance

STAYING HEALTHY

If you suffer from a chronic illness, consult your doctor before your departure. For conditions like epilepsy, diabetes, or heart problems, wear a **Medic Alert Identification Tag** (☎ **800/825-3785;** www.medicalert.org), which will immediately alert doctors to your condition and give them access to your records through Medic Alert's 24-hour hot line. Membership is $35, plus a $15 annual fee.

Pack prescription medications in your carry-on luggage. Carry written prescriptions in generic, not brand-name form, and dispense all prescription medications from their original labeled vials. Also bring along copies of your prescriptions in case you lose your pills or run out.

Contact the **International Association for Medical Assistance to Travelers (IAMAT;** ☎ **716/754-4883** or 416/652-0137; www.sentedex.net/~iamat). This organization offers tips on travel and health concerns in the countries you'll be visiting, and lists many local English-speaking doctors.

TRAVEL INSURANCE

There are three kinds of travel insurance: trip-cancellation, medical, and lost-luggage coverage. **Trip-cancellation insurance** is a good idea if you have paid a large portion of your vacation expenses up front (say, by purchasing a package deal). The other two types of insurance, however, don't make sense for most travelers. Rule number one: Check your existing policies before you buy any additional coverage.

Your existing health insurance should cover you if you get sick while on vacation—though if you belong to an HMO, you should check to see whether you are fully covered when away from home. For independent travel health-insurance providers, see below.

Your homeowner's or renter's insurance should cover stolen luggage. The airlines are responsible for losses up to $2,500 on domestic flights if they lose your luggage (finally upped in early 2000 from the old 1984 limit of $1,250); if you plan to carry anything more valuable than that, keep it in your carry-on bag.

The differences between **travel assistance** and insurance are often blurred, but in general, the former offers on-the-spot assistance and 24-hour hot lines (mostly oriented toward medical problems), while the latter reimburses you for travel problems (medical, travel, or otherwise) after you have filed the paperwork. The coverage you should consider will depend on how much protection is already contained in your existing health insurance or other policies. Some credit- and charge-card companies may insure you against travel accidents if you buy plane, train, or bus tickets with their cards. Before purchasing additional insurance, read your policies and agreements over carefully. Call your insurers or credit-card companies if you have any questions.

Travel Tip

If you're buying a package vacation or tour, don't buy your trip-cancellation insurance from your tour operator—talk about putting all of your eggs in one basket! Buy it from an outside vendor instead.

Some credit cards (American Express and certain gold and platinum Visa and MasterCards, for example) offer automatic **flight insurance** for death or dismemberment in case of an airplane crash at basic limits, and allow you to purchase additional coverage through them.

If you do require additional insurance, try one of the companies listed below. But don't pay for more than you need. If you need only trip-cancellation insurance, don't purchase coverage for lost or stolen property, which should be covered by your homeowner's or renter's policy. Trip-cancellation insurance costs approximately 6% to 8% of the total value of your vacation.

Among the reputable issuers of travel insurance are **Access America** (☎ 800/284-8300; www.accessamerica.com); **Travel Guard International** (☎ 800/826-1300; www.travel-guard.com); and **Travelex Insurance Services** (☎ 888/457-4602; www.travelex-insurance.com).

8 Tips for Travelers with Special Needs

FOR TRAVELERS WITH DISABILITIES   Facilities for travelers with disabilities are certainly above average in Europe, and nearly all modern **hotels** in France now provide rooms designed for persons with disabilities. However, older hotels (unless they've been renovated) may not provide such important features as elevators, special toilet facilities, or ramps for wheelchair access.

The new high-speed **TGV trains** are wheelchair accessible; older trains have special compartments for wheelchair boarding. On the **Paris Métro,** those with disabilities are able to sit in wider seats provided for their comfort. Guide dogs ride free. But some stations don't have escalators or elevators, so these present problems.

There are agencies in the United States and France that can provide advance-planning information. Knowing in advance which hotels, restaurants, and attractions are wheelchair accessible can save you a lot of frustration—firsthand accounts by other travelers with disabilities are the best.

The **Association des Paralysés de France,** 17 bd. Auguste-Blanqui, 75013 Paris (☎ 01-40-78-69-00), is a privately funded organization that provides documentation, moral support, and travel ideas for individuals who use wheelchairs. In addition to the central Paris office, it maintains an office in each of the 90 *départements* of France and can help find accessible hotels, transportation, sightseeing, house rentals, and (in some cases) companionship for paralyzed or partially paralyzed travelers. It's not, however, a travel agency.

Travelers with disabilities may also want to consider joining a tour that caters specifically to them. One of the best operators is **Flying Wheels Travel,** 143 West Bridge (P.O. Box 382), Owatonna, MN 55060 (☎ 800/535-6790). They offer various escorted tours and cruises, with an emphasis on sports, as well as private tours in minivans with lifts.

Other helpful organizations are the **American Foundation for the Blind,** 11 Penn Plaza, Suite 300, New York, NY 10001 (☎ 800/232-5463 or 212/502-7600); **The Lighthouse, Inc.,** 111 E. 59th St., New York, NY 10022 (☎ 800/829-0500 or 212/821-9200; www.lighthouse.org); and the

New York Society for the Deaf, 817 Broadway, 7th floor, New York, NY 10003 (☎ **212/777-3900** TTY/voice; www.nysd.org).

In the United Kingdom, **RADAR** (Royal Association for Disability and Rehabilitation), Unit 12, City Forum, 250 City Rd., London ECIV 8AF (☎ **020/7250-3222;** fax 020/200-0212), publishes holiday "fact packs" (three in all), which sell for £2 each or a set of all three for £5. The first one provides general information, including planning and booking a holiday, insurance, finances, and useful organization and holiday providers. The second outlines transport and equipment, transportation available when going abroad, and equipment for rent. The third deals with specialized accommodations.

Another good resource is the **Holiday Care Service,** 2nd floor, Imperial Buildings, Victoria Road, Horley, Surrey RH6 7PZ, UK (☎ **01293/ 774-535;** fax 01293/784-647), a national charity that advises on accessible accommodations for elderly and persons with disabilities. Once a member, you can receive a newsletter and access to a free reservations network for hotels throughout Britain and, to a lesser degree, Europe and the rest of the world.

FOR GAY & LESBIAN TRAVELERS   Paris vies with London and Amsterdam as Europe's gay and lesbian capital. France is one of the world's most tolerant countries, and Paris, of course, is the center of French gay life, though gay and lesbian establishments exist throughout the country as well, especially on the Riviera.

Before going to France, both lesbians and gay men might want to pick up a copy of *Frommer's Gay & Lesbian Europe.*

"Gay Paree," with one of the world's largest homosexual populations, has dozens of gay clubs, restaurants, organizations, and services. Other than the publications listed below, one of the best sources of information on gay and lesbian activities is **Centre Gai and Lesbien,** 3 rue Keller, 75011 (☎ **01-43-57-21-47;** Métro: Bastille). Well equipped to dispense information, and to coordinate the activities and meetings of gay people from virtually everywhere, it's open daily from 2 to 6pm. Sundays, they adopt a format known as **Le Café Positif,** and feature music, cabaret, and information about AIDS and the care for and prevention of sexually transmitted diseases.

SOS Écoute Gay (☎ **01-44-93-01-02**) is a gay hot line, theoretically designed as a way to creatively counsel persons with gay-related problems— the phone is answered by volunteers, some of whom are not as skilled and helpful as others. A phone counselor responds to calls Monday and Wednesday 8am to 10pm; Tuesday, Thursday, Friday 6 to 8pm.

Another helpful source is **La Maison des Femmes,** 163 rue de Charenton, 12e (☎ **01-43-43-41-13;** Métro: Reuilly-Diderot), offering information about Paris for lesbians and bisexual women and sometimes sponsoring informal dinners and get-togethers. Call any Wednesday from 4 to 7pm for further information.

Gai Pied's publication *Guide Gai* (revised annually) is the best source of information on gay and lesbian clubs, hotels, organizations, and services— even restaurants. Lesbian or bisexual women might also like to pick up a copy of *Lesbia,* if only to check out the ads. These publications and others are available at Paris's largest and best-stocked gay bookstore, **Les Mots à la Bouche,** 6 rue Ste-Croix-de-la-Bretonnerie, 4e (☎ **01-42-78-88-30**). Hours are Monday through Saturday from 11am to 11pm, Sunday from 2 to 8pm. Both French- and English-language publications are available.

If you want help planning your trip, **The International Gay & Lesbian Travel Association** (IGLTA; ☎ **800/448-8550** or 954/776-2626; www.iglta. org), can link you up with the appropriate gay-friendly service organization or tour specialist. With around 1,200 members, it offers quarterly newsletters, marketing mailings, and a membership directory that's updated quarterly. Members are kept informed of gay and gay-friendly hoteliers, tour operators, and airline and cruise-line representatives.

Out and About (☎ **800/929-2268** or 212/645-6922; www.outandabout. com) has been hailed for its "straight" reporting about gay travel. It offers a monthly newsletter packed with good information on the global gay and lesbian scene. There are also two good, biannual English-language gay guidebooks, both focused on gay men but including information for lesbians as well. You can get the *Spartacus International Gay Guide* or *Odysseus* from most gay and lesbian book stores, or order them from Giovanni's Room (☎ **215/923-2960**) or from A Different Light Bookstore (☎ **800/343-4002** or 212/989-4850; www.adlbooks.com). Both lesbians and gays might want to pick up a copy of *Gay Travel A to Z* ($16). *The Ferrari Guides* (www. q-net.com) is yet another very good series of gay and lesbian guidebooks.

General gay and lesbian travel agencies include **Family Abroad** (☎ **800/ 999-5500** or 212/459-1800; gay and lesbian); and **Above and Beyond Tours** (☎ **800/397-2681;** mainly gay men).

FOR SENIORS Many discounts are available in France for seniors—men and women who've reached the "third age," as the French say. For more information, contact the French Government Tourist Office (see "Visitor Information," earlier in this chapter).

At any rail station in the country, seniors (men and women age 60 and older—with proof of age) can obtain **A La Carte Senior.** The pass goes for 285F ($48.45) and is good for a 50% discount on unlimited rail travel throughout 1 year.

There are some restrictions on the carte—for example, you can't use it between 3pm Sunday and noon Monday and from noon Friday to noon Saturday. There's no discount on the Paris network of commuter trains. The carte also delivers reduced prices on certain regional bus lines, as well as half-price admission at state-owned museums.

The French domestic airline **Air France** honors "third agers" by offering a 10% reduction on its regular nonexcursion tariffs. Restrictions do apply, however. Also, discounts of around 10% are offered to passengers age 62 and over on selected Air France international flights. Be sure to ask for the discount when booking, as some restrictions do apply.

Members of the **American Association of Retired Persons (AARP),** 601 E St. NW, Washington, DC 20049 (☎ **800/424-3410;** www.aarp.org), get discounts on hotels, airfares, and car rentals. The AARP offers members a wide range of special benefits, including *Modern Maturity* magazine and a monthly newsletter. If you're not already a member, do yourself a favor and join.

At any rail station in the country, seniors (men and women age 60 and older—with proof of age) can obtain **A La Carte Senior.** The pass goes for 285 F ($45.60) and is good for a 50% discount on unlimited rail travel throughout 1 year.

Golden Companions, P.O. Box 5249, Reno, NV 89513 (☎ **800/ 392-1256**), helps travelers 45-plus find compatible companions through a personal voice-mail service. Contact them for more information.

Grand Circle Travel is one of the hundreds of travel agencies specializing in vacations for seniors (☎ **800/221-2610** or 617/350-7500). Many of these packages, however, are of the tour-bus variety, with free trips thrown in for those who organize groups of 10 or more. Seniors seeking more independent travel should probably consult a regular travel agent. **SAGA International Holidays,** 222 Berkeley St., Boston, MA 02116 (☎ **800/343-0273**), offers inclusive tours for those 50 and older. SAGA also sponsors the more substantial "Road Scholar Tours" (☎ **800/621-2151**), which are fun-loving but with an educational bent.

If you want something more than the average vacation or guided tour, try **Elderhostel** (☎ **877/426-8056;** www.elderhostel.org) or the University of New Hampshire's **Interhostel** (☎ **800/733-9753**), both variations on the same theme: educational travel for senior citizens. On these escorted tours, the days are packed with seminars, lectures, and field trips, and all sightseeing is led by academic experts. The courses in both these programs are ungraded, involve no homework, and often focus on the liberal arts. They're not luxury vacations, but they're fun and fulfilling.

FOR STUDENTS   The best resource for students is the **Council on International Educational Exchange,** or CIEE, 6 Hamilton Place, Boston, MA 02108. They can set you up with an ID card (see below), and their travel branch, **Council Travel Service** (☎ **800/226-8624;** www.counciltravel.com), is the biggest student travel agency operation in the world. It can get you discounts on plane tickets, railpasses, and the like. Ask them for a list of CTS offices in major cities so you can keep the discounts flowing (and aid lines open) as you travel.

From CIEE you can obtain the student traveler's best friend, the $20 **International Student Identity Card** (ISIC). It's the only officially acceptable form of student identification, good for cut rates on railpasses, plane tickets, and other discounts. It also provides you with basic health and life insurance and a 24-hour help line. If you're no longer a student but are still under 26, you can get a GO 25 card from the same people, also for $20, which will get you the insurance and some of the discounts (but not student admission prices in museums).

In Canada, **Travel CUTS,** 200 Ronson St., Ste. 320, Toronto, ONT M9W 5Z9 (☎ **800/667-2887** or 416/614-2887, or 020/7528-6113 in London; www.travelcuts.com), offers similar services. **Usit Campus,** 52 Grosvenor Gardens, London SW1W 0AG (☎ **020/7730-3402;** www.usitcampus.co.uk), opposite Victoria Station, is Britain's leading specialist in student and youth travel.

9 Flying to France from North America

Flying time to Paris is about 7 hours from New York or Washington, D.C., 8 hours from Atlanta or Miami, 9 hours from Chicago, and 11 hours from Los Angeles.

The two Parisian airports—Orly and Charles de Gaulle—are almost even bets in terms of convenience to the city's center, though taxi rides from Orly might take a bit less time than those from de Gaulle. Orly, the older of the two, is 8 miles south of the center, whereas Charles de Gaulle is 14 miles northeast. In April 1996 the last of Air France's flights to Orly from North America was rerouted to Charles de Gaulle (Terminal 2C). U.S. carriers tend to land at both airports in equal measure.

Most airlines divide their year into roughly seasonal slots, with the lowest fares between November 1 and March 13. Shoulder season (October and mid-March to mid-June) is only slightly more expensive. We think it's the ideal time to visit France.

THE MAJOR AIRLINES

American Airlines (☎ 800/433-7300; www.aa.com) offers daily flights to Paris from Dallas/Fort Worth, Chicago, Miami, Boston, and New York.

British Airways (☎ 800/AIRWAYS) offers flights from 18 U.S. cities to Heathrow and Gatwick airports in England. From there, you can book any number of British Airways flights to Paris.

Continental Airlines (☎ 800/231-0856; www.flycontinental.com) provides nonstop flights to Paris from Newark and Houston. Flights from Newark depart daily, while flights from Houston depart four to seven times a week, depending on the season.

Delta Airlines (☎ 800/241-4141; www.delta-air.com) is one of the best choices for those flying to Paris from the southeastern United States or the Midwest. There's a nonstop from Atlanta to Paris every evening. Delta also operates daily nonstop flights from both Cincinnati and New York. Note that Delta is the only airline offering nonstop service from New York to Nice.

TWA (☎ 800/892-4141; www.twa.com) operates daily nonstop service to Paris from New York. In summer, several flights a week from Boston and Washington, D.C., go through New York; several times a week there are nonstop flights from St. Louis; and three times a week there are flights from Los Angeles, connecting in St. Louis or New York. In winter, flights from Los Angeles and Washington are suspended, and flights from St. Louis make brief stopovers in New York or Boston en route.

US Airways (☎ 800/428-4322; www.usairways.com) offers daily nonstop service from Philadelphia to Paris.

The French national carrier, **Air France** (☎ 800/237-2747; www.airfrance.com), offers daily or several-times-a-week flights between Paris and such North American cities as Atlanta, Boston, Chicago, Cincinnati, Houston, Los Angeles, Mexico City, Miami, Montreal, New York, Newark, San Francisco, Toronto, and Washington D.C.

Canadians usually choose **Air Canada** (☎ 800/776-3000 in North America; www.aircanada.ca), which offers daily nonstop flights to Paris from Toronto and Montréal. Two of Air Canada's flights from Toronto are shared with Air France and feature Air France aircraft.

FLYING FOR LESS:
TIPS FOR GETTING THE BEST AIRFARES

1. Watch for **sales.** You'll almost never see them during the peak summer vacation months of July and August, or during the Thanksgiving or Christmas seasons; but at other times, you can get great deals. In the last couple of years, there have been amazing deals on winter flights to Paris. If you already hold a ticket when a sale breaks, it may even pay to exchange your ticket, which usually incurs a charge of between $50 and $150, depending on the airline and the ticket.

2. If your schedule is flexible, ask if you can secure a cheaper fare by **staying an extra day or by flying midweek.** (Many airlines won't volunteer this information.)

3. **Consolidators,** also known as bucket shops, are a good place to find low fares. Consolidators buy seats in bulk from the airlines and then sell them back to the public at prices below even the airlines' discounted rates. Their small boxed ads usually run in the Sunday travel section of your newspaper, at the bottom of the page. **Council Travel** (☎ 800/226-8624; www.counciltravel.com) and **STA Travel** (☎ 800/ 781-4040; www.sta.travel.com) cater especially to young travelers, but their bargain

basement prices are available to people of all ages. **Travel Bargains** (☎ **800/AIR-FARE;** www.1800airfare.com) was formerly owned by TWA but now offers the deepest discounts on many other airlines, with a 4-day advance purchase. Other reliable consolidators include **1-800-FLY-CHEAP** (www.1800flycheap.com); **TFI Tours International** (☎ **800/745-8000** or 212/736-1140), which serves as a clearinghouse for unused seats; or "rebators" such as **Travel Avenue** (☎ **800/333-3335** or 312/876-1116).

4. Book a seat on a **charter flight.** Most charter operators advertise and sell their seats through travel agents, thus making these local professionals your best source of information for available flights. Before deciding to take a charter flight, however, check the restrictions on the ticket: You may be asked to purchase a tour package, to pay in advance, to be amenable if the day of departure is changed, to pay a service charge, to fly on an airline you're not familiar with (this usually is not the case), and to pay harsh penalties if you cancel—but be understanding if the charter doesn't fill up and is canceled up to 10 days before departure. Summer charters fill up more quickly than others and are almost sure to fly, but if you decide on a charter flight, seriously consider cancellation and baggage insurance.

5. **Search for deals on the Web.** It's possible to get some great deals on airfare, hotels, and car rentals via the Internet. See the online directory at the end of this chapter for more information about travel Web sites that can save you money.

   Arthur Frommer's Budget Travel (www.frommers.com) offers detailed information on 200 cities and islands around the world, and up-to-the-minute ways to save dramatically on flights, hotels, car reservations, and cruises.

   Microsoft Expedia (www.expedia.com) offers the "Fare Tracker": You fill out a form on the screen indicating that you're interested in cheap flights from your hometown, and, once a week, they'll e-mail you the best airfare deals on up to three destinations. The site's "Travel Agent" will steer you to bargains on hotels and car rentals, and with the help of hotel and airline seat pinpointers, you can book everything right on line. This site is even useful once you're booked. Before you depart, log on to Expedia for maps and up-to-date travel information, including weather reports and foreign exchange rates.

   Travelocity (www.travelocity.com) is one of the best travel sites out there, especially for finding cheap airfare. In addition to its "Personal Fare Watcher," which notifies you via e-mail of the lowest airfares for up to five different destinations, Travelocity will track the three lowest fares for any routes on any dates in minutes. You can book a flight right then and there, and if you need a rental car or hotel, Travelocity will find you the best deal via the SABRE computer reservations system (another huge travel agent database).

   The Trip (www.thetrip.com) is really geared toward the business traveler, but vacationers-to-be can also use The Trip's exceptionally powerful fare-finding engine, which will e-mail you every week with the best city-to-city airfare deals for as many as 10 routes.

10 Packages & Escorted Tours

Package tours are not necessarily the same thing as escorted tours. They are simply a way of buying your airfare and accommodations at the same time—and they can save you a ton of money. In many cases, a package that includes airfare, hotel, and rental car will cost you less than just the hotel alone if you booked it yourself. That's because packages are sold in bulk to tour operators, who resell them to the public.

It pays to comparison shop among various packages, though. Some packages offer a better class of hotels than others; some provide the same hotels for lower prices. Some feature flights on scheduled airlines whereas others book charters. In some packages, your choices of accommodations and travel days may be limited. Some packages let you choose between escorted vacations and independent vacations; others allow you to add on just a few excursions or escorted day trips (also at prices lower than if you booked them yourself) without booking an entirely escorted tour. The time you spend shopping around will be well rewarded.

For package tours that offer adventure and activity, see "Special-Interest Vacations," earlier in this chapter.

Delta Air Lines, for example, through its tour division (Delta Dream Vacations, ☎ 800/872-7786), offers a full package called "Jolie France," lasting 10 nights and costing from $1,756 to $1,956 per person double occupancy, depending on the season, taking in not only Paris, but some of the regional highlights of France, including Tours, Bordeaux, Carcassonne, Nice, Nîmes, Dijon, and back to Paris. All hotels, airfare from the U.S. East Coast, tours, and breakfasts are included, plus four dinners.

The French Experience, 370 Lexington Ave., Room 812, New York, NY 10017 (☎ 212/986-1115; fax 212/986-3808), offers inexpensive airline tickets to Paris on most scheduled airlines. Several tours use varied types and categories of country inns, hotels, private châteaux, and bed-and-breakfasts. They take reservations for about 30 small hotels in Paris, and arrange short term apartment rentals in the city or farmhouse rentals in the countryside. They also offer all-inclusive packages in Paris as well as prearranged package tours of various regions of France. Any tour can be adapted to suit individual needs.

American Express Vacations (☎ 800/241-1700; www.americanexpress. com) is another option. Check out the **Last Minute Travel Bargains** site, offered in conjunction with **Continental Airlines** (www6.americanexpress. com/travel/lastminutetravel/default.asp), with deeply discounted vacation packages and reduced airline fares that differ from the E-savers bargains that Continental e-mails weekly to subscribers.

Among the airline packages, yet another option includes **American Airlines FlyAway Vacations** (☎ 800/321-2121).

Escorted tours are a different animal. Some people love having all the details taken care of for them; others hate the structure and loss of spontaneity. Before you book, ask hard questions about the cancellation policy, the size of the group, how action-packed the itinerary is, and exactly what's included.

Globus/Cosmos Tours, 5301 S. Federal Circle, Littleton, CO 80123-2980 (☎ 800/338-7092) offers first-class escorted coach tours of various regions of France lasting from 8 to 16 days. Cosmos, a budget branch of Globus, offers escorted tours of about the same length. You must book tours through a travel agent, but you can call the 800 number for brochures.

Tauck Tours, 276 Post Rd. W., Westport, CT 06880 (☎ 800/468-2825), provides superior first-class, fully escorted coach grand tours of France as well as 1-week general tours of specific regions within France. Its 14-day tour of France covering the Normandy landing beaches, the Bayeux Tapestry, and Mont-St-Michel among other places of historic interest costs $3,790 per person, double occupancy (land only), and a 14-day trip beginning in Nice and ending in Paris costs $3,980 per person, double occupancy (land only).

11 Getting There from Elsewhere in Europe

BY PLANE

From London, Air France (☎ **0845/084-5111**) and **British Airways** (☎ **0345/222111** in the U.K. only) fly frequently to Paris with a trip time of only 1 hour. These airlines alone operate up to 17 flights daily from Heathrow, one of the busiest air routes in Europe. Many commercial travelers also use regular flights originating from the London City Airport in the Docklands.

Direct flights to Paris also exist from **other major cities in the U.K.,** such as Manchester, Edinburgh, and Southampton. Contact Air France, British Airways, or **British Midland** (☎ **0870/607-555**) for details.

There are no hard-and-fast rules for British travelers interested in getting the best deals for European flights, but do bear the following points in mind. Daily papers often carry advertisements for companies offering cheap flights. Highly recommended companies include **Trailfinders** (☎ **020/7937-5400**), which sells discounted fares, and **Avro Tours** (☎ **0181/715-0000**), which operates charters. In London, there are many ticket consolidators (who buy inventories of tickets from airlines and then resell them) in the neighborhoods of Earl's Court and Victoria Station that offer cheap fares. CEEFAX, a British television information service (received by many private homes and hotels), presents details of package holidays and flights to Europe and beyond.

You can reach Paris from any **major European capital.** Your best bet would be to fly on the national carrier, Air France, which has more connections into Paris from European capitals than any other airline. From **Dublin,** try **Aer Lingus** (☎ **800/223-6537;** www.aerlingus.com), with the most frequent flights into Paris from Ireland. From **Amsterdam,** the convenient airline for Paris is **KLM** (☎ **800/374-7747;** www.klm.nl).

BY TRAIN

Paris is one of Europe's busiest rail junctions, with trains arriving at and departing from its many stations every few minutes. If you're already in Europe, you may want to go to Paris by train. Even if you don't, the cost is relatively low—especially in comparison to renting a car.

Railpasses as well as individual rail tickets within Europe are available at most travel agencies or at any office of **Rail Europe** (☎ **800/4-EURAIL** in the U.S.) or Eurostar (☎ **800/EUROSTAR** in the U.S.). Their Internet address is www.raileurope.com.

BY BUS

Bus travel to Paris is available from London as well as many other cities throughout the Continent. In the early 1990s, the French government established strong incentives for long-haul buses not to drive into the center of Paris. The arrival and departure point for Europe's largest bus operators, **Eurolines France,** is a 35-minute Métro ride from central Paris, at the terminus of Métro line 3 (Métro: Gallieni), in the eastern suburb of Bagnolet. Despite this inconvenience, many people prefer bus travel. Eurolines France is located at 28 av. du Général-de-Gaulle, 93541 Bagnolet (☎ **08-36-69-52-52**).

Long-haul buses are equipped with toilets, but they also stop at mealtimes for rest and refreshment. The price of a round-trip ticket between Paris and London (a 7-hour trip) is 490 F ($78.40) for passengers 26 or over, and 430 F ($68.80) for passengers under 26.

Because Eurolines does not have a U.S.-based sales agent, most people wait until they reach Europe to buy their tickets. Any European travel agent can

In London, an especially convenient place to buy rail tickets is **Wasteels Ltd.,** opposite Platform 2 in Victoria Station, London SW1V 1JY (☎ **020/ 7834-7066**). It provides railway-related services and information on the pros and cons of various types of fares and railpasses; its staff will probably spend more than the usual amount of time with you in planning your itinerary. Depending on circumstances, Wasteels sometimes charges a £5 ($8.50) fee, but for the information provided the cost might be worth it.

arrange these purchases. If you're traveling to Paris from London, you can contact **Eurolines (U.K.) Ltd.,** 52 Grosvenor Gardens, Victoria, London SW1; or call ☎ **0990/143219** for information or for credit-card sales.

BY CAR

The **major highways** into Paris are the A1 from the north (Great Britain and Benelux); the A13 from Rouen, Normandy, and other points of northwest France; the A10 from Bordeaux, the Pyrénées, France's southwest, and Spain; the A6 from Lyon, the French Alps, the Riviera, and Italy; and the A4 from Metz, Nancy, and Strasbourg in eastern France.

BY FERRY FROM ENGLAND

Ferryboats and hydrofoils operate day and night, in all seasons, with the exception of last-minute cancellations during particularly fierce storms. Many Channel crossings are carefully timed to coincide with the arrival/departure of major trains (especially those between London and Paris). Trains let you off a short walk from the piers. Most ferries carry cars, trucks, and massive amounts of freight, but some hydrofoils take passengers only. The major routes include at least 12 trips a day between Dover or Folkestone and Calais or Boulogne. Hovercraft and hydrofoils make the trip from Dover to Calais, the shortest distance across the Channel, in just 40 minutes during good weather, whereas the slower-moving ferries might take several hours, depending on weather conditions and tides. If you're bringing a car, it's important to make reservations, as space below decks is usually crowded. Timetables can vary depending on weather conditions and many other factors.

The leading operator of ferryboats across the channel is **P&O Stena Lines** (BritRail ☎ **800/247-7268** for reservations within North America, or 0870/600-0611 in England). It operates car and passenger ferries between Portsmouth, England, and Cherbourg, France (three departures a day; 4¼ hours each way during daylight hours, 7 hours each way at night); between Portsmouth and Le Havre, France (three a day; 5½ hours each way). Most popular of all are the routes it operates between Dover and Calais, France (25 sailings a day; 75 minutes each way), costing $41 (U.S.) one-way.

The shortest and by far the most popular route across the Channel is between Calais and Dover. **Hoverspeed** operates at least 12 hovercraft crossings daily; the trip takes 35 minutes. It also runs a SeaCat (a catamaran propelled by jet engines) that takes slightly longer to make the crossing between Boulogne and Folkestone; the SeaCats depart about four times a day on the 55-minute voyage. For reservations and information, call Hoverspeed (☎ **800/677-8585** for reservations in North America or 08705/240-241 in England). Typical one-way fares are 25 F ($4) per person.

If you plan to transport a rental car between England and France, check in advance with the rental company about license and insurance requirements and additional drop-off charges. And be aware that many car-rental companies, for insurance reasons, forbid transport of one of their vehicles over the water between England and France. Transport of a car each way begins at 75 F ($12). A better idea is to ask about a car exchange program (Hertz's is called "Le Swap"), in which you drop off a right-hand drive car and pick up a left-hand drive vehicle at Calais.

UNDER THE CHANNEL

Queen Elizabeth and the late French president François Mitterrand officially opened the Channel Tunnel in 1994, and the *Eurostar Express* now has daily passenger service from London to both Paris and Brussels. The $15 billion tunnel, one of the great engineering feats of our time, is the first link between Britain and the continent since the Ice Age. The 31-mile journey takes 35 minutes, although the actual time spent in the Chunnel is only 19 minutes.

Eurostar tickets, for train service between London and Paris or Brussels, are available through **Rail Europe** (☎ 800/4-EURAIL for information). A one-way first class nonrefundable ticket costs $199, or else $239 if refundable. In second class a nonrefundable one-way ticket goes for $119, or else $159 if refundable.

In London, make reservations for Eurostar at ☎ 0990/300003 (accessible in the United Kingdom only); in Paris at ☎ 01-44-51-06-02; and in the United States at ☎ 800/EUROSTAR. Chunnel train traffic is roughly competitive with air travel, if you calculate door-to-door travel time. Trains leave from London's Waterloo Station and arrive in Paris at Gare du Nord.

LE SHUTTLE   The Chunnel accommodates not only trains, but also passenger cars, charter buses, taxis, and motorcycles. Le Shuttle, a half-mile-long train carrying motor vehicles under the English Channel (☎ 0990/353535 in the U.K.), connects Calais, France, with Folkestone, England, and vice versa. It operates 24 hours a day, 365 days a year, running every 15 minutes during peak travel times and at least once an hour at night.

With Le Shuttle, gone are weather-related delays, seasickness, and a need for reservations. Before boarding Le Shuttle, you stop at a toll booth to pay, and then pass through Immigration for both countries at one time. During the ride, you travel in bright, air-conditioned carriages, remaining inside your car or stepping outside to stretch your legs. An hour later, when you reach France, you simply drive off.

12 Getting Around France

BY TRAIN

With some 50 cities in France linked by the world's fastest trains, you can get from Paris to just about anywhere else in the country in just a few hours. With 24,000 miles of track and about 3,000 stations, SNCF (French National Railroads) is fabled throughout the world for its on-time performance. You can travel first or second class by day and in *couchette* or sleeper by night. Many trains carry dining facilities.

INFORMATION   If you plan much travel on European railroads, get the latest copy of the *Thomas Cook European Timetable of Railroads.* This comprehensive 500-plus-page book documents all Europe's mainline passenger rail services with detail and accuracy. It's available in North America from the **Forsyth Travel Library,** 226 Westchester Ave., White Plains, NY 10604 (☎ **800/367-7984**), at a cost of $27.95, plus $4.95 postage (priority airmail in the U.S. and $6.95 U.S. for shipments to Canada).

In the United States: For more information and to purchase railpasses (see below) before you leave, contact **Rail Europe** at 500 Mamaroneck Ave., Suite 314, Harrison, NY 10528 (☎ **800/677-8585;** fax 914/682-3712).

In Canada: Rail Europe offices are at 2087 Dundas St. E., Suite 105, Mississauga, ON L4X 1M2 (☎ **800/361-7245** or 905/602-4195; fax 905/602-4198).

In London: SNCF maintains offices at **French Railways,** 179 Piccadilly, London W1V 0BA (☎ **0345/48-49-50;** fax 020/7491-9956).

In Paris: For train information or to make reservations call **SNCF** at ☎ **08-36-35-35-35.** You are charged at the rate of 3 F (50¢) per minute to use this service. You can also go to any local travel agency, of course, and book tickets. A simpler way to book tickets is to take advantage of the Billetterie or ticket machines in every train station. If you know your PIN, you can use credit cards such as American Express, MasterCard, and Visa to purchase your ticket.

FRENCH RAIL PASSES   Working cooperatively with SNCF, Air Inter Europe, and Avis, Rail Europe offers three flexible cost-saving railpasses that can reduce travel costs considerably.

The **France Railpass** provides unlimited rail transport throughout France for any 3 days within 1 month, costing $205 in first class and $175 in second. You can purchase up to 6 more days for an extra $30 per person per day. Costs are even more reasonable for two adults traveling together: $328 for first class and $280 in second. Children 4 to 11 travel for half price.

The **France Rail 'n Drive Pass,** available only in North America, combines good value on both rail travel and Avis car rentals and is best used by arriving at a major rail depot, then striking out to explore the countryside by car. It includes the France Railpass (see above), and use of a rental car. A 3-day rail pass (first class) and 2 days' use of the cheapest rental car (with unlimited mileage) is $204 per person (assuming two people traveling together). It's $187 per person for the second-class rail pass and the same car; you can upgrade to a larger car for a supplemental fee. Solo travelers pay from $289 for first class and $255 for second.

EURAILPASSES   For years, many in-the-know travelers have been taking advantage of one of Europe's greatest travel bargains: the Eurailpass, which permits unlimited first-class rail travel in any country in Western Europe except the British Isles (good in Ireland). Passes are for periods as short as 15 days or as long as 3 months and are strictly nontransferable.

The pass is sold only in North America. A Eurailpass is $554 for 15 days, $718 for 21 days, $890 for 1 month, $1,260 for 2 months, and $1,558 for 3 months. Children 3 and under travel free providing they don't occupy a seat (otherwise they're charged half fare); children 4 to 11 are charged half fare. If you're under 26, you can purchase a Eurail Youthpass, entitling you to unlimited second-class

Don't Leave Home Without It

Eurailpasses are sold only in North America. If you don't get one before you leave, you can't get one anywhere in Europe. If you plan to do a lot of rail travel in Europe, make sure you get your pass before you leave.

Remember that a train ticket by itself does not guarantee you a seat; it merely gets you transportation from one place to another. On crowded trains and during busy times of year, you'll have to make a **seat reservation** (and pay for the privilege) if you want to be sure of sitting somewhere other than on top of your luggage. Seat reservations cost $8 per person.

---

travel for $388 for 15 days, $499 for 21 days, $623 for 1 month, $882 for 2 months, and $1,089 for 3 months. Regardless of the pass you buy, you'll have to pay an extra supplement if you want to take a high-speed TGV train anywhere in France.

Seat reservations are required on some trains (and cost an additional $8 per person). Many of the trains have *couchettes* (sleeping cars), which also cost extra. Obviously, the 2- or 3-month traveler gets the greatest economic advantages; the Eurailpass is ideal for such extensive trips. With the pass you can visit all of France's major sights, from Normandy to the Alps, then end your vacation in Norway, for example. Eurailpass holders are entitled to considerable reductions on certain buses and ferries as well.

Travel agents everywhere, and railway agents in such major cities as New York, Montreal, and Los Angeles, sell Eurailpasses. You can also purchase them at the North American offices of CIT Travel Service, the French National Railroads, the German Federal Railroads, and the Swiss Federal Railways.

The **Eurail Flexipass** allows you to visit Europe with more flexibility. It's valid in first class and offers the same privileges as the Eurailpass. However, it provides a number of individual travel days that you can use over a much longer period of consecutive days. That makes it possible to stay in one city for a while without losing days of rail travel. There are two passes: 10 days of travel in 2 months for $654, and 15 days of travel in 2 months for $862.

With many of the same qualifications and restrictions as the previously described Flexipass is a **Eurail Youth Flexipass.** Sold only to travelers under 26, it allows 10 days of travel within 2 months for $458, and 15 days of travel within 2 months for $599.

BY CAR

The most charming châteaux and best country hotels always seem to lie away from the main cities and train stations. You'll find that renting a car is often the best way to travel around France, especially if you plan to explore in depth and not stick to the standard Paris–Nice route.

But frankly, Europe's rail networks are so well developed and so inexpensive, we recommend that you rent a car only for exploring areas little serviced by rail lines, such as Brittany, rural Burgundy, and the Dordogne. Or take trains between cities and rent a car only on the days when you want to explore independently.

Driving time in Europe is largely a matter of conjecture, urgency, and how much sightseeing you do along the way. Driving time from Paris to Geneva is $5^1/2$ hours minimum. It's $2^1/2$ hours from Paris to Rouen, $3^1/2$ hours to Nantes, and 4 hours to Lyon. The driving time from Marseille to Paris is a matter of national pride, and tall tales abound about how rapidly the French can do it. With the accelerator pressed to the floor, you might conceivably make it in 7 hours, but we always make a 2-day journey of it.

RENTALS   Renting a car in France is easy. You'll need to present a passport, a valid driver's license, and a valid credit card. You'll also have to meet the minimum age requirement of the company. (For their least expensive cars, this is 21 at Hertz, 23 at Avis, and 25 at Budget. More expensive cars at any of the above-mentioned companies might require that you be at least 25.) It usually isn't obligatory, at least within France, but certain companies, especially the smaller ones, have at times asked for the presentation of an International Driver's License, even though this is becoming increasingly superfluous in Western Europe.

Note: The best deal is usually a weekly rental with unlimited mileage. All car-rental bills in France are subject to a whopping 19.6% government tax, among the highest in Europe. And though the rental company won't usually mind if you drive your car across the French border—into, say, Germany, Switzerland, Italy, or Spain—it's often expressly forbidden to transport your car on any ferry-boat, including the dozens that ply the waters of the Channel to England.

Unless it's already factored into the rental agreement, an **optional collision-damage waiver (CDW)** carries an extra charge of 110 F to 125 F ($17.60 to $20) per day for the least expensive cars. Buying this will usually eliminate all but $250 of your responsibility in the event of accidental damage to the car. Because most newcomers aren't familiar with local driving customs and conditions, we highly recommend that you buy the CDW, though you should check with your credit-card company first to see if they'll cover this automatically when you rent with their card (they may cover damage to the car but not liability, so make sure you understand this clearly). At some of the companies the CDW won't protect you against the theft of a car, so if this is the case, ask about buying extra theft protection. This cost is 45 F ($7.20) extra per day.

Automatic transmission is considered a luxury in Europe, so if you want it you'll have to pay dearly.

Budget (☎ **800/472-3325** in the U.S. and Canada; www.budgetrentacar.com) maintains about 30 locations in Paris, with its largest branch at 81 av. Kléber, 16e (☎ **01-47-55-61-00;** Métro: Trocadéro). For rentals of more than 7 days, you can pick up a car (at least in most cases) in one French city and drop it off in another, but there are extra charges. Drop-offs in cities within an easy drive of the French border (including Geneva and Frankfurt) incur no extra charge; however, you can arrange drop-offs in other non-French cities for a reasonable surcharge.

Hertz (☎ **800/654-3001** in the U.S. and Canada; www.hertz.com) maintains about 15 locations in Paris, including offices at the city's airports. The main office is at 27 rue St-Ferdinand, 17e (☎ **01-45-74-97-39;** Métro: Argentine). Be sure to ask about any promotional discounts.

Avis (☎ **800/331-2112** in the U.S. and Canada; www.avis.com) has offices at both Paris airports, as well as an inner-city headquarters at 5 rue Bixio, 7e (☎ **01-44-18-10-50;** Métro: École-Militaire), near the Eiffel Tower.

National (☎ **800/227-3876** in the U.S. and Canada; www.nationalcar.com) is represented in Paris by Europcar, whose largest office is at 165 bis rue De Vaugirard (☎ **01-44-38-61-61;** Métro: St.-Sulpre). It has offices at both Paris airports and at about a dozen other locations. Any of its offices can rent you a car on the spot, but to qualify for the lowest rates it's best to reserve in advance from North America.

Two U.S.-based agencies that don't have Paris offices but act as booking agents for Paris-based agencies are **Kemwel Holiday Auto** (☎ **800/678-0678;** www.kemwel.com) and **Auto Europe** (☎ **800/223-5555;**

www.autoeurope.com). These companies can make bookings in the U.S. only, so call before your trip.

GASOLINE Known in France as *essence,* gas is extraordinarily expensive for those accustomed to North American prices. All but the least expensive cars usually require an octane rating that the French classify as essence super, the most expensive variety. Depending on your car, you'll need either leaded (*avec plomb*) or unleaded (*sans plomb*). Filling a medium-size car will cost between $45 and $65.

Beware of the mixture of gasoline and oil sold in certain rural communities called *mélange* or *gasoil;* this mixture is for very old two-cycle engines.

Note: Sometimes you can drive for miles in rural France without encountering a gas station, so don't let your tank get dangerously low.

DRIVING RULES Everyone in the car, in both the front and the back seats, must wear seat belts. Children 11 and under must ride in the back seat. Drivers are supposed to yield to the car on their right, except where signs indicate otherwise, as at traffic circles.

If you violate the speed limits, expect a big fine. Those limits are about 130 kilometers per hour (80 m.p.h.) on expressways, about 100 kilometers per hour (60 m.p.h.) on major national highways, and 90 kilometers per hour (56 m.p.h.) on small country roads. In towns, don't exceed 60 kilometers per hour (37 m.p.h.).

MAPS For France as a whole, most motorists opt for the Michelin map 989. For regions, **Michelin** publishes a series of yellow maps that are quite good. Big travel-book stores in North America carry these maps, and they're commonly available in France (at lower prices). One useful feature of the Michelin map (in this age of congested traffic) is its designations of alternative *routes de dégagement,* which let you skirt big cities and avoid traffic-clogged highways.

Another recommended option is *Frommer's Road Atlas Europe.*

BREAKDOWNS/ASSISTANCE A breakdown is called *une panne* in France, and it's just as frustrating here as anywhere else. Call the police at ☎ 17 anywhere in France and they'll put you in touch with the nearest garage. Most local garages have towing services. If your breakdown occurs on an expressway, find the nearest roadside emergency phone box, pick up the phone, and put a call through. You'll immediately be connected to the nearest breakdown service facility.

BY PLANE

Regrettably, there are very few competitors in the rarefied world of domestic air travel within France. **Air France,** which recently acquired Air Inter Europe, is the 800-pound gorilla in this field, serving about eight cities in France and eight others in Europe. Airfares tend to be much higher than they would be for comparable distances in the U.S., and discounts are few and far between. Sample round-trip fares between Paris and Nice sell for 2,300 F ($368); Paris to Bordeaux is 2,240 F ($358.40); Paris to Toulouse is 2,260 F ($361.60). Air travel time from Paris to most anywhere in France is about an hour.

13 Tips on Accommodations

The French government rates hotels on a one-to-four star system. One-star hotels are budget accommodations; two-star lodgings are quality tourist hotels; three stars go to first-class hotels; four stars are reserved for deluxe accommodations. In some of the lower categories, the rooms may not have private bathrooms; instead, many have what the French call a *cabinet de toilette* (hot and cold running water and maybe a bidet). In such hotels, bathrooms are down the hall. Nearly all hotels in France have central heating, but, in some cases, you might wish the owners would turn it up a little on a cold night.

RELAIS & CHÂTEAUX Now known worldwide, this organization of deluxe and first-class hostelries began in France for visitors seeking the ultimate in hotel living and dining, most often in a traditional atmosphere. Relais & Châteaux establishments (there are about 150 in France) are former castles, abbeys, manor houses, and town houses that've been converted into hostelries or inns and elegant hotels. All have a limited number of rooms, so reservations are imperative. Sometimes these owner-run establishments have pools and tennis courts. The Relais part of the organization refers to inns called relais, meaning "posthouse." These tend to be less luxurious than the châteaux, but they're often quite charming. Top-quality restaurants are *relais gourmands*. Throughout this guide we've listed our favorite Relais & Châteaux, but there are many more.

For an illustrated catalog of these establishments, send $8 to **Relais & Châteaux,** 11 E. 44th St., Suite 704, New York, NY 10017 (for information on and reservations for individual Relais & Châteaux, call ☎ **800/735-2478** or 212/856-0115). Check out their Web site at www.integra.fr/relaischateaux.com.

BED & BREAKFASTS Called **gîtes—chambres d'hôte** in France, these accommodations may be one or several bedrooms on a farm or in a village home. Many of them offer one main meal of the day as well (lunch or dinner).

There are at least 6,000 of these accommodations listed with **La Maison des Gîtes de France et du Tourisme Vert,** 59 rue St-Lazare, 75009 Paris (☎ **01-49-70-75-75**). Sometimes these B&Bs aren't as simple as you might think: instead of a bare-bones farm room, you might be housed in a mansion deep in the French countryside.

In the United States, a good source for this type of accommodation is **The French Experience,** 370 Lexington Ave., Room 812, New York, NY 10017 (☎ **212/986-1115;** fax 212/986-3808). It also rents furnished houses for as short a period as 1 week.

CONDOS, VILLAS, HOUSES & APARTMENTS If you can stay for at least a week and don't mind cooking your own meals and cleaning house, you might want to rent a long-term accommodation. The local French Tourist Board might help you obtain a list of real-estate agencies that represent this type of rental (which tends to be especially popular at ski resorts). In France, one of the best groups of estate agents is the **Fédération Nationale des Agents Immobiliers,** 129 rue du Faubourg St-Honoré, 75008 Paris (☎ **01-44-20-77-00**).

In the United States, **At Home Abroad,** 405 E. 56th St., Apt. 6H, New York, NY 10022-2466 (☎ **212/421-9165;** fax 212/752-1591), specializes in villas on the French Riviera and in the Dordogne as well as places in the Provençal hill towns. Rentals are usually for 2 weeks. For a $25 registration fee (applicable to any rental), they'll send you photographs of the properties and a newsletter.

A worthwhile competitor is **Vacances en Campagne,** British Travel International, P.O. Box 299, Elkton, VA (☎ **800/327-6097;** fax 540/298-2347). Its $4 directory contains information on more than 700 potential rentals across Europe, including France.

If you want to rent an apartment in Paris, the **Barclay International Group,** 150 E. 52nd St., New York, NY 10022 (☎ **800/845-6636**), can give you access to about 3,000 apartments and villas scattered throughout Paris (plus 39 other cities in France), ranging from modest modern units to the most stylish. Units rent from 1 night to up to 6 months; all have TVs and kitchenettes, and many have concierge staffs and lobby-level security. The least-expensive units cost around $90 per night, double occupancy. Incremental discounts are granted for a stay of 1 week or 3 weeks. Rentals must be prepaid in U.S. dollars or by a major U.S. credit or charge card.

Hometours International, Inc., P.O. Box 11503, Knoxville, TN 37939 (☎ **800/367-4668** or 865/690-8484), offers more than 400 moderately priced apartments, apartment hotels, and B&Bs in Paris. On the Riviera, you can rent beautiful villas, all with pools, at reasonable rates. For budget travelers, this organization offers a prepaid voucher program for the Campanile hotels, a chain of about 350 two-star family-run hotels throughout France. Rates begin as low as $90 per night double. This is an excellent alternative to B&B hotels, because some chain members provide a buffet breakfast for only 35 F ($5.60) per person. B&B catalogs for $9 or apartment brochures for free are available from the address above.

HOTEL CHAINS   One good moderately priced choice is the **Mercure** chain: An organization of simple but clean and modern hotels offering attractive values throughout France. Even at the peak of the tourist season, a room at a Mercure in the heart of Paris rents for as little as $95 per night (admittedly, a rarity). For more information on Mercure hotels and a copy of their 100-page directory, call **RESINTER** at ☎ **800/221-4542** in the United States.

Formule 1 hotels are bare-bones and basic but clean and safe, offering rooms for up to three people, for around $30 per night. Built from prefabricated units, these air-conditioned, soundproofed hotels are shipped to a site and reassembled, often on the outskirts of cities like Paris (27 in the suburbs alone). In addition, there's a coterie of 150 of these low-budget hotels throughout the rest of France.

Mercure and Formule 1 are both owned by the French hotel giant Accor, corporate parent of Motel 6, to which Formule 1 bears a resemblance. While you can make a reservation at any member of the Accor group through the RESINTER number above, the chain finds that the low cost of Formule 1 makes it unprofitable and impractical to prereserve (from the States) rooms in the Formule chain. So you'll have to reserve your Formule 1 room on arrival in France. For a directory, write to Formule 1/ETAP Hotels, 6/8 rue du Bois-Briard, 91021 Evry CEDEX (☎ **01-69-36-75-00**).

Other worthwhile economy bets, sometimes with a bit more charm, are the hotels and restaurants belonging to the **Fédération Nationale des Logis de France,** 83 av. d'Italie, 75013 Paris (☎ **01-45-84-70-00**). This is a marketing association of 3,828 hotels, usually simple country inns especially convenient for motorists, most rated one or two stars. The association publishes an annual directory.

14 Tips on Shopping

France is the market of continental Europe—a jumble of products, colors, crafts, and cutting-edge style. Though its retail reputation has grown through fashion and style, the truth is that this is a country where shopping at the local produce market is a quasi-religious experience, where the dime stores are as much fun as (if not more) the major department stores, and where many of the best things in life can be found in a *parapharmacie*—a newfangled concept that marries tons of drugstore/health-care/beauty products with a discount system.

Factory outlets are opening up *droit* and *gauche*, whereas the old factories continue to sell wares straight from their hometown (like Limoges), and the new factories have opened boutiquelike shops to hawk overruns to the public.

Add to all this a tradition of the finest antiques in the world (plus heaps of fun junk and what locals call *brocante*) and you have the makings of a spree even a nonshopper will love.

THE BEST BUYS IN FRANCE

BEAUTY PRODUCTS Regular designer makeup at retail may be the same price in France as in the States—or possibly more expensive in France. But at a "duty-free" (nonairport variety) store or a discounter where you can qualify for *détaxe* (see box, "How to Get Your VAT Refund" later in this chapter), you'll see anywhere from 20% to 45% melt off your bill. Paris offers the most duty-free stores and bigger discounts on name-brand goods, but any city with a tourist business (Nice, Cannes, Monaco, Biarritz) will have at least one discounter. If you know you'll be qualifying for détaxe (i.e., spending more than 1,200 F), ask at each parfumerie you visit until you find one that has the selection you need and the new détaxe program.

CRAFTS The main **faïence** cities are in the north, stretching from Rouen in the northeast to Quimper (for specific shops, see chapter 8) on the Atlantic coast. You'll find **tiles** in the south (check out Salernes), and Moustier Ste-Marie in Provence is known for a specific type of faïence with animals. **Soap making** is an art in the south of France, with soap makers dotting Marseille and Provence. L'Occitane, a Provençal brand, is now sold in its own boutiques in assorted Provence towns and in Paris.

You'll find **copper cooking pots** in northern France, especially in a Normandy village called Villedieu-les-Poêles, 22 miles south of St-Lô, not far from Mont-St-Michel. Copper-lined cookware has been manufactured here since the 1700s, and dozens of stores along the main street sell huge amounts of the stuff every year. To watch the artisans at work, stop by **Les Ateliers du Cuivre et de l'Argent,** 54 rue du Général-Huard (☎ **02-33-51-31-85**). A factory store sells the goods at prices that are considerably less than those within retail stores in such urban centers as Paris. The complex is open Monday to Saturday from 9am to noon, and from 1:30 to 5:30pm. You'll find it just outside of Ville-Dieu-les-Poêles, beside the main road to Mauviel. Northeastern France, near Strasbourg, is the home of **Baccarat crystal,** whereas Burgundy is known for its large hand-carved (and very heavy) pieces of **furniture.**

FASHION You can find knockoffs of the latest trends all over France, at more-than-affordable prices, in the two major dime-store chains. Every major city has a Monoprix (owned by Galeries Lafayette) or Prisunic (owned by Au Printemps); some have both.

If you can't leave France without buying something from that icon Hermès, the sorry news is that you may find better deals outside France; London currently has a better price structure (depending on the rate of exchange for your dollar, of course). You'll qualify for a détaxe refund if you buy a scarf at Hermès, but you'll have to buy three ties or two ties and a pocket square to get a tax break.

SIZE CONVERSION CHART
Women's Clothing

American	6	8	10	12	14	16		
French	36	38	40	42	44	46		
British	8	10	12	14	16	18		

Women's Shoes

American	5	6	7	8	9	10		
French	36	37	38	39	40	41		
British	4	5	6	7	8	9		

Men's Suits

American	34	36	38	40	42	44	46	48
French	44	46	48	50	52	54	56	58
British	34	36	38	40	42	44	46	48

Men's Shirts

American	$14^1/_2$	15	$15^1/_2$	16	$16^1/_2$	17	$17^1/_2$	18
French	37	38	39	41	42	43	44	45
British	$14^1/_2$	15	$15^1/_2$	16	$16^1/_2$	17	$17^1/_2$	18

Men's Shoes

American	7	8	9	10	11	12	13
French	$39^1/_2$	41	42	43	$44^1/_2$	46	47
British	6	7	8	9	10	11	12

FOOD   You can bring into the United States **cheeses** that have aged more than 90 days—this basically means hard and moldy cheeses, not soft and runny ones. No fresh fruit or vegetables are allowed. You'll be safer with **mustards;** Dijon is brimming with choices, but any French grocery store will have a large selection of possibly a dozen choices of the Maille brand.

You can buy **chocolates** in grocery stores, but these are commercial chocolates. If you want to know what everyone's raving about, save up a few francs and head to the chocolatiers in Lyon or Paris, preferably in the cooler months, and begin your own taste test. You should consume handmade fresh chocolate within 3 days. In Paris, the big outlets are **La Maison du Chocolat** and **Christian Constant** (see chapter 4).

KITCHENWARE   Innovative kitchen appliances are promoted all over France, but their electricity requirements aren't compatible with your household current in North America. However, the ubiquitous copper-lined casseroles and thick-walled roasters might last a lifetime once you recover from the shock of their prices. If you happen to be touring Normandy and want to pick up the best copper-lined saucepans available, head for the hamlet of Villedieu-les-Poêles (see "Crafts," above). You can buy used copperware at almost any flea market and then clean it up yourself. Copper polish is sold at markets as well. In Paris, hit rue Montmartre in the 2nd arrondissement (not in Montmartre) for a choice of kitchen and restaurant suppliers that sell to the public.

PERFUME   Note that French perfume lasts longer than the U.S. counterpart of the same scent (it's made with potato alcohol, not grain alcohol) and that most new scents are launched in France before they come to the States. French perfume makers, especially the top-of-the-line designer names (like Chanel and Dior), are cracking down on the recent move toward discounting.

How to Get Your VAT Refund

French sales tax, or VAT (value-added tax), is now a hefty 19.6%, but you can get most of that back if you spend 1,200 F ($190) or more at any participating retailer. Most stores participate, though discount perfume shops usually peg the minimum at 1,200 F net, which actually works out to an equivalent pretax amount of 1,600 F to 1,700 F ($254 to $270). They then deduct the 20% discount so you're back where you started, at 1,200 F. Since this sounds more complicated than it is, ask!

The name of the refund is *détaxe,* meaning exactly what it says. You never really get the full 19.6% back, but you can come close.

After you spend the required minimum amount, ask for your détaxe papers; fill out the forms before you arrive at the airport and allow at least half an hour for standing in line. All refunds are processed at the final point of departure from the EU, so if you're going to another EU country, you don't apply for the refund in France.

Mark the paperwork to request that your refund be applied to your credit card so you aren't stuck with a check in francs that you can't cash. Even if you made the purchase in cash, you can still get the refund put on a credit card. This ensures the best rate of exchange. While you can get cash in some airports, if you don't take the cash in French francs you'll lose money on the transaction.

If you're considering a major purchase, especially one that falls between 1,200 F to 2,000 F ($192 to $320), ask the store policy before you get too involved—or be willing to waive your right to the refund.

Some stores will discount other brands and not these premium ones; some outlets will give a smaller discount on the big names.

Basically, if you don't qualify for détaxe (see "How to Get Your VAT Refund," later in this chapter), you should be able to get a flat 20% discount in duty-free stores in Paris and in major cities in the provinces. The airport offers a 13% discount. Don't buy American brands of fragrance in Europe, even at a duty-free shop—they're more expensive than at home. If a store offers a 10% discount, ask what else you get for free—there could be lots of free samples and maybe a tote bag or promotional kit thrownin that the airport can't match.

PORCELAIN   For delicate porcelains, head for Limoges (in the Limousin), where zillions of factory shops sell local wares and a few seconds. Note that factory shops are always closed from noon to 2pm. In Limoges look for Bernardaud and Raynaud; in nearby Aixe-sur-Vienne there's the Ancienne Manufacture Royale de Limoges (see chapter 20).

For earthenware, or faïence, see "Crafts," above. If driving to the French provinces doesn't suit your itinerary, head for rue de Paradis in Paris, where you'll find several suppliers with massive displays from all the big French factories. You'll eliminate any savings if you have to ship back to the States, but if you can carry a piece with you, you may save 20% to 25%.

WINE & CHAMPAGNE   Searching out unusual vintages from small vintners is great fun. Any wine outlet inventories an overwhelming choice of wines from Bordeaux, Burgundy, Alsace, the Rhône Valley, and Champagne. You'll find lots of sales outlets for exotic burgundies in and around Beaune, Brouilland, Montbard, and Gevrey-Chambertin, and any wine store in Dijon will be amply stocked. If bubbly is your thing, head for Epernay and Reims, where all sorts of champagnes are sold at decent prices—though prices may be no different from those in Paris or in the States, depending on promotions and the time of year (see chapter 9).

While all the big *maisons* sell directly to visitors, they discount only a smidgen and then only for three bottles or for six bottles and no more. Prices in the local hypermarché in Reims or in any branch of the French wine-shop chain Nicolas may rival prices offered by the maisons.

Alsace, Provence, and the Bordeaux region retain thousands of cases of their local vintages for sale (at favorable prices). Bottles of unusual cognacs, often with labels scrawled in the shaky script of an old vintner, are for sale in out-of-the-way corners around southwestern France and in centre-ville Cognac.

If after-dinner liqueurs are your thing, in Normandy you'll find bottles of Calvados (the famous apple-based liqueur) everywhere in the region; out past Rouen you get into apple country and can taste your way to bed (or visit the apple museum if you can't drink and drive).

For information on Customs and how much alcohol you can bring home with you, see "Customs" under "Entry Requirements & Customs Regulations," above.

SHIPPING IT HOME

Shipping costs will possibly double your cost on goods; you'll also pay U.S. duties on the items if they're valued at more than $50. The good news is that détaxe is automatically applied to any item shipped to an American destination—no need to worry about the 1,200 F minimum. However, some stores have a $100 minimum for shipping. You can also walk into any PT&T (post office) and mail home a Jiffy bag or small box of goodies. French do-it-yourself boxes can't be reopened once closed.

Fast Facts: France

For information specifically about Paris, see "Fast Facts: Paris" in chapter 3.

Auto Clubs   The **Association Française des Auto Clubs,** 14 av. de la Grand-Armée, 17e (☎ **01-40-55-43-00;** Métro: Porte-Maillot), provides limited information to members of U.S. auto clubs like the AAA.

Business Hours   Business hours here are erratic, as befits a nation of individualists. Most banks are open Monday through Friday from 9:30am to 4:30pm. Many, particularly in smaller towns or villages, take a lunch break at varying times. Hours are usually posted on the door. Most museums close 1 day a week (often Tuesday), and they're generally closed on national holidays. Usual hours are 9:30am to 5pm. Some museums, particularly the smaller and less-staffed ones, close for lunch from noon to 2pm. Most French museums are open on Saturday; many are closed Sunday morning but open Sunday afternoon. Again, refer to the individual museum listings.

Generally, offices are open Monday through Friday from 9am to 5pm, but always call first. In Paris or other big French cities, stores are open from 9 or 9:30am (but often 10am) to 6 or 7pm without a break for lunch. Some shops, particularly those operated by foreigners, open at

8am and close at 8 or 9pm. In some small stores the lunch break can last 3 hours, beginning at 1pm. This is more common in the south than in the north.

Drugstores If you need one during off-hours, have your concierge get in touch with the nearest **Commissariat de Police.** An agent there will have the address of a nearby pharmacy open 24 hours a day. French law requires that the pharmacies in any given neighborhood display the name and location of the one that remains open all night.

Electricity In general, expect 200 volts, 50 cycles, though you'll encounter 110 and 115 volts in some older establishments. Adapters are needed to fit sockets. Many hotels have two-pin (in some cases, three-pin) sockets for electric razors. It's best to ask your hotel concierge before plugging in any appliance.

Embassies/Consulates If you have a passport, immigration, legal, or other problem, contact your consulate. Call before you go, as they often keep strange hours and observe both French and home-country holidays. The Embassy of the **United States,** at 2 av. Gabriel, 8e (☎ 01-43-12-22-22; Métro: Concorde), is open Monday to Friday from 9am to 6pm. Passports are issued at its consulate at 2 rue St-Florentin (☎ 01-43-12-22-22; Métro: Concorde). Getting a passport replaced costs $55. The Embassy of **Canada** is at 35 av. Montaigne, 8e (☎ 01-44-43-29-00; Métro: F.-D.-Roosevelt or Alma-Marceau), open Monday to Friday from 9am to noon and 2 to 5pm. The Embassy of the **United Kingdom** is at 35 rue Faubourg St-Honore, 8e (☎ 01-44-51-31-00; Métro: Concorde or Madeleine), open Monday to Friday from 9:30am to 1pm and 2:30 to 5pm. The consulate is at 16 rue d'Anjou, 8e (☎ 01-44-66-29-79), and is open Monday to Friday from 9am to noon and 2 to 5pm. The Embassy of **Ireland** is at 12 ave. Foch, 16e, 75116 Paris (☎ 01-44-17-67-00; Métro: Argentine). Hours are Monday to Friday 9:30am to noon and 2:30 to 5:30pm. The Embassy of **Australia** is at 4 rue Jean-Rey, 15e (☎ 01-40-59-33-00; Métro: Bir-Hakeim), open Monday to Friday from 9:15am to noon and 2:30 to 4:30pm. The embassy of **New Zealand** is at 7 ter rue Léonard-de-Vinci, 75116 Paris (☎ 01-45-00-24-11; Métro: Victor Hugo), open Monday to Friday from 9am to 1pm and 2:30 to 6pm. The Embassy of **South Africa** is at 59 quai d'Orsay (☎ 01-53-59-23-23; Métro: Invalides). Hours are Monday to Friday 8:45 to 11am.

Emergencies In an emergency while at a hotel, contact the front desk. Most staffs are trained in dealing with a crisis and will call the police, summon an ambulance, or do whatever is necessary. But if the emergency involves something like a stolen wallet, go to the police station in person. Otherwise, you can get help anywhere in France by calling ☎ 17 for the police or ☎ 18 for the fire department *(pompiers).* For roadside emergencies, see "Getting Around France," earlier in this chapter.

Mail Most post offices in Paris are open Monday through Friday from 8am to 7pm and Saturday from 8am to noon. Allow 5 to 8 days to send or receive mail from your home. Airmail letters within Europe cost 3 F (50¢); to the United States, 4.40 F (70¢). Airmail letters to other European countries cost 3 F (50¢). Airmail letters to Canada cost 4.40 F (70¢), and airmail letters to Australia and New Zealand cost 5.20 F (85¢).

You can exchange money at post offices. Many hotels sell stamps, as do local post offices and cafes displaying a red TABAC sign outside.

Police   Call ☎ **17** anywhere in France.

Rest Rooms   If you're in dire need, duck into a cafe or brasserie to use the lavatory. It's customary to make some small purchase if you do so. Paris Métro stations and underground garages usually contain public rest rooms, but the degree of cleanliness varies. France still has some "hole-in-the-ground" toilets, so be warned.

Safety   Much of the country, particularly central France, the northeast, Normandy, and Brittany, remains relatively safe, even though no place in the world is crime-free. Those intending to visit the south of France, especially the Riviera, should exercise extreme caution—robberies and muggings here are commonplace. It's best to check your baggage into a hotel and then go sightseeing instead of leaving it unguarded in the trunk of a car, which can easily be broken into. Marseille is among the most dangerous French cities.

Taxes   Watch it: You could get burned. As a member of the European Union, France routinely imposes a value-added tax (VAT in English; TVA in French) on many goods and services. The standard VAT on merchandise is 19.6%, including clothing, appliances, liquor, leather goods, shoes, furs, jewelry, perfumes, cameras, and even caviar. Refunds are made for the tax on certain goods and merchandise, but not on services. The minimum purchase is 1,200 F ($192) in the same store for nationals or residents of countries outside the EU. See the "How to Get Your VAT Refund" box earlier in this chapter for details.

Telephone   You'll find public phone booths in cafes, restaurants, Métro stations, post offices, airports, and train stations, and occasionally on the streets. Pay phones accept coins of $^1/_2$ F, 1 F, 2 F, and 5 F; the minimum charge is 2 F (30¢). Pick up the receiver, insert the coin(s), and dial when you hear the tone, pushing the button when there's an answer.

The French also use a *télécarte,* a phone debit card, which you can purchase at rail stations, post offices, and other places. Sold in two versions, it allows you to use either 50 or 120 charge units (depending on the card) by inserting the card into the slot of most public phones. Depending on the type of card you buy, they cost 41 F to 98 F ($6.55 to $15.70).

If possible, avoid making calls from your hotel, as some French establishments double or triple the charges on you.

To call France from North America, dial **011,** then **33** (the country code for all of France), the **area code,** and then the **eight-digit number.** Although French area codes are two digits (the first digit is always a 0), you do not dial the zero when calling from abroad. For example, the Hôtel Négresco (☎ **04-93-16-64-00**) contains the area code for southeastern France (04). **To call long-distance within France,** you simply dial this 10-digit number. But if you call from North America, you would dial ☎ **011-33-4-93-16-64-00.**

To call North America from France, an easy and relatively inexpensive way is to use USA Direct/AT&T WorldConnect. From within France, dial any of the following numbers: ☎ **0800/99-0011, -1011, -1111,** or **-1211.** Now follow the prompt, which will ask you to punch in the number of either your AT&T credit card or a MasterCard or Visa.

Along with the USA, the countries which participate in the system—referred to as WorldConnect—include Canada, the U.K., Ireland, Australia, New Zealand, and South Africa. By punching in the number of the party you want in any of these countries, you'll avoid the surcharges imposed by the hotel operator. At any time, an AT&T operator will be available to help you. The country code for the U.S. and Canada is **1.** Great Britain is **44,** Ireland is **353,** Australia is **61,** New Zealand is **64,** and South Africa is **27.**

For information, dial ☎ **12.**

Time   The French equivalent of daylight saving time lasts from April to September, which puts it 1 hour ahead of French winter time. France is usually 6 hours ahead of U.S. eastern time, except in October, when U.S. clocks are still on daylight time; then France is only 5 hours ahead. The rest of the year, when it's 9am in New York, it's 3pm in France.

Tipping   All bills, as required by law, are supposed to say *service compris,* which means that the tip has been included. But French diners often leave some small change as an additional tip, especially if service has been exceptional.

Here are some general guidelines: for hotel staff, tip 6 F to 10 F (95¢ to $1.60) for every item of baggage the porter carries on arrival and departure, and 10 F ($1.60) per day for the chambermaid. In cafes, service is usually included. Tip taxi drivers 10% to 15% of the amount on the meter. In theaters and restaurants, give cloakroom attendants at least 5 F (80¢) per item. Give rest-room attendants about 2 F (30¢) in nightclubs and such places. Give cinema and theater ushers about 2 F (30¢). For guides for group visits to museums and monuments, 5 to 10 F (80¢ to $1.60) is a reasonable tip.

Water   Drinking water is generally safe, though it's occasionally been known to cause diarrhea. If you ask for water in a restaurant, it'll be served bottled (for which you'll pay) unless you specifically request tap water (*l'eau du robinet*). Your waiter may ask if you'd like your water carbonated (*avec gas*) or without bubbles (*sans gas*).

Planning Your Trip: An Online Directory

Frommer's Online Directory will help you take better advantage of the travel-planning information available online. Section 1 lists general Internet resources that can make any trip easier, such as sites for obtaining the best possible prices on airline tickets. In Section 2 you'll find some top sites specifically for France.

This is not a comprehensive list, but a discriminating selection to get you started. Recognition is given to sites based on their content value and ease of use. Inclusion here is not paid for—unlike some Web-site rankings, which are based on payment. Finally, remember this is a press-time snapshot of leading Web sites; some undoubtedly will have evolved, changed, or moved by the time you read this.

1 Top Travel-Planning Web Sites

By Lynne Bairstow

Lynne Bairstow is the co-author of *Frommer's Mexico*, and the editorial director of *e-com* magazine.

WHY BOOK ONLINE?

Online agencies have come a long way over the past few years, now providing tips for finding the best fare, and giving you suggested dates or times to travel that yield the lowest price if your plans are at all flexible. Other sites even allow you to establish the price you're willing to pay, and they check the airlines' willingness to accept it. However, in some cases, these sites may not always yield the best price. Unlike a travel agent, for example, they may not have access to charter flights offered by wholesalers.

Online booking sites aren't the only places to reserve airline tickets— all major airlines have their own Web sites and often offer incentives (bonus frequent-flyer miles or Net-only discounts, for example) when you buy online or buy an e-ticket.

The new trend is toward conglomerated booking sites. By mid-2000, a consortium of U.S. and European-based airlines is planning to launch an as-yet unnamed Web site that will offer fares lower than those available through travel agents. United, Delta, Northwest, and Continental have initiated this effort, based on their success at selling airline seats on their own sites.

Check Out Frommer's Site

We highly recommend **Arthur Frommer's Budget Travel Online (www. frommers.com)** as an excellent, travel-planning resource. Of course, we're a little biased, but you'll find indispensable travel tips, reviews, monthly vacation giveaways, and online booking. Among the most popular features of this site are the regular "Ask the Expert" bulletin boards, which feature Frommer's authors answering your questions via online postings.

Subscribe to Arthur Frommer's Daily Newsletter (**www.frommers. com/newsletters**) to receive the latest travel bargains and inside travel secrets in your e-mailbox every day. You'll read daily headlines and articles from the dean of travel himself, highlighting last-minute deals on airfares, accommodations, cruises, and package vacations.

Search our Destinations archive (**www.frommers.com/destinations**) of more than 200 domestic and international destinations for great places to stay and dine, and tips on sightseeing. Once you've researched your trip, the online reservation system (**www.frommers.com/booktravelnow**) takes you to Frommer's favorite sites for booking your vacation at affordable prices.

The best of the travel planning sites are now highly personalized; they store your seating preferences, meal preferences, tentative itineraries, and credit-card information, allowing you to quickly plan trips or check agendas.

In many cases, booking your trip online can be better than working with a travel agent. It gives you the widest variety of choices, control, and the 24-hour convenience of planning your trip when you choose. All you need is some time—and often a little patience—and you're likely to find the fun of online travel research will greatly enhance your trip.

WHO SHOULD BOOK ONLINE?

Online booking is best for travelers who want to know as much as possible about their travel options, for those who have flexibility in their travel dates, and for bargain hunters.

One of the biggest successes in online travel for both passengers and airlines is the offer of last-minute specials, such as American Airlines' weekend deals or other Internet-only fares that must be purchased online. Another advantage is that you can cash in on incentives for booking online, such as rebates or bonus frequent-flyer miles.

Business and other frequent travelers also have found numerous benefits in online booking, as the advances in mobile technology provide them with the ability to check flight status, change plans, or get specific directions from hand-held computing devices, mobile phones, and pagers. Some sites will even e-mail or page a passenger if their flight is delayed.

Online booking is increasingly able to accommodate complex itineraries, even for international travel. The pace of evolution on the Net is rapid, so you'll probably find additional features and advancements by the time you visit these sites. The future holds ever-increasing personalization and customization for online travelers.

TRAVEL-PLANNING & BOOKING SITES

The following sites offer domestic and international flight, hotel, and rental car bookings, plus news, destination information, and deals on cruises and vacation packages. Free (one-time) registration is required for booking.

Expedia. expedia.com

Expedia is known as the fastest and, most flexible online travel planner for booking flights, hotels, and rental cars. It offers several ways of obtaining the best possible fares: **Flight Price Matcher** service allows your preferred airline to match an available fare with a competitor; a comprehensive **Fare Compare** area shows the differences in fare categories and airlines; and **Fare Calendar** helps you plan your trip around the best possible fares. Its main limitation is that like many online databases, Expedia focuses on the major airlines and hotel chains, so don't expect to find too many budget airlines or one-of-a-kind B&Bs here.

Personalized features allow you to store your itineraries and receive weekly fare reports on favorite cities. You can also check on the status of flight arrivals and departures, and through MileageMinder, track all of your frequent-flyer accounts.

Expedia also offers packages, cruises, and information on specialized travel (like casino destinations, and adventure, ski, and golf travel). There are also special features for travelers accessing information on mobile devices.

Note: In early 2000, Expedia bought travelscape.com and vacationspot.com, and incorporated these sites into expedia.com.

Travelocity (incorporates Preview Travel). www.travelocity.com; www.previewtravel.com

Frommer's online partner, Travelocity, uses the SABRE system to offer reservations and tickets for more than 400 airlines; you can also reserve and purchase from more than 45,000 hotels and 50 car-rental companies. An exclusive feature of the SABRE system is their **Low Fare Search Engine,** which automatically searches for the three lowest-priced itineraries based on a traveler's criteria. Last-minute deals and consolidator fares are included in the search. If you book with Travelocity, you can select specific seats for your flights with online seat maps, and also view diagrams of the most popular commercial aircraft. Their hotel finder provides street-level location maps and photos of selected hotels.

Travelocity features an inviting interface for booking trips, though the wealth of graphics involved can make the site somewhat slow to load, and any adjustment in your parameters means you'll need to completely start over.

This site also has some very cool tools. With the **Fare Watcher** e-mail feature, you can select up to five routes for which you'll receive e-mail notices when the fare changes by $25 or more. If you own an alphanumeric pager with national access that can receive e-mail, Travelocity's **Flight Paging** can alert you if your flight is delayed. You can also access real-time departure and arrival information on any flight within the SABRE system.

Note to AOL Users: You can book flights, hotels, rental cars and cruises on AOL at keyword: Travel. The booking software is provided by Travelocity/Preview Travel and is similar to the Internet site. Use the AOL "Travelers Advantage" program to earn a 5% rebate on flights, hotel rooms, and car rentals.

TRIP.com. www.trip.com

TRIP.com began as a site geared for business travelers, but its innovative features and highly personalized approach have broadened its appeal to leisure

More people still look online than book online, partly due to fear of putting their credit-card numbers out on the Net. Secure encryption, and increasing experienced buying online, has removed this fear for most travelers. In some cases, however, it's simply easier to buy from a local travel agent who can deliver your tickets to your door (especially if your travel is last-minute or if you have special requests). You can find a flight online and then book it by calling a toll-free number or contacting your travel agent, though this is somewhat less efficient. To be sure you're in secure mode when you book online, look for a little icon of a key (in Netscape) or a padlock (in Internet Explorer) at the bottom of your Web browser.

travelers as well. It is the leading travel site for those using mobile devices to access Internet travel information.

TRIP.com provides the average and lowest fare for the route requested, in addition to the current available fare. An on-site "newsstand" features breaking news on airfare sales and other travel specials. Among its most popular features are Flight TRACKER and intelliTRIP. **Flight TRACKER** allows users to track any commercial flight en route to its destination anywhere in the U.S., while accessing real-time FAA-based flight monitoring data. **intelliTRIP** allows you to identify the best airline, hotel, and rental-car fares in less than 90 seconds.

In addition, TRIP.com offers e-mail notification of flight delays, plus city resource guides, currency converters, and a weekly e-mail newsletter of fare updates, travel tips, and traveler forums.

Yahoo Travel. www.travel.yahoo.com
Yahoo is currently the most popular of the Internet information portals, and its travel site is a comprehensive mix of online booking, daily travel news, and destination information. Their **Best Fares** area offers what it promises, and provides feedback on refining your search if you have flexibility in travel dates or times. There is also an active section of Message Boards for discussions on travel in general, and to specific destinations.

LAST-MINUTE DEALS & OTHER ONLINE BARGAINS

There's nothing airlines hate more than flying with lots of empty seats. The Net has enabled airlines to offer last-minute bargains to entice travelers to fill those seats. Most of these are announced on Tuesday or Wednesday and are valid for travel the following weekend, but some can be booked weeks or months in advance. You can sign up for weekly e-mail alerts at the airlines' own sites (see the box below listing the airlines' Web addresses) or check sites that compile lists of these bargains, such as **Smarter Living** or **WebFlyer** (see below). To make it easier, visit a site that will round up all the deals and send them in one convenient weekly e-mail.

Important Note: See "Flying to France from North America" in chapter 2 for the Web addresses of airlines serving France. These sites offer schedules and flight booking, and most have pages where you can sign up for e-mail alerts for weekend deals and other late-breaking bargains.

✪ 1travel.com. www.1travel.com
Here you'll find deals on domestic and international flights and hotels. 1travel. com's **Saving Alert** compiles last-minute air deals so you don't have to scroll

through multiple e-mail alerts. A feature called "Drive a little using low-fare airlines" helps map out strategies for using alternate airports to find lower fares. And **Farebeater** searches a database that includes published fares, consolidator bargains, and special deals exclusive to 1travel.com. *Note:* The travel agencies listed by 1travel.com have paid for placement.

Bid for Travel. www.bidfortravel.com
Bid for Travel is another of the travel auction sites, similar to Priceline (see below), which are growing in popularity. In addition to airfares, Internet users can place a bid for vacation packages and hotels.

Cheap Tickets. www.cheaptickets.com
Cheap Tickets has exclusive deals that aren't available through more mainstream channels. One caveat about the Cheap Tickets site is that it will offer fare quotes for a route, and later show this fare is not valid for your dates of travel—most other Web sites, such as Expedia, consider your dates of travel before showing what fares are available. Despite its problems, Cheap Tickets can be worth the effort because its fares can be lower than those offered by its competitors.

LastMinuteTravel.com. www.lastminutetravel.com
Suppliers with excess inventory come to this online agency to distribute unsold airline seats, hotel rooms, cruises, and vacation packages. It's got great deals, but an excess of advertisements and slow-loading graphics.

Moment's Notice. www.moments-notice.com
As the name suggests, Moment's Notice specializes in last-minute vacation deals. You can browse for free, but if you want to purchase a trip you have to join Moment's Notice, which costs $25.

✪ Priceline.com. travel.priceline.com
Priceline lets you "name your price" for domestic and international airline tickets and hotel rooms. You select a route and dates, guarantee with a credit card, and make a bid for what you're willing to pay. If one of the airlines in Priceline's database has a fare lower than your bid, your credit card will automatically be charged for a ticket.

But you can't say when you want to fly—you have to accept any flight leaving between 6am and 10pm on the dates you selected, and you may have to make a stopover. No frequent-flyer miles are awarded, and tickets are non-refundable and can't be exchanged for another flight. So if your plans change, you're out of luck. Priceline can be good for travelers who have to take off on short notice (and who are thus unable to qualify for advance purchase discounts). But be sure to shop around first, because if you overbid, you'll be required to purchase the ticket—and Priceline will pocket the difference between what it paid for the ticket and what you bid.

Priceline says that over 35% of all reasonable offers for domestic flights are being filled on the first try, with much higher fill rates on popular routes (New York to San Francisco, for example). They define "reasonable" as not more than 30% below the lowest generally available ,advance-purchase fare for the same route.

SkyAuction.com. www.skyauction.com
An auction site with categories for airfare, travel deals, hotels, and much more.

Smarter Living. www.smarterliving.com
Best known for its e-mail dispatch of weekend deals on 20 airlines, Smarter Living also keeps you posted about last-minute bargains.

Check Your E-mail
While You're on the Road

You don't have to be out of touch just because you don't carry a laptop while you travel. Web browser–based free e-mail programs make it much easier to stay in e-touch.

Just open a freemail account at a browser-based provider, such as **MSN Hotmail** (**hotmail.com**) or **Yahoo! Mail** (**mail.yahoo.com**). AOL users should check out **AOL Netmail** (**aol.com**), and **USA.NET** (**www.usa.net**) comes highly recommended for functionality and security. You can find hints, tips and a mile-long list of freemail providers at www.emailaddresses.com.

Be sure to give your freemail address to the family members, friends, and colleagues with whom you'd like to stay in touch while you're in France. All you'll need to check your freemail account while you're away from home is a Web connection, easily available at Internet cafes, copy shops, and cash- and credit-card Internet-access machines (often available in hotel lobbies or business centers). After logging on, just point the browser to **www.hotmail.com**, **www.yahoo.com**, or the address of any other service you're using. Enter your user name and password, and you'll have access to your mail, both for receiving and sending messages to friends and family back home, for just a few dollars an hour.

The Net Café Guide (www.netcafeguide.com/mapindex.htm) will help you locate Internet cafes at hundreds of locations around the globe.

Travelzoo.com. **www.travelzoo.com**
At this Internet portal, more than 150 travel companies post special deals. It features a Top 20 list of the best deals on the site, selected by its editorial staff each Wednesday night. This list is also available via an e-mailing list, free to those who sign up.

WebFlyer. **www.webflyer.com**
WebFlyer is a comprehensive online resource for frequent flyers and also has an excellent listing of last-minute air deals. Click on "Deal Watch" for a round-up of weekend deals on flights, hotels, and rental cars from domestic and international suppliers.

ONLINE TRAVELER'S TOOLBOX

Exchange Rates. **www.x-rates.com**
See what your dollar, or pound, is worth in French francs.

✪ Foreign Languages for Travelers. **www.travlang.com**
Learn basic terms in more than 70 languages and click on any underlined phrase to hear what it sounds like. (*Note:* Free audio software and speakers are required.) They also offer hotel and airline finders with excellent prices and a simple system to get the listings you are looking for.

InnSite. **www.innsite.com**
Listings for inns and B&Bs around the globe (even a "floating hotel"—a six-cabin barge—moored on Paris's Quai Henri IV.) Find an inn at your destination, have a look at images of the rooms, check prices and availability, and

then send e-mail to the innkeeper if you have further questions. This is an extensive directory of bed and breakfast inns, but only includes listings if the proprietor submitted one. (*Note:* It's free to get an inn listed.) The descriptions are written by the innkeepers, and many link to the inns' own Web sites.

ismap.com. www.ismap.com
Locate almost any address in France with this neat interactive map that identifies nearby points of interest with icons that link to sites with more information.

U.S. Customs Service Traveler Information.
www.customs.ustreas.gov/travel/index.htm

HM Customs & Excise Passenger Enquiries. www.open.gov.uk

Canada Customs and Revenue Agency. www.ccra-adrc.gc.ca

Australian Customs. www.dfat.gov.au

New Zealand Customs Service. www.customs.govt.nz
Planning shopping spree and wondering what you're allowed to bring home? Check the latest regulations at these thorough sites.

Visa ATM Locator. www.visa.com/pd/atm/

MasterCard ATM Locator. www.mastercard.com/atm
Find ATMs in hundreds of cities around the world. Both include maps for some locations and both list airport ATM locations, some with maps.

The Weather Channel. www.weather.com
Weather forecasts for cities around the world.

2 The Top Web Sites for France

By Cheryl Pientka

Most of the following sites give users the option of using English or French. Though many of them will first come up in French, follow the icons for English versions. If it's not evident at first, scroll down to find an American or British flag.

GENERAL SITES FOR FRANCE

Enjoy France. www.enjoyfrance.com
Search for a restaurant, hotel, guest house, or ski resort around the country. Most listings include basic contact information and photos.

✪ FranceWay. www.franceway.com
Full of suggestions for your trip to France. Especially heavy on information about Paris, this guide covers dining, lodging, and transportation. A section called "Prepare Your Trip" offers short articles on duty-free shopping, visa requirements, information for people with disabilities, and a list of French consulates in the U.S.

Maison de la France. www.franceguide.com
The official site of the French Government Tourist office is a practical guide to France with advice on using transportation and finding the accommodation that's right for you. The calendar of events links to other sites, and the Regions section includes brief cultural articles on each part of the country.

Travel France. www.bonjour.com
Pick one of the country's regions and peruse a directory of links to attractions, tour operators, and city tourism offices. Check out the hints for getting

around Paris, learn about events taking place around the country, learn basic French phrases (you'll need to download free RealPlayer).

PARIS GUIDES

Aeroports de Paris. www.paris-airports.com
For the Charles de Gaulle and Orly airports, find, listings of hotels, restaurants, and car rental agencies. The parking map and accessibility information may be helpful for disabled travelers.

Bonjour Paris. www.bparis.com; AOL Keyword: Bonjour; CompuServe: Go: Paris
One of the most comprehensive and fun Web sites about life in Paris today, written from an American expatriate point of view. Hotel recommendations and travel tips for Paris abound. Message boards debate cultural differences between the French and Americans, and offer readers' restaurant, food, and wine picks. The Travel Tips section is especially helpful for new travelers to France.

✪ Paris Pages. www.paris.org
There's so much information on this site that it sometimes takes a while to download. Lodging reviews are organized by area of the city and the monuments that stand nearby. The city guide includes an event calendar, shop listings, map of attractions with details about each, and photo tours.

Paris Tourist Office. www.paris-touristoffice.com
Get a calendar of events, and contact information and the closest Métro stops for museums, lodging, restaurants, and nightlife. Tour parks and gardens and discover Paris's trendy arrondissements.

Paris Zagat. www.zagat.com
You must register (it was free as of this writing) to access this site. Choose Paris from the pull-down menu and see what other travelers have to say about the local cuisine and service.

RATP (Subway and Buses). www.ratp.fr/index.eng.html
Paris Métro and bus maps as well as street maps to the city will help get you around. Download a free version of Adobe Acrobat to view some of the street maps. RATP links to Subway Navigator, which shows you how to use the Métro from one point to another.

Smartweb: Paris. www.smartweb.fr/paris
This city guide shows the big attractions, such as the Louvre and Eiffel Tower, and includes history, photos, admission fees, and hours. Navigate the shopping and gallery listings organized by district and preview the airports' terminals. Click on maps to get the weather and subway information.

PROVENCE & THE FRENCH RIVIERA

Avignon and Provence. www.avignon-et-provence.com
Restaurant reviews (many restaurants provide their menus), museum listings, ideas for outdoor activities, and lots of history about the popes of Avignon, in addition to practical information for emergencies and classified ads.

Beyond the French Riviera. www.beyond.fr
A thorough alphabetical list of villages with maps, directions, and hotel and restaurant information, as well as photos, history, and excursions.

Cannes Online. www.cannes-on-line.com
The city's promotional site includes uncritical hotel listings, a city map, and an events calendar.

Nice. **www.nice-coteazur.org**
The in-depth outline of guided tours around the city makes this site worthwhile. You can also search for a hotel by criteria you select.

✪ **Provence Touristic Guide.** **www.provence.guideweb.com**
Dig into the Leisure and Culture section for pictures, exhibit descriptions, and contact information for museums. A directory of hotels and guest houses includes photos and some online reservations. Visitors can refer to travel guides for wine and antiques.

Provence Web. **www.provenceweb.fr**
Addresses for hotels, restaurants, and activities for 600 towns in Provence and Camargue, Luberon, and Verdon.

Riviera Cote d'Azur. **www.crt-riviera.fr**
Excursions and outdoor activities around the Côte d'Azur are arranged by season. Take a photo tour to see where you might go hiking or four-wheeling. Find out where you can get a Carte Musée Côte d'Azur, the pass good at 62 museums on the Riviera.

St. Tropez Tourism Office. **www.nova.fr/saint-tropez**
Some of the links on this site (most notably restaurants and beaches) had expired at press time. Others are in French or poor English. The site has expanded to include the villages of the surrounding peninsula and has photos and links to the e-mail of hotels and restaurants. Many of the hotels listed are chains, however, and feature other locations in addition to those in St-Tropez.

BORDEAUX & THE ATLANTIC COAST

Bordeaux Office of Tourism. **www.bordeaux-tourisme.com**
Most of the cultural information and travel tips here are fairly general. However, a nice photo gallery in the "City" section shows pictures of Bordeaux's architecture. Information is provided on 82 hotels and 12 restaurants.

Pays Basque.com. **www.paysbasque.com**
Click on the tiny British flag in the top right hand corner of this site to discover the mountains, beaches, towns, restaurants and hotels in the southwest corner of France.

Real South West of France: 123 Voyage. **www.123voyage.com/realsw**
Read lengthy descriptions about villages and attractions throughout the southwest of France. Though the lodging listings are ad-based, they include photos and offer a good idea of what to expect in this beautiful region.

Touradour.com. **www.touradour.com**
Listings for 64 hotels on the Basque coast, and more than 1,100 inland, as well as history of the region, extensive sports and activities, and links to maps and local transportation information. You'll also find lists of addresses for scooter and bike rentals. Restaurants appear in the individual town sections.

Tour of Bordeaux. **www.bordeaux.com**
Wine lovers, get ready. Read up on which wines from the region fit your taste. Also consult the dining and lodging reviews and download free QuickTime VR software to take a virtual tour of town.

BURGUNDY & THE RHONE VALLEY

Burgundy: Land of Great Art and Good Living. **www.burgundy-tourism.com**

Online Directory

A regional map directs wine enthusiasts to the area's vineyards, and photos and brief background on nearby castles show off the local architecture. Information on restaurant and lodging and sports and leisure activities is also provided.

Lyon Convention and Visitors Bureau. www.lyon-france.com
An attractive site with an excellent "City Guide" section includes directions on arriving by car and plane, public transportation, maps, foreign exchange offices, and travel tips.

BRITTANY

Brittany Holiday Guide. www.brittany-guide.com
Thorough descriptions with photos of places of interest, hotels and guest houses, transportation information (including roadwork), history, and an events calendar for the region.

Region Bretagne. www.region-bretagne.fr
Get the basics from the "Tourism" section, then see the "Leisure" section, which includes outdoor activities such as hiking and horseback riding. Otherwise, this site offers little substance in its dining and lodging sections.

NORMANDY

French Tourism Board for Normandy. www.normandy-tourism.org
Hotel descriptions and information on museums and attractions organized by town. Check out the D-Day section that highlights Battle of Normandy places of interest. An interactive parks and gardens list takes you to photos and information about the many gardens in the region. Check out the "Sports & Leisure" section with its details about the region's many golf courses.

✪ **Giverny and Vernon. www.giverny.org**
Visitors to the old stomping grounds of Claude Monet will find loads of useful travel and transportation information at this basic site. Find details on the area's castles, museums, and places of archaeological interest. Don't miss the tips on avoiding the crowds (avoid Sundays and bank holidays).

LOIRE VALLEY

Chateaux and Country. www.chateauxandcountry.com
Scroll down to the bottom of the home page and click on the American flag in the right-hand corner for the English version. A comprehensive site with photos, driving directions, castle hours, and admission prices, and, where applicable, castle lodging prices. Discover the France of the kings by following the "historical journeys" mapped here. You can search for châteaux in five regions of France.

Loire Net. www.loire.net
With photos, descriptions, and reviews, this guide to the Loire Valley shows off the historic châteaux, museums, and other attractions.

West Loire. www.cr-pays-de-la-loire.fr/eng.htm
Pictures of château-accommodations give a nice preview of your trip. Read the brief descriptions of golf courses, local cuisine, spas, and museums.

GETTING AROUND

Rail Europe. www.raileurope.com
Rail Europe lets you buy Eurail, Europass, and Brit Rail railroad passes online, as well as Eurostar tickets to and from London via the Channel Tunnel, rail and drive packages, and point-to-point travel in 35 European countries. Even

if you don't want a railpass, the site offers invaluable first- and second-class fare and schedule information to the most popular European rail routes.

SNCF (Railroad). **www.sncf.fr**

Schedule and fare information for main French and European railroad lines. You can reserve or purchase tickets online and pick up the ticket at a station or ticket vending machine (your credit card is required for this) or have it sent to you.

✪ Subway Navigator. **http://metro.ratp.fr:10001/bin/cities/english**

An amazing site with detailed subway route maps for Paris, Lyon, Marseille, and some other French cities.

3

Settling into Paris

Stroll along the river Seine and the broad tree-lined boulevards, stopping to browse through the chic shops and relax over coffee or wine at the sidewalk cafes; visit the world-renowned museums, monuments, and cathedrals; sample the legendary cuisine; attend an opera or a concert; and enjoy the red-hot nightlife. Despite the turmoil going on behind the scenes, Paris is still the City of Light—and it always manages to live up to its reputation as one of the world's most romantic cities.

Ernest Hemingway referred to the many splendors of Paris as a "moveable feast" and wrote, "There is never any ending to Paris, and the memory of each person who has lived in it differs from that of any other." It's this personal discovery of the city that has always been the most compelling reason for coming here.

1 Orientation

ARRIVING

BY PLANE Paris has two major international airports: Aéroport d'Orly, 8¹/₂ miles south, and Aéroport Roissy-Charles de Gaulle, 14¹/₄ miles northeast of the city. A shuttle (75 F or $12.75) operates between the two airports about every 30 minutes, taking 50 to 75 minutes to make the journey.

Charles de Gaulle Airport (Roissy) At Charles de Gaulle (☎ **01-48-62-22-80**), foreign carriers use Aérogare 1, while Air France wings into Aérogare 2. From Aérogare 1 you take a moving walkway to the passport checkpoint and the Customs area. The two terminals are linked by a shuttle bus (*navette*).

The shuttle bus also transports you to the **Roissy rail station,** from which fast RER trains leave every 15 minutes heading to such Métro stations as Gare du Nord, Châtelet, Luxembourg, Port-Royal, and Denfert-Rochereau. A typical fare from Roissy to any point in central Paris is 62.50 F ($10) in first class, 49 F ($7.85) in second class.

You can also take an **Air France shuttle bus** to central Paris for 75 F ($12). It stops at the Palais des Congrès (Port Maillot), then continues on to place Charles-de-Gaulle-Étoile, where subway lines can carry you farther along to any point in Paris. That ride, depending on traffic, takes between 45 and 55 minutes. The shuttle departs about every 12 minutes between 5:40am and 11pm.

Another option is the **Roissybus,** departing from the airport daily from 5:45am to 11pm and costing 48 F ($7.70) for the 45- to 50-minute ride. Departures are about every 15 minutes, and the bus will take you near the corner of rue Scribe and place de l'Opéra in the heart of Paris.

A **taxi** from Roissy into the city will cost about 220 F ($35.20), but from 8pm to 7am the fares are 40% higher. Long lines of both taxis and passengers form outside each of the airport's terminals and are surprisingly orderly.

Orly Airport   Orly (☎ 01-49-75-15-15) has two terminals—Orly Sud (south) for international flights and Orly Ouest (west) for domestic flights. They're linked by a free shuttle bus.

Air France buses leave from Exit E of Orly Sud and from Exit F of Orly Ouest every 12 minutes between 5:45am and 11pm, heading for Gare des Invalides; fare is 45 F ($7.20). When you're returning to the airport, buses leave the Invalides terminal heading to Orly Sud or Orly Ouest every 15 minutes, taking about 30 minutes.

Another way to get to central Paris is via the free **shuttle bus** that leaves both of Orly's terminals about every 15 minutes for the nearby Métro and RER train station (Pont-de-Rungis/Aéroport-d'Orly). From here, RER trains take 35 minutes for rides into the city center. A trip to Les Invalides, for example, is 47 F ($7.50).

A **taxi** from Orly to the center of Paris costs about 170 F ($27.20), more at night. Don't take a meterless taxi from Orly Sud or Orly Ouest—it's much safer (and usually cheaper) to hire a metered cab from the lines, which are under the scrutiny of a police officer.

BY TRAIN   Paris has six major train stations: **Gare d'Austerlitz,** 55 quai d'Austerlitz, 13e (servicing the southwest with trains to and from the Loire Valley, the Bordeaux country, the Pyrénées, and Spain); **Gare de l'Est,** place du 11-Novembre-1918, 10e (servicing the east with trains to and from Strasbourg, Nancy, Reims, and beyond to Zurich, Basel, Luxembourg, and Austria); **Gare de Lyon,** 20 bd. Diderot, 12e (servicing the southeast with trains to and from the Côte d'Azur [Nice, Cannes, St-Tropez, etc.], Provence, and beyond to Geneva, Lausanne, and Italy); **Gare Montparnasse,** 17 bd. Vaugirard, 15e (servicing the west with trains to and from Brittany); **Gare du Nord,** 18 rue de Dunkerque, 15e (servicing the north with trains to and from London, Holland, Denmark, Belgium, and northern Germany); and **Gare St-Lazare,** 13 rue d'Amsterdam, 8e (servicing the northwest with trains to and from Normandy). Buses operate between the stations. Each of these stations has a Métro stop, making the whole city accessible. Taxis are also available at designated stands—look for the signs that say TÊTE DE STATION. For general train information and to make reservations, call ☎ 08-36-35-35-35 from 7am to 8pm daily.

Note: The stations and the surrounding areas are usually seedy and frequented by pickpockets, hustlers, hookers, and drug addicts. Be alert, especially at night.

BY BUS   Most buses arrive at the **Gare Routière Internationale du Paris-Gallieni,** 28 av. du Général-de-Gaulle, in the suburb of Bagnolet (☎ 01-49-72-51-51; Métro: Gallieni).

BY CAR   Driving in Paris is definitely not recommended. Parking is difficult and traffic dense. If you do drive, remember that Paris is encircled by a ring road called the *périphérique.* Always obtain detailed directions to your destination, including the name of the exit on the périphérique (exits aren't numbered). Avoid rush hours.

Few hotels, except the luxury ones, have garages, but the staff will usually be able to direct you to one nearby.

The major highways into Paris are A1 from the north (Great Britain and Benelux); A13 from Rouen, Normandy, and other points of northwest France; A10 from Spain, the Pyrénées, and the southwest; A6 and A7 from the French Alps, the Riviera, and Italy; and A4 from eastern France.

VISITOR INFORMATION

The **main tourist information office** is at 127 av. des Champs-Elysées, 8e (☎ **08-36-68-31-12;** Métro: George V), where you can secure details about both Paris and the provinces. The office is open daily from 9am to 8pm from April to October, with an annual closing May 1. Between November and March, the office is open daily from 11am to 6pm, with an annual closing December 25.

Welcome Offices in the city's rail stations (except Gare St-Lazare) and at the Eiffel Tower will give you free maps, brochures, and *Paris Selection,* a French-language monthly listing current events and performances.

CITY LAYOUT

Paris is surprisingly compact. Occupying 432 square miles, it's home to more than 10 million people. The river Seine divides Paris into the **Right Bank (Rive Droite)** to the north and the **Left Bank (Rive Gauche)** to the south. These designations make sense when you stand on a bridge and face downstream (west), watching the waters flow out toward the sea—to your right is the north bank, to your left the south. A total of 32 bridges link the Right Bank and the Left Bank, some providing access to the two small islands at the heart of the city—**Île de la Cité,** the city's birthplace and site of Notre-Dame, and **Ile St-Louis,** a moat-guarded oasis of sober 17th-century mansions. These islands can cause some confusion to walkers who think they've just crossed a bridge from one bank to the other, only to find themselves caught up in an almost-medieval maze of narrow streets and old buildings.

The "main street" on the Right Bank is, of course, **avenue des Champs-Elysées,** beginning at the Arc de Triomphe and running to place de la Concorde. Avenue des Champs-Elysées and 11 other avenues radiate like the arms of an asterisk from the Arc de Triomphe, giving it its original name, place de l'Étoile (*étoile* means "star"). It was renamed place Charles-de-Gaulle following the general's death; today it's often referred to as place Charles-de-Gaulle-Étoile.

FINDING AN ADDRESS   Paris is divided into 20 municipal wards called *arrondissements,* each with its own mayor, city hall, police station, and central post office; some even have remnants of market squares. Arrondissements spiral out clockwise from the 1st, which is in the geographical center of the city. The 2nd through the 8th form a ring around the 1st, while the 9th through the 17th form an outer ring around the inner ring. The 18th, 19th, and 20th are at the far northern and eastern reaches of the Right Bank. Arrondissements 5, 6, 7, 13, 14, and 15 are on the Left Bank.

Most city maps are divided by arrondissement, and all addresses include the arrondissement number (written in Roman or Arabic numerals and followed by "e" or "er"). Paris also has its own version of a zip code. The proper mailing address for a certain hotel is written as, for example, "75014 Paris." The last two digits, 14, indicate that the address is in the 14th arrondissement—in this case, Montparnasse.

Numbers on buildings running parallel to the Seine usually follow the course of the river—east to west. On perpendicular streets, numbers onbuildings begin low closer to the river.

MAPS   If you're staying more than 2 or 3 days, purchase an inexpensive pocket-size book called *Paris par arrondissement,* available at all major newsstands and bookshops. These guides provide you with a Métro map, a foldout map of the city, and maps of each arrondissement, with all streets listed and keyed.

The Arrondissements in Brief

Each of Paris's 20 arrondissements possesses a unique style and flavor. Do note, however, that in this guide we cover only those hotels in central Paris; for a wider selection of accommodations in the outer arrondissements, see *Frommer's Paris 2001.*

1er (Musée du Louvre/Les Halles)   One of the world's greatest art museums, the **Louvre** lures hordes to the 1st arrondissement. Here are many elegant addresses, rue de Rivoli, and the **Jeu de Paume** and **Orangerie** museums. Walk through the formal **Jardin des Tuileries,** laid out by Le Nôtre, Louis XIV's gardener. Pause to take in the classic beauty of **place Vendôme.** Jewelers and art dealers are plentiful, and the memories of Chopin are evoked at no. 12 on the square where he died. Zola's "belly of Paris" (Les Halles) is no longer the food-and-meat market; it has become the **Forum des Halles,** a center of shopping, entertainment, and culture.

2e (La Bourse)   Home to the **Bourse (stock exchange),** this Right Bank district lies mainly between the Grands Boulevards and rue Etienne-Marcel. On weekdays the shouts of brokers echo across place de la Bourse until lunchtime, when they continue their hysteria in the district's restaurants. Much of the eastern end of the 2nd is devoted to the **garment district (Le Sentier),** where thousands of garments are sold to buyers from stores all over Europe. If you explore this district, you'll find gems amid the commercialism—none finer than the **Musée Cognacq-Jay,** at 25 bd. des Capucines, which features work by every artist from Watteau to Fragonard.

3e (Le Marais)   This district embraces much of **Le Marais (the Swamp),** one of the best loved of the old Right Bank neighborhoods. Over the centuries kings have called Le Marais home, and its salons have echoed with the witty, often devastating remarks of Racine, Voltaire, Molière, and Mme de Sévigné. Allowed to fall into decay for decades, it has come back in the '90s, with lots of galleries and trendy new boutiques. One of its chief draws today is the **Musée Picasso,** a great repository of 20th-century art. Le Marais is also the center of Paris's hot gay and lesbian scene. Rue des Rosiers, with its Jewish restaurant, remains as a memory of the hundreds of Jewish residents who used to reside in Le Marais.

4e (Île de la Cité/Ile St-Louis & Beaubourg)   It seems as if the 4th has it all: not only the Île de la Cité, with **Notre-Dame,** the **Sainte-Chapelle,** and the **Conciergerie,** but also the Ile St-Louis, with aristocratic town houses, courtyards, and antiques shops. Ile St-Louis, a former cow pasture and dueling ground, is home to 6,000 lucky Louisiens, its permanent residents. Of course, the whole area is touristy and overrun.

The heart of medieval Paris, the 4th evokes memories of Danton and Robespierre, even of Charlotte Corday stabbing Marat in his bath. You get France's finest **bird and flower markets,** plus the **Centre Georges-Pompidou.** After all this pomp and glory, you can retreat to **place des Vosges,** a square of perfect harmony where Victor Hugo penned many masterpieces from 1832 to 1848.

5e (Latin Quarter)   The Quartier Latin is Paris's intellectual soul. Bookstores, schools, churches, smoky jazz clubs, student dives, Roman ruins, publishing houses, and chic boutiques characterize the district. With the founding of the **Sorbonne** in 1253, the quarter got its name because all the students and professors spoke Latin. As the traditional center of "bohemian Paris," it formed the setting for Henry Murger's novel *La Vie Bohème* (later the Puccini opera *La Bohème,* and even later the basis of the Broadway hit *Rent*).

For sure, the old Latin Quarter is gone. Changing times have brought Greek, Moroccan, and Vietnamese immigrants, among others, hustling everything from

Paris by Arrondissement

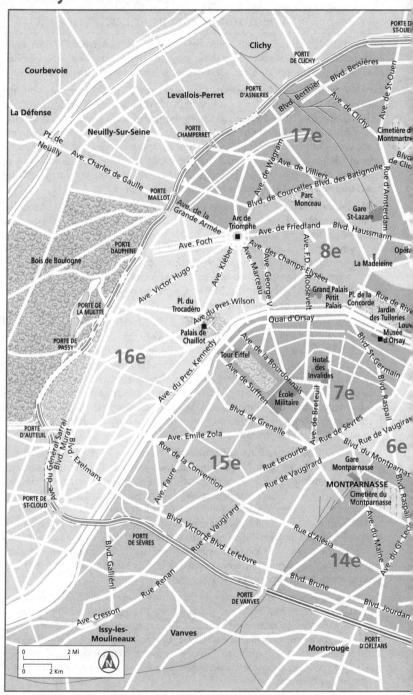

Clichy

Courbevoie

Levallois-Perret

La Défense

PORTE DE CLICHY

PORTE D'ASNIERES

PORTE CHAMPERRET

Neuilly-Sur-Seine

Pt. de Neuilly

Ave. Charles de Gaulle

PORTE MAILLOT

Ave. de la Grande Armée

Blvd. Berthier

Blvd. Bessières

Ave. de Clichy

Ave. de St-Ouen

PORTE D'ST-OUEN

17e

Cimetière d Montmartre

Blvd de Clic

Rue d'Amsterdam

Ave. de Wagram

Ave. de Villiers

Blvd. de Courcelles

Blvd. des Batignolle

Parc Monceau

Gare St-Lazare

Arc de Triomphe

Ave. de Friedland

Blvd. Haussmann

Ave. Foch

Ave. des Champs-Elysées

8e

Opéra

La Madeleine

Bois de Boulogne

PORTE DAUPHINE

Ave. Victor Hugo

Ave. Kléber

Ave. Marceau

Ave. George V

Ave. F.D. Roosevelt

Grand Palais
Petit Palais

Pl. de la Concorde

Rue de Riv

PORTE DE LA MUETTE

Pl. du Trocadéro

Ave. du Pres. Wilson

Quai d'Orsay

Jardin des Tuileries

Louv
Musée d'Orsay

PORTE DE PASSY

Palais de Chaillot

16e

Tour Eiffel

Ave. du Pres. Kennedy

Ave. de la Bourdonnais

Ave. de Suffren

Hotel. des Invalides

Blvd. St-Germain

Blvd. Raspail

7e

PORTE D'AUTEUIL

Ave. du Général Sarrail

Blvd. Murat

Blvd. Exelmans

École Militaire

Blvd. de Grenelle

Ave. de Breteuil

Rue de Sevres

Rue de Vaugirard

6e

Ave. Emile Zola

Rue de la Convention

15e

Rue Lecourbe

Rue de Vaugirard

Blvd. du Montparnas

Gare Montparnasse

MONTPARNASSE
Cimetière du Montparnasse

Blvd. Raspail

PORTE DE ST-CLOUD

Ave. Faure

Blvd. Victor de Vaugirard

Rue de Blvd. Lefebvre

Rue d'Alésia

Ave. du Maine

Ave. du Gl. Lec

14e

Blvd. Galliéni

PORTE DE SEVRES

Rue Renan

Blvd. Brune

Blvd. Jourdan

Ave. Cresson

Issy-les-Moulineaux

Vanves

PORTE DE VANVES

Montrouge

PORTE D'ORLEANS

0   2 Mi

0   2 Km

N

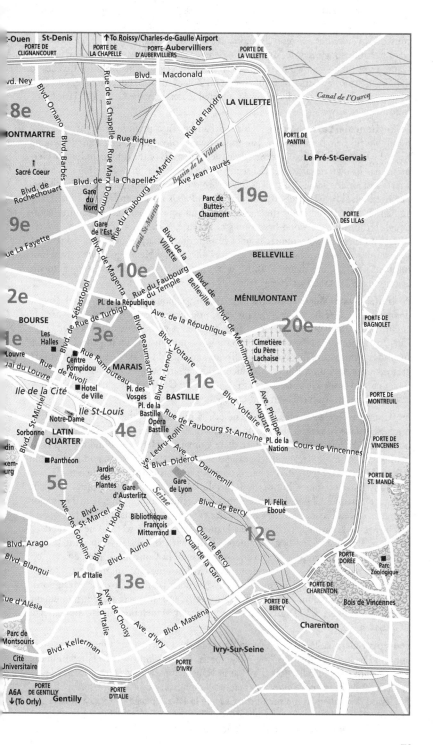

-Ouen St-Denis ↑To Roissy/Charles-de-Gaulle Airport
PORTE DE   PORTE DE   PORTE Aubervilliers   PORTE DE
CLIGNANCOURT   LA CHAPELLE   D'AUBERVILLIERS   LA VILLETTE

vd. Ney   Blvd.   Macdonald
                                                    LA VILLETTE   Canal de l'Ourcq
8e   PORTE DE
MONTMARTRE   PANTIN
                                                    Parc de   Le Pré-St-Gervais
↑ Sacré Coeur   Ave. Jean Jaurès Buttes-
Blvd. de   Bassin de la Villette Chaumont 19e
Rochechouart   Gare   PORTE
9e   du   DES LILAS
                   Nord   BELLEVILLE
ue La Fayette   Gare
                   de l'Est   MÉNILMONTANT
2e   10e   20e   PORTE DE
                                                                                    BAGNOLET
BOURSE   Pl. de la République   Cimetière
1e   Les   Ave. de la République   du Père
         Halles   3e   Lachaise
Louvre   Rue Rambuteau   PORTE DE
         Centre   MONTREUIL
Quai du Louvre   Pompidou MARAIS
Rue de Rivoli   Hotel   Pl. des   BASTILLE   PORTE DE
Ile de la Cité   de Ville   Vosges   11e   VINCENNES
         St-Michel Ile St-Louis Pl. de la
         Notre-Dame   Bastille Rue de Faubourg St-Antoine Pl. de la
Sorbonne LATIN   Opéra   Nation Cours de Vincennes
din   QUARTER 4e   Bastille   PORTE DE
xem-   ST. MANDÉ
urg   Panthéon   Ave. Blvd. Diderot Daumesnil
         5e   Jardin   Gare   PORTE
                   des   de Lyon   DORÉE   Parc
Blvd. Arago   Plantes   Gare   Pl. Félix   Zoologique
Blvd. Blanqui   d'Austerlitz Blvd. de Bercy   Eboué   12e
                   Bibliothèque
                   François
                   Mitterrand   PORTE DE
         Pl. d'Italie 13e   CHARENTON Bois de Vincennes
ue d'Alésia   PORTE DE
Parc de   BERCY   Charenton
Montsouris   Blvd. Kellerman   Ivry-Sur-Seine
Cité
Universitaire
A6A   PORTE   PORTE   PORTE
↓(To Orly) DE GENTILLY D'ITALIE   D'IVRY
       Gentilly

73

couscous to fiery-hot spring rolls and souvlaki. The 5th borders the Seine, so you'll want to stroll along **quai de Montebello,** where vendors sell everything from antique Daumier prints to yellowing copies of Balzac's *Père Goriot.* The 5th also stretches to the **Panthéon,** the resting place of Rousseau, Zola, Hugo, Braille, Voltaire, and Jean Moulin, the Resistance leader who was tortured to death by the Gestapo. Marie Curie is buried here as well.

6e (St-Germain/Luxembourg)   This heartland of Paris publishing is, for some, the most colorful Left Bank quarter. You can see waves of earnest young artists emerging from the **École des Beaux-Arts.** Strolling the boulevards of the 6th, including **St-Germain,** has its own rewards, but the secret of the district lies in discovering its narrow streets and hidden squares as well as the **Jardin du Luxembourg,** a classic French garden overlooked by Marie de Médici's Italianate **Palais du Luxembourg.** To be really authentic, you should stroll these streets with an unwrapped loaf of country sourdough bread from the wood-fired ovens of **Poilâne,** 8 rue du Cherche-Midi. Everywhere you turn you'll encounter famous historic and literary associations, none more so than on **rue Jacob,** where Racine, Wagner, Ingres, and Hemingway once lived (not together). Today's big name is likely to be filmmaker Spike Lee checking into his favorite, La Villa Hôtel, at 29 rue Jacob.

7e (Eiffel Tower/Musée d'Orsay)   Paris's most famous symbol, the **Eiffel Tower,** dominates the Left Bank 7th. The tower is, of course, one of the most recognizable landmarks in the world, but many Parisians hated it when it was unveiled in 1889. The 7th is home to several other imposing monuments, including the **Hôtel des Invalides,** which contains Napoléon's Tomb and the Musée de l'Armée (the world's greatest army museum). But there's much hidden charm as well. Even visitors with no time to discover the 7th at least rush to the **Musée d'Orsay,** the world's premier showcase of 19th-century French art and culture.

8e (Champs-Elysées/Madeleine)   The 8th is the heart of the Right Bank and its prime showcase is **avenue des Champs-Elysées,** linking the **Arc de Triomphe** with the delicate Egyptian obelisk on **place de la Concorde.** Here you'll find the top fashion houses, the most elegant hotels, expensive restaurants and shops, and fashionably attired Parisians. By the 1980s it had become a garish strip, with too much traffic and too many fast-food joints. But in the 1990s the Gaulist mayor of Paris (now president of France), Jacques Chirac, launched a massive cleanup and improvement. The major change has been broadened sidewalks, with new rows of trees planted.

The area is known for having either France's (perhaps the world's) best, grandest, and most impressive: the best restaurant (**Taillevent**), the sexiest strip joint (**Crazy Horse Saloon**), the most splendid square (**place de la Concorde**), the best rooftop cafe (at **La Samaritaine**), the grandest hotel (**Crillon**), the most impressive triumphal arch (**Arc de Triomphe**), the most expensive residential street (**avenue Matignon**), the oldest Métro station (**Franklin-D.-Roosevelt**), and the most ancient monument (**Obelisk of Luxor,** 3,300 years old). Also here is **La Madeleine** church, looking like a Greek temple.

9e (Opéra Garnier/Pigalle)   Everything from the Quartier de l'Opéra to the strip joints of Pigalle (the infamous "Pig Alley" for the GIs of World War II) falls within the 9th. The 9th was radically altered by Baron Haussmann's 19th-century urban redevelopment, and the *grands boulevards* here are among the most obvious of his labors. Boulevard des Italiens is the site of the **Café de la Paix,** opened in 1856 and once the meeting place of Romantic poets like Théophile Gautier and Alfred de Musset. Later, de Gaulle, Dietrich, and two million Americans started showing up.

Another major attraction is the **Folies-Bergère,** where cancan dancers have been kicking since 1868 and such entertainers as Mistinguett, Piaf, and Chevalier have appeared, along with the American Josephine Baker. But more than anything, it was the **Opéra** (now the Opéra Garnier or Palais Garnier), once the haunt of the Phantom, that made the 9th the last hurrah of Second Empire opulence.

10e (Gare du Nord/Gare de l'Est)   Gare du Nord and Gare de l'Est, along with movie theaters, porno houses, and dreary commercial zones, make the 10th one of the least desirable arrondissements in which tourists can spend their time. We always try to avoid the 10th, except for two longtime favorite restaurants: **Brasserie Flo,** 7 cour des Petites-Ecuries (go for *la formidable choucroute*—a heap of sauerkraut garnished with everything); and **Julien,** 16 rue du Faubourg St-Denis (called the poor man's Maxim's because of its belle époque interior and moderate prices).

11e (Opéra Bastille)   For many years this quarter seemed to sink lower and lower. However, the 1989 opening of the **Opéra Bastille** gave it a new lease on life. The "people's opera house" now stands on the landmark **place de la Bastille,** where on July 14, 1789, some 633 Parisians stormed the fortress, seized the ammunition depot, and released the few remaining prisoners.

Even when the district wasn't fashionable, visitors flocked to the most famous brasserie in Paris, **Bofinger,** 5–7 rue de la Bastille, to sample its Alsatian choucroute. (Technically Bofinger lies in the 4th arrondissement, but it has always been associated with place de la Bastille.) What charms exist in the 11th? Whatever is here has to be sought out, including the **Marché place d'Aligre,** a secondhand market in the Middle Eastern food market. Everything is cheap, and though you must search hard for treasures, you'll often find them.

12e (Bois de Vincennes/Gare de Lyon)   Few out-of-towners came here until a French chef opened **Au Trou Gascon.** Then the whole world started showing up. The major attraction is the **Bois de Vincennes,** a sprawling park on the eastern periphery of Paris. It has been a longtime favorite of families who enjoy its zoos and museums, its royal château and boating lakes, and the Parc Floral de Paris, whose springtime rhododendrons and autumn dahlias are among the city's major lures. The dreary **Gare de Lyon** lies in the 12th, but going here is worthwhile even if you don't have to take a train. The attraction is **Le Train Bleue,** the station's restaurant, whose ceiling frescoes and Art Nouveau decor are classified as national artistic treasures— and the food's good, too. The 12th, once a depressing neighborhood, is moving toward a multimillion-dollar resuscitation, including new housing, shops, gardens, and restaurants.

13e (Gare d'Austerlitz)   Centering around the grimy Gare d'Austerlitz, the 13th may have its fans, though we've yet to meet one. British snobs who flitted in and out of the train station were among the first foreign visitors, and they in essence wrote the 13th off as a "dreary working-class district." But there's at least one reason to go here: the **Manufacture des Gobelins,** 42 av. des Gobelins—this is the tapestry factory that made the word *Gobelins* world famous.

14e (Montparnasse)   The northern end of this district is **Montparnasse,** home of the Lost Generation. One of its major monuments, helping set the tone of the neighborhood, is the Rodin statue of Balzac at the junction of boulevard Montparnasse and boulevard Raspail. At this corner are famous **literary cafes** like La Rotonde, Le Sélect, La Dôme, and La Coupole. Perhaps only Gertrude Stein didn't come here (she loathed cafes), but all the other American expatriates, including Hemingway and Fitzgerald, arrived for a drink or four. At 27 rue de Fleurus, Stein and Toklas collected their paint-ings and entertained T. S. Eliot and Matisse. At its southern end, the 14th contains residential neighborhoods filled with well-designed apartment buildings, many con-structed between 1910 and 1940.

15e (Gare Montparnasse/Institut Pasteur)   A mostly residential district beginning at Gare Montparnasse, the 15th stretches west to the Seine. It's the largest arrondisse-ment, but attracts few visitors and has few attractions, except for the **Parc des Expo-sitions** and the **Institut Pasteur.**

16e (Trocadéro/Bois de Boulogne)   Highlights of the 16th are the **Bois de Boulogne, Jardins du Trocadéro, Musée de Balzac, Musée Guimet** (famous for its Asian collections), and the **Cimetière de Passy,** resting place of Manet, Talleyrand, Giraudoux, and Debussy. One of the largest arrondissements, it's known for its well-heeled bourgeoisie, upscale rents, and posh residential boulevards. Prosperous and suitably conservative addresses include **avenue d'Iéna** and **avenue Victor-Hugo;** also prestigious is **avenue Foch,** the widest boulevard, with homes that at various periods were maintained by Aristotle Onassis, the shah of Iran, Debussy, and Prince Rainier of Monaco. The 16th also includes the best place in Paris to view the Eiffel Tower from afar: **place du Trocadéro.**

17e (Parc Monceau/Place Clichy)   Flanking the northern periphery of Paris, the 17th is one of the most spread out arrondissements, incorporating the northern edge of glamorous place de Charles-de-Gaulle-Étoile in the west, the conservatively bour-geois place Wagram at its center, and the relatively tawdry place Clichy in the east. Highlights are **Parc Monceau,** the **Palais des Congrès** (which will be of interest only if you're attending a convention or special exhibit), and the **Porte Maillot Air Termi-nal,** no grand distinction. More exciting than any of those are two great restaurants: **Guy Savoy** and **Michel Rostang** (see "Dining," below).

18e (Montmartre)   The 18th is the most famous outer arrondissement, embracing **Montmartre** and associated with such legendary names as the **Moulin Rouge, Sacré-Coeur,** and **place du Tertre** (a tourist trap if there ever was one). Utrillo was its native son, Renoir lived here, and Toulouse-Lautrec adopted the area as his own. Today place Blanche is known for its prostitutes, and Montmartre is filled with honky-tonks, sou-venir shops, and terrible restaurants. Go for the attractions and *mémoires.* The **Marché aux Puces de Clignancourt** flea market is another landmark.

19e (La Villette)   Visitors come here to what was once the village of La Villette to see the much-publicized angular **Cité des Sciences et de l'Industrie,** a spectacular science museum/park built on a site that for years was devoted to slaughterhouses. Mostly residential, the district is one of the most ethnic in Paris, home of workers from all parts of the former Empire. A highlight is **Les Buttes Chaumont,** a park where kids can enjoy puppet shows and donkey rides.

20e (Père-Lachaise Cemetery)   This district's greatest landmark is the **Père-Lachaise Cemetery,** resting place of Piaf, Proust, Wilde, Duncan, Stein and Toklas, Bernhardt, Colette, Jim Morrison, and many others. Nostalgia buffs sometimes visit Piaf's former neighborhood, Ménilmontant-Belleville, but it has been almost totally bulldozed and rebuilt. The district is now home to many Muslims and hundreds of members of Paris's Sephardic Jewish community, many of whom fled from Algeria or Tunisia. With turbaned men selling dates and grains on the street, this arrondissement seems more North African than French.

2 Getting Around

Paris is a city for strollers, whose greatest joy is rambling through unexpected alleys and squares. If you have a choice, try to make it on your own two feet whenever possible. How else can you rub elbows (literally) with Parisians and experience the real Paris?

BY MÉTRO (SUBWAY)   Easy to use, the Métro (☎ **08-36-68-77-14**) is the most efficient and fastest means of transportation in Paris. Each line is numbered, and the final destination of each line is clearly marked on subway maps, in the underground passageways, and on the train cars.

The Métro runs daily from 5:30am to around 1:15am. It's reasonably safe at any hour, but beware of pickpockets.

To familiarize yourself with Paris's Métro system before you leave, check out the map on the inside front cover of this book. Most stations display a map of the Métro at the entrance. To make sure you catch the correct train, find your destination, then follow the rail line it's on to the end of the route and note the name of the final destination—this final stop is the direction. To find your train in the station, follow the signs labeled with your direction in the passageways until you see it labeled on a train.

Transfer stations are known as *correspondances*—some require long walks; Châtelet is the most difficult—but most trips will require only one transfer. When transferring, follow the bright-orange CORRESPONDENCE signs until you reach the proper platform. Don't follow a SORTIE ("Exit") sign or you'll have to pay another fare to resume your journey.

Many of the larger stations have easy-to-use maps with push-button indicators that light up your route when you press the button for your destination.

On the urban lines, it costs the same to travel to any point: 8 F ($1.30). On the Sceaux, Boissy-St-Léger, and St-Germain-en-Laye lines serving the suburbs, fares are based on distance. A *carnet* is the best buy—10 tickets for 55 F ($8.80).

At the turnstile entrances to the station, insert your ticket and pass through. At some exits tickets are also checked, so hold on to it. There are occasional ticket checks on trains and platforms and in passageways, too.

BY BUS   Buses are much slower than the Métro and the majority run only from 7am to 8:30pm (a few operate until 12:30am, and 10 operate during early-morning hours). Service is limited on Sunday and holidays. Bus and Métro fares are the same, and you

Discount Passes

You can purchase a **Paris-Visite,** a pass valid for 3 or 5 days on the public transport system, including the Métro, buses, and RER (Réseau Express Régional) trains. (The RER has both first- and second-class compartments; the pass lets you travel in first class.) As a bonus, the funicular ride to the top of Montmartre is included. The cost is 55 F ($8.80) for 1 day, 90 F ($14.40) for 2 days, 120 F ($19.20) for 3 days, or 175 F ($28) for 5 days. The card is available at RATP (Régie Autonome des Transports Parisiens) offices, the tourist office, and the main Métro stations; call ☎ **01-44-68-20-20** for information.

There are other discount passes as well, though most are available only to French residents with government ID cards and proof of taxpayer status. One available to temporary visitors is **Carte Mobilis,** which allows unlimited travel on all bus, subway, and RER lines during a 1-day period for 32 F to 72 F ($5.10 to $11.50), depending on the zone. Ask for it at any Métro station.

can use the same carnet tickets on both. Most bus rides require one ticket, but there are some destinations requiring two (never more than two within the city limits).

At certain bus stops, signs list the destinations and numbers of the buses serving that point. Destinations are usually listed north to south and east to west. Most stops along the way are also posted on the sides of the buses. During rush hours you may have to take a ticket from a dispensing machine, indicating your position in the line at the bus stop.

If you intend to use the buses a lot, pick up an RATP bus map at the office on place de la Madeleine, 8e, or at the tourist offices at RATP headquarters, 53 bis quai des Grands-Augustins, 6e. For detailed recorded information in English on bus and Métro routes, call ☎ **08-36-68-41-14.**

The same organization that runs the Métro and the buses, the **RATP** (☎ **08-36-68-77-14**), also offers the **Balabus,** big-windowed orange-and-white motor coaches that, unfortunately, run only during limited hours: Sundays and national holidays from noon to 9pm, April 15 to September only. Itineraries run in both directions between Gare de Lyon and the Grande Arche de La Défense, encompassing some of the city's most beautiful vistas. It's a great deal—two Métro tickets for 16 F ($2.55) will carry you the entire route. You'll recognize the bus and the route it follows by the *Bb* symbol emblazoned on each bus's side and on signs posted beside the route it follows.

BY TAXI   It's impossible to get one at rush hour, so don't even try. Taxi drivers are strongly organized into an effective lobby to keep their number limited to 15,000.

Watch out for the common rip-offs. Always check the meter to make sure you're not paying the previous passenger's fare. Beware of cabs without meters, which often wait outside nightclubs for tipsy patrons, or settle the tab in advance. You can hail regular cabs on the street when their signs read LIBRE. Taxis are easier to find at the many stands near Métro stations.

The flag drops at 14 F ($2.40), and from 7am to 7pm you pay 3.58 F (55¢) per kilometer. From 7pm to 7am, expect to pay 5.94 F (95¢) per kilometer. On airport trips you're not required to pay for the driver's empty return ride.

You're allowed several small pieces of luggage free if they're transported inside and don't weigh more than 5 kilograms (11 pounds). Heavier suitcases carried in the trunk cost 6 F to 10 F (95¢ to $1.60) apiece. Tip 12% to 15%—the latter usually elicits a *merci.* For radio cabs, call ☎ **01-45-85-85-85,** 01-49-36-10-10, or 01-42-70-00-42—note that you'll be charged from the point where the taxi begins the drive to pick you up.

BY BOAT   The **Batobus** (☎ **01-44-11-33-44**) is a 150-passenger ferryboat with big windows. Every day between May and September, the boats operate along the Seine, stopping at five points of interest: from west to east, the **Eiffel Tower, Musée d'Orsay,** the **Louvre, Notre-Dame,** and the **Hôtel de Ville** (from east to west, the order is reversed). Transit from one stop to another is 20 F ($3.20), and departures are about every 30 minutes from 10am to 7pm. Unlike on the Bâteaux-Mouche (see chapter 4), there's no recorded commentary. The Batobus isn't really a sightseeing tour (though the views are panoramic and sometimes inspiring); instead, it offers a way to move from one attraction to another.

Fast Facts: Paris

For additional practical information, see "Fast Facts: France" in chapter 2.

American Express   With a grand Paris office, American Express, 11 rue Scribe, 9e (☎ **01-47-77-77-07;** Métro: Opéra, Chaussée-d'Antin, or Havre-Caumartin;

RER: Auber), is extremely busy with customers buying and cashing traveler's checks (not the best rates for exchange transactions), picking up mail, and solving travel problems. It's open Monday through Friday from 9am to 6pm; the bank is also open Saturday (from 9am to 5:30pm), but the mail-pickup window is closed. A less busy office is at 38 av. de Wagram, 8e (☎ 01-42-27-58-80; Métro: Ternes), open Monday through Friday from 9am to 5pm.

Area Code   There isn't one as North Americans think of it. All French telephone numbers now consist of 10 digits, the first two of which are sort of like an area code. If you're calling anywhere in France from inside France, just dial all 10 digits—no additional codes are needed. If you're calling from the United States, drop the initial 0 (zero). For more, see "Fast Facts: France" in chapter 2.

Currency Exchange   American Express can fill most banking needs. Most banks in Paris are open Monday through Friday from 9am to 4:30pm, but only a few are open Saturday; ask at your hotel for the location of the one nearest you. For the best exchange rate, cash your traveler's checks at banks or foreign-exchange offices, not at shops and hotels. Most post offices will also change traveler's checks or convert currency. Currency exchanges are also found at Paris airports and train stations and along most of the major boulevards like the Champs-Elysées. A small commission is charged.

Some exchange places charge favorable rates to lure you into their stores. For example, **Paris Vision,** 214 rue de Rivoli, 1er (☎ 01-42-86-09-33; Métro: Tuileries), maintains a minibank in the back of a travel agency, open daily from 9am to 2:30pm and 3:30 to 6pm (closes at 4:30pm on Sunday). Its exchange rates are only a fraction less favorable than those offered for very large blocks of money as listed by the Paris stock exchange.

Dentists   For emergency dental service, call ☎ 01-43-37-51-00 Monday through Friday from 8pm to midnight and Saturday and Sunday from 9:30am to midnight. The **American Hospital,** 63 bd. Victor-Hugo, Neuilly (☎ 01-46-41-25-43; Métro: Pont-de-Levallois or Pont-de-Neuilly; Bus: 82), operates a 24-hour English/French clinic on the premises.

Doctors   Some large hotels have a doctor on staff. If yours doesn't, try the **American Hospital,** 63 bd. Victor-Hugo, Neuilly (☎ 01-46-41-25-43; Métro: Pont-de-Levallois or Pont-de-Neuilly; Bus: 82), which operates a 24-hour emergency service. Blue Cross and other American insurance are accepted by their bilingual staff.

Drugstores   After regular hours, have your concierge contact the Commissariat de Police for the nearest 24-hour pharmacy. French law requires one pharmacy in any given neighborhood to stay open 24 hours. You'll find the address posted on the doors or windows of all other drugstores. One of the most central all-nighters is **Pharmacy "les Champs,"** 84 av. des Champs-Elysées, 8e (☎ 01-45-62-02-41; Métro: George-V).

Embassies/Consulates   See "Fast Facts: France" in chapter 2.

Emergencies   For the police, call ☎ 17; to report a fire, call ☎ 18. For an ambulance, call the fire department at ☎ 01-45-78-74-52; a fire vehicle rushes cases to the nearest emergency room. **S.A.M.U.** is an independently operated, privately owned ambulance company; call ☎ 15. In nonemergency situations, you can reach the police at 9 bd. du Palais, 4e (☎ 01-53-71-53-71 or 01-53-73-53-73; Métro: Cité).

Hospitals   See "Doctors," above.

Police   In an emergency, call ☎ **17.** For nonemergency situations, the principal Préfecture is at 9 bd. du Palais, 4e (☎ **01-53-71-53-71;** Métro: Cité).

Safety   Beware of child pickpockets, who roam Paris preying on visitors around such sites as the Louvre, the Eiffel Tower, Notre-Dame, and Montmartre, and who especially like to pick pockets in the Métro, often blocking the entrance and exit to the escalator. A band of these young thieves can clean out your pockets even while you try to fend them off. They'll get very close, sometimes ask for a handout, and deftly help themselves to your money, passport, or whatever. Women should hang on to their purses firmly.

3 Accommodations

Although Paris hotels are shockingly expensive, there is some good news. Scores of lackluster, cheap Paris lodgings, where the wallpaper seemingly wasn't rehung since the twilight of the Napoleonic era, have been newly renovated and offer much better value in the moderate to inexpensive price range. The most outstanding example of this is in the **7th arrondissement,** a normally pricey district of Paris that has emerged with several good-value hotels blossoming from former dives that couldn't be recommended until now.

By now the Paris "season" has almost ceased to exist. Most visitors, at least those from North America, come in July and August. Since many French are on vacation then and trade fairs and conventions come to a halt, there are usually plenty of rooms, even though these months have traditionally been the peak season for European travel. In most hotels, February is just as busy as April or September because of the volume of business travelers and the increasing number of tourists who've learned to take advantage of the off-season discount airfares.

Hot weather doesn't last long in Paris, so most hotels, except the deluxe ones, don't provide air-conditioning. If you're trapped in a Paris garret on a hot summer night, you may have to sweat it out. To avoid the noise problem when you have to open windows, request a room in the back when making a reservation.

Most hotels offer a continental breakfast of coffee, tea, or hot chocolate; a freshly baked croissant and roll; and limited quantities of butter and jam or jelly. Though nowhere near as filling as a traditional English or American breakfast, it does have the advantage of being quick to prepare—it'll be at your door a few moments after you call down for it and can be served at almost any hour. The word "breakfast" in the following entries refers to this continental version.

Note: Service and value-added tax are included in all rates quoted in this book, unless otherwise specified. Also, unless otherwise specified, all hotel rooms come with a private bathroom.

RIGHT BANK: 1ST ARRONDISSEMENT (LOUVRE/LES HALLES)
VERY EXPENSIVE

✪ **Costes.** 239 rue St-Honoré, 75001 Paris. ☎ **01-42-44-50-50.** Fax 01-42-44-50-01. 83 units. A/C MINIBAR TV TEL. 2,250–3,500 F ($360–$560) double; 5,250–5,500 F ($840–$880) suite. AE, DC, MC, V. Métro: Tuileries or Concorde.

Grand style and a location close to some of the most upscale shops in Paris attract lots of chic fashion types to this hotel, some of whom come for meetings in the nearby editorial offices of *Harper's Bazaar.* The five-story, town house–style building was a private home for many years. In 1996, it was richly adorned with the jewel-toned colors, heavy swag curtains, and lavish accessories of the late 19th century (the Napoléon III style). Today, everything about it evokes the rich days of France's Gilded Age, especially the bedrooms. Although small, they're cozy and ornate, and come with a CD player and fax machine. Each unit contains one or two large beds, each with a sumptuous mattress. Bathrooms are fairly spacious, with makeup mirrors, deluxe toiletries, thick towels, and a tub and shower combination.

Dining: Four dining rooms, each with a different decorative theme, and each overlooking the building's Italianate inner courtyard, are chock-a-block with chinoiserie, dried and framed flowers, and 19th-century art. Open daily from noon to 1am, they feature delectable dishes such as grilled scallops and a grilled version of steak tartare with all the spicy ingredients of its original (raw) version.

Amenities: Car-rental desk, concierge, room service, dry cleaning, laundry service, baby-sitting, and gym with steam room, indoor pool, and masseurs/masseuses.

✪ **Hotel de Vendôme.** 1 Place Vendôme, 75001 Paris. ☎ **01-42-60-32-84.** Fax 01-49-27-97-89. E-mail: reservations@hoteldevendome.com. 29 units. A/C MINIBAR TV TEL. 2,800–3,200 F ($448–$512) double; 4,500–5,500 F ($720–$880) suite. AE, DC, MC, V. Métro: Tuilieries or l'Opéra.

Once the home of the Embassy of Texas when that state was a nation, this building dates from 1723 when it was the home of the secretary to Louis XIV. Now it's a jewel box of a hotel that opened in the summer of 1998 at one of the world's most prestigious addresses. Although the sumptuous bedrooms are only moderate in size, you live in opulent comfort here (you ought to for these prices!). The security here is fantastic—for example, when the doorbell rings, you pick up the receiver and press a button, and your caller appears on a small TV. Most of the bedrooms are decorated in a classic Second Empire style with luxurious beds and mattresses, tasteful fabrics, and well-upholstered furnishing. Rare woods go into the hand-carved furnishings. Bathrooms are equally sumptuous, with a tub and shower combination, robes, thick towels, and Guerlain toiletries.

Dining: The hotel restaurant, Café de Vendôme, is directed by Gérard Sallé, who has worked at some of the premier addresses of Paris, including the Bristol and the Plaza Athénée. The cuisine is imaginative, the setting rather austere but elegant.

Amenities: Room service, laundry, concierge.

Hôtel du Louvre. Place André Malraux, 75001 Paris. ☎ **800/888-4747** in the U.S. and Canada, or 01-44-58-38-38. Fax 01-44-58-38-01. www.hoteldulouvre.com. E-mail: hoteldulouvre@hoteldulouvre.com. 195 units. A/C MINIBAR TV TEL. 2050–2800 F ($328–$448) double; 3,000–4,500 F ($480–$720) suite. Ask about mid-winter discounts. AE, CB, DC, MC, V. Parking 100 F ($16). Métro: Palais-Royal.

When Napoléon III inaugurated this hotel in 1855, French journalists described it as "a palace of the people, rising adjacent to the palace of kings." In 1897 Camille Pissarro moved to a room with a view that inspired many of his Parisian landscapes. Set between the Musée du Louvre and the Palais Royal, the hotel has a decor of soaring marble, bronze, and gilt. The rooms are quintessentially Parisian—cozy, soundproof, and filled with souvenirs of the belle époque. Most were renovated between 1996 and 1998. Some of the bedrooms are small but most of them are medium in size—with all elegant fabrics and upholstery, excellent wool carpeting, double glazing, plush and comfortable beds with fine linens and quality mattresses, and traditional wood furniture. The well-maintained bathrooms are medium in size, with thick towels and a hair dryer. Extras include robes and trouser presses. The newer rooms have shower stalls while the older rooms are fitted with large tubs.

Heart of the Right Bank Hotels

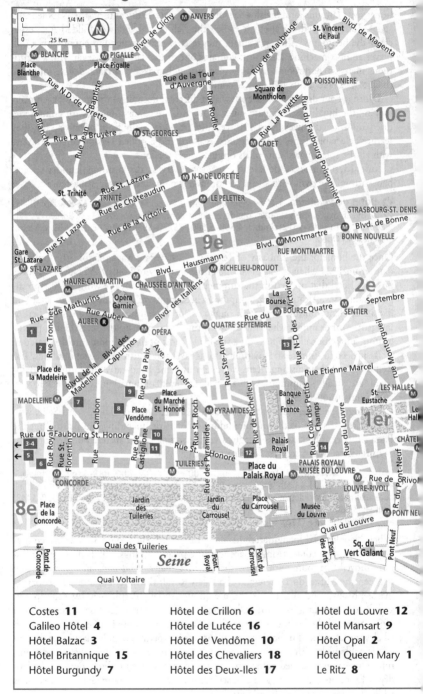

Costes **11**
Galileo Hôtel **4**
Hôtel Balzac **3**
Hôtel Britannique **15**
Hôtel Burgundy **7**

Hôtel de Crillon **6**
Hôtel de Lutéce **16**
Hôtel de Vendôme **10**
Hôtel des Chevaliers **18**
Hôtel des Deux-Iles **17**

Hôtel du Louvre **12**
Hôtel Mansart **9**
Hôtel Opal **2**
Hôtel Queen Mary **1**
Le Ritz **8**

Pavillon de la Reine **19**
Residence Lord Byron **5**
Timhôtel Louvre **14**
Timhôtel Palais Royal **13**

Dining: Le Bar "Defender" is a cozy hideaway, with mahogany trim, Scottish over-tones, and a collection of single-malt whiskies; a pianist plays after dusk. There's also the French Empire Brasserie du Louvre, whose tables extend to the terrace in fine weather.

Amenities: Concierge, room service (24 hours), baby-sitting, laundry, dry cleaning, valet, business center.

Hotel Meurice. 228 rue de Rivoli, Paris 75001. ☎ **01-44-58-10-10.** Fax 01-44-58-10-15. 160 units. A/C MINIBAR TV TEL. 3,500–4,000F ($560–$640) double; from 6,500F ($1,040) suite. Métro: Tuileries or Concorde.

After a spectacular 2-year renovation, the landmark Meurice reopened in mid-2000 better than ever. Since the early 1800s it has been welcoming the royal and the rich and even the radical: The deposed king of Spain, Alfonso XIII, once occupied suite 108; the mad genius Salvador Dalí made the Meurice his headquarters, as did General von Cholritz, the Nazi who ruled Paris during the occupation. The mosaic floors, elaborate plaster ceilings, hand-carved moldings, and Art Nouveau glass roof atop the Winter Garden look like new. Each guest room is individually decorated with period pieces, fine carpets, Italian and French fabrics, rare marbles, and modern features like fax and Internet access. The Louis XVI and Empire styles predominate. Our favorites and the least expensive are the sixth-floor dormer rooms. Some rooms have painted ceilings of puffy clouds and blue skies along with canopied beds.

Dining/Diversions: Le Meurice remains a citadel of haute cuisine, though many of its dishes are lighter (yet still exquisitely flavored) than before. The Fontainebleau Bar is one of the new chic rendezvous places, and the Winter Garden is the most elegant place in Paris for drinks or high tea.

Amenities: Concierge, 24-hour room service, laundry/dry cleaning, secretarial service, new spa with state-of-the-art facilities, fitness area, massage, beauty treatments.

✪ **Le Ritz.** 15 place Vendôme, 75001 Paris. ☎ **800/223-6800** in the U.S. and Canada, or 01-43-16-30-30. Fax 01-43-16-31-78. www.ritzparis.com. E-mail: resa@ritzparis.com. 175 units. A/C MINIBAR TV TEL. 3,600–4,500 F ($576–$720) double; from 6,500 F ($1,040) suite. AE, DC, MC, V. Parking: 230 F ($36.80). Métro: Opéra.

The Ritz is Europe's greatest hotel. This enduring symbol of elegance stands on one of Paris's most beautiful and historic squares. César Ritz, the "little shepherd boy from Niederwald," converted the private Hôtel de Lazun into a luxury hotel that he opened in 1898. With the help of the culinary master Escoffier, he made the Ritz a miracle of luxury living.

In 1979 the Ritz family sold the hotel to the Egyptian businessman Mohamed Al Fayed (Dodi's father), who refurbished it and added a cooking school. (Dodi Al Fayed and Princess Diana were staying here when they set out on their fateful drive through Paris.) Two town houses were annexed, joined by a long arcade lined with miniature display cases representing 125 of the leading boutiques of Paris. The salons are furnished with museum-caliber antiques: gilt pieces, ornate mirrors, Louis XV and Louis XVI furniture, hand-woven tapestries, and 10-foot-high bronze candelabras. The spacious marble-clad bathrooms are among the city's most luxurious, filled with deluxe toiletries, hair dryers, scales, a private phone, cords to summon maids and valets, fluffy peach towels and peach robes, full-length and makeup mirrors, dual basins, and even plumbing hardware that is remarkable, as the hotel has its own workshop to repair and reproduce it. Ever since Edward VII got stuck in a too-narrow bathtub with his plump love of the evening, bathtubs at the Ritz have been deep and big.

Dining/Diversions: The Espadon grill room is one of the finest in Paris. The Ritz Supper Club includes a bar, a salon with a fireplace, a restaurant, and a dance floor. You can order drinks in either the Bar Vendôme or the Bar Hemingway.

Amenities: Concierge, room service (24 hours), laundry, valet, health club (with pool and massage parlor), florist, shops, squash court.

MODERATE

Hôtel Britannique. 20 av. Victoria, 75001 Paris. ☎ **01-42-33-74-59.** Fax 01-42-33-82-65. www.hotel-britannique.fr. E-mail: mailbox@hotel-britannique.fr. 40 units. MINIBAR TV TEL. 790–1,080 F ($126.40–$172.80) double. AE, DC, MC, V. Parking 100 F ($16). Métro: Châtelet.

Cozy, conservatively modern, and plush-looking, this much-renovated 19th-century hotel gets three stars from the French government. It's in the heart of Paris, near Les Halles, the Pompidou Centre, and Notre-Dame. The rooms may be small, but they're spic-and-span, comfortable, soundproof, and well-equipped with safety deposit box, hair dryer, comfortable beds, and satellite TV that gets U.S. and U.K. shows. The reading room is a cozy retreat. The place is not only British in name but seems also to have cultivated an English style of graciousness.

Hôtel Burgundy. 8 rue Duphot, 75001 Paris. ☎ **01-42-60-34-12.** Fax 01-47-03-95-20. www.turquoise.co.uk. 89 units. MINIBAR TV TEL. 980 F ($156.80) double; 1,600 F ($256) suite. AE, DC, MC, V. Métro: Madeleine or Concorde.

The Burgundy is one of the best values in an outrageously expensive neighborhood. This frequently renovated building is a former pension, where Baudelaire wrote some of his eerie poetry in the 1860s. What you'll see today was conceived as two side-by-side town houses in the 1830s. One flourished as a bordello before they were linked by British-born managers, who insisted on using the English name. Radically renovated in 1992, the hotel often hosts many North and South Americans. It features conservatively decorated and very comfortable rooms with cozy-looking decor; efficient, modestly sized bathrooms; and comfortable beds. The **Charles Baudelaire** restaurant is open for lunch and dinner Monday through Friday. There's no bar, but drinks are served in the lobby during restaurant hours. Amenities include limited concierge services, room service from 6:30am to 9:30pm, laundry/dry cleaning, and a conference room.

Hôtel Mansart. 5 rue des Capucines, 75001 Paris. ☎ **01-42-61-50-28.** Fax 01-49-27-97-44. http://paris.hotelguide.net. 57 units. MINIBAR TV TEL. 630–1,020 F ($100.80–$163.20) double; 1,650 F ($264) suite. AE, DC, MC, V. Métro: Opéra or Madeleine.

Designed by its namesake, the 17th-century architect Jules Hardouin-Mansart, this building composes part of the grand ensemble of place Vendôme. After operating as a glorious wreck for many decades, it was radically renovated in 1991 and now offers some of the lowest rates in this pricey neighborhood. The public areas contain Louis-inspired reproductions and startling floor-to-ceiling geometric designs. The small to medium-sized guest rooms are subtly formal and comfortable, though only half a dozen of the suites and most expensive rooms actually overlook the famous square. All have beds with firm, high-quality mattresses, and 20 are air-conditioned. The compact bathrooms have shower stalls and hair dryers. Breakfast, the only meal offered, is served one floor above lobby level.

Timhôtel Louvre. 4 rue Croix des Petits-Champs, 75001 Paris. ☎ **01-42-60-34-86.** Fax 01-42-60-10-39. 56 units. TV TEL. 680–700 F ($108.80–$112) double. AE, DC, MC, V. Métro: Palais-Royal.

This hotel and its sibling, Timhôtel Palais-Royal, are mirror images of each other, at least inside; they're part of a new breed of two-star business-oriented hotel that's cropping up around France. These Timhôtels share the same manager and the same

---

ⓘ Family-Friendly Hotels

Hôtel de Fleurie *(see p. 93)*   In the heart of St-Germain-des-Prés, this has long been a family favorite. You can rent its *chambres familiales*—two connecting rooms with two large beds. Children 12 and under stay free in their parents' room.

Hôtel du Louvre *(see p. 81)*   This hotel has welcomed families to Paris since 1855—well, rich families anyway. It's well situated near the Louvre and the Palais Royal and offers generally spacious rooms, many large enough to accommodate families. Baby-sitting can be arranged.

Timhôtel Louvre *(see p. 85)*   This hotel is especially great for families, as it offers some rooms with four beds; children under 12 are welcome to stay in their parents' room for free.

---

temperament, and though the rooms at Timhôtel Palais-Royal are a bit larger than those here, the Louvre branch is so close to the museum as to be almost irresistible. The ambience is bland and standardized but modern and comfortable, with tiled baths, monochromatic guest rooms, and wall-to-wall carpeting that was upgraded and renovated in 1998. The beds are good with firm mattresses, but the bathrooms are a bit cramped, containing a shower stall. Breakfasts are served rather anonymously from self-service cafeterias.

Timhôtel Palais-Royal is in the 2nd arrondissement, at 3 rue de la Banque, 75002 Paris (☎ **01-42-61-53-90;** fax 01-42-60-05-39; Métro: Bourse); it has 46 rooms and charges the same price as above.

RIGHT BANK: 3RD ARRONDISSEMENT (LE MARAIS)
VERY EXPENSIVE

✪ **Pavillon de la Reine.** 28 place des Vosges, 75003 Paris. ☎ **01-40-29-19-19.** Fax 01-40-29-19-20. www.pavillon-de-la-Reine.com. E-mail: pavillon@clubinternet.fr. 55 units. A/C MINIBAR TV TEL. 1,950–2,150 F ($312–$344) double; 2,150–2,500 F ($344–$400) duplex; 2,600–3,900 F ($416–$624) suite. AE, DC, MC, V. Free parking. Métro: Chemin Vert or Bastille.

Built in 1986, this cream-colored neoclassical villa blends in perfectly with the rest of the neighborhood. You enter through an arcade that opens onto a small formal garden. The Louis XIII decor evokes the heyday of place des Vosges, and wing chairs with flame-stitched upholstery combine with iron-banded Spanish antiques to create a rustic feel. Each guest room is unique; some are duplexes with sleeping lofts above cozy salons. All have a warm decor of weathered beams, reproductions of famous oil paintings, and roomy marble baths with hair dryers and thick towels. Most rooms are of good size, although shape and size varies. The better rooms come with private safes. The preferred rooms are on the upper floors opening onto the romantic Place de Vosges. Quality mattresses and fine linens are used on all the excellent French beds.

Dining: The hotel has an "honesty bar" and a limited 24-hour room-service menu.

Amenities: A receptionist/concierge can arrange massage, dry cleaning, car rentals, and tickets for shows, concerts, and the theater.

MODERATE

Hôtel des Chevaliers. 30 rue de Turenne, 75003 Paris. ☎ **01-42-72-73-47.** Fax 01-42-72-54-10. 24 units. MINIBAR TV TEL. 660–700 F ($105.60–$112) double; 874 F ($139.85) triple. Métro: Chemin-Vert or St-Paul.

Half a block from the northwestern edge of place des Vosges, this carefully renovated hotel occupies a dramatic corner building whose 17th-century vestiges have been elevated into high art. These include the remnants of a stone-sided well in the cellar, a sweeping stone barrel vault that covers the breakfast area, half-timbering that's artfully exposed in the stairwell, and Louis XIII accessories. Each room is comfortable and well maintained, with a safe, a hair dryer, and a decor that's based on modernized interpretations of either Directoire, Louis XV, or XVI style, and in some cases with reproductions of well-known modern paintings. Bathrooms are compact, with stall showers.

RIGHT BANK: 4TH ARRONDISSEMENT (ÎLE DE LA CITE/ILE ST-LOUIS)
MODERATE

✪ **Hôtel de Lutèce.** 65 rue Ile St-Louis, 75004 Paris. ☎ **01-43-26-23-52.** Fax 01-43-29-60-25. www.francehotelreservation.com. 23 units. A/C TV TEL. 900 F ($144) double; 1,100 F ($176) triple. AE, MC, V. Métro: Pont-Marie.

This hotel feels like a country house in Brittany. The lounge, with its old fireplace, is graciously furnished with antiques and contemporary paintings. Each of the individualized guest rooms boasts antiques, adding to a refined atmosphere that attracts celebrities, like the duke and duchess of Bedford. Many of the accommodations, ranging in size from small to medium, were renovated in 1998, with plush French mattresses added. Each room is well maintained, traditional in feeling, and comfortable, with wool carpeting and upholstered chairs. Bathrooms are small but are well-maintained; they have hair dryers. The hotel is comparable in style and amenities to the Deux-Îles (same ownership).

Hôtel des Deux-Îles. 59 rue Ile St-Louis, 75004 Paris. ☎ **01-43-26-13-35.** Fax 01-43-29-60-25. 17 units. TV TEL. 890 F ($142.40) double. AE, MC, V. Métro: Pont-Marie.

This much-restored 17th-century town house is an unpretentious but charming hotel with a great location. Bedrooms are on the small side, but each is fitted with a comfortable French mattress and good linen. Bathrooms are also small, but are tiled and furnished with a hair dryer. A garden of plants and flowers off the lobby leads to a basement breakfast room with a fireplace. Amenities include room service from 7:30am to 8pm and laundry/dry cleaning.

RIGHT BANK: 8TH ARRONDISSEMENT (CHAMPS-ELYSÉES/MADELEINE)
VERY EXPENSIVE

Hôtel Balzac. 6 rue Balzac, 75008 Paris. ☎ **800/457-4000** in the U.S. and Canada, or 01-44-35-18-00. Fax 01-44-35-18-05. E-mail: hotelbalzac@wanadoo.fr. 70 units. A/C MINIBAR TV TEL. 2,200 F ($352) double; from 3,300 F ($528) suite. AE, DC, MC, V. Parking 150 F ($24). Métro: George-V.

If you liken the Crillon or the Ritz to a Rolls-Royce, you could say that the Balzac is like a Bentley. Elegant and discreet, it boasts a well-trained formal staff and comfortable accommodations with modern furniture. The hint of opulence is unmatched by many other hotels in its neighborhood near the upper end of the Champs-Elysées. The hotel opened in 1986 in a belle époque mansion, then was redecorated in 1994 by the famed English designer Nina Campbell. Each room is soundproofed and conceived as a well-upholstered hideaway, with extremely comfortable mattresses and bath accessories. Most rooms range from medium to spacious in size, with double glazing, private safes, mirrored closets, and king-sized beds. Bathrooms are clad in marble, with thick towels, robes, deluxe toiletries, and a hair dryer.

Dining: In November 1996 a prominent spot near the hotel's elegant lobby was rented to the Restaurant Pierre Gagnaire. Its namesake is a promising new chef whose three-star cuisine has impressed critics throughout France.

Amenities: Concierge, room service (24 hours), dry cleaning, express laundry.

✪ **Hôtel de Crillon.** 10 place de la Concorde, 75008 Paris. ☎ **800/241-3333** in the U.S. and Canada, or 01-44-71-15-00. Fax 01-44-71-15-04. www.crillon.com. E-mail: reservations@crillon.com. 160 units. A/C MINIBAR TV TEL. 3,500–4,400 F ($560–$704) double; from 4,950 F ($792) suite. AE, DC, MC, V. Parking 120 F ($19.20). Métro: Concorde.

One of Europe's greatest hotels, the Crillon sits across from the U.S. Embassy. The 200-year-old building, once the palace of the duc de Crillon, has been a hotel since the early 1900s and is now owned by Jean Taittinger of the champagne family. Inside are many preserved architectural details as well as museum-quality antiques and reproductions. The salons boast 17th- and 18th-century tapestries, gilt-and-brocade furniture, chandeliers, fine sculpture, and Louis XVI chests and chairs. The large guest rooms are classically furnished, featuring baths lined with travertine or pink marble, and an overall decor from designer Sonia Rykiel. Beds are opulent with luxury mattresses, elegant fabrics, and fine linens. Some of the accommodations are spectacular, such as the Leonard Bernstein Suite, with one of the maestro's pianos and one of the grandest views of any hotel room in Paris. Baths are sumptuous as well, with deluxe toiletries, marble, dual sinks, hair dryers, robes, thick towels, and, in some, thermal taps.

Dining: You can dine at the elegant Les Ambassadeurs or the more informal L'Obélisque, where menu choices are less experimental. Les Ambassadeurs offers a business lunch Monday to Friday only; the menu dégustation is served at lunch on weekends and every evening. The breakfast menu is one of our favorites in the city.

Amenities: Room service (24 hours), secretarial/translation service, laundry, valet, meeting and conference rooms, garden-style courtyard with restaurant service, shops.

MODERATE

✪ **Galileo Hotel.** 54 rue Galilée, 75008 Paris. ☎ **01-47-20-66-06.** Fax 01-47-20-67-17. 27 units. A/C MINIBAR TV TEL. 950 F ($152) double. AE, C, MC, V. Métro: Étoile or George-V.

For years *Frommer's Paris* has been recommending Hotel des Deux-Îles and Hotel de Lutèce on Ile St-Louis. Now the owners of those hotels, Roland and Elisabeth Buffat, have invaded the 8th arrondissement with their particular boutique-style hotel. A short walk from the Champs-Elysées, the town house hotel is the epitome of French elegance and charm. Bedrooms are medium in size for the most part and a study in understated taste, decorated in various shades of cocoa and beige. The bathrooms are lined with marble. Try, if possible, for units 501 and 502, which are the most spacious and have a glass-covered veranda which can be used even in winter. You're just steps from the Arc de Triomphe and the heart of monumental Paris. For such a tony neighborhood, the prices are quite moderate. Breakfast is the only meal provided.

Hôtel Queen Mary. 9 rue Greffulhe, 75008 Paris. ☎ **01-42-66-40-50.** Fax 01-42-66-94-92. www.hotelqueenmary.com. E-mail: hotelqueenmary@wanadoo.fr. 36 units. A/C MINIBAR TV TEL. 795–1,010 F ($127.20–$161.60) double; 1,450 F ($232) suite. AE, DC, MC, V. Parking 80 F ($12.80). Métro: Madeleine or Havre-Caumartin.

Meticulously renovated both inside and out, this hotel was built around the turn of the century. It's graced with an iron-and-glass canopy, ornate wrought iron, and the kind of detailing you might expect in more expensive hotels. The public rooms have touches of greenery and reproductions of mid 19th–century antiques; each guest room has an upholstered headboard, a comfortable bed, and mahogany furnishings, plus a carafe of sherry. Rooms are a bit on the small side, but they were all fully renovated in 1998. Bathrooms have a tub and shower combination and a hair dryer.

Résidence Lord Byron. 5 rue de Chateaubriand, 75008 Paris. ☎ **01-43-59-89-98.** Fax 01-42-89-46-04. www.escapade-paris.com. E-mail: lord.byron@escapade-paris.com. 31 units. MINIBAR TV TEL. 890–990 F ($142.40–$158.40) double; from 1,390 F ($222.40) suite. AE, DC, MC, V. Parking 75 F ($12). Métro: George V. RER: Étoile.

Just off the Champs-Elysées on a curving street of handsome buildings, Lord Byron may not be as grand as other hotels in the neighborhood, but it is affordable. Correct, unassuming, and a bit staid, it's exactly what repeat clients want and expect: a sense of luxury, solitude, and understatement. It remains a good value for the upscale 8th arrondissement, and is a fine choice for families. Some of the city's major monuments are only a 10-minute walk away. Rooms are small to medium in size. Bathrooms are small (some have showers but not tubs). If you choose to have breakfast at the hotel, you can order it in the dining room or in a shaded inner garden.

INEXPENSIVE

Hôtel Opal. 19 rue Tronchet, 75008 Paris. ☎ **01-42-65-77-97.** Fax 01-49-24-06-58. www.hotels.fr/opal. E-mail: h_opal@club-internet.fr. 36 units. A/C MINIBAR TV TEL. 590–730 F ($94.40–$116.80) double. Extra bed 100 F ($16). AE, DC, V. Parking 130 F ($20.80) nearby. Métro: Madeleine.

This rejuvenated hotel is a real find in the heart of Paris, behind the Madeleine and near the Opéra Garnier. The guest rooms are somewhat cramped but very clean and comfortable, and many of them are air-conditioned. Those on the top floor are reached by a narrow staircase; some have skylights. Most rooms have twin brass beds with a decent mattress. Bathrooms are compact, with hair dryers and stall showers.

RIGHT BANK: 16TH ARRONDISSEMENT (TROCADÉRO/BOIS DE BOULOGNE)

Au Palais de Chaillot Hotel. 35 av. Raymond Poincarré, 75016. 28 units. ☎ **01-53-70-09-09.** Fax 01-53-70-09-08. 28 units. TV TEL. 570 F ($91.20) double, 680 F ($108.80) triple, 640 F ($102.40) junior suite. Métro: Victor-Hugo or Trocadéro.

For years travelers on a budget avoided the high-priced 16th arrondissement. But when two U.S.-trained brothers, Thierry and Cyrille Pien, opened this excellent hotel, frugal visitors arrived on their doorstep. Between the Champs-Elysées and Trocadéro, the town house was restored from top to bottom and the result is a contemporary yet informal style of Parisian chic. Bedrooms come in a variety of shapes and sizes and are furnished with a light touch, with bright colors and wicker. Appointments from mattresses to toiletries are first rate, and half of the accommodations are air conditioned. Numbers 61, 62, and 63 afford partial views of the Eiffel Tower. Reached by elevator, the floors offer room service, and breakfast is served on a small terrace in fair weather. Right outside your door you can go window shopping along avenue Victor-Hugo.

LEFT BANK: 5TH ARRONDISSEMENT (LATIN QUARTER)

EXPENSIVE

Libertel Quartier Latin. 9 rue des Écoles, 75005 Paris. ☎ **800/949-7562** in the U.S., or 01-44-27-06-45. Fax 01-43-25-36-70. www.libertel-hotels.com. 29 units. MINIBAR TV TEL. 1,082 F ($173.10) double; 1,213 F ($194.10) suite. AE, DC, MC, V. Nearby parking 100 F ($16) per night. Métro: Jussieu or Cardinal-Lemoire.

Set within a century-old, six-story hotel in a neighborhood that's crowded with *quartier latin* color, this hotel was given a radical upgrade in 1997, adding a French

Heart of the Left Bank Hotels

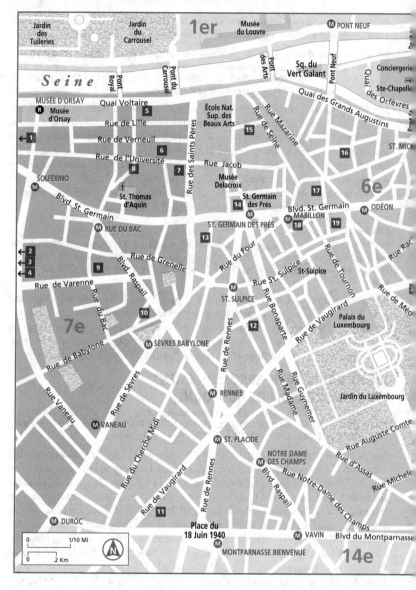

literary theme to each room. Expect a hardworking and articulate staff, and book-lined public rooms that evoke a cozy library. Your room might have a framed portrait of Colette, André Gide, or Jacques Prévert, or framed verses of poetry from writers like Baudelaire. Bedrooms are small and cozy, furnished with traditional wood pieces and modern and comfortable beds with quality mattresses. Bathrooms are small but efficiently organized with adequate shelf space and hair dryers. Breakfast is the only meal served here, but there are lots of restaurants in the surrounding neighborhood.

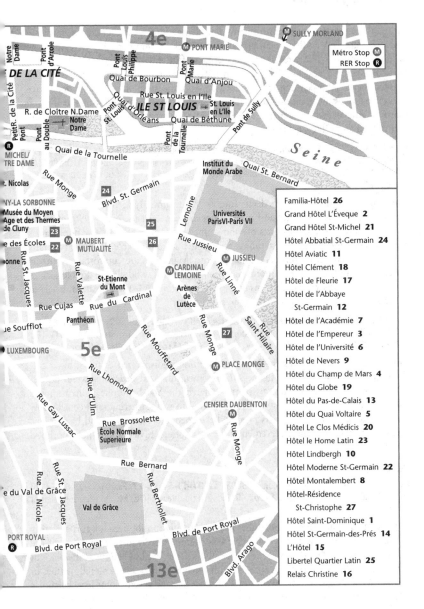

Métro Stop ⓜ
RER Stop ⓡ

Familia-Hôtel **26**
Grand Hôtel L'Éveque **2**
Grand Hôtel St-Michel **21**
Hôtel Abbatial St-Germain **24**
Hôtel Aviatic **11**
Hôtel Clément **18**
Hôtel de Fleurie **17**
Hôtel de l'Abbaye
  St-Germain **12**
Hôtel de l'Académie **7**
Hôtel de l'Empereur **3**
Hôtel de l'Université **6**
Hôtel de Nevers **9**
Hôtel du Champ de Mars **4**
Hôtel du Globe **19**
Hôtel du Pas-de-Calais **13**
Hôtel du Quai Voltaire **5**
Hôtel Le Clos Médicis **20**
Hôtel le Home Latin **23**
Hôtel Lindbergh **10**
Hôtel Moderne St-Germain **22**
Hôtel Montalembert **8**
Hôtel-Résidence
  St-Christophe **27**
Hôtel Saint-Dominique **1**
Hôtel St-Germain-des-Prés **14**
L'Hôtel **15**
Libertel Quartier Latin **25**
Relais Christine **16**

MODERATE

Grand Hôtel St-Michel. 19 rue Cujas, 75005 Paris. ☎ **01-46-33-33-02.** Fax 01-40-46-96-33. http://paris.hotelguide.net. 46 units. MINIBAR TV TEL. 890 F ($142.40) double; 1,400 F ($224) suite. AE, DC, MC, V. Métro: Cluny-La Sorbonne. RER: Luxembourg or St-Michel.

Built in the 19th century, this hotel is larger and more businesslike than many of the smaller town house–style inns nearby. It basks in the reflected glow of the Brazilian dissident Georges Amado, whose memoirs (released in 1996) recorded his 2-year literary sojourn in one of the rooms. In 1997 the hotel completed a renovation and earned three stars from the government. The changes enlarged some rooms, lowering their ceilings and adding such modern amenities as minibars, but retained old-fashioned touches like wrought-iron balconies (fifth floor only). Public rooms are particularly lavish and tasteful, outfitted with oil portraits, rich upholsteries, and a sense of early 19th-century grandeur. Rooms on the sixth (uppermost) floor have interesting views over the rooftops. Each bedroom was fitted with a quality French mattress after a major overhaul. The bathrooms are as small as ever, but are tidily maintained and offer hair dryers.

Hôtel Abbatial St-Germain. 46 bd. St-Germain, 75005 Paris. ☎ **01-46-34-02-12.** Fax 01-43-25-47-73. www.abbatial.com. E-mail: abbatial@hotellerie.net. 43 units. A/C MINIBAR TV TEL. 750–850 F ($120–$136) double. AE, MC, V. Parking 110 F ($17.60). Métro: Maubert-Mutualité.

The origins of this hotel run deep: Interior renovations have revealed such 17th-century touches as dovecotes and massive oaken beams. In the early 1990s a radical restoration brought the six stories of rooms up to modern standards. The public areas are especially appealing. Guest rooms are small but comfortable, furnished in faux Louis XVI, each with a different color scheme. Mattresses are comfortable, but the towels are thin; the small bathrooms have hair dryers. All windows are double-glazed, and the fifth- and sixth-floor rooms enjoy views over Notre-Dame. Breakfast is served beneath the vaulted ceilings of the stone-sided cellar.

Hôtel-Rèsidence St-Christophe. 17 rue Lacépède, 75005 Paris. ☎ **01-43-31-81-54.** Fax 01-43-31-12-54. E-mail: hotelstchristophe@compuserve.com. 31 units. MINIBAR TV TEL. 680 F ($108.80) double. AE, DC, MC, V. Parking 100 F ($16). Métro: Place-Monge.

This hotel, in one of the Latin Quarter's charming undiscovered districts, has a gracious English-speaking staff. All the small to medium-sized bedrooms were successfully renovated in 1998. Millions of francs later, the St-Christophe is inviting and comfortable, with Louis XV–style furniture, wall-to-wall carpeting, and comfortably firm mattresses. The compact bathrooms have adequate shelf space and hair dryers. Breakfast is the only meal served, but the staff offers advice about neighborhood bistros.

INEXPENSIVE

✪ **Familia-Hôtel.** 11 rue des Écoles, 75005. ☎ **01-43-54-55-27.** Fax 01-43-29-61-77. 30 units. MINIBAR TV TEL. 390–595 F ($62.40–$95.20) double. AE, DC, MC, V. Métro: Jussieu or Cardinal Lemoine.

As the name implies, this is a hotel that has been family run for decades. It is currently in the hands of the dynamic young Eric Gaucheron, who is justifiably proud of the many personal touches that make his place unique. He lavishly renovated the place in 1998. The walls of 14 rooms are graced with finely executed sepia-colored frescoes of Parisian scenes, eight rooms have restored stone walls, and seven rooms have balconies with delightful views over the Latin Quarter. All rooms have cable TV (including CNN), hair dryers, and high-quality mattresses, making the hotel more comfortable than most in this category.

✪ **Hôtel Le Home Latin.** 15–17 rue du Sommerard, 75005 Paris. ☎ **01-43-26-25-21.** Fax 01-43-29-87-04. 54 units. TV TEL. 595–650 F ($95.20–$104) double. AE, V. Parking 85 F ($13.60). Métro: St-Michel or Maubert-Mutualité.

This is one of the most famous budget hotels in Paris, known since the 1970s for clean and simple lodgings. Renovations in 1999 made the rooms blandly functional; some of them have small balconies overlooking the street. Rooms, mostly medium in size, have a streamlined look without a lot of frills, though each is fitted with a good, comfortable mattress, usually covered with a flowery spread. The rooms facing the courtyard are quieter than those fronting the street, and the elevator doesn't reach beyond the fifth floor. To make up for the stair climb, the sixth floor's *chambres mansardées* offer a romantic location under the eaves and panoramic views over the rooftops. Bathrooms are tiled, sterile-looking, and efficient, with thin towels.

Hôtel Moderne St-Germain. 33 rue des Écoles, 75005 Paris. ☎ **01-43-54-37-78.** Fax 01-43-29-91-31. www.tulipinn.com. E-mail: hotel@tulipinn.com. 45 units. TV TEL. 590–840 F ($94.40–$134.40) double; 750–1,050 F ($120–$168) triple. AE, DC, MC, V. Parking 170 F ($27.20). Métro: Maubert-Mutualité.

Built in the heart of the Latin Quarter, the Hôtel Moderne was completely renovated in 1998. Its charming owner, Madame Gibon, welcomes guests warmly. The comfortably furnished bedrooms are spotlessly maintained. In the rooms fronting the rue des Écoles, double-glazed aluminum windows hush the traffic. Though the rooms are small, this is still one of the better three-star hotels in the neighborhood. Mattresses are firm, and each bathroom is equipped with a hair dryer. Clients enjoy access to the sauna and Jacuzzi within the Hotel Sully next door.

LEFT BANK: 6TH ARRONDISSEMENT (ST-GERMAIN/LUXEMBOURG)
VERY EXPENSIVE

Relais Christine. 3 rue Christine, 75006 Paris. ☎ **01-40-51-60-80.** Fax 01-40-51-60-81. www.relais-christine.com. E-mail: relaisch@club-internet.fr. 51 units. A/C MINIBAR TV TEL. 1,850–2,350 F ($296–$376) double; 2,450–4,300 F ($392–$688) duplexes and suite. AE, CB, DC, MC, V. Free parking. Métro: Odéon.

Relais Christine welcomes you into what was a 16th-century Augustinian cloister. You enter from a narrow cobblestone street into first a symmetrical courtyard and then an elegant reception area with baroque sculpture and Renaissance antiques. Each guest room is uniquely decorated with wooden beams and Louis XIII–style furnishings. Accents might include massively beamed ceilings, luxurious wall-to-wall carpeting, and marble bathrooms. Mattresses are comfortable. Some of the rooms, which come in a wide range of styles and shapes, are among the most spacious on the Left Bank, with such extras as mirrored closets, plush carpets, thermostats, and in some cases balconies facing the outer courtyard. The least attractive and smallest rooms are those in the interior; they're also dim.

Dining: Off the reception area is a paneled sitting room/bar area ringed with 19th-century portraits and comfortable leather chairs. The breakfast room is in a vaulted cellar; the ancient well and massive central stone column are part of the cloister's former kitchen.

Amenities: Room service (24 hours), laundry, baby-sitting.

EXPENSIVE

✪ **Hôtel de Fleurie.** 32–34 rue Grégoire-de-Tours, 75006 Paris. ☎ **01-53-73-70-00.** Fax 01-53-73-70-20. www.hotel-de-fleurie.tm.fr. E-mail: bonjour@hotel-de-fleurie.tm.fr. 29 units. A/C MINIBAR TV TEL. 1,000–1,350 F ($160–$216) double; 1,700–1,800 F ($272–$288) family room. Children 12 and under stay free in parents' room. AE, DC, MC, V. Métro: Odéon.

Just off boulevard St-Germain on a colorful little street, the Fleurie is one of the best of the "new" old hotels. It was restored to its former glory in 1988, with about half the rooms and bathrooms renovated again in 1999. The hotel has a facade that's studded with spot-lit statuary, recapturing a 17th-century elegance. The stone walls have been exposed in the reception salon, where you check in at a refectory desk. An elevator takes you to well-furnished bedrooms, each with a comfortable bed and a safe. Many of them have elaborate curtains, reproductions of antiques, and a sense of late 19th-century charm. This hotel has long been a family favorite because of the interconnecting doors that open between certain pairs of its rooms, creating *chambres familiales*. Only breakfast is served, although there is a small bar.

Hôtel de l'Abbaye St-Germain. 10 rue Cassette, 75006 Paris. ☎ **01-45-44-38-11.** Fax 01-45-48-07-86. www.hotel-abbaye.com. E-mail: hotel.abbaye@wanadoo.fr. 46 units. A/C TV TEL. 1,160–1,700 F ($185.60–$272) double; 2,300 F ($368) suite. Rates include continental breakfast. AE, MC, V. Métro: St-Sulpice.

Built early in the 18th century as a convent for the Église St-Germain, this charming boutique hotel has brightly colored rooms decorated with traditional furniture like what you'd find in a private club, and touches of sophisticated flair. In front is a small garden, and in back is a verdant courtyard featuring a fountain, raised flower beds, and masses of ivy and climbing vines. If you don't mind paying a little more, one of the most charming rooms has a terrace overlooking the upper floors of neighboring buildings. Mattresses are comfortable.

Dining: Only breakfast is served, but the public areas include a trio of salons and a bar.

Amenities: Car rentals arranged, concierge, room service, dry cleaning, laundry.

Hôtel St-Germain-des-Prés. 36 rue Bonaparte, 75006 Paris. ☎ **01-43-26-00-19.** Fax 01-40-46-83-63. www.hotel-st-ger.com. E-mail: hotelsaintgermain@wanadoo.fr. 30 units. MINIBAR TV TEL. 1,020–1,350 F ($163.20–$216) double; from 1,750 F ($280) suite. Rates include breakfast. MC, V. Métro: St-Germain-des-Prés.

This hotel has an enviable location in the Latin Quarter—behind a well-known Left Bank street near many shops. Each room is small but charming, with antique ceiling beams, a safe, and reasonably comfortable beds. Each received an extensive renovation in 1994 and others were renovated again in the late 1990s. The public areas are severely elegant, with dentil moldings, Louis XIII furnishings, and original stonework. Air-conditioning is available in most, but not all, of the rooms.

✪ **L'Hôtel.** 13 rue des Beaux-Arts, 75006 Paris. ☎ **01-44-41-99-00.** Fax 01-43-25-64-81. www.l-hotel.com. E-mail: reservation@l-hotel.com. 27 units. A/C MINIBAR TV TEL. 600–3,000 F ($96–$480) double; from 1,700 F ($272) suite. AE, DC, MC, V. Métro: St-Germain-des-Prés.

This boutique hotel was once a 19th-century fleabag called the Hôtel d'Alsace, whose major distinction was that Oscar Wilde died here, broke and in despair. But today's guests aren't anywhere near poverty row: now show-business and fashion celebrities march through the lobby. L'Hôtel was the creation of the late French actor Guy-Louis Duboucheron, who established an atmosphere of super-sophistication.

You'll feel like a movie star while bathing in your rosy-pink marble tub. An eclectic collection of antiques that includes Louis XV and Louis XVI, Empire, and Directoire pieces pops up throughout the hotel. The spacious 3,000 F ($480) room contains the original furnishings and memorabilia of Mistinguette, France's legendary stage star, a frequent performer with Maurice Chevalier and his on-again, off-again lover. Her pedestal bed is set in the middle of the room, surrounded everywhere by mirrors, as she liked to see how she looked or "performed" at all times of the day and night. Rooms vary widely in size, style, and price—some are quite small, while others are deluxe rooms fit for the occasional movie star who checks in (though Liz Taylor found *all* the rooms too small for her trunks). Regardless of room assignment, each bed has a plush French mattress and quality linens, along with such extras as non-working fireplaces, private safes, and fabric-covered walls. Clad in marble, the relatively small bathrooms are well equipped with thick towels, deluxe toiletries, a hair dryer, and a bidet; however, about half of them are tiny tub-less nooks.

Dining: Other than breakfast, afternoon tea, and room service (see below), there's no conventional dining within the hotel. Breakfast and tea are served in a greenhouse-style room loaded with plants.

Amenities: Concierge, room service (daily from 6:30am to 11pm), baby-sitting, laundry, and valet services.

MODERATE

Hôtel Aviatic. 105 rue de Vaugirard, 75006 Paris. ☎ **01-53-63-25-50.** Fax 01-53-63-25-55. www.aviatic.fr. E-mail: parishotel@aol.com. 43 units. A/C MINIBAR TV TEL. 780–1,180 F ($124.80–$188.80) double. AE, DC, MC, V. Parking 120 F ($19.20). Métro: Montparnasse-Bienvenue.

This is a bit of old Paris, with a modest inner courtyard and a vine-covered lattice on the walls. It has been a family-run hotel for a century. The reception lounge, with marble columns, brass chandeliers, antiques, and a petit salon, provides an attractive setting. It doesn't have the decorative flair of some of the other 6th arrondissement hotels we've listed, but it offers good comfort and a warm ambience. Completely remodeled, it's in an interesting section of Montparnasse, surrounded by cafes. The staff speaks English. Rooms were renovated in stages throughout the 1990s, and each has a safe, hair dryer, and comfortable bed.

Hôtel du Pas-de-Calais. 59 rue des Sts-Pères, 75006 Paris. ☎ **01-45-48-78-74.** Fax 01-45-44-94-57. E-mail: lepasdecalais@horeca.tm.fr. 41 units. A/C TV TEL. 850–920 F ($136–$147.20) double. AE, DC, MC, V. Parking 200 F ($32). Métro: St-Germain-des-Prés or Sèvres-Babylone.

The five-story Pas-de-Calais was built in the 17th century by the Lavalette family. Its elegant facade, complete with massive wooden doors, has been retained. The romantic novelist Chateaubriand lived here from 1811 to 1814. Its most famous guest was Jean-Paul Sartre, who struggled with the play *Les Mains Sales* (The Red Gloves) in room 41 during the hotel's pre-restoration days. The hotel is a bit weak on style, but as one longtime guest confided, in spite of the updates and renovations, "we still stay here for the memories." Rooms are modern with large baths. Each has been renovated, with new mattresses added, in the past few years. Inner rooms surround a modest courtyard with two garden tables and several trellises. All rooms have safe-deposit boxes. Off the lobby is a comfortable, carpeted sitting room.

Hôtel Le Clos Médicis. 56 rue Monsieur-le-Prince, 75006 Paris. ☎ **01-43-29-10-80.** Fax 01-43-54-26-90. www.closmedicis.com. E-mail: clos_medicis@compuserve.com. 38 units. A/C MINIBAR TV TEL. 790–1,200 F ($126.40–$192) double. AE, CB, DC, MC, V. Parking 150 F ($24). Métro: Odéon. RER: Luxembourg.

In 1994 this hotel opened on the premises of what had been a private home in 1860 and most recently had been a bookstore and a run-down boardinghouse. You'll find a verdant garden with lattices and exposed stone walls, a lobby with modern spotlights and simple furniture, and a multilingual staff. Its location, adjacent to the Jardin du Luxembourg, is a major plus. The warmly colored guest rooms, small to medium in size, are comfortable, with medium-quality mattresses and hair dryers. Breakfast is the only meal served.

INEXPENSIVE

Hôtel Clément. 6 rue Clément, 75006 Paris. ☎ **01-43-26-53-60.** Fax 01-44-07-06-83. E-mail: hotelment@worldnet.fr. 31 units. A/C TV TEL. 560–680 F ($89.60–$108.80) double; 780 F ($124.80) suite. AE, DC, V. Métro: Mabillon.

This hotel sits on a quiet, narrow street, within sight of the twin towers of the Église St-Sulpice. Built in the 1700s, the six-story structure that houses the hotel was stripped down and renovated several years ago into a bright, uncomplicated design. Don't expect deluxe bedrooms; they're simple and small, in some cases not much bigger than the beds they contain. Mattresses are medium quality, but not luxurious, and towels are thin. On the premises is a simple bistro with specialties from the Auvergne.

Hôtel du Globe. 15 rue des Quatre-Vents, 75006 Paris. ☎ **01-46-33-62-69.** Fax 01-46-33-62-69. 15 units. TV TEL. 495–595 F ($79.20–$95.20) double. MC, V. Closed 3 weeks in Aug. Métro: Mabillon, Odéon, or St-Sulpice.

This 17th-century building occupies an evocative street in one of Paris's oldest neighborhoods. Inside, you'll find most of the original stonework and dozens of original timbers and beams. Each room is decorated with individual old-fashioned flair. There's no elevator (you have to lug your suitcases up a very narrow, antique staircase) and no breakfast area (trays are brought to your room).

Insider Tip: The rooms with a tub are almost twice as large as those with a shower stall, so for the extra expense you'll get a lot more than just different plumbing. The largest and most desirable rooms are nos. 1, 12 (with a baldaquin-style bed), 14, 15, and 16. The room without a bathroom is a single at 270 F ($45.90). Mattresses were each custom-made for this hotel, and configured to fit the hotel's inventory of odd-sized but comfortable beds. Towels are relatively thin, but that's usually the case with Parisian hotels of this price range.

LEFT BANK: 7TH ARRONDISSEMENT (EIFFEL TOWER/MUSÉE D'ORSAY)
VERY EXPENSIVE

Hôtel Montalembert. 3 rue de Montalembert, 75007 Paris. ☎ **800/447-7462** in the U.S. and Canada, or 01-45-49-68-68. Fax 01-45-49-69-49. www.montalembert.com. E-mail: welcome@hotel-montalembert.fr. 56 units. A/C MINIBAR TV TEL. 1,800–2,400 F ($288–$384) double; 2,950 F ($472) junior suite; 4,400 F ($704) suite. AE, DC, MC, V. Parking 120 F ($19.20). Métro: Rue-du-Bac.

Unusually elegant for the Left Bank, the Montalembert was built in 1926 in beaux-arts style. In 1989 the hotel, much in need of renovation, was bought by the Hong Kong–based Leo group, whose directors hired one of France's premier architectural designers, Christian Liaigre. Millions of francs later, the hotel reopened in 1992 and was hailed as a smashing restoration. You'll find a sophisticated modern interpretation that borrows elements of Bauhaus and postmodern design in honey beiges, creams, and golds. Half the guest rooms follow the style established in the public rooms; the other half are stylishly but conservatively decorated in Louis-Philippe style. Bedrooms are spacious, except for some standard doubles that are quite small unless you're a very thin supermodel; all have VCRs and safes. Embroidered linens and quality mattresses adorn the large beds, and the bathrooms are elegant with marble vanities, generous shelf space, thick towels, and a hair dryer.

Dining/Diversions: Le Montalembert is favored by area artists, writers, publishers, and antique dealers. The stylish dining room provides excellent service and exceptionally good food based on market-fresh ingredients. Dishes include traditional veal chops slathered with wild mushrooms, along with more inventive fare from the relatively young kitchen staff. Expect crowds for weekday lunches; it thins out at other times. In summer, dining is offered on the terrace. The hotel also has a full-fledged bar and 24-hour room service.

Amenities: The concierge can arrange for practically anything under the sun. Guests have privileges at a nearby health club.

MODERATE

Hôtel de l'Acadèmie. 32 rue des Saints-Pères, 75007 Paris. ☎ **800/246-0041** in the U.S. and Canada, or 01-45-49-80-00. Fax 01-45-49-80-10. www.123europe.com. 34 units. A/C MINIBAR TV TEL. 690–990 F ($110.40–$158.40) double; 1,290–1,590 F ($206.40–$254.40) suite for 2. AE, DC, MC, V. Parking 150 F ($24). Métro: St-Germain-des-Prés.

The exterior walls and old ceiling beams are all that remain of this 17th-century residence of the private guards of the duc de Rohan. In 1999 the hotel was completely renovated to include an elegant reception area, and many yards of stylish fabrics upgraded the decor. The up-to-date guest rooms have Directoire beds with duvets and comfortable mattresses, an Île-de-France decor, and views over the 18th- and 19th-century buildings of the neighborhood. By American standards the rooms are small, but they're normal for Paris. Bathrooms are attractive and functional, often with marble trim, and all with hair dryers. The staff speaks English.

✪ **Hôtel de l'Université.** 22 rue de l'Université, 75007 Paris. ☎ **01-42-61-09-39.** Fax 01-42-60-40-84. www.hoteluniversite.com. 27 units. A/C TV TEL. 900–1,300 F ($144–$208) double. AE, MC, V. Métro: St-Germain-des-Prés.

Long favored by the well-heeled parents of North American students studying in Paris, this hotel enjoys a location in a discreetly upscale neighborhood. It's the love child of Mme Bergmann, who has renovated this 300-year-old town house and filled it with fine antiques. Number 54 is a favorite room, with a rattan bed, period pieces, and a marble bath. Opening onto a courtyard, no. 35 is another charmer, with a fireplace. The most expensive accommodation, at 1,300 F ($234), has a small terrace overlooking the surrounding rooftops. The beds contain elegant linen and tasteful fabrics, along with quality mattresses. Clad in tiles, most of the compact bathrooms have a tub and shower combination, although each is equipped with a hair dryer and adequate shelf space. The bistro-style breakfast room opens onto a courtyard with a fountain.

✪ **Hôtel du Quai-Voltaire.** 19 quai Voltaire, 75007 Paris. ☎ **01-42-61-50-91.** Fax 01-42-61-62-26. 33 units. TV TEL. 670–720 F ($107.20–$115.20) double; 850 F ($136) triple. AE, DC, MC, V. Parking 110 F ($17.60) nearby. Métro: Musée d'Orsay.

Built in the 1600s as an abbey, then transformed into a hotel in 1856, Quai-Voltaire is best known for illustrious guests, including Wilde, Baudelaire, and Wagner; they occupied Rooms 47, 56, and 55, respectively. Camille Pissarro painted Le Pont Royal from the window of his room on the fourth floor. Many rooms in this modest inn have been renovated, and most overlook the bookstalls and boats of the Seine. You can have drinks in the bar or small salon; simple meals (like omelets and salads) can be prepared for those who prefer to eat in. In 1999, the facade of the hotel was painted, as were most of the bedrooms. Mattresses are comfortable and firm, and bathrooms are well designed.

INEXPENSIVE

Grand Hôtel L'Èveque. 29 rue Cler, 75007 Paris. ☎ **01-47-05-49-15.** Fax 01-45-50-49-36. www.hotel-leveque.com. E-mail: info@hotelleveque.com. 50 units. TV TEL. 380–400 F ($60.80–$64) double. AE, MC, V. Métro: École Militaire.

Built in the 1930s, with pastel-colored bedrooms that are vaguely Art Deco, this five-story hotel was recommended by one of travel guru Rick Steves's TV documentaries. Now it's packed with English-speaking guests, many of whom appreciate its proximity to the Eiffel Tower. Each bedroom contains a hair dryer, a small lockbox for valuables, just enough space to be comfortable, and double-insulated windows that overlook either a courtyard in back or the street in front. In 1998, the hotel's interior was completely renovated and repainted. They didn't change the comfortable mattresses, but guests rarely, if ever, complain about them.

Hôtel de l'Empereur. 2 rue Chevert, 75007 Paris. ☎ **01-45-55-88-02.** Fax 01-45-51-88-54. 38 units. MINIBAR TV TEL. 470–530 F ($75.20–$84.80) double. AE, DC, MC, V. Parking 110–150 F ($17.60–$24) across the street. Métro: Latour-Maubourg.

This inexpensive and convenient six-story hotel is across the street from Les Invalides. There's an elevator inside to haul you and your luggage to one of the smallish but attractively decorated bedrooms. In 1998, management renovated the two upper-most floors of this place. Mattresses are not top of the line, but are acceptably comfortable anyway; towels are small and thin. There's no restaurant or bar, but a nearby restaurant sends platters of food to the bedrooms upon request. Built in the early 1700s, the hotel enjoys a loyal group of repeat guests.

Hôtel de Nevers. 83 rue du Bac, 75007 Paris. ☎ **01-45-44-61-30.** Fax 01-42-22-29-47. www.l-gf.com/hotel-de-nevers. 11 units. MINIBAR TV TEL. 450–530 F ($72–$84.80) double. No credit cards. Métro: Rue-du-Bac.

This is one of the most historic choices in an old neighborhood. Between 1627 and 1790 it was a convent for the Soeurs de la Recollette; they were disbanded by the Revolution. (Look for the religious plaque on the stone wall opposite the reception desk.) The building, brought to its present level of modernization in 1983, is presently *classé*, which means that any restoration must respect the original architecture. That precludes an elevator, so you'll have to climb the beautiful but never-ending white staircase. The cozy and pleasant rooms contain a combination of antique and reproduction furniture and medium-quality mattresses. Rooms 10 and 11 are especially sought-after for terraces overlooking either a corner of rue du Bac or a rear courtyard. Bathrooms are small but do the trick, each with a tub and shower combination or else a shower stall, and suitable shelf space.

Hôtel du Champ de Mars. 7 rue du Champ de Mars, 75007 Paris. ☎ **01-45-51-52-30.** Fax 01-45-51-64-36. www.hotel-du-champ-de-mars.com. E-mail: stg@club-internet.fr. 25 units. TV TEL. 430–460 F ($68.80–$73.60) double. AE, DC, MC, V. Parking 100–150 F ($16–$24) in nearby public parking lot. Métro: École Militaire.

Favored by families, this hotel rises five floors above a position close to the park that flanks the base of the Eiffel Tower. Built during the mid-20th century, it offers clean and simple bedrooms that are frilly and pretty. In 1998 most of the bedrooms were renovated and redecorated, retaining their charm, although they're still rather cramped. Most of the mattresses were replaced at that time. Bathrooms are efficiently scaled and modern looking, with adequate shelf space. The most memorable of the public areas is a stone-sided breakfast room.

Hôtel Lindbergh. 5 rue Chomel, 75007 Paris. ☎ **01-45-48-35-53.** Fax 01-45-49-31-48. http://paris.hotelguide.net. 26 units. TV TEL. 510–670 F ($81.60–$107.20) double; 760–860 F ($121.60–$137.60) triple or quad. AE, DC, MC, V. Parking 70 F ($11.20). Métro: Sèvres-Babylone or St-Sulpice.

Constructed between 1880 and 1881, this building was made into a hotel shortly after Charles Lindbergh electrified Paris with his solo flight across the Atlantic in 1927. Between then and the hotel's renovation in 1995, it looked as if little had changed since his famous landing. But today the hotel has streamlined and simple, medium-sized rooms, and lies about a 3-minute walk from St-Germain-des-Prés. Mattresses are comfortable, not too soft. Each bathroom has a hair dryer. Breakfast is the only meal served, but the staff will point out good restaurants nearby (an inexpensive, well-managed bistro, Le Cigale, is a few buildings away). Room service is available daily from 7am to 7pm.

Hôtel Saint-Dominique. 62 rue Saint-Dominique, 75007 Paris. ☎ **01-47-05-51-44.** Fax 01-47-05-81-28. 34 units. MINIBAR TV TEL. 540–580 F ($86.40–$92.80) double. AE, DC, MC, V. Métro: Latour-Maubourg or Invalides.

Part of the charm here is the way three separate buildings have been interconnected through an open-air courtyard. The most main structure originated as a convent during the 18th century, and still features battered ceiling beams and structural timbers (some of them exposed to view) in the reception area. Each building has cozy bedrooms outfitted with French provincial fabrics and patterns. The bedrooms aren't large, but each is warm, simply decorated, and comfortable. Beds usually have wooden headboards, comfortable mattresses, and cramped tiled bathrooms with a hair dryer and relatively thin towels.

NEAR THE AIRPORTS
ORLY

Hilton Paris Orly Airport. Aéroport Orly, 267 Orly Sud, 94544 Val-de-Marne. ☎ **800/445-8667** in the U.S. and Canada, or 01-45-12-45-12. Fax 01-45-12-45-00. www.hilton.com. 359 units. A/C MINIBAR TV TEL. 930 F ($148.80) double; 1,200–1,400 F ($192–$224) suite. AE, DC, MC, V. Parking 90 F ($14.40). Free shuttle bus between the hotel and both Orly terminals; 40-min taxi ride from central Paris, except during rush hours.

Boxy and bland, this airport hotel betrays its 1960s design. Despite that, the Hilton International at Orly remains a solid and well-maintained, but not particularly imaginative, hotel that business travelers from around Europe and the world prefer for its convenience. Try as they might, incoming jets can't penetrate the bedrooms' sound barriers, guaranteeing a decent night's sleep. Bedrooms are outfitted in a chain-hotel international style, and most of the mattresses were replaced in 1998. Bathrooms are predictable and functional.

Dining: The hotel has two restaurants, an upscale restaurant open Monday to Friday for lunch and dinner, and a less expensive bistro that serves lunch and dinner 7 days a week.

Amenities: 24-hour room service, laundry, exercise room and sauna, nearby tennis courts.

ROISSY/CHARLES DE GAULLE

Hôtel Sofitel Paris Aéroport CDG. Aéroport Charles de Gaulle, Zone Central, B.P. 20248, 95713 Roissy. ☎ **800/221-4542** in the U.S. and Canada, or 01-49-19-29-29. Fax 01-49-19-29-00. www.accor.com. 352 units. A/C MINIBAR TV TEL. 980–1,500 F ($156.80–$240) double; from 2,250 F ($360) suite. AE, DC, MC, V. Parking 164 F ($26.25). Free shuttle bus service to and from the airport.

Many international travelers shuttle happily through this bustling but somewhat anonymous member of the nationwide French chain. It rises nine floors above a gray, industrial landscape, and employs a multilingual staff that's accustomed to accommodating constantly arriving and departing international business travelers. Travelers sleep in monochromatic, conservatively international bedrooms that are soundproofed against the all-night roar of jets. Each was renovated in 1998, and many of the older mattresses were replaced.

Dining: International food with French overtones is served at a comfortable restaurant and a bar on the hotel's ground floor.

Amenities: 24-hour room service, a business center, video movies in several different languages, swimming pool and sauna.

4 Dining

Our best piece of advice—even if your budget is lean—is to splurge on one grand classic French meal. (You'll need to make reservations weeks or even months in advance.) A meal at a place such as **La Tour d'Argent, Taillevent, Alain Ducasse,** or **Violin d'Ingres** will be a memory you'll always carry.

Three-star dining remains extremely expensive in Paris. Brace yourself. The $100 main course (*entree* means appetizer in French so don't get them confused) is no longer a novelty, and first courses can sometimes top $50; in the top Michelin-starred dining rooms, the total bill easily tops $175 per person. But you can get around that high price tag in many places by ordering a fixed-price menu, perhaps for a mere $90, or heading for one of the not so celebrated but equally stellar dining rooms—**Pierre Gagnaire,** for example, instead of the almost legendary Alain Ducasse.

A restaurant where most or all main courses cost more than $35, or where a fixed price meal is more than $70, is classified as **Very Expensive.** At an **Expensive** restaurant, most main courses are between $25 and $35, and a complete meal runs between $45 and $70. For a restaurant to be considered **Moderate,** most main courses must cost between $15 and $25, while fixed price meals may be between $25 and $45. At an **Inexpensive** restaurant, main courses are less than $15 and complete dinners can be had for under $25.

One question we're often asked is if you can dine badly in Paris. The answer is an emphatic yes—and increasingly so. We repeatedly get complaints from visitors who cite haughty service and mediocre food dispensed at outrageous prices. Often these complaints are about places catering almost solely to tourists. We'll help you avoid them by sharing our favorite discoveries. While others are fighting it out for a table at one of the less-than-wonderful places along the Champs-Elysées, you might be enjoying finer fare off the beaten track.

Changes are in the Paris air. In the past, suits and ties were a given, and women always wore a smart dress or suit. Well, you can kiss your suits *au revoir*—these days. Except in first-class and deluxe places, dress has become more relaxed. Relaxed doesn't mean sloppy jeans and jogging attire, however. Parisians still value style, even when dressing informally.

Restaurants are still required by law to post their menus outside, so peruse them carefully. The prix-fixe menu still remains a solid choice if you want to have some idea of what your bill will be when it's presented by the waiter (whom, by the way, you should call *monsieur,* not *garçon*).

Part of the fun of a trip to Paris is enjoying the experience of an old-fashioned, family-run bistro. And just when you thought bistros were dying off, new wave chefs are moving in, hoping to revive them with excellent food at affordable prices. A trend that developed in the early 1990s—that of the "baby bistro"—continues into the late 1990s. These babies are reasonably priced spin-offs of some of Paris's ultra-deluxe restaurants. We've recommended some of the best of them, including **Jacques Cagna's Rôtisserie d'en Face.**

RIGHT BANK: 1ST ARRONDISSEMENT (LOUVRE/LES HALLES)
VERY EXPENSIVE

✪ **Carré des Feuillants.** 14 rue de Castiglione (near place Vendôme and the Tuileries). ☎ **01-42-86-82-82.** Reservations required. Main courses 240–280 F ($38.40–$44.80); fixed-price menus 340 F ($54.40) at lunch, 880 F ($140.80) at dinner. AE, DC, MC, V. Mon–Fri

Check, Please

It's considered somewhat provincial these days to request *l'addition* (the bill). Chic Parisians ask for *la note.*

---

noon–2pm; Mon–Sat 7:30–10pm. Closed first 3 weeks in Aug. Métro: Tuileries, Concorde, or Madeleine. FRENCH.

When leading chef Alain Dutournier converted this 17th-century convent into a restaurant, it was an overnight smash. The interior is like a turn-of-the-century bourgeois house with several small salons opening onto a skylit courtyard, across from which is a glass-enclosed kitchen. Dutournier offers a sophisticated re-interpretation of cuisine from France's southwest, based partly on seasonally fresh ingredients and lots of know-how. Examples include roasted veal kidney cooked in its own fat; grilled wood pigeon served with chutney and polenta; fillet of rabbit in a bitter chocolate sauce with quince; and roasted leg of suckling lamb from the Pyrénées with autumn vegetables. Lighter dishes are also available, such as scallops in a crispy coat of parsley-infused puff pastry served with cabbage and truffles. Dessert might include a slice of pistachio cream cake with candied tangerines.

Goumard. 9 rue Duphot. ☎ **01-42-60-36-07.** Reservations recommended. Main courses 190–380 F ($30.40–$60.80); fixed-price lunch 390 F ($62.40); menu gastronomique 780 F ($124.80). AE, DC, MC, V. Tues–Sat 12:30–2:30pm and 7:30–10:30pm. Closed 2 weeks in Aug. Métro: Madeleine or Concorde. SEAFOOD.

Opened in 1872 under a different name ("Restaurant Prunier"), this restaurant is one of the leading seafood restaurants in Paris. There's no meat on the menu, though if you've brought along someone who hates fish, the cooperative staff might be able to offer a limited choice of meat dishes. The decor consists of an unusual collection of Lalique crystal fish that are displayed in artificial "aquariums" lining the walls. Even more unusual are the men's and women's rest rooms, now classified as *monuments historiques* by the French government. (The commodes were designed by the Art Nouveau master cabinetmaker Majorelle around the turn of the century.)

Much of the seafood here is flown in direct from Brittany every day. Examples include a craquant of crayfish in its own herb salad; lobster soup with coconut; a parmentier of crabmeat served with a mousseline of potatoes; fillet of grilled sea wolf served with a fricassée of artichokes and Provençal pistou; and a salad of grilled turbot on a bed of artichokes with tarragon. Especially appealing is poached turbot with hollandaise sauce, served with leeks in vinaigrette. In all these dishes, nothing (no excess butter, spices, or salt) is allowed to interfere with the natural flavor of the sea. Be prepared for some very unusual food here—the staff will help translate the menu items for you.

✪ **Le Grand Véfour.** 17 rue de Beaujolais. ☎ **01-42-96-56-27.** Reservations required. Main courses 300–400 F ($48–$64); fixed-price menus 380–860 F ($60.80–$137.60) at lunch, 860 F ($137.60) at dinner. AE, DC, MC, V. Mon–Fri 12:30–2pm and 8–10:15pm. Métro: Louvreor Pyramides. FRENCH.

This has been a restaurant since the reign of Louis XV—the name has changed, however. The exact date of its opening as the Café de Chartres isn't known, but this place is more than 200 years old. In 1812 it was named after its owner, Jean Véfour, a former chef to a member of the royal family. Napoléon, Danton, Hugo, Colette, and Cocteau have dined here—as the brass plaques on the tables testify. Jean Taittinger, of the champagne family (owner of the Hôtel de Crillon), purchased the restaurant and meticulously restored it to its former glory.

Heart of the Right Bank Restaurants

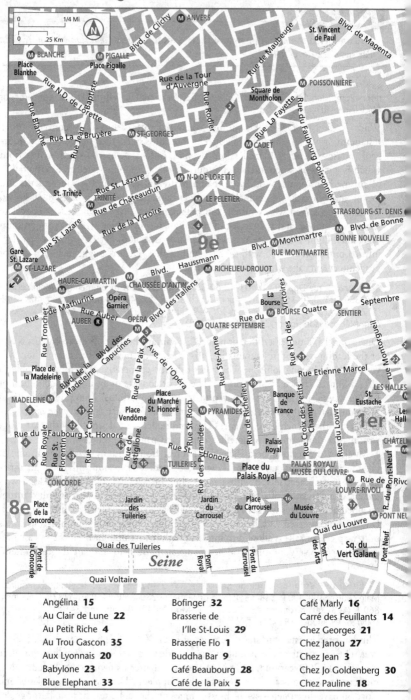

Angélina **15**	Bofinger **32**	Café Marly **16**
Au Clair de Lune **22**	Brasserie de	Carré des Feuillants **14**
Au Petit Riche **4**	l'Ile St-Louis **29**	Chez Georges **21**
Au Trou Gascon **35**	Brasserie Flo **1**	Chez Janou **27**
Aux Lyonnais **20**	Buddha Bar **9**	Chez Jean **3**
Babylone **23**	Café Beaubourg **28**	Chez Jo Goldenberg **30**
Blue Elephant **33**	Café de la Paix **5**	Chez Pauline **18**

Chez Vong **24**	L'Astor **7**	Mansouria **34**
Goumard **12**	Le Fumoir **17**	Maxim's **10**
Il Cortile **11**	Le Grand Véfour **19**	Restaurant Opéra **6**
Joe Allen **25**	Le Train Bleu **35**	Wally Le Saharien **2**
L'Ambassade	Lescure **13**	
d'Auvergne **26**	Lucas-Carton	
L'Ambroisie **31**	(Alain Senderens) **8**	

Dining here is a great gastronomic experience. The chef for the past 8 years, Guy Martin, bases many dishes on recipes from the French Alps. His finest hour is when he does roast lamb in a juice of herbs. Exotic touches also appear in the plate. Ever have cabbage sorbet in a dark chocolate sauce? Other specialties include noisettes of lamb with star anise and Breton lobster. The desserts are often grand, like the *gourmandises au chocolat*, a richness of chocolate served with chocolate sorbet.

EXPENSIVE

Chez Pauline. 5 rue Villedo. ☎ **01-42-96-20-70.** Reservations recommended. Main courses 190–400 F ($30.40–$64); fixed-price menu 220 F ($35.20). AE, DC, MC, V. Mon–Fri 12:15–2:30pm and 7:30–10:30pm, Sat 7:30–10:30pm. Métro: Palais-Royal. BURGUNDIAN/ FRENCH.

Many of its loyal fans say that this is a less expensive (if you stick to the fixed-price menu), less majestic version of Le Grand Véfour. The setting is grand enough to impress a business client and lighthearted enough to attract an impressive roster of celebs. You'll be ushered to a table on one of two levels, amid polished mirrors and red-leather banquettes. The emphasis is on the cuisine of central France, especially Burgundy, as shown by the liberal use of wines in time-honored favorites like a cassoulet of Burgundian snails with bacon and tomatoes; filet of wild duckling with seasonal berries; old-fashioned beef bourguignonne with tagliatelle; and a ragoût of wild hare in an aspic of Pouilly. You'll do well with the roasted Bresse chicken with dauphinois potatoes, or any of the stews that swim with savory morsels of duck, wild boar, and venison. Dessert might include a *clafoutis* of apricots and raspberries lightly sautéed in sugar, or a caramelized version of rice pudding.

MODERATE

Chez Vong. 10 rue de la Grande-Truanderie. ☎ **01-40-26-09-36.** Reservations recommended. Main courses 100–185 F ($16–$29.60); fixed-price lunch 150 F ($24). AE, DC, MC, V. Mon–Sat noon–2:30pm and 7pm–midnight. Métro: Étienne-Marcel. CANTONESE.

This is the kind of place you head for when you've had your fill of grand French cuisine and grander culinary pretensions. The decor is a soothing mixture of green and browns, steeped in a Chinese colonial ambience that evokes the turn-of-the-century era when Shanghai rocked and rolled as one of the most sophisticated settings in Asia. Menu items include shrimps and scallops served with any degree of spiciness you want, including a superheated version with garlic and red peppers; "joyous beef" that mingles sliced filet with pepper sauce; chicken in puff pastry with ginger; and a tempting array of fresh fish dishes. This isn't your average Chinese joint; it's one of the hipster-restaurants-of-the-moment, full of folk from the worlds of entertainment and the arts.

Il Cortile. In the Hotel Castille, 37 rue Cambon. ☎ **01-44-58-45-67.** Reservations recommended. Main courses 100–150 F ($16–$24). AE, DC, MC, V. Mon–Fri noon–2:30pm and 7:30–10:30pm. Métro: Concorde or Madeleine. ITALIAN/MEDITERRANEAN.

Flanking the verdant courtyard of a small, discreetly elegant hotel, in a district known for its fashion powerhouses and grandiose architecture, this is a much-talked-about restaurant whose Italian food is the best in Paris. There are two conservatively modern, beige-and-yellow dining rooms, plus a small courtyard (the Italian staff here refers to it as a *"cortile"*) where tables spill over during clement weather. The cuisine is fresh, inventive, and seasonal. There's an emphasis on items from the north of Italy, as shown by a special promotion of wines of Tuscany and the Piedmont. Look for farfalle pasta with squid ink and fresh shellfish, fettuccine with pistou, grilled swordfish with grilled and skewered vegetables, and an award-winning version of guinea fowl. Spit-roasted, and served with artfully shaped slices of the bird's gizzard, heart, and liver, it is served with polenta. Service is virtually flawless: You'll get the feeling that many members of the Italian-speaking staff consider themselves semi-official ambassadors of goodwill to the Parisians.

Joe Allen. 30 rue Pierre-Lescot. ☎ **01-42-36-70-13.** Reservations recommended for dinner. Main courses 75–140 F ($12–$22.40); fixed-price menus 112–140 F ($17.90–$22.40). AE, MC, V. Daily noon–1am. Métro: Etienne-Marcel. AMERICAN.

Joe Allen long ago invaded Les Halles with his hamburger. Though the New York restaurateur admits "it's a silly idea," it works. After he set the place up, most of his work went into creating the American burger, easily the best in Paris. While listening to the jukebox, you can order savory black-bean soup, spicy chili, juicy sirloin steak, barbecued spareribs, or apple pie. Try the spinach salad topped with creamy Roquefort dressing and sprinkled with crunchy bacon bits and fresh mushrooms. Joe Allen is getting more sophisticated, catering to modern tastes with dishes like grilled salmon with coconut rice and sun-dried tomatoes.

Joe claims that his saloon is the only place in Paris that serves authentic New York cheesecake or real pecan pie. Thanks to French chocolate, he feels that his brownies are better than those in the States. Giving the brownies tough competition are the California chocolate-mousse pie, strawberries Romanoff, and coconut-cream pie. Thanksgiving dinner is becoming a tradition (you'll need a reservation way in advance). On a regular night, if you haven't made a reservation for dinner, expect to wait at the New York bar for at least 30 minutes.

Le Fumoir. 6 rue de l'Amiral Coligny. ☎ **01-42-92-00-24.** Reservations recommended. Main courses 105–120 F ($16.80–$19.20). AE, DC, MC, V. Daily for salads, pastries, and snacks 11am–1am; complete menu daily noon–3pm and 7–11:30pm. Métro: Louvre or Pont Neuf. INTERNATIONAL.

Stylish and breezy, and set in an antique building a few steps from the Louvre, this is an upscale brasserie that's a great vantage point for watching hipster denizens of Paris's arts scene come and go. Currently, it's the hottest place to be seen eating or drinking in Paris today. Within a high-ceilinged setting of warm but somber browns and indirect lighting, you can order salads, pastries, and drinks during the off-hours noted above, and platters of more substantial food during the conventional meal times. Examples include filets of codfish with onions and herbs; sliced rack of veal simmered in its own juices with tarragon; calf's liver with onions; a combination platter of lamb chops with grilled tuna steak; and herring in a mustard-flavored cream sauce.

INEXPENSIVE

Angélina. 226 rue de Rivoli. ☎ **01-42-60-82-00.** Reservations accepted for lunch, not for tea time. Pot of tea for one 35–36 F ($5.60–$5.75); sandwiches and salads 58–98 F ($9.30–$15.70); main courses 68–135 F ($10.90–$21.60). AE, V. Daily 9am–7pm (lunch served 11:45am–3pm). Métro: Tuileries. TEA/LIGHT FARE.

In the high-rent district near the Hôtel Inter-Continental, this *salon de thé* combines glitter and bourgeois respectability. The carpets are red, the ceilings are high, and the gilded accessories have the right amount of patina. For a view (over tea and delicate sandwiches) of the lionesses of the world of haute couture, this place has no equal. Overwrought waitresses bearing silver trays serve light platters, pastries, drinks, and tea or coffee at tiny marble-top tables. Lunch usually offers a salad and a plat du jour like chicken salad, sole meuniére, or poached salmon. The house specialty, designed to go well with a cup of tea, is a Mont Blanc, a combination of chestnut cream and meringue. There are two drawbacks, however: The tearoom is in a section of rue de Rivoli that's getting scuzzy, and the service tends to be a bit snooty.

✪ **Lescure.** 7 rue de Mondovi. ☎ **01-42-60-18-91.** Reservations not accepted. Main courses 26–84 F ($4.15–$13.45); 4-course fixed-price menu 115 F ($18.40). V. Mon–Fri noon–2:15pm and 7–11pm. Closed 3 weeks in Aug. Métro: Concorde. FRENCH.

This minibistro is a major find—it's one of the few reasonably priced restaurants near place de la Concorde. It's animated, fun, irreverent, and very appealing. You'll get a lot for your franc here. The tables on the sidewalk are tiny, and there isn't much room inside, but what this place does have is rustic charm. The kitchen is wide open, and the aroma of drying bay leaves, salami, and garlic pigtails hanging from the ceiling fills the room. Expect *cuisine bourgeoise*—nothing too innovative, just substantial, hearty fare. Perhaps begin with *pâté en croûte* (pâté encased in pastry). Main-course house specialties include *confit de canard* (duckling) and cabbage stuffed with salmon. During autumn and winter, expect a savory repertoire of Gaite dishes such as venison and pheasant. A favorite dessert is one of the chef's fruit tarts.

RIGHT BANK: 2ND ARRONDISSEMENT (LA BOURSE)
MODERATE

Babylone. 34 rue Tiquetonne. ☎ **01-42-33-48-35.** Main courses 75–125 F ($12–$20). V. Daily 8pm–7am. Métro: Etienne-Marcel or Sentier. WEST INDIAN/AFRICAN.

This place honors the French Caribbean island of Guadeloupe, with appetizers like *accras* of codfish and Creole *boudin* (blood sausage) that usually precede such main courses as fricassée of shrimp or chicken or a *colombo* (stew) of baby goat. Look for African masks, touches of zebra skin, and photos of the divas and celebrities (like Stevie Wonder and Jesse Jackson) who have dined here. Some (Diana Ross) you might know; others are sports stars and fashion models better known in France. Don't even think of coming here before dark. After 2am or so, the focus shifts away from the hearty Caribbean soul food toward reggae, jazz, and cocktails.

Chez Georges. 1 rue du Mail. ☎ **01-42-60-07-11.** Reservations required. Main courses 140–165 F ($22.40–$26.40). AE, MC, V. Mon–Sat noon–2:15pm and 7–9:45pm. Closed 3 weeks in Aug. Métro: Bourse. FRENCH.

This bistro is something of a local landmark, opened in 1964 near the Bourse. The place has been run by three generations of the Broillet family—George, the patriarch, founded it, and his son, Bernard, manages it today. Naturally, at lunch it's packed with stock-exchange members. The owners serve what they call *la cuisine typiquement bourgeoise*—"food from our grandmère in the provinces." Waiters bring around bowls of appetizers, such as celery rémoulade, to get you started. You can follow with sweetbreads with morels; duck breast with cêpe mushrooms; a classic cassoulet; or a *pot-au-feu* (beef simmered with vegetables). A delight is filet of sole with a sauce made from Pouilly wine and crème fraîche. Beaujolais goes great with this hearty food.

INEXPENSIVE

Au Clair de Lune. 27 rue Française. ☎ **01-42-33-59-10.** Reservations recommended. Main courses 54–72 F ($8.65–$11.50); fixed-price menu 68 F ($10.90). DC, MC, V. Daily noon–2:30pm and 7:30–11pm. Métro: Etienne-Marcel or Sentier. ALGERIAN/FRENCH.

This neighborhood staple has flourished in the heart of the wholesale garment district since the 1930s. Today you'll dine in a long, narrow room whose walls are hung with colorful Berber carpets; your fellow diners are likely to include many shop workers from the nearby wholesale clothiers. There's always the Algerian staple of couscous on the menu, as well as an array of such oft-changing daily specials as *blanquette de veau* (veal stew), shoulder or rack of lamb, grilled or pan-fried fish, and roast chicken. The portions are large, so bring your appetite. The wines are from throughout France and North Africa.

✪ **Aux Lyonnais.** 32 rue Saint-Marc, 2e. ☎ **01-42-96-65-04.** Reservations required. Main courses 70–90 F ($11.20–$14.40). AE, DC, MC, V. Mon–Sat 11:30am–3pm and 6:30–11:30pm. Métro: Bourse or Richelieu-Drouot. LYONNAIS/FRENCH-TRADITIONAL.

À LYON LE COCHON ES ROI! proclaims the sign. Pig may be king at this fin-de-siècle bistro, but a competent kitchen staff does everything well here. After a meal at this bistro just behind the Bourse (Paris's stock exchange), you'll know why Lyon is called the gastronomic capital of France. If you like your bistros with walls molded with roses and garlands, brass globe lamps, potted palms, and etched glass, Aux Lyonnais is for you.

Chances are you'll enjoy one of your finest regional meals in Paris here. Everything is washed down with Beaujolais. Launch your repast with one of the large Lyonnais sausages, although a favorite opener remains a chicory salad with bacon and slices of hot sausages. Poached eggs in red wine sauce still appear on the menu, as do grilled pig's feet, the eternal favorite around here among the old-timers. Pike dumplings are always prepared to perfection, and served classically in a white butter sauce. The upside-down apple pie with crème fraîche is the dessert of choice.

RIGHT BANK: 3RD ARRONDISSEMENT (LE MARAIS)
MODERATE

L'Ambassade d'Auvergne. 22 rue de Grenier St-Lazare. ☎ **01-42-72-31-22.** Reservations recommended. Main courses 88–120 F ($14.10–$19.20); fixed-price menu 170 F ($27.20). AE, MC, V. Daily noon–2pm and 7:30–10pm. Métro: Rambuteau. AUVERGNE/FRENCH.

ou enter this rustic tavern through a busy bar, with heavy oak beams, hanging hams, and ceramic plates. More than any other Paris restaurant, this favorite showcases the culinary generosity of France's most isolated and slow-to-change region, Auvergne, whose pork products are celebrated throughout France. Examples include a chicory salad with apples and pieces of country ham; pork braised with cabbage, turnips, and white beans; grilled tripe sausages with mashed potatoes and cantal cheese with garlic; and pork jowls with green lentils. Non-pork specialties include pan-fried duck liver with gingerbread; filets of perch steamed with verbena tea; and roasted rack of lamb with wild mushrooms. Dessert might consist of a poached pear with crispy almonds and caramel sauce, or a wine-flavored sorbet.

INEXPENSIVE

Chez Janou. 2 rue Roger-Verlomme. ☎ **01-42-72-28-41.** Reservations recommended. Main courses 68–100 F ($10.90–$16). No credit cards. Daily noon–3pm and 7:30pm–midnight. Métro: Chemin-Vert. PROVENÇAL.

On one of the narrow 17th-century streets behind place des Vosges, this unpretentious bistro operates from a pair of cramped but cozy dining rooms filled with memorabilia from Provence. It includes a covered terrace. Service is brusque and usually somewhat hectic. The menu items include such dishes as *gambas* (large shrimp) with pastis sauce, *brouillade des pleurotes* (baked eggs with oyster mushrooms), velouté of frogs' legs, fondue of ratatouille, au gratin of mussels, and a simple but savory version of *daube Provençale*, which is sometimes compared to pot roast.

RIGHT BANK: 4TH ARRONDISSEMENT (ÎLE DE LA CITÉ/ILE ST-LOUIS)
VERY EXPENSIVE

✪ **L'Ambroisie.** 9 place des Vosges. ☎ **01-42-78-51-45.** Reservations required. Main courses 350–530 F ($56–$84.80). AE, MC, V. Tues–Sat noon–1:30pm and 8–9:30pm. Métro: St-Paul. FRENCH.

Operating out of the most gracious and elegant dining room in the Marais, Bernard Pacaud has been hailed as a culinary genius. One critic once wrote that "this is how Escoffier would be cooking today were he still alive." The crowd of moneyed, cosmopolitan gourmets who flock here don't mind the high prices, but insist on the very best for their pampered palates, and they know that Pacaud delivers. In the words of our dining companion here on our latest rounds, "I was dazed by the deliciousness of it all."

The dishes change seasonally but may include fricassée of Breton lobster with a civet/red-wine sauce; filet of turbot braised with celery served with a julienne of black truffles; and one of our favorites, Bresse chicken roasted with black truffles and truffled vegetables. An award-winning dessert is a *tarte fine soblée* served with chocolate and vanilla flavored ice cream.

MODERATE

Bofinger. 5–7 rue de la Bastille. ☎ **01-42-72-87-82.** Reservations recommended. Main courses 75–196 F ($12–$31.35); fixed-price menu 189 F ($30.25). AE, DC, MC, V. Mon–Fri noon–3pm and 6:30pm–1am, Sat–Sun noon–1am. Métro: Bastille. FRENCH/ALSATIAN.

This is Paris's oldest Alsatian brasserie, tracing its origins back to 1864, and its decor is such a part of the Paris landscape that it has been classified a historic landmark. At night, many opera-goers venture here for beer and sauerkraut. The brasserie offers excellent Alsatian fare in hearty portions. In 1996 the restaurant was acquired by Les Restaurants de Jean Bucher, losing its independent status but gaining a new lease on life—it's now affiliated with La Coupole, Julien, and Brasserie Flo. The menu has been updated, retaining only the most popular dishes (such as sauerkraut and sole meunière). Recent additions have included roast leg of lamb with a fondant of artichoke hearts and a purée of parsley, grilled turbot with a brandade of fennel, and filet of stingray with chives and burnt-butter sauce. Shellfish, including lots of fresh oysters and langoustines, is available in season. Although Bofinger is technically in the 4th arrondissement, it is usually associated with the 11th.

Brasserie de l'Ile St-Louis. 55 quai de Bourbon. ☎ **01-43-54-02-59.** Reservations not accepted. Main courses 85–130 F ($13.60–$20.80). MC, V. Thurs–Tues noon–midnight. Métro: Pont-Marie. FRENCH/ALSATIAN.

This is the kind of retro-chic brasserie where celebrities sometimes turn up for an informal meal. Little about the patina and paneled decor has changed since the 1880s, so the atmosphere can't be matched in more modern nearby competitors. Menu items are flavorful and well prepared, with absolutely no concern for cutting-edge fads and trends. Examples are an always-popular version of Alsatian sauerkraut, cassoulet in the Toulouse style, stingray with a nut-and-butter sauce, calf's liver, and a succulent version of jarret of pork with a warm apple marmalade.

INEXPENSIVE

Chez Jo Goldenberg. 7 rue des Rosiers. ☎ **01-48-87-20-16.** Reservations recommended. Main courses 75–110 F ($12–$17.60). AE, DC, MC, V. Daily noon–1am. Métro: St-Paul. JEWISH/CENTRAL EUROPEAN.

On the "Street of the Rosebushes" this is the best-known restaurant. Albert Goldenberg, the doyen of Jewish restaurateurs in Paris, long ago moved to a restaurant in choicer surroundings (at 69 av. de Wagram, 17e), but his brother, Joseph, has remained here. Dining is on two levels, one reserved for nonsmokers. Look for the collection of samovars and the white fantail pigeon in a wicker cage. Interesting paintings and strolling musicians add to the ambience. The *carpe farcie* (stuffed carp) is a preferred selection, but the beef goulash is also good. We like the eggplant moussaka and the pastrami. The menu also offers Israeli wines, but M. Goldenberg admits that they're not as good as French wine. Live Israeli music is presented every night beginning at 9pm, and during Jewish holidays, such as Pesach, Rosh Hashana, and Yom Kippur, special menus are presented in honor of the event—but only with advance reservations.

RIGHT BANK: 8TH ARRONDISSEMENT (CHAMPS-ELYSÉES/MADELEINE)
VERY EXPENSIVE

Lasserre. 17 av. Franklin-D.-Roosevelt. ☎ **01-43-59-53-43.** Reservations required. Main courses 170–280 F ($27.20–$44.80); fixed-price menu 340 F ($54.40) at lunch, 800 F ($128) at dinner. AE, MC, V. Tues–Sat 12:30–2:30pm, Mon–Sat 7:30–10:30pm. Closed Aug. Métro: Franklin-D.-Roosevelt. FRENCH.

This deluxe restaurant was a simple bistro before World War II. Then came René Lasserre, and today it's one of the few remaining examples of *le grand restaurant à la française*. Behind the front doors are two private dining rooms with a "disappearing wall," plus a reception lounge with Louis XVI furnishings and brocaded walls. You ascend to the second landing in an elevator lined with brocaded silk, where you are seated on a Louis XV salon chair at an exquisite table set with porcelain, gold-edged crystal glasses, and a silver candelabra. The ceiling is pulled back in fair weather to reveal the sky.

The appetizers are among the finest in Paris, including a salad of truffles, a three-meat terrine, and Belon oysters flavored with chablis. The fish selections include the signature filet of sole Club de la Casserole (poached filets served in puff pastry with asparagus tips and asparagus-flavored cream sauce). When you taste the meat and poultry dishes, such as veal kidneys flambée or pigeon André Malraux, you'll think Escoffier is still alive. The best of the spectacular desserts are soufflé Grand Marnier and a selection of three freshly made sorbets of the season. The cellar, with 180,000 bottles of wine, is among Paris's most remarkable.

Lucas-Carton (Alain Senderens). 9 place de la Madeleine. ☎ **01-42-65-22-90.** Fax 01-42-65-06-23. Reservations required several days ahead for lunch, several weeks ahead for dinner. Main courses 240–700 F ($38.40–$112); fixed-price menu 395 F ($63.20) at lunch, 1,300 F ($208) at dinner. AE, DC, MC, V. Tues–Fri noon–2:30pm, Mon–Sat 8–10:15pm. Closed 3 weeks in Aug. Métro: Madeleine. FRENCH.

This landmark was designed by an Englishman, Lucas, and a talented French chef, François Carton. Since Alain Senderens has taken over, he has added some welcomed modern touches. The two dining rooms downstairs and private rooms upstairs are decorated with mirrors, fragrant bouquets, and paneling that has been polished weekly since 1900. Every dish is influenced by Senderens's creative flair. Menu items change seasonally and include polenta with black truffles, foie gras with cabbage, duckling Apicius (roasted with honey and spices), and a delectable *millefeuille* with vanilla sauce. Senderens's latest sensations include lobster roasted with vanilla, and *poularde demi-deuil*—a Bresse hen whose flesh has been scored with black truffles; he says that the resulting black-and-white flesh is "in partial mourning," and it's accompanied by saffron-flavored rice.

Maxim's. 3 rue Royale. ☎ **01-42-65-27-94.** Reservations required. Main courses 225–330 F ($36–$52.80) at lunch, 300–480 F ($48–$76.80) at dinner. AE, DC, MC, V. Mon–Sat 12:30–2pm and 7:30–10pm. Métro: Concorde. FRENCH.

Maxim's is the world's most legendary restaurant and even has clones in cities like New York, Beijing, and Tokyo. It preserves the era of belle époque decor and was a favorite of Edward VII, then the prince of Wales. It was the setting for *The Merry Widow*, so you can be sure the orchestra will play that tune at least once each evening. Much later, Louis Jourdan took Leslie Caron to the restaurant in the musical *Gigi*. Today rich tourists from around the world are likely to occupy once-fabled tables where Onassis wooed Callas. The clothing industry giant Pierre Cardin took over the restaurant in 1981. Although not always available, billi-bi soup (made with mussels, white wine, cream, chopped onions, celery, parsley, and coarsely ground pepper) is a classic opener. Another favorite is sole Albert, flavored with chopped herbs and bread crumbs, plus a large glass of vermouth. For dessert, try the *tarte Tatin*.

✪ **Pierre Gagnaire.** In the Hôtel Balzac, 6 rue Balzac. ☎ **01-44-35-18-25.** Fax 01-44-35-18-37. Reservations imperative (and difficult to make). Main courses 310–460 F ($49.60–$73.60); fixed-price menus 520–950 F ($83.20–$152) at lunch, 950 F ($152) at dinner. AE, DC, MC, V. Mon–Fri 12:30–2:15pm; Sun–Fri 8–10pm. Métro: George-V. FRENCH.

In the town of St-Etienne, Pierre Gagnaire rose to greatness and won coveted three-Michelin-star fame. However, his restaurant went into receivership. When he popped up in Paris, operating on the premises of the Hôtel Balzac, all of Paris tried to make its way to Gagnaire's closely guarded door. The chef is hot, but this shy man, who prefers to remain in the kitchen instead of appearing on TV, is hard to reach. In many cases, his reception doesn't even answer the phone from eager callers wanting a reservation. They're often told by an answering machine to fax a "request" for a table. If you do get through, you'll find it worth the effort.

Gagnaire's menus are seasonally adjusted to take advantage of France's bounty, and he blends flavors and textures in ways that are dazzling. One critic wrote, "Picasso stretched the limits of painting; Gagnaire does it with cooking." Try anything from a menu that changes every 2 months: Examples of the creative panache here include freshwater crayfish cooked tempura-style with thin-sliced flash-seared vegetables and a sweet-and-sour sauce; or turbot cooked in a bag and served with fennel and Provençal lemons. Dessert might be a chocolate soufflé served with a frozen parfait and Sicilian pistachios.

✪ **Taillevent.** 15 rue Lamennais. ☎ **01-44-95-15-01.** Fax 01-42-25-95-18. Reservations required weeks, even months, in advance. Main courses 295–500 F ($47.20–$80). AE, DC, MC, V. Mon–Fri noon–2:30pm and 7–10pm. Closed Aug. Métro: George-V. FRENCH.

Dine in grand 18th-century style in this town house just off the Champs-Elysées. In 1946, when owner Jean Claude Vrinat's father opened the doors, he established one of Paris's outstanding restaurants. The competition is great, but this is our number one dining choice in Paris. The wines are superb, and the service is impeccable. Under chef Philippe Legendre, the menus are deftly balanced between traditional and modern cuisine. You might begin with aspic de foie gras (liver and veal sweetbreads in aspic with slivers of carrots and truffles). Main-dish specialties are cassolette de crayfish from Brittany, and *agneau aux trois cuissons* (feet, breast, and tenderloin of lamb with various sauces). A star dessert is the *fondant aux deux parfumes* (an almond-toffee Bavarian cream covered with chocolate).

EXPENSIVE

Buddha Bar. 8 rue Boissy d'Anglas. ☎ **01-53-05-90-00.** Reservations recommended. Main courses 112–270 F ($17.90–$43.20). AE, MC, V. Mon–Fri noon–3pm, daily 6pm–2am. Métro: Concorde. FRENCH/PACIFIC RIM.

This place is hot, hot, and hot, and it's truly the restaurant of the moment in Paris. Its location on a chic street near the Champs-Elysées and its fashionable fusion of French with Asian and Californian cuisine almost guarantee an uber-trendy crowd.

The cutting-edge menu combines Japanese sashimi, Vietnamese spring rolls, lacquered duck, sautéed shrimp with a black-bean sauce, grilled chicken skewers with orange sauce, and sweet-and-sour spareribs. Many come here just for a drink in the carefully lacquered, hip-looking bar, which is set upstairs from the street-level dining room. In the twin dining rooms dominated by a plaster-and-fiberglass copy of a tranquil and meditating Buddha, and flanked by walls that are lavishly ornamented with Asian castings and carvings, you can revel in one of the most sophisticated cross-cultural medleys in Paris.

✪ **L'Astor.** In the Hôtel Astor, 11 rue d'Astorg. ☎ **01-53-05-05-20.** Reservations recommended. Main courses 110–240 F ($17.60–$38.40); fixed-price menus 298–580 F ($47.70–$92.80). AE, DC, MC, V. Mon–Fri noon–2pm and 7:30–10pm. Métro: St-Augustin. FRENCH.

Have you ever wondered what happens to great French chefs after they retire? If they're lucky (and well funded) enough, they become "culinary consultants," dropping in two or three times a week to keep an eye on what's happening. That's what happened when Joël Robuchon retired from his citadel on avenue Raymond-Poincaré. His replacement is the well-respected Eric Lecerf, a formidable force who's better able than anyone else to step into Robuchon's shoes. The setting, which moved into this hotel dining room early in 1996, is a gray-and-white enclave with a stained-glass ceiling in the Art Deco style.

If you dine here, expect an almost religious devotion to those specialties that were personally developed by Joel Robuchon during his active years here, and a less overwhelming emphasis on newer dishes created and fostered by his replacement. Examples of "classic Robuchon," as pointed out by the staff, include caramelized sea urchins in aspic with a fennel-flavored cream sauce, cannellonis stuffed with eggplant with filets of tuna and olive oil, and spit-roasted Bresse chicken roasted with flap mushrooms. Items created by Lecerf (carpaccio of Breton lobster with olive oil and confit of tomatoes; roasted and braised rack of lamb, supreme of pigeon with cabbage and foie gras) are presented as the creation of a young-blooded, hot new chef following in the footsteps of a master.

Spoon Food & Wine. in the Marignan-Elysée Hotel, 14 rue Marignan. ☎ **01-40-76-34-44.** Reservations recommended. Appetizers, main courses, vegetable side dishes each 65–180 F ($10.40–$28.80). Mon–Fri noon–2:30pm and 7–11:30pm. AE, DC, MC, V. Métro: Franklin-D-Roosevelt. INTERNATIONAL.

The latest culinary statement of *wunderkind* chef Alain Ducasse, which opened in December of 1998, has been hailed as a "restaurant for the millennium," although it's been equally condemned by some Parisian food critics. Surreal, a bit absurd, it's a hypermodern spot, with a claustrophobic dining room that evokes both stylish Paris and stylish California. The cuisine roams the world for inspiration, even focusing on a classic but rather bland American macaroni and cheese. There's even a B.L.T., barbecued ribs, chicken wings, and pastrami. But other dishes evoke Italy, Latin America, Asia, and India. Sometimes the waitstaff doesn't know the national origin of a dish—*youm loumg,* for example, (it's squid and shellfish in a spicy bouillon). Some dishes are more successful than others—the steamed lobster with mango chutney, for example, is a winner. For a "vegetable garden," you can mix and match among 15 ingredients, including iceberg lettuce. For the one basic pasta, you have a selection of five different sauces, so you have great leeway in creating your own meal. Warning: Although a first glance at the menu makes you think this restaurant is moderate in price, your tab can mount very quickly, especially when wine, service, and VAT are added on.

MODERATE

Androuït. 6 rue Arsène-Houssaye. ☎ **01-42-89-95-00.** Reservations required. Main courses 110–280 F ($17.60–$44.80); fixed-price menus 250–300 F ($40–$48); dégustation de fromages 300 F ($48). AE, DC, MC, V. Mon–Fri noon–2:30pm and Mon–Sat 7:30–10pm. Métro: Étoile. FRENCH.

This is one of the world's most unusual restaurants, as cheese is the basic ingredient in most dishes. It all began in 1909, when the founder, M. Androuët, started inviting favored guests down to his cellar to sample cheese and good wine. The idea caught on. Today Androuët is an institution. To accommodate its continued and growing popularity, it moved to new headquarters in spring 1997. Cheese experts, of course, flock here; we've heard one claim that he could tell what the goat ate by the cheese made from its milk. For a first course, the *ravioles de chèvre frais* (ravioli stuffed with fresh goat cheese) is wonderful. A good main dish is *fillet de boeuf cotentin* (beef fillet with Roquefort sauce, flambéed with Calvados). True cheese lovers order the *dégustation de fromages affinés dans nos caves* (a sampling of cheese). There are as many as 120 varieties.

RIGHT BANK: 9TH ARRONDISSEMENT (OPERA GARNIER/PIGALLE)

EXPENSIVE

Restaurant Opéra. In the Grand Hôtel Inter-Continental, place de l'Opéra. ☎ **01-40-07-30-10.** Reservations recommended. Main courses 184–320 F ($29.45–$51.20); fixed-price menus 240–585 F ($38.40–$93.60). AE, DC, MC, V. Mon–Fri noon–2pm and 7:30–10:30pm. Métro: Opéra. FRENCH.

Dine here with the ghosts of Dalí, Josephine Baker, Dietrich, Chevalier, Callas, and Chagall, who often came here while working on the famous ceiling of the nearby Opéra Garnier. On August 25, 1944, de Gaulle placed this restaurant's first food order in a newly freed Paris—cold plate to go. Today you can enjoy a before-dinner drink in the ornate bar before heading for a table in the gilded jewel box of a dining room. Appetizers may include lobster bisque with champagne or deep-fried frogs' legs with tomato and cauliflower in the Greek style. The most sumptuous main courses are sweetbreads fried with pistachios, lemon, and licorice; filet of John Dory with celery; and rack of veal (divided into veal chops and prepared only for two), garnished with wild mushrooms and small new potatoes. Chocoholics will find nirvana with the Tour Chocolat.

MODERATE

✪ **Au Petit Riche.** 25 rue Le Peletier. ☎ **01-47-70-68-68.** Reservations recommended. Main courses 94–135 F ($15.05–$21.60); fixed-price menus 165 F ($26.40) at lunch, 140–180 F ($22.40–$28.80) at dinner. AE, MC, V. Mon–Sat noon–2:15pm and 7pm–midnight. Métro: Le Peletier or Richelieu-Drouot. LOIRE VALLEY (ANJOU).

When it opened in 1865, this bistro was conceived as the food outlet for the grandly ornate Café Riche next door. Today, all that remains is the bistro, serving simple but well-prepared bistro food in an old-fashioned setting. You'll be ushered to one of five "compartments," each of which was crafted for maximum intimacy, with red velour banquettes, ceilings painted with allegorical themes, and accents of brass and frosted glass. The wine list favors Loire Valley vintages that go well with such dishes as *rillettes* and *rillons* (potted fish or meat, especially pork) in a Vouvray wine aspic, poached fish with a buttery white-wine sauce, seasonal game like civet of rabbit, old fashioned blanquette of chicken, and duck breast roasted with green peppercorns.

Chez Jean. 8 rue St-Lazare. ☎ **01-48-78-62-73.** Reservations recommended. Main courses 130–210 F ($20.80–$33.60); fixed-price menu 195 F ($31.20). MC, V. Daily noon–2:30pm and 7–11pm. Métro: Notre-Dame de Lorette or Le Peletier. FRENCH.

There's been a brasserie of one sort or another on this site since 1900, and some specialties here are appropriately old-fashioned. You'll dine in one of two rooms, amid well-oiled pinewood panels and carefully polished copper, feasting on menu items that include some of grandmother's favorites. More modern dishes include risotto with lobster and squid ink, scallops with a fricassée of endive, lamb roasted with basil, a combination of mussels and fennel, and a pavé of duckling served with honey sauce and a fricassée of exotic mushrooms. The menu changes virtually every day, a fact that attracts lots of fans who consider its food a lot more sophisticated than what's featured in your average brasserie.

Wally Le Saharien. 36 rue Rodier. ☎ **01-42-85-51-90.** Reservations recommended. Dinner set-price menu 240 F ($38.40). Main courses all 150 F ($24). MC, V. Tues–Sat noon–2pm and Mon–Sat 7–10pm. Metro: Anvers or Cadet. ALGERIAN.

This place celebrates the spicy, slow-cooked cuisine of the Sahara. The inspiration is southern Algerian, served within a dining room lined with photographs of the desert and tribal artifacts crafted from ceramics, wood, and weavings. The set-price menu that's featured every evening begins with a trio of starters that include a spicy soup, stuffed and grilled sardines, and a savory *pastilla* of pigeon in puff pastry. This can be followed by any of several kinds of couscous, or a succulent *méchouia* (slow-cooked tart) of lamb dusted with an (optional) coating of sugar, according to your tastes. *Merguez*, the cumin-laden spicy sausage of the North African world, is often featured, as are homemade (usually honey-infused) pastries. End your meal with a traditional cup of mint-flavored tea.

RIGHT BANK: 10TH ARRONDISSEMENT (GARE DU NORD/GARE DE L'EST)
MODERATE

Brasserie Flo. 7 cour des Petites-Ecuries, 10e. ☎ **01-47-70-13-59.** Reservations recommended. Main courses 90–168 F ($14.40–$26.90); fixed price menu 138 F ($22.10) at lunch, 189 F ($30.25) at dinner, 142 F ($22.70) late-night supper (after 10pm). AE, DC, MC, V. Daily noon–3pm and 7pm–1:30am. Métro: Château-d'Eau or Strasbourg-St-Denis. ALSATIAN.

This restaurant is in a remote area and a bit hard to find, but once you arrive (after walking through passageway after passageway), you'll see that fin-de-siècle Paris lives on. The restaurant was established in 1860 and has changed its decor very little since. The house specialty is *la formidable choucroute* (a heaping mound of sauerkraut surrounded by boiled ham, bacon, and sausage) for two. It's bountiful in the best tradition of Alsace. The onion soup and sole meunière are always good, as is the warm foie gras and guinea hen with lentils. Look for the *plats du jour* (plates of the day), ranging from roast pigeon to fricassée of veal with sorrel.

RIGHT BANK: 11TH ARRONDISSEMENT (BASTILLE)
MODERATE

Blue Elephant. 43 rue de la Roquette. ☎ **01-47-00-42-00.** Reservations recommended. Main courses 85–160 F ($13.60–$25.60); fixed-price dinner 275 F ($44). AE, DC, MC, V. Sun–Fri noon–2:30pm; Mon–Sat 7pm–midnight; Sun 7–11pm. Métro: Bastille. THAI.

This is the Paris branch of an international chain of Thai restaurants that prides itself on running the best and most stylish Thai restaurant in whatever city they operate. In

Paris they've done it again in a location near the Bastille. The decor evokes an artful version of the jungles of southeast Asia, with a labyrinth of waterfalls, replicas of garden paths, potted plants, and bridges, always interspersed with Thai sculptures and paintings. Menu items are savory, succulent, and infused with lemongrass, curries, and distinctive aromas. Examples include a salad made with a Thai fruit that's larger and more tart than a grapefruit, a pomelo, studded with shrimp and herbs. Other specialties include a salmon soufflé served in banana leaves; chicken in green curry sauce; and a delectable grilled fish served with passion fruit.

Mansouria. 11 rue Faidherbe. ☎ **01-43-71-00-16.** Reservations recommended. Main courses 98–158 F ($15.70–$25.30); fixed-price menus 135 F ($21.60) at lunch, 182–280 F ($29.10–$44.80) at dinner. MC, V. Daily noon–2pm and 7:30–11pm. Métro: Faidherbe-Chaligny. MOROCCAN.

One of the most charming and best-managed Moroccan restaurants in Paris occupies a much-restored building midway between Place de la Bastille and Place de la Nation. The decor of the place combines a minimalist version of futuristic French architecture with bare white walls that are accented only with several sets of antique doors and portals imported from Morocco's sub-Sahara. Intricate and painstaking in their geometric precision, they're artworks in their own right. Menu items are artfully prepared and served with the dignity of ancient traditions. Look for a half-dozen kinds of couscous, including versions made with chicken or with brochettes of beef, and one prepared "in the style of the imperial city of Fez," with lamb, onions, and almonds. *Tagines* are succulent versions of lamb, chicken, or fish cooked slowly with aromatic herbs in clay pots that are carried directly to your table.

RIGHT BANK: 12TH ARRONDISSEMENT (BOIS DE VINCENNES/GARE DE LYON)
EXPENSIVE

Au Trou Gascon. 40 rue Taine. ☎ **01-43-44-34-26.** Reservations required. Main courses 145–165 F ($23.20–$26.40); fixed-price menu 200 F ($32) at lunch, 320 F ($51.20) at dinner. AE, DC, MC, V. Mon–Fri noon–2pm and 7:30–10pm, Sat 7:30–10pm. Closed Aug. Métro: Daumesnil. GASCONY.

Alain Dutournier launched his career in southwestern Gascony, working in the kitchen with his mother and grandmother. His parents mortgaged the inn they owned to allow him to open a turn-of-the-century bistro in an off-the-beaten-track part of the 12th arrondissement, where word soon spread that he was a true artist. Today he has opened another restaurant. The owner's wife, Nicole, is here to greet you, and Dutournier has distinguished himself with an extensive cellar (more than 800 varieties) containing several little-known wines along with an array of Armagnacs. Here you get the true cuisine of Gascony: cassoulet, wild salmon with smoked bacon, foie gras, and Gascon ham farmer's style. We suggest that you order the roasted chicken from the Chalosse region of Landes, served in its own drippings.

MODERATE

Le Train Bleu. In the Gare de Lyon, 12e. ☎ **01-43-43-09-06.** Reservations recommended. Main courses 110–185 F ($17.60–$29.60); fixed-price menu 255 F ($40.80), including wine. AE, DC, MC, V. Daily 11:30am–3pm and 7–11pm. Métro: Gare de Lyon. FRENCH.

To reach this restaurant, climb the ornate double staircase that faces the grimy platforms of the Gare de Lyon. Both restaurant and station were built simultaneously with the Grand Palais, the Pont Alexandre III, and the Petit Palais, as part of the World Exhibition of 1900. As a fitting end to a traveler's long trip, the station's architects

---

A Dining Tip

If a full meal in one of the top spots in Paris is beyond your means, you can still get a peek into this world by dropping into the bar at **Alain Ducasse** and ordering one of the best arrays of tapas in town (Madrid, eat your heart out). Of course, you'll have to put up with a lot of the increasingly hip cigar smoke.

---

designed a restaurant whose decor is classified as a national artistic treasure. Inaugurated by the French president in 1901 and renovated and cleaned at great expense in 1992, the restaurant displays an army of bronze statues, a lavishly frescoed ceiling, mosaics, mirrors, old-fashioned banquettes, and 41 belle époque murals. Each of these celebrates the distant corners of the French-speaking world, which join Paris via its rail network.

Service is fast, attentive, and efficient, in case you're about to catch a train. A formally dressed staff will bring steaming platters of soufflé of brill, escargots in Chablis sauce, steak tartare, loin of lamb Provençal, veal kidneys in mustard sauce, rib of beef for two, and rum cake with raisins. The cuisine is well prepared in a classic French Escoffier manner.

RIGHT BANK: 16TH ARRONDISSEMENT (TROCADERO/BOIS DE BOULOGNE)
VERY EXPENSIVE

✪ **Alain Ducasse.** In Le Parc Hotel. 59 av. Raymond-Poincaré. ☎ **01-47-27-12-27.** Fax 01-47-27-31-22. Reservations required, 6 weeks in advance. Main courses 385–510 F ($61.60–$81.60); fixed-price menus 480 F ($76.80) at lunch, 950–1,490 F ($152–$238.40) at dinner. AE, DC, MC, V. Mon–Fri noon–2pm and 7:45–10pm. Métro: Trocadéro. FRENCH.

The celebrated Monte Carlo chef has taken Paris by storm since taking over the reins here from the great Joël Robuchon (now consultant at L'Astor). This six-star Michelin chef (three for Paris, three for Monte Carlo) divides his time between Paris and Monaco. Why so many stars? Ducasse brilliantly refines and defines produce from every region of France in this restored four-story mansion. On the ground floor is a bar stocked with rare brandies and fine cigars. Taking advantage of his southern roots, Ducasse includes typically Mediterranean dishes on his menu. He serves fish from the French coasts and vegetables from all over France. Though many dishes are light, Ducasse isn't afraid of lard, as in his thick, oozingly delicious slabs of pork grilled to a crisp. He has kept a single Robuchon dish as a tribute: the famed caviar in aspic with cauliflower cream. The food remains sober in presentation, true, precise, and authentic in flavor. Ducasse told us, "The tasting of a dish must leave a remembrance. If nothing remains in the memory of a single guest, I have fooled myself."

The wine list is based on the fine existing cellar left by Robuchon and noted for its classic composition, extensiveness, and high quality. Ducasse has added many new acquisitions from the vineyards of France but has also opened his cellar to young wine growers, including those from Germany, Switzerland, Spain, and Italy.

EXPENSIVE

Jamin. 32 rue de Longchamp. ☎ **01-45-53-00-07.** Fax 01-45-53-00-15. Reservations imperative. Main courses 185–230 F ($29.60–$36.80); fixed-price menus 280–410 F ($44.80–$65.60) at lunch, 410 F ($65.60) at dinner. AE, DC, MC, V. Mon–Fri 12:30–2pm and 7:30–10pm. Métro: Trocadéro. FRENCH.

In the 1980s the great Joël Robuchon became a sensation here. Nowadays, Benoit Guichard, longtime second in command, is in charge. Clearly inspired by his master, he is also an imaginative and inventive chef in his own right. Guichard has chosen pale-green panels and pink banquettes for a soothing backdrop to his short but well-chosen menu. Classic technique and an homage to tradition characterize the cuisine, with offerings like John Dory with celery and fresh ginger, or pigeon sausage with foie gras, pistachios, and mâche lettuce. You might start with ocean-fresh Brittany langoustines married to spaghetti-sized strips of ginger-laced squid. The beef shoulder is so tender it obviously is braised for hours. A particularly earthy dish celebrates various parts of the sow that are usually rejected by most diners; it blends the tail and cheeks of the sow on a platter with walnuts and fresh herbs. Guichard's wife, Marjorie, is on hand, as is his dream team of chefs. Finish off with a tarte Tatin that deserves an award.

MODERATE

La Butte Chaillot. 110 bis av. Kléber. ☎ **01-47-27-88-88.** Reservations recommended. Main courses 98–118 F ($15.70–$18.90); fixed-price menus 150–195 F ($24–$31.20). AE, MC, V. Daily noon–2:30pm and 7pm–midnight. Métro: Trocadéro. FRENCH.

This "baby bistro" showcases the cuisine of high priest Guy Savoy. It draws lots of corporate types from the affluent surrounding neighborhood, who congregate in the congested but posh dining areas. Menu items change weekly (sometimes daily), depending on whatever is in season, and are carefully and artfully packaged. Examples are a sophisticated medley of terrines, codfish steak with herbs, a salad of snails and herbed potatoes, grilled filet of rascasse (scorpion fish) with ginger and lemon, succulent rack of lamb, and roasted rabbit with sage with a compôte of onions, bacon, and mushrooms.

RIGHT BANK: 17TH ARRONDISSEMENT (PARC MONCEAU/PLACE CLICHY)
VERY EXPENSIVE

✪ **Guy Savoy.** 18 rue Troyon. ☎ **01-43-80-40-61.** Fax 01-46-22-43-09. Reservations required a week in advance. Main courses 250–700 F ($40–$112); menu dégustation 980 F ($156.80). AE, MC, V. Mon–Fri noon–2:30pm and 7:30–10:30pm, Sat 7–10:30pm. Métro: Charles-de-Gaulle-Étoile. FRENCH.

Guy Savoy is among Europe's hottest chefs, and this restaurant and its menu bear his signature style. His cooking almost always takes its inspiration from the market. Save your appetite (and a giant wad of francs) and order his nine-course menu dégustation. Perhaps you'll get red mullet and wild asparagus; cassoulet of snails with tarragon; or chicken quenelles (a sort of dumpling) with chicken livers and cream, garnished with black truffles. Depending on when you visit, you may have the pleasure of tasting Savoy's masterfully prepared mallard, venison, or game birds. He's fascinated with mushrooms and has been known to serve as many as a dozen types, especially in autumn. One of his most delectable dishes is fresh oysters in a frozen aspic of their own juices.

✪ **Michel Rostang.** 20 rue Rennequin. ☎ **01-47-63-40-77.** Fax 01-47-63-82-75. Reservations required. Main courses 198–385 F ($31.70–$61.60); fixed-price menus 365–660 F ($58.40–$105.60) at lunch, 660–860 F ($105.60–$137.60) at dinner. AE, MC, V. Mon–Fri 12:30–2:30pm; Mon–Sat 8–10:30pm. Closed 2 weeks in Aug. Métro: Ternes. FRENCH.

Michel Rostang is a creative fifth-generation chef from one of France's most distinguished cooking families. From Grenoble, he eventually came to the 17th arrondissement, where the world soon came to dine at what he modestly calls his "boutique restaurant" seating up to 70. Menu choices may include ravioli filled with goat cheese

🛈 Family-Friendly Restaurants

Crémerie-Restaurant Polidor *(see p. 123)* One of the most popular restaurants on the Left Bank, this reasonably priced dining room is so family-friendly it even calls its food *cuisine familiale*. This might be the best place to introduce your child to French cuisine.

Joe Allen *(see p. 105)* Joe Allen delivers everything from chili to chocolate-mousse pie. This place in Les Halles serves real American cuisine, including the best hamburgers in Paris.

and sprinkled with chervil bought fresh from the market, as well as Bresse chicken, the finest in France. From October to March he prepares quail eggs with sea urchins. On occasion he also concocts a delicate fricassée of sole or duckling cooked in its own blood. One dish worth the trek across town is a galette of artichokes with fresh truffles and duckling foie gras, served in a cream sauce that has been reduced and flavored with vinegar. Wines from the Rhône are available, including Châteauneuf du Pape and Hermitage.

MODERATE

Bistro d'à Côté Flaubert. 10 rue Flaubert. ☎ **01-42-67-05-81.** Reservations recommended. Main courses 98–145 F ($15.70–$23.20); fixed-price menu 150 F ($24) at lunch. AE, MC, V. Daily 12:30–2pm and 7:30–11pm. Métro: Ternes. FRENCH.

This is one of four baby bistros around the city that feature a pared-down, less expensive menu from superstar chef Michel Rostang. Since this branch is next door to the temple where Michel Rostang reigns, it's the most interesting. You'll enter a nostalgically decorated dining area ringed with unusual porcelain and antique copies of Michelin guides, some of which date from 1900. The place is stylishly informal and chic, with a simple menu that's enhanced by daily chalkboard specials. Tantalizing items include ravioli stuffed with pulverized lobster, an upscale version of macaroni laced with Serrano ham, and a *rable de lievre* (rabbit stew) *en cocotte.*

Rôtisserie d'Armaillé. 6 rue d'Armaillé. ☎ **01-42-27-19-20.** Reservations recommended. Fixed-price menus 165 F ($26.40) at lunch, 230 F ($36.80) at dinner. AE, DC, MC, V. Mon–Fri noon–2:30pm and Mon–Sat 7:30–11pm. Métro: Étoile. FRENCH.

The impresario behind this baby bistro is Jacques Cagna, who has been one of the city's top chefs for many years. This chic place, ringed with light wood paneling and banquettes with patterns of pink and green, bustles with businesspeople and the residents and shoppers of this grand neighborhood, which surrounds the place d'Étoile. You have only two options at both lunch and dinner—the 218F meal or the less-expensive 165F meal. Menu choices include flan of wild mushrooms with red-wine sauce, terrine of foie gras, a salad of sweetbreads and crayfish, scorpion fish (rascasse) *en papillote,* and rack of lamb accented with parsley and sage. The artwork features bucolic depictions of the cows, pigs, and lambs that are likely to be among the menu's grilled steaks and chops.

LEFT BANK: 5TH ARRONDISSEMENT (LATIN QUARTER)
VERY EXPENSIVE

✪ **La Tour d'Argent.** 15–17 quai de la Tournelle. ☎ **01-43-54-23-31.** Fax 01-44-07-12-04. Reservations required. Main courses 270–515 F ($43.20–$82.40); fixed-price lunch 400 F ($64). AE, DC, MC, V. Tues–Sun noon–2:30pm and 7:30–10:30pm. Métro: Maubert-Mutualité or Cardinal-LeMoine. CLASSIC FRENCH.

Heart of the Left Bank Restaurants

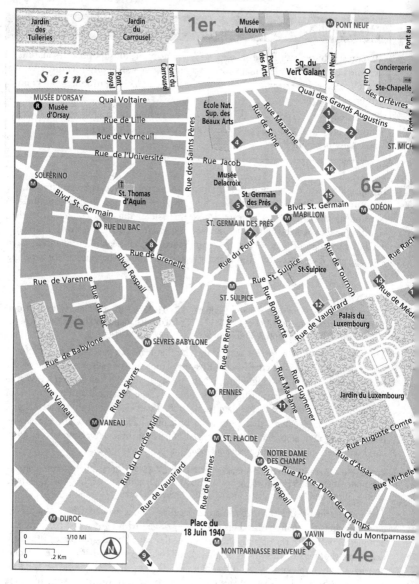

The penthouse Tour d'Argent is a national institution, boasting a panoramic view over the Seine and the apse of Notre-Dame. Although this restaurant's position as the best in Paris has long been taken over by Taillevent and others, dining here remains a major theatrical event. Since the 16th century there has always been a restaurant on this spot. It became famous when it was owned by Frédéric Delair, who purchased the wine cellar of the Café Anglais and began issuing certificates to diners who ordered the house specialty, pressed duck *(caneton)*. Today La Tour d'Argent is under the direction of the debonair Claude Terrail.

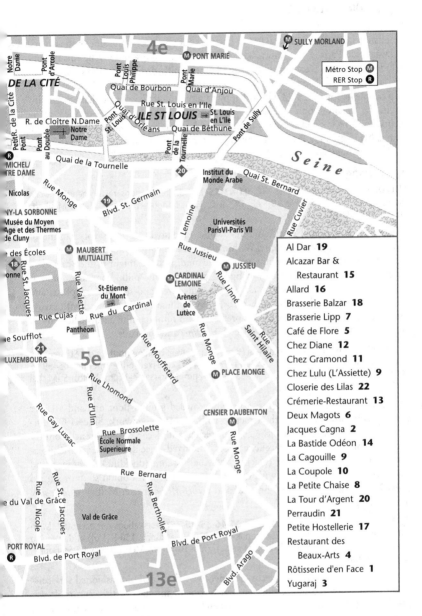

Map Labels

4e

DE LA CITÉ

Métro Stop Ⓜ
RER Stop Ⓡ

SULLY MORLAND

PONT MARIE

Notre Dame

Pont d'Arcole

Pont Louis Philippe

Pont Marie

Quai de Bourbon

Quai d'Anjou

Rue St. Louis en l'Île

ÎLE ST LOUIS

St. Louis en L'Île

R. de la Cité

Petit R. Pont au Double

R. de Cloître N.Dame

Pont St. Louis

Pont St. Louis d'Orléans

Notre Dame

Quai de Béthune

Pont de Sully

MICHEL/ TRE DAME

Quai de la Tournelle

Pont de la Tournelle

Institut du Monde Arabe

Quai St. Bernard

Seine

Nicolas

Rue Monge

20

Rue Cuvier

NY-LA SORBONNE

19

Blvd. St. Germain

Musée du Moyen Age et des Thermes de Cluny

Lemoine

Universités Paris VI-Paris VII

des Écoles

MAUBERT MUTUALITÉ

Rue Jussieu

JUSSIEU

18

Rue St. Jacques

onne

Rue Valette

CARDINAL LEMOINE

Rue Linné

St-Etienne du Mont

Rue du Cardinal

Arènes de Lutèce

Rue Saint Hilaire

Rue Cujas

Panthéon

e Soufflot

21

LUXEMBOURG

5e

Rue Mouffetard

Rue Monge

PLACE MONGE

Rue Lhomond

Rue d'Ulm

CENSIER DAUBENTON

Rue Gay Lussac

Rue Monge

Rue Brossolette

École Normale Superieure

Rue Bernard

e du Val de Grâce

Rue St. Jacques

Rue Nicole

Val de Grâce

Rue Berthollet

PORT ROYAL

Blvd. de Port Royal

Blvd. de Port Royal

Blvd. Arago

13e

Restaurant List

Al Dar **19**
Alcazar Bar & Restaurant **15**
Allard **16**
Brasserie Balzar **18**
Brasserie Lipp **7**
Café de Flore **5**
Chez Diane **12**
Chez Gramond **11**
Chez Lulu (L'Assiette) **9**
Closerie des Lilas **22**
Crémerie-Restaurant **13**
Deux Magots **6**
Jacques Cagna **2**
La Bastide Odéon **14**
La Cagouille **9**
La Coupole **10**
La Petite Chaise **8**
La Tour d'Argent **20**
Perraudin **21**
Petite Hostellerie **17**
Restaurant des Beaux-Arts **4**
Rôtisserie d'en Face **1**
Yugaraj **3**

The cuisine is classically French. New diners often order the duck—it's sensational. Other selections are filet de sole cardinal and filet Tour d'Argent. Begin with the potage (soup) Claudius Burdel made with sorrel, egg yolks, fresh cream, chicken broth, and butter whipped together. For dessert, the *pêches flambées* (flambéed peaches) are marvelous.

MODERATE

Brasserie Balzar. 49 rue des Écoles. ☎ **01-43-54-13-67.** Reservations strongly recommended. Main courses 75–125 F ($12–$20). AE, MC, V. Daily noon–midnight. Métro: Odeon or Cluny-La Sorbonne. FRENCH-TRADITIONAL.

Established in 1898, Brasserie Balzar is battered but cheerful, with some of the friendliest waiters in Paris. The menu makes almost no concessions to nouvelle cuisine, and includes pepper steak, sole meunière, sauerkraut garnished with ham and sausage, pig's feet, and fried calf's liver. The food is decently prepared, and it's clear these dishes still keep people happy. The staff will be happy to serve you if you want to have a full dinner in the midafternoon, accustomed as they are to the odd hours of their many clients. You'll be in good company here: Former patrons have included both Sartre and Camus (who often got into arguments), James Thurber, countless professors from the nearby Sorbonne, and a bevy of English and American journalists.

INEXPENSIVE

Al Dar. 8 rue Frédéric Sauton. ☎ **01-43-25-17-15.** Reservations recommended. Main courses 85–95 F ($13.60–$15.20). AE, DC, MC, V. Daily noon–midnight. Métro: Maubert-Mutualité. LEBANESE.

This is a well-respected restaurant that works hard to bring the savory cuisine of Lebanon to the Paris dining scene. Within a room lined with photographs of Lebanese architecture and scenery at its best, you'll dine on dishes that might include *taboulé,* a refreshing combination of finely chopped parsley, mint, milk, tomatoes, onions, lemon juice, olive oil, and salt; *baba ganush,* pulverized and seasoned eggplant; and *hummus* (pulverized chickpeas with herbs). Any of these can be followed with savory roasted chicken; tender minced lamb prepared with mint, cumin, and Mediterranean herbs; and any of several kinds of delectable *tagines* and couscous.

✪ **La Petite Hostellerie.** 35 rue de la Harpe (a side street running north of bd. St-Germain, just east of bd. St-Michel). ☎ **01-43-54-47-12.** Fixed-price menus 65–89 F ($10.40–$14.25). AE, DC, MC, V. Tues–Sat noon–2pm, Mon–Sat 7–11pm. Métro: St-Michel or Cluny-La Sorbonne. FRENCH.

This place has two dining rooms: a usually crowded ground-floor one and a larger (seating 100) upstairs one with attractive 18th-century woodwork. Since 1902 diners have been coming here for the cozy ambience and decor, decent French country cooking, polite service, and excellent prices. The fixed-price dinner menu might feature favorites like *coq au vin* (chicken in wine), *canard* (duckling) *à l'orange,* and *entrecôte à la moutarde* (steak with mustard sauce). Start with onion soup or stuffed mussels and finish with cheese or salad and *pêches Melba* (peach Melba) or *tarte aux pommes* (apple tart).

✪ **Perraudin.** 157 rue St-Jacques. ☎ **01-46-33-15-75.** Reservations not accepted. Main courses all 62 F ($9.90); fixed-price menus 63 F ($10.10) at lunch, 150 F ($24) at dinner. No credit cards. Tues–Fri noon–2:15pm; Mon–Sat 7:30–10:15pm. Métro: Cluny-La Sorbonne. RER: Luxembourg. FRENCH.

Everything about this place—decor, cuisine, low prices, and old-fashioned service—attempts to replicate the bustling Parisian bistros of the turn of the century. It was Hemingway's favorite restaurant in Paris when he was poor. The walls look as if they've been marinated in tea for about a year; marble-top tables, old mirrors, and posters of Parisian vaudeville of the cancan years complete the picture. You don't make reservations: instead, diners usually drink a glass of kir at the zinc-top bar as they wait. (Tables turn over quickly.) Marie-Christine K'vella and her brother offer old-fashioned dishes that include roast leg of lamb with dauphinois potatoes, beef bourguignon, grilled salmon with sage sauce, and blanquette of veal in white sauce. Any of these might be preceded with onion tart, pumpkin soup, snails, or any of several pâtés or terrines.

LEFT BANK: 6TH ARRONDISSEMENT (ST-GERMAINE/LUXEMBOURG)

VERY EXPENSIVE

✪ **Jacques Cagna.** 14 rue des Grands-Augustins. ☎ **01-43-26-49-39.** Fax 01-43-54-54-48. Reservations required. Main courses 190–350 F ($30.40–$56); fixed-price menus 280–490 F ($44.80–$78.40) at lunch, 490 F ($78.40) at dinner. AE, DC, MC, V. Tues–Fri noon–2pm; Mon–Sat 7:30–10:30pm. Closed 3 weeks in Aug. Métro: St-Michel. FRENCH.

In a 17th-century town house, Jacques Cagna is a place where both the patrons and the food are among the grandest in Paris. Its pinkish-beige interior is filled with massive timbers and 17th-century Dutch paintings. A specialty is the Aberdeen Angus beef, aged for 3 weeks, which Cagna imbues with a rich shallot-flavored sauce. Each dish is sublime: rack of suckling veal with ginger-and-lime sauce, breast of duck with burgundy sauce, line-caught sea bass with caviar in a potato shell, and fried scallops with celery and potatoes in truffle sauce. The menu changes according to the season and the inspiration of the chef. If you're lucky, he'll offer his carpaccio of sea bream with a rémoulade of celery garnished with caviar.

EXPENSIVE

Chez Gramond. 5 rue de Fleurus. ☎ **01-42-22-28-89.** Reservations recommended. Main courses 130–219 F ($20.80–$35.05). MC, V. Mon–Sat noon–2:20pm and 7–10pm. Closed: Aug. Métro: Notre-Dame-des-Champs. FRENCH.

If you want hearty, traditional fare, forget about the trendy places nearby and head to Chez Gramond. It seats only 20 people at a time, each of whom is treated to the savoir-faire of Auvergne-born Jean-Claude Gramond and his charming wife, Jeannine. Menu items are listed the old-fashioned way, in purple ink that's duplicated on an old-timey mimeograph machine in back. Examples include roasted partridge in wine sauce; suckling lamb with sorrel sauce; terrines of foie gras; seared scallops served with butter sauce on a bed of leeks; and a succulent version of lamb stew served with white beans. We always order the soufflé Grand Marnier for dessert. Wines are fairly priced, and presented on a wine list that's carefully compiled and artfully balanced.

Closerie des Lilas. 171 bd. du Montparnasse. ☎ **01-40-51-34-50.** Reservations required in the restaurant. Main courses 120–220 F ($19.20–$35.20) in the restaurant, 90–180 F ($14.40–$28.80) in the brasserie. AE, DC, V. Restaurant daily noon–3pm and 7:30pm–11pm; brasserie daily 11:30am–1am. Métro: Port-Royal or Vavin. FRENCH.

The number of famous people who've dined here watching the fallen leaves blow along the Montparnasse streets is almost countless: Stein and Toklas, Ingres, Henry James, Chateaubriand, Lenin and Trotsky, Proust, Sartre and de Beauvoir, and Whistler. Since getting a seat in the *bateau* (brasserie) section is difficult, you can while away the hours waiting at the bar and ordering the best champagne julep in the world. Once seated in the brasserie, you can select dishes like poached haddock and steak tartare. In the chic restaurant, the cooking is classic. Try the escargots façon Closerie for openers. Of the main-course selections, the *rognons de veau à la moutarde* (veal kidneys with mustard) and the steak tartare are highly recommended.

MODERATE

Alcazar Bar & Restaurant. 62 rue Mazarine. ☎ **01-53-10-19-99.** Reservations recommended. Main courses 95–160 F ($15.20–$25.60); fixed-price lunch 140–160 F ($22.40–$25.60). AE, DC, MC, V. Daily noon–5:30pm and 7pm–1am. Métro: Odéon. FRENCH.

One of Paris's newest high-profile *brasseries de luxe* is this artfully high-tech place funded by British restaurateur and *wunderkind* Sir Terence Conran. (His chain of well-publicized restaurants in London is a textbook example of how to captivate an audience of terminally jaded European foodies.) It has an all-white, futuristic decor within a large, street-level dining room, a busy and hyper-stylish bar one floor above street level, and an upscale bistro menu. Recommended dishes include entrecôte with béarnaise sauce and fried potatoes; Charolais duckling with honey and spices; sashimi and sushi with lime; filet of monkfish with saffron in puff pastry; and a comprehensive collection of shellfish and oysters from the waters of Brittany. Wines are as stylish and diverse as you'd expect, and the clientele tends to include lots of fashionistas clad in black.

✪ **Allard.** 41 rue Saint-André-des-Arts, 6e. ☎ **01-43-26-48-23.** Reservations required. Main courses 120–135 F ($19.20–$21.60); fixed-price menus 150 F ($24) at lunch, 150–200 F ($24–$32) at dinner. AE, DC, MC, V. Mon–Fri 12:30–2:30pm and 7:30–11:30pm. Métro: Saint-Michel or Odéon. FRENCH-TRADITIONAL.

Long missing from this guide, this old-time bistro, established in 1931, is back and as good as ever after a long decline. Once it was the leading bistro of Paris, although today the competition is too great to reclaim that reputation. The street outside was used as the background for George du Maurier's *Trilby*. The corner building housing Allard, with its entrance on 1 rue de l'Éperon, traces its origins back to the days of Marie di Medici and Cardinal Richelieu. In the front room is a zinc bar, a haven preferred by many a celebrated *personnalité* over the years, including movie actor Alain Delon or Madame Pompidou. All the old Allard specialties are still offered, and quality ingredients are deftly handled by the kitchen. Try the snails, foie gras, veal stew, or frogs' legs: all classics. On Mondays we head here for *boeuf à la mode:* no, not beef with ice cream, but braised in red wine with carrots. The cassoulet Toulousain (white bean and meat casserole with goose and other meats), remains one of the Left Bank's bet. We're also fond of the coq au vin served on Wednesdays. This dish of chicken stewed in red wine is fondly recalled from our student days when we frequented Allard. For dessert, we opt for the *tarte tatin,* an upside-down apple pie, if featured.

✪ **Chez Diane.** 25 rue Servandoni. ☎ **01-46-33-12-06.** Reservations recommended for groups of 4 or more. Main courses 100–140 F ($16–$22.40); fixed-price menu 160 F ($25.60). V. Mon–Fri noon–2pm; Mon–Sat 8–11:30pm. Métro: St-Sulpice. FRENCH.

Although its prices say "simple bistro," this place serves a surprisingly chic and sophisticated cuisine. This is a result of the care and dedication of Didier and Diane Derrieux. Designed to accommodate only 40 diners at a time, the place is illuminated with Venetian glass chandeliers and paved with floor tiles manufactured near Aix-en-Provence. The menu changes seasonally and with the inspiration of the owners. Examples are nuggets of wild boar in a honey sauce, minced salmon prepared as a terrine with green peppercorns, and a light-textured adaptation of a dish every French-born diner remembers, *hachis Parmentier* (elegant meat loaf lightened with parsley, chopped onions, and herbs). The fish dishes are likely to include turbot with béarnaise sauce and stingray with caper-flavored butter sauce.

La Bastide Odéon. 7 rue Corneille. ☎ **01-43-26-03-65.** Reservations recommended. Fixed-price menus 152–192 F ($24.30–$30.70). AE, MC, V. Tues–Sat 12:30–2pm and 7:30–10:30pm. Métro: Odéon. RER: Luxembourg. PROVENÇAL.

This brasserie has recently developed into a star. The decor evokes the sunny climes of southern France with its pale-yellow walls, heavy oaken tables, and bouquets of dried wheat and flowers. Chef Gilles Ajuelos prepares a market-based Provençal cuisine that varies according to his inspiration and the available ingredients. The simplest first courses seem the most satisfying, like a platter of sardines and seared sweet peppers with olive oil and pine nuts, grilled eggplant layered with herbs and olive oil, and roast rabbit stuffed with eggplant and served with olive toast and balsamic vinegar. Main courses include wild duckling with pepper sauce, stuffed suckling pig with a gratin of polenta and parmesan, and lambs' feet and giblets prepared in the age-old Provençal style. Pastas (creamy tagliatelle with clams and parsley is especially savory) can be prepared as a starter or a main course. A dessert winner is warm almond pie with prune-and-Armagnac ice cream.

✪ **Rôtisserie d'en Face.** 2 rue Christine. ☎ **01-43-26-40-98.** Reservations recommended. Fixed-price menus 100–160 F ($16–$25.60) at lunch; 230 F ($36.80) at dinner. AE, MC, V. Mon–Fri noon–2:30pm; Mon–Sat 7–11pm. Métro: St-Michel. FRENCH.

This is the most packed baby bistro in Paris, operated by Jacques Cagna, whose vastly more expensive eponymous restaurant is across the street. And this place has earned its popularity, because the food, though simply prepared, is very good, using high-quality ingredients. The place features a postmodern decor with high-tech lighting and black lacquer chairs. Menu items include several types of ravioli, a pâté of duckling en croûte with foie gras, *friture d'éperlans* (tiny fried freshwater fish), smoked Scottish salmon with spinach, and several types of fresh fish and grilled meats. Pork cheeks is based on an old-fashioned recipe passed down to Cagna from his mother. The Barbary duckling in red-wine sauce is incomparable.

Yugaraj. 14 rue Dauphine. ☎ **01-43-26-44-91.** Reservations recommended. Main courses 105–118 F ($16.80–$18.90); fixed-price menus 110–290 F ($17.60–$46.40) at lunch, 180–290 F ($28.80–$46.40) at dinner. AE, DC, MC, V. Tues–Sun noon–2:15pm; daily 7–11pm. Métro: Odéon. INDIAN.

In an old Latin Quarter building, this restaurant serves moderately priced, flavorful food based on the recipes of northern and (to a lesser degree) southern India. Here you can sample the spicy, aromatic tandoori dishes that are all the rage in France. Seafood specialties are usually concocted from warm-water fish from the Seychelles and include species with names like thiof (an Indian Ocean whitefish), capitaine, and bourgeois, prepared Calcutta style, with tomatoes, onions, cumin, coriander, ginger, and garlic. The flavors are spicy and earthy, rich with mint and sometimes touches of yogurt.

INEXPENSIVE

✪ **Crémerie-Restaurant Polidor.** 41 rue Monsieur-le-Prince. ☎ **01-43-26-95-34.** Reservations not accepted. Main courses 40–76 F ($6.40–$12.15); fixed-price menu 55 F ($8.80) at lunch Mon–Fri, 110 F ($17.60) at dinner Mon–Fri. No credit cards. Daily noon–2:30pm; Mon–Sat 7pm–12:30am, Sun 7–11pm. Métro: Odéon. FRENCH.

This little bistro serves *cuisine familiale.* A hangout for students and artists, it opened in 1930 and has barely changed since then. The restaurant's name still contains the word *crémerie,* referring to its specialty: frosted crème desserts. This has become one of the Left Bank's most noted literary bistros; it was André Gide's favorite. Lace curtains and brass hat racks, drawers in the back where repeat customers lock up their cloth napkins, and clay water pitchers on the tables create an old-fashioned atmosphere. Overworked but smiling waitresses serve grandmother's favorite dishes, such as pumpkin soup, snails from Burgundy, rib of beef with onions, rabbit with mustard sauce, and veal in white sauce. The desserts include raspberry and lemon tarts.

Restaurant des Beaux-Arts. 11 rue Bonaparte. ☎ **01-43-26-92-64.** Reservations recommended. Main courses 68–115 F ($10.90–$18.40); fixed-price menu 105 F ($16.80), including wine. MC, V. Daily noon–2:15pm and 7–10:45pm. Métro: St-Germain-des-Prés. FRENCH.

This is Paris's most famous budget restaurant. Does it please everyone? No. Have there been complaints about bad food and service? Some. But is it packed daily? That's for sure. So it must be doing something right, because thousands of hungry diners have come for its low prices, large portions, and robust stick-to-the-ribs dishes, all featured on a fixed-price menu. Tables are upstairs, but if you can get a place on the main floor you can see the steaming pots in the open kitchen. Typical platters are boeuf bourguignon, *navarin d'agneau* (lamb chops cooked with carrots, onions, and tomatoes), *lapin sauce moutarde* (rabbit leg with mustard sauce), trout with saffron sauce, fish soup—plus that dish the French always like, *blanquette de veau* (veal with white sauce).

LEFT BANK: 7TH ARRONDISSEMENT (EIFFEL TOWER/MUSÉE D'ORSAY)
VERY EXPENSIVE

✪ **L'Arpège.** 84 rue de Varenne. ☎ **01-47-05-09-06.** Fax 01-44-18-98-39. Reservations required. Main courses 420–620 F ($67.20–$99.20); fixed-price lunch 490 F ($78.40); menu dégustation 1,400 F ($224). AE, CB, DC, MC, V. Mon–Fri noon–2pm and 7:30–10pm. Métro: Varenne. FRENCH.

Three-star L'Arpège is where Alain Passard prepares his divine specialties. Amid a cultivated decor of etched glass, burnished steel, and monochromatic paintings, you can enjoy dishes that've been heralded as truly innovative. Some of his latest creations are Breton lobster in sweet-and-sour rosemary sauce, scallops prepared with cauliflower and lime-flavored grape sauce, and pan-fried duck with juniper-and-lime sauce, followed by the restaurant's signature dessert, a candied tomato stuffed with 12 kinds of dried and fresh fruit and served with anise-flavored ice cream. The wine list is something to write home about.

EXPENSIVE

✪ **Le Violin d'Ingres.** 135 rue St-Dominique. ☎ **01-45-55-15-05.** Reservations required. Main courses 180–210 F ($28.80–$33.60); fixed-price menu 240 F ($38.40) at lunch, 490 F ($78.40) at dinner. AE, MC, V. Tues–Sat noon–2:30pm and 7–10:30pm. Métro: École Militaire. FRENCH.

Chef/owner Christian Constant is the man of the moment. Those who are fortunate enough to dine in Violin's warm atmosphere of rose-colored wood, soft cream walls, and elegant chintz fabrics rave about the cleverly artistic dishes. They range from a starter of pan-fried foie gras with gingerbread-and-spinach salad to elegant main courses like lobster ravioli with crushed vine-ripened tomatoes, roast veal in a creamy milk sauce with tender spring vegetables, and rotisseried leg of lamb rubbed with fresh garlic and thyme. One memorable dish is a delicate slice of sea bass enfolded in a crust of tiny croûtons, topped with almonds and set on a bed of sweet spinach and encircled by a *ravigote* of capers and a *blancmange* of red mullet. Even his familiar dishes seem new at each tasting. The repertoire goes from classicism to novelty. Constant keeps a well-chosen selection of wine to accompany his satisfying meals. The service is all about understated charm.

MODERATE

La Petite Chaise. 36–38 rue de Grenelle. ☎ **01-42-22-13-35.** Reservations required. Fixed-price menus 125–195 F ($20–$31.20). AE, V. Daily noon–2pm and 7–11pm. Métro: Rue de Bac or Sèvres-Babylone. FRENCH.

This is the oldest restaurant in Paris, established by the baron de la Chaise in 1680 as an inn at the edge of what was then a large hunting preserve. (The baron, according to the restaurant's lore, maintained a series of upstairs bedrooms for mid-afternoon dalliances.) Very Parisian, the "Little Chair" invites you into a world of cramped but attractive tables, old wood paneling, and ornate wall sconces. The only option is a well-priced four-course fixed-price menu with a large choice of dishes. Samplings from the menu may be salad of strips of duck breast on a bed of fresh lettuce, filet of beef prepared with green peppercorns, and a seafood and scallop ragoût with saffron.

LEFT BANK: 14TH ARRONDISSMENT (GARE MONTPARNASSE)
EXPENSIVE
Chez Lulu (L'Assiette). 181 rue du Château, 14e. ☎ **01-43-22-64-86.** Reservations recommended. Main courses 150–200 F ($24–$32); fixed-price menu 200 F ($32). AE, MC, V. Wed–Sun noon–2:30pm and 8–10:30pm. Closed Aug. Métro: Gaité. SOUTHWESTERN FRENCH.

Everything about this place seems to appeal to a nostalgic clientele seeking down-to-earth prices and flavorful food. You'll recognize it by the bordeaux-colored facade and potted plants in the windows. François Mitterrand used to drop in with his cronies for his favorite platters of oysters, crayfish, sea urchins, and clams. The place was a *charcuterie* (pork butcher's shop) in the 1930s, and today it maintains some of its old accessories. Dishes are unashamedly inspired by Paris's long tradition of bistro cuisine, with a few twists. Examples include a salad of chanterelle mushrooms; *rillettes* (a roughly textured pâté) of mackerel; roasted guinea fowl; and desserts made on the premises, including a crumbly version of apple cake served with fresh North African figs. Particularly delicious is a *petit salé* (stew with vegetables) of duckling with wine from the Poitou region of west-central France.

MODERATE
La Cagouille. 10–12 place Brancusi. ☎ **01-43-22-09-01.** Reservations recommended. Main courses 120–180 F ($19.20–$28.80); fixed-price menus 150–250 F ($24–$40). AE, V. Daily noon–2pm and 5:30–10:30pm. Métro: Gaité. FRENCH/CHARENTAIS.

Don't even think of ordering beef at this temple of seafood—the burly and genteel owner, Gérard Allamandou, refuses to allow it to appear on his menu. Everything about this place honors the culinary arts of La Charente, the sandy, flat district that hugs the Atlantic south of Bordeaux. Within a trio of deliberately simple, oak-sheathed dining rooms, with marble-topped tables and minimal decor, you can enjoy seafood that's prepared as simply and naturally as possible. The beauty here lies in the utter simplicity and a strict insistence on fresh ingredients, many of which arrive directly from the Atlantic coasts only a few hours before they are cooked—you won't find any heavy sauces here. Allamandou's preferred fish is red mullet, which might appear sautéed in a bland oil or baked in rock salt from the Île de Ré, or any of several other all-natural dishes that are served with the same lack of pretension as the methods used to cook them. The name of the place derives from the regional symbol of La Charente: the sea snail, whose preparation here is elevated to a fine culinary art. Look for a vast assemblage of all-French, mostly white wines, and at least 150 types of cognac.

5 The Top Cafes

To a Parisian, a cafe is a club/tavern/snack bar. Whatever your pleasure—reading a newspaper, meeting a lover or a friend, doing your homework, writing your memoirs, nibbling at a hard-boiled egg, or drinking yourself into oblivion—you can do it all at a French cafe.

Brasserie Lipp, 151 bd. St-Germain, 6e (☎ **01-45-48-53-91;** Métro: St-Germain-des-Prés), has an upstairs dining room, but it's more fashionable to sit in the back room. For breakfast, order the traditional black coffee and croissants. At lunch or dinner, the house specialty is pork and *choucroute* (sauerkraut)—the best in Paris. Open daily from 9am to 2am, although restaurant service is available only from 11am to 1am—it's fashionable to arrive late.

Across from the Centre Pompidou, the avant-garde **Café Beaubourg,** 100 rue St-Martin, 4e (☎ **01-48-87-63-96;** Métro: Rambuteau or Hôtel-de-Ville), boasts soaring concrete columns and a minimalist decor by the architect Christian de Portzamparc. In summer, tables are set on the sprawling terrace, providing a panoramic view of the neighborhood's goings-on. Open Sunday through Thursday from 8am to 1am and Friday and Saturday from 8am to 2am.

Jean-Paul Sartre often came to **Café de Flore,** 172 bd. St-Germain, 6e (☎ **01-45-48-55-26;** Métro: St-Germain-des-Prés), during the war. It's said that he wrote his trilogy, *Les Chemins de la liberté* (The Roads to Freedom) at these tables. The cafe is still going strong, though the celebrities have moved on. Open daily from 7am to 2am.

Café de la Paix, place de l'Opéra, 9e (☎ **01-40-07-30-20;** Métro: Opéra), has been a popular American enclave since the U.S. troops marched through Paris in their victory parade after World War II. No one can remember de Gaulle dining here, but a messenger arrived and ordered a "tinned" ham for the general's first supper when he returned after the Liberation. Open daily from noon to midnight.

Café Marly, 93 rue de Rivoli, 1er (☎ **01-49-26-06-60;** Métro: Palais-Royal-Musée-du-Louvre), occupies the Louvre's historic cour Napoléon. It's accessible only from a point close to the pyramid and has become a favorite refuge for Parisians escaping the roar of traffic. Anyone is welcome to sit for just a *café au lait* whenever meals aren't being served (11am to 1am). Menu items, served in three Louis-Philippe-style rooms, include club sandwiches, oysters and shellfish, steak *au poivre* (pepper steak), and upscale bistro food. In summer, outdoor tables overlook the majestic courtyard. Open daily from 8am to 2am.

At **La Coupole,** 102 bd. Montparnasse, 14e (☎ **01-43-20-14-20;** Métro: Vavin), the crowd ranges from artists' models to young men dressed like Rasputin. Perhaps order a coffee or cognac VSOP at one of the sidewalk tables. The dining room looks like a railway station and serves food that is sometimes good, sometimes indifferent. But people don't really come here for the cuisine; it's more on the see-and-be-seen circuit. Try the sole meunière, *carré d'agneau* (lamb), or cassoulet. A buffet breakfast is served Monday through Friday from 7:30 to 10:30am. Open daily from 7:30am to 2am.

The legendary **Deux Magots,** 6 place St-Germain-des-Prés, 6e (☎ **01-45-48-55-25;** Métro: St-Germain-des-Prés), is still the hangout for sophisticated neighborhood residents and a favorite for visitors in the summer. Inside are two large Asian statues that give the cafe its name. Open daily from 7:30am to 1:30am.

Fouquet's, 99 av. des Champs-Elysées, 8e (☎ **01-47-23-70-60;** Métro: George-V), is the premier cafe on the Champs-Elysées. The outside tables are separated from the sidewalk by a barricade of potted flowers. Inside is an elegant grill room with leather banquettes and rattan furniture, private banquet rooms, and a restaurant. The cafe and grill room are open daily from 9am to 2am; the restaurant is open daily from noon to 3pm, and 7pm to 1am.

Exploring Paris 4

Paris is one of those cities where taking in the street life—shopping, strolling, and hanging out—should claim as much of your time as sightseeing in churches and museums. A gourmet picnic in the Bois de Boulogne, a sunrise pilgrimage to the Seine, an afternoon of bartering at the flea market—Paris bewitches you with these kinds of experiences. For all the Louvre's beauty, you'll probably remember the Latin Quarter's crooked alleyways better than the 370th oil painting of your visit.

The best way to discover Paris is on foot—and it won't cost you a franc to explore the streets of the City of Light. Walk along the grand avenue des Champs-Elysées, tour the quays of the Seine, wander around Île de la Cité and Île St-Louis, browse the countless shops and stalls, wander through the famous squares and parks. Each turn will open a new vista. If you're an early riser, a stroll through Paris at dawn can be enthralling as you see the city coming to life: Shop fronts are washed clean for the new day, cafes begin serving hot coffee and warm croissants, and vegetable and fruit vendors start setting up their stalls and arranging their produce.

Paris is also a shopper's city—with everything from tony boutiques to colorful street markets. We've covered the best of the best in this chapter.

And for sheer variety, there's nothing like Parisian nightlife. Nowhere else will you find such a huge and mixed bag of nightclubs, bars, dance clubs, cabarets, jazz dives, music halls, and honky-tonks. (For Paris's cafe scene, see chapter 3.)

ORGANIZED TOURS

Before plunging into more detailed sightseeing on your own, you might like to take the most popular get-acquainted tour in Paris: **Cityrama,** 147–149 rue St-Honoré, 1er (☎ **01-44-55-61-00;** Métro: Palais-Royal-Musée-du-Louvre). On a double-decker bus with enough windows for Versailles, you're taken on a leisurely 2-hour ride through the city. Since you don't go inside any attractions, you must settle for a look at the outside of such places as Notre-Dame and the Eiffel Tower, but it'll help you get a feel for the city if this is your first visit. The language barrier is overcome by the individual earphones distributed with commentary in 10 languages. Tours depart daily at 9:30am,

Paris Attractions

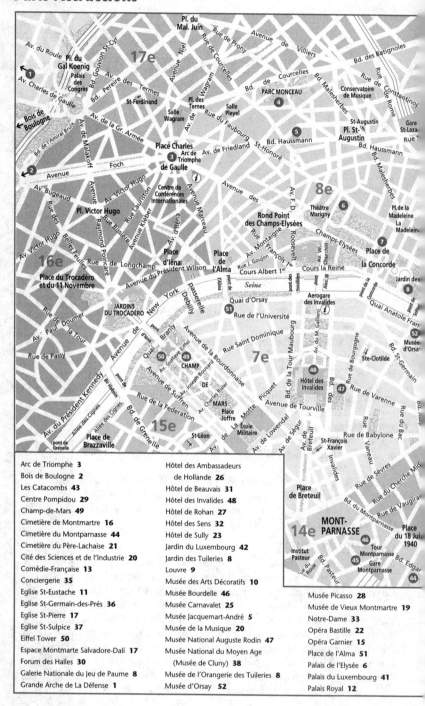

128

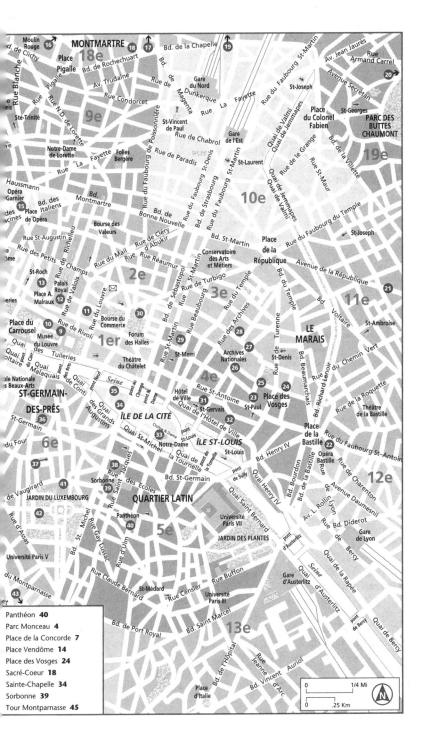

Panthéon **40**
Parc Monceau **4**
Place de la Concorde **7**
Place Vendôme **14**
Place des Vosges **24**
Sacré-Coeur **18**
Sainte-Chapelle **34**
Sorbonne **39**
Tour Montparnasse **45**

10:30am, 1:30pm, and 2:30pm. Throughout the year, there are additional tours every Saturday and Sunday at 11:30am, and between March and October, there are two additional tours every day at 3:30 and 4:30pm. A 2-hour orientation tour is 150 F ($24).

A morning tour with interior visits to Notre-Dame and the Louvre costs 295 F ($47.20). Half-day tours to Versailles at 320 F ($51.20) and half-day tours to Chartres at 275 F ($44) represent good value and remove at least some of the hassle associated with visiting those monuments. A joint ticket that includes both Versailles and Chartres costs 500 F ($80). Another Cityrama offering, a tour of the nighttime illuminations, leaves daily at 10pm in summer or at 7pm in winter and costs 150 F ($24); however, it tends to be tame and touristy.

The same entity that maintains Paris's network of Métros and buses, **RATP** (☎ **08-36-68-41-14**), operates the **Balabus,** a fleet of orange-and-white big-windowed motorcoaches. The only drawback is their limited operating hours: Sundays only, from noon to 9pm (and the afternoons of some national holidays). Itineraries run in both directions between Gare de Lyon and the Grand Arche de La Défense. Three Métro tickets will carry you along the entire route. You'll recognize the bus, and the route it follows, by the *Bb* symbol emblazoned across its side and along signs posted beside the route it follows.

A boat tour on the Seine provides sweeping vistas of the riverbanks and some of the best views of Notre-Dame. Many of the boats have open sundecks, bars, and restaurants. **Bateaux-Mouche** cruises (☎ **01-42-25-96-10** for reservations or **01-40-76-99-99** for schedules; Métro: Alma-Marceau) depart from the Right Bank of the Seine, adjacent to pont de l'Alma, and last about 75 minutes each. Tours leave every day at 20- to 30-minute intervals between May and October, from 10am to 11:30pm. Between November and April, there are at least nine departures every day between 11am and 9pm, with a schedule that changes frequently according to demand and the weather. Fares cost 40 F ($6.40) for adults and 20 F ($3.20) for children ages 5 to 15. Dinner cruises depart every evening at 8:30pm, last 3 hours, and cost between 500 F and 700 F ($80 and $112), depending on which of the fixed-price menus you order. Aboard dinner cruises, jackets and ties are required for men.

The **Batobus** (☎ **01-44-11-33-44**) are 150-passenger ferryboats with big windows suitable for viewing the passing riverfronts. Daily between April and September, they operate east-west along the Seine, stopping at six points en route. Departures occur at 30-minute intervals between 10am and 7pm daily. (The boats don't run between October and March.) Stops include the Eiffel Tower, Musée d'Orsay, points on both the Left Bank and the Right Bank opposite the Louvre, Notre-Dame, and the Hôtel de Ville. These ferries weren't conceived as sightseeing vehicles, and unlike on the *bateaux-mouches,* which are run by a separate outfit, there's no recorded commentary. Fares between any two stops are 20 F ($3.20) for the first segment, and 10 F ($1.60) for each individual segment after that, though frankly we consider the Batobus an expensive way to cross a river that's already crisscrossed with an impressive network of bridges. More appealing is to pay 60 F ($9.60) per adult or 30 F ($4.80) per child 11 and under (children under 3 ride free) for a day ticket that allows you to enter and exit from the boats as many times as you like (and ride as long as you like) during any single day. The views are panoramic and majestic, and the boat allows you to move from one history-rich neighborhood to another without dealing with the Métro or street traffic.

Suggested Itineraries

These itineraries are obviously intended for the first-time visitor, but even those making their 30th trip to Paris will want to revisit attractions like the Louvre, where you could spend every day of your life and always see something new. Use these tips as a guide, not a bible. Paris rewards travelers with guts and independence of mind, those who will pull open the doors to a chapel or an antiquarian's shop not because they're listed on a souvenir map but because they look intrinsically interesting. In Paris, they usually are.

If You Have 1 Day

Get up early and begin walking the streets in the neighborhood of your hotel. The streets of Paris are live theater. Find a little cafe; chances are there'll be one on every block. Go in and order a typical Parisian breakfast of coffee and croissants. If you're a museum and monument junkie and don't dare return home without seeing the "must" sights, know that the two most popular museums are the **Musée du Louvre** and the **Musée d'Orsay.** The three most enduring monuments are the Eiffel Tower, the Arc de Triomphe, and Notre-Dame (which you can see later in the day, since it's not imperative that you go inside). If it's a toss-up between the Louvre and the d'Orsay, we'd make it the Louvre because it holds a greater variety of works. If you feel the need to choose between monuments, we'd make it the **Eiffel Tower** just for the panoramic city view. If you feel your day is too short to visit museums or wait in lines for the tower, we'd suggest you spend most of your time strolling the streets. The most impressive neighborhood is **Île St-Louis,** the most elegant place for a walk in Paris. After exploring this island and its mansions, wander at will through such Left Bank districts as **St-Germain-des-Prés** or the area around **place St-Michel,** the heart of the student quarter. As the sun sets over Paris, head for Notre-Dame, which stands majestically along the banks of the Seine. This is a good place to watch shadows fall over Paris as the lights come on for the night. Afterward, walk along the banks of the **Seine,** where vendors sell books and souvenir prints. Promise yourself a return visit and have dinner in the Left Bank bistro of your choice.

If You Have 2 Days

Take in the glories of the Right Bank. Begin at the **Arc de Triomphe** and stroll down the **Champs-Elysées,** the main boulevard of Paris, until you reach the Egyptian obelisk at **place de la Concorde.** This grand promenade is one of the most famous walks in the world. Place de la Concorde affords terrific views of the Madeleine, the Palais-Bourbon, the Arc de Triomphe, and the Louvre. This is where some of France's most notable figures lost their heads on the guillotine. After all this walking, we suggest a rest stop in the **Jardin des Tuileries,** directly west and adjacent to the Louvre. Give your fee a long rest at lunch in a Right Bank bistro. Then for a total contrast to monumental Paris, go for a walk in the Marais. Our favorite stroll is along the rue des Rosiers, a narrow street that's the heart of the **Jewish community.** And don't miss **place des Vosges.** After a rest at your hotel, select one of the restaurants down in **Montparnasse,** following in Hemingway's footsteps. This area is far livelier at night.

If You Have 3 Days

Many visitors will target the restored **Centre Pompidou** as one of their major sightseeing goals. Others wander the sculpture garden of the **Musée National Auguste-Rodin.** Or if you prefer the **Musée Picasso,** you can use part of the morning to

---

A Time-Saving Tip

Museums require that you check shopping bags and book bags, and sometimes lines for these can be longer than the ticket and admission lines. If you value your time, leave these bags behind or do your shopping afterward. Ask if a museum has more than one coat line; if so, avoid the main one and go to the less-crowded ones.

---

explore a few of the art galleries of the Marais. Following in the trail of Descartes and Mme de Sévigné, select a cafe or restaurant here for lunch. Reserve the afternoon for **Île de la Cité,** where you'll get to see not only Notre-Dame again but also the **Conciergerie,** where Marie Antoinette and others were held captive before they were beheaded. See also the stunning stained glass of **Sainte-Chapelle** in the Palais de Justice. Even if you've been saving money up until now, our final suggestion is that you go all out for one really grand French meal at a fabulous restaurant. It's a memory you'll probably treasure long after you've recovered from paying the tab. After dinner, if your energy holds, you can sample Paris's nightlife—whatever you fancy, the dancers at the **Lido or the Folies-Bergère** or a smoky Left Bank jazz club. If you'd just like to sit and have a drink, Paris has some of the most elegant hotel bars in the world at such places as the **Crillon** and **Plaza Athenée.**

1 The Top Attractions

✪ **Eiffel Tower.** In the Champ-de-Mars, 7e. ☎ **01-44-11-23-23.** Admission: First landing, 22 F ($3.50); second landing, 44 F ($7.05); third landing, 62 F ($9.90); stairs to second landing, 18 F ($2.90). June–Aug, daily 9am–midnight; Sept–May, daily 9:30am–11pm (stairs close at 6:30pm). Métro: École-Militaire or Bir-Hakeim. RER: Champ-de-Mars/Tour-Eiffel.

This may be the single most recognizable structure in the world—it's the symbol of Paris. Weighing 7,000 tons but exerting about the same pressure on the ground as an average-size person sitting in a chair, the tower was never meant to be permanent. It was built for the Universal Exhibition of 1889 by Gustave-Alexandre Eiffel, the engineer whose fame rested mainly on his iron bridges. (He also designed the framework for the Statue of Liberty.)

The tower, including its 55-foot TV antenna, is 1,056 feet tall. On a clear day you can see it from 40 miles away. Its open-framework construction ushered in the almost-unlimited possibilities of steel construction, paving the way for the 20th-century's skyscrapers. Skeptics said it couldn't be built, and Eiffel actually wanted to make it soar higher. For years it remained the tallest man-made structure on earth, until such skyscrapers as the Empire State Building usurped the record. The advent of wireless communication in the early 1890s preserved the tower from destruction.

You can visit the tower in three stages: Taking the elevator to the first landing, you have a view over the rooftops of Paris. Here you'll find a cinema museum and restaurants and a bar open year-round. The second landing provides a panoramic look at the city (on this level is Le Jules Verne restaurant, a great place for lunch or dinner; see below). The third landing offers the most panoramic view, allowing you to identify monuments and buildings. On the ground level, in the eastern and western pillars, you can visit the 1899 elevator machinery when the tower is open.

To get to **Le Jules Verne** (☎ **01-45-55-61-44**), you take a private south foundation elevator. You can enjoy an aperitif in the relaxing piano bar, then take a seat at one of the dining room's tables, all of which provide an inspiring view. The menu changes seasonally, offering fish and meat dishes that range from fillet of turbot with seaweed and buttered sea urchins to veal chops with truffled vegetables. Reservations are recommended.

✪ **Musée du Louvre.** 34–36 quai du Louvre, 1er (entrance: Pyramid/cour Napoléon). ☎ **01-40-20-53-17** or 01-40-20-51-51 for recorded information, or 08-03-80-88-03 for advance credit-card orders. Admission 45 F ($7.20) before 3pm, 26 F ($4.15) after 3pm and all day Sun, free for children 17 and under; free for everyone first Sun of every month. Mon and Wed 9am–9:45pm (Mon, short tour only), Thurs–Sun 9am–6pm. 90-min English-language tours Mon, Wed–Sat at various times of the day for 17 F ($2.70). Free for children 12 and under with museum ticket. Métro: Palais-Royal/Musée du Louvre.

The Louvre is the world's largest palace and one of the world's largest and greatest museums. It's more beautiful than ever since the facade has been thoroughly cleaned. The $1.2 billion Grand Louvre Project is expected to be entirely completed by the end of 2000. Of course, it was supposed to be completed by the end of 1999, so stay tuned. For up-to-the-minute data on what is open or about to open, you can check out the Louvre's Web site at **www.louvre.fr**.

The Louvre's collection is truly staggering. You'll have to resign yourself to missing certain masterpieces here because you won't have the time or stamina to see everything. People on one of those "Paris-in-a-day" tours try to break track records to glimpse the two most famous ladies here: the *Mona Lisa* and the *Venus de Milo*. Those with an extra 5 minutes go in pursuit of *Winged Victory*, that headless statue discovered at Samothrace and dating from about 200 B.C.

To enter the Louvre, you pass through the controversial 71-foot **I. M. Pei glass pyramid** in the courtyard. Commissioned by Mitterrand and completed in 1989, it received mixed reviews. The pyramid allows sunlight to shine on an underground reception area and shelters shops and restaurants that stretch beneath the Jardin du Carrousel. The renovation also increases the Louvre's gallery space by an astonishing 80% and provides underground garages for the tour buses that used to jam rue de Rivoli.

Tips on Tickets: If you don't want to wait in line for tickets at the entrance of the pyramid or use the new automatic ticket machines, you can now order tickets over the phone (see above) with a credit card. You can also order advance tickets (and take a virtual tour of the museum from your desk) at the Web site. Tickets can be mailed to you in the U.S., or you can pick them up at any FNAC location in Paris.

Those with little time should go on one of the **guided tours** (in English), which last about 1¹/₂ hours. These tours start under the pyramid at the station marked ACCEIL DES GROUPES.

The collections are divided into seven departments: Asian antiquities; Egyptian antiquities; Greek, Etruscan, and Roman antiquities; sculpture; paintings; prints and drawings; and objets d'art. In December 1997, President Jacques Chirac inaugurated 107,000 square feet of gallery space, most of it in the eastern Sully wing, including a new presentation of the Louvre's vast collection of Egyptian antiquities. This innovation means 60% more space for the world of the pharaohs, a culture that has fascinated the French since Napoléon's occupation of Egypt in 1798.

New areas also now open include freshly restored and newly occupied rooms of Greek, Etruscan, and Roman antiquities. The Grand Galerie, a 600-foot hall opening onto the Seine, is dedicated to mostly Italian paintings from the 1400s to the 1700s, including works by Raphael and Leonardo da Vinci.

The **Richelieu Wing** houses the museum's collection of northern European and French paintings, along with decorative arts, French sculpture, Oriental antiquities (a rich collection of Islamic art), and the grand salons of Napoléon III. Originally constructed from 1852 to 1857, this wing has been virtually rebuilt. In its 165 rooms, plus three covered courtyards, some 12,000 works of art are displayed. Of the Greek and Roman antiquities, the most notable (aside from *Venus* and *Winged Victory*) are **fragments of the Parthenon's frieze.**

Of course we love Mona and Venus, but our eternal passion burns for Jacques-Louis David's *Portrait of Madame Récamier,* depicting Napoléon's opponent at age 23; on her comfortable sofa, she reclines in the style of classical antiquity. Other favorites of ours are *Ship of Fools* by Hieronymous Bosch, tucked in the Flemish galleries (no one can depict folly and greed more vividly than Bosch); *Four Seasons* by Nicolas Poussin, the canonical work of French classicism; Eugène Delacroix's *Liberty Leading the People,* perhaps the ultimate endorsement of revolution (Louis-Philippe purchased the painting and hid it during his reign); and Paolo Veronese's gigantic *Wedding Feast at Cana,* showing (if nothing else) how stunning colors can be when applied by a master.

When you tire of strolling the galleries, you might like a pick-me-up at the Richelieu Wing's **Café Richelieu** or **Café Marly** (93 rue de Rivoli, 1er; ☎ **01-49-26-06-60**). Boasting Napoléon III opulence, the Marly offers a perfect oasis. Perhaps try a café crème, a club sandwich, a decadent pastry, or something from the upscale bistro menu.

✪ **Musée d'Orsay.** 1 rue de Bellechasse or 62 rue de Lille, 7e. ☎ **01-40-49-48-14.** Admission 40 F ($6.40) adults, 30 F ($4.80) ages 18–24, free for children 17 and under. Tues–Wed and Fri–Sat 10am–6pm, Thurs 10am–9:45pm, Sun 9am–6pm. June 20–Sept 20, opens daily at 9am. Métro: Solférino. RER: Musée-d'Orsay.

The handsome neoclassical Gare d'Orsay train station has been transformed into one of the world's greatest art museums. It contains an important collection devoted to the pivotal years from 1848 to 1914. Across the Seine from the Louvre and the Tuileries, this museum is a repository of works by the Impressionists as well as lesser-known groups like the Symbolists, Pointillists, Realists, and late Romantics. Artists represented include van Gogh, Manet, Monet, Degas, and Renoir. It houses thousands of sculptures and paintings spread across 80 galleries, plus belle époque furniture, photographs, objets d'art, architectural models, and even a cinema.

One of Renoir's most joyous paintings is here: *Moulin de la Galette* (1876). Another celebrated work is by the American James McNeill Whistler—*Arrangement in Gray and Black: Portrait of the Painter's Mother.* The most famous piece in the museum is Manet's 1863 *Déjeuner sur l'herbe* (*Picnic on the Grass*), which created a scandal when it was first exhibited; it depicts a nude woman nonchalantly picnicking with two fully clothed men in a forest. Two years later his *Olympia,* lounging on her bed wearing nothing but a flower in her hair and high-heeled shoes, met the same response.

✪ **Musée National Auguste Rodin.** In the Hôtel Biron, 77 rue de Varenne, 7e. ☎ **01-44-18-61-10.** Admission 28 F ($4.50) adults, 18 F ($2.90) ages 18–25 and seniors 60 and over, free for children 17 and under. Apr–Sept, Tues–Sun 9:30am–5:45pm; Oct–Mar, Tues–Sun 9:30am–4:45pm. Métro: Varenne.

This beautiful house and its gardens are a repository of the work of Auguste Rodin (1840–1917), the undisputed master of French 19th-century sculpture (even though his works were first thought obscene). After his death, the government purchased Rodin's gray-stone 18th-century mansion in Faubourg St-Germain, where he had his studio from 1910 until 1917. The rose gardens were restored to their original splendor, making a perfect setting for Rodin's most memorable works.

In the courtyard are three world-famous creations: *The Gate of Hell, The Thinker,* and *The Burghers of Calais.* Rodin's first major public commission, *The Burghers* commemorated the heroism of six burghers who in 1347 offered themselves as hostages to Edward III in return for his ending the siege of their port. *The Thinker,* in Rodin's own words, "thinks with every muscle of his arms, back, and legs, with his clenched fist and gripping toes." Inside the mansion, the sculptures, plaster casts, reproductions, originals, and sketches reveal the freshness and vitality of that remarkable man. Many of his works appear to be emerging from marble into life. Everybody is drawn to *The Kiss* (of which one critic wrote, "the passion is timeless"). Upstairs are two versions of the celebrated and condemned nude of Balzac, his bulky torso rising from a tree trunk. Included are many versions of his *Monument to Balzac* (a large one stands in the garden), Rodin's last major work. Generally overlooked is a room devoted to Camille Claudel, Rodin's mistress and a towering artist in her own right. His pupil, model, and lover, she created such works as *Maturity, Clotho,* and (donated in 1995) the *Waltz* and the *Gossips.*

The little alley behind the mansion winds its way down to a pond with fountains and flower beds, even sandpits for children. It's one of the most idyllic hidden spots of Paris.

✪ **Musée Picasso.** In the Hôtel Salé, 5 rue de Thorigny, 3e. ☎ **01-42-71-25-21.** Admission 30–38 F ($4.80–$6.10) adults, 20–28 F ($3.20–$4.50) ages 19–25 and seniors over 60, free for children 18 and under. Apr–Sept, Wed–Mon 9:30am–6pm; Oct–Mar, Wed–Mon 9:30am–5pm. Métro: St-Paul, Filles-du-Calvaire, or Chemin-Vert.

When it opened in the beautifully restored Hôtel Salé in the Marais, the press hailed it as a "museum for Picasso's Picassos," meaning those he chose not to sell. Far superior to a similar museum in Barcelona, this museum offers an unparalleled view of the artist's long and varied career and his different periods, including his fabled gaunt blue figures and harlequins. This museum remains one of Paris's most popular attractions. The world's greatest Picasso collection, acquired by the state in lieu of $50 million in inheritance taxes, consists of 203 paintings, 158 sculptures, 16 collages, 19 bas-reliefs, 88 ceramics, and more than 1,500 sketches and 1,600 engravings, plus 30 notebooks. These works span some 75 years of Picasso's life and changing styles.

The range of paintings includes a remarkable 1901 self-portrait and embraces such masterpieces as *Le Baiser* (*The Kiss*), painted at Mougins in 1969. Another masterpiece is *Reclining Nude and the Man with a Guitar.* It's easy to stroll through seeking your own favorite work—ours is the delightfully wicked *Jeune garçon à la langouste* (*Young Man with a Lobster*), painted in Paris in 1941. The museum also owns several intriguing studies for *Les Demoiselles d'Avignon,* the painting that launched Cubism in 1907.

✪ **Notre-Dame.** 6 place du parvis Notre-Dame, 4e. ☎ **01-42-34-56-10.** Admission to cathedral free; towers and crypt 35 F ($5.60) adults, 23 F ($3.70) ages 12–25 and over 60, free for children under 12. Museum and treasury 15 F ($2.40) adults, 10 F ($1.60) ages 12–25 and over 60, free for children under 12. Cathedral daily 8am–6:45pm year-round. Towers and crypt Apr–Sept, daily 9:30am–6pm; Oct–Mar, daily 10am–4:15pm. Museum Wed and Sat–Sun 2:30–6pm. Treasury Mon–Sat 9:30–11:30am and 1–5:45pm. Métro: Cité or St-Michel. RER: St-Michel.

This cathedral is one of the world's most famous houses of worship. For 6 centuries it has stood as a fabled Gothic masterpiece of the Middle Ages. Although many may disagree, we feel that Notre-Dame is more interesting outside than in. You'll have to walk around the entire structure to appreciate more fully this "vast symphony of stone" with its classic flying buttresses. Better yet, cross the bridge to the Left Bank and view it from the quay. Talk about a Kodak moment!

From square parvis, you can view the trio of 13th-century sculpted portals. On the left, the Portal of the Virgin depicts the signs of the zodiac and the Virgin's coronation. The restored central Portal of the Last Judgment is divided into three levels: The first shows Vices and Virtues; the second, Christ and his Apostles; the third, Christ in

Notre-Dame de Paris

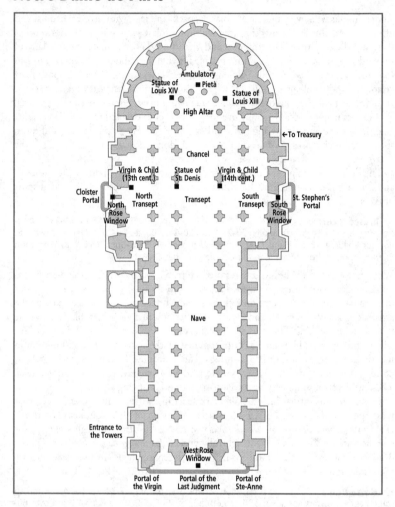

triumph after the Resurrection. On the right is the Portal of Ste. Anne, depicting such scenes as the Virgin enthroned with Child. It's Notre-Dame's most perfect piece of sculpture. Over the central portal is a remarkable rose window, 31 feet in diameter, forming a showcase for a statue of the Virgin and Child. Equally interesting (yet often missed) is the Cloister Portal (around on the left), with its dour-faced 13th-century Virgin, a unique survivor of the many that originally adorned the facade. (Unfortunately, the Child she's holding is decapitated.)

If possible, view the interior at sunset. Of the three giant medallions that warm the austere cathedral, the north rose window in the transept, from the mid-13th century, is best. The interior is typical Gothic, with slender, graceful columns. The carved-stone choir screen from the early 14th century depicts biblical scenes like the Last Supper. Near the altar stands the highly venerated 14th-century Virgin and Child. Behind glass in the treasury is a display of vestments and gold objects, including crowns. Notre-Dame is especially proud of its relic of the True Cross and the Crown of Thorns.

To visit those grimy gargoyles immortalized by Victor Hugo (where Quasimodo lurked and yearned), you have to scale steps leading to the twin square towers, rising to a height of 225 feet. Once here, you can closely inspect those devils (some sticking out their tongues), hobgoblins, and birds of prey.

Approached through a garden behind Notre-Dame is the **Memorial des Martyrs Français de la Déportation,** jutting out on the tip of the Île de la Cité. This memorial honors the French martyrs of World War II, who were deported to camps like Auschwitz and Buchenwald. In blood-red are the words (in French): "Forgive, but don't forget." It's open Monday through Friday from 8:30am to 9:45pm, Saturday and Sunday from 9am to 9:45pm. Admission is free.

2 Musée de Louvre/Les Halles: The 1st Arrondissement (Right Bank)

The first arrondissement is first for a reason: it's where most visitors make a beeline upon arrival in Paris. Several of the city's top attractions are here, including, of course, the **Louvre** (see section 1 of this chapter, "The Top Attractions") and the Tuileries. It's also home to **Les Halles,** for 8 centuries the major wholesale fruit, meat, and vegetable market of Paris. The smock-clad vendors, the carcasses of beef, the baskets of the most appetizing vegetables in the world—all that belongs to the past. Today the action has moved to the modern steel-and-glass structure at Rungis, a suburb near Orly. Here today is **Les Forum des Halles** (Métro: Les Halles; RER: Châtelet-Les Halles), which opened in 1979. This large complex, much of it underground, houses dozens of shops, plus several restaurants and movie theaters.

For many visitors, a night on the town still ends in the wee hours with the traditional bowl of onion soup at Les Halles, usually at **Au Pied de Cochon** (Pig's Foot) or **Au Chien Qui Fume** (Smoking Dog).

There's still much to see in Les Halles, beginning with the **Église St-Eustache,** 2 rue du Jour, 1er (☎ **01-42-36-31-05;** Métro: Les Halles), with another entrance on rue Rambuteau. In the old days, cabbage vendors came here to pray for their produce. The Gothic-Renaissance church dates from the mid-16th century yet wasn't completed until 1637. It has been known for its organ recitals ever since Liszt played here in 1866. Inside is the black marble tomb of Jean-Baptiste Colbert, the minister of state under Louis XIV. A marble statue of the statesman rests on top of his tomb, which is flanked by Coysevox's *Abundance* (a horn of flowers) and J. B. Tuby's *Fidelity.* The church is open from April to September daily from 8am to 8pm, and from October to March daily from 9am to 7pm; mass is at 9:30am, 11am, and 6pm Sunday, and there's also an organ concert Sunday at 5:30pm.

Galerie Nationale du Jeu de Paume. In the Jardin des Tuileries at place de la Concorde, 1er. ☎ **01-42-60-69-69.** Admission 38 F ($6.10) adults, 28 F ($4.50) students, free for visitors 13 and under. Tues noon–9:30pm, Wed–Fri noon–7pm, Sat–Sun 10am–7pm. Métro: Concorde.

Jeu de Paume, in the northeast corner of the Tuileries (see below), was ordered constructed by Napoléon III as a court on which to play *jeu de paume,* a precursor to tennis. For years it was one of Paris's treasured addresses, displaying some of the finest works of the Impressionists. To the regret of many, the collection was hauled off to the Musée d'Orsay in 1986. Following a $12.6-million face-lift, the Second Empire building has been transformed into a new art gallery with state-of-the-art display facilities and a video screening room. There's no permanent collection; every 2 or 3 months a new show is mounted. Sometimes the works of little-known contemporary artists are on display; at other times the exhibition features established artists like Jean Dubuffet.

✪ **Jardin des Tuileries.** Bordering place de la Concorde, 1er. ☎ **01-44-50-75-01.** Métro: Tuileries.

These spectacular, statue-studded gardens are as much a part of Paris as the Seine. They were designed by Le Nôtre, Louis XIV's gardener and planner of the Versailles grounds. About 100 years before that, Catherine de Médici ordered a palace built here, connected to the Louvre; other occupants have included Louis XVI (after he left Versailles) and Napoléon. Twice attacked by enraged Parisians, it was finally burned to the ground in 1871 and never rebuilt. The gardens, however, remain. In orderly French manner, the trees are arranged according to designs and even the paths are arrow-straight. Breaking the sense of order and formality are bubbling fountains.

Seemingly half of Paris can be found in the Tuileries on a warm spring day, listening to the chirping birds and admiring the daffodils and tulips. As you walk toward the Louvre, you'll enter the **Jardin du Carrousel,** dominated by the **Arc de Triomphe du Carrousel,** at the Cour du Carrousel. Pierced with three walkways and supported by marble columns, the monument honors Napoléon's Grande Armée, celebrating its victory at Austerlitz on December 5, 1805. The arch is surmounted by statuary, a chariot, and four bronze horses.

Musée des Arts Décoratifs. In the Palais du Louvre, 107 rue de Rivoli, 1er. ☎ **01-44-55-57-50.** Admission 35 F ($5.60) adults, 25 F ($4) ages 18–25, free for children 17 and under. Tues and Thurs–Fri 11am–6pm, Wed 11am–9pm, Sat–Sun 10am–6pm. Métro: Palais-Royal or Tuileries.

In the northwest wing of the Louvre's Pavillon de Marsan, this museum holds a treasury of furnishings, fabrics, wallpaper, objets d'art, and other items displaying living styles from the Middle Ages to the present. Notable on the first floor are the 1920s Art Deco boudoir, bath, and bedroom done for couturière Jeanne Lanvin by the designer Rateau, plus a prestigious collection of the works donated by Jean Dubuffet. Decorative art from the Middle Ages to the Renaissance is housed on the second floor; rich collections from the 17th, 18th, and 19th centuries occupy the third and fourth floors. The fifth floor has specialized centers, such as wallpaper and drawings, and documentary centers detailing fashion, textiles, toys, crafts, and glass trends.

Palais Royal. Rue St-Honoré, on place du Palais-Royal, 1er. Métro: Palais-Royal/Musée du Louvre.

At the demolished Café Foy in the Palais Royal, the outraged Camille Desmoulins once jumped up on a table and shouted for the mob "to fight to the death." The date was July 13, 1789. The renown of the Palais Royal goes back even farther. The gardens were planted in 1634 for Cardinal Richelieu, who presented them to Louis XIII. In time the property became the residence of the ducs d'Orléans. Philippe-Egalité, a cousin of Louis XVI, built his apartments on the grounds and subsequently rented them to prostitutes. By the 20th century those same apartments were rented by such artists as Cocteau and Colette. (A plaque at 9 rue Beaujolais marks the entrance to her apartment, which she inhabited until her death in 1954.) Today the Palais Royal contains apartments, some discreet shops, and a few great restaurants (such as **Le Grand Véfour;** see chapter 3). Note sculptor Daniel Buren's prison-striped columns, added to the garden in 1986, and Pol Bury's steel-ball sculptures decorating the fountains.

3 Le Marais: The 3rd Arrondissement (Right Bank)

When Paris began to overflow the confines of the Île de la Cité in the 13th century, the citizenry settled in the Marais, the marsh that used to be flooded regularly by the high-rising Seine. By the 17th century the Marais had reached the pinnacle of fashion, becoming the center of aristocratic Paris. At that time, most of its great *hôtels particuliers* (mansions)—many now restored or being spruced up today—were built by the finest craftspeople in France.

In the 18th and 19th centuries, the fashionable deserted the Marais in favor of the expanding Faubourg St-Germain and Faubourg St-Honoré. Industry eventually took over the quarter, and the once-elegant hôtels were turned into tenements. There was talk of demolishing this blighted sector, but in 1962 the alarmed Comité de Sauvegarde du Marais banded together and saved the district. The regeneration of the neighborhood was sparked by the Pompidou Center.

No longer "the Swamp" (its English name), the Marais in the 3rd arrondissement (and part of the 4th) is trendy once again, filled with tiny twisting streets, bars for both gays and straights, and cutting-edge designer shops.

In **place de la Bastille** on July 14, 1789, a mob of Parisians attacked the Bastille and thus sparked the French Revolution. Nothing remains of the historic Bastille, built in 1369, for it was torn down. Many prisoners—some sentenced by Louis XIV for "witchcraft"—were kept within its walls, the best known being the "Man in the Iron Mask." When the fortress was stormed, only seven prisoners were discovered (the marquis de Sade had been transferred to the madhouse 10 days earlier). Authorities had discussed razing it anyway, so the attack was more symbolic than anything else. What it signified, however, and what it started will never be forgotten. Bastille Day is celebrated with great festivity every July 14. In the center of the square is the **Colonne de Juillet** (July Column), which doesn't commemorate the Revolution; rather, it honors the victims of the 1830 July Revolution, which put Louis-Philippe on the throne. The tower is crowned by the God of Liberty, a winged nude with a star emerging from his head.

Not far away, ✪ **place des Vosges,** 4e (Métro: St-Paul or Chemin-Vert), is Paris's oldest square and once its most fashionable. Situated in the heart of the Marais, it was called the Palais Royal in the days of Henri IV, who planned to live here—but his assassin, Ravaillac, had other intentions for him. Henry II was killed while jousting on the square in 1559, in the shadow of the Hôtel des Tournelles. His widow, Catherine de Médici, had the place torn down. Place des Vosges, once a major dueling ground, was one of Europe's first planned squares. Its grand siècle redbrick houses are ornamented with white stone, and its covered arcades allowed people to shop at all times, even in the rain—quite an innovation at the time. In the 18th century chestnut trees were added, sparking a controversy that continues to this day: Critics say that the addition spoils the perspective.

As you stroll the Marais, you might want to seek out the following hôtels: The **Hôtel de Rohan,** 87 rue Vieille-du-Temple (☎ **01-40-27-60-09**), was once occupied by the fourth Cardinal Rohan, who was involved in the scandal that framed Marie Antoinette for buying a priceless diamond necklace. The first Cardinal Rohan, the original occupant, was reputed to be the son of Louis XIV. The main attraction is the amusing 18th-century Salon des Singes (Monkey Room). In the courtyard is a stunning bas-relief of a nude Apollo and four horses against exploding sunbursts. The hotel can be visited only during special exhibitions announced in Paris newspapers.

At 47 rue Vieille-du-Temple is the **Hôtel des Ambassadeurs de Hollande,** where Beaumarchais wrote *The Marriage of Figaro.* It's one of the most splendid mansions in the area—and was never occupied by the Dutch embassy. It's not open to the public.

Although the facade of the 17th-century **Hôtel de Beauvais,** 68 rue François-Miron, was badly damaged during the Revolution, it remains one of the most charming in Paris. A plaque commemorates the fact that Mozart inhabited the mansion in 1763. To visit inside, speak to the Association du Paris Historique, on the ground floor of the building, any afternoon.

Hôtel de Sens, a landmark at 1 rue de Figuier (☎ 01-42-78-14-60), was built from the 1470s to 1519 for the archbishops of Sens. Along with the Hôtel de Cluny on the Left Bank, it's the only domestic architecture remaining from the 15th century. Long after the archbishops had departed in 1605, it was occupied by the scandalous Queen Margot, wife of Henri IV. Her "younger and more virile" new lover slew the discarded one as she looked on in amusement. Today the mansion houses the Bibliothèque Forney. The gate is open Tuesday through Saturday from 1:30 to 8pm.

Work began on the **Hôtel de Bethune-Sully,** 62 rue St-Antoine (☎ 01-44-61-20-00), in 1625. In 1634 it was acquired by the duc de Sully, who had been Henri IV's minister of finance before the king was assassinated in 1610. After a straitlaced life, Sully broke loose in his later years, adorning himself with diamonds and garish rings—and a young bride who had a preference for even younger men. The hôtel was acquired by the government after World War II and now contains the National Office of Historical Monuments and Sites. Recently restored, the relief-studded facade is especially appealing. There's daily admittance to the courtyard and the garden that opens onto place des Vosges.

The most characteristic street in the district is **rue des Rosiers (Street of the Rose-bushes),** one of the most colorful of the streets remaining from the old Jewish quarter. The Star of David shines here, Hebrew letters flash (in neon), couscous is sold from the shops run by Moroccan or Algerian Jews, bearded old men sit in doorways, restaurants serve strictly kosher meals, and signs appeal for Jewish liberation.

Shoppers will delight in such places as **Passage de Retz,** 9 rue Charlot (☎ 01-48-04-37-99), established in 1994, an avante-garde gallery with the most amusing exhibitions in the Marais. At **Hier, Aujourd'hui, and Demain,** 14 rue de Bretagne (☎ 01-42-77-69-02), you'll fall in love with 1930s Art Deco.

The 3rd arrondissement is also home to **The Picasso Museum** (see "The Top Attractions," above).

Musée Carnavalet. 23 rue de Sévigné, 3e. ☎ **01-42-72-21-13.** Admission 35 F ($5.60) adults, 25 F ($4) ages 25 and under and seniors over 60. Tues–Sun 10am–5:40pm. Métro: St-Paul or Chemin-Vert.

The history of Paris comes alive here in intimately personal terms—right down to the chessmen Louis XVI used to distract himself in the days before he went to the guillotine. A renowned Renaissance palace, the hôtel was built in 1544 by Pierre Lescot and Jean Goujon and later acquired by Mme de Carnavalet. The great François Mansart transformed it between 1655 and 1661. It's probably best known because one of history's most famous letter writers, Mme de Sévigné, moved here in 1677. Fanatically devoted to her daughter (until she had to live with her), she poured out nearly every detail of her life in letters, virtually ignoring her son. A native of the Marais, she died at her daughter's château in 1696. It wasn't until 1866 that the city acquired the mansion and turned it into a museum.

4 Where Paris Was Born: Île de la Cité & the 4th Arrondissement

Medieval Paris, that architectural blending of grotesquerie and Gothic beauty, began on this island in the Seine. Explore as much of it as you can, but if you're in a hurry, try to visit at least **Notre-Dame** (see section 1 of this chapter, "The Top Attractions"), the Sainte-Chapelle, and the Conciergerie. The 4th arrondissement is on the right bank, opposite the island.

✪ **Centre Pompidou.** Place Georges-Pompidou, 4e. ☎ **01-44-78-12-33.** Admission 30 F ($4.80) adults, 20 F ($3.20) students, free for children under 13. Special exhibitions 40 F ($6.40) adults, 30 F ($4.80) students, free for children under 13. Wed–Mon 11am–9pm. Métro: Rambuteau, Hôtel-de-Ville, or Châtelet-Les-Halles.

Relaunched in January of 2000, in what was called in the 1970s "the most avant-garde building in the world," the newly restored Pompidou Centre is packing in the art-loving crowds again.

The dream of former president Georges Pompidou, this center for 20th-century art, designed by Richard Rogers and Renzo Piano, opened in 1977 and immediately became the focus of loud controversy. Its bold exoskeletal architecture and the brightly painted pipes and ducts crisscrossing its transparent facade (green for water, red for heat, blue for air, and yellow for electricity) were jarring in the old Beaubourg neighborhood. Perhaps the detractors were right all along—within 20 years the building began to deteriorate so badly that a major restoration was called for.

The Centre Pompidou encompasses four separate attractions:

The **Musée National d'Art Moderne** (National Museum of Modern Art) offers a large collection of 20th-century art. With some 40,000 works, this is the big attraction, although only some 850 works can be displayed at one time. If you want to view some real charmers, see Alexander Calder's 1926 *Josephine Baker,* one of his earlier versions of the mobile, an art form he invented. Marcel Duchamps' *Valise* is a collection of miniature reproductions of his fabled Dada sculptures and drawings; they're displayed in a carrying case. And every time we visit Paris we have to see Salvador Dali's *Portrait of Lenin Dancing on Piano Keys.*

In the **Public Information Library** the public has free access to a million French and foreign books, periodicals, films, records, slides, and microfilms in nearly every area of knowledge. The **Center for Industrial Design** emphasizes the contributions made in the fields of architecture, visual communications, publishing, and community planning; and the **Institute for Research and Coordination of Acoustics/Music** brings together musicians and composers interested in furthering the cause of music, both contemporary and traditional.

Finally, you can also visit a re-creation of the jazz-age studio of Romanian sculptor Brancusi (**l'Atelier Brancusi**), which is configured as a mini-museum that's slightly separate from the rest of the action.

Conciergerie. 1 quai de l'Horloge, 1er. ☎ **01-53-73-78-50.** Admission 35 F ($5.60) adults, 23 F ($3.70) ages 12–25, free for children 11 and under. Apr–Sept, daily 9:30am–6:30pm; Oct–Mar, daily 10am–5pm. Métro: Cité, Châtelet, or St-Michel. RER: St-Michel.

The Conciergerie is the most sinister building in France. Though it had a long, regal history before the Revolution, it's visited today chiefly by those wishing to bask in the Reign of Terror's horrors. The Conciergerie conjures images of the days when tumbrils pulled up daily to haul off the fresh supply of victims to the guillotine.

You approach the Conciergerie through its landmark twin towers, the Tour d'Argent and Tour de César, though the 14th-century vaulted Guard Room is the actual entrance. Also from the 14th century—and even more interesting—is the vast, dark, foreboding Salle des Gens d'Armes (People at Arms), chillingly transformed from the days when the king used it as a banqueting hall.

Few of the prisoners in the Conciergerie's history endured the tortures of Ravaillac, who assassinated Henry IV in 1610. He got the full treatment—pincers in the flesh as well as hot lead and boiling oil poured on him like bathwater. This was also where Marie Antoinette, in failing health and in shock, was brought to await her trial and eventual beheading.

✪ **Sainte-Chapelle.** In the Palais de Justice, 4 bd. du Palais, 1er. ☎ **01-53-73-78-50.** Admission 35 F ($5.60) adults, 25 F ($4) students and children 13–25, free for children 12 and under. Apr–Sept, daily 9:30am–6:30pm; Oct–Mar, daily 10am–5pm. Métro: Cité, St-Michel, or Châtelet-Les-Halles. RER: St-Michel.

Go here if for no other reason than to see one of the world's greatest examples of Flamboyant Gothic architecture—"the pearl among them all," as Proust called it— and brilliantly colored stained-glass windows with a lacelike delicacy, a triumph of transparency. The reds are so red that Parisians have been known to use the phrase "wine the color of Sainte-Chapelle's windows." Sainte-Chapelle is Paris's second most important monument of the Middle Ages (after Notre-Dame), erected to enshrine relics from the First Crusade. These included what were believed to have been the Crown of Thorns, two pieces from the True Cross, and even the Roman lance that pierced the side of Christ. St. Louis (Louis IX) acquired the relics from the emperor of Constantinople and is said to have paid heavily for them, raising money through unscrupulous means.

Viewed on a bright day, the 15 stained-glass windows vividly depicting Bible scenes seem to glow ruby red and Chartres blue. The walls consist almost entirely of the glass. Built in only 5 years, beginning in 1246, the chapel has two levels. You enter through the lower chapel, supported by flying buttresses and ornamented with fleurs-de-lis. The lower chapel was used by the servants of the palace, the upper chamber by the king and his courtiers; the latter is reached by ascending a narrow spiral staircase. At the top you're sure to ooh and aah at the sight.

ANOTHER ISLAND IN THE STREAM: ÎLE ST-LOUIS

As you walk across the iron footbridge from the rear of Notre-Dame, you descend into a world of tree-shaded quays, aristocratic town houses and courtyards, restaurants, and antiques shops.

The Île St-Louis (Métro: Sully-Morland or Pont-Marie), the sibling island of the Île de la Cité, is primarily residential; those who live here fiercely guard their heritage, privileges, and special position. It was originally two "islets," one named Island of the Heifers, until the two islands were ordered joined by Louis XIII. The number of famous people who have occupied these patrician mansions is now legend. Plaques on the facades make it easier to identify them: Madame Curie, for example, lived at 36 quai de Bethune, near pont de la Tournelle, from 1912 until her death in 1934.

The most exciting mansion is the **Hôtel de Lauzun,** built in 1657, at 17 quai d'Anjou; it's named after a 17th-century rogue, the duc de Lauzun, famous lover and on-again/off-again favorite of Louis XIV. The French poet Charles Baudelaire lived here in the 19th century with his "Black Venus," Jeanne Duval. Baudelaire attracted such artists as Delacroix and Courbet to his apartment, which was often filled with the aroma of hashish. Occupying another apartment was the novelist Théophile Gautier ("art for art's sake"), who's remembered today chiefly for his *Mademoiselle de Maupin.*

Voltaire lived in the **Hôtel Lambert,** 2 quai d'Anjou, with his mistress, Emilie de Breteuil, the marquise du Châteley, who had an "understanding" husband. The mansion was built by Louis Le Vau in 1645 for Nicolas Lambert de Thorigny, the president of the Chambre des Comptes. For a century the hotel was the home of the royal family of Poland, the Czartoryskis, who entertained Chopin, among others.

Farther along, at no. 9 quai d'Anjou, is the house where Honoré Daumier, the painter/sculptor/lithographer, lived between 1846 and 1863. From here he satirized the petite bourgeoisie. His caricature of Louis-Philippe netted him a 6-month jail sentence.

5 The Champs-Elysées, Paris's Grand Promenade: The 8th Arrondissement (Right Bank)

In late 1995, after two hard, dusty, and hyperexpensive years of construction, several important improvements in Paris's most prominent triumphal promenade were unveiled. The *contre-allées* (side lanes that had always been clogged with parked cars) were removed (new underground garages alleviate the horrendous parking problem), new lighting was added, the pedestrian sidewalks were widened, and new trees were planted. Now the Grand Promenade truly is grand again . . . except for all those fast-food joints.

✪ **Arc de Triomphe.** Place Charles-de-Gaulle-Étoile, 8e. ☎ **01-55-37-73-77.** Admission 40 F ($6.40) adults, 25 F ($4) ages 12–25, free for children 11 and under. Apr–Sept, daily 9:30am–11pm; Oct–Mar, daily 10am–10:30pm. Métro: Charles-de-Gaulle-Étoile.

Situated at the western end of the Champs-Elysées, the Arc de Triomphe is the largest triumphal arch in the world, about 163 feet high and 147 feet wide. To reach it, don't try crossing the square, the busiest traffic hub in Paris. (Death is certain!) Instead, take the underground passage. With a dozen streets radiating from the "Star," the traffic circle is vehicular roulette.

The arch has witnessed some of France's proudest moments—and some of its more humiliating defeats, notably those of 1871 and 1940. The memory of German troops marching under the arch that had come to symbolize France's glory—who can forget the 1940 newsreel footage of the Frenchman openly weeping as the Nazi stormtroopers goose-stepped down the Champs—is still painful to the French so many years later.

Commissioned by Napoléon in 1806 to commemorate his Grande Armée's victories, the arch wasn't completed until 1836, under Louis-Philippe. Four years later Napoléon's remains—brought from his grave on St. Helena—passed under the arch on their journey to his tomb at the Hôtel des Invalides. Since then it has become the focal point for state funerals. It's also the site of the tomb of the unknown soldier, where an eternal flame is kept burning.

Of the sculptures decorating the monument, the best known is Rude's *Marseillaise,* also called *The Departure of the Volunteers.* J. P. Cortot's *Triumph of Napoléon in 1810,* and the *Resistance of 1814* and *Peace of 1815,* both by Etex, also adorn the facade. The arch is engraved with the names of hundreds of generals (those underlined died in battle) who commanded troops in Napoléonic victories.

You can take an elevator or climb the stairway to the top. Up there is an exhibition hall, with lithographs and photos depicting the arch throughout its history. From the observation deck you have a panoramic view of the Champs-Elysées as well as such landmarks as the Louvre, Eiffel Tower, and Sacré-Coeur.

Where the Royal Heads Rolled

The eastern end of the Champs-Elysées is **place de la Concorde,** an octagonal traffic hub ordered built in 1757 to honor Louis XV. It's one of the world's grandest squares. The statue of the king was torn down in 1792 and the name of the square changed to place de la Révolution. Floodlit at night, it's dominated now by an **Egyptian obelisk** from Luxor, the oldest man-made object in Paris; it was carved circa 1200 B.C. and presented to France in 1829 by the viceroy of Egypt.

During the Reign of Terror, Dr. Guillotin's splendid little invention was erected on this spot, where it claimed thousands of lives—everybody from Louis XVI, who died bravely, to Mme du Barry, who went kicking and screaming all the way. Before the leering crowds, Marie Antoinette, Robespierre, Danton, Mlle Roland, and Charlotte Corday lost their heads here. (You can still lose your life on place de la Concorde—if you try to chance the frantic traffic and cross over.)

For a spectacular sight, look down the Champs-Elysées—the view is framed by Coustou's Marly horses, which once graced the gardens at Louis XIV's Château de Marly (these are copies; the originals are in the Louvre). On the opposite side, the gateway to the Tuileries is flanked by Coysevox's winged horses. On each side of the obelisk are two fountains with bronze-tailed mermaids and bare-breasted sea nymphs. Gray-beige statues ring the square, honoring the cities of France. To symbolize that city's fall to Germany in 1871, the statue of Strasbourg was covered with a black drape that wasn't lifted until the end of World War I. Two of the palaces on place de la Concorde are today the Ministry of the Marine and the deluxe Hôtel de Crillon. They were designed in the 1760s by Jacques-Ange Gabriel.

Musée Jacquemart-André. 158 bd. Haussmann, 8e. ☎ **01-42-89-04-91.** Admission 48 F ($7.70) adults, 37 F ($5.90) ages 7–17, free for children 6 and under. Daily 10am–6pm. Métro: Miromesnil or St-Philippe-du-Roule.

This is the best decorative-arts museum in Paris, though it's no place to take the kids (unless they're aspiring decorators). Give it at least 2 hours. The museum derives from the André family, prominent Protestants in the 19th century. The family's last scion, Edouard André, spent most of his life as an officer in the French army stationed abroad, returning later in his life to marry Nélie Jacquemart, a well-known portraitist of government figures and members of the aristocracy. Together they compiled a collection of rare French 18th-century decorative art and European paintings in an 1850s town house, which they continually upgraded and redecorated according to the fashions of their time.

In 1912 Mme André willed the house and its collections to the Institut de France, which paid for extensive renovations and enlargements that were completed in 1996. The collection's pride are works by Bellini, Carpaccio, and Uccelo, complemented by Houdon busts, Gobelin tapestries, Savonnerie carpets, della Robbia terra-cottas, an awesome collection of antiques, and works by Rembrandt (*The Pilgrim of Emmaus*), van Dyck, Rubens, Watteau, Fragonard, and Boucher. After a major restoration, one of their most outstanding exhibits is three mid-18th-century frescoes by Giambattista Tiepolo; this is the only museum in France with frescoes by the Venetian master. The works—one central fresco and two side panels—depict spectators on balconies viewing

Henri III's arrival in Venice in 1574. Take a break from all the gilded-age opulence with a cup of tea, a salad, or a tart in Mme André's dining room, with 18th-century tapestries.

Palais de l'Elysée. Rue du Faubourg St-Honoré, 8e. Métro: Miromesnil.

The "French White House" occupies a block along fashionable Faubourg St-Honoré and since 1873 has been occupied (officially, if not physically) by the president of France. You can admire the palace from the outside (from a point about a block away) but can't enter without an official invitation. Built in 1718 for the comte d'Evreux, it had many owners before it was purchased by the Republic. It was once owned by Mme de Pompadour. When she "had the supreme delicacy to die discreetly at the age of 43," she bequeathed it to the king. After her divorce from Napoléon, Joséphine lived here. A grand dining hall was built for Napoléon III, and an orangerie (now a winter garden) was constructed for the duchesse du Berry.

Place Vendôme. 8e. Métro: Opéra.

Always aristocratic and often royal, place Vendôme enjoyed its golden age during the Second Empire. Fashion designers—the great ones, such as Worth—introduced the crinoline here. Louis Napoléon lived here, wooing his future empress, Eugénie de Montijo, at the Hôtel du Rhin. In its halcyon days, Strauss waltzes echoed across the plaza. In time, however, they were replaced by cannon fire. The square is dominated by a column crowned by Napoléon. There was a statue of the Sun King here until the Revolution, when it was replaced briefly by *Liberty.*

Then came Napoléon, who ordered that a sort of Trajan's Column be erected in honor of his victory at Austerlitz. It was made of bronze melted from captured Russian and Austrian cannons. After Napoléon's downfall, the statue was replaced by one of Henri IV, everybody's favorite king and every woman's favorite man. Later Napoléon surmounted it again, this time in uniform and without the pose of a Caesar.

The Communards of 1871, who detested royalty and the false promises of emperors, pulled down the statue. Courbet is said to have led the raid. For his part in the drama, he was jailed and fined the cost of restoring the statue. He couldn't pay it, of course, and was forced into exile in Switzerland. Eventually, the statue of Napoléon, wrapped in a Roman toga, finally won out.

6 Montmartre: The 18th Arrondissement (Right Bank)

From the 1880s to just before World War I, Montmartre enjoyed its golden age as the world's best-known art colony, where *la vie de bohème* reigned supreme. Following World War I, the pseudoartists flocked here in droves, with camera-snapping tourists hot on their heels. The real artists had long gone to such places as Montparnasse.

Before its discovery and subsequent chic, Montmartre was a sleepy farming community, with windmills dotting the landscape. Those who find the trek up to Paris's highest elevations too much of a climb may prefer to ride **Le Petit Train de Montmartre,** a miniature train that passes all the major landmarks; it seats 55 passengers and offers English commentary. Board at place du Tertre (at the Église St-Pierre) or place Blanche (near the Moulin Rouge). From June to September, trains run daily from 10am to 10pm; off-season, daily from 10am to 6pm. For information, contact **Promotrain,** 131 rue de Clignancourt, 18e (☎ **01-42-62-24-00**).

The simplest way to reach Montmartre is to take the Métro to Anvers, then walk up rue du Steinkerque to the funicular, which runs to the precincts of Sacré-Coeur every day from 5:30am to 12:30am. Except for Sacré-Coeur (see below), Montmartre has only minor attractions; it's the historic architecture and the atmosphere that are compelling.

Specific attractions to look for include the **Bateau-Lavoir (Boat Warehouse),** place Emile-Goudeau. Although gutted by fire in 1970, it has been reconstructed. Picasso once lived here and, in the winter of 1905 to 1906, painted one of the world's most famous portraits, *The Third Rose* (Gertrude Stein).

Espace Montmartre Salvadore-Dalí, 11 rue Poulbot (☎ **01-42-64-40-10**), presents Dalí's phantasmagorical world with 330 original works, including his 1956 *Don Quixote* lithograph. It's open daily from 10am to 6pm, charging 40 F ($6.40) for adults and 25 F ($4) for children from 8 to 25 years. Free for children under 8.

One of the most famous churches here is the **Église St-Pierre,** rue du Mont-Cenis, originally a Benedictine abbey. The church was consecrated in 1147; two of the columns in the choir stall are the remains of a Roman temple. Among the sculptured works, note the nun with the head of a pig, a symbol of sensual vice. At the entrance are three bronze doors sculpted by Gismondi in 1980: The middle door depicts the life of St. Peter; the left is dedicated to St. Denis, first bishop of Paris; and the right is dedicated to the Holy Virgin.

Musée de Vieux Montmartre, 12 rue Cortot (☎ **01-46-06-61-11**), exhibits a wide collection of mementos. This 17th-century house was once occupied by Dufy, van Gogh, Renoir, and Suzanne Valadon and her son, Utrillo. It's open Tuesday through Sunday from 11am to 6pm. Admission is 25 F ($4) for adults and 20 F ($3.20) for students. Free for children 10 and under.

✪ **Basilique du Sacré-Coeur.** Place St-Pierre, 18e. ☎ **01-53-41-89-00.** Basilica, free; joint ticket to dome and crypt 30 F ($4.80) adults, 16 F ($2.55) students and children. Apr–Sept, daily 9am–7pm; Oct–Mar, daily 9am–6pm. Métro: Abbesses; then take the elevator to the surface and follow the signs to the funiculaire, which goes up to the church for the price of 1 Métro ticket.

Montmartre's crowning achievement is Sacré-Coeur, though the view of Paris from its precincts takes precedence over the basilica itself. Like other Parisian landmarks, it has always been the subject of much controversy. One Parisian called it "a lunatic's confectionery dream." Zola declared it "the basilica of the ridiculous." Sacré-Coeur's supporters included the Jewish poet Max Jacob and the artist Maurice Utrillo, who never tired of drawing and painting it. The two of them came here regularly to pray.

Its gleaming white domes and *campanile* (bell tower) tower over Paris like a Byzantine church of the 12th century. But it's not that old: After France's defeat by the Prussians in 1870, the basilica was planned as an offering to cure the country's misfortunes; rich and poor alike contributed the money to build it. Construction began in 1873, but the church wasn't consecrated until 1919. The interior of the basilica is brilliantly decorated with mosaics, the most striking of which are the ceiling depiction of Christ and the mural of the Passion found at the back of the altar. The crypt contains a relic of what some of the devout believe is a piece of the sacred heart of Christ—hence the church's name.

On a clear day the vista from the dome can extend for 35 miles. You can also walk around the inner dome of the church, peering down like a pigeon (a few will likely be there to keep you company).

Cimetière de Montmartre. 20 av. Rachel (west of the Butte Montmartre and north of bd. de Clichy), 18e. ☎ **01-43-87-64-24.** Sun–Fri 8am–6pm, Sat 8:30am–6pm (closes at 5:30pm in winter). Métro: La Fourche.

Novelist Alexandre Dumas and Russian dancer Vaslav Nijinsky are just a few of the scores of famous composers, writers, and artists interred here. The great Stendhal was

La Grande Arche de La Défense

Designed as the architectural centerpiece of the sprawling futuristic suburb of La Défense, this massive steel-and-masonry arch rises 35 stories. It was built with the blessing of the late François Mitterrand and ringed with soaring office buildings and a circular avenue (*périphérique*), patterned after the one surrounding the more famous Arc de Triomphe. This deliberately overscaled archway is one of the latest major landmarks to dot the Paris skyline, along with the Cité de la Musique in the city's northwestern section. High enough to shelter Notre-Dame below its canopy, the monument was designed as an extension of the panorama that connects the Louvre, Arc de Triomphe du Carrousel, Champs-Elysées, Arc de Triomphe, avenue de la Grande-Armée, and place du Porte-Maillot into a magnificent straight line. An elevator carries you to an observation platform from which you can see the carefully conceived geometry of the street plan.

Note that the netting you'll see has been placed there to catch any falling fragments of the arch. Watch your head.

The arch is located at 1 place du parvis de La Défense, outside the city limits, beyond the 17th arrondissement. To get here, take the RER to La Défense. Call ☎ 01-49-07-27-57 for information. It's open daily from 10am to 6pm. Admission is 53 F ($8.50) adults, 43 F ($6.90) children 6 to 18, free for children 5 and under.

---

buried here, as were Hector Berlioz, Heinrich Heine, Edgar Degas, Jacques Offenbach, and even François Truffaut. We like to pay our respects at the tomb of Alphonsine Plessis, the courtesan on whom Dumas based his Marguerite Gautier in *La Dame aux Camélias*. Émile Zola was interred here, but his corpse was exhumed and taken to the Panthéon in 1908. In the tragic year of 1871, the cemetery became the site of the mass burials of victims of the Siege and the Commune.

7 La Villette: The 19th Arrondissement (Right Bank)

Cité des Sciences et de l'Industrie. La Villette, 30 av. Corentin-Cariou, 19e. ☎ 01-40-05-80-00. Cité Pass (entrance to all exhibits), 50 F ($8), free for children 7 and under; Géode, 57 F ($9.10). Tues–Sun 10am–6pm. Métro: Porte-de-la-Villette.

In 1986, this opened as the world's most expensive ($642 million) science complex, designed to "modernize mentalities" as a first step in the process of modernizing society. The place is so vast, with so many options, that a single visit will give you only an idea of its scope. Some exhibits are couched in an overlay of Gallic humor, including seismographic activity as presented in the comic-strip adventures of a jungle explorer. The silver-skinned Géode (a geodesic dome) shows the closest thing to a 3-D cinema in Europe on the inner surfaces of its curved walls. It's a 112-foot sphere with a 370-seat theater. Explora, a permanent exhibit, is spread over the three upper levels; its displays revolve around four themes: the universe, life, matter, and communication. The Cité also has a multimedia library and a planetarium. An "inventorium" is for children.

At Cinaxe, sophisticated stereo systems and larger-than-normal screens combine to enhance the sensations of the scenes being presented in the film. The experience includes several 10-minute episodes, representing what you'd see, for example, in an airplane flying low over mountains or if you were positioned on the nose cone of a rocket.

The *Argonaut* is a submarine that was originally built in 1905 as part of a scientific experiment and is today a historic machine and a forerunner of the giant nuclear subs whose construction was partially based on ideas developed here. It was disarmed in

1982 and would have been demolished but for its purchase by the Musée de la Villette. Today, it's a somewhat nationalistic source of pride, although it's firmly mounted on concrete and is never submerged.

La Cité des Enfants is divided into two sections: one for ages 3 to 5, the other for ages 6 to 12. This is an adventure playground, with water sports, a butterfly greenhouse, robots, an ant farm, interactive TVs, and even a Techno Cité where kids are given an explanation of the workings of computers and other machines. There are also visual exhibits on such subjects as electricity.

The Cité is in **La Villette** park, Paris's largest city park, with 136 acres of greenery—twice the size of the Tuileries. Here you'll find a belvedere, a video workshop for children, and information about exhibitions and events, along with a cafe and restaurant.

Musée de la Musique. In the Cité de la Musique, 221 av. Jean-Jaurès, 19e. ☎ 01-44-84-44-84. Admission 35 F ($5.60) adults, 25 F ($4) students and seniors 60 and over, 10 F ($1.60) children 17 and under. Visits with commentary, 60 F ($9.60) adults, 45 F ($7.20) students and seniors 60 and over, 20 F ($3.20) children 17 and under. Tues–Thurs noon–6pm, Fri–Sat 10am–7:30pm, Sun 10am–6pm. Métro: Porte-de-Pantin.

Contained in the stone-and-glass Cité de la Musique, this museum serves as a tribute to the rich musical traditions of many ages and cultures. You can view 4,500 instruments, primarily from the 17th century to the present, as well as paintings, engravings, and sculptures that all relate to musical history. One especially appealing section of mandolins, lutes, and zithers evokes music from 400 years ago. It's all here: Cornets disguised as snakes, antique music boxes, and even a postwar electric guitar that Elvis might have collected. As part of the permanent collection, models of the world's great concert halls and interactive display areas give you a chance to hear and better understand the art and technology of musical heritage.

8 The Latin Quarter: The 5th Arrondissement (Left Bank)

This is the Left Bank precinct of the **University of Paris** (a.k.a. the **Sorbonne**), where students meet and fall in love over coffee and croissants. Rabelais called it the *Quartier Latin* because of the students and professors who spoke Latin in the classrooms and on the streets. The sector teems with belly dancers, exotic restaurants (from Vietnamese to Balkan), sidewalk cafes, bookstalls, and *caveaux* (basement nightclubs).

A good starting point is **place St-Michel** (Métro: Pont-St-Michel), where Balzac used to get water from the fountain when he was a youth. This center was the scene of much Resistance fighting in the summer of 1944. The quarter centers on **boulevard St-Michel** ("Boul Mich"), to the south.

La Sorbonne. Bd. St-Michel. Métro: St-Michel.

The University of Paris—everybody calls it the Sorbonne—is one of the most famous institutions in the world. Founded in the 13th century, it had become the most prestigious university in the West by the 14th century, drawing such professors as Thomas Aquinas. Reorganized by Napoléon in 1806, the Sorbonne is today the premier university of France. At first glance from place de la Sorbonne, it may seem architecturally undistinguished; it was rather indiscriminately reconstructed at the turn of the century. Not so the **Église de la Sorbonne,** however, built in 1635 by Le Mercier at the exact center of the Sorbonne. It contains the marble tomb of Cardinal Richelieu, a work by Girardon based on a Le Brun design. At his feet is the remarkable statue *Science in Tears.*

Will you have enough stories to tell your grandchildren

Yahoo! Travel

Musée National du Moyen Age (Musée de Cluny). 6 place Paul-Painlevé, 5e. ☎ **01-53-73-78-00.** Admission 30 F ($4.80) adults, 20 F ($3.20) ages 18–25, free for children 17 and under. Wed–Mon 9:15am–5:45pm. Métro: Cluny-Sorbonne.

There are two reasons to come here: The museum houses the world's finest collection of art from the Middle Ages, including jewelry and tapestries; and it's all displayed in a well-preserved manor house built atop Roman baths. In the cobblestone Cour d'Honneur you can admire the Flamboyant Gothic building with its clinging vines, turreted walls, gargoyles, and dormers with seashell motifs. Along with the Hôtel de Sens in the Marais, this is all that remains in Paris of domestic medieval architecture.

Originally, the Cluny was the mansion of a 15th-century abbot. By 1515 it was the residence of Mary Tudor, the teenage widow of Louis XII and the daughter of Henry VII of England and Elizabeth of York. Seized during the Revolution, it was rented in 1833 to Alexandre du Sommerard, who adorned it with medieval works of art. On his death in 1842, both the building and the collection were bought back by the government.

Most people come primarily to see the **Unicorn Tapestries,** the world's most outstanding tapestries. They were discovered only a century ago in the Château de Boussac in the Auvergne. Five seem to deal with the senses (one depicts a unicorn looking into a mirror held by a dour-faced maiden). The sixth shows a woman under an elaborate tent, her pet dog resting on an embroidered cushion beside her. The lovable unicorn and its friendly companion, a lion, hold back the flaps. The red and green background forms a rich carpet of spring flowers, fruit-laden trees, birds, rabbits, donkeys, dogs, goats, lambs, and monkeys.

Downstairs are the ruins of the Roman baths, dating from around A.D. 200. You wander through a display of Gallic and Roman sculptures and an interesting marble bathtub engraved with lions.

Panthéon. Place du Panthéon, 5e. ☎ **01-44-32-18-00.** Admission 35 F ($5.60) adults, 23 F ($3.70) ages 12–25, free for children 11 and under. Apr–Sept, daily 9:30am–6:30pm; Oct–Mar, daily 10am–6:15pm. (Last entrance 45 minutes before closing.) Métro: Cardinal-Lemoine or Maubert-Mutualité.

Some of the most famous men in the history of France (Victor Hugo, for one) are buried here in austere grandeur, on the crest of the mount of Ste-Geneviève. In 1744 Louis XV made a vow that if he recovered from a mysterious illness, he would build a church to replace the decayed Abbaye de Ste-Geneviève. He recovered—and Mme de Pompadour's brother hired Soufflot for the job. He designed the church in the form of a Greek cross, with a dome reminiscent of St. Paul's Cathedral in London. When Soufflot died, his pupil Rondelet carried out the work, completing the structure 9 years after his master's death.

Following the Revolution, the church was converted into a "Temple of Fame:" ultimately a pantheon for the great men of France. Mirabeau was buried here, though his remains were later removed. Likewise, Marat was only a temporary tenant. However, Voltaire's body was exhumed and placed here—and allowed to remain. In the 19th century the building changed roles so many times—first a church, then a pantheon, again a church—that it was hard to keep its function straight. After Victor Hugo was buried here it became a pantheon once more. Other notable men entombed within include Jean-Jacques Rousseau, Soufflot, Émile Zola, and Louis Braille.

In spring 1995, the ashes of scientist Marie Curie were entombed at the Panthéon, "the first lady so honored in our history for her own merits," in the words of the late François Mitterrand. Madame Curie had once been denied membership in the all-male Academy of Sciences. Another woman, Sophie Bertholet, was buried here first, but only alongside her chemist husband, Marcellin, and not as a personal honor to her.

The finest frescoes, the Puvis de Chavannes, are at the end of the left wall before you enter the crypt. One illustrates Ste. Geneviève bringing supplies to relieve the victims of the famine. The best depicts her white-draped head looking out over moonlit medieval Paris, the city whose patroness she became.

9 St-Germain-des-Prés: The 6th Arrondissement (Left Bank)

This was the postwar home of existentialism, associated with Jean-Paul Sartre, Simone de Beauvoir, Albert Camus, and the intellectual, bohemian crowd that gathered at the Café de Flore, the Brasserie Lipp, and Les Deux-Magots. Among them, the black-clad poet Juliette Greco was known as *la muse de St-Germain-des-Prés,* and to Sartre she was the woman with "millions of poems in her throat." Her long hair and uniform of black slacks, black turtleneck sweater, and sandals launched a fashion trend adopted by young women from Paris to California.

In the 1950s new names appeared—like Françoise Sagan, Gore Vidal, and James Baldwin—but by the 1960s the tourists had become just as firmly entrenched at the cafes. Today St-Germain-des-Prés retains a bohemian street life, full of interesting bookshops, art galleries, *caveaux* (basement) nightclubs, bistros, and coffeehouses.

Église St-Germain-des-Prés. 3 place St-Germain-des-Prés, 6e. ☎ **01-43-25-41-71.** Free admission. Daily 8am–8pm. Métro: St-Germain-des-Prés.

Outside it's a handsome early-17th-century town house; inside it's one of Paris's oldest churches, dating from the 6th century when a Benedictine abbey was founded on the site. Unfortunately, the marble columns in the triforium are all that remain from that period. Restoration of the Chapelle St-Symphorien—the site of a pantheon for Merovingian kings, at the entrance of the church—began in 1981. During that work, unknown Romanesque paintings were discovered on the chapel's triumphal arch. The Romanesque tower, topped by a 19th-century spire, is the most enduring landmark in the village of St-Germain-des-Prés. Its church bells, however, are hardly noticed by the patrons of Deux-Magots across the way.

The Normans nearly destroyed the abbey at least four times. The present building has a Romanesque nave and a Gothic choir with fine capitals. Among the people interred at the church are Descartes (well, his heart at least) and Jean-Casimir, the king of Poland who abdicated his throne.

When you leave the church, turn right onto rue de l'Abbaye and have a look at the 17th-century (and very pink) Palais Abbatial.

Église St-Sulpice. Rue St-Sulpice, 6e. ☎ **01-46-33-21-78.** Free admission. Daily 7:30am–7:30pm. Métro: St-Sulpice.

Pause first on the quiet rue St-Sulpice. The 1844 fountain by Visconti displays the sculpted likenesses of four bishops of the Louis XIV era: Fenelon, Massillon, Bossuet, and Flechier. Work on the church itself, at one time Paris's largest, began in 1646 as

Church Concerts

Église St-Germain-des-Prés stages the most wonderful concerts on the Left Bank, featuring fantastic acoustics and a marvelous medieval atmosphere. The church was built to accommodate an age without microphones, and the sound effects will thrill you. For more information, call ☎ **01-43-25-41-71.** Performances take place on Tuesday and Thursday; arrive about 45 minutes early if you'd like a front-row seat.

part of the Catholic revival then occurring in France. Although the body of the church was completed in 1745, work on the bell towers continued until 1780, when one was finished, the other left incomplete. One of the most notable treasures inside is Servandoni's rococo Chapelle de la Vierge (Chapel of the Madonna), which contains a Pigalle statue of the Virgin. The church houses one of the world's largest organs; it has 6,700 pipes and has been played by such musicians as Charles-Marie Widor and Marcel Dupré.

The main draw at St-Sulpice is the Delacroix frescoes in the Chapel of the Angels (the first on your right as you enter). Seek out his muscular Jacob wrestling (or is he dancing?) with an angel. On the ceiling, St. Michael has his own troubles with the devil, and yet another mural depicts Heliodorus being driven from the temple. Painted in the final years of his life, the frescoes were a high point in the baffling career of Delacroix.

10 The Eiffel Tower/Musée d'Orsay: The 7th Arrondissement (Left Bank)

From place du Trocadéro, you can step between the two curved wings of the Palais de Chaillot and gaze out on a panoramic view. At your feet lie the Jardins du Trocadéro, centered by fountains. Directly in front, pont d'Iéna spans the Seine, leading to the iron immensity of the **Eiffel Tower** (see section 1 of this chapter, "The Top Attractions"). And beyond, stretching as far as your eye can see, is the **Champ-de-Mars,** once a military parade ground but now a garden with arches, grottoes, lakes, and cascades. Also easily combined with these sights are the **Musée d'Orsay** and the **Musée Rodin** (see section 1 of this chapter, "The Top Attractions").

Hôtel des Invalides (Napoléon's Tomb). Place des Invalides, 7e. ☎ **01-44-42-37-72.** Admission to Musée de l'Armée, Napoléon's Tomb, and Musée des Plans-Reliefs (☎ **01-45-51-95-05**) 38 F ($6.10) adults, 28 F ($4.50) children 12–18, free for children 11 and under. Oct–Mar, daily 10am–5pm; Apr–May and Sept, daily 10am–6pm; June–Aug, daily 10am–7pm. Closed Jan 1, May 1, Nov 1, and Dec 25. Métro: Latour-Maubourg, Varenne, or Invalides.

The glory of the French military lives on in the Musée de l'Armée, the world's greatest army museum. It was the Sun King who decided to build the "hotel" to house soldiers who had been disabled by war. It wasn't entirely a benevolent gesture, since these veterans had been injured, crippled, or blinded while fighting Louis's battles. In 1670 this massive building program was launched. Eventually the structure was crowned by a Jules Hardouin-Mansart gilded dome.

The best way to approach the Invalides is by walking from the Right Bank across the turn-of-the-century pont Alexandre-III. Among the collections (begun by a French inspector in 1794) are Viking swords, Burgundian bacinets, 14th-century blunderbusses, Balkan khandjars, American Browning machine guns, war pitchforks, salamander-engraved Renaissance serpentines, musketoons, and grenadiers. As a sardonic touch, there's even General Daumesnil's wooden leg. Outstanding are the suits of armor—especially in the Arsenal—worn by kings and dignitaries, including Louis XIV. The famous "armor suit of the lion" was made for François I. The showcases of swords are among the finest in the world.

Crossing the Cour d'Honneur (Court of Honor), you'll come to Église du Dôme, designed by Hardouin-Mansart for Louis XIV. He began work on the church in 1677, though he died before its completion. The dome is Paris's second-tallest monument. In the Napoléon Chapel is the hearse used at the emperor's funeral on May 9, 1821.

⭐ **Frommer's Favorite Paris Experiences**

Strolling Along the Seine. Lovers still walk hand in hand alongside it, and vendors on its banks still peddle everything from postcards to 100-year-old pornography. Some energetic types walk the full 7-mile stretch of the river, but you may want to confine your stroll to central Paris, passing the Louvre, Notre-Dame, and pont Neuf.

Window Shopping Along the Faubourg St-Honoré. In the 1700s this was home to the wealthiest of Parisians; today it's home to the stores that cater to them. Even if you don't buy anything, you'll enjoy some great window shopping with all the big names, like Hermès, Larouche, Lacroix, Lanvin, Courrèges, Cardin, Saint Laurent, and Lagerfeld.

An Afternoon of Cafe-Sitting. The Parisian cafe is an integral part of the city's life. Even if it means skipping a museum, spend some time at a cafe. Whether you have one small coffee or the most expensive cognac in the house, nobody will hurry you, and you can see how the French really live. See our recommendations in chapter 3.

Taking Afternoon Tea à la Française. Skip London's cucumber-and-watercress sandwiches and get down to the business of rich, luscious desserts like Mont Blanc, that creamy purée of sweetened chestnuts. Try the grandest Parisian tea salon of them all: **Angelina,** 226 rue de Rivoli, 1er (see chapter 3). A close rival is the **Salon de Thé Bernardaud,** 11 rue Royale, 8e (☎ **01-42-66-22-55;** Métro: Concorde), run by the Limoges-based manufacturer of fine porcelain. Tea time here is unique: A staff member presents you with five porcelain patterns and you choose the one in which you'd like your tea served.

Attending an Opera or a Ballet. In 1989 the acoustically perfect Opéra Bastille was inaugurated to compete with the grande dame of Paris's musical scene, the

To accommodate the Tomb of Napoléon—made of red porphyry, with a green granite base—the architect Visconti had to redesign the high altar in 1842. First buried at St. Helena, Napoléon's remains were returned to Paris in 1840 and then locked inside six coffins. Legends abound that not all those parts were buried with Napoléon, notably his penis and his heart. According to Napoléonic scholars, the two doctors who dissected the emperor placed all his body parts in an urn positioned between his legs. Scholars deny the truth of these legends about the missing parts, though one wealthy gentleman in Connecticut frequently exhibits a penis preserved in alcohol, claiming that it was once attached to the emperor. Surrounding the tomb are a dozen Amazonlike figures representing his victories. Almost lampooning the small-ness of the man, everything is made awesome: You'd think a real giant was buried here, not a symbolic one. The statue of Napoléon in his coronation robes stands 8¹/₂ feet tall.

11 Montparnasse: The 14th Arrondissement (Left Bank)

For the Lost Generation, life centered on the literary cafes here. Hangouts like the Dôme, Coupole, Rotonde, and Sélect became legendary. Artists, especially U.S. expatriates, turned their backs on touristy Montmartre. Picasso, Modigliani, and Man Ray came this way, and Hemingway was a popular figure. So was Fitzgerald when he was

Opéra Garnier, which then was reserved for dance only and eventually closed for renovations. Now the Garnier has reopened, and opera has returned to its roco-co splendor. A night here will take you back to the Second Empire, beneath a ceiling by Chagall. Whether for a performance of Bizet or Tharp, check out these two major Paris landmarks. Dress with pomp and circumstance.

Discovering Hidden Montmartre. This is the most touristy part of Paris. But far removed from the area's top draw, Sacré-Coeur, another neighborhood unfolds—that of the true Montmartrois. Wander on any of the backstreets away from the souvenir shops. Arm yourself with a good map and seek out such streets as rue Lepic (refresh yourself at the Lux Bar at no. 12), rue Constance, rue Tholozé (with its view over the rooftops of Paris), lively rue des Abbesses, and rue Germain-Pilon. None of these is famous, none is crowded with hordes of visitors, but each is flanked with buildings whose detailing shows the pride and care that permeates Paris's architecture. You'll discover dozens of other streets on your own.

Checking Out the Marchés. A daily Parisian ritual is ambling through one of the open-air markets to purchase fresh food to be consumed that day—some ripe and properly creamy Camembert or a pumpkin-gold cantaloupe at its peak when consumed before sundown. You can partake of this tradition and gather supplies for a picnic in one of the city's parks. The vendors arrange their wares into a mosaic of vibrant colors. Sanguine, an Italian citrus whose juice is the color of an orange sunset; ruby-red peppers; golden yellow bananas from Martinique—all dazzle the eye. Our favorite market is on rue Montorgeuil, beginning at rue Rambuteau, 1er (Métro: Les-Halles). See "Shopping" later in this chapter for other markets to check out.

poor (when he was in the chips, he hung out at Le Ritz). Faulkner, Isadora Duncan, Miró, Joyce, Ford Madox Ford, and even Trotsky came here.

The life of Montparnasse still centers around its cafes and nightclubs, many only a shadow of what they used to be. Its heart is at the crossroads of boulevards Raspail and du Montparnasse, one of the settings of *The Sun Also Rises.* Rodin's controversial statue of Balzac swathed in a large cape stands guard over the prostitutes who cluster around the pedestal. Balzac seems to be the only one in Montparnasse who doesn't feel the impact of time and change.

Tour Montparnasse. ☎ 01-45-38-52-56. Admission 46 F ($7.35) adults, 38 F ($6.10) seniors, 35 F ($5.60) students, 30 F ($4.80) children 5–14, free for children 4 and under. Apr–Sept, daily 9:30am–11:30pm; Oct–Mar, Mon–Fri 9:30am–10:30pm. Métro: Montparnasse-Bienvenue.

Towering over the entire arrondissement is the Tour Montparnasse, rising 688 feet—like the Eiffel Tower, a landmark on the Paris skyline. Completed in 1973, it was immediately denounced by some critics as "bringing Manhattan to Paris." The city soon passed an ordinance outlawing any further structures of this size in the heart of Paris. Today, the tower houses a mammoth underground shopping mall and even a train station. You can ride an elevator up to the 56th floor, then climb three flights to the rooftop terrace. At viewing tables at the top you can pick out all the landmarks, from Sacré-Coeur and Notre-Dame to the new Défense area in the distance. A bar and restaurant are on the 56th floor.

Cimetière du Montparnasse. 3 bd. Edgar-Quinet, 14e. ☎ **01-44-10-86-50.** Mon–Fri 8am–6pm, Sun 9am–6pm (closes at 5:15pm Nov–Mar). Métro: Edgar-Quinet.

In the shadow of the Tour Montparnasse lies this burial ground of yesterday's celebrities, sadly debris-littered and badly maintained. A map (available to the left of the main gateway) will direct you to the most famous occupants: the shared grave site of Simone de Beauvoir and Jean-Paul Sartre. Others buried here include Samuel Beckett, Guy de Maupassant, Alfred Dreyfus, the auto tycoon André Citroën, Camille Saint-Saëns, and Man Ray.

12 Gare Montparnasse/Institut Pasteur: The 15th Arrondissement (Left Bank)

Musée Bourdelle. 18 rue Antoine-Bourdelle, 15e. ☎ **01-49-54-73-73.** Admission 20 F ($3.20) adults, 25 F ($4) students, 15 F ($2.40) children. Tues–Sun 10am–5:40pm. Métro: Falguière.

Here you can see works by the prime student of Rodin, Antoine Bourdelle (1861–1929). The museum displays the artist's drawings, paintings, and sculptures and lets you wander at will through his studio, garden, and house. The most notable exhibits are the 21 studies he did of Beethoven. The original plaster casts of some of his greatest works are also on display. Though some of the exhibits are badly captioned, you'll still feel the impact of Bourdelle's genius.

13 Parks, Gardens & Cemeteries

See section 2, "Musée de Louvre/Les Halles," for details on the **Tuileries. Cimetière du Montmartre** can be found in section 6, "Montmartre"; the **Cimetière de Montparnasse** is covered earlier in section 11, "Montparnasse."

✪ **Jardin du Luxembourg.** 6e. Métro: Odéon. RER: Luxembourg.

Hemingway told a friend that the Jardin du Luxembourg "kept us from starvation." He related that in his poverty-stricken days in Paris, he wheeled a baby carriage through the gardens because it was known "for the classiness of its pigeons." When the gendarme left to get a glass of wine, the writer would eye his victim, then lure it with corn and snatch it. "We got a little tired of pigeon that year," he confessed, "but they filled many a void."

Before it became a feeding ground for struggling artists in the 1920s, the Luxembourg Gardens knew greater days. They are the finest formal gardens on the Left Bank (some say in all of Paris). Marie de Médici, the much-neglected wife and later widow of the roving Henri IV, ordered the **Palais du Luxembourg** built on this site in 1612. She planned to live here with her "witch" friend, Leonora Galigaï. A Florentine by birth, the regent wanted to create another Pitti Palace, or so she ordered the architect, Salomon de Brosse. She wasn't entirely successful, although the overall effect is most often described as Italianate.

The queen didn't get to enjoy the Luxembourg Palace for very long after it was finished. She was forced into exile by her son, Louis XIII, after he discovered that she was plotting to overthrow him. She died in Cologne in poverty, quite a comedown from the luxury she'd known in the Luxembourg. (Incidentally, the 21 paintings she commissioned from Rubens that glorified her life were intended for her palace but are now in the Louvre.) For 50 F ($8) you can visit the palace the first Sunday of each month at 10:15am. However, you must call ☎ **01-44-61-20-89** to make a reservation. There is no information number for the park itself.

But the main draw here is not the palace but the gardens. For the most part, they're in the classic French style: well groomed and formally laid out, the trees planted in designs. The large central water basin is encircled by urns and statuary—one statue honors Ste. Geneviève, the patroness of Paris, depicted with pigtails reaching to her thighs. Come here to soak in the atmosphere, and bring the kids if you have any. You can sail a toy boat, ride a pony, or attend a Grand Guignol puppet show on occasion. Best of all, play boules with a group of elderly men who aren't afraid of looking like a French cliché from 1928, complete with black berets and Gauloises.

⭐ **Bois de Boulogne.** Porte-Dauphine, 16e. ☎ **01-40-67-90-82.** Métro: Les-Sablons, Porte-Maillot, or Porte-Dauphine.

This is one of the most spectacular parks in Europe. Horse-drawn carriages traverse it, or you can stroll its many hidden pathways. If you had a week to spare, you could spend it all in the Bois de Boulogne and still not see everything.

Porte-Dauphine is the main entrance, but you can take the Métro to Porte-Maillot as well. West of Paris, the park was once a forest kept for royal hunts. In the late 19th century it was very much in vogue: Carriages bearing elegant Parisian damsels with their foppish escorts rumbled along avenue Foch. Nowadays, it's more likely to attract middle-class picnickers.

When Napoléon III gave the grounds to the city in 1852, they were developed by Baron Haussmann. Separating Lac Inférieur from Lac Supérieur is the Carrefour des Cascades (you can stroll under its waterfall). The Lower Lake contains two islands connected by a footbridge. From the east bank, you can take a boat to these idyllic grounds, perhaps stopping at the café-restaurant on one of them. Restaurants in the Bois are numerous, elegant, and expensive. The Pré-Catelan contains a deluxe restaurant of the same name and a Shakespearean theater in a garden said to have been planted with trees mentioned in the bard's plays.

The **Jardin d'Acclimation,** at the northern edge of the Bois de Boulogne, is for children, with a small zoo, an amusement park, and a narrow-gauge railway. Two race-tracks, **Longchamp** and **Auteuil,** are also in the park. The annual Grand Prix is run in June at Longchamp (site of a medieval abbey). The most fashionable Parisians turn out, the women attired in their finest haute couture and hats to die for. To the north of Longchamp is the Grand Cascade, the artificial waterfall of the Bois de Boulogne.

In the 60-acre **Bagatelle Park,** the comte d'Artois (later Charles X), brother-in-law of Marie Antoinette, made a wager with her that he could erect a small palace in less than 3 months. He hired nearly 1,000 craftsmen and irritated the local populace by requisitioning all shipments of stone and plaster arriving through the west gates of Paris. He hired ébenistes, painters, and the Scottish landscape architect Thomas Blaikie—and he won his bet. If you're in Paris in late April, go to the Bagatelle to look at the tulips, if for no other reason. In late May one of the finest and best-known rose collections in all of Europe is in full bloom. If you can, visit also in September, when the light is less harsh than summer, or even in February when, stripped of much of its greenery, the park's true shape can be seen. *Note:* Beware of muggers and knife-carrying prostitutes at night.

Parc Monceau. 8e. ☎ **01-42-27-39-56.** Métro: Monceau or Villiers.

An American expatriate once said that all babies in Parc Monceau were respectable. Whether or not babies like the park, their mothers and nurses seem fond of wheeling their carriages through it. Much of the park is ringed with 18th- and 19th-century mansions, some evoking Proust's *Remembrance of Things Past.* The park was opened to the public during Napoléon III's Second Empire. It was built in 1778 by the

Royal Remains at St-Denis

In the 12th century, Abbot Suger placed an inscription on the bronze doors of St-Denis: "Marvel not at the gold and expense, but at the craftsmanship of the work." The first Gothic building in France that can be dated precisely, St-Denis was the "spiritual defender of the State" during the reign of Louis VI ("The Fat"). The massive facade, with its crenelated parapet on the top similar to the fortifications of a castle, has a rose window. The stained-glass windows, in stunning colors—mauve, purple, blue, and rose—were restored in the 19th century.

St-Denis, the first bishop of Paris, became the patron saint of the French monarchy. Royal burials began here in the sixth century and continued until the Revolution. The sculptures designed for tombs—some two stories high—span the country's artistic development from the Middle Ages to the Renaissance. The guided tour (in French only) takes you through the crypt. François I was entombed at St-Denis. His funeral statue is nude, although he demurely covers himself with his hand. Other kings and queens here include Louis XII and Anne of Brittany, as well as Henri II and Catherine de Médici. However, the Revolutionaries stormed through, smashing many marble faces and dumping royal remains in a lime-filled ditch in the garden. Royal remains were reburied under the main altar during the 19th century. The basilica stands today in a dreary northern suburb of Paris, but it's easily reached by the Métro. Free organ concerts are presented here on Sunday at 11:15am.

The Basilique St-Denis is located at Place de l'Hôtel-de-Ville, 2 rue de Strasbourg (☎ **01-48-09-83-54**). Admission is 32 F ($5.10) for adults and 21 F ($3.35) for seniors and students, free for visitors 11 and under. It's open daily from April through September, and Monday through Saturday during the rest of the year. The closest Métro is St-Denis Basilique.

duc d'Orléans, or Philippe-Egalité, as he became known. Carmontelle designed the park for the duke, who was at the time the richest man in France.

Parc Monceau was laid out with an Egyptian-style obelisk, a medieval dungeon, a thatched alpine farmhouse, a Chinese pagoda, a Roman temple, an enchanted grotto, various chinoiseries, and a waterfall. These fairy-tale touches have largely disappeared except for a pyramid and an oval *naumachie* fringed by a colonnade. Many of the former fantasies have been replaced by solid statuary and monuments, one honoring Chopin. In spring, the red tulips and magnolias alone are worth the airfare to Paris.

✪ **Cimetière du Père-Lachaise.** 16 rue de Repos, 20e. ☎ **01-43-70-70-33.** Mon–Fri 8am–6pm, Sat 8:30am–6pm, Sun 9am–6pm; Nov to early Mar closes 5:30pm. Métro: Père-Lachaise.

When it comes to name-dropping, this cemetery knows no peer—it's been called the "grandest address in Paris." Everybody from Sarah Bernhardt to Oscar Wilde (his tomb by Epstein) was buried here. So were Balzac, Delacroix, and Bizet. The body of Colette was taken here in 1954 (legend has it that cats replenish the red roses always found on her black granite slab), and in time, the "little sparrow," Edith Piaf, would follow. The lover of George Sand, the poet Alfred de Museet, was buried here under a weeping willow. Napoleon's marshals Ney and Masséna were entombed here, as were Chopin and Molière. Marcel Proust's black tombstone rarely lacks a tiny bunch of violets; alas, Proust wished to be buried with his friend/lover, the composer Maurice Ravel, but their families wouldn't allow it.

Some tombs are sentimental favorites: that of American rock star Jim Morrison reportedly draws the most visitors—and causes the most disruption. The great dancer Isadora Duncan came to rest in a "pigeonhole" in the Columbarium, where bodies have been cremated and then "filed." If you search hard enough, you can find the tombs of star-crossed Abélard and Héloïse, the ill-fated lovers of the 12th century. At Père-Lachaise, they've found peace at last. Other famous lovers also rest here: One stone is marked Gertrude Stein on one side, Alice B. Toklas on the other.

Spreading over more than 110 acres, Père-Lachaise was acquired by the city in 1804. Nineteenth-century French sculpture abounds, each family trying to outdo the others in ornamentation and cherubic ostentation. Some French socialists still pay tribute at the Mur des Fédérés, the anonymous gravesite of the Communards who were executed on May 28, 1871. The French who died in the Resistance or in Nazi concentration camps are also honored by several monuments.

Note: A free map is available at the newsstand across from the main entrance; it will help you find the well-known grave sites.

14 Paris Underground

Les Catacombs. 1 place Denfert-Rochereau, 14e. ☎ **01-43-22-47-63.** Admission 33 F ($5.30) adults, 22 F ($3.50) ages 7–25 and students, free for ages 6 and under. Tues–Fri 2–4pm, Sat–Sun 9–11am and 2–4pm. Métro: Denfert-Rochereau.

Every year an estimated 50,000 tourists explore some 1,000 yards of tunnel in these dank Catacombs to look at six million ghoulishly arranged skull-and-crossbones skeletons. First opened to the public in 1810, this "empire of the dead" is now illuminated with overhead electric lights throughout its entire length.

In the Middle Ages the Catacombs were originally quarries, but in 1785 city officials decided to use them as a burial ground. The bones of several million persons were moved here from their previous resting places, since the overcrowded cemeteries were considered health menaces. In 1830 the prefect of Paris closed the Catacombs to the viewing public, considering them obscene and indecent. He maintained that he could not understand the morbid curiosity of civilized people who wanted to gaze upon the bones of the dead. Later, in World War II, the Catacombs were the headquarters of the French Resistance.

The Sewers of Paris (Les Égouts). Pont de l'Alma, 7e. ☎ **01-53-68-27-81.** Admission 25 F ($4) adults, 20 F ($3.20) students and seniors over 60, 15 F ($2.40) ages 5–12, free for children 4 and under. May–Oct, Sat–Wed 11am–5pm; Nov–Apr, Sat–Wed 11am–4pm. Closed 3 weeks in Jan for maintenance. Métro: Alma-Marceau. RER: Pont de l'Alma.

Some sociologists assert that the sophistication of a society can be judged by the way it disposes of waste. If that's true, Paris receives good marks for its mostly invisible network of sewers. Victor Hugo is credited with making these sewers famous in *Les Misérables.* "All dripping with slime, his soul filled with a strange light," Jean Valjean makes his desperate flight through the sewers of Paris. Hugo also wrote, "Paris has beneath it another Paris, a Paris of sewers, which has its own streets, squares, lanes, arteries, and circulation."

In the early Middle Ages, drinking water was taken directly from the Seine, while wastewater was poured onto fields or thrown onto the then-unpaved streets, transforming the urban landscape into a sea of rather smelly mud.

Around 1200, the streets of Paris were paved with cobblestones, with open sewers running down the center of each. These open sewers helped spread the Black Death, which devastated the city. In 1370, a vaulted sewer was built in the rue Montmartre,

---

Memorial to a Princess

Place de l'Alma (Métro: Alma-Marceau) has been turned into a tribute to the late Diana, princess of Wales, who was killed in an auto accident August 31, 1997, in the nearby underpass. The bronze flame in the center is a replication of the flame in the Statue of Liberty and was a 1987 gift by the *International Herald Tribune* to honor Franco-American friendship. Many bouquets and messages are still placed around the flame, which seems to have come to represent the princess. Paris has also opened a nature garden for children in honor of Princess Diana in the Marais, at 21 rue des Blancs-Manteaux.

---

draining effluents directly into a tributary of the Seine. During the reign of Louis XIV improvements were made, but the state of waste disposal in Paris remained deplorable.

During the early 1800s, under the reign of Napoléon I, $18^1/_2$ miles of underground sewer were added beneath the Parisian landscape. By 1850, as the Industrial Revolution made the manufacture of iron pipe and steam-digging equipment more practical, Baron Haussmann developed a system that used separate underground channels for both drinking water and sewage. By 1878, it was 360 miles long. Beginning in 1894, under the guidance of Belgrand, the network was enlarged, and new laws required that discharge of all waste and storm water runoff be funneled into the sewers. Between 1914 and 1977, an additional 600 miles of sewers were added beneath the pavements of a burgeoning Paris.

Today, the city known for its gastronomy boasts some memorable statistics regarding its waste disposal: The network of sewers, one of the world's best, is 1,300 miles long. Within its cavities, it contains freshwater mains, compressed-air pipes, telephone cables, and pneumatic tubes. Every day, 1.2 million cubic meters of wastewater are collected and processed by a plant in the Parisian suburb of Achères. One of the largest in Europe, it's capable of treating more than two million cubic meters of sewage per day.

The *égouts* of the city, as well as telephone and telegraph pneumatic tubes, are constructed around four principal tunnels, one 18 feet wide and 15 feet high. It's like an underground city, with the street names clearly labeled. Further, each branch pipe bears the number of the building to which it is connected. These underground passages are truly mammoth, containing pipes bringing in drinking water and compressed air as well as telephone and telegraph lines.

Tours of the sewers begin at Pont de l'Alma on the Left Bank, where a stairway leads into the bowels of the city. However, you often have to wait in line as much as half an hour. Visiting times might change in bad weather, as a storm can make the sewers dangerous. The tour consists of a movie on sewer history, a visit to a small museum, and a short trip through the maze.

15 Shopping

Shopping is the local pastime of the Parisians; some would even say it reflects the city's very soul. The City of Light is one of the rare places in the world where you don't go anywhere in particular to shop—instead, shopping surrounds you on almost every street. Each walk you take immerses you in uniquely French styles. The windows, stores, people (and yes, even their dogs) brim with energy, creativity, and a sense of visual expression found in few other cities.

You don't have to buy anything to appreciate shopping in Paris—just soak up the art form the French have made of rampant consumerism. Peer in the *vitrines* (display windows), absorb cutting-edge ideas, witness new trends—and take home with you a whole new education in style.

BUSINESS HOURS

Shops are usually open Monday through Saturday from 10am to 7pm, but the hours vary greatly, and Paris doesn't run at full throttle on Monday mornings. Small shops sometimes take a 2-hour lunch break and may not open until after lunch on Mondays. Aside from Monday, while most stores open at 10am weekdays and Saturday, some stores prefer to open at 9:30am or even 11am. Thursday is the best day for late-night shopping, with stores open until 9 or 10pm.

Sunday shopping is currently limited to tourist areas and flea markets, though there's growing demand for full-scale Sunday hours, à la the United States and the United Kingdom. The big department stores are now open for the five Sundays before Christmas; otherwise, they're dead on *dimanche.*

The Carrousel du Louvre, an underground mall adjacent to the Louvre, is open and hopping on Sundays but closed on Mondays. The tourist shops that line rue de Rivoli across from the Louvre are all open on Sundays, as are the antiques villages, assorted flea markets, and several good food markets in the streets. The Virgin Megastore on the Champs-Elysées pays a fine in order to stay open on Sunday. It's *the* teen hangout.

GREAT SHOPPING AREAS

1er & 8e   These two *quartiers* adjoin each other and form the heart of Paris's best Right Bank shopping neighborhood. This area includes the famed **rue du Faubourg St-Honoré,** where the big designer houses are, and **avenue des Champs-Elysées,** where the mass-market and teen scenes are hot. At one end of the 1er is the **Palais Royal**—one of the city's best shopping secrets, where an arcade of boutiques flanks the garden of the former palace.

At the other side of town, at the end of the 8e, lies **avenue Montaigne,** 2 blocks of the fanciest shops in the world, where you simply float from big name to big name; in a few hours you can see everything from **Louis Vuitton** at no. 54 (☎ 01-45-62-47-00) to **Parfums Caron** at 34 (☎ 01-47-23-40-82), selling fabulous perfumes since 1904.

2e   Right behind the Palais Royal lies the **Garment District** (Sentier), as well as a few very upscale shopping secrets like **place des Victoires.** This area also hosts a few old-fashioned *passages,* alleys filled with tiny stores such as **Galerie Vivienne** on rue Vivienne.

3e & 4e   The difference between these two arrondissements gets fuzzy, especially around **place des Vosges,** center stage of the Marais. Even so, they offer several dramatically different shopping experiences.

On the surface, the shopping includes the real-people stretch of **rue de Rivoli** (which becomes **rue St-Antoine**). Two department stores are in this area: **La Samaritaine,** 19 rue de la Monnaie (☎ 01-40-41-20-20), occupies four architecturally noteworthy buildings erected between 1870 and 1927. **BHV** (Bazar de l'Hôtel de Ville), which opened in 1856, has seven floors loaded with merchandise; it lies adjacent to Paris's City Hall at 52–64 rue de Rivoli (☎ 01-42-74-90-00).

Meanwhile, hidden away in the Marais is a medieval warren of tiny, twisting streets chockablock with cutting-edge designers and up-to-the-minute fashions and trends. Start by walking around place des Vosges for art galleries, designer shops, and fabulous little finds, then dive in and get lost in the area leading to the Musée Picasso.

Finally, the 4e is also home of **place de la Bastille,** an up-and-coming area for artists and galleries where the newest entry on the retail scene, the **Viaduc des Arts** (which actually stretches into the 12e), is situated.

6e & 7e   Whereas the 6e is one of the most famous shopping districts in Paris—it's the soul of the Left Bank—much of the really good stuff is hidden in the zone that becomes the wealthy residential 7e. **Rue du Bac,** stretching from the 6e to the 7e in a few blocks, stands for all that wealth and glamour can buy. The street is jammed with art galleries, home-decorating stores, and gourmet-food shops.

9e   To add to the fun of shopping the Right Bank, 9e sneaks in behind 1er, so if you choose not to walk toward the Champs-Elysées and the 8e, you can instead head to the city's big department stores, built in a row along **boulevard Haussmann** in the 9e. Here you'll find not only the two big French icons, **Au Printemps** and **Galeries Lafayette,** but also a large branch of Britain's **Marks & Spencer.**

SHOPPING A TO Z

ANTIQUES   Directly across from the Louvre, ✪ **Le Louvre des Antiquaires,** 2 place du Palais-Royal, 1er (☎ **01-42-97-00-14;** Métro: Palais-Royal), is the largest repository of antiques in central Paris. More than 250 dealers display their wares on three floors. The place specializes in precious objets and small-scale furniture of the type that might have been favored by Mme de Pompadour. You may find 30 matching Baccarat crystal champagne flutes from the 1930s, a Sèvres tea service dated 1773, or a small signed Jean Fouquet pin of gold and diamonds. Too stuffy? No problem. There's always the 1940 Rolex with the aubergine crocodile strap.

Village St-Paul, 23–27 rue St-Paul, 4e (no phone; Métro: St-Paul), isn't an antiques center but a cluster of individual dealers in their own hole-in-the-wall hideout; the rest of the street, stretching from the river to the Marais, is lined with dealers, most of which are closed on Sundays. The Village St-Paul, however, *is* open on Sunday, and hopping. Inside the courtyards and alleys are every dreamer's visions of hidden Paris: many dealers in a courtyard selling furniture and other decorative items in French provincial and, to a much lesser extent, formal styles.

ART   ✪ **Galerie Adrien Maeght,** 42 rue du Bac, 7e (☎ **01-45-48-45-15;** Métro: Rue-du-Bac), is among the most famous names, selling contemporary art on a very fancy Left Bank street. In addition to major works of art, they sell posters beginning at 30 F ($5.10), signed and numbered lithographs from 500 F ($85), and books on art and artists.

The **Viaduc des Arts,** 9–147 av. Daumesnil (between rue de Lyon and av. Diderot), 12e (☎ **01-44-75-80-66;** Métro: Bastille, Ledru-Rollin, Reuilly-Diderot, or Gare-de-Lyon), occupies a long, 2-block stretch from the Bastille Opera to the Gare de Lyon, and features art galleries and artisans in individual boutiques created within the arches of an old train viaduct. As you can tell from the number of Métro stops that serve the address, you can start at one end and work your way to the other, or even start in the middle.

BOOKS   The most famous bookstore on the Left Bank was **Shakespeare and Company,** on rue de l'Odéon, home to the legendary Sylvia Beach, "mother confessor to the Lost Generation." Hemingway, Fitzgerald, and Gertrude Stein were all frequent patrons. Anaïs Nin, the diarist noted for her description of struggling American artists in 1930s Paris, also often stopped in. At one point she helped her companion, Henry Miller, publish *Tropic of Cancer,* a book so notorious in its day that returning Americans trying to slip a copy through Customs often had it confiscated as pornography.

(When times were hard, Nin herself wrote pornography for a dollar a page.) Long ago, the shop moved to 37 rue de la Bücherie, 5e (no telephone; Métro: St-Michel), where expatriates swap books and literary gossip.

Tea and Tattered Pages, 24 rue Mayet, 6e (☎ **01-40-65-94-35;** Métro: Duroc), is one of the largest stores in Paris specializing in used English-language books. Fiction titles on the street level seem to contain an inordinate number of mysteries and crime/suspense titles. Nonfiction, with both biography and some semi-antique travel guides, is arranged by subject in the cellar.

Scattered over two floors of tightly packed inventory, **The Village Voice Book-shop,** 6 rue Princesse, 6e (☎ **01-46-33-36-47;** Métro: Mabillon), specializes in new English-language books from English and American publishers, so it's a favorite among expat Yankees and Brits. The location is near some of the Left Bank gathering places described in Gertrude Stein's *The Autobiography of Alice B. Toklas.* Look for copies of that biography or crime/mystery title you left back home, or even copies of whatever Frommer's guides you might need to continue your journeys around Europe.

W. H. Smith France, 248 rue de Rivoli, 1er (☎ **01-44-77-88-99;** Métro: Concorde), is the French flagship of a chain of English-language bookstores and is France's largest store devoted to English and American books, magazines, and periodicals. You can get the *Times* of London and the Sunday *New York Times,* available every Monday afternoon. There's a fine selection of maps and travel guides, including titles by Frommer's.

CHILDREN'S CLOTHES, SHOES & TOYS   **Au Nain Bleu,** 406 rue St-Honoré, 8e (☎ **01-42-60-39-01;** Métro: Concorde), is the world's fanciest toy store. But don't panic; in addition to the expensive stuff, there are rows of penny candy–style cheaper toys in jars on the first floor.

Bonpoint, 15 rue Royale, 8e (☎ **01-47-42-52-63;** Métro: Concorde), is part of a well-known chain that helps parents transform their darlings into models of well-tailored conspicuous consumption. Though you'll find some garments for real life, the primary allure of the place lies in its tailored, traditional—and very expensive—garments designed by the "Coco Chanel of the children's garment industry," Marie-France Cohen, the company's resident designer. The shop sells clothes for boys and girls ages 1 day to 16 years.

The prices are a whole lot lower at **Dipaki,** 18 rue Vignon, 9e (☎ **01-42-66-24-74;** Métro: Madeleine), which carries selections for toddlers to 12-year-olds. Kids will love the fashions, which are wearable, washable, and affordable. It's only a short walk from place de la Madeleine.

Natalys, 92 av. des Champs-Elysées, 8e (☎ **01-43-59-17-65;** Métro: Franklin-D.-Roosevelt), is part of a French chain with about 15 stores in Paris and many elsewhere. It's an upscale mass-marketer of maternity clothes and garments for kids 1 day to 6 years old. The styles have just enough French panache without going over the top in design or price. There's also a wide inventory of strollers, cribs, bassinets, and car seats. You'll find the place midway between Planet Hollywood and the Lido.

CHINA & CRYSTAL   Purveyor to kings and presidents of France since 1764, ✪ **Baccarat,** 30 bis rue de Paradis, 10e (☎ **01-47-70-64-30;** Métro: Gare-de-l'Est), and 11 place de la Madeleine, 8e (☎ **01-42-65-36-26;** Métro: Madeleine), produces world-renowned full-lead crystal in dinnerware, jewelry, chandeliers, and even statuary. The rue Paradis address is the more historic of the two, while the Madeleine branch is more glamorous but less well stocked; prices are equivalent in both stores. The Madeleine showroom also stocks porcelain and crystal from other manufacturers like Christofle, but the rue Paradis shop carries Baccarat products only.

Lalique, 11 rue Royale, 8e (☎ **01-53-05-12-12;** Métro: Concorde), famous for its clear- and frosted-glass sculpture, Art Deco crystal, and unique perfume bottles, has recently branched out into sales of other types of merchandise—like silk scarves meant to compete with Hermès and leather belts with Lalique buckles.

And then there's ✪ **Limoges-Unic & Madronet,** at 34 and 58 rue de Paradis, 10e (☎ **01-47-70-54-49** or 01-47-70-61-49; Métro: Gare-de-l'Est). In two shops of more or less equal size, a 3-minute walk from each other on the same street, you'll find Limoges china brands and anything else you might need for the table—glass, crystal, and silver. It pays to drop into both stores before making a purchase, as their inventories vary slightly according to the season and the whims of the buyers. They'll ship your purchases, but doing so will severely cut into your savings.

CHOCOLATE   Some of Paris's most sinfully delicious chocolates can be found at **Christian Constant,** 37 rue d'Assas, 6e (☎ **01-53-63-15-15;** Métro: Saint-Placide). Particularly appealing are his combinations of chocolate meringue, chocolate mousse, and bitter chocolate known as *feuilles d'automne* (autumn leaves).

Racks and racks of chocolates are priced individually or by the kilo (2.2 pounds) at **La Maison du Chocolat,** 225 rue du Faubourg St-Honoré, 8e (☎ **01-42-27-39-44;** Métro: Ternes), though it'll cost you nearly or over 500 F ($85) for a kilo. Note the similarity to Hermès when it comes to the wrapping and ribbon (and prices). The chocolate pastries are affordable; the store even has its own chocolate milk! There are five other branches around Paris.

CRAFTS   One of the few regional handcrafts stores in Paris worth going out of your way to find, ✪ **La Tuile à Loup,** 35 rue Daubenton, 5e (☎ **01-47-07-28-90;** Métro: Censier-Daubenton), carries beautiful pottery and faïence from many regions of France. Look for figures of Breton folk on the faïence of Quimper as well as garlands of fruits, leaves, and flowers from the *terre vernissée* (varnished earth, a charming way to define stoneware) from Normandy, Savoy, Alsace, and Provence. Prices begin at 10 F ($1.80) for a sachet of Provençal lavender and climb as high as 4,000 F ($720) for a bulky but undeniably beautiful wall plaque.

DEPARTMENT & DIME STORES   After you've admired the superb architecture of one of Europe's most famous department stores, step inside ✪ **Au Printemps,** 64 bd. Haussmann, 9e (☎ **01-42-82-50-00;** Métro: Havre-Caumartin; RER: Auber), for a view of all it offers. Inside the main building is Printemps de la Mode, which occupies the bulk of the structure, and an affiliated housewares shop, Printemps de la Maison. Don't be fooled by the rows of fragrances in display cases near the entrance—upstairs are floors of wares of every conceivable sort, especially clothing. An affiliated store, under the same management but across the street, is **Brummel,** the menswear division. Directly behind the main store is a branch of **Prisunic,** Printemps's workaday but serviceable dime store, which contains a grocery. Be sure to check out the magnificent stained-glass dome, built in 1923, through which kaleidoscopic light cascades into the sixth-floor cafe. English-speaking interpreters are stationed throughout the store and at the Welcome Desk in the basement of the main building. *Note:* Foreign visitors who show their passport will receive a flat 10% discount.

A two-part department store, **Bon Marché,** 22 and 28 rue de Sèvres, 7e (☎ **01-44-39-80-00;** Métro: Sèvres-Babylone), is on the Left Bank in the midst of all the chic boutiques. Number 28 houses a gourmet grocery store; no. 22 is a source for all your general shopping needs.

✪ **Colette,** 213 rue St-Honoré, 1er (☎ **01-55-35-33-90;** Métro: Palais-Royal), is Paris's new store of the moment, a splendid and swank citadel for à la mode fashion that has made the elegant but staid rue St-Honoré less stuffy. For cutting-edge design, this is the place to go; you'll see fashions by young talents like Marni and Lucien Pellat-Fimet, home furnishings by such designers as Tom Dixon, and even zany Japanese accessories. We'll let you in on a secret: Even if you don't buy any of the merchandise, head for the tea salon downstairs, with its freshly made quiches, salads, and cakes.

At **Galeries Lafayette,** 40 bd. Haussmann, 9e (☎ **01-42-82-34-56;** Métro: Chaussée-d'Antin; RER: Auber), take a minute to stand under "The Dome"—a stained-glass cupola that towers above the arcaded store. Built in 1912, Galeries Lafayette is now divided into several stores: **Galfa** men's store, **Lafayette Sports,** and two other general-merchandise stores, both known simply as **"GL."** Next door is a branch of the dime store **Prisunic,** which the chain also owns. Above Prisunic is one of the fanciest grocery stores in town, **Gourmet Lafayette,** with prices half those at Fauchon.

FASHION: CUTTING-EDGE CHIC   Azzadine Alaïa, 7 rue de Moussy, 4e

(☎ **01-42-72-19-19;** Métro: Hôtel-de-Ville), showcases the collection of the darling of French fashion in the 1970s. Alaïa revived body consciousness and put the ooh-la-la in Paris chic; he specializes in tailored evening dresses. If you can't afford the current collection, try the stock shop around the corner at 18 rue de Verrerie (☎ **01-40-27-85-58**), where last year's leftovers are sold at serious discounts.

Jean-Charles de Castelbajac, 26 rue Madame, 6e (☎ **01-45-48-40-55;** Métro: St-Sulpice), is the bad boy of French fashion, known for flamboyant yet amusing gear in primary colors, often with big bold sayings scribbled across the clothes. His store is in a cluster of designer shops that's great for gawking.

Lolita Lempicka, 14 rue du Faubourg St-Honoré, 8e (☎ **01-49-24-94-01;** Métro: Concorde), formerly of the hidden Marais and the underground fashion scene, went mainstream in the mid-1990s when she established herself on what is arguably the most prestigious shopping street in France. Her style? Very, very feminine, with diaphanous evening dresses of silk mousseline, form-fitting tailored vests, and clingy skirts, many accented with touches of lace.

FASHION: DISCOUNT & RESALE   Anna Lowe, 104 rue du Faubourg St-Honoré,

8e (☎ **01-42-66-11-32;** Métro: Miromesnil), is one of the premier boutiques for the discriminating woman who wishes to purchase a little Chanel or perhaps a Versace . . . at a discount, *bien sur.* Many clothes are runway samples; some have been gently worn. It's next door to stores where the ready-to-wear is much more expensive.

Mendès, 5 rue d'Uzés, 2e (☎ **01-42-36-83-32;** Métro: Grands Boulevards), is open Monday to Saturday 10am to 6pm. In the center of the French garment district, this store mainly sells Yves Saint Laurent, Christian Lacroix, and Montana. Prices, though discounted, can be quite steep and you have to get lucky to find anything worth sighing over.

The inventory at **Réciproque,** 88–123 rue de la Pompe (between av. Victor-Hugo and av. Georges-Mandel), 16e (☎ **01-47-04-30-28;** Métro: Pompe), is scattered over five buildings on rue de la Pompe in a prosperous residential neighborhood. Everything it carries is used, clustered into sections devoted to Chanel, Versace, Lacroix, Mosquino, Hermès, and Mugler. Women will find gowns, business suits, sportswear, and shoes. Men should go to no. 101; the other buildings are for women's apparel. Although everything here has already been worn, in some cases that means only on runways or during photo shoots.

FASHION FLAGSHIPS   If you can't have the sun, the moon, and the stars, at least

buy something with Coco Chanel's initials on it, created in either drop-dead chic, classic Chanel, or in the rather interesting twist given by Karl Lagerfeld. The ✪ **Chanel** boutique is at 31 rue Cambon, 1er (☎ **01-42-86-28-00;** Métro:

Concorde or Tuileries), and 42 av. Montaigne, 8e (☎ **01-47-23-74-12;** Métro: Franklin-D.-Roosevelt).

During the decade (1947–57) that he directed his empire, **Christian Dior,** 11 rue François-1er, 8e (☎ **01-40-73-54-44;** Métro: Franklin-D.-Roosevelt), was the only couturier whose name was known throughout the Western Hemisphere. The house continues to thrive since its reorganization into a small-scale version of a department store. Departments are devoted to men's, women's, and children's clothing; gift items; makeup and perfume; and so on. Unlike some of the other big-name fashion houses, Dior is very approachable.

One of the most instantly recognizable accessories in France is a lavishly opulent silk scarf or tie from ✪ **Hermès,** 24 rue du Faubourg St-Honoré, 8e (☎ **01-40-17-47-17;** Métro: Concorde). You'll find them in abundance, along with virtually everything else (bags, purses, suitcases) endorsed by the legendary saddlemaker, at the flagship branch, which occupies the most prestigious shopping street in France. It also carries beach towels and accessories, dinner plates, clothing for men and women, a large collection of Hermès fragrances, and even a saddle shop.

✪ **Louis Vuitton,** 6 place St-Germain-des-Prés, 6e (☎ **01-45-49-62-32;** Métro: St-Germain-des-Prés), is the most interestingly decorated branch of Vuitton in Paris. Antiques and fine hardwoods evoke the grand age of travel, when steamships and railway cars hauled the affluent off to uncharted destinations. It stocks a wide inventory of purses, suitcases, and trunks with the traditional monogram, plus new lines of Vuitton leather goods crafted from beige-colored cowhide—without any monograms—whose patina darkens with age and the rigors of international travel. The store also sells writing instruments as well as a Carnet du Voyage, a do-it-yourself scrapbook graced with watercolors and space in which to jot down your own memories.

FOOD   At the place de la Madeleine stands one of the most popular sights in the city—not La Madeleine church but ✪ **Fauchon,** 26 place de la Madeleine, 8e (☎ **01-47-42-60-11;** Métro: Madeleine), which offers a wider choice of upscale gourmet products than anyplace else in the world. Distinct areas are devoted to candy, pastries, and bread; fresh fruits and veggies; dry and canned goods; fresh fish and meats; awe-inspiring take-away food that simply requires reheating before a grand dinner party; and wine. If you're hungry (and who wouldn't be after a promenade around Fauchon?), you won't have to resort to munching an apple or opening a package of cookies. There are five restaurants on the premises, ranging from the grand **(Le 30)** to the simple **(Brasserie Fauchon).**

Fauchon's main competitor, **Hédiard,** 21 place de la Madeleine, 8e (☎ **01-43-12-88-77;** Métro: Madeleine), opened in 1854. It was recently renovated and transformed into a series of salons filled with almost Disneyesque displays meant to give the store the look of a turn-of-the-century spice emporium. Upstairs is the solidly reliable **Restaurant de l'Epicerie.**

More intimate than its larger competitors, **Albert Ménès,** 41 bd. Malesherbes, 8e (☎ **01-42-66-95-63;** Métro: St-Augustin or Madeleine), serves the Parisian upper crust with jams, confiture, sugared almonds, teas, and assorted packed gourmet foodstuffs, many from small-scale producers from the provinces. Virtually everything can be shipped or, even better, packed for easy transport. A specialty food basket for the holidays (and saints days) is a status treat and can be made in virtually any price range.

Le Maison du Miel, The House of Honey, at 24 rue Vignon, 9e (☎ **01-47-42-26-70;** Métro: Madeleine, Havre-Caumartin, or Opéra), has been a family tradition since before World War I. The entire store is devoted to products made from honey: honey oil, honey soap, regional varieties of nougat, and certainly various honeys to eat. It's around the corner from Fauchon and worth the walk.

JEWELRY Well-dressed women around the world wear fabulous gemstones from ✪ **Van Cleef & Arpels,** 22 place Vendôme, 1er (☎ **01-53-45-45-45;** Métro: Opéra or Tuileries). One of the firm's distinctive specialties is yellow diamonds whose color resembles amber but whose fire is unmistakably brilliant. Floral motifs, cunningly set into platinum or gold with vibrant hues, are also a trademark.

LEATHER A cult hero in France yet virtually unknown elsewhere, **Didier Lamarthe,** 219 rue St-Honoré, 1er (☎ **01-42-96-09-90;** Métro: Tuileries), is famous for his handbags and small leather goods in funky fashion shades like melon or mint. Sure, he does more conservative colors like navy and black, but if you want the world to know you've been to Paris and that you're totally *branché* (plugged in), spring for one of the more risqué shades.

   Longchamp, 404 rue St-Honoré, 1er (☎ **01-43-16-00-12;** Métro: Concorde), is known for high-quality leather and strong everyday durables that come in basic as well as fashion shades. Except for a handful of men's accessories (briefcases, belts, and ties), most of the inventory is designed for women. Most of the leatherware comes in four colors: black, brown, navy blue, and "Longchamp green."

LINGERIE The undergarments sold and manufactured by **Cadolle,** 14 rue Cambon, 1er (☎ **01-42-60-94-94;** Métro: Concorde), are among the world's most comfortable and opulent. Herminie Cadolle invented the brassiere from premises nearby in 1889, and in 1911 she moved to this location near the former headquarters of Coco Chanel, whose "emaciated" styles she thoroughly disliked. Today the store is managed by her charming great-granddaughters. What's new here? The magic word is corsets, preferably in black, worn with long skirts or slacks and without blouses or jackets, that emphasize the curvaceous lines of full-figured women to their best advantage. Fashioned from everything from velvet to embroidered satins, they're almost guaranteed to turn heads day or night.

MALLS At **Carrousel du Louvre,** 99 rue de Rivoli, 1er (no phone; Métro: Palais-Royal-Musée-du-Louvre), you can combine a convenient location, a fun food court, handy boutiques, and plenty of museum gift shops with a touch of culture. Always mobbed with locals and visitors, this is one of the few venues allowed to stay open on Sundays. The easiest way to get here is to enter straight from rue de Rivoli. There's a Virgin Megastore, the Body Shop, and several big-name boutiques, like Courrèges and Lalique. Check out Diane Claire for the fanciest souvenirs of Paris you've ever seen. A branch of the French Government Tourist Office is next door to Virgin.

   Forget about the street address of **Forum des Halles,** 1–7 rue Pierre-Lescot, 1er (no phone; Métro: Etienne-Marcel or Châtelet-Les-Halles). This mall fills an entire city block where the great old produce market, Les Halles, once stood. Now it's a vast crater of modern metal with layers of boutiques built around a courtyard. There's one of everything here—but the feel is sterile, without a hint of the famous French joie de vivre. It's near the Centre Pompidou if you're in a rush and need access to a lot of stores in a hurry.

MARKETS Artists love to paint the **Marché aux Fleurs,** place Louis-Lépine, on Île de la Cité, 4e (Métro: Cité); photographers love to click away. The stalls are ablaze with color, each a showcase of flowers (most of which escaped the fate of being hauled to the perfume factories of Grasse in the French Riviera). The Flower Market is along the Seine, behind the Tribunal de Commerce. On Sundays, this is a bird market.

   Paris's most famous flea market is actually a grouping of more than a dozen flea markets. ✪ **Marché aux Puces de Clignancourt,** av. de la Porte de Clignancourt (Métro: Porte-de-Clignancourt; then turn left, cross bd. Ney, and walk north on av. de la Porte de Clignancourt), is a complex of 2,500 to 3,000 open stalls and shops in

St-Ouen, a congested suburb just north of the 18th arrondissement. It sells everything from antiques to junk, from new to vintage clothing.

The first clues showing you're here are the stalls of cheap clothing along avenue de la Porte de Clignancourt. As you proceed, various streets will tempt you. Hold off until you get to rue des Rosiers, then turn left. Vendors start bringing out their offerings around 9am and begin taking them in around 6pm. Hours are a tad flexible, depending on weather and crowds. Monday is traditionally the best day for bargain seekers, as there is smaller attendance at the market and a greater desire on the part of the merchants to sell.

First-timers at the flea market always ask two things: "Will I get any real bargains here?" and "Will I get fleeced?" It's all comparative. Obviously, the best buys have been skimmed by dealers (who often have a prearrangement to have items held for them). And it's true that the same merchandise displayed here will sell for less out in the provinces. But from the point of view of the visitor who has only a few days to spend in Paris—and only half a day for shopping—the flea market is worth the experience. Vintage French postcards, old buttons, and bistroware are quite affordable; each market has its own personality and an aura of Parisian glamour that can't be found elsewhere.

Most of the markets have toilets; some have a central office to arrange shipping. Cafes, pizza joints, and even a few real restaurants are scattered throughout. Beware of pickpockets and troublemakers.

Then there's the **Marché aux Puces de la Porte de Vanves,** av. Georges-Lafenestre, 14e (Métro: Porte-de-Vanves). More a giant yard sale than anything serious, this weekend event sprawls along two streets and is actually Paris's best flea market—dealers swear by it. There's little in terms of formal antiques and few large pieces of furniture. You'll do better if you collect old linens, used Hermès scarves, toys, costume jewelry, or perfume bottles. Asking prices tend to be high as dealers prefer to sell to nontourists. On Sundays, there's a food market one street over.

Marché Buci, rue de Buci, 6e (Métro: St-Germain-des-Prés), is a traditional French food market held at the intersection of two streets. It's only 1 block long, but what a block! Seasonal fruits and vegetables dance across tabletops while chickens spin in the rotisserie. One stall is devoted to big bunches of fresh flowers. Avoid Monday mornings, since very little is open then.

MUSIC The chain called **FNAC,** with a branch at 136 rue de Rennes, 6e (☎ **01-49-54-30-00;** Métro: St-Placide), is a mecca for anyone looking for computers, CDs, records and tapes, photography equipment, TVs, and stereo systems. It's known for its wide selection and competitive prices; recordings made by every artist of consequence in Europe and the Americas are readily available. The ticket service sells tickets for most of the entertainment venues and concerts in the city. There are eight other locations in Paris.

The showcase **Virgin Megastore,** 52–60 av. des Champs-Elysées, 8e (☎ **01-49-53-50-00;** Métro: Franklin-D.-Roosevelt), is one of the anchors that helped rejuvenate the Champs-Elysées. Built in a landmark building on the famed strip, it's Paris's largest music store. In addition to the music store, which carries every French and North American release imaginable, the building houses a bookstore and cafe. A ticket-buying service can reserve tickets to plays, concerts, and sporting events. Other branches are in the Carrousel du Louvre (see "Malls," above), at both airports, and in Gare Montparnasse.

PERFUME, COSMETICS & TOILETRIES Just about every working woman around place de la Madeleine shops at **Catherine,** 7 rue Castiglione, 1er (☎ **01-42-61-02-89;** Métro: Concorde). They appreciate its deep discounts and absolute lack of pretension. It resembles a high-volume pharmacy more than a chichi boutique; bottles and *flacons* of perfume move in and out of the expanded premises very fast. You get a 30% discount on most brands of makeup and perfume and a 20% discount on brands like Chanel and Dior.

Parfumerie de la Madeleine, 9 place de la Madeleine, 8e (☎ **01-42-66-52-20;** Métro: Madeleine), offers good discounts off suggested retail, but the amount varies with the brand—10% on Chanel but up to 30% on some others, such as Gucci. There are tons of fragrances and a few designer accessories (ties, belts, handbags, costume jewelry) in this chic shop that since 1995 has been linked to one of France's largest discount perfume chains. Prices are marked with the discount already applied, so it's hard to figure out how much you're actually saving.

Though you can buy its scents in any duty-free or discount parfumerie, we advise you to visit the source of some of the world's most famous perfumes: **Caron,** 34 av. Montaigne, 8e (☎ **01-47-23-40-82;** Métro: Franklin-D.-Roosevelt). Established in 1904, it gained a reputation as the choice of temptresses; the store is small but stylish, boasting old-fashioned glass beakers filled with fragrances. The *Scent of a Woman* that Al Pacino fell in love with was Caron's Fleurs de Rocaille.

A specialist in products for skin and hair, **Annick Goutal,** 14 rue de Castiglione, 1er (☎ **01-42-60-52-82;** Métro: Tuileries), or 12 place St-Sulpice, 6e (same phone; Métro: St-Sulpice), sells everything a person would need to stay young-looking—or at least try. You might want to pop in for herbalized and aromatized shampoos, liquid soaps, bubble bath, oils, and creams.

At the rear of a small courtyard, halfway between place de la Madeleine and the Champs-Elysées, is **Makeup Forever,** 5 rue de la Boetie, 8e (☎ **01-42-66-01-60;** Métro: St-Augustin). Established in the 1980s, its products were quickly endorsed by professional stylists; since then, its allure has only increased among retail clients. The company's purse-sized makeup case, at about 100 F ($18), as well as virtually anything with the brand name, has become a mini-status symbol for French yuppies and fashionable types.

At **Octée,** 12 rue des Quatre-Vents, 6e (☎ **01-46-33-18-77;** Métro: Odéon), the collection of fragrances is color-coded to your personality, skin type, and mood. Prices are surprisingly reasonable, with any scent priced at 185 F ($31.45) for a purse-sized vial. Though most of the scents were conceived for women, a limited number are meant for men, the most popular of which is Black Cedar.

SHOES   The collection of shoes at **Maud Frizon,** 83 rue des Sts-Pères, 6e (☎ **01-45-49-20-59;** Métro: Sèvres-Babylone), is among the city's sexiest and most inventive. Don't come here looking for sensible shoes to go with your tweeds. Footwear is likely to be available in shades like pink, orange, and green, as well as black and brown—in most cases, very, very feminine.

TABLEWARE & MORE   Much about the **Conran Shop,** 117 rue du Bac, 7e (☎ **01-42-84-10-01;** Métro: Sèvres-Babylone), might remind you of an outpost of the British Empire, valiantly imposing British aesthetics and standards on the French-speaking world. Inside, you'll find articles for the home, articles for the kitchen and dining room, glass and crystal vases, fountain pens and stationery, reading material and postcards, and even a selection of chocolates, teas, and coffees. It lies adjacent to the sprawling department-store racks of Bon Marché, at the top of a street known for its collection of charming shops.

Looking for the perfect table accessories to make your dinner party unique? **Geneviève Lethu,** 95 rue de Rennes, 6e (☎ **01-45-44-40-35;** Métro: St-Sulpice), a Provençal designer, has shops all over France, with several in Paris, all selling her clever and colorful designs that seem to reflect what happens when Pottery Barn style goes

French Mediterranean. Prices are moderate. Her goods, filled with energy, style, and charm, are also sold in the major department stores.

WINES **Les Caves Taillevent,** 199 rue du Faubourg St-Honoré, 8e (☎ **01-45-61-14-09**; Métro: Charles-de-Gaulle-Étoile), is a temple to the art of making fine French wine. Associated with one of Paris's grandest restaurants, Taillevent, which is nearby, it occupies the street level and cellar of an antique building in a neighborhood awash with memories of the French empire. Stored here are more than half a million bottles of wine—some at around 26 F ($4.40); others, rare vintages at 20,000 F ($3,400).

16 Paris After Dark

THE PERFORMING ARTS

Announcements of shows, concerts, and operas are plastered on kiosks all over town. You can find listings of what's playing in *Pariscope,* a weekly entertainment guide, or the English-language *Boulevard,* a bimonthly magazine. Performances start later in Paris than in London or New York City—anywhere from 8 to 9pm—and Parisians tend to dine after the theater. (But you may not want to follow suit, since many of the less expensive restaurants close as early as 9pm.)

There are many ticket agencies in Paris, but most are found near the Right Bank hotels. *Avoid them if possible.* You can buy the cheapest tickets at the theater box office. Remember to tip the usher who shows you to your seat in a theater or movie house 3 F (50¢).

For information on and tickets to just about any show and entertainment in Paris (also Dijon, Lyon, and Nice), **Edwards & Edwards** has a New York office if you'd like to make arrangements before you go. It's at 1270 Ave. of the Americas, Suite 2414, New York, NY 10020 (☎ **800/223-6108** or 914/328-2150). It also has an office in Paris at 19 rue des Mathurins, 9e (☎ **01-42-65-39-21**; Métro: Havre-Caumartin). A personal visit isn't necessary; Edwards & Edwards will mail tickets to your home, fax confirmation, or leave tickets at the box office in Paris. There's a markup of 20% (excluding opera and ballet) over box-office price, plus a U.S. handling charge of $8. Hotel and theater packages are also available.

Several agencies sell tickets for cultural events and plays at discounts of up to 50%. One is the **Kiosque Théâtre,** 15 place de la Madeleine, 8e (no phone; Métro: Madeleine), offering leftover tickets for about half price on the day of performance. Tickets for evening performances are sold Tuesday through Friday from 12:30 to 8pm and Saturday from 2 to 8pm. If you'd like to attend a matinee, buy your ticket Saturday 12:30 to 2pm or Sunday from 12:30 to 4pm.

For easy access to tickets for festivals, concerts, and the theater, try one of two locations of the **FNAC** department-store chain: 136 rue de Rennes, 6e (☎ **01-49-54-30-00**; Métro: Montparnasse-Bienvenue), or in the Forum des Halles, 1–7 rue Pierre-Lescot, 1er (☎ **01-40-41-40-00**; Métro: Châtelet-Les-Halles).

THE TOP VENUES

The ✪ **Opéra Garnier,** place de l'Opéra, 9e (☎ **01-40-01-17-89**; Métro: Opéra), is the premier stage for dance and once again for opera. Because of the competition from the Opéra Bastille, the original opera has made great efforts to present more up-to-date works, including choreography by Jerome Robbins, Twyla Tharp, and George Balanchine. This rococo wonder was designed as a contest entry by the young architect Charles Garnier in the heyday of the empire. The facade is adorned with marble

and sculpture, including *The Dance* by Carpeaux. The world's great orchestral, oper-
atic, and ballet companies have performed here. Months of painstaking restorations
have returned the Garnier to its former glory: Its boxes and walls are once again lined
with flowing red and blue damask, the gilt gleams, the ceiling (painted by Marc
Chagall) has been cleaned, and an air-conditioning system has been added. The box
office is open Monday through Saturday from 11am to 6:30pm.

The controversial building known as the ✪ **Opéra Bastille,** place de la Bastille,
120 rue de Lyon (☎ **01-43-43-96-96;** Métro: Bastille), was designed by the Canadian
architect Carlos Ott, with curtains created by fashion designer Issey Miyake. The
showplace was inaugurated in July 1989 (for the Revolution's bicentennial), and on
March 17, 1990, the curtain rose on Hector Berlioz's *Les Troyens.* Since its much-
publicized opening, the opera house has presented masterworks like Mozart's *Marriage
of Figaro* and Tchaikovsky's *Queen of Spades.* The main hall is the largest of any French
opera house, with 2,700 seats, but music critics have lambasted the acoustics. The
building contains two additional concert halls, including an intimate room with only
250 seats, usually used for chamber music. Both traditional opera performances and
symphony concerts are presented here. There are sometimes free concerts on French
holidays; call before your visit.

For the best orchestra performances in France, try **Maison de Radio France,** 116 av.
du Président-Kennedy, 16e (☎ **01-42-30-15-16;** Métro: Passy-Ranelagh), which
offers top-notch concerts with guest conductors. It's the home of the Orchestre Philharmonique de Radio France and the Orchestre National de France. The box office is
open Monday through Saturday from 11am to 6pm.

The Art Deco **Théâtre des Champs-Elysées,** 15 av. Montaigne, 8e (☎ **01-49-
52-50-50;** Métro: Alma-Marceau), which attracts the haute-couture crowd, hosts
both national and international orchestras as well as opera and ballet. The box office
is open Monday through Saturday from 11am to 7pm. Events are held year-round,
except in August.

Théâtre du Châtelet (Théâtre Musical de Paris), 1 place du Châtelet, 1er
(☎ **01-40-28-28-40;** Métro: Châtelet), occupies a neoclassical building near the
Hôtel de Ville. Built in 1862 on the site of an ancient Roman stadium, it's largely
subsidized by the government of Paris and known for its superb acoustics. Opera, classical music, and occasional dance recitals are performed here year-round, except in
July and August. *A warning:* the least expensive seats here are, even in the words of
its administrators, "very, very bad." We recommend you pay a little extra to have far
superior views. The theatre, which is maintained by the City of Paris, was completely
renovated, to much public acclaim, in 1999.

Designed as part of the architectural complex facing the Eiffel Tower, **Théâtre
National de Chaillot,** 1 place du Trocadéro, 16e (☎ **01-53-65-30-00;** Métro:
Trocadéro), is one of the city's largest concert halls, hosting a variety of cultural events
from dance to drama that are announced on billboards out front. The box office is
open Monday through Saturday from 11am to 7pm and Sunday from 11am to 5pm.

Conceived by the Mitterrand administration, **Cité de la Musique,** 221 av. Jean-
Jaurès, 19e (☎ **01-44-84-45-00,** or 01-44-84-44-84 for tickets and information;
Métro: Porte-de-Pantin), has been widely applauded. At the city's northeastern edge
in what used to be a run-down and depressing neighborhood, the $120-million stone-
and-glass structure, designed by the noted architect Christian de Portzamparc, incorporates a network of concert halls, a library/research center for the study of music
from around the world, and a museum. The complex hosts a rich variety of concerts,
ranging from Renaissance to 20th-century programs.

Even those with only a modest understanding of French can still delight in a sparkling production of Molière at the **Comédie-Française,** 2 rue de Richelieu, 1er (☎ **01-44-58-15-15;** Métro: Palais-Royal-Musée-du-Louvre), established to keep the classics alive and promote important contemporary authors. The box office is open daily from 11am to 6pm, but the hall is dark from July 21 to September 5. In 1993 a Left Bank annex was launched, the **Comédie-Française-Théâtre du Vieux-Colombier,** 21 rue du Vieux-Colombier, 4e (☎ **01-44-39-87-00**). Although its repertoire can vary, it's known for presenting some of the most serious French dramas in town.

Charles Aznavour and other big names make frequent appearances in the cavernous **Olympia,** 28 bd. des Capucines, 9e (☎ **01-47-42-25-49;** Métro: Opéra or Madeleine). Yves Montand appeared once—and the performance was sold out 4 months in advance. Today you're more likely to catch Gloria Estefan. A typical lineup might include an English rock group, showy Italian acrobats, a well-known French singer, a dance troupe, an American juggler/comedy team (doing much of their work in English), plus the featured star. A witty emcee and an onstage band provide smooth transitions between acts.

CHANSONNIERS

The *chansonniers* (literally songwriters) provide a bombastic musical satire of the day's events. This combination of parody and burlesque is a time-honored Gallic amusement and a Parisian institution. Songs are often created on the spot, inspired by the "disaster of the day." You'll need to speak French to understand most of the humor.

Au Caveau de la Bolée. 25 rue de l'Hirondelle, 6e. ☎ **01-43-54-62-20.** Fixed-price dinner 260 F ($41.60) Mon–Fri, 300 F ($48) Sat. Cover 150 F ($24) Mon–Sat if you don't order dinner. Métro: St-Michel.

To enter this bawdy boîte, you descend into the catacombs of the early 14th-century Abbey of St-André, once a famous literary cafe that attracted Verlaine and Oscar Wilde, who downed (or drowned in) glass after glass of absinthe here. The singing is loud and bawdy, just the way the young student regulars like it. Occasionally the audience sings along. You'll enjoy this place a lot more if your French is pretty good, but even if it's not, there are enough visuals (magic acts and performances by singers) to amuse. A fixed-price dinner, served Monday through Saturday at 8:30pm, is followed by at least four entertainers, usually comedians. The cabaret starts at 10:30pm, and in lieu of paying admission, you can order dinner. If you've already eaten, you can just order a drink.

✪ **Au Lapin Agile.** 22 rue des Saules, 18e. ☎ **01-46-06-85-87.** Cover (including the first drink) 130 F ($20.80). Tues–Sun 9:15pm–2am. Métro: Lamarck.

Picasso and Utrillo once patronized this little cottage near the top of Montmartre, formerly known as the Café des Assassins. It has been painted by numerous artists, including Utrillo, and was used as a setting for a Steve Martin play. For many decades it has been the heartbeat of French folk music. You'll sit at carved wooden tables in a dimly lit room with walls covered by bohemian memorabilia, listening to French folk tunes, love ballads, army songs, sea chanteys, and music-hall ditties. You're encouraged to sing along, even if it's only the "oui, oui, oui—non, non, non" refrain of "Les Chevaliers de la Table Ronde." The best sing-alongs are on weeknights after tourist season ends.

NIGHTCLUBS & CABARETS

These places are all outrageously expensive, but they provide some of the most lavish, spectacular floor shows anywhere.

Chez Michou. 80 rue des Martyrs, 18e. ☎ **01-46-06-16-04.** Reservations required for dinner. Dinner and show (including aperitif, wine, and coffee) 590 F ($94.40); show only (at bar) 220 F ($35.20). Métro: Pigalle.

The setting is blue, the emcee wears blue, and the spotlights shining on the stage bathe the cross-dressing performers in a celestial blue light. The creative force behind all this is Michou, veteran impresario whose 20-odd belles bear names like Hortensia and DuDuche, and lip-synch their way through revivals of songs by Whitney Houston, Diana Ross, and Tina Turner and such French luminaries as Mireille Mathieu, Sylvie Vartan, "Dorothée," and the immortal Brigitte Bardot.

✪ **Crazy Horse Saloon.** 12 av. George-V, 8e. ☎ **01-47-23-32-32.** Cover (including 2 drinks) 450–560 F ($72–$89.60); dinner spectacle 660 F ($105.60). Métro: George-V or Alma-Marceau.

This sophisticated strip joint has thrived for decades thanks to good choreography and a sly, flirty theme that celebrates and exalts the female form. Each of the numbers features gorgeous girls, girls, girls, all outfitted in outrageous costumes. If you opt for dinner as part of the show, it will be a tasteful, well-prepared event served with flair at Chez Francis, a restaurant under separate management a few steps from the cabaret itself. Shows last for 1³/₄ hours each, and are attended by menfolk, and to a lesser extent, women, from around Europe and the world.

Folies-Bergère. 32 rue Richer, 9e. ☎ **01-44-79-98-98.** Cover 160–350 F ($25.60–$56); dinner and show 370–550 F ($59.20–$88). Métro: Rue-Montmartre or Cadet.

The Folies-Bergère is a Paris institution; foreigners have been flocking here for excitement since 1886. Josephine Baker, the legendary African-American singer who used to throw bananas into the audience, became "the toast of Paris" here. According to legend, the first G.I. to reach Paris at the 1944 Liberation asked for directions to the club.

Don't expect the naughty and slyly permissive skin-and-glitter revue that used to be the trademark of this place. In 1993, that all ended with a radical restoration of the theater and a reopening under new management. The site now functions as a conventional 1,600-seat theater, presenting musical revues filled with a sense of nostalgia for old Paris. You're likely to witness an intriguing, often charming, but not particularly erotic repertoire of songs, mostly in French but sometimes in English, interspersed with the banter of an emcee. A restaurant serves bland fixed-price dinners in an anteroom to the theater. The experience probably isn't worth the staggering cost, but for many a first-timer, a visit to Paris without going to the Folies-Bergère would be no visit at all.

✪ **Lido de Paris.** 116 bis av. des Champs-Elysées, 8e. ☎ **800/227-4884** in the U.S., or 01-40-76-56-10. Shows at 10pm and midnight. Cover 460–560 F ($73.60–$89.60); 8pm dinner dance and 10pm show 815–1,015 F ($130.40–$162.40). Prices include a half bottle of champagne. Métro: George-V.

As it moves into the millennium, the Lido has changed its feathers and modernized its shows; today it competes with the best Las Vegas has to offer. Its $15-million current production, *C'est Magique,* reflects a dramatic reworking of the classic Parisian cabaret show, with eye-popping special effects, water technology using more than 60,000 gallons per minute, and bold new themes, even aerial and aquatic ballet. The show, the most expensive ever produced in Europe, uses 70 performers, $4 million in costumes, and a $2-million lighting design with lasers. There's even an ice rink and swimming pool that magically appear and disappear. The 45 Bluebell Girls, those legendary sensual showgirls, are still here, however. Now that celebrated chef Paul Bocuse is the consultant for the culinary offerings, the cuisine is better than ever.

Moulin Rouge. Place Blanche, 18e. ☎ **01-53-09-82-82.** Cover including champagne 500–560 F ($80–$89.60), dinner and show 790 F ($126.40). For seats at the bar, cover 370 F ($59.20) includes 2 drinks. Dinner nightly at 7pm. Revues presented nightly at 9 and 11pm. Métro: Blanche.

The establishment that Toulouse-Lautrec immortalized in his paintings is still here, but the artist would probably have a hard time recognizing it today. Colette created a scandal here by offering an on-stage kiss to Mme de Morny, but shows today have a hard time shocking 1990s audiences. Try to get a table, as the view is much better on the main floor than from the bar. What's the theme? The strip routines and saucy sexiness of *la belle époque,* and of permissive, promiscuous Paris between the world wars. Handsome men and girls, girls, girls, virtually all of them topless, keep the place going. Dance finales usually include two dozen of the belles ripping loose with a topless can-can.

Villa d'Este. 4 rue Arsène-Houssaye, 8e. ☎ **01-42-56-14-65.** Cover (including first drink) 190 F ($30.40); dinner (including wine) and show 340–750 F ($54.40–$120). Métro: Charles-de-Gaulle-Étoile.

In the past this club booked Amalia Rodrigues, Portugal's leading fadista, and the French chanteuse Juliette Greco. Today you're more likely to hear the French singer François de Guelte or other top talent from Europe and America. Villa d'Este has been around for a long time, and the quality of its offerings remains high. You'll probably hear some of the greatest hits of such beloved French performers as Piaf, Aznavour, Brassens, and Brel.

LE COOL JAZZ

The great jazz revival that long ago swept America is still going strong here, with Dixieland or Chicago rhythms being pounded out in dozens of jazz cellars, mostly called *caveaux.* Most clubs are crowded on the Left Bank near the Seine, between rue Bonaparte and rue St-Jacques.

For the latest details, see *Jazz Hot, Jazz Magazine,* or *Pariscope.*

Au Duc des Lombards. 42 rue des Lombards, 1er. ☎ **01-42-33-22-88.** Cover 80–120 F ($12.80–$19.20). Nightly 9pm–3am. Métro: Châtelet.

Popular, comfortable, and appealing, this jazz club replaced an earlier club and has thrived in a low-key way ever since. Artists begin playing at 9pm and continue (with breaks) for 5 hours, touching on repertoires that include everything from "free jazz" to more traditional forms such as "hard bop." Unlike at many of its competitors, tables can be reserved here, and will usually be held until 10:30pm.

Baiser Salé. 58 rue des Lombards, 1er. ☎ **01-42-33-37-71.** Cover 50–100 F ($8–$16) Wed–Sun, free Mon–Tues. Nightly 6pm–6am. Métro: Châtelet.

Set within a cellar lined with jazz-related paintings, with a large central bar and an ongoing roster of videos that show great jazz moments (Charlie Parker, Miles Davis) of the past, this is an appealing and musically varied jazz club. Everything is very, very mellow and laid-back, with an emphasis on the music. Genres include Afro-Caribbean, Afro-Latino, salsa, merengue, rhythm and blues, and less frequently, fusion. Music is presented nightly from 10:30pm till 3am.

✪ **Le Bilboquet/Club St-Germain.** 13 rue St-Benoît, 6e. ☎ **01-45-48-81-84.** No cover. Métro: St-Germain-des-Prés.

This restaurant/jazz club/piano bar offers some of the best music in Paris. The film *Paris Blues* was shot here. Jazz is played on the upper level in the restaurant,

Le Bilboquet, a wood-paneled room with a copper ceiling, brass-trimmed sunken bar, and Victorian candelabra. The menu is limited but classic French, and a dinner will run you 180 F to 300 F ($28.80 to $48). Under separate management is the downstairs disco, Club St-Germain, which charges no cover (but drinks cost a staggering 100 F [$16]). You can walk from one club to the other but have to buy a new drink each time you change venues.

New Morning. 7–9 rue des Petites-Ecuries, 10e. ☎ **01-45-23-51-41.** Cover 100–180 F ($16–$28.80). Métro: Château-d'Eau.

Jazz maniacs come here to drink, talk, and dance at this enduring club. It's sometimes a scene, attracting such guests as Spike Lee and TAFKAP (The Artist Formerly Known As Prince). The place is especially popular with jazz groups from Central and South Africa.

Slow Club. 130 rue de Rivoli, 1er. ☎ **01-42-33-84-30.** Cover 80–100 F ($12.80–$16). Tues–Thurs 10pm–3am, Fri–Sat 10pm–4am. Métro: Châtelet.

One of the most famous jazz cellars in Europe, capped with medieval ceiling vaults that reverberate the music in an evocative way, this venue hosts a revolving set of jazz artists who tend to focus on New Orleans–style jazz. The hip folks who flock here tend to be in their 30s and early 40s.

DANCE CLUBS

The area around the Église St-Germain-des-Prés is full of dance clubs. They come and go so quickly that last year's Disco Inferno could be a hardware store by the time you get there—but new ones will spring up to take the place of the old. For the most up-to-date information, see *Time Out, Pariscope,* or *L'Officiel des Spectacles.*

La Balajo. 9 rue de Lappe, 11e. ☎ **01-47-00-07-87.** Cover (including first drink) 100 F ($16) Thurs–Sat evenings, 50 F ($8) Sun afternoon. Métro: Bastille.

Established in 1936, this dance club is best remembered as the place where Edith Piaf first won the hearts of thousands of Parisian music lovers. Today Le Balajo is hardly as fashionable, though it continues its big-band traditions on Sunday afternoons, when a crowd mostly aged 45 and up dances to an eclectic mix of World War II-era swing and bebop. Thursday to Saturday nights, the focus is on disco and, to a lesser degree, reggae, salsa, rock, and rap.

La Java. 105 rue du Faubourg du Temple, 11e. ☎ **01-42-02-20-52.** Cover 80 F ($12.80) Thurs, 100 F ($16) Fri–Sat, 40 F ($6.40) Sun. Métro: Belleville.

Once this bal-musette dance hall was one of the most frequented in Paris; Piaf and Maurice Chevalier made their names here. Today, you can still dance the waltz here on what one critic called "Retro fetish night," or perhaps even tango on a Sunday afternoon. Brazilian and Latin themes predominate on some nights. Overall, it's one of the best places in Paris for the old-fashioned pleasures of couples arm-in-arm on a dance floor.

Le New Riverside. 7 rue Grégoire-de-Tours, 6e. ☎ **01-43-54-46-33.** Cover (including first drink) 90 F ($14.40) for men at all times, for women only after midnight Fri–Sat. Métro: St-Michel or Odéon.

This battered Left Bank cellar club attracts droves of jaded veteran club-goers, who appreciate the indestructible premises and the classic rock from the '70s. Expect a crowd aged 25 to 40; women, especially when unaccompanied, are almost always admitted free.

Le Saint. 7 rue St-Severin, 5e. ☎ **01-43-25-50-04.** Cover (including first drink) 60–90 F ($9.60–$14.40). Métro: St-Michel.

Occupying three medieval cellars deep in the university area, this place attracts a crowd in their 20s and 30s who dance (to music from both the U.S. and Europe), drink, and generally soak up the Left Bank student-dive scene. Vacationers will enjoy this fun spot, and its "Young Love Beside the Seine" vibe can be a hoot.

Les Bains. 7 rue du Bourg-l'Abbé, 3e. ☎ **01-48-87-01-80.** Cover (including first drink) 120 F ($19.20). Métro: Réaumur.

This chic spot has been pronounced "in" and "out" many times, but lately it's very in, attracting a good-looking local crowd and growing a bit more gay.

Les Coulisses. 5 rue du Mont-Cenis (place du Tertre), 18e. ☎ **01-42-62-89-99.** Cover 100 F ($16) Fri–Sat; no cover for people who eat in the restaurant. Métro: Abbesses.

There are more tourist traps in Montmartre than anywhere else in Paris, but this fairly new club has some legitimacy, providing a good spot for drinking and dancing in the heart of the district. Its premises combine a basement-level dance club, a first-floor bar, and a restaurant on the second floor. The decor changes all the time, but management usually sticks to baroque and medieval themes. The club stays open until dawn.

Rex Club. 5 bd. Poissonière, 2e. ☎ **01-42-36-83-98.** Cover (including first drink) 50–80 F ($8–$12.80). Métro: Bonne-Nouvelle.

This echoing blue-and-orange space emulates the techno-grunge clubs of London, complete with an international, mood-altered clientele enjoying the kind of music only someone aged 18 to 28 could love. A revolving host of DJs is on hand, including regular appearances by a local techno-circuit celeb, Laurent Garnier.

ROCK & ROLL

Bus Palladium. 6 rue Fontaine, 9e. ☎ **01-53-21-07-33.** Cover 100 F ($16) for men, 100 F ($16) for women Fri–Sat only. Tues–Sat 11pm–6am. Métro: Blanche or Pigalle.

Set in a single room with a very long bar, this rock-and-roll temple has varnished hardwoods and fabric-covered walls that barely absorb the reverberations of nonstop recorded music. You won't find techno, punk-rock, jazz, blues, or soul here. It's rock-and-roll and nothing but rock-and-roll, for hard-core, mostly heterosexual, rock wanna-bes ages 25 to 35. Alcoholic drinks of any kind cost 80 F ($12.80), except for women on Tuesday, when they drink as much as they want for free.

SALSA

Les Étoiles. 61 rue du Château d'Eau, 10e. ☎ **01-47-70-60-56.** Cover 120 F ($19.20) including first drink. Métro: Château d'Eau.

Since 1856, this red-swabbed old-fashioned music hall has shaken with the sound of performers at work and patrons at play. Its newest incarnation is as a restaurant discothèque where the music is exclusively salsa and the food Cubano. Expect simple but hearty portions of fried fish, shredded pork or beef, white rice, beans, and flan, as bands from Venezuela play salsa to a crowd that already knows or quickly learns how to dance to South American rhythms.

WINE BARS

Many Parisians now prefer the wine bar to the traditional cafe or bistro. The food is often better and the ambience more inviting.

Au Sauvignon. 80 rue des Sts-Pères, 7e. ☎ **01-45-48-49-02.** Closed Aug. Métro: Sèvres-Babylone.

This tiny spot has tables overflowing onto a covered terrace and a decor featuring old ceramic tiles and frescoes done by Left Bank artists. Wines range from the cheapest beaujolais to the most expensive Puligny-Montrachet. A glass of wine costs 21 F to 30 F ($3.35 to $4.80), with an additional charge of 2 F (30¢) to consume it at a table. To go with your wine, choose an Auvergne specialty, like goat cheese or a terrine. The fresh Poîlane bread is ideal with the ham, pâté, or goat cheese.

Juveniles. 47 rue de Richelieu, 1er. ☎ **01-42-97-46-49.** Métro: Palais-Royal.

This is a spin-off of one of Paris's most successful wine bars, Willi's (see below), which is nearby. Louder, less formal, more animated, and (at least to wine lovers) more provocative than its older sibling, it prides itself on experimenting with wines. There's no stuffiness at this British-owned spot, where high-quality but less-well-known wines from Spain, France, California, and Australia go for between 19 F to 49 F ($3.05 to $7.85) a glass. Anything you like, including bottles of the "wine of the week," can be hauled away uncorked from a wine boutique on the premises. And if you get hungry, savory tapas-style platters are available for 34 F to 64 F ($5.45 to $10.25).

Les Bacchantes. 21 rue Caumartin, 9e. ☎ **01-42-65-25-35.** Métro: Havre-Caumartin.

This place prides itself on offering more wines by the glass—at least 50—than any other wine bar in Paris; prices range from 13 F to 30 F ($2.05 to $4.80) . It also does a hefty restaurant trade in well-prepared *cuisine bourgeoise.* Its cozy, rustic setting— with massive exposed beams, old-fashioned paneling, and chalkboards announcing both the vintages and the platters—attracts dozens of theater-goers before and after performances at the nearby Théâtre Olympia, as well as anyone interested in carefully chosen vintages from esoteric or small-scale wine makers. Wines derive mainly from France, but you'll also find examples from neighboring countries of Europe.

Willi's Wine Bar. 13 rue des Petits-Champs, 1er. ☎ **01-42-61-05-09.** Métro: Bourse, Louvre, or Palais-Royal.

Journalists and stockbrokers head for this increasingly popular wine bar in the center of the financial district. About 250 kinds of wine are offered, including a dozen "wine specials" you can taste by the glass for 22 F to 81 F ($3.50 to $12.95). Lunch is the busiest time; on quiet evenings you can better enjoy the warm ambience. Daily specials are likely to include lamb brochette with cumin or Lyonnais sausage in truffled vinaigrette, plus a spectacular dessert like chocolate terrine.

BARS & PUBS

Académie de la Bière. 88 bis bd. du Port-Royal, 5e. ☎ **01-43-54-66-65.** Métro: Port-Royal.

The decor is paneled and rustic, an appropriate foil for an "academy" whose curriculum includes studying more than 150 kinds of microbrewed beer. More than half of the dozen on tap are from small breweries in Belgium that deserve to be better known. Mugs or bottles cost 29 F to 43 F ($4.65 to $6.90) each, depending on how esoteric they are. Getting hungry? Snack-style food is available, including platters of mussels, assorted cheeses, and sausages with mustard.

Bar du Crillon. In the Hôtel de Crillon, 10 place de la Concorde, 8e. ☎ **01-44-71-15-00.** Métro: Concorde.

Though some visitors consider the Bar du Crillon too stuffy and self-consciously elegant, the social and literary history of this bar is remarkable. Hemingway set a

After-Dark Diversions:
Dives, Drag & More

On a Paris night, the cheapest entertainment, especially if you're young, is "the show" staged at the southeasterly tip of the Île de la Cité, behind Notre-Dame. Like a Gallic version of the Sundowner Festival in Key West, Florida, it attracts anyone who has ever wanted to try his or her hand at performance art. The entertainment is strictly spontaneous, usually including magicians, fire-eaters, jugglers, mimes, and music-makers from all over the world, performing against the backdrop of the illuminated cathedral. Completely unchoreographed, the setting provides one of the greatest places in Paris to meet other young people.

Where to quench your thirst afterward? Wander over to the **Café-Brasserie St-Regis,** 6 rue Jean-du-Bellay, 4e (☎ **01-43-54-59-41;** Métro: Musée-du-Louvre), for a drink to go. It's on the Île St-Louis, across from pont St-Louis. If you want to linger inside, you can order a plat du jour for around 60 F ($9.60) or a coffee at the bar. But if you're looking for maximum mobility, order a beer in a plastic go cup (*une bière à emporter*), priced at 13 F ($2.10), and take it with you on a stroll around the island. The little cafe is open daily from 7am to 2am.

For another memorable way to see spontaneous Paris in action, take a walk along the Seine after 10pm. Follow the graveled pathway down to the Seine from the Left Bank side of the Pont de Sully, close to the Institut du Monde Arabe, and walk away from Notre-Dame. Joggers come here, saxophone players entertain, and many Parisians show up to dance everything from the cancan to the jitterbug. These dance parties are impromptu and depend on the weather, of course.

Looking for a dive to hang out in until the Métro starts running again at 5am? Try **Sous-Bock Tavern,** 49 rue St-Honoré, 1er (☎ **01-40-26-46-61;** Métro: Pont-Neuf), at the corner of rue du pont-Neuf. A crowd of young beer drinkers gathers here to sample some 400 varieties. If you want a shot of whiskey to accompany your brew, you face a choice of 150 varieties. The tavern is open daily from 11am to 5am. The dish to order here is a platter of mussels—curried, with white wine, or with cream sauce. They go well with the brasserie-style French fries.

If you're looking for some of the best (and most flamboyant) drag in Paris, head to **Madame Arthur,** 75 bis rue des Martyrs, 18e (☎ **01-42-54-40-21;** Métro: Abbesses or Pigalle). It's the longest-running transvestite show in Paris, attracting

climactic scene of *The Sun Also Rises* here, and over the years it has attracted a crowd of diplomats from the nearby U.S. Embassy as well as visiting heiresses, stars, starlets, and wanna-bes. Under its new owner, the Concorde Group, the bar has been redecorated by Sonia Rykiel. Another option down the hall is the Edwardian-style **Jardin d'Hiver,** where, amid potted palms and upscale accessories, you can order tea, cocktails, or coffee.

✪ **Bar Hemingway/Bar Vendôme.** In Le Ritz, 15 place Vendôme, 1er. ☎ **01-43-16-30-30.** Métro: Opéra.

In 1944 during the Liberation of Paris, Ernest Hemingway made history by ordering a drink at the Ritz Bar while gunfire from retreating Nazi soldiers was still audible in the streets. Today, basking in the literary glow, the Ritz commemorates this event with both straight and gay people who find the revue funnier, and more tasteful, than they might have expected. The creative force behind the affair is Madame Arthur, who is no lady, and whose stage name during her shticks as mistress of ceremonies is Chantaline. This place has been here so long that, according to Pigalle lore, it used to welcome the invading armies of Julius Caesar. But despite its detractors (and very few people don't like the nightly ooh-la-la's) it's still going strong, thanks to between 9 and 11 artists whose campy personae bear names like Vungala, Lady Lune, and Miss Badabou. You can visit just to drink, or you can dine from an uncomplicated fixed-price menu. Reservations are strongly advised. The club is open daily from 9 to 10:30pm for dinner, with the show beginning at 10:30pm. Additional shows, according to demand, are on Friday and Saturday at 7pm, with dinner beginning at 6pm. After the last show, around 12:30am, the place is transformed into a disco. Cover (including the first drink) is 165 F ($26.40); or dinner and show 295 F ($47.20) from Sunday to Thursday, and 395 F ($63.20) Friday and Saturday.

Remember Marlon Brando in *Last Tango in Paris?* Relive it at **Le Tango,** 13 rue au Maire, 3e (☎ **01-42-72-17-78;** Métro: Arts-et-Métiers). It's a dive with bordello décor, but you can tango and dance to various salsa and zouk music originating from the French Caribbean to Africa. The club attracts those in their 20s and 30s. The cover costs 40 F ($6.40) .

What's one of the most fun and trendy things to do in Paris today? Put on your red dancing shoes and head for **La Guinguette Pirate,** quai de la Gare, 13e (☎ **01-44-24-89-89;** Métro: Quai-de-la-Gare), a Chinese junk moored off the banks of the Seine. This is the 1990s version of the fabled *guinguette* (riverbordering cafe). Some of the best jazz, zouk, and live salsa are waiting to enthrall you. The cover is 50 F ($8).

Looking for a sophisticated, laid-back spot? Consider a drink at the **Sanz-Sans,** 49 rue du Faubourg St-Antoine, 4e (☎ **01-44-75-78-78;** Métro: Bastille). Expect the children of prominent Parisians to mingle freely at this multiracial playground, set within a richly upholstered, red-velvet duplex. Lots of cruising goes on in the stairway or on the back-room couches where the margaritas slide down constantly. The later it gets, the sexier the scene. No cover.

bookish memorabilia, rows of newspapers, and stiff drinks. Look for the bar's entrance, and homages to other writers such as Proust, near the hotel's rue Cambon entrance. If you develop a thirst in the daytime, when the Bar Hemingway isn't open, head for the Bar Vendôme, which is near the hotel's main (place Vendôme) entrance. The setting there is just as cozy and woodsy, albeit a bit more grand.

The China Club. 50 rue de Charenton, 12e. ☎ **01-43-43-82-02.** Métro: Bastille.

Designed to recall France's 19th-century colonies in Asia (on the ground floor) and England's empire in India (upstairs), the China Club offers a chance to chitchat or flirt with the singles who crowd into the street-level bar, then escape to a quieter setting upstairs. You'll see regulars from the worlds of fashion and the arts, along with nightcappers from the nearby Opéra Bastille. There's a Chinese restaurant on the street level; a scattering of books, newspapers, and chessboards upstairs; and a more animated (and occasionally raucous) bar in the cellar.

✪ **Harry's New York Bar.** 5 rue Daunou, 2e. ☎ **01-42-61-71-14.** Métro: Opéra or Pyramides.

Sank roo doe noo, as the ads tell you to instruct your cabdriver, is the most famous bar in Europe—quite possibly in the world. Opened on Thanksgiving Day 1911 by an expat named MacElhone, it's the spot where members of the World War I ambulance corps drank themselves silly. In addition to being Hemingway's favorite bar, Harry's is legendary for other reasons: the white lady and sidecar cocktails were invented here in 1919 and 1931, respectively, and it's also the alleged birthplace of the Bloody Mary and the headquarters of a loosely organized fraternity of drinkers known as the International Bar Flies (IBF). Harry's has stayed in the family: MacElhone's bilingual grandson, Duncan, now owns and runs it.

The place's historic core is the street-level bar, where CEOs and office workers loosen their ties on more or less equal footing. Daytime crowds draw from the neighborhood's insurance, banking, and travel industries; evening crowds include pre- and post-theater groupies and night owls who aren't bothered by the gritty setting and deliberately unflattering lighting. A softer, somewhat less macho ambience reigns in the cellar, where a pianist provides music every night from 10pm to 2am.

Le Bar de l'Hôtel. In L'Hôtel, 13 rue des Beaux-Arts, 6e. ☎ **01-44-41-99-00.** Métro: St-Germain-des-Prés.

This is the city's most romantic bar, located in a hotel on the Left Bank. Oscar Wilde checked out long ago, but the odd celebrity still shows up: We were once 15 minutes into a conversation before realizing we were speaking to French actress Jeanne Moreau. Drinks are expertly mixed, the place is sleek and chic, and conversations are held at a discreet murmur. There's no better place for a romantic rendezvous.

Le Floridita. 19 rue de Presbourg, 16e. ☎ **01-45-00-84-84.** Métro: Étoile.

Some aspects of this place might remind you of Cuba before Castro, including the macho brown and green decor that evokes a private men's club. The name was inspired by a long-ago bar in Havana. You can drink Cuba libres, cognac, or endless cups of coffee, or eat platters of food priced at 80 F to 130 F ($12.80 to $20.80). Men and women puff away at cigars. Cafe and cigar service are every Monday to Saturday from 10:30am to 2am; meals are served Monday to Saturday from noon to 2pm and from 8 to 11:15pm.

Le Forum. 4 bd. Malesherbes, 8e. ☎ **01-42-65-37-86.** Métro: Madeleine.

Its regulars, who include international business travelers, compare this place to a private club in London—probably because of the carefully polished oak paneling and ornate stucco as well as the list of single-malt whiskeys, among the most comprehensive in town. Cocktails, anyone? The drink menu lists more than 150 choices.

Le Fumoir. 6 rue de l'Amiral Coligny, 1er. ☎ **01-42-92-00-24.** Métro: Louvre-Rivoli.

In a neighborhood not known for exotic nightlife, this bar encourages a kind of classy raucousness from a well-traveled crowd that either lives or works nearby. The decor is a lot like that of an English library. A Danish chef prepares an international menu featuring meal-sized salads (the one with scallops and lobster is particularly savory); roasted codfish with zucchini; and roasted beef in red wine sauce. More popular than the food are the stiff martinis, the selection of wines and beers, and the dozen or so types of cigars, some of them from Cuba. It's open daily from 11am to 2am.

Le Web Bar. 32 rue de Picardie, 3e. ☎ **01-42-72-66-55.** Métro: Temple.

Le Web Bar taps gleefully into the computer age. It occupies a three-story space at the eastern edge of the Marais that echoes with the sound of people talking and schmoozing with each other, or e-mailing their friends back home. There's a restaurant on street level, 25 computers one floor up, and a top-floor art gallery. And to keep things perking, there's some kind of live music every night beginning around 7pm. Beer costs 18 F ($3.05); a plat du jour averages 50 F ($8.50); and use of the somewhat battered computers is free. Menu items stress comfort food like boeuf bourguignonne. If you want to check out the site prior to your arrival, its Web site address is www. ethernite.com. It's open daily from 8am till 2am.

Pub St-Germain-des-Prés. 17 rue de l'Ancienne-Comédie, 6e. ☎ **01-43-29-38-70.** Métro: Odéon.

With nine rooms and 650 seats, this is the largest pub in France, offering 450 brands of beer—don't ask your server to name them all—26 of them on draft. The deliberately tacky decor, which has seen a lot of beer swilled and spilled since its installation, consists of leather booths, faded gilt-framed mirrors, hanging lamps, and a stuffed parrot in a gilded cage. It gets *really* fun between 10:30pm and 4am, when live rock turns everything louder, sudsier, and rowdier.

GAY & LESBIAN CLUBS

Gay life is centered around Les Halles and Le Marais, with the greatest concentration of gay and lesbian clubs, restaurants, bars, and shops between the Hôtel-de-Ville and Rambuteau Métro stops. Gay dance clubs come and go so fast that even the magazines devoted somewhat to their pursuit—*3 Keller* and *Exit,* both distributed free in the gay bars and bookstores—have a hard time keeping up. *Lesbia,* a monthly national lesbian magazine, focuses on women's issues.

✪ **Banana Café.** 13 rue de la Ferronnerie, 1er. ☎ **01-42-33-35-31.** Métro: Châtelet-Les-Halles.

This is the most popular gay bar in the Marais, a required stop for gay Europeans (mostly male) visiting or doing business in Paris. Occupying two floors of a 19th-century building, it has walls the color of an overripe banana, dim lighting, and a well-publicized policy of raising drink prices after 10pm, when the joint becomes really interesting. On theme nights such as Valentine's Day, expect the entire premises to be plastered with pink crêpe paper. There's a street-level bar and a dance floor in the cellar that features a live pianist and recorded music. On many nights, go-go dancers perform in the cellar.

Bar Hotel Central. 33 rue Vieille-du-Temple, 4e. ☎ **01-48-87-99-33.** Métro: Hôtel-de-Ville.

Bar Hotel Central is one of the leading bars for men in the Hôtel-de-Ville area. The club has opened a small hotel upstairs. Both the bar and its hotel are in a 300-year-old building in the heart of the Marais. The hotel caters mostly to gay men, less frequently to lesbians.

La Champmeslé. 4 rue Chabanais, 2e. ☎ **01-42-96-85-20.** Métro: Pyramides or Bourse.

With dim lighting, background music, and comfortable banquettes, La Champmeslé offers a cozy meeting place for women, and to a much, much lesser extent (about 5%), "well-behaved" men. Paris's leading women's bar is housed in a 300-year-old building with exposed stone, ceiling beams, and 1950s-style furnishings. Every Thursday night, one of the premier lesbian events in Paris, a cabaret, begins at 10pm (with the same cover and drink prices as on any other day).

Le Bar. 5 rue de la Ferronerie, 1er. ☎ **01-40-41-00-10.** Métro: Châtelet.

Covering the street level and cellar of a sprawling building in a neighborhood known for its serious pickup scene, this is the largest gay bar in Paris. You'll find three bars on the premises, and an ambience that's more sexually charged and explicit in the cellar than on the street level. The average age of most patrons is around 32, and the majority are gay and male.

Le Pulp. 25 bd. Poissonnière, 2e. ☎ **01-40-26-01-93.** Métro: Rue-Montmartre.

This is one of the most popular (and most fun) lesbian discos in Paris, welcoming women of all ages. After a change in management, the club's seedy past is now a distant memory; today this replica of a late 19th-century French music hall is trendy and chic, with all types of cutting-edge music. It's best to show up before midnight. What to do if you're a gay male who wants to hang out with the girls? Head for the side entrance, where a "separate but equal facility" called Le Scorp welcomes gay guys into a roughly equivalent place that, alas, never manages to be as much fun as Le Queen.

✪ **Le Queen.** 102 av. des Champs-Elysées, 8e. ☎ **01-53-89-08-90.** No cover Tues–Thurs and Sun, 50 F ($8) Mon, 100 F ($16) Fri–Sat. Métro: Franklin-D.-Roosevelt.

Should you miss gay life à la New York, follow the flashing purple sign near the corner of avenue George-V. This place is often mobbed, primarily by gay men and, to a much lesser degree, chic women who work in the fashion and film industries. Look for drag shows, muscle shows, striptease from danseurs who gyrate atop the bars, and everything from Monday '70s-style disco nights to Tuesday-night foam parties (only in summer), when cascades of mousse descend onto the dance floor. Go very, very late: the place stays open until 6 or 7am, but doesn't even open until midnight.

TIMBUKTU   KALAMAZOO

AT&T Direct® Service

The easy way to call home from anywhere.

Global
connection
with the AT&T
Network
AT&T
direct
service

or the easy way to call home, take the attached wallet guide.

Make Learning Fun & Easy

With IDG Books Worldwide

Frommer's

WEBSTER'S
NEW WORLD™

Betty Crocker's

the
Unofficial Guide®

CliffsNotes™
www.cliffsnotes.com

BURPEE®

ARCO®

GUIDE TO
A HAPPY HEALTHY PET™

HOWELL
BOOK
HOUSE™

WEIGHT WATCHERS®

Available at your local bookstores

Side Trips from Paris: Versailles, Chartres & the Best of Île de France

Château de Versailles, the Cathédrale Notre-Dame de Chartres, and the Palais de Fontainebleau draw countless tour buses. They're the stars of the Île de France and need no selling from us. However, some lesser-known but equally stunning spots in this greenbelt around Paris may not be as familiar to you.

Many people know of this region through the paintings of Corot, Renoir, Degas, Monet, and Cézanne. Here you'll find everything from Romanesque ruins, Gothic cathedrals, and feudal castles to splendid 18th-century châteaux, enormous forests like Fontainebleau and Chantilly, sleepy villages, and even an African game reserve. To top it off, there's Disneyland Paris if your kids just have to see Mickey and Minnie with a Gallic twist.

Everything described in this chapter can be seen on a day trip from Paris or as an overnight excursion.

1 Versailles

13 miles SW of Paris, 44 miles NE of Chartres

Back in the grand siècle, all you needed was a sword, a hat, and a bribe for the guard at the gate. Providing you didn't look as if you had smallpox, you'd be admitted to the precincts of the Château de Versailles, where you could stroll through salon after glittering salon, where you could watch the Sun King at his banquet table, gossiping, dancing, plotting, flirting. Louis XIV was accorded about as much privacy as an institution.

Today Versailles needs the return of Louis XIV and his fat treasury. You wouldn't believe it to look at the glittering Hall of Mirrors, but Versailles is down-at-the-heels. It suffers from a lack of funds, which translates into a shortage of security forces. At Versailles today you get to see only half its treasures; the rest are closed to the public, including the Musée de France, with its 6,000 paintings and 2,000 statues. Some 3.2 million visitors arrive annually, and on average they spend 2 hours here.

ESSENTIALS

GETTING THERE To get to Versailles **by train** from Paris, catch the RER line C at the Gare d'Austerlitz, St-Michel, Musée d'Orsay, Invalides, Pont-de-l'Alma, Champ-de-Mars, or Javel station and take it to the Versailles Rive Gauche station, from which you can walk or take a shuttle bus to the château. The 35 F ($5.60) round-trip takes about 35 to 40 minutes; Eurailpass holders travel free on the train, but pay 20 F ($3.20) for a ride on the shuttle bus. Regular SNCF trains also make the run from central Paris to Versailles: One set of trains departs from the Gare St-Lazare for the Versailles Rive Droite RER station; another set of trains departs from the Gare Montparnasse for Versailles Chantiers station, a 15-minute walk from the château (you can take bus B from Versailles Chantiers to the château for 8 F ($1.35) each way if you don't want to make this walk).

If you're **driving,** exit the périphérique on N10 (or avenue du Général-Leclerc), which will take you straight to Versailles; park on place d'Armes in front of the château.

VISITOR INFORMATION   The **Office de Tourisme** is at 7 rue des Réservoirs (☎ **01-39-24-88-88;** fax 01-39-24-88-89).

EVENING SPECTACLES   The French government offers a program of evening fireworks and illuminated fountains, designated as Les Fêtes de Nuit de Versailles (Rêve de Roi), on 7 to 10 scattered dates throughout the summer. Two hundred actors in period costume portray Louis XVI and members of his *ancien régime* court. In July, the 90-minute shows begin at 10:30pm; during August and September, they start at 9:30pm. Spectators sit on bleachers clustered at the palace's boulevard de la Reine entrance, adjacent to the Fountain (Bassin) of Neptune. The most desirable seats cost 250 F ($40); standing room sells for 70 F ($11.20). Gates to the bleacher area open 90 minutes before showtime. For more information call ☎ **01-30-83-78-88.**

Tickets can be purchased in advance at the tourist office in Versailles—inquire by phone, fax, or mail, or in central Paris at any branch of the FNAC department stores. (For FNAC locations near your hotel, see "Paris After Dark," in chapter 4; or call FNAC's central phone number, ☎ **01-55-21-57-93.**) You can also take your chances and buy tickets an hour prior to the event itself from a kiosk adjacent to the boulevard de la Reine entrance to the bleachers.

SUNDAY-AFTERNOON PROMENADES IN THE PARK

Every Sunday between early April and mid-October, and every Saturday between early July and late August, between 11am and noon, and again between 3:30 and 5:30pm, the government broadcasts classical music throughout the park and opens all the valves of every fountain at Versailles. The effect during these Grandes Eaux Musicales duplicates the landscaping vision of the 18th-century architects who designed Versailles. You won't be confined to a seat within a bleacher for this midday event, but rather, you'll be encouraged to walk freely around the park, enjoying the unusual juxtapositions of grand architecture with lavish waterworks and music by Mozart, Haydn, and such French-born composers as Couperin, Charpentier, and Delalande. The cost of admission to the park during these events costs 25 F ($4) per person. Call ☎ **01-30-83-78-88** for general information about any of the nighttime or Sunday afternoon spectacles on the grounds surrounding the palace.

EXPLORING THE CHÂTEAU & GARDENS

✪ **Château de Versailles.** ☎ **01-30-83-78-00.** Palace, 45 F ($7.20) adults, 35 F ($5.60) adults after 3:30pm and for ages 18–25, free for seniors 60 and over; Grand Trianon, 25 F ($4) adults, 15 F ($2.40) adults after 3:30pm and for ages 18–25; Petit Trianon, 15 F ($2.40) adults, 10 F ($1.60) adults after 3:30pm and for ages 18–25. Everything free for children 17 and under. May 2–Sept 30, Tues–Sun 9am–6:30pm (until 5:30pm the rest of the year). Trianons maintain same closing hours, but open at 10am. Grounds daily dawn–dusk.

Within 50 years the Château de Versailles was transformed from Louis XIII's simple hunting lodge into an extravagant palace. Begun in 1661, the construction of the

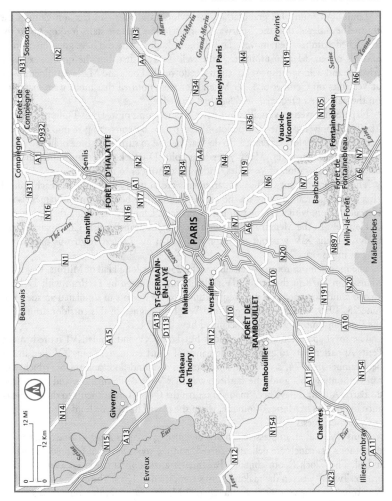

château involved 32,000 to 45,000 workmen, some of whom had to drain marshes and move forests. Louis XIV set out to build a palace that would be the envy of all Europe, and he created a symbol of pomp and opulence that was to be copied, yet never quite duplicated, all over Europe and even in America.

So he could keep an eye on the nobles of France (and with good reason), Louis XIV summoned them to live at his court. Here he amused them with constant entertainment and lavish banquets. To some he awarded such tasks as holding the hem of his ermine-lined robe. While the aristocrats frivolously played away their lives, often in silly intrigues and games, the peasants on the estates sowed the seeds of the Revolution.

When Louis XIV died in 1715, he was succeeded by his great-grandson, Louis XV, who continued the outrageous pomp, though he is said to have predicted the outcome: "Après nous le déluge" (After us the deluge). His wife, Marie Leczinska, was shocked by the blatant immorality at Versailles.

Louis XVI found his grandfather's behavior scandalous—in fact, on gaining the throne he ordered that the "stairway of indiscretion" (secret stairs leading up to the king's bedchamber) be removed. This dull, weak king (who did have good intentions) and his queen, Marie Antoinette, were well liked at first, but the queen's excessive frivolity and wild spending soon led to her downfall. Louis and Marie Antoinette were at Versailles on October 6, 1789, when they were notified that mobs were marching on the palace. As predicted, *le déluge* had arrived.

Napoléon stayed at Versailles but never seemed fond of it. Louis-Philippe (reigned 1830–48) prevented the destruction of the palace by converting it into a museum dedicated to the glory of France. To do that, he had to surrender some of his own not-so-hard-earned currency. Many years later John D. Rockefeller contributed heavily toward the restoration of Versailles, and work continues to this day.

The six magnificent Grands Appartements are in the Louis XIV style, each named after the allegorical painting on the room's ceiling. The best known and largest is the Hercules Salon, with a ceiling painted by François Lemoine, depicting the Apotheosis of Hercules. In the Mercury Salon (with a ceiling by Jean-Baptiste Champaigne), the body of Louis XIV was put on display in 1715; his 72-year reign was one of the longest in history.

The most famous room at Versailles is the 236-foot-long Hall of Mirrors. Begun by Mansart in 1678 in the Louis XIV style, it was decorated by Le Brun with 17 large arched windows matched by corresponding beveled mirrors in simulated arcades. On June 28, 1919, the treaty ending World War I was signed in this corridor. Ironically, the German Empire was also proclaimed here in 1871.

The royal apartments were for show, but Louis XV and Louis XVI retired to the Petits Appartements to escape the demands of court etiquette. Louis XV died in his bedchamber in 1774, a victim of smallpox. In a second-floor apartment, which you can visit only with a guide, he stashed away first Mme de Pompadour and then Mme du Barry. Attempts have been made to return the Queen's Apartments to their appearance in the days of Marie Antoinette, when she played her harpsichord in front of specially invited guests.

Louis XVI had an impressive Library, designed by Jacques-Ange Gabriel, which was sumptuous. Its panels are delicately carved, and the room has been restored and refurnished. The Clock Room contains Passement's astronomical clock, encased in gilded bronze. Twenty years in the making, it was completed in 1753. The clock is supposed to keep time until the year 9999. At the age of 7 Mozart played for the court in this room.

Gabriel designed the Opéra for Louis XV in 1748, though it wasn't completed until 1770. In its heyday it took 3,000 candles to light the place. With gold-and-white harmony, Hardouin-Mansart built the Royal Chapel in 1699, dying before its completion. Louis XVI, when still the dauphin (crown prince), married Marie Antoinette here in 1770. At this arranged marriage, both the bride and the groom were teenagers.

Spread across 250 acres, the Gardens of Versailles were laid out by the great landscape artist André Le Nôtre. At the peak of their glory, 1,400 fountains spewed forth. *The Buffet* is an exceptional one, having been designed by Mansart. One fountain depicts Apollo in his chariot pulled by four horses, surrounded by tritons emerging from the water to light the world. Le Nôtre created a Garden of Eden using ornamental lakes and canals, geometrically designed flower beds, and avenues bordered with statuary. On the mile-long Grand Canal, Louis XV—imagining he was in Venice—used to take gondola rides with his favorite of the moment.

A long walk across the park will take you to the Grand Trianon, in pink-and-white marble, designed by Hardouin-Mansart for Louis XIV in 1687. Traditionally it has been a place where France has lodged important guests, though de Gaulle wanted

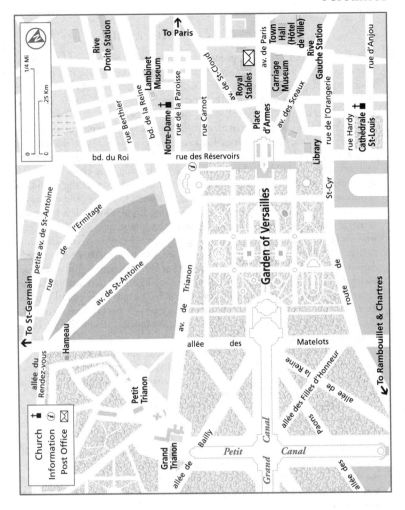

to turn it into a weekend retreat. Nixon once slept here in the room where Mme de Pompadour died. Mme de Maintenon also slept here, as did Napoléon. The original furnishings are gone, of course, with mostly Empire pieces there today.

Gabriel, the designer of place de la Concorde in Paris, built the Petit Trianon in 1768 for Louis XV. Louis used it for his trysts with Mme du Barry. In time, Marie Antoinette adopted it as her favorite residence, a place to escape the rigid life at the main palace. Many of the current furnishings, including a few in her rather modest bedchamber, belonged to the ill-fated queen.

On Christmas night of 1999, one of the worst storms in France's history destroyed some 10,000 historic trees on the grounds of the Château de Versailles. Blowing in at 100 mph, wind gusts uprooted 80% of the trees planted mostly during the 18th and 19th centuries. These included pines from Corsica planted during the reign of Napoléon, tulip trees sent over from Virginia, and a pair of junipers planted in honor of Marie-Antoinette. Versailles had never undergone such a natural catastrophe, and it will take years to rebuild the park.

Peaches & Peas Fit for a King

Between 1682 and 1789 (except for 8 years during the minority of Louis XV), Versailles housed a royal entourage of 3,000 people. To feed them, the sprawling kitchens employed a permanent staff of 2,000. Without benefit of running water or electricity, they labored over the banquets that became day-to-day rituals at the most glorious court since the collapse of ancient Rome.

The fruits and vegetables that arrayed the royal tables were produced on-site, in *Les Potagers du Roi* (the King's Kitchen Gardens). Surprisingly, the gardens have survived and can be found a 10-minute walk south of the château's main entrance, at 6 rue du Hardy, behind an industrial-looking gate. Here, 23 acres of fertile earth are arranged into parterres and terraces as formal as the legendary showcases devoted, during the royal tenure, to flowers, fountains, and statuary.

Meals at Versailles were quite a ritual. The king almost always dined in state, alone, at a table visible to hundreds of observers and, in some cases, other diners, who sat in order of rank. Fortunately for gastronomic historians, there are many detailed accounts of what Louis XIV ingested and how much he consumed: Addicted to salads, he ate prodigious amounts of basil, purslane, mint, and wood sorrel. He loved melons, figs, and pears. He found peaches so desirable that he rarely waited to cut and peel them, preferring to let the juices flow liberally down his royal chin. The culinary rage, however, was peas—imported from Genoa for the first time in 1660. According to Mme de Maintenon, Louis XIV's second wife, the entire court was obsessed with "impatience to eat them."

Today Les Potagers du Roi are maintained by about half a dozen gardeners under the direction of the École Nationale du Paysage. It manages to intersperse the fruits and vegetables once favored by the monarchs with experimental breeds and hundreds of splendidly espaliered fruit trees.

The kitchen gardens can be visited only between April and November, every Saturday and Sunday from 10am to 5pm. Adults pay 40 F ($6.40); persons under 18 pay 20 F ($3.20). Look for the entrance at 6 rue Hardy (☎ **01-39-24-62-00**), about a quarter-mile south of the palace itself. Free guided tours of the garden, in French, each last an hour, and depart every hour on the hour during the above-mentioned open hours. On the premises is a kiosk, where the fruits and vegetables grown within the gardens are for sale, as they would be at any farmer's market.

ACCOMMODATIONS
EXPENSIVE

✪ **Hôtel Trianon Palace.** 1 bd. de la Reine, 78000 Versailles. ☎ **800/228-3000** in the U.S., or 01-30-84-38-00. Fax 01-39-49-00-77. www.westin.com. E-mail: trian@westin.com. 200 units. MINIBAR TV TEL. 1,200–2,300 F ($192–$368) double; 3,500–3,900 F ($560–$624) suite. AE, DC, DISC, MC, V. Free parking.

This hotel was built in the grandest of styles available in 1910, on land that had sheltered a Capucine monastery during the heyday of the *ancien régime*. In 1919 this was the headquarters of the peace conference where Woodrow Wilson, Lloyd George, Georges Clemenceau, and other world leaders gathered. Since then, clients have included John D. Rockefeller, Gabriele d'Annunzio, Queen Elizabeth II, and Marlene Dietrich, who made nationwide headlines by entering the dining room wearing pants. Today, the hotel dwarfs all the competition in town, especially the new Sofitel Château de Versailles. A classically designed palace with stately charm, whose space is supplemented with a circa 1990 annex (Le Pavillon) that's connected to the original structure via an underground tunnel, it's set in a 5-acre garden bordering those of the Trianons at Versailles. Japanese owners restored the place in the early 1990s to the tune of $60 million. Public rooms are, quite simply, splendid. Accommodations in both buildings are decorated in rich fabrics, in traditional styles with reference to château living, and a mixture of genuine antiques and fine reproductions. Mattresses, bath amenities, and electronic accessories are top-of-the-line, without equal at any other hotel in Versailles.

Dining/Diversions: Breakfast is served in the sumptuous Salle Clemenceau, where the Treaty of Versailles was negotiated. Chef Gérard Vié, the finest in Versailles, operates his world-class Les Trois Marchés (see below), whose soaring windows overlook the park. You can dine less expensively by ordering a menu du jour in the Café Trianon, or in a smaller space, Les Petites Marches, where Chesterfield sofas create an ambience similar to that of an upscale tearoom. The Marie-Antoinette Piano Bar features live music daily after 6pm, occasionally with featured jazz performers.

Amenities: 24-hour room service, baby-sitting, laundry, health club, indoor pool, tennis courts. The hotel has joined with Givenchy, one of the top names in French beauty care, to create an outstanding spa, with many treatments and services available.

MODERATE

Novotel Versailles Le Chesnay. 4 bd. St-Antoine, 78150 Le Chesnay. ☎ **01-39-54-96-96.** Fax 01-39-54-94-40. E-mail: h1022@accor-hotels.com. 105 units. A/C MINIBAR TV TEL. 650–750 F ($104–$120) double. Children 16 and under stay free in parents' room. AE, DC, MC, V. Parking 50 F ($8).

A 15-minute walk north from one of the side wings of the château, this hotel, built in 1988 as part of a nationwide chain, has a modern facade with columns and large windows. It's a good price and a convenient choice. The rooms are practical and all are identical except for four that are equipped for the disabled. Each was renovated, with improvements to the comfort levels, and replacements of the mattresses, in 1998. There's a restaurant and a bar, but the food is mediocre.

INEXPENSIVE

Hôtel Paris. 14 av. de Paris, 78000 Versailles. ☎ **01-39-50-56-00.** Fax 01-39-50-21-83. 38 units, 35 with bathroom. TV TEL. 220 F ($35.20) double without bathroom, 360–400 F ($57.60–$64) double with bathroom. AE, DC, MC, V.

This is the best deal in town. The Paris is a somewhat nondescript wood-and-stucco hotel that was built late in the 19th century and has been modernized into a clean, well-maintained, if not particularly exciting design. The price is hard to beat, especially because of its great location, a 15-minute walk west of the château. Even the cheapest rooms have showers and sinks (although no toilets). The cheapest of the rooms with private baths are the best value; if you upgrade to the 400 F ($64) rate, all you'll get is a bathtub instead of a stall shower. Most rooms are a bit small, but reasonably comfortable, with good mattresses. The staff is helpful.

Relais Mercure Versailles Château. 19 rue Philippe-de-Dangeau, 78000 Versailles. ☎ **800/221-4542** for reservations in the U.S. and Canada, or 01-39-50-44-10. Fax 01-39-50-65-11. www.mercure-versailles.com. E-mail: hotel@mercure-versailles.com. 60 units. TV TEL. 510 F ($81.60) double. AE, DC, MC, V. Parking 50 F ($8).

The interior of this 18th-century Mansard-style building (a 10-minute walk from the château) was completely gutted in 1994, leaving only the awesomely thick walls. The stately chain hotel that now stands here provides all the modern comforts, but very few frills. Mattresses are first rate, however. The service is brisk and efficient, very much what you'd expect. Breakfast is the only meal served.

DINING
VERY EXPENSIVE

✪ **Les Trois Marchés.** In the Hôtel Trianon Palace, 1 bd. de la Reine. ☎ **01-30-84-38-40.** Reservations required. Fixed-price menus 350 F ($56) Mon–Fri at lunch, otherwise 625–825 F ($100–$132). AE, DC, MC, V. Daily noon–2pm and 7:30–10pm. Closed Aug. FRENCH.

The food here is of the highest order—and so are the prices. Chef Gérard Vié, known for the inventiveness of his cuisine bourgeoise, serves the finest food in Versailles. His soaring greenhouse-inspired dining room is remarkable for its generous expanses of glass and its intimate size (only 55 seats). In summer, you can dine under the canopy on the front terrace. Begin with the delectable lobster salad flavored with fresh herbs and served with an onion soufflé; the foie gras of duckling; a galette of potatoes with bacon, chardonnay, and sevruga caviar; or the delightful citrus-flavored scallop bisque. The chef is a great innovator, especially when it comes to main courses: pigeon roasted and flavored with rosé and accompanied with celeriac and truffles, or fillet of sea bass with a "cake" of eggplant. If you can't choose a single dessert, opt for the signature assortment. Note that some people have found the staff a bit too stiff and patronizing.

MODERATE

La Flottille. In the Parc du Château. ☎ **01-39-51-41-58.** Reservations recommended. Restaurant, main courses 98–120 F ($15.70–$19.20); fixed-price menu 135 F ($21.60). Brasserie, snacks 60–80 F ($9.60–$12.80). AE, MC, V. Restaurant, daily noon–3:30pm; brasserie, daily 8:30am–7pm for coffee, ice cream, and snacks. FRENCH.

This place was built around 1896 as a bar for the laborers who maintained the gardens surrounding the château. Today, the only restaurant inside the park occupies an enviable position at the head of the Grand Canal, with a sweeping view over some of Europe's most famous landscaping. Tables for lunch are placed outside in warm weather, and there's also a charming pavilion-inspired dining room. A brasserie/snack bar serves sandwiches, omelets, crêpes, salads, and ice cream. At lunch most people prefer the dining room, where unpretentious menu specialties include snail-stuffed ravioli with chablis sauce, sweetbreads braised in port, fillet of beef in sauce *périgourdine* (with truffles), and a ballotine of chicken "in the old-fashioned style."

Le Potager du Roy. 1 rue du Maréchal-Joffre. ☎ **01-39-50-35-34.** Reservations required. Fixed-price menu 135 F ($21.60) at lunch, 179 F ($28.65) at dinner. AE, MC, V. Tues–Fri noon–2:30pm; Tues–Sat 7–10:30pm. FRENCH.

Philippe Letourneur has emerged as a formidably talented chef after spending years perfecting a distinctive cuisine and now adding novelty to the oft-jaded dining scene in Versailles. Letourneur rotates his skillfully prepared menu with the seasons. Examples are foie gras with a vegetable-flavored vinaigrette, roasted duck with a navarin of vegetables, ragoût of macaroni with a persillade of snails, roasted codfish with roasted peppers in the style of Provence, and supreme of turbot braised with fresh endives and herbs. Looking for something unusual and more earthy? Try the fondant of pork jowls with a confit of fresh vegetables.

INEXPENSIVE

✪ **Le Quai No. 1.** 1 av. de St-Cloud. ☎ **01-39-50-42-26.** Reservations required. Main courses 85 F ($13.60); fixed-price menus 110 F ($17.60) at lunch, and 140–185 F ($22.40–$29.60) at dinner. MC, V. Tues–Sun noon–2:30pm; Tues–Sat 7:30–11pm. SEAFOOD/FRENCH.

This is the relatively informal seafood bistro associated with the much grander, much more expensive Les Trois Marchés (see above). Mega-chef Gérard Vié is the creative force here, lending his credentials, and his glamour, to the 18th-century building overlooking the western facade of France's most famous château. The dining room is decorated with lithographs and wood paneling; there's also a summer terrace. Though the cuisine isn't opulent, it's charming, very French, and reasonable in price and dependable in presentation. The fixed-price menus make Le Quai a dining bargain in high-priced Versailles. Specialties are seafood sauerkraut, seafood paella, bouillabaisse, and home-smoked salmon. The chef recommends the *plateau de fruits de mer.* Carnivores appreciate the three meat-based main courses, the best of which are magrêt of duckling dressed with aged vinegar, and navarin of lamb. Care and imagination go into the cuisine, and the service is professional and polite. An enduringly popular platter is an upscale version of surf and turf: grilled Breton lobster and a sizzling sirloin, just like you'd expect in North America.

2 The Forest of Rambouillet

34 miles SW of Paris, 26 miles NE of Chartres

Georges Pompidou used to visit the château here, as did Louis XVI and Charles de Gaulle. Dating from 1375, it's surrounded by a park in one of the most famous forests in France, with more than 47,000 acres of greenery stretching from the valley of the Eure to the high valley of Chevreuse, the latter rich in medieval and royal abbeys. The lakes, deer, and even wild boar are some of the attractions of this beautiful area.

ESSENTIALS

GETTING THERE **Trains** depart from Paris's Gare Montparnasse every 20 minutes throughout the day. One-way passage costs 41 F ($6.55) for a ride of about 35 minutes. For train information and schedules, contact La Gare de Rambouillet, place Prud'homme (☎ **01-53-90-20-20**).

VISITOR INFORMATION The **Office de Tourisme** is at the Hôtel de Ville, place de la Libération (☎ **01-34-83-21-21**).

SEEING THE CHÂTEAU

Château de Rambouillet. Parc du Château. ☎ **01-34-83-00-25.** Admission 32 F ($5.10) adults, 21 F ($3.35) students 12–25, free for children 11 and under. Apr–Sept, Wed–Mon 10–11:30am and 2–4:30pm; Oct–Mar, Wed–Mon 10am–11:30am and 2–3:30pm.

This is one of the royal châteaux of France, though it offers no serious competition to Fontainebleau or Versailles. François I, the Chevalier King, died of a fever at Rambouillet in 1547 at the age of 52. When the château was later occupied by the comte de Toulouse, Rambouillet was often visited by Louis XV, who was amused (in more ways than one) by the comte's witty and high-spirited wife. Louis XVI acquired the château, but his wife, Marie Antoinette, was bored with the place and called it "the toad."

Napoléon's second wife, Marie-Louise, came here in 1814, after leaving him. She was on her way to Vienna with the exiled king of Rome, her son, Napoléon II. A sad Napoléon slept here shortly before leaving on the long voyage into exile at St. Helena.

In 1830 Charles X, Louis XVI's brother, abdicated after the July Revolution. Following that, Rambouillet became privately owned. At one time it was a fashionable restaurant, attracting Parisians, who could also go for rides in gondolas. Napoléon III, however, returned it to the Crown. In 1897 it was designated as a residence for the presidents of the Republic. Superb woodwork is used throughout, and the walls are adorned with tapestries, many dating from the era of Louis XV.

Today it's used as a vacation retreat by the president. When the president is not in residence, the rooms of the château can be visited on a self-guided tour. And although there are no guided tours of the 30,000-acre Rambouillet forest, you can pick up a map at the tourist office and go hiking, biking, or driving through it.

ACCOMMODATIONS

Hotel Amarys. Lieu-Dit la Louvière, rue de la Louvière, 78120 Rambouillet. ☎ **01-34-85-62-62.** Fax 01-30-59-23-57. 66 units. TV TEL. 285–310 F ($45.60–$49.60) double. AE, DC, MC, V. Exit from N10 at the Dampierre Chevreuse exit.

Built in 1988, this stone-fronted building sits in the famous forest about half a mile north of the town center. This affordable hotel, which caters mainly to business travelers, offers comfortable and distinguished rooms. The bathrooms are boxy and motel-standard. There's an outdoor heated pool, a tennis court, and a restaurant serving fixed-price menus, priced from 78 F to 98 F ($12.50 to $15.70). The restaurant is open daily from noon to 2pm and 7:30 to 10pm.

DINING

La Poste. 101 av. du Général-de-Gaulle. ☎ **01-34-83-03-01.** Reservations recommended Sat–Sun. Main courses 119–158 F ($19.05–$25.30); fixed-price menus 125–195 F ($20–$31.20). AE, CB, V. Tues–Thurs and Sat noon–2pm; Tues–Sun 7–10pm. FRENCH.

On a street corner in the town's historic center, across from the Sous-Préfecture de Police, this restaurant has been serving food since the mid-19th century, when it was a coaching inn. The two dining rooms have rustic beams and old-fashioned accents that complement the flavorful but old-fashioned food, such as homemade terrines of foie gras and freshly made pastries. Main courses of note are fricasée of chicken with crayfish, and noisettes of lamb with copious amounts of red wine and herbs. A particularly flavorful dish is fillet of beef with a Périgueux sauce of madeira and foie gras.

3 The Glorious Cathedral of Chartres

60 miles SW of Paris, 47 miles NW of Orléans

Many observers feel that medieval architecture reached its pinnacle in the world-renowned cathedral at Chartres. Come to see its architecture, its sculpture, and—most of all—its stained glass, which gave the world a new color, Chartres blue.

The ancient town of Chartres also played a role in World War II. There's even a monument to Jean Moulin, the great Resistance hero and friend of de Gaulle. Under torture, he refused to sign a document stating that French troops committed atrocities. The Gestapo killed him in 1943 (today he's buried in the Panthéon in Paris). From the cathedral, head down rue du Cheval-Blanc until it becomes rue Jean-Moulin (the monument is up ahead on your right). Other street names also commemorate the World War II Resistance, including boulevard de le Résistance.

ESSENTIALS

GETTING THERE   From Paris's Gare Montparnasse, **trains** run directly to Chartres, taking less than an hour. Tickets cost 144 F ($23.05) round-trip. Call ☎ 08-36-35-35-35 for information. If you're **driving,** take A10/A11 southwest from the périphérique and follow the signs to Le Mans and Chartres (the Chartres exit is clearly marked).

VISITOR INFORMATION   The **Office de Tourisme** is on place de la Cathédrale (☎ 02-37-18-26-26).

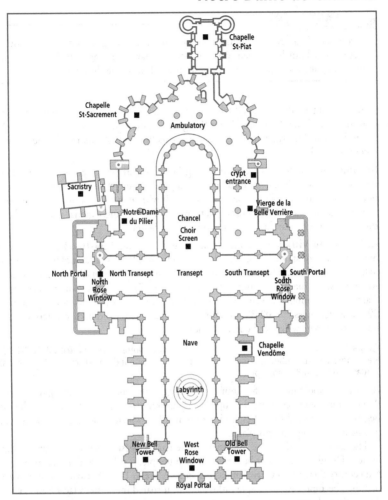

SEEING THE CATHEDRAL & EXPLORING THE TOWN

THE TOWN If time remains after you tour the cathedral (see below), you may want to explore the medieval cobblestone streets of the *Vieux Quartiers* (Old Town). Next door to the cathedral is the **Musée des Beaux-Arts de Chartres,** 29 Cloître Notre-Dame (☎ **02-37-36-41-39**), open Wednesday through Monday from 10am to noon and 2 to 5pm October 31 to May 2; 10am to noon and 2 to 6pm the rest of the year. Admission is 15 F ($2.40) for adults and 7.50 F ($1.20) for children. Installed in a former episcopal palace, the building at times competes with its exhibitions. One part dates from the 15th century and encompasses a courtyard. The permanent collection of paintings covers mainly the 16th to the 20th century, offering the works of old masters like Zurbarán, Watteau, and Brosamer. Of particular interest is David Ténier's *Le Concert.*

A Free Concert

If you visit Chartres on a Sunday afternoon in July and August, note that the church features free hour-long organ concerts every Sunday beginning at 4:45pm, when the filtered light makes the cathedral's western windows come thrillingly alive.

At the foot of the cathedral, the lanes contain gabled houses. Humped bridges span the Eure River. From the Bouju Bridge, you can see the lofty spires in the background. Try to find rue Chantault, which boasts houses with colorful facades; one is 8 centuries old.

Shopping in Town   Your best shopping bet in Chartres is place des Épars. This pedestrian area is home to most of the apparel shops, even some haute couture boutiques. Along rue Noël-Balay is a small mall with about 15 shops you might find interesting, especially if it's raining. Many of the shops selling regional items are along the narrow streets that fan southeast from the cathedral.

At **Galerie du Vitrail,** 17 Cloître Notre-Dame (☎ **02-37-36-10-03**), you'll find a huge selection of stained glass for sale—all illuminated in its radiant glory by natural light or light boxes. These works of art come in every size and style. **Lassaussois Antiquités,** 17 rue des Changes (☎ **02-37-21-37-74**), specializes in antique objets d'art and contemporary furnishings. If antique lace is your passion, stop by **Ariane,** 39 rue des Changes (☎ **02-37-21-20-68**), which also sells handmade sweaters, elegant linens, costume jewelry, and children's clothing.

✪ **Cathédrale Notre-Dame de Chartres.** 16 Cloître Notre-Dame. ☎ **02-37-21-56-33.** Free admission to cathedral (see below for tour, crypt, and tower charges). Mon–Sat 7:30am–7pm, Sun 8:30am–7pm.

Reportedly, Rodin once sat for hours on the edge of the sidewalk, admiring this cathedral's Romanesque sculpture. His opinion: Chartres is the French Acropolis. When it began to rain, a kind soul offered him an umbrella—which he declined, so transfixed was he by the magic of this place.

The cathedral's origins are uncertain; some have suggested that it grew up over an ancient Druid site that later became a Roman temple. It is known that as early as the 4th century there was a Christian basilica here. A fire in 1194 destroyed most of what had then become a Romanesque cathedral, but it spared the western facade and crypt. The cathedral you see today dates principally from the 13th century, when it was rebuilt with the combined efforts and contributions of kings, princes, churchmen, and pilgrims from all over Europe. One of the world's greatest High Gothic cathedrals, it was the first to use flying buttresses.

French sculpture in the 12th century broke into full bloom when the Royal Portal was added. It's a landmark in Romanesque art. The sculptured bodies are elongated, often formalized beyond reality, in their long, flowing robes. But the faces are amazingly (for the time) lifelike, occasionally betraying Mona Lisa smiles. In the central tympanum, Christ is shown at the Second Coming, with his descent depicted on the right, his ascent on the left. Before entering, stop to admire the Royal Portal and then walk around to both the North Portal and the South Portal, each dating from the 13th century. They depict such biblical scenes as the expulsion of Adam and Eve from the Garden of Eden.

Inside is a celebrated choir screen (parclose screen); work on it began in the 16th century and lasted until 1714. The niches, 40 in all, contain statues illustrating scenes from the life of the Madonna and Christ—everything from the massacre of the innocents to the coronation of the Virgin.

To Taste a Madeleine

And suddenly the memory returns. The taste was that of the little crumb of madeleine which on Sunday mornings at Combray (because on those mornings I did not go out before church-time), when I went to say good day to her in her bedroom, my aunt Léonie used to give me, dipping it first in her own cup of real or of lime-flower tea.

—Marcel Proust, *Remembrance of Things Past*

Illiers-Combray, a small town 54 miles southwest of Paris and 15 miles southwest of Chartres, was once known simply as Illiers. Then Proust groupies started to come and signs were posted: ILLIERS, ILLIERS, LE COMBRAY DE MARCEL PROUST. Illiers was and is a real town, but Marcel Proust in his imagination made it world famous as Combray in his masterpiece, *À la recherche du temps perdu* (*Remembrance of Things Past*). So today the town is known as Illiers-Combray.

It was the taste of a luscious little madeleine that launched Proust on his immortal recollection. To this day hundreds of his readers from all over the world flock to the pastry shops in Illiers-Combray to eat a madeleine or two dipped in lime-flower tea. Following the Proustian labyrinth, you can explore the gardens, streets, and houses he wrote about so richly and had frequently visited until he was 13. The town is epitomized by its Église St-Jacques, where Proust as a boy placed hawthorn on the altar, and which he later referred to in his novels as l'Église St-Hilaire.

Some members of Proust's family had lived in Illiers for centuries. His grandfather, François, was born here on rue du Cheval-Blanc. At 11 place du Marché, just opposite the church, he ran a small candle shop. His daughter, Elisabeth, married Jules Amiot, who ran a shop a few doors away. Down from Paris, young Marcel would visit his aunt at 4 rue du St-Esprit, which has been renamed rue du Docteur-Proust, honoring Marcel's grandfather.

Musée Marcel Proust/Maison de Tante Léonie, 4 rue du Docteur-Proust (☎ 02-37-24-30-97), contains the world's most concentrated dose of memorabilia associated with Proust and the objects and memories that helped spark his creative vision. In his novels, this was Aunt Léonie's home, filled with antimacassars and antiques, and typical of the solid bourgeois comforts of its day. Upstairs you can see the pair of bedrooms where the young Marcel and his Aunt Léonie slept. Today, they contain souvenirs of key episodes in his novels. Also important is a meticulously crafted re-creation of the Salon Rouge, which Proust maintained in his second-to-last residence, at 102 Bd. Haussmann, Paris 8e, filled with furniture owned by his parents and grandparents. The museum can be visited only as part of French-language guided tours that are conducted at 2:30 and 4pm, every Tuesday to Sunday. Participation in the tour costs 30 F ($4.80) for adults, 20 F ($3.20) for students. It's free for children under 12. Closed mid-December to mid-January.

In the center of town, a sign will guide you to further Proustian sights, each of which is open 24 hours a day without charge.

But few rushed visitors ever notice the screen: They're too transfixed by the light from the stained glass. Covering an expanse of more than 3,000 square yards, the glass is without peer in the world and is truly mystical. It was spared in both world wars because of a decision to remove it painstakingly piece by piece. Most of the stained glass dates from the 12th and 13th centuries.

It's difficult to single out one panel or window of special merit—and depending on the position of the sun, the images all change constantly, as if in a kaleidoscope—however, an exceptional one is the 12th-century *Vierge de la Belle Verrière* (*Virgin of the Beautiful Window*) on the south side. Of course, there are three fiery rose windows, but you couldn't miss those even if you tried.

The nave—the widest in France—still contains its ancient labyrinth. The wooden *Notre-Dame du Pilier* (*Our Lady of the Pillar*), to the left of the choir, dates from the 14th century. The crypt was built over 2 centuries, beginning in the 9th. Enshrined within is *Notre-Dame de Sous Terre* (*Our Lady of the Crypt*), a 1976 Madonna that replaced one destroyed during the Revolution.

Try to get a tour conducted by Malcolm Miller (☎ **02-37-28-15-58;** fax 02-37-28-33-03), an Englishman who has spent 3 decades studying the cathedral and giving tours in English. His rare blend of scholarship, enthusiasm, and humor will help you understand and appreciate the cathedral. He usually conducts 75-minute tours at noon and 2:45pm Monday through Saturday for a fee of 40 F ($6.40) per person. Tours are cancelled in the event of pilgrimages, religious celebrations, and large-scale funerals. French-language tours at 35 F ($5.60) are conducted at 10:30am and 3pm from Easter to October and at 2:30pm the rest of the year.

If you're fit enough, don't miss the opportunity, especially in summer, to climb to the top of the tower. Open the same hours as the cathedral, except for a lunch closing between noon and 2pm, it costs 25 F ($4) for adults and 15 F ($2.40) for students. You can visit the crypt, gloomy and somber but rich with medieval history, only as part of a French-language tour conducted whenever there's enough demand. The cost is 11 F ($1.75) per person.

ACCOMMODATIONS

Grand Monarque Best Western. 22 place des Epars, 28005 Chartres. ☎ **800/528-1234** in the U.S., or 02-37-21-00-72. Fax 02-37-36-34-18. 54 units. MINIBAR TV TEL. 615–740 F ($98.40–$118.40) double; 1,120–1,350 F ($179.20–$216) suite. AE, DC, MC, V. Parking 50 F ($8).

The leading hotel of Chartres is housed in a classical building enclosing a courtyard. Functioning as an inn almost since its original construction, and greatly expanded over the centuries, it still attracts guests who enjoy its old-world charm—such as Art Nouveau stained glass and Louis XV chairs in the dining room. The guest rooms are decorated with reproductions of antiques; most have sitting areas. There is solid and reliable comfort here, including fine mattresses, but not great style. The hotel also has an old-fashioned, unremarkable restaurant.

Hôtel de la Poste. 3 rue du Général-Koenig, 28003 Chartres. ☎ **02-37-21-04-27.** Fax 02-37-36-42-17. E-mail: hotelposte.chartres@wanadoo.fr. 57 units. TV TEL. 315–350 F ($50.40–$56) double. AE, DC, MC, V. Parking 40 F ($6.40).

A member of the Logis de France chain, this modest hotel in the center of town offers one of the best values in Chartres—even though it's short on charm. The rooms are soundproofed, comfortably furnished with wall-to-wall carpeting and comfortable mattresses. Bathrooms are cramped with shower stalls and rather thin towels, but the price is unbeatable in Chartres. The surprise here is the good food served at affordable prices, and one of the town's finest wine cellars. Set menus range in price from 85 F to 170 F ($13.60 to $27.20), and are served daily at both lunch and dinner. The one drawback: group tours often flood the hotel.

DINING

Note that the restaurant at the Hôtel de la Poste (see above) serves good, reasonably priced food.

✪ **La Truie qui File (Choukroune).** Place Poissonnerie. ☎ **02-37-21-53-90.** Reservations recommended. Fixed-price menu 220 F ($35.20). AE, MC, V. Tues–Sun noon–2pm; Tues–Sat 7:30–9:30pm. Closed Aug. FRENCH.

At last Chartres has a restaurant worthy of some of the more stellar choices in Paris. The blue-and-yellow decor of this place includes modern furniture and art that's set beneath the venerable ceiling beams of a building erected in the 15th century. That, coupled with the savory cuisine of Gilles and Geneviève Choukroune, create a combination that usually bustles with good cheer and repeat visitors. The only option on the menu is a fixed-price menu with five choices for the starter, main course, and dessert. Menu items change with the season and the inspiration of the chef, but are likely to include foie gras with spice bread, a combination of crayfish and snails in a blanquette, oxtail stewed in Loire valley wine, and roasted scallops with coriander oil. The signature dessert combines fresh clementines with cumin. The cookery aims to please and does so admirably. Cooking times are unerringly accurate, and there is a certain charm and fragrance to every dish.

Le Buisson Ardent. 10 rue au Lait. ☎ **02-37-34-04-66.** Reservations recommended. Main courses 88–135 F ($14.10–$21.60); fixed-price menus 138–250 F ($22.10–$40). MC, V. Thurs–Tues noon–2pm, and 7:30–9:30pm. FRENCH.

In a charming 300-year-old house in the most historic section of town, this restaurant is one floor above street level in the shadow of the cathedral. From its location you might expect it to be a tourist trap, but it isn't, and it steadfastly refuses to follow many of the fads that sweep through restaurants in nearby Paris. The fixed-price menus change about once a month and, like the À la carte dishes, are based on strictly fresh meats, produce, and fish. Best-sellers are escalope of warm foie gras with apples and Calvados and émincée of roasted pigeon with sweetbreads and honey sauce. A dessert specialty is crispy hot pineapples with an orange and passion fruit salad.

CHARTRES AFTER DARK

For a formal evening of theater or modern dance, try the **Théâtre Municipal,** 1 place de Ravenne (☎ **02-37-18-27-27**), which offers presentations from September to June. From time to time you can catch a jazz or rock concert here as well. **Forum de la Madeleine,** 1 Mail Jean-de-Dunois (☎ **02-37-88-45-00**), presents lighter fare and usually has a busier performance season.

For a relaxing drink, try **La Bodega,** 20 place des Halles (☎ **02-37-36-05-05**). It has one of the best selections of beer in town, with a Cuban/salsa atmosphere and live entertainment on weekends. For dancing the night away, go to **Le Privilège,** 1 place St-Pierre (☎ **02-37-35-52-02**), where you'll find a wide range of dance music from zouk to funk and even disco.

4 Barbizon: The School of Rousseau

35 miles SE of Paris, 6 miles NW of Fontainebleau

In the 19th century the Barbizon school of painting gained world renown. This village on the edge of the Forest of Fontainebleau was a refuge for artists like Rousseau, Millet, and Corot, many of whom couldn't find acceptance in the more conservative Paris salons. In Barbizon they turned to nature for inspiration and painted more realistic pastoral scenes, without nude nymphs and dancing fauns. These artists attracted a school of lesser painters, including Daubigny and Diaz. Charles Jacques, Decamps, Paul Huet, Troyon, and many others followed. Today Barbizon attracts fashionable Parisians—often off the record—for le weekend. Some complain about its outrageous prices, but others just enjoy Barbizon's sunshine and clean air. Even with hordes of art galleries and souvenir shops, the town still retains much of its traditional atmosphere.

ESSENTIALS

GETTING THERE　Barbizon doesn't have a railway station of its own, so the most direct **train route** involves traveling from Paris to Fontainebleau (see below), and from there, taking one of only two buses a day that double back a few miles to Barbizon. The round-trip fare to Fontainebleau is 94 F ($15.05). Bus fare to Barbizon costs 13 F ($2.10) each way. For information and schedules, call ☎ **01-64-23-71-11.**

VISITOR INFORMATION　The **Office de Tourisme** is at 55 Grande-Rue (☎ **01-60-66-41-87**).

BARBIZON MUSEUMS

Maison et Atelier de Jean-François Millet. 29 Grande-Rue. ☎ **01-60-66-21-55.** Free admission. Wed–Sat and Mon 10am–12:30pm and 2–5:30pm.

This museum stands adjacent to the Hostellerie Les Pléiades (see below). Its premises are devoted to the best-known Barbizon painter, who settled here in 1849. Millet painted religious, classical, and especially peasant subjects. See his etching of *The Man with the Hoe,* as well as some of his original furnishings.

Musée Ganne. 92 Grande-Rue. ☎ **01-60-66-22-27.** Admission 25 F ($4), 13 F ($2.10) for students, free for children under 12. Apr–Oct, Wed–Mon 10am–12:30pm and 2–6pm; Nov–Mar, Wed–Mon 10am–12:30pm and 2–5pm.

The inn that housed most of the Barbizon artists during their late 19th-century sojourns here was L'Auberge du Père-Gannes. In the mid-1990s, through collaboration with Paris's Musée d'Orsay, it was transformed into the Musée Ganne, a showcase for Rousseau, the founder of the Barbizon school, who began painting landscapes directly from nature (novel at the time) and settled in Barbizon in the 1840s.

ACCOMMODATIONS

✪ **Hostellerie du Bas-Bréau.** 22 Grande-Rue, 77630 Barbizon. ☎ **01-60-66-40-05.** Fax 01-60-69-22-89. www.relaischateaux.fr/basbreau. E-mail: basbreau@relaischateaux.fr. 20 units. MINIBAR TV TEL. 950–1,500 F ($152–$240) double; 1,700–2,800 F ($272–$448) suite. AE, MC, V.

Dwarfing all the local competition, this member of Relais & Châteaux is one of France's great old inns, set amid shade trees and courtyards. In the 1830s many famous artists and writers stayed here, notably Robert Louis Stevenson, who scattered anecdotes of the inn throughout his novels. Napoléon III and his empress, Eugénie, came here for a day in 1868 to purchase some paintings from the Barbizon school.

　　The hotel is furnished in lustrous provincial antiques and fantastic reproductions. In the colder months, guests gather around the brick fireplace in the living room. The guest rooms have antiques and comfortable mattresses. The rooms in the rear building open directly onto semiprivate terraces.

　　Dining: Whether in the courtyard or the old-world dining room, you can enjoy specialties like the choicest and tenderest cuts of beef, followed by cold raspberry soufflé. In summer you can order good-tasting fish dishes flavored with herbs from the hotel's own garden, or veal kidney with fresh spinach and a confit of shallots. During the brisk autumn you'll find wild game on the menu, none finer than the specialty of the house: *pâté chaud de grouse* (a gamey Scottish grouse pâté wrapped in puff pastry and coated with a clear brown sauce).

Hostellerie La Clé d'Or. 73 Grande-Rue, 77360 Barbizon. ☎ **01-60-66-40-96.** Fax 01-60-66-42-71. 17 units. MINIBAR TV TEL. 470 F ($75.20) double; 870 F ($139.20) suite. AE, DC, MC, V.

Encircled by a stone wall, the grounds of this 100-year-old hotel include a large garden and an intimate stone terrace full of plants that flower in a wash of pinks and yellows during spring and summer. The terrace leads directly to many of the rooms, which are all modern but mainly quite small, with upholstered chairs and simple tables. Other rooms provide a bit more architectural flair and sport A-frame ceilings with exposed heavy wooden beams. Note that in some rooms a color-coordinated curtain of sorts has been used in lieu of a bathroom door. Bedrooms were each renovated in 1996, and mattresses were replaced in 1998. Bathrooms are small, with minimal shelf space. The hotel has a cozy English-style bar where you can relax with a drink before or after dinner; fixed-price menus—170 F or 230 F ($27.20 or $36.80)—are always available at the on-site French restaurant.

Hostellerie Les Pléiades. 21 Grande-Rue, 77630 Barbizon. ☎ **01-60-66-40-25.** Fax 01-60-66-41-68. E-mail: les.pleiades.barbizon@wanadoo.fr. 23 units. TV TEL. 320–550 F ($51.20–$88) double. AE, DC, MC, V. Free parking.

Les Pléiades combines antique decor with modern comforts in the former home of the respected 19th-century landscape painter Charles François Daubigny, creating a cozy, conservative, and homey atmosphere. It's also the seat of a series of art, music, and history conferences, which attract important politicians, artists, and writers. Bedrooms come in various shapes and sizes but each is fitted with a firm mattress. The place is run and directed by the town's local historian, Roger S. Karampournis, and his wife, Yolande.

   Dining: Before Karampournis bought the place 14 years ago, he was a dishwasher near the fish piers in Boston and later managed several PX operations for U.S. soldiers in Europe. Today, he supervises a team of high-quality, hardworking chefs who prepare French food with flair and style. Examples include roasted lobster; a ragoût of scallops; veal kidneys with mustard sauce; and fillet of beef with green peppercorns. Set menus in the well-recommended restaurant cost 185 F or 235 F ($29.60 or $37.60).

DINING

We also recommend the restaurants at the Hostellerie du Bas-Bréau and Hostellerie Les Pléiades (see "Accommodations," above).

Le Relais. 2 av. Charles-de-Gaulle. ☎ **01-60-66-40-28.** Reservations recommended on weekends. Main courses 86–110 F ($13.75–$17.60); fixed-price menus 110–210 F ($17.60–$33.60) Mon–Sat, 160–210 F ($25.60–$33.60) Sun. MC, V. Thurs–Tues noon–2:30pm; Thurs–Mon 7–9:30pm. Closed 1 week at Christmas and last week of Aug. FRENCH.

Many people prefer dining at this down-to-earth, comfortable restaurant to dining at the more pricey inns, such as the Bas-Bréau. Consistently offering excellent value, Le Relais is a corner tavern in a building boasting 300-year-old walls, with a provincial dining room centering on a small fireplace. In sunny weather, tables are set in the rear yard, with a trellis, an arbor, and trees. Typical menu choices are *quenelle* (a kind of dumpling) *de brochet,* roast quail with prunes, an excellent coq au vin, breast of duckling with cherries or seasonal fruit, grilled beef, and in autumn, different preparations of venison, rabbit, and pheasant.

5 Fontainebleau—Refuge of Kings

37 miles S of Paris, 46 miles NE of Orléans

Napoléon called the Palais de Fontainebleau the house of the centuries. Much of French history has taken place behind its walls, perhaps none more memorable than when Napoléon stood on the horseshoe-shaped exterior staircase and bade farewell to his army before his departure to exile on Elba. That scene has been the subject of countless paintings, including Vernet's *Les Adieux.*

Set in 50,000 acres of verdant forest, Fontainebleau today remains a country retreat for Parisians, even for those who have seen the château a dozen times. Visitors come to enjoy the grounds for horseback riding, picnicking, and hiking. Not as crowded with tourists, it's more peaceful here than Versailles.

ESSENTIALS

GETTING THERE   Trains to Fontainebleau depart from the Gare de Lyon in Paris. The trip takes between 45 and 60 minutes each way and costs 94 F ($15.05) round-trip. Fontainebleau's railway station lies 2 miles from the château, within the suburb of Avon. A local bus (it's marked simply "Château") makes the trip to the château at 15-minute intervals every Monday to Saturday, and at 30-minute intervals every Sunday, for 10 F ($1.60) each way.

By car, from the périphérique, take A6 south from Paris, exit onto N191, and follow the signs.

VISITOR INFORMATION   The **Office de Tourisme** is at 4 rue Royale in Fontainebleau (☎ **01-60-74-99-99**).

SEEING THE CHÂTEAU & GARDENS

✪ **Musée National du Château de Fontainebleau.** ☎ **01-60-71-50-70.** Combination ticket including the grand appartements and the Chinese Museum 35 F ($5.60) adults, 23 F ($3.70) students 18–25. Ticket to appartements and the Napoléonic rooms 16 F ($2.55) adults, 12 F ($1.90) students 18–25, free for children 17 and under. July–Aug, Wed–Mon 9:30am–6pm; Sept–June, Wed–Mon 9:30am–12:30pm and 2–5pm.

Napoléon joined in the grand parade of French rulers who used the Palais de Fontainebleau as a resort, hunting in its magnificent forest. Under François I (reigned 1515–47) the hunting lodge here was enlarged into a royal palace (as at Versailles under Louis XIV), much in the Italian Renaissance style the king admired. The style got botched up, but many artists, including Cellini, came from Italy to work for the French monarch.

Under François I's patronage, the School of Fontainebleau (led by the painters Rosso Fiorentino and Primaticcio) increased in prestige. These two artists adorned one of the most outstanding rooms at Fontainebleau: the 210-foot-long Gallery of François I. (The restorers under Louis-Philippe didn't completely succeed in ruining it.) Surrounded by pomp, François I walked the length of his gallery while artisans tried to tempt him with their wares, job seekers asked favors, and scented courtesans tried to lure him from the duchesse d'Étampes. The stucco-framed panels depict such scenes as Jupiter (portrayed as a bull) carrying off Europa, the Nymph of Fontainebleau (with a lecherous dog peering through the reeds), and the monarch holding a pomegranate, a symbol of unity. However, the frames compete with the pictures. Everywhere is the salamander, symbol of the Chevalier King.

If it's true that François I built Fontainebleau for his mistress, then Henri II, his successor, left a fitting memorial to the woman he loved, Diane de Poitiers. Sometimes called the Gallery of Henri II, the Ballroom is in the Mannerist style, the second

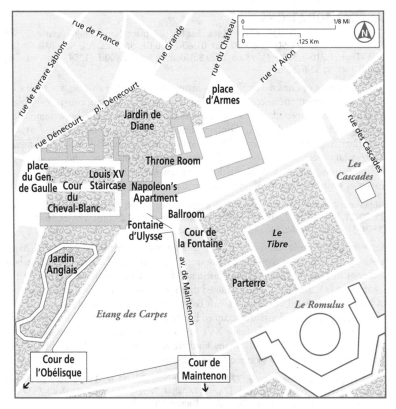

splendid interior of the château. The monograms H & D are interlaced in the decoration (the king didn't believe in keeping his affection for Diane a secret). At one end of the room is a monumental fireplace supported by two bronze satyrs, reproduced in 1966 (the originals were melted down in the Revolution). A series of frescoes, painted between 1550 and 1558, depicts mythological subjects.

An architectural curiosity is the richly adorned Louis XV Staircase. Originally the ceiling was decorated by Primaticcio for the bedroom of the duchesse d'Étampes. When an architect added the stairway, he simply ripped out her bedroom floor and used the ceiling to cover the stairway. Of the Italian frescoes that were preserved, one depicts the Queen of the Amazons climbing into Alexander the Great's bed.

Fontainebleau found renewed glory under Napoléon. You can wander around much of the palace on your own, visiting sites that evoke his 19th-century imperial heyday. They include the throne room, the room where he abdicated his rulership of France (the abdication document displayed is a copy), his offices, his monumental bedroom (look for his symbol, a bee), and his bathroom. Some of the smaller rooms, especially those containing his personal mementos and artifacts, are accessible by guided tour only. The furnishings in the grand apartments of Napoléon and Joséphine are marvelous.

Musée Chinois or Chinese Museum holds the Empress Eugénie's private collection of stunning Chinese treasures, including Far Eastern porcelain, jade, and crystal.

After your long trek through the palace, visit the gardens and, especially, the carp pond; the gardens, however, are only a prelude to the Forest of Fontainebleau and not nearly as spectacular as those surrounding Versailles.

ACCOMMODATIONS

✪ **Hôtel de l'Aigle-Noir (The Black Eagle).** 27 place Napoléon-Bonaparte, 77300 Fontainebleau. ☎ **01-60-74-60-00.** Fax 01-60-74-60-01. 56 units. A/C MINIBAR TV TEL. Mon–Thurs 1,210–1,380 F ($193.60–$220.80) double; from 2,400 F ($384) suite. AE, DC, MC, V. Parking 55 F ($8.80).

Once the home of Cardinal de Retz, this mansion opposite the château was built with a formal courtyard entrance, using a high iron grille and pillars crowned by black eagles. It was converted into a hotel in 1720 and has recently been remodeled, making it the finest lodgings in Fontainebleau, far superior in amenities and style to the Hôtel Napoléon (see below). The rooms are decorated with Louis XVI, Empire, or Restoration-era antiques or reproductions with plush mattresses and elegant bathroom amenities. Have a drink in the Napoléon III–style piano bar before dinner. Facilities include indoor pool, gymnasium, sauna, and underground garage.

Hôtel de Londres. 1 place du Général de Gaulle, 77300 Fontainebleau. ☎ **01-64-22-20-21.** Fax 01-60-72-39-16. www.hoteldelondres.com. 12 units. TV TEL. 650–850 F ($104–$136) double. AE, MC, V. Closed Christmas to Jan 10.

Set behind a historic 1830s-era façade, and owned and managed by several hard-working generations of the same family since 1932, this hotel enjoys one of the best locations in town for anyone who's fascinated by the renaissance architecture of the Château of Fontainebleau. It's positioned directly in front of the *Cour des Adieux,* site of Napoléon's farewell to his troops, just before his exile to the Isle of Elba. Only two of the building's three floors are occupied by the hotel, but each of the rooms is tastefully, even cozily outfitted in Louis XVI furniture and tones of soft blues and reds. Other than breakfast, no meals of any kind are served in this hotel, but the Colombier family will direct you to any of several nearby restaurants.

Hôtel Napoléon. 9 rue Grande, 77300 Fontainebleau. ☎ **01-60-39-50-50.** Fax 01-64-22-20-87. www.concorde-hotels.com. 57 units. MINIBAR TV TEL. 740–860 F ($118.40–$137.60) double; 1,200 F ($192) suite. AE, DC, MC, V. Parking 50 F ($8).

This classically designed hotel—the number-two choice in Fontainebleau—is a short walk from the château. The lobby has Oriental rugs, big arched windows overlooking the street, and a garden tearoom. An inviting bar off the reception area has an ornate oval ceiling, Louis-Philippe chairs, and a neoclassical fireplace. The rooms are filled with reproductions of antiques and eye-catching flowered headboards. All are comfortable, but those facing the courtyard are larger and more tranquil. Mattresses were replaced throughout the hotel in 1998, and ongoing maintenance has kept each unit freshly painted.

Dining: Since the Napoléon is so close to the château, many visitors dine in its first-class restaurant, La Table des Maréchaux—the food is among the finest served in Fontainebleau.

DINING

In addition to the options below, **La Table des Maréchaux** in the Hôtel Napoléon (see above) is a superb choice.

Le Caveau des Ducs. 24 rue de Ferrare. ☎ **01-64-22-05-05.** Reservations recommended. Main courses 95–130 F ($15.20–$20.80); fixed-price menus 125–250 F ($20–$40). AE, MC, V. Daily noon–2pm and 7–10pm. FRENCH.

Deep underground, beneath a series of 17th-century stone vaults built by the same masons who laid the cobblestones of rue de Ferrare upstairs, this reasonably priced restaurant occupies what once was a storage cellar for the nearby château. The decor is traditional, with lots of wood and flickering candles, and the staff helpful. The food is simple, but the setting is dramatic. Menu items include staples like snails in garlic butter, roast leg of lamb with garlic-and-rosemary sauce, and virtually everything that can be concocted from the body of a duck (terrines, magrêt, and confits). The fillet of rumpsteak is quite tasty, especially when served with brie sauce, as are the platters of sole, crayfish tails, and salmon on a bed of pasta. Especially flavorful are strips of veal in a morel-studded cream sauce on a bed of fresh pasta.

✪ **Le François-1er.** 3 rue Royale. ☎ **01-64-22-24-68.** Reservations required. Main courses 75–125 F ($12–$20); fixed-price menus 160–250 F ($25.60–$40). AE, DC, MC, V. Mon–Sat noon–2:30pm and 7:30–10pm, Sun noon–2:30pm. FRENCH.

The premier dining choice for Fontainebleau has Louis XIII decor, wine-making memorabilia, and walls that the owners think are about 200 years old. If weather permits, sit on the terrace overlooking the château and the cour des Adieux. In game season, the menu includes hare, roebuck, duck liver, and partridge. Other choices may be cold salmon with *cèpes* (flap mushrooms), *rognon de veau* (veal kidneys) with mustard sauce, and a salad of baby scallops with crayfish. The cuisine is meticulous, with an undeniable flair. The *magrêt de canard* (duck) flavored with cassis is delicious.

6 Vaux-le-Vicomte: Life Before Versailles

29 miles SE of Paris, 12 miles NE of Fontainebleau

Though it's so close to Paris, it's tough to reach Vaux-le-Vicomte without a car. Once you get here, allow 2 hours to see the château. By car, take N-6 southeast from Paris to Melun, which is 3³/₄ miles west of the château. By train, you'll need to take the 45-minute ride from Gare de Lyon to Melun first and then take one of the taxis lining up at the railway station for the 4-mile ride to Vaux-le-Vicomte. A rail ticket costs 86 F ($13.75) round-trip. For information call ☎ **01-53-90-20-20.**

SEEING THE CHÂTEAU

✪ **Château de Vaux-le-Vicomte.** 77950 Maincy. ☎ **01-64-14-41-90.** www.vaux-le-vicomte.com Admission 63 F ($10.10) adults, 49 F ($7.85) children 6–15, free for children 5 and under. Mid-Mar to mid-Nov, daily 10am–6pm. Closed mid-Nov to mid-Mar.

The château was built in 1656 for Nicolas Fouquet, Louis XIV's ill-fated finance minister. Louis wasn't at all pleased that Fouquet was able to live so extravagantly here, hosting banquets that rivaled the king's. Then Louis discovered that Fouquet had embezzled funds from the country's treasury, and the king was not amused. Fouquet was swiftly arrested, and then Louis hired the same artists and architects who had built Vaux-le-Vicomte to begin the grand task of creating Versailles. If you visit both you'll see the striking similarities between the two.

The view of the château from the main gate reveals the splendor of 17th-century France. On the south side, a majestic staircase sweeps toward the formal gardens, designed by Le Nôtre. The grand canal, flanked by waterfalls, divides the lush greenery. The château's interior, now a private residence, is completely furnished and decorated with 17th-century pieces. The great entrance hall leads to 12 state rooms, including the oval rotunda. Many of the rooms are hung with Gobelin tapestries and decorated with painted ceiling and wall panels by Le Brun, with sculpture by Girardon. A self-guided tour of the interior includes Fouquet's personal suite, the huge basement with its wine cellar, the servants' dining room, and the copper-filled kitchen.

Included in the price of admission is entrance to the château's carriage museum (Musée des Équipages), which is housed in the stables. The carriages are of three types—for country, for town, and for sports and hunting. Some 25 perfectly restored 18th- and 19th-century carriages are on display, each accessorized with mannequin horses and people. Hours are the same as those of the château itself.

From May to mid-October, candlelight evenings (Des Soirées à Chandelles) are held every Thursday and Saturday between 8pm and midnight. During those events, all electricity is cut off to the château, and thousands of candles are lit both within the château and within its surrounding gardens. The effect has been called mystical—a memorable re-creation of the way of life that prevailed during the building's heyday. Cost of admission during the candlelit evenings is 80 F ($12.80) for adults, 70 F ($11.20) for students and children ages 6 to 15, and free for children 5 and under.

DINING

Auberge de Crisenoy. Grande Rue, Crisenoy. ☎ **01-64-38-83-06.** Reservations recommended. Main courses 85–140 F ($13.60–$22.40); fixed-price menus 165–225 F ($26.40–$36). AE. Thurs–Tues noon–3pm and 7:30–9:30pm. From Vaux-le-Vicomte, follow N36 toward Meaux for $1^1/_2$ miles. FRENCH.

Though it's near Vaux-le-Vicomte, this auberge does more business with locals from Melun than with visitors. Behind the solid stone walls of a former private home, the two dining rooms (on separate floors) overlook a garden. The menu items are based on modern interpretations of French classics and change every 3 weeks. Examples include oysters in puff pastry with asparagus coulis; warm foie gras with a purée of figs; and a well-seasoned cassolette of crayfish with spinach and mussels, served in a copper pot placed directly on the table.

Le Table Saint-Just. Rue de la Libération, in the nearby village of Vaux-le-Pénil. ☎ **01-64-52-09-09.** Reservations recommended. Main courses 95–150 F ($15.20–$24); fixed-price menus 145–280 F ($23.20–$44.80). Mon–Fri noon–1:30pm; Tues–Sat 7:30–9:30pm. Closed Aug. AE, V. From the château of Vaux-le-Vicomte, drive $3^1/_2$ miles west, following the signs to Melun, then to Maincy, then to Vaux-le-Pénil. FRENCH.

This restaurant's charm derives from its nearness to the château, and from its location in a 17th-century farmhouse whose original masonry and artfully crafted structural beams are exposed to view within the high-ceilinged dining room. The place is run by Isabelle and Fabrice Vitu, who supervise the dining room and kitchen, respectively, of this well-respected place. Menu items change with the seasons, but might include foie gras in puff pastry, served with a confit of celery and acidified apples; lobster with red wine sauce; and a roasted rack of lamb with a moussaka of fresh vegetables.

7 Disneyland Paris

20 miles E of Paris

After provoking some of the most enthusiastic and controversial reactions in recent French history, the multimillion-dollar Euro Disney Resort opened in 1992 as one of the world's most lavish theme parks. Conceived on a scale rivaling that of Versailles, the project didn't begin auspiciously: European journalists delighted in belittling it and accused it of everything from cultural imperialism to the death knell of French culture.

But after goodly amounts of public relations and financial juggling, the resort is now on track. Disneyland Paris (the name change was also a boon) has become France's number-one tourist attraction, with 50 million annual visitors. Disney surpasses the Eiffel Tower and the Louvre in the number of visitors and accounts for 4% of the French tourism industry's foreign currency sales. Figures reveal that 40% of the visitors are French, half of them from Paris. Disneyland Paris looks, tastes, and feels like its parents in California and Florida—except for the $10 cheeseburgers *"avec pommes frites."*

Situated on a 5,000-acre site (about one-fifth the size of Paris) in the suburb of Marne-la-Vallée, with a European flair, the park incorporates the most successful elements of its Disney predecessors.

ESSENTIALS

GETTING THERE   The resort is linked to the RER commuter express **rail network** (Line A), which maintains a stop within walking distance of the theme park. Board the RER at such inner-city Paris stops as Charles-de-Gaulle-Étoile, Châtelet-Les Halles, or Nation. Get off at Line A's last stop, Marne-la-Vallée/Chessy, 45 minutes from central Paris. The round-trip fare costs 80 F ($12.80). Trains run daily, every 10 to 20 minutes from 5:30am to midnight.

Shuttle buses connect Orly and Charles de Gaulle airports with each hotel in the resort. Buses depart the airports at intervals of 30 to 45 minutes, depending on the time of day and day of the year. One-way transport to the park from either airport costs 85 F ($13.60) per person.

If you're **driving,** take A4 east from Paris and get off at Exit 14, where it's marked Parc Euro Disneyland. Guest parking at any of the thousands of spaces begins at 40 F ($6.40) per day. A series of interconnected moving sidewalks speeds up pedestrian transit from the parking areas to the entrance to the park. Parking is free for guests of any of the hotels in the resort.

VISITOR INFORMATION   All the hotels we recommend offer general information about the theme park. For details about Disney and for reservations at any of the resort hotels, contact the Disneyland Paris Guest Relations Office, located in City Hall on Main Street, USA (☎ **01-60-30-60-53** in English or 01-60-30-60-30 in French; www.disneylandparis.com). For general information about Disneyland Paris and specific details about the many other attractions and monuments in the Île de France and the rest of the country, contact the Maison du Tourism, Disney Village (B.P. 77705), Marne-la-Vallée CEDEX 4 (☎ **01-60-43-33-33**).

ADMISSION   Depending on season: 1 day, 165 F to 220 F ($26.40 to $35.20) for adults and 135 F to 170 F ($21.60 to $27.20) for children 3 to 12; 2 days, 320 F to 420 F ($51.20 to $67.20) for adults and 260 F to 330 F ($41.60 to $52.80) for children; children 2 and under enter free. Peak season is mid-June to mid-September as well as Christmas and Easter weeks. Entrance to Village Disney is free, though there's usually a cover charge to enter the dance clubs.

HOURS   July and August, the park is open daily from 9am to 11pm; September through June, Monday to Friday from 10am to 6pm and Saturday and Sunday from 9am to 8pm. Opening and closing hours vary with the weather and the season. It's usually good to phone the information office (see above).

EXPLORING DISNEYLAND

Disneyland Paris is a total vacation destination. Clustered into one enormous unit, the Disneyland Park includes five "lands" of entertainment, six massive well-designed hotels, a campground, an entertainment center (Festival Disney), a 27-hole golf course, and dozens of restaurants, shows, and shops.

Visitors from all over Europe stroll amid an abundance of flower beds, trees, reflecting ponds, fountains, and a large artificial lake flanked with hotels (see below). An army of smiling employees and Disney characters—many of whom are multilingual, including Buffalo Bill, Mickey and Minnie Mouse, and of course, the French-born

Caribbean pirate Jean Laffite—are on hand to greet and delight the thousands of *enfants.*

Main Street, U.S.A., is replete with horse-drawn carriages and street-corner barber-shop quartets. Steam-powered railway cars embark from the Main Street Station for a trip through a Grand Canyon diorama to **Frontierland,** with its paddle-wheel steamers reminiscent of Mark Twain's Mississippi River. Other attractions are a petting zoo called the Critter Corral at the Cottonwood Creek Ranch and the Lucky Nugget Saloon, whose inspiration comes from the gold-rush era; ironically, the steps and costumes of the cancan show originated in the cabarets of turn-of-the-century Paris.

The park's steam trains chug past **Adventureland**—with its swashbuckling 18th-century pirates, tree house of the Swiss Family Robinson, and reenacted *Arabian Nights* legends—to **Fantasyland.** Here you'll find the park's symbol, the Sleeping Beauty Castle (*Le Château de la Belle au Bois Dormant*), whose soaring pinnacles and turrets are an idealized (and spectacular) interpretation of the châteaux of France. Parading in its shadow are time-tested but Europeanized versions of *Blanche neige et les sept nains* (Snow White and the Seven Dwarfs), Peter Pan, Dumbo, Alice (from Wonderland), the Mad Hatter's Teacups, and Sir Lancelot's Magic Carousel.

Visions of the future are exhibited at **Discoveryland,** whose tributes to human invention and imagination are drawn from the works of Leonardo da Vinci, Jules Verne, H. G. Wells, the modern masters of science fiction, and the *Star Wars* series.

As Disney continues to churn out animated blockbusters, look for all their newest stars to appear in the theme park. You'll see characters from *Aladdin, The Lion King, Pocahontas,* and *Toy Story.*

In addition to the theme park, Disney maintains the **Village Disney** entertainment center. Illuminated inside by a spectacular gridwork of lights suspended 60 feet above ground, the complex contains dance clubs, shops, restaurants (one of which offers a dinner spectacle, *Buffalo Bill's Wild West Show*), bars for adults trying to escape their children for a while, a French Government Tourist Office, a post office, and a marina.

ACCOMMODATIONS

The resort contains six hotels, each evoking a different theme but all sharing a reservations service. For more information in North America, call ☎ **407/934-7639.** For information or reservations in France, contact the Central Reservations Office, Euro Disney S.C.A. (B.P. 105), F-77777 Marne-la-Vallée CEDEX 4 (☎ **01-60-30-60-30**). In correspondence, Euro Disney Resort (not Disneyland Paris) remains the official designation. For travelers with Internet access, all Disneyland Paris hotels can be reached through one Web site: www.disneylandparis.com.

✪ **Disneyland Hotel.** Euro Disney Resort, B.P. 105, F-77777 Marne-la-Vallée CEDEX 4. ☎ **01-60-45-65-00.** Fax 01-60-45-65-33. 496 units. A/C MINIBAR TV TEL. 1,600–3,840 F ($256–$614.40) double; 4,135–19,380 F ($661.60–$3,100.80) suite. AE, CB, DC, DISC, MC, V. Rates include breakfast. Children stay free in parents' room.

The flagship hotel of the resort, positioned at the entrance, resembles a massive Victorian resort hotel, with red-tile turrets and jutting balconies. The guest rooms are plushly and conservatively furnished and contain private safes. The generously proportioned accommodations evoke the image of Disney with cartoon depictions and a candy stripe decor. Some rooms have armchairs that convert to day beds. The luxury bathrooms have hair dryers, marble vanities, and twin basins. On the "Castle Club" floor, free newspapers, all-day beverages, and access to a well-equipped private lounge are provided.

Dining/Diversions: The hotel has three restaurants (The California Grill is recommended under "Dining," below) and two bars.

Amenities: Room service; laundry; baby-sitting; health club with indoor/outdoor pool, whirlpool, and sauna.

Hotel Cheyenne & Hotel Santa Fe. Euro Disney Resort, B.P. 115, F-77777 Marne-la-Vallée CEDEX 4. ☎ **01-60-45-62-00** for the Cheyenne or **01-60-45-78-00** for the Santa Fe. Fax 01-60-45-62-33 for the Cheyenne or 01-60-45-78-33 for the Santa Fe. 2,000 units. TV TEL. 1,100–1,760 F ($176–$281.60) double in Hotel Santa Fe; 1,200–1,850 F ($192–$296) double in Hotel Cheyenne. AE, DC, DISC, MC, V. Rates include a 2-day pass and breakfast.

Adjacent to each other, these are the least expensive places to stay at the resort (except for the campgrounds). They're near a re-creation of Texas's Rio Grande and evoke the Old West. The Cheyenne accommodates visitors in 14 two-story buildings along Desperado Street, whereas the Santa Fe, sporting a desert theme, encompasses four "nature trails" winding among 42 adobe-style pueblos. These are the least elegant of all the Disney hotel properties, although beds have firm mattresses and the comfort level is still high. The only drawback for parents is the lack of a pool. Tex-Mex specialties are offered at La Cantina (Santa Fe), while barbecue and smokehouse specialties predominate at the Chuck Wagon Café (Cheyenne).

Newport Bay Club. Euro Disney Resort, B.P. 105, F-77777 Marne-la-Vallée CEDEX 4. ☎ **01-60-45-55-00.** Fax 01-60-45-55-33. 1,098 units. A/C MINIBAR TV TEL. 1,520–2,160 F ($243.20–$345.60) double; from 2,970 F ($475.20) suite. AE, DC, MC, V. Rates include a 2-day pass and breakfast.

This hotel is designed with a central cupola, jutting balconies, and a large front porch with comfortable rocking chairs. Ringed by verdant lawns, it's inspired by a turn-of-the-century resort hotel in New England. Each nautically decorated room receives closed-circuit movies. Guest rooms come in various shapes and sizes; the most spacious rooms are the corner units. Amenities include private safes, phones with voice mail, and two double beds or one king-size, each with quality mattresses and fine linen. Some accommodations are reserved for nonsmokers, and others are suited for those with disabilities. Bathrooms are roomy with generous shelf space, deluxe toiletries, and a tub and shower combination. The upscale Yacht Club and less formal Cape Cod are the dining choices. Facilities include a lakeside promenade, a croquet lawn, a glassed-in pool pavilion, an outdoor pool, and a health club with sun beds and a sauna.

DINING

There are at least 45 restaurants and snack bars in the resort, each trying to please thousands of European and North American palates. Here are two recommendations:

Auberge de Cendrillon. In Fantasyland. ☎ **01-64-74-24-02.** Reservations recommended. Main courses 110–140 F ($17.60–$22.40); fixed-price menu 175 F ($28). AE, DC, DISC, MC, V. Thurs–Mon 11:30am to 90 minutes before the park closes. FRENCH.

The most visible and whimsical French restaurant at the resort is a fairy-tale version of Cinderella's sumptuous country inn, with a glass couch in the center. A master of ceremonies, in a plumed tricorne hat and an embroidered tunic and lace ruffles, welcomes you. Try the warm goat-cheese salad with lardons or the smoked-salmon platter for an appetizer. If you don't choose one of the fixed-price meals, you can order from the limited but excellent à la carte menu. Perhaps you'll settle happily for poultry in puff pastry, loin of lamb roasted with mustard, or sautéed medaillons of veal. The only drawback to this place is its location in the theme park, limiting its accessibility to its seasonal schedules. Lunches are usually easier to arrange than dinners.

The California Grill. In the Disneyland Hotel. ☎ **01-60-45-65-00.** Reservations required. Main courses 55–205 F ($8.80–$32.80); children's menu from 85 F ($13.60). AE, DC, DISC, MC, V. Sun–Fri 7–11pm, Sat 6–11pm. CALIFORNIAN/FRENCH.

Focusing on the lighter specialties for which the Golden State is famous, with many concessions to French palates and French tastes, this airy and elegant restaurant manages to gracefully accommodate both adults and children. Specialties include oysters with leeks and salmon; foie gras with roasted red peppers; roasted pigeon with braised Chinese cabbage and black-rice vinegar; and salmon roasted over beechwood, served with walnut oil, sage sauce, asparagus, and a fricassée of mushrooms. Children will appreciate "Mickey's Pizzas," spaghetti Bolognese, and grilled ham with French fries. *Note:* If you're looking for a quiet, mostly adult venue, go here as late as your hunger pangs will allow.

8 Provins: City of Roses

50 miles SE of Paris, 30 miles E of Melun

Feudal Provins, the "city of roses," is one of this region's most interesting towns. Historic, romantic, and beautiful, Provins soared to the pinnacle of its power and prosperity in the Middle Ages, then fell to ruin in the Hundred Years' War (1337–1453). Given its proximity to Paris, it's surprising that Provins today remains so relatively little known by foreigners.

Once it was the third town of France, after Paris and Rouen, and its Champagne Fair rivaled that of Troyes. But it sits high and dry today with its memories. The city is also known for its Damask Rose, brought back from the Crusades by Thibault IV. When the duke of Lancaster, through marriage, became the comte de Provins, he included the rose in his coat-of-arms. A century and a half later the red rose of Lancaster confronted the white rose of York in the War of the Roses.

If you're looking for a particular green tree to sit under, within the medieval core of Provins, head for Le Jardin Garnier and its "Allées d'Aligre." A flat, symmetrically laid out city park bounded by the Rue des Jacobins, the Allées d'Aligre, the Avenue de Verdun, and the Rue Saint-Thibault, adjacent to the Église Ste-Croix, it offers the kind of verdant space that encourages quiet reflection, and views stretching up to the city's *Ville Haute.*

ESSENTIALS
GETTING THERE   **Trains** depart from Paris's Gare de l'Est six times a day. The trip is 80 minutes each way (a bit longer if a transfer is required en route in the town of Longueville). Tickets cost 122 F ($19.50) round-trip. For information and schedule, call ☎ **01-53-90-20-20.**

VISITOR INFORMATION   The **Maison du Visiteur** (tourist office) is on chemin de Villecran (☎ **01-64-60-26-26**), adjacent to the entrance to the medieval ramparts.

EXPLORING THE TOWN
With its towers and bastions, Provins was surrounded in the 13th century by ramparts that protected it from the vast plains of Brie. The once-mighty fortifications are so well preserved that scholars refer to Provins as the "Carcassonne of the North." The best site for viewing these ramparts is the **Porte Jouy,** on the Upper Town's northwestern edge, at the terminus of rue de Jouy. A staircase rises to the top. Though the ramparts no longer make a full circuit of the town, you can still promenade along the top, enjoying a composite of military, secular, and ecclesiastical architecture from the Middle Ages. Entrance is free, and you can climb anytime you want.

Ville Haute (Upper Town) is perched on a promontory, and Ville Basse (Lower Town) is crossed by two rivers, the Durteint and the Voulzie, the latter an effluent of the Seine.

Tour César. Rue de la Pie. ☎ **01-64-60-26-26.** Admission 17 F ($2.70) adults, 10 F ($1.60) children 5–12, free for children 4 and under. Nov 1–Apr 2, daily 2–5pm; Apr 3–Oct 31, daily 2–6pm.

This 12th-century tower is the pride of the town. Since the 17th century it has functioned as the bell tower for the nearby Église St-Quiriace. When a fire destroyed the bell tower of St-Quiriace in the 17th century, the church was rebuilt with a vaguely baroque-looking dome, according to the fashion of the time, and the role of the bell tower was transferred to the Tour César. In 1998, its masonry was restored at great expense as part of a general overhaul of Provins's historic monuments.

The adjoining Église St-Quiriace was constructed in the 12th and 13th centuries, then rebuilt in the 17th. It contains a majestic, primitive Gothic choir and a modern dome. Joan of Arc stopped here on her way to Orléans. The church is open day and night. For July and August there is a guided tour. For information, call the tourist office. Admission is free.

Grange-aux-Dîmes (Tythe Barn). Rue St-Jean. ☎ **01-64-60-26-26.** Admission to exhibition 22 F ($3.50) adults, 14 F ($2.25) children. June–Aug, Mon–Fri 11am–6pm, Sat–Sun and holidays 10am–8pm; Apr–May and Sept–Oct, Mon–Fri 2–6pm, Sat–Sun 11am–6pm; Nov–Mar, Sat–Sun and holidays 2–5pm.

This historic building was used first as a covered marketplace for the medieval merchants who sold their goods here, then as lodgings for the merchants who traveled from far away. Later it was a warehouse for the tithes the Catholic church extracted from the corps of its faithful. In 1995 a permanent exhibition was added: Provins aux Temps des Foires de Champagne (Provins During the Trade Fairs of Champagne).

Les Souterrains de Provins (The Tunnels of Provins). Tours begin from the Hôtel-Dieu (Town Hall) on rue de Jouy. The tourist office (see above) will provide information. Guided tour 22 F ($3.50) adults, 14 F ($2.25) children. Spring and autumn tours, Sat–Sun and holidays 11am–6pm, Mon–Fri 1 tour at 2:30pm; June–Aug tours, Mon–Fri 2–6pm, Sat–Sun 11am–6pm; Winter tours, Sat–Sun and holidays at 2, 3, and 4pm.

The bedrock below the medieval streets of Provins is the site of a mysterious network of underground passageways that interconnect more than 150 separate subterranean "rooms." Many of these spaces are listed by the French government as historically important because of their graceful medieval architecture; others are more crude, with vaulting that was chiseled randomly out of the bedrock. Town historians don't completely understand the long-ago function of these tunnels. Possible explanations of why they were dug, between the 12th and the 13th century, include the following: A particular type of mineral was extracted from the porous soil for the treatment of the textiles manufactured during that era; the tunnels were used to escape enemy forces during sieges; they were used to conceal treasures; or they were used as a secret meeting place for Freemasons. A guided tour of the labyrinth begins and ends at the Hôtel-Dieu and requires 45 minutes.

DINING

Le Médiéval. 6 place Honoré-de-Balzac. ☎ **01-64-00-01-19.** Reservations recommended. Main courses 75–145 F ($12–$23.20); fixed-price menu 98 F ($15.70). AE, CB, V. Tues–Sun noon–2pm; Tues–Sat 7–9:30pm. FRENCH.

In a turn-of-the-century building in the Ville Basse's commercial center, this worthwhile restaurant has served thousands of meals during its long life. There are two dining rooms, one outfitted with big windows like a greenhouse, the other more con-fined and cozy. Since it hired a new, forward-thinking chef, Maria de Luz, in the late 1990s, its menu began to incorporate items that were more sophisticated than they had been during its more conservative past. Look for such tried-and-true favorites as warm shrimp cocktail and goat cheese salad on warm croutons, snails in butter-garlic sauce, and fillet of beef with morels. Also look for more unusual dishes such as terrine of venison, a mousseline of lobster, braised turbot with morels, and a mixture of chopped beef fillet served with foie gras of duckling. And if you want something really authentic to the region, and if you're really adventurous, consider the old-fashioned chitterling sausages (andouillettes) braised in the style of Troyes with mustard-flavored cream sauce.

9 Malmaison: Love Nest of Joséphine

10 miles W of Paris, 3 miles NW of St-Cloud

In the 9th century the Normanslanded in this area and devastated the countryside, hence the name of this Paris suburb, which translates to "bad house." History abounds at the country retreat, the Château de Malmaison.

EXPLORING THE CHÂTEAU

Musée National du Château de Malmaison. Av. du Château. ☎ **01-41-29-05-55.** Admission to Malmaison, which includes entrance to Bois Préau (if it's open), 30 F ($4.80) Mon and Wed–Sat; 20 F ($3.20) Sun, free for children 17 and under and students. May–July, Mon and Wed–Fri10am–5:45pm, Sat–Sun 10am–6pm; Apr and Aug–Sept, Mon and Wed–Fri 10am–12:30pm and 1:30–5:45pm, Sat–Sun 10am–6pm. Free tours Mon and Wed–Fri at 10am, 2pm, and 3:30pm, every 15 minutes Sat–Sun. (Bois-Préau will reopen after renovations sometime in 2001.) Take the RER A-1 line to La Défense. Transfer to bus no. 258 for the 6-mile ride to the château (Stop: Château).

Few other sites in France carry as strong a dose of the intimate moments of Napoléon Bonaparte, albeit within a period of his life that wasn't noted for its marital happiness. Construction on the château, used as a country retreat far removed from the Tuileries or Compiègne (other Napoleonic residences), began in 1622. It was purchased in 1799 by Napoléon's wife, Joséphine, who had it restored and fashionably decorated as a love nest. She then enlarged the estate (but not the château). Popular references to Malmaison as having been a lepers' sanitarium are unfounded.

Today Malmaison is filled with mementos from Napoléon's euphoric early days as a general shortly after the Revolution and during his rise to power as first consul of France. The veranda and council room were obviously inspired by the tent he occu-pied on his military campaigns and are filled with Empire furnishings. His study and desk are exhibited in the library. Marie-Louise, his second wife, took Napoléon's books with her when she left France; they were later purchased by an English couple who presented them to the museum here. Most of the furnishings are originals; some came from the Tuileries and St-Cloud. Napoléon always attached a sentimental importance to Malmaison, and he spent a week here before his departure for St. Helena.

Many of the portraits and sculptures immortalize a Napoleonic deity—for example, David's equestrian portrait of the emperor and also a flattering portrait of Joséphine by Gérard.

After her divorce in 1809 (she couldn't bear Napoléon an heir), Joséphine retired here and was passionately devoted to her roses until her sudden death in 1814 at the age of 51. The bed in which Joséphine died is exhibited, as is her toilette kit, including her toothbrush.

Also here is the small Château de Bois-Prau (follow the signs through the park, a 5-minute walk from the main building). Built in 1700 and acquired by Joséphine in 1810, it's smaller, darker, sadder, and less architecturally distinguished than Malmaison. The château (more of a villa since its reconstruction in 1854) is a museum/shrine to the emperor's exile on the isolated Atlantic outpost of St. Helena, after his fall from grace. For better coverage of the years between his rise to power (as exhibited at Malmaison) and his disgrace and death on St. Helena, see the Napoleonic museum in Fontainebleau (above).

10 The Remarkable Zoo of Château de Thoiry

25 miles W of Paris

✪ **Château et Parc Zoologique de Thoiry.** 78770 Thoiry-en-Yvelines. ☎ **01-34-87-52-25.** Admission château, 38 F ($6.10) adults, 30 F ($4.80) children 3–12, free for children 2 and under; reserve or gardens, 105 F ($16.80) adults, 79 F ($12.65) children 3–12, free for children 2 and under. Park, Apr–Oct, daily 10am–6pm; Nov–Mar, daily 10am–5pm. The Château, Mar–Oct, Mon–Sat 10am–6pm, Sun 10am–8pm. Take the Autoroute de l'Ouest (A13) toward Dreux, exiting at Bois-d'Arcy. Then get on N12, following the signs on D11 to Thoiry.

This major attraction drew more visitors in a single year than the Louvre or Versailles. The 16th-century château, owned by the vicomte de La Panouse family (now run by son Paul and his wife, Annabelle), displays two unpublished Chopin waltzes, antique furniture, and more than 343 handwritten letters of French or European kings, as well as the original financial records of France from 1745 to 1750. But these aren't as much a draw as the Parc Zoologique.

The château's grounds have been turned into a game reserve with elephants, giraffes, zebras, monkeys, rhinoceroses, alligators, lions, tigers, kangaroos, bears, and wolves—more than 1,000 animals and birds roam at liberty. The reserve and park cover 300 acres of the 1,200-acre estate.

In the French gardens you can see llamas, Asian deer and sheep, and many types of birds, including flamingos and cranes. In the tiger park a promenade has been designed above the tigers. In addition, in the basement of the château is a vivarium. Paul and Annabelle are also restoring the 300 acres of 17th-, 18th-, and 19th-century gardens as well as creating new ones.

To see the animal farm you can drive your own car, providing it isn't a convertible (an uncovered car may be dangerous). The park is most crowded on weekends, but if you want to avoid the crush, visit on Saturday or Sunday morning.

ACCOMMODATIONS & DINING

Hôtel de l'Étoile. 38 rue de la porte St-Martin, 78770 Thoiry. ☎ **01-34-87-40-21.** Fax 01-34-87-49-57. 12 units. TV TEL. 245–325 F ($39.20–$52) double. AE, DC, MC, V. Free parking.

This appealing rustic hotel was built more than 200 years ago and retains many of its original wall and ceiling beams, and much of its original masonry. Bedrooms were renovated in the late 1990s. The premises contain a fountain shaped like a dolphin, and there's a particularly worthy on-site restaurant featuring conservative, time-tested French cuisine. Expect to pay 120 F to 170 F ($19.20 to $27.20) for a fixed-price meal.

11 Giverny: In the Footsteps of Monet

50 miles NW of Paris

On the border between Normandy and the Île de France, the Claude Monet Foundation is where the great painter lived for 43 years. The restored house and its gardens are open to the public.

ESSENTIALS

GETTING THERE   If you're going by **train,** take the Paris-Rouen line (Paris-St-Lazare) to the Vernon station. A **taxi** can take you the 3 miles to Giverny. **Bus tours** are operated from Paris by American Express (☎ **01-42-27-58-80**) and Cityrama (☎ **01-44-55-61-00**).

If you're **driving,** take the Autoroute de l'Ouest (Port de St-Cloud) toward Rouen. Leave the autoroute at Bonnières, then cross the Seine on the Bonnières Bridge. From here, a direct road with signs will bring you to Giverny. Expect about an hour of driving and try to avoid weekends.

Another way is to leave the highway at the Bonnières exit and go toward Vernon. Once here, cross the bridge over the Seine and follow the signs to Giverny or Gasny (Giverny is before Gasny). This is easier than going through Bonnières, where there aren't many signs.

SHOW ME THE MONET

✪ **Claude Monet Foundation.** Rue Claude-Monet Parc Gasny. ☎ **02-32-51-28-21.** Reservations required. Admission 35 F ($5.60) adults, 20 F ($3.20) children. Gardens only, 25 F ($4) adults, 10 F ($1.60) children. Apr–Oct, Tues–Sun 10am–6pm. Closed Nov–Mar.

Born in 1840, the French Impressionist was a brilliant innovator, excelling in presenting the effects of light at different times of the day. In fact, some critics claim that he "invented light." His series of paintings of the Rouen cathedral and of water lilies, which one critic called "vertical interpretations of horizontal lines," are just a few of his masterpieces.

Monet first came to Giverny in 1883. Many of his friends used to visit him here at Le Pressoir, including Clemenceau, Cézanne, Rodin, Renoir, Degas, and Sisley. When Monet died in 1926, his son, Michel, inherited the house, but left it abandoned until it decayed into ruins. The gardens became almost a jungle, inhabited by river rats. In 1966 Michel died and left it to the Académie des Beaux-Arts. It wasn't until 1977 that Gerald van der Kemp, who restored Versailles, decided to work on Giverny. A large part of it was restored with gifts from U.S. benefactors, especially the late Lila Acheson Wallace, former head of *Reader's Digest,* who contributed $1 million.

You can stroll through the garden and view the thousands of flowers, including the *nymphéas.* The Japanese bridge, hung with wisteria, leads to a dreamy setting of weeping willows and rhododendrons. Monet's studio barge was installed on the pond.

DINING

Auberge du Vieux Moulin. 21 rue de la Falaise. ☎ **02-32-51-46-15.** Main courses 72–95 F ($11.50–$15.20); fixed-price menus 128–148 F ($20.50–$23.70). MC, V. Tues–Sun noon–3pm and 7:30–10pm. Closed Jan. FRENCH.

This is a convenient lunch stop for visitors to the Monet house, in a stone building with a pair of flowering terraces. The Boudeau family maintains a series of cozy dining rooms filled with original Impressionist paintings. Since you can walk here from the museum in about 5 minutes, leave your car in the museum lot. Specialties include escalope of salmon with sorrel sauce, chicken fillet garnished with shrimp, and aiguillettes of duckling with peaches. The kitchen doesn't pretend that the food is anything more than good, hearty country fare with a dash of panache. The charm of the staff helps a lot, too.

12 Chantilly—A Day at the Races

26 miles N of Paris, 31 miles SE of Beauvais

This is a resort town for Parisians who want a quick getaway for le weekend. Known for its frothy whipped cream and its black lace, it also draws visitors to its racetrack and château. The first two Sundays in June are the highlight of the turf season, bringing out an exceedingly fashionable crowd.

Two of the great horse races of France, Le Prix du Jockey Club (conducted the first Sunday in June) and the Prix Diane-Herès (conducted the second Sunday in June), take place at the Hippodrome de Chantilly. Thoroughbreds from as far away as Kentucky and Brunei, as well as mounts sponsored by the old and new fortunes of Europe, compete in a very civil format that's broadcast around France and talked about in horse circles around the world. On race days, as many as 30 trains depart from Paris's Gare du Nord for Chantilly, where they are met with free shuttle buses to the track. Buses also depart on race days from Place de la République and Porte de St-Cloud, on a schedule that coincides with the beginning and end of the races. Call ☎ 01-49-10-20-30 for more information.

ESSENTIALS

GETTING THERE   **Trains** depart frequently for Chantilly from the Gare du Nord in Paris; the ride takes about 30 minutes; cost is 84 F ($13.45) round-trip. Alternatively, RER line D will get you from metro stop Châtelet-Les Halles to Chantilly in about 45 minutes.

VISITOR INFORMATION   The **Office de Tourisme** is at 60 av. du Maréchal-Joffre (☎ **03-44-57-08-58**).

TOURING THE CHÂTEAU & MUSEUMS

✪ **Château de Chantilly/Musée Condé.** ☎ **03-44-62-62-62.** Admission 42 F ($6.70) adults, 37 F ($5.90) students 12–18, 15 F ($2.40) children 3–11. Mar–Oct, Wed–Mon 10am–6pm; Nov–Feb, Wed–Mon 10:30am–12:45pm and 2–5pm. Admission includes guided tour.

Once the seat of the grand Condé, a princely cousin of Louis XIV and head of the Bourbon-Condé dynasty, the Château de Chantilly and the Musée Condé (within the château) are on an artificial carp-stocked lake. You approach via the same forested drive that Louis XIV, with hundreds of guests, rode along for a banquet prepared by Vatel, one of the best-known French chefs. (One day when the fish didn't arrive on time, Vatel committed suicide.) The château is French Renaissance, with gables and domed towers, but part was rebuilt in the 19th century. It's skirted by a romantic forest once filled with stag and boar.

In 1886 the château's owner, the duc d'Aumale, bequeathed the park and palace to the Institut de France, along with his fabulous art collection and library. The château houses sumptuous furnishings as well as works by artists like Memling, van Dyck, Botticelli, Poussin, Watteau, Ingres, Delacroix, Corot, Rubens, and Vernet. See especially Raphael's *Madonna of Lorette, Virgin of the House d'Orléans,* and *Three Graces* (sometimes called the *Three Ages of Woman*). The foremost French painter of the 15th century, Jean Fouquet, is represented here by a series of about 40 miniatures. A copy of the rose diamond that received worldwide attention when it was stolen in 1926 is on display in the jewel collection. One of the most celebrated Condé library acquisitions is the Limbourg brothers' *Très Riches Heures du Duc de Berry,* a 15th-century illuminated manuscript illustrating the months of the year.

The château was built about 1560 by Jean Bullant for one of the members of the Montmorency family. The stables (see below), a hallmark of French 18th-century architecture, were constructed to house 240 horses, with adjacent kennels for 500 hounds. If you have time, take a walk in the garden laid out by Le Nôtre. A hamlet of rustic cottages and the Maison de Sylvie, a graceful building constructed in 1604 and rebuilt by Maria-Felice Orsini, are in the park. You can just visit the garden for 17 F ($2.70) if you don't want to see the château (Musee).

Les Grandes Écuries/Musée Vivant du Cheval. 7 rue du Connétable. ☎ **03-44-57-40-40.** Admission 50 F ($8). Sept–Apr, Wed–Mon 10:30am–6:30pm; May–June, daily 10:30am–6:30pm; July–Aug, Wed–Mon 10:30am–6:30pm, Tues 2–5pm. Equestrian displays Apr–Oct, daily 11:30am, 3:30pm, and 5:15pm; Nov–Mar, 3:30pm.

This museum occupies the restored *Grandes Écuries,* the stables built between 1719 and 1735 for Louis-Henri, prince de Bourbon and prince de Condé, who occupied the château. Besides being fond of horses, he believed in reincarnation and expected to come back as a horse in his next life; therefore, he built the stables fit for a king.

The stables and an adjoining kennel fell into ruin over time, but they've now been restored as a museum of the living horse, with thoroughbreds housed alongside old breeds of draft horses, Arabs and Hispano-Arabs, and farm horses. Yves Bienaimé, the certified riding instructor who established the museum, presents exhibitions tracing the horse's association with humans, as well as a blacksmith shop and displays of saddles, equipment for the care of horses, and horse-race memorabilia.

The three daily equestrian displays (from April to October) last about half an hour and explain how the horse is ridden and trained. A restaurant on the premises, Le Carrousel Gourmand (☎ 03-44-57-19-77), features the specialties of Picardy, and does so exceedingly well. Reservations are required.

ACCOMMODATIONS

Best Western Hôtel du Parc. 36 av. du Maréchal-Joffre, 60500 Chantilly. ☎ **800/528-1234** or 03-44-58-20-00. Fax 03-44-57-31-10. 57 units. TV TEL. 500 F ($80) double. AE, DC, MC, V. Parking 50 F ($8) day.

This modern hotel is in the center of town, close to a host of restaurants and sights. The contemporary-styled spacious lobby, dominated by sharp angles of mirror and chrome, gives way to a more inviting English-style bar with plenty of dark wood and leather. The medium-size guest rooms have built-in furnishings and sliding glass doors that open onto private balconies. Mattresses here have seen better days. Overall, expect a no-frills experience that's pleasant but nothing special.

Château de Chaumontel. 21 rue André-Vassord, 95270 Chaumontel. ☎ **01-34-71-00-30.** Fax 01-34-71-26-97. www.chateau-de-chaumontel.com. E-mail: chateau-de-chaumontel@wanadoo.fr. 20 units. TV TEL. 980–1,010 F ($156.80–$161.60) double; 1,290 F ($206.40) suite. Rates include half board. AE, MC, V. Take N16 south for 4 miles.

Northeast of Luzarches and south of Chantilly is this hotel/restaurant from the late 16th century. Accented with conical towers and slate roofs, it has had many aristocratic owners and was once the hunting lodge of the prince de Condé, who lived at Chantilly. In 1956 it was turned into a hotel, with well-furnished rooms. The decor ranges from rooms with high, sloping ceilings trussed with massive antique beams, to elegant replicas of the kind of room you'd find within a privately owned manor house. Surrounded by a moat and a verdant landscape dotted with wildflowers, the château is about as evocative a site as any in this region. The rustic dining room serves excellent meals every day from noon to 3pm and from 7 to 11pm, offering specialties like crabs' legs, filet mignon, and eggplant and caviar. There's an independently owned Indian restaurant on-site.

Château de la Tour. Chemin de la Chaussée, 60270 Chantilly-Gouvieux. ☎ **03-44-62-38-38.** Fax 03-44-57-31-97. www.lechateaudelatour.wanadoo.fr. E-mail: chateau. reception@wanadoo.fr. 41 units. MINIBAR TV TEL. 690–930 F ($110.40–$148.80) double. AE, DC, MC, V. Free parking.

This turn-of-the-century château and its 12-acre park was built as a weekend getaway by a wealthy Parisian banking family. During World War II it became the home of the German l'État Major, and in 1946 it was transformed into a luxury hotel. The likes of Edith Piaf, Tino Rossi, and Jean Gabin would meet and mingle with friends in the restaurant. Today many celebrities and sports personalities still frequent the château. In 1990 a new wing was added, giving you the opportunity to choose rooms with a modern flavor or a more traditional ambience. In either case, all rooms are large and have hardwood floors, high ceilings, and first-class furnishings. All the mattresses in the hotel's newer wing, and all but a handful within the hotel's older core, are high quality. You can also enjoy haute French cuisine every day at lunch and dinner at set meals priced at 210 F to 290 F ($33.60 to $46.40) each. The grand dining room has parquet floors and two wood-burning fireplaces. Other amenities include a tennis court, an outdoor pool, and access to a nearby entrepreneur specializing in mountain-bike rentals.

DINING

The restaurant at the Château de la Tour (see above) is open to the public.

La Ferme de Condé. 42 av. du Maréchal Joffre. ☎ **03-44-57-32-31.** Reservations recommended. Main courses 70–115 F ($11.20–$18.40); fixed-price menus 98–125 F ($15.70–$20). DC, MC, V. Daily noon–2:30pm and 7–10:15pm. FRENCH.

The most appealing restaurant in Chantilly occupies the stone-sided premises of what was built about a century ago as an Anglican church, on the northern periphery of town, about a mile north of the château. Today, it's the most popular restaurant in town, thanks to excellent food and a rustic, informal decor that works as a pleasant contrast to the buildings soaring vertically. Coziness derives from a collection of antique farm implements, racks of wine bottles, and well-preserved barrels. Cuisine is artfully old-fashioned, with almost daily variations, based on seasonal ingredients and the inspiration of the chef. Examples include a terrine *de basse cour,* which combines poultry, rabbit, and duck in the same way that a 19th-century matriarch might have pulled whatever animals she had been raising from her barnyard (*basse cour*) as raw ingredients for the week's terrine. There's also a succulent version of suckling pig roasted on a spit and served with fresh thyme and veal kidneys in a mustard-flavored cream sauce. Also look for a fricasée of scallops with white wine and herbs; and salmon *verdurette,* served with cream sauce and fresh local herbs.

13 Senlis

32 miles S of Paris, 62 miles S of Amiens

Today sleepy Senlis, which some Parisians treat as a suburb of Paris, remains a quiet township surrounded by forests. No history has been made here in a long time, but its memories are many and regal. Barbarians no longer threaten its walls as they did in the 3rd century; and gone, too, are all those kings of France, from Clovis to Louis XIV, who either passed through or took up temporary residence here. You can tie a visit to this northern French town with a trek to nearby Chantilly (below). Today the core of Vieux Senlis is an archaeological garden that attracts visitors from all over the world.

ESSENTIALS

GETTING THERE   Take any of the approximately 20 **trains** that depart every day from Paris's Gare du Nord for Chantilly (see above). In front of the railway station in Chantilly, bus no. 15 (it's marked "Senlis") maintains departures that are timed to coincide with the arrival of trains from Paris. Round-trip fares from the Gare du Nord to the center of Senlis, combining transits aboard both the bus and train, cost 98 F ($15.70) per person. Total travel time from downtown Paris to the heart of Senlis takes between 45 and 60 minutes.

VISITOR INFORMATION   The **Office de Tourisme** is on place parvis Notre-Dame (☎ **03-44-53-06-40**).

SEEING THE SIGHTS

Medieval streets loaded with antique masonry, evocative portals and doorways include the rue du Chat-Harét, from the center of which there's a view over the ruined château and the Gallo-Roman foundations it sits on. There's also the rue des Cordelier, site of a (since demolished) medieval convent. Nos. 14 and 10 along that street are particularly beautiful and old, but neither can be visited.

Cathédrale Notre-Dame de Senlis. Place parvis Notre-Dame. ☎ **03-44-53-01-59** in the town center. Free admission. Daily 8am–7pm.

Notre-Dame has a graceful 13th-century spire that towers 256 feet and dominates the countryside for miles around. The severe western facade contrasts with the Flamboyant Gothic southern portal. A fire swept over the structure in 1504 and much rebuilding followed. A 19th-century decorative overlay was applied to the original Gothic structure, which was begun in 1153. Before entering, walk around to the western porch to see the sculptures. Depicted in stone is an unusual calendar of the seasons, along with scenes showing the ascension of the Virgin and the entombment. The builders of the main portal imitated the work at Chartres. In the forecourt are memorials to Joan of Arc and Marshal Foch.

Château Royal et Parc and Musée de la Vénerie (Hunting Museum). ☎ **03-44-53-06-40**, ext. 1315. Admission 16 F ($2.55) adults, 8 F ($1.30) students, free for children 16 and under. Wed 2–6pm, Thurs–Mon 10am–noon and 2–5pm. All visits of the Musée de la Vénerie only include an obligatory guided tour, in French, that begins every hour, on the hour, during the opening hours listed above. Closed mid-Dec to Jan.

A short walk away from the Cathédrale, you'll find the Château Royal et Parc. Built on the ruins of a Roman palace, the castle followed the outline of the Gallo-Roman walls, some of the best preserved in all of France. Once inhabited by such monarchs as Henri II and Catherine de Médici, the château (now in ruins) encloses a complex of buildings. Of the 28 towers originally constructed against the Gallo-Roman walls, only 16 remain. One ruin houses the King's Chamber, the boudoir of French monarchs since the time of Clovis. In the complex is the Prieuré St-Mauritius, a priory that not only honors a saint but also was founded by one, Louis IX.

The Musée de la Vénerie (Hunting Museum), in the Château Royal, is housed in an 18th-century prior's building in the middle of the garden and displays hunting-related works of art from the 15th century to the present—paintings, drawings, engravings, old hunting suits, arms, horns, and trophies.

Musée d'Art de Senlis. Place Notre-Dame. ☎ **03-44-53-00-80.** Admission 16 F ($2.55) adults, 8 F ($1.30) for students under 25, free for local residents and for anyone under 16. Wed 2–6pm, Thurs–Mon 10am–noon and 2–6pm. Nov–Jan, closes 5pm.

No other site in Senlis depicts the ancient Roman occupation of Gaul in such vivid terms. Set within the partially Gothic former home of the local bishop, and inaugurated in 1989, it contains most of the archaeological artifacts of the Gallo-Romans discovered in the region. It also contains rare sculptures and church art from the Middle Ages. One floor above street level, you'll find paintings, some by local artists painting in an untrained style that art historians refer to as "naive," executed between the 17th and 20th centuries.

ACCOMMODATIONS

Hostellerie de la Porte Bellon. 51 rue Bellon, 60300 Senlis. ☎ **03-44-53-03-05.** Fax 03-44-53-29-94. 20 units. MINIBAR TV TEL. 400 F ($64) double; 990 F ($158.40) 3-bedroom suite for up to 6. MC, V. Closed Dec 21–Jan 5.

This stately looking but relatively inexpensive hotel and restaurant was originally built as a convent 300 years ago, and later functioned as a coaching inn for the lodging of mail carriages. Set within a short walk east of Senlis's historic core, it has three floors of big-windowed bedrooms, and a facade that's dotted with old-fashioned shutters, window boxes filled with pansies and geraniums, and prefacing the entrance, an unusual 19th-century glass vestibule inspired by an English greenhouse. Bedrooms have comfortable mattresses, but are a bit Spartan despite the cheerful wallpaper. Many of the rooms were renovated during the mid-to-late 1990s. The establishment's restaurant offers set menus priced at 135 F ($21.60) and 190 F ($30.40), some charmingly rustic accessories, and a massive fireplace. It's open daily for both lunch and dinner.

DINING

The restaurant at the Hostellerie de la Porte Bellon (see above) is open to the public.

Vieille Auberge. 8 rue Long Filet. ☎ **03-44-60-95-50.** Reservations recommended Fri–Sat. Main courses 85–110 F ($13.60–$17.60); fixed-price menus 114–169 F ($18.25–$27.05). AE, DC, MC, V. Daily noon–2pm; Mon–Sat 7–10pm. FRENCH.

This is the town's best restaurant. Each dining room, with its stone walls and heavy tables, has been coordinated with simple fabrics and candlelight to create a refined rustic ambience. During warm months, a small terrace functions as another dining area. The attentive staff takes an unmistakable pride in serving classically French dishes, which may include such favorites as monkfish tournedos in a piquant pepper sauce, fillet of beef in a country wine sauce and accompanied by a vegetable crêpe, and duck fillet with foie gras and whole-grain mustard sauce. Even though the cuisine isn't worth a special drive from Paris, the restaurant is nevertheless memorable for its atmosphere and perfectly prepared dishes.

14 Compiègne

50 miles N of Paris, 20 miles NE of Senlis

A visit to this Oise River valley town is usually combined with an excursion to Senlis (see above). The most famous dance step of all time was photographed in a forest about 4 miles from town: Hitler's "jig of joy" on June 22, 1940, which heralded the ultimate humiliation of France and shocked the world.

Like Senlis, this is another town north of Paris that still lives for its memories—not all of them pleasant. Many Parisians visit not for the attractions, but for the 35,000-acre Forest of Compiègne. With its majestic vistas, venerable trees, and ponds, it merits exploration, especially the colorful little villages of St-Jean-aux-Bois and Vieux-Moulin.

ESSENTIALS

GETTING THERE   There are frequent **rail connections** from the Gare du Nord in Paris. The ride takes 50 minutes. The station is across the river from the town center. A ticket costs 140 F ($22.40) round-trip. If you're **driving,** take the northern Paris-Lille motorway (A1 or the less convenient E15) for 50 miles.

VISITOR INFORMATION   The **Office de Tourisme** is on place Hôtel-de-Ville (☎ **03-44-40-01-00**).

SEEING THE SIGHTS

An imposing statue of Joan of Arc, who was taken prisoner at Compiègne by the Burgundians on May 23, 1430, before she was turned over to the English, stands in the town square.

Musée National du Château de Compiègne. Place du Palais. ☎ **03-44-38-47-00.** Admission (including the museums) 35 F ($5.60) adults, 23 F ($3.70) students, free for children under 18. Wed–Mon 10am–5:15pm.

In the town's heyday, royalty and the two Bonaparte emperors flocked here. But this wasn't always a place of pageantry. Louis XIV once said: "In Versailles, I live in the style befitting a monarch. In Fontainebleau, more like a prince. At Compiègne, like a peasant." But the Sun King returned again and again. His successor, Louis XV, started rebuilding the château, based on plans by Gabriel. The king died before work was completed, but Louis XVI and Marie Antoinette continued to expand it.

Napoléon's second wife, Marie-Louise, arrived at Compiègne to marry him, and in a dining room, which you can visit only on the guided tour, she had her first meal with the emperor. Accounts maintain that she was paralyzed with fear of this older man (Napoléon was in his 40s, she was 19). After dinner, he seduced her and is said to have only increased her fears.

It wasn't until the Second Empire that Compiègne reached its pinnacle of success. Under Napoléon III and Eugénie, the autumnal hunting season was the occasion for gala balls and parties, some allegedly lasting 10 days without a break. It was the "golden age:" Women in elegant hooped gowns danced with their escorts to Strauss waltzes, Offenbach's operas echoed through the chambers and salons, and Eugénie, who fancied herself an actress, performed in the palace theater for her guests.

On the guided tour you'll see the gold-and-scarlet Empire Room, where Napoléon spent many a troubled night. His library, known for its secret door, is also on the tour. In the Queen's Chamber, the "horn of plenty" bed was used by Marie-Louise. The furniture is by Jacob, and the saccharine nude on the ceiling by Girodet. Dubois decorated the charming Salon of Flowers, and the largest room, the Ball Gallery, was adorned by Girodet. In the park, Napoléon ordered the gardeners to create a green bower to remind Marie-Louise of the one at Schönbrunn in Vienna, where she grew up.

Various wings of the château contain a handful of museums, entrance to which is included in the château admission. They include the Musée National de la Voiture (National Automobile Museum), which exhibits about 150 vehicles: everything from Ben-Hur chariots to bicycles to a Citroën "chain-track" vehicle. About 10 of the vehicles are gas-powered antique autos; another 40 are exotic forms of horse-drawn carriages. The château also contains a series of rooms defined as either the Musée de l'Imperatrice Eugénie, the Musée du Second Empire, or the Musée Napoléon III, according to whomever happens to be talking about it at the time. It's devoted to sculpture, paintings (including some by Carpeaux), and furniture, as well as mementos and documents showcasing life, politics, values, and morals of France's Industrial Revolution and its Gilded Age.

Musée de la Figurine Historique (Museum of Historical Figurines). Place de l'Hôtel-de-Ville. ☎ **03-44-40-72-55.** Admission 12 F ($1.90) adults; 6 F (95¢) students, seniors, children. Tues–Sat 9am–noon and 2–6pm, Sun 2–6pm. Nov–Feb, closes 5pm.

One of Compiègne's finest monuments is the Flamboyant Gothic Hôtel de Ville. Built from 1499 to 1503, with a landmark belfry that's visible from far away, it houses a unique museum of great interest to students of the wars that have raged across northern France. The Museum of Historical Figurines offers a unique collection of about 100,000 tin soldiers, from a Louis XIV trumpeter to a soldier from World War II. The Battle of Waterloo, staged in miniature form on a landscape with thousands of figurines, is depicted in all its gore.

Château de Pierrefonds. In the Forêt de Compiègne. ☎ **03-44-42-72-72.** Admission 32 F ($5.10) adults, 21 F ($3.35) students 18–26, free for children under 18. May–Aug, daily 10am–5:15pm; Sept–Apr, daily 10am–12:30pm and 2–5:15pm.

One of the Compiègne forest's most evocative medieval buildings lies $7^1/_2$ miles north of Compiègne. (To reach it from the town center, follow the signs to Soissons.) Originally built in the 1100s as a château-fortress, it was later bought by Napoléon, who intended to transform it into one of his private homes. Surrounded with a moat, it boasts a feudal look, with rounded towers capped by funnel-shaped pointed roofs. Artifacts from the Middle Ages are displayed within its interior. Save time for a stroll through the tiny village, Pierrefonds, at the base of the château. Here, half-timbered houses evoke the life of the château's medieval heyday.

Wagon de l'Armistice (Wagon du Maréchal-Foch). Route de Soissons in the village of Rethondes. ☎ **03-44-85-14-18.** Admission 10 F ($1.60) adults, 6 F (95¢) children 7–14, free for children 6 and under. Apr to mid-Oct, Wed–Mon 9am–12:15pm and 2–6:15pm; mid-Oct to Mar, Wed–Mon 9am–11:45am and 2–5:30pm.

In 1940, at the peak of his power, in one of the most ironic twists of fate in European history, Hitler forced the vanquished French to capitulate in the same rail coach where German officials signed the Armistice on November 11, 1918. The then-triumphant Nazis transported the coach to Berlin, and then to Ordüff in the Thuringian Forest, where it was destroyed by an Allied bomb in April of 1945. In Compiègne's suburb of Rethondes, 4 miles to the south, you can visit a replica that retells the events of both 1918 and 1940 in graphic detail, assisted by newspapers, photos, maps, and slide shows.

ACCOMMODATIONS

The **Rôtisserie du Chat Qui Tourne** (see "Dining," below) also rents rooms.

Au Relais Napoléon. Av. de l'Europe, 60200 Compiègne. ☎ **03-44-20-11-11.** Fax 03-44-20-41-60. E-mail: au.relais@wanadoo.fr. 47 units. TV TEL. 415 F ($66.40) double. AE, DC, MC, V. Free parking. Head west on av. Berthelot, which becomes av. de l'Europe, a 10-min. trip.

This modern hotel outside of town is near sports complexes and the border of the forest, surrounded by a sunny terrace, green lawns, and even a small vineyard. The interior is First Empire style, with honeycomb ceilings, tiled floors, and dark woodwork. The medium-size guest rooms offer a relaxing ambience with rich colored walls, reproduction furniture, and firm mattresses. The elegant bar is open 24 hours, and the air-conditioned restaurant, which is open for lunch and dinner every day except Sunday night, provides fixed-price meals from 98 F to 280 F ($16.65 to $47.60) each.

Hostellerie du Royal-Lieu. 9 rue de Senlis, 60200 Compiègne. ☎ **03-44-20-10-24.** Fax 03-44-86-82-27. 26 units. TV TEL. 495 F ($79.20) double; 655 F ($104.80) suite. AE, DC, MC, V. Follow the signs southwest toward Senlis until you reach rue de Senlis, a 5-min drive east from the town center.

Monsieur and Madame Bonechi have carefully decorated the rooms in this rambling half-timbered inn about 1¼ miles from town. They have names like Madame de Pompadour, Madame Butterfly, and La Goulue; less fancifully named rooms are done in a scattering of different "Louis" periods or Empire style. Bedrooms are medium in size and sleekly designed, often with excellent mattresses. The tiled bathrooms are tidily organized with adequate shelf space, a shower and tub combination, and medium-size towels. Both the rooms and the restaurant's terrace look out over an immaculate garden. Meals in the elegantly rustic, recently enlarged and renovated dining room may include four-fish stew with red butter, brochette of quail with black olives and polenta, and fillet of beef with morels in cream sauce or with foie gras. Dessert soufflés are available if you order them 30 minutes in advance. Meals are served daily at lunch and dinner. (Closed Sunday night during winter.)

DINING

Note that the restaurants in both hotels above are open to the public.

Rôtisserie du Chat Qui Tourne. In the Hôtel de France, 17 rue Eugène-Floquet, 60200 Compiègne. ☎ **03-44-40-02-74.** Reservations recommended. Main courses 78–220 F ($12.50–$35.20); fixed-price menus 135–220 F ($21.60–$35.20). MC, V. Daily noon–2:15pm and 7:15–9:15pm. FRENCH.

The name, "Inn of the Cat That Turns the Spit," dates from 1665. The bar and a traditional country inn-style dining room are downstairs. Madame Robert, the proprietor, believes in judicious cooking and careful seasoning and prices her table d'hôte menus to appeal to a wide range of budgets. The *menu gastronomique* is likely to include *foie gras de canard* (duck), then *cassolette de Roguens* (veal kidneys), followed by either *poulet rôti* (roast chicken) *à la broche* or tournedos of salmon with wild mushrooms, and finally a cheese and a dessert.

Madame Robert also rents 22 clean and well-maintained rooms, each with bathroom, TV, phone, and comfortable beds outfitted with flowered bedcovers. Doubles are 165 F to 385 F ($26.40 to $61.60).

The Loire Valley **6**

Bordered by vineyards, the winding Loire Valley cuts through the land of castles deep in France's heart. Crusaders returning to their medieval quarters here brought news of the opulence of the East, and soon they began rethinking their surroundings. Later, word came from neighboring Italy of a great artistic flowering led by Leonardo da Vinci and Michelangelo. So when royalty and nobility built châteaux throughout this valley during the French Renaissance, sumptuousness was uppermost in their minds. An era of excessive pomp reigned until Henri IV moved his court to Paris, marking the Loire's decline.

The Loire is blessed with abundant attractions—ranging from medieval, Renaissance, and classical châteaux to Romanesque and Gothic churches to treasures like the Apocalypse Tapestries. There's even the castle that inspired the fairy tale *Sleeping Beauty.* Our warnings about driving in Paris do not apply to the Loire Valley. Although there's train service to some of the towns, renting a car is the best way to see this region.

REGIONAL CUISINE Patricia Wells, author of *The Food Lover's Guide to France,* has said that the Loire's cuisine reminds her "of the daffodil days of spring and blue skies of summer." Particularly superb are rose-fleshed salmon caught in the Loire River, often served with sorrel. The region's rivers are stocked with other fish as well, including pike, carp, shad, and mullet.

Various types of *rillettes* (potted pork) begin most meals. Gourmets highly prize *pâté d'alouettes* (lark pâté) and *matelote d'anguille* (stewed eel). From the mushroom-rich Sologne emerges wild boar, along with deer, miniature quail, hare, pheasant, and mallard duck. Two popular poultry dishes are chicken casserole in red-wine sauce and spit-roasted capon.

The valley's Atlantic side produces an astonishing variety of grapes, used to make wines ranging from dry to lusciously sweet, and from still to sparkling and fruity. The best whites are Vouvray (ideal with Loire salmon) and Montlouis. Red Anjou wines, including Rouge de Cabernet and Saumur-Champigny, have a slight raspberry flavor. Dry Sancerre wines, with plenty of backbone, are wonderful with the Loire's fabled goat cheese and whitewater fish.

The Loire Valley

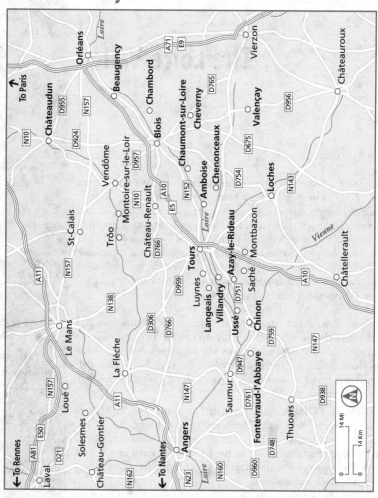

1 Orléans

74 miles SW of Paris, 45 miles SE of Chartres

After suffering heavy damage in World War II, many Orléans neighborhoods were rebuilt in dull postwar styles, so visitors who hope to see how it looked when the Maid of Orléans was here are likely to be disappointed. There are still many rewarding sights, though, and a jazz festival held the first week of July significantly livens the place up. Today, this city of 200,000 has lost a lot of its former importance to Tours, but signs of urban restoration bring hope for the city's future.

ESSENTIALS

GETTING THERE **Ten trains** per day arrive from Paris's Gare d'Austerlitz (trip time: 1¼ hours); there are also a dozen connections from Tours (trip time: 1¼ hours). The one-way fare from Paris is 91 F ($14.55); from Tours it's also 91 F ($14.55).

Orléans lies on the road between Paris and Tours. If you're **driving** from Paris, take A10 south; from Tours, take A10 north.

VISITOR INFORMATION   The **Office de Tourisme** is on place Albert-1er (☎ **02-38-24-05-05**).

EXPLORING THE TOWN

Orléans is the chief town of Loiret, on the Loire, and beneficiary of countless associations with the French aristocracy—even giving its name to ducs and duchesses who influenced the course of the nation's history. Joan of Arc relieved the city in 1429 from attacks by the Burgundians and the English. That deliverance is celebrated every year on May 8, the anniversary of her victory. An equestrian statue of Jeanne d'Arc stands in place du Martroi, which was created by Foyatier in 1855. From the square, you can drive down rue Royal (rebuilt in 18th-century style) across pont George-V (erected in 1760). After crossing the bridge, you'll have a good view of the town. A simple cross marks the site of the Fort des Tourelles, which Joan of Arc and her men captured.

If you're looking for a unique gift indigenous to the area, go to **La Chocolaterie Royale,** 53 rue Royale (☎ **02-38-53-93-43**), where you'll find jars of *cotignac,* an apricot-colored jelly made from quince. While in the store, you can also stock up on fine handmade chocolate.

Near rue Royale is place du Châtelet, with its many boutiques, including a Galeries Lafayette. Look for fashionable clothing, jewelry, books, and leather goods. For antiques, walk along rue de Bourgogne, where you'll find a host of dealers offering everything from objets d'art to furniture.

Cathédrale Ste-Croix. Place Ste-Croix. ☎ **02-38-77-87-50.** Free admission, but you should tip the guide. Daily 10am–noon and 2–5pm (May–Sept closes 6pm). Guided visits, in French only, can be arranged by the tourist office for 25 F ($4) per person. May–Sept, tours at 3, 4, and 5pm.

Begun in 1287 in the High Gothic period, the cathedral was burned by the Huguenots in 1568. The first stone on the present building was laid by Henri IV in 1601, and work continued until 1829. The cathedral boasts an excellent 17th-century organ and some magnificent woodwork from the early 18th century in its chancel, the masterpiece of Jules Hardouin-Mansart and other artists of Louis XIV. You'll need to take the guided tour to see the chancel, the crypt, and the treasury, with its Byzantine enamels, goldwork from the 15th and 16th centuries, and Limoges enamels.

Hôtel Groslot. Place de l'Étape (northwest of the cathedral). ☎ **02-38-79-22-30.** Free admission. July–Sept, Sun–Fri 9am–7pm, Sat 5–9pm; Oct–June, Mon–Fri 10am–noon and 2–6pm, Sat 5–6pm.

This Renaissance mansion was begun in 1550 and embellished in the 19th century. François II (first husband of Mary, Queen of Scots) lived in it during the fall of 1560 and died here on December 5. Between the Revolution and the mid-1970s, it functioned as the town hall until it was replaced with something less dramatic but more functional. Despite that, marriage ceremonies, performed by the town's civil magistrates, still occur here. Romance is nothing new to this building: It was here that Charles IX met his lovely Marie Touchet. The statue of Joan of Arc praying (at the foot of the flight of steps) was the work of Louis Philippe's daughter, Princesse Marie d'Orléans. In the garden you can see the remains of the 15th-century Chapelle St-Jacques.

Église St-Aignan. Place St-Aignan. (no phone; ask at tourist office). July–Sept, Sun–Fri 9am–7pm, Sat 5–9pm; Oct–June, Sun–Fri 10am–noon and 2–6pm, Sat 5–6pm.

One of the most frequently altered churches in the Loire Valley, St-Aignan was consecrated in 1509 in the form you see today. It's noted for possessing one of France's earliest vaulted hall crypts, complete with polychromed capitals. Scholars of pre-Romanesque art view the place with passionate interest, for its 10th- and 11th-century aesthetics are exceptionally rare. Above ground, the church's Renaissance-era choir and transept remain, but the nave was burned by the Protestants during the Wars of Religion. In a gilded carved-wood shrine are the remains of the church's patron saint.

Musée des Beaux-Arts. 1 rue Fernand-Rabier. ☎ **02-38-79-21-55.** Admission 20 F ($3.20) adults, 10 F ($1.60) children. Sun and Tues 11am–6pm, Wed 10am–8pm, Thurs–Sat 10am–6pm.

This is primarily a picture gallery of French and (to a lesser degree) Dutch and Flemish works from the 16th to the late 19th centuries. Some of the works once hung in Cardinal Richelieu's château. The collection includes busts by Pigalle and a fine array of portraits, including one of Mme de Pompadour. Among non-French works, the undisputed star is a lovely Velásquez commemorating the Apostle St. Thomas.

ACCOMMODATIONS

Hôtel d'Arc. 37 rue de la République, 45000 Orléans. ☎ **02-38-53-10-94.** Fax 02-38-81-77-47. 35 units. MINIBAR TV TEL. 350 F ($56) double. AE, DC, MC, V.

This hotel, with its ornate Art Deco facade, sits in the middle of the historic town center and is close to just about everything. Most rooms are of average size, with functional, built-in furnishings and good mattresses on the beds. Bathrooms are only of modest size, but each comes with a tub and shower. Most rooms are peaceful, but avoid those that face rue de la République, as they tend to be somewhat noisy. Although the hotel has no restaurant, it does serve breakfast in an ornate room with a carved marble fireplace.

Hôtel Mercure Orléans. 44–46 quai Barentin, 45000 Orléans. ☎ **02-38-62-17-39.** Fax 02-38-53-95-34. 108 units. A/C MINIBAR TV TEL. 630 F ($100.80) double. AE, DC, MC, V.

Along the river, adjacent to pont Joffre, this modern eight-floor bandbox structure is within walking distance of place du Martroi and its Joan of Arc statue. Though rather impersonal—it's favored by businesspeople—it offers the best and most comfortable rooms in the city, each recently repainted and refurbished. Most rooms are chain format in style and of medium size, but each is fitted with a comfortable bed with a firm mattress. There's a heated pool, and a restaurant/bar, Le Gourmandin, serves straightforward French and Loire Valley specialties, with fixed-price menus at 145 F to 300 F ($23.20 to $48) each.

Hôtel St-Martin. 52 bd. Alexandre-Martin, 45000 Orléans. ☎ **02-38-62-47-47.** Fax 02-38-81-13-28. 22 units, 13 with bathroom. 150 F ($24) double without bathroom, 250–310 F ($40–$49.60) double with bathroom. AE, DC, V.

If you prefer simplicity over opulence and think of a hotel room only as a place to sleep and shower, then this is the place for you. The 80-year-old three-story building has spacious rooms, sparsely furnished with firm mattresses and built-in armoires. Half are blessed with windows that look out onto the private garden behind the hotel, where you can sit and enjoy a refreshing nonalcoholic drink.

Orléans

To Chartres & Paris
To Etampes
place de Gambetta
Gare
bd. de Verdun
place Albert-1er
Bus Station
Parc Louis Pasteur
rue E. Vignat
rue Jules Lemaître
rue du faubourg St-Vincent
rue Bannier
rue de la République
rue de la Bretonnerie
rue d'Alsace-Lorraine
bd. de Aléxandre Martin
rue R. Chollet
bd. A. Briand
rue Bellebat
bd. St-Euverte
place de l'Etape
rue d'Escures
place du Martroi
Hôtel Groslot
rue Dupanloup
rue du Bourdon Blanc
place du Gén de Gaulle
rue Jeanne d'Arc
place Ste-Croix
place Abbé Desnoyes
Cathédrale Ste-Croix
Musée Historique
Musée des Beaux-Arts
rue de Bourgogne
rue de Bourgogne
Maison de Jeanne d'Arc
rue Royale
rue de la Tour Neuve
To Sens & Gien
place du Châtelet
Nouvelle Halle
Eglise St-Aignan
quai Cypierre
quai du Châtelet
quai du Fort-Alleaume
To Blois & Tours
pont George-V
L o i r e

Church
Information
Post Office

0   1/4 Mi
0   .25 Km

N

DINING

La Poutrière. 8–10 rue de la Brêche. ☎ **02-38-66-02-30.** Reservations required. Main courses 140–600 F ($22.40–$96); fixed-price menus 228–320 F ($36.50–$51.20). AE, MC, V. Tues–Sun noon–2pm; Tues–Sat 7:30–9:30pm. Closed Dec 24–Jan 15. FRENCH.

This 18th-century restaurant occupies an antique, much renovated farmhouse on the relatively underpopulated left bank of the Loire. Beneath heavy ceiling beams, you can enjoy specialties from the talented chef Simon Lebras, such as a lobster "cake," veal kidneys with sauterne sauce, salmon with Bourgeuil wine, Loire valley fish and game, pan-fried scallops stuffed either with truffles or foie gras (and sometimes both). Any of these might be accompanied with a particularly succulent ragoût of wild mushrooms. The apple tart served with apricot-flavored sorbet makes a worthy dessert. Be prepared for a staff that speaks absolutely no English and seems a little awkward with international guests.

✪ **Les Antiquaires.** 2–4 rue au Lin. ☎ **02-38-53-52-35.** Reservations required. Main courses 90–152 F ($14.40–$24.30); fixed-price menu 220 F ($35.20). AE, DC, MC, V. Tues–Sun noon–2:30pm; Tues–Sat 7:30–10pm. Closed 1 week in Jan. FRENCH.

This rustically elegant stone-sided mansion on a narrow street near the river was built in the 1300s during the time of Joan of Arc. The original ceiling beams are highlighted within a rust-colored environment that's cozy, warm, and appealing. Owners Philippe and Pascale Bardau, cooking and tending the dining room, respectively, create a virtually flawless cuisine based on modern interpretations of traditional French recipes, each of which changes with the seasons. Savor the Loire Valley's abundance of wild game, if you're lucky enough to arrive in autumn or winter, in dishes like an estouffade of wild boar with red-wine sauce. In springtime, look for dishes such as ravioli of fresh morels with asparagus tips; roasted baby goat served with tagliatelle and sweet garlic sauce; fried fillets of sandre with slices of chitterling sausages and fried fillets of eel; and an orange-and-Grand-Marnier-flavored soufflé served with sorbet in puff pastry. Everything is very creative here, and the staff is most attentive.

ORLÉANS AFTER DARK

You'll find most of the after-dark action in this town in the bars along rue de Bourgogne and the handful of places that spill over onto rue Bannier. A trendy young crowd dances and drinks the night away at the **George V,** Les Halles Châtelet (☎ **02-38-53-08-79**). A few streets over is one of the better jazz clubs, **Paxton's Head,** 264 rue de Bourgogne (☎ **02-38-81-23-29**), with a down-home English pub feel. The mid-20s crowd enjoys a live comedian every night at the **Majestic Café,** 2 rue des Trois-Maries (☎ **02-38-54-68-68**); housed in a 13th-century building, it looks like a church on the inside with its stone walls and vaulted ceilings. If you like to drink beer and shoot pool or billiards, head for **Bar Darlington,** 3 rue du Colombier (☎ **02-38-54-67-98**), where there's a real easygoing ambience.

2 Châteaudun

64 miles SW of Paris, 27 miles SW of Chartres

Austere and foreboding, **Château de Châteaudun,** place Jean-de-Dunois (☎ **02-37-94-02-90**), rises on a stonebound table over a tributary of the Loire. Although begun in the Middle Ages, the château is a mix of medieval and Renaissance architecture, with towering chimneys and dormers. After a fire in the 18th century, Hardouin, Louis XV's architect, directed the town's near-total reconstruction and indiscreetly turned the castle over to the homeless, who stripped it of its finery. In 1935, the government acquired the fortress and launched a major restoration. Even today it's not richly furnished, but fine tapestries depicting scenes like the worship of the golden calf now cover its walls. The château's most admirable features are two carved staircases. Inside the Sainte-Chapelle, dating from the Middle Ages, are more than a dozen 15th-century robed statues.

The château is open daily, April to September from 9:30am to 6pm and October to March from 10am to 12:30pm and 2 to 5pm. Admission is 32 F ($5.10) for adults, 21 F ($3.35) for ages 18 to 24, and free for children 17 and under.

ESSENTIALS

GETTING THERE   Buses run frequently from Chartres, and there are about a half-dozen trains per day, departing from Paris's Gare d'Austerlitz, charging around 100 F ($16) each way, and arriving 90 minutes later in Châteaudun. The Office de Tourisme, 1 rue de Luynes (☎ **02-37-45-22-46**), keeps schedules and provides information. If you're driving from Paris, head southwest along the A10 autoroute, and exit at Phivars. Then take the N10, following the signs for Châteaudun.

ACCOMMODATIONS

Hôtel de Beauce. 50 rue Jallans, 28200 Châteaudun. ☎ **02-37-45-14-75.** Fax 02-37-45-87-53. 24 units, 18 with bathroom. TV TEL. 160 F ($25.60) double without bathroom, 270 F ($43.20) double with bathroom. MC, V. Closed Sun and Dec 20–Jan 10. Parking 26 F ($4.15).

This clean, modern hotel is utterly without pretense. Built in the 1950s, it's set in a quiet residential neighborhood about a 2-minute walk from the edge of town. Though it lacks a restaurant, it does have a small cocktail lounge for guests only. The rooms are furnished in a simple contemporary style. Between 1996 and 1999, most of the mattresses in this hotel were replaced with up-to-date new ones.

Hôtel St-Michel. 28 place du 18-Octobre and 5 rue Péan, 28200 Châteaudun. ☎ **02-37-45-15-70.** Fax 02-37-45-83-39. www.groupcitotel.com/hotels/michel.html. 19 units, 15 with bathroom. TV TEL. 185–220 F ($29.60–$35.20) double without bathroom, 250–310 F ($40–$49.60) double with bathroom. AE, DC, V. Parking 28 F ($4.50).

This hotel's tradition of welcoming overnight guests extends to the early 19th century, when it served as a coaching inn. Today, under the direction of Pierre Le Menestrel, and with the help of his hardworking staff and the stellar location on the town's main square, this is one of the best hotels around. Bedrooms, which have been undergoing renovations since the early 1990s, are simply furnished and comfortable, with high-quality mattresses. Breakfast is served in the lounge, in your room, or in the greenhouse-style winter garden. There's no restaurant on the premises, but there's a sauna and a small gym.

3 Beaugency

93 miles SW of Paris, 53 miles NE of Tours

Situated on the right bank of the Loire, the town of Beaugency boasts a 14th-century bridge that's unusual because each of its 26 arches is in a different style. The heart of this ancient Loire Valley town is an archaeological garden called the City of the Lords, named after the counts who enjoyed great power in the Middle Ages. A major event in medieval Europe took place here: the 1152 annulment of the marriage between Eleanor of Aquitaine and her fourth cousin, Louis VII. This remarkable woman later became queen consort of Henry II of England, bringing southwestern France as her dowry. She was also the mother of Richard the Lion-Hearted. (These events are retold in the movie *The Lion in Winter;* Katharine Hepburn won an Oscar for her portrayal of Eleanor.)

The 15th-century **Château Dunois,** 2 place Dunois (☎ **02-38-44-55-23**), contains a folklore museum of the Orléans district. The collection includes antique toys, hairpieces, furniture, costumes, paintings, and sculpture found in the district. The museum is open Wednesday through Monday from 10am to noon and 2 to 5pm (to 6:30pm in summer). Admission is 22 F ($3.50) for adults, 10 F ($1.60) for children 6 to 17, free for children 5 and under. Near the château is the Voûte St-George (St. George's Vault), a gate of the former castle of the Lords of Beaugency, which opened from the fortress onto the Rû Valley and the lower part of town.

Église Notre-Dame would have been a good example of 12th-century Romanesque architecture if Gothic touches hadn't been added. Originally, it was attached to a Benedictine abbey. Nearby is the Tour St-Firmin, all that remains of a church that once stood on place St-Firmin. A trio of bells is sheltered in this tower, whose spire rises 180 feet. From here you'll have a panoramic view of the river valley.

In the archaeological garden, the Hôtel-Dieu (hospital) is one of the oldest buildings in Beaugency, dating to the 11th century. The Église St-Etienne, also from the 11th century, is one of the oldest churches of France, and the Tour César is a fine example of the period's military art.

ESSENTIALS

GETTING THERE   If you're **driving** from Blois to Beaugency, take D951 northeast. About **20 trains** per day run between Beaugency and either Blois or Orléans;

each trip takes 20 minutes and costs from 32 F ($5.10) one-way. For railway information, call ☎ **08-36-35-35-35.** From Orléans there are about eight buses a day making the trip to Beaugency.

VISITOR INFORMATION The **Office de Tourisme** is at 3 place du Dr.-Hyvernaud (☎ **02-38-44-54-42**).

ACCOMMODATIONS & DINING

✪ **Abbaye de Beaugency.** 2 quai de l'Abbaye, 45190 Beaugency. ☎ **02-38-44-67-35.** Fax 02-38-44-87-92. 17 units. TV TEL. 530–580 F ($84.80–$92.80) double. AE, DC, MC, V.

This three-star hotel offers the finest and most historic accommodations in Beaugency, dwarfing the competition. Built in 1640 as an Augustinian monastery, it retains the stone window and door frames of its original construction, and an elegant brick facade that might remind you of a château in its own right. Functioning as a hotel since 1935, it occupies a small tract of land beside the Loire, within view of the town's oldest bridge. Guest rooms are large and bright and have ceilings. In some rooms, the big, modern bathrooms are simply separated by a curtain.

Dining: The restaurant, which is open daily for lunch and dinner, is known for such classic Loire Valley dishes as whitefish with mushroom cream sauce. Game is a specialty in season. Fixed-price menus begin at 190 F ($32.30).

La Tonnellerie. 12 rue des Eaux-Bleues, Tavers, 45190 Beaugency. ☎ **02-38-44-68-15.** Fax 02-38-44-10-01. E-mail: tonnellerie@club-internet.fr. 20 units. TV TEL. 480–990 F ($76.80–$158.40) double; 990–1,290 F ($158.40–$206.40) apt or suite. AE, MC, V. Take A10, exit at Beaugency, then take N152 to Beaugency/Tavers.

This longtime favorite offers comfortable, soothingly traditional rooms in a pleasant old house with a garden and pool. Rooms are simply furnished but still comfortable, with firm mattresses; bathrooms are small, usually with shower stalls. The Pouey family can arrange visits to the château, a game of golf, hiking, cycling, or a trip to a winery.

Dining: The inn is also known for its food, with foie gras, duck, and monkfish among the specialties, plus a good choice of Loire Valley wines. Main courses range from 145 F to 260 F ($23.20 to $41.60).

4 Chambord

118 miles SW of Paris, 11 miles E of Blois

When François I used to say, "Come on up to my place," he meant the ✪ **Château de Chambord,** 41250 Bracieux (☎ **02-54-50-40-40**), not Fontainebleau or Blois. Some 2,000 construction workers began to piece together "the pile" in 1519. What emerged after 20 years was the pinnacle of the French Renaissance, the largest château in the Loire Valley. It was ready for the visit of Charles V of Germany, who was welcomed by nymphets in transparent veils gently tossing wildflowers in his path. French monarchs like Henri II and Catherine de Médici, Louis XIII, and Henri III came and went from Chambord, but none developed an affection for it to match François I's. The state acquired Chambord in 1932.

The château is set in a park of more than 13,000 acres, enclosed by a wall stretching some 20 miles. Chambord's facade is dominated by four monumental towers. The keep has a spectacular terrace from which the ladies of the court used to watch the return of their men from the hunt. The three-story keep also encloses a corkscrew staircase, superimposed so that one person may descend at one end and a second ascend at the other without ever meeting. The apartments of Louis XIV, including his redecorated bedchamber, are also in the keep.

The 440-room château is open daily: January through March and October through December from 9am to 5:15pm; April through June, it closes at 6:15pm; and July and August it closes at 7:15pm. Admission is 40 F ($6.40) for adults and 25 F ($4) for ages 12 to 25. It's free for children 11 and under. At the tourist office you can pick up tickets for the *son-et-lumière* presentation in summer, called *Jours et Siècles* (Days and Centuries), but check the times. A ticket costs 50 F ($8).

The château is illuminated every evening throughout the year for 4 hours beginning at nightfall. One of the highlights of a visit here is returning at night to watch the illuminations.

ESSENTIALS

GETTING THERE   It's best to **drive** to Chambord. Take the D951 northeast from Blois to Ménars, turning onto the rural road to Chambord. You can also rent a bicycle in Blois and cycle the 11 miles to Chambord, or take one of the organized tours to Chambord leaving from Blois in summer. From June 15 to September 15, **Point Bus,** 2 place Victor Hugo (☎ **02-54-78-15-66**), operates a bus service to Chambord, leaving Blois at 9:10am and again at 1:20pm with returns at 1 and 6:10pm.

VISITOR INFORMATION   The **Office de Tourisme** is on place St-Michel (☎ **02-54-20-34-86**).

ACCOMMODATIONS & DINING

Hôtel du Grand-St-Michel. 103 place St-Michel, 41250 Chambord, Bracieux. ☎ **02-54-20-31-31.** Fax 02-54-20-36-40. 39 units. TV TEL. 350–450 F ($56–$72) double. MC, V. Closed Nov 14–Dec 20.

The oldest part of this inn, in full view of the château, is the reception area, which was conceived in the 1500s as the kennel for the hounds that used to accompany the French king on his hunting treks through the forests of the Loire Valley. Most of the bedrooms are in modern wings added during the 20th century. Particularly dramatic are the front rooms overlooking the château, whose panorama is especially dramatic when floodlit at night. Accommodations are modern, uninspired, and plain but comfortable, with bland furnishings but acceptably comfortable mattresses.

Dining: The on-site restaurant provides fixed-price meals at 98 F and 135 F ($15.70 and $21.60). In summer, food is served outdoors, beneath an awning, overlooking the nearby historic architecture. Menu specialties don't often rise to the caliber of the wines within the cellar, but high points include a stew of wild boar (in late autumn and winter); breast of duckling in a green peppercorn sauce; and several of the local pâtés and terrines, including the coarsely textured and very flavorful rillettes of local pork.

5 Blois

112 miles SW of Paris, 37 miles NE of Tours

This little town of 55,000 people at the gateway to the Valley of the Loire receives a half-million visitors yearly, primarily to visit its notorious château (see "Exploring the Town & the Château," below). If time remains after a visit to the château, you might want to walk around the old town itself. It is a beautiful piece of living history, with narrow cobblestone streets and well-restored white houses with blue slate roofs and red-brick chimneys. Blois (pronounce it "Blwah") enjoys a scenic setting on the right bank of the Loire, its buildings hugging a hillside overlooking the river. Some of its "streets" are mere alleyways originally laid out in the Middle Ages, or lanes are linked by a series of stairs.

ESSENTIALS

GETTING THERE   The Paris-Austerlitz line via Orléans delivers **six trains** per day from Paris (trip time: 2 hours), costing 180 F ($28.80) one-way. From Tours, five trains arrive per day (trip time: 30 minutes), at a cost of 65 F ($10.40) one-way. From Amboise, 10 trains arrive per day (trip time: 20 minutes), costing 50 F ($8) one-way. For train information and schedules, call ☎ **08-36-35-35-35.** The train station is at place de la Gare. Once here you can take buses operated by T.L.C., route de Vendôme (☎ **02-54-58-55-44**), to tour various châteaux in the area, including Chambord, Chaumont, Chenonceau, and Amboise. Buses depart from the train station but only from June to September.

If you're **driving** from Tours, take RN152 east to Blois.

VISITOR INFORMATION   The **Office de Tourisme** is in the Pavillon Anne-de-Bretagne, 3 av. Jean-Laigret (☎ **02-54-90-41-41**).

EXPLORING THE TOWN & THE CHÂTEAU

If you have time for shopping, head for the area around rue St-Martin and rue du Commerce. Shops here offer high-end items like quality clothing, perfumes, shoes, and jewelry. For contemporary art, watercolors, and oils, visit Art Cadre, 18 rue Denis-Papin (☎ **02-54-74-80-10**). If you're in the market for a one-of-a-kind piece of jewelry or want to have something created to suit your tastes, go to the master jeweler **Philippe Denies,** 3 rue St-Martin (☎ **02-54-74-78-24**). If you prefer antique jewelry, stop by **Antebellum,** 12 rue St-Lubin (☎ **02-54-78-38-78**), and browse through its selection of precious and semiprecious stone jewelry set in gold and silver. For something a little less serious, stop at **Le Paradis des Enfants,** 2 rue des Trois-Clefs (☎ **02-54-78-09-68**), where you'll find toys in every shape and size imaginable. And if you want to acquire a historically accurate copy of the medieval tapestries you might have admired at some of the nearby châteaux, you'll find a wide range at Tapisserie Langlois, **Voûte du Château** (☎ **02-54-78-04-43**). Tapestries cost from 500 F to 10,000 F ($80 to $1,600), depending on their size and intricacy.

✪ **Château de Blois.** ☎ **02-54-90-33-33.** Admission 35 F ($5.60) adults, 25 F ($4) students 6–20, 20 F ($3.20) children under 6. July–Aug, daily 9am–7:30pm; mid-Mar to June and Sept, daily 9am–6:30pm; mid-Oct to mid-Mar, daily 9am–12:30pm and 2–5pm.

A wound in battle earned him the name *Balafré* (Scarface), but he was quite a ladies' man. In fact, on the cold misty morning of December 23, 1588, the duc de Guise had just left a warm bed and the arms of one of Catherine de Médici's ladies-in-waiting (and courtesans skilled at political intrigue). His archrival, King Henri III, had summoned him, but when the duke arrived, Henri was nowhere to be seen; only the king's minions were about. The guards moved menacingly toward the duke with daggers. Wounded, the duke made for the door, where more guards awaited him. Staggering, he fell to the floor in a pool of his own blood. Only then did Henri emerge from behind the curtains. "Mon Dieu," he reputedly exclaimed, "he's taller dead than alive!" The body couldn't be shown: The duke was too popular. Quartered, it was burned in a fireplace.

The murder of the duc de Guise is only one of the memories evoked by the Château de Blois, begun in the 13th century by the comtes de Blois. Blois reached the apex of its power and prestige in 1515 century, when François I moved the royal residence to the chateau. For that reason, Blois is often called the "Versailles of the Renaissance," the second capital of France, and the "city of kings." However, Blois soon became a palace of exile. Louis XIII banished his interfering mother, Marie de Médici, to the chateau here, but she escaped by sliding into the moat down a mound of dirt left by the builders.

If you stand in the courtyard, you'll find the château is like an illustrated storybook of French architecture. The Hall of the Estates-General is a beautiful 13th-century work; the Charles d'Orléans gallery was actually built by Louis XII from 1498 to 1501, as was the Louis XII wing. The Gaston d'Orléans wing was constructed by Mansart between 1635 and 1637. Most remarkable is the François I wing, a French Renaissance masterpiece, containing a spiral staircase with elaborately ornamented balustrades and the king's symbol, the salamander. In the Louis XII wing, seek out paintings by Antoine Caron, Henri III's court painter, depicting Thomas More's persecution.

The château presents a *son-et-lumière* (sound-and-light) show in French from May to September, beginning in most cases at 10:30pm, but in rare instances, including throughout the month of May, at 9:30 or 10:15pm, depending on the school calendar. As a taped lecture is played, colored lights and dramatic readings, in French, evoke the age in which the château was built. Participation in the sound and light show costs 60 F ($9.60) for adults and 30 F ($4.80) for children 7 to 15. Free for children 6 and under.

ACCOMMODATIONS

Note that some of the best rooms in town are found at **Le Médicis** (see "Dining," below).

Holiday Inn Garden Court. 26 av. Maunoury, 41000 Blois. ☎ **800/465-4329** in the U.S., or 02-54-55-44-88. Fax 02-54-74-57-97. E-mail: holibloi@imaginet.fr. 78 units. MINIBAR TV TEL. 460–560 F ($73.60–$89.60) double. Children 12 and under stay free in parents' room. AE, DC, MC, V. Bus: 1.

This leading three-star hotel, built in 1996 in the commercial heart of town, has all the modern amenities as well as a respect for traditional charm. The rooms are furnished with a contemporary flair and a chain-hotel instinct for standardized comfort. There's a well-managed restaurant on-site, La Vallière, where fixed-price meals cost from 98 F to 140 F ($15.70 to $22.40) each.

Hôtel Le Savoie. 6–8 rue du Dr.-Ducoux, 41000 Blois. ☎ **02-54-74-32-21.** Fax 02-54-74-29-58. 26 units. TV TEL. 230–280 F ($36.80–$44.80) double. MC, V.

This modern hotel has made every effort to keep itself inviting. It all begins with the courteous staff, who greet you the moment you enter the long, narrow reception area. Though the guest rooms tend to be small, they're nonetheless quiet and relaxing, with comfortable beds and small but well-organized bathrooms. Bedrooms are cozy and clean, with flowered upholsteries and touches of charm. In the morning, a breakfast buffet is set up in the bright dining room with its wall of windows looking out onto the surrounding residences.

Mercure Centre. 28 quai St-Jean, 41000 Blois. ☎ **02-54-56-66-66.** Fax 02-54-56-67-00. www.mercure-blois.fr. E-mail: mercure-blois@wanadoo.fr. 96 units. A/C MINIBAR TV TEL. 600–615 F ($96–$98.40) double; 650–700 F ($104–$112) suite. AE, CB, DC, MC, V. Parking 40 F ($6.40).

This is the best-located hotel in Blois, along the quays of the Loire, a 5-minute walk from the château. The larger-than-expected rooms boast contemporary furniture, soothing colors, and big windows. Bedrooms never rise above their Mercure chain format and are very roadside motel in look, but they are roomy and soundproof and equipped with alarm clocks and satellite TVs. Bathrooms are clad entirely in marble. The greenhouse-style lobby leads into a pleasant restaurant, where meals are served daily. The duplex suites all feature private terraces and views of the river. On the premises are an exercise room and an indoor pool.

DINING

Le Médicis. 2 allée François-1er, 41000 Blois. ☎ **02-54-43-94-04.** Fax 02-54-42-04-05. E-mail: christiangaranger@wanadoo.fr. Reservations required. Main courses 80–165 F ($12.80–$26.40); fixed-price menus 115–275 F ($18.25–$43.65). AE, DC, MC, V. Daily noon–2pm and 7–10pm. Closed Jan. FRENCH.

Christian and Annick Garanger maintain the most sophisticated inn in Blois—ideal for a gourmet meal or an overnight stop. Typical main courses are fillet steak with truffle sauce, scampi ravioli with saffron sauce, and sea bass cooked on a hot slate placed directly atop your table. Dessert brings chocolate in many manifestations. Some dishes aren't recommended for those with high cholesterol.

In addition, the Garangers rent 12 elegant rooms, each with bathroom and sometimes charming decor. Doubles cost 480 F to 600 F ($76.80 to $96), and the suite goes for 700 F ($112).

✪ **Rendezvous des Pêcheurs.** 27 rue du Foix. ☎ **02-54-74-67-48.** Reservations recommended. Main courses 96–130 F ($15.35–$20.80); fixed-price menu 150 F ($24). MC, V. Tues–Sat noon–2pm; Mon–Sat 7:30–10pm. Closed 1 week in Feb and 3 weeks in Aug. FRENCH.

This restaurant occupies a small 16th-century house near the Église St-Nicolas, a 5-minute walk south of the château, beside the quays of the Loire. Chef Eric Reithler prepares only two meat dishes (pigeon and veal kidneys), which appear alongside a much longer roster of popular seafood dishes. Some dishes may seem deceptively simple, but the result is usually a taste sensation. The menu changes daily according to the availability of fish in the markets; sea urchins raw from the shell is a favorite. Other savory specialties include crisp-skinned stingray fillet with wild herbs and foie gras, or fillet of sea bass roasted with shellfish and lardons that are caramelized in Loire Valley red wine.

BLOIS AFTER DARK

Although Blois doesn't offer the booming nightlife that you can find in France's larger towns, there's still a healthy selection of clubs. If you prefer the pubs, saunter on down to the fun and friendly **Pub Mancini,** 1 rue du Puits-Châtel (☎ **02-54-78-04-36**), with its 100 brands of beer and 40 brands of whiskey; or **Riverside,** 3 rue Henri-Drussy (☎ **02-54-78-33-79**).

Our particular favorite is **Le Boucchanier,** Promenade du Mail (☎ **02-54-74-37-23**). Set aboard a coal barge that's permanently moored to the side of the river, it has a nautical decor inspired by the fishing traditions of the Loire Valley, stiff drinks, and an ambience that's better suited than any other in town for making and developing dialogues with strangers. Specialties include ice cream, cocktails, and every night after around 9:30pm, disco dancing. There's no cover. Beer costs 25 F ($4) each.

6 Cheverny

119 miles SW of Paris, 12 miles SE of Blois

The upper crust still heads to the Sologne area for the hunt, just as if the 17th century had never ended. However, 20th-century realities—like formidable taxes—can't be entirely avoided, so the **Château de Cheverny** (☎ **02-54-79-96-29**) must open some of its rooms for visitors. At least that keeps the tax collector at bay and the hounds fed in winter.

Unlike most of the Loire châteaux, Cheverny is actually occupied by the descendants of the original owner, the vicomte de Sigalas. The family's lineage can be traced back to Henri Hurault, the son of the chancellor of Henri III and Henri IV, who built the first château here in 1634. Upon finding his wife, Françoise, carrying on with a page, he killed the page and offered his spouse two choices: She could swallow poison or have his sword plunged into her heart. She elected the less bloody method. Perhaps to erase the memory, he had the castle torn down and the present one built for his second wife. Designed in classic Louis XIII style, it boasts square pavilions flanking the central pile.

Inside, you'll be impressed by the antique furnishings, tapestries, decorations, and objets d'art. A 17th-century French artist, Jean Mosnier, decorated the fireplace with motifs from the legend of Adonis. The Guards' Room contains a collection of medieval armor; also on display is a Gobelin tapestry depicting the abduction of Helen of Troy. In the king's bedchamber, another Gobelin tapestry traces the trials of Ulysses. Most impressive, however, is a stone stairway of carved fruit and flowers.

The château is open daily: November through February from 9:30am to noon and 2:15 to 5pm; in March, the last part of September, and October it closes at 5:30pm; in April and May at 6:30pm; and from June to mid-September at 6:45pm. Admission is 34 F ($5.45) for adults and 17 F ($2.70) for children 7 to 14. It's free for children 6 and under.

ESSENTIALS

GETTING THERE   Cheverny is 12 miles south of Blois, along D765. It's best reached by car or on an organized bus tour from Blois. From the railway station at Blois, there's a bus that departs for Cheverny once a day, at noon, returning to Blois 4 hours later, according to an oft-changing schedule that varies by the season and the day of the week. Frankly, most visitors find it a lot easier to take their own car or a taxi from the railway station at Blois.

ACCOMMODATIONS & DINING

Hôtel St-Hubert. Rue Nationale, 41700 Cour-Cheverny. ☎ **02-54-79-96-60.** Fax 02-54-79-21-17. Main courses 85–160 F ($13.60–$25.60); fixed-price menus 80–280 F ($12.80–$44.80). MC, V. Thurs–Tues 12:15–2pm and 7:30–9:30pm. Closed Jan 10–Feb 17 and Sun night off-season. FRENCH.

About 800 yards from the château, this roadside inn was built in the provincial style in the 1950s, using age-old techniques and a local stone (*le bourré*) that grows whiter with its exposure to the sun. The kindly owner/chef, Jean-Claude Pillaut, refuses to use anything but fresh ingredients, most of them local. The least expensive menu may include terrine of quail, pike-perch (sandre) with beurre blanc, a selection of cheese, and a homemade fruit tart. The most expensive may offer lobster or fresh spring asparagus, an aiguillette of duckling prepared with grapes, or wild boar with a creamy house signature sauce. Game is featured in season. The chef recommends the fillet of beef Rossini, a flavorful blend of prime beef fillet and foie gras.

Most visitors pass through Cour-Cheverny on a day trip, but it's also possible to spend the night. The Saint-Hubert offers 19 comfortable rooms with bathroom, charging 200 F to 320 F ($32 to $51.20) for a double.

Les Trois Marchands. Place de l'Église, 41700 Cour-Cheverny. ☎ **02-54-79-96-44.** Fax 02-54-79-25-60. Main courses 70–185 F ($11.20–$29.60); fixed-price menus 127–260 F ($20.30–$41.60). AE, DC, MC, V. Tues–Sun noon–2pm and 7:30–9:15pm. Closed Feb–Mar 15. FRENCH.

This much-renovated coaching inn, more comfortable than the St-Hubert, has been handed down for many generations from father to son. Today the three-story building sports awnings, a mansard roof, a glassed-in courtyard, and sidewalk tables with umbrellas. In the attractive tavern-style dining room, the menu almost always includes frogs' legs with *fines herbes,* fish cooked in a salt crust, fresh asparagus in mousseline sauce, and a *panaché* of sweetbreads and kidneys prepared with port wine.

The inn also rents 35 well-furnished, comfortable rooms, 20 with bathroom, all with TV and telephone. A double with bathroom is 260 F to 350 F ($41.60 to $56); a double without goes for 180 F ($28.80). Free parking.

7 Valençay

145 miles SW of Paris, 35 miles S of Blois

One of the Loire's handsomest Renaissance châteaux, the **Château de Valençay** (☎ **02-54-00-10-66**) was acquired in 1803 by Talleyrand on the orders of Napoléon, who wanted his shrewd minister of foreign affairs to receive dignitaries in style. In 1838, Talleyrand was buried at Valençay, and the château passed on to his nephew, Louis de Talleyrand-Périgord. Valençay was built in 1550 by the d'Estampes family. The dungeon and great west tower are of this period, as is the main body of the build-ing, but other wings were added in the 17th and 18th centuries. The effect is grandiose—almost too much so—with domes, chimneys, and turrets.

The private apartments are open to the public; they're sumptuously furnished, mostly in the Empire style but with Louis XV and Louis XVI trappings as well. A star-footed table in the main drawing room is said to have been the one on which the Final Agreement of the Congress of Vienna was signed in June 1815 (Talleyrand repre-sented France).

Visits to Valençay are more detailed (and last about 45 minutes longer) than those to other châteaux in the valley. The Musée de Talleyrand that used to stand on the premises is now closed, but some of the collection is displayed in the new rooms of the castle. In the park is a museum of 60 antique cars (ca. 1890 to 1950). After your visit to the main buildings, you can walk through the garden and deer park. On the grounds are many exotic birds, including flamingos.

Admission to the castle, car museum, and park costs 49 F ($7.85) for adults; 37 F ($5.90) for students, children 17 and under, and seniors. It's open daily April through June and September through October from 10am to 6pm; daily July and August from 9:30am to 6:30pm; and on Saturday, Sunday, and school holidays November through March 2 to 5pm.

ESSENTIALS

GETTING THERE   If you're **driving** from Tours, take N76 east, turning south on D956 to Valençay. From Blois, follow D956 south. There are frequent **SNCF rail connections** from Blois. For train information and schedules, call ☎ **08-36-35-35-35.**

VISITOR INFORMATION   The **Office de Tourisme** is on route de Blois (☎ **02-54-00-04-42**).

ACCOMMODATIONS & DINING

✪ **Hôtel d'Espagne.** 9 rue du Château, 36600 Valençay. ☎ **02-54-00-00-02.** Fax 02-54-00-12-63. 14 units. TV TEL. 450–600 F ($72–$96) double; 900 F ($144) suite. AE, DC, MC, V. Closed Feb. Parking 25 F ($4).

This former coaching inn has a wide-arched entrance leading to a U-shaped building whose stone walls ring a flagstone-covered courtyard. The hotel was named after the prince of Spain, who was imprisoned for a while in the nearby Château de Valençay during Napoléon's reign. Monsieur and Madame Fourré and their family provide an old-world ambience and a first-class kitchen; the family has maintained a smooth operation since 1875. The unique guest rooms are each named after an ancestral manor house in the region. Yours might feature authentic Empire, Louis XV, or Louis XVI decor. Bedrooms are beautifully kept and comfortable, with quality mattresses and fine linen resting on the French beds.

Meals are served in either the dining room or gardens Tuesday through Sunday; specialties include noisettes of lamb in tarragon and sweetbreads with morels. Within the hotel's dining room, fixed-price menus range from 180 F to 260 F ($28.80 to $41.60).

8 Chaumont-sur-Loire

124 miles SW of Paris, 25 miles E of Tours

On the morning when Diane de Poitiers crossed the drawbridge, the ✪ **Château de Chaumont** (☎ **02-54-51-26-26**) looked fiercely grim, with its battlements and pepper-pot turrets crowning the towers. Henri II, her lover, had recently died. The king had given her Chenonceau, but his angry widow, Catherine de Médici, forced her to trade her favorite château for Chaumont. Inside, portraits reveal that Diane truly deserved her reputation as forever beautiful. Another portrait—of Catherine looking like a devout nun—invites unfavorable comparisons.

Chaumont (Burning Mount) was built during the reign of Louis XII by Charles d'Amboise. Overlooking the Loire, it's approached by a long walk up from the village through a tree-studded park. It was privately owned until the state acquired it in 1938. The castle spans the period between the Middle Ages and the Renaissance, and its prize exhibit is a rare collection of medallions by the Italian artist, Nini. A guest of the château for a while, he made medallion portraits of kings, queens, and nobles—even Benjamin Franklin, who once visited. In the bedroom once occupied by Catherine de Médici, you can see a rare portrait of the Italian-born queen, painted when she was young. The superstitious Catherine always kept her astrologer, Cosimo Ruggieri, at her beck and call, housing him in one of the tower rooms (a portrait of him remains). He reportedly foretold the disasters awaiting her sons, including Henri III. In Ruggieri's room, an unusual tapestry depicts Medusa with a flying horse escaping from her head.

The château is open daily January through mid-March and October through December from 10am to 4:30pm; mid-March to September, it's open daily 9:30am to 6pm. Admission is 32 F ($5.10) for adults and 21 F ($3.35) for children 12 to 17. Free for children 11 and under.

ESSENTIALS

GETTING THERE   Seventeen **trains** per day travel to Chaumont every day from both Blois (trip time: 15 minutes) and Tours (trip time: about 45 minutes). One-way fares are 20 F ($3.20) from Blois or 46 F ($7.35) from Tours. The railway station servicing Chaumont is in Onzain, 1¹/₂ miles north of the château, a pleasant walk. For transportation information, call ☎ **08-36-35-35-35.**

VISITOR INFORMATION   The **Office de Tourisme** is on rue du Maréchal-Leclerc (☎ **02-54-20-91-73**).

ACCOMMODATIONS & DINING

Domaine des Hauts de Loire. Rte. d'Herbault, 41150 Onzain. ☎ **02-54-20-72-57.**
Fax 02-54-20-77-32. www.relaischateau.fr/hauts-loire. E-mail: hauts-loire@relaischateau.fr.
35 units. MINIBAR TV TEL. 700–1,500 F ($112–$240) double; from 1,850 F ($296) suite.
AE, DC, MC, V. From Chaumont, cross pont de Chaumont and follow rte. d'Herbault through
the hamlet of Onzain.

Less than 2 miles from the château, on the opposite side of the Loire, this Relais &
Châteaux is a stately manor house built in 1840 by the prosperous owner of a Paris-
based newspaper. It's the most appealing stop in the neighborhood, with a roster of
Louis Philippe–style guest rooms. About half the accommodations are in a half-
timbered annex that was once a stable. Bedrooms come in various sizes and dimensions, each fitted with fine linen and a quality mattress. Bathrooms are tiled with
shower and tubs, and adequate shelf space.

   Dining: The stately dining room once hosted the parties of one of France's most
influential newspaper owners; it's now open, daily for lunch and dinner, to nonguests
who phone in advance. It serves well-prepared food that knowledgeable locals often
drive many miles to enjoy. Fixed-price menus for 320 F to 700 F ($51.20 to $112)
include a salad of marinated eel with shallot-flavored vinaigrette; congealed oysters on
a layered sheet of sardines; fillet of sole with black pepper and watercress; roasted
fillet of Loire Valley whitefish (sandre) served with parsley-flavored cream sauce and
cabbage stuffed with a compote of snails; and the ultimate Loire valley main course, a
fillet of smoked eel prepared with Vouvray wine.

9 Amboise

136 miles SW of Paris, 22 miles E of Tours

On the banks of the Loire, Amboise is located in the center of vineyards known as
Touraine-Amboise. Unlike commercial Tours, this is still a real Renaissance town.
That's the good news. The bad news: Because the town is so beautiful, it's overrun by
tour buses, especially in summer. Many townspeople still talk about Mick Jagger's
recent purchase of a small nearby château. A much earlier resident of Amboise
was Leonardo da Vinci, the quintessential Renaissance man, who spent his last years
in this city.

ESSENTIALS

GETTING THERE   Amboise lies on the main Paris-Blois-Tours rail line, with 14
trains per day arriving from both Tours and Blois. The trip from Tours takes only
20 minutes and costs 30 F ($4.80) one-way; the trip from Blois lasts just 20 minutes,
at a one-way cost of 34 F ($5.45). About five conventional trains depart from Paris's
Gare d'Austerlitz every day from Paris (trip time: 2¹/₂ hours), and several high-speed
TGV trains depart from the Gare Montparnasse every day for the village of St-Pierre-
des-Corps, less than a mile from Tours. From St-Pierre-des-Corps you can transfer
onto a conventional train bound for Amboise. Fares from Paris to Amboise, depending on which route and which method you opt for, cost from 142 F to 263 F ($22.70
to $42.10) each way. For railway information, call ☎ **08-36-35-35-35.**
   If you prefer to travel to Amboise by bus, **Autocars de Touraine,** which operates
out of the Gare Routière (☎ **02-47-05-30-49**) in Tours, just across from the town's
railway station, runs about a half-dozen buses every day between Tours and Amboise.
Each takes about 40 minutes for the trip, and costs 13 F ($2.10) each way.
   If you're driving from Tours, take N152 east to D32 and then turn south, following the signs to Amboise.

VISITOR INFORMATION   The **Office de Tourisme** is on quai du Général-de-Gaulle (☎ **02-47-57-09-28**).

SEEING THE SIGHTS

✪ **Château d'Amboise.** ☎ **02-47-57-00-98.** Admission 40 F ($6.40) adults, 33 F ($5.30) students, 21 F ($3.35) children. July–Aug, daily 9am–7:30pm; Apr–June, daily 9am–6:30pm; Sept–Oct, daily 9am–6pm; Nov–Mar, daily 9am–noon and 1:30–5:30pm.

This 15th-century château, which dominates the town, was the first in France to reflect the Italian Renaissance. A combination of both Gothic and Renaissance styles, it is mainly associated with Charles VIII, who built it on a rocky spur separating the valleys of the Loire and the Amasse.

You enter via a ramp that opens onto a panoramic terrace fronting the river. At one time, this terrace was surrounded by buildings; fêtes were staged in the enclosed court-yard. The castle fell into decline during the Revolution, and today only about a quarter remains of this once-sprawling edifice. You first come to the Flamboyant Gothic Chapelle de St-Hubert, distinguished by its lacelike tracery.

Today, tapestries cover the walls of the château's grandly furnished rooms. The *Logis du Roi* (king's apartment) escaped destruction and can be visited. It was built against the Tour des Minimes (it's also known as the Tour des Cavaliers) and was noteworthy for its ramp that horsemen could ride up. The other notable tower is the Heurtault, which is broader than the Minimes, with thicker walls.

Clos-Lucé. 2 rue de Clos-Lucé. ☎ **02-47-57-62-88.** Admission 39 F ($6.25) adults, 32 F ($5.10) for students, 20 F ($3.20) for children 6–15, free for children under 6. Daily 9am–6pm. Closed Dec 25.

Set within a 2-mile walk from the base of Amboise's château, this brick-and-stone building was constructed in the 1400s, and later served as a private retreat for Anne de Bretagne, who, according to legend, spent a lot of her time here praying and meditating. Later François I installed "the great master in all forms of art and science," Leonardo himself. Venerated by the Chevalier King, Leonardo (da Vinci, not di Caprio) lived here for 3 years, until his death in 1519. (Those paintings of Leonardo dying in François's arms are probably symbolic; the king was supposedly out of town at the time.) Today, the site functions as a small-scale museum, offering insights into the life of Leonardo da Vinci and a sense of the decorative arts of this era.

ATTRACTIONS ON THE OUTSKIRTS

The region around Amboise has recently been accented with attractions which resemble a mix of Disney's Animal Kingdom and the court of the Renaissance kings. The most frequently visited of them lies 6 miles west of Amboise, the **Aquarium de Touraine, Parc des Mini-Châteaux** (☎ **02-47-23-44-44**). Opened in 1994, it contains tanks and aquariums whose water surface covers more than 4,000 square yards. Within them, more than 10,000 freshwater and saltwater fish, including about a half-dozen sharks, live within replicas of their natural habitats. Entrance to the aquarium costs 59 F ($9.45) for adults and 39 F ($6.25) for children under 16. At the same address (and same phone) is the Parc des Mini-Châteaux, where small-scale replicas of France's most famous castles have each been built at $^1/_{25}$ the size of the originals. Chambord, for example, is reduced to a maximum height of less than 11 feet. It's all very patriotic—sort of a learning game that teaches French schoolchildren about the glories of their native *patrimoine*, and which provides architecture enthusiasts with an easy-to-compare overall digest of some of the most celebrated architecture in Europe. Entrance costs 65 F ($10.40) for adults and 45 F ($7.20) for children. Hours for both of these sites vary widely from week to week, according to the seasons and any special exhibition that might be conducted at the time of your visit, so it's best to call in advance of your arrival to reconfirm the hours. To get here from Amboise, follow the signs to Tours, and travel along RD751 along the southern bank of the Loire. The aquarium lies a half mile beyond the village of Lussault-sur-Loire, and it's clearly marked on the highway.

ACCOMMODATIONS

Belle-Vue. 12 quai Charles-Guinot, 37400 Amboise. ☎ **02-47-57-02-26.** Fax 02-47-30-51-23. 32 units. TV TEL. 420 F ($67.20) double. MC, V. Closed Nov 15–Mar 15.

This modest inn lies at the bridge crossing the Loire at the foot of the château. It features rows of French doors and outdoor tables on two levels, shaded by umbrellas in summer. The interior lounges are well maintained; modernized guest rooms are comfortably furnished with bland contemporary furniture that's vaguely based on French traditions, with reasonably comfortable beds. Try to stay in the main building rather than in the somewhat less convenient annex across the river. Views from the establishment's front windows look out over the river-fronting boulevard and the buildings surrounding the railway station on the Loire's far side. Breakfast is the only meal served.

Hostellerie du Château-de-Pray. Route de Chargé (D751), 37400 Amboise. ☎ **02-47-57-23-67.** Fax 02-47-57-32-50. www.chateauxethotels.com. E-mail: chateaudepray@ wanadoo.fr. 19 units. TV TEL. 490–850 F ($78.40–$136) double; 750–990 F ($120–$158.40) suite. Half board 225 F ($36) per person extra. AE, DC, V. Closed Jan 2–Feb 10.

From its position above parterres surveying the Loire in a park about a mile east of the town center, this château, which was built in stages between 1250 and 1650, resembles a tower-flanked castle on the Rhine. Inside you'll find antlers, hunting trophies, antiques, and a paneled drawing room with a fireplace and a collection of antique oils. The recently renovated rooms are stylishly conservative. Although the four rooms within the annex have the same amenities and comfort levels as those within the main building, they aren't as convenient. In 1998, the hotel added an outdoor swimming pool within its garden.

Dining: Open to nonguests, the hotel restaurant offers fixed-price menus of excellent quality priced at 155 F, 225 F, and 305 F ($24.80, $36, and $48.80). In summer, diners can sit on a terrace overlooking formal gardens. The menu might include grilled salmon with beurre blanc, lobster cannelloni, noisettes of baby lamb with sage, or roast rabbit with wine sauce.

✪ **Le Choiseul.** 36 quai Charles-Guinot, 37400 Amboise. ☎ **02-47-30-45-45.** Fax 02-47-30-46-10. www.choiseul.com. E-mail: admin@choiseul.com. 32 units. MINIBAR TV TEL. 930–1,450 F ($148.80–$232) double; 1,130–1,950 F ($180.80–$312) suite. MC, V. Closed mid-Dec to late Jan.

This Relais & Châteaux is Amboise's finest hotel, with a nearly impeccable 18th-century pedigree. Named after its original owner, the duc de Choiseul (finance minister to Louis XV), the hotel encompasses its namesake's original house and two other old buildings. The grandest rooms are in what was built as a convent for an obscure French religious sect (Les Minimes). All rooms are luxurious; although recently modernized, they have retained their old-world charm. Sixteen are air-conditioned. Beds are top-notch and very comfortable.

Dining: The formal dining room, the best in town, offers views of the Loire and of flowering garden terraces; nonguests who phone ahead are welcome. It's open daily from noon to 2pm and 7 to 9:30pm. Fixed-price menus range from 290 F to 500 F ($46.40 to $80). The cuisine, presented with seamless style, utilizes only the freshest and highest-quality products; even the bread is homemade. The service is impeccable, and the wine list is the best in the area.

Amenities: Outdoor pool, tennis court within a 10-minute walk, Ping-Pong table.

✪ **Le Fleuray.** 37530 Cangey. ☎ **02-47-56-09-25.** Fax 02-47-56-93-97. www.lefleurayhotel. com. E-mail: lefleurayhotel@wanadoo.fr. 14 units. TEL. 375–550 F ($60–$88) double. MC, V. Free parking. From Amboise, take the N152 NE of town, following the signs to Blois. Turn onto the D74, direction Cangey, which you'll reach after a total distance from Amboise of $7^1/_2$ miles.

One of the most genuinely appealing country-house hotels in the region is this well-maintained, pink-stucco manor house administered by English expatriates Peter and Hazel Newington. Built in the mid-1800s as the centerpiece for a large farm, it's a marvel of country-living grandeur, partly because of the masses of flowering geraniums, marigolds, and flowering vines that drape themselves over the masonry during warm weather. Mick Jagger has already discovered the place; he stays here whenever he feels a 19th nervous breakdown coming on. Bedrooms are cozy, homey, and elegant, dotted with antique accessories and modern conveniences whose combination might remind you of an elegant but not terribly formal country house in England. Bathrooms are compact and well organized.

There's a restaurant on the premises that, frankly, would be a mistake for you to miss during your stay here; local residents flock here for the excellent food. Menu items include local dates stuffed with warm Roquefort cheese; pork pâté with onions and chutney; Creole style chicken in a curry-flavored cream sauce garnished with pineapples; and breast of chicken with a mushroom and cognac-flavored cream sauce. Fixed-price meals cost 155 F to 210 F ($24.80 to $33.60); the restaurant is open nightly for dinner, from 7 to 11pm.

DINING

The finest dining choice is **Le Choiseul.** The dining room at **Le Fleuray** is also excellent (see "Accommodations," above).

Le Manoir St-Thomas. Place Richelieu. ☎ **02-47-57-22-52.** Reservations required. Fixed-price menus 175–295 F ($28–$47.20). AE, DC, MC, V. Wed–Sat noon–2:30pm, Tues–Sat 7:15–9:30pm. Closed Jan 15–Mar 15 and Sun evenings in winter. FRENCH.

The best food in town outside Le Choiseul is served at this steep-gabled, stately looking Renaissance house, set in a pleasant garden in the shadow of the château. The dining room is richly decorated with a polychrome ceiling and massive stone fireplace. Owner/chef François Le Coz's specialties include truffles with smoked foie gras, supreme of pheasant with figs and grapes, and red mullet fillet with cream of sweet-pepper sauce. The tender saddle of hare is perfectly flavored.

10 Chenonceaux

139 miles SW of Paris, 16 miles E of Tours

A Renaissance masterpiece, the ✪ **Château de Chenonceau** (☎ **02-47-23-90-07**) is best known for the *dames de Chenonceau,* who once occupied it. (Note that the village, whose year-round population is less than 300, is spelled with a final x, but the château isn't.)

In 1547, Henri II gave Chenonceau to his mistress, Diane de Poitiers, 20 years his senior. For a time this remarkable woman was virtually queen of France, infuriating Henri's dour wife, Catherine de Médici. Diane's critics accused her of using magic to preserve her celebrated beauty and to keep Henri's attentions from waning. Apparently

Henri's love for Diane continued unabated, although she was in her 60s when he died in a jousting tournament in 1559.

Upon Henri's death, Catherine became regent of France (her eldest son was still a child) and wasted no time in forcing Diane to return the jewelry Henri had given her and abandon her beloved Chenonceau. Catherine added her own touches to Chenonceau, building a two-story gallery across the bridge—obviously inspired by her native Florence.

Today, Chenonceau is one of the most remarkable castles in France because of the way it spans an entire river. The way that the waters of the Cher river surge and foam beneath its vaulted medieval foundations has been described as mystical by thousands of visitors, many of whom consider it their favorite château in all of France.

Many of the château's walls are covered with Gobelin tapestries, including one depicting a woman pouring water over the back of an angry dragon. The chapel contains a delicate marble *Virgin and Child* by Murillo as well as portraits of Catherine de Médici in her traditional black and white, looking like Whistler's mother. There's even a portrait of the stern Catherine in the former bedroom of her rival, Diane de Poitiers, obviously disapproving of the action that took place here between Diane and Henri II. In François I's Renaissance bedchamber, the most interesting portrait is that of Diane as the huntress Diana.

The history of Chenonceau is related in 15 tableaux in the **Musée de Cire** (wax museum), which is located within a Renaissance-era annex a few steps from the château. Open during the same hours as the château, it charges an admission fee of 10 F ($1.70) for adults, students, and children. Diane de Poitiers, who, among other accomplishments, introduced the artichoke to France, is depicted in three tableaux. One portrays Catherine de Médici tossing out her husband's mistress.

The château is open daily, March 16 to September 15 from 9am to 7pm; September 16 to 30 from 9am to 6:30pm; March 1 to 15 and October 1 to 15 from 9am to 6pm; February 16 to 28 and October 16 to 31 from 9am to 5:30pm; February 1 to 15 and November 1 to 15 from 9am to 5pm; and November 16 to January 31 from 9am to 4:30pm. Admission is 50 F ($8) for adults, 40 F ($6.40) for children 7 to 15, and free for children 6 and under.

The château presents a *son-et-lumière* (sound-and-light) show called *Au Temps des Dames de Chenonceau* (*In the Days of the Ladies of Chenonceau*) every night during July and August. Shows begin promptly at 10:15pm; tickets cost 50 F ($8) for adults and 35 F ($5.60) for children 7 to 15; children 6 and under enter free.

ESSENTIALS

GETTING THERE   There are four daily trains from Tours to Chenonceaux (trip time: 30 minutes), costing 32 F ($5.10) one-way. The train deposits you directly at the base of the château; from there, you can either walk or take a taxi.

VISITOR INFORMATION   The Syndicat d'Initiative (tourist office) is at 1 rue Bretonneau (☎ **02-47-23-94-45**), open Easter to September.

ACCOMMODATIONS

Hôtel du Bon-Laboureur et du Château. 6 rue du Dr. Bretonneau, Chenonceaux, 37150 Bléré. ☎ **02-47-23-90-02.** Fax 02-47-23-82-01. E-mail: bon-laboureur.fr@lemel.fr. 29 units. TV TEL. 350–700 F ($56–$112) double; 850–1,000 F ($136–$160) suite. AE, DC, MC, V.

This country inn, with an ivy-covered facade and tall chimneys, is within walking distance of the château and is your best bet for a comfortable night's sleep and good food. The rear garden has a little guest house, plus formally planted roses. Founded in 1880, the hotel maintains the flavor of that era, thanks to thick walls, solid masonry, and a scattering of antiques. In 1998 bedrooms received particular attention and upgrades. Most are small, especially those on the upper floors. Bathrooms are also small. The place is noted for its restaurant, which, ironically, receives notably fewer bus groups than many of its competitors within the region. In fair weather, tables are set up within the courtyard, amid trees and flowering shrubs. Fixed-price menus in the restaurant cost 155 F to 315 F ($24.80 to $50.40) each. On the premises is a heated outdoor swimming pool.

☼ **La Roseraie.** 7 rue du Dr.-Bretonneau, 37150 Chenonceaux. ☎ **02-47-23-90-09.** Fax 02-47-23-91-59. www.charminghotel.com. E-mail: lfiorito@aol.com. 16 units. TV TEL. 280–480 F ($44.80–$76.80) double; from 900 F ($144) suite. Feb–Mar and mid-Oct through Nov, rates include breakfast; Apr to mid-Oct, breakfast 38 F ($6.10). AE, DC, MC, V. Closed Dec and Jan.

You'll find the most charming hotel in Chenonceaux on the main street, across from the post office, in a late-19th-century building covered with streams of clinging ivy-like vines. Until its decline after the death of its longtime owner in 1955, the French government used it as a stop during the official visits of such VIPs as Harry Truman, Winston Churchill, and Franklin D. Roosevelt. In 1993, after decades of neglect, its fortunes were reversed by the hotelier Laurent Fiorito, who radically upgraded its guest rooms, bathrooms, and gardens and reinstated the tradition of carefully supervised cuisine. There's a heated pool on the property.

The restaurant serves some of the finest meals in town at lunch and dinner daily. Fixed-price menus range from 98 F to 170 F ($15.70 to $27.20) and include such specialties as *foie gras maison* and a delicious version of rumpsteak prepared with cassis.

DINING

Note that **La Renaudière** (24 rue du Dr.-Bretonneau; ☎ **02-47-23-90-04**) and **La Roseraie** (see above) boast very good restaurants.

Au Gâteau Breton. 16 rue du Dr.-Bretonneau. ☎ **02-47-23-90-14.** Reservations required July–Aug. Fixed-price menus 60–115 F ($9.60–$18.40). MC, V. May–Sept, daily noon–2:30pm and Thurs–Mon 7–9:30pm; Oct–Apr, Thurs–Tues 11:30am–2:30pm and Thurs–Mon 7–9:30pm. FRENCH.

A short walk from the town's château, this is a refreshing place for dinner or tea, especially in summer, when the terrace provides a close-up view of the garden. Gravel paths run among beds of pink geraniums and lilacs, and bright canopies and umbrellas offer shade. The chef offers home cooking that's sometimes enhanced with the fruit-based liqueurs (cherry, strawberry, and other flavors) made at the nearby Fraise d'Or distillery. Specialties include small chitterling sausages of Tours, chicken with Armagnac sauce, and blood sausage with apples, a highly touted local favorite.

11 Tours

144 miles SW of Paris, 70 miles SW of Orléans

Though it doesn't boast a major château, Tours, at the junction of the Loire and Cher rivers, is the traditional center for exploring the valley. The devout en route to Santiago de Compostela in northwest Spain once stopped off here to pay homage at the tomb of St. Martin, the Apostle of Gaul, who was bishop of Tours in the 4th century. One of the most significant conflicts in world history, the 732 Battle of Tours, checked the Arab advance into Gaul.

With a population of 130,000, Tours is a major city, known for its fine food and wine. Because many of its buildings were bombed in World War II, ugly 20th-century apartment towers have taken the place of stately châteaux. However, since Tours is at the doorstep of some of the most magnificent châteaux in France, it makes a good base from which to explore. Most Loire Valley towns are rather sleepy, but Tours is where the action is centered, as you'll see by its noisy streets and cafes. One-quarter of the residents are students, who add a vibrant, active touch to a soulless commercial enclave.

ESSENTIALS

GETTING THERE   Tours is a 55-minute **TGV train** ride from Paris's Montparnasse. Nearly 10 trains per day make this run, costing 207 F to 264 F ($33.10 to $42.25) one-way. Trains arrive at place du Maréchal-Leclerc, 3 rue Edouard-Vaillant (☎ **08-36-35-35-35** for information and schedules). If you're **driving,** take highway A10 to Tours.

VISITOR INFORMATION   The **Office de Tourisme** is at 78 rue Bernard-Palissy (☎ **02-47-70-37-37**).

EXPLORING THE CITY

The heart of town is place Jean-Jaurès. The principal street (the valley's Champs-Elysées) is rue Nationale, running north to the Loire River. Head west along rue du Commerce and rue du Grand-Marché to reach Vieux Tours/Vieille Ville (Old Town).

In the pedestrian area of rue de Bordeaux, starting essentially to the right of the magnificent train station (when you're facing the station) and running to rue Nationale, you'll find dozens of mall-type shops and department stores selling clothes, shoes, jewelry, leather goods, and the like. Up rue Nationale toward the river are more stores, a little more upscale when it comes to clothing, as well as a small modern mall with chain boutiques. Rue Nationale continues all the way across the river, but turn left on rue du Commerce toward the old town center. You'll want to explore this district's small streets and courtyards for regional specialties, books, toys, and craft items. A hotbed for antiques is east of rue Nationale (toward the cathedral), along rue de la Scellerie. If you like to search through secondhand items, place de la Victoire is the place to be every Wednesday and Saturday from 7am to 5pm for an open-air flea market.

Cathédrale St-Gatien. 5 place de la Cathédrale. ☎ **02-47-71-21-00.** Free admission. Daily 9am–7pm.

This cathedral, which honors a 3rd-century evangelist, has a Flamboyant Gothic facade flanked by towers with bases from the 12th century, though the lanterns are Renaissance. The choir is from the 13th century, with new additions built each century through the 16th. Sheltered inside is the handsome 16th-century tomb of Charles VIII and Anne de Bretagne's two children. Some of the glorious stained-glass windows are from the 13th century.

Musée des Beaux-Arts. 18 place François-Sicard. ☎ **02-47-05-68-73.** Admission 30 F ($4.80) adults, 15 F ($2.40) children under 16. Wed–Mon 9am–12:45pm and 2–6pm.

This fine provincial museum is housed in the Palais des Archevêques, which would be worth a visit just to see its lovely rooms and gardens. However, there are old masters as well, including works by Degas, Delacroix, Rembrandt, and Boucher. The impressive sculpture collection includes works by Houdon and Bourdelle. You can tour the gardens for free daily from 7am to 8:30pm.

Musée de l'Historial de la Touraine (Musée Grévin). Château Royal, 25 av. André-Malraux. ☎ **02-47-61-02-95.** Admission 35 F ($5.60) adults, 16 F ($2.55) children 7–15, free for children 6 and under. July–Aug, daily 9am–6:30pm; May 16–June and Sept–Oct, daily 9am–noon and 2–6pm; Nov–Mar 15, daily 2–5:30pm.

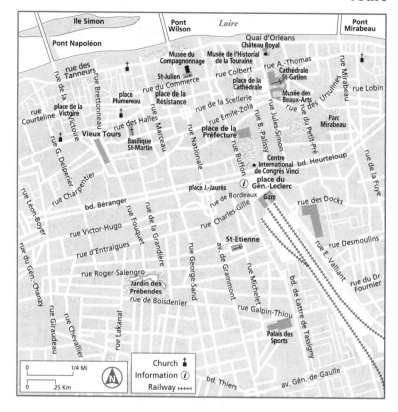

This museum traces the tormented tides of change that have swept over the Loire Valley. It depicts the region's history in 31 moderately kitschy but forcefully evocative scenes with 165 wax figures. They follow 1,500 years of interaction between locals and such personalities as Charlemagne and his queen, Luitgarde; St. Martin and assorted bishops; Clovis, king of the Visigoths; and Joan of Arc. Other scenes simulate the grisly death of Henry V and the hangings of the Huguenots during the Wars of Religion.

ACCOMMODATIONS

The most sumptuous rooms, as well as the finest cuisine, are found at the **Parc de Belmont** (see "Château Belmont," under "Dining," below).

Best Western Le Central. 21 rue Berthelot, 37000 Tours. ☎ **800/528-1234** in the U.S., or 02-47-05-46-44. Fax 02-47-66-10-26. www.tours-online.com. E-mail: bestwestern. centralhotel@wanadoo.fr. 40 units, 38 with bathroom, 2 with sink and bidet only. MINIBAR TV TEL. 165 F ($26.40) double with sink and bidet only, 400–500 F ($64–$80) double with bathroom. AE, DC, MC, V. Parking 40 F ($6.40). Bus: 1, 4, or 5.

There are enough old-fashioned touches in this turn-of-the-century hotel to add an undeniable charm. All dowdiness was erased in 1998, thanks to a complete overhaul of the upper corridors and the bedrooms. Set off the city's main boulevard, within walking distance of both the river and the cathedral, the hotel is surrounded by gardens, lawns, and trees. Bedrooms evoke nostalgia for bygone eras, thanks to a vague combination of styles. Rooms come in a variety of shapes and sizes, from small to spacious, each with a good mattress resting on a comfortable French bed. A rejuvenation of the plumbing has improved the small bathrooms. The Tremouilles family are the owners, maintaining two formal but comfortable salons outfitted with reproductions of 18th- and 19th-century furniture.

Clarion Hôtel de l'Univers. 5 bd. Heurteloup, 37000 Tours. ☎ **800/252-7466** in the U.S., or 02-47-05-37-12. Fax 02-47-61-51-80. 85 units. TV TEL. 880 F ($14.80) double. AE, DC, MC, V. Parking 55 F ($8.80). Bus: 1, 4, or 5.

This highly regarded hotel on the main artery of Tours is the oldest in town and has hosted Edison, Hemingway, and the former kings of Spain, Portugal, and Romania. The rooms are decorated with both modern and art deco pieces and comfortable but worn mattresses. The small bathrooms have stall showers and hair dryers. La Touraine, the main dining room (open daily), serves excellent meals from a fixed-price menu priced at 140 F ($22.40).

Hôtel du Manoir. 2 rue Traversière, 37000 Tours. ☎ **02-47-05-37-37.** Fax 02-47-05-16-00. 20 units. TV TEL. 290 F ($46.40) double. DC, MC, V. Parking 15 F ($2.40) per day.

On a quiet street near the train station and many shops and restaurants, this renovated 19th-century residence is a comfortable place to stay. The cheerful reception area, with its marble tile and rich woodwork, is a good indication of the quality of the guest rooms. Though small to average in size, all units have big windows that let in lots of light, affording views of the residential neighborhood or the hotel's courtyard. Most have simple furnishings and mattresses dating from 1992, but a few showcase decorative touches like wall sconces, antique armoires, and custom bed linens.

DINING
VERY EXPENSIVE

Château Belmont (Jean Bardet). 57 rue Groison, 37100 Tours. ☎ **02-47-41-41-11.** Fax 02-47-51-68-72. Reservations recommended. Main courses 220–420 F ($35.20–$67.20); fixed-price menus 250–750 F ($40–$120). AE, DC, MC, V. Apr–Oct, Tues–Sun noon–2pm, daily 7:30–9:30pm; Nov–Mar, Tues–Sun noon–2pm, Tues–Sat 7:30 9:30pm. FRENCH.

This fine restaurant showcases the creations of two-Michelin-star chef Jean Bardet, who considers meals here "an orchestration of wines, alcohol, food, and cigars." You need not partake of all four elements, however, to enjoy one of the region's best meals, although Bardet does take great pains to get to know his wines and cigars. In this way, he continues to learn how their roles subtly influence each of his dishes. Favorites include wild duck with chanterelle and exotic mushrooms served in chanterelle-cream sauce; roasted breast of pigeon with sweet potato purée, grilled almonds, and bitter oranges; and stew of Breton lobster and shellfish seasoned with fresh ginger and lime. The dining rooms, with black-and-gold Napoléon III furnishings, look out onto the surrounding 7¹/₂ acres of English gardens and park.

Fresh flowers are a staple year-round and fireplaces warm the three dining rooms in cooler months. That's helpful, because the welcome you receive here can often be chilly. Staff can be off-putting, and even if you're able to win them over with your charm, a subtle sense of Gallic *froideur* has elicited an occasional complaint.

The rest of this 19th-century château has been transformed into a luxurious hotel and is the domain of Bardet's wife, Sophie. The spacious guest rooms are individually decorated and invite relaxation with their soft pastel walls, high ceilings, cozy fireplaces, antique furnishings, and superb mattresses. Some even have private balconies that look out onto the gardens. A double ranges from 750 F to 1,200 F ($120 to $192); suites begin at 1,500 F to 1,900 F ($240 to $304).

EXPENSIVE

✪ **La Roche le Roy.** 55 rte. St-Avertin. ☎ **02-47-27-22-00.** Reservations recommended. Main courses 120–185 F ($19.20–$29.60); fixed-price menus 175–380 F ($28–$60.80) at lunch, 240–380 F ($38.40–$60.80) at dinner. AE, MC, V. Tues–Sat 12:15–1:45pm and 7–10pm. Closed the first week in Aug and 2 weeks in Feb. From the center of town, take av. Pompidou south (follow signs to St-Avertin-Vierzon). The road crosses a bridge, but doesn't change names. The restaurant is beside that road, on the southern periphery of Tours. FRENCH.

One of the hottest chefs in town, Alain Couturier blends new and old culinary techniques at this restaurant housed in a 15th-century manor 2 miles south of the town center. Couturier's repertoire includes scalloped foie gras with lentils, fresh cod with saffron cream, and panfried scallops with a truffle vinaigrette. His masterpiece is suprême of pigeon with "roughly textured" sauce, and a matelote of eel with chinon wine. For dessert, try his mélange of seasonal fruit with sabayon made from Vouvray Valley wine, or a hot orange soufflé.

MODERATE

✪ **La Rôtisserie Tourangelle.** 23 rue du Commerce. ☎ **02-47-05-71-21.** Reservations required. Main courses 95–125 F ($15.20–$20); fixed-price menus 95–300 F ($15.20–$48). AE, DC, MC, V. Tues–Sat 12:15–1:45pm and 7:15–9:30pm, Sun noon–1:45pm. Bus: 1, 4, or 5. FRENCH.

This local favorite offers solidly reliable traditional food and a staff that refuses to be hurried. In summer you can dine on a terrace overlooking a garden, but there's not much to see. It's better to concentrate on the changing menu, which may include homemade foie gras, blinis stuffed with snails, and chitterling sausages with a shallot-flavored cream sauce and Vouvray wine; duckling glazed with a wine-based jam; an old-fashioned rabbit stew with a mushroom-studded lasagne served with goat cheese; and a confit of quail with a walnut, raisin, and apple salad. Also consider a slice of chateaubriand with foie gras, a cocoa-flavored pepper sauce, and mashed potatoes studded with chunks of bacon.

INEXPENSIVE

Le Relais Buré. 1 place de la Résistance. ☎ **02-47-05-67-74.** Main courses 68–115 F ($10.90–$18.40); fixed-price menu 130 F ($20.80). AE, DC, MC, V. Daily noon–2pm and 7pm–midnight. Bus: 1 or 5. FRENCH.

This loud and likeable upscale brasserie, which is only a 5-minute walk east of the center of Tours, specializes in shellfish and regional recipes. It has a busy bar and a front terrace, with tables scattered inside on the street level and mezzanine. Menu items include six well-flavored versions of sauerkraut (including the traditional version and a more imaginative variation with seafood), a wide choice of grilled meats (like peppery steak au poivre), and a jarret of pork. Begin your meal with foie gras or smoked salmon, both prepared in-house, and end with one of the tempting array of desserts. If the cassolette of scallops appears as a special offering of the day, go for it.

Les Tuffeaux. 19 rue Lavoisier. ☎ **02-47-47-19-89.** Reservations required. Main courses 85–110 F ($13.60–$17.60); fixed-price menus 115 F, 155 F, and 200 F ($18.40, $24.80, and $32). AE, MC, V. Tues–Sat noon–1:45pm; Mon–Sat 7–9:30pm. Bus: 1, 4, or 5. FRENCH.

This 18th-century house contains one of the best restaurants in Tours, although the cuisine at La Rôtisserie Tourangelle (see above) has a slight edge. Menu items change about once a month, depending on the inspiration of chef Gildas Marsollier, who faithfully prepares a roster of French classics, but who also experiments with noisettes of roasted rabbit with bacon and almonds, supreme of pike-perch, fricassée of chicken livers with raspberry vinegar, and braised turbot with a gratinated *viennoise* of Comté cheese. Roasted fillet of pigeon with pink grapefruit is an enduring favorite. The 115 F ($18.40) fixed-price menu is the best restaurant bargain in town, but note that it isn't available on Saturday.

NEARBY ACCOMMODATIONS & DINING

✪ **Château d'Artigny.** Rte. d'Azay-le-Rideau (the D-17), 37250 Montbazon. ☎ **02-47-34-30-30.** Fax 02-47-34-30-39. www.chateaux-hotels.com. E-mail: artigny@wanadoo.fr. 53 units. MINIBAR TV TEL. 1,200–1,800 F ($192–$288) double; 2,400–3,200 F ($384–$512) suite. Half board 460 F ($73.60) per person extra. AE, DC, MC, V. Closed Dec 3–Jan 13. From Tours, take N10 south for 7 miles to Montbazon, then take D17 a mile southeast.

Set about a mile west of the hamlet of Montbazon, this château was built between 1912 and 1920 for the perfume and cosmetic king François Coty, who lived and entertained lavishly here. The 18th-century Italianate design was inspired by an obscure villa, the Château de Champlatreux, near Paris. Set in a forest, overlooking formal French gardens, this château is a fascinating combination of Jazz Age ostentation and the 18th-century French aesthetic. The drawing room and corridors are lavishly furnished with fine antiques, Louis XV-style chairs, and bronze statuary. The grounds contain acres of private park and a large formal garden with reflecting pool.

Guest rooms are outfitted in various period styles, sometimes with marble wall sheathings, as well as many antiques, comfortable mattresses, and all the perks of upscale country living. Only 33 of the accommodations are in the main building; 23 others are within three annexes that were originally built as a chapel, a gatehouse, and a mill, respectively.

Dining: Superb cuisine is served in the moss-green and gilt dining room. Non-residents are welcome to dine here daily from 12:30 to 2pm and 7:30 to 9:15pm. Menu items are predictably elegant and upscale, and extremely well-prepared. Examples include a ravioli of shrimp perfumed with linden-leaf tea and ginger; grilled turbot with curried tomatoes and essence of coriander; and sea bass roasted with chanterelles.

Château de Beaulieu. 67 rue de Beaulieu, 37300 Joué-les-Tours. ☎ **02-47-53-20-26.** Fax 02-47-53-84-20. 19 units. A/C MINIBAR TV TEL. 490–780 F ($78.40–$124.80) double. Half board 900–1,250 F ($144–$200) for 2. AE, MC, V. Take D86 from Tours, then D207 for Beaulieu, 4^1/2 miles southwest of Tours.

At this secluded 17th-century country estate's restaurant and three-star hotel, you can experience the lifestyle of another era. Beyond the formal entrance, a double curving stairway leads to the reception hall. The rooms have mahogany and chestnut furniture, decorative fireplaces, and good plumbing. Nine are in the château (we recommend these); the others, a bit more sterile, are housed in a recently constructed pavilion nearby. All the rooms come with an elegant French bed equipped with a comfortable mattress.

Dining: The owner, Jean-Pierre Lozay, is an excellent chef, so at least try to visit for a meal within the high-ceilinged, very formal dining room. French windows open onto views of the gardens. Fixed-price menus run 225 F to 400 F ($36 to $64), and à la carte meals feature traditional French specialties. Reservations are recommended.

Amenities: A park with public pool (open from July to September) and four tennis courts are across the road; a terrace also overlooks the garden.

TOURS AFTER DARK

Long a student town, Tours has a lively young population that demands a hip night scene. Even during summer, when most students have fled the city, the younger crowd still rules the hot spots. Place Plumereau (often shortened to "place Plume"), a large square of medieval buildings, now houses a riot of restaurants and bars. During the warmer months, the square explodes with tables and umbrellas, which quickly fill with people who like to see and be seen. This is definitely the cruisy place to begin an evening out.

The most interesting clubs in and around place Plumereau include **Blues Rock Café,** 24 rue de la Monnaie (☎ **02-47-61-57-97**), with its classically American memorabilia and young crowd. One enduringly popular place is the three-level bar at **37 rue Briçonnet** (☎ **02-47-05-77-17**), whose tiers bear the names Le Louis XIV (the most formal and straight-laced), Le Duc (the most jazz-oriented), and Le Pharaon (the one in the cellar that plays the most disco). And perhaps the hottest place in town is **L'Excalibur,** 35 rue Briçonnet (☎ **02-47-64-76-78**), with its disco beat and ultramodern video system. An alternative disco, with a clientele of all ages, many of whom drive in from throughout the surrounding countryside, is **Le Pyms,** 170 av. de Grammont (☎ **02-47-66-22-22**), which is open every night except Monday from 10:30pm till at least 4am.

If you're young and gay and you like to dance, check out **Club 71 la Gamme,** 71 rue Georges-Courteline (☎ **02-47-37-01-54**). You'll want to drive here or walk in a group, as it's on a rather dark street in the middle of a somewhat run-down neighborhood. Inside, though, is a lively disco with a local male crowd that really packs the place on weekends. The dance floor, at the far end of the club, has plenty of mirrors, flashing lights, and smoke.

12 Loches

160 miles SW of Paris, 25 miles SE of Tours

Forever linked to legendary beauty Agnès Sorel, Loches is the *cité médiévale* of the valley, situated in the hills on the banks of the Indre. Known as the acropolis of the Loire, the château and its satellite buildings form a complex called the ✪ **Cité Royale.** The House of Anjou, from which the Plantagenets descended, owned the castle from 886 to 1205. The kings of France occupied it from the mid-13th century until Charles IX became king in 1560.

Château de Loches, 5 place Charles-VII (☎ **02-47-59-01-32**), is remembered for the *belle des belles* (beauty of beauties), Agnès Sorel. Inside is her tomb, where two angels guard her velvet cushion. In 1777, the tomb was opened, but all that remained of the dazzling 15th-century beauty were a set of dentures and some locks of hair. Maid of honor to Isabelle de Lorraine, she was singled out by Charles VII to be his mistress and had great influence on the king until her mysterious death. Afterward, Fouquet painted her as a practically topless Virgin Mary, with a disgruntled Charles VII looking on. (The original masterpiece is in Antwerp, but the château has a copy.) The château also contains the oratory of Anne de Bretagne, decorated with sculpted ermine tails. One of its most outstanding treasures is *The Passion* triptych (1485) from the Fouquet school.

You can visit the château without a guide daily, July to mid-September from 9am to 7pm, mid-March to June and the last 2 weeks of September from 9:30am to 6pm, and October to mid-March from 9:30am to noon and 2 to 5pm. The dungeon opens 30 minutes after the castle and closes 1 hour after the castle. One ticket for both costs 32 F ($5.10) for adults, 17 F ($2.70) for children between 7 and 18 years old. Free for ages 6 and under.

The château is the site of a *son-et-lumière* (sound-and-light) show depicting the exploits of *Le Chevalier au Loup* (The Wolf-Knight: "a Fairy Tale from the Age of Chivalry") about 21 times during July and August, beginning promptly at 10pm. It includes a cast of about a hundred local residents wearing medieval costumes, mingling history, lore, and legend into a highly entertaining program that's conducted entirely in French. Adults pay 70 F ($11.20). Schedules vary and are announced only a few months prior to the event, so contact the tourist office of Loches (see above) if you're interested in attending.

You can visit the ancient keep (*donjon*), reached along the mail du Donjon, of the comtes d'Anjou during the same hours as the château. The Round Tower of Louis XI contains rooms formerly used for torture; a favorite method involved suspending the victim in an iron cage. In the 15th century the duke of Milan, Ludovico Sforza, was imprisoned in the Martelet, and he painted frescoes on the walls to pass the time; he died here in 1508.

Nearby, the Romanesque **Collegiale St-Ours** (Collegiate Church of St. Ours), 1 rue Thomas-Pactius (☎ **02-47-59-02-36**), spans the 10th to the 15th centuries. Its portal is richly decorated with sculpted figures, unfortunately damaged but still attractive. Monumental stone pyramids (*dubes*) surmount the nave; the carving on the west door is exceptional. The church is open daily, year-round from 9am to 7pm, except during class.

Finally, you may want to walk the ramparts and enjoy the view of the town, including a 15th-century gate and Renaissance inns.

ESSENTIALS

GETTING THERE   Between 6 and 10 buses run here daily from Tours, costing 45 F ($7.20) for the one-way, 50-minute trip. If you drive from Tours, take N143 southeast to Loches.

VISITOR INFORMATION   The **Office de Tourisme** is near the bus station on place Wermelskirchen, which is referred to on some, but not all, maps as place de la Marne (☎ **02-47-91-82-82**).

ACCOMMODATIONS & DINING

✪ **Grand Hôtel de France.** 6 rue Picois, 37600 Loches. ☎ **02-47-59-00-32.** Fax 02-47-59-28-66. 19 units. TV TEL. 295–365 F ($47.20–$58.40) double. DC, V. Closed Jan 5–Feb 13. Parking 27 F ($4.30).

This charmingly French hotel functioned as a postal relay station in the mid-1800s. In 1932, three floors were built atop its original core, and in 1997 and 1998, rooms were upgraded, repainted, and redecorated with new amenities that included mattresses for all the beds. Many rooms overlook an inner courtyard. The rates are low for the region, and English is spoken. Enjoy your meals in the petite dining room with paneling and crystal, or under parasols in the courtyard.

Dining: Four excellent fixed-price meals are offered: 87 F, 118 F, 170 F, and 260 F ($13.90, $18.90, $27.20, and $41.60). The restaurant is open daily in July and August but is closed Sunday nights and Mondays the rest of the year.

Hôtel George-Sand. 39 rue Quintefol, 37600 Loches. ☎ **02-47-59-39-74.** Fax 02-47-91-55-75. 20 units. TV TEL. 270–450 F ($43.20–$72) double; 600 F ($96) suite. MC, V. Parking 25 F ($4).

Loaded with faithful reproductions of medieval tapestries, this tastefully decorated inn, a 5-minute walk from the town center and a few steps from the base of the château, dates from the 15th century. George Sand used to stash her luggage here before trekking up the hill to visit her lover, Chopin, who resided in the town's château. The family-owned inn was completely renovated in 1995, and many of the mattresses were replaced in 1998. Several of the rooms look out over a tributary of the Indre; the quieter ones are at the rear.

Dining: This Logis de France hotel has a restaurant with a view of the Indre. À la carte dishes feature Touraine cuisine, including fondue of goat with confit of leeks, fillet of pike-perch (a river fish) in beurre blanc sauce, and breast of duck George Sand. The food is very good, and all pastries are baked fresh on the premises daily. Fixed-price menus cost from 100 F to 245 F ($16 to $39.20).

13 Villandry

157 miles SW of Paris, 20 miles NE of Chinon, 11 miles W of Tours, 5 miles E of Azay-le-Rideau

The extravagant 16th-century-style gardens of the Renaissance ✪ **Château de Villandry,** 37510 Villandry (☎ **02-47-50-02-09**), are celebrated throughout the Touraine. Forming a trio of superimposed cloisters with a water garden on the highest level, the gardens were purchased in a decaying state and restored by the Spanish doctor/scientist Joachim Carvallo, the grandfather of the present owner.

The grounds contain $10^1/_2$ miles of boxwood sculpture, which the gardeners must cut to style in only 2 weeks each September. Every square of the gardens is like a geometric mosaic. The borders represent the many faces of love: tender, tragic (represented by daggers), and crazy (evoked by a labyrinth that doesn't go anywhere). Pink tulips and dahlias suggest sweet love; red, tragic; and yellow, unfaithful. Crazy love is symbolized by all colors. The vine arbors, citrus hedges, and shady walks keep six men busy full time. One garden contains all the common French vegetables except the potato, which wasn't known in France in the 16th century.

Originally, a feudal castle stood at Villandry, but in 1536 Jean Lebreton, François I's chancellor, built the present château, whose buildings form a U and are surrounded by a two-sided moat. Near the gardens is a terrace from which you can see the small village and its 12th-century church.

Admission to the gardens, including a tour of the château, costs 45 F ($7.20) for adults, 38 F ($6.10) for children. A separate visit to the gardens, without a guide, costs 33 F ($5.30) for adults, 26 F ($4.15) for children. The château is open from mid-February to mid-November, and guided tours in French only (English leaflets are available) are conducted daily from 9am to 5:30pm. The gardens are open daily from 9am to sunset.

There is no train service to Villandry. The nearest train connection is the run from Tours to the town of Savonnières. From Savonnières, you can walk along the Loire for 2 miles to reach Villandry, rent a bike at the train station, or take a taxi. You can also drive, following D7 from Tours.

ACCOMMODATIONS & DINING

Le Cheval Rouge. Villandry, 37510 Joué-les-Tours. ☎ **02-47-50-02-07.** Fax 02-47-50-08-77. Reservations recommended. Main courses, 80–120 F ($12.80–$19.20). Fixed-price menus 95–180 F ($15.20–$28.80). MC, V. Tues–Sun noon–2pm and 7:30–9pm. Closed Feb to mid-Mar. FRENCH.

Despite the uptight management and stiff welcome, this is the major lunch choice near the château. Many of the famous gardens of the château are visible from the dining-room windows, and the Cher flows 100 yards away. Specialties include lobster Thermidor and medaillons of veal with morels. The food is fine, but this probably won't be one of your most memorable meals in the Loire.

This inn also rents 20 comfortable rooms, 18 with bathroom. A double goes for 230 F to 280 F ($36.80 to $44.80).

14 Langeais

161 miles SW of Paris, 16 miles W of Tours

Château de Langeais, 37130 Langeais (☎ **02-47-96-72-60**), is a true medieval fortress, a formidable gray pile that dominates the town. It's one of the few châteaux actually on the Loire. The facade is forbidding, but once you cross the drawbridge and go inside, you'll find the apartments so richly decorated that the severe effect is softened. The castle dates from the 9th century, when the dreaded Black Falcon erected the first dungeon in Europe, the ruins of which remain to this day. The present structure was built in 1465. The interior is well preserved and furnished thanks to Jacques Siegfried, who not only restored it over 20 years but also bequeathed it to the Institut de France in 1904.

On December 6, 1491, Anne de Bretagne "arrived at Langeais carried in a litter decked with gold cloth, dressed in a gown of black trimmed with sable. Her wedding gown of gold cloth was ornamented with 160 sables." Her marriage to Charles VIII was to be Langeais's golden hour. Their symbols—scallops, fleurs-de-lis, and ermine—set the motif for the Guard Room, while seven tapestries known as the Valiant Knights cover the walls of the Wedding Chamber.

In a bedchamber known sardonically as "the Crucifixion," the 15th-century black-oak four-poster bed is reputed to be one of the earliest known. The room takes its odd name from a tapestry of the Virgin and St. John standing on flower-bedecked ground. A rare Flemish tapestry hangs in the Monsieur's Room. The Chapel Hall was built by joining two stories under a ceiling of Gothic arches. In the Luini Room is a large 1522 fresco by that artist, removed from a chapel on Lake Maggiore, Italy; it depicts St. Francis of Assisi and St. Elizabeth of Hungary with Mary and Joseph. The Byzantine Virgin in the Drawing Room is thought to be an early work of Cimabue, the Florentine artist. Finally, the Tapestry of the Thousand Flowers is an ageless celebration of spring, a joyous riot of growth, a symbol of life's renewal.

The château is open daily, July 15 to August from 9am to 9pm, April 1 to July 14 and September 1 to 30 from 9am to 6:30pm, October 1 to November 2 from 9am to 12:30pm and 2 to 6:30pm, and November 3 to March 31 from 9am to noon and 2 to 5pm (closed Christmas). Admission is 40 F ($6.40) for adults, 35 F ($5.60) for seniors, and 25 F ($4) for children.

ESSENTIALS

GETTING THERE   **Eighteen trains** per day make a stop here en route from either Tours or Saumur. For train schedules and information, call ☎ **08-36-35-35-39.** If you **drive** from Tours, take N152 southwest to Langeais.

VISITOR INFORMATION   The **Bureau du Tourisme** is at place du 14 Julliet (☎ **02-47-96-58-22**).

ACCOMMODATIONS & DINING

Errard Hosten et Restaurant Langeais (Logis de France). 2 rue Gambetta, 37130 Langeais. ☎ **02-47-96-82-12.** Fax 02-47-96-56-72. 10 units. 280–450 F ($44.80–$72) double; 550 F ($88) suite. AE, MC, V. Closed Feb 15–Mar 15. Parking 30 F ($4.80).

This ivy-draped country inn offers an informal atmosphere and excellent food. The restaurant is expensive (and has received many honors), but the hotel charges reasonable rates for its well-furnished, comfortable rooms. Rooms range in size from small to medium, each with a good mattress and fine linen. Guests dine indoors or at tables set in the open courtyard under umbrellas and flowering trees. The *menu de prestige* includes a matelote of eel with Bourgueil red wine, or *homard* (lobster) *Cardinal.* The desserts may include soufflé au Grand-Marnier. A meal costs 125 F to 245 F ($20 to $39.20). The restaurant is open for lunch Tuesday through Sunday and for dinner Tuesday through Saturday.

La Duchesse Anne. 10 rue de Tours, 37130 Langeais. ☎ **02-47-96-82-03.** Fax 02-47-96-68-60. 15 units, 11 with bathroom. TV TEL. 230 F ($36.80) double without bathroom, 310 F ($49.60) double with bathroom. MC, V.

On the eastern outskirts of town, this hotel was conceived in the 18th century as a coaching inn, providing food and shelter for people and horses. The clean rooms are simply furnished but comfortable. They come in a variety of sizes and shapes, each fitted with a good mattress and fine linen on a comfortable bed. Garden tables are set out for dining. The cuisine reflects the traditions of the Loire Valley and includes flavorful but not experimental dishes such as fresh salmon with beurre blanc sauce or guinea fowl with Bourgueil wine sauce. Fixed-price meals range from 82 F to 215 F ($13.10 to $34.40). From April to October, the restaurant is open for lunch and dinner daily; the rest of the year, it's closed Friday night, Saturday at lunch, and Sunday night.

15 Azay-le-Rideau

162 miles SW of Paris, 13 miles SW of Tours

Its machicolated towers and blue-slate roof pierced with dormers shimmer in the moat, creating a reflection like one in a Monet painting. But the defensive medieval look is all for show: The Renaissance ✪ **Château d'Azay-le-Rideau,** 37190 Azay-le-Rideau (☎ **02-47-45-42-04**), was created as a residence at an idyllic spot on the Indre River. Gilles Berthelot, François I's finance minister, commissioned the castle while his spendthrift wife, Philippa, supervised its construction. So elegant was the creation that the Chevalier King grew immensely jealous. In time Berthelot was accused of misappropriation of funds and forced to flee, and the château reverted to the king. He didn't live here, however, but granted it to "friends of the Crown." It became the property of the state in 1905.

Before entering, circle the château and note the perfect proportions of the crowning achievement of the Renaissance in the Touraine. Check out its most fancifully ornate feature, the bay enclosing a grand stairway with a straight flight of steps. The Renaissance interior is a virtual museum.

From the second-floor Royal Chamber, look out at the gardens. This bedroom, also known as the Green Room, is believed to have sheltered Louis XIII. The adjoining Red Chamber contains a portrait gallery that includes a *Lady in Red* and Diane de Poitiers (Henri II's favorite) in her bath.

The château is open daily, July to August from 9am to 7pm, April to June and September to October from 9:30am to 6pm, and November to March from 9:30am to 12:30pm and 2 to 5:30pm. Admission is 35 F ($5.60) for adults and 23 F ($3.70) for children.

The château presents a nightly *son-et-lumière* (sound-and-light) show from May to July at 10:30pm, in August at 10pm, and in September at 9:30pm. Shows begin promptly, with tickets costing 60 F ($9.60) for adults and 35 F ($5.60) for children.

Three miles east of Azay-le-Rideau (take D17), you can visit the hamlet of **Saché,** the hometown of Honoré de Balzac, where he wrote *The Lily of the Valley.* Of particular interest to literary fans of the great writer is the **Musée Balzac,** in the Château de Saché, 37190 Saché (☎ **02-47-26-86-50**), which contains the writer's bedrooms preserved as they were when he lived here.

A collection of Balzac's scribblings, first editions, etchings, letters, political cartoons, and even a copy of Rodin's famous sculpture of the controversial writer are on display. The castle is open from July to August, daily from 10am to 6:30pm; March 15 to May 14 and in September, daily from 9:30am to noon and 2 to 6pm; May 15 to June 30, daily from 10am to 6pm; February to March 14 and in October and November, daily from 9:30am to noon and 2 to 5pm. Admission is 24 F ($3.85) for adults, 13 F ($2.10) for children 7 to 18, 17 F ($2.70) for students and seniors, and free for children 6 and under.

ESSENTIALS

GETTING THERE   To reach Azay-le-Rideau, take the **train** from either Tours or Chinon. Trip time is about 30 minutes from either; one-way fare is 27 F ($4.30). Both Tours and Chinon have express service to Paris. For SNCF bus and rail schedules to Azay-le-Rideau from virtually anywhere, call ☎ **08-36-35-35-35.** If you're **driving** from Tours, take D759 southwest to Azay-le-Rideau.

VISITOR INFORMATION   The **Syndicat d'Initiative** (tourist office) is on place de l'Europe (☎ **02-47-45-44-40**).

ACCOMMODATIONS

Le Grand Monarque. 3 place de la République, 37190 Azay-le-Rideau. ☎ **02-47-45-40-08.** Fax 02-47-45-46-25. 26 units. TV TEL. 440–650 F ($70.40–$104) double. AE, MC, V. Closed Dec 15–Jan 31. Parking 40 F ($6.40).

The exterior of this hotel—conveniently located less than 500 feet from the château—is covered by a coat of lush ivy that seems to protect the interior from the modern world. As you enter the rustic French manor house with its dark exposed ceiling beams, you'll be transported back to a different era. The large guest rooms are accented with deep-red tones and outfitted with antique furnishings and very comfortable mattresses. Bathrooms are well maintained. In 1999, the hotel's government rating was increased from two-star to three-star status, thanks to significant renovations and improvements. You can enjoy a casual evening in the lounge area or in the hotel restaurant's warm dining room, whose fireplace you'd expect to see in the château across the way. During warmer months, guests can also dine out on the private courtyard terrace. The restaurant here is genuinely superb, thanks to the cuisine of a talented young chef, Fréderic Arnault, whose fixed-price menus range from 155 F to 285 F ($24.80 to $45.60). Look for specialties that include a terrine of stingray with celery, a steak of mullet prepared with the local wine of Azay, braised pig's foot served with veal drippings, and a kettle of crayfish prepared with a bouillon of exotic mushrooms.

DINING

We also recommend the restaurant at Le Grand Monarque (see above).

L'Aigle d'Or. 10 av. Ade[a]laïde-Riché. ☎ **02-47-45-24-58.** Reservations recommended. Main courses 80–115 F ($12.80–$18.40); fixed-price menus 105 F ($16.80) at lunch, 155–255 F ($24.80–$40.80) at dinner. MC, V. Thurs–Tues noon–2pm and 7:30–9:30pm. Closed Feb, 2 weeks in Nov, and Sun and Tues nights off-season. FRENCH.

This longtime favorite offers an often charming welcome, professional service, and a reputation for superb food that's rivaled only by Le Grand Monarque (see above). Menu items are likely to include cream of white bean soup with strips of duckling, warm oysters with a fondue of leeks in champagne sauce, fried scallops with endive and orange-flavored butter, and noisettes of venison with juniper berries. Dessert might be a frozen parfait of chestnut confit with chocolate sauce.

16 Chinon

176 miles SW of Paris, 30 miles SW of Tours, 19 miles SW of Langeais

Remember in the film *Joan of Arc* when Ingrid Bergman sought out the dauphin as he tried to conceal himself among his courtiers? The action took place in real life at the Château de Chinon, one of the oldest fortress-châteaux in France. Charles VII, mockingly known as the King of Bourges, centered his government at Chinon from 1429 to 1450. In 1429, with the English besieging Orléans, the Maid of Orléans, that "messenger from God," prevailed upon the weak dauphin to give her an army. The rest is history. The seat of French power stayed at Chinon until the end of the Hundred Years War.

Today Chinon remains a tranquil little village known mainly for the delightful red wine produced here. After you visit the attractions, we recommend taking a long walk along the Vienne River; definitely stop to taste the wine at one of Chinon's terraced cafes.

ESSENTIALS

GETTING THERE   Three trains arrive daily from Tours (trip time: 1 hour), costing 46 F ($7.35) one-way. For tickets and train information, call ☎ 08-36-35-35-35 in Tours. If you're driving from Tours, take D759 southwest through Azay-le-Rideau to Chinon.

VISITOR INFORMATION   The Office de Tourisme is at Place Hoffheim (☎ 02-47-93-17-85).

SPECIAL EVENTS   The best time to visit is the first weekend in August, for the celebrated Marché Médiéval (☎ 02-47-93-17-85 for information). This fair, marked by overtones of both the Middle Ages and the Renaissance, celebrates native son Rabelais with presentations of early music along with arts and crafts. The food is bountiful, and the wine flows freely as the whole town devotes itself to revelry.

SEEING THE TOWN & CHÂTEAU

Situated on the banks of the Vienne, the town of Chinon consists of winding streets and turreted houses, many built in the 15th and 16th centuries in the heyday of the court. For the best view, drive across the river and turn right onto quai Danton. From that vantage point you'll have the best perspective, seeing the castle in relation to the village and the river. The gables and towers make Chinon look like a toy village. The most typical street is rue Voltaire, lined with 15th- and 16th-century town houses. At no. 44, Richard the Lion-Hearted died on April 6, 1199, from a mortal wound suffered during the siege of Chalus in Limousin. The Grand Carroi, in the heart of Chinon, served as the crossroads of the Middle Ages.

In between châteaux visits and vineyard tastings, you may want to pop into **Fleurisson Production,** 5 rue de l'Olive (☎ 02-47-93-21-79). Expect a French twist to their grapes—they make not vino but jam (*confiture de vin*). Ask about purchasing products at the vineyard.

Chinon is also famous for its wines, which crop up on prestigious lists around the world. These are sold in supermarkets and wine shops throughout the region, but the two most interesting stores are maintained by families who have been in the business longer than anyone can remember. At **Caves Plouzeau,** 94 rue Haute-St-Maurice (☎ 02-47-93-16-34), the 12th-century cellars were dug to provide building blocks for the foundations of the nearby château. The present management dates from 1929; bottles of red or white are 30 F to 45 F ($4.80 to $7.20). You're welcome to climb down to the massive cellars, whose presence in the center of urban Chinon is a medieval oddity even by French standards. It's open for wine sales and visits from April to September Tuesday through Saturday from 9:30am to noon and 2 to 6pm, and Sunday from 10am to 2pm.

The cellars at ✪ **Couly-Dutheil,** 12 rue Diderot (☎ **02-47-97-20-20**), are suitably medieval, many carved into the rock undulating through the area's forests. This company produces largely Chinon wines (mostly reds), though they're justifiably proud of the Borgeuil and St-Nicolas de Borgeuil, whose popularity in the North American market has grown in recent years. Tours of the caves and a *dégustation des vins* require an advance phone call and cost 25 F ($4) per person. Visits are conducted Monday through Friday from 8am to noon and 2 to 5:45pm.

Château de Chinon. ☎ **02-47-93-13-45.** Admission 28 F ($4.50) adults, 19 F ($3.05) children. July–Aug, daily 9am–7pm; Mar 15–June and Sept, daily 9am–6pm; Oct, daily 9am–5pm; Nov 1–Mar 14, daily 9am–noon and 2–5pm.

The château consists of three separate buildings, two of which have been partially restored (they're still missing roofs). One of the restored buildings, Château du Milieu, dates from the 11th to the 15th centuries and contains the keep and clock tower, which houses a museum of Joan of Arc. The other, Château du Coudray, is separated from Château du Milieu by a moat, and contains the Tour du Coudray, where Joan of Arc once stayed. In the 14th century, the Knights Templar were imprisoned here (they're responsible for the graffiti) before meeting their violent deaths. Some of the grim walls from other dilapidated edifices remain, although many buildings—including the Great Hall where Joan of Arc sought out the dauphin—have been torn down; among the most destructive owners were the heirs of Cardinal Richelieu.

Musée de la Devinière. La Devinière, on D117 near N751. ☎ **02-47-95-91-18.** Admission 24 F ($3.85) adults; 17 F ($2.70) children, students 11–25, and seniors; free for children 10 and under. Tickets for theatrical performances 50 F ($8). Jan 1–Mar 13 and Oct 1–Dec 31, daily 9:30am–12:30pm and 2–5pm; Mar 14–Apr 30, daily 9:30am–12:30pm and 2–6pm; May 1–Sept 14, daily 10am–7pm.To reach it from Chinon, follow the road signs pointing to Saumur and the D117.

The most famous son of Chinon, François Rabelais, the earthy and often bawdy Renaissance writer, walked the streets of Chinon, and lived in a substantial dwelling on rue de la Lamproie. (A plaque marks the spot where his father practiced law and maintained a prosperous home and office.) The above-mentioned site, in the suburb of La Devinière, 3^1/$_2$ miles west of Chinon, was an isolated cottage at the time of his birth. It was maintained, because of local superstition and custom, for the sole purpose of delivering the children of the Rabelais clan into the world.

The ground-floor rooms house literary works, prints, and documents of Rabelais and his contemporaries, thoroughly retracing the Rabelaisian era. Throughout the year, the museum hosts special events such as shows by local artists, displays of 16th-century clothing, and (in the courtyard at night) performances that bring to life some of Rabelais's own works.

ACCOMMODATIONS

Chris' Hôtel. 12 place Jeanne d'Arc, 37500 Chinon. ☎ **02-47-93-36-92.** Fax 02-47-98-48-92. www.chris-hotel.fr. E-mail: info@chris-hotel.fr. 33 units. TV TEL. 220–430 F ($35.20–$68.80) double. AE, DC, MC, V.

This well-run hotel is housed in a 19th-century building near the town's historic district. Many rooms offer views of the castle and river; most are furnished in Louis XV style, and all have modern amenities and reasonably comfortable mattresses. Bathrooms are small but efficiently organized. Breakfast is the only meal served.

Hostellerie Gargantua. 73 rue Voltaire, 37500 Chinon. ☎ **02-47-93-04-71.** fax 02-47-93-08-02. 9 units. TEL. 400–600 F ($64–$96) double. MC, V. Free parking.

This 15th-century mansion features a terrace with a château view. Try to stop here for at least a meal, served formally in a stylish medieval hall; on weekends the staff dons medieval attire. You can sample Loire sandre prepared with Chinon wine, or duckling with dried pears and smoked lard, followed by a medley of seasonal red fruits in puff pastry. We're not as fond of the food as we once were, and the staff is somewhat blasé about details, but the place is still recommendable. Bedrooms have been slowly renovated over the years, but management hasn't replaced the mattresses frequently enough. Bathrooms are old-fashioned but still in working order.

Hôtel Diderot. 4 rue Buffon, 37500 Chinon. ☎ **02-47-93-18-87.** Fax 02-47-93-37-10. 27 units. TEL. 310–410 F ($49.60–$65.60) double. AE, DC, MC, V.

This sprawling aristocratic house from the 1700s has a calm elegance about it. With its high black-slate roof and white-limestone walls, the hotel still maintains a regal air. The friendly staff helps you settle into the large guest rooms, which feature hardwood floors, exposed beams, antique furniture, and cushy mattresses. A sense of the past is preserved in the rough-hewn exposed beams and supports, the 18th-century staircase, and the 15th-century fireplace in the dining room, where breakfast is served. As an added bonus, you have use of a private garden and patio.

DINING

✪ **Au Plaisir Gourmand.** 2 rue Parmentier. ☎ **02-47-93-20-48.** Reservations required. Main courses 80–150 F ($12.80–$24); fixed-price menus 175–340 F ($28–$54.40). AE, V. Tues–Sun noon–2pm; Tues–Sat 7:30–9:30pm. Closed Feb. FRENCH.

The area's premier restaurant is owned by Jean-Claude Rigollet, who used to direct the chefs at the fabled Templiers in Les Bézards. His restaurant, at the foot of the château in the old section of town, offers an intimate dining room with a limited number of tables in a charming 18th-century building. Menu items might include roast rabbit in aspic with foie-gras sauce, or sandre in beurre blanc sauce. For dessert, try prunes stuffed in puff pastry. Fine wines (especially those from Chinon) accompany the chef's refined, subtle cuisine, and only the finest and freshest produce is used.

NEARBY ACCOMMODATIONS & DINING

✪ **Château de Marçay.** Marçay, 37500 Chinon. ☎ **02-47-93-03-47.** Fax 02-47-93-45-33. www.relaischateaux.fr/marcay. E-mail: marcay@relaischateaux.fr. 34 units. TV TEL. 660–1,380 F ($105.60–$220.80) double; 1,680 F ($268.80) suite. Extra bed 160 F ($25.60). AE, DC, MC, V. Closed 6 weeks mid-Jan to mid-Mar. Take D116 for 4^1/2 miles southwest of Chinon.

This Relais & Châteaux began in the 1100s as a fortress and changed to its present form during the Renaissance. Remarkably, it remained untouched during the region's civil wars. The centerpiece of the wine-producing hamlet of Marçay, it's sumptuously decorated throughout. The main building houses the more opulent lodgings, while a handful of less expensive, less dramatic rooms are located in a nondescript annex a short walk away. Regardless of room assignment, each comes with a comfortable bed and mattress. Menu specialties change with the season, and the chef works hard to maintain high standards. There's a panoramic view from the garden terrace and dining room, where the decor is elegantly rustic. There's also a swimming pool and tennis courts on the premises.

Manoir de la Giraudière. Beaumont-en-Veron, 37420 Avoine. ☎ **02-47-58-40-36.** Fax 02-47-58-46-06. www.hotels-france.com/giraudiere. E-mail: giraudiere@hotels-france. com. 25 units. TV TEL. 200–390 F ($32–$62.40) double; 490–590 F ($78.40–$94.40) suite. AE, MC, V. Head 3 miles west of Chinon along D749 toward Bourgueil.

Built during the mid-1600s, this elegant manor house resembles a small château because of its use of *tuffeau* (the beige-colored stone used to build the residences of many of the French monarchs). Set in a 6-acre park surrounded by hundreds of acres of fields and forests, this two-star choice offers classic decor and modern comforts. Each good-size room comes with a fine bed and quality linen. Air-conditioning isn't necessary because the very thick walls act as natural insulation against the heat and cold. Note the 17th-century *pigeonnière* (dovecote) that doubles as a salon during warm weather.

The hotel's restaurant closes for three weeks at Christmas; otherwise, it's open daily for lunch and dinner. Fixed-price menus range from 120 F to 230 F ($19.20 to $36.80) and feature dishes like crêpinette of pig's foot with braised cabbage and juniper-berry sauce, confit of duckling served with quince, a "duet" of local fresh-water fish with sage, and an eggplant "caviar" with essence of fresh green peppers.

17 Ussé

183 miles SW of Paris, 9 miles NE of Chinon

At the edge of the hauntingly dark forest of Chinon, **Château d'Ussé** (☎ **02-47-95-54-05**) was the inspiration for Perrault's legend of *The Sleeping Beauty* (*La Belle au bois dormant*). Conceived as a medieval fortress, the complex of steeples, turrets, towers, chimneys, and dormers was erected at the dawn of the Renaissance on a hill overlooking the Indre River. Two powerful families—the Bueil and the d'Espinay—lived here in the 15th and 16th centuries. The terraces, laden with orange trees, were laid out in the 18th century. When the need for a fortified château had passed, the north wing was demolished, opening up a greater view.

The château was later owned by the duc de Duras and then by Mme de la Roche-jacquelin; its present owner, the marquis de Blacas, has opened many rooms to the public. The guided tour begins in the Renaissance chapel, with its sculptured portal and handsome stalls. You then proceed to the royal apartments, which are furnished with tapestries and antiques like a four-poster bed draped in red damask. One gallery displays an extensive collection of swords and rifles. A spiral stairway leads to a tower with a panoramic view of the river and a waxwork Sleeping Beauty waiting for her prince to come.

ESSENTIALS

The château is open daily February to October 9am to 6:30pm; it's closed from November to January. Admission is 59 F ($9.45) for adults, 19 F ($3.05) for children 8 to 17, and free for children 7 and under. The château is best visited by car or on an organized bus tour from Tours. If you're **driving** from Tours or Villandry, follow D7 to Ussé.

18 Fontevraud-l'Abbaye

189 miles SW of Paris, 10 miles SE of Saumur

You'll find the Plantagenet dynasty of England buried in the **Abbaye Royale de Fontevraud** (☎ **02-41-51-71-41**). Why here? These monarchs, whose male line ended in 1485, were also the comtes d'Anjou, and they left instructions that they be buried in their native soil.

In the 12th-century Romanesque church—boasting four Byzantine domes—are the remains of two English kings or princes, including Henry II of England, the first Plantagenet king, and his wife, Eleanor of Aquitaine, the most famous woman of the Middle Ages. Her crusading son, Richard the Lion-Hearted, was also entombed here. The Plantagenet line ended with the death of Richard III at the 1485 Battle of Bosworth. The tombs fared badly in the Revolution as mobs invaded the church, desecrating the sarcophagi and scattering their contents on the floor.

More interesting than the tombs, however, is the octagonal Tour d'Evraud, the last remaining Romanesque kitchen in France. A group of apsides, crowned by conically roofed turrets, surrounds the tower. A pyramid tops the conglomeration, capped by an open-air lantern tower pierced with lancets.

The abbey was founded in 1099 by Robert d'Arbrissel, who spent much of his life as a recluse. His abbey was like a public-welfare commune, liberal in its admission policies. One part, for example, was occupied by aristocratic ladies, many banished from court, including discarded mistresses of kings. The four youngest daughters of Louis XV were educated there as well.

The abbey is open daily, June to September from 9am to 7pm, and from October to May every day from 9:30am to noon and 2 to 5:30pm. Admission is 35 F ($5.60) for adults, 22 F ($3.50) for ages 12 to 25, and free for ages 11 and under.

ESSENTIALS

GETTING THERE   If you're **driving,** take N147 about 2[bf]1/2 miles from the village of Montsoreau. Four **buses** run daily from Saumur, costing 14 F ($2.25) for the 30-minute, one-way trip.

VISITOR INFORMATION   The **Office de Tourisme** is at the Chapelle Ste-Catherine (☎ **02-41-51-79-45**), open May 15 to September 30.

ACCOMMODATIONS

Hostellerie du Prieuré St-Lazare. 49590 Fontevraud-l'Abbaye. ☎ **02-41-51-73-16.** Fax 02-41-51-75-50. www.abbeyhotelfontevraud.com. E-mail: prieure.stlazare@wanadoo.fr. 52 units. MINIBAR TV TEL. 450–490 F ($72–$78.40) double; 670 F ($107.20) triple. AE, MC, V. Closed Nov 15–Mar 15.

This is one of the most unusual hotels in Europe, set on 11th-century foundations within the perimeter of the legendary Abbaye Royale, in what functioned long ago as cells for penitent monks. It became a hotel in 1990. The guest rooms are well maintained and monastically simple, with white walls, modern furniture, and exposed sections of cream-colored tuffeau, the easy-to-carve rock that was used to build the abbey during the early Middle Ages.

Dining: On the premises is Le Cloître, a restaurant housed in a panoramic enclosure of the 11th-century medieval cloister. Fixed-price lunch and dinner menus, 98 F to 290 F ($15.70 to $46.40), are served daily.

DINING

Another choice is the restaurant at the **Hostellerie du Prieuré St-Lazare** (see above).

✪ **La Licorne.** Allée Ste-Catherine. ☎ **02-41-51-72-49.** Reservations required. Main courses 80–170 F ($12.80–$27.20); fixed-price menus 130–280 F ($20.80–$44.80). AE, DC, MC, V. Tues–Sun noon–1:30pm and Tues–Sat 7–9pm. Closed 2 weeks in Jan. FRENCH.

For the perfect combination of medieval history and culinary sensuality, visit the nearby abbey and then dine at this 30-seat restaurant set on a linden-lined walkway between the abbey and a nearby parish church. Its symmetrical proportions and neoclassical pilasters, built in the 1700s just before what the owners refer to as "La Révolution," evoke the *ancien régime* at its most graceful and opulent. In summer, guests dine in the garden or in the elegantly rustic dining room. Chef Jean-Michel Bezille's menu almost always includes fillet of beef flavored with smoked pork and shallots, roasted sandre with Szechuan peppers, crayfish-stuffed ravioli with morel sauce, fillet of salmon with vanilla sauce, and luscious desserts like warm chocolate tart with pears and lemon-butter sauce.

19 Angers

179 miles SW of Paris, 55 miles E of Nantes

Once the capital of Anjou, Angers straddles the Maine River at the western end of the Loire Valley. Though it suffered extensive damage in World War II, it has been considerably restored, blending provincial charm with a suggestion of sophistication. The bustling regional center is often used as a base for exploring the château district to the west. With its skyscrapers and industrial complexes, it hardly suggests a sleepy Loire town; its preponderance of young people, including some 25,000 college students, keeps this vital city of 225,000 jumping until late at night.

ESSENTIALS

GETTING THERE　　Twelve **trains** per day leave Paris's Gare de Montparnasse for the 90-minute trip; cost is 243 F ($38.90) one-way. From Saumur, 12 trains per day make the 30-minute trip to Angers; a one-way ticket costs 42 F ($6.70). From Tours, seven trains per day make the 75-minute trip; a one-way trip is 83 F ($13.30). The Angers train station, at place de la Gare, is a convenient walk from the château. For train information and schedules, call ☎ **08-36-35-35-35.**

　　If you're **driving** from Tours, take N152 southwest to Saumur, turning west on D952.

VISITOR INFORMATION　　The **Office de Tourisme** is on place du Président-Kennedy (☎ 02-41-23-51-11).

SEEING THE SIGHTS

If you have some time for shopping, wander to the pedestrian zone in the center of town. The boutiques and small shops here sell everything from clothes and shoes to jewelry and books. For regional specialty items, head to **La Maison du Vin,** 5 place du Président-Kennedy (☎ **02-41-88-81-13**), where you can learn about the area's many vineyards, taste their wares, and buy a bottle or two for gifts or an afternoon picnic. Another libation that's unique to Angers is Cointreau. **La Distillerie Cointreau,** rue Croix-Blanche in nearby St-Barthélémy d'Anjou (☎ **02-41-30-50-50**), has a showroom where you can sample and stock up on this citrusy liqueur. To reach it from the center of Angers, follow the signs first to Paris, then to Cholet, then to St-Barthélémy. It's closed in January.

Château d'Angers.　☎　**02-41-87-43-47.** Fax 02-41-87-17-50. Admission 35 F ($5.60) adults, 23 F ($3.70) seniors and students 19–25, free for children 18 and under. June–Sept 15, daily 9:30am–7pm; Sept 16–May, daily 10am–5pm.

The moated Château d'Angers, dating from the 9th century, was once the home of the comtes d'Anjou. The notorious Black Falcon lived here, and in time the Plantagenets also took up residence. From 1230–38, the outer walls and 17 massive towers were built, creating a formidable fortress well prepared to withstand invaders. The château was favored by Good King René, during whose reign a brilliant court life flourished here until he was forced to surrender Anjou to Louis XI. Louis XIV turned the château into a prison, dispatching his finance minister, Fouquet, to a cell here. During World War II, the Nazis used the castle as a munitions depot, which explains why Allied planes bombed it in 1944.

Visit the castle if only to see the ✪ **Apocalypse Tapestries.** This series of tapestries wasn't always so highly regarded—they once served as a canopy for orange trees, protecting the fruit from unfavorable weather; they were also used to cover the damaged walls of a church. Woven in Paris by Nicolas Bataille from cartoons by Jean de Bruges around 1375 for Louis I of Anjou, they were purchased for only a nominal sum in the 19th century. The series of 77 pieces, illustrating the book of St. John, stretch a distance of 335 feet. One scene is called *La Grande prostituée;* another shows Babylon invaded by demons; yet another depicts a peace scene of two multiheaded monsters holding up a fleur-de-lis.

After seeing the tapestries, you can tour the fortress, including the courtyard of the nobles, prison cells, ramparts, windmill tower, 15th-century chapel, and royal apartments.

Cathédrale St-Maurice. Place Freppel. ☎ **02-41-87-58-45.** Free admission, but donation appreciated. Daily 9am–7pm, sometimes longer for special events.

The cathedral dates mostly from the 12th and 13th centuries; the main tower, however, is from the 16th century. The statues on the portal represent everybody from the Queen of Sheba to David at the harp. *Christ Enthroned* is depicted on the tympanum; the symbols, such as the lion for St. Mark, represent the Evangelists. The stained-glass windows from the 12th through the 16th centuries have made the cathedral famous. The oldest one illustrates the martyrdom of St. Vincent (the most unusual is of the former St. Christopher with the head of a dog). All of the Apocalypse Tapestries were once shown here; now only a few remain, with the majority on display in the nearby château. The 12th-century nave, considered a landmark in cathedral architecture, is a clear, coherent plan that's a work of harmonious beauty, the start of the Plantagenet architecture. If you're interested in a guided tour (offered in English in July and August), call the church's presbytery (see the number above). Tours are conducted erratically, often by an associate of the church itself, and usually with much charm and humor.

ACCOMMODATIONS

Hôtel d'Anjou. 1 bd. Foch, 49100 Angers. ☎ **800/528-1234** in the U.S., or 02-41-88-24-82. Fax 02-41-87-22-21. 51 units. MINIBAR TV TEL. 480–680 F ($76.80–$108.80) double. AE, DC, MC, V. Parking 45 F ($7.20).

This four-story hotel, on the main boulevard next to a large park, is clearly the best choice, plus it offers reasonable rates. The management claims that it opts to retain its three-star status, even though its size and comfort levels match those of four-star hotels in regions nearby. Room decor and size vary widely by price: The most expensive ones have upholstered walls, antiques or convincing reproductions, and carefully coordinated colors and fabrics; the less expensive rooms are comfortable but a lot more prosaic. Each of the cozy, high-ceilinged bedrooms have good carpets and new upholsteries.

Dining: La Salamandre is the best restaurant in town, charging 130 F to 210 F ($20.80 to $33.60) for fixed-price menus; you'll dine amid carefully maintained paneling, a valuable antique tapestry, and a wood-burning fireplace inspired by the Renaissance. Meals, served Monday through Saturday from noon to 3pm and 7:30 to 10pm, offer regional specialties and fresh Loire Valley fish.

Hôtel de France. 8 place de la Gare, 49100 Angers. ☎ **02-41-88-49-42.** Fax 02-41-86-76-70. E-mail: hotel.de.france.anjou@wanadoo.fr. 57 units. MINIBAR TV TEL. 400–600 F ($64–$96) double. AE, DC, MC, V. Parking 40 F ($6.40).

This 19th-century hotel—one of the most respected in town—has been run by the Bouyer family since 1893. It's the preferred choice near the railway station. In 1998, about three-quarters of the bedrooms were renovated, with new upholsteries, curtains, and fresh paint. Mattresses are reasonably comfortable and the rooms are sound-proofed, but only four are air-conditioned (it can get hot on a summer night). The restaurant, Les Plantagenets, serves reliable fixed-price meals.

Hôtel du Mail. 8–10 rue des Ursules, 49100 Angers. ☎ **02-41-25-05-25.** Fax 02-41-86-91-20. www.destination-anjou.com/mail. E-mail: hoteldumailangers@minitel.net. 26 units. MINIBAR TV TEL. 285–335 F ($45.60–$53.60) double. AE, DC, MC, V. Parking 20 F ($3.20).

The peaceful, relaxing atmosphere of this hotel becomes apparent the moment you set eyes on the stately three-story 17th-century mansion. The owners have gone to great lengths to restore the large guest rooms, each individually decorated with reproduction antiques and comfortable mattresses. You can enjoy breakfast in either the spacious dining room with its hardwood floors or the garden courtyard under the lime trees.

DINING

Hôtel d'Anjou (see above) boasts the town's best restaurant.

La Rose d'Or. 21 rue Delaâge. ☎ **02-41-88-38-38.** Reservations recommended. Fixed-price menus 110–180 F ($17.60–$28.80). MC, V. Tues–Sun noon–1:30pm; Tues–Sat 7–9pm. MC, V. FRENCH.

Conveniently located midway between the château and the railway station, La Rose d'Or serves a tried-and-true French menu that includes many of the staples of the traditional French repertoire. Examples include fillet of zander cooked in Loire Valley wine; entrecôte of beef marinated in red Borgeuil wine; fillet of skate (stingray) with Roquefort sauce; and a succulent roasted duckling that's stuffed with homemade foie gras. The pink-and-gray dining room is formal-looking, with Louis XVI furniture and glittering chandeliers. The Halet family is your host.

Provence Caffé. 9 place du Ralliement. ☎ **02-41-87-44-15.** Reservations recommended. Main courses 85 F ($13.60); fixed-price menus 98–149 F ($15.70–$23.85). AE, MC, V. Tues–Sat noon–2pm and 7–10pm. PROVENÇAL.

This restaurant opened in 1994; ever since, it has celebrated the herbs, spices, and seafood of Provence here in the colder and foggier climes of the Loire Valley. The decor features bright tawny tones of yellow, bundles of herbs, and souvenirs of the Mediterranean; the ambience is unstuffy and sunny. Menu items include risotto, either with asparagus and basil or with snails, a bourride of monkfish, a ballotine of chicken with ratatouille, and grilled sea bass marinated in pastis.

ANGERS AFTER DARK

If you head to place du Ralliement and its fountain or rue St-Laud with its many bars and cafes, you'll find yourself in the center of Angers's nightlife. But for a great night of beer drinking with your friends, go to **Le Kent,** an Irish pub at 7 place Ste-Croix (☎ **02-41-87-88-55**), where you can choose from some 50 varieties of beer and 70 brands of whiskey. If you prefer quantity to quality when it comes to beer, stop by **Le Spirit Factory,** 14 rue Bressigny (☎ **02-41-88-50-10**). Just walk in and order *un mètre,* and for 98 F ($15.70), you'll be served a meter-long wooden feeding trough full of beer (enough for 10 glasses), which many guests share with friends. If you've never had the pleasure of drinking a meter of beer before, here's a bit of etiquette: fill your drinking glass using the spout on the end of the trough and don't try to slurp your beer from the top, as that's *trop gauche,* even for this place.

If a night of dancing seems the perfect antidote to a diet of château-gazing, consider **Disco Le Boléro,** rue Saint-Laud, adjacent to the Place de Ralliement (☎ **02-41-88-61-19**). It's open only on Thursday, Friday, and Saturday nights from 10pm till dawn. There's no entrance charge, but beer costs around 50 F ($8). The club attracts a lot of singles (or at least those temporarily unattached), ranging in age from 25 to 45.

7

Normandy & Mont-St-Michel

Ten centuries have passed since the Vikings invaded the province of Normandy. The early Scandinavians might have come to ravish the land, but they stayed to cultivate it. The Normans produced great soldiers, none more famous than William the Conqueror, who defeated the forces of King Harold at the Battle of Hastings in 1066. The English and the French continued to do battle on and off for 700 years—a rivalry that came to a head at the 1815 Battle of Waterloo.

Much of Normandy was later ravaged in the 1944 invasion that began on a June morning when airborne troops parachuted down into Ste-Mère-Église and Bénouville-sur-Orne. The largest armada ever assembled was responsible for a momentous saga: the reconquest of continental Europe from the Nazis. Today many come to Normandy just to see the D-Day beachheads.

Some of this province may remind you of a Millet landscape, with cattle grazing sleepily in verdant fields and wood-framed houses alongside modern buildings. Not far from the Seine you'll come on the hamlet where Monet painted his water lilies. Here and there you can still find stained-glass windows and Gothic architecture that miraculously survived the bombardments; however, many great buildings were leveled to the ground. And Normandy's wide beaches may attract families, but in August the Deauville sands draw the chicest of the chic from Europe and North America.

REGIONAL CUISINE Normandy is the land of the three Cs: cider, Calvados, and Camembert. Butter, cream, and other dairy products with such accompaniments as pear or apple cider and fiery apple brandy make up a large part of the diet. Norman cream is velvety in texture and ivory in color. The region's *sauce normande* might be called a plain white sauce anywhere else, but here it takes on added allure because of its richer taste.

Certain Norman towns and regions are associated with certain dishes—tripe a la Caen, sole from Dieppe, duck from Rouen, and soufflélike omelets from Mont-St-Michel. Auge Valley chicken, though not as highly praised as that of Bresse, also has a place in the diet. Locals adore *andouillet* (tripe sausage) from Vire, mussels from Isigny, oysters from Courseulles, cockles from Honfleur, and lobsters from La Hague. Highly prized lamb (*pré salé*) is raised on the salt meadows of Normandy.

The supple, fragrant cow's-milk Camembert, sold in a wooden box since 1880, is joined by other cheeses of the area, including

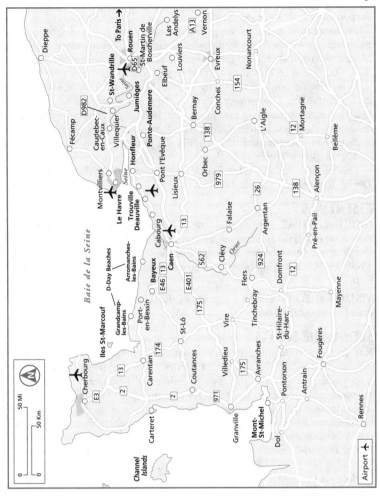

Pont-L'Evêque. Brillat-Savarin, with a high fat content of 75%, was invented in the 1930s by the cheese merchant Henri Androuët.

Normans consume cider at nearly every meal. **Bon bère** is the term for true cider, and sometimes it's so strong that it must be diluted with water. It takes 12 to 15 years to bring Calvados to taste perfection (in America Calvados may be called applejack). Many a Norman finishes a meal with black coffee and a glass of this strong drink, which is also used to flavor main courses.

1 Rouen

84 miles NW of Paris, 55 E of Le Havre

The capital of Normandy, Rouen is the north's second most important center. It's also a hub of commerce, the fifth-largest port in France. Rouen is a bustling, vibrant place, bursting with activity generated by an explosion of industrial businesses connected to the port and a lively scene generated by students at nearby universities and art schools. Today it's a city of half a million people holding memories of its former occupants, including the writers Pierre Corneille and Gustave Flaubert, along with Claude Monet, who endlessly painted the Cathédrale de Notre-Dame here, and even Joan of Arc ("Oh, Rouen, art thou then my final resting place?").

Victor Hugo called Rouen "the city of a hundred spires." Half of it was destroyed during World War II, mostly by Allied bombers, and many Rouennais were killed. During the reconstruction of the old quarters, some of the almost-forgotten crafts of the Middle Ages were revived. On the Seine, the city is rich in historic associations: William the Conqueror died here in 1087, and Joan of Arc was burned at the stake on place du Vieux-Marché in 1431.

The Seine, as in Paris, splits Rouen into a *Rive Gauche* (Left Bank) and *Rive Droite* (Right Bank). The old city is on the right bank.

ESSENTIALS

GETTING THERE   From Paris's Gare St-Lazare, **trains** leave for Rouen about once every hour (trip time: 70 minutes), costing from 103 F ($16.50) one-way. The rail station is at rue Jeanne d'Arc. For train information and schedules, call ☎ **08-36-35-35-35**. When **driving** from Paris, take A13 northwest to Rouen (trip time: 1¹/₂ hours).

VISITOR INFORMATION   The **Office de Tourisme** is at 25 place de la Cathédrale (☎ **02-32-08-32-40**).

SEEING THE SIGHTS

Rue du Gros-Horloge (Street of the Great Clock) runs between the cathedral and place du Vieux-Marché. Now a pedestrian mall, it's named for an ornate gilt Renaissance clock mounted on an arch, Rouen's most popular monument. The arch bridges the street and is connected to a Louis XV fountain with a bevy of cherubs and a bell tower. At night the bells still toll a curfew. In the past, the inside of the belfry could be visited for a view of the iron clockworks and the bells. Unfortunately, it will be closed for renovations throughout most of 2000. On the chance that it's open, however, at the time of your visit in 2001, call either the tourist office or the Musée des Beaux-Arts (see below) for up-to-date information about visiting hours.

Place du Vieux-Marché (Old Marketplace) is where Joan of Arc was executed for heresy. Tied to a stake, she was burned alive on a pyre set by the English on May 30, 1431. Her ashes were gathered and tossed into the Seine. A modern church displaying stained-glass windows from St-Vincent sits in the center of a monumental complex in the square; beside it a bronze cross marks the position of St. Joan's stake.

✪ **Cathédrale Notre-Dame de Rouen.** Place de la Cathédrale. Free admission. Mon–Sat 8am–6pm, Sun 7:30am–6pm. Closed during mass and on bank holidays.

Rouen's cathedral was immortalized by Monet in a series of Impressionist paintings of the three-portal facade with its galaxy of statues. The main door, Porte Central, is embellished with sculptures (some decapitated) depicting the Tree of Jesus. It's flanked by the 12th-century Porte St-Jean and Porte St-Etienne. Consecrated in 1063, the cathedral, a symphony of lacy stonework, was last reconstructed after the bombings of World War II. Two soaring towers distinguish it: Tour de Beurre was financed by the faithful willing to pay in exchange for the privilege of eating butter during Lent and is a masterpiece of the Flamboyant Gothic style. Containing a carillon of 56 bells, the three-story Tour Lanterne (Lantern Tower)—built in 1877 and utilizing 740 tons of iron and bronze—rises to almost 500 feet.

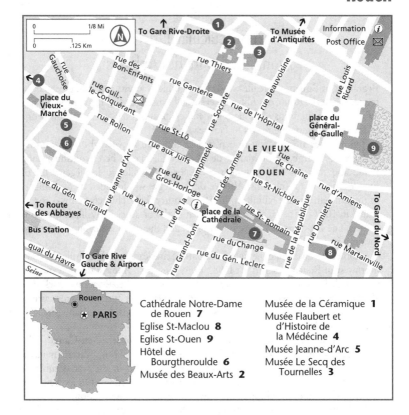

The cathedral's interior is fairly uniform. The nave has 11 bays; the choir is a masterpiece of harmony, with 14 soaring pillars. The Booksellers' Stairway, in the north wing of the transept, is adorned with a large rose window with stained glass that dates in part from the 1500s. The 13th-century chancel is beautiful, with relatively simple lines. Especially interesting is the **Chapelle de la Vierge,** adorned with the Renaissance tombs of the cardinals d'Amboise as well as Jean de Brézé. Also entombed inside was the heart of Richard the Lion-Hearted, a token of his affection for the people of Rouen.

Behind the cathedral is the **Palais de l'Archevêché** (Archbishop's Palace), which was bombed in the war. Now it stands naked against the sky. The broken arches and rosette windows witnessed the trial of Joan of Arc in 1431, and her rehabilitation was proclaimed here in 1456.

Église St-Maclou. Behind the cathedral, at 3 rue Dutuit. ☎ **02-35-71-71-72.** Mon–Sat 10am–noon and 2–6pm, Sun 3–6pm. Closed Jan 1, May 1, July 14, and Nov 11.

St-Maclou was built in the Flamboyant Gothic style, with a step-gabled porch and handsome cloisters, and is known for the remarkable 16th-century panels on its doors. Our favorite (to the left) is the *Portail des Fontaines* (Portal of the Fonts). The church was constructed in 1200, rebuilt in 1432, and finally consecrated in 1521, though its lantern tower is from the 19th century. It sits on a square of old Norman crooked-timbered buildings. Inside, pictures dating from June 4, 1944, document St-Maclou's destruction.

A Spectacular Drive
Along the Route des Abbayes

Beginning at Rouen, the Seine winds through black forests and lush green coun-tryside along the Route des Abbayes, eventually ending at Le Havre. As you make your way past the ruins of monasteries and châteaux, you'll agree that this is one of the most memorable routes in France.

Ten minutes after leaving Rouen (via D982), you arrive at the 11th-century **Abbaye St-George,** in St-Martin de Boscherville. From here, continue along D982 and then on D65 around the Seine for 12 miles to Jumièges. One of France's most beautiful ruins, **Abbaye de Jumièges** was founded by St. Philbert in the 7th century and rebuilt in the 10th century. The abbey church was conse-crated in 1067 by the archbishop of Rouen in the presence of William the Con-queror. The 100-foot-high nave is complete, and the porch is surrounded by two towers 150 feet high.

Another 10 miles along the right bank of the Seine leads to St-Wandrille, 33 miles northwest of Rouen (reached via D982 from Jumièges). **Abbaye de St-Wandrille** was founded in 649. Over the centuries the abbey has suffered various attacks (by Vikings, among others), and today nothing remains of the 7th-century monastery. A huge 18th-century blue gate frames the entrance, and inside you can visit clois-ters from the 14th to the 16th century.

From St-Wandrille, continue for 2 miles or so to **Caudebec-en-Caux,** set in an amphitheater along the Seine. Nearly destroyed in World War II, it has a Gothic church from the 15th century that was spared in the war bombings. Henri IV considered it the handsomest chapel in his kingdom. On its west side is a trio of Flamboyant Gothic doorways, crowned by a rose window.

Drive west around the north bank of the Seine to **Villequier,** a tranquil village whose early 19th-century manor house now functions as a reasonably priced 29-room hotel charging 350 F to 400 F ($56 to $64) for a double room. For infor-mation and reservations, contact the **Château-Hotel de Villequier,** 76490 Villequier (☎ **02-35-95-94-10**). Regrettably, breakfast is the only meal served. It was in this town that Victor Hugo lost his daughter, along with her husband, in a seasonal tidal wave. You can visit the **Musée Victor-Hugo,** on quai Victor-Hugo (☎ **02-35-56-78-31**). It has the manuscript of his poem "Contempla-tions," and original excerpts from Hugo's manuscript of *The Hunchback of Notre Dame.* The museum is open Wednesday to Monday, March to October from 10am to 12:30pm and 2 to 6pm (it closes at 5pm from November to February). Adults pay 20 F ($3.20). It's free for students and for anyone under 18.

Some 33 miles to the west, along D81 and N182, you reach **Le Havre,** France's major Atlantic port. The city was the target of more than 170 bombings during World War II, but its recovery was amazing. From here you can take boat tours to Trouville and Deauville, a pair of lovely, chic resorts.

Église St-Ouen. Place du Général-de-Gaulle. Mar–Oct, Wed–Mon 10am–12:30pm and 2–6pm; Nov–Feb, Wed and Sat–Sun 10am–12:30pm and 2–4pm.

This church is the outgrowth of a 7th-century Benedictine abbey. Flanked by four tur-rets, its 375-foot octagonal lantern tower is called "the ducal crown of Normandy."

One of the best-known Gothic buildings in France, the church represents the work of 5 centuries. Its nave is from the 15th century, its choir from the 14th (but with 18th-century railings), and its remarkable stained glass from the 14th to the 16th. On May 23, 1431, Joan of Arc was taken to the cemetery here, where officials sentenced her to be burned at the stake unless she recanted. She signed an abjuration, thus condemning herself to life imprisonment, but that sentence was later revoked.

Hôtel de Bourgtheroulde. 15 place de la Pucelle (Square of the Maid). ☎ **02-35-08-64-00.** Courtyard visits Mon–Fri 8am–6pm. Closed Sat and Sun except for special exhibitions. Call for details.

This building, one of the most frequently showcased Gothic buildings of Rouen, functions as the headquarters of a local bank, Crédit Industrielle de Normandie (C.I.N.). Built in the 15th century by William the Red, then enlarged during the Renaissance, it's noteworthy for an interior courtyard, which is the only part you can visit regularly. In the courtyard, whose ageless architecture warrants a brief visit, look back at the octagonal stair tower. The left gallery is entirely Renaissance.

Musée des Beaux-Arts. Place Verdel. ☎ **02-35-71-28-40.** Admission 20 F ($3.20) adults, 13 F ($2.10) students, free for children 18 and under. Wed–Mon 10am–6pm.

This is one of France's most important provincial museums, with more than 65 rooms containing a retrospective of French art that ranges from medieval primitives to 20th-century contemporary paintings. Inside, you'll find portraits by David, plus works by Delacroix and Ingres (seek out his *La Belle Zélie*). A Gérard David retable, *La Vierge et les saints* (*The Virgin and the Saints*), is a masterpiece. One salon is devoted to Géricault, including a portrait of Delacroix. Other works are by Veronese, Velásquez, Caravaggio, Rubens, Poussin, Fragonard, and Corot, and several paintings are by Impressionists like Monet, including several versions of his Rouen Cathedral.

Musée de la Céramique. 1 rue Faucon. ☎ **02-35-07-31-74.** Admission 15 F ($2.40) adults, 10 F ($1.60) students, free for children under 18. Wed–Mon 10am–1pm and 2–6pm.

One of the greatest treasures here is the 17th-century Rouen faïence, which because of the unique color of the local clay, has a distinctive dull Indian red color. The exhibits provide a showcase for the talents of Masseot Abaquesne, the premier French artist in faïence and of the specific Rouen-style production (1650–1780). An exceptional showcase is devoted to chinoiserie from 1699 to 1745.

Musée Le Secq des Tournelles (Wrought Ironworks Museum). Rue Jacques-Villon. ☎ **02-35-88-42-92.** Admission 15 F ($2.40) adults, 10 F ($1.60) students, free for children under 18. Wed–Mon 10am–1pm and 2–6pm.

Housed in the 15th-century Église St-Laurent, this museum showcases an art form for which the Normans have been famous for centuries. Its collection ranges from what the press once called "forthright masculine forging to lacy feminine filigree, from Roman keys to the needlepoint balustrade that graced Mme de Pompadour's country mansion." A Parisian aristocrat, Le Secq des Tournelles, began the collection in 1870. So passionately was he devoted to it that his wife divorced him, charging alienation of affection. Donated to the city of Rouen, the collection now has some 14,000 pieces.

Musée Flaubert et d'Histoire de la Médécine. In the Hôtel-Dieu, 51 rue de Lecat. ☎ **02-35-15-59-95.** Admission 15 F ($2.40) adults, free for students and children. Tues–Sat 10am–noon and 2–6pm. Closed holidays.

Gustave Flaubert, author of *Madame Bovary,* was born in the director's quarters of Rouen's public hospital (his father was the director). Flaubert spent his first 25 years in the city; the room where he was born in 1821 is still intact. In addition, family furniture and medical paraphernalia are displayed. Only a glass door separated the Flauberts from the ward and its moaning patients.

Musée Jeanne-d'Arc. 33 place du Vieux-Marché. ☎ **02-35-88-02-70.** Admission 25 F ($4) adults, 13 F ($2.10) children and students. May–Sept 15, daily 9:30am–7pm; Sept 16–Apr, daily 10am–noon and 2–6:30pm.

The life and martyrdom of Joan of Arc, France's national heroine, are traced here. In a vaulted cellar are dioramas and waxworks as well as commentary in four languages, depicting the main stages of her life—from Domrémy, where she was born, to her burning at the stake on the square near the museum's entrance. The site also contains a research library on her life and the politics of her era.

SHOPPING

Rouen was once one of France's major producers of the fine decorative ceramic ware known as *faïence de Rouen.* Examples of both antique and contemporary faïence still abound, and it's worth picking up one or two pieces for your home or even as gifts. For contemporary faïence, your best bet is the shop of **Michel Carpentier,** 26 rue St-Romain (☎ **02-35-88-77-47**), where his artisans carry on the tradition of making faïence de Rouen.

Another Rouen specialty to keep on the lookout for while exploring area antiques shops is *coffret de Rouen.* These little hand-painted wooden boxes were all the rage during the 18th and 19th centuries. The original versions continue to be popular, but watch out for modern forgeries.

Rouen has also become an antiques capital. The best hunting ground is in Vieux Rouen (the Old Town) along **rue Eau-de-Robec, place Barthélémy, rue Damiette,** and **rue St-Romain.** The first Saturday of every month you can find an **antiques fair** on rue Eau-de-Robec. The city also has two **flea markets,** one on Saturday and Sunday at place St-Mare and the other on Thursday at place des Emmurés. Medium- and large-scale antiques auctions take place throughout the year at the **Salles des Ventes,** 25 rue du Général-Giraud (☎ **02-35-71-13-50**) and 20 rue de la Croix-de-Fer (☎ **02-35-98-73-49**).

Other antiques shops worth visiting are **M. Bertran,** 108 rue Molière (☎ **02-35-98-24-06**), with a good selection of 18th- and 19th-century paintings; **E. Bertran,** 110 rue Molière (☎ **02-35-70-79-96**), with its collection of antique books dating back to the 1400s; **Antic St-Maclou,** 178 rue Martainville (☎ **02-35-89-52-61**), a 20-year-old shop specializing in estate jewelry and silver; **P. Chasset,** 12 rue de la Croix-de-Fer (☎ **02-35-70-59-97**), where you'll find toys and gaming cards from the 1700s and 1800s as well as bottles and glassware. You'll find watercolors by local artists, as well as antique Norman and English engravings, at **Atelier St-Romain,** 28 rue St-Romain (☎ **02-35-88-76-17**).

Lovers of chocolate will find a veritable paradise at **La Chocolatière,** 18 rue Guillaume-le-Conquérant (☎ **02-35-71-00-79**). If hats are your thing, head for **Monique,** 58 rue St-Romain (☎ **02-35-98-07-03**). Here hats run the gamut from funky to refined and elegant—and you won't be paying Parisian prices.

ACCOMMODATIONS

✪ **Hôtel Cardinal.** 1 place de la Cathédrale, 76000 Rouen. ☎ **02-35-70-24-42.** Fax 02-35-89-75-14. 20 units. TV TEL. 305–395 F ($48.80–$63.20) double. MC, V. Parking 31 F ($4.95) nearby.

You couldn't find a more ideally located hotel as affordable as this one. It's right across from the cathedral (imagine waking up to the view of this ancient majesty and the surrounding half-timbered buildings each morning) and in the middle of a neighborhood known for antiques stores, art galleries, and fine dining. With this much to do, you won't mind the hotel's simplicity. The rooms are business-class plain with built-in furnishings and color schemes in whites and beiges. The small breakfast room takes advantage of natural sun shining through the multicolored windows.

Hôtel de Bordeaux. 9 place de la République, 76000 Rouen. ☎ **02-35-71-93-58.** Fax 02-35-71-92-15. E-mail: interhotel.rouen@wanadoo.fr. 48 units. TV TEL. 300–340 F ($48–$54.40) double. AE, DC, MC, V.

Practically on the banks of the Seine, this hotel provides medium-size rooms with standard built-in furnishings. Most rooms were renovated in the late 1990s. Each is acceptably comfortable albeit just a wee bit sterile-looking, thanks to the hotel's boxy, somewhat uninspired architecture. They all have views of either the town's medieval rooftops or the cathedral. Accommodations on the upper floors get the bonus of a river view. The hotel has an intimate breakfast room that can, at times, overflow with an assortment of healthy green plants. In the reception/sitting area, with its mahogany furniture, guests congregate before setting out on a day of adventure, shopping, and sightseeing.

Hôtel de Dieppe. Place Bernard-Tissot, 76000 Rouen. ☎ **800/528-1234** in the U.S. and Canada, or 02-35-71-96-00. Fax 02-35-89-65-21. E-mail: hotel.Dieppe@wanadoo.fr. 41 units. TV TEL. 530–630 F ($84.80–$100.80) double. AE, DC, MC, V. Bus: 1, 3, 5, 7, or 10.

This Best Western across from the train station has been run by the Gueret family since 1880. Though modernized, it's still a traditional French inn. The only problem might be the noise, but the double-glazed windows help; after 10pm the last train from Paris arrives and the area quiets down. The rooms are done in either period or contemporary styling and are fairly compact. Each is outfitted with a firm mattress and fine linen on a comfortable bed. In Le Quatre Saisons, the adjoining rôtisserie, which is open daily from noon to 2pm and 7:30 to 10pm, you can enjoy dishes such as duckling *à la presse* and sole poached in red wine. The on-site bar, Le Dieppe, is open daily till midnight.

Hôtel de la Cathédrale. 12 rue St-Romain, 76000 Rouen. ☎ **02-35-71-57-95.** Fax 02-35-70-15-54. 24 units. TV TEL. 310–370 F ($49.60–$59.20) double. MC, V. Parking 31 F ($4.95) nearby. Bus: 1, 3, 5, 7, or 10.

Built around a timbered and cobble-covered courtyard, this hotel is on a pedestrian street midway between the cathedral and the Église St-Maclou, opposite the Archbishop's Palace where Joan of Arc was tried. The recently remodeled rooms are well maintained and tastefully furnished, accessible by both stairs and an elevator. Breakfast is the only meal served.

Hôtel Le Viking. 21 quai du Havre, 76000 Rouen. ☎ **02-35-70-34-95.** Fax 02-35-89-97-12. www.leviking.com. E-mail: leviking@normandnet.fr. 37 units. TV TEL. 295–325 F ($47.20–$52) double. AE, DC, MC, V. Parking 45 F ($7.20). Bus: 1, 3, 5, 7, or 10.

On a riverbank overlooking the Seine, this seven-story hotel is in a white-sided concrete building. The traffic noise can be bad at times, but the front rooms open onto charming river views. In July and August reserve well in advance, since it's usually packed. The accommodations are a little small but still comfortable. Each comes with a fairly comfortable bed, though the mattresses appear a bit thin. Breakfast is the only meal served.

Mercure Centre. Rue de la Croix-de-Fer, 76000 Rouen. ☎ **02-35-52-69-52.** Fax 02-35-89-41-46. 125 units. A/C MINIBAR TV TEL. 480–590 F ($76.80–$94.40) double; 890–990 F ($142.40–$158.40) suite. AE, DC, MC, V. Parking 50 F ($8). Métro: Place-Foch.

In a town of lackluster hotels, the Mercure is a fine choice for an overnight stay, but don't expect anything romantic. The functionally designed rooms, all almost exactly identical to those in hundreds of other Mercure hotels across Europe, are clean and well maintained, though perhaps a tad small. Nonetheless, each contains comfortable beds with good mattresses. There's a bar on the premises, but breakfast is the only meal served.

DINING

✪ **Gill.** 9 quai de la Bourse. ☎ **02-35-71-16-14.** Reservations recommended. Main courses 145–195 F ($23.20–$31.20); fixed-price menus 220–420 F ($35.20–$67.20). AE, DC, MC, V. May–Sept, Tues–Sat noon–2pm and 5:45–9:45pm; Oct–Apr, Wed–Sun noon–2pm, Tues–Sat 5:45–9:45pm. Métro: Théâtre-des-Arts. Closed 3 weeks in Aug. FRENCH.

The best place in town is located just beside the traffic of the Seine's quays. The uncluttered modern decor with high-tech accessories is an appropriate backdrop for the sophisticated cuisine of Gilles Tournadre, who believes in exemplary ingredients and innovation, in a classic context. Who can resist the ravioli stuffed with foie gras and served in a bouillon sprinkled with fresh truffles? What about a terrine of artichoke flavored with fresh truffles, roasted white turbot with fresh asparagus flavored with Parmesan, or fillet of sea bass with smoked salmon in red-wine sauce? The lobster fricassée with fresh mushrooms "from the woods" is another winning selection. Save room for the Calvados soufflé. It's a winner!

Les Nymphéas. 9 rue de la Pie. ☎ **02-35-89-26-69.** Reservations recommended. Main courses 150–260 F ($24–$41.60); fixed-price menus 165–380 F ($26.40–$60.80). AE, DC, MC, V. Tues–Sun noon–1:45pm; Tues–Sat 7:15–9:30pm. FRENCH.

One of the most appealing restaurants in Rouen bears the name of a favorite painting by Monet (*Water Lilies*), which the owners selected when their restaurant was established in 1991. The setting is a 16th-century half-timbered house that fits gracefully into the centrally located neighborhood (Place du Vieux-Marché) that contains it. It features a sophisticated and savory cuisine by owner and chef Patrice Kukurudz and service directed by his wife Thérèse. The restaurant is celebrated for its warm foie gras; wild duckling Rouennais style, served with wild mushrooms and caramelized onions; and a *civet* (stew) of lobster with sauterne. Also look for veal chops with "*garniture bourgeois*" which includes long-simmered versions of pearl onions, bacon, and potatoes. An award-winning dessert that richly evokes the countryside of Normandy is a warm soufflé flavored with apples and Calvados.

✪ **Maison Dufour.** 67 bis rue St-Nicholas. ☎ **02-35-71-90-62.** Reservations required. Main courses 80–160 F ($12.80–$25.60); fixed-price menus 89–230 F ($14.25–$36.80) at lunch, 120–230 F ($19.20–$36.80) at dinner. AE, MC, V. Tues–Sun noon–2pm; Tues–Sat 7–9:30pm. Métro: Palais de Justice. NORMAN.

One of Normandy's best-preserved 15th-century inns has flourished under four generations of the Dufour family since 1906. The three street-level dining rooms are decorated with copper pots, wood carvings, lavish curtains, and engravings. The food, reflecting Normandy's culinary traditions, is so outstanding it's hard to single out specialties. However, the home-smoked salmon, *canard* (duckling) *rouennais,* John Dory in cider sauce, and sole normande are exemplary. The most appropriate dessert is a Calvados-flavored soufflé or a thin but wide slice of apple tart.

Pascaline. 5 rue de la Poterne. ☎ **02-35-89-67-44.** Reservations recommended. Main courses 59–82 F ($9.45–$13.10); fixed-price menus (Mon–Fri only) 69 F ($11.05) at lunch, 76.50–99 F ($12.25–$15.85) at dinner. V. Daily noon–2:30pm and 7:30–11:30pm. Métro: Place du Polais de Justice. FRENCH.

This informal bistro with a turn-of-the-century decor is often filled with regulars, though it's not as atmospheric or charming as the Brasserie de la Grande Poste. The cheapest fixed-price menus represent some of the best bargains in town. Menu items include seafood dishes like pavé of monkfish with roughly textured mustard sauce, a savory *pot-au-feu maison,* navarin of monkfish, tenderloin steaks, and cassoulet toulousain. Don't come for refined cuisine—instead, you can expect hearty and time-tested old favorites. Thursday night is especially appealing here, as management provides a live jazz and swing band.

ROUEN AFTER DARK

The citizens of Rouen usually start their nights on the town at a pub or cafe. The better ones frequented by 25- to 45-year-olds are the always-crowded **Café Leffe,** 36 place des Carmes (☎ **02-35-71-93-30**); and **La Taverne St-Amand,** 11 rue St-Amand (☎ **02-35-88-51-34**), with a friendly environment perfect for enjoying a mug or two of the best Irish, Belgian, and German beers around. Across the street from the Taverne St-Amande, at 16 rue St-Amand, is an even smaller tavern, **La Bohème** (no phone), that offers a cozy, sometimes alcohol-sodden publike ambience that can be both friendly and spontaneously charming. Many students call the **Underground Tavern,** 26 rue des Champs-Maillets (☎ **02-35-98-44-84**), their home away from home. This place has both a street-level bar and an underground bar outfitted in wood and British bric-a-brac.

WINE BAR   If beer drinking doesn't turn you on, try **Le Petit Zinc,** 20 place du Vieux-Marché (☎ **02-35-89-39-69**). This bistro-style wine bar, with its early 1900s retro decor, has one of the best wine selections in town. Of course, you can order Norman cider as well.

DISCO   At **Le Kiosk,** 43 bd. de Verdun (☎ **02-35-88-54-50**), twenty-somethings rule the dance floor. Paying a cover of 95 F ($15.20) will get you into the hard-edged techno music and psychedelic light action.

GAY & LESBIAN BARS   **Le Bloc House,** 138 rue Beauvoisine (☎ **02-35-07-71-97**), attracts a très cool crowd of mostly gay males from their 20s to their 40s who prefer the James Dean look. There's a full bar and lots of distractions, including house and techno dance music, pinball machines, video screens, billiards, and dartboards. **L'Opium,** 2 rue Malherbe (☎ **02-35-03-29-36**), open only on Friday, Saturday, and Sunday nights, is where the hip young gay and lesbian crowd comes to be seen and dance. Drag shows are popular every Sunday night. The cover is 50 F ($8). The modern **Le Traxx,** 4 bis bd. Ferdinand-de-Lesseps (☎ **02-32-10-12-02**), attracts its share of young, well-connected gays and lesbians. It's known for killer light shows, intense techno, and a wild crowd until the wee hours. Here you'll pay 40 F to 60 F ($6.40 to $9.60) to get in, depending on the time and day of your arrival. The price includes one drink.

MUSIC   Rouen also has its cultural side. **Théâtre des Arts,** 7 rue du Dr.-Rambert (☎ **02-35-71-41-36**), has a very busy schedule of classical and contemporary operas. A variety of musical concerts are hosted at the **Église St-Maclou,** 3 rue Dutuit, and the **Église St-Ouen,** place du Général-de-Gaulle. One or both of these churches is scheduled to be closed for renovations in parts of 2001. You can obtain current concert schedules, as well as alternative venues for the concerts that would have been conducted in the churches, from the Office de Tourisme (see above).

2 Honfleur

125 miles NW of Paris, 39 miles NE of Caen

At the mouth of the Seine, opposite Le Havre, Honfleur is one of Normandy's most charming fishing ports. Having miraculously escaped damage in World War II, the port today looks like an antique, although it's a working one. Thanks to the pont de Normande suspension bridge, which links it directly to Le Havre, visitors are now flocking here. Honfleur is actually 500 years older than Le Havre, dating from the 11th century. Early in the 17th century, colonists set out for Québec in Canada. The township has long been favored by artists, including Daubigny, Corot, and Monet.

ESSENTIALS

GETTING THERE   If you're **driving** in from Pont l'Evêque or other points south (including Paris), D579 leads to the major boulevard, rue de la République. Follow it until it ends at the town center. Driving time from Paris is $2^{1}/_{2}$ hours.

There's no direct **train** service to Honfleur. From Paris, take one of five trains per day from Gare St-Lazare for the town of Lisieux. From there, buses coordinated to leave shortly after the arrival of the trains continue the last 45 minutes onto Honfleur. From Rouen, take the train to Le Havre and transfer to a bus for the last 30-minute leg. Bus fare for either of the above routes is 42.50 F ($6.80) each way. Three **Bus Verts** per day connect Caen and Honfleur (trip time: 2 hours), costing 69 F to 86 F ($11.05 to $13.75) one-way. Call ☎ **02-31-89-28-41** for information and schedules.

VISITOR INFORMATION   The **Office de Tourisme** is on place Arthur-Boudin (☎ **02-31-89-23-30**).

SEEING THE TOWN

From place de la Porte-de-Rouen you can begin your tour of the town, which should take about an hour. Stroll along the **Vieux Bassin,** the old harbor, which has fishing boats and slate-roofed narrow houses. The former governor's house, **Lieutenance,** on the north side of the basin, which today contains the administrative body of the nearby port, dates from the 16th century. Nearby is the **Église Ste-Catherine,** Place Ste.-Catherine (☎ **02-31-89-11-93**), built by shipbuilders entirely of timber in the 15th century. The church's belfry stands on the other side of the street and is also of wood. Open daily 9am to noon and 2 to 6pm.

   Musée Eugène-Boudin, place Erik-Satie (☎ **02-31-89-54-00**), has a good collection of the painters who flocked to this port when Impressionism was born. The largest collection is of the pastels and paintings of Boudin, of course. It's open March 15 to September, Wednesday to Monday from 10am to noon and 2 to 6pm; October to March 14, Monday and Wednesday to Friday from 2:30 to 5pm and Saturday and Sunday from 10am to noon and 2 to 5pm. Admission is 26 F ($4.15).

   Musée du Vieux Honfleur, quai St-Etienne (☎ **02-31-89-14-12**), celebrates the unique cultural and aesthetic contribution of Normandy to the rest of Europe. Inside, you'll find old furniture, in some cases going back to the 17th century, lace headdresses, embroideries, candle-making equipment, and farm implements, as well as several rooms outfitted with period art and antiques. Entrance costs 25 F ($4) for adults, 15 F ($2.40) for students and persons under 18. Entrance is free for children under 10. From April till June and during all of September, it's open Tuesday to Sunday from 10am to noon, and from 2 to 6pm. During July and August, it's open daily from 10am to 1pm and 2 to 6:30pm. And from October to mid-November, and from mid-February to March, it's open Tuesday to Friday from 2 to 5:30pm, and Saturday and

Sunday from 10am to noon and from 2 to 5:30pm. From mid-November to mid-February, it's closed.

ACCOMMODATIONS

Restaurant/Hôtel L'Absinthe (see "Dining" below) also rents rooms.

Castel Albertine. 19 cours Albert-Manuel, 14600 Honfleur. ☎ **02-31-98-85-56.** Fax 02-31-98-83-18. www.honfleurhotels.com. E-mail: info@honfleurhotels.com. 26 units. TV TEL. 420–620 F ($67.20–$99.20) double; 630 F ($100.80) suite. AE, DC, MC, V.

Great care was taken to maintain the character of this stately home of Albert Sorel, a 19th-century historian/scholar, into a handsome, welcoming hotel. Its reception area is a unique greenhouse room linking the main house to its modern built-to-look-old addition—one that retains the architectural integrity of the estate. All the individually decorated rooms have antique reproduction furnishings, soft colors, and floor-to-ceiling windows that open up on views of gardens and century-old trees. Each was renovated in 1999 and each has a comfortable mattress. Many contain king-size beds. The airy breakfast room, with its light pine hardwood floor and furniture, is bathed in the morning sun. You can also enjoy the hotel's Finnish sauna with its multijet shower.

✪ Hostellerie Lechat. 3 place Ste-Catherine, 14600 Honfleur. ☎ **02-31-14-49-49.** Fax 02-31-89-28-61. E-mail: lechat@mail.cpod.fr. 23 units. TV TEL. 450–540 F ($72–$86.40) double; 850 F ($136) suite. AE, DC, MC, V. Closed Jan–Feb 15. Bus: 20 or 50.

Parts of this hotel near the port date from the 16th century, and an undeniable sense of old-fashioned coziness abounds. The comfortably furnished rooms, though modest, are fine for an overnight stop. Each has comfortable mattresses and 19th-century decor.

The rustic **restaurant** offers an array of seafood, like sole, salmon, and turbot, and an unusual and popular dish that combines fresh cod with chitterling sausages. The chef also does some superb terrines and an award-winning chicken breast with almonds and a confit of lemon zest. The restaurant is closed on Wednesday evening and all day Thursday. During January, it's open only on Saturday night, presumably to profit from the stream of Parisians seeking weekend getaways. Fixed-price menus cost from 155 F to 240 F ($24.80 to $38.40).

✪ La Ferme St-Simeon. Route Adolphe-Marais, 14600 Honfleur. ☎ **02-31-81-78-00.** Fax 02-31-89-48-48. E-mail: simeon@relaischateaux.fr. 34 units. MINIBAR TV TEL. 1,460–3,510 F ($233.60–$561.60) double; 3,510–5,900 F ($561.60–$944) suite. AE, V.

An old cider press is the focal point of this 17th-century half-timbered slate house, which has become one of Normandy's most elegant inns. The shimmering water of the English Channel drew artists to this hilltop inn, said to be where Impressionism was born in the 19th century. Much of the hotel has terra-cotta floors, carved wood, and copper and faïence touches. The guest rooms are decorated in an 18th-century style.

Dining: Food is served in the restaurant or on the terrace, with a view of the Seine estuary and Le Havre. The classic yet simple cuisine is superb: try the chausson of lobster, fricassée of rice and kidneys, or sole normande. Fixed-price menus cost 240 F to 590 F ($38.40 to $94.40) at lunch, and 420 F to 590 F ($67.20 to $94.40) at dinner.

Amenities: Heated indoor pool, sauna, solarium, fitness center, whirlpool.

DINING

L'Assiette Gourmande. 2 quai des Passagers. ☎ **02-31-89-24-88.** Reservations required. Main courses 150–300 F ($24–$48); fixed-price menus 170–450 F ($27.20–$72). AE, DC, MC, V. Tues–Sun noon–2:15pm and 7–9:45pm. FRENCH.

Although this well-respected restaurant, located along the medieval port, is still popular, the quality has fallen recently. On the street level of the Cheval Blanc hotel, with which it's not associated, it's the domain of Gérard and Anne-Marie Bonnefoy, who serve oft-repeated dishes such as omelet au gratin studded with lobster chunks, escalope of warm foie gras with lentil-flavored cream sauce, roasted crayfish with a marinade of two vegetables, and roasted turbot with essence of chicken. Be sure to leave room for the *petit gâteau moelleux au chocolat* (very moist, deliberately overcooked chocolate-fudge cake).

Restaurant/Hôtel L'Absinthe. 10 quai de la Quarantaine, 14600 Honfleur. ☎ **02-31-89-39-00.** Reservations required. Main courses 150–300 F ($24–$48); fixed-price menus 175–380 F ($28–$60.80). DC, MC, V. Daily 12:15–2:15pm and 7:15–9:15pm. Bus: 20 or 50. FRENCH.

This tavern—named for the drink preferred by many 19th-century writers in Honfleur—is known by practically everyone in town for its beautiful decor, extravagant portions, and well-prepared savory cuisine. It has two dining rooms—one from the 17th century, one from the 15th. Owner Antoine Ceffrey will probably make an appearance in the dining rooms before the end of your meal. Menu choices may be veal kidneys with Calvados, baked turbot with pepper sauce, and attractive desserts like assorted fresh fruit with essence of raspberries.

   If the food is so good that you can't bear to leave, you can rent one of the six simple but comfortable rooms (or the suite). All have satellite TV and phone. A double is 550 F to 750 F ($88 to $120), and the suite is 1,350 F ($216). Parking is available for 40 F ($6.40).

3 Deauville

128 miles NW of Paris, 29 miles NE of Caen

Deauville has been associated with the rich and famous since it was founded as an upscale resort in 1859 by the duc de Morny, Napoléon III's half-brother. In 1913 it entered sartorial history when Coco Chanel launched her career here by opening a boutique selling tiny hats that challenged the current fashion of huge-brimmed hats loaded with flowers and fruit. (Coco's point of view: "How can the mind breathe under those things?")

ESSENTIALS

GETTING THERE   There are between 6 to 10 daily **rail** connections from Paris's Gare St-Lazare (trip time: 2^1/$_2$ hours), costing from 145 F ($23.20) one-way. The rail depot is between Trouville and Deauville, south of the town. **Bus Verts du Calvados** (☎ 08-01-21-42-14) serves the lower Normandy coast from Caen to Le Havre. When **driving** from Paris (trip time: 2^1/$_2$ hours), take A13 west to Pont L'Evêque. From here follow N177 traveling east to Deauville.

VISITOR INFORMATION   The Office de Tourisme is on place de la Mairie (☎ 02-31-14-40-00).

SPECIAL EVENTS   For a week in early September the Deauville Film Festival honors movies made in the United States only. Actors, producers, directors, and writers flock here and briefly eclipse the high rollers at the casinos and the horse-race/polo crowd. For information call the tourist office.

EXPLORING THE RESORT

Coco Chanel cultivated a tradition of elegance that still survives here in Deauville, as well as in its smaller and less prestigious neighbor, Trouville, on the opposite bank of the Toques (see below). Don't expect flashiness—in its own way, restrained and ever-so-polite Deauville is the most British seaside resort in France.

However, in its heart Deauville is less English than French, Parisian in particular. It has even been dubbed Paris's 21st arrondissement. Don't come here looking for medieval France. The aura is Edwardian. The crowds tend to be more urban and hip than the folk at resorts, say, near La Rochelle or in the remote stretches of Brittany. None of this comes cheaply—Deauville is stylish and not (by anyone's definition of the word) inexpensive.

With its golf courses, casinos, deluxe hotels, La Touques and Clairefontaine racetracks, regattas, yachting harbor, polo grounds, and tennis courts, Deauville is still a formidable contender for the business of the smart set. Looking for a particularly charming place to stroll through the town? Head for the shop-lined **rue Eugène-Colas, place Morny** (named in honor of the resort's founding patriarch), and **rue des Villas** (lined with expansive and expensive holiday homes built by the well-heeled during France's gilded age).

BEACHES   Expect to spend time on Deauville's boardwalk, **Les Planches,** a wooden plank promenade running parallel to the beach; its edges are lined with formal beauxarts or half-timbered Norman-inspired architecture. In summer, especially August, parasols dot the beach, and oiled bodies stretch out and seemingly cover every inch of sand.

The resort's only beach is **Plage de Deauville,** a long strip of sand that's part of Plage Fleurie. Flowers don't actually grow from the sand, but its name was part of a successful 19th-century marketing ploy developed by entrepreneurs to attract Parisians and even, to a lesser extent, the English. Allegedly, its borders harbored some fragile flowers long before the mobs of sunbathers, high tides, and building sprees buried them forever, but today, if they bloom at all, they appear during April and May, when most people aren't likely to be here.

If you're looking for a specifically gay and nudist beach, you'll have to drive 24 miles from Deauville toward Caen, to **Merville-France-Ville,** but considering how permissive most Deauville fans are, many gays feel perfectly comfortable remaining here.

Access to every beach in Normandy is free, although at least within Deauville itself, you'll pay about 8 F ($1.35) per hour for parking in any of the many public parking lots beside the sea.

GOLF   On Mont Canisy, Deauville's **New-Golf Club** (☎ **02-31-14-24-24,** see below) offers a tranquil country setting tinged by the sea's salty tang. The par-71, 18-hole course rolls through 6,490 yards of rapid greens and difficult roughs, with sweeping views of the Auge valley and the sea, and the par-36, nine-hole course runs 3,315 yards through a typically lush wooded setting. In addition, there's an indoor driving range, a putting green, a practice bunker, available instruction from three professionals, and a clubhouse with not only a bar and restaurant but also an exclusive line of golfing gear. A franchise of the Lucien Barrière chain of resorts, hotels, and casinos, the facility includes a palatial half-timbered hotel (see below). Greens fees for hotel residents are 250 F to 500 F ($40 to $80) on Saturday and Sunday and 180 F to 300 F ($28.80 to $48) Monday through Friday. Nonguests pay a supplement of 10% above those rates.

HORSE RACES   Take a break from the sun and sand to watch the horse races, but only from late June to early September. There's at least one racing event held every afternoon, either a race at 2pm or a polo match at 3pm. The venues are the **Hippodrome de Deauville La Touques,** boulevard Mauger (☎ **02-31-14-20-00**), in the heart of town, near the Mairie de Deauville (Town Hall); or the **Hippodrome de**

Deauville Clairefontaine, route de Clairefontaine (☎ **02-31-14-69-00**), a bit farther afield but still within the city limits.

SHOPPING   This seaside town has a pedestrian shopping area between the polo
field and the port; the main drags are rue Mirabeau, rue Albert-Fracasse, and the west
end of avenue de la République. At **La Ferme Normande,** 13 rue Breney
(☎ **02-31-88-17-86**), or **La Cave de Deauville,** 48 rue Mirabeau
(☎ **02-31-87-35-36**), you'll be able to find a great selection of apple ciders, cheeses,
Calvados, and the aperitif known as pommeau.

For an overview of the agrarian bounty derived from the fertility of Norman soil,
head for the **open-air market (Marché Publique)** that's conducted in the Place du
Marché, immediately adjacent to the very central Place Morny. From June to mid-
September, it's open daily from 8am till 1pm. The rest of the year, it's conducted only
on Tuesday, Friday, and Saturday mornings from 8am to 1pm. In addition to fruits,
vegetables, poultry, cider, wine, and cheeses, you'll find cookware, porcelain table settings, and cutlery for sale.

ACCOMMODATIONS
EXPENSIVE

Hôtel du Golf. At New-Golf Club, Mont Canisy, St-Arnoult 14800 Deauville. ☎ **02-31-
14-24-00.** Fax 02-31-14-24-01. E-mail: hoteldugolf@lucienbarriere.com. 178 units. MINIBAR
TV TEL. 920–1,790 F ($147.20–$286.40) double; 1,800–3,200 F ($288–$512) suite. AE, DC,
MC, V. Closed Nov–Dec 20 and late Jan–Mar 15. From Deauville, take D278 south for $1^1/_2$
miles.

Golfers naturally gravitate to this colossal half-timbered hotel created by the Lucien
Barrière chain in the late 1980s. Lavishly outfitted in an English country-house style,
it's one of the few hotels in Normandy with its own golf course. If the links aren't your
thing, however, you might consider the Normandy or Le Royal instead. The accommodations here come in a wide range of sizes; some have balconies. The older rooms
aren't as good as the more recently renovated ones; those in back open onto the links,
but those in front have better views of the Channel. The best rooms are called Prestige, featuring antique-style furnishings and French windows, along with spacious
baths and balconies. Each unit comes with elegant linen and fine mattresses on the
quality beds.

Dining: A glass-enclosed dining room, La Pommeraie, encircles a veranda, offering
views of the Channel. The food doesn't rate a trip here but is competently prepared in
the international style. Simple but sporty lunches are served year-round in the club
house on the golf course. Poolside barbecues are a summer feature.

Amenities: Heated pool, sauna, three tennis courts, 27-hole golf course, room service, laundry, bicycles (free), fitness room.

✪ **Hôtel Normandy.** 38 rue Jean-Mermoz, 14800 Deauville. ☎ **02-31-98-66-22.** Fax
02-31-98-66-23. www.lucienbarriere.com. E-mail: normandy@lucienbarriere.com. 303 units.
MINIBAR TV TEL. 1,190–2,400 F ($190.40–$384) double; 2,460–6,000 F ($393.60–$960)
suite. AE, DC, MC, V. Free outside parking, 100 F ($16) in garage.

Resembling a Norman village, with turrets, gables, and windows piercing sloping
roofs, this year-round hotel is near the casino, in a park of well-manicured shrubs and
flowers. It's Deauville's best, and also its most legendary, though some discriminating
people prefer Le Royal. The interior is as warm and comfortable as a rambling country house, with chandeliers and Oriental carpeting. Activities revolve around the main
rotunda, which is encircled by a marble colonnade. The rooms are in a constant state
of refurbishment. The sloping ceilings make the fourth-floor units feel cramped. The

rooms are chicly styled and come in a range of shapes and sizes, with many luxuries such as deluxe mattresses, double glazing, mirrored closets, and ample space. Many evoke the era of Louis XV.

Dining: La Belle Epoque captivates the glamour of turn-of-the-century Deauville.

Amenities: Heated indoor pool, sauna, fitness room, steam room, tennis courts, miniature-golf course, room service, laundry, safes, nursery.

✪ **Le Royal.** Bd. Eugène-Cornuché, 14800 Deauville. ☎ **02-31-98-66-33.** Fax 02-31-98-66-34. www.lucienbarriere.com/deauville. E-mail: royal@lucienbarriere.com. 270 units. MINIBAR TV TEL. 1,300–2,900 F ($208–$464) double; from 2,100–15,000 F ($336– $2,400) suite. AE, DC, MC, V. Closed Nov to mid-Mar.

Le Royal adjoins the casino and fronts a block-wide park near the Channel. An ideal place for a holiday, it rises like a regal palace, with columns and exposed timbers. The accommodations range from sumptuous suites to cozy little nooks. Most of the two dozen rooms were recently renovated, with designer fabrics, thick rugs, and comfortable mattresses. The rooms on the upper floors open onto the most panoramic views.

Dining: L'Etrier is the chic choice for dining; Le Côte Royal offers buffets at lunch and dinner. The chef often creates innovative dishes. There's also terrace dining in summer.

Amenities: Heated outdoor pool, beach, sauna, two recreation rooms, bicycle rental, health club, room service, valet parking.

INEXPENSIVE

Hôtel Ibis. 9 quai de la Marine, 14800 Deauville. ☎ **02-31-14-50-00.** Fax 02-31-14-50-05. E-mail: ho795@accor-hotels.com. 95 units. TV TEL. 335–495 F ($53.60–$79.20) double; 635–800 F ($101.60–$128) duplex suite for 2 to 6. AE, DC, MC, V. Parking 39 F ($6.25).

Built in the mid-1980s as part of a nationwide chain, the Ibis is scenically located and offers some of the best values of any hotel in Deauville. The modern building overlooks the harbor. The rooms are comfortable but done in a rather dull chain style. Each was renovated during the late 1990s, and each has acceptably comfortable, but not particularly plush, beds. The restaurant offers a traditional French menu.

Hôtel Le Trophée. 81 rue du Général-Leclerc, 14800 Deauville. ☎ **02-31-88-45-86.** Fax 02-31-88-07-94. 24 units. MINIBAR TV TEL. 400–580 F ($64–$92.80) double; 680–980 F ($108.80–$156.80) suite. AE, DC, MC, V. Parking 50 F ($8).

This modern replica of a half-timbered medieval building is in the middle of Deauville, 500 feet from the beach. The rooms, with nondescript contemporary furniture, are on the small side. But they have private balconies overlooking the shopping streets. The roof of the hotel has been converted into a sun terrace and provides a bird's-eye view of the town as well as a more private tanning area than the beach. The intimate restaurant serves breakfast and three fixed-price menus as well as daily specials. If you plan on taking one or more of your meals here, eat at least one under the stars in the patio courtyard garden.

✪ **L'Augeval.** 15 av. Hocquart-de-Turtot, 14800 Deauville. ☎ **02-31-81-13-18.** Fax 02-31-81-00-40. 32 units. MINIBAR TV TEL. 440–870 F ($70.40–$139.20) double; 890–1,400 F ($142.40–$224) suite. AE, DC, MC, V. Parking 50 F ($8).

Across from the racetrack and mere blocks from the beach and casino, this rare gem provides you with a great mix of city flair and country charm. The three-story brick-and-stone former private villa was built in the early 1900s and sits in the middle of well-kept lawns and gardens. You can walk out the back of the hotel and take a dip in the heated pool or have a drink on the garden patio. The guest rooms range from medium to spacious and are outfitted with overstuffed armchairs and sofas. The public areas include a bar and dining room, both with tall stone and brick vaulted ceilings, plus an exercise room. Fixed-price menus in the hotel restaurant cost from 140 F to 380 F ($22.40 to $60.80).

DINING

Chez Miocque. 81 rue Eugène-Colas. ☎ **02-31-88-09-52.** Reservations recommended. Main courses 100–180 F ($16–$28.80). MC, V. May–Oct, daily 9am–midnight; mid-Feb to Apr and Nov–Dec, Fri–Mon noon–3pm and 7pm–midnight. Closed Jan 1 to mid-Feb. FRENCH.

Irreverent and hip, this cafe near the casino and the resort's boutiques does a bustling business at its sidewalk tables. The owner, known simply as Jack, speaks English and will welcome you for lunch or dinner or provide a convivial bar-type setting if you just want to stop in for a drink. Set below a brightly striped awning, the place serves hearty brasserie-style food, including succulent lamb stew with spring vegetables, fillet of skate with cream-based caper sauce, mussels in white-wine sauce, and steaks. The portions are filling, and the atmosphere can be lively. The dish of the day is always from the sea.

✪ **Le Ciro's.** Promenade des Planches. ☎ **02-31-14-31-14.** Reservations required. Main courses 90–350 F ($14.40–$56); fixed-price menu 195 F ($31.20). AE, DC, MC, V. Daily noon–2:30pm, and 7:30–10:30pm. Jan–Mar closed Tues night and all day Wed. Also closed 2 weeks in Jan. FRENCH/SEAFOOD.

Hot on the resort's social scene, Le Ciro's serves Deauville's best seafood. It's expensive, but it's worth it. As you enter, you can make your lobster selection from the bubbling tank. Or wait while the kitchen prepares something from its stock of delectable oysters and mussels. If you want a bit of everything, ask for the *plateau de fruits de mer*, with lobster and various oysters and clams. The most expensive item is grilled lobster. For an elaborate appetizer, we recommend a tartare of sea bass and salmon, or lobster salad with truffles. A marmite of scallops with sweet sauterne wine and saffron makes a superb main course. Classics like grilled beef filet with béarnaise and grilled lamb cutlets with thyme are also offered. The collection of Bordeaux wine is exceptional. The ambience here is airy, elegant, stylish, and evocative of the belle époque heyday of Deauville at its most appealing.

✪ **Le Spinnaker.** 52 rue Mirabeau. ☎ **02-31-88-24-40.** Reservations required. Main courses 140–310 F ($22.40–$49.60); fixed-price menus 170–250 F ($27.20–$40). AE, DC, MC, V. Apr–Sept, Tues–Sun 12:30–2:30pm and 7:30–10pm; Oct–Mar, Wed–Sun 12:30–2:30pm and 7:30–10pm. Closed Jan. NORMAN.

Directed by the owner/chef, Pascal Angenard, this charming yellow-and-white restaurant features regional cuisine and is filled with English chintz. The menu specialties are ultrafresh and richly satisfying, like terrine of foie gras with four spices, roast lobster with cider vinegar and cream-enriched potatoes, slow-cooked baby veal flank, and a succulent tart with hot apples. Pascal recommends the roast turbot flavored with shallots en confit. A fine array of wines can accompany your meal. There are nights when a dish here or there might not always be sublime, but usually most are excellent.

DEAUVILLE AFTER DARK

Opened in 1912, the **Casino de Deauville,** rue Edmond-Blanc (☎ **02-31-14-31-14**), is one of France's premier casinos. Its original belle époque core has been expanded with a theater, a nightclub, two restaurants (Brunnel and le Cercle), and an extensive collection of slot machines (*machines à sous*). Jackets (but not ties) are required for men after 8pm.

The casino makes an important distinction between the areas devoted to slot machines and more formal and elegant areas containing such time-honored games as roulette, baccarat, chemin de fer, 21, and poker. Areas containing slot machines are open daily from 11am to 2am (to 3am Friday and Saturday), are accessible without cost or fee, and have no dress code. The more elegant and formal areas containing *"les jeux traditionnels"* are open every day at 4pm and close between 3 and 4am, depending on business and the day of the week. Entrance to the more formal (and more interesting) areas costs 70 F ($11.20) per person. Men are requested to wear jackets (ties not required) in the formal areas of the casino. The most interesting nights here are Friday and Saturday, when all the restaurants and the cabaret theater are open. The theater presents glittering, moderately titillating shows at 10:30pm on Friday and Saturday. Entrance is 160 F ($25.60) per person.

If it's a dance club you're looking for, head to the **Y Club,** 14 bis rue Désiré-le-Hoc (☎ **02-31-88-30-91**), with its high-energy dance scene, or the **Snake Pit Club,** 13 rue Albert-Fracasse (☎ **02-31-88-17-64**), where the energy level is a little less intense but by no means sleepy. If you want to say you've played miniature golf in France, stop by for a round at **Bar du Golf Miniature,** boulevard de la Mer (☎ **02-31-98-40-56**), with its sophisticated little bar alongside that attracts a varied crowd. On Friday nights a DJ spins the tunes. An alternative choice for salsa, merengue, and reggae is the **Brok Café,** 14 avenue du Général-de-Gaulle (☎ **02-31-81-30-81**). And if you want to re-create an almost Paleolithic sense of the restrained but decadent ambience of the 1970s, consider an hour or two within **Le Régine's,** inside Deauville's casino, rue Edmond-Blanc (☎ **02-31-14-31-14**).

An alternative spot for dancing, 3 miles from Deauville, is **Dancing Les Planches,** Le Bois Lauret, Blonville (☎ **02-31-87-58-09**). Here you'll find up-to-date music, an active dance floor, billiard tables, even an outdoor swimming pool flanking a warm-weather bar.

4 Trouville

128 miles NW of Paris, 27 miles NE of Caen

Across the Touques River from its more fashionable (and more expensive) rival, Deauville, Trouville feels like a fisher's port, something like the more charming Honfleur, but with fewer boutiques and art galleries. Don't expect the grand beaux-arts atmosphere of Deauville—Trouville is much more low-key. It's also less dependent on resort francs than its neighbor, for when the sea bathers leave the splendid sands to return to Paris or wherever, Trouville lives on—its resident population of fishers sees to that.

ESSENTIALS

GETTING THERE   There are **rail** connections from Gare St-Lazare in Paris to Trouville (see the Deauville section earlier in this chapter). **Bus Verts du Calvados** services Trouville, Deauville, and much of the surrounding region, linking those towns with the rest of Normandy. For information about bus departures and fares in and out of Trouville, call the **Gare Routière** (☎ **08-01-21-42-14**). If you're traveling by **car** from Deauville, simply travel west along D180 to Trouville.

VISITOR INFORMATION   The **Office de Tourisme** is at 32 quai Fernand-Moureaux (☎ **02-31-14-60-70**).

EXPLORING THE TOWN

In the heyday of Napoléon III, during the 1860s, boulevardiers used to bring wives and families to Trouville and stash their mistresses in the then-fledgling, and decidedly unstylish, Deauville, which was just beginning to emerge from what was at the time a marsh. Consequently, whereas Deauville is a planned city, with straight avenues and a sense of industrial-age orderliness, the narrow and labyrinthine alleyways of Trouville hint at its origins as a medieval fishing port.

Our recommendation? Stamp around Trouville, enjoying its low-key charm, and when you tire of it, join the caravan of traffic that heads across the river to the bright lights and glamour of Deauville (see above).

Trouville's main **shopping streets** are quai Fernand-Moureaux, rue des Bains, some sections of which are off-limits to conventional traffic, and to a lesser degree, the rue du Général-de-Gaulle, which has a greater concentration of everyday shops such as food outlets and hardware stores. And although the rue des Bains has its share of fashion boutiques and clothing stores, greater numbers of stylish shops lie within the neighboring resort of Deauville.

Les Planches is a rambling stretch of seafront boardwalk dotted with concessions on one side and a view of the sea on the other. Expect lots of flesh sprawled on the sands before you in midsummer in various states of undress—this is France. There's only one beach, **Plage de Trouville,** though when you've tired of it, you'll only have to cross the river to the Plage de Deauville. On Trouville's seafront promenade is the **Piscine de Trouville,** Promenade des Planches (☎ **02-31-88-89-81**), a freshwater pool that gets very, very crowded in summer. An alternative option for pool swimming is at Deauville, just across the river. There, the **Piscine Olympique,** Bord de Mer (☎ **02-31-88-89-81**), offers a larger alternative, albeit with seawater rather than fresh water. Entrance to either pool costs 32 F ($5.10) for adults, 23 F ($3.70) for children under 16, and both are open between late May and mid-September from 10am to 7pm.

ACCOMMODATIONS

Hôtel Carmen. 24 rue Carnot, 14360 Trouville. ☎ **02-31-88-35-43.** Fax 02-31-88-08-03. 16 units, 15 with bathroom. MINIBAR TV TEL. 250 F ($40) double without bathroom, 380–460 F ($60.80–$73.60) double with bathroom. Half-board 240 F ($38.40) extra per person. AE, DC, MC, V.

This highly recommended Logis de France consists of two connected late-18th-century villas, one designed by a cousin of Georges Bizet. The management prefers that you take the half-board plan (breakfast and dinner). It's run by the Bude family, whom some guests find a bit bourgeois. The rooms are simply furnished, some overlooking a flower-filled courtyard. Rooms come in a variety of sizes; although most of them are rather small, they are fitted with a comfortable mattress on a good bed. The restaurant is open daily. Fixed-price menus in the hotel's **restaurant** cost from 95 F to 180 F ($15.20 to $28.80).

Le Beach Hotel. 1 quai Albert-1er, 14360 Trouville. ☎ **02-31-98-12-00.** Fax 02-31-87-30-29. 118 units. TV TEL. 585–690 F ($93.60–$110.40) double; from 990 F ($158.40) suite. AE, DC, MC, V. Closed Jan 4–28. Parking 50 F ($8).

This hotel emerges out of the lackluster lot as the resort's top accommodation, only 150 feet from the beach, facing Trouville harbor. Although a poor relation to the palace hotels of Deauville, it offers grand comfort at a more affordable price. Its average-size rooms have modern furniture, comfortable beds, and fabrics with sunny tropical island colors, plus ocean views. Most bathrooms only have showers instead of complete combination tub and shower baths. You can mingle in the bar and sample the excellent Norman and international cuisine in the hotel's **restaurant,** which features fixed-price menus. You can even sip a fruity drink with a little umbrella in it while sunning on the deck or taking a dip in the pool.

DINING

La Petite Auberge. 7 rue Carnot. ☎ **02-31-88-11-07.** Reservations required. Fixed-price menus 132–260 F ($21.10–$41.60). AE, MC, V. Daily noon–2:30pm and 7–10pm. Sept–June closed Tues–Wed. FRENCH.

If you want something inexpensive without sacrificing quality, head to this Norman bistro a block from the casino. Try the *soupe de poissons* (fish soup), one of the finest along the Flower Coast, or the seafood pot-au-feu, featuring fillet of sole, scallops, monkfish, and salmon beautifully simmered together. You can also order grilled beef and stuffed rabbit braised in cider. Since there are only 30 seats, reservations are vital in summer.

✪ **Les Vapeurs.** 160 bd. Fernand-Moureaux. ☎ **02-31-88-15-24.** Reservations recommended. Main courses 100–180 F ($16–$28.80). AE, MC, V. Daily noon–1am. FRENCH/SEAFOOD.

This Art Deco brasserie, one of the most popular on the Norman coast, is frequented by stylish Parisians on le weekend. Established in 1926, this has been called the Brasserie Lipp of Normandy. The windows face the port, and in warm weather you can dine at sidewalk tables. Seafood is the specialty: A wide range of shrimp, mussels laced with cream, crinkle-shelled oysters, and fish is served. Sauerkraut is also popular.

TROUVILLE AFTER DARK

If the casino in Deauville is too stuffy for your tastes, you'll feel more comfortable in the smaller, less grand, less architecturally distinctive sibling in Trouville, **Louisiane Follies,** place du Maréchal-Foch (☎ **02-31-87-75-00**). Here you can try your hand at Lady Luck in a more New Orleans–style environment, with areas that add to the city-of-sin feel, like a blues/jazz bar and small-scale replica of a section of Bourbon Street. Entrance to the area containing slot machines is free. That area is open daily from 10am to between 2 and 4am, depending on the day of the week and business. Entrance to the more formal area containing roulette and blackjack tables costs 70 F ($11.90) per person. The formal area is open daily from 4pm till between 2 and 4am, depending on the day of the week and business. Trouville's leading nightclub and disco, **L'Embellie,** lies within the casino as well. Open nightly, it charges 100 F ($16) for entrance, and includes one free drink. Unlike in Deauville, men aren't required to wear jackets and ties here, but no tennis shoes are allowed.

5 Caen

148 miles NW of Paris, 74 miles SE of Cherbourg

On the banks of the Orne, the port of Caen suffered great damage in the Allied invasion of Normandy in 1944. Nearly three-quarters of its buildings, 10,000 in all, were destroyed, though the twin abbeys founded by William the Conqueror and his wife, Mathilda, were spared. The city today is essentially modern and has many broad avenues and new apartment buildings. Completely different from Deauville and Trouville, this capital of Lower Normandy is bustling, congested, and commercial (it's a major rail and ferry junction). The resident student population of 30,000 and the hordes of international travelers have made this city more cosmopolitan than ever.

ESSENTIALS

GETTING THERE   From Paris's Gare St-Lazare, 13 **trains** per day arrive in Caen (trip time: 2¹/₂ hours), costing from 174 F ($27.85) one-way. There are also six trains from Rouen (trip time: 1³/₄ hours), costing from 114 F ($18.25) one-way. When **driving** from Paris, travel west along A13 to Caen (driving time: 2¹/₂ hours).

VISITOR INFORMATION   The **Office de Tourisme** is on place St-Pierre in the 16th-century Hôtel d'Escoville (☎ **02-31-27-14-14**).

EXPLORING THE CITY

Caen has several good boutique-lined shopping streets, like **boulevard du Maréchal-Leclerc, rue St-Pierre,** and **rue de Strasbourg. Antiques** hunters should check out the shops along rue Ecuyère and rue Commerçantes, as well as the antiques show held at the **Parc aux Expositions,** rue Joseph-Philippon (☎ **02-31-29-99-99**), each year during early December. The **markets** at place St-Sauveur on Friday mornings and place Courtonne on Sunday mornings also sell various secondhand articles.

For reproduction antique furniture that can be built to meet your specific needs, visit **La Reine Matilde,** 47 rue St-Jean (☎ **02-31-85-45-52**); it also sells decorative items, including a wide selection of bed linens and curtains. If you need to pick up some gift items, **Le Chocolatier Hotot,** 13 rue St-Pierre (☎ **02-31-86-31-90**), has a cornucopia of chocolate products as well as local jams and jellies; or you may want to stop by **Folklore,** 7 rue de Geole (☎ **02-31-86-34-13**), where you can find many regional items, like pottery, ciders, faïence, and decorative plates.

For objets and paintings, check out **L'Atelier,** 33 rue Montoir-Poissonnerie (☎ **02-31-44-49-38**), which showcases many local artisans, dealing in all crafts media. And if you're in the mood for browsing through worthy inventories of wine and *eaux-de-vie* deriving from throughout France, head for **Nicolas,** rue Bellivet 10 (☎ **02-31-85-24-19**).

Abbaye aux Dames. Place de la Reine-Mathilde. ☎ **02-31-06-98-98.** Free admission. Daily 2–5:30pm. Free guided 1-hour tour of choir, transept, and crypt (in French) daily at 2:30 and 4pm.

Founded by Mathilda, this abbey embraces Église de la Trinité, which is flanked by Romanesque towers. Its spires were destroyed in the Hundred Years War and never rebuilt. In the 12th-century choir is the tomb of Queen Mathilda; note the ribbed vaulting.

Abbaye aux Hommes. Esplanade Jean-Marie-Louvel. ☎ **02-31-30-42-81.** Open for self-guided visits, without charge, daily 8:15am–7:30pm. Tours (in French) daily at 9:30 and 11am and 2:30 and 4pm for 10 F ($1.60) for adults, 5 F (80¢) for students, free for anyone under 18.

Founded by William and Mathilda, the abbey is adjacent to the Église St-Etienne, which you enter on place Monseigneur-des-Hameaux. During the height of the Allied invasion, denizens of Caen flocked to St-Etienne for protection. The church is dominated by twin 276-foot Romanesque towers; its 15th-century spires helped earn Caen the appellation "city of spires." A marble slab inside the high altar commemorates the site of William's tomb. The Huguenots destroyed the tomb in an uprising in 1562, save for a hip bone that was recovered. However, during the Revolution the last of William's dust was scattered to the wind. The hand-carved wooden doors and elaborately sculpted wrought-iron staircase are exceptional. From the cloisters you get a good view of the two towers of St-Etienne.

✪ **Caen Memorial (Le Mémorial de Caen).** Esplanade Dwight-Eisenhower. ☎ **02-31-06-06-44.** Admission 74 F ($11.85) adults; 65 F ($10.40) for students and anyone ages 10–18; free to World War II veterans, war disabled, war widows, and children under 10. Daily 9am–6pm (open till 9pm from mid-July to mid-Aug). Closed Christmas, Jan 1–18, and Jan 24–25.

The memorial stands 10 minutes from the Pegasus Bridge and 15 minutes from the landing beaches. The museum presents a journey through history from 1918 to the present, recalling the unfolding and the meaning of World War II. It's also an ideal place to relax with walks through International Park; to have brunch, tea, a cold buffet, or a drink in the restaurant; or to browse through the boutique for that special souvenir. Expect to spend at least 2¹/₂ hours at this site—anyone intrigued by 20th-century European history will be fascinated by the display here.

ACCOMMODATIONS

Note that **Le Dauphin** (see "Dining," below) also rents rooms.

Holiday Inn. Place du Maréchal-Foch, 14000 Caen. ☎ **800/465-4329** in the U.S., or 02-31-27-57-57. Fax 02-31-27-57-58. www.holiday-inn.com. 92 units. TV TEL. 560–695 F ($89.60–$111.20) double. AE, DC, MC, V. Bus: 1, 3, 4, 10, or 11.

Across from the racecourse and opposite an angel-capped monument to a military hero, this hotel was built before World War II but was enlarged and modernized in 1991 when it adopted the Holiday Inn logo. Today it's the best hotel in town, with a flavor that's French and international. The guest rooms are predictable, comfortable, and well maintained. Bedrooms are tastefully and discreetly decorated in chain-hotel style, with modern contemporary furniture and comfortable beds.

The Holiday Inn offers a cozy bar favored by Americans visiting the D-Day beaches, plus a restaurant, Le Rabelais. Fixed-price menus, priced at 145 F to 215 F ($23.20 to $34.40) feature meals the 16th-century writer and Chinon native might have enjoyed in his day.

Hôtel Bristol. 31 rue du 11-November, 14000 Caen. ☎ **02-31-84-59-76.** Fax 02-31-52-29-28. 25 units. TV TEL. 230–260 F ($36.80–$41.60) double. Rates include continental breakfast. DC, MC, V. Bus: 12.

Built shortly after the devastating bombings of World War II and renovated in 1992, this hotel is on a block of modern apartments and shops, not far from the park. Consider the Bristol more a bare-bones stopover hotel than a charming inn. The price is fair, however. Bedrooms are small but are well kept, each with a comfortable bed. Breakfast is the only meal served.

Hôtel de France. 10 rue de la Gare, 14000 Caen. ☎ **02-31-52-16-99.** Fax 02-31-83-23-16. 47 units. TV TEL. 200–300 F ($32–$48) double. MC, V. Free parking.

The exterior of this six-story brick building is plain but still reflects a bit of charm. Maybe it's the window boxes outside every room or the French door–style windows that swing open to let breezes in. The rooms are functional with simple furnishings, but many make a statement with their strong colors, such as deep fuchsia with metallic blues, for example. Mattresses are a bit thin but still reasonably comfortable, especially at this price. The public areas have a provincial charm. This hotel is a favorite with tour groups (often World War II veterans) and offers a restaurant that serves only these groups.

Hôtel des Quatrans. 17 rue Gémare, 14300 Caen. ☎ **02-31-86-25-57.** Fax 02-31-85-27-80. 36 units. TV TEL. 260–270 F ($41.60–$43.20) double. V. Free parking. Bus: 2 or 7.

This agreeable and unpretentious hotel was built after the devastations of World War II, and thanks to continual renovations, it remains one of Caen's best bargains. Don't expect luxury: The hotel has four floors and no elevator; rooms are old-fashioned, are simply furnished, and offer only the most basic amenities. Mattresses aren't particularly plush, towels are a bit threadbare, but at these prices, who can complain? Breakfast is the only meal served, at 35 F ($5.60).

Hôtel Royal. 1 place de la République, 14000 Caen. ☎ **02-31-86-55-33.** Fax 02-31-79-89-44. 43 units. TV TEL. 290–330 F ($46.40–$52.80) double. AE, MC, V. Free parking.

The original Hôtel Royal was built in 1794 but destroyed 150 years later during a World War II bombing raid. The new hotel was built several years later on the site of the original, and today it's surrounded by a busy commercial area of shops and restaurants as well as more tranquil pedestrian streets. The last renovation, completed in 1998, brought all the rooms up to an acceptable level of comfort, though space is a bit cramped. The public areas include a standard restaurant, open only for breakfast, and a small lobby/sitting area that has an austere look but opens onto place de la République.

ACCOMMODATIONS NEARBY

Relais Château d'Audrieu. 14250 Audrieu. ☎ **02-31-80-21-52.** Fax 02-31-80-24-73. www.relaischateaux.fr/audrieu. E-mail: chateaudaudrieu@mail.cpod.fr. 30 units. TV TEL. 790–1,450 F ($126.40–$232) double; 2,150–2,300 F ($344–$368) suite. AE, MC, V. Closed Nov 30–Feb 14. From Caen, take N13 for 11 miles, then D158 for 2 miles to Audrieu.

This château in a 50-acre park offers some of the most luxurious accommodations near Caen. It was built of local stone (*pierre de Caen*) at the beginning of the 18th century. During the Allied invasion of Normandy, some of the fiercest fighting took place right around this hotel. Notice the gashes and wounds in the trees in the surrounding park. The château functioned as a private home until 1976, when it was transformed into this stately hotel. The rooms are lovely and well appointed, usually with antiques, each with a carefully planned unique style. Beds are elegantly appointed with deluxe mattresses, tasteful linens, and elegant fabrics.

Dining: Dinner here may include bouillon of duckling with cider or croustade of oysters with beet-flavored vinaigrette. Fixed-price menus range from 285 F to 520 F ($45.60 to $83.20). The restaurant, but not the hotel, is closed on Monday.

DINING

✪ **La Bourride.** 15–17 rue du Vaugueux. ☎ **02-31-93-50-76.** Reservations required. Main courses 140–230 F ($22.40–$36.80); fixed-price menus 340–620 F ($54.40–$99.20). AE, DC, MC, V. Tues–Sat noon–2pm and 7:30–10pm. Closed 3 weeks in Jan, 2 weeks in late Aug. Bus: 1, 3, 4, 10, or 11. NORMAN.

This restaurant serves Caen's best food. The namesake bourride is concocted from five kinds of fish, delicately seasoned and simmered under the expert eye of Michel Bruneau. The place occupies a beautiful 17th-century house near the château, and its dining room has thick stone walls and a magnificent Renaissance fireplace. The service includes tactful advice on wines to accompany any of the specialties, such as roasted pigeon with vanilla essence and salt. Their signature dessert, which draws directly on the culinary traditions of Normandy, is *pommes, pommes, pommes,* which includes at least four variations of apples, all served on the same dessert plate. On it, look for tarte tatin, apple sorbet, aumônière of apples, and a surprise apple dish as well, all of it linked to Normandy's fixation on the apple and all its derivatives.

Le Dauphin. 29 rue Gémare, 14300 Caen. ☎ **02-31-86-22-26.** Fax 02-31-86-35-14. Reservations required. Main courses 75–105 F ($12–$16.80); fixed-price menus 110–310 F ($17.60–$49.60). AE, DC, MC, V. Sun–Fri noon–2:30pm; Mon–Sat 7:30–9:30pm. Hotel and restaurant closed 2 weeks in Feb; restaurant also closed July 17–Aug 6. FRENCH.

Although this establishment traces its history back to the Middle Ages, much of which you'll see today dates from a comprehensive restoration and reconstruction during the 1950s. All ingredients are market fresh; owners Stephane and Sylvie Pugnat prepare interesting items like ragoût of lobster with fresh pasta; sweetbreads forester style; a gratin of oysters with a fondue of leeks; an émincé of sole with fresh spinach; and a chartreuse of partridge with crispy potatoes and slices of foie gras.

Le Dauphin also offers 22 well-furnished, richly accessorized guest rooms, each with comfortable beds, for 430 F to 480 F ($68.80 to $76.80) for a double, and 600 F ($96) for a suite.

A NEARBY CHOICE

✪ **Le Manoir d'Hastings.** Av. Côte-de-Nacre, 14970 Bénouville. ☎ **02-31-44-62-43.** Fax 02-31-44-76-18. Reservations required. Main courses 80–130 F ($12.80–$20.80); fixed-price menus 125–390 F ($20–$62.40) at lunch, 170–390 F ($27.20–$62.40) at dinner. AE, DC, MC, V. Sun 12:30–2pm, Tues–Sat 12:30–2pm and 7–9:30pm. From Caen, follow the signs north for Ouistreham, then turn off onto RD35. Stay on this road for 6^1/₂ miles, following the signs to Bayeux and Bénouville; the manor is next to the village church. FRENCH.

This restaurant occupies a converted 17th-century monastery with an enclosed Norman garden. It's one of Normandy's most famous and charming inns (and a magnet for Parisians seeking a rustically elegant weekend getaway). The owners, José and Carole Aparicio, focus much of their attention on the sophisticated *cuisine moderne* that emerges with panache from their kitchens. Many dishes are twists on traditional Norman favorites, like cider-cooked lobster with Nantua sauce, delicately flavored sea bass, and fillet of monkfish poached in port. Beef fillets are stuffed with foie gras and scallops braised in an old-fashioned apple-based liqueur, Pommeau. Other choices include a mousseline of scallops with basil-flavored cream sauce; and fillets of turbot and sea bass served on the same platter drenched in champagne sauce. For dessert, try the tarte normande flambéed with Calvados.

The manor also offers 15 handsome rooms in a stone-sided annex. Each has a garden view, bathroom, TV, minibar, and phone. A double goes for 500 F to 800 F ($80 to $128). Each of the rooms was overhauled and upgraded in the late 1990s, with improvements in the mattresses, furnishings, and fabrics. The hotel lies very close to Pegasus Bridge, one of the first strategic targets liberated by Allied soldiers after the invasion of Normandy in 1944.

CAEN AFTER DARK

Take a walk down rue de Bras, rue St-Pierre, and the north end of rue Vaugueux to take a look at the action. If you want to connect with the hip 18-to-35 crowd, go to **Le Chic,** rue des Prairiers St-Gilles (☎ **02-31-94-48-72**), where disco music begins at 10:30pm, and where you're likely to get a hint of the various scandals and infidelities that might be blossoming within this otherwise quiet Norman town. Another dance club is **Joy's/Le Paradis,** 10 rue de Strasbourg (☎ **02-31-85-40-40**), with a frenetic crowd and a techno beat.

A couple of the better pubs/bars are **Pub Concorde,** 7 rue Montoir-Poissonnerie (☎ **02-31-93-61-29**), with more than 150 beers to choose from, and **Le Dakota,** 54 rue de Bernières (☎ **02-31-50-05-25**). **Café des Beaux-Arts,** 88 rue de Geôle

(☎ **02-31-86-43-21**), has become the hang-out-and-hang-about place where you can talk, play pinball, and listen to jazz, reggae, and salsa. There's no attitude here, just good music and fun people.

The town's most visible and popular gay bar is **Le Cabaret Joyeux,** place du 36e Régiment d'Infanterie (☎ **02-31-34-99-00**). It's open nightly 11pm till as late as 5am.

6 Bayeux

166 miles NW of Paris, 16 miles NW of Caen

The ducs de Normandie sent their sons to this Viking settlement to learn the Norse language. Bayeux has changed a lot since, but miraculously it was spared from bombardment in 1944. This was the first French town liberated, and the citizens of Bayeux gave de Gaulle an enthusiastic welcome when he arrived on June 14. Today the sleepy town is filled with timbered houses, stone mansions, and cobblestone streets.

Visitors wanting to explore sites associated with "the longest day" flood the town today, as many memorials (not to mention the beaches) are only 6 to 12 miles away. The cozy little streets are lined with shops, many selling World War II memorabilia, and more postcards and T-shirts than you'll ever need.

ESSENTIALS

GETTING THERE   Between 6 and 14 **trains** depart daily from Paris's Gare St-Lazare (depending on the season and the day of the week), for the 2¹/₂-hour trip to Bayeux (costing 188 F/$30.10 each way). Most of these trains stop in Caen en route. Travel time between Caen and Bayeux is about 20 minutes, and costs 42 F ($6.70) each way. When **driving** to Bayeux from Paris (driving time: 3 hours), simply take E-46 west from Caen.

VISITOR INFORMATION   The **Office de Tourisme** is at pont St-Jean (☎ **02-31-51-28-28**).

SPECIAL EVENTS   The town goes wild with **Fêtes Médiévales** the first weekend in July, when Bayeux has 2 complete days of lunacy and revelry, filling the streets with wine and song outside the cathedral.

SEEING THE SIGHTS

✪ **Musée de la Tapisserie de Bayeux.** Centre Guillaume-le-Conquérant, 13 rue de Nesmond. ☎ **02-31-51-25-50.** Admission 40 F ($6.40) adults, 16 F ($2.55) students, free for children 9 and under. May–Aug, daily 9am–7pm; mid-Mar to Apr and Sept 1 to mid-Oct, daily 9am–6:30pm; mid-Oct to mid-Mar, daily 9:30am–12:30pm and 2–6pm.

Here you'll find the Bayeux tapestry—the most famous tapestry in the world. Actually, it's an embroidery on a band of linen, 231 feet long and 20 inches wide, depicting some 58 scenes in 8 colors. Contrary to legend, it wasn't made by Queen Mathilda but was probably commissioned in Kent and created by unknown embroiderers between 1066 and 1077. The first recorded mention of the embroidery was in 1476, when it was explained that it was used to decorate the nave of the Cathédrale Notre-Dame de Bayeux.

Housed in a Plexiglas case, the embroidery tells the story of the conquest of England by William the Conqueror, including such scenes as the coronation of Harold as the Saxon king of England, Harold returning from his journey to Normandy, the surrender of Dinan, Harold being told of the apparition of a comet (a portent of misfortune), William dressed for war, and the death of Harold. The decorative borders include scenes from *Aesop's Fables.*

Admission to this museum also gets you into two less significant museums, the **Musée Baron Gérard,** Place de la Liberté (☎ **02-31-92-14-21**), and the **Musée de l'Art Sacré,** 6 rue Lambert le Forestier (☎ **02-31-92-73-80**), each within 200 yards of the main attraction. Both are open daily 10am to 12:30pm and 2 to 7pm (to 6pm in winter) and exhibit local examples of regional lacework, religious statues, and religious and secular paintings.

Musée Memorial de la Bataille de Normandie. Bd. Fabian-Ware. ☎ **02-31-21-85-11.** Admission 33 F ($5.30) adults, 16 F ($2.55) children, free for children under 10. May–Sept 15, daily 9:30am–6:30pm; Sept 16–Apr, daily 10am–12:30pm and 2–6pm. Closed last 2 weeks in Jan.

Across from the cemetery, this museum deals exclusively with the military and human history of the Battle of Normandy (June 6 to August 22, 1944). Within a low-slung building designed like a bunker are 440 feet of window and film displays, plus a diorama. Wax soldiers in their uniforms, along with the tanks and guns used to win the battle, are exhibited.

Notre-Dame de Bayeux. Rue du Bienvenu. ☎ **02-31-92-01-85.** Free admission. Daily 9am–6pm (to 7pm July–Aug).

The cathedral was consecrated in 1077, but partially destroyed in 1105. Romanesque towers left over from that church rise on the western side. The central tower is from the 15th century, with an even later top. The nave is a fine example of Norman Romanesque style. Rich in sculpture, the 13th-century choir, a perfect example of Norman Gothic style, has handsome Renaissance stalls. The crypt was built in the 11th century and then sealed. Its existence remained unknown until 1412.

ACCOMMODATIONS

Family Home. 39 rue du Général-de-Dais, 14400 Bayeux. ☎ **02-31-92-15-22.** Fax 02-31-92-55-72. E-mail: family-home@wanadoo.fr. 13 units. 190 F ($30.40) double. Rates include breakfast. AE, MC, V.

In the town center, this 16th-century presbytery, now a privately owned hotel, encompasses four interconnected buildings. The rooms are furnished with Norman antiques, and you can cook your own meals in the kitchen. Madame Lefèvre also serves large and varied meals of Normandy specialties at a long communal table for 65 F ($10.40), including wine. The wine served is a smooth Anjou red produced by Mme Lefèvre's family at their own vineyards. Rooms are renovated at regular intervals, most recently a few years ago. Accommodations are a bit old fashioned but each contains a soft, comfortable bed.

Hôtel Clarine-Churchill. 14 rue St-Jean, 14404 Bayeux. ☎ **02-31-21-31-80.** Fax 02-31-21-41-66. 32 units. TV TEL. 380–560 F ($60.80–$89.60) double; 560–730 F ($89.60–$116.80) suite. AE, DC, MC, V. Closed Nov 15–Mar 1.

Built in 1850, this hotel sits in the heart of the old town on a quiet pedestrian street near lots of boutiques, restaurants, and historic sites. The rooms are somewhat cramped but thoughtfully appointed with delicate Louis XVI reproductions. Each was renovated with new curtains, carpets, and paint jobs in 1998. The rooms are enhanced by large windows that look out onto panoramic views of black slate rooftops and Bayeux's 11th-century cathedral. The hotel wraps around a private courtyard that has been turned into a glassed-in patio dining room for its independently managed restaurant—a cheery environment in which to wake up over morning coffee and croissants. Evening meals filled with Norman specialties are also served here.

Hôtel d'Argouges. 21 rue St-Patrice, 14402 Bayeux. ☎ **02-31-92-88-86.** Fax 02-31-92-69-16. E-mail: dargouges@aol.com. 25 units. MINIBAR TV TEL. 390–460 F ($62.40–$73.60) double. AE, DC, MC, V. Free parking.

Madame Auregan has handsomely restored a pair of interconnected 18th-century town houses, with exposed beams, thick walls, and sloping ceilings. In good weather, you can enjoy the pleasant garden. Bedrooms are comfortable, intimate, and cozy. Breakfast is the only meal served, but there are at least three restaurants within a 2-minute walk.

Hôtel de Luxembourg. 25 rue Bouchers, 14403 Bayeux. ☎ **800/528-1234** in the U.S. and Canada, or 02-31-92-00-04. Fax 02-31-92-54-26. 22 units. MINIBAR TV TEL. 495–615 F ($79.20–$98.40) double; from 950 F ($152) suite. AE, MC, V.

After Le Lion d'Or (below), this Best Western is the area's finest hotel. The completely restored interior has terrazzo floors and a decor combining neoclassical and Art Deco. Bedrooms range in size from small to medium, and each has been thoroughly over-hauled with an eye to modern comfort, including very firm mattresses and fine linen on the beds. The Luxembourg contains a richly decorated bar, an elegant **restaurant,** and an elevator. Fixed-price menus run 118 F to 295 F ($18.90 to $47.20).

✪ **Le Lion d'Or.** 71 rue St-Jean, 14400 Bayeux. ☎ **02-31-92-06-90.** Fax 02-31-22-15-64. E-mail: lion-d-or.bayeux@wanadoo.fr. 25 units. MINIBAR TV TEL. 420–630 F ($67.20–$100.80) double; 630–945 F ($100.80–$151.20) suite. AE, DC, MC, V. Closed Dec 20–Jan 20.

This old-world hotel, the best in town, has an open courtyard with lush flower boxes decorating the facade. The personalized guest rooms are set back from the street. As befits this old inn, bedrooms come in various shapes and sizes. Guests are required to take at least one meal. But this shouldn't be a problem, since the traditional cuisine is inspired by the region's bounty, like homemade Normandy sausage, mushroom-stuffed chicken with creamy Pommeau sauce, and sole fillet with cider-butter sauce. Normandy cheese or warm apple tart with creamy Calvados sauce perfectly tops off a meal. There are lots of reasonably priced wines. Fixed-price menus cost 105 F ($16.80) for lunch (Monday through Saturday) and from 150 F to 230 F ($24 to $36.80) for dinner.

7 The D-Day Beaches

Arromanches-les-Bains: 169 miles NW of Paris, 6¹/₂ miles NW of Bayeux; Grandcamp-Maisy (near Omaha Beach): 186 miles NW of Paris, 35 miles NW of Caen

During a rainy week in early June, 1944, the greatest armada ever known—soldiers and sailors, warships, landing craft, tugboats, jeeps, whatever—assembled along the southern coast of England. At 9:15pm on June 5, the BBC announced to the French Resistance that the invasion was imminent, signaling the underground to start dyna-miting the railways. Before midnight, Allied planes began bombing the Norman coast fortifications. By 1:30am on June 6 (known forever after as "the longest day"), mem-bers of the 101st Airborne were parachuting to the ground on German-occupied French soil. At 6:30am the Americans began landing on the heavily fortified beaches, code-named Utah and Omaha. An hour later British and Canadian forces made beachheads at Juno, Gold, and Sword.

The Nazis had mocked Churchill's promise in 1943 to liberate France "before the fall of the autumn leaves." When the invasion did come, it was swift, sudden, and a surprise to the formidable "Atlantic wall." Today aging veterans from Canada, the

United States, and Britain walk with their children and grandchildren across the beaches where "Czech hedgehogs," "Belgian grills," pillboxes, and "Rommel asparagus" once stood.

ESSENTIALS

GETTING THERE   The best way to get to the D-Day beaches is to **drive,** as public transportation is unreliable. The trip takes about 3 hours from Paris. Take A-13 west to Caen, continuing west on E46 to Bayeux. From Bayeux, travel north along D6 until you reach the coast at Port-en-Bessin. From here, D514 runs along the coastline; D-Day sites are generally west of Port-en-Bessin. Parking is not a problem, as there are designated areas all along the roadway, most of them free. The best days to visit are during the week, as weekends (especially in summer) can be a bit overcrowded with tourists and sunbathers alike.

Bus service from Bayeux is very uneven and almost always involves long delays. **Bus Verts** (☎ **02-31-92-02-92**) heads for Port-en-Bessin and points west along the coast, and no. 74 buses offer service to Arromanches and other points in the east. Bus no. 70 travels west from Bayeux to points west of town, towards Omaha Beach and the American cemetery.

VISITOR INFORMATION   The **Office de Tourisme** is at 4 rue du Maréchal-Joffre, Arromanches-les-Bains (☎ **02-31-21-47-56**), open April to September.

RELIVING THE LONGEST DAY

Start out your exploration of the D-Day beaches at the modest seaside resort of **Arromanches-les-Bains.** In June 1944 it was a fishing port, until it was taken by the 50th British Division. Towed across the English Channel, a mammoth prefabricated port known as Winston was installed to supply the Allied forces. "Victory could not have been achieved without it," said Eisenhower. The wreckage of that artificial harbor—known as Mulberry—lies right off the beach, *la plage du débarquement.* The **Musée du Débarquement,** place du 6-Juin (☎ **02-31-22-34-31**), features relief maps, working models, a cinema, and photographs, plus a diorama of the landing, with an English commentary. Admission is 35 F ($5.60) for adults and 20 F ($3.20) for students and children. From May to September, it's open daily from 9am to 6:30pm. From October to April, it's open daily from 10am to 12:30pm and 1:30 to 5pm.

Moving along the coast, you arrive at **Omaha Beach,** where you can still see the war wreckage. "Hanging on by their toenails," the men of the 1st and 29th American Divisions occupied the beach that June day. The code-name Omaha became famous throughout the world, though up to then the beaches had been called St-Laurent, Vierville-sur-Mer, and Colleville. A monument commemorates the heroism of the invaders. Covering some 173 acres at Omaha Beach, the **Normandy American Cemetery** (☎ **02-31-51-62-00**) is filled with Latin crosses and Stars of David in Lasa marble. The remains of 9,386 American military dead were buried here on territory now owned by the United States, a gift from the French nation. The cemetery is open from 9am to 5pm daily (until 6pm in summer).

Farther along the coast you'll see the jagged lime cliffs of the **Pointe du Hoc.** A cross honors a group of American Rangers, led by Lt.-Col. James Rudder, who scaled the cliffs using hooks to get at the pillboxes. The scars of war are more visible here than at any other point along the beach. Much farther along the Cotentin Peninsula is **Utah Beach,** where the 4th U.S. Infantry Division landed at 6:30am. The landing force was nearly 2 miles south of its intended destination, but, fortunately, Nazi defenses were weak at this point. By midday the infantry had completely cleared the beach. A U.S. monument commemorates their heroism.

Nearby, you can visit the sleepy but historic hamlet of **Sainte-Mère-Église,** which was virtually unknown outside of France until the night of June 5 and 6, when paratroopers dropped from the sky above the town. They were from the 82nd U.S. Airborne Division, under the command of Gen. Matthew B. Ridgeway. Members of the 101st U.S. Airborne Division, commanded by Gen. M. B. Taylor, were also involved. Also in Ste-Mère-Église is Kilometer "0" on the Liberty Highway, marking the first of the milestones the American armies reached on their way to Metz and Bastogne.

There's a **tourist office** (☎ **02-33-21-00-33**), maintaining infrequent and irregular hours, even in the peak of midsummer.

ACCOMMODATIONS & DINING

Hôtel Duguesclin. 4 quai Crampon, 14450 Grandcamp-Maisy. ☎ **02-31-22-64-22.** Fax 02-31-22-34-79. Reservations recommended. Main courses 55–130 F ($8.80–$20.80); fixed-price menus 65–175 F ($10.40–$28). AE, MC, V. Daily noon–2pm and 7–9pm. Closed Jan 15–Feb 15 and 1 week in Oct. Free parking. FRENCH.

We recommend this three-story Norman inn, built in 1932 and repaired after the ravages of World War II, for lunch or even for an overnight. The fish soup, grilled scallops, Norman sole (if available), and grilled turbot with white butter are excellent. Everything tastes better with the dining room's country bread and Norman butter.

The hotel rents 31 simple but comfortable rooms, 25 with bathroom and all with TV. A double without bathroom is 175 F to 190 F ($28 to $30.40), and a double with bathroom goes for 200 F to 300 F ($32 to $48). About half of the bedrooms are in a cozy and comfortable annex, built in 1981. Throughout the hotel, improvements are made to the bedrooms virtually every year, with care devoted to the quality of the mattresses.

La Marée. 5 quai Henri Chéron. ☎ **02-31-21-41-00.** Reservations required. Main courses 85–155 F ($13.60–$24.80); fixed-price menus 98–198 F ($15.70–$31.70). AE, DC, MC, V. Daily 12:30–2:30pm and 7–9:30pm. Closed Dec–Feb. NORMAN.

Set beside the port, this small, nautically decorated restaurant in a 1920s building is ideal for seafood devotees. Only fish that are caught within *La Manche* (the English Channel) or within a reasonable distance out in the Atlantic are served here, guaranteeing an authentically local culinary experience. First, try the fresh oysters, then perhaps the grilled turbot served with oysters from the nearby coast. Sea bass served with bacon and herbs is excellent, as is the sole à la Normande, in a herb-flavored cream sauce. During clement weather, the dining room expands onto an outdoor terrace dotted with potted shrubs and flowers.

8 Mont-St-Michel

201 miles W of Paris, 80 miles SW of Caen, 47 miles E of Dinan, 30 miles E of St-Malo

One of Europe's great attractions, the island of ✪ **Mont-St-Michel** is surrounded by massive walls measuring more than half a mile in circumference. Connected to the shore by a causeway, it crowns a rocky islet at the border between Normandy and Brittany. The rock is 260 feet high.

ESSENTIALS

GETTING THERE   The best way to reach the isolated Mont-St-Michel is to **drive.** The best route involves going from Caen along N175 southwest to Pontorson, then taking E3 north to Mont-St-Michel. Total driving time from Paris is about 4¹/₂ hours.

There are no direct trains between Paris and Mont-St-Michel. The best way to get there is to take the high-speed **TGV train** from Paris's Gare Montparnasse to Rennes,

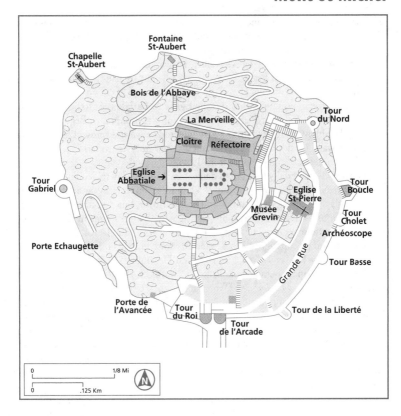

where you can transfer to the **bus** service provided by **Les Couriers Bretons** (☎ **02-99-19-70-70** for reservations and information) for the 75-minute transfer to Mont-St-Michel. Depending on the season, there are between two and five bus departures from Rennes a day, most of which are configured to correspond to the arrival times in Rennes of the TGV. The same company also operates buses, between two and five a day, a 75-minute ride, to Mont-St-Michel from Saint Malo.

VISITOR INFORMATION   The **Office de Tourisme** is in the Corps de Garde des Bourgeois (the Old Guard Room of the Bourgeois), at the left of the town gates (☎ **02-33-60-14-30**). The tourist office is closed two weekends (Saturday and Sunday) in January, and two weekends in February. Otherwise, it's open daily throughout the year.

EXPLORING MONT-ST-MICHEL

You'll have a steep climb up Grande Rue, lined with 15th- and 16th-century houses, to reach the **abbey** (☎ **02-33-89-80-00**). Those who make it to the top can begin their exploration of the Marvel of the West. In the 8th century an oratory was founded on the spot by St. Aubert, the bishop of Avranches. It was replaced by a Benedictine monastery, founded in 966 by Richard I. That met with destruction by fire in 1203. Large parts of the abbey were financed by Philip Augustus in the 13th century.

Ramparts encircle the church and a three-tiered ensemble of 13th-century buildings called **La Merveille** that rise dramatically to the pointed spire of the abbey church.

This terraced complex is one of Europe's most important Gothic monuments, a citadel from which the concept of an independent France was nurtured during the darkest years of the English occupation of Aquitaine.

On the second terrace of La Merveille, midway up the rock, is one of Mont-St-Michel's largest and most beautiful rooms, a 13th-century banquet hall known as the **Salle des Chevaliers.**

Crowning the mountain's summit is the **Église Abbatiale** (not to be confused with the less important Église St-Pierre lower down on the mountain). Begun in the 11th century, the abbey church consists of a Romanesque nave and transept, plus a choir in the Flamboyant Gothic style. The rectangular refectory is from 1212, the cloisters with their columns of pink granite from 1225.

The abbey is open daily (with mass daily at 12:15pm): May to September from 9am to 5:30pm and October to April from 9:30am to 4:30pm. Many visitors opt to wander through the multi-leveled compound on their own, but if you're interested, there are guided tours—most in French, but occasionally there are some in English—on an extremely erratic schedule. The cost of any tour is 40 F ($6.40) for adults, 25 F ($4) for students and persons ages 12 to 25, and free for children 11 and under. Everything is closed January 1, May 1, Nov 1 and 11, and December 25.

The **Archeoscope,** chemin de la Ronde (☎ **02-33-48-09-37**), is a small theater that presents *L'Eau et La Lumière* (Water and Light), celebrating the legend and lore associated with the construction of Mont-St-Michel and its role as a preserver of French medieval nationalism during an era when most of France was swallowed up by foreign invaders. Shows are presented at intervals that begin every 30 to 60 minutes between 9:30am and 5:30pm, based on the season and demand, and last for 30 minutes each. An unusual diversion is the adjacent **Musée Maritime et Archéologique,** Grande Rue (☎ **02-33-60-14-09**), showcasing the marine crafts of civilizations throughout history and the world, information on the ecology of the local tidal flats, and illustrations of the French government's plans, beginning on a grand scale sometime during the lifetime of this edition, to reactivate the tidal cleansing of the nearby marshes. Finally, the **Musée Grevin** (Musée Historique de Mont-St-Michel), chemin de la Ronde (☎ **02-33-60-14-09**), traces the history of the abbey. Admission to each

---

Sign of the Tides

Mont-St-Michel historically has been noted for its tides, the highest on the Continent, measuring at certain times of the year a 50-foot difference between high and low tide. Unsuspecting visitors wandering across the sands (notorious for quicksands) have been trapped as the sea rushes toward the mont at a speed comparable to that of a galloping horse. However, the bay around the abbey has silted, not only because of the causeway *(la digue)* but also because of various barriers and dikes erected. Today tides engulf the island less and less frequently. France will spend $110 million over the next few years replacing the mile-long causeway "La Digue" with a bridge so water can lap freely around the mont. Parking lots will be moved farther away from the abbey, and ecology experts will work to encourage bird and marine life in the air and water. Ecological and engineering studies for the construction of the bridge, and appropriate means of rendering the surrounding marshlands more hospitable to bird and wildlife, began in the mid-1990s. Actual construction of the new bridge, which will be followed by the demolition of the causeway, is tentatively scheduled to begin late in 2000.

of these attractions is 45 F ($7.20), and 20 F ($3.20) for persons under 16, but a combined ticket that's valid for all three attractions costs 75 F ($12) for adults, and 45 F ($7.20) for children under 16. Each is open daily from 9am to 5:30pm (last entrance). Note that locals regard these "attractions" as tourist traps, preferring to concentrate on the architectural and symbolic majesty of La Merveille instead.

ACCOMMODATIONS & DINING

Hôtel du Mouton-Blanc. Grande Rue, 50116 Mont-St-Michel. ☎ **02-33-60-14-08.** Fax 02-33-60-05-62. 15 units. TEL. 390 F ($62.40) double. AE, MC, V. Closed Jan.

In a pair of buildings, parts of which date from the 14th century, this inn stands halfway between the sea and the basilica and has been accepting guests since the 1700s. The lower floors contain the restaurant; the simple double rooms are upstairs. Bedrooms are relatively small but cozy, each a welcome haven against the Atlantic chill in winter and the hordes of visitors on the narrow alleyways nearby in summer. Tables are set in a Norman-style dining room accented with stone and roughly textured wood and on a terrace overlooking the sea. As in most restaurants here, popular dishes include omelets, along with fruits de mer, mussels in cream sauce, several preparations of lobster, and roast pork in cider sauce. Fixed-price menus, priced from 70 F to 255 F ($11.20 to $40.80), are served daily at lunch and dinner.

La Mère Poulard. Grande Rue, 50116 Mont-St-Michel. ☎ **02-33-60-14-01.** www.mere-poulard.fr. Reservations recommended. Main courses 98–190 F ($15.70–$30.40); fixed-price menus 250–350 F ($40–$56). AE, DC, MC, V. Daily noon–10pm. NORMAN.

This country inn is a shrine to those who revere the omelet that Annette Poulard created in 1888 when the hotel was founded. It's under the same ownership as Terrasses Poulard (see below). Her secret has been passed on to the inn's operators: The beaten eggs are cooked over an oak hearth fire in a long-handled copper skillet (you can buy one of these skillets, if you'd like to bring one home). The frothy mixture really creates more of an open-fire soufflé than an omelet. Other specialties are *agneau du pré salé* (lamb) raised on the saltwater marshes near the foundations of the abbey, and an array of fish, including lobster.

The guest house rents 27 rooms with TV, phone, minibar, and hair dryer; however, we recommend that you opt for one of the other hotels recommended here, and come here strictly for the omelet. A double ranges from 500 F to 950 F ($80 to $152); the hotel's suite costs 1,600 F ($256), double occupancy.

Les Terrasses Poulard. Grande Rue, 50116 Mont-St-Michel. ☎ **02-33-60-14-09.** Fax 02-33-60-37-31. www.mere-poulard.fr. E-mail: mere.poularde.mtstmichel@wanadoo. 29 units. MINIBAR TV TEL. 300–900 F ($48–$144) double. AE, DC, MC, V.

This inn was formed when two village houses—one medieval, the other built in the 1800s—were united. Today the hotel is one of the best in town, with an English-speaking staff and cozy bedrooms with comfortable beds. The rates depend on the view: pedestrian traffic on the main street, the village, or the medieval ramparts. The largest and most expensive rooms have fireplaces. The **restaurant,** which is open every day throughout the year for lunch and dinner, offers a sweeping view over the bay to accompany its seafood and regional Norman specialties.

8 Brittany

In this ancient northwestern province, many Bretons stubbornly cling to their traditions. Deep in l'Argoat (the interior), many older folks quietly live in stone farmhouses, just as their grandparents did, and on special occasions the women still wear the trademark starched-lace headdresses. The Breton language is still spoken, but it's better understood by the Welsh and Cornish than by the French. Sadly, it may die out altogether, despite attempts by folklore groups to keep it alive.

Nearly every village and hamlet has its own *pardon,* a religious festival that sometimes attracts thousands of pilgrims in traditional dress. The best-known ones are on May 19 at Treguier (honoring St. Yves), on the second Sunday in July at Locronan (honoring St. Ronan), on July 26 at St-Anne-d'Auray (honoring the "mothers of Bretons"), and on September 8 at Le Folgoet (honoring *ar foll coat*— "idiot of the forest").

Traditionally, the province is divided into Haute-Bretagne and Basse-Bretagne. The rocky coastline, some 750 miles long, is studded with promontories, coves, and beaches. Like the prow of a ship, Brittany projects into the sea. The interior, however, is a land of sleepy hamlets, stone farmhouses, and moors covered with yellow broom and purple heather. We suggest that first-time visitors to the craggy peninsula stick to the coast, where you can see salt-meadow sheep grazing on pastureland whipped by sea breezes. If you're coming from Mont-St-Michel in Normandy, you can easily use St-Malo, Dinan, or Dinard as a base. Visitors coming from the château country of the Loire can explore the south Brittany coastline.

Brittany is a beach resort region. Many French families come here simply to go to the beach. British tourists frequent the resort of Dinard, although the water here is often choppy and cold, albeit with high waves sometimes suitable for surfing. If you're coming to Brittany just to go to the beach, La Baule in the south is warmer, with a great beach, tranquil waters, gourmet restaurants, and the finest hotels in Brittany.

REGIONAL CUISINE   Breton cuisine derives its excellence from the flavors and freshness of its ingredients rather than from the skill of its preparation. Seafood is abundant: Oysters, shellfish, barnacles, and crabs from the Breton coastline are famous throughout France. Many

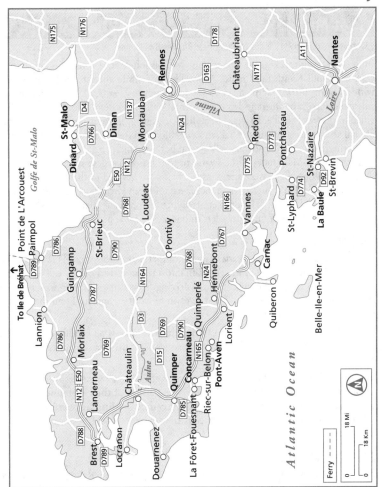

are served raw, especially Belon oysters, as appetizers (on a bed of seaweed with lemon/onion sauce and white wine).

Other regional specialties are *homard* (lobster) in cream sauce, grilled, or *à l'armoricaine;* salmon *en brochet;* trout and *l'alose,* excellent with one of the Loire's fruity whites; and lamb and mutton, raised on the salt marshes. *Gigot à la bretonne* (leg of lamb), traditionally served with white beans, is one of France's great dishes. The ducklings of Nantes and chickens of Rennes are succulent, as are the strawberries of Plougastel.

Brittany is closely associated with crêpes, those delectable thin pancakes served plain, sweet, or salted and often filled with jam, cheese, ham, salad, or eggs. Most villages have their own crêperie, some of which sell crêpes right on the street.

The only famous wine produced in Brittany is muscadet, cultivated near Nantes, an excellent complement to seafood.

1 St-Malo

257 miles W of Paris, 43 miles N of Rennes, 8 miles E of Dinard

Built on a granite rock in the Channel, St-Malo is joined to the mainland by a causeway. It's popular with the English, especially those from the Channel Islands, and, with its warm brown sands, makes a modest claim to be a beach resort. The peninsula curves like a boomerang around a natural harbor whose interior has been subdivided into several smaller basins. The walled city, one of the most impressive examples of civil architecture in Brittany, radiates outward from the town's château and its spiritual centerpiece, the Cathédrale St-Vincent, both of which lie near the peninsula's tip. The curse of St-Malo today is the swarm of tour buses that descend upon it, the passengers engulfing the narrow streets as souvenirs are hawked to them. There's charm here, even though it's "merely the mock," having been virtually rebuilt after damage caused by World War II. The problem is trying to appreciate that charm while being trampled by millions of other travelers intent on the same pursuit.

ESSENTIALS

GETTING THERE   From Paris's Gare Montparnasse, about nine TGV **trains** per day make the journey via Rennes. For train information and schedules, call ☎ **08-36-35-35-35.** Trip time is 3 hours. If you're **driving** from Paris, take A13 west to Caen, continuing southwest along N175 to the town of Miniac Morvan. From there, travel north on N137 directly to St. Malo.

VISITOR INFORMATION   The **Office de Tourisme** is on esplanade St-Vincent (☎ **02-99-56-64-48**). A valid passport is necessary for the hydrofoil or car-ferry trips and tours to the Channel Islands.

SPECIAL EVENTS   One of the most important Breton *pardons* (festivals) is held at St-Malo in late January and early February: the **Pardon of the Newfoundland Fishing Fleet** (*Pardon de St-Ouen*). The town's **Festival de la Musique Sacrée,** from mid-July to mid-August, offers evening concerts from time to time. Check with the Office de Tourisme for complete details.

EXPLORING THE CITY

For the best view of the bay and the islets at the mouth of the Rance, walk along the ramparts. These walls were built over a period of centuries, some parts of them from the 14th century. However, they were mainly reconstructed in the 17th century, then restored in the 19th. You can begin at the 15th-century **Porte St-Vincent.**

At the harbor, you can book tours of the **Channel Islands.** Hydrofoils leave for the English island of Jersey (a passport is necessary, of course).

At low tide, you can take a 25-minute stroll to the **Île du Grand-Bé,** the site of the tomb of Chateaubriand, "deserted by others and completely surrounded by storms." The tomb, marked by a cross, is simple, unlike the man it honors, but the view of the Emerald Coast from here makes up for it.

Called the Bastille of the West, the severe and forbidding-looking **Château de St-Malo,** Porte St-Vincent (☎ **02-99-40-71-57**), and its towers shelter the **Musée de l'Histoire de St-Malo,** which is filled with insights into the role of St-Malo within Brittany and the rest of France, as well as souvenirs of the once-notorious locally-based pirates Duguay-Trouin and Surcouf, the most famous of the St-Malo privateers. You can visit Tuesday through Sunday from 10am to noon and 2 to 6pm. Admission costs 27 F ($4.30) for adults and 13.50 F ($2.15) for students and children 18 and under.

It's open daily from 10am to noon and from 2 to 6pm (closed Mondays, October to March). Free guided tours, conducted in English, are available on an as-needed basis, in July and August only.

After your visit to the château, try to carve out some time for wandering aimlessly through the narrow streets and alleyways of St-Malo's historic core. Memories of the town's origins as a medieval fishing village confront you at nearly every turn.

St-Malo's **Cathédrale St-Vincent,** 12 rue St-Benoît (☎ **02-99-40-82-31**), is known for its 1160 nave vault. It's of the Angevin or Plantagenet style, elegantly marking the transition between Romanesque and Gothic. The cathedral also has a Renaissance west facade, with additions from the 18th century and a 15th-century tower. The 14th-century choir is surmounted by a triforium with trefoiled arches and flanked by chapels. It's open daily from 8am to 7pm.

BEACHES   As you drive along the coast, you'll find long stretches of sand interspersed with rocky outcroppings that suggest fortresses protecting the rest of Brittany from Atlantic storms. You can swim virtually wherever you like (beware of undertows in these storm-tossed waters!), but if you're staying in St-Malo, the two best beaches are **Plage du Bon Secours,** near the northern tip of the Vieille Ville, and **La Grande Plage du Sillon,** a longer stretch of tawny sand that begins at the eastern perimeter of the Vieille Ville.

SHOPPING   If you're in St-Malo on Tuesday or Friday between 8am and 12:30pm, and want to experience a great Breton **market,** head for the Place de la Poissonerie and the Halles au Blé, in the heart of the old city. You can't miss the activity, the bustle, and the hawking of country-fresh produce, cheeses, fish, and dozens of household items, including dishware, cooking utensils, and handcrafts.

For **boutique shopping,** head for rue St-Vincent, rue Porcon, rue Broussaus, and rue de Dinan. Here you'll find everything from the trendy to the trashy. In particular, check out **Vêtements Marin-Marine,** 5 Grand' Rue (☎ **02-99-40-90-32**), for quality men's and women's fashions that include, of course, those great Breton wool sweaters, one of the town's best buys. For last-minute souvenir shopping, stop by **Aux Délices Malouins,** 12 rue St-Vincent (☎ **02-99-40-55-22**).

For a rich selection of Breton handcrafts, head for **Le Comptoir de Bretagne,** 3 rue Broussais (☎ **02-99-40-89-69**). In addition to hand-painted stoneware, books, sheet music and Gaelic CDs, you'll also find handmade Breton lace, Celtic souvenirs, and traditional food items that include almond-flavored pastries and sugar-coated galettes.

ACCOMMODATIONS

Hôtel Central. 6 Grand' Rue, 35400 St-Malo. ☎ **02-99-40-87-70.** Fax 02-99-40-47-57. E-mail:centralvw@aol.com. 46 units. MINIBAR TV TEL. 600–800 F ($96–$128) double; 980 F ($156.80) suite. Half board 170 F ($27.20) per person extra. AE, DC, MC, V. Parking 60 F ($9.60).

On a street near the harbor, this hotel is the best of a fairly lackluster lot. It offers well-planned albeit standardized rooms, each renovated during the 1990s. The structure you see today was rebuilt of granite blocks after the bombings of World War II, like much of the neighborhood surrounding it. Don't expect old-time touches; the furnishings are all contemporary. One of the most compelling reasons to stay here is the food: **La Pêcharie restaurant** serves wonderful seafood as part of set menus priced at 115 F to 280 F ($18.40 to $44.80). Before dinner, enjoy a drink in the cozy bar.

Hôtel de France et de Chateaubriand. Place Chateaubriand, 35412 St-Malo. ☎ **02-99-56-66-52.** Fax 02-99-40-10-04. E-mail: hotel.france.chateaubriand@wanadoo.fr. 80 units. TV TEL. 434–496 F ($69.45–$79.35) double. AE, DC, MC, V. Parking 50 F ($8).

This hotel, within the walls of old St-Malo, is a masterpiece of Napoléon III architecture. Guest rooms run from comfortably cozy to spacious and feature such details as cove moldings, ornate plaster ceiling reliefs, and chandeliers. All contain period reproductions, and most have panoramic ocean views. Each was renovated sometime during the 1990s. In the chic bar, with gold-trimmed Corinthian columns, you can chat over drinks, play billiards, and listen to the baby grand. A restaurant with four sumptuous dining rooms serves breakfast, lunch, and dinner, but it's closed January and February. Two less formal dining alternatives are the sunny courtyard terrace and the sidewalk cafe tables in front of the hotel.

Hôtel de la Cité. Place Vauban, 35412 St-Malo. ☎ **02-99-40-55-40.** Fax 02-99-40-10-04. 41 units. TV TEL. 510–551 F ($81.60–$88.15) double; 854–1,162 F ($136.65–$185.90) suite. AE, DC, MC, V. Parking 50 F ($8).

You'd never guess that this inn is new. It was built in 18th-century style following the plan of the building that once stood here. The contemporary interior, however, is no match for the richly embellished facade. Like most modern chain hotels, it offers solid comforts but is short on style. The rooms are well laid out, however, ranging from rather cramped to most spacious. Those on the top floor do break away from the norm with their angled ceilings. As a saving grace, many rooms open onto views of the often turbulent ocean. The hotel also has an elegant breakfast room and a small bar.

DINING

✪ **À la Duchesse Anne.** 5 place Guy-La-Chambre. ☎ **02-99-40-85-33.** Reservations required. Main courses 100–140 F ($16–$22.40). V. May–Nov, Thurs–Tues 12:15–1:30pm and 7:15–9:15pm. Closed Dec–Jan. FRENCH.

This leading restaurant, built into the ramparts, offers summer dining under a large canopy amid hydrangeas. Try the fish specialties. The fish soup with chunks of fresh seafood, spiced and cooked in an iron pot, is excellent, as are the Cancale oysters. Main courses include grilled turbot with beurre blanc and pepper steak. The equally tempting desserts may include the *fantaisie du chocolat,* several chocolate-based desserts artfully arranged on a platter. Year after year, this choice delivers the finest food in town.

Le Chalut. 8 rue de la Corne-de-Cerf. ☎ **02-99-56-71-58.** Reservations required. Main courses 110–180 F ($17.60–$28.80); fixed-price menus 100–270 F ($16–$43.20). AE, V. Wed–Sun 12:15–1:30pm; Tues–Sat 7:15–9:30pm (also Sun night in summer). FRENCH.

The decor here is nautical, with green and blue throughout. Chef Jean-Philippe Foucat's flavorful cuisine, based on fresh ingredients, includes a tart containing layers of salmon and scallops, bound together with lime juice; John Dory with wild mushrooms, essence of lobster, and coriander; and a particularly succulent version of line-caught sea bass with sherry sauce and braised endive. For dessert, try the gâteau of bitter chocolate with almond paste or the feuillet of red seasonal berries. The only complaint we've heard is that the place is touristy, but that's the curse of St-Malo in general.

ST-MALO AFTER DARK

For a full evening of dinner, dancing, and gambling, experience the **Casino,** 2 chaussée du Sillon (☎ **02-99-40-64-09**). Here you can take in a show, enjoy a dinner concert, and even trip the light fantastic at the casino's disco, City's Club. The dress code is informally elegant. Admission is 60 F ($9.60) Monday to Friday and 70 F ($11.20) on weekends, including one drink.

Bar La Belle Epoque, 11 rue de Dinan (☎ **02-99-40-82-23**), attracts a 20-and-over crowd with its inviting setting, complete with a fireplace that heats things up on cooler nights. Play a game of darts, study the exhibits of local artists' work, or, during the weekend, enjoy live music while sipping a drink.

If you're out on a pub crawl, hunt for **Le O'Flaherty's,** 18 rue des Cordiers (☎ **02-99-56-87-54**), where you can experience a real Irish pub with a French twist. They serve at least six different draft beers and more than 40 brands of whiskey.

2 Dinard

259 miles W of Paris, 14 miles N of Dinan

Dinard (not to be confused with its inland neighbor Dinan) sits on a rocky promontory at the top of the Rance River, opposite St-Malo (see above). Ferries ply the waters between the two resorts. Turn-of-the-century Victorian-Gothic villas, many now hotels, overlook the sea, and gardens and parks abound. Dinard today seems to have passed its prime, though a number of modern buildings dot the landscape. The old is still best here; for a look at what the Edwardians admired, go down the pointe de la Vicomte at the resort's southern tip or stroll along the promenade. You'll expect to see Maurice Chevalier in top hat and cane appear at any moment.

One of France's best-known resorts, Dinard offers safe, well-sheltered bathing and bracingly healthful sea air in La Manche (The Sleeve, the term given centuries ago to a body of water claimed by the British as the English Channel). During Queen Victoria's time, this town became popular with the Channel-crossing English, who wanted a continental holiday that was "not too foreign."

ESSENTIALS
GETTING THERE   If you **drive,** simply take D186 west from St-Malo to Dinard. SNCF **trains** travel only as far as St-Malo; from there, you'll have to take one of the dozen buses that depart from the St-Malo rail station daily for the 20-minute ride to Dinard. For **bus information,** call Compagnie T.I.V. (☎ **02-99-40-83-33**). Buses arrive from many large cities in Brittany, including Rennes and St-Malo. Between May and September, a **ferry** maintained by the **Emeraud-Lines** (☎ **02-99-46-10-45**) makes one daily trip from Dinan to Dinard. A **taxi** ride to Dinard from St-Malo is a particularly useful option, costing 100 F ($16) during the day and around 150 F ($24) on national holidays or any evening after 7pm. For taxi information, call (☎ **02-99-46-75-75**).

VISITOR INFORMATION   The Office de Tourisme is at 2 bd. Féart (☎ **02-99-46-94-12**).

SPECIAL EVENTS   From mid-June to mid-September there's *musique-et-lumière* wherein floodlights and recorded jazz, pop, or classical music add drama to walks along the city's seafront Promenade du Clair-de-Lune.

ENJOYING THE RESORT
Dinard's main beach is **Plage de l'Écluse** or **La Grande Plage,** the strip of sand between the seaward-jutting peninsulas that define the edges of the old town. Favored by families and vacationers, it's crowded on hot days. Smaller and somewhat more isolated, and accessible after a 20-minute hike east from Dinard that'll take you through the village of St-Enogat, is **Plage de St-Enogat.** There's also **Plage du Prieuré,** a 10-minute walk from the center; you may or may not like the many trees that shade the

sand. Because there's such a difference in elevation between high and low tides here, the municipality has built swimming pool-style basins along the Plage de L'Écluse and the Plage de St-Enogat beaches as a means of catching seawater during high tides. Most people, however, trek along the salt flats during low tides to bathe in the sea.

Looking for a bona-fide pool that's covered, heated, filled with sea water, and open year-round? Head for the **Piscine Olympique,** boulevard du Président-Wilson (☎ **02-99-46-22-77**). Entrance is 25 F ($4) for adults, 16 F ($2.55) for children ages 5 to 16, free for ages 5 and under. From July to mid-September, it's open Monday through Saturday from 10am to 12:30pm and 3 to 7:30pm, and on Sunday to 6:30pm. The rest of the year, it runs on a schedule that varies according to the agendas of local school groups and swim teams.

GOLF   About 5 miles from Dinard is a par-68, 18-hole golf course, **Le Dinard Golf,** at St-Briac (☎ **02-99-88-32-07**), one of the finest in Brittany. It's set on sandy, windy terrain studded with tough grasses and durable trees and shrubs. You'll have to reserve your tee-off time in advance and present a membership card from a golf course in your hometown. Greens fees are 200 F to 320 F ($32 to $51.20) per person, depending on the season. A limited number of clubs can be rented, but it's wiser to bring your own.

SHOPPING   For the usual selection of shops and boutiques selling men's and women's clothes, antiques, shoes, and jewelry, concentrate on **rue du Maréchal-Leclerc, rue Levavasseur,** and **boulevard du Président-Wilson.** Your best bet is the **Galerie Line Boutique,** 13 bd. du Président-Wilson (☎ **02-99-46-11-21**). The art gallery scene offers you a chance to pick up some unique pieces at affordable prices. The owner of the **Atelier du Prince Noir,** 70 av. George-V (☎ **02-99-46-29-99**), travels the country seeking talented artists for exhibitions in her gallery. In this 15th-century medieval house you'll find a wide range of paintings and sculptures from some of the most talented artists in France. The gallery is closed from October to April. An equally worthwhile shopping destination is **Marinette,** 29 rue Jacques-Cartier (☎ **02-99-46-82-88**), whose premises originally functioned as a Protestant church. Within an artfully old-fashioned and high-ceilinged set of antique-looking showrooms, you'll find inventories of porcelain, stoneware, kitchen utensils, gift items, and fresh flowers.

ACCOMMODATIONS

Note that **Altaïr** and **Le Prieuré** (see "Dining," below) also rent rooms.

Grand Hôtel de Dinard. 46 av. George-V, 35801 Dinard. ☎ **02-99-88-26-26.** Fax 02-99-88-26-27. 66 units. MINIBAR TV TEL. 820–1,680 F ($131.20–$268.80) double; from 1,580 F ($252.80) suite. AE, DC, MC, V. Closed late Oct–late Mar.

Dinard's largest hotel, a member of the nationwide Lucien Barrière chain, was built in 1859. Its location, just a 2-minute walk from the town center, commands an excellent view of the harbor. It rises in two wings, separated from each other by a heated outdoor pool. Most rooms have balconies and are furnished with traditional pieces. The inviting bar is a popular spot before and after dinner. Fine meals, with generous portions, are offered in the dignified in-house **restaurant, the George V.**

✪ **Hôtel de la Reine-Hortense.** 19 rue de la Malouine, 35800 Dinard. ☎ **02-99-46-54-31.** Fax 02-99-88-15-88. E-mail: reine.hortense@wanadoo.fr. 10 units. TV TEL. 980–1,200 F ($156.80–$192) double; 1,800–2,200 F ($288–$352) suite. AE, DC, MC, V.

This hotel on the beach was built in 1860 as a retreat for one of the Russian-born courtiers of Holland-based Queen Hortense de Beauharnais, daughter of Joséphine de

Beauharnais (who went on to marry Napoléon) and mother of Napoléon III. It offers glamorously outfitted public salons and many guest rooms decorated in either Louis XV or Napoléon III style. Most have private balconies, all have comfortable beds and a deep-seated sense of nostalgia. One high-ceilinged room even has Hortense's silver-plated bathtub, dating from the early 19th century. Breakfast is the only meal served.

Under the same management as the Hortense, the 4-room **Castel Eugénie** next door charges the same rates. About a decade old, it's well appointed and comfortable.

Hôtel Printania. 5 av. George-V, 35800 Dinard. ☎ **02-99-46-13-07.** Fax 02-99-46-26-32. E-mail: Printania@wanadoo.fr. 59 units. TV TEL. 350–460 F ($56–$73.60) double. Half board 280–380 F ($44.80–$60.80) per person. AE, MC, V. Closed mid-Nov to mid-Mar.

On August 15, 1944, this Breton hotel was damaged in a bombing raid, but the debris was removed in time for the Allied victory. The Printania draws many repeat guests, among them writers and artists. The main villa boasts terraces and a glassed-in veranda with potted palms, while the sitting room has carved-oak furniture, old clocks, and provincial chairs. The old-fashioned guest rooms contain antiques and Breton decorations. Some, but not all, contain *des lits Bretons* (Brittany-style beds), wherein the occupant is surrounded either with curtains or paneled doors for additional coziness and protection from the howling winds outside. Dinner here combines superb cookery with a view of the coast; the restaurant specializes in seafood and various shellfish, and the waitresses wear traditional Breton costumes.

DINING

Another choice is the restaurant at **Hôtel de Dinard** (see "Accommodations," above).

Altaïr. 18 bd. Féart, 35800 Dinard. ☎ **02-99-46-13-58.** Fax 02-99-88-20-49. Reservations recommended. Main courses 90–175 F ($14.40–$28); fixed-price menus 95–200 F ($15.20–$32). AE, DC, MC, V. Sun noon–2pm, Mon–Sat noon–2pm and 7–9:30pm. Winter, closed Mon. FRENCH.

Patrick Leménager, who operates the intimate Altaïr, serves excellent cuisine that includes sea scallops in puff pastry with coriander sauce; fresh salmon with herbs; ravioli with oysters, pulverized crayfish, and herbs; and duck breast with apple-and-honey sauce, followed by gratin of red fruits. The portions are generous, and most prices are a good value for the area. In warm weather, you may dine alfresco on the terrace.

The Altaïr also rents 21 standard rooms with bathroom and TV. Each was renovated in the late 1990s. Mattresses are up-to-date and very comfortable. Bathrooms are up-to-date and well maintained. A double is 250 F to 490 F ($40 to $78.40) per person with half board.

Le Prieuré. 1 place du Général-de-Gaulle, 35800 Dinard. ☎ **02-99-46-13-74.** Fax 02-99-46-81-90. Reservations recommended. Main courses 75–130 F ($12–$20.80); fixed-price menus 98–200 F ($15.70–$32). MC, V. Tues–Sun 12:30–2pm; Tues–Sat 7:30–9pm. Closed Jan and 1 week in late Sept. SEAFOOD.

Diners at this family-style, turn-of-the-century seafood restaurant are greeted by a lively room full of seafaring bric-a-brac. Come here with a hearty appetite and you'll be rewarded with dishes like sautéed sole in beurre blanc with baby potatoes, grilled salmon with a stir-fry of seasonal vegetables, sauerkraut of fish and even a beef fillet topped with a rich black-pepper sauce. Desserts like the ever-popular crème caramel and the commendable wine list round out the menu.

The food here is straightforward, generously portioned, and richly traditional, with no newfangled ideas from faraway Paris. One of the most appealing parts involves the view that sweeps out from the hotel over the La Rance estuary. Le Prieuré also rents

An Idyll on an Île

Île de Bréhat is home to some 500 hearty people who live most of the year isolated from others—until the summer crowds arrive to see their lovely island. The tiny island (actually two islands, Île Nord and Île Sud, linked by a bridge) is in the Golfe de St-Malo, north of Paimpol. A visit to Bréhat is an offbeat adventure, even to the French.

Walking is the primary activity here, and it's possible to stroll the marked footpaths around the islands in a day. Cars aren't allowed, except those used by the police and fire departments. Some tractor-driven carts carry visitors on a 5-mile circuit of Bréhat, charging 38 F ($6.10) for the 45-minute jaunt. A number of places rent bikes, but one isn't necessary.

The rich flora here astonishes many visitors, who get off the ferry expecting a windswept Channel island—only to discover a more Mediterranean clime. Flower gardens are in full summer bloom, though both the gardens and houses appear tiny because of the scarcity of land. At the highest point, Chapelle St-Michel, you'll be rewarded with a panoramic view.

If you need information, there's a little summer tourist office at Le Bourg, place du Bourg (☎ **02-96-20-04-15**). It is open from mid-June to mid-September.

Paimpol can be reached by **driving** on D768 west from Dinard to Lamballe; then E50 west to Plérin; then D786 north to Paimpol. To reach the island, take D789 3 miles north of Paimpol, where the peninsula ends dramatically at the pink-granite Pointe de l'Arcouest. A **CAT bus** from Paimpol (about 5 to 10 per day) makes the 10-minute run to the point for a one-way fare of 14 F ($2.25). Once here, catch one of the **ferries** operated by **Les Vedettes de Bréhat** (☎ **02-96-55-73-47** for schedules), which will take you to the Île de Bréhat year round. Ferries depart about every 30 minutes in summer, two or three per day in off-season, costing 40 F ($6.40) round-trip. Visitors in April, May, June, and September will find the island pleasantly less crowded.

8 small guest rooms, each priced at 290 F ($46.40) for a double. Each is simply outfitted with the bare essentials of a bed, an armoire, a chair or two, a phone, a TV, and a cramped private bathroom.

DINARD AFTER DARK

Like many of Brittany's seaside towns, Dinard has a **Municipal Casino,** boulevard du Président-Wilson (☎ **02-99-16-30-30**). It's liveliest from Easter to late October, when all its facilities, including a room for roulette and blackjack, are open. The rest of the year, only the slot machines are in operation. Regardless of season, the hours are Sunday through Thursday from 10am to 3am and Friday and Saturday from 10am to 4am. Admission is free, and the management encourages men to wear ties, especially in the roulette and blackjack areas. Also on the premises is **La Brasserie de la Mer,** open year-round, daily from noon to 2:30pm and 7pm to midnight. An alternative choice is Dinard's newest contender, **Le Metro-Dôme,** Le Haut-Chemin (no phone), which has earned the loyalty of many local residents thanks to a good selection of wine and an amiable ambience that encourages conviviality.

In the evenings from June to September, the **promenade du Clair-de-Lune** attracts a huge crowd of strollers for the *musique-et-lumière,* when the buildings and flowers along the promenade are illuminated and musical groups of just about every ilk—from rock to blues to jazz—perform.

3 Dinan

246 miles W of Paris, 32 miles NW of Rennes

Once a stronghold of the ducs de Bretagne, Dinan is one of the best-preserved towns of Brittany, characterized by houses built on stilts over the sidewalks. The 18th-century granite dwellings provide sharp contrast to the medieval timbered houses in this walled town with a once-fortified château. Dinan today remains one of Brittany's prettiest towns, with a tranquil population of 14,000—it's not overrun like St-Malo.

ESSENTIALS

GETTING THERE   Although Dinan has a railway station, at this writing, the SNCF, because of budgetary constraints, had opted to avoid sending **trains** here. Consequently, railway passengers usually opt to travel to either Rennes, Dinard, or St-Malo, and from there, transfer to any of the SNCF **buses** (about five a day from each) that line up in front of the railway stations in those towns for ongoing transit to Dinan. For information about bus service into Dinan, call the town's Gare Routière (☎ **02-96-39-21-05**). If you're **driving** from Dinard, take highway D166 south to Dinan.

VISITOR INFORMATION   The Office de Tourisme is at 6 rue de l'Horloge (☎ **02-96-39-75-40**).

SPECIAL EVENTS   The most activity you'll ever see here occurs during the last weekend in July, during the 3-day **Fêtes des Remparts,** a celebration held in Dinan in even-numbered years. Duels from the Age of Chivalry are staged, and locals don medieval apparel for raucous carousing in the streets of the city's historic core. During odd-numbered years, the venue is transferred to Dinan's sibling city, Québec, Canada.

EXPLORING THE TOWN

For a panoramic view of the valley, head for the **Jardin Anglais** (English Garden), a terraced garden that huddles up to the ramparts. A Gothic-style bridge spans the Rance River; it was damaged in World War II but has since been restored. Dinan's most typical and one of its most appealing streets is the sloping **rue du Jerzual,** flanked with some buildings dating from the 15th century. The street ends at the **Porte du Jerzual,** a 13th- and 14th-century gate. **Rue du Petit-Fort** contains a number of 15th-century *maisons.*

Dominating the old city's medieval ramparts, **Château de Dinan Musée Du Château,** rue du Château (☎ **02-96-39-45-20**), contains a 14th-century keep and a 15th-century tower, built to withstand lengthy sieges. Within the stones you'll see the space for the portcullis and the drawbridge. Inside you can view an exhibition of the architecture and art of the city, including locally carved sculpture from the 12th to the 15th centuries. Admission costs 25 F ($4) for adults, and 10 F ($1.60) for children between 12 and 18. Entrance is free for children under 12. Between June and mid-October, the castle and its museum are open daily from 10am to 6:30pm. From mid-October to mid-November it's open Wednesday to Monday from 10am to noon. During December, February, and March, it's open Wednesday to Monday from 1:30 to 5:30pm. During April and May, it's open Wednesday to Monday from 10am to noon and from 2 to 6pm. It's completely closed during January.

The old city's **Tour de l'Horloge** (clock tower), on rue de l'Horloge, (☎ **02-96-39-22-43**) now classified a historic monument, boasts a clock made in 1498 and a great bell donated by Anne de Bretagne in 1507. You'll have a panoramic view of medieval Dinan from the 75-foot belfry. Admission is 18 F ($2.90) for adults and 12 F ($1.90) for children. The belfry is open daily from 10am to 5:30pm, June 15 to September 15.

The heart of Bertrand du Guesclin, who defended the town when the duke of Lancaster threatened it in 1359, was entombed in a place of honor in the **Basilique St-Sauveur,** place St-Sauveur (no phone); note the basilica's Romanesque portals and ornamented chapels. It's open daily from 9am to 7pm.

REGIONAL CRAFTS   Dinan has attracted groups of craftspeople and artists for at least 20 years. The densest concentration of artists' studios lie along either side of the **rue du Jerzual** and the **rue de la Port,** where art objects are laboriously crafted from glass, wood, silk, leather, clay. You might be able to buy a crafts item directly from the artisan who produced it, although that tends to be time-consuming, and you won't be able to compare objects or prices from other artisans. And frankly, very few artisans are willing to confront an uncertain buyer of their wares. A wiser, more efficient idea is to visit galleries that stock and sell art objects from a wide assortment of the town's artisans. Two of the best of them include **Galerie St-Sauveur,** 12 rue de la Port (☎ **02-96-85-26-62**); and **Galerie La Phonographe,** 2 rue de la Port (☎ **02-96-39-38-38**), where wide cross-sections of paintings and crafts help provide a perspective on the state of crafts and the visual arts in Dinan.

ACCOMMODATIONS

Hôtel Arvor. 5 rue Pavie, 22100 Dinan. ☎ **02-96-39-21-22.** Fax 02-96-39-83-09. 23 units. TV TEL. 280–380 F ($44.80–$60.80) double. AE, MC, V.

This is an unpretentious, comfortable, and relatively inexpensive hotel set within a former 14th-century Jacobin convent. The entrepreneur who conducted its restoration in the early 1990s is Stephane Pierre, who manages the place today. During the renovation process, most of the building's interior was demolished and rebuilt. The result is a series of clean and comfortable, contemporary-looking bedrooms, painted anew in pastel colors in the late 1990s, that retain none of their original medieval characteristics, but provide a safe and cozy haven within one of Dinan's oldest neighborhoods. Breakfast is the only meal served, but many inviting restaurants lie within a short walk.

✪ **Hôtel d'Avaugour.** 1 place du Champs-Clos, 22100 Dinan. ☎ **02-96-39-07-49.** Fax 02-96-85-43-04. E-mail: avavgour.hotel@wanadoo.fr. 24 units. TV TEL. 420–850 F ($67.20–$136) double; 900–1,600 F ($144–$256) suite. AE, DC, MC, V.

It's hard to believe that what was once a gutted pair of stone-fronted buildings has been transformed into Dinan's best, most up-to-date hotel. The rooms boast new fabrics inspired by traditional French 18th-century design and furniture reflecting the heritage of Dinan. Half of the units overlook the square; the others face the rear garden and were renovated in 1998. Bedrooms are attractively decorated with a great attention paid to detail, reflecting the historic charm of the area. Many are canopied, and each comes with thick soft mattresses.

DINING

✪ **Chez La Mère Pourcel.** 3 place des Merciers. ☎ **02-96-39-03-80.** Reservations recommended. Main courses 100–155 F ($16–$24.80); fixed-price menus 97 F ($15.50) (lunch only Mon–Fri), otherwise 168–395 F ($26.90–$63.20). AE, DC, MC, V. Daily noon–2pm and 7:15–10pm. Closed Feb; Mar–June and Sept–Jan, closed for dinner Sun and all day Mon. FRENCH.

This restaurant enjoys an outstanding reputation for regional food and an ambience that's artfully old-fashioned and cozy. The menu, as in olden days, is defined by the season, with many concessions made to the chef's inspiration of the moment. Examples include slightly smoked foie gras of duckling served with rhubarb; grilled codfish with a garlic-flavored mayonnaise; grilled and oven-baked wild turbot, served with coconut and essence of shellfish; and a traditional version of whole roasted and de-boned pigeon with apples, prunes, foie gras, and chopped cabbage. Many clients opt to skip the desserts in favor of the well-chosen cheeses, many of which come from small local producers, and many of which are almost sinfully creamy.

A particularly unctuous experience involves ordering the "Discovery Menu" (*Menu Découverte*), priced at 395 F ($63.20), wherein five courses will "surprise you" with whatever seasonal ingredients the chefs and buyers were able to procure in local markets. This is prepared for a minimum of two diners at a time.

La Caravelle. 14 place Duclos. ☎ **02-96-39-00-11.** Reservations required. Main courses 150–350 F ($24–$56); fixed-price menus 140–260 F ($22.40–$41.60). AE, MC, V. Daily noon–2pm and 7–9:30pm. Closed Nov 12–Dec 3; Dec–July, closed Wed. FRENCH.

We used to hail Jean-Claude Marmion as the most inventive chef in Dinan. He still serves wonderful food, and his 140 F ($22.40) menu is the town's best value, but some of the magic has gone now that he prepares only time-tested dishes. Specialties are scallops with flap mushrooms; John Dory with caramelized onions and a brochette of barnacles; and sweetbreads with flap mushrooms and bacon. In season, Marmion prepares fine game dishes like jugged hare and rabbit. When the first of the spring turnips come in, he uses them with a veal fillet often served with onion compote.

DINAN AFTER DARK

The densest concentration of cafes and bars in Dinan line either side of the **rue de la Cordonnerie,** which was informally nicknamed by long-ago sailors as **La rue de la Soif** ("the street where you go when you're thirsty"). Two of the most folklorically appealing include **Le Bistrot d'en Bas,** 20 rue Haute-Voie (☎ **02-96-85-44-00**), where many vintages of wine are sold by the glass along with an appealing assortment of *tartines* (open-faced sandwiches) made with cheeses, meats, and pâtés. For a site where there's likely to be guitar music, and sometimes singing, provided by the owners and staff, head for **La Truie Qui File** ("The Sow That's Trying to Escape"), 14 rue de la Cordonnerie (☎ **02-36-39-72-29**). Here, stiff drinks and a sense of bemused camaraderie will help warm even the stormiest of Breton nights.

4 Quimper

342 miles W of Paris, 127 miles NW of Rennes

The town that pottery built, Quimper, at the meeting of the Odet and Steir rivers, is the historic capital of Brittany's most traditional region, La Cornouaille. Today its faïence decorates tables from Europe to America. Skilled artisans have been turning out Quimper ware since the 17th century, using bold provincial designs. You can tour one of the ateliers during your stay; inquire at the tourist office (see below). Today's Quimper is rather smug and bourgeois, home to some 65,000 Quimperois, who walk narrow streets miraculously spared from World War II damage.

ESSENTIALS

GETTING THERE   Two or three regular **trains** from Paris arrive daily (trip time: 7¹/₂ hours). The speedier TGV has 12 trains per day from Paris (trip time: 4 to 5 hours). Fifteen trains also arrive from Rennes (trip time: 3 hours). For train information and schedules, call ☎ 08-36-35-35-35. If you **drive** to Quimper, the best route is from Rennes, taking E50/N12 west to just outside the town of Montauban and continuing west along N164 to the town of Châteaulin in western France. From Châteaulin, head south along N165 to Quimper.

VISITOR INFORMATION   The Office de Tourisme is on place de la Résistance (☎ 02-98-53-04-05).

SPECIAL EVENTS   During 6 days in late July, the **Festival de Cornouaille** adds a traditional flavor to the nightlife scene with Celtic and Breton concerts held throughout the city. For detailed information, contact the Office de Tourisme.

EXPLORING THE TOWN

In some quarters, Quimper still maintains its old-world atmosphere, with charming footbridges spanning the rivers. At place St-Corentin is the landmark **Cathédrale St-Corentin** (☎ 02-98-95-06-19), characterized by two towers that climb 250 feet. The cathedral was built between the 13th and the 15th centuries; the spires weren't added until the 19th. Inside, note the exceptional 15th-century stained glass. It's open daily from 9am to 6:30pm.

Also on the square is the **Musée des Beaux-Arts,** 40 place St-Corentin (☎ 02-98-95-45-20), with a collection that includes Rubens, Boucher, Fragonard, and Corot, plus an exceptional exhibit from the Pont-Aven school (Bernard, Sérusier, Lacombe, Maufra, Denis). Admission is 25 F ($4) for adults and 15 F ($2.40) for those under 26, free for children under 12. The gallery is open in July and August, daily from 10am to 7pm; September to June, Wednesday through Monday from 10am to noon and 2 to 6pm.

When artisans from Rouen and other parts of France settled in Quimper, the city became forever associated with ceramics. The most typical are white ceramics painted in blue and yellow with Breton figures, fruits, and flowers.

SHOPPING

The chunky blue and yellow porcelain produced in Quimper is arguably the most frequently recognized and the most popular French porcelain sold outside of France. Although newer designs are sometimes proposed, and merchandized, the most consistently popular patterns feature either a male *Breton* or a female *Bretonne,* both in profile and both in traditional Breton costume, each reeking of bucolic charm and simplicity. Today, that folkloric 19th-century design is rigidly copyrighted and fiercely protected. In 1984, after the near-bankruptcy of one of Quimper's largest stoneware factories, it was consolidated with three competitors under the same Dutch-American ownership. Thanks to his intervention in the preservation of a Breton folk tradition, the new, Connecticut-based owner, Paul Janssens, is viewed as something of a local hero.

The best shopping streets are **rue Kereron** and **rue du Parc,** where you'll find all kinds of quintessentially Breton products, including pottery, dolls and puppets, clothing made from regional cloth and wool, jewelry, metal and wooden crafts, lace, and even those beautiful Breton costumes.

One of the three sites where the stoneware is produced is open for tours. Between 9am and 4:30pm every Monday to Friday, between five and seven tours a day depart from the visitors' information center of **H.B.-Henriot Faïenceries de Quimper,** rue Haute, Quartier Locmaria (☎ 02-98-90-09-36). Tours each last between 40 and 45 minutes, are conducted in either English or French (or both), and cost 20 F ($3.20) for adults and 10 F ($1.60) for persons ages 8 to 14. It's free for children ages 7 and under. On the premises is a factory store selling the most complete inventories of Quimper porcelain in the world. You can invest in either first-run (nearly perfect) pieces, or slightly discounted "seconds," wherein the flaws are so small as to be nearly imperceptible. Anything you buy can be shipped.

For other Breton pottery and fine pieces of the faïence once heavily produced in this area, visit **François le Villec**, 4 rue du Roi-Gradlon (☎ **02-98-95-31-54**). Here you'll find quality tablecloths as well as other household linens. With some 2 decades of experience and more than 1,200 square feet of showroom, **Le Grenier**, 60 rue du Pres-ident Sadate (☎ **02-98-52-04-60**), is a treasure trove of antique furniture, bibelots, and paintings.

Another worthwhile choice for the acquisition of Breton art objects and artwork is **La Galerie le Cornet â Dés**, 1 rue Ste-Thérèse (☎ **02-98-53-37-51**), where inven-tories of hand-painted porcelain and both antique and contemporary paintings will try to seduce you with their taste and appeal.

ACCOMMODATIONS

La Tour d'Auvergne. 13 rue des Réguaires, 29000 Quimper. ☎ **02-98-95-08-70.** Fax 02-98-95-17-31. www.la-tour-dauvergne.fr. E-mail: latourdauvergne@wanadoo.fr. 38 units. TV TEL. 510–610 F ($81.60–$97.60) double. AE, DC, MC, V. Free parking.

Although they're small and overlook a not particularly picturesque area in the town center, about 200 yards from the cathedral, the rooms at this 19th-century coaching inn represent good value for Quimper. Each double has a private bathroom and rela-tively new mattresses. Bathrooms are small but efficiently organized. The present owner's grandparents bought the hotel in 1927, and one part or another has been ren-ovated every year since.

One of the main attractions here is the kitchen's Breton cuisine. Fixed-price menus are 148 F to 300 F ($23.70 to $48). Menu items may include tian of monkfish with Basmati rice and vegetable "caviar," saddle of rabbit with mustard sauce, and croustil-lant of crayfish and scallops with tarragon sauce.

Novotel. 17 rue Dupoher, pont de Poulguinan, 29000 Quimper. ☎ **02-98-90-46-26.** Fax 02-98-53-01-96. www.novotel.com. 92 units. A/C MINIBAR TV TEL. 530–600 F ($84.80–$96) double. 2 children ages 16 and under can stay free in parents' room and get a free breakfast. AE, DC, MC, V. From the town center, follow the signs to route Pont-l'Abbé.

In a garden about a mile southwest of the town center, the Novotel, despite its bland-ness, is your best choice here. Built in the early 1980s with comfortable, carefully stan-dardized rooms, it boasts a Breton-style slate roof that would be the envy of any homeowner. It's ideal for motoring families (the pool is a magnet in summer) and is the best business-oriented hotel in the region. Each of its chain hotel–style rooms has lots of space, plus a writing desk and comfortable and up-to-date mattresses.

DINING

Another good dining choice is the restaurant at **La Tour d'Auvergne** (see above).

✪ **Le Capucin Gourmand.** 29 rue des Réguaires. ☎ **02-98-95-43-12.** Reservations required in summer. Main courses 87–155 F ($13.90–$24.80); fixed-price menus 100–360 F ($16–$57.60). AE, DC, V. Tues–Sun noon–2pm; Tues–Sat 7–10pm. FRENCH.

This popular restaurant offers the area's finest dining. Delightful appetizers may include foie gras in a terrine, a dozen Breton oysters, or a succulent plate of ravioli filled with basil-flavored lobster. For your main course, opt for a *blanquette* of turbot with langoustines and artichokes or fillet of sole with fresh basil. Breton lamb appears frequently, usually roasted and served in a made-from-scratch sauce, perhaps flavored with leeks. The chef's secret involves giving familiar dishes a new twist by adding an unexpected ingredient or two.

NEARBY ACCOMMODATIONS & DINING

In an orchard district 8 miles from Quimper, the sleepy village of **La Forêt-Fouesnant** produces the best cider in the province and is home to one of Brittany's finest manor houses. Take N783 and turn off at the clearly marked sign. Free parking.

✪ **Manoir du Stang.** 29940 La Forêt-Fouesnant. ☎ and fax **02-98-56-97-37.** 24 units. TEL. 600–1,000 F ($96–$160) double. No credit cards. Closed Oct–Apr. Drive a mile north of the village center and follow the signs from N783; access is by private road.

To get to this 16th-century ivy-covered manor, you travel down a tree-lined avenue and under a stone tower gate into a courtyard. On your right is a formal garden; raised stone terraces lead to 25 acres of rolling woodland. This is the domain of M. and Mme Guy Hubert, who provide gracious living in period rooms. Guests stay either in the main building or in the even older but less desirable annex with a circular stone staircase. Your room is likely to be furnished with silk and fine antiques. One luxury here is the maid who brings your breakfast on a tray each morning. The restaurant's specialties are grilled lobster with tarragon, côte of beef with green peppercorns, *fruits de mer* (seafood), and oysters house style. Fixed-price menus cost 180 F ($28.80) each, and are served only to residents and their guests.

QUIMPER AFTER DARK

A trip down **rue Ste-Catherine** will lead to some of the best nightspots. The steadfastly Celtic bar, the **Céili Pub,** 4 rue Aristide-Briand (☎ **02-98-95-17-61**), was recently renovated and has lots of polished wood, regional music, and happy people—join in a game of darts with any of the regulars. **St. Andrew's Pub,** 11 place Styvel (☎ **02-98-53-34-49**), with its wood-and-leather interior and 44 varieties of beer and 37 varieties of whiskey, attracts a large number of Brits and Americans.

The young and stylish flock to **Les Naïades Discothèque,** boulevard Créac'h Gwen (☎ **02-98-53-32-30**), where you can dance to the latest tunes (there's sometimes a 50 F ($8) cover). **Le Coffee Shop,** 26 rue du Frout (☎ **02-98-95-43-30**), has a cool gay and lesbian crowd that unwinds to disco and techno.

5 Concarneau

335 miles W of Paris, 58 miles SE of Brest

This port is a favorite of painters, who never tire of capturing on canvas the subtleties of the fishing fleet in the harbor. It's also our favorite of the coast communities—primarily because it doesn't depend on tourists for its livelihood. In fact, its canneries today produce nearly three-quarters of all the tuna consumed in France. Walk along the quays here, especially in the late evening, and watch the rustic Breton fishers unload their catch; later, join them for a pint of potent cider in the taverns.

ESSENTIALS

GETTING THERE   There's no passenger rail service to Concarneau. If you're **driving,** the town is 13 miles southeast of Quimper along D783. A Caoudal **bus** (☎ **02-98-56-96-72**) runs from Quimper to Concarneau (trip time: 40 minutes). A different bus runs 8 to 10 times per day from Resporden to Concarneau (trip time: 20 minutes).

VISITOR INFORMATION   The **Office de Tourisme** is on quai d'Aiguillon (☎ **02-98-97-01-44**).

EXPLORING THE AREA

The town is built on three sides of a natural harbor whose innermost sheltered section is the Nouveau Port. In the center of the harbor, connected to its westernmost edge by a bridge, is the heavily fortified Ville-Close, an ancient hamlet surrounded by ramparts, some from the 14th century. From the quay, cross the bridge and descend into the town. Admittedly, souvenir shops have taken over, but don't let that spoil it for you. You can easily spend an hour wandering the winding alleys, gazing up at the towers, peering at the stone houses, and pausing in the secluded squares. For a splendid view of the port, walk the ramparts—it's free. Walks are possible mid-April to mid-June, daily from 10am to 6pm; and mid-June to mid-September, daily from 10am to 9:30pm. Access to the ramparts is closed between December and February, or whenever freezing rain causes them to be slippery, and costs 5 F (80¢) per person.

Also in the old town is a fishing museum, **Musée de la Pêche**, rue Vauban (☎ **02-98-97-10-20**). Its 17th-century building contains ship models and exhibits tracing the development of the fishing industry throughout the world; you can also view the preserved ship *Hemerica*. Admission costs 36 F ($5.75) for adults, and 24 F ($3.85) for children under 15. Year-round hours are daily from 10am to noon and 2 to 6pm. It's closed during 3 weeks in January.

BEACHES   Concarneau's largest and most beautiful beach, popular with families, is **Plage des Sables Blancs,** near the historic core. Within a 10-minute walk is **Plage de Cornouaille** and two small beaches, **Plage des Dames** and **Plage de Rodel,** where you'll find fewer families with children. The wide-open **Plage du Cabellou,** 3 miles west of town, is less congested than the others.

SEA EXCURSIONS   Boat rides are usually fine between June and September, but they're downright treacherous the rest of the year, when storms that have been brewing in the central Atlantic unleash their forces onto the battered coastline. During clement midsummer periods, you can arrange deep-sea fishing with the captain of the *Santa Maria* (☎ **02-98-50-69-01**). For **boat excursions** to anywhere along the coastline of southern Brittany, contact **Vedettes Glenn** (☎ **02-98-97-10-31**), Vedettes de l'Odet (☎ **02-99-57-00-58**), or **Vedettes Taxis** (☎ **02-99-50-72-12**).

ACCOMMODATIONS

Hotel Les Halles. Place de l'Hotel de Ville, 29900 Concarneau. ☎ **02-98-97-11-41.** Fax 02-98-50-58-54. 23 units. TV TEL. 260–350 F ($41.60–$56) double. AE, DC, MC, V.

It's rated only two stars by the local tourist board, and there isn't a lot of historic charm associated with this three-story, cement-sided 1960s-era hotel. Yet it's affordable and warm, with bedrooms that are cozier than you might have thought, and a location less than 150 yards west of the Vauban-designed fortifications encircling Concarneau's historic core. Rooms are upgraded frequently, each with a different, discreetly contemporary decor, and an eye for practicality. The city's covered food market (Les Halles, open daily from around 8am to around 1pm) lies within a short walk. Breakfast is the only meal served.

DINING

La Coquille. 1 rue du Moros, at Nouveau Port. ☎ **02-98-97-08-52.** Reservations required Sat–Sun and in summer. Main courses 100–150 F ($16–$24); fixed-price menus 150–420 F ($24–$67.20). AE, DC, MC, V. Tues–Sun 12:30–1:30pm; Tues–Sat 7:30–9:30pm. Closed Jan. FRENCH.

This 30-year-old restaurant occupies one end of a stone-sided harborfront building; guests dine in a trio of rooms with exposed stone walls and ceiling beams. La Coquille serves primarily seafood, particularly lobster. Much of the food is prepared simply because the fish is always so fresh and succulent, although a particularly excellent dish is scallop tart with shellfish and cream sauce. The service is bistro style (no great compliment), with a cheerful, somewhat old-fashioned kind of panache that's enhanced by the harbor view.

NEARBY ACCOMMODATIONS & DINING

On the outskirts of the once-fortified town of **Hennebont,** 35 miles west of Concarneau, is the most delightful hotel in all of southern Brittany.

✪ **Château de Locguénolé.** Route de Port-Louis, 56700 Hennebont. ☎ **02-97-76-76-76.** Fax 02-97-76-82-35. E-mail: locguenole@relaischateaux.fr. 22 units. MINIBAR TV TEL. 680–1,650 F ($108.80–$264) double; 1,950–2,400 F ($312–$384) suite. AE, DC, MC, V. Closed Jan 2–Feb 11. From Hennebont, follow the prominent signs to the château, 3 miles south.

This country estate in a 250-acre private park has been owned by the same family for more than 500 years. Now a Relais & Châteaux, with views over rugged coastline and an inlet, it's filled with antiques, tapestries, and paintings. The rooms vary widely in size and furnishings, but each has harmonious colors and, season permitting, sprays of flowers. The converted maids' rooms are smaller than the others yet still charming; some units are in a converted Breton cottage.

Dining: Even if you can't stay here, consider taking a meal in the dining hall. Specialties are fillet of beef with foie gras, *suprême de barbue* (brill) with cider and leeks, and grilled salmon. Another specialty is a thick slice of sole served with a bouillon of artichokes and oysters. There's also a creamy, fig-flavored custard with black raisins and vanilla ice cream. Fixed-price menus range from 190 F to 520 F ($30.40 to $83.20).

Amenities: Outdoor pool heated from May to October, sauna and steam bath, free use of mountain bikes.

6 Pont-Aven

324 miles W of Paris, 20 miles SE of Quimper, 10 miles S of Concarneau

Paul Gauguin loved this peaceful village with its little white houses along the gently flowing Aven River. In the late 19th century, many painters followed him here, including Maurice Denis, Paul Sérusier, and Emile Bernard. The artistic theories and techniques developed here at the time have been known ever since as the School of Pont-Aven.

Before leaving for Tahiti, Gauguin painted *The Yellow Christ* and *La Belle Angèle* here. Within the 16th-century **Chapelle de Trémalo,** less than a mile north from the town center, you can admire the crucifix that inspired two of Gauguin's paintings, *The Yellow Christ* (hanging today in the Albright-Knox Art Gallery in Buffalo, New York), and *Self-Portrait with the Yellow Christ,* which hangs today in the Musée d'Orsay. Every year, the local branch of the Société de Peinture organizes an exhibition of paintings, usually in the chapel, by other members of the School of Pont-Aven. The Chapel of Trémalo is on private land, and is privately owned; the only phone contact any casual visitor can have with it is through the Pont-Aven tourist office. The owners unlock the chapel (its location is clearly signposted) every morning at 9am, and close it between 7 and 8:30pm, depending on their whim and the season. In addition, there's a neighbor, semi-guardian, who appears magically to survey any possible danger.

Entrance is free. The only address for the place is Chapelle de Trémalo, lieu-dit Trémalo. (no phone).

ESSENTIALS

GETTING THERE   From Quimperlé, **drive** west along D783 toward Concarneau. SNCF **rail lines** stop at Quimperlé, where you can transfer to one of six daily **buses** for the 30-minute ride to Pont-Aven. Cost is 20 F ($3.20) each way. For train information, call either the Pont-Aven tourist office (see below) or ☎ **08-36-35-35-35.**

VISITOR INFORMATION   The **Office de Tourisme** is on place de l'Hôtel-de-Ville (☎ **02-98-06-04-70**).

ACCOMMODATIONS & DINING

✪ **Le Moulin de Rosmadec.** 29123 Pont-Aven. ☎ **02-98-06-00-22.** Reservations recommended. Main courses 120–250 F ($19.20–$40); fixed-price menus 165–298 F ($26.40–$47.70); menu tradition (with oysters and lobster) 398 F ($63.70). MC, V. Thurs–Tues 12:30–2pm and 7:30–9pm. Closed Feb, Nov 15–Dec 1; Sept–June closed Sun night. Free parking. FRENCH.

For a charming setting, nothing in Brittany compares to this 15th-century reconstructed stone mill. Meals are served in a bilevel dining room with antique furniture or, in good weather, on a flower-filled "island" terrace. The owners, M. and Mme Sebilleau, serve carefully prepared food, with specialties like trout with almonds, sole suprême with champagne, grilled lobster with tarragon, and duck breast with cassis. The fish dishes are especially sublime.

The Moulin also rents four comfortable rooms, at 480 F ($76.80) for a double. Because of the hotel's location at the end of a quiet cul-de-sac in the heart of the village, rooms are quiet and calm. Each is impeccably clean, with comfortable mattresses and well-organized bathrooms.

7 Carnac

302 miles W of Paris, 23 miles SE of Lorient, 62 miles SE of Quimper

In May and June, the fields here are resplendent with golden broom. Aside from being a seaside resort, Carnac is home to the most important prehistoric sites in northern France: the hundreds of huge stones in the ✪ **Field of Megaliths** (six alignments), whose arrangement and placement remain a mystery. These enigmatic stones date from Neolithic times. Many of them are set up in parallel rows. The exact purpose of these stones has been debated by scholars for centuries, although most theories suggest they had astronomical or religious significance to the ancient people of the area. One common belief is that some of the stones marked burial sites lost to antiquity. Some of these menhirs, or standing stones, rise to a height of 60 feet.

The park is open to unguided, individual visits daily from October 1 to April 1; admission is free. When the busy summer months come, the park is open only for guided tours, restricted to groups of 25 at a time, with a limit of 180 for the entire day. Tours are offered by the visitors' center on-site, costing 32.50 F ($5.55). Tours last 90 minutes. Before heading here, call ☎ **02-97-52-89-99** to find out when group visits are scheduled and if the quota of visitors has been filled.

At Carnac Ville, **Musée de Préhistoire,** 10 place de la Chapelle (☎ **02-97-52-22-04**), displays collections from 450,000 B.C. to the 8th century. Admission is 30 F ($4.80) for adults and 15 F ($2.40) for children 10 to 18, free for children 9 and under. The museum is open June 15 to September 15, daily from 10am to 6:30pm; September 16 to June 14, Wednesday through Monday from 10am to noon

The Wild Wild Coast

If you take D768 south from Carnac and follow it onto the peninsula (formerly an island) connected to the mainland by a narrow strip of alluvial deposits, you'll come to the port of **Quiberon,** with its white-sand beach. You'll probably see the rugged Breton fishers hauling in their sardine catch.

This entire coast—the **Côte Sauvage,** or Wild Coast—is dramatic and rugged; the ocean breaks with fury against the reefs. Northern winds, especially in winter, lash across the dunes, shaving the short pines that grow here. On the landward side, however, the beach is calm and relatively protected.

Ten miles west of Brittany's tormented shoreline is **Belle-Île-en-Mer,** an outpost of sand, rock, and twisted vegetation that the French love for summer holidays. Depending on the season, 4 to 12 ferries depart daily for this island from Port Maria in Quiberon (☎ 02-97-31-80-01). The trip takes 45 minutes and costs 112 F ($17.90) round-trip for adults, 69 F ($11.05) round-trip for children. In summer, you must reserve space on board for your car. The ferry docks at **Le Palais,** a fortified 16th-century port that serves as the island's chief window to the rest of France. Storm-wracked and eerie, the local topography contains rocky cliffs; a reef-fringed west coast; the **Grotte de l'Apothicairerie,** a cave (which is closed to visitors) whose name derives from pendulous stalactites shaped like apothecary jars; and a general sense of isolation, despite a scattering of hotels and seasonal restaurants. A drive around the island's periphery is about 35 miles, each rife with bracing Atlantic sights, breezes, and smells.

In the days before he was jailed for embezzlement, the Sun King's finance minister, Nicolas Fouquet, the inspirational force behind Vaux-le-Vicomte, erected a

and 2 to 6pm; and October to May, Wednesday through Monday from 10am to noon and 2 to 5pm.

Even if Carnac didn't possess these prehistoric monuments, its pine-studded sand dunes would be worth the trip. Protected by the Quiberon Peninsula, **Carnac-Plage** is a family resort beside the ocean and alongside the waterfront boulevard de la Plage.

The center of Carnac is about half a mile from the sea. From the main square, rue du Tumulus leads north from the center of town to the **Tumulus St-Michel,** a Celtic burial chamber three-quarters of a mile from the center. Visitation has been halted until 2003 for an archaeological dig.

SHOPPING   Carnac has two **shopping** areas: one along the beachfront called Carnac-Plage and the other about 1¹/₂ miles inland in Carnac proper. Along the beachfront, you'll run into your fair share of touristy souvenir shops, but venture down avenue des Druids and avenue de l'Atlantique for more specialized galleries and antiques stores. Other good areas are rue St-Cornély and place de l'Église, with a host of clothing and shoe stores, antiques dealers, and jewelry and fine gift items.

For a real treat, visit **L'Enfant d'Armor,** 2 place de l'Église (☎ 02-97-52-06-87), which offers a vast array of regional Breton embroidery. It's open only from April to September. **Kryso,** 10 rue St-Cornély (☎ 02-97-52-28-31), sells unique creations of jewelry that combine silver and semiprecious and precious stones, as well as mother-of-pearl. They can also design pieces to meet your particular tastes. Finally, go to **Clémentine,** avenue de l'Atlantique (☎ 02-97-52-96-34), if you're in the market for fine-quality French household linens and dishware.

château on this island. Much later the "Divine" Sarah Bernhardt spent many pleasant summers here in a 17th-century fortress that was "always swarming with guests."

You'll find excellent accommodations in **Port de Goulphar,** one of the most
char-ming spots on Belle-Île. It's on the southern shore, on a narrow inlet framed
by cliffs. Certainly the standout, and the only four-star hotel on the island, is
the Relais & Châteaux **Castel Clara,** Port de Goulphar, 56360 Bangor (☎ **02-97-
31-84-21;** fax 02-97-31-51-69; www.relaischateaux.fr/castelclara; e-mail:
castelclara@relaischateaux.fr). Containing 43 units and set 2 miles from the center
of Bangor, it was built in the early 1970s in a bay-windowed style that permits maximum visibility of the rugged terrain and seascapes nearby. Few other places along
the coast provide such a sense of isolated peace accompanied by ideal service and
first-class cuisine.

The rooms are monochromatic, comfortable, and well furnished, with TV,
phone, and balcony facing the sea. The chef takes pride in his achievements,
and the menu is a good showcase for his talents, particularly the seafood. Sea
bass, for example, might be steamed over seaweed, then served with a beurre
blanc sauce. The hotel also offers a large terrace with a solarium around a heated seawater pool. Depending on the season, rates for two occupants (including
half board) range from 1,440 F to 2,110 F ($230.40 to $337.60) for a double
and from 2,890 F to 3,900 F ($462.40 to $624) for a suite. Family-style apartments without kitchens, which are nothing more complicated than two conventional bedrooms interconnected together, cost 2,100 F to 2,900 F ($336 to
$464), with half-board included. American Express, MasterCard, and Visa are
accepted. The hotel is closed November 15 to February 15.

ESSENTIALS

GETTING THERE Driving is the most convenient way to get to Carnac. From
Lorient, take N165 east to Auray, turning south on D768 to Carnac.

Public transport links are possible but inconvenient. Nine TIM **buses** (call
☎ 02-97-47-29-64 in Vannes or 02-97-24-26-20 in Auray for schedules) run to
Carnac from Quiberon (trip time: 30 minutes). There are also at least nine TIM buses
from Auray to Carnac (trip time: 30 minutes). SNCF **trains** will take you as far as
Plouharnel, and from here you can catch one of seven buses per day (trip time: 5 minutes). For train information and schedules, call ☎ 08-36-35-35-35.

VISITOR INFORMATION The **Office de Tourisme,** on avenue des Druides
(☎ 02-97-52-13-52), is open all year.

ACCOMMODATIONS & DINING

Hôtel Lann-Roz. 36 av. de la Poste, 56340 Carnac. ☎ **02-97-52-10-48.** Fax
02-97-52-24-36. E-mail: hotel-lann-roz@infornie.fr. 14 units. TV TEL. 660–700 F ($105.60–
$112) double. MC, V. Rates include half board. Closed Jan; Sept–May closed Mon nights.

Within walking distance of the water, this oasis for the budget-minded is surrounded
by a garden and lawns. Lann-Roz is managed by the friendly Mme Le Calvez, who
will invite you to have a drink on the veranda. In the typical Breton dining room, the
chef serves generous portions of regional food. Most of the menu items are derived
from local culinary traditions, and are concocted with locally produced ingredients.

Examples include fresh Breton tuna with basil and fresh noodles; a *rillette* (chunky terrine) of fish with shrimp and beurre blanc; house-smoked salmon with a creamy chive sauce; and a platter containing both veal chops and veal kidneys, prepared "in the style of Madame." Dessert might be a flaky slice of cherry tart. Fixed-price meals range from 100 F to 235 F ($16 to $37.60). You don't have to be a guest to dine here.

Hôtel Le Diana. 21 bd. de la Plage, 56340 Carnac Plage. ☎ **02-97-52-05-38.** Fax 02-97-52-87-91. www.ot.carnac.fr. E-mail: diana@ot-carnac.fr. 32 units. MINIBAR TV TEL. 590–1,230 F ($94.40–$196.80) double; 1,150–1,750 F ($184–$280) suite. AE, DC, MC, V. Closed Oct 4–Easter.

Located on the most popular beach, the Diana is the most reliable and comfortable hotel in Carnac and better than its chief rival, the nearby Novotel. On the terrace, you can sip drinks and watch the crashing waves. The spacious, contemporary guest rooms contain balconies facing the sea, comfortable beds, and summery, airy-looking furniture. The hotel restaurant also faces the sea and serves standard seafood fare. There's a gym, a sauna, and a solarium on the premises, and a swimming pool flanked with a bar. Bicycles are loaned without charge to guests, and two minigolf courses are within easy reach.

CARNAC AFTER DARK

Sleepy Carnac doesn't stay up very late, but a few places are worth checking out. The **Whiskey Club,** 8 av. des Druides (☎ 02-97-52-10-52), operates in an old stone house with two floors devoted to entertainment. The first floor offers an atmosphere conducive to casual conversation over drinks; the second floor is home to dancing and loud music. **Les Chandelles,** avenue de l'Atlantique (☎ 02-97-52-90-98), manages to pull together a young, flashy crowd. The club plays mainly disco and charges a 60 F ($9.60) cover. As with most discos in France, no jeans or sneakers are allowed. The professional crowd gathers at **Petit Bedon,** 106 av. des Druides (☎ 02-97-52-11-62). With its exotic mixture of African and Mexican decor, this is the place for dancing to the classic rock of the 1960s. Though there's no cover here, a beer will set you back a hefty 50 F ($8). There's also a restaurant on-site.

8 La Baule

281 miles W of Paris, 49 miles NW of Nantes

Founded during the Victorian seaside craze, La Baule remains as inviting as the Gulf Stream that warms the waters of its 5-mile crescent of white-sand beach. Occupying the Côte d'Amour (Coast of Love), it competes with Biarritz today as the Atlantic coast's most fashionable resort. But La Baule is still essentially French, drawing only a small number of foreigners.

The gambler François André founded the casino and major resort hotels here. Pines grow on the dunes, and villas on the outskirts draw the wealthy chic from late June to mid-September; if you arrive at any other time you might have La Baule all to yourself. While the movie stars and flashy rich go to Deauville or Cannes, La Baule draws a more middle-class crowd; however, the more reserved wealthy still come here—as the yachts in the harbor testify.

The town itself is north of a popular stretch of beachfront. The two main boulevards run roughly parallel through the long, narrow town; the one closer to the ocean changes its name six times—at its most famous point, it's called boulevard de l'Océan.

Other than a rock outcropping much weathered by Atlantic storms, the beaches here are clean and sandy bottomed, providing safe swimming and lots of options for admiring flesh in all states of fitness and differing degrees of preservation.

Avenue du Général-de-Gaulle and avenue Louis-Lajarrige have the best collection of shops and boutiques. Next to the casino on esplanade de François-André, you'll hit the shopping jackpot: a mini-mall with 40 or so French chain stores and boutiques.

ESSENTIALS

GETTING THERE   If you're **driving** from Nantes, take N165 northwest to Savenay, continuing west along D773 to La Baule. The **train** trip from Nantes is about an hour. Get off at the most central inner-city station, La Baule-Escoublac, or the more easterly and remote La Baule-Les Pins. For train information and schedules, call ☎ **08-36-35-35-35.**

VISITOR INFORMATION   The Office de Tourisme is at 8 place de la Victoire (☎ **02-40-24-34-44**).

ACCOMMODATIONS

EXPENSIVE

✪ **Castel Marie-Louise.** 1 av. Andrieu, 44504 La Baule. ☎ **02-40-11-48-38.** Fax 02-40-11-48-35. www.relaischateaux.fr/marielouise. E-mail: marielouise@relaischateaux.fr. 31 units. MINIBAR TV TEL. 890–2,500 F ($142.40–$400) double; 1,900–3,000 F ($304–$480) suite. Half board 360 F ($57.60) extra per person. AE, DC, MC, V. Closed Nov to mid-Dec.

This turn-of-the-century Breton manor offers grand living in an oceanfront pine park. The public rooms are furnished in French provincial style, with tapestries of stylized animals. Each accommodation was renovated during the late 1990s; none of the mattresses are older than 5 or 6 years old, and many are much newer than that. Most upper-floor guest rooms come with a balcony; two are in a tower. Their furnishings reflect several styles: Louis XV, Directoire, and rustic.

Dining: The excellent chef is reason enough to stay here, and even if you aren't a guest you may want to stop in for a meal of regional-based fare that dares to be different. Specialties are lobster and home-smoked salmon. You might want to begin with Breton oysters. Fixed-price menus range from 260 F to 480 F ($41.60 to $76.80).

Amenities: Water sports, tennis. Golf (guests receive a 30% discount) is a 15-minute drive away. Nearby is the Thalgo La Baule Thalassotherapy Centre, with gym, sauna, solarium, and steam room.

MODERATE

Hôtel Alexandra. 3 bd. René-Dubois, 44500 La Baule. ☎ **02-40-60-30-06.** Fax 02-40-24-57-09. 36 units. TV TEL. 440–820 F ($70.40–$131.20) double. AE, DC, MC, V. Closed Dec–Feb. Free parking.

Built in 1966 adjacent to the beach, the Alexandra boasts eight floors of modern rooms with balconies. There's an open-air terrace with umbrellas and sidewalk tables, plus planters of flowers and greenery. The ninth-floor solarium is a popular spot for drinks and coffee. The dining room has a view of the ocean and the lounge is intimate. Note that the rooms here are basic, even by the admission of the staff, and completely unfrilly, the kind of boxy, functional decor where you can bring in sand and seashells and no one will mind.

Hôtel Bellevue-Plage. 27 bd. de l'Océan, 44500 La Baule. ☎ **02-40-60-28-55.** Fax 02-40-60-10-18. www.hotel-bellevue-plage.fr. E-mail: hotel@hotel-bellevue-plage.fr. 35 units. TV TEL. 380–890 F ($60.80–$142.40) double. AE, DC, MC, V. Closed mid-Nov to mid-Feb.

This hotel, which many prefer to the Alexandra, is more reliable than exciting, with a tranquil position in the center of the shoreline curving around the bay. Frequent renovations have removed many of the original Art Deco features, leaving a modern, somewhat banal decor that's appropriate for a beach hotel. Guests gravitate to the rooftop solarium and the ground floor restaurant with its sweeping view. The staff behaves correctly, albeit in ways that some consider anonymous and somewhat detached. You'll find a beach, sailboats for rent, and access to spa facilities.

INEXPENSIVE

Hôtel La Palmeraie. 7 allée des Cormorans, 44500 La Baule. ☎ **02-40-60-24-41.** Fax 02-40-42-73-71. 23 units. TV TEL. 400–550 F ($64–$88) double. Half board (required July–Aug) 430 F ($68.80) per person extra. AE, DC, MC, V. Closed Oct–Apr 1.

In high-priced La Baule, this is a charmer. Built in the 1930s and renovated in the 1990s, it's named after eight large palms that thrive in the garden, thanks to the mild climate. Decorated in festive pink and white, La Palmeraie is near a beach and luxuriant with flowers in summer. The rooms are attractively decorated, often with English-style pieces. Each has comfortable mattresses, a high ceiling, and dignified (sometimes antique) furniture. The only drawback: the soundproofed rooms aren't all that soundproof. Half board is obligatory in July and August; the food, however, is hardly in the league of that at the first-class hotels. The management and staff are helpful and even friendly.

DINING

Another fine dining choice is the restaurant at the **Castel Marie-Louise** (see "Accommodations," above).

La Marcanderie. 5 av. d'Agen. ☎ **02-40-24-03-12.** Reservations required. Main courses 80–180 F ($12.80–$28.80); fixed-price menus 160–340 F ($25.60–$54.40). AE, DC, MC, V. Sun noon–2pm, Mon–Sat noon–2pm and 7:30–10pm. Sept–June, closed Mon. FRENCH.

In 1989, the award-winning chef Jean-Luc Giraud and his wife Marie-Claire transformed a ratty-looking stable into La Baule's finest restaurant. Since then, hundreds of locals, up to 50 at a time, have dined within this elegantly rustic half-timbered lodge. There's something two-fisted and attractively gutsy about this place. Sometimes, particularly if the restaurant is full, you'll have to wait quite a while between courses. The savory and satisfying cuisine utilizes only the finest ingredients. Try the shellfish ravioli, or the terrine of foie gras with a confit of onions followed by fillet mignon of lamb served with a fricassée of wild mushrooms, or the breast of pigeon steamed in cabbage-flavored bouillon. The grilled turbot is flavored with Giraud's variation of a Choron sauce, with butter, shallots, tarragon, vinegar, and a secret process that's unique to his kitchens. The array of after-dinner cheeses is comprehensive, with some unusual local varieties made within a few kilometers of the restaurant. Desserts are appropriately lush and esoteric.

LA BAULE AFTER DARK

The most visible nighttime venue in town is the **Casino,** esplanade de François-André (☎ **02-40-11-48-28**), some areas of which are relatively stylish, but which can't compete with the glamour and high stakes at Deauville. No entrance fee is charged to the area containing the slot machines, which is accessible daily, year-round, from 10am to 4am. There is a fee, however—70 F ($11.20)—for entrance to the area containing the *jeux traditionnels* of blackjack, roulette, and poker. That area is accessible only between May and September, every evening from 9pm till 5am. The casino is the site of a sometimes crowded in-house disco, **L'Indiana** (☎ **02-40-11-48-28**), which is open every night between June and September from 11:30pm till dawn, and every

Wednesday to Sunday otherwise from 11:30pm till dawn. Entrance costs 70 F ($11.20) and includes the first drink.

A stroll down avenue du Général-de-Gaulle or avenue Maréchale-de-Lattre-de-Tassigny will uncover any number of interesting bars and pubs. One of the most appealing is **Le Bax,** 12 avenue de Pavie (☎ **02-40-60-90-00**), a bar where newcomers usually feel welcome within a cozy environment that survives despite the oft-changing seasonal clientele. Other choices include **Safari,** 157 av. du Général-de-Gaulle (☎ **02-40-24-14-46**); **Le Sailor,** 305 av. Maréchale-de-Lattre-de-Tassigny (☎ **02-40-60-24-49**); and **Antidote,** 104 av. du Général-de-Gaulle (☎ **02-40-11-04-03**).

9 Nantes

239 miles W of Paris, 202 miles N of Bordeaux

Nantes is Brittany's largest town, although in spirit it seems to belong more to the Loire Valley's châteaux country. The mouth of the Loire is 30 miles away, and here it divides into several branches. A commercial/industrial city, Nantes is a busy port that suffered great damage in World War II. It's best known for the Edict of Nantes, issued by Henri IV in 1598, guaranteeing religious freedom to Protestants (it was later revoked). Many famous people, from Molière to Stendhal, have lived here. But Nantes hardly lives off its illustrious past. Now home to dozens of high-tech industries, it has some 30,000 college students and a bustling population of half a million who welcome you as you make a stop between Brittany and points south or east in the Loire Valley.

Built on the largest of three islands in the Loire, the city expanded in the Middle Ages to the northern edge of the river, where its center lies today. The most prominent building is the **Château des Ducs de Bretagne,** which rises several hundred feet from a wide boulevard, the main artery of Nantes: quai de la Fosse. At one end of this boulevard is the train station; at the other are the promenades beside the Loire.

ESSENTIALS

GETTING THERE   If you're **driving,** take the A11 highway from Paris to Nantes. About 20 **trains** leave Paris, usually from Gare Montparnasse, for Nantes every day. The trip takes between 2 and 5¹/₂ hours, depending on the number of stops. The world's fastest train (300 m.p.h.), the TGV Atlantique from Paris to Rennes and Nantes, is the best connection. Trains also make the 3- to 4-hour trip from Bordeaux about 10 times a day. For train information and schedules, call ☎ **08-36-35-35-35.**

VISITOR INFORMATION   The **Office de Tourisme** is at place du Commerce (☎ **02-40-20-60-00**).

EXPLORING THE CITY

Cathédrale St-Pierre. Place St-Pierre. ☎ **02-40-47-84-64.** Free admission. Summer, daily 9am–7pm; off-season, daily 9am–6pm.

Begun in 1434, this cathedral wasn't finished until the end of the 19th century. But after all that it has remained architecturally harmonious—a rare feat. Two square towers dominate the facade, but the 335-foot-long interior is more impressive. Its pièce de résistance, however, is Michel Colomb's Renaissance tomb of François II, duc de Bretagne, and his second wife, Marguerite de Foix. Another impressive work is the tomb of Gen. Juchault de Lamoricière, a native of Nantes and a great African campaigner; the sculptor Paul Dubois completed the tomb in 1879. After a 1972 fire destroyed the roof (rebuilt in 1975), the interior was restored. The white walls and pillars contrast with the rich colors of the stained-glass windows. The crypt, from the 11th century, shelters a museum of religions, although at press time it remains closed to the public due to terrorist threats.

Château des Ducs de Bretagne. 4 place Marc-Elder. ☎ **02-40-41-56-56.** Admission 20 F ($3.20) adults, 20 F ($3.20) students, free for children 17 and under. July–Aug, daily 10am–6pm; Sept–June, Wed–Mon 10am–noon and 2–6pm.

Between the cathedral and the Loire is Nantes' second major sight, where the Edict of Nantes was discussed and signed. The castle was constructed in the 9th or 10th century, enlarged in the 13th century, destroyed, and then rebuilt into more or less its present shape by François II in 1466. His daughter, Anne de Bretagne, continued the work. The castle is flanked by large towers and a bastion and contains a formally symmetrical section (the Grand Gouvernement) built during the 17th and 18th centuries. The duchesse du Berry, royal courtesan, was imprisoned here, as was Gilles de Retz ("Bluebeard"), one of France's most notorious mass murderers.

The castle's rich collections are being shaped into a museum of the history of Nantes from the 17th century to the present day. Currently, special exhibitions are staged at the château pending completion of the museum.

Musée des Beaux-Arts de Nantes. 10 rue Georges-Clemenceau, east of place du Maréchal-Foch. ☎ **02-40-41-65-65.** Admission 20 F ($3.20) adults; 10 F ($1.60) students, children, and seniors. Free first Sun of the month and Fri 6–9pm. Mon and Wed–Thurs 10am–6pm, Fri 10am–9pm, Sat–Sun 11am–6pm.

In one of western France's most interesting provincial galleries, you'll find an unusually fine collection of sculptures and paintings from the 12th to the late 19th centuries. The street level is devoted to mostly French modern or contemporary art created since 1900, with special emphasis on painters from the 1950s and 1960s.

Musée Thomas-Dobrée. 18 rue Voltaire. ☎ **02-40-71-03-50.** Admission 20 F ($3.20) adults; 10 F ($1.60) children, students, and seniors. Tues–Sun 10am–noon and 1:30–5:30pm.

This 19th-century neo-Romanesque mansion was built by Thomas Dobrée, an important collector and traveler, whose fortune derived from the whaling fortune that his parents left him in 1850. It stands in the town center, adjacent to the 15th-century manor of Jean V, where the bishops of Nantes occasionally lived. Inside, you'll find Dobrée's varied and eclectic collection, gathered during the height of France's gilded age, including prehistoric and medieval antiquities, Flemish paintings from the 15th century, many ecclesiastical relics, paintings by masters like Dürer, many art objects from India, and the Dobrée family jewels. The collection, along with the building that contains it, was deeded to the city of Nantes after the death of M. Dobrée in 1894.

Musée Jules Verne de Nantes. 3 rue de l'Hermitage. ☎ **02-40-69-72-52.** Admission 10 F ($1.60) adults, 5 F (80¢) children and seniors. Mon and Wed–Sat 10am–noon and 2–5pm, Sun 2–5pm.

The novelist Jules Verne (*Journey to the Center of the Earth, Around the World in Eighty Days*) was born in Nantes in 1828, and literary fans seek out his house at 4 rue de Clisson in the Île-Feydeau. This museum is filled with memorabilia and objects inspired by his writings, from ink spots to a "magic" lantern with glass slides.

SHOPPING

Nantes overflows with shops and boutiques. The principal shopping streets are **rue du Calvaire, rue Crebillon, rue Boileau, rue d'Orléans, rue de la Marne, rue de Verdun,** and **passage Pommeraye.** Most of these encompass the shopping districts

Nantes

Cathédrale St-Pierre **4**
Château des Ducs de Bretagne **3**
Musée des Beaux-Arts de Nantes **5**
Musée Jules Verne de Nantes **1**
Musée Thomas Dobrée **2**

Church †
Information ⓘ
Post Office ✉

around place Graslin, place Royale, the château, and the cathedral. One of the prime areas for antiques is around place Aristide-Briand and rue Mercoeur.

The more interesting antiques dealers include **Antique Bijoux,** 21 rue Mercoeur (☎ **02-40-35-60-84**), specializing in antique and secondhand jewelry; **Jean-Yves Coue,** 7 rue Mercoeur (☎ **02-40-08-29-95**), dealing in antique primitive art from Africa, South and Central America, and the Pacific basin; and **L'Ecritoire Antiquités,** 12 rue Jean-Jaurès (☎ **02-40-47-78-18**), offering 18th- and 19th-century furniture and decorative pieces like historic mantels. **Robin Soustre,** 18 rue Mercoeur (☎ **02-40-48-51-79**), sells 19th-century furniture, usually mahogany, and antique porcelain. **Librairie Brocante du Palais,** 28 rue Jean-Jaurès (☎ **02-40-48-43-64**), sells engravings and antique books; and **Antiquité du Bouffay,** 17 rue de la Juiverie (☎ **02-40-12-11-87**), sells small-scale art objects and antique furniture.

For other unique gifts, check out the stores of two talented master artisans: **Maison Devineau,** 2 place Ste-Croix (☎ **02-40-47-19-59**), which brings the art of wax-working to a new level, "growing" bushels of fruits and vegetables from liquid wax; and **Georges Gautier,** 9 rue de la Fosse (☎ **02-40-48-23-19**), where you'll find the town's best chocolates.

ACCOMMODATIONS

Hôtel Graslin. 1 rue Piron, 44000 Nantes. ☎ **02-40-69-72-91.** Fax 02-40-69-04-44. 47 units. TV TEL. 350–400 F ($56–$64) double. AE, DC, MC, V.

In the center of town, Graslin is on a steep old street near the harbor. The owner-managers, M. and Mme Roche, have given it many homelike touches, so it now offers more for the money than almost any other hotel in its price category. The comfortable rooms, each with a safe, are decorated blandly and functionally; eight contain mini-bars. Overall, there's a definite lassitude and boredom to this hotel, but the price is good, and the beds are reasonably comfortable.

✪ **L'Hôtel.** 6 rue Henri-IV, 44000 Nantes. ☎ **02-40-29-30-31.** Fax 02-40-29-00-95. 31 units. TV TEL. 360–420 F ($57.60–$67.20) double. AE, DC, MC, V. Parking 45 F ($7.20).

Within sight of the château and the cathedral, this hotel is, for the price, a perfect base in Nantes. Built in the early 1980s, the place is neat and modern but still manages to maintain an inviting atmosphere. The rooms range from medium to large in size and boast firm beds, rich colors, and contemporary furnishings. Some accommodations even have their own private balconies looking out over the château, while others open onto a small garden and terrace. Rooms were renovated in the late 1990s, and many of the mattresses were upgraded at that time. You'll find a paneled sitting area with overstuffed couches and chairs next to the reception desk, as well as a softly lit breakfast room with terrace views.

Mercure Beaulieu. Île-Beaulieu, 44200 Nantes-Beaulieu. ☎ **02-40-95-95-95.** Fax 02-40-48-23-83. www.mercure.com. 102 units. A/C MINIBAR TV TEL. 545–620 F ($87.20–$99.20) double; 850 F ($136) suite. AE, DC, MC, V. Free parking. Follow the blue NOVOTEL signs from any of the major traffic arteries in the city to a point 2 miles south of the town center.

Situated on an island in the Loire, the Mercure offers well-furnished, soundproofed chambers. If you prefer contemporary comforts to historic charm, you'll be satisfied by the up-to-date amenities and the alert, hardworking staff who know how to welcome international guests. The bedrooms were renovated in 2000. The restaurant/bar, Le Nautilus, offers a wide choice of seafood dishes. Facilities include a heated outdoor pool and tennis courts.

DINING

L'Atlantide. Centre des Salorges, 16 quai Ernest-Renaud. ☎ **02-40-73-23-23.** Reservations required. Main courses 140–160 F ($22.40–$25.60); fixed-price menus 144–350 F ($23.05–$56) at lunch, 200–350 F ($32–$56) at dinner. AE, V. Mon–Fri noon–2:30pm; Mon–Sat 7–10:30pm. Closed Aug 3–31. FRENCH.

On the fourth floor of the complex that houses the city's chamber of commerce, this panoramic restaurant, with views sweeping out over the semi-industrial landscapes that surround it, serves the finest cuisine in the area. The world-renowned designer Jean-Pierre Wilmotte created a nautical-looking enclave of pale hardwoods with lots of mirrors, but it's the innovative cooking of Jean-Yves Gueho that draws patrons. Menu items, steeped in the traditions of both the Loire Valley and the Breton coast, may include lobster salad with a crispy mixture of potatoes and olives; potato and herb tart capped with foie gras; Breton turbot with shellfish; and braised sweetbreads with Anjou wine. The cellar is known for some of the finest vintages of Loire Valley wine anywhere, with special emphasis on Anjous and muscadets.

La Cigale. 4 place Graslin. ☎ **02-51-84-94-94.** Reservations recommended. Main courses 69–92 F ($11.05–$14.70); fixed-price menus 75–135 F ($12–$21.60) at lunch, 100–150 F ($16–$24) at dinner. MC, V. Daily 11:45am–12:30am. Bus: 11 or 34. FRENCH/SEAFOOD.

This is Nantes' most historic and charming brasserie, decorated in a gracefully sprawling belle époque style that has changed little since the place opened in 1895 across from the landmark Théâtre Graslin. Menu items might include heaping platters of fresh shellfish, *confit des cuisses de canard* (duckling), an array of grilled steaks, and fresh scallops with green peppers and emulsified butter. It's usually quite loud, and the staff members tend to be overworked.

Villa Mon Rêve. Route des Bords-de-Loire, Basse-Goulaine. ☎ **02-40-03-55-50.** Reservations recommended. Fixed-price menus 158–298 F ($25.30–$47.70). AE, DC, MC, V. Daily noon–2pm and 7–9:30pm. Closed 2 weeks in early Nov and 2 weeks in Feb. Take D751 5 miles east of Nantes. FRENCH.

This restaurant, housed in a stone-sided, late-19th-century villa built by a prosperous producer of fruits and vegetables, is set in a 1-acre garden awash in summer with rose beds. Chef Gérard Ryngel and his wife, Cécile, took over Mon Rêve in 1979. Monsieur Ryngel's repertoire includes both regional specialties and his own creations: wild duck with Bourgueil wine sauce, sandre from the Loire with beurre blanc, an unusual combination of veal sweetbreads with crayfish, gazpacho studded with chunks of lobster, and frogs' legs with local white wine. Especially unusual is roasted challons duckling served with caramelized muscadet wine. The vast wine list features more than 40 locally produced wines.

NANTES AFTER DARK

When the sun goes down, this town turns into one big party. Head over to **place du Bouffay** and **place du Pilori,** where you'll find lots of atmospheric cafes and pubs, many with live music and plenty of fun people. A younger crowd rules **rue Scribe** like Louis XIV throwing a party at Versailles.

To beat that unshakable urge to check your e-mail before committing to an evening of fun, stop by **CyberHouse,** 8 quai de Versailles (☎ 02-40-12-11-84); you'll pay 1 F (15¢) per minute to hook up to the Internet and 13 F ($2.10) for a beer. Afterward, catch some live blues, jazz, or rock at **Le Pub Univers,** 16 rue Jean-Jacques-Rousseau (☎ 02-40-73-49-55); or **Quai West,** 17 quai François Mitterand (☎ 02-40-47-68-45), where you'll find techno and disco music all night long. A great piano bar complete with dance floor and occasional jazz concerts is **Le Tie Break,** 1 rue des Petites-Ecuries (☎ 02-40-47-77-00).

The pump-it-up dance scene has a huge following of everyone from students to seniors. **Balapapa,** 24 quai François-Mitterrand (☎ 02-40-48-40-29), has a real cabaret feel in both its dance rooms. It plays an eclectic mix ranging from big band to funk and attracts a crowd just as diverse. The cover is 90 F ($14.40). The over-30 crowd heads to the vintage 1970s disco **L'Evasion,** 3 rue de l'Emery (☎ 02-40-47-99-84). Other discos that keep their dance floors packed are **New's,** place Émile-Zola (☎ 02-40-58-01-04); **Le Royal Club Privé,** 7 rue des Salorges (☎ 02-40-69-11-10); and **Wilton's Club,** 23 rue de Rieux (☎ 02-40-12-01-13). Don't wear blue jeans to any of these places, and be prepared to pay 45 F to 60 F ($7.20 to $9.60) to get in.

The perennial favorite with gays and lesbians is **Le Plein Sud,** 2 rue Prémion (☎ 02-40-47-06-03), where people come to meet and talk in a friendly atmosphere that welcomes everything from leather to lace. A lesbian bar worth a look is **Le Second Soufflé,** 1 rue Kervégan (☎ 02-40-20-14-20). **Le Temps d'Aimer,** 14 rue Alexandre-Fourny (☎ 02-40-89-48-60), is gay-friendly, though not exclusively gay. This medium-size disco with its small dance floor attracts a pretty sophisticated crowd. The most you'll pay to get in is 60 F to 80 F ($9.60 to $12.80). The basement of **News** is another gay discotheque called **Le Privilége,** place Émile-Zola (☎ 02-40-58-01-04). It's the favorite place for techno music lovers.

9

The Champagne Country

In about 3 days, you can take the Autoroute de l'Est (N3) from Paris and explore a region of beautiful cathedrals, historic battlefields, fantastic food, and world-famous vineyards, topping your tour with a heady glass or two of bubbly. On one of the three Routes du Champagne, you can drive to the wine-producing center of Epernay, then on to Reims, some 90 miles northeast of Paris. After visiting Reims and its cathedral, you can leave on Route 31 east, heading toward Verdun, of World War I fame.

REGIONAL CUISINE   Champagne's wine overshadows its cuisine, though several culinary specialties are unique to the district. Most are simple, hearty recipes developed over the centuries in country homes, using pork, beef, fish, and the area's fresh vegetables.

The tang and bite of the sparkling wines dissolve—in the most appetizing of ways—some of the flavorful grease and oils that are part of the local charcuteries and pâtés. Specialties include pork or sheep *andouillettes* (chitterlings) from Bar-sur-Aube and Bar-sur-Seine, pig's feet from Ste-Menehould, and an endless variety of pâtés made from offal, which many North Americans would never consider eating. A *matelote* is a fish stew, generally prepared with freshwater fish and red or white wine. The matelotes here usually employ champagne and carp, pike, and trout.

Most of the area's cheeses are made from cows' milk. The most famous are the *maroilles*, aged collectively (so their skins turn a terra-cotta red) in communal cellars. Some maroilles are sprinkled with tarragon, pepper, and paprika and aged 2 months to produce the strong, aromatic Boulette d'Avesnes, which the French consume with beer. One cheese enjoying popularity in North America is Brie de Melun or Brie de Meaux—the best varieties are made in Champagne, preferably near Meaux.

The largest champagne producer here is Moët et Chandon, though there are excellent smaller vintners like Krug, Roederer, Böllinger, and Veuve Clicquot. Some of the still (nonsparkling) wines from the region, including blanc de blancs, are famous as well.

1 La Ferté-sous-Jouarre

41 miles E of Paris, 51 miles SW of Reims

In the village of Jouarre, 2 miles south of Ferté-sous-Jouarre, you can visit a 12th-century Benedictine abbey and explore one of the oldest

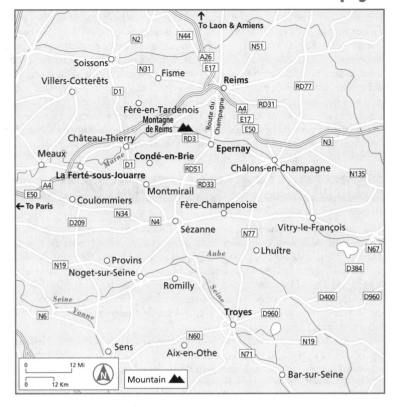

crypts in France. At the **Tour de l'Abbaye de Jouarre,** 6 rue Montmorin (☎ **01-60-22-64-54**), those interested in medieval history will appreciate the preserved documents referring to the Royal Abbey of Jouarre as well as the stones in the Merovingian crypt, which evoke the 7th century. There's also a collection of prehistoric artifacts, remnants of the Roman occupation, and sculptural fragments. The crypt and tower are open Wednesday through Monday from 9am to noon and 2 to 5pm (until 6pm May through October). Admission to the crypt and tower is 30 F ($4.80); to the crypt only, it's 20 F ($3.20), and to the tower only, 15 F ($2.40).

ESSENTIALS

GETTING THERE   If you're **driving,** take N3 along the Marne. About 10 **trains** per day make the 55-minute run from Paris's Gare de l'Est, stopping at Ferté-sous-Jouarre. From there, it's a brief taxi ride 2 miles south to Jouarre and its abbey.

VISITOR INFORMATION   The most comprehensive and best equipped **Office de Tourisme** is adjacent to the tower and the abbey, at place de la Tour (☎ **01-60-22-64-54**), in Jouarre. There's also a **Syndicat d'Initiative** (tourist office) is at 26 place de l'Hôtel-de-Ville (☎ **01-60-22-63-43**) in Ferté-sous-Jouarre.

ACCOMMODATIONS

Château des Bondons. Rte. D70 (Rte. Det Montménard). 77260 La Ferté-sous-Jouarre. 14 units. MINIBAR TV TEL. 500–850 F ($80–$136) double; 1,100 F ($176) suite. AE, DC, MC, V. Follow the signs to Montménard, and drive along D70 for 1¹/₂ miles east of the town center.

Surrounded by a 60-acre park and forest, this château was built around the time of the French Revolution. Not much of the furniture is original to the building, but overall, a sense of the English aesthetic, complete with chintz-patterned curtains and upholsteries and British antiques, fill many of the public areas. Bedrooms are most comfortable, and, as befits a château, come in a variety of shapes and sizes, filled with both old and new furnishings. Members of the Busconi family have proudly framed photographs of the château from the early 20th-century, some of which convey the grandeur that used to be the norm around here. There's even a literary link: Novelist Geôrges Ohnet wrote a popular novel, *Le Maître de Forge,* in the château's library. Other than breakfast, no full-fledged meals are served, but room-service is available most hours of the day and evening, focusing exclusively on salads and cold platters.

2 Château-Thierry

56 miles E of Paris, 6 miles SW of Reims

An industrial town on the Marne's right bank, Château-Thierry contains the ruins of a castle believed to have been constructed for the Frankish king Thierry IV. Château-Thierry gained fame for being the farthest point reached by the German offensive in the summer of 1918. Under heavy bombardment, French forces were aided by the Second and Third Divisions of the American Expeditionary Force. The Battlefields of the Marne are a mile west of town; here, thousands of Allied soldiers who died fighting in World War I are buried. Atop Hill 204 stands a monument honoring American troops who lost their lives.

Château-Thierry is also where the poet/fable writer Jean de la Fontaine (1621–95) was born, in a stone-sided house built in 1452. Today it contains one of France's most oft-visited literary shrines, the **Musée Jean-de-la-Fontaine,** 12 rue Jean de la Fontaine (☎ 03-23-69-05-60). Located a few steps from place de l'Hôtel-de-Ville, it contains a collection of his mementos, including many editions of his works from the Charles-Henri Genot collection, plus paintings and engravings from the 17th to the 20th centuries. Copies of his fables (allegorical barnyard stories depicting the foibles of humans) and *contes* (short stories that are usually a lot racier than his fables) are for sale in the museum bookshop. Hours are Wednesday through Monday from 10am to noon and 2 to 6pm. Admission is 19 F ($3.05) for adults and 10 F ($1.60) for children. Admission is free on Wednesday.

If you're interested in World War I relics, head 5 miles northwest of Château-Thierry to the **Bois de Belleau** (Belleau Wood). The Battle of Belleau Wood marked the second clash between American and German troops in World War I and demonstrated the bravery of the U.S. soldiers in modern warfare. After a bitter 2-week struggle, the woods were taken by the Second Division of the U.S. Expeditionary Force under Maj.-Gen. Omar Bundy. Though the Germans suffered many losses and some 1,650 prisoners were taken, U.S. casualties were appalling: Nearly 7,585 soldiers and 285 officers were wounded, killed, or missing in action.

In 1923, the battleground was dedicated as a memorial to the men who gave their lives here. The **American cemetery** (also known as Le Cimetière de Belleau; ☎ 03-23-70-70-90) contains 2,288 graves. You'll also see a chapel that was damaged in World War II.

ESSENTIALS

GETTING THERE   If you're **driving,** take A4 southwest from Reims or northeast from La Ferté-sous-Jouarre. There are frequent local **trains** from Paris and Reims. For information and schedules, call ☎ 08-36-35-35-35.

VISITOR INFORMATION   The **Office de Tourisme** is at 11 rue Vallée (☎ **03-23-83-10-14**).

ACCOMMODATIONS

Hôtel Île-de-France. Rte. de Soissons, 02400 Château-Thierry. ☎ **03-23-69-10-12.** Fax 03-23-83-49-70. www.perso.wanadoo.fr/hotel.ile-de-france/. 50 units. TV TEL. 350F ($59.50) double. AE, DC, MC, V.

This elegant modern hotel is the leading choice in this area of not-so-hot options. Set in a park overlooking the green Marne Valley, near the ruins of the town's château, the four-story structure boasts balconies and dormers, a view of the town, and well-maintained rooms furnished in contemporary style each with comfortable mattresses. The restaurant is not particularly noteworthy. Fixed-price menus range from 98 F to 248 F ($15.70 to $39.70).

DINING

Auberge Jean-de-la-Fontaine. 10 rue des Filoirs. ☎ **03-23-83-63-89.** Reservations required. Main courses 60–95 F ($9.60–$15.20); fixed-price menu (including aperitif, wine, and coffee) 200 F ($32). AE, DC, MC, V. Tues–Sun 12:30–2pm; Tues–Sat 7:30–9:30pm. Closed Jan 5–18 and first 3 weeks of Aug. FRENCH.

This restaurant is filled with paintings on wood panels dedicated to the fables of Jean de la Fontaine. The menu changes every 3 weeks but may include dishes like a gâteau of sea crabs *"printanier"* with fresh asparagus and new baby vegetables; an appetizer that showcases the duck "in all its states," combining a portion of traditional duck breast with a taste of smoked duck thigh with a confit of gizzards and a slice of home-made duck liver. Main courses include a warm pâté of freshwater sandre with Breton lobster, or a supreme of guinea fowl with coriander sauce. A typical regional dish might be a fricassée of chicken flavored with champagne.

3 Condé-en-Brie

55 miles E of Paris, 15 miles W of Epernay

West of Epernay, **Château de Condé,** Rue du Château, 02330 Condé-en-Brie (☎ **03-23-82-42-25**), was inherited in 1814 by the comte de Sade and remained in his family until 1983. The Sade name was besmirched by the infamous marquis, an innovative writer (*Justine, Juliette, The 120 Days of Sodom*) whose sexual practices as described in his works gave us the word *sadism.*

The castle was built in the late 12th century by Enguerran of Coucy. A part of the old keep still remains—two big rooms with great chimneys and thick walls. The castle was reconstructed in the Renaissance style at the beginning of the 16th century by Cardinal de Bourbon, a member of the royal family. His nephew, Louis de Bourbon, called himself the prince de Condé, most likely because he had many fond childhood memories of the place. After sustaining damage in the early 18th century, the château was rebuilt yet again—this time for the marquis de La Faye. The Italian architect Servandoni invited artists like Boucher and Watteau to do frescoes and paintings, which you can still see today. Servandoni decorated the largest room, making it a theater hall for music and entertainment. The present castle is an exceptional ensemble, with its paintings, woodwork, chimneys, and so-called Versailles floor.

In 1994, the new owners, the de Rocheforts, discovered several Watteau paintings concealed behind mirrors installed during the 18th century. Now, at the push of a button, the mirrors open to reveal the previously hidden treasures.

Admission is 36 F ($5.75) for adults and 18 F ($2.90) for children 14 and under. The castle is open for tours from June to September, daily at 2:30, 3:30, 4:30, and 5:30pm. In May, it's open only on Sundays and bank holidays at the same hours.

GETTING THERE   If you're traveling between Château-Thierry and Epernay on N3, head south at Dormans and follow the signs to Condé-en-Brie.

4 Reims

89 miles E of Paris, 28 miles NW of Châlons-en-Champagne

Reims (pronounced *Rahns*), an ancient Roman city, was important at the time Caesar conquered Gaul. French kings traditionally came here to be crowned, and it's said that the French nation was born here in A.D. 498. Joan of Arc escorted Charles VII here in 1429, kissing the silly man's feet. But don't let this ancient background mislead you: As you approach Reims you'll pass through prefabricated suburbs that look like apartment-house blocks in Eastern Europe. There are gems in Reims, including the cathedral, of course, but you must seek them out.

Most visitors come to Reims because it's the center of a wine-growing district whose bubbly is present at celebrations all over the world. The city today, with a population of 185,000, is filled with swank restaurants, ritzy champagne houses, large squares, and long tree-lined avenues. The champagne bottled here is the lightest and subtlest in flavor of the world's wines. Make an effort to linger, exploring the vineyards and wine cellars, the Gothic monuments, and the battlefields (the Germans occupied Reims in 1870, 1914, and 1940).

ESSENTIALS
GETTING THERE   If you're **driving** from Paris to Reims, take A4 east. **Trains** depart from Paris's Gare de L'Est Station every 2 hours (trip time: 1¹/₂ hours). There are also five trains per day from Strasbourg (trip time: 4 hours). For train information and schedules, call ☎ **08-36-35-35-35.**

VISITOR INFORMATION   The **Office de Tourisme** is at 2 rue Guillaume-de-Machault (☎ **03-26-77-45-25**).

SEEING THE SIGHTS
✪ **Cathédrale Notre-Dame de Reims.** Place du Cardinal-Luçon. ☎ **03-26-47-55-34.** Free admission. Mon–Sat 7am–7:30pm, Sun 8:30am–7pm.

This is one of the world's most famous cathedrals. It was restored after World War I, largely by U.S. contributions from John D. Rockefeller; mercifully, it escaped World War II relatively unharmed. Built on the site of a church that burned to the ground in 1211, it was intended as a sanctuary where French kings would be anointed. St. Rémi, the bishop of Reims, baptized Clovis, the pagan king of the Franks, here in 496. All of the kings of France from Louis the Pious (son of Charles the Great) in 815 to Charles X in 1825 were crowned here.

Laden with statuettes, its three western facade portals are spectacular. A rose window above the central portal is dedicated to the Virgin. The right portal portrays the Apocalypse and the Last Judgment; the left, martyrs and saints. At the western facade's northern door is a smiling angel. Lit by lancet windows, the immense nave has many bays. Beside the cathedral is the treasury with a 12th-century chalice for the communion of French monarchs and a talisman supposedly containing a relic of the True Cross that Charlemagne is said to have worn. From the interior of the cathedral, you can visit Palais du Tau, the ancient residence of the bishop of Reims, now a museum.

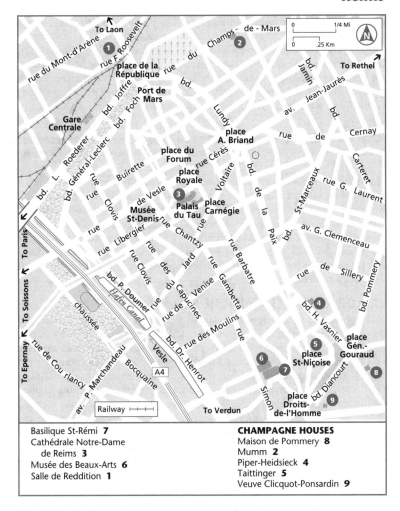

Basilique St-Rémi **7**	**CHAMPAGNE HOUSES**
Cathédrale Notre-Dame	Maison de Pommery **8**
de Reims **3**	Mumm **2**
Musée des Beaux-Arts **6**	Piper-Heidsieck **4**
Salle de Reddition **1**	Taittinger **5**
	Veuve Clicquot-Ponsardin **9**

Salle de Reddition. 12 rue Franklin-D.-Roosevelt. ☎ **03-26-47-84-19.** Admission 10 F ($1.60). Wed–Mon 10am–noon and 2–6pm. Closed May 1 and July 14.

On May 7, 1945, the Germans surrendered to General Eisenhower in this structure, which was once a little schoolhouse near the railroad tracks. The walls of the room are lined with maps of the rail routes, exactly as they were on the day of surrender.

Basilique St-Rémi. 53 rue St-Simon. ☎ **03-26-85-23-36.** Admission 10 F ($1.60) adults, free for children and students. Mon–Fri 2–6:30pm, Sat–Sun 2–7pm.

The Basilique St-Rémi is the oldest church in Reims, dating from 1007. Unfortunately, it is often unfavorably compared to the more spectacular cathedral. It is, however, an example of medieval French masonry at its most classic. Housed within the Basilica complex is the former royal abbey of St-Rémi, who was once the guardian of the holy ampula used to anoint the kings of France. The abbey now functions as a fascinating museum with an extensive collection covering the history of Reims, regional archaeology, and military history. The architect Louis Duroché designed the majestic ornamental front of the main quadrangle as well as the Grand Staircase (1778), where you can admire one of the official portraits of the young Louis XV in his coronation robes. It also contains a grand Romanesque nave leading to a magnificent choir crowned with massive pointed arches. The nave, the transepts, one of the towers, and the aisles date from the 11th century; the portal of the south transept is in Flamboyant early 16th–century style. Some of the stained glass in the apse is from the 13th century. The tomb of St. Rémi is elaborately carved with Renaissance figures and columns.

Musée des Beaux-Arts. 8 rue Chanzy. ☎ **03-26-47-28-44.** Admission 10 F ($1.60) adults, free for children under 12 and students. Wed–Mon 10am–noon and 2–6pm. Closed Jan 1, May 1, July 14, Nov 1 and 11, and Dec 25.

Housed in the 18th-century buildings belonging to the old Abbaye St-Denis, this fine provincial art gallery contains more than a dozen portraits of German princes of the Reformation by both "the Elder" and "the Younger" Cranach; the museum has owned this remarkable collection since it opened in 1795. You can see the *Toiles Peintes* (light painting on rough linen) that date from the 15th and 16th centuries and depict the *Passion du Christ* and *Vengeance du Christ*. Paintings and fine furniture from the 17th and 18th centuries are in the Salles Diancourt and Jamot-Neveux. There's an excellent series of 26 of Corot's tree-shaded walks.

EXPLORING THE CHAMPAGNE CELLARS

Many of the vast ✪ **champagne cellars** of Reims extend for miles through chalky deposits. In fact, during the German siege of 1914 and throughout the war, people lived in them and even published a daily paper there. Although the cellars are open all year, they're most interesting during the fall grape harvest. After that, the wine is fermented in vats in the caves, then is bottled with a small amount of sugar and natural yeast. The yeast feeds on the sugar and causes a second fermentation to take place—thus producing those fabulous bubbles. The wine growers wait until the sparkle has "taken," as they say, before they remove the bottles to racks or pulpits. For about 3 months, *remueurs* are paid just to turn them a fraction every day, which brings the impurities (dead yeast cells and other matter) toward the cork. Eventually these sediments are removed and the wine is given its proper dosage (sugar dissolved in wine), depending on the desired sweetness. The process takes 4 or 5 years and is carried out in caves that are usually 100 feet deep and kept at a constant 50°F.

Maison de Pommery. Place du Général-Gouraud. ☎ **03-26-61-62-56.** Admission 40 F ($6.40), free for children 15 and under. Apr–Oct, daily 9am–7pm; Nov–Mar, Mon–Fri 10am–6pm. Call in advance to book your visit.

Among the most visited cellars are those under the Gothic-style buildings and spacious gardens of the Maison de Pommery. A magnificent 116-step stairway leads to a maze of galleries dug into the chalk that are more than 11 miles long and about 100 feet below ground. Various stages of champagne making are shown.

Mumm. 34 rue du Champ-de-Mars. ☎ **03-26-49-59-70.** Tours in English 25 F ($4), free for children. Mar–Oct, daily 9–11am and 2–5pm; Nov–Feb, Mon–Fri 9–11am and 2–5pm, Sat–Sun and holidays 2–5pm.

A visit here includes a video show and a cellar tour; a small museum exhibits casks and the ancient tools of a vintner. Champagne is available for purchase in the gift shop.

Piper-Heidsieck. 51 bd. Henri-Vasnier. ☎ **03-26-84-43-44.** Admission 40 F ($6.40). Daily 9–11:45am and 2–5:15pm. Dec–Feb, closed Tues–Wed.

Champagne: The Fizz & the Fun

The love of that effervescent mystery called champagne is certainly nothing new. During the Renaissance, the only thing François I of France and Henry VIII of England could agree on was a preference for bubbly. Napoléon carted along cases of the stuff to his battlefronts. Casanova used it to liven up his legendary seductions, Mme de Pompadour employed it to tempt the Sun King, and Tallyrand imported cases of it to the Congress of Vienna for a different sort of seduction—procuring more favorable peace terms.

We all owe a toast or two to Dom Pérignon, that Benedictine monk (1638–1715) who initiated the technique of adding cane sugar and natural yeast to the still wine to cause it, after years of fermentation, to foam. Without a complicated series of additives, double fermentations, cooling at precise temperatures, and turnings and twistings, champagne would be plain old table wine. Without the fizz, where would be the fun?

The best champagne grapes are grown in a network of vineyards that meander like narrow ribbons along the bottomlands south of Reims. French vintners consider the best regions the Côte des Blancs, Montagne de Reims, and Vallée de la Marne; these are also the names for the three Routes du Champagne, signposted wine roads extending through the area.

The association of this bubbling wine with glamour, romance, and celebration is a triumph of marketing. Off the record, Burgundy's vintners will remind oenophiles that it takes a lot more work, with a greater chance of failure from uncontrollable variables, to produce a great bottle of still red than a jeroboam of sparkling Veuve Clicquot.

Nonetheless, the fascination with real champagne remains fervent, as shown by the spectacular increase in worldwide consumption of the stuff since Leslie Caron and Louis Jourdan sang about "The Night They Invented Champagne" in the 1958 movie *Gigi*.

And now a word about the word *champagne*. Since the days of the grand époque, when dandies drank bubbly out of ladies' slippers and beauties bathed in the stuff, the misuse of that word has aroused the wrath of even such venerable personages as the Veuve Clicquot herself. By law, only champagne made in France's Champagne region can be called champagne. Bubbly made in any other area of France must be categorized as sparkling wine produced via the *méthode champenoise*. In the U.S., each state has its own laws about this—in one state you can call your bubbly champagne and in another you cannot. But don't dare try that in France, as you'll face lengthy litigation. Just ask Yves Saint Laurent, who once had the effrontery to name a new perfume he'd invented Champagne.

This firm—one of the oldest champagne houses in the world—was established in 1785. Here you explore the cellars in an electric-powered car (five occupants at a time) known as *une nacelle* and enjoy a tasting at the end of the tour.

✪ **Taittinger.** 9 place St-Niçoise. ☎ **03-26-85-84-33.** Admission 35 F ($5.60). Mon–Fri 9:30am–noon and 2–4:30pm, Sat–Sun 9–11am and 2–5pm. Dec–Feb, closed weekends.

Taittinger is a grand *marque* of French champagne, one of the few whose ownership is controlled by members of the family that founded it in 1930. It's one of the most visitor-friendly of the champagne houses. The Romanesque cellars were dug from the site of Gallo-Roman chalk mines in use between the 4th and 13th centuries. Tours—including a film presentation, a guided cellar visit, and a surprisingly rich set of anecdotes about Reims, the champagne-making process, and Taittinger family lore—last about an hour.

Veuve Clicquot-Ponsardin. 1 place des Droits-de-l'Homme. ☎ **03-26-89-54-41.** Free admission. Apr–Oct, Mon–Sat; Nov–Mar, Mon–Fri (call for an appointment).

You can visit part of the 16 miles of underground galleries on guided tours at Veuve Clicquot-Ponsardin. The highlight is the screening of a film about one of Champagne's grande dames, the Veuve Clicquot (Widow Clicquot).

SHOPPING

The main shopping district is conveniently located around the cathedral. Nearby streets to shop are the very long **rue de Vesle,** the **cours Langlet,** and the **place Drouet d'Erlon.**

Of course, you'll definitely want to include bottles of champagne on your shopping list. Many people opt to visit one of the major champagne houses in town; others get in their car and drive along the **Routes du Champagne,** three signposted wine roads that cover the region. This is where you'll find more of the smaller champagne makers. When you're making the rounds along these roads, be aware that most champagne houses prefer you to take their tour and not just stop in their shops. If you do take the tour, you'll at least get a glass of bubbly at the end. When purchasing here, be aware that the bottles are priced individually, but you can get discounts if you buy three or six bottles at a time. However, if you're looking for a good deal, you may want to buy at stores in town such as **Le Marché aux Vins, Pérandel,** 3 place Léon-Bourgeois (☎ **03-26-40-12-12**), where you can choose from a very large selection of not only local champagnes but also other wines. For complete information on the champagne houses in and around Reims, contact the Office de Tourisme.

Another specialty here is the light and delicious little cookie known as *biscuit de Reims.* Two of the best places to find them are **La Maison Fossier,** 25 cours Langlet (☎ **03-26-47-59-84**), and **Boutique Nominee,** place du Parvis (☎ **03-26-40-43-85**). For chocolate and candied specialties, try **La Petite Friande,** 15 cours Langlet (☎ **03-26-47-50-44**), where you can purchase liqueur-filled chocolate champagne bubbles and corks.

Parc des Expositions, route de Châlons-en-Champagne (2½ miles east of Reims), hosts a flea market the first Sunday of every month except August. On the first weekend of April there's a huge "Euro" flea market, with more than 500 vendors, in the same location. The organization responsible for these events is **Artcom/Puces de Reims,** 82 rue Jacquart (☎ **03-26-02-04-06**).

ACCOMMODATIONS
EXPENSIVE

✪ **Boyer-les-Crayères.** 64 bd. Henri-Vasnier, 51100 Reims. ☎ **03-26-82-80-80.** Fax 03-26-82-65-52. www.gerardboyer.com. E-mail: crayeres@relaischateaux.fr. 19 units. A/C MINIBAR TV TEL. 1,490–2,150 F ($238.40–$344) double; 2,150–2,550 F ($344–$408) suite. AE, DC, MC, V. Closed Dec 22–Jan 12.

There's no better place to stay or dine than at this hotel, which occupies one of the finest châteaux in eastern France. Set in a 14-acre park, it boasts 18-foot ceilings, burnished paneling, and luxurious furnishings. The rooms, with terraces and all the amenities, are individually decorated in a sophisticated country-manor style, and are usually available when a champagne mogul isn't in residence.

Dining: The hotel's restaurant is one of the greatest in the area. World-famous chef Gérard Boyer imbues each dish with his culinary imprint. One of his masterpieces is *salade du Père-Maurice,* with green beans, artichoke hearts, lemon, foie gras, truffles, and lobster. Other dishes, each spectacular, include turbot steak studded with truffles and served with foie gras, and salsify braised in champagne and served with a truffle-flavored cream sauce. Dessert might be an American-inspired brownie served with almond-flavored chocolate truffles, accompanied with ice cream flavored with caramelized peanuts and a caramelized walnut sauce. Reservations are required a few days in advance for weekday dinners, at least a month in advance for weekend dinners.

Amenities: A masseur or hairdresser can be sent to your room.

Les Templiers. 22 rue des Templiers, 51100 Reims. ☎ **03-26-88-55-08.** Fax 03-26-47-80-60. E-mail: hotel.templiers@wanadoo.fr. 17 units. A/C MINIBAR TV TEL. 1,200–1,400 F ($192–$224) double; 1,800 F ($288) suite. AE, DC, MC, V. Bus: G or H.

This hotel, just a short walk from the cathedral, may be small, but it's your best inner-city bet. A restored 1800s Mock-Gothic house, the place exhibits taste and sensitivity, with antiques, ornate ceilings, and hand-carved woodwork creating an inviting ambience. The rooms continue the 19th-century allure with color-coordinated fabrics and bold print wallcoverings. Each comes with a quality French mattress and a comfortable bed.

Dining: Breakfast, the only meal served, can be taken in your room, beside an indoor pool, or on the new terrace.

Amenities: Room service, laundry/dry cleaning, concierge.

MODERATE

L'Assiette Champenoise. 40 av. Paul-Vaillant-Couturier, 51430 Tinqueux. ☎ **03-26-84-64-64.** Fax 03-26-04-15-69. www.chateau-muire.com. E-mail: assiette.champenoise@wanadoo.fr. 62 units. MINIBAR TV TEL. 585–770 F ($93.60–$123.20) double; 1,100 F ($176) suite. AE, DC, MC, V. Free parking. From Reims, take A4 west toward Paris and exit at "Sortie 22-Tinqueux"; av. Paul-Vaillant-Couturier will lead you directly to Tinqueux.

About 4 miles from Reims, this is the second-best hotel/restaurant in the area. Built in the 1970s among century-old trees, it occupies part of what was once a private Norman estate. Rooms are attractively furnished and well maintained in a combination of French traditional and modern style. Many people come here just to enjoy the cooking of Jean-Pierre Lallement, who is assisted by his wife, Colette; his son, Arnaud; and Arnaud's wife, Maryanne. In their artfully rustic **dining room,** the cuisine covers a medley of conservative classics, some with an innovative twist. Try the fillet of beef with marrow sauce and red wine, John Dory with ragoût of vegetables, or grilled duck liver with fondue of tomatoes. Homemade foie gras is always a reliable starter. Fixed-price menus range from 295 F to 495 F ($47.20 to $79.20).

INEXPENSIVE

Best Western Hôtel de la Paix. 9 rue Buirette, 51100 Reims. ☎ **800/528-1234** in the U.S., or 03-26-40-04-08. Fax 03-26-47-75-04. www.bestwestern.com. E-mail: bw.lapaix@wanadoo.fr. 106 units. MINIBAR TV TEL. 460 F ($73.60) double; 690 F ($110.40) junior suite for 2–3. AE, DC, MC, V. Parking 50 F ($8). Bus: G or H.

Conveniently located between the train station and the cathedral, this is the only modern hotel in France that owns a medieval chapel (built for Benedictine nuns in the 1200s) overlooking its garden and pool. Constructed in 1946, it has been thoroughly enlarged since then into the pleasant chain-hotel format you'll see today. The rooms are contemporary and well maintained, and many are air-conditioned. Furnishings are a bit sterile but the beds are comfortable, each with a fine mattress and good linen. The hotel's **Taverne du Maître Kanter** serves excellent meals daily between noon and midnight. The cuisine might include sauerkrauts, fish, grills, oysters, and casseroles.

Grand Hôtel du Nord. 75 place Drouet-d'Erlon, 51100 Reims. ☎ **03-26-47-39-03.** Fax 03-26-40-92-26. E-mail: grandhoteldunord-reims@wanadoo.fr. 50 units. MINIBAR TV TEL. 295–330 F ($47.20–$52.80) double. AE, DC, MC, V. Parking 30 F ($4.80). Bus: G or H. Take A4 (A26) motorway and exit at Reims-Centre.

This recently renovated old-fashioned hotel offers comfortably decorated rooms. Rooms range from small to medium, each fitted with comfortable beds and fine mattresses. Two steps from the entrance, the liveliness of place Drouet-d'Erlon unfolds with its many boutiques, cafe terraces, and cinemas. You're also near the cathedral, the basilica, and various museums.

Grand Hôtel L'Univers. 41 bd. Foch, 51100 Reims. ☎ **03-26-88-68-08.** Fax 03-26-40-95-61. www.ebc.fr/hotel-univers. E-mail: hotel-univers@ebc.net. 42 units. TV TEL. 425–480 F ($68–$76.80) double. AE, DC, MC, V.

In the heart of Reims and across from the train station, this five-story modern hotel has small-to average-size rooms outfitted in a basic manner, with a simple desk and chair along with a firm bed. Since this area can get rather noisy, all the rooms fortunately have double-pane windows to block out the street "ambience." You can have breakfast in the American-style bar or dinner in the hotel's small but elegant restaurant, which specializes in traditional French cuisine and offers fixed-price menus.

Mercure Reims Cathédrale. 31 bd. Paul-Doumer, 51100 Reims. ☎ **03-26-84-49-49.** Fax 03-26-84-49-84. E-mail: h1248@accor-hotels.com. 126 units. A/C MINIBAR TV TEL. 570 F ($91.20) double; 790–890 F ($126.40–$142.40) suite. AE, DC, MC, V. Parking 50 F ($8).

This hotel, a member of a national chain, sits on the banks of the Marne Canal, a 5-minute walk from the town center. It's near the entrance to the autoroute, so it's easy to find. The good-size rooms have all the modern conveniences, and some have views of a scenic waterway. Furnishings are in a standard motel style; each comfortable bed boasts a fine mattress and linen. Les Ombrages restaurant serves French specialties nightly to 10pm.

DINING

Boyer-les-Crayéres and **L'Assiette Champenoise** (see "Accommodations," above) both contain excellent restaurants.

Le Chardonnay. 184 av. d'Epernay. ☎ **03-26-06-08-60.** Reservations recommended. Main courses 90–175 F ($14.40–$28); fixed-price menus 150–420 F ($24–$67.20); "menu champagne" for 2 (including a bottle of a "champagne de marque") 880 F ($140.80). AE, DC, MC, V. Sun–Fri noon–2:30pm; Mon–Sat 7:30–10pm. Drive 4 miles south of Reims's center, following the signs to Epernay. FRENCH.

This cozy enterprise serves superb cuisine in a much-restored turn-of-the-century building managed by members of the Lange family. You're likely to be greeted by Chantal and Delphine, the mother-daughter team that oversees the dining room, which overlooks a flowering courtyard. The cuisine is remarkably consistent from week to week, with sauces often based on a generous use of local wines. Examples include roasted rabbit with foie gras, fillet of veal stuffed with truffles and cooked in a clay pot, and nuggets of venison in a red wine and mushroom sauce.

Le Vigneron. Place Paul-Jamot. ☎ **03-26-79-86-86.** Reservations recommended. Main courses 80–140 F ($12.80–$22.40); fixed-price menus 150–260 F ($24–$41.60). DC, MC, V. Mon–Fri 11:30am–2:30pm and 5:30–10pm. Closed Aug 1–15 and Dec 23–Jan 2. CHAMPENOISE.

At this sophisticated, low-key restaurant, the cuisine is firmly rooted in the traditions of Champagne: Much of the cuisine is laced with one or another of the region's delectable wines. Wine experts grab the carte even before glancing at the menu. With 650 choices, it includes some museum-quality vintages, such as a Pol Roger 1892 (not for sale at any price) and a Veuve Clicquot 1923. Hervé Liegent and the charming staff offer such specialties as a fillet of trout from the Marne, prepared with crayfish sauce, and poached eggs with a sauce made with *maroilles* (a mild locally fermented cheese). A superb dessert is the *biscuits roses de Reims* served with a liqueur (*marc*) distilled from sparkling champagne. Try to step into the restaurant's small-scale museum, maintained in honor of the vintner's art, before you leave.

NEARBY ACCOMMODATIONS & DINING

✪ **Château de Fère.** Rte. de Fismes (D967), 02130 Fère-en-Tardenois. ☎ **03-23-82-21-13.** Fax 03-23-82-37-81. Reservations required. Main courses 95–230 F ($15.20–$36.80); fixed-price menus 180 F ($28.80) at lunch Mon–Fri, 290–480 F ($46.40–$76.80) at lunch (weekends) and dinner. AE, DC, MC, V. Daily noon–2:30 and 7:30–9pm. Closed Jan. FRENCH.

Set in a park, this fabulous restaurant occupies a restored 16th-century crenellated château with turrets. The only restaurant in Champagne that's superior to it in cuisine is Boyer-les-Crayères. In summer, begin your repast in the sunny garden, sipping an aperitif or a glass of champagne with juice from freshly crushed raspberries. The owners oversee every detail and serve imaginative meals, with specialties like foie gras of duckling with a confit of ginger and a sauce made from the sweet dessert wine "Muscats de Venise"; nuggets of suckling lamb cooked in a truffle-and-parsley-flavored crust, and deliberately undercooked Scottish salmon served in a lemon-flavored sweet-and-sour sauce. The desserts are mouthwatering, but we prefer to order the *boulette d'Avesnes,* a cone of cheese flecked with herbs and crushed peppercorns and coated with paprika.

Also available here are 19 luxuriously furnished guest rooms and six suites, each with bathroom, minibar, TV, and phone. The doubles cost 80 F to 1,250 F ($12.80 to $200); the suites, 1,200 F to 1,950 F ($192 to $312).

To get here from Reims, take E46 northwest toward Soissons. At the town of Fismes, take D367 southwest toward Fère-en-Tardenois and follow the signs to the Château de Fère. About 1 1/2 miles north of the restaurant and guest house, you'll see the ruins of a 12th-century fortified castle—also called the Château de Fère. The trip to the ruins or the restaurant should take 35 minutes.

REIMS AFTER DARK

Reims has the best and most vibrant nightlife in the entire Champagne region. The best place to start is place Drouet-d'Erlon, home to Reims's premier clubs. This is a university town, so for the most part students rule the night. Just follow them to the best venues.

For a beer, head to **The Glue Pot,** 49 place Drouet-d'Erlon (☎ **03-26-47-36-46**), with its heavy dose of noise and rowdy students; **Au Bureau,** 80 place Drouet-d'Erlon (☎ **03-26-40-33-06**), where a mixed-age crowd congregates in a typically Irish pub that has more than 120 brands of beer; or the exotic **Au Lion de Belfort,**

37 place Drouet-d'Erlon (☎ **03-26-47-48-17**), where stuffed heads of hippos, elephants, and the like keep watch over the young patrons. For a more sedate bar experience, try **L'Escalier,** 7 rue de Chativesle (☎ **03-26-84-95-14**), where the atmosphere is more conducive to striking up conversation with both locals and other tourists.

The best dance floors in town are **Le Boss,** 17 rue Lesage (☎ **03-26-88-33-83**), where techno is king and disco is dead; **Aquarium,** 93 bd. Général Leclerc (☎ **03-26-47-34-29**), attracting a mixed-age crowd of 25- to 40-year-olds; and **Le Tigre,** 2 bis av. Georges-Clemenceau (☎ **03-26-82-64-00**), with its decor of old French cars placed like artwork against the brick walls and mirrors. The fave of young gays and lesbians is **Les Lilas Club,** 75 rue des Courcelles (☎ **03-26-47-02-81**). Everybody wears jeans; cover to any of these dance clubs is 50 F ($8).

Another activity that always draws a crowd is the free laser show on the exterior walls of the cathedral on Saturday nights in July and August. For details call the **Centre National Arts et Technologies** (☎ **03-26-06-58-00**). If you want to enjoy an evening of stage performance, **Comédie de Reims,** chaussée Bocquaine (☎ **03-26-48-49-00**), has a varied and full schedule, with tickets costing 100 F ($16) adults, 70 F ($11.20) seniors, and 30 F ($4.80) for students.

5 Laon & Amiens: Side Trips from Reims

Laon: 28 miles NW of Reims, 74 miles SE of Amiens, 86 miles NE of Paris; Amiens: 68 miles NW of Reims, 75 miles N of Paris, 71 miles SW of Lille

North Americans tend to overlook France's northern region, but savvy travelers know that this pristine area offers restful alternatives to the densely populated tourist meccas of Paris and the Riviera. The landscape of this low-lying region, adjacent to Belgium's border, will be familiar to admirers of Matisse, who found much inspiration here. Amiens and Laon are the area's major draws.

From Reims, **Laon** would be a logical first stop, particularly for those traveling by rail who will have to transfer here anyway en route to Amiens. This site is the north's most intriguing due to its history and setting. Over the years, it has witnessed much turbulence from its perch on an isolated ridge 328 feet above the plain and the Ardon River.

Amiens, on the Somme River, has subsisted as a textile center since medieval days. It was once the ancient capital of Picardy, and its old town is a warren of jumbled streets and intersecting canals. Today, Amiens is renowned for its Gothic cathedral, one of the finest in France.

Beyond Amiens and Laon, the heavily forested **Ardennes** attracts lovers of nature and French poetry alike. Rimbaud lived and wrote here; other writers such as Victor Hugo, George Sand, and Alexandre Dumas also expounded on its beauty in their writings. The sandy beaches of **Le Touquet-Paris-Plage** are the most fashionable and best equipped of the many resorts along the Channel. A mini-Monte Carlo, it was dubbed the "playground of kings" in the days before World War II. Many other stops merit a look if you have the time.

LAON

Arguably the single most intriguing town in the north of France, Laon is perched on an isolated ridge that rises 328 feet above the plain and the Ardon River. The capital of the *département* of Aisne, Laon has had a long, turbulent history, due in large part to its remarkable location.

ESSENTIALS

GETTING THERE   If you're **driving** from Reims, go 28 miles on A26 north directly to Laon. **Trains** arrive from Paris's Gare du Nord at least 15 times a day (trip time: $1^1/2$ to 2 hours). Other trains arrive from Reims seven times a day (trip time: about 45 minutes). For train information and schedules, call ☎ **08-36-35-35-85.**

VISITOR INFORMATION   The **Office de Tourisme** is on place du Parvis (☎ **03-23-20-28-62**).

SEEING THE SIGHTS

The Romans, recognizing Laon's strategic value early on, had it fortified. It was later besieged by Vandals, Burgundians, Franks, and many others. German troops entered Laon in 1870 and again in the summer of 1914, holding it until the end of World War I. The town is still surrounded by medieval ramparts, regarded by many as the single most rewarding attraction in the north. They appear to have survived intact from the Middle Ages and provide a ready-made itinerary for touring Laon. They aren't structurally sound enough to be climbed on so they must be admired from below.

You don't have to huff and puff as you head from Laon's Basse Ville to its Haute Ville, thanks to a cable-operated tram, **Poma 2000** (☎ **03-23-79-07-59**), that shuttles passengers up and down the rocky hill at 3-minute intervals. It departs from the rail station on place de la Gare and ascends to the Hôtel-de-Ville on place du Général-Leclerc. The tram operates Monday through Saturday from 7am to 8pm. The cost is 6.40 F ($1) one-way and 6.50 F ($1.05) round-trip.

Cathédrale Notre-Dame de Laon. 8 rue du Cloître, off place Aubry. ☎ 03-23- 20-26-54. Free admission. Daily 8:30am to 6:30pm.

Most visitors head first to this famous cathedral with the huge carved oxen on its facade. Having escaped World War I relatively unharmed, it stands on the same spot where an ancient basilica stood until it was destroyed by fire in 1111. The structure has six towers, four of which are complete. Inside are stained glass, some panels dating from the 13th century, and an 18th-century choir grille. Tours are conducted from Easter to October on weekends only at 3pm. The cost is 35 F ($5.60) and can be arranged through the tourist office.

After visiting the cathedral, stroll down the pedestrians-only **rue Châtelaine,** Laon's major shopping street.

Musée Archéologique Municipal. 32 rue George-Ermant. ☎ **03-23-20-19-87.** Admission 20 F ($3.20) adults, 15 F ($2.40) students and children. Wed–Mon 10am–noon and 2–6pm (to 5pm Oct–Apr).

This museum was founded in 1861 and remained rather sleepy until 1937, when a collection of 1,700 artifacts (mainly from Greece, Rome, Egypt, Cyprus, and Asia Minor) was added, as well as a collection of French painting and sculpture.

ACCOMMODATIONS

Hostellerie St-Vincent. 29 av. Charles-de-Gaulle, 02000 Laon. ☎ **03-23-23-42-43.** Fax 03-23-79-22-55. 47 units. TV TEL. 305 F ($48.80) double. AE, MC, V.

At the edge of the city, near the point where the road from Reims (A26) enters the Basse Ville, this simple two-star hotel is the most modern and comfortable in town, with basic but comfortable guest rooms. The restaurant is noted for its good food, served in a setting accented by lots of plants and a serpentine staircase that acts as the focal point of the dining room. Meals are served from noon to 2:30pm and 7 to 9:30pm; closed Saturday at lunch and Sunday night.

Hôtel de la Bannière de France. 11 rue Franklin-D.-Roosevelt, 02000 Laon. ☎ **03-23-23-21-44.** Fax 03-23-23-31-56. www.leisureplanet.com. E-mail: hotel.banniere.de.france@wanadoo.fr. 18 units. TV TEL. 460 F ($73.60) double. Rates include breakfast. AE, CB, DC, MC, V. Closed May 1 and Dec 20–Jan 20. Parking 35 F ($5.60).

This revered hotel, built in 1685, is located in the most historic part of Laon, Haute Ville. Despite its antique-looking facade, its interior has been completely modernized, though an attempt was made to maintain the ambience of a traditional French hotel. The rooms are small but comfortably furnished and cozy. The personality of the owner, Paul Lefevre, is most obvious in the traditional restaurant, open daily from noon to 2pm and 6:30 to 9:30pm. The flavorful menu items include trout poached in champagne, sole *à la normande,* and a delicious version of chocolate profiteroles. Fixed-price menus range from 93 F to 325 F ($14.90 to $52).

DINING

Hostellerie St-Vincent and **Hôtel de la Bannière de France** (see "Accommodations," above) both contain very good restaurants.

Brasserie du Parvis. Place du Parvis. ☎ **03-23-20-27-27.** Reservations recommended. Main courses 39–89 F ($6.25–$14.25); fixed-price menus 65–150 F ($10.40–$24). Daily 11:30am–3:30pm and 6–11pm. MC, V. PICARD/FRENCH.

The allure here is the location directly opposite the main facade of the Cathedral of Laon. When the weather is warm, the outdoor tables, facing the church, are hard to snag. Inside, the owners redecorate frequently, always focusing on whatever festival or calendar event happens to be in the minds of local residents, including eclipses of the sun or moon, local music or medieval festivals, etc. Menu items include a *ficelle Picard,* a kind of crêpe made with ham and mushrooms; a pungent tart of local maroilles cheese; T-bone steak with béarnaise sauce; and a very ethnic version of chitterling sausages, *les andouillettes de Troyes* with mustard sauce. More appetizing, at least to many North American palates, is a chicken cutlet with a mushroom-flavored cream sauce.

AMIENS

A major textile center since medieval days, Amiens was the ancient capital of Picardy, set on the south bank of the Somme, where it divides into a complex series of canals and irrigation networks. Its old town, a jumble of narrow streets crisscrossed by canals, is run-down and seedy but still worth exploring. The city's focal point is its world-famous Gothic cathedral, one of France's finest. The edge of the modern town begins several blocks south of the cathedral, around the Tour Perret.

ESSENTIALS

GETTING THERE   If you're **driving** from Reims, take A26 north 28 miles to Laon, then travel west on N44 to N32, which becomes D934 en route to Amiens. The distance traveled is 68 miles; however, the trek may take you more than $1^1/_2$ hours because of the country roads you'll be traversing after you exit A26. Amiens is adjacent to the main autoroute (A1) connecting Paris with Lille. Driving time from Paris is about 90 minutes. Drivers coming from the northern suburbs of Paris usually prefer to take A16, which passes near Amiens on its way to Calais.

Reaching Amiens by **train** from Reims requires a transfer in Laon (which you can explore before continuing on; see above) or Tergnier. Trains are relatively infrequent—only three a day—and take 80 minutes to 3 hours, depending on the schedule.

Many visitors come here straight from Paris, for Amiens sits astride the main rail lines connecting Paris's Gare du Nord with Lille. Depending on the season, four or five trains a day make the trip, taking 65 minutes each way. The rail station in Amiens is at place Alphonse-Fiquet, a 10-minute walk from the old town. For train information and schedules, call ☎ **08-36-35-35-35.**

VISITOR INFORMATION   The **Office de Tourisme** is at 6 bis rue Dusevel (☎ **03-22-71-60-50**).

SEEING THE SIGHTS

Julius Caesar himself praised the fertility of the fields around Amiens. During the Middle Ages, **Les Hortillonnages,** an expanse of almost 600 acres at the eastern edge of the historic core, was set aside for the cultivation of pears, carrots, turnips, and all kinds of herbs and vegetables. Irrigated by a web of canals fed by the Somme, the district is still a commercial garden, producing ample amounts of foodstuffs. Not too long ago, the harvest was floated on barges and in shallow-bottomed boats to the Quai Bélu, near the cathedral, for sale to consumers. Although today the produce is hauled from the fields into the town center by truck and not by boat, the ritual retains its medieval name, the **Marché sur l'Eau,** although locals are increasingly referring to it as **Marché St-Leu.** The tradition continues every Thursday and Saturday from 8 to 11am, when the river's quays are transformed into a huge outdoor vegetable market.

A few paces north of the cathedral, straddling both banks of the Somme, is a cluster of carefully restored 13th- and 14th-century houses arranged within a labyrinth of narrow cobblestone streets. Known as the **Quartier St-Leu,** this is a neighborhood of gift shops, antiques shops, art galleries, boutiques, and cafes.

Jules Verne, author of *20,000 Leagues Under the Sea* and *Journey to the Center of the Earth,* is buried in Amiens, and you may want to visit him at the **Cimetière de la Madeleine,** rue St-Maurice, about half a mile northwest of the town center. His beaux-arts tomb bears a representation of Verne as if physically rising from the dead. The cemetery is open daily from 9am to 7pm. Verne's home is located at 2 rue Charles-Dubois ☎ **03-22-45-37-84.** It's now a research center documenting his life and literary achievements; admission for members of the general public, however, is not encouraged.

✪ **Cathédrale Notre-Dame d'Amiens.** Place Notre-Dame. ☎ **03-22-71-60-50.** Admission 30 F ($4.80). Easter–Oct, daily 8:30am–7pm; Nov–Mar, daily 8:30am–noon and 2–5pm (till 6pm on Sat).

At 469 feet long, this cathedral is the largest church in France. It was begun in 1220 to the plans of Robert de Luzarches and completed around 1270. Its original purpose was to house the head of St. John the Baptist, brought back from the Crusades in 1206. Two unequal towers were added later—the south one in 1366, the north one in 1402. The renowned architect Viollet-le-Duc restored the cathedral in the 1850s.

The Amiens cathedral is the crowning example of French Gothic architecture. In John Ruskin's rhapsodical *Bible of Amiens* (1884), which Proust translated into French, he extolled the door arches. The three portals of the west front are lavishly decorated, important examples of Gothic cathedral sculpture. The portals are surmounted by two galleries. The upper one contains 22 statues of kings; the large rose window is from the 16th century.

Inside are beautifully carved stalls and a Flamboyant Gothic choir screen. These stalls with some 3,500 figures were made by local artisans in the early 16th century. The interior is held up by 126 slender pillars, the zenith of the High Gothic in the north of France. The cathedral somehow managed to escape destruction in World War II. In 1996, the *Portail de la Mère-Dieu* (Portal of the Mother of God), to the right of the cathedral's main entrance as you look over the facade, was restored at enormous expense.

Musée de Picardie. 48 rue de la République. ☎ **03-22-97-14-00.** Admission 20 F ($3.20) adults, 12 F ($1.90) students and children. Temporary exhibitions may require a 20–35 F ($3.20–$5.60) surcharge. Tues–Sun 10am–12:30pm and 2–6pm.

This museum occupies a building constructed from 1855 to 1867. The palace of the Napoleonic dynasty, inaugurated by Napoléon III, is divided into three sections, including one devoted to archaeology. Other sections include exhibits on the Roman occupation of Gaul, the Merovingian era, ancient Greece, and Egypt. One collection documents the Middle Ages with ivories, enamels, art objects, and sculpture. The sculpture and painting collection traces the European schools from the 16th to the 20th centuries, with works by El Greco, Maurice Quentin de La Tour, Guardi, and Tiepolo. Fragonard's *Les Lavandières* is his most beautiful work here.

ACCOMMODATIONS

Note that **Le Prieuré** also rents rooms.

Hôtel Le Carlton. 42 rue de Noyon, 80000 Amiens. ☎ **03-22-97-72-22.** Fax 03-22-97-72-00. 25 units. TV TEL. 400–640 F ($64–$102.40) double; 1,000 F ($160) suite. AE, DC, MC, V.

From a glance at this hotel's Napoléon III architecture, you'll immediately see that this is Amiens's stellar choice. Though it's geared toward business travelers, the rooms are luxurious, with rich furniture and murals of turn-of-the-century cityscapes. Appointments include well-maintained bedrooms, with quality mattresses and fine linens resting on comfortable beds. The public areas include a reception area, English bar, and deluxe brasserie-style restaurant. All have the elegant style of polished dark woods and deep hunter-green and burgundy walls. Menus range from 69 F to 105 F ($11.05 to $16.80).

Relais Mercure. Amiens Cathedrale, 17–19 place au Feurre, 8000 Amiens. ☎ **03-22-22-00-20.** Fax 03-22-91-86-57. 47 units. TV TEL. 480–510 F ($76.80–$81.60) double. AE, DC, MC, V. Free parking.

This hotel lies directly opposite the main facade of Amiens' most legendary building, the cathedral. It was purchased by France's biggest hotel conglomerate in 1997, and radically upgraded a year later. The renovation managed to preserve the stately facade and some of the antique beams in many of its bedrooms, while giving the interior a clean, unfussy, modern look. The pricier rooms contain cramped but cozy sitting areas; the less expensive units are smaller and more functional. Some have windows overlooking the cathedral. Rooms rarely rise above that of a good standard motel, but come with comfortable beds and fine mattresses. Overall, the place provides good value, an unbeatable location, and the cost-consciousness of the Accor group. A woodsy-looking pub on the premises serves coffee and drinks but no food. Other than breakfast, no meals of any kind are served.

DINING

Les Marissons. 68 rue des Marissons. ☎ **03-22-92-96-66.** Reservations recommended. Main courses 125–158 F ($20–$25.30); fixed-price menus 120–295 F ($19.20–$47.20). AE, DC, MC, V. Mon–Fri noon–2pm; Mon–Sat 7–10pm. Closed Dec 20–Jan 5. FRENCH.

Two or three places around town match the quality of the food here, but none of them offers such a charming antique setting. The restaurant sits in a heavily timbered 15th-century building that's adjacent to one of the city's oldest bridges (pont de la Dodane). The cuisine is elegantly and flavorfully presented by chef Antoine Benoit and is defined as a celebration of Picardy. Menu specialties include pâté made from local ducklings, roast lamb *pré-salé* from the salt marshes off the English Channel, scallops baked in their shells, and succulent sea bass prepared whole and presented with morels. In summer you can dine on the terrace in the garden.

AMIENS AFTER DARK

Try the **Riverside Café,** place du Don (☎ **03-22-92-50-30**), with its movie posters and photos of 1960s American icons filling the walls and an active young crowd filling the seats; or the **Café Expo Vents et Marées,** 48 rue du Don (☎ **03-22-92-37-78**), where you can absorb the fusion of rock, alcohol, and comic strips—exhibits of original art boards from France's most famous strips. You'll find the largest number of nightspots around quai Bélu.

If you're big on musical events, head for a place next to the train station: **Le Grand Wazoo,** 5 rue Vulfran-Warmé (☎ **03-22-91-64-91**). Named in honor of Frank Zappa, this cool club with its exotic Arab decor draws a mixed crowd intent on listening to local musicians as well as groups famous throughout the continent. Concerts are generally scheduled on Fridays and Saturdays and range from techno and reggae to punk rock. Tickets cost from 10 F to 40 F ($1.60 to $6.40).

While you're checking out the nightlife along the canal area, stop in the old medieval house that's home to the traditional wine bar **La Queue de Vache** (the Cow's Tail), 51 quai Bélu (☎ **03-22-91-38-91**), where you'll be gregariously welcomed and immediately drawn into the heady atmosphere of half-timbered walls, fireplaces, live jazz, and (on occasion) accordion music. It's the ideal setting in which to drink good French wine and sample rich, chewy country breads along with aromatic French cheeses.

For dancing, your best bet is **Le Nemo,** 9 rue des Francs-Mûriers (☎ **03-22-97-96-71**), with its spacious interior and majestic frescoes of dolphins and marine life. The mainly young, hip crowd pays as much as 35 F ($5.60) to dive in here. Alternatively, the town's newest disco, **Le Triplex,** 14 rue des Archers (☎ **03-22-92-94-80**), welcomes a clientele mostly aged 28 to 45. A theme bar, **Le Texas Café,** 13 rue des Francs-Mûriers (☎ **03-22-72-19-79**), offers a roster of stiff drinks and a karaoke machine. And if you're gay and on the loose in Amiens, **Les Vaches Folles,** rue de la Dodane, in the Quartier St-Leu (no phone), will offer the chance to meet and talk with like-minded folk who might have dropped in for an after-dinner drink or to hear some music.

6 Epernay

87 miles E of Paris, 16 miles S of Reims

On the left bank of the Marne, Epernay rivals Reims as a center for champagne. Although it only has one-sixth of Reims's population, Epernay today produces nearly as much champagne as its larger sibling. It boasts an estimated 200 miles or more of cellars and tunnels, a veritable warren for storing champagne. These caves are vast vaults cut into the chalk rock on which the town is built. Represented in Epernay are such champagne companies as Moët et Chandon (the largest), Pol Roger, Mercier, and de Castellane.

Epernay's main boulevards are the elegant residential avenue de Champagne, rue Mercier, and rue de Reims, all radiating from place de la République. Two important squares in the narrow streets of the commercial district are place Hughes-Plomb and place des Arcades.

Epernay has been either destroyed or burned nearly two dozen times, as it lay in the path of invading armies, particularly from Germany. Few of its old buildings are left.

However, check out avenue de Champagne for its neoclassical villas and Victorian town houses.

ESSENTIALS

GETTING THERE   If you're **driving** to Epernay from Reims, head south on E51. Thirteen **trains** per day arrive from Paris (trip time: 1¼ hours); there are also 13 trains per day from Reims (trip time: 20 minutes). For train information and schedules, call ☎ **08-36-35-35-35.** The major **bus** link is STDM Trans-Champagne (☎ **03-26-65-17-07** in Epernay for schedules), operating four buses per day Monday through Saturday between Châlons-en-Champagne and Epernay (trip time: 45 minutes); a one-way fare is 34 F ($5.45).

VISITOR INFORMATION   The **Office de Tourisme** is at 7 av. de Champagne (☎ **03-26-53-33-00**).

EXPLORING THE TOWN

Boutiques and shops abound in the pedestrian district of **place des Arcades** and **rue du Général-Leclerc, rue St-Martin,** and **rue Port Lucas.** Here you'll find art galleries, gift shops, and stores selling clothes, antiques, books, and regional food items.

Of course, you may want to stock up on some vintages. You can go to the individual houses along avenue de Champagne—places like **Moët et Chandon,** 18 av. de Champagne (☎ **03-26-51-20-20**); and **Mercier,** 70 av. de Champagne (☎ **03-26-51-22-22**)—or try one of the champagne stores that represent a variety of houses. One of the best is **La Cave Salvatori,** 11 rue Flodoard (☎ **03-26-55-32-32**). More unusual is **La Boutique Achille Princier,** 9 rue Jean-Chandon-Moët (☎ **03-26-54-04-06**), which sells only the well-respected yet rather obscure brand of champagne, Achille Princier.

For an antiques dealer with a wide inventory of antique and semi-antique items, head for **Antiquités Gallice,** 9 rue Gallice (☎ **03-26-54-23-84**), where absolute gems can be found scattered amid the bric-a-brac from many of the attics of old houses throughout the Champagne district.

For champagne gift items like flutes and corks as well as table decorations and linens, visit **La Boutique de Sophie,** 33 rue du Général-Leclerc (☎ **03-26-54-48-56**); **La Boutique Fromm,** 33 rue St-Thibault (☎ **03-26-55-25-64**); and **Camaieu,** 12 rue du Professeur-Langevin (☎ **03-26-51-83-83**). For regional antiques from the 18th and 19th centuries, try **Bonne Époque,** 106 av. Foch (☎ **03-26-54-11-39**).

Moët et Chandon Champagne Cellars. 18 av. de Champagne. ☎ **03-26-51-20-20.** Admission 40 F ($6.40). Daily 9:30–11:30am and 2–4:30pm. Closed holidays.

An expert staff member gives guided tours in English, describing the champagne-making process and filling you in on champagne lore: Napoléon, a friend of Jean-Rémy Moët, used to stop by here for thousands of bottles on his way to the battlefront. The only time he didn't take a supply with him was at Waterloo—and look what happened there. At the end of the tour you're given a complimentary glass of bubbly. No appointment is necessary, except for large groups.

Mercier. 70 av. de Champagne. ☎ **03-26-51-22-22.** Admission 30 F ($4.80). Mon–Fri 9:30–11:30am and 2–4:30pm, Sat–Sun 9:30–11:30am and 2–5pm. Dec–Feb, closed Tues–Wed.

Since Mercier is near Moët et Chandon, you can visit them both on the same day. In the middle of the vineyard, Mercier conducts tours in English of its 11 miles of

Impressions ————————————————————————————

Brothers, brothers, come quickly! I am drinking stars!

—Dom Pérignon

———————————————————————————————————————

tunnels from laser-guided trains. The caves contain one of the world's largest wooden barrels, with a capacity of more than 200,000 bottles. No appointment is necessary if there are fewer than 10 in your group.

ACCOMMODATIONS

Note that **Les Berceaux** (see "Dining," below) also rents rooms.

Best Western Hôtel de Champagne. 30 rue Eugène-Mercier, 51200 Epernay. ☎ **800/ 528-1234** in the U.S., or 03-26-53-10-60. Fax 03-26-51-94-63. www.bw-hotel-champagne. com. E-mail: info@bw-hotel-champagne.com. 33 units. MINIBAR TV TEL. 480–550 F ($76.80– $88) double. AE, MC, DC, V. Free parking.

Built in the 1970s about 200 yards from the Moët et Chandon showroom, near place de la République, this simple inn is one of the best of a modest lot in the town itself. Some rooms are outfitted in modern style; others look vaguely inspired by Louis XV. A generous buffet breakfast is served every morning.

✪ **Royal Champagne.** 51160 Champillon Belevue. ☎ **03-26-52-87-11.** Fax 03-26-52-89-69. www.relaischateaux.com. E-mail: royalchampagne@wanadoo.fr. 29 units. MINIBAR TV TEL. 880–1,350 F ($140.80–$216) double; 1,500–1,800 F ($240–$288) suite. AE, DC, MC, V. Drive 4 miles from Epernay toward Reims on the Route du Vignoble (N2051); the hotel is in the hamlet of Champillon.

Constructed around what was originally built in the 1700s as a relay station for the French postal system, this historic hotel is a member of the prestigious Relais & Châteaux chain. The establishment's historic core contains the reception, bar, and dining facilities; guest rooms are in town house–style accommodations set edge to edge overlooking the nearby vineyards. The units are artfully rustic and very comfortable, exemplifying the coziness of wine-country living. Each comes with a sumptuous bed with luxury mattresses and fine linen.

The food is exceptional, with specialties like lobster ragoût, John Dory with a purée of celery and a truffle-flavored cream sauce, and roast lamb with garlic. The chef Christophe Pufosser is known for classic dishes with an innovative twist. The fixed-price menus cost 300 F and 500 F ($48 and $80); expect to spend 500 F ($80) for an entire à la carte meal.

DINING

Note that the food at **Royal Champagne** (see "Accommodations," above) is also excellent.

Les Berceaux. 13 rue Berceaux, 51200 Epernay. ☎ **03-26-55-28-84.** Fax 03-26-55-10-36. Reservations recommended. Main courses 150–180 F ($24–$28.80); fixed-price menus 140 F ($22.40) at lunch Tues–Fri, 250–330 F ($40–$52.80) at dinner. AE, DC, MC, V. Tues–Sun noon–2:30pm; Tues–Sat 7–9:30pm. CHAMPENOIS.

Owner and veteran chef Patrick Michelon serves generous portions of flavorful and relatively conservative Champenois cuisine. The menus change seasonally but always feature fresh produce (from the region whenever possible) and superior cuts of fish, meat, and game in season. Particularly scrumptious are such dishes as roasted leg of lamb with an herb-flavored wine sauce; snails in champagne sauce; and a galette of guinea fowl in puff pastry, served with potatoes. Local wines, especially champagne, are showcased. There's a wine bar on the premises where you can sample an assortment of the local vintages by the glass. If it errs at all, this place tends to be a wee bit pretentious and self-important, a flaw that you might best be able to overcome with a touch of humor. There are also 29 comfortably furnished bedrooms available upstairs, each with TV and telephone, comfortable mattresses, adequately thick towels, and decorative references to the champagne industry. A double with bath costs 390 F to 450 F ($62.40 to $72).

EPERNAY AFTER DARK

Start out with a stop at the chic cafe/bar **Le Progrès,** 5 place de la République (☎ **03-26-55-22-72**). This popular place lets you loosen up before the real festivities get under way. For a simple glass of wine or even Scotch (something you don't see enough of in this wine-crazed region of France), consider a visit to **Le Chriss Bar,** 38 rue de Suzanne (☎ **03-26-54-38-47**). Something that rocks and rolls a bit later into the night, sometimes with a live singer or musical act, is **Le Garden Club,** 5 av. Foch (☎ **03-26-54-20-30**), which has an atmosphere more in tune with Paris. Le **Tap-Too,** 5 rue du Près Dimanche (☎ **03-26-51-56-10**), attracts all ages and types to its four dance halls and six bars together in one big warehouse. For live concerts and the occasional lighthearted theatrical performance, head over to the two-story American-style bar/pub **La Marmite Swing,** 160 av. Foch (☎ **03-26-54-17-72**). Most acts take the stage on Friday and Saturday evenings, but the place continues to sizzle during the rest of the week as high-energy partyers work the crowd against a backdrop of techno and rock. For performance nights, expect to pay a cover upward of 60 F ($9.60).

Alsace-Lorraine 10

The provinces of Alsace and Lorraine, with ancient capitals at Strasbourg and Nancy, respectively, have been much disputed by Germany and France. Alsace has been called "the least French of French provinces," more reminiscent of the Black Forest across the Rhine. In fact, it became German from 1870 until after World War I and then was ruled by Hitler from 1940 to 1944. These days, both provinces are back under French control, though they remain somewhat independent.

In the Vosges mountains you can follow **La Route des Crêtes** (Crest Road) or skirt along the foothills, visiting the wine towns of Alsace. In its cities and cathedrals, the castle-dotted landscape evokes memories of a great past and (in battle monuments or scars) sometimes military glory or defeat. Lorraine is Joan of Arc country, and many of its towns still suggest their heritage from the Middle Ages.

There is no clear-cut dividing line that exactly delineates Alsace from Lorraine. Alsace is more German, forming a fertile watershed between the mountains of the Vosges and the Black Forest of Germany. Lorraine, with its gently rolling landscape, is a poorer cousin and appears more French in character.

REGIONAL CUISINE   The ample use of pork and goose fat in Alsatian dishes gives the cuisine a distinctive flavor. Alsace is a leader in the production of pâtés, with more than 40 varieties, so you really must visit a local *charcuterie* (delicatessen) for a sampling. Don't miss the richly flavorful pâté de foie gras (goose-liver pâté).

In Lorraine, the joyful excesses of cholesterol are even more exaggerated. In addition to butter and loads of cream, local chefs use large quantities of salted lard. Even local pot-au-feu (known as *une potes*) replaces beef with salted lard and local pork sausages.

Other regional specialties are *choucroute* (sauerkraut) with sausages, salted ham, pork chops, or (in deluxe versions) truffles; chicken with Riesling; trout in cream, with Riesling, or simply fried (*au bleu*); Alsatian *kouglof* (made with almonds, dried raisins, sugar, milk, flour, and eggs); and a simple tart made with flour, milk, and sugar called *un ramequin*.

The most famous Alsatian beer is Kronenbourg, which you'll find in thousands of bars throughout France. There are more than 90 varieties of Alsatian wines, traditionally drunk from slender flutes whose glass is sometimes colored blue or green. The most celebrated Alsatian varieties are Riesling, gewürztraminer (traminer), and pinot blanc.

Alsace-Lorraine

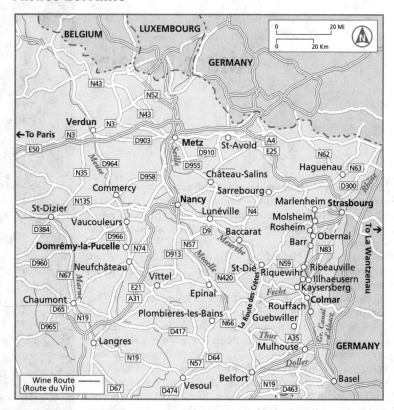

1 Strasbourg

303 miles SE of Paris, 135 miles SW of Frankfurt

The capital of Alsace, Strasbourg is one of France's greatest cities and is also the birthplace of pâté de foie gras. And it was in Strasbourg that Rouget de Lisle first sang "La Marseillaise" (the French national anthem).

Strasbourg is one of France's most important ports, being only 2 miles west of the Rhine. In addition to being host to the Council of Europe, Strasbourg is the meeting place of the European Parliament, which convenes at the Palais de l'Europe.

In 1871, Strasbourg was absorbed by Germany and made the capital of the imperial territory of Alsace-Lorraine, but it reverted to France in 1918. One street is a perfect illustration of the city's identity crisis: More than a century ago it was avenue Napoléon. In 1871, it became Kaiser-Wilhelmstrasse, then turned into boulevard de la République in 1918. In 1940, it became Adolf-Hitler-Strasse, then ended up as avenue du Général-de-Gaulle in 1945.

One of the most happening cities of France, Strasbourg today is the seat of the University of Strasbourg, once attended by the likes of Goethe, Napoléon, and Pasteur. Today some 40,000 students follow in their footsteps.

ESSENTIALS

GETTING THERE The **Strasbourg-Entzheim Airport** (☎ **03-88-64-67-67**), 9 miles southwest of the center, receives daily flights from many major European cities, including Paris, London, Rome, and Frankfurt. You can get from the airport to the center of town by using a well-defined combination of shuttle buses and city trams. They run at 30-minute intervals during the morning and every 15 minutes in the afternoon. The cost of 27 F ($4.30) each way involves taking a shuttle bus to the south side of Strasbourg, to a junction point known as Baggersee. From there, you'll continue to the town center via a tram line. Combined travel time is between 35 and 40 minutes each way. For information, call **Autocars C.T.S.B** (☎ **03-88-77-70-70**).

Strasbourg is also a major railway junction. At least nine **trains** a day arrive from Paris's Gare de l'Est (trip time: 4 hours). From Nancy, there are 13 trains per day (trip time: 90 minutes). For railway information and schedules, call ☎ **08-36-35-35-35.**

By **car,** the giant N83 highway, with many lanes, crosses the plain of Alsace and becomes at times the A35 expressway. It links Strasbourg with Colmar and Mulhouse.

VISITOR INFORMATION   The **Office de Tourisme** is on place de la Cathédrale (☎ **03-88-52-28-28**).

SPECIAL EVENTS   **Wolf Music,** 24 rue de la Mésange (☎ **03-88-32-43-10**), puts on two summer festivals: the classical **Festival International de Musique** in June and the **Festival de Jazz** (☎ **03-88-15-29-19** for information) in the first week of July. Both feature performances by internationally acclaimed artists and always draw a large crowd despite the hefty ticket prices of 130 F to 420 F ($20.80 to $67.20); tickets go on sale in mid-April. The **Festival International des Musiques d'Aujourd'hui** is organized by the association Musica (☎ **03-88-23-47-23**). It takes place from the end of September to the first week of October and combines contemporary music concerts with movies and modern opera performances. Tickets are 80 F to 110 F ($12.80 to $17.60) and go on sale at the end of June.

SEEING THE SIGHTS

Despite war damage, much remains of Old Strasbourg, including covered bridges and towers from its former fortifications, plus many 15th- and 17th-century dwellings with painted wooden fronts and carved beams.

The city's traffic hub is **place Kléber,** dating from the 15th century. Sit here with a tankard of Alsatian beer and slowly get to know Strasbourg. The bronze statue in the center is of J. B. Kléber, born in Strasbourg in 1753; he became one of Napoléon's most noted generals and was buried under the monument. Apparently his presence offended the Nazis, who removed the statue in 1940. However, this Alsatian bronze was restored to its proper place in 1945 at the Liberation.

Next, take rue des Grandes-Arcades southeast to **place Gutenberg,** one of the city's oldest squares and formerly a *marché aux herbes.* The central statue (1840) by David d'Angers is of Gutenberg, who perfected his printing press in Strasbourg in the winter of 1436 to 1437. The former town hall, now the **Hôtel du Commerce,** was built in 1582 and is one of the most significant Renaissance buildings in all Alsace.

La Petite France is the most interesting quarter of Strasbourg. Its 16th-century houses are mirrored in the waters of the Ill River. In "Little France," old roofs with gray tiles have sheltered families for ages, and the cross-beamed facades with their roughly carved rafters are in typical Alsatian style. Rue du Bain-aux-Plantes is of particular interest. An island in the middle of the river is cut by four canals—for a good view, walk along rue des Moulins, branching off from rue du Bain-aux-Plantes.

✪ **Cathédrale Notre-Dame de Strasbourg.** Place de la Cathédrale. ☎ **03-88-21-43-34,** or 03-88-21-43-30 for the precise times of all the masses and offices. Tower 20 F ($3.20) adults, 10 F ($1.60) children. Tower July–Aug, daily 8:30am–7pm. (You may have to wait to climb the tower.) Close-up views of the clock available noon–12:30pm for 5 F (80¢); tickets on sale daily in the south portal from 11:30am.

Exploring Strasbourg by Boat

One of the most romantic ways to spend your time in Strasbourg is to take an excursion on the **Ill River,** leaving from the Palais de Rohan near the cathedral. Daytime outings operate year-round, but night excursions are offered only from May to October. The 75-minute cruise is 41 F ($6.55) for adults and 20.50 F ($3.30) for children and includes a prerecorded running commentary (in English and in French) on the history of the region. Between April and November, rides depart at 30-minute intervals every day between 9:30am and 9pm. Between December and March, there are departures only at 10:30am, 1pm, 2:30pm, and 4pm. Information is provided by the Strasbourg-Fluvial, 15 rue de Nantes (☎ **03-88-84-13-13**).

The city's crowning glory stands proudly, an outstanding example of Gothic architecture, representing a harmonious transition from the Romanesque. Construction began on it in 1176. The pyramidal tower in rose-colored stone was completed in 1439; at 469 feet, it's the tallest one dating from medieval times. This cathedral is still used for Roman Catholic worship services. Religious ceremonies, particularly on feast days, meld perfectly with the historic majesty of this place. The tower can be visited by individual tourists only during the summer. The Office du Tourisme (see above) organizes tours for groups; call them for the schedule.

Four large counterforts divide the main facade into three vertical parts and two horizontal galleries. Note the great **rose window,** which looks like real stone lace. The facade is rich in sculptural decoration: On the portal of the south transept, the *Coronation and Death of the Virgin* in one of the two tympana is the finest such medieval work. In the north transept, see also the facade of the **Chapelle St-Laurence,** a stunning achievement of the late Gothic German style.

A Romanesque **crypt** lies under the chancel, which is covered with square stonework. The central stained-glass window is the work of Max Ingrand. The **nave** is majestic, with windows depicting emperors and kings on the north Strasbourg aisle. Five chapels are grouped around the transept, including one built in 1500 in the Flamboyant Gothic style. In the south transept stands the **Angel Pillar,** illustrating the Last Judgment, with angels lowering their trumpets.

The **astronomical clock** was built between 1547 and 1574. It stopped working during the Revolution, and from 1838 to 1842 the mechanism was replaced. The clock is wound once a week. People flock to see its 12:30pm show of allegorical figures. On Sunday Apollo drives his sun horses, on Thursday you see Jupiter and his eagle, and so on. The main body of the clock has a planetarium based on the theories of Copernicus.

Église St-Thomas. Rue Martin-Luther (along rue St-Thomas, near pont St-Thomas). ☎ **03-88-32-14-46.** Free admission. Mar–Oct, daily 10am–noon and 2–6pm; Nov–Dec, daily 10am–noon and 2–5pm. Closed Jan–Feb.

Built between 1230 and 1330, this Protestant church boasts five naves. It contains the mausoleum of Maréchal de Saxe, a masterpiece of French art by Pigalle (1777).

Musée Alsacien. 23 quai St-Nicolas. ☎ **03-88-35-55-36.** Admission 20 F ($3.20) adults, 10 F ($1.60) students, free for children. Mon and Wed–Sat 10am–noon and 1:30–6pm, Sun 10am–5pm.

This occupies three mansions from the 16th and 17th centuries and is like a living textbook of the folklore and customs of Alsace, containing arts, crafts, and tools of the old province.

Strasbourg

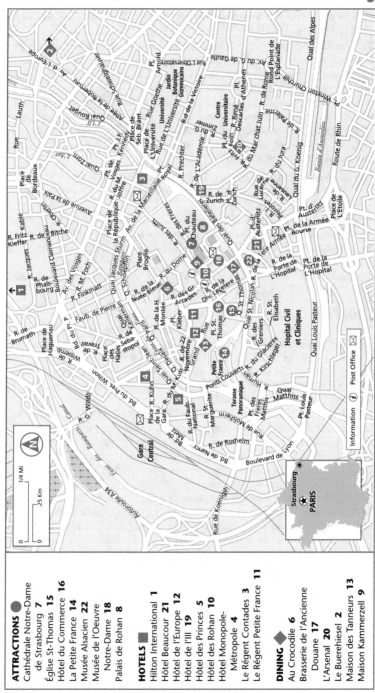

345

Musée de l'Oeuvre Notre-Dame. 3 place du Château. ☎ **03-88-52-50-00.** Admission 20 F ($3.20) adults, 10 F ($1.60) children. Tues–Sun 10am–6pm.

The museum illustrates the art of the Middle Ages and Renaissance in Strasbourg and surrounding Alsace. Some of the pieces were once displayed in the cathedral, where copies have been substituted. The most celebrated prize is a circa-1070 stained-glass head of Christ from a window said to have been at Wissembourg. There's also a stained-glass window depicting an emperor from around 1200. The medieval sculpture is of great interest, as are the works of Strasbourg goldsmiths from the 16th and 17th centuries. The winding staircase and interior are in the pure Renaissance style. The 13th-century hall contains the loveliest sculptures from the cathedral, including the wise and foolish virgins from 1280.

Palais de Rohan. 2 place du Château. ☎ **03-88-52-50-00.** Admission 20 F ($3.20) adults, 10 F ($1.60) students, free for children 15 and under. Mon and Wed–Sat 10am–noon and 1:30–6pm, Sun 10am–5pm.

This palace, located south of the cathedral, was built from 1732 to 1742. It's an example of supreme elegance and proportion. Noted for its facades and rococo interior, it's one of the crowning design achievements in eastern France. On the first floor is a fine-arts museum (Musée des Beaux Arts), with works by Rubens, Rembrandt, Van Dyck, El Greco, Goya, Watteau, Renoir, and Monet. A decorative-arts museum exhibits ceramics and the original machinery of the cathedral's first astronomical clock.

SHOPPING

Strasbourg overflows with antiques shops, artisans, craftspeople, and beer makers. Every well-accessorized home in Alsace stocks at least some of the napkins, aprons, tablecloths, and tea and bath towels of the Beauvillé textile mills, one of eastern France's largest producers. One of its premier outlets is **Nappes d'Alsace,** 6 rue Mercière (☎ **03-88-22-69-29**). Very close to the cathedral, this store has one of the widest selections of textiles in town.

Bastian, 22–24 place de la Cathédrale (☎ **03-88-32-45-93**), specializes in the 18th- and 19th-century ceramic tureens that Alsace produced with charm and abundance. Look for ragoût pots in the form of a cabbage, a trout, a boar's head, or a turkey, brightly painted in appetizing colors. There's also a selection of Louis XV and Louis XVI furniture, crafted in the region during the 18th and 19th centuries, that follows Parisian models from the same era.

Bastian's main competitor is **Antiquités de l'Ill,** 23 quai des Bateliers (☎ **03-88-36-96-84**), in a Renaissance-style 17th-century building across from the Palais de Rohan. Standout items are polychromed Alsatian antiques (especially 18th- and 19th-century armoires and chests of drawers), Louis- and Directoire-style furnishings, and statues and antique paintings.

More affordable and accessible is **Arts et Collections d'Alsace,** 18 quai des Bateliers (☎ **03-88-14-03-77**). This outlet sells copies of articles found exclusively in Alsatian museums or prestigious private collections. Look for articles in wood, glass, stone, and ceramics. A name you're likely to encounter is Soufflenheim, a provincial rococo pattern named after the Alsatian village where the style originated.

If you're looking for ceramics and pottery, consider an excursion 17 miles north to this village. Ceramics and pottery have been staples of the economy here since the Bronze Age, and Soufflenheim contains at least 15 factory outlets selling cake molds, tureens, saucers and cups, and dinnerware sets, usually in rustic patterns of enduring charm. One of the most prominent of the outlets belongs to local manufacturer

Gérard Wehrling, 64 rue de Haguenau (☎ **03-88-86-65-25**). Selling directly to visitors, it's known for pottery that can withstand the rigors of modern ovens, microwaves, and freezers. Expect to pay about 300 F ($48) for a large casserole.

If you're driving around, you may want to check out the nearby villages of Obernai, Illhauesern, Ribeauville, and Schiltigheim (the last is beer-drinking territory; the others offer country wares, antiques, warrenlike old-fashioned streets, and pure charm).

ACCOMMODATIONS
EXPENSIVE

Hilton International Strasbourg. Av. Herrenschmidt, 67000 Strasbourg. ☎ **800/445-8667** in the U.S. and Canada, or 03-88-37-10-10. Fax 03-88-36-83-27. www.hilton_strasbourg.com. E-mail: sales_Strasbourg@hilton.com. 246 units. A/C MINIBAR TV TEL. 1,200–1,700 F ($192–$272) double; from 2,700 F ($432) suite. AE, DC, MC, V. Parking 65–85 F ($10.40–$13.60). Take the Strasbourg-Centre exit from the autoroute and follow signs to the Wacken, Palais des Congrès, and Palais de l'Europe.

The seven-story Hilton International is quite luxurious. The steel-and-glass hotel stands over a university complex and is opposite the Palais de la Musique et des Congrès. Five kinds of Iberian marble were used in the decor, much of it chosen to resemble the ruddy sandstone of the famous cathedral, visible from the hotel. The guest rooms contain tasteful artwork and spacious marble-trimmed bathrooms; some are suitable for nonsmokers or persons with disabilities. Rooms are medium to spacious, with quality mattresses and fine linens.

Dining/Diversions: Live music and guests ranging from heads of state to international visitors make the hotel's Bugatti Bar the town's social center. The moderately priced Le Jardin du Tivoli offers a buffet at all three meals. Some evenings are devoted to special themes, like seafood, Italian, or vegetarian. There's also a brasserie and a buffet, and La Table du Chef, open for lunch from Monday to Saturday.

Amenities: 24-hour room service, dry cleaning/laundry, boutique, interpretive/secretarial facilities.

☼ Le Régent Petite France. 5 rue des Moulins, 67000 Strasbourg. ☎ **800/223-5652** in the U.S. and Canada, or 03-88-76-43-43. Fax 03-88-76-43-76. www.regent-hotels.com. E-mail: rpf@regent-hotels.com. 72 units. 1,280–1,650 F ($204.80–$264) double; 2,000–2,600 F ($320–$416) suite. AE, DC, MC, V.

This is the first serious challenger in years to the Hilton. Many guests check in here for its more comfortable rooms and more intriguing atmosphere. This site on the banks of the Ill was once an ice factory, and many of its old steam machines were wisely kept in place as artifacts of a vanished era. The large marble lobby sets the design note, with summery ice-cream colors, potted palms, and paintings. Guest rooms come in various sizes, the best of which are quite spacious and open onto river views. The luxurious beds are among the city's finest. The staff is one of the most professional in Strasbourg.

Dining: The river-view restaurant, Au Pont Tournant, serves fine Alsatian cuisine.

Amenities: Jacuzzi, sauna, concierge, room service, dry cleaning/laundry, fitness club.

MODERATE

Hôtel Beaucour. 5 rue Bouchers, 67000 Strasbourg. ☎ **03-88-76-72-00.** Fax 03-88-76-72-60. www.hotel-beaucour.com. E-mail: beaucour@hotel-beaucour.com. 49 units. A/C MINIBAR TV TEL. 780 F ($124.80) double; from 950 F ($152) suite. AE, DC, MC, V. Parking 45 F ($7.20).

This three-star hotel is geared mainly to business travelers, but anyone will find it ideal. At the end of a private street a few blocks east of the cathedral, it occupies a 17th-century building with lots of timbered ceilings and is the city's most tranquil hotel. Both the rooms and the suites harmoniously blend modern and traditional furnishings; every room has a whirlpool tub, a fax hookup, and computer connections. Furnishings are in a standard international style, but quite comfortable, with deluxe mattresses. The hotel maintains an affiliation with three restaurants a short walk away. The concierge, who seems to know all the city's secrets, will gladly make reservations for you.

Hôtel de l'Europe. 38–40 rue du Fosse-des-Tanneurs, 67000 Strasbourg. ☎ **03-88-32-17-88.** Fax 03-88-75-65-45. www.hotel-europe.com. E-mail: info@hotel-europe.com. 60 units. MINIBAR TV TEL. 610–950 F ($97.60–$152) double. AE, DC, MC, V. Parking 70 F ($11.20).

Behind a half-timbered facade a 3-minute walk west of the cathedral, this is one of the best-located three-star hotels in town. Its roots go back to the 15th century, when it functioned as a coaching inn; it was later enlarged with the annexation of an 18th-century house next door. Frequently renovated, it's comfortable and unpretentious, with an elevator and all the electronic gadgets you might want. About a third of the rooms are air-conditioned. They run the gamut from glossily modern to a half-timbered fantasy directly under the roof (no. 404), where steeply angled beams evoke the original construction. There's no in-house restaurant, but room service is available 24 hours.

☼ Hôtel des Rohan. 17–19 rue du Maroquin, 67000 Strasbourg. ☎ **03-88-32-85-11.** Fax 03-88-75-65-37. www.hotel-rohan.com. E-mail: info@hotel-rohan.com. 36 units. A/C MINIBAR TV TEL. 795 F ($127.20) double. AE, DC, MC, V.

In the pedestrian-only zone, 50 yards from the cathedral, this is one of the city's best values, with nearby underground parking. The hotel is within walking distance of the Palais des Rohan. It offers a choice of elegantly furnished rooms, the cheapest of which are small and have a French bed called a *matrimonial*, which is a standard double bed. Large and more classic rooms have either a large double bed or twin beds. Each comes with a good mattress.

Hôtel Monopole-Métropole. 16 rue Kuhn, 67000 Strasbourg. ☎ **800/528-1234** in the U.S., or 03-88-14-39-14. Fax 03-88-32-82-55. www.bw-monopole.com. E-mail: info@bw-monopole.com. 90 units. MINIBAR TV TEL. 585–800 F ($93.60–$128) double. AE, DC, MC, V. Parking 60 F ($9.60).

Monopole-Métropole is on a quiet street corner near the train station and has a modern lobby with a scattering of antiques, among them a 17th-century carved armoire and a bronze statue of a night watchman. An extension of the salon displays oil portraits of 18th-century Alsatian personalities and glass cases with pewter tankards and brass candlesticks. Breakfast (the only meal served) is presented in the high-ceilinged Alsatian-style dining room. Each guest room is unique; many contain Louis-Philippe antiques. The bedrooms are most comfortable, especially in the selection of mattresses and white crisp linen. Léon and Monique Siegel are the proprietors; members of their family have owned this place since 1919.

☼ Le Régent Contades. 8 av. de la Liberté, 67000 Strasbourg. ☎ **03-88-15-05-05.** Fax 03-88-15-05-15. www.regent-hotels.com. E-mail: re@regent-hotels.com. 45 units. A/C MINIBAR TV TEL. 695–1,390 F ($111.20–$222.40) double; 1,650–2,200 F ($264–$352) suite. AE, DC, MC, V.

Our favorite moderately priced choice in Strasbourg is this glorified B&B, housed in a regal three-story structure with dormers, close to both the cathedral and the Rhine.

Diplomats often guard it as a secret address, but the secret is out. The hostelry is stylish and fashionable and has an intelligent and helpful staff. The guest rooms are alluring, furnished with classic style. The most spacious are in a new wing offering 14 accommodations. Breakfast is the only meal served, though 24-hour room service is available. Amenities include a sauna and solarium.

INEXPENSIVE

Hôtel de l'Ill. 8 rue des Bateliers, 67000 Strasbourg. ☎ **03-88-36-20-01.** Fax 03-88-35-30-03. 27 units. TV TEL. 250–370 F ($40–$59.20) double. MC, V. Parking 45 F ($7.20). Bus: 10 direct from the train station.

A 5-minute walk from the cathedral, this two-star hotel is a good value. An inviting little place, it offers quiet, comfortably furnished rooms. Each is in either a modern or an Alsatian traditional style. Smoking and non-smoking rooms are available. Those at the rear contain a private terrace or balcony, opening onto a view of neighboring gardens. Even though the bedrooms don't have a lot of room, you get good comfort here, especially in the beds which have quality mattresses and good linen. The breakfast room is decorated Laura Ashley–style, well, except for the cuckoo clock, that is.

Hôtel des Princes. 33 rue Geiler, Conseil de l'Europe, 67000 Strasbourg. ☎ **03-88-61-55-19.** Fax 03-88-41-10-92. www.strasbourg.com/hotel-princes. E-mail: princes@strasbourg.com. 43 units. TV TEL. 450–580 F ($72–$92.80) double. AE, MC, V. Bus: 20.

A 15-minute walk from the center of town, the Hôtel des Princes has received a three-star government rating and is one of the best values in the city. The management is helpful, and the rooms are furnished comfortably but simply. A continental breakfast is the only meal served.

DINING
VERY EXPENSIVE

✪ **Au Crocodile.** 10 rue de l'Outre. ☎ **03-88-32-13-02.** Reservations required. Main courses 195–385 F ($31.20–$61.60); fixed-price menus 310–450 F ($49.60–$72) at lunch, 460–740 F ($73.60–$118.40) at dinner. AE, DC, MC, V. Tues–Sat noon–1:45pm and 7–9:30pm. Closed the last 3 weeks of July and Dec 24–Jan 8. ALSATIAN.

A beautifully skylit restaurant, Au Crocodile serves some of the most inventive food in Strasbourg. If we awarded more than one star, we'd give this one three. There are only two restaurants in this entire region of France to equal it: Buerehiesel (below) and the Auberge de l'Ill (see section 3, "Colmar," in this chapter). Chef Emile Jung offers a wide array of dishes. Some of the best include a duck liver terrine fried with rhubarb and ginger; a confit of quail with foie gras of duckling; red snapper encased in a crust of confit of lemon and served with stewed artichokes; and a crispy guinea fowl with spinach and truffles. The menu continues to be charged with energy and inventiveness. Our major problem with the place comes only when the bill (or *la note*, as the French say) does, especially when you indulge in those high-priced wines.

✪ **Le Buerehiesel.** 4 parc de l'Orangerie. ☎ **03-88-45-56-65.** Reservations required. Main courses 290–420 F ($46.40–$67.20); fixed-price menus 520–790 F ($83.20–$126.40). AE, DC, MC, V. Thurs–Mon noon–2pm and 7:30–9:30pm. Closed 1 week in Dec, 1 week in Jan, 1 week in Feb, and first 2 weeks in Aug. FRENCH.

Also known as Le Restaurant Westermann, Buerehiesel is famous for Antoine Westermann's *cuisine moderne*, as well as for the restaurant's prime location. It's in l'Orangerie, a beautiful park at the end of the allée de la Robertsau that was planned by the landscape artist Le Nôtre, who gave it to Joséphine during her marriage to Napoléon. Main courses might include sole and lobster *à la nage* (cooked in court bouillon and flavored with herbs). Of special merit is a whole Bresse chicken whose preparation varies according to the season and the inspiration of the chef. A mid-winter preparation might be with truffles and herbs; in summer, it might come with a medley of potatoes, artichoke hearts, confit of lemon, and rosemary. We cannot praise the cuisine too highly. Distantly remembered recipes are brought down from the attic and recycled here in innovative and exciting ways. Even though the place elevates stuffiness to an art form, the movers and shakers of the European Union seem to lap it up.

MODERATE

L'Arsenal. 11 rue de l'Abreuvoir. ☎ **03-88-35-03-69.** Reservations required. Main courses 80–130 F ($12.80–$20.80); fixed-price menus 145–250 F ($23.20–$40). AE, DC, MC, V. Tues–Fri noon–2pm; Mon–Sat 7:15–9:30pm. Closed Aug 1–21. ALSATIAN.

This pleasant Alsatian restaurant is in a historic building and often counts European Parliament members among its patrons. The inventive regional menu changes often but may feature young rabbit and goose liver in jelly, veal escalope and calf's feet in red-wine sauce, or carp filets of zandar and salmon on a bed of sauerkraut. A specialty of the house is *kouglhof* with escargots—normally this pastry is sweet, but the chef here makes it salted with snails.

Maison des Tanneurs. 42 rue du Bain-aux-Plantes. ☎ **03-88-32-79-70.** Reservations required. Main courses 125–170 F ($20–$27.20); fixed-price menus 235–285 F ($37.60–$45.60). AE, DC, MC, V. Tues–Sat noon–2:15pm and 7:15–10pm (also open for Sun lunches in Dec). Closed 3 weeks in mid-summer. ALSATIAN.

This restaurant stands on a typical street in the Petite France quarter; inside, the over-worked staff sometimes rushes frantically from one task to another. Flowers and Alsatian antiques create a warm atmosphere, and the dining terrace opens onto the canal. It has been called La Maison de la Choucroute, as the sauerkraut-and-pork platter is a specialty, the finest in the area. But the chef prepares many other dishes as well, including an extravagant parfait of foie gras with fresh truffles. Main courses we recommend are crayfish tails in court bouillon, guinea fowl with green peppercorns served on a bed of sauerkraut, and *coq au Riesling* (chicken cooked in white wine and served with noodles).

Maison Kammerzell. 16 place de la Cathédrale. ☎ **03-88-32-42-14.** Reservations required. Main courses 89–155 F ($14.25–$24.80); fixed-price menus 184–295 F ($29.45–$47.20). AE, DC, MC, V. Daily noon–2:30pm and 7–11pm. ALSATIAN.

The gingerbread Maison Kammerzell is a sightseeing attraction as well as a fantastic restaurant. The carved-wood framework was constructed during the Renaissance; the overhanging stories were built in 1589. We suggest *la choucroute formidable* (for two), the Alsatian specialty prepared with goose fat and Riesling wine, as well as Strasbourg sausages and smoked breast of pork. The owner, Guy-Pierre Baumann, also offers guinea hen with mushrooms, medaillon of young wild boar, filet of beef Vigneronne with vegetables, and other regional dishes.

A recent concession to modern cuisine is the chef's version of sauerkraut with fish. Families will want to take advantage of the free meals for children under 10 every day at lunch. The policy has made the place immensely popular with big broods; if you want to eat your sauerkraut in peace and quiet, come for dinner.

INEXPENSIVE

✪ **Brasserie de l'Ancienne Douane.** 6 rue de la Douane. ☎ **03-88-15-78-78.** Reservations recommended. Main courses 73–110 F ($11.70–$17.60); fixed-price menus 85–125 F ($13.60–$20); children's menu 48 F ($7.70). AE, DC, MC, V. Daily 11:30am–11pm. ALSATIAN.

This is the largest and most colorful dining spot in Strasbourg. Established as part of a historic renovation, it offers 600 seats indoors and 200 seats on a terrace. From the outside, along a street in the oldest part of town, you'll see the arcades of the lower floor and the small windows of the stone facade. The high-ceilinged rooms are somewhat formal, with Teutonic chairs and heavily timbered ceilings. Among the Alsatian specialties are the well-known "sauerkraut of the Customs officers" and the foie gras of Strasbourg. Chicken in Riesling with Alsatian noodles, onion pie, and ham knuckle with potato salad and horseradish also are popular dishes.

NEARBY DINING

Instead of dining in Strasbourg, many visitors drive north $7^1/_2$ miles to the village of La Wantzenau, which has very good restaurants. From Strasbourg, take D468, which runs along the west bank of the Rhine.

✪ **À la Barrière.** 3 rte. de Strasbourg, 67610 la Wantzenau. ☎ **03-88-96-20-23.** Reservations required. Main courses 85–175 F ($13.60–$28); fixed-price menus 260–400 F ($41.60–$64). AE, DC, MC, V. Thurs–Mon noon–2:30pm and 7–9:30pm. Closed Feb and Aug 7–30. FRENCH.

This restaurant is a 5-minute walk from the center of La Wantzenau. In a restrained Art Deco interior, the chefs prepare a sophisticated cuisine. The menu might include fillet of sole with scallops and scampi in ginger sauce, roast rack of lamb with a potato casserole, white ocean fish with celery and tomatoes, and salmon steaks with sorrel. In autumn the game dishes (especially pheasant and venison) are excellent.

STRASBOURG AFTER DARK

For family fun in July and August, head to La Petite France and its ponts Converts around 9 or 10pm for *Les Nuits de Strass*—a water-show spectacular with fountains, lasers, music, and entertainers. Another bastion of outdoor entertainment is **place de la Cathédrale,** where you can find an astonishing assortment of street performers and artists. For a chance to see folk-dancing troupes from the world over, go to the **Palais des Rohan** around 8:30pm in summer. From mid-July to about August 8, additional open-air folkloric dances are presented within La Petite France every Monday at 8pm in the places des Tripiers, every Tuesday at 8pm in the place Benjamin Zix, and every Wednesday in the place du Marché aux Chochons de Lait. Performance dates vary, so check with the Office de Tourisme (see "Essentials," above) for a precise schedule.

PERFORMING ARTS   For opera and ballet, try the **Opéra du Rhin,** 19 place Broglie (☎ 03-88-75-48-01); tickets range from 70 F to 330 F ($11.20 to $52.80). The **Orchestre Philharmonique de Strasbourg** gives concerts at the Palais de la Musique et des Congrès, place de Bordeaux (☎ **03-88-15-09-00**). Tickets cost 125 F to 245 F ($20 to $39.20). The **Théâtre National de Strasbourg** plays a busy schedule at 1 av. de la Marseillaise (☎ **03-88-24-88-24**). Tickets cost 140 F ($22.40).

CLUBS   For the **club scene,** head over to the streets surrounding place de la Cathédrale: rue des Frères, rue des Soeurs, and rue de la Croix. For jazz and blues, your best bets are **Gayot,** 18 rue des Frères (☎ 03-88-36-31-88), with occasional guest performers; and the more refined though still sultry **Le Bistro Piano Bar,** 30 rue des Tonneliers (☎ **03-88-23-02-71**), with a jazz piano player and free concerts Wednesday, Friday, and Saturday. **Café des Anges,** 5 rue Ste-Catherine (☎ **03-88-37-12-67**), provides an underground dance floor converted from an old wine cellar as well as a ground-level bar area. The dance club never has a cover charge.

    Le Seven, 25 rue des Tonneliers (no phone), has a below-street-level dance floor that features any type of music but disco. The place stays packed with a stylish crowd between 20 and 35. Cover charges range between 35 F and 50 F ($5.60 and $8).

One of the biggest and most visible discos in the region lies 4¹/₂ miles north of Strasbourg. (To reach it, follow the signs to Wantzenau.) It's **Le Chalet,** 376 rte. de Wantzenau (☎ **03-88-31-18-31**), where a 55 F ($8.80) entrance fee buys the first drink, and the right to parade at will between two distinctively different sections. One is designed for techno, heavy-metal fans, another for less harsh dance music with a good mix of some of the disco classics from the 1980s. Regardless of which section you move into, the contrast usually contributes to a good time, and the huge size of the place guarantees that you'll at least find someone you can talk to.

GAY NIGHTLIFE   Gays and lesbians should head for either of the following sites: **Le Sous-Sol,** 1 rue du Miroir (☎ **03-88-22-22-23**), most of whose clients are men; and **Le Monte Carl',** 1 quai Turkheim (☎ **03-88-22-35-02**), which attracts a mixed gay crowd with a somewhat higher percentage of lesbians.

2 La Route du Vin (Wine Road)

The fastest route between Strasbourg and Colmar, 42 miles to the south, is the N83. But if you've got time to spare, the famous *Route du Vin* (Wine Road) makes a rewarding experience. It rolls through 60 of charming villages, many illuminated on summer nights for your viewing pleasure. Along the way are country inns if you'd like to sample some of the wine, take a leisurely lunch or dinner, or rent a room for the night.

The Wine Road runs along the Vosges foothills, with medieval towers and feudal ruins evoking faded pageantry. Of course, the slopes, sometimes reaching a height of 1,450 feet, are covered with vines, as there's an estimated 50,000 acres of vineyards along this road. Some 30,000 families earn their living tending the grapes. The best time to go is for the harvest in September and October.

The traditional route starts at Marlenheim; signs are posted all along the way, so it's hard to get lost.

MARLENHEIM

This agreeable wine town, noted for its Vorlauf red wine, is 13 miles due west of Strasbourg on N4. You might want to visit it even if you can't take the drive the full length of the Wine Road, as it offers an excellent inn.

ACCOMMODATIONS & DINING

✪ **Le Cerf.** 30 rue du Général-de-Gaulle, 67520 Marlenheim. ☎ **03-88-87-73-73.** Fax 03-88-87-68-08. www.lecerf.com. E-mail: info@lecerf.com. 17 units. TEL. 550–850 F ($88–$136) double; 1,250 F ($200) suite. AE, DC, MC, V. Free parking.

In the heart of this medieval village, occupying a half-timbered building at least 300 years old, this hotel offers pleasantly furnished rooms adjoining an excellent restaurant.

Dining: Robert Husser and his son, Michel, will feed you specialties like fresh foie gras, cassoulet of lobster, ballotine of quail (autumn only) with sweetbreads, oysters cooked in court bouillon and flavored with herbs, and roast turbot with vegetables. One of the most charming offerings is an all-Alsatian fixed-price meal for 450 F ($72). Other fixed-price meals begin at 250 F ($40) at lunch during the week. Regular fixed-price menus are 350 F to 600 F ($56 to $96). The restaurant is open Thursday through Monday, noon to 2:15pm and 7 to 9:30pm.

WANGEN

One of the many jewels along the route, Wangen (18.6 miles from Strasbourg) contains a city gate crowned by a tower and twisting narrow streets. It's one of the most typical of the Alsatian wine towns. The road from Wangen winds down to Molsheim.

MOLSHEIM

One of the 10 free cities of Alsace, called the "Decapolis," Molsheim (15^1/$_2$ miles from Strasbourg) retains its old ramparts and a Gothic/Renaissance church built from 1614 to 1619. Its *Alte Metzig* (town hall) was erected by the Guild of Butchers and is a most interesting sight, with its turret, gargoyles, loggia, and belfry housing a clock with allegorical figures striking the hour. The local **Office de Tourisme** is at 17 place de l'Hôtel de Ville (☎ **03-88-38-11-61**).

ROSHEIM

Nestled behind medieval fortifications, this old wine-producing town (19^1/$_4$ miles from Strasbourg) is another of the 10 free Alsatian cities. It has a 12th-century Romanesque house and the Église St-Pierre et St-Paul, also Romanesque, from 2 centuries later; it's dominated by an octagonal tower. Medieval walls and gate towers evoke Rosheim's past. The **Office de Tourisme** is at place de la République (☎ **03-88-50-75-38**).

OBERNAI

The patron saint of Alsace, Obernai, was born here. Located 20 miles from Strasbourg, and with old timbered houses and a colorful marketplace, **place du Marché,** this is one of the most interesting stopovers on the Wine Route. There's a market on Thursdays from 8am to noon; go early. **Place de l'Étoile** is decked out in flowers, and the Hôtel de Ville has a delightful loggia (inside you can see the council chamber). An old watchtower, the **Tour de la Chapelle,** is from the 13th and 16th centuries. The town's six-pail **fountain** is one of the most spectacular in Alsace. The **Office de Tourisme** is at place du Beffroi (☎ **03-88-95-64-13**).

ACCOMMODATIONS & DINING

Le Parc. 169 rte. d'Ottrott, 67210 Obernai. ☎ **03-88-95-50-08.** Fax 03-88-95-37-29. www.hotel-du-parc.com. E-mail: leparc@imaginet.fr. 56 units. A/C TV TEL. 620–965 F ($99.20–$154.40) double; 1,000–1,680 F ($160–$268.80) suite. AE, MC, V. Closed June 29–July 11 and Dec 8–Jan 6.

This contemporary hotel, most recently renovated in 1999, offers fine dining and many of the facilities you'd find in a health spa, with a decorative motif and architectural style of traditional Alsatian. It's located in a verdant park. City dwellers seeking some R&R appreciate the well-furnished, spacious rooms. There's a good restaurant here with three dining rooms. The food depends on what's available in the local markets and may include monkfish with mushrooms, duckling with apples and *cèpes* (flap mushrooms), salad of foie gras, salmon in red-wine sauce, and rich fruit desserts. Fixed-price menus are 385 F ($61.60). The dining rooms are closed Sunday night and Monday; there's also La Stube, an informal brasserie serving mostly Alsatian specialties. Amenities include a hot tub, sauna, steam room, indoor and outdoor pools, and fitness center.

BARR

The grapes for some of the finest Alsatian wines, sylvaner and gewürztraminer, are harvested here. The castles of Landsberg and Andlau stand high above the town. Barr (23 miles from Strasbourg) has many pleasant old timbered houses and a charming **place de l'Hôtel-de-Ville** with a town hall from 1640.

MITTELBERGHEIM

This is a special village. Its place de l'Hôtel-de-Ville is bordered by houses in the Renaissance style.

La Formidable Choucroute

There's no single recipe and no universal preparation, even in Alsace, but *choucroute garnie à l'alsacienne* is the dish most often associated with the province. Best consumed when the leaves start falling, it's a hearty dish intended to fortify hardworking bodies against the coming winter. You'll know autumn is at hand when you see signs in restaurants announcing "Nouvelle Choucroute": the season's first batch of cabbage marinated for weeks in herbs and salt brine, with hints of crunchiness and acidity permeating the healthful fibers. Added zest comes from juniper berries, caraway seeds, freshly ground pepper, bouquet garni, bacon fat, and (in truly classic versions) a dollop or two of goose fat.

Choucroute and its perfect accompaniment, Riesling, are both products of Alsace. Potatoes and cabbage are produced locally and can be stored in barrels in a cool cellar through a long cropless winter. Since the Middle Ages, local farmers have produced vast amounts of pork products, some traditionally smoked over fir or cherrywood fires to impart the earthy taste that permeates the shredded cabbage. The sanitized version you'll likely encounter in restaurants will include only the choicest cuts of pork (a variety of chops, sausages, knuckles, and offal keeps even the most jaded diner from growing bored). Earthier, more traditional versions that many Alsatians are likely to remember from their childhoods include pork brains, entrails, feet, ears, tail, and pork-liver dumplings. Regardless of the ingredients, many diners find the result nothing less than *formidable.*

So how does a connoisseur identify the best choucroute? A worthy version is easy to digest, is free of excess grease and/or acidity, and doesn't float on a lake of juices. The dish should be cooked carefully so the potatoes don't turn to mush; and the meat and marinated cabbage should gracefully blend so they coordinate with the flavors of an Alsatian Riesling. (Enjoying it with a hearty glass or two of beer is a dignified alternative, but if you opt for other types of liquid accompaniments, you're likely to be labeled an infidel.)

How can you tell whether the sauerkraut you're eating is authentically strasbourgeoise or the rip-off version served in Germany? The difference is in the sausage, which any charcuterie within 40 miles of either side of the Rhine could identify as *vraiment alsacien* (frankfurters best consumed with beer and mustard).

Riesling is the king of Alsatian wine, with its exquisitely perfumed bouquet. Other regional wines are chasselas, knipperle, sylvaner, pinot blanc (one of the oldest), muscat, pinot gris, pinot auxerrois, traminer, and gewürztraminer.

ACCOMMODATIONS & DINING

Winstub Gilg. 1 rte. du Vin, Mittelbergheim, 67140 Barr. ☎ **03-88-08-91-37.** Fax 03-88-08-45-17. 15 units. TV TEL. 275–420 F ($44–$67.20) double. AE, DC, MC, V.

This is an excellent inn. Though parts of the building date from 1614, its architectural showpiece is a two-story stone staircase, classified a historic monument, which was carved by the medieval stonemasons who worked on the cathedral at Strasbourg. The rooms are attractively furnished.

Dining: Chef Georges Gilg and his son-in-law, Vincent Reusché, attract a loyal following with regional specialties like onion tart, sauerkraut, and foie gras in brioche. Their main courses include stewed kidneys and sweetbreads and duck with oranges. In season, they're likely to offer roast pheasant with grapes and fillet of roebuck. Fixed-price menus cost 105 F to 380 F ($16.80 to $60.80) each. The restaurant (but not the hotel) is closed all day Tuesday and Wednesday, during all of January, and from June 21 to July 8.

ANDLAU

This gardenlike resort, located 26 miles from Strasbourg, was once the site of an abbey dating from 887, founded by the disgraced wife of Emperor Charles the Fat. It has now faded into history, but a church remains that dates from the 12th century. In the tympanum are noteworthy Romanesque carvings. **The Office de Tourisme** (☎ **03-88-08-22-57**) is located at 5 rue du Général-de-Gaulle.

DINING

Au Boeuf Rouge. 6 rue du Dr.-Stoltz. ☎ **03-88-08-96-26.** Reservations recommended. Main courses 95–160 F ($15.20–$25.60); fixed-price menus 110–205 F ($17.60–$32.80). AE, DC, MC, V. Fri–Wed 11am–2:30pm; Fri–Tues 6:30–9:30pm. Closed Jan 10–28 and 2 weeks between June and July. FRENCH.

This place was originally conceived as a relay station for the French postal services. Today, it's a bustling and unpretentious bistro, with a busy bar area and a comfortably battered, much-used dining room. Its menu features classic and time-tested specialties that include homemade terrines, gamecock, fresh fish, a wide array of meats, and a tempting dessert cart. This place doesn't offer the most innovative cookery on the wine trail, but it's reliable and consistent. The chef knows how to impress most palates without reverting to ostentation. There's also a wine stube (tavern) on site. From March to October, you can dine out on the terrace in front of the restaurant in the traditional Parisian cafe style.

DAMBACH

In the midst of its well-known vineyards, Dambach (30 miles from Strasbourg) is one of the delights of the Wine Route. Its timbered houses are gabled with galleries, and many contain oriels. Wrought-iron shop signs still tell you if a place is a bakery or a butcher. The town has ramparts and three fortified gates. A short drive from the town leads to the **Chapelle St-Sebastian,** with a 15th-century ossuary. **The Office de Tourisme** (☎ **03-88-92-61-00**) is located in La Mairie (Town Hall).

SÉLESTAT

After passing through Chatenois, you'll reach Sélestat (32 miles from Strasbourg). This was once a free city, a center of the Renaissance, and the seat of a great school. Towered battlements enclose the town. The **Bibliothèque Humaniste,** 1 rue de la Biblio-thèque (☎ **03-88-58-07-20**), houses a rare collection of manuscripts, including Sainte-Foy's *Book of Miracles.* It's open Monday and Wednesday to Friday from 9am to noon and 2 to 6pm and Saturday from 9am to noon (July and August, Saturday and Sunday also 2 to 5pm); admission is 20 F ($3.20) for adults, 10 F ($1.60) for students, free for children 12 and under.

The Gothic **Église St-George** has some fine stained glass and a gilded and painted stone pulpit. You should also try to visit the 12th-century **Église Ste-Foy,** built of red sandstone in the Romanesque style. One of the town's most noteworthy Renaissance buildings is the **Maison de Stephan Ziegler.**

The **Office de Tourisme** is in La Commanderie St-Jean, boulevard du Général-Leclerc (☎ **03-88-58-87-20**).

From Sélestat you can take a detour about 2,500 feet up on an isolated peak to **Château Haut-Koenigsbourg** (☎ **03-88-82-50-60**), a 15th-century castle, which is the largest in Alsace and treats you to an eagle's-nest view. It once belonged to the Hohenstaufens. During the Thirty Years' War the Swedes dismantled it, but it was rebuilt in 1901 after it was presented to Kaiser Wilhelm II. Admission is 40 F ($6.40) for adults, 25 F ($4) for students and ages 18 to 25, free for children 17 and under. It's open May to June and September daily 9am to 6pm; March through April and October daily 9am to noon and 1 to 5:30pm; February 6 to 28 and November through February daily 9:30am to noon and 1 to 4:30pm; July to August 9am to 6:30pm.

DINING

✪ **La Couronne.** 45 rue de Sélestat-Baldenheim. ☎ **03-88-85-32-22.** Reservations required. Main courses 90–160 F ($14.40–$25.60); fixed-price menus 190–410 F ($30.40–$65.60). AE, MC, V. Tues–Sun noon–2pm; Tues–Sat 7–9pm. Closed first week in Jan and last 2 weeks in July. From Sélestat, go 5^1/2 miles east on D21; when the road forks, go to the right, taking D209 to the village of Baldenheim. FRENCH.

This family-run place serves dishes reflecting the bounty of Alsace, prepared with considerable finesse. A flower-filled vestibule near the entrance leads to a trio of pleasant dining rooms. Menu choices may include noisettes of roebuck (midsummer to Christmas), ragoût of fish, foie gras, *omble chevalier* (the elusive whitefish from Lake Geneva) with sauerkraut and cumin-laced potatoes, and traditional sandre.

BERGHEIM

Renowned for its wines, this town (54 miles from Strasbourg) has kept part of its 15th-century fortifications. You can see timbered Alsatian houses and a Gothic church.

RIBEAUVILLÉ

At the foot of vine-clad hills, Ribeauvillé (53 miles from Strasbourg) is charming, with old shop signs, pierced balconies, turrets, and flower-decorated houses. See its Renaissance fountain and **Hôtel de Ville,** on place de la Mairie, which has a collection of silver-gilt medieval and Renaissance tankards known as *hanaps.* (These are showcased only from May to September, Tuesday to Friday at 10am, 11am, 1:45pm, and 2:30pm, as part of free guided tours.) Also of interest is the **Tour des Bouchers,** a "butchers' tower" of the 13th and 16th centuries, whose interior is closed to the public. The town is noted for its Riesling and traminer wines. In September, a "Day of the Strolling Fiddlers" fair is held here.

The **Office de Tourisme** is at 1 rue de Pierre de Coubertin (☎ **03-89-73-62-22**).

ACCOMMODATIONS & DINING

✪ **Clos St-Vincent.** Rte. de Bergheim, 68150 Ribeauvillé. ☎ **03-89-73-67-65.** Fax 03-89-73-32-20. E-mail: closvincent@aol.com. 15 units. MINIBAR TV TEL. 780–1,050 F ($124.80–$168) double; from 1,200 F ($192) suite. Rates include breakfast. MC, V.

This hotel is one of the most elegant dining and lodging choices along Route du Vin. Most of the individually decorated rooms have a balcony or terrace, but you get much more than a lovely view of the Haut-Rhin vineyards and summer roses. Bedrooms, ranging in size from medium to large, are furnished with grand comfort in mind; each has a deluxe mattress covered in fine linen.

Dining: Bertrand Chapotin's food is exceptional: hot duck liver with nuts, turbot with sorrel, roebuck (in season) in hot sauce, and veal kidneys in pinot noir. Of course, the wines are smooth, especially the Riesling and gewürztraminer, which seem to be the most popular. The fixed-price menu costs 270 F ($43.20).

RIQUEWIHR

This town (55 miles from Strasbourg), surrounded by some of the finest vineyards in Alsace, appears much as it did in the 16th century. With well-preserved walls and towers and great wine presses and old wells, it's one of the most rewarding targets along the route. You can see many Gothic and Renaissance houses, with wooden balconies, voluted gables, and elaborately carved doors and windows. Its most interesting are **Maison Liebrich** (1535), **Maison Preiss-Zimmer** (1686), and **Maison Kiener** (1574). Try to peer into some of the galleried courtyards, where time seems frozen. **Tour de Dolder** (Dolder Belfry Tower), straddling an arch through which you can pass, is from 1291. Nearby, the pentagonal **Tour des Voleurs** (Tower of Thieves, often called "the robbers' tower") contains a torture chamber. The château of the duke of Württemberg, from 1539 (now called the **Musée d'Histoire des P.T.T. d'Alsace** or Alsace Postal History Museum; ☎ **03-89-47-93-80**), offers a museum devoted to postal and telecommunications history.

The **Office de Tourisme** is shared with Ribeauvillé at 1 rue de Pierre de Coubertin (☎ **03-89-49-08-40**), in Ribeauvillé.

DINING

Auberge du Schoenenbourg. 2 rue de la Piscine. ☎ **03-89-47-92-28.** Reservations required. Main courses 140–185 F ($22.40–$29.60); fixed-price menus 190–420 F ($30.40–$67.20). AE, MC, V. Sun noon–2pm; daily 7–9:30pm. Nov–Apr and Jan 9–Feb 12, closed Wed.

We highly recommend the food served here. You'll dine in a garden completely surrounded by vineyards at the edge of the village. The cuisine of François Kiener offers a delectable array of tantalizingly prepared fare. *Foie gras maison* is de rigeur, but salmon soufflé with sabayon truffles is an elegant surprise. Perhaps try the panache of fish with sorrel or ravioli of snails with poppy seeds, or the tournedos in puff pastry with mushrooms and foie gras. Especially flavorful is a platter containing portions of both smoked salmon and fresh salmon, served with a creamy horseradish sauce and white, herb-flavored sauerkraut.

KIENTZHEIM

Kientzheim is known for its wine, two castles, timber-framed houses, and walls from the Middle Ages. From here, it's just a short drive to Kaysersberg, also known for its vineyards.

KAYSERSBERG

Once a free city of the empire, Kaysersberg (58 miles from Strasbourg) lies at the mouth of the Weiss Valley, between two vine-covered slopes; it's crowned by a feudal castle ruined in the Thirty Years' War. From one of the many ornately carved bridges, you can see the city's medieval fortifications stretching along the top of one of the nearby hills. Many of the houses are Gothic and Renaissance, and most have prominent half timbering, lots of wrought-iron accents, small leaded windows, and multiple designs carved into the reddish sandstone that seems to have been the principal building material.

In the cafes you'll hear a combination of French and Alsatian. The language is usually determined by the age of the speaker—the older ones remain faithful to the dialect of their grandparents. Dr. Albert Schweitzer was born here in 1875; his house is near the fortified bridge over the Weiss. You can visit the **Centre Culturel Albert-Schweitzer** from June to October, daily from 9am to noon and 2 to 6pm.

The **Office de Tourisme** is at 31 rue du Geibourg (☎ **03-89-78-22-78**).

ACCOMMODATIONS & DINING

Au Lion d'Or. 66 rue du Général-de-Gaulle. ☎ **03-89-47-11-16.** Reservations required. Main courses 75–150 F ($12–$24); fixed-price menus 79–260 F ($12.65–$41.60). AE, MC, V. Thurs–Tues noon–2:30pm and 6:30–9:30pm. Closed Jan; Dec–Apr, closed Wed–Thurs. FRENCH.

This restaurant boasts an exceptionally beautiful decor. A carved lion's head is set into the oak door leading into the restaurant, which has a beamed ceiling, stone detailing, brass chandeliers, and a massive fireplace. If you eat at an outdoor table, you'll have a view of one of Alsace's prettiest streets. The food, a medley of typical Alsatian dishes, is reliable and quite fine; it's true to the flavors of the region. Sauerkraut, served either in its traditional meat-and potato form, or with fish, is an enduring specialty and a favorite with the loyal clientele.

✪ **Chambard.** 9–13 rue du Général-de-Gaulle, 68240 Kaysersberg. ☎ **03-89-47-10-17.** Fax 03-89-47-35-03. Reservations required. Main courses 140–220 F ($22.40–$35.20); fixed-price menus 250–450 F ($40–$72). AE, MC, V. Tues 7–9:30pm, Wed–Sun noon–2pm and 7–9:30pm. Closed Jan 1–7 and Mar 5–30. FRENCH.

The regional cuisine here is so good it's well worth planning your wine tour to include a stopover. Chambard is the domain of Pierre Irmann, a chef of unusual versatility and imagination. You'll recognize the restaurant—the finest in town—by the gilded wrought-iron sign above the cobblestones. Inside you'll find a rustic ambience, with exposed stone and polished wood. The cuisine is impeccably flavored, and very sophisticated, often accompanied by sauces that have been pronounced as divine by many reputable critics, and with wines that might be suggested by Mr. Irmann's charming wife, Marinette. Examples include a sausage-shaped portion of homemade foie gras; a *pot-au-feu* of goose liver served in its own confit, and a succulent version of an entire sole baked in the oven and served in an herb-flavored butter sauce.

The Chambard offers a 20-room hotel annex built in 1981 to match the other buildings on the street. It has a massive Renaissance fireplace that was transported from another building. A double is 650 F to 750 F ($104 to $120).

AMMERSCHWIHR

This is a good stop to cap off your Wine Road tour, near the outskirts of Colmar (49 miles from Strasbourg). Once a free city of the empire, Ammerschwihr was almost destroyed in 1944 battles but has been reconstructed in the traditional style. More and more travelers stop off here to sample the wine, especially Käferkopf. Check out its trio of gate towers, 16th-century parish church, and remains of early fortifications.

ACCOMMODATIONS & DINING

À l'Arbre Vert. 7 rue des Cigognes, 68770 Ammerschwihr. ☎ **03-89-47-12-23.** Fax 03-89-78-27-21. 17 units. TV TEL. 380 F ($60.80) double. Half board 290–370 F ($46.40–$59.20) per person extra. AE, DC, MC, V. Nov–Apr, restaurant closed Mon dinner and all day Tues.

If you want to call it an evening before you go on to Colmar, À l'Arbre Vert is a charming place to stay. Its public rooms are delightfully decorated, though the guest rooms are rather plain. The inn also serves very good Alsatian specialties in its restaurant, where you can dine even if you aren't staying at the hotel. Fixed-price meals go for 105 to 230 F ($16.80 to $36.80).

✪ **Aux Armes de France.** 1 Grand Rue, 68770 Ammerschwihr. ☎ **03-89-47-10-12.** Fax 03-89-47-38-12. Reservations required. Main courses 180–290 F ($28.80–$46.40); fixed-price menus 380–480 F ($60.80–$76.80); menu dégustation 520 F ($83.20). AE, DC, DISC, MC, V. Fri–Tues noon–2pm and 7–9pm. FRENCH.

This is the best restaurant along the Wine Road. Although you can rent a room here (doubles go for 380 F to 480 F [$60.80 to $76.80]), the real reason to come is the cuisine. In a flower-filled setting, Philippe Gaertner and his staff receive many French and German gourmands. A specialty is fresh foie gras served in its own golden aspic. Main courses include classics with imaginative variations: for example, roebuck (in season) in hot sauce and lobster fricassée with cream and truffles. Their spicy duckling is particularly savory, as is the fillet of sole with fresh noodles. Their terrine of lobster and calf's head in aspic (they call it a *presskopf,* and we've never seen it in any restaurant in France) is particularly sought after by curious and adventurous gastronomes.

ROUFFACH

Rouffach is south of Colmar. It's included here because of the excellent vineyard **Clos St-Landelin** (☎ 03-89-78-58-00). It's on the Route du Vin, at the intersection of RN83 route de Soultzmatt. Rouffach is sheltered by one of the highest of the Vosges mountains, Grand-Ballon, which stops the winds that bring rain. That makes for a dry climate and a special grape. A clerical estate from the 6th century until the Revolution and celebrated over the centuries for the quality of wine it produces, Clos St-Landelin covers 40 acres at the southern end of the Vorbourg Grand Gru area. Its steep slopes call for terrace cultivation.

Ironically, the soil that produces these famous wines is anything but fertile. Loaded with pebbles and high in alkalines, sand, and limestone, it produces low-yield, scraggly vines whose fruit (depending on where the vines are planted and how they're exposed to the sun) is used to make superb Rieslings, gewürztraminers, and pinot noirs. Since 1648 the Muré family has owned the vineyards, which today sprawl across 62 acres. In their cellar is the oldest wine press in Alsace, from the 13th century. They welcome visitors and speak English.

3 Colmar

273 miles SE of Paris, 87 miles SE of Nancy, 44 miles SW of Strasbourg

One of the most attractive towns in Alsace, Colmar is filled with many medieval and early Renaissance buildings, with half-timbered structures, sculptured gables, and gracious loggias. Tiny gardens and wash houses surround many of the homes. Its old quarter looks more German than French, filled with streets of unexpected twists and turns. As a gateway to the Rhine country, Colmar is a major stopover south from Strasbourg. It's the third-largest town in Alsace, near the vine-covered slopes of the southern Vosges.

Colmar today has been so well restored that it's now Alsace's most beautiful city, far more so than Strasbourg. By walking its streets you'll find it hard to tell that Colmar was hard hit in two world wars.

ESSENTIALS

GETTING THERE   If you're **driving,** take N83 from Strasbourg; trip time is 1 hour. Because of Colmar's narrow streets, we suggest that you park in the Champ-de-Mars northeast of the rail station, and then walk a few blocks east to the old city.

Railway lines link Colmar to Nancy, Strasbourg, and Mulhouse, as well as to Germany via Freiburg, across the Rhine. Nine trains per day arrive from Paris (trip time: 6 hours). For train information and schedules, call ☎ 08-36-35-35-35.

VISITOR INFORMATION   The **Office de Tourisme** is at 4 rue des Unterlinden (☎ 03-89-20-68-92).

For information about winery visits, contact the **CIVA (Alsace Wine Committee),** Maison du Vin d'Alsace, 12 av. de la Foire-aux-Vins (☎ **03-89-20-16-20**). The CIVA office is usually open Monday to Friday from 9am to noon and 2 to 5pm. Make your arrangements far in advance.

SPECIAL EVENTS   Alsatian **folk dances** take place on Tuesday at 8:30pm on place de l'Ancienne-Douane from mid-May to mid-September. If you want to listen to classical music, try the **Festival International de Musique de Colmar** during the first 2 weeks in July, when 24 concerts are held in various venues around the city such as churches and public monuments. Les Mardis de la Collégiale at place de la Cathédrale (☎ **03-89-24-52-27**) offers **organ and instrumental concerts** every Tuesday at 8:45pm from the end of July to mid-September. And **L'Été Musical** (☎ **03-89-20-29-01**) presents instrumental classical concerts once a week during August at the Église St-Pierre. Tickets for any of these range from 100 F to 120 F ($16 to $19.20), and you can get complete information at the Office de Tourisme.

SEEING THE SIGHTS

Colmar boasts lots of historic houses, many of them half-timbered and, at least in summer, accented with geranium-draped window boxes. One of the most beautiful is the **Maison Pfister,** 11 rue des Marchands at the corner of rue Mercière, a civic building erected in 1537 with wooden balconies. On the ground floor is a wine boutique owned by a major Alsace wine grower, **Mure,** proprietor of the vineyard Clos St-Landelin. (A cursory glance of its exterior may be all you'll get, as this isn't a public *maison*.)

If you take pont St-Pierre over the Lauch River, you'll have an excellent view of Old Colmar and can explore the section known as **Petite Venise** because it's filled with canals.

SHOPPING   If you're up for a little shopping, head for the old town of Colmar, in particular rue de Clefs, Grand Rue, rue des Têtes, and rue des Marchands.

Antiques abound in Colmar, and you'll find a large grouping of stores in the old town, especially along rue des Marchands. Shops that deserve particular attention are **Fontaine,** 26 rue des Marchands (☎ **03-89-23-95-87**), offering collections of metal and wood toys; **Gelsmar Dany,** 32 rue des Marchands (☎ **03-89-23-30-41**), specializing in antique furniture; and **Antiquités Guy Caffard,** 56 rue des Marchands (☎ **03-89-41-31-78**), with its mishmash of furniture, currency, postcards, books, toys, bibelots, and the like. Also worth noting are **Lire & Chiner,** 36 rue des Marchands (☎ **03-89-24-16-78**), and **Antiquité Arcana,** 13 place l'Ancienne Douane (☎ **03-89-41-59-81**). For reproductions of objects found in Strasbourg's Alsacien Museum, such as glassware, jewelry, fabrics, and pottery, go to **Arts et Collections d'Alsace,** 1 rue des Tanneurs (☎ **03-89-24-09-78**).

WINERIES   Since Colmar is one of the gateways into the wine-producing Rhine country, local wine is one of the best purchases you can make. If you don't have the time to head out to the vineyards along the Wine Road, stop in at **Cave du Musée,** 11 rue Kléber (☎ **03-89-23-85-29**), for one of the largest selections of wines and liqueurs from the region as well as the rest of France.

However, if you have a car, you can drive to one of the most historic vineyards in Alsace-Lorraine. ✪ **Domaines Schlumberger,** at Guebwiller (where it's signposted), lies 16 miles southwest of Colmar. The cellars, established by the Schlumberger family beginning in 1810, are an unusual combination of early-19th-century brickwork and modern stainless steel. A visit here will go far in enhancing your understanding of the subtle differences between wines produced by the seven varieties of grape cultivated in Alsace. Each of these—including Rieslings, gewürztraminers, muscats, sylvaners, and pinots (blancs, gris, noir)—is produced with enduring success by the Schlumberger vineyards. Views of the vineyards and the tasting rooms are available without an appointment, but tours of the cellars are conducted only whenever a staff member isn't too busy to provide one. Call (☎ **03-89-74-85-75**) before you go to find out when that might be.

Église des Dominicains. Place des Dominicains. ☎ **03-89-24-46-57.** Admission 8 F ($1.30) adults, 6 F (95¢) students, free for children. Apr–June and Sept–Dec, daily 10am–1pm and 3–6pm; July–Aug, daily 10am–6pm. Closed Jan–Mar.

This church contains one of the most famous artistic treasures of Colmar: Martin Schongauer's painting *Virgin of the Rosebush* (1473), all gold, red, and white, with fluttering birds. Look for it in the choir.

Église St-Martin. Place de la Cathédrale. ☎ **03-89-41-27-20.** Free admission. Daily 8am–6pm. Closed to casual visitors during mass.

In the heart of Old Colmar is a collegiate church begun in 1230 on the site of a Romanesque church. It has a notable choir erected by William of Marburg in 1350 and is crowned by a steeple rising to a height of 232 feet.

Musée Bartholdi. 30 rue des Marchands. ☎ **03-89-41-90-60.** Admission 20 F ($3.20) adults, 15 F ($2.40) children 12–18, free for children 11 and under. Wed–Mon 10am–noon and 2–6pm. Closed Jan–Feb.

Statue of Liberty sculptor Frédéric-Auguste Bartholdi was born in Colmar in 1834. In this small memento-filled museum, which is the house where he was born, there are Statue of Liberty rooms containing plans and scale models, as well as documents in connection with its construction and other works regarding U.S. history. Bartholdi's Paris apartment, with furniture and memorabilia, has been reconstructed here. The museum supplements its exhibits with water and oil paintings of Egyptian scenes this diversified talent captured during his travels in 1856.

✪ Musée d'Unterlinden (Under the Linden Trees). Place d'Unterlinden. ☎ **03-89-41-89-23.** Admission 35 F ($5.60) adults, 30 F ($4.80) seniors, 25 F ($4) students and children 12–17, free for children 11 and under. Apr–Oct, daily 9am–6pm; Nov–Mar, Wed–Mon 10am–5pm. Closed on national holidays.

This former Dominican convent (1232), the chief seat of Rhenish mysticism in the 14th and 15th centuries, was converted to a museum around 1850, and it's been a treasure house of the art and history of Alsace ever since.

The jewel of its collection is the **Issenheim Altarpiece (Le Retable d'Issenheim),** painted by the Würzburg-born Matthias Grünewald, "the most furious of realists," around 1515. His colors glow and his fantasy will overwhelm you. One of the most exciting works in the history of German art, it's an immense altar screen with two-sided folding wing pieces—designed to show first the Crucifixion, then the Incarnation, framed by the Annunciation and the Resurrection. The carved altar screen depicts St. Anthony visiting the hermit St. Paul; it also reveals the Temptation of St. Anthony, the most beguiling part of a work that contains some ghastly misshapen birds, weird monsters, and loathsome animals. The demon of the plague, for example, is depicted with a swollen belly and purple skin, his body blotched with boils, a diabolical grin on his horrible face.

The museum has other attractions as well, including the magnificent altarpiece of Jean d'Orlier by Martin Schongauer (ca. 1470), a large collection of religious wood carvings and stained glass from the 14th to the 18th centuries, and Gallo-Roman lapidary collections, including funeral slabs. Its armory collection includes ancient arms from the Romanesque to the Renaissance, featuring halberds and crossbows.

ACCOMMODATIONS

Rooms are also available in the **Hôtel des Têtes** (see "Dining," below).

Grand Hôtel Bristol. 7 place de la Gare, 68000 Colmar. ☎ **03-89-23-5959.** Fax 03-89-23-92-26. www.grand-hotel-bristol.fr. E-mail: reservation@grand-hotel-bristol.fr. 70 units. MINIBAR TV TEL. 430F–750 F ($68.80–$120) double. AE, DC, MC, V.

This red sandstone hotel is the traditional first-class choice. Right at the train station, it provides well-maintained rooms with both modern and provincial decor. Rooms are rather standardized and not quite as grand as the name of the hotel suggests.

✪ **Hostellerie le Maréchal.** 4–5 place des Six-Montagnes-Noires, 68000 Colmar. ☎ **03-89-41-60-32.** Fax 03-89-24-59-40. www.romantikhotels.com/colmar. E-mail: marechal@rmcnet.fr. 30 units. A/C MINIBAR TV TEL. 600–1,400 F ($96–$224) double; 1,500–1,600 F ($240–$256) suite. AE, MC, V.

This hotel, the most tranquil in town, was formed when three 16th-century houses were joined. You climb a wide staircase to reach the rooms, most of which are air-conditioned. In the east wing is a small partially timbered room with a sloping ceiling. Rooms are generally small but neatly organized, with functional beds with firm mattresses. There's a winter restaurant with a welcoming fireplace; in summer the restaurant is moved to the terrace where you can enjoy a water view. You can feast on stuffed quail, good beef and veal dishes, and lamb Provençal—all accompanied by Tokay and Alsatian wines. Fixed-price menus range from 200 F to 430 F ($32 to $68.80).

Le Colombier. 7 rue Turenne, 68000 Colmar. ☎ **03-89-23-96-00.** Fax 03-89-23-97-27. 24 units. A/C MINIBAR TV TEL. 560–1,100 F ($89.60–$176) double; 1,260–1,470 F ($201.60–$235.20) suite. AE, DC, MC, V.

In 1994, after a 2-year renovation, what had been a 14th-century half-timbered ruin was transformed into an appealing combination of old and new. The furnishings are streamlined, and the staff is engaging and helpful. But for the fact that it doesn't have a restaurant (breakfast is the only meal served), this three-star hotel would be worthy of four-star status. With the exception of the cozy room beneath the steeply pitched pinnacle of the roofline, the guest rooms are high-ceilinged and come in a variety of sizes and shapes that were determined by the original layout. Each contains a safe and a comfortable mattress and fine linen, plus a small but tidily arranged bathroom. Some rooms overlook the canals of the surrounding Petite Venise neighborhood; others open onto a half-timbered courtyard.

DINING

✪ **Fer Rouge.** 52 Grand' Rue. ☎ **03-89-41-37-24.** Reservations required. Main courses 185–250 F ($29.60–$40); fixed-price menus 295–395 F ($47.20–$63.20); menu dégustation 530 F ($84.80). AE, DC, MC, V. Mon–Sat noon–2:15pm and 7:15–10pm. Closed Jan. FRENCH/ALSATIAN.

In a black-and-white half-timbered building on a cobblestone square in Colmar's historic core, Au Fer Rouge has stained- and bottle-glass windows and window boxes that overflow with geraniums in summer. Inside, carved oak beams and brass and copper decorations provide a setting straight out of a Teutonic folktale. The owner, Patrick Fulgraff, has departed from the typical Alsatian fare in favor of more inventive styles. His specialties are scallops served with bacon and a pulverized essence of mussels, bound together with butter-sautéed endives; breast of pigeon smothered in "country-style cabbage" served with potatoes and port sauce; and breast of wild duckling grilled with its skin and served with a *parmentier* of its own thighs in a red wine sauce and with wild mushrooms. A particularly succulent dessert is a slice of thin apple tart with cinnamon-flavored cream sauce and fresh-made vanilla ice cream.

✪ **Maison des Têtes.** In the Hôtel des Têtes, 19 rue des Têtes, 68000 Colmar. ☎ **03-89-24-43-43.** Reservations required. Main courses 92–150 F ($14.70–$24); fixed-price menus 169–229 F ($27.05–$36.65); menu dégustation 350 F ($56). AE, DC, MC, V. Sun noon–2pm, Tues–Sat noon–2pm and 7–9:30pm. FRENCH.

This Colmar monument, named for the sculptured heads on its stone facade, is reached via a covered cobblestone drive and an open courtyard. The dining rooms are decorated with aged-wood beams and paneling, Art Nouveau lighting fixtures, and stained-glass and leaded windows. The food is excellent, including traditional foie gras with truffles, *choucroute* (sauerkraut), seasonal roebuck with morels, roasted duck with two spices, and fresh trout or Rhine salmon braised in Riesling. The Alsatian wines are sublime.

Hôtel des Têtes offers 18 nicely furnished rooms, all with minibar, TV, phone, coffee-making facilities, and hair dryer, and some with Jacuzzi. The rates are 570 F to 695 F ($91.20 to $111.20) for a double; the three suites are 1,400 F ($224) each.

NEARBY ACCOMMODATIONS & DINING

Gourmets flock to Illhaeusern, 11 miles from Colmar, east of the N83 highway, for one important reason—to dine at the Auberge de l'Ill, one of France's greatest restaurants. The signs for the restaurant, beside the main highway, are difficult to miss.

✪ **Auberge de l'Ill.** Rte. de Collonges, 68970 Illhaeusern. ☎ **03-89-71-89-00.** Fax 03-89-71-82-83. Reservations required, sometimes 6 weeks in advance on summer weekends. Main courses 145–300 F ($23.20–$48); fixed-price menu 790 F ($126.40). AE, DC, MC, V. Wed–Sun noon–2pm and 7–9:30pm. Closed Feb. FRENCH.

Run by the Haeberlin brothers in what used to be their family's 19th-century farm-house, Auberge de l'Ill combines the finest-quality Alsatian specialties with cuisine moderne and classic offerings. You can take your aperitif or coffee under the weeping willows in a beautiful garden, with a river view. The house is furnished with antiques, polished silver hollowware, and Buffet paintings. Chef Paul Haeberlin takes dishes of Alsatian origin and makes them into *grande cuisine—matelotes* (small glazed onions) in Riesling, eel stewed in Riesling, and an inventive foie gras. His partridge, pheasant, and duckling are among the best in Europe. Two unsurpassed choices that may be offered are his braised slices of pheasant and partridge served with a winey game sauce, chestnuts, wild mushrooms, and Breton cornmeal; and his salmon soufflé. Some dishes require 24-hour notice, so inquire when you make reservations.

You can spend the night at the restaurant's air-conditioned **Hôtel de Berges** (☎ **03-89-71-87-87;** fax 03-89-71-87-88) in a delightfully furnished and sumptuously comfortable room (11 in all), overlooking the Ill River. A double costs 1,350 F to 1,550 F ($216 to $248).

COLMAR AFTER DARK

Head for the smoky and seductive **Haricot Rouge,** 6 place de la Cathédrale (☎ **03-89-41-74-13**), where rock concerts pull people in especially Wednesday and Thursday nights, when live music is featured; or the local version of the Hard Rock Cafe known as **Rock Café,** 6 rue des Trois-Epis (☎ **03-89-24-05-36**). Both places attract a cool crowd flaunting a little bit of a rough edge. For a softer atmosphere, try the piano bar **Louisiana Club,** 3A rue Berthe-Molly (☎ **03-89-24-94-18**), where you can groove to authentic blues and jazz. If you can imagine a French version of a country/western bar, mosey on down to the **Country Bar,** 9 rte. d'Ingersheim

(☎ **03-89-41-48-47**), with its barnyard country dance floor and ample supply of big belt buckles, cowboy boots, and ten-gallon hats. If you would prefer to boogie the night away in a more conventional-style disco, try the newly opened **Le Jet-Set,** 221 Rte. de Rouffach (☎ **03-89-24-55-46**).

4 La Route des Crêtes

From Basel to Mainz, a distance of some 150 miles, the Vosges mountain range stretches along the west side of the Rhine Valley, bearing a great similarity to the Black Forest of Germany. Many German and French families spend their summer vacation exploring the Vosges. However, those with less time may want to settle for a quick look at these ancient mountains that once formed the boundary between France and Germany. The Vosges are filled with tall hardwood and fir trees and traversed by a network of twisting roads with hairpin curves. Deep in these mountain forests is the closest that France comes to having a wilderness.

EXPLORING THE AREA

You can explore the mountains by heading west from Strasbourg, but you can take a more interesting route from Colmar. From that ancient Alsatian town, you can explore some of the highest of the southern Vosges with their remarkable beauty. La Route des Crêtes (Crest Road) begins at **Col du Bonhomme,** to the west of Colmar. It was devised by the French High Command during World War I to carry supplies over the mountainous front. From Col du Bonhomme you can strike out along this magnificent road, once the object of such bitter fighting but today a series of panoramic vistas, including one of the Black Forest.

By **Col de la Schlucht** you'll have climbed 4,905 feet. Schlucht is a winter/summer resort, one of the most beautiful spots in the Vosges—with a panoramic view of the Valley of Münster and the slopes of Hohneck. As you skirt the edge of this glacier-carved valley, you'll be in the midst of a land of pine groves with a necklace of lakes. You may want to turn off the main road and go exploring in several directions, the scenery is that tempting. But if you're still on the Crest Road, you can circle **Hohneck,** one of the highest peaks at 5,300 feet, dominating the Wildenstein Dam of the Bresse winter-sports station.

At **Markstein** you'll come into another pleasant summer/winter resort. From here, take N430 and then D10 to **Münster,** where the savory cheese is made. You go via the Petit-Ballon, a landscape of forest and mountain meadows with lots of grazing cows. Finally, at **Grand-Ballon** you'll have attained the highest point you can reach by car in the Vosges, 4,662 feet. From here you can get out of your car and go for a walk. If it's a clear day, you'll be able to see the Jura, with the French Alps beyond, and can gaze on a lovely panorama of the Black Forest.

ACCOMMODATIONS & DINING IN MÜNSTER

Au Chêne Voltaire. Rte. du Chêne-Voltaire, at Luttenbach, 68140 Münster. ☎ **03-89-77-31-74.** Fax 03-89-77-45-71. 19 units, 15 with bathroom. TEL. 270 F ($43.20) double without bathroom, 300 F ($48) double with bathroom. AE, DC, MC, V. Take D10 less than 1¹/₂ miles southwest from the center of Münster.

This chalet-style inn, built in 1939 and renovated many times since, lies in an isolated section of the forest. The modern but no-frills rooms are in a separate building from the rustic core that contains the popular restaurant. The hotel isn't a destination in and of itself; it's just good to keep in mind if you need to rest for the night before pressing on your way in the morning. Facilities include a sauna and a solarium. You can dine here even if you're not staying at the hotel. Fixed-price menus range from 105 F to 165 F ($16.80 to $26.40).

5 Nancy

230 miles SE of Paris, 92 miles W of Strasbourg

Nancy, in the northeastern corner of France, was the capital of old Lorraine. The city was built around a fortified castle on a rock in the swampland near the Meurthe River. The important canal a few blocks east of the historic center connects the Marne to the Rhine. It once rivaled Paris as the center for Art Nouveau.

The city is serenely beautiful, with a historic tradition, a cuisine, and an architecture all its own. And it has three faces: the medieval alleys and towers around the old Palais Ducal where Charles II received Joan of Arc, the rococo golden gates and frivolous fountains, and the spreading dull modern sections with their university and industry.

With a population of 100,000, Nancy remains the hub of commerce and politics in Lorraine. The seat of the third-largest scientific university in France, it's a center of mining, engineering, metallurgy, and finance. Its 30,000 students, who have a passion for *le cool jazz,* keep Nancy jumping at night.

ESSENTIALS

GETTING THERE   Trains from Strasbourg arrive every 30 minutes (trip time: 1 hour); trains from Paris's Gare de l'Est pull in about every hour (trip time: 3 hours). For train information and schedules, call ☎ **08-36-35-35-35.**

When **driving** to Nancy from Paris, follow N4 east (trip time: 4 hours).

VISITOR INFORMATION   The **Office de Tourisme** is at place Stanislas (☎ **03-83-35-22-41**).

SPECIAL EVENTS   Serious jazz lovers come to town for a 2-week period in mid-October to attend the best-publicized music festival in Nancy, **Jazz Pulsations.** There is some kind of jazz presentation every night around sundown during the above-mentioned period, conducted within a tent that's erected in the Parc de la Pépinière, a very short walk from the Place Stanislas. Tickets range in price from 100 F to 150 F ($16 to $24). For information and ticket sales, call ☎ **03-83-35-40-86.**

SEEING THE SIGHTS

The most monumental square in eastern France and the heart of Nancy is ✪ **place Stanislas,** named for Stanislaus Leczinski, the last of the ducs de Lorraine, ex-king of Poland, and father-in-law of Louis XV. His 18th-century building programs transformed Nancy into one of Europe's most palatial cities. The square stands between Nancy's two most notable neighborhoods: the **Ville Vieille,** which occupies the medieval core in the northwest, centered around the cathedral, Grande-Rue, and the labyrinth of narrow meandering streets that funnel into it; and the **Ville Neuve,** in the southeast. Built in the 16th and 17th centuries, when streets were laid out in generally straight lines, Ville Neuve is centered on rue St-Jean.

Place Stanislas was laid out from 1752 to 1760 to the designs of Emmanuel Héré. Its ironwork gates are magnificent. Grilles stand at each corner, and two enclose fountains, the Neptune and the Amphitrite. The most imposing building on the square is the **Hôtel de Ville** (town hall); if you ask permission of the security guard at the entrance, you might be allowed into the building's majestic foyer to admire its grandiose inner staircase. It's edged with one of the wrought-iron masterpieces of eastern France, an 80-foot forged-iron balustrade with a single-piece handrail, the masterpiece of Jean Lamour, who designed the square's screens and fountains. You can also visit the Town Hall, during July and August only, for a brief nocturnal display of the building's showcase salons. The civic authorities unlock the doors for public visits every evening between 10:30 and 11pm for a fee of 10 F ($1.60) per person. On the square's eastern side is the also-recommended **Musée des Beaux-Arts** (see below).

Arc de Triomphe, constructed by Stanislas from 1754 to 1756 to honor Louis XV, brings you to the long rectangular place de la Carrière, a tree-lined promenade leading to the **Palais du Gouvernement,** built in 1760. This governmental palace adjoins the **Palais Ducal,** built in 1502 in the Gothic style with Flamboyant balconies.

Église des Cordeliers. 66 Grande-Rue. ☎ **03-83-32-18-74.** Admission 20 F ($3.20), 15 F ($2.40) students and children under 12. Cumulative ticket for the church and the Musée Historique Lorrain, 30 F ($4.80) adults, 20 F ($3.20) students and children. May–Sept, Wed–Mon 10am–6pm; Oct–Apr, Wed–Mon 10am–noon and 2–5pm.

This church, with a round chapel based on a design for Florence's Medici, contains the burial monuments of the ducs de Lorraine. The most notable are those of René II (1509), attributed to Mansuy Gauvain, and his second wife, Philippa of Gueldres, by Ligier Richier. The octagonal ducal chapel (1607) holds the baroque sarcophagi. The convent houses the **Musée des Arts et Traditions Populaires,** which has antiques, porcelain, and reconstructed interiors of regional *maisons*.

Musée de l'École de Nancy. 38 rue Sergent-Blandan. ☎ **03-83-40-14-86.** Admission 30 F ($4.80). Mon 2–6pm, Wed–Sun 10:30am–6pm. Guided tours available (in French) Fri, Sat, and Sun at 3pm for 40 F ($6.40) extra.

Housed appropriately in a stunning turn-of-the-century building is a museum displaying the works of Emile Gallé, the greatest artist of the Nancy style. See, in particular, Gallé's celebrated "Dawn and Dusk" bed and our favorite, the well-known "mushroom lamp." Works by Eugènc Vallin, another outstanding artist, are also on display.

Musée des Beaux-Arts. 3 place Stanislas. ☎ **03-83-85-30-72.** Admission 35 F ($5.60) adults, 20 F ($3.20) students and children. Wed–Mon 10am–6pm.

Built in the 1700s, this is an outstanding regional art museum, encompassing the Collection Galilée, works displayed in Paris between 1919 and 1930. Its collection boasts a Manet portrait of the wife of Napoléon III's dentist—remarkable because of its brilliance and intensity, and because Manet portraits are rare. There are also works by Delacroix, Utrillo, Modigliani, Boucher, and Rubens. The Italians, like Perugino, Caravaggio, Ribera, and Tintoretto, are also represented.

✪ **Musée Historique Lorrain.** In the Palais Ducal, 64 Grande-Rue. ☎ **03-83-32-18-74.** Admission 20 F ($3.20) adults, 15 F ($2.40) students and children. Cumulative ticket for the museum and Eglise des Cordeliers 30 F ($4.80) adults, 20 F ($3.20) students and children. May–Sept, Wed–Mon 10am–6pm; Oct–Apr, Wed–Mon 10am–noon and 2–5pm.

This is one of France's great museums, covering the art and history of the Lorraine region from ancient times. The first floor devotes an entire room to the work of Jacques Callot, the noted engraver who was born in Nancy in 1592. Galerie des Cerfs displays intricately woven tapestries. You'll also find a vast collection of 17th-century Lorraine masterpieces by Jacques Beljlange, Jacques Callot, Georges de la Tour, and Claude Deruet, from when the duchy was known as a cultural center. The museum also has a room portraying eastern France's Jewish history.

Nancy

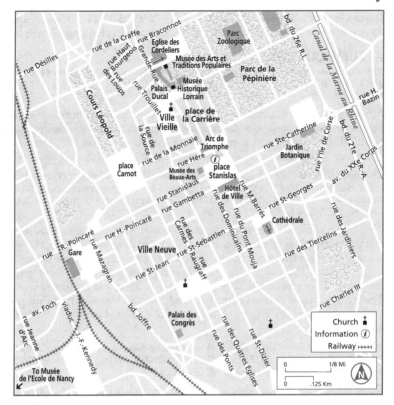

SHOPPING

For glitz and glamour, your first stops should be along **rue Gambetta** and **rue des Dominicains,** where exclusive boutiques carry the best names in fashion and perfume. Along **rue St-Dizier** you'll run across more down-to-earth shops selling clothes, shoes, jewelry, and leather goods at more affordable prices. The old town is home to small boutiques that sell antiques, arts and crafts, books, and bric-a-brac, as well as some clothing and jewelry.

For chic women's clothing and accessories, including the finest in handbags and shoes, try **Vanessa,** 14 place St-Epvre (☎ **03-83-32-85-88**), or **Signatures,** 39 rue St-Jean (☎ **03-83-32-93-30**). From the sophisticated to the trendy, men of class, or their partners who want them to dress the part, seek out **Alto Stratus,** 34 rue des Dominicains (☎ **03-83-30-17-33**), and **Ecce Homo,** 2 bis rue d'Amerval (☎ **03-83-32-12-82**).

Many of Nancy's antique shops specialize in Art Nouveau. Visit **Jean Claude Jantzen,** 13 rue Stanislas (☎ **03-83-35-20-79**), for the best pieces. If you'd like a more modern objet d'art, consider **Galerie Ovadia,** 14 Grande-Rue (☎ **03-83-37-93-32**), with its offerings by contemporary masters of painting, sculpture, and intensely colorful mixed-media collages; and **Galerie Art International,** 17 rue d'Amerval (☎ **03-83-35-06-83**), where you can choose from Lalique crystal, brightly colored vases and boxes known as Emaux de Longwy, and an assortment of lamps.

Daum Glassworks Showroom, place Stanislaus (☎ **03-83-32-14-55**), offers exquisite crystal, especially items of the world-famous transparent-colored *pâte de verre.*

ACCOMMODATIONS

Albert-1er-Astoria. 3 rue de l'Armée-Patton, 54000 Nancy. ☎ **03-83-40-31-24.** Fax 03-83-28-47-78. 85 units. TV TEL. 300–395 F ($48–$63.20) double. AE, DC, MC, V. Parking 35 F ($5.60).

Across from the railway station, this well-equipped hotel is run in a businesslike manner. Guests stay here mainly for the price and central location. It offers comfortable if not exactly plush rooms, with angular furniture and relatively comfortable mattresses. There is also a very pleasant garden in which to relax. Breakfast is the only meal served.

✪ **Grand Hôtel de la Reine.** 2 place Stanislas, 54000 Nancy. ☎ **800/777-4182** in the U.S. and Canada, or 03-83-35-03-01. Fax 03-83-32-86-04. http://netlondon.hotelbook.com. 48 units. A/C MINIBAR TV TEL. 830–1,600 F ($132.80–$256) double; from 2,200 F ($352) suite. AE, DC, MC, V. Parking 70 F ($11.20).

This 18th-century mansion was built simultaneously with the monumental square that contains it and so figures prominently in the town's historic framework. The hotel is one of the showplaces of the upscale Concorde chain, operators of such bastions of luxury as Paris's Hôtel de Crillon. The Louis XV–style guest rooms boast draped testers over the comfortable beds, Venetian-style chandeliers, and gilt-framed mirrors. The Stanislas restaurant serves both classic and modern dishes as part of fixed-price meals ranging from 180 F to 370 F ($28.80 to $59.20), and the waiters are formal and considerate.

Hôtel Mercure Nancy Centre Thiers. 11 rue Raymond-Poincaré, 54000 Nancy. ☎ **03-83-39-75-75.** Fax 03-83-32-78-17. 192 units. A/C MINIBAR TV TEL. 595–655 F ($95.20–$104.80) double; 1,000 F ($160) suite. AE, DC, MC, V.

Rising above every other building in Nancy, this streamlined seven-story hotel caters to both business travelers and visitors. Functional and efficient, with a hardworking staff, it's a top choice for Nancy but lacks the style of the Grand Hôtel de la Reine. The rooms are outfitted in the chain-format style that nonetheless offers comfort, predictability, and warmth, with firm comfortable mattresses and sound functional bathrooms with plenty of regularly replaced towels.

The hotel has two restaurants on the premises: the upscale choice, La Toison d'Or, and a less formal, somewhat more raucous brasserie, Le Rendez-Vous. Both offer cuisine inspired by Lorraine and the rest of France.

DINING

The **Hôtel Mercure Nancy Centre Thiers** and **Grand Hôtel de la Reine** (see "Accommodations," above) also have decent restaurants.

✪ **Le Capucin Gourmand.** 31 rue Gambetta. ☎ **03-83-35-26-98.** Reservations required. Main courses 96–176 F ($15.35–$28.15). Fixed-price menu 140–320 F ($22.40–$51.20). AE, MC, V. Tues–Sun noon–2pm and Tues–Sat 7:30–10pm. Closed 2 weeks in Feb and 3 weeks in Aug. FRENCH.

Chef Hervé Fourrière, a veteran of culinary apprenticeships at many of the grandest restaurants in France, is the owner of this gastronomic citadel that's outfitted with many different examples of the hand-blown glass that's a trademark of the region. A massive glass chandelier overlooks the otherwise modern setting. Menu items include slices of panfried foie gras served on a bed of lentils, a cream of Canadian lobster soup served with truffle-stuffed ravioli, roasted pigeon in sherry sauce, a quartet of braised saltwater fish served with a confit of vegetables, and red snapper and scallops with finely chopped vegetables.

Les Pissenlits (The Dandelions). 27 rue des Ponts. ☎ **03-83-37-43-97.** Reservations recommended. Main courses 50–99 F ($8–$15.85); fixed-price menus 99–149 F ($15.85–$23.85). MC, V. Tues–Sat 11:45am–2pm and 7:15–10:30pm. FRENCH.

In 1998, the well-respected owners of one of Nancy's most upscale restaurants reconfigured their image into that of a simpler, more cost-conscious brasserie. Today, the food served here is simple but flavorful, artfully prepared, and relatively inexpensive. Chef Jean-Luc Mengin's specialties are likely to include a matelot of freshwater zander with shallots; a dandelion salad with bacon and a creamy vinaigrette sauce; sweetbreads with morels; and aiguillettes of duckling with a spice-flavored honey sauce. The chef's wife, Danièle, is one of the few fully accredited female wine stewards in France. The dining room is filled with Art Nouveau antiques, many of them crafted in Nancy.

Restaurant Le Foy. 1 place Stanislas. ☎ **03-83-32-21-44.** Reservations recommended. Main courses 85–130 F ($13.60–$20.80); fixed-price menus 120–320 F ($19.20–$51.20). AE, MC, V. Thurs–Tues noon–2pm, Mon and Thurs–Sat 7–9:30pm. Closed Feb 15–Mar 10 and July 15–Aug 9. FRENCH.

This restaurant occupies the second floor of a building that's part of the 18th-century borders of place Stanislaus. Outfitted with exposed timbers and Louis XIII furnishings, it sits above, but is completely independent of, a simple brasserie/cafe (Café Foy) that occupies the building's street level but serves much less appealing food. Menu items include a stylish roster of such dishes as roasted rabbit with violet-flavored mustard sauce, foie gras (a specialty of the house), crispy duck with braised cabbage, fried crayfish with a concasse of tomatoes, lasagne of frogs' legs and calamari in foie gras flavored butter, and a local freshwater fish (sandre) baked in a potato crust. Try a dessert that's both unusual and heavenly: honey mousse cake prepared with brandy.

NANCY AFTER DARK

As night approaches, most of the student population heads to the old town. **Le Blue Note,** 3 rue des Michottes (☎ **03-83-30-31-18**), has a room reserved for weekly rock performances, a laid-back piano bar, a fireplace room with comfy armchairs, and an upbeat and rowdy beer hall. A cover of 60 F ($9.60) is charged on concert nights.

For a pub experience, go to the **Be Happy Bar,** 23 rue Gustave-Simon (☎ **03-83-35-56-41**), with 12 brands of beer on tap. It's got an English flavor, and it's full of colorful characters playing games and guzzling beer well into the night. Nancy's most popular dance clubs are **Les Caves du Roi,** 9 place Stanislas (☎ **03-83-35-24-14**), with its industrial techno crowd flailing around in the chrome-and-metallic space; and the wine-cellar-turned-rock-dance-club called **Métro,** 1 rue du Général-Hoche (☎ **03-83-40-25-13**). Covers at both of these dance clubs range from 20 F to 50 F ($3.20 to $8), depending on the night and the entertainment.

6 Domrémy-la-Pucelle

275 miles SE of Paris, 6¹/₂ miles NW of Neufchâteau

A pilgrimage center attracting tourists from all over the world, Domrémy is a plain village that would have slumbered in obscurity except for the fact that Joan of Arc was born here in 1412. Here she heard the voices and saw the visions that led her to play out her historic role as the heroine of France.

A residence traditionally considered her family's house, near the church, is known as **Maison Natale de Jeanne d'Arc,** 2 rue de la Basilique (☎ **03-29-06-95-86**). Here you can see the bleak chamber where she was born. A museum beside the house shows a film depicting St. Joan's life. You can visit the house Wednesday to Monday: April to September from 9am to noon and 1:30 to 6pm, and October to March from 9:30am to noon and 2 to 5pm. Admission is 20 F ($3.20) for adults, 10 F ($1.60) for children 6 to 10, and free for children 5 and under.

Adjacent to the museum, on rue Principale, is **Église St-Rémi,** a much-reconstructed building whose 12th-century origins have mostly been masked by more recent repairs. All that remains from the age of Joan of Arc is a baptismal font and some stonework. Above the village, on a slope of the Bois-Chenu, is a monument steeped in turn-of-the-century French nationalism, the **Basilique du Bois-Chenu,** which was begun in 1881 and consecrated in 1926.

GETTING THERE   If you're coming **by car,** take N4 southeast of Paris to Toul, and from there A31 south toward Neufchâteau/Charmes. Then take N74 southwest (signposted in the direction of Neufchâteau). At Neufchâteau follow D164 northwest to Coussey. From here, take D53 into Domrémy.

There is no train station in Domrémy—you must take one of four **trains** daily going to either Nancy or Toul where bus and rail connections can be made to Neufchâteau. From here, there are three **buses** running daily to Domrémy. The cost of a one-way ticket is 16 F ($2.55). For bus information call **Autocars Cariane** (☎ **03-29-94-15-54**). You can also take a taxi for about 100 F ($16) (☎ **03-29-06-12-13**).

7 Verdun

162 miles E of Paris, 41 miles W of Metz

Built on both banks of the Meuse and intersected by a complicated series of canals, Verdun has an old section, the Ville Haute on the east bank, which includes the cathedral and episcopal palace. Today stone houses clustered on narrow cobblestone streets give Verdun a medieval appearance.

But most visitors come to see the famous World War I battlefields, 2 miles east of the town, off N3 toward Metz.

ESSENTIALS

GETTING THERE   Four or five **trains** (sometimes fewer) arrive daily from Paris's Gare de l'Est; you'll have to change at Châlons-en-Champagne. Several daily trains also arrive from Metz, after a change at Conflans. For train information and schedules, call ☎ **08-36-35-35-35.**

Driving is easy, since Verdun is several miles north of the Paris-Strasbourg autoroute (A4).

VISITOR INFORMATION   The **Office de Tourisme,** place de la Nation (☎ **03-29-86-14-18**), is closed on bank holidays only.

TOURING THE BATTLEFIELDS

At this garrison town in eastern France, Maréchal Pétain said, "They shall not pass!" And they didn't. Verdun is where the Allies held out against a massive assault by the German army in World War I. Near the end of the war, 600,000 to 800,000 French and German soldiers died battling over a few miles along the muddy Meuse between Paris and the Rhine. Two monuments commemorate these tragic events: Rodin's *Defense* and Boucher's *To Victory and the Dead.*

A tour of the battlefields is called the ***Circuit des Forts,*** covering the main fortifications. On the Meuse's right bank, this is a good 20-mile run, taking in **Fort Vaux,** where Raynal staged a heroic defense after sending his last message by carrier pigeon. After passing a vast **French cemetery** of 16,000 graves, an endless field of crosses, you arrive at the **Ossuaire de Douaumont,** where the bones of those literally blown to bits were embedded. Nearby at the mostly underground **Fort de Douaumont,** the "hell of Verdun" was unleashed. From the roof you can look out at a vast field of corroded tops of "pillboxes." Then you proceed to the **Tranchée des Baïonettes** (Trench of Bayonets). Bayonets of French soldiers instantly entombed by a shell burst form this unique memorial.

Within a few paces of the Tranchée des Baïonettes you'll see the extremely dignified (ca. 1967) premises of the **Mémorial de Verdun,** Fleury Devant Douaumont (☎ **03-29-84-35-34**), a museum that commemorates the weapons, uniforms, photographs, and geography of one of the most painful and bloody battles of World War I. From April to mid-September, it's open daily from 9am to 6pm. From February to March and again from mid-September to mid-December, it's open daily from 9am to noon and from 2 to 6pm. It's closed the rest of the year. Entrance costs 30 F ($4.80) for adults and students; 15 F ($2.40) children 11 to 16, free for children 10 and under.

The other tour, *Circuit Rive Gauche,* is about a 60-mile run and takes in the **Butte de Montfaucon,** a hill on which Americans erected a memorial tower, and the **Cimetière Américain at Romagne,** with some 15,000 graves.

Because of inadequate public transportation, only visitors with cars should attempt to make these circuits.

ACCOMMODATIONS & DINING

Château des Monthairons. Rte. D34, 55320 Dieue-sur-Meuse. ☎ **03-29-87-78-55.** Fax 03-29-87-73-49. www.chateaudesmonthairons.fr. E-mail: chateaudesmonthairons@wanadoo.fr. 20 units. MINIBAR TV TEL. 450–890 F ($72–$142.40) double; 990–1,200 F ($158.40–$192) suite. AE, DC, MC, V. Drive 7^1/$_2$ miles south of Verdun on D334.

This hotel, operated by the Thouvenin family, occupies an 1857 château crafted of chiseled blocks of pale stone. As you would expect from a château, rooms come in a variety of shapes and sizes. All of them, however, are fitted with luxury mattresses and quality linen. Bathrooms boast generous shelf space, thick towels, and a tub and shower combination. The grounds contain a pair of 15th-century chapels, a nesting ground for herons, and opportunities for canoeing and fishing.

In summer the dining room serves meals Tuesday to Sunday from noon to 4pm and 7:30 to 9:30pm; closed Sunday night to Tuesday at dinner from November to March 15. Fixed-price menus are 185 F to 450 F ($29.60 to $72) and include pigeon soufflé with truffles, scallops with basil-cream sauce, and roast lobster with risotto and Thai herbs.

✪ **Le Coq Hardi.** 8 av. de la Victoire, 55100 Verdun. ☎ **03-29-86-36-36.** Fax 03-29-86-09-21. www.coq-hardi.com. E-mail: coq.hardi@wanadoo.fr. 35 units. TV TEL. 470–790 F ($75.20–$126.40) double; from 1,200 F ($192) suite. AE, MC, V. Parking 68 F ($10.90).

This is our favorite hotel in town, composed of four connected 18th-century houses near the Meuse. The interior contains church pews and antiques and a Renaissance fireplace. Most of the well-maintained rooms have been decorated in regional style. Each has a comfortable, relatively new mattress and efficient but small bathrooms.

Dining: This hotel serves the best food in town in a dining room with a painted ceiling, Louis XIII chairs, and two deactivated World War I bombshells at its entrance. Menu specialties are *salade Coq Hardi* with green mustard and pine nuts, Challons duck, cassolette of snails in champagne, and various preparations of foie gras. Fixed-price menus range from 210 F to 475 F ($33.60 to $76).

Burgundy

Vineyard castles and ancient churches mark the landscape of Burgundy, which is the land of the good life for those who savor fine cuisine and wines served in historic surroundings. Burgundy was once an incredibly powerful independent province, its famed Valois dukes spreading their might across all of Europe from 1363 to 1477. In preserving its shaky independence, Burgundy weathered many struggles, notably under Charles the Bold, who was always in conflict with Louis XI. When Charles died in 1477, Louis invaded and annexed the duchy. Nonetheless, the Habsburgs still maintained their claims to it. Even after its reunion with France, Burgundy suffered many more upheavals, including its ravaging during the Franco-Spanish wars beginning in 1636. Peace did not finally come to the region until 1678.

At the time of the Revolution, Burgundy disappeared as a political entity, and it was subdivided into the *départements* of France, Yonne, Saône-et-Loire, and Côte-d'Or. The ducs de Bourgogne are but a dim memory now, but they left a legacy of vintage red and white wines to please and excite the palate. The six major wine-growing regions of Burgundy are Chablis, Côte de Nuits, Côte de Beaune, Côte de Chalon, Mâconnais, and Nivernais.

REGIONAL CUISINE   For centuries the cuisine of Burgundy has been appreciated for the freshness and variety of its ingredients and the skill and finesse of its native chefs. Many Roman historians, Charles VI, Escoffier, and Brillat-Savarin (who was born in the Burgundian town of Bugey) have praised the food and wine of Burgundy. There's something about the mild climate, adequate rainfall, and nutrient-rich soil that produces some of the most excellent beef (especially of the rare Charolais breed), mushrooms, grapes, fish, wild game, snails, fruit, and vegetables in Europe. The cuisine seems to have been invented for healthy appetites, and the typical Bourguignonne has been defined as someone who's both a gourmet and a gourmand.

Any sauce created with a dose of wine added to it (at least in Burgundy) is called *une meurette*, and there are lots listed as accompaniments to main courses on menus in the province. These *meurettes*, whether bound with butter and flour or strongly spiced with quantities of herbs and (occasionally) the blood of the slaughtered animal, are enormously flavorful and seem to make whatever wine you happen to be drinking taste even better. In the same vein, any cut of meat

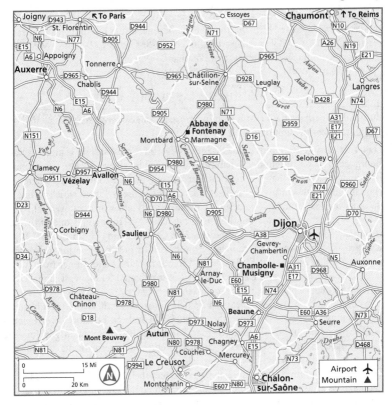

prepared *à la bourguignonne* is usually braised and then served with a sauce concocted from wine (usually red), onions, mushrooms, and (except if it's served with fish) lardons.

One major specialty is a succulent species of snail, cooked in the shell and flavored with garlic and butter. Other recipes handed down for generations are *coq au vin* (chicken flavored with red wine, brandy, pulverized chicken livers, and blood), and chicken or ham cooked *en sauce* (made traditionally with white wine and cream) or *au sang* (with blood sauce, lard, and baby onions).

The region also produces fine cheese, which is sold in wine bars across Europe, most visibly the goat cheese *crottin de chavignol,* made in the district of Sancerre along with the superb white wine of the same name. The cheese and the wine accompany each other splendidly. Another is the blue-veined Gex, which has a flavor similar to Roquefort. All of the famous Epoisses cheeses are made in the Yonne valley.

Almost everyone appreciates the flavor of Dijon mustard, called the "king of French condiments." Any menu item followed by the adjective *dijonnaise* will have a sauce containing a liberal dose of that mustard. It's estimated that Dijon produces nearly three-quarters of the mustard consumed in France.

And, of course, there are Burgundy's wines. Consisting of only 2% of all the wines produced in France (only one-third the production of all the wines of Bordeaux), they include vintages sought the world over. The best are those from the Côte d'Or, a narrow strip of gravel-studded soil usually divided into family-owned plots of fewer than

40 acres, which lies between Dijon and Santenay. In the Côte d'Or, the two major categories are the Côte de Nuits and the Côte de Beaune. Other burgundy categories are Gevrey-Chambertin, Chambolle-Musigny, Nuits-St-Georges, Beaune, Meursault, Chassagne-Montrachet, Santenay, and Pommard.

Exploring the Region by Car

Burgundy is perhaps the finest region in France to tour by car. Here's a suggested way to link together the best of the region.

Day 1   Begin at Burgundy's northwestern edge, in **Chablis.** The capital of Basse Bourgogne (Lower Burgundy), Chablis is surrounded by vineyards. The town is more famous for its wine than for its monuments, but it does contain two interesting churches: the 12th-century Église St-Martin and the Église St-Pierre, which retains little of its original Romanesque design. Chablis is really not worth an overnight stop, though 9 miles to the east along D965, in the hamlet of **Tonnere,** is one of the best restaurants in the province: ✪ **Saint-Père,** 2 av. G. Pompidon (☎ **03-86-55-12-84**). It's open daily for lunch and dinner, yet most visitors prefer it as a lunch stopover. Menus cost at 72 F to 230 F ($11.50 to $36.80) for lunch and dinner from 124 F ($19.85) on weekends. After a meal, backtrack for about 15 miles east along D965 (passing through Chablis en route) to **Auxerre.**

Scene of many pivotal moments in French history, Auxerre is the site of one of France's most impressive churches, the Gothic **Cathédrale St-Etienne.** If you're looking for truly fine dining, drive north for 17 miles to the hamlet of **Joigny** for **À la Côte St-Jacques** (see section 1 in this chapter). Return to Auxerre for the night or stay over in Joigny if you wish.

Day 2   Drive south from Auxerre along N151 and then east on D951 to the hilltop hamlet of **Vézelay**—if there's any Romanesque church in France that's a must-see, it's the one here. Marvel at the severe majesty of a pilgrimage site consecrated to Mary Magdalene. Ordinances encourage you to park at the bottom of the village and climb the sloping cobblestone main street. A luxurious ending to your day is at the base of the hill on which the famous church sits: ✪ **L'Espérance,** St-Père-sous-Vézelay (☎ **03-86-33-39-10**), is one of the best restaurants in the world. It's closed all day Tuesday and Wednesday at lunch, however, so you may want to plan your itinerary accordingly.

You have the option now of spending the night in Vézelay, driving 6 miles east on D957 to the densely forested town of **Avallon,** or continuing south for 35 miles on well-signposted country roads to **Château-Chinon.** Wherever you opt to spend the night, plan on an early-morning departure the following day.

Day 3   From Château-Chinon, drive east 20 miles on D978 to visit one of the oldest towns in France, **Autun.** En route, you might wish to take the following detour: heading east on D978 toward Autun, turn right (south) at the town of Arleuf, going right onto D500. At a fork, turn right to Glux and then follow the arrows to Mont Beuvray via D18. You reach the summit through D274. After 2 miles of climbing you'll be at **Oppidum of Bibracte,** home of the Eduens, a Gallic tribe. At this altitude of 2,800 feet, Vercingetorix organized the Gauls to fight Caesar's legions in A.D. 52. From here you'll have a splendid view of Autun and Mont St-Vincent. If the weather is clear, you can see the Jura and snowy Mont Blanc. Leave Mont Beuvray via D274 and continue northeast to Autun.

At Autun, you'll find a historic town loaded with ruins left by the ancient Romans, as well as a hilltop cathedral built in 1120 to hold the remains of St. Lazarus. Spend the night here.

Day 4   Start your day early, prepared for brief tours of various châteaux, feudal fortresses, vineyards, and other historic sites. Your route will be loaded with appealing detours, so be as flexible as possible as you negotiate your way through a labyrinth of well-marked country roads leading toward Beaune.

Leave Autun on D973 east. After 6 miles, turn left onto D326 toward Sully. Here you'll find the **Château de Sully,** once known as the Fontainebleau of Burgundy; it's closed to the public, but a view from the outside might satisfy you. The gardens are open from Easter to September, daily from 8am to 6pm. Leave Sully, following the road signs to the small village of Nolay. Three miles past Nolay you'll reach the **Château de La Rochepot** (☎ **03-80-21-71-37**), a medieval-style fortress built during the Renaissance. It's open daily: April 1 to June 30 from 10 to 11:30am and 2 to 5:30pm; July to August from 10am to noon and 2 to 6pm; September from 10 to 11:30am and 2 to 5:30pm; and October from 10 to 11:30am and 2 to 4:30pm. Closed November to March. Admission is 34 F ($5.45) for adults, 16 F ($2.55) for children.

Now head toward **Beaune** on D973, passing near some of the best-known **vineyards:** Chassagne-Montrachet, Puligny-Montrachet, Meursault, Auxey Duresses, Volnay, and Pommard. En route, perhaps stop at a restaurant whose setting is as interesting as its food. **Chagny,** 27 miles east of Autun and 11 miles southwest of Beaune, rarely attracts sightseers; gourmands from all over stop in for a meal at **Lameloise,** 36 place d'Armes (☎ **03-85-87-65-65**). It offers choices like lamb fillet in a rice crêpe, Bresse pigeon cooked in a bladder, hot lemon soufflé, and one of the broadest spectrums of burgundies anywhere in France. Reservations are required. Closed all day Wednesday and Thursday and on Tuesday at lunch.

Continue north to Beaune on D973, which will soon change to N74. You'll pass villages like Aloxe-Corton, where Charlemagne once owned vineyards, and Comblanchien. In Vougeot you can visit the **Château du Clos-de-Vougeot** (☎ **03-80-62-86-09**), surrounded by France's most celebrated vineyards. The Renaissance château is associated with the Brotherhood of the Knights of Tastevin, an organization revived in 1934 along medieval lines; it maintains a 12th-century cellar, open for visits April to September, daily from 9am to 7pm (off-season, daily from 9 to 11:30am and 2 to 5pm). Admission is 20 F ($3.20).

Resume north on N74, then branch off onto D122, which will take you through the scenic hamlet of Chambolle Musigny, then to Morey St-Denis and the site of your overnight stay, historic **Gevrey-Chambertin.** It marks the beginning of the Côte de Nuits district, source of some of the world's most prestigious wines. Our favorite places to stay are **Arts et Terroirs** (☎ **03-80-34-30-76**) and **Hôtel Les Grands Crus** (☎ **03-80-34-34-15**), both of which rent simple rooms for under $90 a night. For dinner, you might try **La Rôtisserie du Chambertin** (☎ **03-80-34-33-20**) on Rue Chambertin for regional classics like *coq au vin,* or ✪ **Les Millésimes** (☎ **03-80-51-84-24**) at 25 rue de l'Église (at rue de Meixville) for a special night out, especially if you're a wine connoisseur.

Days 5 to 8   Continue north the remaining short distance to **Dijon,** home to some of the region's most spectacular architecture. Use Dijon as your base for several interesting side trips.

SIDE TRIPS FROM DIJON   Leave Dijon on A38 northwest toward Paris. You'll be traveling along a good road in the Vallée de l'Ouche, alongside the Burgundy Canal. At pont de Pany, on the outskirts of Sombernon, exit onto a local highway (D905) and continue northwest. On your left lies the artificial lake of Grosbois. The scenery is typical of agricultural France, with isolated farms, woods, and pastures.

You pass through Vitteaux and just before the next village, Posanges, stands a feudal château. You can't visit it, but it's worth a picture. Continue on D905 for a few miles until you come to a railroad crossing. On your left is another old castle, now part of a private farm. The next village you reach along D905 is Pouillenay. Follow the signs for a short detour to the hamlet of **Flavigny-sur-Ozerain.** Park your car outside the walls and walk through the old streets.

Leave Flavigny and follow the signs for a few miles on country roads to **Alise-Ste-Reine,** the site of the camp of Alesia, where Caesar wiped out a concentration of Gallic soldiers. Here, Millet sculpted a bronze statue of Vercingetorix. You can explore the excavated ruins of a Roman-Gallic town and visit the **Musée Alesia,** rue de l'Hôpital (☎ **03-80-96-10-95**); it's open June 30 to September 3, daily from 9am to 7pm; March 25 to June 30 and September 8 to November 5, daily from 10am to 6pm (closed November 5 to March 20). Admission is 28 F ($4.50) for adults and 18 F ($2.90) for students and children. Alise-Ste-Reine honors a Christian girl who was decapitated for refusing to marry a Roman governor, Olibrius. As late as the 17th century, a fountain at the site of the beheading was said to have curative powers.

After Alise-Ste-Reine, you can head back to the village of Les Laumes, a railroad center. Before entering the village, make a U-turn to the right and take N454 to Baigneux-les-Juifs. After the village of Grésigny, on your left is a farm-fortress surrounded by water.

One mile farther, turn right toward the **Château de Bussy-Rabutin.** Roger de Rabutin, cousin of Mme de Sévigné, ridiculed Louis XIV's court, for which he spent 6 years in the Bastille. The château, with two round towers, has survived mostly intact, including the interior decoration. The gardens and park are attributed to Le Nôtre. It's open Wednesday to Monday: April to September from 9am to noon and 2 to 6pm and October to March from 10am to noon and 2 to 5pm.

Going back to Grésigny, turn right before the farm-fortress, then go left. Outside the village, turn right again toward Menetreux Le Pitois. You're now off the main road and into the real countryside. Once back on D905, head on to **Montbard,** hometown of George-Louis Leclerc, comte de Buffon, one of the 18th century's greatest naturalists and author of *L'Histoire naturelle,* a 44-volume encyclopedia. The scientist's home is on display, as well as a minimuseum of his life and work. The town is also the site of a pleasant hotel/restaurant, the **Hôtel de l'Ecu,** 7 rue Auguste-Carré (☎ **03-80-92-11-66**), where moderately priced meals are prepared in what was during the 1700s a postal relay station.

Continue east for another 6 miles to Marmagne, then turn left on D32 and head toward the **Abbaye de Fontenay** (☎ **03-80-92-15-00**). Isolated in a valley, Fontenay is one of Europe's most unspoiled 12th-century Cistercian abbeys. It was classified as a World Heritage Site by UNESCO in 1981 and is open daily from 10am to noon and 2 to 6pm (to 5pm in winter). Admission is 47 F ($7.50) for adults and 24 F ($3.85) for children and students.

1 Auxerre

103 miles SE of Paris, 92 miles NW of Dijon

Auxerre was founded by the Gauls and enlarged by the Romans. On a hill overlooking the Yonne River, it's the capital of Lower Burgundy and the center of vineyards, some of which produce chablis. Joan of Arc spent several days here in 1429. Napoléon met Maréchal Ney here on March 17, 1815, on the former emperor's return from Elba. Louis XVIII had sent Ney to stop Napoléon, but Ney embraced him and turned his army against the king. For that gesture, Ney was later shot in Paris.

The handsome city of Auxerre is a sleepy, dreamy kind of place today, as you'll agree if you spend an afternoon with the Auxerrois reading a newspaper in a cafe. Its population of 42,000 will often admit that not a lot is happening around here these days—and that's how they'd like to keep it.

ESSENTIALS

GETTING THERE   Many visitors **drive** here, since Auxerre is near A6/E1 (Autoroute du Soleil).

Many of the **trains** traveling between Paris and Lyon stop at Auxerre. There are 12 departures per day from Paris and nine from Lyon; trip time is 2 hours from either city. For train information and schedules, call ☎ **08-36-35-35-35.**

VISITOR INFORMATION   The **Office de Tourisme** is at 1–2 quai de la République (☎ **03-86-52-06-19**).

TOURING THE CATHEDRAL

The railway station lies at the eastern edge of town, about a mile from the historic center. Most of Auxerre is on the opposite (western) bank of the Yonne River. Its heart is between place du Maréchal-Leclerc (where you'll find the Hôtel de Ville) and the Cathédrale St-Etienne.

Cathédrale St-Etienne. ☎ 03-86-52-23-29. Admission 25 F ($4). Daily 9am–6pm.

Pay a visit to the Flamboyant Gothic Cathédrale St-Etienne, begun in the 13th century but not completed until the 16th. The front facade is remarkable, with sculptured portals. The stained glass, some of it original, is famous. In the crypt, all that remains of the Romanesque church that stood on this site, you can see 11th-century frescoes.

Every Sunday in July and August you can attend an organ concert from 5 to 6pm; admission is free. And daily, June to August from 10pm to 11:10pm and in September from 9:30pm to 10:40pm, there's a sound-and-light show here depicting the history of the church. It's presented in English, French, and German for 35 F ($5.60) for adults, free for children 13 and under.

ACCOMMODATIONS

Hôtel Le Maxime. 2 quai de la Marine, 89000 Auxerre. ☎ **03-86-52-14-19.** Fax 03-86-52-21-70. 25 units. TV TEL. 480 F ($76.80) double. AE, DC, MC, V. Parking 20 F ($3.20).

This family-run hotel contains attractive rooms, many with views of the river Yonne or the old city. Most retain their original wall and ceiling beams. You can take breakfast in your room or in the quiet salon, amid Oriental rugs, polished paneling, and a sense of the gentility of an earlier era.

Hôtel Normandie. 41 bd. Vauban, 89000 Auxerre. ☎ **03-86-52-57-80.** Fax 03-86-51-54-33. www.acom.fr/normandie. E-mail: normandie@acom.fr. 47 units. TV TEL. 295–420 F ($47.20–$67.20) double. AE, DC, MC, V. Parking 27 F ($4.30).

This centrally located hotel offers traditional hospitality, combining antique furnishings with modern amenities. The tranquil and comfortably furnished rooms open onto garden views. There's overnight parking for 30 cars, plus a complete gymnasium, sauna, bar, terrace, and room service with hot and cold dishes anytime.

✪ **Le Parc des Maréchaux.** 6 av. Foch, 89000 Auxerre. ☎ **03-86-51-43-77.** Fax 03-86-51-31-72. 25 units. MINIBAR TV TEL. 495–550F ($79.20–$88) double; 600F ($96) triple or quad. AE, DC, MC, V.

An absolute gem that completely outshines the competition, this was a private residence in the 19th century, set in its own 1-acre park. It's the most secluded choice in

Colette: An Unlikely Literary Heroine

"C'est Colette! C'est un miracle!"

That's what her fans had to say, and Colette's fans included the poet Stephen Koch (he claimed that she was the only writer who got it right when writing about sex), Proust, Updike, Woolf, Gide, and her beloved friend Cocteau. Auden compared her favorably to Tolstoy.

Born in 1873 to a one-legged, once-bankrupt tax collector from Provence and raised in the obscure Burgundian village of St-Sauveur-en-Puisaye, Sidonie Gabrielle Colette was an unlikely literary heroine. As a schoolgirl, Colette fell for a would-be writer twice her age—known as Willy, pseudonym of Henri Gauthier-Villars—and married him at age 20. He exposed her to the murky world of Paris society and imposed a rigid writing discipline, frequently locking her in a room until she finished a designated number of pages. Those pages were eventually compiled into four novellas known as the *Claudine* series. Published at yearly intervals between 1900 and 1903 under her husband's pseudonym, each was based on the experiences of a *libertine ingenue,* with an acute preoccupation for evoking the sounds, tastes, textures, colors, and interactions of that era's beautiful people. They began to explore a theme that Colette returned to again and again, with exquisite sensitivity: the pleasures and pains of love, permeated with a mix of naïveté and cunning.

In 1910 she divorced Willy and did a stint as a vaudeville entertainer in a Paris music hall. Later that year she was writing for *Le Matin,* whose editor in chief was Henri de Jouvenel, whom she married in 1912. That partnership produced a daughter, Colette de Jouvenel (or Bel Gazou, "beautiful warbler," as her mother called her), and lasted until 1925. Then Colette met and married her third and final husband, Maurice Goudeket.

Two of Colette's most enduring works are *Chéri* (1920), the story of a semicrazed youthful survivor of World War I who initiates a love affair with an older woman, and *Gigi* (1945), about a young girl reared to become a Parisian courtesan by two sophisticated and aging sisters. This work gained even more popularity when Hollywood made it into a musical starring Leslie Caron and Louis Jourdan in 1958.

The former country girl's official awards eventually included membership in the Belgian Royal Academy (1935), France's Académie Goncourt (elected a

the area: on the western outskirts of town, surrounded by century-old trees. The guest rooms are christened with the names of the sometimes obscure 19th-century *maréchals* of France. Decor of the public areas and the cocktail lounge is French Empire; bedrooms are less coherent in their decor, with a mixture of contemporary and Empire predominating. The only bona fide meal served here is breakfast, although a limited roster of hot food can be served, on special request, in either your bedroom or in one of the salons, at prices that range from 20 F to 65 F ($3.20 to $10.40) à la carte or fixed-price menu at 100 F ($16) per platter.

DINING

Le Jardin Gourmand. 56 bd. Vauban. ☎ **03-86-51-53-52.** Reservations required. Main courses 80–150 F ($12.80–$24); fixed-price menus 150–280 F ($24–$44.80). AE, MC, V. Thurs–Mon noon–2pm and 7:30–9:30pm. Closed 2 weeks in late Mar and 3 weeks in Sept. FRENCH.

member in 1945, elected president in 1949), and the French Légion d'Honneur (elected a member in 1920, elected Grand Officer in 1953)—honors that until then had rarely been granted to women.

Literary fans around the world mourned the passing of Colette in 1954. In Paris they shouted "Gigi!" or "Chéri!" as her body traveled from an elaborate ceremony in the courtyard of the Palais Royal to the Cimetière du Père-Lachaise, to be buried with honors near Oscar Wilde and other literary icons.

Today you can pay homage to Colette by journeying to the village of St-Sauveur-en-Puisaye, where you can visit the **Musée Colette** (☎ **03-86-45-61-95**). It's open April to October, Wednesday to Monday from 10am to 6pm; November to March, Saturday and Sunday from 2 to 6pm. Admission is 28 F ($4.50) for adults or 10 F ($1.60) for students and children 10 and under.

Colette fans from around the world—led by her daughter and only child—helped establish the museum. Her daughter died in 1981, long before the shrine opened in 1995. Photographs in the museum serve as a guidebook to Colette's life. Pictured are Colette with her trio of husbands and even her lesbian lover, the marquise de Belboeuf. (Colette came out of the closet long before it was fashionable to do so.) One photograph depicts her going up in a balloon over Paris for *Le Matin*. She's seen with many of the leading legends of her day, including Sarah Bernhardt.

One room is a trompe-l'oeil copy of Colette's apartment in the Palais Royal (not open to the public) in Paris. You can also watch a 50-minute 1951 film of Colette in which she appears with Cocteau.

What comes as a surprise is that at a tearoom here you can order, among other items, *fra,* that salt cheese tart so beloved by Colette. Colette's other favorite Burgundian pastries are made fresh daily and served here, including a pastry called *gâteau à six cornes* culled from a recipe of Colette's.

To reach the village, take the Autoroute du Soleil (A6) south from Paris heading toward Lyon but exit at Joigny. Follow the signs for Toucy, where you go in the direction of Orléans-St-Fargeau. At the Toucy exit, St-Sauveur-en-Puisayne is signposted. If you're already in Auxerre, take D965 to Toucy.

The most sophisticated and charming restaurant in town specializes in *cuisine moderne du marché,* using the freshest ingredients within artfully presented menu items that change, often radically, eight times a year. The setting is a 10-minute walk from the cathedral, within an antique house. In summer, a retractable awning shades an outdoor terrace from the harsh summer sun. Pierre Boussereau (chef) and Olivier Laplaine (sommelier/maître-d'hotel) are devoted to cultivating fresh salad greens and herbs from their own on-site garden, used to garnish such platters as a *carpaccio* of duck liver with, among others, *cornes de cerf* (stag's horn) and *pourpier d'Asie* (Asian purple-leaf). Other menu items might include a steak of calf's liver served with a thickened veal stock and fresh cardamon; roasted scallops served with the essence of pulverized pea pods; and a fillet of red mullet served with a sauce made from thickened fish stock and star anise.

NEARBY ACCOMMODATIONS & DINING

✪ **À la Côte St-Jacques.** 14 Faubourg de Paris (N6), 89300 Joigny. ☎ **03-86-62-09-70.** Fax 03-86-91-49-70. Reservations required. Main courses 160–430 F ($25.60–$68.80); fixed-price menus 380–900 F ($60.80–$144) at lunch, 780–900 F ($124.80–$144) at dinner. AE, DC, MC, V. Daily 12:15–2:45pm and 7:15–9:45pm. From Auxerre, head north on N6 (toward Sens) for 17 miles. FRENCH.

Jean-Michel Lorain and his wife, Brigitte, are the directors of this top-echelon Relais & Châteaux. The 300-year-old foundation and 19th-century design contribute to the atmosphere in what is one of the region's most luxurious hotels and restaurants. In addition to the main building, there's a luxurious annex across the N6 highway that's connected to it via an underground tunnel fashioned from rocks salvaged from old buildings nearby. In one of the elegant dining rooms that has welcomed such stars as Catherine Deneuve, you can enjoy specialties like a terrine of Brittany oysters; smoked sea bass served with Servruga caviar; Bresse chicken steamed in champagne; and turbot cooked in salt crust, served with a creamy medley of leeks and peas, and with a emulsion of liquefied bitter almonds.

The hotel rents 25 **rooms,** priced at 790 F to 2,750 F ($126.40 to $440) per night depending on size and views over the river. Each has ultra-comfortable mattresses, well-designed bathrooms, TV, phone, minibar, air-conditioning, and a conservatively contemporary decor. On the premises are a heated indoor pool and a sauna.

2 Vézelay

135 miles SE of Paris, 32 miles S of Auxerre

Vézelay, a living museum of French antiquity, stands frozen in time. For many, the town is the high point of their trip through Burgundy. Because it contained what was believed to be the tomb of St. Mary Magdalene, that "beloved and pardoned sinner," it was once one of the great pilgrimage sites of the Christian world.

Today the medieval charm of Vézelay is widely known throughout France, and the town is virtually overrun with visitors in summer. The hordes are especially thick on July 22, the official day of homage to La Madeleine.

ESSENTIALS

GETTING THERE   When **driving** from Paris, take A6 south to Auxerre, then continue south along N151 to Clamency, turning east along D951 to Vézelay.

Trains travel from Auxerre to nearby Sermizelles, where a bus makes the run to Vézelay only on Saturday at noon. For train information and schedules, call ☎ 08-36-35-35-35. Then take a taxi for the 15-minute trip.

VISITOR INFORMATION   The **Office de Tourisme** is on rue St-Pierre (☎ 03-86-33-23-69), open daily April to September and Friday to Wednesday October to March.

EXPLORING THE TOWN

On a hill 360 feet above the countryside, Vézelay is known for its ramparts and houses with sculptured doorways, corbeled staircases, and mullioned windows. The site was originally an abbey founded by Girart de Roussillon, a comte de Bourgogne (troubadours were fond of singing of his exploits). It was consecrated in 878 by Pope John VIII.

On March 31, 1146, St. Bernard preached the Second Crusade there; in 1190 the town was the rendezvous point for the Third Crusade, drawing such personages as

Richard the Lion-Hearted and King Philippe-Auguste of France. Later, St. Louis of France came here several times on pilgrimages.

Park outside the town hall and walk through the medieval streets lined with 15th-, 16th-, and 18th-century houses, past flower-filled gardens.

Basilique Ste-Madeleine. ☎ **03-86-33-39-50.** Free admission. July–Aug, daily 7am–7pm; Sept–June, daily sunrise–sunset. Parking 10 F ($1.70).

Built in the 12th century, France's largest and most famous Romanesque church is only 10 yards shorter than Notre-Dame de Paris. You enter the narthex, a vestibule of large dimensions, about 4,000 square feet. Raise your eyes to the famous doorway depicting Christ giving the apostles the Holy Spirit. From the Romanesque nave, with its alternately white and gray stone of the traverse arches, you discover the light Gothic chancel. It's possible to visit the Carolingian crypt, where the tomb of Mary Magdalene formerly rested (today it contains some of her relics). There's a panoramic view from the back terrace.

SHOPPING   Most of Vézelay's shops line either side of **rue St-Etienne** and **rue St-Pierre.** You'll find an assortment of stores selling religious books and statuary, including **Jerusalem,** 78 rue St-Pierre (☎ **03-86-33-37-43**), and **Le Magasin du Pélerin,** place de la Basilique (☎ **03-86-33-29-14**). For one-of-a-kind pieces by local craftspeople and artists, go to **Atelier Marie-Noëlle,** 69 rue St-Pierre (☎ **03-86-33-26-02**), offering rich, colorful weavings and silk decorations; **Galerie Lieber,** 14 rue St-Etienne (☎ **03-86-33-33-90**), which specializes in handmade jewelry using semiprecious and precious stones in both heavy and delicate settings of silver and gold; and **Jacques d'Aubres,** rue St-Etienne (☎ **03-86-33-22-32**), with his unique textiles as well as stone and metal sculptures. You may also want to pick up a bottle or two of Vézelay wine at **La Vézelienne,** route de Nanchèvres in St-Père-sous-Vézelay (☎ **03-86-33-29-62**).

ACCOMMODATIONS

L'Espérance (see "Dining," below) also rents luxurious rooms.

Le Compostelle. Place du Champ-de-Foire, 89450 Vézelay. ☎ **03-86-33-28-63.** Fax 03-86-33-34-34. 18 units. TV TEL. 275–335 F ($46.75–$56.95) double. AE, MC, V. Closed Jan.

This unpretentious and pleasant hotel occupies a late-19th-century building that was radically renovated in 1991. It's in the center of town, midway up the hill leading to the basilica, evoking in some ways a country house in England. It's the best of the simpler and more affordable inns in town. Breakfast is the only meal served.

Poste et Lion d'Or. Place du Champ-de-Foire, 89450 Vézelay. ☎ **03-86-33-21-23.** Fax 03-86-32-30-92. 39 units. TV TEL. 320–600 F ($51.20–$96) double. AE, DC, MC, V. Closed mid-Nov to mid-Mar. Parking 40 F ($6.40).

A local historic monument on the main square, at the bottom of the hill that rises to the basilica, this hotel was built in the 17th century as a postal station. With a terrace and small garden, the Poste et Lion d'Or is a first-class place with surprisingly reasonable rates. Bedrooms are conservatively outfitted in a functional yet respectable way. Other than L'Espérance, which is in the countryside, it's the finest address in town, but only slightly better than Le Pontot.

The food is exceptional, especially the escargots de Bourgogne in chablis and stuffed trout with herbs. Fixed-price menus cost 118 F to 230 F ($18.90 to $36.80). It's classic Burgundian—nothing experimental here. The restaurant is closed all day Monday and Tuesday at lunch.

Résidence-Hôtel Le Pontot. Place du Pontot, 89450 Vézelay. ☎ **03-86-33-24-40.** Fax 03-86-33-30-05. 11 units. TEL. 620–920 F ($99.20–$147.20) double; 820–1,050 F ($131.20–$168) suite. DC, MC, V. Closed Nov–Easter. Parking 50 F ($8).

Near the basilica, this tastefully renovated medieval structure is Vézelay's other leading hotel. The rooms are decorated in a romantic French style—at times not to everyone's taste but a lovely attempt at creating a cozy, homelike environment. Room size ranges from small to spacious, and beds are quite elegant, each with a good mattress and quality linen. It has a charming walled garden for breakfast and bar service but no restaurant. English is spoken.

DINING

✪ **L'Espérance.** St-Père-sous-Vézelay, 89450 Vézelay. ☎ **03-86-33-39-10.** Fax 03-86-33-26-15. www.relaischateaux.fr/esperance. E-Mail: marcimeneau@wanadoo.fr. Reservations recommended. Main courses 300–600 F ($48–$96); fixed-price menus 600–950 F ($96–$152) at lunch Mon–Fri. Closed Feb. Take D957 1¹/₂ miles south of Vézelay. FRENCH.

Few other restaurants in Burgundy have been as richly or as frequently analyzed, assessed, and gossiped about as L'Espérance. Its acquisition and loss of Michelin accolades (its ratings traditionally bounce between two and three stars) are usually reported breathlessly in the national press. Each acquisition of an additional star prompts a flow of traffic from foodies as far away as Paris, while the loss of a star prompts speculation that the quality is slipping. Through it all, it never loses the support of its loyal fans. At this writing, this legendary restaurant has just been demoted to the "mere mortal" (but much sought-after) status of a two-star monument, but it still elicits our fervent loyalty.

The restaurant has the feel of a prosperous, old-fashioned farm and bakery compound; it simultaneously emanates Burgundian wholesomeness and Parisian chic. It's set in a fertile valley at the base of the most famous hill in Burgundy—the one that's capped with the majestic church of Vézelay. Marc Meneau is the self-taught chef and creative force behind the cuisine here; his wife Françoise is an adept hostess who's never fazed at welcoming movie stars or government leaders. Flagstone floors and big windows overlooking a garden create a foil for superb cuisine. Menu items change frequently but are likely to include an "ambrosia" of poultry with truffles and foie gras; oysters in a seawater-flavored aspic; a cream of truffle soup with an infusion of green olives; and a galette of new potatoes with caviar.

On the premises are 34 well-maintained and extremely comfortable rooms. Each evokes French country living at its best. Doubles cost 750 F to 1,400 F ($120 to $224); suites 1,700 F to 2,500 F ($272 to $400). If there's a flaw here at all, it involves a somewhat overworked and occasionally pedantic staff, who struggle valiantly with the flow of traffic generated by the place's fame.

3 Avallon

133 miles SE of Paris, 32 miles SE of Auxerre

This old fortified town is shielded behind its ancient ramparts, upon which you can stroll. A medieval atmosphere still permeates Avallon, where you'll find many 15th- and 16th-century houses. At the town gate on Grande Rue Aristide-Briand is a clock tower from 1460. The Romanesque **Église St-Lazarus** dates from the 12th century and has two interesting doorways. The church is said to have received the head of St. Lazarus in 1000, thus turning Avallon into a pilgrimage site. Today Avallon is mainly visited for its fabulous food.

ESSENTIALS

GETTING THERE   To reach Avallon by **car,** travel south from Paris along A6 to Auxerre; from Auxerre, take N6 south to Avallon.

Ten **trains** arrive daily from Paris (trip time: 2 hours), and eight trains pull in from Dijon daily (trip time: 3 hours). For train information and schedules, call ☎ 08-36-35-35-35. **Buses** run from the railway junction of Montbard (a stop on the TGV lines from Paris) for Avallon, in ways that are timed to coincide with the arrival of trains (about three a day). With the train and the bus combined, via Montbard, travel time from Paris is about 2 hours. For bus information, contact the railway station in Avallon at ☎ 03-86-34-01-01.

VISITOR INFORMATION   The **Office de Tourisme** is at 4–6 rue Bocquillot (☎ 03-86-34-14-19).

ACCOMMODATIONS & DINING

✪ **Château de Vault-de-Lugny.** A Vault-de-Lugny, 89200 Avallon. ☎ **03-86-34-07-86.** Fax 03-86-34-16-36. www.ila-chateau.com/lugny. E-mail: lugny@transeo.fr. 13 units. MINI-BAR TV TEL. 950–1,400 F ($152–$224) double; 2,300–2,800 F ($368–$448) suite. Rates include breakfast. AE, MC, V. Closed Nov 13–Mar 17. Take D957 from Avallon; turn right in Pontaubert (after the church) and follow the signs to the château; Vault-de-Lugny is about 2 miles away.

At this château halfway between Avallon and Vézelay, Matherat Audan and his daughter, Elisabeth, welcome you. This 16th-century château is encircled by a moat, and on the grounds are a fortress tower and peacocks. Personal service is a hallmark (two staff members to every guest). The rooms and suites are often sumptuous, with half-tester or canopied beds with comfortable mattresses, plus antique furnishings and fireplaces. You can order cocktails in an ornate salon and then proceed to dinner by candlelight.

Dining: Market-fresh ingredients are the hallmark of the cuisine. A special bourguignon meal is offered nightly, consisting of typical regional dishes. Favorites include a homemade beef terrine in aspic jelly, snails with butter and garlic, a regional beef stew, and cheese and a *carte des desserts*. A more elaborate *menu gourmand* is also offered nightly: perhaps fresh scampi roasted with green beans and artichoke hearts, duck foie gras, homemade ravioli, fresh turbot or sole, prime beef steak with pepper sauce, or traditional *coq au vin*, followed by cheese and dessert.

Moulin des Ruats. Vallée du Cousin, 89200 Avallon. ☎ **03-86-34-97-00.** Fax 03-86-31-65-47. www.hostellerie-moulin-ruats.fr. E-mail: hostellerie.dumoulin.desrauts@wanadoo.fr. 24 units. TV TEL. 380–680 F ($60.80–$108.80) double. AE, DC, MC, V. Closed Nov 15–Feb 17; Mon–Tues closed lunch. Take D427 2 miles outside town.

This country inn on the banks of the Cousin is enchanting. Rooms are simultaneously rustic and modern. The elegant restaurant, with a terrace, serves an excellent menu of freshwater fish and boasts a fine wine list. The restaurant is outstanding, certainly more impressive than the hotel it's in. The meals are discreetly balanced, and everything has a certain zest and flavor. A reasonably priced fixed-price meal here, at 155 F ($24.80), might include a dozen Burgundian snails with garlic-flavored parsley sauce; a "farmers salad" with semi-soft goat cheese and supreme of chicken; a stewpot of Mediterranean hogfish with essence of shellfish; and a homemade pastry.

4 Autun

182 miles SE of Paris, 53 miles SW of Dijon, 30 miles W of Beaune, 37 miles SE of Auxerre

Deep in burgundy country, Autun is one of the oldest towns in France. In the days of the Roman Empire it was called "the other Rome." Some relics still stand, including the remains of the largest theater in Gaul, the Théâtre Romain, holding some 15,000 spectators. It was nearly 500 feet in diameter. Outside the town you can see the quadrangular tower of the Temple de Janus rising incongruously 80 feet over the plain.

Today Autun is a thriving provincial town of some 20,000 people. But because it's off the beaten track, the hordes go elsewhere. Still, it has its memories, even of Napoléon, who studied here in 1779 at the military academy (today the Lycée Bonaparte).

ESSENTIALS

GETTING THERE   If you're **driving,** take D944 south from Avallon to the town of Château-Chinon. Then follow D978 east right into Autun.

Autun has its own railway station; however, it isn't used very frequently. Consequently, many rail passengers find it more convenient to take one of the 10 **trains** a day from Paris (Gare de Lyon) or the eight trains a day from Lyon to the larger railway junction of Montchanin-le-Creusot, 25 miles to the south. From there they take a 45-minute bus connection to Autun, priced at around 50 F ($8) each way. In Autun, **buses** arrive at a parking lot adjacent to the railway station on Avenue de la République. For more bus information, call ☎ **03-85-86-92-55.** For further railway information, call the railway station in Autun at either ☎ **03-85-52-28-01** or the national SNCF information line at ☎ **08-36-35-35-35.**

VISITOR INFORMATION   The **Office de Tourisme** is at 2 av. Charles-de-Gaulle (☎ **03-85-86-80-38**).

SEEING THE SIGHTS

Once Autun was an important link on the road from Lyon to Boulogne, as reflected by the 55-foot high **Porte d'Arroux,** with its two large archways now used for cars and two smaller ones for pedestrians. Also exceptional is the **Porte St-André** (St. Andrew's Gate), about a quarter of a mile northwest of the Roman theater. Rising 65 feet, it too has four doorways and is surmounted by a gallery of 10 arcades.

Cathédrale St-Lazare. Place St-Louis. ☎ **03-85-52-12-37.** Free admission. Daily 8am–6pm (till 7pm July–Aug).

On the highest point in Autun, the cathedral was built in 1120 to house the relics of St. Lazarus. On the facade, the tympanum in the central portal depicts the *Last Judgment*—a triumph of Romanesque sculpture. Inside, a painting by Ingres depicts the martyrdom of St. Symphorien, who was killed in Autun. In the 1860s, Viollet-le-Duc, the architect who restored (sometimes with controversial results) some of the major monuments of France, had to double the size of some of the columns supporting the cathedral's roof to avoid a collapse of the structure. New capitals matching the Romanesque style of the original building were crafted for placement atop the new columns. The original capitals, however, are now on display, more or less at eye level, in the Salle Capitulaire, one flight above street level. Especially noteworthy are *La Reveil des Mages* (The Awakening of the Magi) and *La Fuite en Egypte* (The Flight into Egypt).

Musée Rolin. 3 rue des Bancs. ☎ **03-85-52-09-76.** Admission 20 F ($3.20) adults, 10 F ($1.60) students and children. Apr–Sept, Wed–Sun 9:30am–noon and 1:30–7pm; Oct–Mar, Wed–Sun 10am–noon and 2–5pm.

This 15th-century mansion was built for Nicolas Rolin (b. 1380), who became a famous lawyer in his day. An easy walk from the cathedral, the museum displays a fine collection of Burgundian Romanesque sculpture, as well as paintings and archaeological mementos. From the original Rolin collection are exhibited the *Nativity* by the Maître de Moulins, along with a statue that's a masterpiece of 15th-century work, *Our Lady of Autun* (La Vierge d'Autun, also known as La Vierge Bulliot after the benefactor who donated the original statue back to the cathedral in 1948).

NEARBY ATTRACTIONS

If you have a car, after visiting Autun you can tour one of Burgundy's finest wineries. ✪ **Domaine Protheau** (☎ **03-85-98-99-10**), Château d'Etoyes, lies at Mercurey, 25 miles southeast along D978. Among the selections are at least two appellations contrôlées, so you'll have a chance to immerse yourself in the subtle differences among reds (both pinot noirs and burgundies), whites, and rosés produced under the auspices of both Rully and Mercurey. The headquarters of the organization, founded in the 1740s, is a château built in the late 1700s and early 1800s. Free tours of the sprawling cellars and explanations of the various vintages it produces are offered, in French and halting English, daily from 9am to 6pm (call ahead to confirm). A *dégustation des vins* and the opportunity to haul a bottle or two away with you are included in every visit.

Two miles away, you can visit the **Château de Rully,** site of the **Domaine de la Bressande** (☎ **03-85-87-20-89**), a well-respected producer of white and, to a lesser extent, red burgundies. Originally built in the 12th-century as a stronghold for the comte de Ternay, it offers tours. The owner prefers you visit the château as part of a group; cost is 30 F ($4.80) per person. Individuals can visit between mid-July and mid-September daily at 3pm. This visit costs only 15 F ($2.40) and is more limited than the group tour.

ACCOMMODATIONS & DINING

Hostellerie du Vieux Moulin. Porte d'Arroux, 71400 Autun. ☎ **03-85-52-10-90.** Fax 03-85-86-32-15. 16 units. TEL. 250–380 F ($40–$60.80) double. AE, MC, V. Closed Dec–Feb.

This fine hotel, a 10-minute walk north of the town center, contains Autun's best restaurant. At the edge of the Arroux River, within the stone walls of what was built in the 1870s as a grain mill, it boasts a warm ambience, a scattering of 19th-century regional antiques, and simple but clean rooms. Each is accented with reminders of the winemaking trade.

Dining: In summer you can sit at a table overlooking the garden and the stream that abuts it. Fixed-price menus range from 150 F to 250 F ($24 to $40). Menu items include fillet of local sandre (whitefish) with basil-flavored cream sauce, Charolais beef simmered in red wine, and tournedos Tallyrand (the namesake was a local bishop, not the politician, and the dish is flavored with shallots and red wine). An appropriate starter? Consider the fricassée of snails *forestière* with wild mushrooms and cream sauce. Naturally any of dozens of red burgundies can accompany your meal. From June to September, the dining room is open daily from noon to 2pm and 7:30 to 9pm. The rest of the year, it's closed Sunday night and all day Monday.

Hôtel des Ursulines. 14 rue Rivault, 71400 Autun. ☎ **03-85-86-58-58.** Fax 03-85-86-23-07. www.ursulines.fr. E-mail: welcome@hotelursulines.fr. 43 units. A/C MINIBAR TV TEL. 400–595 F ($64–$95.20) double; 820 F ($131.20) suite. AE, MC, DC, V.

The best hotel in Autun, the Ursulines (in a former convent) offers attractively decorated rooms with views of the countryside and the distant Morvan mountains. Accommodations vary in shape and size; each comes with a fine mattress and quality linen.

The hotel is also known for its cuisine. The results are sometimes more interesting than the menu suggests. The wine list needs expanding.

5 Beaune

196 miles SE of Paris, 24 miles SW of Dijon

This is the capital of the Burgundy Wine Country and also one of the best-preserved medieval cities in the district, with a girdle of ramparts. Its history goes back more than 2,000 years. Beaune was a Gallic sanctuary, then later a Roman town. Until the 14th century it was the residence of the ducs de Bourgogne. When the last duke, Charles the Bold, died in 1477, Beaune was annexed by Louis XI. Visited today for its art, architecture, wines, and Burgundian cuisine, Beaune is a thriving town of some 20,000.

ESSENTIALS

GETTING THERE   If you're **driving,** note that Beaune is a few miles from the junction of four superhighways that fan out—A6, A31, A36, and N6.

Beaune has good railway connections with Dijon, Lyon, and Paris. From Paris, there are four TGV **trains** per day (trip time: 2 hours); from Lyon, seven trains arrive per day (trip time: 1¹/₂ hours); and from Dijon, 22 trains per day (trip time: 25 minutes). For train information and schedules, call ☎ **08-36-35-35-35.**

VISITOR INFORMATION   The **Office de Tourisme** is on rue de l'Hôtel-Dieu (☎ **03-80-26-21-30**).

SPECIAL EVENTS   The town comes to life on the third Sunday in November, when wine buyers and oenophiles from all over the world descend on the medieval old town for a 3-day festival and wine auction called **Les Trois Glorieuses.** The town is packed with wineries offering free *dégustations*—and also packed with tourists visiting the labyrinth of caves or wine cellars. With all the free spirits (both kinds), visitors crowding the streets on summer nights are more than a bit tipsy. It's a fun, sometimes funky, and always colorful event that really puts you in the mood to buy a lot of wine.

EXPLORING THE TOWN

North of the Hôtel-Dieu, the **Collégiale Notre-Dame** on Place du Général Leclerc (☎ **03-80-26-22-70**) is an 1120 Burgundian Romanesque church. Some remarkable tapestries illustrating scenes from the life of Mary are displayed in the sanctuary. You can view them from Easter to Christmas.

Musée de l'Hôtel-Dieu. Rue de l'Hôtel-Dieu. ☎ **03-80-24-45-00.** Admission 32 F ($5.10) adults, 25 F ($4) children. Apr–Nov 19, daily 9am–6:30pm; Nov 20–Mar, daily 9–11:30am and 2–5:30pm.

One of the town's most visible antique buildings is the Hôtel-Dieu. Formally a hospital, it thrived during the Middle Ages thanks to its ownership and maintenance of an order of nuns who were associated with the famous vineyards of Aloxe-Corton and Meursault. It functioned as a working hospital until 1970, and some sections of it are still devoted to a retirement home. It's now the home of the Musée de l'Hôtel-Dieu, displaying Flemish-Burgundian art such as Rogier van der Weyden's 1443 polyptych *The Last Judgment.* In the Chambre des Pauvres (Room of the Poor) you'll find painted, broken-barrel, timbered vaulting, with mostly authentic furnishings.

Musée des Beaux-Arts et Musée Marey. In the Hôtel de Ville (town hall), rue de l'Hôtel de Ville. ☎ **03-80-24-56-92.** Free admission if you've paid for admission to the Musée du Vin (below). Daily 2–6pm. Closed Nov–Mar (except open on the 3rd weekend in Nov).

This museum contains a rich Gallo-Roman archaeological section. The main gallery of paintings has works from the 16th to the 19th century, like Flemish primitives and many paintings by Felix Ziem, a precursor of the Impressionist school. Sculptures from the Middle Ages and the Renaissance are also displayed. A larger part of the museum honors the Beaune physiologist Etienne Jules Marey, who discovered the principles of the cinema long before 1895.

Musée du Vin de Bourgogne. Rue d'Enfer. ☎ **03-80-22-08-19.** Admission 25 F ($4) adults, 15 F ($2.40) students and children, free for children 11 and under. Wed–Mon 9:30am–6pm.

Housed in the former mansion of the ducs de Bourgogne, the Musée du Vin de Bourgogne traces the evolution of the region's wine making. The collection of tools, objets d'art, and documents is contained in 15th- and 16th-century rooms. A collection of winepresses is displayed in a 14th-century press house.

SHOPPING   The best commercial shopping streets are **rue de Lorraine, rue d'Alsace, rue Mauffoux,** and **place de la Madeleine.** For smaller boutiques, stroll down the pedestrian **rue Carnot** and **rue Monge.** For antiques, concentrate your efforts around **place de la Halle.**

FOR WINE LOVERS   Beaune is one of the best towns in the region for sampling and buying famous Burgundy wines. In one of the town's more extraordinary wine cellars, you can tour, taste, and buy these hearty wines. **Marché aux Vins,** rue Nicolas-Rolin (☎ **03-80-25-08-20**), is housed in a 14th-century church. Its cellars are set in and among the ancient tombs, under the floor of the church, and hold 18 wines. Another cellar, **Caves Patriarche Père et Fils,** 7 rue du Collège (☎ **03-80-24-53-78**), is under the former Convent of the Visitandines with individual cellars from the 13th, 16th, and 17th centuries. You can choose from between 12 and 18 vintages here. A tour and tasting at any of the cellars is 50 F ($8).

ACCOMMODATIONS

Hostellerie de Bretonnière. 43 rue de Faubourg Bretonnière, 21200 Beaune. ☎ **03-80-22-15-77.** Fax 03-80-22-72-54. www.bretonnier.hotel.com. 24 units. TV TEL. 440 F ($70.40) double. AE, DC, MC, V. Free parking.

This is the best bargain in town: It's well run, with clean and quiet rooms, and it's conveniently located only a 5-minute walk from the center of town. The accommodations in the rear are the cheapest and most tranquil, though most visitors prefer those overlooking the garden. Rooms are a bit small, with good mattresses, but they're still comfortably adequate for an overnight stopover. There's no restaurant, but a continental breakfast is available.

Hôtel de la Poste. 1 bd. Georges-Clemenceau, 21200 Beaune. ☎ **03-80-22-08-11.** Fax 03-80-24-19-71. www.hoteldelapostebeaune.com. E-mail: francoise.stratigos@wanadoo.fr. 30 units. A/C MINIBAR TV TEL. 700–1,100 F ($112–$176) double; 1,250–1,500 F ($200–$240) suite. AE, DC, MC, V. Parking 50 F ($8).

Outside the town fortifications, this traditional hotel has been completely renovated. The rooms overlook either the ramparts or the vineyards; some have brass beds, with firm, comfortable mattresses and air-conditioning. Menu specialties at the hotel's **restaurant, La Saint-Christophe,** include chicken fricassée with tarragon, and sole in court bouillon with white butter. The restaurant is closed Sunday all day and Monday at lunch. The bar and restaurant are in the belle époque style.

✪ **Hôtel Le Cep.** 27 rue Maufoux, 21206 Beaune. ☎ **03-80-22-35-48.** Fax 03-80-22-76-80. www.slh.com/hotelcep. 57 units. A/C MINIBAR TV TEL. 800–1,200 F ($128– $192) double; 1,500–1,800 F ($240–$288) suite for 2. AE, CB, DC, MC, V. Parking 50 F ($8).

The chic spot for oenophiles visiting Beaune is this mansion in the town center, fit enough for the ducs de Bourgogne. All the charm, grace, and style of Burgundy are reflected in this once-private residence. Each room is individually decorated and named after a Grand Cru wine of the Côte-d'Or vineyards. Our favorites are the Chambre Montrachet and the Chambre Meloisey. Beaune's loveliest courtyard is here, with arcades and sculptured Renaissance stone medallions. A magnificent tower housing one of the city's most beautiful stone staircases rises from here.

A former wine cellar, Le Cellier is the breakfast room (no other meals are served). Beaune's finest restaurant, Bernard Morillon (see below), is next door.

DINING

Hôtel de la Poste (see "Accommodations," above) also has a good restaurant.

✪ **Bernard Morillon.** 31 rue Maufoux. ☎ **03-80-24-12-06.** Reservations recommended. Main courses 120–220 F ($19.20–$35.20); fixed-price menus 180–480 F ($28.80–$76.80). AE, DC, DISC, MC, V. Tues 7:30–10pm, Wed–Sun noon–2pm and 7–10pm. Closed 3 weeks in Jan. FRENCH.

You'll dine here in a Directoire/Louis XV room on specialties like gratin of crayfish tails, an unusual version of *pigeonneau* made with fish served with a *fumet* of red wine, Bresse chicken with Gevrey-Chambertin wine, and deboned Bresse pigeon stuffed with foie gras and truffles. Bernard Morillon has a distinctive style and his food always pleases. The desserts are sumptuous. To find a better restaurant, you'll have to journey outside town to the Hostellerie de Levernois (see below).

Relais de Saulx. 6 rue Louis-Very. ☎ **03-80-22-01-35.** Reservations required for large groups. Main courses 140–170 F ($22.40–$27.20); fixed-price menus 120–330 F ($19.20–$52.80). MC, V. Tues–Fri noon–2pm; Mon–Sat 7–9:30pm. Closed 3 weeks in Dec. FRENCH.

In a 200-year-old stone-trimmed building named after one of the ancient and noble families of the Beaune region, Relais de Saulx is decorated with heavy timbers, oil paintings, and all the accessories you'd expect from one of the region's most respected restaurants. Chef Jean-Louis Monnoir, assisted by his wife, Christiane, prepares a sophisticated combination of traditional Bourguignon cuisine and up-to-date adaptations. Ongoing staples are Bresse chicken with a morel sauce, rack of lamb studded with rosemary and mountain herbs, stuffed cabbages braised with snails, lobster garnished with a sauce derived from the carapaces of shellfish, and roast pigeon whose sauces and garnishes vary according to the season (like baby asparagus tips in springtime and a wine-dark game sauce in winter). Monnoir's presentation is excellent and sometimes flavors elicit gasps of delight. The skillfully compiled wine list includes many unusual local vintages.

NEARBY ACCOMMODATIONS & DINING

✪ **Hostellerie de Levernois.** Rte. de Verdun-sur-le-Doubs, Levernois, 21200 Beaune. ☎ **03-80-24-73-58.** Fax 03-80-22-78-00. E-mail: levernois@relaischateaux.fr. Reservations required. Main courses 150–300 F ($24–$48); fixed-price menus 200–680 F ($32–$108.80) at lunch Mon–Fri, 330–680 F ($52.80–$108.80) at lunch Sat–Sun, 395–535 F ($63.20–$85.60) at dinner. AE, DC, MC, V. Summer, Wed–Mon noon–2pm, Mon–Sat 7–9:30pm; off-season, Thurs–Mon noon–2pm, Wed–Mon 7–9:30pm. Closed Mar 1–Mar 15. Take D970 south of Beaune for 2 miles, following the signs for Lons le Saunier. FRENCH.

Jean Crotet and his sons, Christophe and Guillaume, offer grand cuisine in a stone-sided *maison bourgeoise* from the 1800s, set in an 8-acre park. Two of the trademark dishes here are salmon smoked on the grounds, and a delicious version of snails in puff pastry with a purée of watercress. Three kinds of fish arranged on the same platter, drenched with a garlic-tinged cream sauce, makes a worthy and memorable main course, as does a "canon" of roasted lamb with truffle sauce. There isn't a major emphasis on virtuoso techniques, just a powerful knowledge of first-class ingredients and what to do with them.

The inn also rents 15 carefully decorated **rooms and a suite,** each with TV and phone, in a well-designed modern annex. Doubles cost 950 F to 1,100 F ($152 to $176); the suite goes for 1,900 F ($304).

BEAUNE AFTER DARK

Your best bets for a good time out on the town are the local nightclubs and discos. To hear some solid jazz and rock and maybe even flirt with some of the locals, step over to the **Cotton Bar,** 164 rte. de Dijon (☎ **03-80-24-69-48**), which fills up early with a 30-plus crowd that seems to complete the retro ambience. If you've had enough of wine tasting and feel more in the mood for an ale or two, try the English-style **Pickwick's Pub,** 2 rue Notre-Dame (☎ **03-80-24-72-59**). For a little piano bar and karaoke, try **Why Not,** 74 rue de Faubourg-Madeleine (☎ **03-80-22-64-74**). For a more jolting, electric evening, head over to **Opéra-Night,** rue du Beaumarché (☎ **03-80-24-10-11**), with its booming house music, immense dance floor, strobe lights, and mirrors revealing every angle imaginable. This is one of the hottest places in town, so expect to pay a 60 F ($9.60) cover.

6 Dijon

194 miles SE of Paris, 199 miles NE of Lyon

Dijon is known overseas mainly for its mustard. In the center of the Côte d'Or, it's the ancient capital of Burgundy. In this town, good food is always accompanied by great wine. Between meals you can enjoy Dijon's art and architecture.

The first impression, especially if you arrive at the rail station, is misleading. You'll think Dijon today is a dreary modern city. Not so. Press on to the medieval core only a few blocks away. Many old streets and buildings have been restored. The once and future mayor, Robert Poujade (first elected in 1971), was the minister of environment in the Pompidou government (1969–74), and he thinks he's still back at his old job, wildly planting trees everywhere.

ESSENTIALS

GETTING THERE   The best way to reach Dijon is to **drive.** From Paris, follow A6 southeast to the town of Pouilly-en-Auxois, then east along A38 into Dijon.

Dijon also has excellent rail and bus connections to the rest of Europe. A total of 25 **trains** arrive from Paris each day (trip time: 1³/₄ hours). Trains arrive from Lyon every hour (trip time: 2 hours). For train information and schedules, call ☎ **08-36-35-35-35.**

VISITOR INFORMATION   The **Office de Tourisme** is on place Darcy (☎ **03-80-44-11-44**).

SPECIAL EVENTS   Between the end of June and the beginning of August, the streets of Dijon go through a lively renaissance when Estivade comes to town. This festival uses the city's streets as a stage for folk dances, music, and theatrical art that never fails to be a big hit. You can get a complete schedule of events from either the city tourist office (see above) or from La Mairie (town hall; ☎ **03-80-74-51-51**).

SEEING THE SIGHTS

One of the most historic buildings in this ancient province is the **Palais des Ducs et des États de Bourgogne,** which symbolizes perfectly the proudly independent (or semi-independent, depending on the era) status of this fertile region. Capped with an elaborate tile roof, it's a solid complex built in stages from the 1300s to the 1800s, all of it arranged around a trio of spacious courtyards. The oldest section, only part of which you can visit (see below), is the **Ancien Palais des Ducs de Bourgogne,** erected in the 12th century and rebuilt in the 14th. The newer section is the **Palais des États de Bourgogne,** constructed between the 17th and 18th centuries as a meeting place for the equivalent of a Burgundian parliament (it struggled unsuccessfully to retain the duchy's semi-independent status against encroachments from the French monarchy). Today, as the palace is Dijon's *la mairie* (town hall), all of its newer section and a substantial part of its older section are reserved for the municipal government and can't be visited. However, there's a fine museum in the building that we highly recommend, the **Musée des Beaux-Arts** (see below).

A mile from the center of town on N5 stands the **Chartreuse de Champmol,** the Carthusian monastery built by Philip the Bold as a burial place; it's now a psychiatric hospital. Much of it was destroyed during the Revolution, but you can see the Moses Fountain in the gardens designed by Sluter at the end of the 14th century. The Gothic entrance is superb.

Musée Archéologique, 5 rue du Dr-Maret (☎ 03-80-30-88-54), contains the rather dusty findings unearthed from Dijon's many archaeological digs. A medieval nunnery, **L'Ancien Couvent des Bernardines,** 17 rue Ste-Anne (☎ 03-80-44-12-69), is home to two separate museums. The convent's chapel is the site of the Musée d'Arts Sacrés, devoted to sacred art objects culled from various regional churches. The convent's severely dignified cloister contains the **Musée de la Vie Bourguignonne** (also known as the Musée Perrin de Puycousin), which celebrates folkloric costumes, farm implements, and even some of the 19th- and early 20th-century storefronts removed from Dijon's commercial center. All three of the above-mentioned museums charge 18 F ($2.90) for adults, 9 F ($1.45) for students and children under 12. Each is open Wednesday to Monday from 10am to noon, and from 2 to 6pm.

Musée des Beaux-Arts. In the Palais des Ducs et des États de Bourgogne, cour de Bar. ☎ **03-80-74-52-70.** Admission 22 F ($3.50) adults, 10 F ($1.60) seniors, free for students and children 17 and under, free for everyone on Sun. Wed–Mon 10am–6pm.

The part of the older palace that you can visit contains one of France's oldest and richest museums. It boasts exceptional sculpture, ducal kitchens from the mid-1400s (with great chimneypieces), a collection of European paintings from the 14th to the 19th century, and modern French paintings and sculptures. Take special note of the Salle des Gardes, the banqueting hall of the old palace built by Philip the Good. The tomb of Philip the Bold was created between 1385 and 1411 and is one of the best in France: a reclining figure rests on a slab of black marble, surrounded by 41 mourners.

Musée Magnin. 4 rue des Bons-Enfants. ☎ **03-80-67-11-10.** Admission 16 F ($2.55) adults, 12 F ($1.90) children and students, free for children under 12. Tues–Sun 10am–noon and 2–6pm.

Built in the 19th century as the opulent home of an arts-conscious member of the grande bourgeoisie, it was willed, along with all its contents, to the city of Dijon as a museum following the death of the family's last descendant. It contains an eclectic display of 19th-century antiques and art objects, as well as a collection of paintings accumulated by, or painted by, the former owners.

SHOPPING

Your shopping list might include robust regional wines, Dijon mustard, antiques, and the black-currant cordial called cassis (try a splash in champagne for a Kir Royale).

L'Ancien Couvent de Bernardines **5**
Ancien Palais des Ducs de Bourgogne **2**
Musée Archéologique **1**
Musée des Beaux-Arts **3**
Musée Magnin **4**
Palais des États de Bourgogne **2**

The best streets to hone in on are **rue de la Liberté, rue du Bourg, rue Bossuet,** and **rue Verrerie,** the latter for antiques.

Dijon hosts a flea market, **Le Broe du Forum,** the last Sunday of every month at the Forum, rue du Général-Delaborde (☎ **03-80-74-31-23**), beginning at 9am and running through the afternoon. There's also a market at **Les Halles Centrales** in the rue Odebert, where fruits, vegetables, and all kinds of foodstuffs are sold every Tuesday, Thursday, and Friday from 8am to noon, and every Saturday from 8am to around 5pm. A completely separate merchandizing effort that specializes in used clothing, kitchen utensils, housewares, and flea-market castoffs, **Les Marchés autour des Halles,** operates along the market's periphery every Tuesday and Friday morning, from 8am to around noon, and every Saturday from 8am to around 5pm.

For the ideal picnic lunch, begin at the mustard shop of **La Boutique Maille,** 32 rue de la Liberté (☎ **03-80-30-41-02**), to purchase a supply of that world-famous condiment; head over to **Au Pain d'Autrefois,** 47 rue du Bourg (☎ **03-80-30-47-92**), for a baguette or round of your favorite chewy French country bread; move on to **La Boucherie Nouvelle,** 27 rue Pasteur (☎ **03-80-66-37-10**), to choose one of its many selections of mouthwatering deli meats; follow that with a visit to the **Crémerie Porcheret,** 18 rue Bannelier (☎ **03-80-30-21-05**), to pick up several varieties of regional cheeses, including the heavenly citeaux, made by a group of brothers at a nearby monastery; then finish off at one of the three locations of **Mulot et Petitjean,** 1 place Notre-Dame, 16 rue de la Liberté, or 13 place Bossuet (☎ **03-80-30-07-10**), where you can pick up a bottle of wine and a gingerbread for dessert. Another excellent source for wines is **Nicot,** rue J.-J.-Rousseau (☎ **03-80-73-29-88**).

For antiques, try **Monique Buisson,** 21 rue Verrerie (☎ **03-80-30-31-19**), where you'll find a good collection of regional furniture from the 1700s; **Dubard,** 25 bis rue Verrerie (☎ **03-80-30-50-81**), carrying 18th-century decorative antiques as well as contemporary upholstery fabrics; and **Au Vieux Dijon,** 8 rue Verrerie (☎ **03-80-31-89-08**), with its assortment of 18th- and 19th-century vases, bibelots, and more refined examples of Burgundian furniture. Other recommended stops are **Galerie 6,** 6 rue Auguste-Comte (☎ **03-80-71-68-46**), offering a wide selection of antique paintings from the 1600s to the 1800s; and **Aux Occasions,** 29 rue Auguste-Comte (☎ **03-80-73-55-13**), where you can browse through a multitude of mainly English antiques from the 1800s as well as handmade Oriental rugs, both old and new. Also appealing is **Antiquaires Golmard,** 3 rue Auguste Comte (☎ **03-80-67-14-15**), which specializes in objects originating from the many private estates in the region.

ACCOMMODATIONS

La Toison d'Or (see "Dining," below) also rents rooms.

Hostellerie du Chapeau-Rouge. 5 rue Michelet, 21000 Dijon. ☎ **800/528-1234** in the U.S. and Canada, or 03-80-50-88-88. Fax 03-80-50-88-89. www.bestwestern.com. E-mail: chapeau.rouge@wanadoo.fr. 30 units. A/C MINIBAR TV TEL. 870 F ($139.20) double; 1,200 F ($192) suite. AE, DC, MC, V. Parking 21 F ($3.35).

This Dijon landmark, with an acclaimed restaurant, is the town's best address. The hotel is filled with 19th-century antiques and has rooms with modern conveniences and comfortable furnishings: All of the bedrooms are air-conditioned, and all of the bathrooms have Jacuzzis. Each accommodation comes with excellent mattresses, comfortable beds, and small and well-organized private bathrooms.

Since no other hotel **restaurant** here serves comparable food, you may want to visit even if you're not a guest. The hotel has a supercharged chef who serves Burgundian favorites but has also broken new ground with mouthwatering fare, the specialties depending on what's good in any given season. Examples include sardines stuffed with marinated salmon and fresh algae, served with a salad of mâche; a confit of quail with a parmentier of its own gizzards; a chopped and sautéed steak of roe venison; and a panfried mixture of scallops with Jerusalem artichokes.

Hôtel Ibis Central. 3 place Grangier, 21000 Dijon. ☎ **03-80-30-44-00.** Fax 03-80-30-77-12. 90 units. TV TEL. 385–425 F ($61.60–$68) double. AE, DC, MC, V. Parking 45 F ($7.20).

On a busy downtown square, this hotel was built in 1930 and renovated by the Ibis chain into a streamlined design in the late 1980s. It doesn't have the atmosphere and charm of some Dijon hotels, but we recommend it for its economy and its simple but businesslike and comfortable rooms. Bedrooms were all renovated in 1998, with comfortable new mattresses added and improvements to the upholsteries, paint, and decor. The Central Grill Rôtisserie offers candlelit dinners and a panoramic view of Dijon (closed Sunday). A fixed-price menu costs 139 F ($22.25).

Hôtel Sofitel-La Cloche. 14 place Darcy, 21000 Dijon. ☎ **03-80-30-12-32.** Fax 03-80-30-04-15. E-mail: h1202@accov-hotels.com. 68 units. A/C MINIBAR TV TEL. 890–1,250 F ($142.40–$200) double; 1,600–2,000 F ($256–$320) suite. AE, DC, MC, V. Free parking.

This 15th-century historic monument, renovated in neoclassical style, is in the center of town. The sophisticated interior features Oriental rugs and a pink-and-gray marble floor. The lobby bar is one of the most elegant places in town, with a view of the garden shared by an adjoining glassed-in tearoom. Though of chain format, the rooms are among the most elegant and comfortable in town. Most are medium in size; each has fine linen and a quality mattress.

✪ **Hôtel Wilson.** Place Wilson. ☎ **03-80-66-82-50.** Fax 03-80-36-41-54. 27 units. TV TEL. 400–510 F ($64–$81.60) double. AE, MC, V.

Our favorite nest in Dijon, opening onto a very pleasant square, is this *ancien relais de poste* from the 17th century. The coaching inn has been tastefully restored. Although it has been completely modernized with traditional Burgundian wood furniture, many of the old wooden and time-darkened ceiling beams have been exposed, adding a hard-to-come-by charm. A bonus is the neighboring **restaurant, Thiebert,** which serves a delectable French cuisine and is known for its wine cellar, which is especially rich in burgundies.

DINING

The Hostellerie du Chapeau-Rouge (see above) boasts a marvelous restaurant.

La Toison d'Or. 18 rue Ste-Anne, 21000 Dijon. ☎ **03-80-30-73-52.** Fax 03-80-30-95-51. E-mail: Hotel-libertel-philippe-le-bon@wanadoo.fr. Reservations required. Main courses 85–170 F ($13.60–$27.20); fixed-price menus 170–270 F ($27.20–$43.20) for dinner. AE, DC, MC, V. Mon–Sat noon–1:30pm and 7–9:30pm. FRENCH.

This elegant and rather grand restaurant is accessible via an antique courtyard. On offer is traditional food that's hearty and satisfying, in a style somewhere between old-fashioned and conservatively modern. Amid stone walls, Oriental carpets, and Louis XII chairs, you'll enjoy specialties that include foie gras of duckling in puff pastry, served with a compôte of figs; a galette of snails and mushrooms with parsley, artfully arranged around a stylish-looking circle of potatoes; and scallops and crayfish tails in a nage of spring vegetables and ginger. Fillet of roasted lamb, served with an assortment of different mushrooms, is invariably excellent.

On the premises of this restaurant, but with a style decor and architecture that's much more modern, is a simple 29-room hotel, **Libertel Philippe-le-Bon** (same address and phone), where each double contains bathroom, minibar, TV, phone, comfortable mattresses, and efficient but compact bathrooms. Doubles rent for 450 F to 524 F ($72 to $83.85) per night.

✪ **Le Pré aux Clercs.** 13 place de la Libération. ☎ **03-80-38-05-05.** Reservations required. Main courses 120–200 F ($19.20–$32); fixed-price menus 200–500 F ($32–$80) at lunch, 260–500 F ($41.60–$80) at dinner. AE, DC, MC, V. Tues–Sun noon–2pm; Tues–Sat 7:30–9:30pm. BURGUNDIAN/FRENCH.

In an 18th-century house across from the Palais des Ducs, this is one of Burgundy's finest restaurants, with a reputation that dates back to 1833. Its chef/owner, Jean-Pierre Billoux, assisted by his wife, Marie Françoise, prepares deceptively simple meals that have won acclaim. Menu items might include roast chicken steeped in liquefied almonds, terrine of pigeon, or thick-sliced fillet of sole on a bed of tomato. Some recently sampled and more innovative dishes are John Dory with thyme oil and confit of fennel, and a charlotte of duck with spice bread. The array of wines will be a joy to any connoisseur.

NEARBY DINING

✪ **Joël Perreaut's Restaurant des Gourmets.** 8 rue Puits-de-Têt, 21160 Marsannay-la-Côte. ☎ **03-80-52-16-32.** Reservations required. Main courses 140–250 F ($22.40–$40); fixed-price menus 160–280 F ($25.60–$44.80); menu dégustation 440 F ($70.40). AE, DC, MC, V. Wed–Sun noon–2pm; Tues–Sat 7–9:30pm. Closed last week of Jan and first week of Feb, and the first 10 days of Aug. Drive 6 miles south of Dijon on R.N. 17, following the signs for Beaune and then Marsannay-la-Côte. FRENCH.

This restaurant is ample justification for journeying outside Dijon to a charming medieval village. After Joël and Nicole Perreaut added an annex, modern kitchens, and a dining room, the place became well known as one of Burgundy's best restaurants. Within a modern-looking, gray-toned dining room whose large, sun-flooded windows overlook a verdant garden, you can enjoy a seasonally changing menu that might include profiteroles of snails with fresh mint sauce; a Moroccan-inspired pastilla of mullet with aromatic spices; a cross-cut section of veal cooked for 7 hours with orange segments and served with parmesan cheese; and veal sweetbreads with a red wine sauce and a purée of mushrooms. The cellar contains more than 600 wines, many of them burgundies from major as well as lesser-known, small-scale wineries whose value might not be immediately obvious.

DIJON AFTER DARK

CAFES   Begin at one of the many cafes or brasseries lining place Zola, rue des Godrans, place du Théâtre, or place Darcy, including the **Concorde,** 2 place Darcy (☎ **03-80-30-69-43**); **Brasserie du Théâtre,** 1 bis place du Théâtre (☎ **03-80-67-11-62**); and **La Comédie,** 3 place du Théâtre (☎ **03-80-67-11-22**). All quickly fill up with young people who like to start the evening with a drink and a cruisy look at others.

BARS   For a 30s-and-40s crowd who like to mingle in the low-key atmosphere of a piano bar, try **Hunky Dory,** 5 av. Foch (☎ **03-80-53-17-24**); **Le Messire,** 3 rue Jules-Mercier (☎ **03-80-30-16-40**); or the two-floored **Le Cintra,** 13 av. Foch (☎ **03-80-53-19-53**), with its piano bar up above and a cramped little disco down below. If the warm, welcoming, boisterous (and often sloshed) atmosphere of an Irish pub is what you're needing, head over to **Le Kilkenny,** 1 rue Auguste-Perdrix (☎ **03-80-30-02-48**). Or for a more British spin, try **Le Brighton,** 33 rue Auguste-Comte (☎ **03-80-73-59-32**), where you'll find a south-of-the-border dance club downstairs.

DISCOS   Two popular discos offering the generic dance music and club atmosphere are **Le Rio,** 9 av. Maréchal Foch (☎ **03-80-43-50-23**), and **Le Klapton,** 5 rue Dauphine (☎ **03-80-50-06-54**). And for a dance venue that might appeal to a more sedate local crowd, try **Le Privé,** 20 avenue Garibaldi (☎ **03-80-73-39-57**), where there is a greater emphasis on slower, more romantic music. Other high-octane dance floors are at **L'An Fer,** 8 rue Pierre-Marceau (☎ **03-80-70-03-69**), with its 60 F ($9.60) cover charge, gay/straight crowd, and Métro station decor complete with billboards; and **Le Grizzli,** 131 av. Gustave-Eiffel (☎ **03-80-43-19-91**), where guys always pay the 40 F ($6.40) cover, but women get in free on Friday.

PERFORMING ARTS   The opera season in Dijon stretches from the middle of October to May. The city's premier venue is at the **Grand Théâtre de Dijon,** 2 rue Longepierre (☎ **03-80-68-46-40** for information on opera, operettes, dance recitals, and concerts). The city's second most-visible cultural venue is the **Théâtre National Dijon-Bourgogne,** rue Monge (☎ **03-80-30-12-12**). Tickets for performances at either theater range from 100 F to 250 F ($16 to $40).

7 Saulieu

155 miles SE of Paris, 47 miles NW of Beaune

The town of Saulieu is fairly interesting, but its food placed it on the international map. On the boundaries of Morvan and Auxois, Saulieu has enjoyed a reputation for cooking since the 17th century. Even Mme de Sévigné praised it in her letters. So did Rabelais.

The main sight is the **Basilique St-Andoche,** on place de la Fontaine (☎ 03-80-64-07-03), which has some interesting decorated capitals. Next door in the art museum, the **Musée François-Pompon,** place de la Fontaine at rue Sallier (☎ 03-80- 64-19-51), you can see many works by François Pompon, the well-known sculptor of animals whose works are featured in Paris's Musée d'Orsay. Pompon's large statue of a bull stands on a plaza off the N6 at the entrance to Saulieu. Other objects featured within the museum include archaeological remnants from the Gallo-Roman era, sacred medieval art, and old tools showing some aspect of life in Burgundy several centuries ago. The museum is open from March to November, Wednesday to Monday from 10am to 12:30pm and 2 to 6pm. Admission costs 20 F ($3.20) for adults, 15 F ($2.40) for children ages 12 to 16, and is free for children 9 and under.

ESSENTIALS
GETTING THERE   **Drive** along N80 from Montbard or N6 from Paris or Lyon.

The **rail** station is northeast of the town center. For train information and schedules, call ☎ 08-36-35-35-35. Passengers coming from Paris sometimes opt to take the TGV from the Gare de Lyon, getting off in Montbard, 30 miles to the north. From Montbard, a series of **buses** carry passengers on to Saulieu about three times a day. For bus and rail information, call the **Gare SNCF** in Saulieu at (☎ 03-80-64-19-31).

VISITOR INFORMATION   The **Office du Tourisme** is at 24 rue d'Argentine (☎ 03-80-64-00-21).

ACCOMMODATIONS & DINING
✪ **Bernard Loiseau-La Côte d'Or.** 21210 Saulieu. ☎ **03-80-90-53-53.** Fax 03-80-64-08-92. www.bernard-loiseau.com. E-mail: loiseau@relaischateaux.fr. 33 units. 880–2,200 F ($140.80–$352) double; from 1,950–2,800 F ($312–$448) suite. AE, DC, MC, V.

This former stagecoach stop is an excellent choice, with one of the best-known restaurants in France. If you want to stay overnight, you'll find guest rooms with everything from Empire to Louis XV decor. Your bed will be complete with a comfortable mattress, but the bed itself is likely to be 200 years old.

Dining: Chef Alexandre Dumaine, the man who made this a world-famous restaurant, is long gone, but the inventive Bernard Loiseau works hard to maintain his standards. (According to most critics, Loiseau has surpassed all previous standards, becoming one of Europe's culinary stars.) The cooking is less traditional, leaning away from heavy sauces to *cuisine légère.* The emphasis is on bringing out maximum taste with no excess fat or sugar. All the great burgundies are on the wine list. Fixed-price dinners are 490 F to 980 F ($78.40 to $156.80), with a fixed-price lunch during the week at 490 F ($78.40).

Hôtel de la Poste. 1 rue Grillot, 21210 Saulieu. ☎ **03-80-64-05-67.** Fax 03-80-64-10-82. www.hoteldelaposte.com. E-mail: @hotelposte.com. 48 units. A/C MINIBAR TV TEL. 355–595 F ($56.80–$95.20) double. AE, DC, MC, V.

Originally a 17th-century postal relay station, Hôtel de la Poste has been completely renovated by Guy Virlouvet. Each of the rooms was renovated late in 1998. New mattresses were added, and the bathrooms were spruced up.

Dining: In the dining room, where antique timbers have been artfully exposed, specialties include escalope of sea perch with baby vegetables, shrimp with saffron and asparagus tips, fillet of Charolais beef with marrow sauce, and kidneys in a sauce of aged mustard. Menus, served to guests and nonguests alike, cost 108 F to 350 F ($17.30 to $56). Service is daily from noon to 2:30pm and 7 to 10:30pm.

12 The Rhône Valley

The Rhône is as mighty as the Saône is peaceful, and these two great rivers form a part of the French countryside that travelers often head through only briefly, glimpsing it out of their car windows as they rush south to the Riviera on the thundering Mediterranean Express. But this land of mountains and rivers, linked by a good road network, invites more exploration than that: It's beaujolais country, home to the city of Lyon, a fabulous stop for gourmets, and boasts Roman ruins, charming villages, castles, and even the Grand Canyon of France.

It was from the Rhône Valley that Greco-Roman architecture and art made their way to the Loire Valley, the château country, and finally to Paris. The district abounds in time-mellowed inns and gourmet restaurants, offering a cuisine that's among the finest in the world.

REGIONAL CUISINE Lyon and environs are the gastronomic capital of France. Excellent ingredients are readily available nearby—the best chicken and beef in France (from Bresse and Charolais, respectively), freshwater fish from the high lakes of the Savoy, and game from the dense forests.

Regional specialties are *quenelles de brochet* (pulverized brochet—a local whitefish—fashioned into cigar-shaped cylinders, served with white butter); Lyonnais sausages; many preparations of chicken, especially garnished with truffles; and a full array of pâtés and terrines, often made from wild game. One excellent dish is *pommes de terres lyonnaises* (sautéed potatoes with onions).

As for wines, the vineyards along the Rhône are some of the oldest in France, established by the ancient Greeks. The better wines are sold under the names of the specific villages that produce them: Côtes-du-Rhône Ardèche, Côtes-du-Rhône Gigondas, Tavel, Châteauneuf-du-Pape, Muscat de Baumes-de-Venise, Condrieu, and Beaujolais. Among them, beaujolais is the premier young wine of France. It's intended for early consumption—the annual release of a year's vintage is truly a national event.

1 Lyon

268 miles SE of Paris, 193 miles N of Marseille

At the junction of the turbulent Rhône and the tranquil Saône, a crossroads of Western Europe, Lyon is the third-largest city in France. The city proper has a population of 400,000, with more than a million others spread across a large urban area. Lyon is the center of a vast

The Rhône Valley

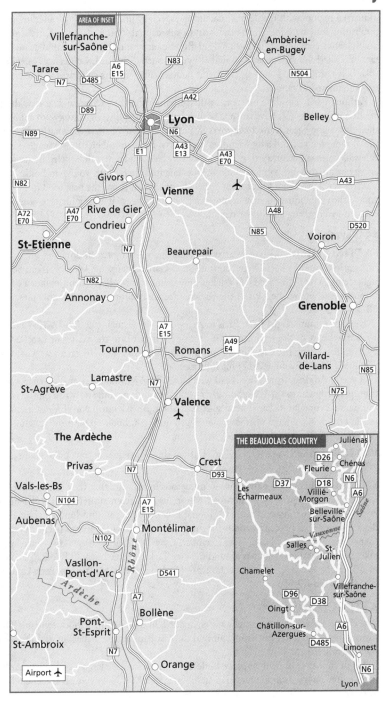

AREA OF INSET

Villefranche-sur-Saône

Tarare

N7

A6
E15

D485

D89

N83

N89

Ambèrieu-en-Bugey

N504

A42

Lyon

N6

Belley

E1

A43
E13

A43
E70

Givors

N82

Vienne

A47
E70

Rive de Gier

A72
E70

Condrieu

St-Etienne

N7

Beaurepair

A48

N85

D520

Voiron

N82

Annonay

Grenoble

A7
E15

A49
E4

Tournon

Romans

Villard-de-Lans

N85

Lamastre

N7

St-Agrève

Valence

N75

The Ardèche

THE BEAUJOLAIS COUNTRY

Juliénas

Privas

N7

Crest

D93

D26

Fleurie

Chénas

Vals-les-Bs

N104

Les Echarmeaux

D37

D18

N6

Villié-Morgon

A6

Aubenas

N102

Belleville-sur-Saône

Saône

A7
E15

Montélimar

Salles

St-Julien

Vauxonne

Vasllon-Pont-d'Arc

Rhône

D541

Chamelet

Villefranche-sur-Saône

Ardèche

A7

D96

D38

Bollène

Oingt

A6

Pont-St-Esprit

Châtillon-sur-Azergues

D485

Limonest

St-Ambroix

N7

Orange

N6

Lyon

Airport ✈

industrial region, with textile manufacturing especially important. It's a leader in book publishing and banking and is the world's silk capital. Some of the country's most highly rated restaurants, including Paul Bocuse, are found in and around Lyon. In fact, it's called the gastronomic capital of France. Such dishes as Lyon sausage, *quenelles* (fish balls), and tripe Lyonnais are world famous. The region's succulent Bresse poultry is the best in France.

Although you can dine better here than in any other French provincial city, there are disadvantages. You have to cope with urban sprawl and smog, along with some of the hottest and most humid summers in France. In spite of these drawbacks, Lyon is much more relaxed and a lot friendlier than Paris. Parks in full bloom, skyscrapers and sidewalk cafes, a great transport system, concert halls, and a nightlife fueled by student energy await you in Lyon today, along with talented chefs, both young and old.

Lyon is the best base for exploring the Rhone region. It has the best food in France and, although industrial and commercial on its fringes, it has a historic core not equaled by anything else in the region.

ESSENTIALS

GETTING THERE   If you're arriving from the north by **train,** don't get off at the first station, Gare La Part-Dieu; continue on to Gare de Perrache, where you can begin sightseeing. The high-speed TGV takes only 2 hours from Paris. Lyon makes a good stopover en route to the Alps or the Riviera. For train information and schedules, call **08-36-35-35-35.**

It's a 45-minute **flight** from Paris to Aéroport Lyon-Satolas (☎ **04-72-22-72-21**), 15¹/₂ miles east of the city. Buses run from the airport into the center of Lyon every 20 minutes during the day. The 45-minute trip costs 48 F ($7.70) each way. Call **Cie Satobus** (☎ **04-72-68-72-17**) for information.

If you're **driving,** from Nice, head west along E1/A7 toward Aix-en-Provence, continuing northwest toward Avignon. Bypass the city and continue north along the same route into Lyon. From Paris, head southeast along A8/E1 into Lyon. From Grenoble to the French Alps, head northeast along A48 until you hook up with the junction of A43, which will take you northeast into Lyon.

VISITOR INFORMATION   The **Office de Tourisme** is on place Bellecour (☎ **04-72-77-69-69**).

SPECIAL EVENTS   Festivals are so numerous in this city that they can become an everyday event, especially in summer. Music festivals reign supreme, with the most popular one occurring on France's National Day of Music, around June 21. This Fête de la Musique has become famous for turning the streets of Lyon into packed performance spaces for local bands. In December, the Festival de Musique du Vieux-Lyon takes place in various churches around the city. Tickets range from 75 F to 225 F ($12 to $36). For details, contact the festival's headquarters at 5 place du Petit-Collège (☎ **04-78-38-09-09**).

ATTRACTIONS

The city sprawls over many square miles, divided, like Paris, into arrondissements. The historic heart straddles the Saône, around the east bank's place Bellecour and the west bank's Primatiale St-Jean.

Begin your tour of Lyon at **place Bellecour,** one of France's largest and most charming squares. A handsome equestrian statue of Louis XIV looks out on the encircling 18th-century buildings.

Lyon

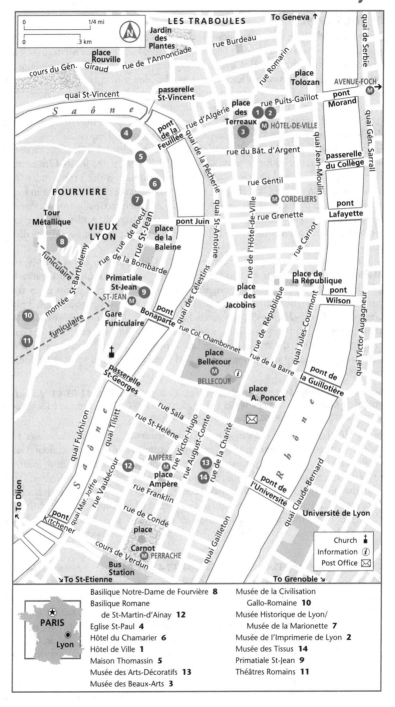

LES TRABOULES

To Geneva ↑

quai de Serbie

Jardin des Plantes

place Rouville

rue Burdeau

rue de l'Annonciade

cours du Gén. Giraud

rue Romarin

place Tolozan

AVENUE-FOCH Ⓜ

quai St-Vincent

passerelle St-Vincent

S a ô n e

pont de la Feuillée

rue d'Algérie

rue Puits-Gaillot

pont Morand

place des Terreaux

place des

Ⓜ HÔTEL-DE-VILLE

passerelle du Collège

quai Gén. Sarrall

① **②**

③

quai de la Pêcherie

rue du Bât. d'Argent

④

⑤

⑥

⑦

rue Gentil

quai Jean-Moulin

Ⓜ CORDELIERS

rue de l'Hôtel-de-Ville

pont Lafayette

FOURVIERE

Tour Métallique

rue de Boeuf

rue St-Jean

pont Juin

rue Grenette

VIEUX LYON

⑧

place de la Baleine

quai St-Antoine

rue Carnot

rue de la Bombarde

Primatiale St-Jean

⑨

quai des Célestins

place des Jacobins

place de la République

pont Wilson

ST-JEAN Ⓜ

rue de République

quai Victor Augagneur

⑩

montée St-Barthélemy

funiculaire

pont Bonaparte

Gare Funiculaire

rue Col. Chambonnet

quai Jules-Courmont

⑪

funiculaire

✝

R h ô n e

passerelle St-Georges

place Bellecour

Ⓜ BELLECOUR ⓘ

rue de la Barre

pont de la Guillotière

place A. Poncet

quai Fulchiron

rue Sala

rue St-Hélène

rue Victor-Hugo

rue August-Comte

rue de la Charité

✉

S a ô n e

quai Tilsitt

AMPÉRE

Ⓜ

⑫

place Ampère

⑬

⑭

pont de l'Université

rue Mar. Joffre

rue Vaubécour

rue Franklin

quai Claude-Bernard

Université de Lyon

rue de Condé

place

← To Dijon

pont Kitchener

quai Gailleton

cours de Verdun

Carnot

Ⓜ PERRACHE

Bus Station

Church	✝
Information	ⓘ
Post Office	✉

↓To St-Etienne

To Grenoble ↘

PARIS

★

Lyon ●

Basilique Notre-Dame de Fourvière **8**
Basilique Romane de St-Martin-d'Ainay **12**
Eglise St-Paul **4**
Hôtel du Chamarier **6**
Hôtel de Ville **1**
Maison Thomassin **5**
Musée des Arts-Décoratifs **13**
Musée des Beaux-Arts **3**

Musée de la Civilisation Gallo-Romaine **10**
Musée Historique de Lyon/ Musée de la Marionette **7**
Musée de l'Imprimerie de Lyon **2**
Musée des Tissus **14**
Primatiale St-Jean **9**
Théâtres Romains **11**

In Vieux Lyon

From place Bellecour, walk across pont Bonaparte to the right bank of the Saône River
and ✪ **Vieux Lyon** (you can also take bus no. 1 or 31, or take the Métro from elsewhere in the city to get here). Covering about a square mile, Old Lyon contains an
amazing collection of medieval and Renaissance buildings. Many of these houses were
built five stories high by thriving merchants to show off their new wealth. After years
as a slum, the area is now fashionable, attracting antiques dealers, artisans, weavers,
sculptors, and painters, who never tire of depicting scenes along the characteristic **rue
du Boeuf,** one of the most interesting streets for walking and exploring.

Your first stop should be the **Primatiale St-Jean** (see below). South of the cathedral
is the **Manécanterie,** 70 rue St-Jean (☎ **04-78-92-82-29**), noted for its 12th-century
Romanesque facade and its role as a dormitory beginning in the 11th century. The
boys who sang in the medieval choir lived here, making it the oldest residence in Lyon.

North of the cathedral is the most historically and architecturally evocative neighborhood of Old Lyon, with narrow streets, spiral stairs, hanging gardens, soaring towers, and unusual courtyards whose balconies seem to sit precariously atop medieval
pilings or columns.

While in Vieux Lyon, try to see the exceptional Gothic arcades of the 16th-century
Maison Thomassin, place du Change, and the 16th-century **Hôtel du Chamarier,**
37 rue St-Jean, where Mme de Sévigné lived. You can admire but not enter these
buildings. The neighborhood also contains the awesomely old **Église St-Paul,** 3 place
Gerson (☎ **04-78-28-34-45**), consecrated in A.D. 549. A rebuilding began in 1084
after its destruction by the Saracens. Its distinctive octagonal lantern tower was completed in the 1100s, the rest of the premises in the 13th century. You can visit Monday through Saturday from noon to 6pm and Sunday from 2 to 6pm. Admission is
free.

Musée Historique de Lyon. 1 place du Petit-Collège. ☎ **04-78 42-03-61.** Admission
(including Musée de la Marionette) 25 F ($4) adults, 13 F ($2.10) students, free for children
17 and under. Both museums, Wed–Mon 10:45am–6pm.

In the Hôtel de Gadagne, an early-16th-century residence, you'll find the Musée Historique de Lyon, with interesting Romanesque sculptures on the ground floor. Other
exhibits are 18th-century Lyonnais furniture and pottery, antique ceramics from the
town of Nevers, a pewter collection, and numerous paintings and engravings of Lyon.

In the same building is the **Musée de la Marionette** (same phone), which has three
puppets by Laurent Mourguet, creator of Guignol, the best known French marionette
character. The museum also has marionettes from other parts of France (including
Amiens, Lille, and Aix-en-Provence) and important collections from around the
world.

Primatiale St-Jean. Place St-Jean. ☎ **04-78-42-11-04.** Free admission. Mon–Fri
8am–noon and 2–7:30pm, Sat 2–7:30pm, Sun 8–5pm.

The cathedral was built between the 12th and the 15th centuries. Its apse is a masterpiece of Lyonnais Romanesque. The exceptional stained-glass windows are from the
12th to the 15th centuries. A highlight is the Flamboyant Gothic chapel of the Bourbons. On the front portals are medallions depicting the signs of the zodiac, the Creation, and the life of St. John. The cathedral's 16th-century Swiss astronomical clock
is intricate and beautiful; it announces the hour daily at noon, 2pm, and 3pm in
grand style: a rooster crows and angels herald the event. The treasury, on the right of
the cathedral, was closed for renovation at press time but might be open when you
visit.

IN FOURVIÈRE HILL

Rising to the west of Vieux Lyon on the west bank of the Saône is **Colline de Fourvière (Fourvière Hill).** This richly wooded hill—on which numerous convents, colleges, hospitals, two Roman theaters, and a superb Gallo-Roman museum have been established—affords a panoramic vista of Lyon, with its many bridges across two rivers, the rooftops of the medieval town, and (in clear weather) a view of the country-side extending to the snow-capped Alps.

Enthroned on its summit is the gaudy 19th-century **Basilique Notre-Dame de Fourvière,** 8 place de Fourvière (☎ **04-78-25-51-82**), rising fortresslike with four octagonal towers and crenellated walls. Its interior is covered with richly colored mosaics; adjoining it is an ancient chapel. The belfry is surmounted by a gilded statue of the Virgin. Admission is free, and it's open daily from 6:30am to 7pm.

Jardin du Rosaire extends on the hillside between the basilica and the 13th-century **Primatiale St-Jean.** They're open daily between 7am and 7pm and provide a pleasant walk. You'll see a vast shelter for up to 200 pilgrims. An elevator takes you to the top of the towers, and two funiculars service the hill.

In a park south of the basilica are the excavated **Théâtres Romains,** Montée de Fourvière, a Roman theater/odeum at 6 rue de l'Antiquaille. The theater is the most ancient in France, built by order of Augustus in 17 to 15 B.C. and greatly expanded during the reign of Hadrian. The odeum, reserved for musical performances, apparently was once sumptuously decorated. Its orchestra floor, for example, contains mosaics of such materials as brightly colored marble and porphyry. The third building in the sanctuary was dedicated in A.D. 160 to the goddess Cybele, or Sibella, whose cult originated in Asia Minor. All that remains are the foundations, though they seem to dominate the theater (175 feet by 284 feet).

An altar dedicated to a bull cult and a monumental marble statue of the goddess are shown in the **Musée de la Civilisation Gallo-Romaine,** 17 rue Cléberg (☎ **04-72-38-81-90**), a few steps from the archaeological site. The museum's collection of Gallo-Roman artifacts is the finest in France outside Paris. The site is open Wednesday through Sunday from 9:30am to noon and 2 to 6pm. Admission costs 20 F ($3.20) for adults, free for children 12 and under. Guides are available on Sundays and holidays from 2 to 6pm. Performances are given at both theaters in summer.

ELSEWHERE AROUND THE CITY

In addition to the sites listed below, you might also check out the **Basilique Romane de St-Martin-d'Ainay,** 11 rue Bourgelat (☎ **04-78-37-48-97**) south of place Belle-cour, near place Ampère. Lyon's oldest church dates from 1107. Admission is free, and it's open daily from 8:30 to 11:30am and 3 to 6:30pm. The rue de l'Hôtel-de-Ville extends north from place Bellecour to **place des Terreaux,** dominated by the 1746 **Hôtel de Ville,** one of the most beautiful in Europe. The outside is dark and rather severe; the interior is brilliant, but alas, it is closed to the public.

Musée de l'Imprimerie de Lyon. 13 rue de la Poulaillerie. ☎ **04-78-37-65-98.** Admission 25 F ($4) adults, 13 F ($2.10) students, free for children under 17. Wed–Sun 9:30am–noon and 2–6pm.

Occupying a 15th-century mansion, this museum is devoted to Lyon's role in the world of printing. Exhibits include a page from a Gutenberg Bible, 17th- to 20th-century presses, 16th- to 19th-century woodcuts, and many engravings. This is one of the most important printing museums in Europe, ranking with those at Mainz and Antwerp. It has a collection of books dating from "all epochs," including incunabula, books printed before Easter 1500.

Musée des Arts-Décoratifs. 30 rue de la Charité. ☎ **04-78-38-42-00.** Combined admission for this museum and Musée des Tissus 30 F ($4.80) adults, 15 F ($2.40) students, free for children 18 and under. Tues–Sun 10am–noon and 2–5:30pm.

In the 1739 Lacroix-Laval mansion built by Soufflot (architect of the Panthéon in Paris), the Musée des Arts-Décoratifs contains furniture and objets d'art, mostly from the 17th and 18th centuries. The medieval and Renaissance periods are also represented. Look for a rare five-octave clavecin by Donzelague, the great 18th-century creator of musical instruments.

Musée des Beaux-Arts. 20 place des Terreaux. ☎ **04-72-10-17-40.** Admission 25 F ($4) adults, 13 F ($2.10) students, free for children 17 and under. Wed–Sun 10:30am–6pm.

On the south side of the square stands the Palais des Arts (also called the Musée de St-Pierre). This former Benedictine abbey was built between 1659 and 1685 in the Italian baroque style. Today it contains the Musée des Beaux-Arts. Radically renovated in 1998, it contains an outstanding collection of paintings and sculpture. You enter via a charming courtyard graced with statuary and shade trees. The ground floor houses a display of 14th-century paintings. The collection also includes Etruscan, Egyptian, Phoenician, Sumerian, and Persian art. See, in particular, Perugino's altarpiece. The top floor is one of France's richest 19th-century collections, devoted to works by artists from Veronese, Tintoretto, and Rubens to Braque, Bonnard, and Picasso. Be sure to see Joseph Chinard's bust of Mme Récamier, the captivating Lyon beauty who charmed Napoleonic Paris by merely reclining, and the Fantin-Latour masterpiece *Reading.*

Musée des Tissus. 34 rue de la Charité. ☎ **04-78-38-42-00.** Combined admission for this museum and Musée des Arts-Décoratifs 30 F ($4.80) adults, 15 F ($2.40) students, free for children 18 and under. Tues–Sun 10am–5:30pm.

Next door to the Musée des Arts-Décoratifs is an even more interesting collection, housed in the 1730 Palais de Villeroy. On view are priceless fabrics from all over the world, spanning 2,000 years. Some of the finest fabrics made in Lyon from the 18th century to the present are displayed. The 15th- and 16th-century textiles embroidered with religious motifs are noteworthy, as are the 17th-century Persian carpets. Seek out the partridge-motif brocade for Marie Antoinette's bedchamber at Versailles, as well as a brocaded satin woven for Queen Victoria of 150 colors with birds of paradise and orchids.

OUTSIDE THE HEART OF THE CITY

One of Lyon's grandest archaeological sites, though quite minor in world terms, is **Amphithéâtre des Trois-Gauls,** rue du Jardin-des-Plantes, Croix-Rousse (no phone), in Lyon's 4th arrondissement, near the city's northern perimeter. Regrettably you can view the site only from the outside. At the time of its construction, it was the centerpiece of Condate, an ancient Gallic village, near the junction of the Rhône and Saône, that predated the arrival of the Roman legions by several centuries. According to scattered historic accounts, delegates from 60 tribes from throughout Gaul met here in the earliest known example of a French parliamentary system. Based on those dimly remembered events, France's 2,000th anniversary was celebrated in Lyon in 1989.

On the opposite side of the Rhône, you'll have the chance to explore Lyon's largest public park and garden, the 260-acre **Parc de la Tête d'Or** (☎ **04-78-89-53-52).** Its largest (but by no means only) entrance is on boulevard des Belges. It opened in 1857 with all the fountains, pedestrian walkways, and ornamental statues you'd expect from Lyon's showcase park. Surrounded by wealthy residential neighborhoods, the park has a lake, illuminated fountains, a little zoo, a botanical garden with green-houses, and a rose garden with some 100,000 plants. It's open throughout the year during daylight hours, and during May and June, it's particularly renowned for its profusion of roses.

At **Rochetaillée-sur-Saône,** 7 miles north of Lyon on D433, the **Musée Français de l'Automobile "Henri Malartre"** is housed in the Château de Rochetaillée, 645 chemin du Musée (☎ **04-78-22-18-80**). Established by a wealthy benefactor (Henri Malartre) and taken over as a public museum by the city of Lyon in 1960, the collection includes 100 cars dating back to 1890, 65 motorcycles from 1903 and after, and 40 cycles dating back to 1848. The château is surrounded by a large park. Admission to the museum and château is 35 F ($5.60), free for children 18 and under. Both are open Tuesday to Sunday from 9am to 5pm.

SHOPPING

Since this is the third-largest city in France, you'll find a full array of shopping options. For small boutiques, art galleries, and local artists' studios and workshops, head to Vieux Lyon and the area around **rue Mercière** and **quai St-Antoine.** For antiques, concentrate around **rue Auguste-Comte** as it approaches place Bellecour. And consider venturing to the **Cité des Antiquaires,** 117 bd. Stalingrad (☎ **04-72-44-91-98**), with more than 100 antiques dealers.

Lyon remains a bastion for fashion: everything from the cutting edge to the classically elegant. While the densest concentrations of retail shops in Lyon lie along the **rue Victor Hugo, rue de la République,** and **rue Emile Zola,** many of the hyper-upscale fashion boutiques are set on either side of the **rue du Président Edouard Herriot.**

For chic couture that rivals anything you'll find in Paris, try **George Rech,** 59 rue du Président Herriot (☎ **04-78-37-82-90**). And for a concentration of more than 200 interesting shops and boutiques set side by side, wander down the walkways of the largest shopping center in Lyon, the **Centre Commercial de la Part-Dieu,** 17 rue du Dr. Bouchut (☎ **04-72-60-60-62**). Though not the major silk center of yesteryear, Lyon still hangs on to several silk manufacturers; and for a good selection of silk scarves, ties, sashes, and squares, try **La Maison des Canuts,** 10–12 rue d'Ivry (☎ **04-78-28-62-04**), as well as the famous Parisian supplier **Hermès,** 56 rue du Président-Herriot (☎ **04-78-42-25-14**).

For a thoroughly Lyonnais gift, keep your eye out for **marionettes de Lyon.** These intricately crafted puppets are art forms in their own right, and at their best, each is permeated with a distinctive personality. Some of the best craftsmanship, and the widest selection, is available at **Atelier de Guignol,** 4 place du Change (☎ **04-78-29-33-37**); **Boutique Cardelli,** 6 rue St-Jean (☎ **04-78-37-01-67**); and **Maison de Guignol,** 60 rue du Lac (☎ **04-78-60-11-91**).

Bernachon, 42 cours Franklin-Roosevelt (☎ **04-78-24-37-98**), is home to Lyon's best chocolates and pastries. Here you'll find 30 varieties of bite-size pastries known as mini-gâteaux, 30 varieties of petits fours, and even dark, rich chocolates lightly dusted with 24-karat gold. Also at the Bernachon store is a small restaurant/tearoom called **Bernachon Passion.** Just down the way, you'll find **Bocuse & Bernachon,** 46 cours Franklin-Roosevelt (☎ **04-72-74-46-19**), a well-respected union that sells both the chocolates of Bernachon and the upscale food products endorsed by gastronomic superstar Paul Bocuse in a format that local wits describe as "a marriage of the sweet with the salted."

ACCOMMODATIONS

Alain Chapel (see "Dining," below) also rents rooms.

EXPENSIVE

✪ **Cour des Loges.** 6 rue du Boeuf, 69005 Vieux Lyon. ☎ **04-72-77-44-44.**
Fax 04-72-40-93-61. www.courdesloges.com. E-mail: contact@courdesloges.com. 63 units.
A/C MINIBAR TV TEL. 1,300–1,900 F ($208–$304) double; 2,300–3,000 F ($368–$480) suite.
AE, DC, MC, V. Parking 120 F ($19.20). Métro: St-Jean.

This four-star luxury hotel in Old Lyon occupies several houses from the 14th to the
17th centuries. It offers beautifully furnished rooms and suites. Most units face gardens, the square, or a large sunlit lobby. The staff is courteous, highly efficient, and
the most savvy in Lyon.

   Dining: The restaurant serves excellent food in an elegant setting; there are also
lounges and a wine cellar.

   Amenities: Roman-style indoor pool, Jacuzzi, sauna, terraced gardens, garage, valet,
24-hour room service. Each room has a TV with foreign channels and a VCR.

MODERATE

Best Western Hôtel des Beaux-Arts. 75 rue du Président-Herriot, 69002 Lyon. ☎ **800/
528-1234** in the U.S., or 04-78-38-09-50. Fax 04-78-42-19-19. www.hotelbeauxarts.fr.
E-mail: hotelbeauxarts@shb.fr. 75 units. A/C MINIBAR TV TEL. 530–720 F ($84.80–$115.20)
double; 810 F ($129.60) suite. AE, DC, MC, V. Métro: Cordelier.

This has long been one of the leading moderately priced choices in central Lyon. The
lobby evokes the 1930s more than the rooms, which, although comfortable, are for the
most part outfitted in businesslike modern style. Since this is a noisy part of the
city, double glazing on the windows helps shut out traffic sounds; the quieter rooms
are in the rear. A large breakfast is the only meal served, though you may prefer having croissants and coffee at one of the cafes along place Bellecour.

✪ **Grand Hôtel Château Perrache.** 12 cours de Verdun, 69002 Lyon. ☎ **800/
MERCURE** or 04-72-77-15-00. Fax 04-78-37-06-56. E-mail: H1292@accor-hotels.com. 117
units. A/C MINIBAR TV TEL. 840–940 F ($134.40–$150.40) double. AE, DC, MC, V. Métro:
Perrache.

This hotel near the Perrache train station offers some of Lyon's best rooms, with plush
fabrics and inviting colors. The hotel is a monument to Art Nouveau and even has a
winter garden. **Les Belles Saisons,** the house restaurant, does more than just cater to
the tired business traveler who doesn't want to leave the premises at night. Its finely
honed cuisine is often innovative and features continental and regional dishes.

Hôtel Globe et Cécil. 21 rue Gasparin, 69002 Lyon. ☎ **04-78-42-58-95.** Fax
04-72-41-99-06. 58 units. A/C TV TEL. 360–750 F ($57.60–$120) double. Rates include breakfast. AE, DC, MC, V. Parking 65 F ($10.40). Métro: Bellecour.

Near place Bellecour, this hotel is a good value for Lyon, not only because of its location but also because of its attentive staff. The rooms are comfortable, attractively furnished, and individually decorated. Breakfast is the only meal served, but many dining
places are nearby.

INEXPENSIVE

✪ **Hôtel Bayard.** 23 place Bellecour, 69002 Lyon. ☎ **04-78-37-39-64.** Fax
04-72-40-95-51. E-mail: hotelbayard@aol.com. 15 units. TV TEL. 403–493 F ($64.50–$78.90)
double. AE, DC, MC, V. Parking 50–65 F ($8–$10.40). Métro: Bellecour.

The foundations of this very dignified town house date from the 16th century, and,
although the walls are much more recent, bedrooms inside are each outfitted in a style

inspired by a distinctive period of French history. You'll enter the place via a narrow hallway, and climb one flight up for the reception area. Don't be put off by the staff, either, who appear rather nonchalant.

Hôtel Bellecordière. 18 rue Bellecordière, 69002 Lyon. ☎ **04-78-42-27-78.** Fax 04-72-40-92-27. 45 units. TV TEL. 310 F ($49.60) double. AE, MC, V. Métro: Bellecour.

A savvy gourmet traveler we know always stays at this nondescript two-star hotel, preferring to spend her money on Lyon's restaurants. The small accommodations are no-frills, and at their worst, a bit depressing. Breakfast is the only meal served, although many worthwhile restaurants are within a short walk.

Le Résidence. 18 rue Victor-Hugo, 69002 Lyon. ☎ **04-78-42-63-28.** Fax 04-78-42-85-76. E-mail: hotel-la-residence@wanadoo.fr. 67 units. TV TEL. 330–360 F ($52.80–$57.60) double. AE, DC, MC, V. Métro: Bellecour.

Long a favorite with budget travelers, this hotel is at the corner of a pedestrian zone in the center of Lyon. Beyond an ornate 19th-century facade, the rooms are comfortably but not spectacularly furnished. For the price, however, they offer one of the best values in this rather overpriced city. Breakfast is the only meal served, but many fine restaurants are literally outside the door, as is some of the finest shopping. Many members of the staff speak English and are filled with helpful advice.

DINING

The food in Lyon is among the finest in the world—with prices to match. However, we've found that a person of moderate means can often afford the most reasonable fixed-price menus even in the city's priciest choices.

VERY EXPENSIVE

✪ **Alain Chapel.** N83 Mionnay, 01390 St-André-de-Corcy. ☎ **04-78-91-82-02.** Fax 04-78-91-82-37. E-mail: chapel@relaischateaux.fr. Reservations required. Main courses 200–300 F ($32–$48); fixed-price menus 380 F ($60.80) at lunch Wed–Fri, 595–800 F ($95.20–$128) at dinner. AE, DC, MC, V. Tues 7:30–10:30pm, Wed–Sun 12:30–1:30pm and 7:30–9:30pm. Closed Jan. Take N83 12^1/$_2$ miles north of Lyon. FRENCH.

This Relais Gourmand occupies a 19th-century postal station that has evolved after years of architectural improvements into a comfortable, conservatively stylish place. Alain Chapel was one of the world's premier chefs, and after his death many people claimed that the stellar reputation of his restaurant would tarnish; but under Philippe Jousse (who trained under Chapel), that hasn't been the case. Jousse, assisted by M. Chapel's widow, continues to maintain the image of Lyon as a gastronomic capital, with perhaps a bit less emphasis on the media hype and cutting-edge glamour of his predecessor.

   Menu items change with the seasons but are likely to include a lasagne of foie gras with flap mushrooms; wild mallard duckling served in a stewpot with potatoes; and a salad of walnut oil and chicken livers. A particularly succulent and hearty main course includes stuffed and braised oxtail with creamed leeks and a side dish containing the oxtail's herb-enriched consommé. When the menu at this place suggests "some country cheeses" as a follow-up for the rest of the meal, expect a particularly appealing assortment of unusual local cheeses whose presentation is charming.

   Also offered are 14 beautiful **rooms,** priced at 650 F to 850 F ($104 to $136) double.

Léon de Lyon. 1 rue Pleney. ☎ **04-72-10-11-12.** Reservations required. Main courses 250–300 F ($40–$48); fixed-price menus 290 F ($46.40) at lunch, 590–800 F ($94.40–$128) at dinner. AE, DC, MC, V. Tues–Sat noon–2pm and 7:30–10pm. Closed Aug 1–17. Métro: Hôtel-de-Ville. FRENCH.

Upstairs in what was once a private home, tables are placed in a series of small rooms decorated with culinary artifacts which have welcomed many a famous guest, from Charles Aznavour to Bill Clinton. The atmosphere may be traditional and typical, but the food isn't. The owner, Jean-Paul Lacombe, has been called a daring challenger to the top chefs of Lyon, serving both regional and modern cuisine with innovative flair. His brilliant use of Lyonnais offal might scare off the timid but will please the dedicated gastronome. Offerings might include pheasant soup with foie gras and red beans, pike *quenelles* (fish balls), or lobster with asparagus. Seasonal offerings include snails bubbling in butter. More challenging fare includes terrine of sweetbreads with spinach and even Bresse chicken with truffles. His sorbets made with fresh fruits are a perfect ending.

✪ **Paul Bocuse.** Pont de Collonges, Collonges-au-Mont-d'Or. ☎ **04-72-42-90-90.** Reservations required as far in advance as possible. Main courses 200–300 F ($32–$48); fixed-price menus 690 F ($110.40) at lunch Mon–Fri, 550–810 F ($88–$129.60) at dinner. AE, DC, MC, V. Daily noon–1:30pm and 7:30–9:30pm. Take N433 5¹/₂ miles north of Lyon. LYONNAISE.

Paul Bocuse is one of the world's most famous contemporary chefs. You can see for yourself at his restaurant on the banks of the Saône at Collonges-au-Mont-d'Or. He specializes in regional cuisine, though long ago he was the leading exponent of nouvelle cuisine (which he later called "a joke"). Since Bocuse (now in his 70s) is gone at least part of the time, the chefs he leaves behind must carry on with the mass production (for up to 180 diners at a time) of the signature dishes the master created and on which there isn't a lot of variation.

In one of the three dining rooms lined with oil paintings, perhaps begin with the famous black truffle soup, then try one of the most enduring dishes in the Bocuse repertoire: the perfumey Bresse chicken cooked in a pig's bladder. Newer options include a gratin of Breton lobster, red snapper in a crusty potato shell, and roast pigeon in puff pastry with baby cabbage leaves and foie gras.

If you want to take more away with you than just a satisfied appetite, a boutique on the premises sells Bocuse's preferred versions of wine, cognac (vintage Bocuse X.O.), jams and jellies, coffees and teas, and cookbooks, all of which most prominently display his image and logo.

Note: You can't miss this place. In the mid-1990s, tired of the conventional facades that shelter most French restaurants, M. Bocuse commissioned a local artist to paint the history of French cuisine, in cartoon form, on the outside of his restaurant. The tale begins in the 1700s and proceeds through the years to its "defining moment" as interpreted in a depiction of Bocuse himself.

EXPENSIVE

✪ **La Mère Brazier.** 12 rue Royale. ☎ **04-78-28-15-49.** Reservations required. Main courses 120–250 F ($19.20–$40); fixed-price menus 280 F and 330 F ($44.80 and $52.80); business menu (Mon–Fri) 190 F ($30.40). AE, DC, MC, V. Wed–Fri noon–2pm; Wed–Sat 7:30–10pm. Closed Apr 23–May 3 and July 22–Aug 22. Métro: Hôtel-de-Ville. FRENCH.

This restaurant near pont Morand has grown from a 1921 lunch spot for silk workers to an internationally known gourmet restaurant that draws connoisseurs. It's managed by Carmen and Jacotte Brazier—the daughter-in-law and one of the granddaughters of the founding mother, Mme Brazier. The simple decor and wood paneling make an attractive setting for a leisurely lunch or an outstanding supper. Here you can order some excellent regional dishes, accompanied by such local wines as Mâcon, Juliénas, Morgon, Chiroubles, and virtually every Côte du Rhone ever bottled. Appetizers include artichoke hearts stuffed with foie gras as well as smoked Nordic salmon. Specialties are *volaille de Bresse demi-deuil* (boiled chicken with truffles under the skin,

Beaucoup Bocuse

A resurgence in interest in chef Paul Bocuse swept across Lyon in 1994 when he bought the ○ **Brasserie Le Nord,** 18 rue Neuve (☎ **04-72-10-69-69**), a turn-of-the-century brasserie the master once worked in as a teenager. Menu prices here—about 180 F ($28.80) per person for a meal with wine and coffee—signaled that the last of the truly great chefs had finally decided to go for the mass market. And we're definitely not complaining! It's the most popular restaurant in town, particularly with the bankers and merchants who seem to pack the place at lunch. A short while after, Bocuse opened a twin of Le Nord, **Brasserie Le Sud,** place Antonin-Poncet (☎ **04-72-77-80-00**), specializing in the cuisine of the French-speaking Mediterranean. Then again in 1998, he opened **Brasserie de l'Est,** 11 place Jules-Ferry (☎ **04-37-24-25-26**), offering a cuisine that incorporates the best of the Nord and the Sud, with a hint of Alsace and Lorraine thrown in for good measure. No prizes for guessing the name of his next brasserie if and when it opens.

At least some of the success of these brasseries stems from the Bocuse name, for he is the most prominent and enduring grand chef in France. His almost mythical restaurant in the Lyon suburb of Collanges-au-Mont-d'Or (see our review, above) has earned a trio of Michelin stars (the top rating) every year since 1965. Less secure chefs might tremble at the thought of the public scrutiny this involves, fearing that the laurels thrown by culinary critics will be ripped away later. But Bocuse, with his irrepressible ego, seems to thrill year after year to the notion that he's without parallel.

So will the master be here when you drop in his brasserie? Not necessarily. He may not even be found at Collanges-au-Mont-d'Or—or even in Lyon. Since creating some of the most award-winning dishes in Europe (black truffle soup, fil-let of sea bass *en croûte,* chicken cooked in a pig's bladder), Bocuse has launched his own line of vacuum-packed foods, endorsed a string of bakeries in Japan, pur-chased a beaujolais vineyard, become interested in the French Pavilion at Walt Disney World's Epcot Center in Florida, and helped develop a collection of CDs (Matins et Câlins) designed to soothe the grumpy after-effects of too much wine and foie gras. He's in demand everywhere from Chicago to Tokyo, and virtually every agent in Hollywood salivates at the thought of getting him to endorse any-thing and everything—from T-shirts to slotted spoons.

His team, however, quickly assures the press and diners alike that although "temporarily absent," Bocuse is present "in spirit." And in this case the spirit, as priests have affirmed for many years, is invariably stronger than the flesh.

served with vegetables, rice, and bouillon) and superbly smooth *quenelles de brochet* (pike) au gratin. More extravagant fare includes lobster Belle Aurore or *à la nage.* The service is solicitous.

MODERATE

La Tassée. 20 rue de la Charité. ☎ **04-72-77-79-00.** Main courses 75–190 F ($12–$30.40); fixed-price menus 160–280 F ($25.60–$44.80). AE, DC, V. Mon–Sat noon–2:30pm and 7:15–10:15pm. Métro: Bellecour. FRENCH.

The chef here isn't interested in fancy frills, but believes in serving good food at prices most people can afford. Huge portions are dished out, and you might be offered anything from strips of tripe with onions to game or sole. On a recent visit, we arrived just when the beaujolais nouveau had come in—a major event. The dining room boasts noteworthy 19th-century frescoes.

Le Bistrot de Lyon. 64 rue Mercière. ☎ **04-78-38-47-47.** Main courses 67–120 F ($10.70–$19.20); fixed-price menus 135–250 F ($21.60–$40). AE, MC, V. Daily noon–2:30pm and 7pm–1am. Métro: Cordelier. FRENCH.

This place stays hopping until the wee hours. It stands on a street of bistros, with several wine bars mixed in. The setting is elegant and traditional, with marble-topped tables. You might want to stick to classic Lyonnais fare, like poached eggs in red-wine sauce and pot-au-feu, a stew with fresh vegetables. Another classic is braised chicken with herbs, white wine, and heaps of fresh pasta. And for the truly adventurous, you can always immerse yourself in such ultra-earthy and eminently savory Lyonnais classics like braised pig's feet stuffed with oxtail and foie gras.

INEXPENSIVE

Café des Fédérations. 8 rue Major-Martin. ☎ **04-78-28-26-00.** Reservations recommended. Fixed-price menu 118 F ($18.90) at lunch, 148 F ($23.70) at dinner. V. Mon–Fri 10am–11pm. Closed Aug. Métro: Hôtel de Ville. FRENCH.

This is one of the busiest, most animated, and sometimes most amusingly raucous bistros in Lyon. It's open only on weekdays, catering to the office-worker crowd. It's operated with panache by a team of hardworking employees who would probably perform beautifully in the trenches of a war zone. All meals are set, fixed-price menus offering a selection of appetizers, main courses, and desserts. Each evokes old-time Lyonnais cuisine at its least pretentious, with such options as a green salad with bacon and croutons; eggs *en meurette* (poached in red wine); *andouillette* (chitterling sausages) served with a *gratin dauphinois;* veal kidneys in mustard sauce, pork chops, and several kinds of sausage, usually with *pommes de terre dauphinoise*.

Le Borsalino. 42 rue Pierre-Corneille. ☎ **04-78-52-19-13.** Reservations recommended. Main courses 60–85 F ($9.60–$13.60); fixed-price menus 85–120 F ($13.60–$19.20). AE, DC, MC, V. Mon–Sat 11:30am–2:30pm and 7:30–10pm. Métro: Avenue-Foch. FRENCH/LYONNAIS.

When a grander, more pretentious restaurant went out of business on this site in 1998, this less expensive newcomer quickly moved in and began attracting a loyal clientele. The theme of the place involves hats, about 300 of which are displayed on shelves or dangle from the walls and ceilings. And as a means of more deeply entrenching the theme, management offers a free apéritif to anyone actually wearing a hat. (In the first months of its opening, the gag within Lyon involved showing up here wearing everything from a paper bag to a watering can, defining it as a hat, and receiving the free cocktail.) Menu items are based on old-fashioned French cuisine, and include strips of herb-marinated pork in puff pastry; frogs' legs with parsley and garlic; scallops with anise; salads of foie gras; and pepper steaks. We admit that the venue is a bit theme-ish, but it's all good-natured and good fun, the cuisine is actually rather good, and the prices are reasonable.

LYON AFTER DARK

This cosmopolitan hub of entertainment and culture offers many options. At a newsstand, buy a copy of the weekly guide *Lyon-Poche,* which lists all the cultural happenings around town from bars and theaters to classical concerts.

For the theater or opera buff, Lyon's **Théâtre des Célestins,** 4 rue Charles-Dullin (☎ **04-72-77-40-00**), is the premier venue for comedy and drama; and the **Opéra,** place de la Comédie (☎ **04-72-00-45-45**), always has a lively and diverse season.

For the best pubs in town, go to the **Smoking Dog,** 16 rue Lainerie (☎ 04-78-28-38-27), a happy neighborhood bar with a mixed-age crowd; or **The Barrel House,** 13 rue Ste-Catherine (☎ 04-78-29-20-40), filled with a younger, English-speaking crowd bent on drinking themselves under the table and having a good time to boot.

Rock-and-rollers head over to the old train station to one of the newest clubs, **Millennium,** 13 place J.-Ferry (☎ 04-72-74-04-41), with its up-and-coming yuppies. Another club to check out is **Le Box-Office,** 30 bd. Eugène-Deruelle (☎ 04-78-95-37-02), with its brash techno crew. Cover charges to these clubs range from 60 F to 100 F ($9.60 to $16). For jazz enthusiasts, give a listen to what has become a Lyon jazz and blues swing tradition, **Le Hot Club,** 26 rue Lanterne (☎ 04-78-39-54-74).

Surprisingly, in a city this size there are no exclusively gay and lesbian discos; the closest thing is a gay-friendly dance club called **Le Show-Biz,** 112 quai Pierre-Scize (☎ 04-72-00-22-55), with its smoke machines, flashing lights, mirrors, and average cover of 60 F ($10.20). It's a fun and safe place to let your hair down and burn off some calories. The macho leather crowd hangs out at **Bar des Traboules,** 86 Grande Rue de la Croix-Rousse (☎ 04-78-29-20-09). Bars include **Le Verre à Soi,** 25 rue des Capucins (☎ 04-78-28-92-44), with a mixed gay and lesbian crowd; **Le Broadway,** 9 rue Terraille (☎ 04-78-39-50-54), with an older crowd of men and women who enjoy a theme night every 2 weeks or so; and the popular **Le Bar du Centre,** 3 rue Simon-Maupin (☎ 04-78-37-40-18), where a guy can relax, have a drink, and strike up a conversation with what one of the bartenders called "the hottest men in Lyon."

2 The Beaujolais Country

The vineyards of Beaujolais start about 25 miles north of Lyon. This wine-producing region is small—only 40 miles long and less than 10 miles wide—yet it's one of the most famous areas in the nation and has become increasingly known throughout the world because of the beaujolais craze that began in Paris some 30 years ago. The United States is now one of the three big world markets for beaujolais. In an average year, this region produces 30 million gallons of wine, more than 190 million bottles.

Most people don't come to the Beaujolais country to visit specific sites but rather to drink the wine. There are around 180 châteaux scattered throughout this part of France, and at many of them, you can sample and/or buy bottles of the beaujolais.

This region is a colorful and prosperous rural part of France, with vineyards on sun-lit hillsides, pleasant golden cottages where the vine growers live, and historic houses and castles. It has been called the Land of the Golden Stones. Don't expect many architectural monuments, though.

Unlike Alsace with its Route du Vin, the Beaujolais country doesn't have a clearly defined route. You can branch off in many directions, stopping at whatever point or wine cellar intrigues you. Don't be worried about losing your way after meandering off the A6 superhighway. This is one of the easiest parts of eastern France to negotiate; the road signs are very clear. If you're in doubt at any time, simply follow the signs to the region's capital and commercial center, Villefranche-sur-Saône.

However, if you're pressed for time, you can tie the highlights together in a one-way drive, beginning at the region's southern terminus, **Villefranche,** which you can access from A6 running between Mâcon and Lyon. (If you're heading north to south, follow the drive in reverse order, beginning in Juliénas, accessible from A6.)

Start in **Villefranche,** marked as its own exit off A6. After an excursion west on D38 to **Bagnol-en-Beaujolais,** return to Villefranche. From there, take the meandering D504 and D20, which make sharp bends toward the east en route to

St-Julien-sous-Montmelas. From St-Julien, take D19 to **Salles-en-Beaujolais.** From Salles, take D62 and D19 to **Belleville-sur-Saône.** From here, follow D37 and D68 to **Villié-Morgon.** From Villié-Morgon take D68 and D266 to **Juliénas.**

VILLEFRANCHE-SUR-SAÔNE—CAPITAL OF BEAUJOLAIS

In Villefranche-sur-Saône we advise you to go to the **Office du Tourisme,** 290 rue de Thizy, not far from the marketplace (☎ **04-74-87-27-40**), open Monday through Saturday from 9am to noon and 1:30 to 6:30pm (open Sundays from 9am to noon in July and August only). Here you can pick up a booklet on the Beaujolais country containing a regional map and many itineraries; it also lists some 30 villages and the wine-tasting cellars open to the public.

BAGNOLS-EN-BEAUJOLAIS

To reach Bagnols from Villefranche, head west on D38.

ACCOMMODATIONS & DINING

✪ **Château de Bagnols-en-Beaujolais.** 69620 Bagnols. ☎ **04-74-71-40-00.** Fax 04-74-71-40-49. www.bagnols.com. E-mail: chateaubagnols@compuserve.com. 20 units. TV TEL. 2,200–3,800 F ($352–$608) double; from 6,000 F ($960) suite. AE, DC, MC, V. Closed Jan 2–Mar 30.

This is lordly living on a grand, super-expensive scale. France's premier château/hotel, this Renaissance ruin has been restored by 400 artisans and craftspeople for Helen Hamlyn and her husband, the publisher/philanthropist Paul Hamlyn, who spent between $6 and $12 million on the project. The mansion is filled with antiques, wall paintings, and art, much from the 17th century. The rooms and suites are sumptuous; one suite is named for Mme de Sévigné, who spent a restless night here in 1673. The rooms are individually decorated, with wall paintings and frescos. The antique beds are hung with period velvets. The sheets are of pure embroidered linen, and the luxurious down pillows and comfortable mattresses beckon the weary traveler. The bathrooms are also individually designed generally with tiled floors, brass fittings, and plenty of soft, fluffy towels. This place is not for the young and restless—there's no gym or tennis courts, for example. Elegant continental fare is served in the Guards Room.

ST-JULIEN-SOUS-MONTMELAS

This charming village is 6¹⁄₂ miles northwest of Villefranche (take D504, then D20). It was the home of Claude Bernard, the father of physiology, who was born here in 1813. The small stone house in which he lived—now the **Musée Claude-Bernard Hameau de Chatenay** (☎ **04-74-67-51-44**)—contains mementos of the great scholar, like instruments and books that belonged to him. The museum is open Wednesday through Sunday from 10am to noon and 2 to 6pm. Admission is 15 F ($2.40) for adults and 10 F ($1.60) for students and children. Closed in March.

SALLES-EN-BEAUJOLAIS

If you want specific sites to visit in the area, we suggest the **Église de Salles Arbuis-sonnas** (☎ **04-74-67-51-50**). Begun in A.D. 1090 and completed at last in the 1700s, this religious hideaway is mostly Romanesque, with an occasional Gothic overlay, especially in its doorways. Notice the Salle Capitulaire, where the ornate capitals of columns from throughout its long history are proudly displayed. The church is open daily, May to September from 9am to 7pm and October to April from 9am to 6pm. Admission is free. From St-Julien take D19 a short distance to Salles.

BELLEVILLE-SUR-SAÔNE

For an excellent dining experience, drive north from Salles on D19 and D62 to Belleville-sur-Saône.

DINING

Le Rhône au Rhin. 10 av. du Port. ☎ **04-74-66-16-23.** Reservations required. Main courses 75–110 F ($12–$17.60); fixed-price menus 98–265 F ($15.70–$42.40). MC, V. Tues–Sun noon–2pm; Tues–Sat 7–9:30pm. FRENCH.

Chef Michel Debize operates this out-of-the-way restaurant almost as a self-imposed refuge from the urban mania of more congested regions of France. Consequently, you'll get the feeling that if he doesn't like you, he won't necessarily deal with you. All of that is forgotten, however, once you try the well-flavored cuisine and align yourself with his escapist dream. Menu items change with the seasons and might include a terrine of foie gras with apples served in puff pastry; a tartare of raw salmon with lime juice; and a duo of salmon and crayfish in a potato galette. An unusual main course includes frogs' legs and chicken fermier with morel-flavored cream sauce. This restaurant doesn't attract the media attention it once did, but we think its cuisine remains as fine as ever.

VILLIÉ-MORGON

If you'd like another dining choice in the Beaujolais country, we suggest driving west from Belleville-sur-Saône on D37, then north on D18 to Villié-Morgon. This village, along with the carefully delineated region around it, contains around 250 wine producers. Their product, at its best, is usually judged one of the greatest Beaujolais wines in France.

In the basement of the Hôtel de Ville (town hall), place de l'Hôtel-de-Ville, is the **Caveau de Morgon** (☎ **04-74-04-20-99**), which assembles and "marries" a selection of the Villié-Morgon region's best wines into a well-respected brand name (Caveau de Morgon) whose marketing savvy benefits wine growers and consumers alike. (Whatever you do, don't use the word "blend" to describe this company's product, as it's usually received with something akin to horror.) The cellar is open for tours and sales daily from 9am to noon and 2 to 7pm (closed January 1 to 15). Admission is free. The town hall that contains it, incidentally, was built during the late 1600s, destroyed during the Revolution, and reconstructed and modified several times since.

JULIÉNAS

Wines are also a reason to travel north on D266 and D68 to Juliénas. This village produces a full-bodied, robust wine. People here go to the **Cellier dans l'Ancien Église** (☎ **04-74-04-41-43**), the old church cellar, to sip the wine. A statue of Bacchus with some scantily clad and tipsy girlfriends looks on from what used to be the altar. It's open daily from 10am to noon and 2:30 to 6:30pm (closed Tuesdays from October to June 1). Admission is 5 F (85¢).

3 Roanne

242 miles SE of Paris, 54 miles NW of Lyon

This industrial town on the left bank of the Loire is often visited from Lyon or Vichy because it contains one of France's greatest three-star restaurants, the Hôtel-Restaurant Troisgros (see "Dining," below).

There's also a worthwhile museum. In a stately neoclassic mansion built at the end of the 18th century, **Musée Joseph-Déchelette**, 22 rue Anatole-France

(☎ 04-77-23-68-77), offers an exceptional display of Italian and French earthenware from the 16th, 17th, 18th, and 20th centuries, as well as earthenware produced in Roanne from the 16th to the 19th centuries. This is the most important privately endowed museum in this part of France. Admission is 20 F ($3.20); hours are Wednesday through Monday from 10am to noon and 2 to 6pm. On Sunday, the museum is open only in the afternoon, and on Friday, there is no noontime break.

ESSENTIALS

GETTING THERE　There are **train** and to a lesser extent **bus** connections from nearby cities, notably Lyon; the train is a lot more convenient. For train information and schedules, call ☎ **08-36-35-35-35.** By train, Roanne lies 3 hours from Paris but only 1 hour from Lyon. If you're **driving,** simply follow N7 northwest from Lyon to Roanne. From Paris, follow A6 south to the town of Nemours, continuing southwest along N7.

VISITOR INFORMATION　The **Office de Tourisme** is on 1 cours de la République (☎ **04-77-71-51-77**).

DINING

✪ **Hôtel-Restaurant Troisgros.** Place de la Gare, 42300 Roanne. ☎ **04-77-71-66-97.** Fax 04-77-70-39-77. Reservations required. Main courses 200–450 F ($32–$72); fixed-price menus 690–830 F ($110.40–$132.80). AE, DC, MC, V. Thurs–Mon noon–1:30pm and 7:30–9:30pm. June–Sept, open Tues for lunch. Closed 3 weeks Feb–Mar and 2 weeks in Aug. FRENCH.

This restaurant first acquired its legendary reputation in the 1950s, and it has factored into the itineraries of globetrotting foodies, visiting heads of state, and any very wealthy people touring the region around Lyon. Come here with a respect for both the French *grande bourgeoisie* and the enduring appeal of French culinary finesse. Don't expect anything too wild and crazy. The place is simply too conservative and too devoted to impeccably tailored service for anything radical or provocative.

Decorated in neutral colors and lined with contemporary artworks, the restaurant features superb cuisine at astronomical prices. Pierre (the father) and Michel (the son) Troisgros are the current bearers of the Troisgros flame, jointly presenting a celebration of the bounty of the Lyonnais countryside. Dishes include warm oysters in butter sauce; fried foie gras served with marinated eggplant; frogs' legs with a remoulade of cumin and celery; salmon with sage sauce; and fillets of beef served with Fleurie wine and bone marrow. For dessert, ask to see one of the best assortments of esoteric cheeses in the region or perhaps enjoy a pralien soufflé.

NEARBY DINING & ACCOMMODATIONS

In the satellite village of **Le Coteau** you'll find several worthy restaurants. These two are our favorites. To reach Le Coteau, take N7 2 miles from the center of Roanne.

✪ **Auberge Costelloise.** 2 av. de la Libération, Le Coteau. ☎ **04-77-68-12-71.** Reservations required. Main courses 90–180 F ($14.40–$28.80); fixed-price menus 130–370 F ($20.80–$59.20). AE, MC, V. Tues–Sat noon–1:30pm and 7:45–9:15pm. Closed Jan 2–10 and Aug 7–15. FRENCH.

Chef Daniel Alex and his wife, Solange, provide what this region needs: an attractive restaurant with fine cuisine and reasonable prices. Choose from one of the fixed-price à la carte menus, which change weekly; the cheapest one isn't available on Saturday night. Popular dishes are gâteau of chicken livers with essence of shrimp, sole fillet with confit of leeks, and foie gras. You can order fine vintages of Burgundian wines by the pitcher. This is the place to head when you can't afford the dazzling but expensive food at Troisgros.

Hôtel Restaurant Artaud. 133 av. de la Libération, 42120 Le Coteau. ☎ **04-77-68-46-44.** Fax 04-77-72-23-50. Reservations recommended. Main courses 49–120 F ($7.85–$19.20); fixed-price menus 98–240 F ($15.70–$38.40). AE, DC, V. Tues–Sat noon–2pm; Mon–Sat 7:30–9pm. Closed July 30–Aug 21. FRENCH.

In an elegant dining room, Nicole and Alain Artaud offer traditional French cuisine. Choices include monkfish salad with saffron, beef from local farms, and a variety of desserts. There's also a good selection of French wines.

The hotel offers 25 well-appointed **rooms** with satellite TV; a double runs from 300 F to 480 F ($48 to $76.80).

4 Pérouges

288 miles SE of Paris, 22 miles NE of Lyon

The Middle Ages live on. Saved from demolition by a courageous mayor in 1909 and preserved by the government, this village of craftspeople often attracts movie crews; *The Three Musketeers* (1973), starring Michael York, and *Monsieur Vincent* (1948) were filmed here. The town sits on what has been called an "isolated throne," atop a hill northeast of Lyon.

Follow rue du Prince, once the main business street, to place des Tilleuls, at the center of which is the *Arbre de la Liberté* (Tree of Liberty) planted in 1792 to honor the Revolution. Nearby, within what was originally built in the 14th century as a private home, is the **Musée du Vieux-Pérouges,** place de la Halle (☎ **04-74-61-00-88**), displaying such artifacts as hand looms. From Easter to November 1, it's open daily from 10am to noon and 2 to 6pm; the rest of the year, it's open only on Saturdays and Sundays (same hours, in midwinter it might be closed if the weather is bad). Admission is 15 F ($2.40). This price includes access to the museum and, through adjoining doors, to one of the finest houses in the village, **the Maison des Princes de Savoie,** with its watchtower (**La Tour de Guet**) and a replica of a 13th-century garden, the **Jardin de Hortulus.**

Wander at your leisure through the town, soaking in the atmosphere of a stone-built village that's virtually unchanged since the birth of the modern age. During the 13th century, weaving was the principal industry here, and linen merchants sold their wares under the Gothic arcades and galleries on either side of the town's streets. In the eastern sector of **rue des Rondes** are many stone houses of former hand weavers. The stone hooks on the facades were for newly woven pieces of linen.

ESSENTIALS

GETTING THERE   It's easiest to **drive** to Pérouges, though the signs for the town, especially at night, are confusing. From Lyon, take Route 84 northeast and exit near Meximieux.

VISITOR INFORMATION   The **Comité de Defense et de Conservation du Vieux-Pérouges** (a fancy name for the tourist office) is in the Hostellerie du Vieux-Pérouges, place des Tilleuls (☎ **04-74-61-00-88**).

ACCOMMODATIONS & DINING

✪ **Hostellerie du Vieux-Pérouges.** Place des Tilleuls, 01800 Pérouges. ☎ **04-74-61-00-88.** Fax 04-74-34-77-90. 28 units. TV TEL. 550–1,050 F ($88–$168) double. AE, MC, V. Free parking.

This is a treasure in a lavishly restored group of 13th-century timbered buildings. Georges Thibaut runs a museum-caliber inn furnished with polished antiques, cupboards with pewter plates, iron lanterns hanging from medieval beams, glistening refectory dining tables, and stone fireplaces.

Dining: The restaurant is run in association with Le Manoir, where guests are accommodated. The food is exceptional, especially when it's served with the local sparkling wine, Montagnieu, which has been compared to Asti-Spumante. Specialties are *terrine truffée Brillat-Savarin* (stuffed fillets of carp), *écrevisses* (crayfish) *pérougiennes,* and *galette pérougienne à la crème* (a dessert crêpe). After dinner, ask for a unique liqueur made from a recipe from the Middle Ages: Ypocras. Fixed-price meals cost 170 F to 200 F ($27.20 to $32).

5 Bourg-en-Bresse

264 miles SE of Paris, 38 miles NE of Lyon

The ancient capital of Bresse, this farming/business center lies on the border between Burgundy and the Jura and offers fabulous food.

ESSENTIALS

GETTING THERE   Bourg-en-Bresse is easily accessible by **train** from Paris, Lyon, and Dijon. Fifteen TGV trains arrive from Paris's Gare de Lyon each day (trip time: 2 hours), and from Lyon, 10 trains arrive per day (trip time: 40 to 80 minutes depending on the train). From Dijon, five trains arrive per day (trip time: 2 hours). For train information and schedules, call ☎ **08-36-35-35-35.**

If you're **driving** from Lyon, take A42 or N83 for the 35- to 45-minute trip; from Dijon, follow A31 to Mâcon and then switch to A40 for the 2-hour drive.

VISITOR INFORMATION   The **Office de Tourisme** is at 6 av. Alsace-Lorraine (☎ **04-74-22-49-40**).

SEEING THE SIGHTS

If you have time, visit the **Église Notre-Dame,** off place Carriat. Begun in 1505, it contains some finely carved 16th-century stalls. It still acts as a functioning church complete with a resident priest. If you'd like to wander around town, check out the **15th-century houses** on rue du Palais and rue Gambetta.

✪ **Église de Brou.** 63 bd. de Brou. ☎ **04-74-22-83-83.** Admission to church, cloisters, and museum 35 F ($5.60) adults, 23 F ($3.70) ages 12–25, free for children 11 and under. Apr to mid-June, daily 9am–12:30pm and 2–6:30pm; mid-June to Sept, daily 9am–6:30pm; Oct–Mar, daily 9am–noon and 2–5pm. Closed Jan 1, May 1, Nov 1 and 11, and Dec 25.

Art lovers will want to stop at the Église de Brou to see its magnificent royal tombs. One of the great artistic treasures of France, this Flamboyant Gothic monastery was built between 1506 and 1532 (the three cloisters between 1506 and 1512, the church between 1513 and 1532) for Margaret of Austria, the ill-fated daughter of Emperor Maximilian. Over the ornate Renaissance doorway, the tympanum depicts Margaret and her "handsome duke," Philibert, who died when he caught cold on a hunting expedition. The initials of Philibert (sometimes known as "the Fair") and Margaret are linked by love knots. The nave and its double aisles are admirable. Look for the ornate rood screen, decorated with basket-handle arching. Ask a guide for a tour of the choir, which is rich in decorative detail; the 74 choir stalls were made of oak in just 2 years by Flemish sculptors and local craftsmen. Vast sums of money were spent in 1998 and 1999 repairing the roof and some of the stonework.

The tombs form the church's treasure. The Carrara marble statues are of Philibert, who died in 1504, and Margaret, who remained faithful to his memory until her death in 1530. Another tomb is that of Marguerite de Bourbon, mother of Philibert and grandmother of François I, who died in 1483. See also the stained-glass windows inspired by a Dürer engraving and an alabaster retable depicting *The Seven Joys of the Madonna.*

Medieval and Renaissance art is not the only allure at this monument. Expositions of modern art are sometimes conducted inside.

ACCOMMODATIONS

Hôtel du Prieuré. 49–51 bd. de Brou, 01000 Bourg-en-Bresse. ☎ **04-74-22-44-60.** Fax 04-74-22-71-07. E-mail: hotelduprieure@wanadoo.fr. 14 units. TV TEL. 380–560 F ($60.80–$89.60) double; 720 F ($115.20) suite. AE, DC. Free parking.

Owned by sisters Mmes Alby and Guerrin, this is the town's most gracious hotel. Its angled exterior is surrounded by an acre of carefully planned gardens and 400-year-old stone walls. The place is especially alluring in spring, when forsythia, lilacs, roses, and Japanese cherries fill the air with perfume. Most guest rooms are large and tranquil, each outfitted in Louis XV, Louis XVI, or French country rustic style.

Le Logis de Brou. 132 bd. de Brou, 01000 Bourg-en-Bresse. ☎ **04-74-22-11-55.** Fax 04-74-22-37-30. www.citotel.com/hotels/logir.html. 30 units. TV TEL. 400 F ($64) double. AE, MC, V. Parking 50 F ($8).

This is actually a much better hotel than its boxlike exterior suggests. The fully refurbished and soundproofed four-story building has landscaped grounds and is near the busy road running in front of the church. Guests register in a lobby with a raised hearth. Each comfortably furnished guest room contains well-crafted reproductions of antique furniture.

DINING

Auberge Bressane. 166 bd. de Brou. ☎ **04-74-22-22-68.** Reservations recommended. Main courses 98–300 F ($15.70–$48); fixed-price menus 98–350 F ($15.70–$56). AE, DC, MC, V. Daily noon–1:30pm and 7:15–9:45pm. FRENCH.

Bresse poultry is the best in France, and chef Jean-Pierre Vullin specializes in succulent *volaille de Bresse,* served five ways, including a delectable version in cream sauce with morels. Of course, the chef knows how to prepare other dishes equally well: You might enjoy a gâteau of chicken liver, crayfish gratin, or sea bass with fresh basil, accompanied by regional wines like Seyssel and Montagnieu. The staff, although not intentionally difficult, may appear slightly aloof.

✪ **Au Chalet de Brou.** 168 bd. de Brou. ☎ **04-74-22-26-28.** Reservations recommended. Main courses 75–130 F ($12–$20.80); fixed-price menus 85–195 F ($13.60–$31.20). MC, V. Sat–Thurs noon–2pm; Sat–Wed 7–9:30pm. Closed Dec 23–Jan 23. FRENCH.

You'll find flavorful but relatively inexpensive food in this small-scale, unpretentious restaurant across from the village's most famous church. Specialties include a "cake" of chicken livers served with essence of tomato; quenelle of pike-perch with lobster sauce; frogs' legs in parsley sauce; and the all-time rave, any of at least a half-dozen kinds of Bresse chicken, served with your choice of a morel-flavored cream sauce; with raspberry vinegar; or with a chardonnay sauce. Some purists (including us) opt for it simply grilled so you can appreciate the unadorned flavor of the bird in its own drippings. Dessert might include an apple tart presented, according to your choice, hot or semifrozen. This isn't the region's most glamorous or cutting-edge restaurant, but the prices are more than fair and the food is well prepared.

6 Vienne

304 miles SE of Paris, 19 miles S of Lyon

Serious gastronomes know Vienne because it boasts one of France's leading restaurants, La Pyramide. But even if you can't afford the haute cuisine served there, you may want to visit Vienne for its sights. Situated on the left bank of the Rhône, it's a wine center and the southernmost Burgundian town.

ESSENTIALS

GETTING THERE   **Rail** lines connect Vienne with the rest of France. Some trips require a transfer in nearby Lyon. For train information and schedules, call ☎ **08-36-35-35-39.** Buses from Lyon arrive about eight times a day, taking about an hour for the transit. For **bus** information, contact Vienne's Gare Routière (☎ **04-74-85-18-51**), which lies adjacent to the railway station.

If you're **driving** from Lyon, take either N7 (which is more direct) or A7, an expressway that meanders along the banks of the Rhône River.

VISITOR INFORMATION   The **Office de Tourisme** is at 3 cours Brillier (☎ **04-74-53-80-30**).

SPECIAL EVENTS   During the first 2 weeks in July, Vienne comes to life with some of the biggest names in jazz during its annual **Festival du Jazz à Vienne.** Such notables as B. B. King, Sonny Rollins, the Count Basie Orchestra, Eric Clapton, and even Little Richard have played here. Tickets range from 150 F ($25.50) for single performances up to 600 F ($102) for seven concerts. You can get tickets and complete information from the **Théâtre de Vienne,** 4 rue Chantelouve (☎ **04-74-85-00-05**).

SEEING THE SIGHTS

Vienne contains many embellishments from its past, making it a *ville romaine et médiévale.* Near the center of town on place du Palais is the **Temple d'Auguste et de Livie,** inviting comparisons with the Maison Carrée at Nîmes. It was ordered built by Roman emperor Claudius and turned into a temple of reason during the Revolution. Another outstanding monument is the small Pyramide du Cirque Romain, part of the Roman circus. Rising 52 feet, it rests on a portico with four arches and is sometimes known as the tomb of Pilate.

Take rue Clémentine to the **Cathédrale St-Maurice,** place St-Maurice (☎ **04-74-85-60-28**), which dates from the 12th century even though it wasn't completed until the 15th. It has three aisles but no transepts. Its west front is built in the Flamboyant Gothic style, and inside are many fine Romanesque sculptures.

In the southern part of town near the river stands the **Église St-Pierre,** at place St-Pierre (☎ **04-74-85-20-35**), a landmark that traces its origins to the 5th century, making it one of the oldest medieval churches in France. It contains a **Musée Lapidaire** (☎ **04-74-85-50-42**), displaying architectural fragments and sculptures found in local excavations. The museum is open from April 1 to October 31, Tuesday through Sunday from 9:30am to 1pm and 2 to 6pm; the rest of the year, it's open Tuesday through Saturday from 9:30am to 12:30pm and 2 to 5pm, and Sunday from 2 to 6pm. Admission is 11 F ($1.75).

A large **Théâtre Romain,** 7 rue du Cirque (☎ **04-74-85-39-23**), has been excavated east of town at the foot of Mont Pipet. Once theatrical spectacles were staged here for an audience of thousands. You can visit from April 1 to August 31, daily from 9:30am to 1pm and 2 to 6pm; the rest of the year, Tuesday through Saturday from

9:30am to 12:30pm and 2 to 5pm, and Sunday from 1:30 to 5:30pm. Admission is 12 F ($1.90).

If you have time to make a side trip about an hour south, in the tiny village of **Hauteville** you'll find one of the world's strangest pieces of architecture, the **Palais du Facteur Cheval** (Palace of the Mailman Cheval; ☎ **04-75-68-81-19**). It represents the lifelong work of a French postman, Ferdinand Cheval; built of stone and concrete and elaborately decorated, often with clamshells, it's a highly unusual, highly eccentric palace of fantasy in a high-walled garden. During his lifetime, M. Cheval was ridiculed by his neighbors as a crackpot, but his palace has since been declared a national monument and a tribute to the aesthetic value, or mania, of the French individual. The work was finished in 1912, when Cheval was 76; he died 13 years later. The north end of the facade is in massive rococo style. The turreted tower is 35 feet tall, and the entire building is 85 feet long. The elaborate sculptural decorations include animals such as leopards and artifacts such as Roman vases. Admission costs 30 F ($4.80) per adult, 20 F ($3.20) for children 6 to 16. The palace is open daily, mid-April to mid-September from 9am to 7pm, February to mid-April and mid-September to November from 9:30am to 5:30pm, and in December and January from 10am to 4:30pm; closed Christmas and New Year's days.

ACCOMMODATIONS

La Pyramide Fernand-Point (see "Dining," below) also offers rooms.

✪ **Hostellerie Beau-Rivage.** 2 rue de Beau-Rivage, 69420 Condrieu. ☎ **04-74-56-82-82.** Fax 04-74-59-59-36. 25 units. MINIBAR TV TEL. 550–850 F ($88–$136) double. AE, V, DC. From Vienne, cross the Rhône on N86, then head south $7^1/2$ miles; pass through Condrieu and, on the southern outskirts, look for signs on the left.

A Relais du Silence, this place originated around 1900 as a simple inn that offered food and wine to fishermen who traveled from Lyon to the well-stocked waters of this section of the Rhône. Since then, it has evolved into a stylish, nostalgic enclave of old-fashioned charm. The rooms are well furnished and, in some cases, discreetly grand and larger than you might expect.

The fast-flowing Rhône passes by the dining terrace. The cuisine is exceptional and traditional. One fixed-price menu (available only at lunch) is 180 F ($28.80); the others (available anytime) range from 370F to 670 F ($59.20 to $107.20). Try *quenelles* (fish balls) of pike; stuffed snails with new potatoes; and an intensely cultivated suprême of pigeon served on a platter with a confit of pigeon, roasted foie gras, and turnips. Also appealing are smoked salmon blinis and mousseline of lobster with chervil. The Côtes du Rhône wines complement the food well.

DINING

✪ **La Pyramide Fernand-Point.** 14 bd. Fernand-Point, 38200 Vienne. ☎ **04-74-53-01-96.** Fax 04-74-85-69-73. www.relaischateaux.fr/pyramide. E-mail: pyramide.f.point@wanadoo.fr. Reservations required. Main courses 270–320 F ($43.20–$51.20); fixed-price menus 480–680 F ($76.80–$108.80). AE, DC, MC, V. Thurs–Mon 12:30–1:30pm and 7:30–9:30pm. Closed Feb. FRENCH.

This is the area's premier place to stay and/or dine, and for many it's their preferred stopover between Paris and the Riviera. The restaurant perpetuates the memory of a superb chef, Fernand Point. Through the continuing efforts of Patrick Henriroux, many of Point's secrets have been preserved, especially his sauces, touted as the best in the country. Menus change seasonally, but regardless of when you arrive, the cuisine is imaginative, cerebral, and destined to create lots of dialogue. Examples include a watercress and zander soup garnished with braised endive; peppered and roasted duckling with red cabbage, wild mushrooms, and liqueur-soaked grapes; a parfait of foie gras with spices and a fruit-and-vegetable salad garnished with aged sherry dressing; suckling veal in puff pastry, served with truffles and braised salsify; and slice of John Dory wrapped in Parma ham, soya-flavored endive, and a Tabasco-flavored sabayon. The cheese platter here is absolutely wonderful, and desserts are as artfully caloric, and as stylish, as anything else in the Rhône valley. The chef can appeal to the tastes of both traditionalists and adventurers.

The hotel offers 21 air-conditioned **rooms and four suites,** all modern and decorated with oak. Doubles are 1,080 F ($172.80); suites go for 1,380 F ($220.80).

Le Bec Fin. 7 place St-Maurice. ☎ **04-74-85-76-72.** Reservations required. Main courses 80–170 F ($12.80–$27.20); fixed-price menus 98–300 F ($15.70–$48). AE, V. Tues–Sun noon–2pm, Tues–Sat 7–9:30pm. FRENCH.

The best-prepared and most generously served fixed-price meals in town are available in this rustic setting near the cathedral. À la carte specialties are somewhat more sophisticated, including salads laced with all the region's delicacies (foie gras, smoked duckling, and the like), breast of duckling with a truffled sauce, fillet of turbot, and monkfish with saffron.

7 Valence

417 miles SE of Paris, 62 miles S of Lyon

Valence stands on the left bank of the Rhône between Lyon and Avignon. A former Roman colony, it later became the capital of the Duchy of Valentinois, set up by Louis XII in 1493 for Cesare Borgia.

Today, Valence is the market town and the major distribution point for the mammoth fruit and vegetable market of the Rhône Valley. Perhaps it's altogether fitting that François Rabelais, who wrote of gargantuan appetites in his lusty prose, spent time here as a student.

You can climb the ruined château atop the white stone **Mont Crussol.** The ruins date from the 12th century. A view of this castle is possible from the esplanade of the Champ de Mars. Valence is still the home of the Arsenal, one of France's oldest gunpowder factories.

The most interesting sight here is the **Cathédrale St-Apollinaire,** Place de Ormeaux (☎ **04-75-43-13-32**), consecrated by Urban II in 1095, though it's been much restored since. Built in the Auvergnat-Romanesque style, the cathedral is on place des Clercs in the center of town. The choir contains the tomb of Pope Pius VI, who died here a prisoner at the end of the 18th century. It's open daily from 8am to 7pm.

Adjoining the cathedral is the **Musée Municipal,** 4 place des Ormeaux (☎ **04-75-79-20-80**), noted for its nearly 100 red-chalk drawings by Hubert Robert done in the 18th century. It also has a number of Greco-Roman artifacts. It's open daily from 2 to 6pm. On Wednesday, Saturday, and Sunday it is also open 9am to noon. Admission is 15 F ($2.40), free for children 15 and under.

On the north side of the square, on Grand-Rue, you'll pass **Maison des Têtes,** built in 1532 with sculpted heads of Homer, Hippocrates, Aristotle, and other Greeks.

ESSENTIALS

GETTING THERE   There are fast and easy **rail** and highway connections from Lyon, Grenoble, and Marseille. For train information and schedules, call ☎ **08-36-35-35-35.** If you're **driving** to Valence from Lyon, take A7 south. From Grenoble, follow E711 to outside the town of Voreppe, heading southwest along E713, merging to W532 into Valence. From Marseilles, follow A7 north.

VISITOR INFORMATION   The **Office de Tourisme** is at parvis de la Gare (☎ 04-75-44-90-40).

ACCOMMODATIONS & DINING

✪ **Hotel-Restaurant Pic.** 285 av. Victor-Hugo. ☎ **04-75-44-15-32.** Fax 04-75-40-96-03. www.pic-valence.com. E-mail: pic@relaischateaux.fr. Reservations required. Main courses 150–320 F ($24–$51.20); fixed-price menus 290–340 F ($46.40–$54.40) at lunch, 490–890 F ($78.40–$142.40) at dinner. AE, DC, MC, V. Sun noon–2:30pm, Mon–Tues and Thurs–Sat noon–2:30pm and 8–9:30pm. Closed 2 weeks in Jan. FRENCH.

This is the least known of France's great three-star restaurants. Both the cooking and the wine list are exceptional, the latter featuring regional selections like Hermitage, St-Péray, and Côtes du Rhône. Alain Pic took over as chef when his renowned father, Jacques, died in 1992, and he continues to perform admirably. This charming villa has a flower-garden courtyard and a dining room with big tables and ample chairs. Appetizers include ballotine of squab, pâté de foie gras, and breast of small game bird. For a main course we recommend the sea bass filet in velvety velouté, crowned by caviar; chicken cooked in a pig's bladder; or lamb stew with basil, sweetbreads, and kidneys. In season, one of the chef's masterpieces is tender noisettes of venison in a wine-dark sauce as light as chiffon. The desserts are a rapturous experience, from the grapefruit sorbet to the cold orange soufflé.

Pic also rents 13 well-furnished **doubles,** costing 750 F to 1,500 F ($120 to $240).

8 The Ardèche

The Ardèche region began to draw significant numbers of foreign visitors only about a decade ago. Until then it was almost unknown beyond the French borders, bypassed in favor of regions with more and better monuments and museums. Its wines aren't the finest in France and its cuisine is the kind of fortifying country fare that nourishes the body but doesn't win awards. Though many districts of France contain buildings that have inspired architects around the world, the Ardèche is limited to stone-sided structures of rustic but not grandiloquent charm. But as urbanites and visitors began seeking the pleasures of escapes to the wilderness or adventures like kayaking down sublimely beautiful cliff-edged canyons, the Ardèche finally came of age.

The Ardèche occupies the eastern flank of the Massif Central (see chapter 20), a landscape of jagged, much-eroded granite and limestone highlands that ramble down to the western bank of the Rhône. It isn't the highest or most dramatic region—that honor goes to the Alps, whose peaks rise as much as three times higher. Although it defines itself as Le Midi (its southern border lies less than 25 and 31 miles from Avignon and Nîmes, respectively), its culture and landscape are more firmly rooted in the rugged uplands of France's central highlands.

Through its territory flow the streams and rivers that drain the snow and rain of the Massif Central. They include rivers with names like Ligne, Fontolière, Lignon, Tanargue, and, most important, Ardèche. They flow beside, around, and through rocky ravines, ancient lava flows, feudal ruins, and stone-sided villages perched in high-altitude sites originally chosen for their medieval ease of defense.

The most famous and oft-visited section of the Ardèche is its southern extremity, with granite-sided ravines 1,000 feet deep, gouged by millions of springtime floodings of the Ardèche River—no wonder it's called the Grand Canyon of France. This area draws thousands of tourists who, often with their children, take driving tours along the highways flanking the ravines.

We recommend that you stop in the southern Ardèche to admire the gorges only briefly, say, for a morning's drive. It's better to spend the night in the less touristy northern reaches of the Ardèche than to stay amid the honky-tonk commercialism that sometimes pervades the southern reaches.

In the northern Ardèche, in the 28 miles of hills and valleys separating the hamlets of Vals-les-Bains and Lamastre, is a soft and civilized wilderness, with landscapes that have been devoted to grape growing, sheep herding, and (more recently) hill trekking.

Vallon-Pont-d'Arc, the gateway to the gorges, was defined by one writer as a Gallic version of Gatlinburg, Tennessee. (For your overnight stop, we suggest you continue even further north to the more picturesque towns of Vals-les-Bains or Lamastre.)

If you want to kayak in the gorges, go between early April and late November, when the waters are green and sluggish and safer than during the floods of winter and spring. You'll find at least three dozen rental agencies for everything from plastic kayaks to horses in Vallon-Pont-d'Arc. One of the best outfitters is **Adventure Canoë,** place du Marché (B.P. 27), 07150 Vallon-Pont-d'Arc (☎ 04-75-37-18-14), which arranges rentals of canoes and kayaks for rides through the gorges. A 3-hour *mini-descente* costs 200 F ($32) for two participants riding a 4-mile route from Vallon-Pont-d'Arc to the downstream hamlet of Chames, or 100 F ($16) for a kayak for one. A full-day *grande descente* for two riding a 19-mile downstream route from Vallon-Pont-d'Arc to St-Martin d'Ardèche costs 340 F ($54.40) for two or 170 F ($27.20) for one. A 2-day trip is 490 F ($78.40) for two or 245 F ($39.20) for one. Prices include transport by minivan back to Vallon-Pont-d'Arc at the end of the ride. Lunch is not included, so bring your own picnic. The makings for this are available at dozens of bakeries and delicatessens near each point of origin.

Despite the appeal of kayaking, most travelers stick with driving along the upper summits of the gorges.

VALS-LES-BAINS

27 miles W of Montélimar, 86 miles SW of Lyon

In a depression of the valley of the Volane River, Vals-les-Bains is surrounded by about 150 freshwater springs whose existence was discovered relatively recently—around 1600. Scientists have never really understood why each spring contains a different percentage of minerals: Most contain bicarbonate of soda, others are almost tasteless, and one—*La Source Dominique*—has such a high percentage of iron and arsenic that it's poisonous. Waters from Dominique are piped away from the town center; others are funneled into a Station Thérmale adjacent to the town's casino.

From a position in the park outside the Station Thérmale, a *source intermittante* erupts, Old Faithful-style, to a height of around 25 feet every 6 hours or so. Small crowds gather for eruptions at 5:30 and 11:30am and 5:30 and 11:30pm.

A few steps away, the belle époque casino, **Parc Thermal** (☎ 04-75-38-77-77), is open daily from noon to 3am; entrance is free. The only casino between Lyon and Aigues-Mortes, it's mobbed on weekends by local farmers and their families playing either roulette or the slot machines, the only options offered. It's not at all glamorous; this isn't Monte Carlo. There's a bistro-style theme restaurant, Le Hollywood, on the premises; it's open nightly from 7pm to midnight. There's also a 600-seat theater for occasional plays or concerts, plus a movie theater.

Other than the surrounding scenery, the town's most unusual site is about 14 miles south, beside the highway to Privas. A ruined feudal château once stood here; it was

The Grand Canyon of France

Measuring no more than 119 miles in length, the Ardèche isn't the longest, mightiest, or most influential river in France, but it flows faster, with more geological after-effects, than any other. Originating on the eastern edge of the Massif Central at about 5,000 feet above sea level, the Ardèche descends faster, over a shorter distance, than any of its mightier competitors. (In some sections it falls as much as 3 feet for every half mile of its length, positively vertiginous by comparison with such relatively placid rivers as the Seine and the Loire.) These changes in altitude, combined with cycles of heavy rainfall and drought, result in what's the most temperamental and changeable waterway in France.

The resulting ebbs and flows have created the Grand Canyon of France. Littered with alluvial deposits, strewn in ravines whose depth sometimes exceeds 950 feet, the river's lower extremity (its final 36 miles, before the waters dump into the Rhône) is one of the country's most unusual geological areas. A **panoramic road (D290)** runs along a rim of these canyons, providing views over an arid landscape of grasses, toughened trees, drought-resistant shrubs, and some of the most distinctively eroded deposits of granite, limestone, and basalt in Europe.

If you drive along this route, expect the type of cheap motels, family-fun emporiums, and fast-food joints you'd see near Yellowstone Park in the United States. There's no denying, however, the basic beauty of the site, which you can admire from a series of belvederes along the highway. The highway runs in a meandering line that's approximately parallel to the bluffs and corniches of the river's northwestern edge. Many of the belvederes have brown-and-white signs that encourage motorists to stop and walk for a few minutes along some of the well-marked footpaths.

The route, which you can traverse in a few hours even if you stop frequently for sightseeing, stretches southeast to northwest between the towns of Vallon-Pont-d'Arc and Pont St-Esprit. Since the meandering corniche roads are a challenge to drive, be extra-careful. In particular, stay on the lookout for other vehicles weaving frighteningly out of their lanes as the drivers and passengers crane their necks to admire the scenery and furiously snap photos.

richly embellished and enlarged in the 1700s and served as the home of the comtes du Valentinois. Ironically, it escaped the ravages of the Revolution only to fall into ruin in 1820, when its bankrupt owners sold its accessories and architectural ornaments to pay their debts. Today only the 16th-century entrance gate remains relatively unharmed. The views over the confluence of two ravines and the valley below are worth the detour.

ACCOMMODATIONS

Grand Hôtel des Bains. 3 Montée de l'Hôtel-des-Bains, 07600 Vals-les-Bains. ☎ **04-75-37-42-13.** Fax 04-75-37-67-02. E-mail: grand.hotel.des.bains@wanadoo.fr. 63 units. TV TEL. 420–480 F ($67.20–$76.80) double; 600–730 F ($96–$116.80) suite. AE, DC, MC, V. Closed Dec–Mar.

This is the largest and best hotel in town, with a central wing built in 1860 in anticipation of a visit from Empress Eugénie. (Alas, Eugénie, finding she was comfortable in the nearby resort of Vichy, canceled her visit.) Despite the snub, the hotel added two additional wings in 1870 and has survived ever since, partly because of a cordial staff and well-maintained, conservatively furnished rooms. The **restaurant** charges 150 F to 333 F ($24 to $53.30) for fixed-price menus, served daily at lunch and dinner.

Hôtel de l'Europe. 86 rue Jean-Jaurès, 07600 Vals-les-Bains. ☎ **04-75-37-43-94.** Fax 04-75-94-66-62. www.ardeche-hotel.com. E-mail: info@ardeche-hotel.com. 32 units. TV TEL. 260–350 F ($41.60–$56) double. AE, V.

Built to house well-heeled patrons of the adjacent spa in 1805 and enlarged and modernized many times since, this hotel retains memories of yesteryear's grandeur. Bedrooms are large, high-ceilinged, and just dowdy enough to remind you of *la Belle France* of another era. The staff is as courtly and well-mannered as the old-fashioned setting seems to require. On the premises is a functional, not-at-all-glittery **restaurant.** Menu specialties include stuffed trout; duck breast with honey sauce; and homemade foie gras. Fixed-price menus range from a bargain 65 F to 175 F ($10.40 to $28).

DINING

Restaurant Mireille. 3 rue Jean-Jaurès. ☎ **04-75-37-49-06.** Reservations recommended. Fixed-price menus 85–160 F ($13.60–$25.60). V. Thurs–Tues noon–2pm; Thurs–Mon 7–9pm. Closed 2 weeks in Apr and 2 weeks in Sept. FRENCH.

Containing only 26 seats, this restaurant occupies the space below vaulted stone ceilings that for centuries sheltered a herd of goats. Known for its earthy warmth, the restaurant serves carefully calibrated cuisine with an ambitious menu. It includes local mousse of flap mushrooms with scallops, and fillet of turbot with white butter.

LAMASTRE

26 miles N of Vals-les-Bains, 18 miles W of Valence

Near the Ardèche's northern frontier, the charming hamlet of Lamastre is known for its light industry (shoes, camping gear, furniture, and light machine tools). Many connoisseurs of Ardèche architecture view it as the most unaltered and evocative village in the district. Its most important site is its church, in Macheville, in the upper part of the village. Built of pink Romanesque stone, it boasts portions dating from the 12th century and is the frequent site of weddings, one of which you might get to view.

Don't expect lots of nightlife or razzle-dazzle here. Most visitors use the town as a base for striking out on nature walks and hikes through the surrounding hills and valleys. A network of brown-and-white signs clearly marks each trail.

ACCOMMODATIONS & DINING

Château d'Urbilhac. Rte. de Vernoux, 07270 Lamastre. ☎ **04-75-06-42-11.** Fax 04-75-06-52-75. 12 units. TEL. 1,300 F ($208) double. Rates include half board. AE, DC, V. Closed Sept 30–May 1. From the center of Lamastre, follow the signs to the château about 1 mile south.

This is the only château in the Ardèche. Built in the 1500s, it was renovated in the 19th century and is sheathed in pink stucco. Rated three stars, it boasts a large outdoor pool and tennis court. Its owner, Mme Marcelle Xampero, prepares evening meals and maintains the 115 acres around the building. The restaurant is usually closed at lunch except to hotel residents, and even at night, nonresidents should phone in advance before their arrival.

Hôtel du Midi. Place Seignobos, 07270 Lamastre. ☎ **04-75-06-41-50.** Fax 04-75-06-49-75. 12 units. TV TEL. 465–520 F ($74.40–$83.20) double. AE, DC, DISC, MC, V. Closed Jan–Feb.

Built in 1925, with slightly faded rooms that retain a vague Art Deco allure, this place has been used as an overnight stop for both Charles de Gaulle and Elizabeth Bowes-Lyon, the Queen Mother of England.

Dining: Maintained by members of the Perrier family, this place is well known for its restaurant, which serves fixed-price menus for 185 F to 470 F ($29.60 to $75.20). Lunch and dinner are offered Tuesday through Sunday (not Sunday night). The food is among the region's best, including many updated takes on regional traditions.

13 The French Alps

No part of France has more dramatic scenery than the Alps, for the western ramparts of these mountains and their foothills are truly majestic. From the Mediterranean in the south to the Rhine in the north, they stretch along the southeastern flank of France. The skiing here has no equal in Europe, not even in Switzerland. Some of the resorts are legendary, like **Chamonix-Mont Blanc,** the historic capital of alpine skiing, with its 12-mile Vallée Blanche run. Mont Blanc, at 15,780 snowy feet, is the highest mountain in Western Europe.

Most of this chapter covers the area known as the Savoy (Savoie), taking in the French lake district, including the largest alpine lake, which the French share with Switzerland. The French call it Lac Léman, but it's known as Lake Geneva in English.

From January to March, skiers flock to Chamonix-Mont Blanc, Megève, Val d'Isère, and Courchevel 1850; from July to September, spa fans head to Evian-les-Bains and Aix-les-Bains. Grenoble, the capital of the French Alps, is the gateway. It's just 30 minutes by car from the Grenoble-St-Geoirs airport, 40 minutes from the Lyon-Satolas international airport, and 90 minutes from Geneva's Cointrin airport. The city is also connected with the Paris-Lyon-Marseille motorway on the west and to the Chambéry-Geneva motorway on the east.

REGIONAL CUISINE   The cuisine of the Savoy is robust and straightforward, well suited to the active lifestyle of the people. Most recipes depend on the region's superb raw ingredients: fresh produce, eggs, fish, meats, and—most important—cheese and milk.

Cheese making, a process developed over thousands of years as a means of preserving the proteins and nutrients of milk, was carefully fine-tuned in the Savoy (where cows and goats thrived on the grasses of the alpine meadows). The region's most famous cheese is a form of especially savory Gruyère known as beaufort, which, though similar to Emmenthal "Swiss" cheese, has hardly any holes. Aged for up to 2 years, it's at its best when made from milk produced between June and September, when the aroma of herbs and flowers is especially pungent. Another famous cheese is reblochon, a slightly bitter semihard cheese that gourmets insist must be fermented at high altitude to achieve its full flavor. Another name for reblochon, in Savoyard dialect, is *tôme* (cheese) *de Savoie.*

Those who appreciate the pungent taste of goat cheese search out the most famous Savoyard chèvre: St-Marcellin or (as its devoted aficionados call it) petit St-Marcellin. Once made solely from the milk

The French Alps

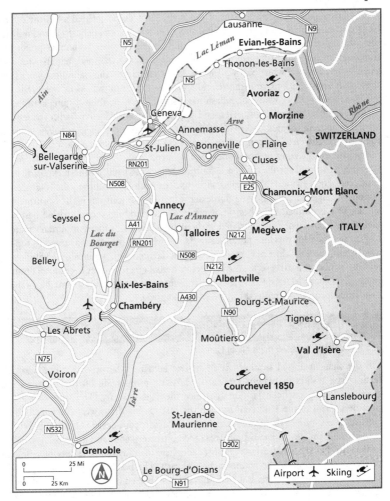

of alpine goats, it's now based on a combination of cows' and goats' milk; its exterior is firm and supple, but its interior runs with sweet creamy goodness. You'll find cheese fondue on almost every menu of the region.

The Savoy and its neighbor, the Dauphine, are most famous for the ways cheese and milk are used to augment the flavors of other dishes. There's much confusion in the non-French world about the meaning of *au gratin*. A concept developed in some of the most rugged countryside here (the isolated Vercors southwest of Grenoble), it refers to the crusty top (not the ingredients) formed when certain ingredients are baked in a certain type of flat (usually oval) dish. "Au gratin" might be the most famous culinary concept to come out of the region and is seen today on menus throughout the world. It usually implies the addition of cheese: A *gratin dauphinoise*, for example, is a baked casserole of sliced potatoes, usually with onions, cream, cheese, and sometimes eggs. A *gratin Savoyard* substitutes beef bouillon for the cream, omits the eggs, and sometimes adds cheese.

The freshwater lakes and streams of the Savoy have always yielded a healthy catch, like trout, carp, grayling, pike, eel, perch, and a famous regional delicacy found only in the cold alpine lakes of France and Switzerland, omble chevalier. In one recipe for the thousands of unnamed tiny fish, too small to fillet, they're seasoned, batter-fried, and usually served with a white Savoyard wine. As for vegetables, the traditional greens are those that endure a long growing season amid the alpine snows. Most notable is the spikey-leafed cardoon, whose firm flesh has inspired many methods of preparation.

The region's smoked hams, pâtés, and sausages (sometimes served with red lentils) are delicious, and the rich chocolate confections whipped up in elegant bakeries reflect the tastes of citizens who can permit themselves the extra calories—at this high altitude, outdoor activities make calories easy to burn.

As for wines and spirits, the gentle foothills benefiting from southern exposure have produced good wines, although—with one exception—nothing like the world-famous vintages of Burgundy or Bordeaux. The most famous red is the Montmélian, similar to a beaujolais. The best-known white is a sparkling Seyssel, whose best vintages have been favorably compared with champagne. As in many mountain regions of Europe, the Alps produce potent eaux-de-vie, which is usually consumed to top off a full evening meal. Most celebrated is Gentian, flavored with a blue alpine wildflower, and the famous Chartreuse, whose distinctive herbal green tint has become a common noun. The local Marc de Savoie is a deceivingly potent residue from the brandy-distillation process guaranteed to give you a hangover.

1 Evian-les-Bains

358 miles SW of Paris, 26 miles NE of Geneva

On the château-dotted southern shore of Lac Léman, Evian-les-Bains is one of the leading spa resorts in eastern France. Its lakeside promenade lined with trees and sweeping lawns has been fashionable since the 19th century. The waters of Evian became famous in the 18th century, and the first spa buildings were erected in 1839. Bottled Evian, one of the great French table waters, is considered beneficial for everything from baby's formula and salt-free diets to treating gout and arthritis.

Back in the days when Marcel Proust came here to enjoy the belle époque grandeur of the town, Evian was the haunt of the very rich. The hotel where Proust stayed, the Splendid, is no longer here, but he fashioned his "Balbec baths" after those of Evian. Today the spa, with its long lakefront promenade and elegant casino, attracts a broader range of clients—it's not just for the rich anymore.

In addition to its **spa buildings,** Evian offers an imposing **Ville des Congrès** (convention hall), earning the resort the title of "city of conventions." In summer the **Nautical Center** on the lake is a popular attraction; it has a 328-foot pool with a diving stage, solarium, restaurant, bar, and children's paddling pool.

The major excursion from Evian is a boat trip on Lake Geneva offered by the **Compagnie Générale de Navigation,** a Lausanne-based outfit whose agent in Evian is the Office du Baigneur, place du Port (☎ **04-50-70-73-20**). Either contact them directly or head for the Office de Tourisme (see below) to pick up a schedule of prices and hours—in summer, night cruises are also offered. If you want to see it all, you can tour both the Haut-Lac and the Grand-Lac. The quickest and most heavily booked of all trips is the crossing from Evian to Ouchy-Lausanne, Switzerland, on the north side.

Crescent-shaped **Lake Geneva** is the largest lake in central Europe (since this name only touches a small part of Geneva, the name Lac Léman was revived in the 18th century). Taking in an area of approximately 225 square miles, the lake is formed by the Rhône and is noted for its unusual blueness.

Driving the Route des Grandes Alpes

Evian could be a starting point for the 460-mile drive to Nice along the **Route des Grandes Alpes.** This is one of Europe's great drives, linking Lake Geneva with the Riviera and crossing 35 passes along the way. Leaping from valley to valley, it's open from end to end only during summer, as many passes are closed in winter.

It's possible to make the drive in 2 days, but why? The charm of this journey involves stopping at scenic highlights along the way, including Chamonix, Megève, and Val d'Isère. The most dramatic pass is the **Galibier Pass** (Col du Galibier) at 8,686 feet, marking the dividing line between the northern and southern parts of the French Alps.

En route to Nice you'll pass through such towns as St-Veran, at 6,530 feet the highest community in Europe; Entrevaux, once a fortress town marking the dividing line between Upper Provence and the Alps; and Touet-sur-Var, a village filled with tall narrow houses constructed directly against the towering rocky slope.

ESSENTIALS

GETTING THERE   Evian-les-Bains is easily reached from Geneva by **train.** In Geneva, the Gare des Eaux-Vives, on the eastern edge of the city on avenue de la Gare des Eaux-Vives, serves Evian-les Bains. For train information and schedules, call ☎ 08-36-35-35-35. Evian can also be reached from Geneva by one of the popular **ferries** (CGN) that depart from quai du Mont-Blanc at the foot of the rue des Alpes or from Le Jardin Anglais. From May 28 to September 21, one ferry a day departs Geneva daily at 9am, arriving in Evian at 11:45am. The return from Evian is at 5:50pm daily, with an arrival in Geneva at 8:45pm. A first-class one-way ticket costs 156 F ($24.95), a second-class ticket 116 F ($18.55). For ferry information and schedules, call ☎ 022/312-52-23.

If you're **driving** from Geneva, take N5 heading east along the southern rim of the lake. From Paris, take the A6 south. Before Macon, signs point to the turnoff for Thonon-Evian. At Thonon, N5 leads to Evian. Anticipate 5¹/₂ hours for trip time, although this can vary greatly depending on traffic conditions.

VISITOR INFORMATION   The **Office de Tourisme** is on place d'Allinges (☎ 04-50-75-04-26).

TAKING THE WATERS AT EVIAN

The clear, cold waters at Evian, legendary for their health and beauty-inducing benefits, attract a distinguished clientele of visitors who possess both the time and money to appreciate them.

For the most luxurious way to immerse yourself in the resort's hydro-rituals, check into either of these two hotels, both of which maintain (private) spa facilities that are open only to well-heeled residents: **Hotel Royal,** Rive Sud du Lac de Genève (☎ 04-50-26-85-00), and **Hotel Ermitage,** route Abondance (☎ 04-50-26-85-00), offer the most expensive packages, and are adept at pampering the bodies, souls, and egos of their world-class patrons.

More reasonably priced are the spa facilities at **Les Thermes de Evian,** place de la Libération, BP 21, Evian CEDEX (☎ 04-50-75-02-30). It's located adjacent to Débarcadère, just uphill from the edge of the lake. The spa treatments here are on a more democratic basis, and they do not restrict access. The hotel spas are more likely to place an emphasis on beauty regimes and stress therapies, while the public facilities contain a broader range of services, including facilities for tanning, massage, and skin and beauty care (but no facilities for overnight guests).

For 340 F ($54.40), you can indulge yourself with a *journée thermale*, which provides access to exercise rooms and classes, saunas, steam baths, floods of water from the Evian springs, and two massage sessions. You can also spend up to 1,000 F ($160) extra per day on additional massage, health, and beauty regimes, depending on your time and inclination. The facilities are open Monday to Saturday from 9am to 8:30pm, with a 1-hour break between 1:30 and 2:30pm.

ACCOMMODATIONS

Note that the **Hôtel-Restaurant Le Bourgogne** (see below) also rents rooms.

☉ Hôtel de la Verniaz et ses Chalets. Av. Verniaz, à Neuvecelle, 74500 Evian-les-Bains. ☎ **04-50-75-04-90.** Fax 04-50-70-78-92. www.relaischateaux.fr/verniaz. E-mail: verniaz@relaischateaux.fr. 33 units, 5 chalets. MINIBAR TV TEL. 600–1,300 F ($96–$208) double; 1,500–2,600 F ($240–$416) suite; 1,100–2,300 F ($176–$368) chalet. AE, DC, MC, V. Closed mid-Nov to mid-Feb.

This glamorous country house stands on a hillside with a panoramic view of woods, water, and the Alps. The well-furnished rooms, complete with amenities, are in either the main house or one of the separate chalets; the chalets have their own gardens and more privacy, but they cost a small fortune. Throughout the hotel, you'll find comfortable, even plush, accommodations.

Dining: Within the hotel's dining room, the chefs turn out dishes for the discriminating palate, including omble chevalier, that fabled fish of Lake Geneva, served with a mousseline sauce; or herb-flavored alpine lamb.

☉ Hôtel Les Prés Fleuris. Rte. de Thollon, 74500 Evian-les-Bains. ☎ **04-50-75-29-14.** Fax 04-50-74-68-75. 12 units. MINIBAR TV TEL. 900–1,050 F ($144–$168) double; 1,200–1,600 F ($192–$256) junior suite. AE, MC, V. Closed Oct to mid-May.

Beside a high-altitude alpine lake 5 miles east of Evian, this Relais & Châteaux occupies a white villa that evolved from a farmhouse built in 1842. In summer, flower boxes are affixed to the windows and balconies, and the glass walls capitalize on the view. Each room is richly furnished, often with antiques or reproductions. Tables and wrought-iron chairs are set under the trees for meals in fair weather.

Dining: M. and Mme Roger Frossard serve exceptional food, using deluxe ingredients such as delectable Bresse chicken, enhanced with fresh herbs. The fricassée of meadow mushrooms is sublime. Nonguests must make reservations, as this is a popular place. The service can often be off-putting.

Hotel Oasis. 11 bd. du Bennevy, 74500 Evian-les-Bains. ☎ **04-50-75-13-38.** Fax 04-50-74-90-30. www.oasis-hotel.com. 20 units. TV TEL. 350–450 F ($56–$72) double. MC, V. Closed mid-Oct to mid-Mar.

This is a large, generously proportioned country house with a modest two-star rating and correspondingly modest prices. It lies about a 5-minute drive from the edge of the lake, in a verdant 1-acre park with an outdoor swimming pool. Bedrooms are modest, but comfortably furnished with nondescript contemporary furniture, each with a comfortable mattress. There's a restaurant on the premises, open daily for lunch and dinner; it serves solid, conservative food (including fillets of lake perch or *fera* served either meunière style or grilled) as part of fixed-price menus priced at 90 F to 180 F ($14.40 to $28.80) each.

DINING

The restaurant at the **Hôtel Les Prés Fleuris** (see above) is a marvelous dining choice.

Hôtel-Restaurant Le Bourgogne. Place Charles-Cottet, 74500 Evian-les-Bains. ☎ **04-50-75-01-05.** Fax 04-50-75-04-05. www.Evian.hotels.com/hbourgogne.htm. Reservations required. Main courses 69–130 F ($11.05–$20.80); fixed-price menus 150–225 F ($24–$36). AE, DC, MC, V. Daily noon–2pm and 7:30–10pm. FRENCH.

Come here if you want a delectable meal, impeccable service, an attractive setting, and excellent wine. Regional wines featured are Crépy and Rousette. Menu choices in the restaurant and less formal brasserie are likely to include the inevitable house version of foie gras, beef in peppercorn poivrade sauce, émincé of duckling with caramelized peaches served on a bed of braised cabbage, and a poached version of the omble chevalier (local whitefish) with whiskey sauce. Items in the brasserie are flavorful and unpretentious, like robust portions of cassoulets, terrines of oxtail or salmon, magrêts of duckling, and steaks.

The inn also offers 31 comfortable rooms, each with television and telephone, costing 400 F to 520 F ($64 to $83.20).

EVIAN-LES-BAINS AFTER DARK

In the town center is the **Casino Royal Evian,** domaine du Royal Club Evian, on the south bank of Lake Geneva (☎ **04-50-26-87-87**), patronized heavily by the Swiss from across the lake. Charging 70 F ($11.20) admission, it offers blackjack, baccarat, and roulette, among other games, and has its own disco (Le Flash) that's open nightly from June to September, Friday and Saturday nights from October to May. Hours are 10:30pm to 5am, and admission is 60 F ($9.60), including first drink. The casino's slot machine area offers more than 250 slot, roller, and video-poker machines and one of the largest machines in the world, the "Jumbo." The Jackpot Bar is open until the casino closes. Jackets are preferred (though not required) at the casino, but not at the disco.

2 Annecy

334 miles SE of Paris, 35 miles SE of Geneva, 85 miles E of Lyon

On Lac d'Annecy, the jewel of the Savoy Alps, the resort of Annecy makes the best base for touring the Haute-Savoie, of which it's the capital. The former seat of the comtes de Genève, and before that a Gallo-Roman town, Annecy opens onto one of the best views of lakes and mountains in the French Alps. Since the 1980s, this has become a booming urban center with a savvy city government that has prompted industry yet preserved its natural setting as well. In summer, its lakefront promenade is crowded and active.

ESSENTIALS

GETTING THERE   Annecy is near a network of highways, so many people **drive** here. From Paris, take A6 southeast to Beaune where you connect with A6/N6 south to Mâcon-Nord. From here, follow A40 southeast to Seyssel, connecting with N508 going southeast into Annecy. Allow 5 hours at least for this trip. From Geneva, follow A40W to St. Julien, linking with the N201 south into Annecy. Trip time is only 30 minutes.

A car is useful but not essential in the Alps. Annecy also has **railway** and **bus** service from Geneva, Grenoble, and Lyon. Nine trains per day arrive from Grenoble (trip time: 2 hours); about 10 trains pull in daily from Paris (trip time: 3 hours and

40 minutes). For train information and schedules, call ☎ **08-36-35-35-35.** There's also a nearby **airport** (☎ **04-50-27-30-06**) in the hamlet of Meythet that receives flights from Paris on Air Liberté airlines (☎ **04-50-27-30-06**).

VISITOR INFORMATION   The **Office de Tourisme** is at 1 rue Jean-Jaurès (☎ **04-50-45-00-33**).

SEEING THE SIGHTS

Built around the river Thiou, Annecy has been called the Venice of the Alps because of the canals that cut through the old part of town, **Vieil Annecy.** You can explore the arcaded streets of the old town, where Jean-Jacques Rousseau arrived in 1728.

After seeing Annecy, consider a trek to the **Gorges du Fier,** a dramatic river gorge 6 miles to the west. To reach it, take either a train or a bus from in front of Annecy's rail station, getting off at the hamlet of Poisy. From there, you'll have to walk about a mile; follow the clearly marked signs. This striking gorge is one of the most interesting sights in the French Alps. A gangway takes you through a winding gully, varying from 10 to 30 feet wide. The gully was cut by the torrent through the rock and over breathtaking depths; you'll hear the roar of the river at the bottom. Emerging from this labyrinth, you'll be greeted by a huge expanse of boulders. You can visit the gorge from June 15 to September 10, daily from 9am to 7pm; March 15 to June 14 and September 11 to October 15, daily from 9am to noon and 2 to 6pm. The site is closed to the public between October 15 and March 15. A hike through its well-signposted depths takes less than an hour and costs 27 F ($4.30) for adults and 16 F ($2.55) for children. Call ☎ **04-50-46-23-07** for more information.

You can also take a cruise on the ice-blue lake for which the town is famous. Tours of **Lac d'Annecy,** from Easter to the end of September, usually last 1 to 2 hours. A tour that makes stops at every significant village around the lake's edge lasts $1^3/4$ hours and costs 72 F ($11.50) per person. During July and August, there are three boat tours daily, allowing you to get off at whatever port you want, explore the town and environs, and pick up the next boat for a return before nightfall to Annecy. Inquire at the Office de Tourisme (see above) about various possibilities, or call the **Compagnie des Bateaux du Lac d'Annecy** (☎ **04-50-51-08-40**) for more information.

Château de Montrottier. 74330 Lovagny. ☎ **04-50-46-23-02.** Admission 30 F ($4.80) adults, 25 F ($4) students, and 20 F ($3.20) children. Wed–Mon 10am–noon and 2–6pm. Closed Oct 15–Mar 15.

Within walking distance of the gorges is the 13th- and 14th-century Château de Montrottier. A once-feudal citadel that was partially protected by the surrounding rugged geology, its tower offers a panoramic view of Mont Blanc. Inside, a small museum showcases pottery, Asian costumes, armor, tapestries, and antiques, as well as some bronze bas-reliefs from the 16th century.

Musée Château d'Annecy. ☎ **04-50-33-87-30.** Admission 30 F ($4.80) adults, 10 F ($1.60) students and children 11–16, free for children 10 and under. June–Sept, daily 10am–6pm; Oct–May, Wed–Mon 10am–noon and 2–6pm.

This forbidding gray-stone monument, whose 12th-century pinnacle is known as the Queen's Tower, dominates the resort. It was in this castle that the comtes de Genève took refuge from their enemies in the 13th century. The château contains a museum of regional artifacts that include alpine furniture, religious art, oil paintings, and modern art. A section is devoted to the geology and marine life of the region's deep, cold lakes.

ACCOMMODATIONS

Note that the **Auberge de l'Eridan** (see "Dining") also rents rooms.

Au Faisan Doré. 34 av. d'Albigny, 74000 Annecy. ☎ **04-50-23-02-46.** Fax 04-50-23-11-10. www.lac-annecy.com. E-mail: ancytour@cybercable.tm.fr. 40 units. TV TEL. 350–490 F ($56–$78.40) double. AE, DC, MC, V. Closed Dec 20–Feb 1. Parking 50 F ($8).

Near the casino at the end of a tree-lined lakefront boulevard, this three-star hotel is only 2 minutes on foot from the lake and Imperial Park. Owned and run by the Clavel family since 1919, it's a member of the Logis de France chain, which caters to families. The public and private rooms follow the decor of the Haute Savoy. Each guest room is cozy and comfortable, but not extravagant. The chef serves three fixed-price menus in the adjacent restaurant.

Demeure de Chavoire. 71 rte. d'Annecy, 74290 Veyrier-du-Lac. ☎ **04-50-60-04-38.** Fax 04-50-60-05-36. 13 units. MINIBAR TV TEL. 800–1,150 F ($128–$184) double; 1,200–1,650 F ($192–$264) suite. AE, DC, MC, V. From Annecy, follow the signs to Chavoires and Talloires.

One of the most charming accommodations in the area is at Chavoires, about 2 miles west of Annecy. It's intimate and cozy, brightly decorated with well-chosen Savoy antiques. Large doors lead to the gardens overlooking the lake. The rooms have names rather than numbers, and each is uniquely decorated. Thoughtful extras such as fruit in the rooms make this a deserving selection—plus it's more tranquil than the hotels in the center of Annecy. Mattresses are of high quality and comfortable; bathrooms are cramped but efficient. The helpful staff will direct you to nearby restaurants.

Hôtel du Nord. 24 rue Sommeiller, 74000 Annecy. ☎ **04-50-45-08-78.** Fax 04-50-51-22-04. www.citotel.com/hotels/nord.html. E-mail: annecy-hotel-du-nord@wanadoo.fr. 30 units. TV TEL. 268–338 F ($42.90–$54.10) double. AE, MC, V.

A two-star hotel in the center of Annecy, the continually renovated du Nord is one of the better bargains here—just minutes from the train station and Lac d'Annecy. The staff is extremely helpful and speaks English. You'll appreciate the cleanliness and modernity of the soundproofed rooms; some are air-conditioned as well. Each is fitted with a comfortable bed and a fine mattress. Breakfast is the only meal served, but the staff will direct you to nearby reasonably priced restaurants.

DINING

✪ **Auberge de l'Eridan.** 13 vieille rte. des Pensières, 74290 Veyrier-du-Lac. ☎ **04-50-60-24-00.** Fax 04-50-60-23-63. Reservations required. Main courses 295–435 F ($47.20–$69.60); fixed-price menu 385 F ($61.60) at lunch Tues–Fri, 795–1,095 F ($127.20–$175.20) at dinner. AE, DC, MC, V. Daily noon–1:30pm, Tues–Sat 7:30–9:30pm. Closed Dec 6–Mar; Sept 2 to mid-June, closed for dinner Sun–Mon. From Annecy's lakefront blvd., follow the signs to Veyrier-du-Lac, Chavoires, and Talloires. FRENCH.

Famous throughout France because of the excellent and unusual cuisine of the owner, Marc Veyrat-Durebex, this world-class restaurant occupies a romanticized version of a Savoyard château at the edge of the lake in the village of Veyrier-du-Lac, about a mile from Annecy. Guests dine in a posh room with ceiling frescoes. Menu choices include ravioli of vegetables flavored with rare alpine herbs gathered by M. Veyrat-Durebex and his team in the mountains. Also recommended are pike-perch sausage, crayfish poached with bitter almonds, and poached sea bass with caviar.

The meals are prepared by an iconoclastic chef who has been dubbed *"l'Enfant Terrible"* of upscale alpine cuisine. What you'll get is likely to be a unique dining experience in the Alps, filled with an almost ritualistic set of protocols regarding how to consume a meal properly. Fortunately, a crew of ultra-sophisticated waitstaff, headed by English-speaking Hervé Audibert, is here to advise the order in which a meal should be consumed. For example, a "declination of local cheeses" consists of three large ravioli, each stuffed with a different cheese (a mild cow cheese, a pungent goat cheese, and a very strong blue cheese, eaten in ascending order of strength). Ensuing platters artfully contrast warm pâté of foie gras accompanied by mountain bayberries with a cold terrine of foie gras served with a combination of figs and bitter orange slices.

Especially interesting is rabbit served "in the style of yesterday and today" that showcases the evolution of cuisine from old-fashioned (a portion cooked in the rabbit's own blood) to modern (a portion of minced rabbit served in a contemporary presentation with a purée of celery) on a single platter. Desserts include a miniature chestnut cake served with essence of truffles. The wine list is excellent, and so is the wine steward.

The Auberge also rents some obscenely expensive **furnished rooms.** Rates are 1,950 F to 3,250 F ($312 to $520) double; suites go for 3,250 F to 3,650 F ($520 to $584).

Le Belvédère. 7 chemin du Belvédère, 7400 Annecy. ☎ **04-50-45-04-90.** Fax 04-50-45-67-25. Reservations recommended. Main courses 125–175 F ($20–$28); fixed-price menus 170–300 F ($27.20–$48). AE, MC, V. Tues–Sun 12:30–2:15pm; Tues–Sat 8–9:30pm. From downtown Annecy, follow the signs leading uphill to Le Semnoz. FRENCH/SEAFOOD.

This is one of the most appealing reasonably priced restaurants in town, run by hard-working owners/chefs Jean-Louis and Michelle Aubeneau since 1969. On a belvedere above Annecy, about a mile west of the town center, it provides views that extend up to 5 miles over mountains and lakes. Menu items include a salad of Breton lobster with freshwater crayfish and strips of foie gras; or a platter containing scallops and red mullet with shellfish-flavored butter sauce. The cheese board here is something francophiles tend to become enthusiastic about (a staff member will explain the origins of each selection on it). Dessert might include a "trilogy" of tropical-flavored sorbets.

The restaurant maintains 10 simple **guest rooms;** they're much less opulent than the restaurant. (They're often used spontaneously by diners who discover they've had too much wine at dinner and prefer not to drive home.) The six rooms with bathroom are 240 F ($38.40) for one or two occupants; the four rooms without bathroom are 200 F ($32).

Le Clos des Sens. 13 rue Jean-Mermoz, Annecy-le-Vieux. ☎ **04-50-23-07-90.** Reservations recommended. Main courses 100–180 F ($16–$28.80); fixed-price menus 198–380 F ($31.70–$60.80). AE, DC, MC, V. Tues–Fri and Sun noon–1:30pm; Tues–Sat 7:30–9:30pm. FRENCH/SAVOYARD.

The charm of this place derives from cuisine based on local ingredients and inspiration, and a decor salvaged from several Savoyard chalets. The street-level introduction to this place is a contemporary-looking, warmly outfitted bar; in the upstairs dining room, the food is elaborate, savory, and geared to the cold-weather climate that surrounds you within this high-altitude city. Menu items include a consommé of shrimp studded with chunks of firm crayfish meat, panfried crayfish served with a sauce made from the yellow wine of the Jura, sea bass with a barigoule of artichoke hearts and confit of tomatoes, and a succulent version of local pork chops served with a long-simmered cocotte of vegetables.

ANNECY AFTER DARK

In the old town, you'll find an assortment of bars, cafes, pubs, and (in warmer months) street dances, fairs, and even carnivals. A calmer alternative is an evening of theater or dance at the **Théâtre d'Annecy,** 1 rue Jean-Jaurès (☎ **04-50-33-44-11**), where tickets cost 80 F to 170 F ($12.80 to $27.20).

If a long day of activities has left you thirsty, try **Le Roi Arthur,** 14 rue Perrière (☎ **04-50-51-27-06**), where you can mingle with 20-somethings. A traditional Irish pub, **Le Captain Pub,** 11 rue Pont-Morenc (☎ **04-50-45-79-80**), has a selection of hearty dark ales on tap. **Le Vieux Necy,** 3 rue Filaterie (☎ **04-50-45-01-57**), attracts a younger, more boisterous crowd.

The best piano bar in town is **Le Duo,** 104 av. de Genève (☎ **04-50-57-01-46**), an ideal spot for quiet conversations. And if you're gay and looking for fun on the high alps, Annecy's two most visible and popular gay bars are the **Comedy Café and Night Bar,** 13 rue Royale, Galerie des Sorbiers (☎ **04-50-52-82-83**); and **Happy People Disco,** rue Carnot (no phone), where some of the most animated dancing takes place amongst a mix of both locals and visitors.

Among dance clubs, the lively **Le Pop Plage,** 30 av. d'Albigny (☎ **04-50-23-12-86**), pulls in an older, more sophisticated crowd than **Le Garage,** rue Sommellier (☎ **04-50-45-69-40**), where the entrance fee of generally around 75 F ($12) buys the first drink and the chance to dance the night away. Both places are bastions of techno and rock and can charge a cover of as much as 100 F ($16) on Fridays and Saturdays. Le Pop Plage is open in summer only.

For the most elegant evening on the town, head for the swank **Casino de l'Impérial,** 32 av. d'Albigny (☎ **04-50-09-30-00**), part of the belle époque Impérial Palace hotel on a peninsula jutting out into Lake Annecy. Entrance into the gaming rooms costs 70 F ($11.90), and requires the presentation of a passport. It's open daily from 8:30pm to 2am (till 4am on Friday and Saturday). The area reserved for slot machines (where admission is free) is open daily 24 hours.

3 Talloires

342 miles SE of Paris, 20 miles N of Albertville, 8 miles S of Annecy

The charming village of Talloires—it dates back to 866—is old enough to appear on lists of territories once controlled by Lothar II, great-grandson of Charlemagne. Chalk cliffs surround a pleasant bay, and at the lower end a wooden promontory encloses a small port. An 18-hole golf course and water sports like boating, swimming, water-skiing, and fishing make this a favorite spot with French vacationers. Talloires is also a great stop for gourmet types, boasting one of France's great restaurants, Auberge du Père-Bise, and a Benedictine abbey founded in the 11th century but now transformed into the deluxe Hôtel de l'Abbaye.

ESSENTIALS

GETTING THERE   From Annecy (see above), you can reach Talloires by **driving** south along N508 (on the western shore of Lac d'Annecy) for 8 miles. There are also about eight daily **buses** from Annecy to Talloires, which take 35 minutes and cost 14.50 F ($2.30) each way. In Talloires, buses stop in front of the town's only post office. For information about bus routes in and out of Talloires, call the Gare Routière in Annecy at ☎ **04-50-45-08-12.**

VISITOR INFORMATION   The **Office de Tourisme** is on rue André-Theuriet (☎ **04-50-60-70-64**).

ACCOMMODATIONS

Auberge du Père-Bise and **Villa des Fleurs** (see "Dining," below) also rent luxurious rooms.

Hôtel de l'Abbaye. Rte. du Port, 74290 Talloires. ☎ **04-50-60-77-33.** Fax 04-50-60-78-81. www.abbaye-talloires.com. E-mail: abbaye@talloires.com. 32 units. TV TEL. 740–1,700 F ($118.40–$272) double; 1,390–1,900 F ($222.40–$304) suite. AE, DC, MC, V. Closed Mar and Nov–Feb 1.

This place was built in the 1500s as a Benedictine monastery but has functioned as a hotel almost continuously since the Revolution. With close-up views of the lake, it makes for a memorable stop even though it doesn't equal the cuisine or the luxury of the Auberge du Père-Bise (see below). Then again, it's a lot more affordable. The secluded hotel is rich with beamed ceilings, antique portraits, leather chairs, formal French gardens, and richly carved balustrades. The great corridors lead to converted guest rooms. No two are alike. Suspended wooden balconies lead to a second level of rooms. The tasteful, well-chosen furnishings include all the Louis periods as well as Directoire and Empire. In 1999, the hotel was tastefully and thoroughly renovated, with attention spent on upgrading the terraces, the decorations in the bedrooms, and the quality of the mattresses. Overall, the site is extremely pleasant for an escape from urban life. In summer, the **restaurant** expands onto a lakefront terrace shaded by trees.

DINING

✪ **Auberge du Père-Bise.** Rte. du Port, Bord du Lac, 74290 Talloires. ☎ **04-50-60-72-01.** Fax 04-50-60-73-05. Reservations required. Main courses 220–365 F ($35.20–$58.40); fixed-price menus 490–820 F ($78.40–$131.20). AE, DC, MC, V. May–Oct, daily noon–2pm and 7–9pm. Closed Nov 15–Feb 12; Feb 13–Apr and Nov 1–15, closed Tues and lunch on Wed. FRENCH.

Since the 1950s, when millionaires and starlets were drawn here like iron filings to a magnet (and when being a millionaire meant something), Auberge du Père-Bise has radiated style and charm. A chalet built beside the lake in 1901 and renovated many times since (most recently in 1996), it's one of France's most acclaimed—and astronomically expensive—restaurants. Today it's directed by Sophie Bise, granddaughter of the patriarch who established it. The elegant dining room has sparkling silverware and bowls of flowers, but in fair weather you can dine under a vine-covered pergola and enjoy the view of mountains and lake. The kitchen excels at traditional dishes like mousse of goose foie gras, delicate young lamb, and gratin of crayfish tails.

The inn also offers 31 **guest rooms** and 3 suites, each with a minibar, TV, and phone; they cost 1,200 F to 2,500 F ($192 to $400) for a double, 3,000 F ($480) for a suite. Because this place is so popular and intimate, it's wise to make reservations at least 2 months in advance, especially in summer.

Villa des Fleurs. Rte. du Port, 74290 Talloires. ☎ **04-50-60-71-14.** Fax 04-50-60-74-06. Reservations required. Main courses 115–165 F ($18.40–$26.40); fixed-price menus 150–290 F ($24–$46.40). AE, V. Tues–Sun noon–2pm and 7–9pm. Closed Nov 15–Dec 15; Nov–May, closed Mon. FRENCH.

This attractive *restaurant avec chambres* should be better known, as it's the best place in Talloires for the price. The proprietors, Marie-France and Charles Jaegler, serve wonderfully prepared meals, which often include *salade landaise* with foie gras and fillet of fera, a fish that lives only in Lac Annecy. The dining room overlooks the water.

Eight simply **furnished rooms** are available for rent, each with minibar, phone, and Victorian-era decor. Doubles cost 490 F to 610 F ($78.40 to $97.60) and are at the top of a winding staircase—there's no elevator.

4 Aix-les-Bains

332 miles SE of Paris, 21 miles SW of Annecy, 10 miles N of Chambéry

On the eastern edge of Lac du Bourget, modern Aix-les-Bains is the most fashionable (and largest) spa in eastern France. The hot springs, which offered comfort to the Romans, are said to be useful for treating rheumatism.

ESSENTIALS

GETTING THERE   Some 20 **trains** per day arrive from Paris (trip time: 3¹/₂ hours); 10 trains pull in from Annecy (trip time: 30 minutes). For information and schedules, call ☎ **08-36-35-35-35. Buses** pull into Aix from Nice usually only once a day. For information about bus routes in and around the French Alps, call the Gare Routière in Chambéry at ☎ **04-79-69-11-88.** If you're **driving** to Aix-les-Bains from Annecy, follow R.N. 201 south.

VISITOR INFORMATION   The **Office de Tourisme** et Syndicat d'Initiative is on place Maurice Mollard (☎ **04-79-35-05-92**).

SEEING THE SIGHTS

The spa is well equipped for visitors: It contains flower gardens, a casino (the Palais de Savoie), a racecourse, a golf course, and Lac du Bourget, which has a beach. **Thermes Nationaux,** place Maurice Mollard (☎ **04-79-35-38-50**), lies in the center of town, near the casino, the Temple of Diana, and the Hôtel de Ville (town hall). Closer to the lake, a long string of flower beds and ornamental shrubs border the town's famous waterside promenades, where you can take a lovely stroll.

Regular steamer service takes you on a beautiful 4-hour **boat ride on Lac du Bourget.** A different 4-hour trip up most of the length of the Canal de Savière (which links the lake with the waters of the Rhône) is conducted between March and November, either daily or four times a week, depending on the season, for a price of 100 F ($16) per person. For information about departure times (which change almost weekly throughout the season), contact the local ferryboat operator, **Les Bateaux d'Aix** (☎ **04-79-63-45-00**). Boats depart from the piers of Grand Port, in the center of town. You can also take a bus ride from Aix to the small town of Revard, at 5,080 feet, where you'll be rewarded with a panoramic view of Mont Blanc. For bus information, contact **Trans Savoir** (☎ **04-79-35-21-74**).

Abbaye d'Hautecombe. 73310 St-Pierre de Curtille. ☎ **04-79-54-26-12.** Tours are free, but donations are welcome. 30-min. self-guided tours with tape recorder, in English and French, depart at 6-min. intervals Wed–Mon 10–11:30am and 2–5pm. You can reach the abbey by car or boat, with 2–5 steamers leaving daily Easter–Oct. To board, go to the landing stage at Aix-les-Bains. The round-trip fare is 60 F ($9.60) for the half-hour trip each way. See Les Bateaux d'Aix above for steamer information.

This is the spiritual centerpiece of the French Alps and the mausoleum of many of the princes of the House of Savoy. It was built by a succession of monks from the Cîteaux, Cistercian, and Benedictine orders beginning in the 1100s and stands on a promontory jutting into the western edge of Lac du Bourget, almost directly across the water from Aix-les-Bains. Before the 1500s, at least 40 members of the royal family of the Savoy were buried here.

After years of neglect, the church was reconstructed and lavishly embellished during the 19th century by Charles-Felix, king of Sardinia, in what is called the Troubadour Gothic style. The fervently religious ecumenical community occupying the abbey organizes seminars, welcomes short- or medium-term devotees, and perpetuates the tradition of worship maintained on this site since the 12th century. Sincere pilgrims are welcome to attend the daily mass at noon.

Musée Faure. 10 bd. des Côtes. ☎ **04-79-61-06-57.** Admission 20 F ($3.20). Wed–Mon 10am–noon and 1:30–6pm.

This is the town's most interesting museum, with a modern-art collection that includes sculptures by Rodin and works by Degas, Corot, and Cézanne. It's situated on a hill overlooking the lake and the town.

Thermes Nationaux d'Aix-les-Bains. Place Maurice-Mollard. ☎ **04-79-35-38-50.** Tours 26 F ($4.15) Apr–Oct, Tues–Sat at 3pm (closed holidays).

The original structure for the Thermes Nationaux d'Aix-les-Bains was begun in 1857 by Victor Emmanuel II; the New Baths, launched in 1934, were expanded and renovated in 1972. To visit, go to the caretaker at the entrance opposite the Hôtel de Ville, the former château of the marquises of Aix in the 16th century. Before you enter the baths, you can visit the thermal caves. In the center of the spa are two Roman remains: a Temple of Diana and the 30-foot-tall triumphal Arch of Campanus. Of special interest are the mosaic-covered compartments that were reserved as changing booths for members of the royal families of Europe. If historic origins don't appeal to you, feel free just to relax and bask in the warm waters.

ACCOMMODATIONS

Note that **Hôtel-Restaurant Davat** (see "Dining," below) also rents rooms.

Hostellerie Le Manoir. 37 rue Georges-1er, 73100 Aix-les-Bains. ☎ **04-79-61-44-00.** Fax 04-79-35-67-67. 73 units. TV TEL. 395–835 F ($63.20–$133.60) double. AE, DC, MC, V. Closed Dec 25 Jan 1.

This architecturally interesting site—it was a stable until the present owners transformed it into a hotel in 1968—includes shutters, an overhanging roof, and paths weaving through turn-of-the-century gardens with outdoor furniture placed under shade trees. You can order breakfast or dinner on a terrace bordering the garden. Most of the public rooms, as well as the guest rooms, open onto terraces. The decor is traditional, with antique and provincial furniture. Facilities include an indoor pool, a Turkish bath, and a sauna.

Hôtel Ariana. Av. de Marlioz, à Marlioz, 73100 Aix-les-Bains. ☎ **04-79-61-79-79.** Fax 04-79-61-79-00. 60 units. A/C MINIBAR TV TEL. 425–720 F ($68–$115.20) double. AE, DC, V.

The Ariana caters to a spa-oriented crowd that enjoys taking quiet walks through the surrounding park. The stylized loggia-dotted glass exterior opens into an Art Deco interior highlighted by contrasting metal, wood, and fabrics, plus plenty of white marble and antique reproductions. Tunnel-like glass walkways connect it to the hotel's main core; facilities include two indoor pools, a sauna, and a health center. The guest rooms are quite comfortable, though small. Café Adelaïde functions as both a cafe and a restaurant, offering fine classic dishes.

DINING

Hôtel-Restaurant Davat. Au Grand Port, 73100 Aix-les-Bains. ☎ **04-79-63-40-40.** Reservations required. Main courses 85–120 F ($13.60–$19.20); fixed-price menus 90–240 F ($14.40–$38.40). AE, MC, V. Mon noon–1:30pm, Tues–Wed and Fri–Sun noon–1:30pm and 7–9:30pm. Closed Nov–Mar. FRENCH.

You'll enjoy the traditional cooking, gracious service, and selection of regional wines here. This is not only a leading restaurant but also an excellent moderately priced place to stay, where the chief attraction is the beautiful flower garden. The 20 **rooms** are simply furnished and begin at 230 F ($36.80) for a double.

Restaurant du Casino Grand Cercle. Rue du Casino. ☎ **04-79-35-16-16.** Reservations recommended. Fixed-price menu, including entrance to the casino and 70 F ($11.20) worth of roulette tokens 250 F ($40). AE, DC, MC, V. Daily 8pm–midnight. FRENCH.

Few other settings within Aix-les-Bains provide as rich a beaux-arts environment as this restaurant, set within the town's casino. It occupies a corner of the area reserved for blackjack and roulette, giving diners a close-up view of the exhilaration of gamblers testing their luck. More impressive is the view that soars overhead. Surely the most elaborate ceiling in the Alps is covered with the 1880s mosaics by Italian artist Salviati. Alas, the food is not as elaborate; instead, anticipate conservative but flavorful preparations of veal, beef, chicken, and a scattering of terrines, soups, and salads. But in terms of a theme-oriented dinner that's associated with more glitter than anything else in town, the place is without equal.

5 Grenoble

352 miles SE of Paris, 34 miles S of Chambéry, 64 miles SE of Lyon

Because this city, the ancient capital of the Dauphine, is the commercial, intellectual, and tourist center of the Alps, it's a major stop for travelers (including those driving between the Riviera and Geneva).

A sports capital in both winter and summer, it also attracts many foreign students—its university has the largest summer-session program in Europe. Founded in 1339, the University of Grenoble today has a student body of some 40,000 and is the heart of intellectual life in the region. With an overall population of some 400,000, this town is also home to four other universities with a large influx of English and American students, giving it a cosmopolitan air.

ESSENTIALS

GETTING THERE   An important rail and bus junction, Grenoble is easily accessible from Paris and all the cities in this chapter. About 11 **trains** per day arrive from Paris (trip time: 3 hours); trains arrive almost every hour from Chambéry (trip time: 30 minutes). For train information and schedules, call ☎ **08-36-35-35-35.**

Grenoble's *Aéroport de St-Étienne de Saint-Geoirs* (☎ **04-76-65-48-48**) is 24 miles northwest of the city center. Air France has a virtual monopoly on scheduled service, though there are charters from England, Turkey, Israel, and the Czech Republic. Five Air France flights per day leave from Orly Ouest; flight time is just under an hour and cost is about 2,000 F ($320) round-trip. A shuttle bus meets every flight at the airport and takes passengers to and from Grenoble's center. Cost is 75 F ($12) each way. For information on flights and bus transit to and from the airport, call the airport phone number listed above. A taxi from the airport to the town center costs around 350 F ($56).

You can also fly into Lyon, which has many more flights per day. **Satobus** (☎ **04-72-68-72-17**) meets most flights at the Lyon airport and takes passengers to Grenoble. Travel time is an hour; cost is 80 F ($12.80) trip each way.

If you're **driving,** take A6 from Paris to Lyon, then continue the rest of the way along A48 into Grenoble. Depending on conditions, the entire drive should take from 6 to 7 hours.

VISITOR INFORMATION Designed by the architect A. Wogenscky and constructed in 1968, the **Maison de la Culture,** 14 rue Paul Claudel (☎ 04-76-51-33-71), is a combined theatre, dance recital space, and concert hall in the residential neighborhood of Malherbe. Within the same building is the **Office de Tourisme,** 14 rue de la République (☎ 04-76-42-41-41). The center is open Tuesday through Saturday from 1 to 7pm (closed part of August).

SEEING THE SIGHTS

Grenoble lies near the junction of the Isère and Drac rivers. Most of the city is on the south bank of the Isère, though its most impressive monument, the **Fort de la Bastille,** stands in relative isolation on a rocky hilltop on the north bank (a cable car will carry you from the south bank's quai Stéphane-Jay across the river to the top of the fort). The center of Grenoble's historic section is the **Palais de Justice** and **place St-André.** The more modern part of town is southeast, centered on the contemporary **Hôtel de Ville** (town hall) and the nearby **Tour Perret.**

Begin at **place Grenette,** where you can enjoy a drink or an espresso at any of the many cafes. This square enjoys many associations with Grenoble-born Stendhal, who wrote such masterpieces as *The Red and the Black* and *The Charterhouse of Parma.* It was here that Antoine Berthet, supposedly the model for Stendhal's Julien Grel, was executed for attempted murder in 1827.

Enjoy a ride on the **Téléférique de la Bastille** (☎ 04-76-44-33-65), high-swinging **cable cars** that haul you over the rocky banks of the Isère River and its valley. In winter, between November and mid-March, the cable car operates daily from 10:30am to 6:30pm (every Monday, it begins operating at 11am). The rest of the year, it operates daily from 9am to between midnight and 12:30am, depending on the season, except for Monday mornings, when operations begin at 11am. The cable car is completely closed for 2 weeks in January. A round-trip ticket costs 35 F ($5.60) for adults, 28 F ($4.50) for students, and 22 F ($3.50) for persons ages 5 to 18. Children under 5 ride free. From the belvedere where you land, you'll have a panoramic view of the city and the mountains that surround it. You can return to the city center on foot, a walk of about an hour. From points along the footpaths leading downhill, signs point the way to various city parks en route, including the Parc de la Bastille, the Parc Guy-Pape, and the Jardin des Dauphins.

Musée Dauphinois. 30 rue Maurice-Gignoux. ☎ **04-76-85-19-01.** Admission 20 F ($3.20) adults, 10 F ($1.60) children 12–16, free for children 12 and under. May–Oct, Wed–Mon 10am–7pm; Nov–Apr, Wed–Mon 10am–6pm. Closed Jan 1, May 1, and Dec 25.

Housed in a 17th-century convent and enhanced by the cloister, gardens, and baroque chapel, the museum lies across the Isère in the Ste-Marie-d'en-Haut section of town. A collection of ethnographic and historic mementos of the Dauphine is displayed, along with folk arts and crafts.

Musée de Peinture et de Sculpture. 5 place de Lavalette. ☎ **04-76-63-44-44.** Admission 25 F ($4) adults; 15 F ($2.40) children, students, and seniors. Wed 11am–10pm and Thurs–Mon 11am–7pm.

Founded in 1796, this is one of the country's oldest art museums. It was the first French museum to focus on modern art, a fact appreciated by Picasso, who donated his *Femme Lisant* in 1921. Flemish and Italian Renaissance works are displayed, although it's the Impressionist paintings that generate the most interest. Note in particular Matisse's *Intérieur aux aubergines* and Léger's *Le Remorqueur.* Ernst, Klee, Bonnard, Monet, Rouault—they're all here.

ACCOMMODATIONS

Hôtel d'Angleterre. 5 place Victor-Hugo, 38000 Grenoble. ☎ **04-76-87-37-21.** Fax 04-76-50-94-10. www.hotel-angleterre.fr. E-mail: hotel-angleterre@hotel-angleterre.fr. 66 units. A/C MINIBAR TV TEL. 520–720 F ($83.20–$115.20) double. AE, DC, MC, V. Parking 10 F ($1.60).

This hotel, located in the center of Grenoble, has tall windows and wrought-iron balconies; it opens onto a pleasant square with huge chestnut trees. Inside, the stylish salons boast wood-grained walls and ceilings and tropical plants. Some rooms look out on the Vercors Massif. Breakfast is the only meal served.

Hôtel Lesdiguières. 122 cours de la Libération, 38000 Grenoble. ☎ **04-76-96-55-36.** Fax 04-76-48-10-13. 36 units. TV TEL. 400 F ($64) double. AE, DC, MC, V. Closed Sat–Sun and all school holidays. Parking 40 F ($6.40).

This imposing gray-brown stucco building, surrounded by a spacious lawn, is a training ground for the local hotel school, so the receptionist, porters, and restaurant staff are all members of the most recent graduating class. Inside, you'll find well-furnished guest rooms and sunny public areas filled with Louis XIII chairs and Oriental rugs. Most rooms are standard in size, and rather functionally furnished, although each comes with a comfortable mattress. A stay here can have its own brand of charm, as the staff here probably works harder to impress than their more jaded counterparts elsewhere. The drawbacks are weekend closings and shutdowns during school holidays, most notably from early July to late September.

Hôtel Trianon. 3 rue Pierre-Arthaud, 38000 Grenoble. ☎ **04-76-46-21-62.** Fax 04-76-46-37-56. 38 units. www.hotel-trianon.com. E-mail: info@hotel-trianon.com. TV TEL. 289–425 F ($46.25–$68) double. AE, DC, MC, V. Parking 35 F ($5.60).

Few other hotels in town have as effectively masked a banal 1950s design with such a dose of historic decorative styles. Trianon caters to business travelers during the week; it's a comfortable, well-managed hotel that survives on more than just tourism. The rates are reduced on weekends, when business is slower. The rooms are somewhat cramped but cozy, furnished with just about every Louis style; a handful are done in a "shepherd" style that evokes a folkloric grange in the Alps. You'll find this popular two-star hotel a short walk south of the pedestrians-only district in the town center, near a well-known school, the Lycée Champollion.

DINING

Le Berlioz. 4 rue Strasbourg. ☎ **04-76-56-22-39.** Reservations required. Main courses 70–160 F ($11.20–$25.60); fixed-price menus 120–340 F ($19.20–$54.40). AE, DC, DISC, MC, V. Mon–Fri noon–2pm; Mon–Sat 7:30–10:30pm. Closed Aug. FRENCH.

Talented chef Françoise Legras, who has won much local acclaim, offers a gourmet tour of France by featuring a different menu with regional specialties every month. Try, for example, medaillons of monkfish in a red pepper cream sauce, beef Charolais steak with a shallot sauce, or the fillet of duck breast with a raspberry vinegar sauce and assorted baby vegetables.

Restaurant Pique-Pierre. Rte. Historique de Stendahl (N75), St-Martin-le-Vinoux. ☎ **04-76-46-12-88.** Reservations recommended. Main courses 60–120 F ($9.60–$19.20); fixed-price menus 150–260 F ($24–$41.60). AE, MC, V. Tues–Sun noon–2pm; Tues–Sat 7–10pm. Closed Aug. Bus 33. FRENCH.

One of the town's most appealing restaurants is this bastion of culinary finesse, about a mile north of the town center, set within a pleasant garden. Sheathed in burnished paneling, even on its ceiling, it offers a roster of oft-changing and delectable food

In Pursuit of Chartreuse:
A Side Trip from Grenoble

Local monks are the custodians of the secret formula for the liqueur known as Chartreuse, which Maréchal d'Estrées gave them in 1605. It was an elixir involving the distillation of 130 herbs, believed to have been originated by an anonymous alchemist.

Eventually the formula found its way to **La Grande Chartreuse** (charterhouse), founded in 1084 about 20 miles north of Grenoble. The monastery is no longer open to the public, but you're allowed to visit the **Musée de la Correrie,** 38380 St-Pierre-de-Chartreuse (☎ **04-76-88-60-45**), housed in a 15th-century building at the head of the valley about 1¹/₂ miles from the monastery. Admission to the museum costs 15 F ($2.40) for adults and 10 F ($1.60) for children. From April through June and September through October, it's open daily from 10am to noon and 2 to 6pm. In July and August hours are daily 9:30am to 6:30pm; it's closed the rest of the year. This unusual museum provides a glimpse into a monk's life; the sound you'll hear is chanting.

Even more interesting is a trip to **Voiron,** about 20 miles west of the monastery, where you can visit the **Caves de la Grande Chartreuse,** 10 bd. Edgar-Kofler (☎ **04-76-05-81-77**), the distillery where the famed Chartreuse is made. To reach the distillery from the monastery, follow the signs to Saint-Laurent du Pont, and then follow the signs to Voiron. Free tours are possible in July and August, daily from 9am to 5pm; Easter to June and in September and October, daily from 9 to 11:30am and 2 to 6:30pm; and November to Easter, Monday through Friday from 9 to 11:30am and 2 to 5:30pm. Dressed in chartreuse green, a guide will show you the copper stills and take you to the cellar, filled with gargantuan oak casks in which the liqueur matures for several years. At the end of the tour, you'll get a free taste of the yellow or fiery green Chartreuse or of a new product. You can also purchase bottles at a shop on the premises. It's said that only three monks and the father procurator have access to the formula.

Before you head out into the Massif de la Chartreuse, where the monastery and distillery lie, obtain a good detailed map from the tourist office in Grenoble.

items that include such dishes as seafood salad with salmon and mussels, roasted pigeon in a foie gras sauce, fillet of bar with a mushroom-flavored vinaigrette, and roasted fillet of duckling with a red wine sauce. A dessert list incorporates 10 tempting, often fattening, desserts, a favorite of which is a semi-solid, bittersweet chocolate tarte.

GRENOBLE AFTER DARK

To get things started, all you have to do is walk to **place St-André, place aux Herbes,** or **place de Gordes.** On a good night, these squares overflow with young people, whose energy level builds in anticipation of an irrepressible explosion of dancing and serious partying.

You may want to pace yourself, though, starting out on the sedate side at the **Cybernet Café,** 3 rue Bayard (☎ **04-76-51-73-18**). Here you'll find an unusual mix of soft candlelight and flea-market finds like car parts, signs, and bedposts, all interspersed between state-of-the-art computers. You'll pay 30 F ($4.80) for 30 minutes of time online. Then you might check out **La Soupe aux Choux,** 7 rte. de Lyon (☎ **04-76-87-05-67**), for an evening of jazz. Two popular sports pubs that host a wild crowd of students are **Le Couche Tard,** 1 rue Palais (☎ **04-76-44-18-79**), and **The London Pub,** 11 rue Brocherie (☎ **04-76-44-41-90**). L'Entre-Pôt, 8 rue Auguste-Gemin (☎ **04-76-48-21-48**), is a die-hard rock club famed for its live concerts.

For a great outdoor party, check out **Le Saxo,** 5 place d'Agier (☎ **04-76-51-06-01**). Its big patio, with killer speakers blasting out techno and rock well into the early morning, has the feeling of a college frat party. If you're really pumped up and need to cut loose on the dance floor, bop on over to **Le Mae Vas,** 1 rue Lamartine (☎ **04-76-87-23-48**), where the young rule the scene. The cover is 50 F ($8).

A restaurant frequented by gays is **La Crêperie,** place de Metz (☎ **04-76-87-55-89**). The town's most animated gay disco is **Le Georges V,** 124 cour Berriat (no phone), which does most of its business every Thursday to Sunday beginning around 10:30pm.

6 Courchevel 1850

393 miles SE of Paris, 32 miles SE of Albertville, 60 miles SE of Chambéry

Courchevel has been called a resort of "high taste, high fashion, and high profile," a chic spot where multimillion-dollar chalets sit perched on pristine pine-covered slopes. Skiers and geographers know of it as part of Les Trois Vallées, sometimes called "the skiing supermarket of France." The resort, with 1,400 acres of ski runs, employs as many workers in winter as in summer, many of whom do nothing more than manicure and maintain the top-notch ski conditions. Courchevel 1850 has excellent resorts and superb hotels—with price tags to match, so it largely draws the super-rich. Travelers on average budgets should avoid the place and head for more reasonably priced resorts in winter, especially Chamonix (see below).

Courchevel maintains three ski schools with a staff of 450 instructors, a labyrinth of chairlifts, and more than 200 ski runs, which are excellent in the intermediate and advanced categories. Also in Les Trois Vallées are the less well-known resorts of Méribel, Les Menuires, and Val Thorens, which you should avoid unless you direly need to save money. Courchevel consists of four planned ski towns, each marked by its elevation in meters. Thus there's less fashionable Courchevel 1300 (Le Prez), Courchevel 1550, and Courchevel 1650. Crowning them all is Courchevel 1850.

Courchevel 1850 is the most attractive ski mecca in the French Alps, a position once held by Megève. It's also the focal point of a chair-hoist network crisscrossing the region. At the center of one of the largest ski areas in the world, Courchevel was built at the base of a soaring alpine amphitheater whose deep snowfalls last longer than those at most other resorts because it faces the north winds. Expect reliable snow conditions throughout the winter, perfectly groomed runs, vertical cliffs, and enough wide runs to appease the intermediate skier as well. The glacier skiing alone draws experts from around the world. The whole complex of Les Trois Vallées is one vast ski circus.

SKI PASSES A 1-day ski pass for Courchevel alone costs 188 F ($30.10), but a 1-day pass to the facilities of Les Trois Vallées goes for 225 F ($36). A 3-day pass costs 536 F ($85.75) for Courchevel or 662 F ($105.90) for Les Trois Vallées.

ESSENTIALS
GETTING THERE Courchevel 1850 is the last stop on a steep alpine road that dead-ends at the village center. Roads are kept open all year, but during winter

Le Snowboarding

Snowboarding ("Le Snowboarding" in French) is indulged and accepted at even the grandest alpine resorts of France. For safety reasons, the *pistes* for snowboards are specifically designated areas that are segregated from conventional ski runs. In the case of Courchevel, the site is identified as *Le Snowpark*. Peppered with all the moguls, hillocks, and obstacles a snowboarder would expect, it straddles the side of *La Piste des Chenus*, running parallel to conventional ski runs and accessible via la Telecabine des Chenus. Snowboarding is still a newcomer to the winter sports scene here, but as long as its participants don't do things too obviously unsafe or disruptive, the sport and its adherents are tolerated, albeit as something of a fad and novelty. Most of the other ski resorts in the French Alps have added half-pipes and other trails exclusively for snowboarders.

snowstorms, driving can be treacherous. To go any higher, you'll have to take a cable car from the center of town. Most visitors drive here (you'll need snow tires and chains), but some buses link the city to railway junctions farther down the mountain. If you're **driving** from Paris, you can take A6 to Lyon, then A42 to Chambéry, then A430 to Albertville. At Albertville, get on N90 to Moutiers, then follow the narrow roads 915 and 75 into Courchevel.

The nearest **train** station is in Moutiers Salins. From Paris, five trains per day leave for Moutiers. The TGV, a high-speed train, covers the distance from Paris to Chambéry in about 3 hours. In Chambéry, you must transfer to another train going to Moutiers. From the train station in Moutiers, you can catch the **bus** that takes you along the final lap of the journey into Courchevel. There are five buses per day Monday through Friday and 15 per day on Saturday and Sunday.

The nearest **international airport** is at Geneva. From here, you can catch a bus to Courchevel. There are three buses Monday through Friday and eight on Saturday and Sunday. It's a 4-hour ride, costing 355 F ($56.80) one-way. If you land at the airport at Lyon, there are three to five buses a day running to Courchevel; the 4-hour trip costs 270 F ($43.20) one-way.

VISITOR INFORMATION   The **Office de Tourisme** is at La Croisette (☎ **04-79-08-00-29**).

ACCOMMODATIONS
EXPENSIVE

✪ **Hôtel Bellecôte.** Rte. de Bellecôte, 73120 Courchevel 1850. ☎ **04-79-08-10-19.** Fax 04-79-08-17-16. www.h.bellecote.com. 53 units. MINIBAR TV TEL. 1,270–1,680 F ($203.20–$268.80) per person double; 2,470–2,960 F ($395.20–$473.60) per person suite. Rates include half board. AE, DC, MC, V. Closed mid-Apr to Dec 20.

This seven-story chalet is known for its collection of unusual antiques. Bored with traditional alpine motifs, founder Roger Toussaint scoured the bazaars of Afghanistan and the Himalayas for an array of fascinating objects that lend exotic warmth to the wood-sheathed walls and ceilings. Each room contains plush accessories as well as Far or Middle Eastern carved wooden objects. Bedrooms are warmly outfitted with lots of varnished paneling.

Dining: Full meals in the elegant dining room include cassolette of sweetbreads with flap mushrooms, frogs' legs Provençal, and chicken with morels. The impressive luncheon buffet table has a dazzling array of seafood, like crayfish and urchins, followed by sauerkraut with pork. The most flavorful *fondant au chocolat* in the Alps is served here. Lunch and dinner are offered daily.

Amenities: Indoor pool, direct access to the slopes, fitness center, hairdresser, and ski-rental shop.

✪ **La Sivolière.** Quartier Les Chenus, 73120 Courchevel 1850. ☎ **04-79-08-08-33.** Fax 04-79-08-15-73. www.hotel-la-sivoliere.com. 32 units. TV TEL. 890–2,500 F ($142.40–$400) double; 2,600 F ($416) suite. AE, MC, V. Closed May–late Nov. Parking 90 F ($14.40).

The secret of La Sivolière's success is the owner, Madeleine Cattelin, who has a rich knowledge of and appreciation for her native Savoy. The hotel was constructed in the 1970s by her husband, a building contractor, who used lots of pinewood boards and artfully rustic lichen-covered boulders. It's set near a small forest (*une sivolière*) in a sunny position near the ski slopes. Each guest room contains tasteful furnishings and a sense of alpine warmth.

Dining: You're invited to enjoy a richly laden afternoon tea table. There's no formal menu in the dining rooms; you're likely to get such dishes as magrêt of duck with crêpes. Lunch and dinner are served daily; nonguests should make reservations.

Amenities: Free access to sauna, steam bath, and exercise room.

Le Chabichou. Quartier Les Chenus, 73120 Courchevel 1850. ☎ **04-79-08-00-55.** Fax 04-79-08-33-58. www.courchevel.com/chabichou. E-mail: chabi@chorchevel.com. 42 units. TV TEL. 900–1,720 F ($144–$275.20) per person double. Rates include half board. AE, DC, MC, V. Closed Apr 18–June 30 and Sept–Nov.

Within easy walking distance of many bars and clubs, this is one of the town's finest hotels, boasting a superb restaurant (see "Dining," below). Most of the guest rooms in this gingerbread-trimmed chalet are large and well furnished; their daring modern design might not appeal to everyone, however. Beds offer grand alpine comfort, with quality mattresses and fine linens.

Amenities: Sauna, Jacuzzi, and exercise room.

Les Ducs de Savoie. Au Jardin Alpin, 73120 Courchevel 1850. ☎ **04-79-08-03-00.** Fax 04-79-08-16-30. www.ducssavoie.com. E-mail: lesducs@aol.com. 70 units. TV TEL. 890–1,720 F ($142.40–$275.20) per person double. Rates include half board. AE, MC, V. Closed Apr 16–Dec 20. Parking 70 F ($11.20).

This hotel, one of the largest at Courchevel, has elaborately scrolled pinewood and often rows of picturesque icicles hanging from the protruding eaves. There's a covered garage, plus an indoor pool with walls intricately chiseled from mountain flagstones. The hotel has spacious, pleasant rooms, each with a terrace. Evoking an alpine theme, the recently modernized guest rooms are furnished with soft, comfortable beds. The hotels lies a few feet from the Téléski of the Jardin Alpin, and you can ski directly to the hotel's vestibule at the end of the day.

Dining/Diversions: In the lobby bar, the stone base deliberately retains its mountain lichens. Fireplaces add to the conviviality of the good food, drinks, and lively conversation.

MODERATE

Courcheneige. Rue Nogentil, 73120 Courchevel 1850. ☎ **04-79-08-02-59.** Fax 04-79-08-11-79. www.skifrance.fr/73227/courch/courch-a-htm. E-mail: courcheneige. courchevel_laposte.fr. 83 units. TV TEL. 545–875 F ($87.20–$140) per person. Rates include half board. AE, V.

A moderately priced choice, at least for Courchevel, this hotel is well located at the heart of the slopes. Built like a chalet with sun-seeking balconies, its rooms for the most part open onto panoramas of the enveloping mountain ranges, including l'Aiguille du Fruit. From the precincts of this hotel, you can virtually ski from your doorstep. Regardless of how violently cold it is outside, it is warm and cozy inside, especially in the art-filled and elegantly decorated public rooms, which often contain antiques. Some of the rooms are large enough for families of five. The cooking is excellent, with alpine and international dishes, sometimes served outdoors on the terrace. On-site facilities include a fitness center with Jacuzzi and sauna, along with an exercise room and solarium.

DINING

✪ **Chalet des Pierres.** Au Jardin Alpin. ☎ **04-79-08-18-61.** Reservations required. Main courses 150–225 F ($24–$36); fixed-price menus 300–600 F ($48–$96) at dinner. AE, MC, V. Daily 11:45am–5pm, Wed–Sat 7:30–10pm. Closed late Apr–early Dec. FRENCH/SAVOYARD.

This one is the best of the several lunch restaurants scattered over the ski slopes. Accented with weathered planking and warmed with open hearths, it sits in the middle of the Verdon slope, a few paces from the whizzing path of skiers. Lunch is served on a sun terrace, but most visitors gravitate to the rustic two-story interior, where blazing fireplaces, hunting trophies, and a hip international crowd contribute to the charm of the place. Meals often include an array of air-dried alpine meat and sausages, the best *pommes frites* (French fries) in Courchevel, pepper steak, rack of lamb, and *plats du jour* (plates of the day). Two particularly appealing dishes are a tart of Beauford cheese, and a leg of lamb that's suspended, the traditional way, from a string within the chimney and left to slowly cook in the smoke from the smoldering fire.

La Bergerie. Quartier Nogentile. ☎ **04-79-08-24-70.** Reservations required. Main courses 70–160 F ($11.20–$25.60); plat du jour (lunch) 140 F ($22.40). AE, V. Restaurant, daily noon–3pm and Tues–Sat 8–10pm; bar and cafe, daily 10am–midnight. Closed late Apr to mid-Dec. FRENCH.

Its uneven flagstone steps, stacks of carefully split firewood, and roughly weathered pine logs and planks testify to La Bergerie's 1830s origins as a shepherd's hut. A low-ceilinged dining room on the ground floor contains a dance floor and live entertainment. The ambience is warm, charming, and outdoorsy. Typical and well-prepared menu items are scallops in shallot butter, fondue bourguignonne, and raclette from cheese imported from small-scale producers in Switzerland. An especially refined platter that usually meets with success is pâté of salmon that's smoked, poached, and grilled, then served with lemon-and-caviar *crème fraîche*.

✪ **Le Bateau Ivre.** In the Hôtel Pomme-de-Pin, quartier Les Chenus. ☎ **04-79-08-36-88.** Reservations required. Main courses 150–190 F ($24–$30.40); fixed-price menus 250–560 F ($40–$89.60) at lunch, 350–510 F ($56–$81.60) at dinner. AE, DC, V. Daily 12:30–2:15pm and 7:30–10pm. Closed Apr–Dec 20. FRENCH.

This restaurant, one of the greatest in the French Alps, is on the sixth floor of a hotel that's poised in the upper reaches of the resort and consequently offers a panoramic view over the town and slopes. Its fine reputation is the result of the dedicated efforts of the Jacob family, who prepare such dishes as polenta and escalopes of foie gras in vinaigrette and fricassée of lobster and truffles; especially delectable is succulent rack of lamb with black olives and artichokes, John Dory with red pepper oil, and scallops scented with gentian, an alpine flower.

✪ **Le Chabichou.** Quartier Les Chenus. ☎ **04-79-08-00-55.** Reservations required. Main courses 120–280 F ($19.20–$44.80); fixed-price menus 340–680 F ($54.40–$108.80). Skier's lunch 180 F ($28.80) (Mon–Sat only). AE, DC, MC, V. Daily noon–2pm and 8–10pm. Closed Apr 18–June 30 and Sept 15–Nov. FRENCH.

This is the second-best restaurant in town (only Le Bateau Ivre, above, is better). Le Chabichou is on the lobby level of the hotel of the same name. Michel and Maryse Rochedy acquired a reputation for their delectable cuisine at their similarly named (but no longer existing) restaurant in St-Tropez. Big windows here showcase a view of the snow. The menu lists a number of superlative dishes, like oyster soup with wild mushrooms, magrêt of duckling with honey sauce, alpine curry, and a parmentier of confit of duckling with caramelized potatoes.

COURCHEVEL AFTER DARK
As a chic but seasonal resort, Courchevel offers nightlife that roars into the wee hours during midwinter but is reduced to a pale shadow of itself as the snows begin to melt. You'll never have to walk far from the center to sample the fun, as the area around **La Croisette** (departure point for most of the ski lifts) contains lots of restaurants, bars, and dance clubs that come and go constantly. Here are some nightspots that have survived for a while:

Les Caves de Courchevel, Porte de Courchevel (☎ 04-79-08-12-74), attracts an upscale crowd. A mock Tyrolean facade of weathered wood hides a club evoking a medieval cloister, with stone arches and columns. Full meals in the restaurant, open nightly from 11pm to 4am, begin at 250 F ($40). It's open December to April only, daily from 6pm to 6am.

La Grange, rue Park-City (☎ 04-79-08-37-99), is an informal spot for music and dancing. If a spectacle is being staged on the night of your visit, the doors may open earlier. Drinks start at a hefty 100 F ($16)! It's open December to April 15 only, daily from 11pm to 4am. The closest thing in town to a British pub is **Rhumerie Le Calico,** Au Forum (☎ 04-79-08-20-28). A cozy, convivially claustrophobic "Night Bar" that features a blazing fireplace, a singer, and a changing series of instrumentalists is **Le Grenier,** rue Park City (☎ 04-79-08-36-47). Both are open only from December to April.

7 Megève

372 miles SE of Paris, 45 miles SE of Geneva

Megève is famous as a summer resort set amid pine forests, foothills, and mountain streams. But it's even better known in winter as a charming, cosmopolitan ski resort, with more than 180 miles of downhill runs plus nearly 50 miles of cross-country trails.

The old village, with its turreted houses gathered around a 17th-century church, suggests what Megève looked like at the turn of the century. After 1920, however, the new town came along and started attracting people who like to go to the mountains for fun, especially skiers. People who have made Megève their winter home have included several prominent members of the Rothschild family, the most visible of whom, Mme Nadine de Rothschild, has an interest in the well-known Mont d'Arbois hotel. Hubert de Givenchy claims that the big draw of Megève is its *parfum d'authenticité,* from its scent of wood smoke to the sounds of heels and hooves clopping on cobblestones.

The interesting center contains **place de l'Église** and its famous hotel, the **Mont-Blanc,** south of the main arteries that cut through the valley. Rita Hayworth and Prince Aly Kahn were photographed nuzzling at this hotel in the 1950s. Some of the resort's hotels and one of its most important cable-car depots are in the village of **Mont d'Arbois,** about a mile east of the center of Megève, at the end of a steep, narrow, and winding road. (In winter it's unwise to drive up that road without chains on your snow tires.)

Two Megève Highlights

If you have the stamina, take the 9-mile footpath called the **Way of the Cross,** which begins at the edge of town and links more than a dozen country rustic chapels from the mid–19th century.

Nothing is more memorable in Megève than the annual **Foire de la Croix,** a fair on the first Saturday of September, marking the return of the herds from the high alpine pastures. You can also taste the rich farmers' bounty at dozens of stands at the fair. It's been a tradition here since 1282.

Tennis, horseback riding, and cable railways add to the attractions, with wide views of the Mont Blanc area from the top of each ski lift. The range of amusements includes a casino, nightclubs, dance clubs, and shows. Megève has more diversions than almost any of the French winter-sports resorts and is a social center of international status.

ESSENTIALS

GETTING THERE   Air France and Swissair both service Geneva's **Cointrin Airport** (☎ 022/717-71-11) with a plethora of flights from all over Europe. Round-trip flights between Geneva and Paris cost from 1,800 F to 2,300 F ($288 to $368) each way. The airport is 43 miles to the southeast, from which there's bus service four times a day direct from the airport to Megève. The 90-minute transit costs 210 F ($33.60) per person. For information, contact Megève's tourist office (see below) or **Borini & Cie** (☎ 04-50-21-18-24).

Many visitors come by **train;** get off at the hamlet of Sallanches, 8 miles away. From Sallanches, about 10 buses every day make the trip to Megève for a price of 40 F ($6.40) each way. Your journey from Paris to Megève will be faster on Saturday or Sunday, when the high-speed TGV travels directly to Sallanches, with stops en route, taking about 5$^{1}/_{2}$ hours. Monday through Friday, the TGV goes only as far as Annecy, after which travelers transfer onto slower trains for the continuation of their trip into Sallanches. Total trip time is around 7$^{1}/_{2}$ hours. For train information, contact Megève's tourist office (below) or the SNCF at ☎ 08-36-35-35-35.

Buses pull into town from other resorts throughout the alps at the Autogare SNCF (also known as the Gare Routière de Megève), beside the highway running through the town center. For bus information of all kinds, call ☎ 04-50-21-23-42.

If you're **driving** to Megève from Paris, take A6 southeast to Mâcon, connecting to the A40 east to St-Gervais, following N212 south straight into Megève. *Be alert:* Winter driving conditions can be perilous. Make sure your car has snow tires and chains.

VISITOR INFORMATION   The **Office de Tourisme** is on rue Monseigneur-Conseil (☎ 04-50-21-27-28).

ACTIVE PURSUITS ON THE SLOPES & BEYOND

You can take a chair hoist to **Mont d'Arbois,** at 6,000 feet, where a panorama unfolds for you, including not only Mont Blanc but also the Fis and Aravis massifs. Cable service operates from June 17 to September 5 every half hour from 9am to 6pm. To reach the station, take route Edmond de Rothschild from the resort's center, going past the golf course. The mountain was developed in the 1920s by members of the Rothschild family, whose search for solitude led them to this scenic outpost. Today Mont d'Arbois is a pocket of poshness in an already posh resort.

From 11am to 6am, the center of the old village of Megève is closed to traffic, except for pedestrians and sledges. You can shop at your leisure—some 200 trades-people await, ranging from a cobbler to an antiques dealer, plus many boutiques.

The Ski School, 176 rue de la Poste (☎ **04-50-21-00-97**), is one of Europe's fore-most, with 250 instructors for adults and 32 for children. Classes include the com-plete French skiing method, modern ski techniques, monosurf-acrobatic skiing, cross-country skiing, and ski touring. The school is open from December 20 to the end of April, daily from 9am to 7pm.

Another option is the **École de Ski Internationale,** 3001 Route Edmond de Roth-schild (☎ **04-50-58-78-88**), which offers much the same facilities.

Much improvement has been made in recent years in sports facilities, including a Chamois gondola, which takes skiers to the mountain from the center of town; the Rocharbois cable car, linking the two major ski areas of Mont d'Arbois and Roche-brune; and the addition of a gondola and chairlift at the Rochebrune massif. Skiing here appeals to both intermediates and experts. A 3-day ski pass costs from 460 F to 511 F ($73.60 to $81.75).

Megève Palais des Sports et des Congrès (Sports Palace and Assembly Hall), route du Jaillet (☎ **04-50-21-15-71**), was built in 1968 as the town's showcase for ice sports, swimming, tennis, conventions, political meetings, concerts, shows, and gala festivals. It contains two pools with a solarium, saunas, an indoor Olympic-size skat-ing rink open throughout summer, a curling track, a body-building room, a bar, a restaurant, a gymnasium, tennis courts, an auditorium, conference rooms, and an exhibition gallery. Hours change with the seasons and any special competitions occur-ring inside, though in most cases it's open daily from 2:30 to 7:30pm. Annual clos-ings occur during May and June.

ACCOMMODATIONS
VERY EXPENSIVE

Chalet du Mont-d'Arbois. Rte. du Mont-d'Arbois, 74120 Megève. ☎ **04-50-21-25-03.** Fax 04-50-21-24-79. www.silicone.fr/arbois. E-mail: arbois@silicone.fr. 20 units. TV TEL. Win-ter 2,400–4,240 F ($384–$678.40) double; off-season 1,900–2,240 F ($304–$358.40) dou-ble. Rates include breakfast. Half board 320 F ($51.20) per person extra. AE, DC, MC, V. Closed Apr–June and Sept 30–Dec 15.

Built in 1928 by a Rothschild matriarch, in a design emulating Switzerland's fanciful chalets, this is the most opulent and stylish small-scale resort on the mountain. Bed-rooms are spacious, sunny, and sumptuous. Firm mattresses are sheathed in fine linens. The public rooms are the grandest in Megève, with roaring fireplaces, beamed ceilings, alpine antiques, and silver-plated replicas of alert deer. During part of the season, the hotel might be filled with friends of Mme Nadine de Rothschild, a novelist/autobiographer whose advice on how a woman should treat her husband became a best-seller in France.

Le Fer à Cheval. 36 rte. du Crêt-d'Arbois, 74120 Megève. ☎ **04-50-21-30-39.** Fax 04-50-93-07-60. 47 units. TV TEL. 1,520–1,960 F ($243.20–$313.60) double; 2,520 F ($403.20) suite for 2. Rates include half board. AE, MC, V. Closed Apr 9–June and Sept 10–Dec 15.

This is the finest hotel in the center of the village. The rooms are beautifully main-tained and have traditional styling, with quality mattresses and linens. For the most part they are spacious and sun-flooded, each opening onto a view.

Dining: Even if you don't stay here, you can enjoy the **restaurant,** decked out with wood to evoke an old-fashioned Savoy atmosphere. Guests often gather for tea around a wood-and-stone fireplace, where they can also enjoy good-tasting alpine meals.

Amenities: In summer a pool draws guests to the beautiful garden; the sauna and Jacuzzi are winter lures.

✪ **Les Fermes de Marie.** Chemin de Riante Colline, 74120 Megève. ☎ **04-50-93-03-10.** Fax 04-50-93-09-84. www.fermesdemarie.com. E-mail: contact@fermesdemarie.com. 60 units, 5 chalets. Winter, 1,880–2,600 F ($300.80–$416) double, from 3,800 F ($608) suite or chalet for 2; off-season, 1,600–2,400 F ($256–$384) double, from 3,300 F ($528) suite or chalet for 2. Rates include half board. AE, MC, V.

In 1989, the Sibuet family opened a hotel with a style that had not been seen before in Megève. The remnants of at least 20 antique barns and crumbling chalets were reassembled, then discreetly modernized in a desirable location at the eastern edge of the resort. The result is a compound of appealing, comfortable buildings loaded with atmosphere and eccentricities. The folkloric theme extends to the guest rooms, which look like attractive alpine cabins. As you lie down for the night in your deluxe bed, you'll know you're experiencing the grandest comfort at the resort.

Dining: The hotel contains **three restaurants:** Le Gastronomique, dining site for most guests on half-board plans; Le Restaurant du Fromage, which serves fondues; and La Rôtisserie, a baronial enclave with lots of rustic glamour.

Amenities: Spa, indoor pool.

MODERATE

Le Rond Point d'Arbois. 111 rte. Edmond de Rothschild, 74120 Megève. ☎ **04-50-21-17-50.** Fax 04-50-58-90-24. 13 units. TV TEL. 310–460 F ($49.60–$73.60) per person double. AE, MC, V. Closed May. Free parking on street. At the edge of town, at the bottom of the road that meanders uphill to the ski slopes of the Mont d'Arbois.

In many ways this hotel, built between the world wars, is more evocative than many of its modern competitors. It's not about glamour; rather, it's a welcoming two-star family-run place with functional but comfortable guest rooms. Rooms range from small to medium; each comes with a comfortable bed and fine linens. About half of the guests opt for the reasonably priced half-board plan, served in a simple but cozy setting near a lounge with a blazing fireplace. The cuisine is old-fashioned and hearty, featuring high-altitude Savoyard specialties.

INEXPENSIVE

✪ **Hôtel Gai Soleil.** Rue du Crêt-du-Midi, 74120 Megève. ☎ **04-50-21-00-70.** Fax 04-50-58-74-50. www.le-gai-soleil.fr. E-mail: le-gai-soleil.fr. 21 units. TV TEL. 320–500 F ($51.20–$80) double. Discounts of 20%–50% for children, depending on age. AE, DC, MC, V. Parking 25 F ($4).

This choice boasts a charming setting at the base of hills at the eastern edge of town, midway between Megève's center and the Rochbrune slopes. Its design was inspired by a Swiss chalet, except for the broad staircase that sweeps down to the front. In back there's a heated outdoor pool; within is a cozy, warm, and colorful interior with lots of exposed wood and well-upholstered comfort. Your host, Mr. Martinez, works hard to make guests comfortable. The cozy, clean rooms are highlighted with varnished pine; however, they're not very large and aren't accessible via elevator. Mattresses here, however, are particularly comfortable, having been replaced in 1998. Fixed-price menus, featuring traditional Savoyard cuisine, cost around 135 F ($21.60).

DINING

You might also try the restaurant at **Le Fer à Cheval** (see "Accommodations," above).

Chalet du Mont-d'Arbois. 447 Chemin de la Rocaille. ☎ **04-50-21-25-03.** Reservations required. Main courses 130–350 F ($20.80–$56); fixed-price menus 280–450 F ($44.80–$72).

AE, MC, V. Daily noon–2pm and 7:30–10pm. Closed Apr 6–June 11 and Oct to mid-Dec. FRENCH.

Richly decorated, and often cited in French fashion magazines as one of the most elegant sites in Megève, this restaurant is known for the spit-roasted meats whose flavors and spices go well in this high-altitude, bracing climate. Accumulated mementos of the owners, the Rothschilds, and their association with some of the greatest vineyards in the world, are scattered artfully throughout. Savory items include foie gras of duckling, omble chevalier (a local freshwater fish) meunière, spit-roasted turbot served with shellfish-studded risotto, and a dish that never fails to please: spit-roasted Bresse chicken served in its own drippings.

Le Prieuré. Place de l'Église. ☎ **04-50-21-01-79.** Reservations required. Main courses 95–280 F ($15.20–$44.80); fixed-price menus 119–197 F ($19.05–$31.50). AE, DC, V. Daily noon–10:30pm. Closed June–July 1, Nov, and Mon off-season. FRENCH.

Le Prieuré offers traditional French cooking, with specialties like foie gras de canard and salad made from crab, mussels, and lake fish. An excellent appetizer is fresh melon with locally cured ham, which can be followed by grilled bass fillet with fennel or magrêt of duckling flavored with peaches. For dessert, try the tasty apple pie. The restaurant is frequently cited as one of the best dining choices outside the hotels.

Les Enfants Terribles. In the Hôtel du Mont-Blanc, place de l'Église. ☎ **04-50-58-76-69.** Reservations required. Main courses 60–152 F ($9.60–$24.30); fixed-price menu 120–150 F ($19.20–$24). AE, DC. Wed–Mon noon–3pm and 7–11pm. Closed 3 weeks in Apr–May and Oct. FRENCH.

In the bar adjoining this acclaimed restaurant, Jean Cocteau painted wall frescoes that gave the place its name. Today, though far from being the most glamorous restaurant in town, it's one of the more fun, ripe with the shenanigans of young vacationers and snow bunnies. Warmly outfitted with wood panels and rustic artifacts, it serves generous portions of dishes that include escalope of veal Savoyard, sole meunière, and fillet of beef with a sauce of mustard, ground black pepper, and flambéed cognac. Locals predicted that the place would cease to be chic after its 1995 overhaul, but the jury's still out. Stop in for nostalgia of the naughty old days of France and judge for yourself.

Restaurant Michel Gaudin. Carrefour d'Arly. ☎ **04-50-21-02-18.** Reservations recommended. Main courses 75–195 F ($12–$31.20); fixed-price menus 120–400 F ($19.20–$64). MC, V. Dec–Apr and July–Sept, daily noon–2:30pm and 7–10:30pm; May, June, and Oct–Nov, Thurs–Sun noon–2:30pm and 7–10:30pm. FRENCH.

This restaurant in the center of Megève benefits from the experience of its Brittany-born owner and namesake. M. Gaudin trained for many years with two of the most spectacularly prestigious restaurants of France, Taillevent in Paris and Troisgros near Lyon. The conservative-looking, wood-paneled interior is less important than the well-flavored cuisine that's produced inside, usually under the supervision of Monique Gaudin. Menu items focus on the conservative and the savory, and include such hearty culinary staples as terrine of foie gras; rack of lamb in the Breton style, in honor of the owners' home; smoked salmon; and a house specialty of roasted pigeon with spicy sauce.

MEGÈVE AFTER DARK

This town is a hotbed of intimate clubs and bars for après-ski fun. The absolute ultimate is a little jazz club by the name of **Club de Jazz des 5 Rues,** rue du Comte-de-Capré (☎ **04-50-21-24-36**), the popular rendezvous for such jazz notables as Claude Luter and Claude Bolling; unfortunately, it's open only during the peak winter season. However, if you're out and about looking to spot the rich and famous, head for the **Casino,** 115 av. Charles-Feige (☎ **04-50-93-01-83**), or its piano bar, **Palo Alto,** av. Charles-Feige (☎ **04-50-93-01-83**), where you might run into members of the French jet set. For the 18- to 25-year-old dance scene, stop by the underground disco **Le Pallas,** route Edmond de Rothschild (☎ **04-50-91-82-70**), where a steep 90 F ($14.40) cover gains you entrance to this techno/rock hot spot.

8 Chamonix-Mont Blanc

381 miles SE of Paris, 58 miles E of Annecy

At an altitude of 3,422 feet, Chamonix is the historic capital of alpine skiing. This is the resort to choose if you're not a millionaire. Site of the first winter Olympic Games in 1924, Chamonix huddles in a valley almost at the junction of France, Italy, and Switzerland. Dedicated skiers all over the world know of its 12-mile **Vallée Blanche run,** one of Europe's most rugged and certainly its longest. Thrill seekers also flock here for mountain climbing and hang gliding.

A charming old-fashioned mountain town, Chamonix has a most thrilling backdrop, ✪ **Mont Blanc,** Western Europe's highest mountain at 15,780 feet. When two Englishmen, Windham and Pococke, first visited Chamonix in 1740, they were thrilled with its location and later wrote a travel book that advertised the village around the world. On August 7, 1786, Jacques Balmat became the first man to climb the mountain, destroying the myth that no one could spend a night up there and survive. In the old quarter of town a memorial to this brave pioneer stands in front of the village church.

Scheduled to reopen in 2001, the 7-mile **Mont Blanc Tunnel** (☎ **04-50-53-06-15**), made Chamonix a major stop along one of Europe's busiest highways. By going underground, the tunnel provides the easiest way to get past the mountains to Italy; motorists now stop here even if they aren't interested in winter skiing or summer mountain climbing. Toll rates depend on the distance between the axles of your vehicle: It's 145 F ($23.20) one-way for a small car and 195 F ($31.20) for a big car or caravan trailer. Round-trip tickets are a significant discount, at 180 F and 240 F ($28.80 and $38.40), respectively. But you must return within 3 days of buying them.

Because of its exceptional equipment —gondolas, cable cars, and chairlifts— Chamonix is one of Europe's major sports resorts, attracting an international crowd.

Chamonix sprawls in a narrow strip along both banks of the Arve River. Its casino, its rail and bus stations, and most of its restaurants and nightlife are in the town center. Cable cars reach into the mountains from the town's edge. Locals refer to Les Praz, Les Bossons, Les Moussoux, and Les Pélerins as satellite villages within Greater Chamonix, though technically Chamonix refers to only a carefully delineated section around place de l'Église.

ESSENTIALS

GETTING THERE   Most (but not all) **trains** coming from other parts of France or Switzerland require a transfer in such nearby villages as St-Gervais (in France) or Martigny (in Switzerland). Through either of those towns, passengers are routed here from Aix-les-Bains, Annecy, Lyon, and Chambéry and, farther afield, Paris and Geneva. There are two connections from Paris every 24 hours (trip time: 8 hours); from Lyon, there are six rail links per day (trip time: 4 hours). For more information and schedules for trains throughout France, call ☎ **08-36-35-35-35.**

In any season there's at least one daily **bus** from Annecy and Grenoble, and from the Geneva airport, there are between two and six buses a day, depending on the season, charging 188 F ($30.10) each way. Buses arrive and depart from a spot adjacent to the railway station when they arrive in Chamonix. For reservations and information, call Cie S.A.T. at ☎ **04-50-53-01-15.**

If you're **driving,** you probably won't have to worry about road conditions: Since Chamonix lies on a main road link between Italy and the Mont Blanc Tunnel, conditions are excellent throughout the year. Even after a severe snowstorm, roads are quickly swept clean of heavy snow. Motorists from Paris can follow A6 toward Lyon, taking the A40 toward Geneva. Before Geneva, turn south along A40 leading into Chamonix.

GETTING AROUND   Within Chamonix, a local network of small-scale buses (*navettes,* usually brightly painted in yellow and blue) make frequent runs from strategic points within the town to many of the *téléphériques* (cable cars) and villages up and down the valley. Transit on any of them is usually included in the price of any lift ticket, but for nonskiers and summer visitors the cost is 7.50 F ($1.20) for each 3-mile sector you travel. For information, contact **Chambus** at ☎ **04-50-53-38-03.**

VISITOR INFORMATION   Chamonix's **Office de Tourisme** is on place du Triangle-de-l'Amitié (☎ **04-50-53-00-24**).

SPECIAL EVENTS   If you're here from mid-July to August, you may want to attend the classical and jazz concerts during the **Semaines Musicales du Mont-Blanc.** Concerts take place at the Grand Salle of "The Majestic," allée du Majestic, which was built during the *Belle Époque* as a particularly opulent hotel, and later transformed into private apartments. Tickets to the events cost 75 F to 150 F ($12 to $24), and are available along with program schedules from the Office de Tourisme.

SKIING

With the highest mountain in western Europe as a backdrop, this is an area for the highly skilled skier. Regrettably, none of the five main ski areas spread along the valley floor are connected by lifts, and lines at the most popular areas are the longest in the alpine world. Weather and snow conditions create crevasses and avalanches that may close whole ski sections for days, even threatening parts of the resort itself.

Skiing is not actually on Mont Blanc but on the shoulders and slopes across the valley facing this giant mountain. Vertical drops can be spectacular—with lift-serviced hills rising to as much as 10,500 feet. Glacier skiing begins at 12,465 feet. This is not for the beginner or timid intermediate skiers, who should head for the satellite resorts of Les Houches or Le Tour. World-class skiers come here to face the daunting challenges of the high snows of Brévant, La Flégère, and especially Les Grands Monets, that fierce north-facing wall of snow that stretches about 3 city blocks wide.

A 1-day ski pass costs 142 F ($22.70) and can be used only in the Brévant area. A better investment is the Chamski Pass, good for at least five major areas, for 241 F ($38.55) for 1 day or 589 F ($94.25) for 3 days.

SEEING THE AREA BY CABLE CAR

The belvederes you can reach from Chamonix by cable car or mountain railway are famous. For information about these rides, contact the **Société Touristique du Mont-Blanc,** 100 Parking de l'Aiguille du Midi, 74400 Chamonix (☎ **04-50-53-30-80**).

In the heart of town, you can board a cable car heading for the **Aiguille du Midi** and on to Italy—a harrowing journey. The first stage, a 9-minute run to the Plan des Aiguilles at an altitude of 7,544 feet, isn't so alarming. But the second stage, to an altitude of 12,602 feet, the Aiguille du Midi station, may make your heart leap, especially when the car rises 2,000 feet between towers. At the summit, you'll be 1,110 yards from

Mont Blanc's peak. The belvedere affords a commanding view of the Aiguilles of Chamonix and Vallée Blanche, the largest glacier in continental Europe (9.3 miles long and 3.7 miles wide). You also have a 125-mile view of the Jura and the French, Swiss, and Italian Alps.

You leave the tram station along a chasm-spanning narrow bridge leading to the third cable car and the glacial fields that lie beyond. Or you can end your journey at Aiguille du Midi and return to Chamonix. Generally the cable cars operate year-round: in summer, daily from 6am to 5pm, leaving at least every 10 minutes; in winter, daily from 8am to 4pm, leaving every 10 minutes. The first stage, to Plan des Aiguilles, costs 85 F ($13.60) round-trip, increasing to 200 F ($32) per person for a round-trip from Chamonix to Aiguille du Midi.

You then cross over high mountains and pass jagged needles of rock and ice bathed in dazzling light. The final trip to **Pointe Helbronner** in Italy—at 11,355 feet— requires a passport if you want to leave the station and descend on two more cable cars to the village of Courmayeur. From here you can go to nearby Entrèves to dine at La Maison de Filippo, a "chalet of gluttony." The round-trip from Chamonix to Pointe Helbronner is 300 F ($48); the cable car operates from mid-May to mid-October only.

Another aerial cableway takes you up to **Brévent**, at 8,284 feet. From here you'll have a first-rate (frontal) view of Mont Blanc and the Aiguilles de Chamonix. The trip takes about 1¹/₂ hours round-trip. Cable cars operate year-round, from 8am to 5pm. Summer departures are at least every half hour. A round-trip costs 82 F ($13.10).

Yet another aerial journey takes you to **Le Montenvers** (☎ **04-50-53-12-54**), at 6,276 feet. From the belvedere at the end of the cable-car run you'll have a view of the 4-mile-long *mer de glace* (sea of ice, or glacier). Aiguille du Dru is a rock climb notorious for its difficulty. The trip takes 1¹/₂ hours, including a return by rail. Departures are 8am to 6pm in summer, until 4:30pm off-season. The round-trip fare is 76 F ($12.15) per person, and service is usually year-round.

You can also visit a cave, **La Grotte de Glace,** hollowed out of the mer de glace; a cable car connects it with the upper resort of Montenvers, and the trip takes just 3 minutes. Train, cable car, and a visit to the cave cost 112 F ($17.90).

ACCOMMODATIONS

Au Bon Coin. 80 av. de l'Aiguille-du-Midi, 74400 Chamonix. ☎ **04-50-53-15-67.** Fax 04-50-53-51-51. 20 units, 16 with bathroom. TEL. 282 F ($45.10) double without bathroom, 384 F ($61.45) double with bathroom. MC, V. Closed May–June and Oct–Dec 18. Free parking.

This two-star hotel is very French alpine. It has comfortable modern rooms, often with views of the mountainside. In autumn the colors are spectacular. The accommodations also feature terraces where you can soak up the sun, even in winter. Bedrooms range in size from small to medium, each equipped with a comfortable bed and a firm mattress. The chalet is tranquil, especially in the garden.

Chalet Hôtel Le Chantel. 391 rte. des Pecles, 74400 Chamonix. ☎ **04-50-53-02-54.** Fax 04-50-53-54-52. 7 units. TEL. 358–488 F ($57.30–$78.10) double. Rates include breakfast. MC, V.

Within a 30-minute walk west from the city hall, this white-stucco hotel evokes a Swiss chalet with its dark-stained wood, balconies, and mountain panoramas. Originally built as a vacation home in 1952, it benefits from the care and attention of its owners, Peter and Françoise Schmid, who have added decorative touches akin to what you'd expect in a private home. The cozy knotty-pine paneled rooms are small but have fine alpine comfort, each with a good bed and a comfortable mattress. Breakfast is the only meal served.

Hôtel de l'Arve. 60 impasse des Anémones, 74400 Chamonix. ☎ **04-50-53-02-31.** Fax 04-50-53-56-92. www.hotelarve-chamonix.com. E-mail: contact@hotelarve-chamonix.com. 39 units, 35 with bathroom. 264–362 F ($42.25–$57.90) double without bathroom, 400–549 F ($64–$87.85) double with bathroom. Half board 120 F ($19.20) per person extra. AE, DC, MC, V. Closed Nov–Dec 20.

Originally a cafe around the turn of the century, this place expanded into a comfortable, unpretentious two-star hotel. Most of its stucco-fronted facade dates from the 1960s, and the interior is a simple kind of setting where furniture and accessories are well chosen, childproof, and much used. Furnishings in the small to medium-size bedrooms are functional, the mattresses a bit worn but still serviceable. This is a simple place that offers warmth and comfort, a friendly welcome, an appreciation for the great outdoors, and lovely views from many of the rooms over the rocky banks of the Arve, which flows nearby. The setting is particularly convenient, just a 5-minute walk from the town hall.

✪ **Le Hameau Albert 1er.** 119 impasse Montenvers, 74402 Chamonix. ☎ **04-50-53-05-09.** Fax 04-50-55-95-48. www.hameaualbert.fr. E-mail: infos@hameaualbert.fr. 41 units. MINIBAR TV TEL. Main building, 820–1,650 F ($131.20–$264) double; La Ferme, 1,700–3,500 F ($272–$560) double. AE, DC, MC, V. Closed Nov 2–Dec 3.

This hotel is an enlarged alpine chalet, ringed by a garden and private residences. Each of the well-furnished rooms offers a mountain view; several also feature private balconies. Facilities include an outdoor pool, tennis court, sauna, and Jacuzzi. Accommodations in the older chalet have welcomed guests for four generations; deluxe newer rooms in the addition, La Ferme, are more spacious and contain fireplaces, a Jacuzzi, and a large balcony opening onto a view of Mont-Blanc. Regardless of room assignment, you'll find a snug alpine retreat, with good beds equipped with fine linen and quality mattresses.

You can dine in one of three elegant rooms, outfitted with Oriental carpets and 18th-century chests. (See below for a complete review of the restaurant.) A copper-topped bar is in the lobby.

DINING

Bartavel. 26 cours du Bartavel (impasse du Vox). ☎ **04-50-53-97-19.** Main courses 75–95 F ($12–$15.20). AE, DC, MC, V. Thurs–Tues 11am–midnight. ITALIAN.

Decorated much like a tavern you'd expect to find in Italy, this restaurant offers a wide range of pastas and salads, plus a medley of rib-sticking platters designed to go well with cold air and high altitudes. Menu items include grilled steaks and chops, escalopes milanese or pizzaiola, and an array of simple desserts. Beer and wine flow liberally. Bartavel attracts a good share of outdoor enthusiasts, who appreciate its copious portions and reasonable prices.

La Casa Valerio. 88 rue du Lyret. ☎ **04-50-55-93-40.** Reservations not necessary. Pizzas, pastas, platters 50–60 F ($8–$9.60). AE, DC, MC, V. Daily noon–2am. ITALIAN.

Prefaced with a cozy bar that's filled with Chianti bottles and alpine souvenirs, this restaurant is known for the best pizza in the region, as well as many of the freshest pastas. It's the good-natured domain of long-time Chamonix resident Valerio Comazetto, whose clients have followed him from restaurant to restaurant over the past 2 decades. You might enjoy tapas at the bar before proceeding upstairs to the cozy dining room, where red and white-checkered tablecloths set the trattoria motif. You'll find a complete range of pizzas, many redolent of Mediterranean herbs, and up to 40 kinds of fresh-made pastas, including succulent versions with salmon and thin-sliced *jambon de Parme.* More substantial dishes include a Roman version of *ossobucco* (braised veal shanks), grilled calamari, mussels in white wine sauce, and perfectly grilled steaks.

Le Chaudron. 79 rue des Moulins. ☎ **04-50-53-40-34.** Reservations recommended. Main courses 180–250 F ($28.80–$40); fixed-price menu 130 F ($20.80). AE, MC, V. Daily 7pm–midnight. Closed June and Oct–Nov. FRENCH.

There are a lot of fancier places in town, but for good value, honest cooking, and fine mountain ingredients, Le Chaudron emerges near the top of our list. Chef Pierre Osterberger cooks right in front of you, and you're sure to appreciate his specialties, which include house-style sweetbreads, several robust beef dishes, and fondues, as well as many salads and desserts. The cellar is filled with well-chosen wines, including Château Mouton-Rothschild and Château Latour.

Restaurant Albert 1er. in the Hameau Albert 1er hotel, 119 impasse du Montenvers. ☎ **04-50-53-05-09.** Reservations recommended. Main courses 185–240 F ($29.60–$38.40); fixed-price menus 190–550 F ($30.40–$88) at lunch, 220–550 F ($35.20–$88) at dinner. AE, DC, MC, V. Fri–Mon and Wed 12:30–2pm; daily 7:30–9:30pm. FRENCH.

Although the hotel complex that contains this establishment features other, newer, eateries, this is the culinary star. You'll dine in one of a trio of cozily decorated dining rooms, which have bay windows opening onto views of Mont Blanc and walls accented with rustic artifacts and antique farm implements. Begin with master chef Pierre Carrier's broth (*fumet*) of wild mushrooms garnished with ravioli stuffed with foie gras. Appealing entrees include sweet onions cooked in rock salt, locally smoked salmon prepared with a caviar-flavored cream sauce, and a savory blanquette of lamb studded with fresh morels. Try the classic honey ice cream with a raspberry coulis—there's nothing more succulent on the dessert menu. In summer, dine alfresco in the garden.

Restaurant Matafan. In the Hôtel Mont-Blanc, 62 allée du Majéstic. ☎ **04-50-53-05-64.** Reservations required. Main courses 130–200 F ($20.80–$32); fixed-price menu 310 F ($49.60). AE, DC, MC, V. Daily noon–2pm and 7–10pm. Closed Oct 15–Dec 15. FRENCH.

This stellar restaurant has a decor of soft pastels and hand-woven tapestries, arranged around a central pentagonal fireplace. Specialties change seasonally but may include omble chevalier (lake fish) meunière, rack of lamb roasted with herbs (for two), and sinful desserts. Many of the dishes are inspired by Savoy cooking but with a refined touch. The excellent cellar contains more than 500 wines, many reasonably priced. In summer you can lunch next to the pool in the garden.

CHAMONIX AFTER DARK

Nightlife in Chamonix runs the gamut from the classical and sublime to the campy and riotous. You'll find the highest concentration of bars and pubs along **rue des Moulins** and **rue Paccard,** including the sexy, high-energy, predominantly young **Dick's Tea Bar,** rue des Moulins (☎ **04-50-53-19-10**), which occupies the premises of a converted water mill in the town center; and the British bastion, **Mill Street Bar,** 123 rue des Moulins (☎ **04-50-55-80-92**), with its tables spilling onto the sidewalk and English-language après-ski stories floating about. For the more mature and sedate crowd, enjoy the mellow atmosphere at **Le Blue Night** Disco, 22 Rue Paccard (☎ **04-50-53-63-52**), where the dance floor occupies a very old vaulted cellar, and the music is at such a level to allow conversation. The **Casino,** 12 place H.-B.-de-Saussure (☎ **04-50-53-07-65**), offers evenings of chance at the slot machines and roulette and blackjack tables.

9 Val d'Isère

413 miles SE of Paris, 73 miles E of Albertville, 81 miles E of Chambéry

Set in an open valley, and originally conceived as a hunting station for the ducs de Savoie, Val d'Isère (6,068 feet above sea level) has grown into the centerpiece for some of Europe's most spectacular skiing. Less snobbish and exhibitionist than Courchevel and less old-fashioned than Megève, it's a youthful, rather brash resort where virtually everyone comes to enjoy active, outdoor pursuits. Its fans compare it favorably to Chamonix, which—despite the allure of nearby Mont Blanc and some superb (mostly expert) skiing—seems to be burdened with longer lift lines and a less accessible layout of its network of ski lifts and slopes. In 1992, Val d'Isère hosted most of the men's downhill racing events for the winter Olympics, which were head-quartered at Albertville.

ESSENTIALS

GETTING THERE & AROUND   Driving is the preferred way to get to and around Val d'Isère. Most visitors traveling by car come from Albertville, accessible by superhighway from Paris. From Albertville, follow the signs to Moutiers. From Moutiers, take RN202 to Bourg-St-Maurice (36 miles) and continue for another 19 miles to Val d'Isère. The meandering RN202 is panoramic and breathtaking—for both its views and its lack of guard rails along some sections. During snowfalls, chains on your tires are required. When you get to the resort, we strongly advise you to park your car and not use it again until you're ready to leave. Parking problems here are legendary, and without chains you'll risk getting stuck during snowfalls. You can walk to virtually anywhere in town faster than you can drive.

Almost two dozen red-and-white Train Rouge **shuttle buses,** each with a capacity of 100 people and their equipment, connect the hamlets at either end of the valley (Daille and Fornet) to the center of Val d'Isère. The central terminus is the Rond-Point des Pistes. Transit is free. During summer, service is available only during July and August.

Parking lots and garages are scattered judiciously around the valley, and clearly marked. Each of them charges around 80 F ($12.80) per day, or 330 F to 450 F ($52.80 to $72) per week, depending on the season and the size of your car.

Nearby **airports** include Cointrin outside Geneva (☎ **022/717-71-11**), Lyon-Satolas (☎ **04-72-22-72-21**), Grenoble (☎ **04-76-65-48-48**), and Chambéry (☎ **04-79-54-49-54**). Bus and limo service are available from any airport via Cars Martin (☎ **04-79-06-00-42**).

The nearest **railway** station is at Bourg-St-Maurice (☎ **04-79-07-10-10**), an alpine village 19 miles west of Val d'Isère. For train information and schedules, call ☎ **08-36-35-35-35**. From here, **buses** maintained by **Cars Martin** (☎ **04-79-07-04-49**) depart between four and 10 times a day, depending on the season, and cost 65 F ($10.40) each way. If that's inconvenient, you can take a **taxi** from Bourg-St-Maurice for a one-way fare of about 420 F ($67.20) for up to four passengers. (Call **Altitude Taxis** at ☎ **04-79-41-14-15** or arrange the pickup in advance with your hotel.)

VISITOR INFORMATION   The resort's **Office de Tourisme,** Rue Principale B.P. 228, 73150 Val d'Isère (☎ **04-79-06-06-60**), is a font of information on outdoor activities.

The widest spectrum of information on sports in town is available from the **Club des Sports (Sports Department),** B.P. 61, 73152 Val d'Isère (☎ **04-79-06-03-49**).

FUN ON & OFF THE SLOPES

As recently as 1930, Val d'Isère was little more than a French-speaking mountain village near the Italian frontier, with a church and a handful of slate and stone houses accessible to the rest of the world only via mule track. Today the town is a mass of urban sprawl whose boundaries are defined by high avalanche-prone walls that rise steeply up to altitudes where snow is common even during spring and autumn. It's bisected by a gravel-bottomed mountain stream, La Tarentaise. The resort's developed (some say overdeveloped) sections sprawl along either side of the highest road in Europe, RN202.

Don't expect a pristine-looking alpine village, like the picture-perfect Swiss resort of Zermatt. In Val d'Isère, traffic roars through the town center. Clusters of cheap restaurants, crêperies, and more than 125 stores and outlets line either side of the road. Since 1983, however, some of the worst of the town's architectural sins have been corrected, thanks to tighter building codes and greater emphasis on traditional chalet-style architecture.

Access to Val d'Isère, less than 6 miles from the Italian border, is inconvenient and time-consuming. Parking is a nightmare during busy seasons, and the medieval cluster of stone farm buildings that comprised the original hamlet were long ago pushed into the background in the region's sometimes hysterical rush to modernize. But despite the commercialism, the town hums with the sense that its visitors are really here to enjoy skiing. And few other European resorts can boast as logical a layout for a far-flung network of ski slopes.

Val d'Isère is the focal point for a network of satellite resorts scattered around the nearby valleys, including the architecturally uninspired Tignes (6,888 feet above sea level), whose layout is divided into at least four resort-style villages. The most stylish and prosperous of these is Val Claret; less fortunate and successful are Tignes le Lac, Tignes les Boisses, and Tignes les Brévières.

Guarding one entrance to Val d'Isère is La Daille, a resort of mostly high-rise condos and time-shares. Standing sentry to the other is the medieval hamlet of Le Fornet, best known as the departure point for gondolas leading over a mountain ridge to the Pissaillas Glacier and another network of ski trails, the Système de Solaise. All these satellites, however, lack the cachet and diversity of Val d'Isère's nightlife and dining. Public transport via the Train Rouge can pick you up and deposit you at the departure point to the terminus of virtually any ski lift or trail in the region.

Val d'Isère is legendary for its "death-defying" chutes and its off-piste walls. These slopes, of course, are for the experts, but the intermediate skier of moderate skills will also find open snowfields. The best place for intermediates is Tignes, with its wide variety of runs, including the Grande Motte at 11,150 feet. Skiers find enough variety here to stay 2 weeks and never repeat the slopes that stretch from the Pissaillas Glacier far above Val d'Isère to Tignes Les Brévières four valleys away.

There are only a few marked expert runs; it's the more accessible off-piste areas that lure experts from all over Europe and the U.S. Most of these runs can be reached after short traverses from the Bellevarde, Solaiwse, and Fornet cable cars in Val d'Isère and the Grande Motte cable car in Val Claret.

Golden Boy

Val d'Isère is the hometown of the legendary Jean-Claude Killy, who swept the gold in all three downhill skiing events (slalom, giant slalom, and downhill) at the 1968 Olympics held in nearby Grenoble.

Year-Round Skiing

Though snow melts on the rock faces around town, in summer exposing the gray bedrock, icy granules remain skiable year-round on the Pissaillas. The glacier is accessible via the Fornet cable car, on the northwestern (uppermost) edges of town. The tourist office considers the ski conditions safe and suitable only between June 28 and August 17. A lift ticket costs 153 F ($24.50) for half a day, 220 F ($35.20) for a full day, and 405 F ($64.80) for 2 days. Note that these prices do not include medical and accident insurance, a limited policy which can be purchased for a supplement of 15 F ($2.40) per day. Access to the glacier from Val Disole requires two cable-car transfers. For information, contact **Ski Lifts,** B.P. 269, 73155 Val d'Isère (☎ **04-79-06-00-35**). Officially, the resort's sports activities slow down or stop altogether every year between early May and late June, and from early September to mid-November.

At least a dozen **ski schools** flourish during winter. One of the largest and busiest is the **École de Ski Français** (French National Ski School), B.P. 265, 73155 Val d'Isère (☎ **04-79-06-02-34**), with 280 ski guides and teachers. Somewhat more personalized is **Snow Fun,** B.P. 287, 73150 Val d'Isère (☎ **04-79-06-16-79**), with 60 guides. Purists usually gravitate to **Top Ski,** galerie des Cimes (B.P. 41), 73153 Val d'Isère (☎ **04-79-06-14-80**), a small but choice outfit with 12 extremely well-trained guides who cater exclusively to alpine connoisseurs who want to ski off-piste (away from the officially recognized and maintained ski trails).

ACCOMMODATIONS

The staff at **Val Hôtel,** B.P. 73, 73153 Val d'Isère (☎ **04-79-06-18-90;** fax 04-79-06-11-88), the resort's central reservations network, can reserve accommodations for you.

Hôtel Altitude. Rte. de la Balme, 73150 Val d'Isère. ☎ **04-79-06-12-55.** Fax 04-79-41-11-09. www.skifrance.fr73304/altitude/. E-mail: altitude-valdisere@laposte.fr. 40 units. TV TEL. Winter 1,360–1,440 F ($217.60–$230.40) double; summer 760–900 F ($121.60–$144) double. Rates include half board. V. Closed May 6–June 30 and Sept 9–Dec 5.

This frequently renovated and oft-modernized chalet was built in the 1970s in true Savoyard style. Because of the similarity of their names, it's frequently confused with the four-star Hôtel Latitude nearby. The three-star Altitude is comfortable and cozy, a short walk south of the town center, so you'll be able to escape the madding crowd. Many of the guests return year after year, occupying elegantly appointed bedrooms with quality mattresses and fine linens.

Dining: On the premises is **Le Restaurant,** with well-prepared, straightforward food, several open fireplaces, and a bar.

Amenities: In summer, the hotel opens its outdoor pool and sundeck; a sauna and steam bath are open year-round.

♦ **Hôtel Christiania.** B.P. 48, 73152 Val d'Isère. ☎ **04-79-06-08-25.** Fax 04-79-41-11-10. www.hotel-christiania.com. E-mail: welcome@hotel-christiania.com. 69 units. TV TEL. 667–1,207 F ($106.70–$193.10) per person double; 1,237–2,327 F ($197.90–$372.30) per person suite. Rates include half board. AE, MC, V. Closed May–Dec 5.

This stylishly designed 1949 chalet was almost completely rebuilt in 1991. Today it's the best hotel in a town filled with worthy contenders. Homage to its original design appears at unexpected moments, most obviously in the *Sputnik*-style furniture a decorator incorporated into a sunken lobby that's otherwise ringed with exposed stone, varnished pine, and blazing fireplaces. The guest rooms are deliberately cozy, with lots of pine trim and alpine touches. The mattresses are comfortable and the towels thick.

Dining: Le Christiania restaurant welcomes guests and nonguests. It's open only from early December to late April, daily for lunch and dinner.

Amenities: Room service (24 hours), baby-sitting, concierge. State-of-the-art fitness center with indoor pool, sauna, Turkish baths, exercise areas, massage facilities.

Hôtel Mercure Village. B.P. 45, 73152 Val d'Isère. ☎ **04-79-06-12-93.** Fax 04-79-41-11-12. 45 units. TV TEL. 620–1,740 F ($99.20–$278.40) double; 980–2,140 F ($156.80–$342.40) suite for 2. Rates include breakfast. AE, DC, MC, V. Closed May 7–June 15. Parking 80 F ($12.80).

The success of this chain hotel is based on its relatively reasonable rates and its deliberate lack of the ostentation and glitter that permeate many of Val d'Isère's properties. Don't judge its charm by its rather uninspired four-story chalet-style exterior: inside are enough alpine touches to evoke a bit of nostalgia. In the public areas are pinewood paneling and flowered curtains. The guest rooms are simpler and rather angular but still feature touches of varnished pine. The hotel is in the town center, with easy access to the chairlifts and the nightlife.

Dining: Well-prepared meals are served in generous portions in the rustic **La Spatule,** specializing in Savoyard cuisine. Those who opt for half-board plans use **Le Potager,** a room that's more formal and appealing than what you'd find in most members of the Mercure chain. Room service is available during regular meal hours in the two restaurants.

DINING

La Grande Ourse. Sur le Front de Neige, adjacent to the church. ☎ **04-79-06-00-19.** Reservations recommended at dinner. Main courses 90–160 F ($14.40–$25.60) at dinner; fixed-price menu 125 F ($20) at lunch, 255 F ($40.80) at dinner. AE, DC, V. Daily noon–3pm and 7:30–9:30pm. Closed May 5–Nov 30. SAVOYARD.

Although it's open for lunch, this restaurant doesn't take on its trademark coziness until after nightfall, when flickering candles and a blazing fireplace permeate the place with lots of Savoyard charm. It was built in 1937 by Jean Fautrier, an important painter who's almost unknown outside France. The place's name derives from a mural he painted of the zodiac, part of which features a large female bear. Menu items at lunch include grilled meats, pastas, salads, and simple but fortifying dishes of the day. Evening menus offer more sophisticated fare, like roast rack of lamb with herbs, lobster ravioli, Savoyard fondue with three cheeses, and escalope of foie gras with purple artichokes. Dessert may be a tarte fine with apples or a Gallic version of a North American brownie.

La Vieille Maison. Vieux Village, La Daille. ☎ **04-79-06-11-76.** Reservations recommended. Main courses 73–99 F ($11.70–$15.85). AE, MC, V. Daily 7–9:30pm. Closed May–June and Sept–Nov. SAVOYARD.

Amid cozy but relatively new buildings in the satellite hamlet of La Daille, this former farmhouse is one of the valley's oldest chalets. Constructed 300 years ago, it has lots of exposed stone, and a cozy decor that's ripe with old-fashioned Savoyard charm. Menu items are based on traditional Savoyard themes, specializing in hearty cold-weather dishes like fondues and raclettes, many of which are prepared only for a minimum of two to four diners. Other choices are fillet mignon with lemon and sour cream, and the signature specialty, Vieille Maison-style veal stuffed with ham and slathered with cheese. Hands-on chefs sometimes opt for La Viande à l'Auze—a super-hot slab of rock is placed directly on your table so you can sizzle your beef strips yourself.

There Was an Olympiad Around Here Somewhere

The 1992 Winter Olympics were held in Albertville, but you'd hardly know it these days. Even during the games, the town was little more than the administrative headquarters for an event that encompassed all of the Savoy region. The official name of those games (*Les Jeux d'Albertville et de La Savoie*) was chosen to downplay Albertville, and to raise awareness of such Savoy resorts as Menuires, La Plagne, and Les Saisies. (It didn't do much good; they're still little-visited by foreigners.)

Today, few vestiges of the 1992 games remain in their original form within Albertville. The town is a phenomenally dull railway and highway junction, and because of its location in a valley, not even particularly panoramic. It's proud of the way it either demolished or transformed many of the Olympic structures into new uses, and 1992 is spoken of with nostalgia. Albertville's most visible monument to the 1992 games is the metal-sheathed **Halle Olympique,** Avenue de Winnenden (☎ **04-79-32-84-11**), but frankly, we don't consider it a hot tourist ticket.

ACCOMMODATIONS & DINING

The unpretentious rail and highway junction of **Albertville** lies within **La Vallée de la Tarantaise,** a sinuous valley that climbs upward along a distance of 53 miles along Route 90. Route 90 extends from low-lying Albertville (at around 1,200 feet above sea level) and eventually branches into **La Vallée d'Isère,** whose focal point is the resort of Val d'Isère. Most visitors travel between the two points by car, although about five trains a day go uphill between Albertville and Bourg-St-Maurice. At Bourg-St-Maurice, a bus, whose departure is timed to coincide with the arrival of trains, continues for another 18 miles uphill to Val d'Isère. Train passengers should expect total transit time of between 60 and 90 minutes, depending on the day of the week, and a one-way fare around 95 F ($15.20).

✪ **Hôtel Million.** 8 place de la Liberté, 73200 Albertville. ☎ **04-79-32-25-15.** Fax 04-79-32-25-36. Reservations recommended. Main courses 150–260 F ($24–$41.60); fixed-price menus 150–550 F ($24–$88). AE, DC, MC, V. Tues–Sun noon–2pm; Tues–Sat 7:45–9:30pm. FRENCH.

Set back from the main road through town, the Hôtel Million was established in 1770 by an ancestor of Philippe Million, the current owner and chef whose cuisine did much to put Albertville on the gourmet map. It's housed in a white building with strong horizontal lines and gables on a flagstone-covered square; the anterooms have authentic 19th-century decor, while the spacious dining room itself has high ceilings and conservatively classic furnishings. Some of the traditional dishes featured on the menu derive from popular Savoy tastes of the 19th century, in particular the frogs' legs, freshwater fish from Lake Annecy, and freshwater crayfish. Other choices include a fillet of *fera* (a white fish found in Alpine lakes) served with wild celery and herb-flavored butter; Bresse veal; sweetbreads with truffle sauce; and roasted rack of veal served with a fricassée of artichokes.

Although the establishment is best known for its restaurant, which attracts both gastronomes and sports enthusiasts, it also contains 26 attractive and unpretentious **guest rooms.** Outfitted in rustic alpine style, each contains a private bathroom, TV, and phone, and more space than you might imagine. Friday and Saturday nights between December and April are the most expensive, when doubles rent for 550 F to 600 F ($88 to $96) a night. The rest of the year, doubles range from 350 F to 400 F ($56 to $64). Parking is free outside, or 50 F to 70 F ($8 to $11.20) inside.

VAL D'ISÈRE AFTER DARK

The resort has its share of bars that come and go every season with the arrival and departure of the snow. Most are in the town's pedestrian zone or adjacent to **rue Principale.** One of the most reliable bars is **L'Aventure** (☎ 04-79-06-20-82). For an attractive-looking crowd, head for **Café Face,** rue Principale (☎ 04-79-06-04-93). If you want to go dancing, there are two discos, both mobbed in winter and dead during spring and autumn: **Dick's Tea Bar** (☎ 04-79-06-14-87), which also opens half-heartedly during July and August but only on evenings when business might justify the effort; and **Club 21** (☎ 04-79-06-04-93), open only in winter. Admission to both is around 75 F ($12) and includes the first drink.

Provence: In the Footsteps of Cézanne & van Gogh

Provence has been called a bridge between the past and the present, where yesterday blends with today in a quiet, often melancholy way. Peter Mayle's best-selling *A Year in Provence* and *Toujours Provence* have played no small part in the burgeoning popularity of this sunny corner of southern France.

The Greeks and Romans first filled the landscape with cities boasting Hellenic theaters, Roman baths, amphitheaters, and triumphal arches. These were followed in medieval times by Romanesque fortresses and Gothic cathedrals. In the 19th century, the light and landscapes here attracted illustrious painters like Cézanne and van Gogh.

Provence has its own language and its own customs. The region is bounded on the north by the Dauphine, on the west by the Rhône, on the east by the Alps, and on the south by the Mediterranean. In the following chapter, we'll focus on the part of Provence known as the glittering Côte d'Azur or French Riviera.

For more extensive coverage of this region, see *Frommer's Provence & the Riviera.*

REGIONAL CUISINE   Part of the charm of Provence lies in its distinctive cuisine, which successfully marries the traditions of the mountains and the seaside. The earliest contributors to this were the ancient Italians, for strong comparisons can be made between the Provençal and the Italian emphasis on fresh fish and vegetables, olive oil, and garlic.

The best of Provençal produce includes melons from Cavaillon and elongated tube-shaped onions known as *éschalotes-bananes.* The most famous vegetable dish is *ratatouille,* a stew of tomatoes, garlic, eggplant, zucchini, onions, and peppers, liberally sprinkled with olive oil and black pepper. A slightly different version is *soupe au pistou,* with the addition of basil, pounded garlic, vermicelli, string beans, and grilled tomatoes.

Each town along the Provence coast seems to have a fish-stew specialty. In Nice, stockfish is used in *stocaficada. Bourride* is made with whitefish, garlic, onions, tomatoes, herbs, egg yolks, saffron, and grated orange rind. Toulon has its *esquinado,* with saltwater crabs, vinegar, water, and pulverized mussels. And the best and most authentic *bouillabaisse* is from Marseille.

Several Provençal meat dishes are welcome substitutes for the ubiquitous fish: *daube de boeuf* (beef stew); *fricassée de pintade* (guinea fowl), perhaps served with a mild purée of sweet garlic; and *fricassée* or *ragoût de cabri* (goat). Provence boasts scores of savory cheeses, among them Picadon, Pélardon, and St-Félicien; dozens of pastries and breads; and many scented honeys.

The regional wines are almost as diverse as the cuisine. They include the vast family of the Côtes-du-Rhône, Gigondas, Châteauneuf-du-Pape, and Château de Fonsalette.

1 Orange

409 miles S of Paris, 34 miles NE of Nîmes, 75 miles NW of Marseille, 16 miles S of Avignon

Orange gets its name from the days when it was a dependency of the Dutch House of Orange-Nassau, not because it's set in a citrus belt. Actually, the last orange grove departed 2,000 years ago. The juice that flows in Orange today comes from its fabled vineyards, which turn out a Côtes du Rhône vintage. Many caves are spread throughout the district, some of which offer *dégustations* to paying customers. (The tourist office will provide you with a list.)

Overlooking the Valley of the Rhône, today's Orange, with a somewhat sleepy population of about 30,000, boasts Europe's third-largest extant triumphal arch and best-preserved Roman theater. Louis XIV, who toyed with the idea of moving the theater to Versailles, said: "It is the finest wall in my kingdom." UNESCO has placed the arch on its World Cultural and Natural Heritage List in the hope that it can be preserved "forever."

ESSENTIALS

GETTING THERE   Orange sits on some of the major French north-south rail and highway arteries, making arrivals by train, bus, or car convenient. Some 20 **trains** per day arrive from Avignon (trip time: 17 minutes), at a one-way fare of around 32 F ($5.10). From Marseille there are 14 trains per day (trip time: 1¹/₂ hours), at around 116 F ($18.55) one-way. From Paris there are 14 trains per day (trip time: 4¹/₂ hours) by TGV, which will be direct or require a transfer at either Valence, Lyon, or Montélimar and ongoing transit by conventional train into Orange; a one-way fare is 362 F ($57.90). For rail information and schedules, call ☎ **08-36-35-35-35.** For information about bus routes and schedules, contact the **Gare Routière** (☎ **04-90-34-15-59**), located on the Place Pourtoules, just behind the Théâtre Antique.

If you're **driving** to Orange from Paris, take A6 south to Lyon, then connect with A7 into Orange. The 425-mile drive takes 5¹/₂ to 6¹/₂ hours.

VISITOR INFORMATION   The **Office de Tourisme** is on cours Aristide-Briand (☎ **04-90-34-70-88**).

SPECIAL EVENTS   From mid-July to mid-August, a drama, dance, and music festival called **Les Chorégies d'Orange** takes place at the Théâtre Antique, one of the most historically evocative ancient theaters in Europe. For information or tickets, visit the permanent office on place Sylvain, adjacent to the antique theater; or call ☎ **04-90-34-24-24;** or log onto www.choregies.asso.fr. Recent events here have included *Tristan und Isolde* (presented in vocal and orchestral form, but without costumes), *Turandot,* and *Lucia di Lammermoor.* The blockbuster event of 1999 involved presentations of both *Norma* and *La Traviata.* There are only six performances throughout the entire month-long festival.

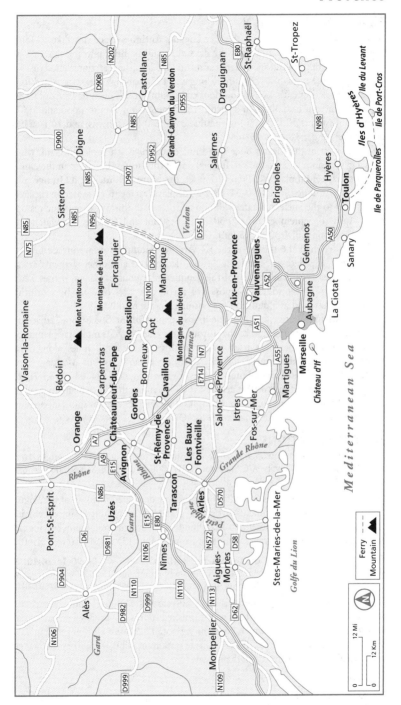

Ferry
Mountain

12 Mi
12 Km

EXPLORING THE TOWN

In the southern part of town, the ✪ **Théâtre Antique,** place des Frères-Mounet (☎ **04-90-51-17-60**), dates from the days of Augustus. Built into the side of a hill, it once held 8,000 spectators in tiered seats divided into three sections based on class. Carefully restored, the nearly 350-foot-long and 125-foot-high theater is noted for its fine acoustics. Today it's used for outdoor entertainment. It's open daily, April to September from 9am to 6:30pm and October to March from 9am to noon and 1:30 to 5pm. Admission is 30 F ($4.80) for adults, 25 F ($4) for students, and 10 F ($1.60) for children under 18.

To the west of the theater once stood one of the biggest temples in Gaul, which, with a gymnasium and the theater, formed one of the greatest buildings in the empire. Across the street on place des Frères-Mounet, the **Musée Municipal d'Orange,** place du Théâtre-Antique (☎ **04-90-51-18-24**), displays fragments excavated in the arena. Your ticket to the ancient theater will also admit you to this museum, which is open daily, April to September from 9:30am to 7:30pm and October to March from 9:30am to noon and 1:30 to 5:30pm.

Even older than the theater is the ✪ **Arc de Triomphe** on avenue de l'Arc-de-Triomphe. It has decayed, but its sculptural decorations and other elements are still fairly well preserved. Built to honor the conquering legions of Caesar, it rises 72 feet and is nearly 70 feet wide. Composed of a trio of arches held up by Corinthian columns, it was used as a dungeon for prisoners in the Middle Ages.

Before leaving Orange, head for the hilltop park, **Colline St-Eutrope,** adjacent to the Théâtre Antique for a view of the surrounding valley with its mulberry plantations.

After exploring the town itself, you can drive south for 8 miles along A9 to **Châteauneuf-du-Pape,** where you can have lunch (any day but Monday) at the **Hostellerie du Château des Fines-Roches,** route d'Avignon (☎ **04-90-83-70-23**). Although it was built in the 19th century, it looks feudal, thanks to its many medieval features. If you're pressing on to Avignon, it's only another 8 miles south along any of at least three highways (each marked AVIGNON).

ACCOMMODATIONS

Hôtel Louvre et Terminus. 89 av. Frédéric-Mistral, 84100 Orange. ☎ **04-90-34-10-08.** Fax 04-90-34-68-71. 32 units. A/C MINIBAR TV TEL. 300–410 F ($48–$65.60) double; 650 F ($104) suite. AE, DC, MC, V. Parking 30 F ($4.80) in garage.

Surrounded by a garden terrace, this conservatively decorated member of the Logis de France chain offers good value. Don't expect grandeur: Everything is simple, efficient, and rather brusque. The hotel also has a modest but worthy restaurant, serving both lunch and dinner. Fixed-price menus cost from 88 F to 135 F ($14.10 to $21.60).

Mercure Orange. 80 rte. de Caderousse, 84100 Orange. ☎ **04-90-34-24-10.** Fax 04-90-34-85-48. 99 units. MINIBAR TV TEL. 490–650 F ($78.40–$104) double. AE, DC, MC, V. Drive ^{1}/$_2$ mile west of the city center, following the directions to Caderousse. Free parking.

This comfortable, modern hotel is in a 20-year-old building whose wings curve around a landscaped courtyard. Its well-furnished rooms are arranged around a series of gardens, the largest of which contains a pool. They were all renovated in 1999. Fixed-price menus are served in the poolside restaurant. This is your best bet for general overnight comfort far from the crowds.

DINING

Le Parvis. 3 cours Pourtoules. ☎ **04-90-34-82-00.** Reservations required. Main courses 65–110 F ($10.40–$17.60); fixed-price menus 128–180 F ($20.50–$28.80). AE, DC, MC, V. Tues–Sun noon–2:30pm; Tues–Sat 7:30–9:15pm. Closed Nov. FRENCH.

Shopping for *Brocante* in Provence

There's a big difference between antiques and fun old junk in France. They even have different names. If you're into serious purchases, you may want to stick to regular and well-established antiques stores, which are found in great abundance all over France, though concentrated mainly in Paris, naturally.

But if you prefer something more affordable, and your idea of fun is a flea market or yard sale, then you really want *brocante*. You'll find brocante throughout France; your best bet is to head to the regular market in town on a specific day (the markets in Cannes are a good example; see chapter 15).

If you find yourself in Provence on a Sunday, head out bright and early (9am) for **Isle-sur-la-Sorgue,** a small village that specializes in brocante. The town is 14 miles east of Avignon, 7 miles north of Cavaillon, and 26 miles south of Orange. There's a brocante market on both Saturday and Sunday, but Sunday is much more fun because there's also a food market. *Warning:* Everything is over by 1pm.

If you're driving, try grabbing a parking space alongside the supermarket, Marché U. The town gets jammed, especially on Sunday. The Sorgue River isn't much bigger than a canal—the heart of town lies on the far side of the river, spanned by many footbridges. The brocante is on the near side of the river, a little farther downstream from the Marché U. If you drive by and shrug at the small number of dealers who are actually outside in the street and on the curb, be aware that every building on the side of the street facing the river hosts a warehouse filled with more dealers and more loot.

Although the prices here aren't the lowest in France, this is a serious market. The market and stores offer top goods, frequently sold to dealers, and shipping can be arranged.

For lunch, there's (surprisingly for such a small place) a Michelin-starred restaurant: **La Prévôté,** 4 rue J.-J.-Rousseau (☎ **04-90-38-57-29**). You should make your reservation even before arriving in town. In the rear of a flower-filled courtyard, chef Roland Mercier wows shoppers and locals with sublime cuisine. His cannelloni filled with fresh salmon and goat cheese is reason enough to cross the river. His tender and perfectly cooked duckling is flavored with honey from bees that flew over Provençal fields of lavender. The pièce de résistance is his hot chocolate tart. Fixed-price menus cost 135 F to 320 F ($21.60 to $51.20) at lunch, and 230 F to 320 F ($36.80 to $51.20) at dinner. Closed November, Sunday nights from October to June, and Mondays year-round.

Jean-Michel Berengier sets the best table in Orange, though the dining room is rather austere. He bases his cuisine not only on well-selected vegetables but also on the best ingredients from "mountain or sea." Try his escalope of braised sea bass with fennel or asparagus or his roasted sea bass with bacon and celeriac. A year-round can't-miss dish is the foie gras, which could be flavorfully followed by lamb whose preparation varies according to the season. (The staff prides itself on dozens of preparations.) The service is efficient and polite. A special children's menu is offered for 60 F ($9.60).

NEARBY ACCOMMODATIONS & DINING

✪ **Château de Rochegude.** 26790 Rochegude. ☎ **04-75-97-21-10.** Fax 04-75-04-89-87. www.chateauderochegude.com. 29 units. A/C MINIBAR TV TEL. 700–2,000 F ($112–$320) double; 2,000–3,000 F ($320–$480) suite. AE, DC, MC, V. Closed Jan–Feb. Free parking. It lies 8 miles north of Orange; take D976, following the signs toward Gap and Rochegude.

This Relais & Châteaux stands on 25 acres of parkland. The stone castle is at the edge of a hill, surrounded by Rhône vineyards. The 12th-century turreted residence has been renovated by a series of distinguished owners, ranging from the pope to the dauphin. The current owners have made many 20th-century additions, but ancient touches still survive. Each room is done in a traditional Provençal style, with fabrics and furniture influenced by the region's 18th- and 19th-century traditions. As befits a château, bedrooms come in many shapes and sizes, some quite spacious. Each has a sumptuous bed with quality mattresses, fine linen, and elegant fabrics.

Dining: The food and service are exceptional. You can enjoy meals surrounded by flowering plants in the stately dining room. There are also a barbecue by the pool and sunny terraces where refreshments are served. In the restaurant, fixed-price menus range from 200 F to 550 F ($32 to $88). This latter is for a dining experience richly highlighted by truffles.

2 Avignon

425 miles S of Paris, 50 miles NW of Aix-en-Provence, 66 miles NW of Marseille

In the 14th century, Avignon was the capital of Christendom. The pope lived here during what the Romans called the Babylonian Captivity. The legacy left by that court of splendor and magnificence makes Avignon one of the most interesting and beautiful of Europe's medieval cities.

Today this walled city of some 100,000 residents is a major stopover on the route from Paris to the Mediterranean. Lately, it has become increasingly known as a cultural center. Artists and painters in growing numbers have been moving here, especially to rue des Teinturiers. Experimental theaters, painting galleries, and cinemas have brought increasing diversity to the inner city. The popes are long gone, but life goes on exceedingly well.

ESSENTIALS

GETTING THERE   There's frequent **train** service to Avignon. The TGV trains from Paris arrive at the Gare SNCF, on the bd. Saint-Roche, 21 times per day (trip time: 3^1/$_2$ hours), and 12 trains per day arrive from Marseille (trip time: 1^1/$_2$ hours). For rail information and schedules, call ☎ **08-36-35-35-35.** Avignon is also a junction for **buses** coming from areas throughout the region. For bus information, contact the Gare Routière, bd. St-Michel (☎ **04-90-82-07-35**).

If you're **driving** to Avignon from Paris, take A6 south to Lyon; once there, follow A7 south to Avignon.

VISITOR INFORMATION   The **Office de Tourisme** is at 41 cours Jean-Jaurès (☎ **04-32-76-32-74**).

SPECIAL EVENTS   The biggest celebration is the famous Festival d'Avignon, held annually over 3 weeks in July. Groups from all over the world are attracted to the festival, which focuses on avant-garde theater, dance, and music. Part of the fun is the bacchanalia that takes place nightly in the streets. Predictably, the prices for hotel rooms and meals skyrocket, so reservations must be made far in advance. Local authorities also crack down on festival-induced vagrancy. For information about dates, tickets, and cultural venues, contact the **Bureaux du Festival,** 8 bis rue de Mons, 84000 Avignon (☎ **04-90-27-66-50**).

Avignon

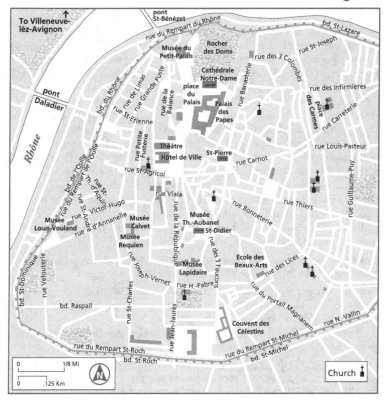

SEEING THE SIGHTS

Even more famous than the papal residency is the ditty *"Sur le pont d'Avignon, l'on y danse, l'on y danse,"* echoing through every French nursery and around the world. Ironically, **pont St-Bénézet** was far too narrow for the *danse* of the rhyme. Spanning the Rhône and connecting Avignon with Villeneuve-lèz-Avignon, the bridge is now a fragmented ruin, with only four of its original 22 arches. According to legend, it was inspired by a vision a shepherd named Bénézet had while tending his flock. Actually, the bridge was built between 1177 and 1185 and suffered various disasters from then on. (In 1669 half the bridge toppled into the river.) On one of the piers is the two-story **Chapelle St-Nicolas**—one story in Romanesque style, the other in Gothic. The remains of the bridge are open daily from 9am to 6:30pm. Admission is 18 F ($2.90) for adults and 9 F ($1.45) for students and seniors.

✪ **Palais des Papes.** Place du Palais. ☎ **04-90-27-50-74.** Admission 45 F ($7.20) adults; 36 F ($5.75) students, children, and seniors. 10 F ($1.60) supplement for special exhibitions. Apr–Oct, daily 9am–7pm (until 9pm in July); Nov–Mar, daily 9:30am–5:45pm (till 6:30pm last 2 weeks of Mar). Guided tours in English given whenever there's enough demand, for 45 F ($7.20) adults, 36 F ($5.75) children and students.

Dominating Avignon from a hilltop is one of the most famous, or notorious (depending on your point of view), palaces in the Christian world. Headquarters of a schismatic group of cardinals who came close to toppling the authority of the popes in

Rome (see the box on "A Tale of Two Papal Cities"), this combination fortress-showplace is the monument most frequently associated with Avignon. You're shown through on a guided tour (usually lasting 50 minutes), which can be somewhat monotonous, as most of the rooms have been stripped of their once-legendary finery. The exception is the **Chapelle St-Jean,** known for its beautiful frescoes attributed to the school of Matteo Giovanetti and painted between 1345 and 1348. These frescoes present scenes from the life of John the Baptist and John the Evangelist. More Giovanetti frescoes can be found above the Chapelle St-Jean in the Chapelle St-Martial. The frescoes depict the miracles of St. Martial, the patron saint of Limousin.

The **Grand Tinel** (banquet hall) is about 135 feet long and 30 feet wide; the pope's table stood on the southern side. The **pope's bedroom** is on the first floor of the Tour des Anges. Its walls are entirely decorated in tempera foliage on which birds and squirrels perch. Birdcages are painted in the recesses of the windows. In a secular vein, the **Studium (Stag Room)**—the study of Clement VI—was frescoed in 1343 with hunting scenes. Added under the same Clement, who had a taste for grandeur, the **Grande Audience** (Great Audience Hall) contains frescoes of the prophets, also attributed to Giovanetti and painted in 1352.

Cathédrale Notre-Dame des Doms. Place du Palais. ☎ 04-90-86-81-01. Free admission. Hours vary with religious ceremonies, but are generally daily 9am to 6pm.

Near the palace is the 12th-century Cathédrale Notre-Dame des Doms, containing the Flamboyant Gothic tomb of some of the apostate popes. Crowning the top is a gilded statue of the Virgin from the 19th century.

From the cathedral, enter the **promenade du Rocher-des-Doms** to stroll through its garden and enjoy the view across the Rhône to Villeneuve-lèz-Avignon.

✪ **La Fondation Angladon-Dubrujeaud.** 5 rue Laboureur. ☎ 04-90-82-29-03. Admission 30 F ($4.80) adults, 20 F ($3.20) students and ages 14–18, 10 F ($1.60) ages 7–13, free for children under 7. Tues–Sun 1–6:30pm (until 6pm off-season).

It's been decades since the death of Jacques Doucet, the belle époque dandy, dilettante, and renowned designer of Parisian haute couture, but his magnificent collection of art is now on view to the general public. When not designing, Doucet collected the early works of a number of young artists, among them Picasso, Braque, Max Jacob, and Marcel Duchamp. Today you can wander through Doucet's former abode, viewing canvases by Cézanne, Sisley, Degas, and Modigliani (with his pink-shirted woman); rare antiques; 16th-century Buddhas; and Louis XVI chairs designed by Jacob. Doucet died in 1929 at the age of 76, his fortune so diminished that his nephew paid for his funeral, but his rich legacy lives on here.

Musée Calvet. 65 rue Joseph-Vernet. ☎ 04-90-86-33-84. Admission 30 F ($4.80) adults, 15 F ($2.40) students, free for children 17 and under. June–Sept, Wed–Mon 10am–7pm; Oct–May, Wed–Mon 10am–1pm and 2–6pm.

Housed in an 18th-century mansion, the fine- and decorative-arts collections feature the works of Vernet, David, Corot, Manet, and Soutine, plus the most extensive collection of ancient silverware in provincial museums. Our favorite oil is by Brueghel the Younger, *Le Cortège nuptial (The Bridal Procession)*. Look for a copy of Bosch's *Adoration of the Magi* as well.

Musée Lapidaire. 18 rue de la République. ☎ 04-90-85-75-38. Admission 10 F ($1.60) adults, 5 F (80¢) students 12–18, free for children. Wed–Mon 10am–1pm and 2–6pm.

Housed in a 17th-century Jesuit church is this important collection of Gallo-Roman sculptures. This museum has been called a veritable junkyard of antiquity. Gargoyles,

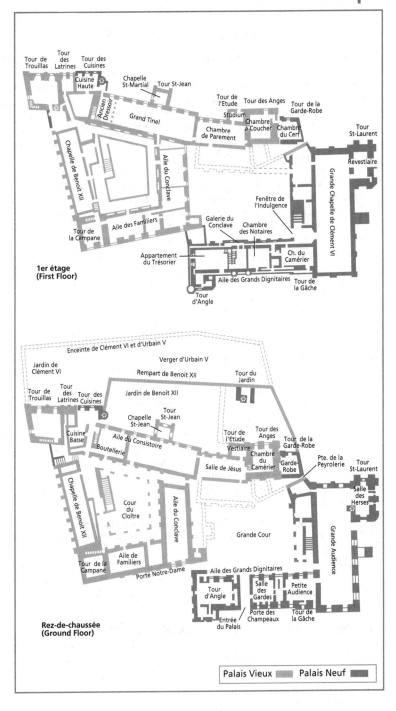

**1er étage
(First Floor)**

Tour de Trouillas
Tour des Latrines
Tour des Cuisines
Cuisine Haute
Chapelle St-Martial
Tour St-Jean
Ancien Dressoir
Grand Tinel
Tour de l'Etude
Tour des Anges
Tour de la Garde-Robe
Studium
Chambre à Coucher
Chambre du Cerf
Tour St-Laurent
Chambre de Parement
Revestiaire
Chapelle de Benoit XII
Aile du Conclave
Grande Chapelle de Clément VI
Fenêtre de l'Indulgence
Tour de la Campane
Aile des Familiers
Galerie du Conclave
Chambre des Notaires
Appartement du Trésorier
Ch. du Camérier
Tour d'Angle
Aile des Grands Dignitaires
Tour de la Gâche

**Rez-de-chaussée
(Ground Floor)**

Enceinte de Clément VI et d'Urbain V
Jardin de Clément VI
Verger d'Urbain V
Rempart de Benoit XII
Tour du Jardin
Tour de Trouillas
Tour des Latrines
Tour des Cuisines
Jardin de Benoit XII
Cuisine Basse
Chapelle St-Jean
Tour St-Jean
Aile du Consistoire
Boutellerie
Tour de l'Etude
Tour des Anges
Tour de la Garde-Robe
Vestiaire
Chambre du Camérier
Garde-Robe
Pte. de la Peyrolerie
Tour St-Laurent
Salle de Jésus
Salle des Herses
Chapelle de Benoit XII
Cour du Cloître
Aile du Conclave
Grande Cour
Grande Audience
Tour de la Campane
Aile de Familiers
Porte Notre-Dame
Aile des Grands Dignitaires
Tour d'Angle
Salle des Gardes
Petite Audience
Entrée du Palais
Porte des Champeaux
Tour de la Gâche

Palais Vieux   Palais Neuf

469

A Tale of Two Papal Cities

In 1309, an ill Pope Clement V arrived in Avignon and prepared to live out the rest of his days here as a guest of the Dominicans, making him the first of seven consecutive popes to live here, rather than in Rome. Clement was succeeded in the spring of 1314 by John XXII, who, unlike the previous Roman popes, chose to live modestly in the Episcopal Palace. When Benedict XII took over, he enlarged and rebuilt the palace. Clement VI, who followed, built an even more elaborate extension called the New Palace. During the 70 years that the papacy resided in Avignon, art and culture flourished—as did vice. Prostitutes blatantly went about peddling their wares in front of cardinals, rich merchants were robbed, and innocent pilgrims from the hinterlands were brutally tricked and swindled. The ramparts (still standing) around Avignon were built at this time. They are characterized by their machicolated battlements, turrets, and old gates.

Pope Gregory XI, who succeeded Urban V in 1362, built no shrines to himself in Avignon. Instead, he returned the papacy to Rome in 1378, setting off the Great Schism, during which one pope ruled in Rome and another (often referred to as an antipope) ruled in Avignon. The Schism continued for four popes and four antipopes until the 1417 election of Martin V produced an undisputed pope.

Gallic and Roman statues, and broken pillars confront you at every turn. Of course, most of these pieces have known greater glory and placement (often in temples), so you'll have to use your imagination to conjure up the full splendor they once enjoyed.

Musée Louis-Vouland. 17 rue Victor-Hugo. ☎ **04-90-86-03-79.** Admission 20 F ($3.20) adults, 10 F ($1.60) students. May–Oct, Tues–Sat 10am–noon and 2–6pm; Nov–Apr, Tues–Sat 2–6pm.

This collection, devoted to 17th- and 18th-century fine arts, is housed in a 19th-century mansion that opens onto a lovely garden. Avignon's greatest treasure trove of lavish antiques and objets d'art includes Sèvres porcelain, the comtesse du Barry's tea set, great tapestries from Aubusson and Gobelin, Persian rugs, antique clocks, glittering chandeliers, and commodes to equal those at Versailles. Our favorites are the Louis XV inkpots with silver rats holding the lids.

Musée du Petit-Palais. Place du Palais. ☎ **04-90-86-44-58.** Admission 30 F ($4.80) adults, 15 F ($2.40) students, free for children 18 and under. Wed–Mon 9:30am–1pm and 2–5:30pm.

The museum contains an important collection of paintings from the Italian schools from the 13th to the 16th centuries, including works from Florence, Venice, Siena, and Lombardy. In addition, salons display 15th-century paintings done in Avignon, and several galleries are devoted to Roman and Gothic sculptures.

STEPPING BACK IN TIME IN VILLENEUVE-LÈZ-AVIGNON

The modern world is impinging on Avignon, but across the Rhône at Villeneuve-lèz-Avignon the Middle Ages slumber on. When the popes lived in exile at Avignon, wealthy cardinals built palaces (*livrées*) across the river. Many visitors prefer to stay or dine here rather than in Avignon.

In addition to the sights below, you might visit the **Église Notre-Dame,** place Meissonier, founded in 1333 by Cardinal Arnaud de Via. Its proudest possession is a

14th-century ivory Virgin, one of the great French treasures. It's open April to September from 10am to 12:30pm and 3 to 7pm, and October to March from 10am to noon and 2 to 5:30pm. From mid-September to mid-June, it's closed on Mondays. It's closed through February. Admission is free, but to visit its cloisters, adults must pay 7 F ($1.10); students and ages 12 to 17 pay 5 F (80¢).

Chartreuse du Val-de-Bénédiction. 60 rue de la République. ☎ **04-90-15-24-24.** Admission 32 F ($5.10) adults, free for children 18 and under. Daily 9am–6:30pm.

Inside France's largest Carthusian monastery, built in 1352, you'll find a church, three cloisters, rows of cells that housed the medieval monks, and rooms depicting aspects of their daily lives. Part of the complex is devoted to a publicly and privately endowed workshop (the Centre National d'Écritures et du Spectacle) for painters and writers who live in the monastic cells rent-free for up to a year to pursue their craft. Exhibitions of photography and painting are presented throughout the year.

Pope Innocent VI (whose tomb you can view) founded this charterhouse, which became the country's most powerful. Inside one of the chapels, a remarkable *Coronation of the Virgin* by Enguerrand Charonton is enshrined; painted in 1453, the masterpiece contains a fringed bottom that's Bosch-like in its horror, representing the denizens of hell. The 12th-century graveyard cloister is lined with cells where the former fathers prayed and meditated.

Fort St-André. Mont Andaon. ☎ **04-90-25-45-35.** Admission 25 F ($4) adults, 15 F ($2.40) students and ages 18–25, free for children under 17. Apr–Sept 9, daily 10am–1pm and 2–6pm; Oct–Mar, daily 10am–1pm and 2–5pm.

Crowning the town is the Fort St-André, founded in 1360 by Jean-le-Bon to serve as a symbol of might to the pontifical powers across the river. The Abbaye St-André, now privately owned, was installed in the 18th century. You can visit the formal garden encircling the mansion, a tranquil setting with a rose-trellis colonnade, fountains, and flowers.

Tour Philippe le Bel. Rue Montée-de-la-Tour. ☎ **04-90-27-49-68.** Admission 10 F ($1.60) adults, 6 F (95¢) students and ages 12–17, free for children 12 and under. Apr–Sept, daily 10am–12:30pm and 3–7pm; Oct–Mar, Tues–Sun 10am–12:30pm and 3–7pm. Closed Feb.

The tower was constructed by Philippe the Fair in the 13th century, when Villeneuve became a French possession; it served as a gateway to the kingdom standing at the intersection of avenue Gabriel-Péri. If you're game and have the stamina, you can climb to the top for a panoramic view of Avignon and the Rhône Valley.

SHOPPING

Since the 1960s, **Antiquités Bourret,** 5 rue Limas (☎ **04-90-86-65-02**), has earned a reputation as a repository for 18th- and 19th-century Provençal antiques. **Véronique Pichon,** place Crillon (☎ **04-90-85-89-00**), is the newest branch of a porcelain manufacturer whose colorful products have been a regional fixture since the 1700s. Manufactured in the nearby town of Uzès, the tableware, decorative urns, statues, and lamps are priced well enough to be shipped virtually anywhere.

The Avignon branch of **Les Olivades,** 28 rue des Marchants (☎ **04-90-86-13-42**), is one of the most visible of a chain of outlets associated in the States with Pierre Deux. Look for fabrics by the yard, bedcovers, slipcovers, draperies, and tablecloths. The fabrics, printed in a factory only 6 miles from Avignon, feature intricate designs in colors inspired by 19th-century models as well as Créole designs with butterflies, pineapples, bananas, and flowers. The idea behind **Les Indiens de Nîmes,** 4 rue Joseph-Vernet (☎ **04-90-86-32-05**), is to duplicate 18th- and 19th-century

Provençal fabric patterns. They're sold by the meter as well as in clothing for men, women, and children. Also available are kitchenware and a selection of furniture inspired by Provence and the steamy wetlands west of Marseille.

The clothing at **Souleiado,** 5 rue Joseph-Vernet (☎ **04-90-86-47-67**), derives from a Provençal model, and even the Provençal name (meaning "first ray of sunshine after a storm") evokes a spirit on which the owners want to capitalize. Most, but not all, of the clothing is for women. Fabrics are also sold by the meter.

Hervé Baume, 19 rue Petite Fusterie (☎ **04-90-86-37-66**), is for those who'd like to set a table like that encountered in Provence. This place is stocked with merchandise including such modern classics as handblown crystal hurricane lamps. The place is piled high with a little bit of everything—from Directoire dinner services to French folk art.

Jaffier-Parsi, 42 rue des Fourbisseurs (☎ **04-90-86-08-85**), is known for its copper saucepans shipped from the Norman town of Villedieu-les-Poêles, which has been making them since the Middle Ages.

If you're desperate for a pot-bellied tureen for your *aïgo boulido,* that regional garlic soup, head for **Terre è provence,** 26 rue République (☎ **04-90-85-56-45**). You can also pick up wonderful kitsch here—perhaps terra-cotta plates decorated with three-dimensional cicadas.

ACCOMMODATIONS
VERY EXPENSIVE

✪ **La Mirande.** 4 place Amirande, 84000 Avignon. ☎ **04-90-85-93-93.** Fax 04-90-86-26-85. www.la-mirande.fr. E-mail: mirande@la-mirande.fr. 20 units. A/C MINIBAR TV TEL. 1,700–2,600 F ($272–$416) double; 3,700 F ($592) suite. AE, DC, V.

In the heart of Avignon (behind the Palais des Papes), this restored 700-year-old town house is one of France's grand little luxuries, far better than anything else in town. The hotel treats you to 2 centuries of decorative art: from the 1700s Salon Chinois to the Salon Rouge, its striped walls in Rothschild red. In 1987 the house was acquired by Achim and Hannelore Stein, who, with their son and daughter and a Paris decorator, transformed it into a citadel of opulence. The most sought-out room is no. 20, whose lavish decor opens directly onto the garden. But all the rooms are stunning, with huge bathtubs. The exquisite taste of the decorators is reflected in every individually designed bedroom, most of which are quite spacious. Rooms have bedside controls, hand-printed fabrics on the walls, antiques, and art, along with deluxe mattresses and fine linens.

Dining: The restaurant, among the finest in Avignon, deserves its one Michelin star. Chef Daniel Hébet has a light, sophisticated touch, with fixed-price menus at 240 F to 480 F ($38.40 to $76.80). The restaurant is open every day between June and September for both lunch and dinner. From October to May, it's closed every Tuesday, all day, and every Wednesday at lunch.

Amenities: Room service, concierge, laundry/dry cleaning.

EXPENSIVE

Hôtel d'Europe. 12 place Grillon, 84000 Avignon. ☎ **04-90-14-76-76.** Fax 04-90-85-43-66. www.hotel-d-europe.fr. E-mail: reservations@hotel-d-europe.fr. 47 units. A/C TV TEL. 690–2,200 F ($110.40–$352) double; 3,000–3,300 F ($480–$528) suite. AE, DC, MC, V. Parking 60 F ($9.60).

The vine-covered Hôtel d'Europe has been in operation since 1799. You enter through a courtyard, where tables are set in the warmer months. The grand hall and salons boast tastefully arranged antiques and decorative elements. The good-size guest rooms have handsome decorations and period furnishings. Three suites are perched on the roof with views of the Palais des Papes. In some twin-bedded rooms the beds are a bit narrow. But overall, beds are comfortable, with touches of Gallic charm.

Dining: Its restaurant, La Vieille Fontaine, is one of the best and most distinguished in Avignon. Meals are served in elegant dining rooms or a charming inner courtyard. Fixed-price menus cost 285 F to 420 F ($45.60 to $67.20). The wine list is impressive but celestial in price.

Amenities: Business services, room service, laundry/dry cleaning, swimming pool; tennis can be arranged.

MODERATE

✪ **Clarion Hotel Cloître Saint-Louis.** 20 rue Portail Boquier, 84000 Avignon. ☎ 04-90-27-55-55. Fax 04-90-82-24-01. www.cloitre-saint-louis.com. E-mail: hotel@cloitre-saint-louis.com. 80 units. A/C MINIBAR TV TEL. 550–1,300 F ($88–$208) double; 1,000–1,700 F ($160–$272) suite. AE, MC, V.

This unusual hotel is housed in a former Jesuit school that was built in the late 1580s. Today, much of the original premises remain, including the grand baroque facade, the wrap-around arcades, and the soaring ceiling vaults. It's amazing to think about all the hammering and drumming that went into constructing this venerable building. Public areas have many of the original, intensely vertical lines. Bedrooms are more functional, however; they're the rather dull-looking result of several severe renovations. Some have sliding glass doors overlooking the patio. Outbuildings and new constructions include a chapel from 1611, and a new wing designed by world-class architect Jean Nouvel, whose most visible triumph was the new wing of Paris's Institut du Monde Arabe. Rooms range from medium to spacious in size; each has sleek modern lines without a lot of frilly extras.

INEXPENSIVE

Hôtel d'Angleterre. 29 bd. Raspail, 84000 Avignon. ☎ 04-90-86-34-31. Fax 04-90-86-86-74. www.hotelangleterre.fr. 40 units, 39 with bathroom. TV TEL. 190 F ($30.40) double without bathroom, 300–360 F ($48–$57.60) double with bathroom. DC, MC, V. Closed Dec 20–Jan 20. Free parking.

In the heart of Avignon, this Art Deco structure is the city's best budget hotel. The rooms are comfortably but basically furnished. Breakfast is the only meal served.

Hôtel Danieli. 17 rue de la République, 84000 Avignon. ☎ 04-90-86-46-82. Fax 04-90-27-09-24. www.avignonetprovence.com/fr/danieli. 29 units. TV TEL. 320–470 F ($51.20–$75.20) double. AE, DC, MC, V. Parking 50 F ($8).

This hotel's Italian influence is clear in its arches, chiseled stone, tile floors, and baronial stone staircase. Built during the reign of Napoléon I, it's classified as a historic monument in its own right. Its small, informal public rooms are outfitted mostly in antiques acquired by the history-conscious owner. The guest rooms, however, have mostly painted bamboo furnishings. Unless special arrangements are made for a group (and this hotel accepts many), breakfast is the only meal served.

Hôtel de l'Atelier. 5 rue de la Foire, 30400 Villeneuve-lèz-Avignon. ☎ 04-90-25-01-84. Fax 04-90-25-80-06. E-mail: hotel.latelier@libertisurf.fr. 19 units. TV TEL. 250–460 F ($40–$73.60) double. AE, DC, MC, V. Free parking on street, 25 F ($4) in nearby garage.

Villeneuve's budget offering is this 16th-century village house that has preserved much of its original style. Inside is a tiny duplex lounge with a large stone fireplace. Outside, a sun-filled rear garden, with potted orange and fig trees, provides fruit for breakfast. The immaculate accommodations are comfortable and informal, but a bit dowdy. In the old bourgeois dining room, a continental breakfast is the only meal served.

DINING

Brunel. 46 rue de La Balance. ☎ **04-90-85-24-83.** Reservations required. Main courses 140–182 F ($22.40–$29.10); fixed-price menus 158–380 F ($25.30–$60.80). MC, V. Mon–Sat noon–1:30pm; Tues–Sat 7:30–9:30pm. PROVENÇAL.

This elegant, air-conditioned, flower-filled restaurant is in the historic heart of Avignon. Managed by the Brunel family, it offers such specialties as warm pâté of duckling and breast of duckling with apples. The chef prepares a superb plate of wild mushroom–stuffed ravioli served with roasted foie gras. The grilled John Dory is accompanied by artichoke hearts, and even the lowly pigs' feet emerge with a sublime taste. The desserts are excellent and prepared fresh daily. Feel free to order house wines by the carafe.

✪ **Christian Etienne.** 10 rue Mons. ☎ **04-90-86-16-50.** Reservations recommended. Main courses 170–210 F ($27.20–$33.60); fixed-price menus 170–500 F ($27.20–$80). AE, DC, MC, V. Jan–June and Aug–Dec, Tues–Fri noon–2:30pm and 7:30–10:30pm, Sat–Sun 8–10:30pm; July, daily noon–2:30pm and 8–10:30pm. PROVENÇAL.

The stone house containing this restaurant was built in 1180, around the same time as the Palais des Papes (next door). The owner, Christian Etienne, continues to reach new culinary heights. Understandably, he's become the star chef of Avignon. His dining room contains early 15th-century frescoes honoring the marriage of Anne de Bretagne to the French king in 1491. Several of the fixed-price menus present specific themes: The two 320 F ($51.20) menus feature only tomatoes or vegetables, respectively; the 430 F ($68.80) menu offers preparations of lobster; and the 500 F ($80) menu relies on the chef's discretion (*menu confiance*) to come up with unique combinations. Note for strict vegetarians: The vegetable menus are among the most creative of their kind but aren't completely devoid of meat. They're flavored with small amounts of meat or fish or, sometimes, meat drippings. In summer, look for a vegetable menu where every course is based on ripe tomatoes; the main course is a mousse of lamb, eggplants, tomatoes, and herbs. À la carte specialties include fillet of red snapper with a black-olive coulis, rack of lamb with fresh thyme and garlic essence, and a dessert specialty of fennel sorbet with saffron-flavored English cream sauce.

Hiély-Lucullus. 5 rue de la République. ☎ **04-90-86-17-07.** Reservations required. Fixed-price menus 130–220 F ($20.80–$35.20). MC, V. Thurs–Mon noon–1:30pm; Wed–Mon 7:30–9:30pm. Closed 1 week in June and 2 weeks in Jan. FRENCH.

Before the arrival of Christian Etienne, this Relais Gourmand used to reign supreme in Avignon. It's still going strong and richly deserves its star, even if it's no longer as trendy as it was. The town's most fabled chef, Pierre Hiély, has retired, though he drops in occasionally to check on how his former sous chef, André Chaussy, is doing. He's doing just fine and is still offering those reasonably priced fixed-price menus (no à la carte). You'll find a similar culinary style, with occasional creative touches. Try one of his special appetizers, like *petite marmite du pêcheur,* a savory fish soup ringed with black mussels. A main-dish specialty is *pintadeau* (young guinea hen) with peaches, roasted salted cod fish with olive oil, and juniper berries. The *pièce de résistance* is *agneau des Alpilles grillé* (grilled alpine lamb). Carafe wines include Tavel Rosé and Châteauneuf-du-Pape.

La Fourchette. 7 rue Racine. ☎ **04-90-85-20-93.** Fixed-price menus 100–150 F ($16–$24) at lunch, 150 F ($24) at dinner. MC, V. Mon–Fri 12:30–2pm and 7:30–9:30pm. Closed Aug 5–29. FRENCH.

This bistro offers creative cooking at a moderate price. There are two dining rooms, one like a summer house with walls of glass, the other more like a tavern with oak beams. You might begin with fresh sardines flavored with citrus, ravioli filled with haddock, or a parfait of chicken livers with a spinach flan and a confiture of onions. For a main course we'd recommend the blanquette of monkfish with endives or daube of beef prepared in the local style with a gratin of macaroni.

AVIGNON AFTER DARK

Near the Palais des Papes is **Le Grand Café,** La Manutention (☎ **04-90-86-86-77**), a restaurant/bar/cafe that might quickly become your favorite watering hole. The dancing standby is **Les Ambassadeurs,** 27 rue Bancasse (☎ **04-90-86-31-55**), which is more animated than its more subdued competitor, **Piano Bar Le Blues,** 25 rue Carnot (☎ **04-90-85-79-71**); the cover at both is 10 F ($2). Near Le Blues is a restaurant, **Red Zone,** 27 rue Carnot (☎ **04-90-27-02-44**), whose bar area is the site of live performances from whatever band happens to be in town.

Winning the award for having the most unpronounceable name is **Le Woolloomoolloo** (it means "Black Kangaroo" in an Aboriginal dialect of Australia), 16 bis rue des Teinturiers (☎ **04-90-85-28-44**). Here a bar and cafe complement a separate room devoted to the cuisine of France and a changing roster of cuisines from Asia, Africa, and South America. An alternative choice is **Bokao's Café,** 9 quai St-Lazare (☎ **04-90-82-47-95**), which offers both a restaurant and a disco as diversions during long sultry nights in Avignon. The most viable option for lesbians and gays is **L'Esclav,** 12 rue de Limas (☎ **04-90-85-14-91**), a bar and disco that's the focal point of the city's gay community.

3 St-Rémy-de-Provence

438 miles S of Paris, 16 miles NE of Arles, 12 miles S of Avignon, 8 miles N of Les Baux

Nostradamus, the famous French physician/astrologer, was born here in 1503. Although he has many fans today, he does have detractors, like those who denounce the astrologer and his more than 600 obscure verses as psychotic.

St-Rémy is more closely associated with van Gogh. He committed himself to an asylum here in 1889 after cutting off his left ear. Between moods of despair, he painted such works as *Olive Trees* and *Cypresses.*

Come to sleepy St-Rémy today not only for its memories and sights but also for a glimpse of small-town Provençal life that you won't find in Aix or Avignon. It's a market town of considerable charm that draws the occasional visiting celebrity trying to escape the spotlight.

ESSENTIALS

GETTING THERE   Local **buses** from Avignon take 45 minutes and cost around 36 F ($5.75) one-way. In St-Rémy, buses pull into the place de la République, in the town center. For bus information and schedules, call ☎ **04-90-14-59-00.**

If you're **driving,** head south from Avignon along D571.

VISITOR INFORMATION   The **Office de Tourisme** is on place Jean-Jaurès (☎ **04-90-92-05-22**).

SEEING THE SIGHTS

Monastère St-Paul-de-Mausolée. Av. Edgar-le-Roy. ☎ **04-90-92-77-00.** Admission 15 F ($2.40) adults, 10 F ($1.60) students and ages 12–16, free for children under 12. Cloisters, June–Sept, Tues–Sun 9:30am–6:30pm; Oct–May, Tues–Fri 11am–5pm.

You can visit the 12th-century cloisters of the asylum van Gogh made famous in his paintings. Now a psychiatric hospital, the former monastery is east of D5, a short drive north of Glanum (see below). You can't visit the cell where the artist was confined from 1889 to 1890, but it's still worth coming here to explore the Romanesque chapel and cloisters with their circular arches and columns, which have beautifully carved capitals. On your way to the church, you'll see a bust of van Gogh.

Musée Archéologique. In the Hôtel de Sade, rue du Parage. ☎ **04-90-92-64-04.** Admission 20 F ($3.20) adults, 15 F ($2.40) students 12–17, free for children 11 and under. Jan, by appointment only; Feb–Mar, daily 10am–noon and 2–5pm; Apr–Sept, daily 10am–noon and 2–7pm; Oct–Dec, daily 10am–noon and 2–5pm.

In the center of St-Rémy, the Musée Archéologique displays both sculptures and bronzes from the ancient Roman excavations at nearby Glanum.

Ruines de Glanum. Av. Vincent-van-Gogh (a mile south of St-Rémy on D5). ☎ **04-90-92-23-79.** Admission 32 F ($5.10) adults, 21 F ($3.35) students and ages 12–25, free for children 11 and under. Apr–Sept, daily 9am–7pm; Oct–Mar, daily 9am–noon and 2–5pm. From the town center, follow the signs to Les Antiques.

A Gallo-Roman settlement thrived here during the final days of the Roman Empire. Its historic monuments include a triumphal arch dating from the time of Julius Caesar, and a cenotaph called the Mausolée des Jules. Garlanded with sculptured fruits and flowers, the arch dates from 20 B.C. and is the oldest in Provence. The mausoleum was raised to honor the grandsons of Augustus and is the only extant monument of its type. In the area are entire streets and foundations of private residences from the 1st-century town. Some remains are from a Gallo-Greek town from the 2nd century B.C.

ACCOMMODATIONS

✪ **Château de Roussan.** Rte. de Tarascon, 13210 St-Rémy-de-Provence. ☎ **04-90-92-11-63.** Fax 04-90-92-50-59. E-mail: chateau.de.roussan@wanadoo.fr. 21 units. TEL. 460–790 F ($73.60–$126.40) double. AE, MC, V.

Although there are other château hotels in the district that are more lavish and stylish, this one is more evocative of another time and place. This château's most famous resident, the Renaissance psychic Nostradamus, lived in a rustic outbuilding a few steps from the front door. Today you pass beneath an archway of 300-year-old trees leading to the neoclassical facade, which was constructed of softly colored local stone in 1701. Most bedrooms are spacious, the mattresses well worn but still comfortable enough. As you wander around the grounds the history here will envelop you, especially when you come on the baroque sculptures lining the basin, fed by a stream. The restaurant, open daily for lunch and dinner, serves fixed-price menus. A fixed-price menu costs 165 F to 180 F ($26.40 to $28.80) each. Be warned that the staff here can be off-putting, but the rampant sense of mysticism and historical importance of the place usually compensates for any Gallic crabbiness they might exhibit.

✪ **Hôtel Château des Alpilles.** Ancienne Rte. du Grès, 13210 St-Rémy-de-Provence. ☎ **04-90-92-03-33.** Fax 04-90-92-45-17. E-mail: chateau.alpilles@wanadoo.fr. 21 units. MINIBAR TV TEL. 1,000–1,250 F ($160–$200) double; 1,520–2,100 F ($243.20–$336) suite. AE, DC, MC, V. Closed Jan 5–Feb 15 and Nov 20–Dec 18.

When she converted this mansion in 1980, Françoise Bon wanted to create a "house for paying friends." When it was built in 1827 by the Pichot family, it housed Chateaubriand and a host of other luminaries. To reach it, you pass beneath the 300-year-old trees that surround the neoclassic exterior. The spacious rooms have combined the best of an antique framework with plush upholstery, rich carpeting, and vibrant colors. Each boasts whimsical accessories, like a pair of porcelain panthers flanking one of the carved mantels, and travertine-trimmed baths with large windows.

Some lie within a gracefully renovated 19th-century annex, and are just as comfortable as those within the main house. Mme Bon has installed an elevator, though you may prefer to descend the massive stone staircase. In the garden the château has an outdoor pool, two tennis courts, a sauna, and a grill where you can order lunch in summer. In the evening, fixed-price menus cost 210 F ($33.60) each.

Hôtel du Soleil. 35 av. Pasteur, 13210 St-Rémy-de-Provence. ☎ **04-90-92-00-63.** Fax 04-90-92-61-07. E-mail: hotelsoleil@pacwan.fr. 24 units. TV TEL. 350–387 F ($56–$61.90) double. AE, DC, MC, V. Free parking.

There's something wonderfully appealing about the masses of ivy that cascade down the facade of this hotel, which is only a 4-minute walk south of the town center. It's set in a pleasant garden with venerable trees and a wrought-iron gazebo. Inside, the rich assortment of ceiling beams and Provençale accessories evokes the region around you. Bedrooms are simple but convenient, with tasteful settings and comfortable beds. You'll want to spend part of your time beside the swimming pool, ringed by chaise longues. Breakfast is the only meal served here.

Les Antiques. 15 av. Pasteur, 13210 St-Rémy-de-Provence. ☎ **04-90-92-03-02.** Fax 04-90-92-50-40. 27 units. MINIBAR TEL. 380–810 F ($60.80–$129.60) double. AE, DC, MC, V. Closed mid-Oct to Mar.

This moderately priced stylish 19th-century villa is in a 7-acre park with a pool. It contains an elegant reception lounge, which opens onto several salons, and all furnishings are Napoléon III. Some of the accommodations are in a private modern pavilion, with direct access to the garden. The rooms are handsomely furnished, usually in pastels and sometimes with flowered wallpapers. Those in the modern pavilion are more comfortable and larger, even though they don't have as much character as those in the main building. In summer you're served breakfast (the only meal) in what used to be the Orangerie.

✪ Vallon de Valrugues. Chemin Canto-Cigalo, 13210 St-Rémy-de-Provence. ☎ **04-90-92-04-40.** Fax 04-90-92-44-01. www.valrugues-cassagne.com. 53 units. MINIBAR TEL. 780–1,650 F ($123–$262) double; 5,300 F ($841) suite. AE, CB, DC, MC, V. Free parking.

Surrounded by a park, this Mediterranean hotel has the best accommodations and restaurant in town. The owners, Françoise and Jean-Michel Gallon, offer beautifully furnished rooms and suites, all with built-in safes. The rooms have recently been enlarged and renovated, with new marble baths.

Dining: The dining terrace alone may compete with the cuisine, which is winning praise for innovative light dishes, such as John Dory with truffles and frozen nougat with a confit of fruits.

Amenities: Pool, tennis courts, sauna, gym, golf putting green. Horseback riding ring with instructors (for which you pay extra).

DINING

Another great dining choice is the restaurant at **Vallon de Valrugues** (see above).

Bar/Hôtel/Restaurant des Arts. 32 bd. Victor-Hugo, 13210 St-Rémy-de-Provence. ☎ **04-90-92-08-50.** Reservations recommended. Main courses 80–140 F ($12.80–$22.40); fixed-price menus 120–145 F ($19.20–$23.20). AE, DC, MC, V. Wed–Mon noon–2pm and 7:30–9:30pm. Closed Feb and Nov 1–12. FRENCH.

This old-style cafe/restaurant evokes the earthy pleasures of *gitanes* and *pastis,* and in many ways it hasn't changed a lot since the days of Albert Camus. The wait for dinner can be as long as 45 minutes, so you may want to spend some time in the bar, with its wooden tables, pine paneling, copper pots, and slightly faded decor. Don't expect cutting-edge cuisine or modern points of view, as everything about this place, including the accents of the all-Provençal staff, is immersed in the Midi of long ago. The menu lists specialties like rabbit terrine, pepper steak with champagne, tournedos with madeira and mushrooms, duckling in orange sauce, and three preparations of trout. *Warning:* Always call before heading here and don't take the opening hours above too literally. The aging owner reserves the right to close whenever she is tired.

La Maison Jaune. 15 rue Carnot. ☎ **04-90-92-56-14.** Reservations recommended. Fixed-price menus 120–305 F ($19.20–$48.80) at lunch, 180–305 F ($28.80–$48.80) at dinner. MC, V. June–Sept, Wed–Sun noon–2pm and Tues–Sun 7:30–9:30pm; Oct–May, Tues–Sat noon–2pm and Mon–Sat 7:30–9:30pm. FRENCH/PROVENÇAL

One of the most competent and enduringly popular restaurants in St-Remy lies within the former home of a wealthy, 18th-century merchant. Today, in a pair of dining rooms scattered over two floors of the yellow-fronted building, you'll appreciate cuisine prepared and served with flair by François and Catherine Perraud. An additional 35 seats are available during clement weather on an outdoor terrace overlooking the Hôtel de Sade. Menu items include pigeon roasted in wine from Les Baux; grilled sardines served with candied lemon and raw fennel; artichoke hearts marinated in white wine and offered with tomatoes; and a succulent version of roasted rack of lamb served with a tapenade of black olives and anchovies.

4 Arles

450 miles S of Paris, 22 miles SW of Avignon, 55 miles NW of Marseille

Arles has been called the soul of Provence. Art lovers, archaeologists, and historians are attracted to this town on the Rhône. Many of its scenes, painted so luminously by van Gogh in his declining years, remain to delight. The great Dutch painter left Paris for Arles in 1888, the same year he cut off part of his left ear. But he was to paint some of his most celebrated works in this Provençal town, including *Starry Night, The Bridge at Arles, Sunflowers,* and *L'Arlésienne.*

The Greeks are said to have founded Arles in the 6th century B.C. Julius Caesar established a Roman colony here in 46 B.C. Under Roman rule, Arles prospered. Constantine the Great named it the second capital of his empire in 306, when it was known as "the little Rome of the Gauls." It wasn't until 1481 that Arles was incorporated into France.

Though Arles doesn't possess quite as much charm as Aix-en-Provence, it's still rewarding to visit, with first-rate museums, excellent restaurants, and summer festivals. The city today isn't quite as lovely as it was when Picasso came here, but it has enough of the antique charm of Provence to keep the appeal alive.

ESSENTIALS
GETTING THERE   Since Arles lies on the Paris-Marseille and the Bordeaux-St-Raphaël rail lines, frequent connections from most cities of France pass through here. Ten **trains** per day arrive from Avignon (trip time: 20 minutes); 10 per day from Marseille (trip time: 1 hour); and 10 per day from Aix-en-Provence (trip time: 1³/₄ hours). For rail information and schedules, call ☎ **08-36-35-35-35.**

There are about four **buses** per day from Aix-en-Provence (trip time: 1³/₄ hours). For bus information and schedules, call ☎ **04-90-49-38-01.**

If you're **driving,** head south along D570 from Avignon.

VISITOR INFORMATION   The **Office de Tourisme,** where you can buy a billet global (see below), is on the esplanade des Lices (☎ **04-90-18-41-20**).

Le Olé

Bullfights in Arles are relatively infrequent, and they don't generate as much excitement or passion as they do in Spain. They are conducted only about five weekends a year, and only between Easter and late September. The bull is killed only on the Easter *corridas* (a cathartic reference to the death of Christ?); otherwise the bull is not killed, making the ritual less bloody than the Spanish version. Most bullfights begin around 5pm, though the Easter event begins at 11am. A seat on the worn stone benches of the Roman amphitheater costs 90 F to 500 F ($14.40 to $80). Tickets are usually available at the amphitheater a few hours before the beginning of every bullfight. For advance ticket sales via credit card, call ☎ **04-90-96-03-70.**

EXPLORING THE TOWN

Go to the tourist office (see "Essentials," above), where you can purchase a **billet global,** the all-inclusive pass that admits you to the town's museums, Roman monuments, and all the major attractions, at a cost of 60 F ($9.60) for adults and 40 F ($6.40) for children.

Arles is full of monuments from Roman times. The general vicinity of the old Roman forum is occupied by **place du Forum,** shaded by plane trees. The Café de Nuit, immortalized by van Gogh, once stood on this square. You can see two Corinthian columns and pediment fragments from a temple at the corner of the Hôtel Nord-Pinus. South of here is **place de la République,** the principal plaza, dominated by a 50-foot-tall blue porphyry obelisk. On the north is the impressive **Hôtel de Ville** (town hall) from 1673, built to Mansart's plans and surmounted by a Renaissance belfry.

The city's two great classical monuments are the **Théâtre Antique,** rue du Cloître (☎ **04-90-49-36-25**), and the Amphitheater (Les Arènes). The Roman theater, begun by Augustus in the 1st century, was mostly destroyed; only two Corinthian columns remain. The theater was where the *Venus of Arles* was discovered in 1651. Take rue de la Calade from the city hall. Admission is 17 F ($2.70) for adults and 12 F ($1.90) for children. It's open daily from 9am to 12:30pm and 2 to 5:30pm.

Nearby, the **Amphitheater (Les Arènes),** rond-point des Arènes (☎ **04-90-49-36-86**), also built in the 1st century, seats almost 25,000 and still hosts bullfights in summer. The government warns you to visit the old monument at your own risk, as the stone steps are uneven, and much of the masonry is worn down to the point where it might be a problem for older travelers or for those with disabilities. For a good view, you can climb the three towers that remain from medieval times, when the amphitheater was turned into a fortress. Both the theater and Les Arènes are open daily, April 1 to September 31 from 10am to 12:30pm and 2 to 4:30pm; the rest of the year, daily from 10 to 11:30am and 2 to 4pm. Admission is 15 F ($2.40) for adults and 9 F ($1.45)for children.

In an isolated position 7$^1/_2$ miles north of Arles, **Les Olivades Factory Store,** chemin des Indienneurs, St-Etienne-du-Grès (☎ **04-90-49-19-19**), sits beside the road leading to Tarascon. Because of the wide array of art objects and fabrics inspired by the traditions of Provence, a trek out here is worth your while. Fabric by the yard, dresses, shirts for men and women, and table linens are all available at retail outlets of the Olivades chain throughout Provence, but the selection here is better and a bit cheaper.

Église St-Trophime. On the east side of place de la République. ☎ **04-90-96-07-38.** Church, free; cloister, 15 F ($2.40) adults, 9 F ($1.45) students and children. Church, daily 8:30–6:30pm; cloister, mid-June to mid-Sept, daily 9am–12:30pm and 2–7pm.

This church is noted for its 12th-century portal, one of the finest achievements of the southern Romanesque style. Frederick Barbarossa was crowned king of Arles here in 1178. In the pediment, Christ is surrounded by the symbols of the Evangelists. The cloister, in both the Gothic and Romanesque styles, is noted for its medieval carvings.

Les Alyscamps. Rue Pierre-Renaudel. ☎ **04-90-49-36-87.** Admission 15 F ($2.40) adults, 9 F ($1.45) children. Mid-Sept to mid-June, daily 9am–12:30pm and 2–7pm; mid-June to mid-Sept, daily 9am–7pm.

Perhaps the most memorable sight in Arles, this was once a necropolis established by the Romans. After being converted into a Christian burial ground in the 4th century, it became a setting for legends in epic medieval poetry and was even mentioned in Dante's *Inferno.* Today it's lined with poplars and the remaining sarcophagi. Arlesiens escape here to enjoy a respite from the heat.

Musée de l'Arles Antique. Presqu'île du Cirque Romain. ☎ **04-90-18-88-88.** Admission 35 F ($5.60) adults, 25 F ($4) students, free for children under 12. Apr–Sept 15, daily 9am–7pm; Sept 16–Mar, daily 10–3pm.

Half a mile south of the town center, you'll find one of the world's most famous collections of Roman Christian sarcophagi, plus a rich ensemble of sculptures, mosaics, and inscriptions from the Augustinian period to the 6th century A.D. Eleven detailed models show ancient monuments of the region as they existed in the past.

Musée Réattu. 10 rue du Grand-Prieuré. ☎ **04-90-49-37-58.** Admission 15 F ($2.40) adults, 9 F ($1.45) children, free for children under 12. Mar, daily 10am–12:30pm and 2–7pm; Apr–Sept, daily 9am–12:30pm and 2–7pm; Oct, daily 10am–12:30pm and 2–6:30pm; Nov–Feb, 10am–12:30pm and 2–5:30pm.

This collection of the local painter Jacques Réattu has been updated with more recent works, including etchings and drawings by Picasso. Other works are by Alechinsky, Dufy, and Zadkine. Note the Arras tapestries from the 16th century.

Museon Arlaten. 29 rue de la République. ☎ **04-90-96-08-23.** Admission 25 F ($4) adults, 20 F ($3.20) children, free for children under 12. Apr–Oct, daily 9am–noon and 2–6:30pm; Nov–Mar, Tues–Sun 9am–noon and 2–5pm.

You'll notice that the name of this museum is written in Provençal style. It was founded by Frédéric Mistral, the Provençal poet and leader of a movement to establish modern Provençal as a literary language, using the money from his Nobel Prize for literature in 1904. This is really a folklore museum, with regional costumes, portraits, furniture, dolls, a music salon, and one room devoted to mementos of Mistral. Among its curiosities is a letter (in French) from President Theodore Roosevelt to Mistral, bearing the letterhead of the Maison Blanche in Washington, D.C.

ACCOMMODATIONS

✪ **Grand Hotel Nord Pinus.** Place du Forum, 13200 Arles. ☎ **04-90-93-44-44.** Fax 04-90-93-34-00. www.nord-pinus.com. E-mail: info@nordpinus.com. 23 units. MINIBAR TV TEL. 840–990 F ($134.40–$158.40) double; 1,700 F ($272) suite. AE, MC, V. Parking 50 F ($8) per night.

Few other hotels in Arles manage to evoke Provence's 19th-century charm as effectively as this one. Occupying an antique town house on a tree-lined square in the heart of town, it has public rooms filled with antiques, an ornate staircase lined with graceful wrought-iron balustrades, and many of the trappings you might have expected

In Search of van Gogh's "Different Light"

What strikes me here is the transparency of the air.

—Vincent van Gogh

Provence attracted artists long before the Impressionists found refuge here. During the pope's residency at Avignon, a flood of Italian artists frescoed the papal palace in a style worthy of St. Peter's, and even after their departure, Provençal monarchs like King René imported painters from Flanders and Burgundy to adorn his public buildings. This continued through the 18th and 19th centuries, as painters drew inspiration from the dazzling light of Provence. Still, it wasn't until the age of the Impressionists that Provence really became known for its role in nurturing artists.

The Dutch-born Vincent van Gogh (1853–90) moved to Arles in 1888 and spent 2 years migrating through the historic towns of Les Baux, St-Rémy, and Stes-Maries, recording through the filter of his neuroses dozens of Impressionistic scenes now prized by museums everywhere. His search, he said, was for "a different light," and when he found it, he created masterpieces like *Starry Night, Cypresses, Olive Trees,* and *Boats Along the Beach.*

Van Gogh wasn't alone in his pursuit of Provençal light: Gauguin joined him 8 months after his arrival and soon thereafter engaged him in a violent quarrel, which reduced the Dutchman to a morbid depression that sent him to a local sanitarium. Within 2 years van Gogh returned to Paris, where he committed suicide in July 1890.

Things went somewhat better for Cézanne, who was familiar with the beauties of Provence thanks to his childhood in Aix-en-Provence. He infuriated his father, a prominent Provençal banker, by abandoning his studies to pursue painting. Later, his theories about line and color were publicized around the world. Although he migrated to Paris, he rarely set foot outside Provence from 1890 until his death, in 1904. Some critics have asserted that Cézanne's later years were devoted to one obsession: recording the line, color, and texture of Montagne-St-Victoire, a rocky knoll a few hours' horse ride east of Aix. He painted it more than 60 times without ever grasping its essence the way he'd hoped. The bulk of the Provençal mountain, however, as well as the way shadows moved across its rocky planes, was decisive in affecting the Cubists, whose work Cézanne directly influenced.

within an upscale private home. In a range of shapes and sizes, bedrooms are glamorous, even theatrical, filled with rich upholsteries and thick curtains strewn artfully beside the oversized French doors. You can't help but notice that many bullfighters and artists have stayed here. Their photographs and framed artworks decorate many of the public areas. The on-site bar/restaurant is open daily for dinner.

✪ **Hôtel Calendal.** 5 rue Porte de Laure, 13200 Arles. ☎ **04-90-96-11-89.** Fax 04-90-96-05-84. 38 units. TEL. 290–450 F ($46.40–$72) double. AE, DC, MC, V. Bus: 4.

Because of its reasonable rates, the Calendal has long been a bargain hunter's favorite. On a quiet square not far from the arena, it offers recently renovated rooms with bright colors, high ceilings, and a sense of spaciousness. Some even have a collection of antiques. Most have views over the hotel's delightful garden filled with palms and palmettos. There's a restaurant with a limited menu featuring omelets, soups, and platters inspired by the cuisine of France and Provence.

Hôtel Jules César et Restaurant Lou Marquês. 9 bd. des Lices, 13631 Arles CEDEX. ☎ **04-90-52-52-52.** Fax 04-90-52-52-53. www.hotel-julescesar.fr. E-mail: julescesar@calvaner.net. 58 units. MINIBAR TV TEL. 850–1,250 F ($136–$200) double; from 1,500 F ($240) suite. AE, DC, MC, V. Closed Nov 12–Dec 23. Parking 65 F ($10.40).

In the center of Arles, this 17th-century former Carmelite convent has been skillfully transformed into a stately country hotel, with the best restaurant in Arles. Though this is a noisy neighborhood, most rooms face the quiet, unspoiled cloister. The decoration is luxurious, with antique Provençal furnishings the owner finds at auctions throughout the countryside. You wake to the scent of roses and the sounds of birds singing.

Throughout, you'll find a curious blend of antique neoclassic architecture and postmodern amenities. Rooms have recently been renewed with fresh carpeting and curtains. The interior rooms are the most tranquil but also the darkest. Bright fabrics enliven them, however. Most downstairs rooms are spacious. And although the upstairs rooms are small, they have a certain old-world charm. Some of the rooms are in modern extensions, and, although spacious and comfortable, lack character.

The **restaurant, Lou Marquês,** has tables outside on the front terrace. The food is extremely fresh. From the à la carte menu, we recommend *bourride à la Provençale* or Arles lamb. Fixed-price menus are 210 F to 380 F ($33.60 to $60.80), with à la carte dinners averaging 300 F ($48).

Hôtel Le Cloître. 16 rue du Cloître, 13200 Arles. ☎ **04-90-96-29-50.** Fax 04-90-96-02-88. E-mail: hotel_cloitre@hotelmail.com. 30 units. TEL. 270–310 F ($43.20–$49.60) double; 400–450 F ($64–$72) triple. AE, MC, V. Closed Nov–Mar 15. Parking 30 F ($4.80). Bus: 4.

This hotel, between the ancient theater and the cloister, is a great value. Originally part of a 12th-century cloister, it still has its original Romanesque vaultings. Throughout the site, you'll find a richly Provençal atmosphere, pleasant rooms with high ceilings and subtle references to the building's antique origins, and lots of charm. Some, but not all, of the rooms have their own TV sets. There's also a public TV lounge.

DINING

For a truly elegant meal, consider dining at the **Restaurant Lou Marquês** at the Hôtel Jules César (see "Accommodations," above).

El Quinto Toro. 12 rue de la Liberté. ☎ **04-90-49-62-29.** Reservations recommended in summer. Main courses 50–80 F ($8–$12.80). AE, V. Thurs–Tues noon–2:30pm and 7–10:30pm. PROVENÇAL/SPANISH.

Set within a few steps of the Place du Forum, and outfitted with a decor inspired by the *corrida* (bullfights) that are held in and around Arles, this is a well-managed restaurant with no more than 30 seats and a following of local fans. Some of the best food is grilled over live coals that waft aromas from the busy kitchens into the dining rooms. You might begin with a platter of Spanish tapas, then follow with generous slabs of duck breast or fresh fish, both grilled and both succulent. A noteworthy specialty, not widely available, is a slab of wood-grilled bull steak from the Camargue. The owners pride themselves on the earthy simplicity of their cusine, and don't provide fancy sauces, preferring instead to emphasize the natural juices and flavors of the meat of fish. A wide selection of French and Spanish wines and beers accompany your meal.

Le Vaccarès. Place du Forum, 9 rue Favorin. ☎ **04-90-96-06-17.** Reservations required. Main courses 100–145 F ($16–$23.20); fixed-price menus 150–320 F ($24–$51.20). AE, MC, V.

Tues–Sat noon–2pm and 7:30–9:30pm, Sun noon–2pm. Closed Jan 15–Feb 15; July–Aug, closed Sun. PROVENÇAL.

Le Vaccarès offers southern French elegance and the finest food in town, in a setting whose outdoor terrace (used during good weather) opens onto the market of Arles. Its staff and two generations of the Dumas family use unusual ingredients to create innovative Provençal dishes. Specialties are sauté of lamb with basil; poached sea wolf with confit of lemon and orange; mussels with fresh herbs; croquette of squid; sea-devil soup; steamed sea bass in an elegantly simple way, garnished only with olive oil; and émincé of beef with Châteauneuf. The selection of wines is impressive (especially the Rhône Valley and Var).

ARLES AFTER DARK

Because of its relatively small population (around 50,000), Arles doesn't offer as rich a panoply of nightlife options as Aix-en-Provence, Avignon, Nice, or Marseille. The town's most appealing choice is the bar/cafe/music hall **Cargo de Nuit,** 7 av. Sadi-Carnot, route pour Barriol (☎ **04-90-49-55-99**). For a cover ranging from 30 F to 100 F ($4.80 to $16), you'll get a dose of recorded blues, salsa, reggae, and Cubano music and access to a sprawling bar and a restaurant that does everything it can to break what might have become too constant a diet of southern French cooking.

Two good options farther from the city center, particularly for those in their 40s and 50s, are the very large **Le Krystal,** route de Pont-de-Crau (☎ **04-90-98-32-40**), about 6 miles south of Arles. The town's most animated cafe, where most of the available single people go, is **Le Café van Gogh,** 11 place du Forum (☎ **04-90-96-44-56**). Overlooking the most attractive plaza in Arles, it features live music and an ambience that the almost-young and the restless refer to as *super-chouette* or "super cool."

5 Les Baux

444 miles S of Paris, 12 miles NE of Arles, 50 miles N of Marseille and the Mediterranean

Cardinal Richelieu called Les Baux a nesting place for eagles. In its lonely position high on a windswept plateau overlooking the southern Alpilles, Les Baux is a mere ghost of its former self. It was once the citadel of powerful seigneurs who ruled with an iron fist and sent their conquering armies as far as Albania. In medieval times, troubadours from all over the continent came to this "court of love," where they recited Western Europe's earliest-known vernacular poetry. Eventually, the notorious "Scourge of Provence" ruled Les Baux, sending his men throughout the land to kidnap people. If no one was willing to pay ransom for one of his victims, the poor wretch was forced to walk a gangplank over the cliff's edge.

Fed up with the rebellions against Louis XIII in 1632, Richelieu commanded his armies to destroy Les Baux. Today the castle and ramparts are a mere shell, though you can see remains of great Renaissance mansions. Although foreboding, the dry countryside around Les Baux, which is nestled in a valley surrounded by mysterious, shadowy rock formations, offers its own fascination. Vertical ravines lie on either side of the town. Vineyards—officially classified as Coteaux d'Aix-en-Provence—surround Les Baux, facing the Alpilles. If you follow the signposted route des vin, you can motor through the vineyards in an afternoon, perhaps stopping off at various growers' estates.

ESSENTIALS

GETTING THERE   From Arles there are six **buses** daily from March to September, but only one bus per day from October to February (trip time: 30 minutes). The fare

Les Baux with a View

For the greatest drive in the area, take the panorama route along D27 for about half a mile and bear right along a steep road. From this rocky promontory you'll have the most spectacular view of Les Baux and even, in the far distance, Arles and Camargue.

---

is 32 F ($5.45) one-way. For bus information and schedules, call ☎ **04-90-49-38-01** in Arles.

If you're **driving** from Arles, take N570 north and D5 east to Les Baux; from Marseille, head north along A7 to Salon-de-Provence and from here travel D5 west.

VISITOR INFORMATION   The **Office de Tourisme** is on Rue Frédéric Mistral (☎ **04-90-54-34-39**).

EXPLORING THE AREA

This is one of the most dramatic towns in Provence. You can wander through feudal ruins, called "La Ville Morte" (Ghost Village), which lie at the northern end of town. The site of this former castle or citadel covers an area at least five times that of Les Baux itself. As you stand at the ruins of the former castle, you can look out over the Valley of Hell (*Val d'Enfer*) and even see the Mediterranean in the distance.

You can reach the castle ruins at the bottom of the town by walking up **rue du Château,** which leads into the **Château des Baux** (☎ **04-90-54-55-56**). Allow at least an hour to explore the ruins. You enter the citadel compound by going through the **Hôtel de la Tour du Brau,** which houses the Musée du Château. The "Hôtel," which in this case refers to a private mansion, was the old residence of the powerful Tour de Brau family. The museum has exhibits related to the history of Les Baux, which will help you understand the other ruins within the compound. Models of the fortress as it existed in medieval times explain how the site has evolved architecturally.

After leaving the Hôtel de la Tour du Brau, you're free to wander at will through the citadel ruins, taking in such sites as the ruined chapel of St-Blaise (now housing a little museum devoted to the olive), replicas of medieval siege engines, various grottoes used for storage or lodgings in the Middle Ages, the skeleton of a hospital built in the 16th century, a cemetery, and finally, the **Tour Sarrisin** (Saracen Tower) which offers a panoramic view of the village and the citadel compound. Admission to the castle is 37 F ($5.90) for adults, 28 F ($4.50) for students, and 20 F ($3.20) ages 7 to 17; free ages 6 and under. The site is open daily 9am to 8:30pm in July and August; daily 9am to 7pm in March and September to October; or daily 10am to 5:30pm during other months.

In the village itself you can explore the **Yves Brauyer Museum,** at the intersection of rue de la Calade and rue de l'Église (☎ **04-90-54-36-99**). The museum is devoted to a retrospective collection of the works of Yves Brayer (1907–1990), a figurative painter and Les Baux's famous native son (he's buried in the village cemetery). He painted scenes of Italy, Morocco, and Spain, including many bullfighting scenes. The museum is open daily April to October 10am to 6:30pm. Otherwise, hours are daily 10am to noon and 2 to 5:30pm. Admission is 20 F ($3.20) adults, 10 F ($1.60) students and children under 12.

Cathêdrale d'Images (☎ **04-90-54-38-65**) is one of the most remarkable cathedrals in Provence. It lies a quarter-mile north of the village and can be reached along Route duVal d'Enfer. On the outside, you can marvel at the fact that the cathedral is carved out of the stone mountain. But it's just as amazing inside, where the limestone surfaces of the large rooms and pillars become three-dimensional screens for a bizarre audio-visual show. Hundreds of projectors splash engaging images from all directions. The site was created by photographer Albert Plecy in 1977. The site is open daily in summer from 10am to 7pm, but closed from mid-January to March 4. Admission is 43 F ($6.90) for adults, and 27 F ($4.30) for children under 18.

Musée des Santons is located in the town's **Ancien Hotel de Ville,** place Louis Jou (no phone). Originally built in the 16th century as a chapel, "La Chapelle des Péni-tents Blancs," it displays antique and idiosyncratic wood carvings, each representing a different saint or legend. It's open April to October daily from 9am to 6:30pm, and November to March daily from 10am to 5:30pm.

Head up to the much-praised **Place St-Vincent** for a sweeping view over the *Vallon de la Fontaine.* This is also the site of the much-respected **Église St-Vincent** (no phone), which is open April to October daily from 9am to 6:30pm, and November to March daily from 10am to 5:30pm.

Its campanile is called *La Lanterne des Morts* (*Lantern of the Dead*). The windows were a gift from Rainier of Monaco, when he was the Marquis des Baux, during the 1980s. They are modern, based on designs of French artist Max Ingrand.

The Renaissance-era **Hôtel de Manville,** rue Frédéric Mistral, was built in the 16th century as a private mansion. Today, it functions as the **Mairie (Town Hall)** of Les Baux. You can visit its courtyard (its hours are the same as Musée des Santons, see above). **Fondation Louis Jou** lies within the Renaissance-era **Hôtel Jean-de-Brion,** rue Frédéric Mistral (☎ **04-90-69-88-03** or **04-90-54-34-17**). It can be visited only after making a specific request, and it does not maintain specific hours. Inside is an inventory of **engravings and serigraphs** by the recently departed artist Louis Jou.

ACCOMMODATIONS

La Riboto de Taven (see "Dining," below) has two rooms for rent.

Auberge de la Benvengudo. Vallon de l'Arcoule, rte. d'Arles, 13520 Les Baux. ☎ **04-90-54-32-54.** Fax 04-90-54-42-58. 26 units. A/C TV TEL. 630–800 F ($100–$127) double; 990 F ($157) suite. AE, MC, V. Closed Nov–Mar 15. Take RD78 for a mile southwest of Les Baux, following the signs to Arles.

This auberge gives you the opportunity to spend the night in a tastefully converted 19th-century farmhouse surrounded by sculptured shrubbery, towering trees, and parasol pines. Extras include a pool, a tennis court, and an expansive terrace filled with the scent of lavender and thyme. Rooms are about equally divided between the original building, above the restaurant, and an attractive stone-sided annex. Regardless of their location, bedrooms are sunny, well-maintained, and clean. They've all been recently renovated. Each has a private terrace or balcony, and in some cases, an antique four-poster bed. The inn offers a delectable **menu** that includes a fillet of hogfish with saffron, fillet of red mullet with a concasse of tomatoes, grilled lamb chops with rata-touille, Mediterranean sole fillet fried with rosemary, and osso buco Provençal. The fixed-price menu costs 260 F ($41.60), but the options offered change daily. There's also an exceptional à la carte menu. Lunch is available in the summer.

Hostellerie de la Reine-Jeanne. Grand-Rue, 13520 Les Baux. ☎ **04-90-54-32-06.** Fax 04-90-54-32-33. 10 units. TEL. 280–380 F ($44.80–$60.80) double. MC, V. Closed Nov 15–Feb 15 (open during the Christmas holidays). Free parking.

This warm, well-scrubbed inn is the best bargain in Les Baux. You enter through a typical provincial French bistro. All the rooms are Spartan but comfortable. Three even have their own terraces. Bathrooms are cramped, with a shower stall only, and the towels are rather thin. Fixed-price menus are sumptuously prepared by the chef.

✪ **La Cabro d'Or.** 13520 Les Baux de Provence. ☎ **04-90-54-33-21.** Fax 04-90-54-45-98. www.lacabrodor.com. E-mail: cabrodor@relaischateaux.fr. 31 units. A/C MINIBAR TV TEL. 845–1,235 F ($135.20–$197.60) double; from 1,870 F ($299.20) suite. Off-season, prices about 25% lower. Breakfast 85 F ($13.60) extra per person; half board 400 F ($64) extra per person. AE, DC, MC, V.

This is the less famous, less celebrated sibling of the also-recommended L'Oustau de Baumanière, which lies less than a half-mile away. The original building, a low-slung Provençal farmhouse, dates from the 18th century. In these five low-slung, stone-built buildings, you'll find some of the most comfortable accommodations in the region. The rooms' decor of unusual art and antiques evokes old-time Provence. Some rooms have sweeping views over the surrounding countryside.

Dining: The in-house restaurant sits in a much-altered agrarian building from the 1800s. The massive ceiling beams are works of art in their own right. The restaurant is flanked by a vine-covered terrace with views of an ornamental pond, a garden, and a rocky and barren landscape that has been compared to the surface of the moon.

Amenities: Swimming pool and two tennis courts.

✪ **L'Oustau de Baumanière.** Les Baux, 13520 Maussane-les-Alpilles. ☎ **04-90-54-33-07.** Fax 04-90-54-40-46. www.oustaudebaumaniere.com. E-mail: oustau@relaischateaux.fr. 22 units. A/C MINIBAR TV TEL. 1,400–1,500 F ($224–$240) double; 2,200 F ($352) suite. AE, DC, MC, V. Closed Jan 3–Mar 4; Nov–Apr 1, hotel and restaurant closed Wed.

This Relais & Châteaux is one of southern France's most legendary hotels. Raymond Thuilier bought this Provençal farmhouse in 1945 and by the 1950s and '60s it was a rendezvous for the glitterati. Today, under the management of the founder's grandson, Jean-André Charial, it's not as glitzy. But the three stone houses, each draped in flowering vines, set in a valley, still charm the guests. The plush guest rooms evoke the 16th and 17th centuries. All the accommodations contain large sitting areas, and no two are alike. If there's no room in the main building, the hotel will assign you to one of the three annexes. If this is the case, request Le Manor; it's the most appealing.

Dining: In the stone-vaulted dining room, the chef serves specialties like ravioli of truffles with leeks, and a *rossini* (stuffed with foie gras) of veal with fresh truffles. The award-winning *gigot d'agneau* (lamb) *en croûte* has become this place's trademark and is particularly succulent. For dessert, consider a soufflé of red fruits. The restaurant is open daily from noon to 3pm and 7:30pm to midnight, except between November 1 and early April, when both the hotel and its restaurant are closed all day Wednesday. Reservations are essential. Fixed-price menus cost from 495 F to 750 F ($79.20 to $120).

Amenities: Outdoor pool, concierge, room service, laundry/dry cleaning. Tennis courts and golf course are a half mile and 3 miles respectively from the hotel.

DINING

L'Oustau de Baumanière (see "Accommodations," above) boasts an excellent dining room.

La Riboto de Taven. Le Val d'Enfer, 13520 Les Baux. ☎ **04-90-54-34-23.** Fax 04-90-54-38-88. Reservations required. Main courses 150–190 F ($24–$30.40); fixed-price menus 220–450 F ($35.20–$72) at lunch, 300–450 F ($48–$72) at dinner. AE, DC, MC, V. Tues noon–2pm, Thurs–Mon noon–2pm and 7:30–10pm. Closed Jan 3–Mar 15. FRENCH.

This 1835 farmhouse outside the medieval section of town has been owned by two generations of the Novi family. In summer you can sit outdoors at the beautifully laid tables, one of which is a millstone. Menu items may include sea bass in olive oil, fricassée of mussels flavored with basil, and lamb en croûte with olives—plus homemade desserts. The cuisine is a personal statement of Jean-Pierre Novi, whose cookery is filled with brawny flavors and the heady perfumes of Provençal herbs.

It's also possible to rent two **rooms** large enough to be suites, each at 1,100 F ($176), breakfast included.

6 Aix-en-Provence

469 miles S of Paris, 50 miles SE of Avignon, 20 miles N of Marseille, 109 miles W of Nice

Founded in 122 B.C. by a Roman general, Caius Sextius Calvinus, who named it Aquae Sextiae after himself, Aix (pronounced "ex") was first a Roman military outpost and then a civilian colony, the administrative capital of a province of the late Roman Empire, the seat of an archbishop, and the official residence of the medieval comtes de Provence. After the union of Provence with France, Aix remained a judicial and administrative headquarters until the Revolution.

The celebrated son of this old capital city of Provence, Paul Cézanne, immortalized the countryside nearby. Just as he saw it, Montagne Ste-Victoire looms over the town today, though a string of high-rises has now cropped up on the landscape. The most charming center in all Provence, this faded university town was once a seat of aristocracy, its streets walked by counts and kings.

Today this city of some 150,000 is reasonably quiet in winter but active and bustling when the summer hordes pour in. Many of the local population are international students. (The Université d'Aix dates from 1413.) Today Émile Zola's absinthe has given way to pastis in the many cafes scattered throughout the town. Summer is especially lively because of the frequent cultural events, ranging from opera to jazz, staged here from June to August. Increasingly, Aix is becoming a bedroom community for urbanites fleeing Marseille after 5pm.

ESSENTIALS

GETTING THERE   As a rail and highway junction, the city is easily accessible, with **trains** arriving hourly from Marseille (trip time: 40 minutes). For rail information and schedules, call ☎ **08-36-35-35-35.**

Several independent **bus** companies service the routes into Aix-en-Provence. Call the **Gare Routière,** rue Lapierre (☎ **04-42-27-17-91**), for information about the various routes and companies. SATAP (☎ **04-42-26-23-78**) specializes in routes from Aix to Avignon, operating up to four buses a day between those two cities.

If you're **driving** from Marseille, take A51 north to Aix-en-Provence; from Avignon, travel A7 south to Senas and follow N7 southeast to Aix-en-Provence.

VISITOR INFORMATION   The **Office de Tourisme** is at 2 place du Général-de-Gaulle (☎ **04-42-16-11-61**).

SPECIAL EVENTS   Aix is more closely geared to music and its performance than virtually any other city in the south of France. It offers at least four midsummer festivals that showcase concerts, opera, and dance. They include the **Saison d'Aix** (June to August), which focuses on symphonic and chamber music, and a well-attended **Jazz Festival** (June 28 to July 11) that attracts musicians from all over the world. For information on either of these, call the **Office des Fêtes et de la Culture,** Espace Forbin, Cours Gambetta (☎ **04-42-63-06-75**).

Aix From the Eyes of Cézanne

The best experience in Aix is a walk along the carefully signposted ✪ **route de Cézanne** (D17), which winds eastward through the Provençal countryside toward Ste-Victoire. From the east end of cours Mirabeau, take rue du Maréchal-Joffre across boulevard Carnot to boulevard des Poilus, which becomes avenue des Écoles-Militaires and finally D17. The stretch between Aix and the hamlet of Le Tholonet is full of twists and turns where Cézanne often set up his easel to paint. The entire route makes a lovely 3½-mile stroll. Le Tholonet has a cafe or two where you can refresh yourself while waiting for one of the frequent buses back to Aix.

Also noteworthy is the **Festival International de Danse** (July 11 to 23), attracting classical and modern dance troupes from throughout Europe and the world. For information, call ☎ **04-42-96-05-01.**

EXPLORING THE AREA

Aix's main street, ✪ **cours Mirabeau,** is one of Europe's most beautiful. Plane trees stretch their branches across the top like an umbrella, shading it from the hot Provençal sun and filtering the light into shadows that play on the rococo fountains below. Shops and sidewalk cafes line one side of the street; richly embellished sandstone *hôtels particuliers* (mansions) from the 17th and 18th centuries fill the other. The street begins at the 1860 landmark fountain on place de la Libération, which honors Mirabeau, the revolutionary and statesman.

After touring Aix, you might consider a side trip to the **Château de Vauvenarges,** site of Pablo Picasso's last home. Reach it from Aix by driving 10 miles east on D10. You can't visit the château's interior, but Picasso and one of his wives, Jacqueline Roche, are buried nearby. If you opt for a day trip from Aix, you might appreciate a meal at **Au Moulin de Provence,** rue des Maquisards (☎ **04-42-66-02-22**).

Atelier de Cézanne. 9 av. Paul-Cézanne (outside town). ☎ **04-42-21-06-53.** Admission 25 F ($4) adults, 10 F ($1.60) students, free for children 16 and under. Daily 10am–noon and 2–6pm (till 5pm Oct–Mar).

Cézanne was considered the major forerunner of Cubism. This is where he worked. Surrounded by a wall, the house was restored by American admirers. Repaired again in 1970, it remains much as Cézanne left it in 1906, "his coat hanging on the wall, his easel with an unfinished picture waiting for a touch of the master's brush," as Thomas R. Parker wrote.

Cathédrale St-Sauveur. Place des Martyrs de la Résistance. ☎ **04-42-23-45-65.** Free admission. Daily 7:30am–noon and 2–6pm.

The cathedral of Aix is dedicated to Christ under the title St-Sauveur (Holy Savior or Redeemer). Its Baptistery dates from the 4th and 5th centuries, but the architectural complex as a whole has seen many additions. It contains a brilliant 15th-century Nicolas Froment triptych, *The Burning Bush.* One side depicts the Virgin and Child; the other, Good King René and his second wife, Jeanne de Laval. Masses are conducted every Sunday at 9am, 10:30am, and 7pm.

Chapelle Penitents-gris (Chapelle des Bourras). 15 rue Lieutaud. ☎ **04-42-26-26-72.** Free admission (donations welcome). July–Aug, Sat 4:30–6pm; Sept–June, Sat 2:30–4:30pm.

This 16th-century chapel honoring St. Joseph was built on the ancient Roman Aurelian road linking Rome and Spain. The chapel was restored by Herbert Maza, founder

Aix-en-Provence

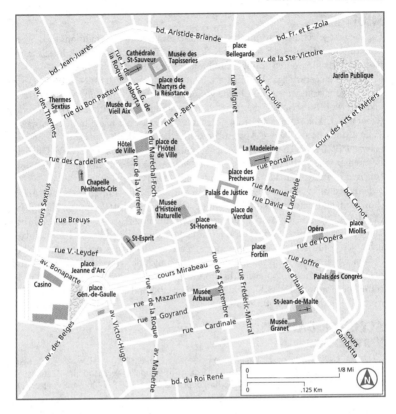

and former president of the Institute for American Universities. If you can't visit during the limited opening hours on Saturdays, you might call M. Borricand, rector of a group of local ecclesiastics, who will arrange a rendezvous upon request.

Musée Granet (Musée des Beaux-Arts). Place St-Jean-de-Malte (up rue Cardinale). ☎ **04-42-38-14-70.** Admission 10 F ($1.60) . Wed–Mon 10am–noon and 2:30–6pm.

This museum owns eight paintings by Cézanne, none of them major. The great painter had a famously antagonistic relationship with the people of Aix—so much so that a former director of the museum once claimed that the galleries "would never be sullied by a Cézanne." Housed in the former center of the Knights of Malta, the museum contains works by van Dyck, van Loo, and Rigaud; portraits by Pierre and François Puget; and (the most interesting) a *Jupiter and Thetis* by Ingres. Ingres also did an 1807 portrait of the museum's namesake, François Marius Granet.

Musée des Tapisseries. 28 place des Martyrs de la Résistance. ☎ **04-42-23-09-91.** Admission 10 F ($1.60), free for ages 25 and under. Wed–Mon 10am–noon and 2–6pm.

Three series of tapestries from the 17th and 18th centuries line the gilded walls of this former archbishop's palace. *The History of Don Quixote* by Natoire, *The Russian Games* by Leprince, and *The Grotesques* by Monnoyer were collected by archbishops to decorate the palace. The museum also exhibits rare furnishings from the 17th and 18th centuries.

SHOPPING

For the best selection of art objects and fabrics inspired by the traditions of Provence, head for **Les Olivades,** 15 rue Marius-Reinaud (☎ **04-42-38-33-66**). It sells tasteful fabrics, shirts for women and men, fashionable dresses, and table linens.

Opened a century ago, **Bechard,** 12 cours Mirabeau (☎ **04-42-26-06-78**), is the most famous bakery in town. On the ground floor of a building on the main street, it takes its work so seriously that it refers to its underground kitchens as a *laboratoire* (laboratory). The pastries are truly delectable, in most cases made fresh every day.

La Boutique du Pays d'Aix, in the Office de Tourisme, 2 place du Général-de-Gaulle (☎ **04-42-16-11-61**), carries a wide selection of *santons* (carved figurines inspired by the Nativity of Jesus), locally woven textiles and carvings, and *calissons* (sugared confections made with almonds and a confit of melon).

Founded in 1934 on a busy boulevard about half a mile from the center of Aix, the showroom and factory of **Santons Fouque,** 65 cours Gambetta, route de Nice, R.N. 7 (☎ **04-42-26-33-38**), stocks the largest assortment of *santons* in Aix. More than 1,800 figurines are cast in terra-cotta, finished by hand, then decorated with oil-based paint according to 18th-century models. Each of the trades practiced in medieval Provence is represented in the inventories, which include grizzled but awestruck shoe-makers, barrel makers, coppersmiths, ironsmiths, and rope makers, each poised to welcome the newborn Jesus. Depending on their size and complexity, figurines range from 22 F to 560 F ($3.50 to $89.60).

ACCOMMODATIONS
VERY EXPENSIVE

✪ **Villa Gallici.** Av. de la Violette (impasse des Grands Pins), 13100 Aix-en-Provence. ☎ **04-42-23-29-23.** Fax 04-42-96-30-45. E-mail: villagallici@wanadoo.fr. 22 units. A/C MINIBAR TV TEL. 1,000–2,500 F ($160–$400) double; 2,500–3,050 F ($400–$488) suite. AE, DC, MC, V.

This elegant, relentlessly chic inn is the most stylishly decorated hotel in Aix. The rooms speak of subtlety and charm. They're richly infused with the decorative traditions of Aix; some boast a private terrace or garden. The villa sits in a large enclosed garden in the heart of town, close to one of the best restaurants, Le Clos de la Violette (see "Dining," below). It's only a 5-minute walk to the town center. Despite its grand reputation as a place that requires ironbound advance reservations, and a place where famous people bask in sybaritic anonymity, some of the staff is not as well trained or as well informed as they might be. But that is only a minor distraction in an otherwise well-orchestrated symphony.

Dining: The airy in-house restaurant is open daily for lunch and dinner.

Amenities: A limited array of spa facilities, plus a swimming pool.

EXPENSIVE

Hôtel des Augustins. 3 rue de la Masse, 13100 Aix-en-Provence. ☎ **04-42-27-28-59.** Fax 04-42-26-74-87. 29 units. A/C MINIBAR TV TEL. 600–1,500 F ($96–$240) double. AE, DC, V. Nearby parking 50 F ($8).

Converted from the 12th-century Grands Augustins Convent, this hotel has been beautifully restored, with ribbed-vault ceilings, stained-glass windows, stone walls, terra-cotta floors, and Louis XIII furnishings. The reception desk is in a chapel, and oil paintings and watercolors decorate the public rooms. The hotel has a private garage on the other side of place de la Rotonde. This site won a place in history by sheltering an excommunicated Martin Luther on his return from Rome. In 1892 it was transformed from a church to a hotel. Bedrooms are outfitted in a severe kind of monastic dignity, with dark-grained wooden furniture, high ceilings, and references to the medieval decor of the building's original function. There's no full-fledged restaurant on the premises; breakfast is the only meal served.

MODERATE

Grand Hôtel Nègre Coste. 33 cours Mirabeau, 13100 Aix-en-Provence. ☎ **04-42-27-74-22.** Fax 04-42-26-80-93. 37 units. A/C TV TEL. 420–750 F ($67.20–$120) double. AE, DC, V. Parking 50 F ($8).

This hotel, a former 18th-century town house, is so popular with the dozens of musicians who flock to Aix for the summer music festivals that it's usually difficult to get a room at any price. Such popularity is understandable. Outside, flowers cascade from jardinières and windows are surrounded with 18th-century carvings. Inside, there's a wide staircase, marble portrait busts, and a Provençal armoire. The medium-size and soundproof rooms contain interesting antiques. The higher floors overlook either cours Mirabeau or the old city.

INEXPENSIVE

✪ **Hôtel des Quatre Dauphins.** 54 rue Roux Alphéran, 13100 Aix-en-Provence. ☎ **04-42-38-16-39.** Fax 04-42-38-60-19. 13 units. TV TEL. 335–420 F ($53.60–$67.20) double. MC, V. Nearby parking 55 F ($8.80).

This hotel is housed in a five-story private town house from the 18th century. It's a short walk from the place des Quatre Dauphins and the cours Mirabeau. Today, despite frequent modernizations, some of the original motifs remain. The medium-size bedrooms were recently refurbished in a simplified Provençal style, sometimes with painted ceiling beams and casement windows that overlook the street outside. Space is not overly abundant. You can have breakfast in your room or in a small breakfast salon.

✪ **Hôtel La Caravelle.** 29 bd. du Roi-René (at cours Mirabeau), 13100 Aix-en-Provence. ☎ **04-42-21-53-05.** Fax 04-42-96-55-46. 32 units. A/C TV TEL. 300–330 F ($48–$52.80) double. AE, DC, MC, V.

This conservatively furnished three-star hotel with a bas-relief of a three-masted caravelle on the beige stucco facade is only a 3-minute walk from the center of town. The hotel is run by M. and Mme Henri Denis, who offer a continuing tradition of warm hospitality. One nice touch is the breakfast they serve in the stone-floored lobby. The majority of the rooms were restored between 1995 and 1998; they have double-glazed windows to help muffle the noise. Most bathrooms have a shower only.

Novotel Aix Point de l'Arc. Périphérique Sud, arc de Méyran, 13100 Aix-en-Provence. ☎ **800/221-4542** in the U.S., or 04-42-16-09-09. Fax 04-42-26-00-09. www.accor.com. 80 units. A/C MINIBAR TV TEL. 520 F ($83.20) double. AE, DC, MC, V. Take the ring road 2 miles south of the town center (exit at Aix-Est 3 Sautets).

You'll find this clean, chain hotel at the end of a labyrinthine but well-marked route. The large rooms have been designed for European business travelers or traveling families in summer. The hotel offers one of the most pleasant dining rooms in the suburbs, Côté Jardin, with big windows overlooking Rivière Arc de Méyran and an ivy-covered forest. There's an outdoor pool in the garden.

If this hotel is full, rooms are usually available at its twin, **Novotel Aix-Beaumanoir,** périphérique Sud, 13100 Aix-en-Provence (☎ **04-42-91-15-15;** fax 04-42-38-46-41). Set less than 500 yards away, it has its own outdoor pool, an in-house restaurant, and 102 rooms. Rooms and rates in both hotels are almost exactly the same.

DINING
VERY EXPENSIVE

Le Clos de la Violette. In the Villa Gallici, 10 av. de la Violette. ☎ 04-42-23-30-71. Reservations required. Main courses 185–270 F ($29.60–$43.20); fixed-price menus 300–600 F ($48–$96) at lunch, 600 F ($96) at dinner. AE, V. Mon 7:30–9:30pm, Tues–Sat noon–1:30pm and 7:30–9:30pm. FRENCH. Closed 2 weeks in Nov and 1 week in Feb.

In an elegant residential neighborhood, which most visitors reach by taxi, Le Clos de la Violette is a creative and innovative restaurant. Fortunately, the food is better than the attention span of the sometimes inexperienced staff. This imposing Provençal villa has an octagonal reception area and several modern dining rooms. Menu items are stylish and seasonal, and include a medley of dishes richly tuned to the flavors of Provence. Examples include local goat cheese in puff pastry, with a confit of fresh celery; braised sea wolf with beignets of fennel; warm onion brioche with a fig-flavored vinaigrette and balsamic vinegar; roasted Provençal lamb in puff pastry. An absolutely superb dessert might be a "celebration" of Provençal figs, presented as an artfully arranged platter containing a galette of figs, a tart of figs, a parfait of figs, and a sorbet of figs.

MODERATE

Chez Maxime. 12 place Ramus. ☎ 04-42-26-28-51. Reservations recommended. Main courses 85–160 F ($13.60–$25.60); fixed-price menus 38–270 F ($6.10–$43.20) at lunch, 135–270 F ($21.60–$43.20) at dinner. MC, V. Mon 8–11pm, Tues–Sat noon–2pm and 8–11pm. Closed Jan 15–31. GRILLS/PROVENÇAL.

In the pedestrian zone, this likable restaurant reflects the skills and personality of its owner, Felix Maxime. You can eat on the terrace on the sidewalk in front or in the wood-trimmed stone dining room. To experience the true flavors of Provence, order the *tian* appetizer: layers of eggplant, peppers, and Mediterranean herbs in a terracotta pot, infused with garlic and olive oil, and baked until bubbly. Another superb beginning is *rillettes* (similar to a roughly textured pâté) of sea wolf with a garlicky *rouille* mayonnaise. Specialties include as many as 19 kinds of grilled meat or fish, cooked over an oak-burning fire, and several preparations of lamb. The wine list features more than 500 vintages, many of them esoteric bottles from the region.

✪ Le Bistro Latin. 18 rue de la Couronne. ☎ 04-42-38-22-88. Reservations recommended. Fixed-price menus 75–95 F ($12–$15.20) at lunch Tues–Fri, 129–189 F ($20.65–$30.25) at dinner. MC, V. Tues–Sat noon–2pm; Mon–Sat 7–10:30pm. PROVENÇAL.

The best little bistro in Aix-en-Provence (for the price) is run by Bruno Ungaro and his partner, Gilles Holtz, who pride themselves on their fixed-price menus. They offer two intimate dining rooms: a street-level room and another in the cellar, decorated in Greco-Latin style. The staff is young and enthusiastic. Provençal music plays in the background. Try the chartreuse of mussels, one of the meat dishes with spinach-and-saffron/cream sauce, or crêpe of hare with basil sauce. We've enjoyed the classic cuisine on all our visits, particularly the scampi risotto.

Trattoria Chez Antoine Côte Cour. 19 rue Mirabeau. ☎ 04-42-93-12-51. Reservations recommended. Main courses 65–140 F ($10.40–$22.40). DC, MC, V. Tues–Sat noon–2:30pm; Mon–Sat 7:30pm–midnight. PROVENÇAL/ITALIAN.

In 1997 this popular trattoria moved into new quarters—an 18th-century town house a few steps from place Rotonde—and managed to lure most of its regulars along. These include Emanuel Ungaro and many film and fashion types who mingle smoothly with old-time "Aixers." Despite the grandeur of the setting, the ambience is deliberately unpretentious, even jovial. Crusty bread and small pots of aromatic purées (anchovy and basil) are placed at your table as you sit down. A simple wine, such as Côtes du Rhône, will go nicely with the kind of hearty Mediterranean food that's de rigueur. Examples are a memorable version of pastas (pasta Romano flavored with calf's liver, flap mushrooms, and tomato sauce), osso buco (veal shank layered with salty ham), a selection of *légumes farcies* (such as eggplant and zucchini stuffed with minced meat and herbs), and at least half a dozen kinds of fresh fish.

AIX AFTER DARK

Aix is one of Provence's largest towns (after Marseille and Nice), and a university town to boot, making it a hotspot for animated nightlife.

Rockers head for **Le Mistral,** 3 rue Frédéric-Mistral (☎ **04-42-38-16-49**), where techno and house music blare long and loud. Its slightly more subdued competitor, **Le Richelm,** 24 rue de la Verrerie (☎ **04-42-23-49-29**), plays the same music but sometimes dips into 1970s and 1980s disco. Nearby is a woodsy-looking English pub that plays rock videos, **Bugsy,** 25 rue de la Verrerie (☎ **04-42-38-25-22**), where the good times are punctuated with bouts at billiard tables.

Less competitive and favored by those over 30 is the **Scat Club,** 11 rue de la Verrerie (☎ **04-42-23-00-23**), where a live pianist and a live jazz trio provide music (jazz, soul, blues, and rock-and-roll). Its most similar rival is **Hot Brass,** chemin de la Pleine des Vergueiers (☎ **04-42-21-05-57**), attracting lots of off-duty photographers, artists, actors, and literary types who appreciate the drinks and live music. Both these places boast two floors, each with its own bar, and live acts that include healthy doses of rhythm and blues.

If you're a university student or want to act like one, head for the **Jungle Café,** 4 bd. Carnot (☎ **04-42-21-47-44**), where live music enhances an everyday preoccupation with dating and mating.

7 Marseille

479 miles S of Paris, 116 miles SW of Nice, 19 miles S of Aix-en-Provence

Bustling Marseille, with more than a million inhabitants, is the second-largest city in France (its population surpassed that of Lyon in the early 1990s) and France's premier port. It's been called France's New Orleans. A crossroads of world traffic—Dumas called it "the meeting place of the entire world"—the city is ancient, founded by Greeks from the city of Phocaea, near present-day Izmir, Turkey, in the 6th century B.C. The city is a place of unique sounds, smells, and sights. It has seen wars and much destruction, but trade has always been its raison d'être.

Perhaps its most common association is with the national anthem of France, "La Marseillaise." During the Revolution, 500 volunteers marched to Paris, singing this rousing song along the way. The rest is history.

Although in many respects Marseille is big and sprawling, dirty and slumlike in many places, there's much elegance and charm here as well. The **Vieux Port,** the old harbor, is especially colorful, somehow compensating for the dreary industrial dockland nearby. Marseille has always symbolized danger and intrigue, and that reputation is somewhat justified. It's also the home of thousands of North and sub-Saharan Africans, creating a lively medley of races and creeds. One-quarter of the population of Marseille is of North African descent.

Marseille today actually occupies twice the amount of land space as Paris, and its age-old problems remain, including a drug industry, smuggling, corruption (often at the highest levels), the Mafia, and racial tension. Unemployment, as always, is on the rise. But in lieu of all these difficulties, it's a bustling, always-fascinating city unlike any other in France. A city official proclaimed recently that "Marseille is the unbeloved child of France. It's attached to France, but has the collective consciousness of an Italian city-state, like Genoa or Venice."

ESSENTIALS

GETTING THERE   The Marseille **airport** (☎ 04-42-14-14-14), 18 miles north of the center, receives international flights from all over Europe. From the airport, blue-and-white minivans (*navettes*) make the trip from a point in front of the arrivals hall to Marseille's St-Charles rail station, near the Vieux-Port, for a one-way fee of 45 F ($8.10) per person. The minivans run daily at 20-minute intervals, from 6:20am to 10:50pm.

Marseille has **train** connections from hundreds of European cities, with especially good connections to and from Italy. The city is also the terminus for the TGV bullet train, which departs daily from Paris's Gare de Lyon (trip time: 4³/₄ hours). Local trains leave Paris almost every hour, making a number of stops before reaching Marseille. For information and schedules, call ☎ **08-36-35-35-35. Buses** pull into Marseille at the Gare Routière, on the place Victor Hugo (☎ **04-91-08-16-40**), adjacent to the St. Charles railway station.

If you're **driving** from Paris, follow A6 south to Lyon; then continue south along A7 to Marseille. The drive takes about 7 hours.

GETTING AROUND   Parking and car safety are such potential hazards in Marseille that your wisest bet is to put your car in a garage and rely on public transportation during your visit here. The city is sprawling, and public transportation will help you avoid the hassle of traffic.

Marseille is serviced by **Métro** lines 1 and 2, both of which stop at the main train station, Gare St-Charles, place Victor Hugo (☎ **08-36-35-35-35**). The Métro runs daily from 5am to 9pm. At the tourist office, pick up a free brochure outlining the public transportation routes of Marseille. If you're going to be in Marseille for 2 or 3 days, purchase a **Carte Liberté** for 50 F ($8) . These tickets are available from **RTM,** 6–8 rue de Fabres (☎ **04-91-91-92-10**), open Monday to Friday from 8:30am to 6pm and Saturday from 9am to 5:30pm. Otherwise, you can purchase tickets at Métro and bus stops, costing 8 F ($1.30) for a ride good for 70 minutes. After that, you need another ticket.

If you can't face the hassle of public transportation, call **Taxi Plus** at ☎ **04-91-03-60-03** or **Marseille Taxi** at ☎ **04-91-02-20-20.**

VISITOR INFORMATION   The **Office de Tourisme** (Métro: Vieux-Port) is at 4 La Canebière (☎ **04-91-13-89-00**).

SEEING THE SIGHTS

Many visitors never bother to visit the museums, preferring to absorb the life of the city on its busy streets and at its sidewalk cafes, particularly those along the main street, **La Canebière.** Known as "can of beer" to World War II GIs, it's the heart and soul of Marseille, even if it is the seediest main street in France. Lined with hotels, shops, and restaurants, the street is filled with sailors of every nation and people of every nationality, especially Algerians. (In fact, some 100,000 North Africans live in the city and its tenement suburbs, often in communities that resemble *souks*.)

Canebière winds down to the **Vieux-Port,** dominated by the massive neoclassical forts of St-Jean and St-Nicholas. The port is filled with fishing craft and yachts and ringed with seafood restaurants. For a panoramic view, head for the **Parc du Pharo,** a

Marseille

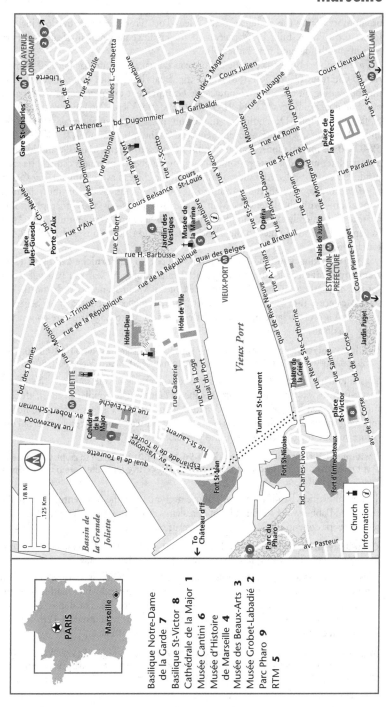

Basilique Notre-Dame
de la Garde 7
Basilique St-Victor 8
Cathédrale de la Major 1
Musée Cantini 6
Musée d'Histoire
de Marseille 4
Musée des Beaux-Arts 3
Musée Grobet-Labadié 2
Parc Pharo 9
RTM 5

promontory facing the entrance to the Vieux-Port. From a terrace overlooking the Château du Pharo, built by Napoléon III for his Eugénie, you can clearly see Fort St-Jean and the old and new cathedrals.

From quai des Belges at the Vieux-Port you can take a motorboat for a 20-minute ride to **Château d'If** for 50 F ($8) round-trip. Boats leave about every 60 to 90 minutes depending on the season. Contact the **Groupement des Armateurs Côtiers;** its office on quai des Belges (☎ **04-91-55-50-09;** Métro: Vieux-Port) is open daily from 6:30am to 6:30pm. Depending on the season, boats depart at intervals between 60 and 90 minutes. On the sparsely vegetated island of Château d'If (☎ **04-91-59-02-30** for information), François I built a fortress to defend Marseille and its port. The site later housed a state prison; carvings by Huguenot prisoners can still be seen inside some of the cells. Alexandre Dumas used the château as a setting for *The Count of Monte Cristo,* though the adventure never really took place. Its most famous association—with the legendary Man in the Iron Mask—is also apocryphal. The château is open daily except Monday from 9am to 5:30pm (it's open until 7pm April to September). Admittance to the island costs 25 F ($4) for adults and 15 F ($2.40) for children.

If you're driving, continue along from the old port to the **corniche Président-J.-F.-Kennedy,** a promenade running for about 3 miles along the sea. You pass villas and gardens along the way and have a good view of the Mediterranean. To the north, the **Port Moderne,** the "gateway to the East," is man-made. Its construction began in 1844, and a century later the Germans destroyed it. Motorboat trips are conducted along the docks.

Basilique Notre-Dame-de-la-Garde. Rue Fort-du-Sanctuaire. ☎ **04-91-13-40-80.** Free admission. Daily 7am–7pm (until 8pm mid-June to mid-Sept). Métro: Vieux-Port. Bus: 60.

This landmark church crowns a limestone rock overlooking the southern side of the Vieux-Port. It was built in the Romanesque-Byzantine style popular in the 19th century and topped by a 30-foot gilded statue of the Virgin. Visitors come here not so much for the church as for the view—best seen at sunset—from its terrace. Spread out before you are the city, the islands, and the sea.

Basilique St-Victor. Place St-Victor. ☎ **04-96-11-22-60.** Admission to crypt 10 F ($1.60). Crypt daily 10am–7pm. Head west along quai de Rive-Neuve (near the Gare du Vieux-Port). Métro: Vieux-Port.

This semifortified basilica was built above a crypt from the 5th century, when the church and abbey were founded by St. Cassianus. You can visit the crypt, which also reflects work done in the 10th and 11th centuries.

Cathédrale de la Major. Place de la Major. ☎ **04-91-90-53-57.** Free admission. Daily 9am–noon; Tues–Thurs 2–5:30pm; Fri–Sat–Sun 2:30–6pm. Métro: Joliette.

This was one of the largest cathedrals (some 450 feet long) built in Europe in the 19th century. Its interior is adorned with mosaic floors and red-and-white marble banners, and the exterior is in a bastardized Romanesque-Byzantine style. The domes and cupolas may remind you of Istanbul. This vast pile has almost swallowed its 12th-century Romanesque predecessor built on the ruins of a Temple of Diana.

Musée Cantini. 19 rue Grignan. ☎ **04-91-54-77-75.** Admission 18 F ($2.90) adults, 10 F ($1.60) students, free for seniors and children 10 and under. June–Sept, Tues–Sun 11am–6pm; Oct–May, Tues–Sun 10am–5pm. Métro: Estrangin Préfecture.

The temporary exhibitions of contemporary art staged here are often as good as the permanent collection. This museum is devoted to modern art, with masterpieces by

Derain, Marquet, Ernst, Masson, Balthus, and others. It also owns a selection of works by important young international artists.

Musée des Beaux-Arts. In Palais Longchamp, on place Bernex. ☎ **04-91-14-59-30.** Admission 12 F ($1.90) adults, 6 F (95¢) students and ages 12–18, free for children under 10. June 15–Sept 15, Tues–Sun 10am–7pm; Sept 16–June 14, Tues–Sun 10am–5pm. Métro: Cinq av. Longchamp or Réfomés.

One of the most scenic sights is Palais Longchamp, with its spectacular fountain and colonnade, built during the Second Empire. This museum, housed in a northern wing of the palace, displays a vast array of paintings from the 16th to the 19th centuries. They include works by Corot, Millet, Ingres, David, and Rubens. Particularly interesting is a gallery of Pierre Puget sculpture. One salon is devoted to Honoré Daumier, born in Marseille in 1808.

Musée d'Histoire de Marseille. Centre Bourse, square Belsunce. ☎ **04-91-90-42-22.** Admission 12 F ($1.90) adults, 6 F (95¢) students and ages 11–18, free for children under 10. Mon–Sat noon–7pm. Métro: Vieux-Port.

You're allowed to wander through an archaeological garden where excavations are still going on, as scholars attempt to learn more about the ancient town of Massalia, founded by Greek sailors. Of course, many of the exhibits, such as old coins and fragments of pottery, only suggest their former glory. To help you more fully realize the era, you're aided by audiovisual exhibits and a free exhibition room. A medieval quarter of potters has been discovered, and the Louis XIV town is open to the public. You can also see what's left of a Roman wreck that was excavated from the site.

Musée Grobet-Labadié. 140 bd. Longchamp. ☎ **04-91-62-21-82.** Admission 12 F ($1.90) adults, 6 F (95¢) students and ages 11–18, free for children under 11. Oct–May, Tues–Sun 10am–5pm; June–Sept, Tues–Sun 11am–6pm. Métro: Réfomés.

This private collection, bequeathed to the city in 1919, includes exquisite Louis XV and Louis XVI furniture, as well as an outstanding collection of medieval Burgundian and Provençal sculpture. Other exhibits are 17th-century Gobelin tapestries; 15th- to 19th-century German, Italian, French, and Flemish paintings; and 16th- and 17th-century Italian and French faïence.

SHOPPING

Only Paris and Lyon can compete with Marseille in the breadth and diversity of merchandise. Your best bet is a trip to the **Vieux Port** and the streets surrounding it for a view of the folkloric things that literally pop out of the boutiques. Many are loaded with souvenirs like crèche-style *santons* (carved wooden figurines of saints appropriate for display at Christmas). But the best place for acquiring these artifacts is just above the Vieux Port, behind the Théâtre National de la Criée. At **Ateliers Marcel Carbonel,** 47 rue Neuve-Ste-Catherine (☎ 04-91-54-26-58), more than 600 Nativity-related figures, available in half a dozen sizes, sell at prices beginning at 60 F ($9.60).

Bring any photo to the artists at **Amandine,** 69 bd. Eugène-Pierre (☎ 04-91-47-00-83), and they'll frost a cake with an amazingly accurate facsimile. If you don't have a favorite snapshot with you, choose from their roster of artfully rich cakes, emblazoned with scenes of the Vieux Port or whatever. A more traditional inventory of pastries and chocolates can be found at **Puyricard,** 25 rue Francis-Davso (☎ 04-91-54-26-25), with another location at 155 rue Jean-Mermoz (☎ 04-91-77-94-11). The treats available here include chocolates stuffed either with almond paste (*pâté d'amande*) or *confits de fruits.*

Since medieval times, Marseille has thrived on the legend of Les Trois Maries—three saints named Mary, including everyone's favorite ex-sinner, Mary Magdalene.

Assisted by awakened-from-the-dead St. Lazarus, they reportedly came ashore at a point near Marseille to Christianize ancient Provence. In commemoration of their voyage, small boat-shaped cookies (*les navettes*) flavored with secret ingredients that include tons of orange zest, orange-flower water, and sugar, are forever associated with Marseille. They're sold throughout the city, most notably at **Le Four des Navettes,** 136 rue Sainte (☎ **04-91-33-32-12**). Opened in 1791, it sells the boat-shaped cookies for 45 F ($7.20) per dozen and does very little else except perpetuate the city's most cherished (and dubious) medieval myth and ferociously guard the secret of how the pastries are made.

Antiques from around Provence are sold at **Galerie Wulfram-Puget,** 39 rue de Lodi (☎ **04-91-76-42-85**), and **Antiquités François-Décamp,** 302 rue Paradis (☎ **04-91-81-18-00**). For hats, at **Felio,** 4 place Gabriel-Péri (☎ **04-91-90-32-67**), you'll find large-brimmed numbers that would have thrilled ladies of the belle époque. There's a selection of *casquettes Marseillaises* (developed for men as protection from the *soleil du Midi*) and berets that begin at 150 F ($24).

All the souvenir shops along the pedestrian **rue St-Féréol,** running perpendicular to La Canebière, sell folkloric replicas of handcrafts from Old Provence, including the cream-colored or pale-green bars of the city's local soap, savon de Marseille. Infused with a healthy dollop of olive oil, it's known for its kindness to skin dried out by the sun and mistral. A large selection of the stuff is available at **La Savonnerie du Sérail,** 50 Bd. Anatle de la Forge (☎ **04-91-98-28-25**).

Looking for something that approximates, with a Provençal accent, the aura of a sun-flooded mall in California? Head for the most talked-about real-estate development in the city's recent history, **L'Escale Borély,** avenue Mendès-France. Only a 25-minute trip (take the Métro to rond-point du Prado, then transfer to bus no. 19) south of Marseille, it incorporates shops, cafes, bars, and restaurants. For more on L'Escale Borély, see "Marseille After Dark," below.

You don't normally think of Marseille as a place to go to shop for fashion, but the local fashion industry is booming. The fashion center is along **Cours Julien,** where you'll find dozens of boutiques and ateliers. Much of the clothing reflects North African influences, although there is a vast array of French styles as well. The basic style of much of this clothing at the millennium is rich, brocaded, and ethnic—cut chic and close to the body.

ACCOMMODATIONS
VERY EXPENSIVE
✪ **L'Hôtel Le Petit Nice.** Corniche Président-J.-F.-Kennedy/Anse-de-Maldormé, 13007 Marseille. ☎ **04-91-59-25-92.** Fax 04-91-59-28-08. www.petitnice-passedat.com. E-mail: hotel@petitnice-passedat.com. 15 units. A/C MINIBAR TV TEL. 1,200–2,600 F ($192–$416) double; 4,300–5,500 F ($688–$880) suite. AE, DC, MC, V. Parking 100 F ($16) in garage; free in supervised outdoor parking lot. Métro: Vieux-Port.

This hotel, the best in Marseille, opened in 1917, when the Passédat family joined two suburban villas. The narrow approach will take you past what looks like a row of private villas, in a secluded area below the street paralleling the beach. The spacious Marina Wing across from the main building offers individually decorated bedrooms in the antique style, each opening onto sea views. The rooms in the main house are more modern and avant-garde. Four units were inspired by the Cubist movement, with posh geometric appointments and bright colors.

Dining: The restaurant is beautiful, with a view of the Marseille shore and the rocky islands off its coast. In summer, dinner is served in the garden facing the sea. It's run by Jean-Paul Passédat and Gerald, his son, whose imaginative culinary successes include sliced sea wolf in the old-fashioned style of the Passédat's family matriarch, Lucy; a vinaigrette of rascasse (hogfish); and sea devil with saffron and garlic. They run the finest restaurant in Marseille, a city where dinner often means a bowl of fish soup or a plate of couscous. The restaurant is open daily from May 18 to October; off-season it's closed all day Sunday and Monday. Fixed-price menus cost 350 F to 650 F ($56 to $104) at lunch and 620 F ($99.20) at dinner.

Amenities: Seawater pool and solarium.

EXPENSIVE

Sofitel Marseille Vieux-Port. 36 bd. Charles-Livon, 13007 Marseille. ☎ **04-91-15-59-00.** Fax 04-91-15-59-50. www.sofitel.com. E-mail: Ho542@accor-hotels.com. 130 units. A/C MINIBAR TV TEL. 1,090–1,780 F ($174.40–$284.80) double; 2,700–4,000 F ($432–$640) suite. AE, DC, MC, V. Parking 70 F ($11.20). Métro: Vieux-Port.

This seven-story Sofitel stands above the massive embankments of the old port. Though having none of the charm, grace, or atmosphere of the above-mentioned Le Petit Nice, it's the choice address among the city's chain hotels, and a good value. Some of the rooms have the best panoramic views of the port of Old Marseille; others look out on the boulevard and traffic. They're all fairly generous in size, up-to-date, comfortable, and furnished in a Provence style. In 1987 its owner, the Accor hotel giant, turned over 90 rooms to a new three-star Novotel (below). Today two entrances, staffs, and dining/drinking facilities coexist in the same building.

Dining: There's an elegant bar, and Les Trois Forts, a restaurant with views of the harbor and its defenses. Meals are served daily from noon to 2pm and 7 to 10:30pm.

Amenities: Pool.

MODERATE

La Résidence du Vieux-Port. 18 quai du Port, 13001 Marseille. ☎ **04-91-91-91-22.** Fax 04-91-56-60-88. 41 units. A/C MINIBAR TV TEL. 580–690 F ($92.80–$110.40) double; 810–1,250 F ($129.60–$200) suite. AE, DC, MC, V. Parking 30 F ($4.80). Métro: Vieux-Port.

This old hotel with a touch of raffish charm has an unbeatable location: directly beside a harbor that was valued by the ancient Phoenicians. The guest rooms have loggia-style terraces opening onto the port; they're simple but serviceable. There's a cafe and a breakfast room on the second floor; a bar is behind the lobby.

Novotel Vieux-Port. 36 bd. Charles-Livon, 13007 Marseille. ☎ **04-96-14-41-11.** Fax 04-91-31-15-48. E-mail: H0911@accor-hotels.com. 90 units. A/C MINIBAR TV TEL. 610–710 F ($97.60–$113.60) double. AE, DC, MC, V. Parking 45 F ($7.20). Métro: Vieux-Port.

This Novotel was carved out of the more upscale and more expensive Sofitel (see above) in 1987. Bedrooms here are outfitted in a chain-hotel format that has been perfected and fine-tuned at hundreds of other locations around France. Services are less extensive, amenities are less plush, and spaces are a bit more cramped, than those at the Sofitel, but in light of the fact that this is one of the most reasonably priced, good-value hotels in town, no one seems to mind. The limited number of rooms overlooking the old port tend to fill up first. The lattice-decorated restaurant (Côte Jardin) serves solid and basic meals, daily from 6am to midnight.

INEXPENSIVE

Hôtel Mascotte. 5 la Canebière, 13001 Marseille. ☎ **04-91-90-61-61.** Fax 04-91-90-95-61. 45 units. A/C TV TEL. 455–550 F ($72.80–$88) double. AE, MC, V. Parking 110 F ($17.60) a day in nearby public lot.

Everything about this hotel evokes the tenuous grandeur of 19th-century port life in Marseille. It's located less than 2 blocks from the inner sanctums of the Vieux-Port, in the heart of town. The sun and mistrals of many, many seasons have battered the beaux-arts facade decorated with ornate corbels and cornices. Inside, a series of renovations have stripped the bedrooms of some of their old-fashioned charm, but left behind clean, efficient, soundproofed spaces that are sometimes larger than you might expect. Breakfast is the only meal served, but considering the many dining options within the surrounding neighborhood, no one seems to care.

New Hôtel Bompard. 2 rue des Flots-Bleus, 13007 Marseille. ☎ **04-91-52-10-93.** Fax 04-91-31-02-14. www.new-hotel.com. E-mail: marseillebompard@new-hotel.com. 46 units. A/C MINIBAR TV TEL. 490–500 F ($78.40–$80) double. Free parking. Bus: 61 or 83.

This is a tranquil retreat, set atop a cliff along the corniche, about 1½ miles east of Vieux Port. Partly because of its elegant garden, it might remind you of a well-appointed private home. Bedrooms have conservatively traditional furniture, tasteful and subdued color schemes, and balconies or terraces overlooking the grounds.

DINING
EXPENSIVE

✪ **Le Miramar.** 12 Quai du Port. ☎ **04-91-91-10-40.** Reservations recommended. Main courses 170–230 F ($27.20–$36.80); bouillabaisse 280 F ($44.80) per person (minimum 2 diners). AE, DC, MC, V. Mon–Sat noon–2pm and 7:15–10pm. Closed 2 weeks in Jan and 3 weeks in Aug. Métro: Vieux-Port/Hôtel de Ville. SEAFOOD.

Since the mid-1960s, aficionados of bouillabaisse have been flocking here. There is no finer dining choice in Marseille today than this restaurant. Savoring the bouillabaisse delights here will be one of the culinary highlights of your trip. It's hard to imagine that this was once a rough-and-tumble recipe favored by local fisherfolk. It was actually devised by Marseille fishermen as a way of using the least desirable portion of their catch. Actually it's two dishes, beginning with a saffron-tinted soup followed by the fish poached in the soup. It's consumed with *lashing a rouille*, a sauce of red chilies, garlic, olive oil, egg yolk, and cayenne. The version served here involves lots of labor and just as much costly seafood. The chef here considers rascasse or hogfish essential to bouillabaisse, although he views lobster as a "silly frill that adds nothing to the soup but plenty to the bill." The setting is a large, big-windowed room with frescoes of underwater life. It's linked to an outdoor terrace that overlooks Marseille's most famous church, Notre-Dame-de-la-Garde.

MODERATE

Au Pescadou. 19 place Castellane. ☎ **04-91-78-36-01.** Reservations recommended. Main courses 90–120 F ($14.40–$19.20); bouillabaisse 238 F ($38.10) per person; fixed-price menus 132 F ($21.10) at lunch Mon–Fri, 188 F ($30.10) at dinner. AE, MC, V. Mon–Sat noon–2pm and 7–11pm, Sun noon–2pm. Closed July–Aug. Métro: Castellane. SEAFOOD.

One of Marseille's finest seafood restaurants is maintained by three multilingual sons of the original owner, Barthélémy Mennella. Beside a busy traffic circle downtown, it overlooks a fountain, an obelisk, and a sidewalk display of fresh oysters. For an appetizer, try almond-stuffed mussels or "hors d'oeuvres of the fisherman." Main-dish specialties are bouillabaisse, *gigot de lotte* (monkfish stewed in cream sauce with fresh vegetables), and scallops cooked with morels.

Adjacent to the main restaurant, and under the same management, is an informal newcomer, **La Brasserie Mille Colonnes,** 21 Place Castellane (☎ 04-91-78-18-10). Bustling and gregarious, it serves platters of grilled fish as well as such non-fish dishes as blanquettes of veal, steak, pizzaiola, and pastas. Full meals, without wine, rarely exceed 140 F ($22.40); and *plats du jour* cost from 55 F to 68 F ($8.80 to $10.90).

○ **Les Arcenaulx.** 25 cours d'Estienne d'orves. ☎ **04-91-59-80-30.** Reservations recommended. Main courses 70–110 F ($11.20–$17.60); fixed-price menus 155–295 F ($24.80–$47.20). AE, DC, MC, V. Mon–Sat noon–2pm and 8–11:30pm. Métro: Vieux-Port. PROVENÇAL.

These bulky stone premises were warehouses built by the navies of Louis XIV. Close to the water near the Vieux Port, they contain this restaurant as well as two bookstores (one for French classics, one for modern titles), all directed by the hardworking and charming sisters, Simone and Jeanne Laffitte. Look for authentic and hearty Provençal cuisine with a Marseillais accent in dishes that include a *baudroie* (kettle of seasonal fish) *à la Raimu*—named for a popular 20th-century actor, it's equivalent to bouillabaisse. Equally tempting are artichokes *barigoule* (loaded with aromatic spices and olive oil), a charlotte of crabs, and a worthy assortment of *petites légumes farcies* (slit-open Provençal vegetables stuffed with chopped meat and herbs).

Les Echevins. 44 rue Sainte. ☎ **04-96-11-03-11.** Reservations recommended. Main courses 110–185 F ($17.60–$29.60); fixed-price menus 120–300 F ($19.20–$48). AE, DC, MC, V. Mon–Fri noon–2:30pm and 7:30–11:30pm, Sat 7:30–11:30pm. Métro: Vieux-Port. PROVENÇAL/SOUTHWESTERN FRENCH.

On the opposite side of the same building that contains Les Arcenaulx (see above), this restaurant occupies what was built as a dorm for the prisoners who were forced to row the ornamental barges of Louis XIV during his rare inspections of Marseille's harbor facilities. Today the setting contains crystal chandeliers, plush carpets, an enviable collection of antiques, and massive rocks and thick beams. You'll get a lot for your money, as the owners insist on using fresh ingredients prepared at the last possible minute, and charge relatively reasonable prices. Provençal dishes include a succulent version of baked sea wolf that's prepared as simply as possible—just with herbs and olive oil. There's also roast codfish with aïoli and a succulent version of *baudroie* (a simpler version of bouillabaisse).

INEXPENSIVE

Chez Angèle. 50 rue Caisserie. ☎ **04-91-90-63-35.** Reservations recommended. Pizzas, pastas, and salads 60–95 F ($9.60–$15.20); fixed-price menu 100 F ($16). AE, MC, V. Mon–Fri noon–2:30pm; daily 7–11pm. Closed July 20–Aug 20. Métro: Vieux-Port. PROVENÇAL/ PIZZA. On the route between Marseille and Aix.

A local friend guided us here, and though most of Marseille's cheap eating places aren't recommendable, this one is worthwhile if you're watching your francs. Small and unpretentious, with a raffish kind of amiability from the owner, it defines itself as a pizzeria-restaurant, with a menu that's much more comprehensive than the average pizzeria's. You can get pizza (the versions with pistou, fresh seafood, or cèpe mushrooms are among the best) or well-prepared ravioli, tagliatelle, osso buco, and grilled versions of shrimp, squid, and daurade Provençal style. If you're looking for something really ethnic, ask for Francis's version of *pieds et paquets,* a country recipe savored by locals that includes equal portions of grilled sheep's foot and sheep's intestines stuffed with garlic-flavored breadcrumbs, herbs, and chopped vegetables.

MARSEILLE AFTER DARK

You can get an amusing (and relatively harmless) exposure to the town's saltiness during a walk around the **Vieux Port,** where a medley of cafes and restaurants angle their sightlines for the best possible view of the harbor. Select any of them that strikes your fancy (or just park yourself by the waterfront for a view of the passing parade). But for a sure bet, head to **Brasserie Vieux-Port New-York,** 33 quai des Belges (☎ **04-91-33-91-79**). A wide roster of Marseille's arts community will probably join you.

Escale Borély, avenue Mendès-France, is a modern-day equivalent of the Vieux Port. It's a waterfront development south of the town center, only 20 minutes away by Métro. About a dozen cafes as well as restaurants of every possible ilk present a wide choice of cuisines, views of in-line skaters on the promenade in front, and the potential for dialogues with friendly strangers. An especially worthwhile place here is **L'Assiette Marine** (☎ **04-91-22-06-21**), a seafood restaurant with a separate bar area where fresh oysters, clams, and chilled lobster might accompany your drink.

Unless the air-conditioning is very powerful, Marseille's dance clubs produce a lot of sweat. The best of them is the **Café de la Plage,** in the above-mentioned Escale Borély (☎ **04-91-71-21-76**), where a 35-and-under crowd dance in an environment that's safer and healthier than many of its competitors'. Closer to the Vieux Port, you can dance and drink at the **Metal Café,** 20 rue Fortia (☎ **04-91-54-03-03**), where 20- to 50-year-olds listen to music that's been recently released in London and Los Angeles; or try the nearby **Trolley Bus,** 24 quai de Rive-Neuve (☎ **04-91-54-30-45**). Trolley Bus is best known for its techno, house, retro music, hip-hop, jazz, and salsa. Also very appealing, if only because people here seem to have more fun than at the usual run-of-the-mill pastis dive, is **Pêle-Mêle,** 8 place aux Huiles (☎ **04-91-54-85-26**), a many-faceted bar/disco/cafe and host of occasional live music.

If you miss free-form modern jazz and don't mind taking your chances in the less-than-completely-savory neighborhood adjacent to the city's rail station (La Gare St-Charles—a taxi here and back is recommended), consider dropping into **La Cave à Jazz,** rue Bernard-du-Bois (☎ **04-91-39-28-28**).

A cabaret that presents views of sexy performers, broad humor, and occasional instances of political satire within a context that also includes a restaurant is **Le Chocolat Théâtre**, 59 cours Julien (☎ **04-91-42-19-29**). The venue and hours change week by week, so phone in advance for an insight into whatever the format is on the night of your arrival.

The gay scene here isn't as interesting as it is in Nice, though there are quite a number of gay bars. **MP Bar,** 10 rue Beauveau (☎ **04-91-33-64-79**), is *le gay bar* in Marseille. It is open nightly from 6pm to sunrise. **L'Enigme,** 22 rue Beauvau (☎ **04-91-33-79-20**), attracts a crowd whose average age is 18 to 35. It offers dance music daily from 7pm to sunrise. The youth-conscious **New Can Can,** 3–5 rue Sénac (☎ **04-91-48-59-76**), is an enormous venue that's everybody's favorite dance emporium every Thursday to Sunday, from around 11pm till dawn. An alternative gay bar and disco, conveniently located in the sultry and central neighborhood near the Vieux Port, is **Le Crazy,** rue du Chantier (no phone). Clients have known one another since forever, and a sailor or student from abroad will probably not buy his own drinks for very long. Its bar area and dance floor are especially busy every night from around 3am to sunrise.

8 Toulon

519 miles S of Paris, 79 miles SW of Cannes, 42 miles E of Marseille

This fortress and modern town is the principal naval base of France: the headquarters of the Mediterranean fleet, with hundreds of sailors wandering the streets. It's not as seedy, but also not as intriguing, as Marseilles. A beautiful harbor, it's surrounded by hills and crowned by forts, protected on the east by a large breakwater and on the west by the great peninsula of Cap Sicié. Separated by the breakwater, the outer roads are known as the Grande Rade and the inner roads the Petite Rade. A winter resort colony lies on the outskirts. Like Marseilles, Toulon has a large Arab population from North Africa. Note that there's racial tension here, worsened by the closing of the shipbuilding yards.

Park your vehicle underground at place de la Liberté, then go along boulevard des Strasbourg, turning right onto rue Berthelot. This will take you into the pedestrian-only area in the core of the old city. It's filled with shops, hotels, restaurants, and cobblestone streets (but it can be dangerous at night). The best beach, **Plage du Mourillon,** is 1¼ miles east of the heart of town.

ESSENTIALS

GETTING THERE & GETTING AROUND Trains arrive from Marseille about every 30 minutes (trip time: 1 hour). If you're on the Riviera, frequent trains arrive from Nice (trip time: 2 hours) and from Cannes (trip time: 80 minutes). For rail information and schedules, call ☎ **08-36-35-35-35.**

Three **buses** per day arrive from Aix-en-Provence (trip time: 75 minutes). For bus information and schedules, call either **Cie Sodetrav** (☎ **04-94-12-55-12**) or **Littoral Cars** (☎ **04-94-74-01-35**); they service Toulon.

If you're **driving** from Marseille, take A50 east to Toulon. When you arrive in Toulon, it's best to park your car and get around on foot, as the *vieille ville* (old town) and most of the attractions are easy to reach. A municipal bus system serves the town as well. Tickets cost 8 F ($1.30); a map of bus routes is available at the tourist office.

VISITOR INFORMATION The **Office de Tourisme** is at place Raimu (☎ **04-94-18-53-00**).

EXPLORING THE TOWN

In **Vieux Toulon,** between the harbor and boulevard des Strasbourg (the main axis of town), are many remains of the port's former days. Visit the **Poissonerie,** the typical covered market, bustling in the morning with fishmongers and buyers. Another colorful market, the **Marché,** spills over onto the narrow streets around cours Lafayette. Also in old Toulon is the **Cathédrale Ste-Marie-Majeure,** built in the Romanesque style in the 11th and 12th centuries, then much expanded in the 17th. Its badly lit nave is Gothic; the belfry and facade are from the 18th century. It's open daily 8am to 6pm.

In contrast to the cathedral, tall modern buildings line quai Stalingrad, opening onto **Vieille d'Arse.** On place Puget, look for the *atlantes* (caryatids), figures of men used as columns. These interesting figures support a balcony at the **Hôtel de Ville** (city hall) and are also included in the facade of the naval museum.

Musée de la Marine, place du Ingénieur-Général-Monsenergue (☎ **04-94-02-02-01**), contains many figureheads and ship models. It's open in July and August, Wednesday to Monday from 9:30am to noon and 3 to 7pm, September to June Wednesday through Monday from 9:30am to noon and 2 to 6pm. Admission is 29 F ($4.65) for adults and 19 F ($3.05) for students and children. **Musée de Toulon,** 113 bd. du Maréchal-Leclerc (☎ **04-94-36-81-00**), displays works from the 16th century to the present. There's a particularly good collection of Provençal and Italian paintings, as well as religious works. The latest acquisitions include New Realism pieces and minimalist art. It's open daily from 1 to 6pm; admission is free.

Once you've covered the top attractions, we suggest taking a drive, an hour or two before sunset, along the **corniche du Mont-Faron.** It's a scenic boulevard along the lower slopes of Mont Faron, providing views of the busy port, the town, the cliffs, and, in the distance, the Mediterranean.

Earlier in the day, consider boarding a **téléphérique** (funicular) near the Altéa La Tour Blanche Hôtel (☎ **04-94-92-68-25**). It operates Tuesday to Sunday from 9:30 to 11:45am and 2:15 to 6:30pm; cost is 38 F ($6.10) for adults and 25 F ($4) for children round-trip. It is not in service during windy conditions. At the top, enjoy the view and then visit the **Memorial du Débarquement en Provence,** Mont Faron (☎ **04-94-88-08-09**), which documents, among other exhibits, the Allied landings in Provence in 1944. It's open in summer daily from 9:30 to 11:45am and 2:30 to 5:45pm, in winter Tuesday through Sunday from 9:15 to 11:45am and 2 to 4:45pm. Admission is 25 F ($4) for adults, 10 F ($1.60) for children 5 to 12, and free for children 4 and under.

ACCOMMODATIONS

Hôtel La Corniche. 1 littoral Frédéric-Mistral (at Le Mourillon), 83000 Toulon. ☎ **800/ 528-1234** in the U.S., or 04-94-41-35-12. Fax 04-94-41-24-58. 23 units. A/C MINIBAR TV TEL. 450–700 F ($72–$112) double; 750–920 F ($120–$147.20) suite. AE, DC, MC, V. Parking 40 F ($6.40). Bus: 3, 13, or 23.

An attractive hotel with an interior garden, La Corniche offers a pleasant staff, two restaurants, and comfortable accommodations. The rooms with sea views and loggias are the most expensive. The rooms are decorated in Provençal style. The hotel lies near the beach, in the neighborhood known as Le Mourillon, a 15-minute walk from the congested commercial center of Toulon.

Ironically, the more formal of the **two restaurants** here is referred to as the **Bistro** and features a trio of pine trees growing upward through the roof and a large bay window overlooking the port. The simpler restaurant is the cramped but cozy **Rôtisserie,** which is under a different management. Both emphasize fish dishes.

New Hôtel Tour Blanche. Bd. de l'Amiral-Vence, 83200 Toulon. ☎ **04-94-24-41-57.** Fax 04-94-22-42-25. www.new-hotel.com. E-mail: toulontourblanche@new-hotel.com. 91 units. A/C MINIBAR TV TEL. 440–490 F ($70.40–$78.40) double. AE, DC, MC, V. Free parking. Bus: 40. From the town center, follow the signs to the Mont Faron téléphérique and you'll pass the hotel en route.

With excellent modernized accommodations, attractive gardens with terraces, and a pool, this seven-story hotel is the best in Toulon. It lies in the rocky hills about a half-mile north of the center of town, a position that contributes to sweeping views of the port and sea from even the lower floors. Many rooms, especially those overlooking the bay, have balconies, and each is comfortably and simply outfitted in an international modern style.

The **restaurant, Les Terrasses,** offers a panoramic view, fixed-price menus at 100 F to 180 F ($16 to $28.80) each, and food and wine whose selection is inspired by the culinary traditions of Provence and the Midi.

DINING

✪ **La Chamade.** 25 rue Denfert-Rochereau. ☎ **04-94-92-28-58.** Reservations recommended. Fixed-price menu 195 F ($31.20). AE, MC, V. Mon–Fri noon–2:30pm and 7–9:30pm, Sat 7–9:30pm. Closed Aug 1–25. Bus: 1 or 21. FRENCH.

In the town center, in a relatively nondescript building whose thick walls hint at its age, this restaurant simplified its culinary format in 1996 by offering only one option: a fixed-price menu that includes an ever-changing choice of three appetizers, three main courses, and three desserts. The chef, Francis Bonneau, is the former disciple of some of the grandest restaurants of Paris and Brittany. Menu items change with the seasons, but might include stuffed and deep-fried zucchini blossoms, fillet of sea bass with basil-flavored butter sauce, and roast whitefish garnished with ham and risotto with local herbs. Desserts often include a craqueline of dates served with gentian, a herb that flourishes on Provence's arid hillsides; or frozen custard garnished with local strawberries marinated in red wine.

TOULON AFTER DARK

A town that's the temporary home of thousands of French and foreign sailors is bound to have a nightlife scene that's earthier, and a bit raunchier, than equivalent-sized towns elsewhere. An appealingly rough-and-ready bar that sports stiff drinks, live music, and a complete lack of pretension is **Le Bar 113,** 113 Avenue de Infanterie de la Marine (☎ **04-94-03-42-41**). Adjacent to the port is the **Bar La Lampa,** Port de Toulon (☎ **04-94-03-06-09**), where tapas and live music accompany copious amounts of beer and glasses of wine or whiskey. An even less formal hangout is **Bar à Thym,** 32 bd. Cuneo (☎ **04-94-41-90-10**), where everybody seems to drink beer, gossip, and listen to live music. Toulon is also home to one of the Azure Coast's best-known gay discos, **Boy's Paradise,** 1 bd. Pierre-Toesca (☎ **04-94-09-35-90**), near the city's railway station, where groups of gay men include a scattering of off-duty French sailors and to a lesser degree, gay women.

But if you feel claustrophobic in a town noted for its heavy industry and want more resorty outlets, you might be happy at Hyère, about 16 miles east of Toulon, where there's an upscale disco, **Le Fou du Roy,** in the Casino des Palmiers (☎ **04-94-12-80-80**). About 9 miles west of Toulon, in the small port town of Sanary, **Mai-Tai,** route de Bandol (☎ **04-94-74-23-92**), appeals to dancers under age 30.

15 The French Riviera

Each resort on the Riviera, known as the Côte d'Azur, offers its own unique flavor and special charms. This narrow strip of fabled real estate, which is less than 125 miles long and is located between the Mediterranean and a trio of mountain ranges, has always attracted the jet set, with its clear skies, blue waters, and orange groves.

A trail of modern artists captivated by the brilliant light and setting of the Côte d'Azur has left a rich heritage: Matisse in his chapel at Vence, Cocteau at Menton and Villefranche, Picasso at Antibes and seemingly everywhere else, Léger at Biot, Renoir at Cagnes, and Bonnard at Le Cannet. The best collection of all is at the Maeght Foundation in St-Paul-de-Vence.

The Riviera's high season used to be winter and spring only. However, with changing tastes, July and August have long been the most crowded, and reservations are imperative. The average summer temperature is 75°F; the average winter temperature, 49°F.

The corniches of the Riviera, depicted in countless films, stretch from Nice to Menton. The Alps here drop into the Mediterranean, and roads were carved along the way. The lower road, about 20 miles long, is the Corniche Inférieure. Along this road are the ports of Villefranche, Cap-Ferrat, Beaulieu, and Cap-Martin. The 19-mile long Moyenne Corniche (Middle Road), built between World War I and the beginning of World War II, also runs from Nice to Menton, winding spectacularly in and out of tunnels and through mountains. The highlight is at mountaintop Eze. The Grande Corniche—the most panoramic—was ordered built by Napoléon in 1806. La Turbie and Le Vistaero are the principal towns along the 20-mile stretch, which reaches more than 1,600 feet high at Col d'Eze.

Note: For more extensive coverage of this region, check out the book *Frommer's Provence & the Riviera.*

REGIONAL CUISINE   In the 19th century an undeveloped coastal strip of eastern Provence was deemed "the Riviera." Technically, the Riviera is part of Provence, and all the culinary traditions of that region (see chapter 14) apply here, albeit in slightly diluted forms.

On the Riviera you'll find high-toned bastions of French cuisine right alongside budget joints catering to the latest culinary fads, juxtaposed in sometimes-uncomfortable proximity. Outside Paris, the Riviera has more different types of restaurants and greater numbers of theme restaurants than anywhere else in France. So expect to find Provençal cuisine, with a generous dose of international sophistication.

The French Riviera

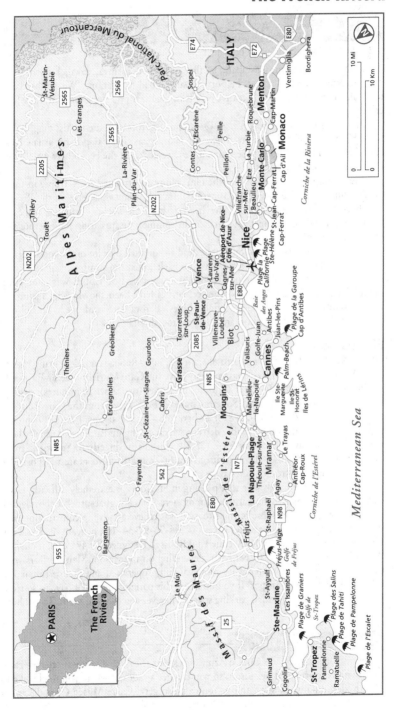

1   St-Tropez

543 miles S of Paris, 47 miles SW of Cannes

An air of hedonism runs rampant in this sun-kissed carnival town, but the true Tropezian resents the fact that the port has such a bad reputation. "We can be classy too," one native has insisted. Creative people in the lively arts along with ordinary folk create a varied mixture.

Brigitte Bardot's *And God Created Woman* put St-Tropez on the tourist map, but it has a history as well. Colette lived here for many years. Even the diarist Anaïs Nin, confidante of Henry Miller, posed for a little cheesecake on the beach here in 1939 in a Dorothy Lamour–style bathing suit.

Artists, composers, novelists, and the film colony are attracted to St-Tropez in summer. Trailing them is a parade of humanity unmatched anywhere else on the Riviera for sheer flamboyance. Some of the most fashionable yachts, bringing some of the most chic people around, anchor here in summer, disappearing long before the dreaded mistral of winter.

In 1995 Bardot pronounced St-Tropez dead—"squatted by a lot of no-goods, drug-heads, and villains." She swore she'd never go back, at least in summer. But 1997 saw her return, as headlines in France flashed the news that St-Tropez was "hot once again." Not only Bardot but also other celebrities have been showing up, including Oprah Winfrey, Don Johnson, Quincy Jones, Barbra Streisand, Jack Nicholson, Robert De Niro, and even Elton and Sly (not together!).

ESSENTIALS

GETTING THERE   The nearest rail station is in St-Raphaël, a neighboring resort; at the Vieux Port, four or five **boats** per day leave the **Gare Maritime de St-Raphaël,** rue Pierre-Auble (☎ **04-94-95-17-46**), for St-Tropez (trip time: 50 minutes), costing 60 F ($9.60) each way. Some 15 Sodetrav **buses** per day, leave from the Gare Routière in St-Raphaël (☎ **04-94-95-24-82**), and go to St-Tropez, taking $1^1/_2$ to $2^1/_4$ hours, depending on the bus and the traffic density, which during midsummer is usually horrendous. A one-way ticket costs 55 F ($8.80). Buses run directly to St-Tropez from Toulon and Hyères. Buses also run directly to St-Tropez from its nearest airport, the airport at Toulon-Hyères 35 miles away.

If you **drive,** note in advance that parking in St-Tropez is extremely difficult, especially in summer, when the carnival atmosphere virtually guarantees a shortage of parking spots. In 1998, some of the situation was relieved with the construction of a multi-storied parking lot, **Parc des Lices** (☎ **04-94-97-34-46**), beneath the Place des Lices, whose entrance is on the Avenue Paul Roussel. Designed for 471 cars, it charges 8 F to 13 F ($1.30 to $2.10) per hour, depending on the season. Many visitors with expensive cars prefer this site, as it's more carefully supervised and guarded than any other parking lot in St-Tropez. If you don't use this parking lot, you'll have to squeeze your car into impossibly small parking spaces wherever you can find them. **To get here**

Surfing on the Riviera

Before your tour of the Côte d'Azur, check out the Web site **www.crt-riviera.fr.** Activities are arranged by season, so you can get an idea of where you might like to go hiking, biking, or sunbathing. You can also get a **Carte Musée Côte d'Azur,** a pass good at 62 museums on the Riviera.

St-Tropez

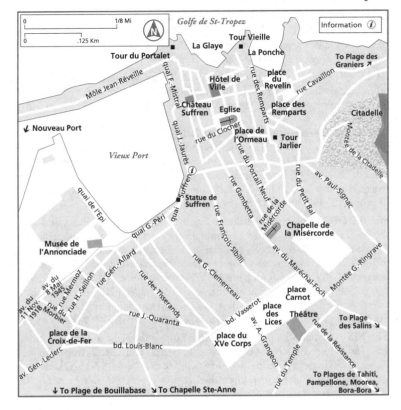

from Cannes, drive southwest along the coastal highway (RD98), turning eastward when you see the signs pointing to St-Tropez.

VISITOR INFORMATION The **Office de Tourisme** is on quai Jean-Jaurès (☎ **04-94-97-45-21**).

A DAY AT THE BEACH

The hottest Riviera beaches are at St-Tropez. The best for families are those closest to the center, including the amusingly named **Plage de la Bouillabaisse** and **Plage des Graniers.** The more daring are the 6-mile sandy crescents at **Plage des Salins** and **Plage de Pampellone,** beginning some 2 miles from the town center and best reached by bike (see below) if you're not driving. Called "notoriously decadent," ✪ **Plage de Tahiti** occupies the north end of the 3¹/₂-mile-long Pampellone, lined with concessions, cafes, and restaurants. It's a strip of golden sand that has long been favored by exhibitionists wearing next to nothing (or truly nothing) and cruising shamelessly. If you ever wanted to go topless, this is the place to do it. Vive la France!

OUTDOOR PURSUITS

BIKING The largest outfitter for bikes and motor scooters is **Louis Mas,** 5 rue Josef-Quaranta (☎ **04-94-97-00-60**). You'll be required to leave a deposit of 1,000 F ($160), payable with a major credit card, plus 48 F ($7.70) per hour for a bike, 190 F to 275 F ($30.40 to $44) per hour for a motor scooter, depending on its size.

BOATING   The highly recommended **Suncap Company,** 15 quai de Suffren (☎ 04-94-97-11-23), rents boats from 18 to 40 feet long. The smallest can be rented to qualified sailors without a captain, but the larger ones come with a captain at the helm. Prices begin at 3,000 F ($480) per day.

GOLF   The nearest golf course, at the edge of Ste-Maxime, across the bay from St-Tropez, is the **Golf Club de Beauvallon,** boulevard des Collines (☎ 04-94-96-16-98), a popular 18-hole course. Greens fees are 250 F to 300 F ($40 to $48) for 18 holes.

Sprawling over a rocky, vertiginous landscape that requires a golf cart and a lot of physical labor is the Don Harradine-designed **Golf de Ste-Maxime-Plaza,** route du Débarquement, Ste-Maxime (☎ 04-94-55-02-02). Built in 1991 with the four-star Plaza de Ste-Maxime, it welcomes nonguests; phone to reserve tee-off times. Greens fees for 18 holes are 250 F to 280 F ($40 to $44.80) per person; cart rental (capacity of two) is 125 F ($20) per 18 holes.

SCUBA DIVING   A team of dive enthusiasts who are ready, willing, and able to show you the watery azure-colored depths off the coast of St-Tropez operate from the *Octopussy* I and II. Both boats are aluminum-sided, yellow-painted dive boats, built in the 1990s. They're based year-round in St-Tropez's Nouveau Port. Experienced divers pay 230 F ($36.80) for a one-tank *"exploration"* dive, and novices are charged 250 F ($40) for a *baptème,* that includes one-on-one supervision from a monitor and a descent to a depth of around 15 feet. For reservations and information, call or write Les *Octopussys,* Quartier de Berteau, Gassin, 83990 St-Tropez (☎ 04-94-56-53-10).

TENNIS   Anyone who phones in advance can use the eight courts (both artificial grass and "Quick," a form of concrete) at the **Tennis-Club de St-Tropez,** route des Plages, in St-Tropez's industrial zone of St-Claude (☎ 04-94-97-15-52), about half a mile from the resort's center. Open throughout the year, the courts rent for 100 F ($16) per hour from 10am to 5pm and 130 F ($20.80) per hour after 5pm.

SHOPPING

Choses, quai Jean-Jaurès (☎ 04-94-97-03-44), is a women's clothing store typical (but stocked better than some others) of the hundreds of middle-bracket, whimsically nonchalant shops that thrive along the Riviera. Its specialty is clingy and often provocative T-shirt dresses.

Galeries Tropéziennes, 56 rue Gambetta (☎ 04-94-97-02-21), crowds hundreds of unusual gift items—some worthwhile, some rather silly—and textiles into its rambling showrooms near place des Lices. The inspiration is Mediterranean, breezy and sophisticated.

In a resort that's increasingly loaded with purveyors of suntan lotion, touristy souvenirs, and T-shirts, **Jacqueline Thienot,** 12 rue Georges-Clemenceau (☎ 04-94-97-05-70), maintains an inventory of Provençal antiques that's prized by dealers from as far away as Paris. The one-room shop is in a late18th-century building that shows the 18th- and 19th-century antiques to their best advantage. Also sold are antique examples of Provençal wrought iron and rustic farm and homemaker's implements.

SEEING THE SIGHTS

Château Suffren is east from the port at the top end of quai Jean-Jaurès. Now home to occasional art exhibits, it was built in 980 by Comte Guillame I of Provence.

Near the junction of quai Suffren and quai Jean-Jaurès stands the bronze *Statue de Suffren,* paying tribute to Vice-Admiral Pierre André de Suffren. This St-Tropez hometown boy became one of the greatest sailors of 18th-century France, though he's largely forgotten today. And in the Vieille Ville, one of the most interesting streets is **rue de la Misércorde.** It's lined with boxy-looking stone houses, with artsy boutiques. This street evokes medieval St-Tropez better than any other street in town. At the corner of rue Gambetta is the **Chapelle de la Misércorde,** with a blue, green, and gold tile roof.

Two miles from St-Tropez, **Port Grimaud** makes an interesting outing. From St-Tropez, drive 3 miles west on A98 to Route 98, then 1 mile north to the Port Grimaud exit. If you approach the village at dusk, when it's softly bathed in Riviera pastels, it'll look like some old hamlet, perhaps from the 16th century. But this is a mirage. Port Grimaud is the dream fulfillment of its promoter, François Spoerry, who carved it out of marshland and dug canals. Flanking these canals, fingers of land extend from the main square to the sea. The homes are Provençal style, many with Italianate window arches. Boat owners can anchor right at their doorsteps. One newspaper called the port "the most magnificent fake since Disneyland."

Musée de l'Annonciade (Musée St-Tropez). Place Grammont. ☎ **04-94-97-04-01.** Admission 30 F ($4.80) adults, 15 F ($2.40) children. June–Sept, Wed–Mon 10am–noon and 3–7pm; Oct and Dec–May, Wed–Mon 10am–noon and 2–6pm. Closed Nov.

Near the harbor, this museum was installed in the former chapel of the Annonciade. It boasts one of the finest modern art collections on the Riviera. Many of the artists, including Paul Signac, depicted the port of St-Tropez. The collection includes such works as Van Dongen's yellow-faced *Women of the Balustrade* and paintings and sculpture by Bonnard, Matisse, Braque, Dufy, Utrillo, Seurat, Derain, and Maillol.

ACCOMMODATIONS
VERY EXPENSIVE

✪ **Hôtel Byblos.** Av. Paul-Signac, 83990 St-Tropez. ☎ **800/223-6800** in the U.S., or 04-94-56-68-00. Fax 04-94-56-68-01. www.byblos.com. E-mail: saint-tropez@byblos.com. 102 units, 10 duplex suites. A/C MINIBAR TV TEL. 1,750–3,350 F ($280–$536) double; from 6,450 F ($1,032) suite; from 4,900 F ($784) duplex suite. AE, DC, MC, V. Closed Oct 15–Easter. Parking 150 F ($24) in garage.

The builder said he created "an anti-hotel, a place like home." That's true if your home resembles a palace in Beirut with salons decorated with Phoenician gold statues from 3000 B.C. On a hill above the harbor, this deluxe complex has intimate patios and courtyards and seductive retreats filled with antiques and rare decorative objects, including polychrome carved woodwork on the walls, marquetry floors, and a Persian-rug ceiling. Every room is unique. Unusual features, for example, might be a fireplace on a raised hearth or a bed recessed on a dais. Bedrooms range from medium in size to spacious, often with high ceilings and antiques or reproductions. Each room is filled with a luxury mattress on an elegant French bed. Some, but not all units, have such special features as four-posters with seductive furry spreads or sunken whirlpool baths. Le Hameau contains 10 duplex suites built around a small courtyard with an outdoor spa. Some rooms have balconies overlooking an inner courtyard; others open onto a terrace of flowers.

Dining/Diversions: You can dine by the pool at Les Arcades, enjoying Provençal food, or try an Italian restaurant offering an antipasti buffet, many pasta courses, and other typical fare from France's neighbor. Later in the evening you can dance on a circular floor surrounded by bas-relief columns in the hotel's nightclub, Caves du Roy. There are also two bars.

Amenities: 24-hour room service, same-day laundry/valet, beauty salon, high-fashion pool, sauna.

Hôtel Le Yaca. 1 bd. d'Aumale, 83900 St-Tropez. ☎ **04-94-55-81-00.** Fax 04-94-97-58-50. www.hotel-le-yaca.fr. 27 units. A/C MINIBAR TV TEL. 1,500–2,350 F ($240–$376) double; 3,300–5,400 F ($528–$864) suite. AE, DC, MC, V. Closed Oct–Easter. Parking 100 F ($16).

Built in 1722 off a narrow street in the old part of town, this was the first hotel in St-Tropez. Colette lived here in 1927, and before that it was the home of pre-impressionists like Paul Signac. The high-ceilinged reception area boasts a view of an inner courtyard filled with flowers. Many of the rooms also have views of this courtyard. Some are on the upper floor, with handmade terra-cotta floor tiles and massive ceiling timbers. Each has a comfortable bed, dignified and utilitarian furniture, and high ceilings.

Dining/Diversions: The in-house restaurant, Le Patio, is open only for dinner. Fixed-price menus cost around 235 F ($37.60) each, and feature a list of food items that vary according to the season and the inspiration of the chef.

Amenities: Heated pool in the garden, 24-hour room service, carefully landscaped courtyard whose architecture might remind you of antique Andalusia.

EXPENSIVE

Hôtel La Ponche. 3 rue des Remparts, 83990 St-Tropez. ☎ **04-94-97-02-53.** Fax 04-94-97-78-61. www.laponche.com. E-mail: hotel@laponche.com. 18 units. A/C MINIBAR TV TEL. 800F–1,900F ($136–$323) double. AE, MC, V. Closed Nov–Mar 15.

Overlooking the old fishing port, this has long been a cherished address, run by the same family for more than half a century. The hotel is filled with the original, airy paintings of Jacques Cordier, which adds to the elegant atmosphere. Each room has been newly redecorated and is well equipped, opening onto views of the sea. There are two or three rooms per floor. Sun-colored walls with subtle lighting evoke a homelike feeling. Beds are elegantly appointed with beautiful linen and quality mattresses.

Dining: The hotel restaurant is big on Provençal charm and cuisine. A sophisticated crowd can be found on its terrace almost any night in fair weather.

MODERATE

Hôtel Ermitage. Av. Paul-Signac, 83990 St-Tropez. ☎ **04-94-97-52-33.** Fax 04-94-97-10-43. 26 units. TV TEL. 690–990 F ($110.40–$158.40) double. AE, DC, MC, V.

Attractively isolated amid the rocky heights of St-Tropez, this hotel was built in the 19th century as a private villa. Today its red-tile roof and green shutters shelter a plush hideaway. A walled garden is illuminated at night, and a cozy corner bar near a wood-burning fireplace takes the chill out of blustery evenings. The guest rooms are pleasantly but simply furnished. Breakfast is the only meal served.

Hôtel La Tartane. Rte. des Salins, 83990 St-Tropez. ☎ **04-94-97-21-23.** Fax 04-94-97-09-16. E-mail: hotellatartane@wanadoo.fr. 14 units. A/C MINIBAR TV TEL. 650–1,000 F ($104–$160) double. AE, DC, V. Closed Oct–Mar.

This small-scale hotel is midway between the center of St-Tropez and the Plage des Salins, about a 3-minute drive from each. There's a heated, stone-rimmed pool set into the garden, attractively furnished public rooms with terra-cotta floors, and an attentive management that works hard to keep everything pulled together. The guest rooms are bungalows surrounding the pool. Amenities such as hair dryers are lacking.

Breakfasts are elaborate and attractive, lunch is offered between 1 and 3pm, and dinner is 7:30 to 9:30pm. Fresh grilled fish from the Mediterranean is the specialty. Dinner prices begin at 220 F ($35.20). There's also room service from 8am to 11pm.

Hôtel Sube. 15 quai Suffren, 83900 St-Tropez. ☎ **04-94-97-30-04.** Fax 04-94-54-89-08. E-mail: sube@nova.fr. 30 units. A/C TV TEL. 890–1,500 F ($142.40–$240) double in the high season; 590–990 F ($94.40–$158.40) double in the low season. AE, DC, MC, V. Parking nearby 200 F ($32).

If you want to be right on the port, this should be your first choice. It was originally established in 1800 as a way station and hotel for the French postal services. It's directly over the Café de Paris in the center of a shopping arcade. The two-story lounge has a beamed ceiling and a glass front, allowing a great view of the harbor activity. The lounge is furnished with a 10-foot-high fireplace and provincial chairs. The bedrooms are very small and decorated in a provincial style, as well. Rooms are not particularly large, but they're comfortable and clean, and carry the added allure of being in the very heart of everything in St-Tropez. The more expensive rooms have nice views overlooking the port.

DINING

Chez Maggi. 7 rue Sibille. ☎ **04-94-97-16-12.** Reservations recommended. Fixed-price menu 175 F ($28). MC, V. Daily 8pm–3am. Closed Nov–Mar. PROVENÇAL/ITALIAN.

This restaurant retained the name it was given by two women during its earlier incarnation as a lesbian bar. Since its acquisition by the present owners, it has emerged as St-Tropez's most flamboyant gay restaurant/bar. At least half its floor space is devoted to a very busy bar, where patrons tend to range from 25 to 35 and whose turf extends out onto the pavement in front. There are no tables in front. Consequently, cruising at Chez Maggi, in the words of loyal patrons, is *très crazee* and seems to extend for blocks in every direction, spilling over into the confines of Chez Joseph.

   Meals are served in an adjoining dining room. Menu items include chicken salad with ginger, goat-cheese salad, *petits farcis provençaux* (local vegetables stuffed with minced meat and herbs), brochettes of sea bass with lemon sauce, and a well-recommended chicken curry with coconut milk, capers, and cucumbers.

L'Echalotte. 35 rue Allard. ☎ **04-94-54-83-26.** Reservations recommended in summer. Main courses 80–140 F ($12.80–$22.40); fixed-price menus 105–160 F ($16.80–$25.60). AE, MC, V. Thurs 8–11:30pm, Fri–Wed 12:30–2pm and 8–11:30pm. Closed Nov 15–Dec 15. FRENCH.

This charming restaurant, with a tiny garden and simple but clean dining room and tables that extend onto a veranda (weather permitting), serves consistently good food for moderate prices. Because of demand, the tables may be difficult to get, especially in peak summer weeks. The cuisine is solid, including grilled veal kidneys, crayfish with drawn-butter sauce, fillet of turbot with truffles, and some of the classic dishes of southwestern France, like three preparations of foie gras and magrêt of duckling. The menu includes several species of fish, like sea bass and daurade royale, which can be cooked in a salt crust.

Le Girelier. Quai Jean-Jaurès. ☎ **04-94-97-03-87.** Main courses 135–500 F ($21.60–$80); fixed-price menu 200 F ($32). AE, DC, MC, V. Daily noon–2pm and 7–11pm. Closed Jan–Mar and Nov 11–Dec 15. PROVENÇAL.

The Rouets own this portside restaurant whose blue-and-white color scheme has become its own kind of trademark. They serve well-prepared grilled fish in many versions, as well as bouillabaisse, served only for two. Also available is brochette of monkfish, a kettle of mussels, and *pipérade* (a Basque omelet with pimientos, garlic, and tomatoes).

☼ **Les Mouscardins.** 1 rue Portalet. ☎ **04-94-97-01-53.** Reservations required. Main courses 100–300 F ($16–$48); fixed-price menus 135–210 F ($21.60–$33.60). AE, MC, V. Daily noon–2:30pm and 7:30–11:30pm. Closed 2 weeks in Nov, and for lunch mid-Nov to mid-Mar. FRENCH.

At the end of St-Tropez's harbor, this restaurant has won awards for culinary perfection. The dining room is in formal Provençal style with an adjoining sunroom under a canopy. The menu includes classic Mediterranean dishes. We recommend the *moules* (mussels) marinières for our appetizer. The two celebrated fish stews of the Côte d'Azur are offered: *bourride provençale* and bouillabaisse. The fish dishes are excellent, particularly the sauté of monkfish, wild mushrooms, and green beans. The dessert specialties are soufflés made with Grand Marnier or Cointreau.

ST-TROPEZ AFTER DARK

On the lobby level of the Hôtel Byblos, **Les Caves du Roy,** avenue Paul-Signac (☎ **04-94-97-16-02**), is the most self-consciously chic nightclub in St-Tropez. It's the kind of place where Aristotle Onassis would camp out. Entrance is free, but drink prices begin at a whopping 120 F ($19.20).

Le Papagayo, in the Résidence du Nouveau-Port, rue Gambetta (☎ **04-94-97-07-56**), is one of the largest nightclubs in town, with two floors, three bars, and lots of attractive women and men from throughout the area. The decor was inspired by the psychedelic 1960s. Entrance is 110 F ($17.60) and includes the first drink.

Le Pigeonnier, 13 rue de la Ponche (☎ **04-94-97-84-26**), rocks, rolls, and welcomes a crowd that's 80% to 85% gay, male, and between the ages of 20 and 50. Most of the socializing revolves around the long and narrow bar, where menfolk from all over Europe seem to enjoy chitchatting. There's also a dance floor. Entrance is 90 F ($14.40) and includes your first drink.

Located below the Hôtel Sube, the **Café de Paris,** sur le Port (☎ **04-94-97-00-56**), is one of the most consistently popular hangouts. An attempt has been made to glorify a utilitarian room with turn-of-the-century globe lights, an occasional 19th-century bronze artifact, masses of artificial flowers, and a long zinc bar. The crowd is irreverent and animated. Busy even in winter, after the yachting crowd departs, it's open daily.

The reporter Leslie Maitland aptly captured the kind of crowd attracted to **Café Sénéquier,** sur le Port (☎ **04-94-97-00-90**). "What else can one do but gawk at a tall, well-dressed young woman who appears *comme il faut* at Sénéquier's with a large white rat perched upon her shoulder, with which she occasionally exchanges little kisses, while casually chatting with her friends."

For a **gay hotspot,** check out the action at **Chez Maggi** (see "Dining," above).

2 La Napoule-Plage

560 miles S of Paris, 5 miles W of Cannes

This secluded resort is on the sandy beaches of the Golfe de la Napoule. In 1919 the once-obscure fishing village was a paradise for the eccentric sculptor Henry Clews and his wife, Marie, an architect. Fleeing America's "charlatans," whom he believed had profited from World War I, this New York banker's son emphasized the fairy-tale qualities of his new home. His house is now the **Musée Henry-Clews**—an inscription over the entrance reads "once upon a time."

Château de la Napoule, boulevard Henry-Clews (☎ **04-93-49-95-05**), was rebuilt from the ruins of a medieval château. Clews covered the capitals and lintels with his own grotesque menagerie—scorpions, pelicans, gnomes, monkeys, lizards—the revelations of a tortured mind. Women, feminism, and old age are recurring themes in the sculptor's work, as exemplified by the distorted suffragette depicted in his *Cat Woman*. The artist admired chivalry and dignity in man as represented by *Don Quixote*—to whom he likened himself. Clews died in Switzerland in 1937, and his body was returned to La Napoule for burial. Marie Clews later opened the château to the public as a testimonial to the inspiration of her husband. You can visit on a guided French-English language tour, conducted March through October Wednesday to Monday at 3 and 4pm. In July and August, there is an extra tour at 5pm. It costs 25 F ($4) for adults and 20 F ($3.20) for children. Free for children under 5.

ESSENTIALS

GETTING THERE   La Mandelieu Napoule-Plage lies on the **bus** and **train** routes between Cannes and St-Raphaël. For information and schedules, call ☎ **08-36-35-35-35.** If you're **driving,** take A8 west from Cannes.

VISITOR INFORMATION   The **Office de Tourisme** is at 274 bd. Henry-Clews (☎ **04-93-49-95-31**).

ACCOMMODATIONS

✪ **Ermitage du Riou.** Bd. Henry-Clews, 06210 La Napoule. ☎ **04-93-49-95-56.** Fax 04-92-97-69-05. www.ermitage-du-riou.fr. E-mail: hotel@ermitage-du-riou.fr. 43 units. A/C MINIBAR TV TEL. 735–1,795 F ($117.60–$287.20) double; 2,020–3,130 F ($323.20–$500.80) suite. AE, DC, MC, V.

This old Provençal house, the most tranquil choice at the resort, was turned into a sea-side hotel in 1952. It borders the Riou River and the Cannes-Mandelieu international golf club. The rooms are furnished in Provençal style with genuine furniture and ancient paintings. The most expensive rooms have private safes. Rooms range in size from medium to spacious, each fitted with an elegant bed with a quality mattress and fine linen. Views are of either the sea or the golf course. The **restaurant,** boasting a wood ceiling with beams, features seafood, with meals beginning at 240 F ($38.40). There's also a pool, solarium, garden, and sauna.

La Calanque. Av. Henry-Clews, 06210 La Napoule. ☎ **04-93-49-95-11.** Fax 04-93-49-67-44. 17 units. TEL. 320–570 F ($51.20–$91.20) double (rates include half board). MC, V. Closed Nov–Mar.

The foundations of this charming hotel date from the Roman Empire, when an aristocrat built a villa here. The present hotel, run by the same family since 1942, looks like a hacienda, with salmon-colored stucco walls and shutters. Bedrooms range from small to medium, each with a comfortable mattress. The hotel's **restaurant** spills onto a terrace and offers some of the cheapest fixed-price meals in La Napoule, at 85 F to 145 F ($13.60 to $23.20). Nonguests are welcome.

Royal Hôtel Casino. 605 av. du Général-de-Gaulle, 06212 Mandelieu La Napoule. ☎ **04-92-97-70-06.** Fax 04-92-97-70-49. www.royal-hotel-casino.com. E-mail: h1168@accor-hotels.com. 110 units. A/C MINIBAR TV TEL. 1,050–2,150 F ($168–$344) double; 2,000–12,000 F ($320–$1,920) suite. CB, DC, MC, V. Parking 60 F ($9.60).

This Las Vegas–style hotel is on the beach near a man-made harbor, about 5 miles from Cannes. It was the first French hotel to include a casino and the last (just before the building codes changed) to be allowed to have a casino directly on the beach. The hotel was purchased in the mid-1990s by the Accor group. It has one of the most dramatically contemporary designs on the Côte d'Azur, with plush touches, warm shades, and lots of marble. Most of the attractive modern rooms are angled toward a view of the sea. Those facing the street are likely to be noisy, despite soundproofing. **Le Féréol** is recommended under "Dining," below. An informal cafe (Le Poker) serves both Tex-Mex and specialties of Provence; a nightclub offers live music. The casino (open daily from 11am to 4am) offers blackjack, craps, and roulette. Facilities include a pool, tennis courts, a sauna, a private beach, and easy access to an 18-hole golf course.

DINING

The restaurant at **La Calanque** (see "Accommodations," above) is open to nonguests.

Le Féréol. In the Royal Hôtel Casino, 605 av. du Général-de-Gaulle. ☎ **04-92-97-70-00.** Reservations recommended. Main courses 100–185 F ($16–$29.60); buffet lunch (June–Sept only) 215 F ($34.40); fixed-price menu 260 F ($41.60) at dinner. AE, DC, MC, V. Daily noon–2:30pm (to 3:30pm July–Aug) and 7–10:30pm (to 11pm July–Aug). FRENCH.

This well-designed restaurant services most of the culinary needs of the largest hotel (and the only casino) in town. Outfitted in a nautical style that includes some of the seagoing accessories of an upscale yacht, it offers one of the most impressive lunch buffets in the neighborhood. At night the place is candlelit and more elegant, and the view through bay windows over the pool is more soothing. Menu items include foie gras, scampi tails fried with ginger, zucchini flowers with mousseline of lobster, mignon of veal with Parma ham and tarragon sauce, sole braised with shrimp, and an émincé of duckling baked under puff pastry with cèpe mushrooms. The dessert buffet lays out a wide array of sophisticated pastries, some light and fruity summer dishes, others designed as irresistible temptations for chocoholics.

✪ **L'Oasis.** Rue Honoré-Carle. ☎ **04-93-49-95-52.** Reservations required. Main courses 240–270 F ($38.40–$43.20); fixed-price menus 320–700 F ($50.80–$111.10) at lunch (including wine), fixed-price menus 250–700 F ($39.70–$111.10) at lunch or dinner (without wine). AE, CB, DC, MC, V. Daily noon–2pm and 7:30–10pm. FRENCH.

At the entrance to the harbor of La Napoule, in a 40-year-old house with a lovely garden and an unusual re-creation of a mock-medieval cloister, this restaurant became world famous under the tutelage of the now-retired Louis Outhier. Today, his protege Stéphane Raimbault prepares the most sophisticated cuisine in La Napoule. Because Raimbault cooked in Japan for 9 years, many of his dishes are of the "East Meets West" variety. Menu choices might include roasted saddle of monkfish and risotto of squid with an ink sauce; medaillons of veal and duck in a muscat wine and grape sauce; and a roasted Dover sole with parsley *scorzonera*. The wine cellar houses one of the finest collections of Provençal wines anywhere. Regrettably, there can be rocky moments here thanks to a staff that could be more helpful. On the bright side, in the summer, meals are served in the shade of the plane trees in the garden.

3 Cannes

562 miles S of Paris, 101 miles E of Marseille, 16 miles SW of Nice

When Coco Chanel went here and got a suntan, returning to Paris bronzed, she startled the milk-white society ladies. However, they quickly began copying her. Today the bronzed bodies—clad in nearly nonexistent swimsuits—that line the sandy beaches of this chic resort continue the late fashion designer's example.

ESSENTIALS

GETTING THERE   Cannes is connected to each of the Mediterranean resorts, Paris, and the rest of France by rail and bus lines. **Trains** arrive frequently throughout

Cannes

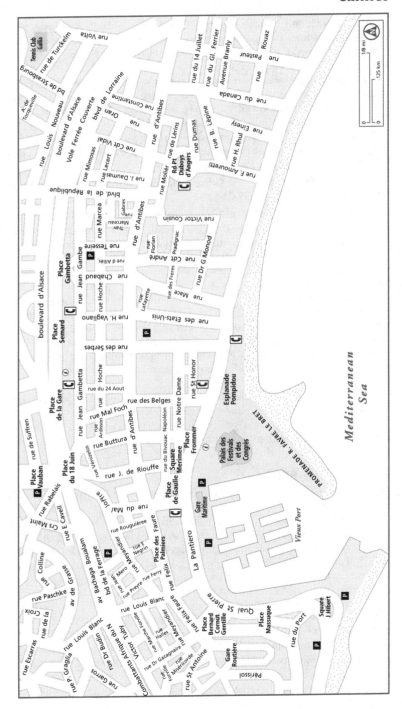

Mediterranean Sea

the day. Cannes is only 15 minutes by train from Antibes, and only 35 minutes from Nice. The TGV from Paris going via Marseille also services Cannes. (Transit from Paris to Cannes via TGV takes only about 3 breathless hours.) For rail information and schedules, call ☎ **08-36-35-35-35.**

The Nice **international airport** is a 20-minute drive northeast. **Buses** pick up passengers at the airport every 40 minutes during the day, delivering them in Cannes at the Gare Routière, place Bernard Cornut-Gentille (☎ **04-93-45-20-08**). Service to Cannes is also available from Antibes at the rate of one bus every half an hour.

By **car,** Cannes can be easily approached by two cities along the Riviera. From Marseille, take A51 north to Aix-en-Provence, continuing along A8 east to Cannes. From Nice, follow A8 southwest to Cannes.

VISITOR INFORMATION   The **Office de Tourisme** is in the Palais des Festivals, bd. de la Croisette (☎ **04-93-39-24-53**).

SPECIAL EVENTS   Cannes is at its most frenzied at the end of May, during the **International Film Festival** at the Palais des Festivals on promenade de la Croisette. It attracts not only film stars but also their hangers-on, as well as seemingly every photographer in the world. On the seafront boulevards, flashbulbs pop as the stars and wanna-bes emerge and pose and pose and pose. You've got a better chance of being named prime minister of France than you do of attending one of the major screenings at Cannes. (Hotel rooms and tables at restaurants are equally scarce during the festival.) But the people-watching is fabulous. If you somehow find yourself here at the right time, you can join the thousands of others who line up in front of the Palais des Festivals, a.k.a. "the bunker," where the premieres are held. With paparazzi shouting and shooting away, and a guard of gendarmes holding back the fans, the guests parade along the red carpet into the building, stopping for a moment or two to strike a pose and chat with a journalist. *C'est Cannes!*

You may also be able to get tickets for some of the lesser films, which play 24 hours. For information, see "France Calendar of Events" in Chapter 2.

From international regattas, to galas, concours d'élégance, and even a Mimosa Festival in February—something's always happening at Cannes, except in November, traditionally a dead month.

A DAY AT THE BEACH

Beachgoing in Cannes has more to do with exhibitionism and voyeurism than with actual swimming.

Plage de la Croisette extends between the Vieux Port and the Port Canto. Though the beaches along this billion-dollar stretch of sand aren't in the strictest sense private, they're *payante,* meaning that you must pay between 90 F and 100 F ($14.40 and $16). You don't need to be a guest of the Noga Hilton, Martinez, Carlton, or Majestic to use the beaches associated with those hotels, though if you are you'll usually get a 50% discount. Each beach is separated from its neighbors by a wooden barricade that stops several feet from the sea, making it easy for you to stroll from one to another.

Why should you pay a fee at all? Well, it includes a full day's use of a mattress, a chaise lounge (the seafront isn't particularly sandy or even soft, covered as it is with pebbles and dark-gray shingle), and a parasol, as well as easy access to freshwater showers and kiosks selling beverages. There are also outdoor restaurants where no one minds if you appear in your bathing suit.

For nostalgia's sake, our favorite beach is the one associated with the **Carlton** (see "Accommodations" below)—it was the first beach we ever went to, as teenagers, in Cannes. The relative merits of each of the 20 or so beaches along La Croisette vary daily depending on the crowd. And since every beach here allows topless bathing (although you must keep your bottom covered), you're likely to find the same forms of décolletage along the entire strip.

Looking for a free public beach where you'll have to survive without rentable chaises or parasols? Head for **Plage du Midi,** sometimes called Midi Plage, just west of the Vieux Port (☎ 04-93-39-92-74), or **Plage Gazagnaire,** just east of the Port Canto (no phone). Here you'll find greater numbers of families with children and lots of caravan-type vehicles parked nearby.

OUTDOOR PURSUITS

BICYCLING & MOTOR-SCOOTERING   Despite the roaring traffic, the flat landscapes between Cannes and such satellite resorts as La Napoule are well suited for riding a bike or motor scooter. **Alliance Location de Cannes,** 9 rue des Frères Pradignac (☎ 04-93-94-61-94), rents pedal bikes for 62 F ($9.90) per day and requires a 1,000 F ($160) deposit (payable with American Express, MasterCard, or Visa). Motor scooters rent for 175 F to 200 F ($28 to $32) per day and require a deposit of 4,000 F to 10,000 F ($640 to $1,600) per day, depending on their value. None of the motor scooters rented here requires a driver's license or special permit.

BOATING   In an annex of the Hôtel Latitude, **New Boat,** rue de la Laiterie (☎ 04-93-93-12-34), is in Mandelieu, 4 miles west of Cannes. With a good reputation and a hardworking staff, it maintains a flotilla of powerboats and small yachts, ranging from 12 to 46 feet long. These rent, usually with a staff included for navigation and safety, from 3,500 F ($560) per day.

GOLF   One of the region's most challenging and interesting courses, ✪ **Country-Club de Cannes-Mougins,** 175 rte. d'Antibes, Mougins (☎ 04-93-75-79-13), 4 miles north of Cannes, was a 1976 reconfiguration by Dye & Ellis of an overly plain course laid out in the 1920s. Noted for the olive trees and cypresses that adorn a relatively flat terrain, it has many water traps and a deceptively tricky layout loaded with technical challenges. It has a par of 72 and a much-envied role, since 1981, as host to the Cannes-Mougins Open, an important stop on the PGA European Tour. The course is open to anyone (with proof of his or her handicap) willing to pay greens fees of 400 F to 450 F ($64 to $72), depending on the day of the week. An electric golf cart rents for 280 F ($44.80), and golf clubs can be rented for 150 F ($24) per set. Reservations are recommended.

SWIMMING   Most of the larger hotels in Cannes have their own pools. In addition, the **Complexe Sportif Montfleury,** 23 av. Beauséjour (☎ 04-93-38-75-78), boasts a large modern pool that's about 100 feet long. Anyone who pays the entrance fee of 25 F ($4) can spend the entire day lounging beside it.

TENNIS   Its 10 tennis courts are one of the highlights of the **Complexe Sportif Montfleury,** 23 av. Beauséjour (☎ 04-93-38-75-78). You'll find eight hard courts, at 80 F ($12.80) per hour, and two clay courts, at 100 F ($16) per hour.

SHOPPING

Cannes competes more successfully than many of its neighbors in a highly commercial blend of resort-style leisure, luxury glamour, and media glitz. So you're likely to find branch outlets of virtually every stylish Paris retailer.

There's every big-name designer you can think of (Saint Laurent, Rykiel, Hermès) as well as big-name designers you've never heard of (Claude Bonucci, Basile, and Durrani)—but, more importantly, there are real-people shops; resale shops for gently worn star-studded castoffs; two flea markets for fun junk; and a fruit, flower, and vegetable market.

ANTIQUES   In the Casino Croisette (also called the Palm Beach Casino) on La Croisette, Cannes hosts one of France's most prestigious **antiques salons,** conducted biannually during week-long periods in mid-July and late December or early January. Its organizers absolutely refuse to include low- or even middle-bracket merchandise. This is serious—not for the gilt-free crowd—with lots of 18th- and early 19th-century stuff that might've appealed to the mistresses of various kings and emperors. Admission is 70 F ($11.20) per person. A bevy of satellite services is available at this event, like crating and freighting and flying whatever you buy to wherever you want it sent. For dates and information, call or write the **Association des Antiquaires de Cannes,** 6 rue de Foresta, 06300 Nice (☎ 04-93-26-11-01).

Looking for top-notch antiques dealers whose merchandise will wow you? Two of the city's most noteworthy dealers are **Hubert Herpin,** 20 rue Macé (☎ 04-93-39-56-18), and **Marc Franc,** 142 rue d'Antibes (☎ 04-93-43-86-43). Within each of the above-mentioned stores, you'll find a wide selection of bronze and marble statues, marquetry, and 18th- and 19th-century furniture.

CHOCOLATE & JELLIED FRUITS   There are several famous chocolatiers in Cannes—try **Maiffret,** 31 rue d'Antibes (☎ 04-93-39-08-29)—but the real local specialty is *fruits confits* (jellied fruits, also called crystallized fruits), which became the rage in the 1880s. Maiffret sells these as well, especially in summer, when the chocolates tend to melt. Pâtés and confits of fruit, some of which decorate cakes and tarts, are also sold as desirable confections. Look for the Provençal national confection, *calissons,* crafted from almonds, a confit of melon, and sugar. A block away is **Chez Bruno,** 50 rue d'Antibes (☎ 04-93-39-26-63). Opened in 1929 and maintained today by a matriarchal descendant of its founder, the shop is famous throughout Provence for *fruits confits* as well as its glazed chestnuts (*marrons glacés*), made fresh daily.

DEPARTMENT STORES   Near the train station in the heart of Cannes, **Galeries Lafayette** has a small branch at 6 rue du Maréchal-Foch (☎ 04-93-39-27-55). It's noted for the self-consciously upscale fashion available in carefully arranged interiors.

DESIGNER SHOPS   Most of the big names in designer fashion, for both men and women, line **promenade de la Croisette,** known as **La Croisette,** the main drag facing the sea. These stores are all in a row, stretching from the Hôtel Carlton almost to the Palais des Festivals, with the best names closest to the high-rise **Gray-d'Albion,** 17 La Croisette (☎ 04-92-99-79-79), which is both a mall and a hotel (how convenient). The stores in the Gray-d'Albion mall include **Hermès** and **Souleiado.** The mall is broken into two parts, so you go outdoors from the first part of the building and then enter again for the second part. It serves as the shopper's secret cutaway from the primary expensive shopping street, La Croisette, to the less expensive shopping street, **rue d'Antibes.**

You'll find a few more designer shops inside the posh hotels lining La Croisette: **Alexandra,** rond-point duboys d'Angers (☎ 04-93-38-41-29), is the fanciest boutique in town for a mixture of designers and for the kind of service demanded by stars and local ladies who lunch. In the words of the owners, *"pour la ville, le soir, et les cérémonies."* Here you'll find garments by Mori, Givenchy, Rochas, Lacroix, and Montana. Find it by ducking around to the back end of the Noga Hilton.

FLEA MARKETS   Things are a lot less elevated at Cannes' two regular flea markets. Casual, dusty, and to an increasing degree filled with the castaways of various estate sales, the **Marché Forville,** conducted in the neighborhood of the same name, near the Palais des Festivals, is a battered stucco structure with a roof and a few arches but no sides. Between Tuesday and Sunday, it's the fruit, vegetable, and flower market that supplies the raw materials for dozens of grand restaurants. But Monday is *brocante* day, when the market fills with offhanded, sometimes strident antiques dealers selling everything from grandmère's dishes to bone-handled carving knives.

Every Saturday, a somewhat disorganized and invariably busy **flea market** is held outdoors, along the edges of the allée de la Liberté, across from the Palais des Festivals. Exact hours depend on the whims of whatever dealer happens to feel compelled to haul in a cache of merchandise, but they usually begin around 8am and run out of steam by around 4:30pm. *Note:* The vendors at the two flea markets may or may not be the same.

FOOD Of the many streets that will attract with rustic and authentic Provençal allure, the most appealing of these, and the one lined with the greatest density of old-fashioned emporiums selling wine, olives, herbs, and oils, is the **rue Meynadier.**

A charmingly old-fashioned shop, **Cannolive,** 16–20 rue Vénizelos (☎ 04-93-39-08-19), is owned by the Raynaud family, who founded the place in 1880. It sells Provençal olives and their by-products—purées (*tapenades*) that connoisseurs refer to as "Provençal caviar," black "olives de Nice," and green "olives de Provence," as well as three grades of olive oil from several regional producers. Oils and food products are dispensed from no. 16, but gift items (fabrics, porcelain, and Provençal souvenirs) are sold next door.

MARKETS At the edge of the Quartier Suquet, the **Marché Forville** is the town's primary fruit, flower, and vegetable market. On Monday it's a *brocante* market. See "Flea Markets," above.

PERFUME The best shop is **Bouteille,** 59 rue d'Antibes (☎ 04-93-39-05-16), but it's also the most expensive. Its prices are high because it stocks more brands, has a wider selection, gives away many more free samples, and presents you with a tote bag. A selection of other perfume shops dots rue d'Antibes. Any may feature your favorite fragrance in a promotional deal (they rotate the deals). A final option for the reasonably priced perfumes is the boutiques associated with the previously recommended Hôtel Gray-d'Albion.

SEEING THE SIGHTS

Cannes is sheltered by hills. For many visitors, it might as well consist of only one street, **promenade de la Croisette** (or just La Croisette), curving along the coast and split by islands of palms and flowers.

A port of call for cruise liners, the seafront of Cannes is lined with hotels, apartment houses, and chic boutiques. Many of the bigger hotels, some dating from the 19th century, claim part of the beaches for the private use of their guests. But there are also public areas. Above the harbor, the old town of Cannes sits on Suquet Hill, where you'll see the 14th-century **Tour de Suquet,** which the English dubbed the Lord's Tower.

Nearby is the **Musée de la Castre,** in the Château de la Castre, Le Suquet (☎ 04-93-38-55-26), containing paintings, sculpture, examples of decorative arts, and a section on ethnography. The latter includes relics and objects from everywhere from the Pacific islands to Southeast Asia, including both Peruvian and Maya pottery. There's also a gallery devoted to relics of ancient Mediterranean civilizations, from the Greeks to the Romans, from the Cypriots to the Egyptians. Five rooms are devoted to

19th-century paintings. The museum is open Wednesday to Monday: April to June from 10am to noon and 2 to 6pm, July to September from 10am to noon and 3 to 7pm, and October to March from 10am to noon and 2 to 5pm. Admission is 10 F ($1.60), free for students and children.

FERRYING TO THE ÎLES DE LÉRINS

Across the bay from Cannes, the Lérins Islands are the most interesting excursion from the port. Ferryboats depart at 30-minute intervals throughout the day, beginning at 7:30am and lasting until 30 minutes before sundown. The largest of the ferryboat companies in Cannes is **Compagnies Estérel-Chanteclair** (☎ **04-93-39-11-82**), but other contenders include **Cie Horizon 4** (☎ **04-93-99-15-09**); **Compagnie Maritime Cannoise** (☎ **04-93-38-66-33**); and **Trans-Côte d'Azur** (☎ **04-92-98-71-30**). Departures are from the Gare Maritime des Îles, 06400 Cannes. Round-trip passage costs 50 F ($8) per person.

Île Ste-Marguerite is named after St. Honorat's sister, Ste. Marguerite, who lived here with a group of nuns in the 5th century. Today this is a youth center whose members (when they aren't sailing and diving) are dedicated to the restoration of the fort. From the dock where the boat lands, you can stroll along the island (signs point the way) to the Fort de l'Île, built by Spanish troops from 1635 to 1637.

Below is the 1st-century B.C. Roman town where the unlucky man immortalized in *The Man in the Iron Mask* was imprisoned. One of French history's most perplexing mysteries is the identity of the prisoner of Louis XIV who arrived at Ste-Marguerite in 1698, wearing the *masque due fer*. Dumas fanned the legend that he was a brother of Louis XIV, and it has even been suggested that the prisoner and a mysterious woman had a son who went to Corsica and "founded" the Bonaparte family. However, the most common theory is that the prisoner was a servant of the superintendent, Fouquet, named Eustache Dauger. At any rate, he died in the Bastille in Paris in 1703.

You can visit his cell at Ste-Marguerite, in which every visitor seemingly has written his or her name. As you stand listening to the sound of the sea, you realize what a forlorn outpost this was.

Musée de la Mer, Fort Royal (☎ **04-93-38-55-26**), traces the history of the island, displaying artifacts of Ligurian, Roman, and Arab civilizations, plus the remains discovered by excavations. These include paintings, mosaics, and ceramics. Regardless of the season, the museum is open Wednesday to Monday, October to March from 10:30am to 12:15pm and 2:15 to 4:30pm; April to June, from 10:30am to 12:15pm, and 2:15 to 5:30pm; and July to September, from 10:30am to 12:15pm, and 2:15 to 6:30pm. Admission costs 10 F ($1.60) for adults, free for children and students.

ÎLE ST-HONORAT

Only a mile long, but richer in history than any of its sibling islands, the Île St-Honorat is the site of a working monastery whose origins go back to the 5th century. Today, the **Abbaye de St-Honorat,** Les Îles de Lérins, 06400 Cannes (☎ **04-92-99-54-00**), boasts a combination of medieval ruins and early 20th-century ecclesiastical buildings, and a permanent community of about 30 Cistercian monks. Under carefully controlled circumstances, if space is available, well-intentioned outsiders can visit and spend the night, but only in circumstances associated with prayer and meditation. Most visitors opt to avoid the monastery, wandering through the pine forests on the island's western side, and sunbathing on its beaches.

ACCOMMODATIONS
VERY EXPENSIVE

✪ Hôtel Carlton Intercontinental. 58 bd. de la Croisette, 06400 Cannes. ☎ **800/ 327-0200** in the U.S., or 04-93-06-40-06. Fax 04-93-06-40-25. www.interconti.com. E-mail: cannes@interconti.com. 354 units. A/C MINIBAR TV TEL. 1,040–4,090 F ($166.40–$654.40) double; from 6,490 F ($1,038.40) suite. AE, DC, MC, V. Parking 180 F ($28.80).

Cynics say that one of the most amusing sights in Cannes is the view from under the vaguely Art Deco grand gate of the Carlton. Here you'll see vehicles of every description pulling up to drop off huge amounts of baggage and vast numbers of oh-so-fashionable (and sometimes not-so-fashionable) guests. It's the epitome of luxury and has become such a part of the city's heartbeat that to ignore it would be to miss the resort's spirit. The twin gray domes at either end of the facade are often the first things recognized by starlets planning their grand entrances, grand exits, and grand scenes in the hotel's public and private rooms.

Shortly after it was built in 1912, the Carlton attracted the most prominent members of Europe's *haut monde,* including royalty. They were followed decades later by battalions of the most important screen stars. Today the hotel is more democratic, hosting lots of conventions and motor-coach tour groups; however, in summer (especially during the film festival) the public rooms still are filled with all the voyeuristic and exhibitionistic fervor that seems so much a part of the Riviera. Bedrooms are plush, and a bit airier than you might expect. The most spacious rooms are in the west wing, and many upper-floor rooms open onto waterfront balconies.

Dining/Diversions: The hotel contains four restaurants. The one offering the most intensely cultivated cuisine is La Belle Otéro, on the seventh floor, followed by the elegant but less spectacular Restaurant du Casino and Restaurant de la Côte, which was renovated in 1997. A ground-floor Brasserie doles out less expensive fare, and at the waterfront Restaurant de la Plage, virtually everyone seems to arrive in *maillots de bain* (bathing suits).

Amenities: Private beach, health club with spa facilities, glass-roofed indoor pool.

Hôtel Gray-d'Albion. 38 rue des Serbes, 06400 Cannes. ☎ **04-92-99-79-79.** Fax 04-93-99-26-10. www.lucienbarrere.com. E-mail: graydalbion@lucienbarriere.com. 189 units. A/C MINIBAR TV TEL. High season, 1,320–2,020 F ($211.20–$323.20) double, 4,620–8,120 F ($739.20–$1,299.20) suite, low season, 920–1,520 F ($147.20–$243.20) double, 2,920–4,670 F ($467.20–$747.20) suite. AE, DC, MC, V.

The smallest of the major hotels here isn't on La Croisette. But the rooms are still outfitted with all the luxury a modern hotel can offer. In fact, some critics consider the Gray-d'Albion among the most luxurious hotels in all of France. Groups form a large part of its clientele, but it also caters to the individual guest. Rooms on the eighth and ninth floors have views of the Mediterranean. All bedrooms are fairly standardized and medium in size, blending both contemporary and traditional furnishings along with such amenities as private safes and bedside controls. Each room has a balcony but the views aren't notable.

Dining: Dining selections include Le Royal Gray and a beach-club restaurant.
Amenities: Beauty salon/massage facility, room service from 6:30am to midnight.

Hôtel Martinez. 73 bd. de la Croisette, 06400 Cannes. ☎ **04-92-98-73-00.** Fax 04-93-39-67-82. www.hotel-martinez.com. E-mail: martinez@concorde-hotels.com. 430 units. A/C MINIBAR TV TEL. 1,300–4,800 F ($208–$768) double; from 2,750 F ($440) suite. AE, DC, MC, V. Parking 160 F ($25.60).

When this landmark Art Deco hotel was built in the 1930s, it rivaled any other hotel along the coast in sheer size alone. Over the years, however, it fell into disrepair, and closed and reopened several times. But in 1982 the Concorde chain returned the hotel and its restaurants to their former luster, and today it competes with the Carlton and Noga Hilton. Despite its grandeur, the hotel is a little too convention-oriented for our tastes, but the rooms remain in good shape. The aim of the decor was a Roaring Twenties style, and all units boast private safes, marble baths with thick towels, wood furnishings, tasteful carpets, quality mattresses, and pastel fabrics.

Dining/Diversions: La Palme d'Or is among the finest restaurants in Cannes (see "Dining," below). The poolside restaurant, L'Orangerie, serves light, low-calorie meals in a decor of azure and white lattices.

Amenities: 24-hour room service, same-day laundry/valet, private beach, waterskiing school, cabanas, octagonal pool, seven tennis courts.

Noga Hilton Cannes. 50 bd. de la Croisette, 06414 Cannes. ☎ **800-445-8667** in the U.S., or 04-92-99-70-00. Fax 04-92-99-70-11. www.hilton.com. 229 units. A/C MINIBAR TV TEL. 1,690–3,990 F ($270.40–$638.40) double; 2,500–8,500 F ($400–$1,360) suite. AE, DC, MC, V.

The owners were able to procure one of Cannes's most sought-after building sites, the lot occupied by the old (since demolished) Palais des Festivals. Finished in 1992, the Hilton was the first major palace hotel to open in Cannes since the 1930s. This six-story deluxe place, with massive amounts of exposed glass, boasts a contemporary design mimicking the best aspects of its older twin, the lakefront Noga Hilton in Geneva. You register in a soaring lobby sheathed with a semitranslucent white marble. The guest rooms are stylish, containing impeccable soundproofing and all the electronic accessories you'll ever need. Rooms are all alike; the difference in rates is based on the view of the sea. Many of the appointments evoke a 1930s aura, all with private safes, balconies, bedside controls, and luxury mattresses. The Prestige Rooms have very large beds and elegant carpeting. Less desirable units are called Cityview and Gardenview rooms. There are six rooms for persons with disabilities, and 21 for non-smokers.

Dining/Diversions: The most expensive dining venue is La Scala, a smart restaurant with its own piano bar one floor above lobby level. It specializes in the cuisines of the Riviera—both French and Italian. Less grand is the Brasserie Le Grand Bleu. La Plage is an informal lunch restaurant on the beach. There's also a casino and an 825-seat theater for cabarets and conventions.

Amenities: 24-hour room service, baby-sitting, health club with sauna, outdoor pool, shopping arcade with about 30 boutiques, waterfront pier for mooring yachts, business center, access to nearby golf course.

MODERATE

Hôtel Côté Sud. 6 rue Lecerf, 06400 Cannes. ☎ **04-93-38-69-54.** Fax 04-92-98-68-30. www.cotesud.net. E-mail: cotesudg@aol.com. 15 units. A/C MINIBAR TV TEL. 450–650 F ($72–$104) double; 710–910 F ($113.60–$145.60) suite. AE, DC, MC, V. Parking 30 F ($4.80).

Set on a quiet commercial street about 4 blocks from the seafront, this small hotel occupies the second floor of a four-story apartment building constructed in the '70s. In 1998, it was renovated and upgraded by its owner, Brice Guëlle, who lives on the premises and runs a tight ship. Bedrooms are well maintained, furnished unpretentiously but comfortable, and are relatively affordable in high-priced Cannes. Breakfast is the only meal served, although there are many inexpensive bistros in the neighborhood.

Hotel Splendid. Allée de la Liberté (4 and 6 rue Félix-faure), 06400 Cannes. ☎ **04-93-99-53-11.** Fax 04-93-99-55-02. 64 units. A/C TV TEL. 612–1,092 F ($97.90–$174.70) double; 1,200–1,500 F ($192–$240) suite. Rates include continental breakfast. AE, DC, MC, V. Parking 40 F ($6.40).

This is a good, conservative choice, and a favorite of academicians, politicians, actors, and musicians. Opened in 1871, it's one of the oldest hotels in Cannes. An ornate white building with sinuous wrought-iron accents and an old-fashioned staff, the Splendid looks out onto the sea, the old port, and a park. The rooms boast antique furniture and paintings as well as videos; about half of them have kitchenettes. The more expensive rooms have sea views. Each comes with a good mattress and a small but efficient bathroom with a shower/tub combination.

Hôtel Victoria. Rond-point Duboys-d'Angers, 06400 Cannes. ☎ **04-93-99-36-36.** Fax 04-93-38-03-91. E-mail: hotelvictoria@aol.com. 25 units. A/C MINIBAR TV TEL. 790–1,200 F ($126.40–$192) double. AE, DC, MC, V. Closed Nov–Dec. Parking 80 F ($12.80).

The Victoria, a stylish modern hotel in the heart of Cannes, offers accommodations with period reproductions and refrigerators. Nearly half the rooms have balconies overlooking the small park and the hotel pool. Bedspreads of silk and padded headboards with quality mattresses evoke a boudoir quality. The accommodations facing the park cost a little more but are well worth it. After a day on the beach, guests congregate in the paneled bar and sink comfortably into the couches and armchairs.

INEXPENSIVE

Hôtel de Provence. 9 rue Molière, 06400 Cannes. ☎ **04-93-38-44-35.** Fax 04-93-39-63-14. www.hotel-de-provence.com. E-mail: contact@hotel-de-provence.com. 30 units. A/C MINIBAR TV TEL. 420–530 F ($67.20–$84.80) double. AE, MC, V. Parking 60 F ($9.60).

Built in the 1930s and renovated in 1992, this hotel is small scale and unpretentious—a distinct contrast to the intensely stylish larger hotels with which it competes. Most of the rooms have private balconies, and many overlook the carefully tended shrubs and palms of the hotel's walled garden. Bedrooms are showing their age but still offer fine comfort, and for Cannes this is a remarkable bargain. In warm weather, breakfast is served under the vines and flowers of an arbor.

Hôtel Villa de l'Olivier. 5 rue des Tambourinaires, 064000 Cannes. ☎ **04-93-39-53-28.** Fax 04-93-39-55-85. www.hotelolivier.com. E-mail: reception@hotelolivier.com. 24 units. A/C TV TEL. 490–740 F ($78.40–$118.40) double; 1,600 F ($256) suite. AE, DC, MC, V. Parking 60 F ($9.60).

Small, charming, and personalized, with a low-key family management style, this well-positioned hotel originated in the 1930s as a private villa. In the 1960s, it was transformed into a hotel, and a six-unit annex was built within the garden. Today, you'll find buildings with lots of glass overlooking a kidney-shaped swimming pool, and a decor that combines aspects of the French colonial tropics and Provence. Throughout, you'll find lots of potted plants and a breezy indoor-outdoor motif that many guests find both appealing and relaxing. Bedrooms are outfitted with upholstered walls, each in a different color and pattern, and lots of Provençal accessories.

DINING
VERY EXPENSIVE

✪ **La Palme d'Or.** In the Hôtel Martinez, 73 bd. de la Croisette. ☎ **04-92-98-74-14.** Reservations required. Main courses 250–480 F ($40–$76.80); fixed-price menus 295 F ($47.20) at lunch Mon–Sat, 390–850 F ($62.40–$136) at dinner. AE, DC, MC, V. Wed–Sun

12:30–2pm and 7:30–10:30pm (also Tues 7:30–10:30pm mid-June to mid-Sept). Closed Nov 20–Dec 20. FRENCH.

When this hotel was renovated by the Taittinger family (of champagne fame), one of their primary concerns was to establish a restaurant that could rival the tough competition in Cannes. And they've succeeded. The result is this light wood-paneled, Art Deco marvel with bay windows, a winter garden theme, and outdoor and enclosed terraces overlooking the pool, the sea, and La Croisette. Menu items change with the seasons but are likely to include warm foie gras with fondue of rhubarb; fillets of fried red mullet with a beignet of potatoes, zucchini, and an olive-cream sauce; or a medley of crayfish, clams, and squid marinated in peppered citrus sauce. A modernized version of a Niçoise staple includes three parts of a rabbit with rosemary sauce, fresh vegetables, and chickpea rosettes. The most appealing dessert is wild strawberries from nearby Carros, with a Grand Marnier–flavored nage and a "cream sauce of frozen milk." The service is sensitive, sophisticated, and worldly, without being stiff.

EXPENSIVE

Gaston-Gastounette. 7 quai St-Pierre. ☎ **04-93-39-49-44.** Reservations required. Main courses 160–300 F ($25.60–$48); fixed-price menu 125–170 F ($20–$27.20) at lunch, 200 F ($32) at dinner. AE, DC, MC, V. Daily noon–2pm and 7–11pm. Closed Dec 1–20. FRENCH.

This is the best restaurant for views of the marina. Located in the old port, it has a stucco exterior with oak moldings and big windows and a sidewalk terrace surrounded by flowers. Inside you'll be served any of three different bouillabaisses, ranging from full-flown authentic stewpots that are meals in their own right, to less daunting versions designed merely as an appetizer. Other choices include baby turbot with hollandaise sauce; fillets of John Dory with wild mushrooms; an unusual Japanese–style broth flavored with monkfish, saltwater salmon, and chives; and a succulent platter of fried mixed fish served with basil-flavored butter sauce. Profiteroles with hot chocolate sauce make a memorable dessert.

○ **La Mère Besson.** 13 rue des Frères-Pradignac. ☎ **04-93-39-59-24.** Reservations required. Main courses 75–120 F ($12–$19.20); fixed-price menus 140–170 F ($22.40–$27.20) at dinner. AE, DC, MC, V. Mon–Sat 12:15–2pm and 7:30–10:30pm. FRENCH.

The culinary traditions of the late Mère Besson, who opened her restaurant in the 1930s, are carried on in one of Cannes's favorite places. All the specialties are prepared with respect for Provençal traditions and skill, especially some dishes that are served up in great steaming portions. Most delectable is *estouffade Provençal* (beef braised with red wine and rich stock flavored with garlic, onions, herbs, and mushrooms). You can also sample an old-fashioned platter with codfish, fresh vegetables, and dollops of the famous garlic mayonnaise (aïoli) that Provence produces by the tubful. Other specialties are fish soup, a *bourride Provençale* (a form of thick fish and vegetable stew), and shoulder of lamb with Provençal herbs and a purée of garlic.

Le Festival. 55 bd. de la Croisette. ☎ **04-93-38-04-81.** Reservations required. Main courses 150–300 F ($24–$48); fixed-price menus from 195 F ($31.20). AE, DC, MC, V. Daily 11:30am–3pm and 7:30–10pm. Closed Nov 20–Dec 26. FRENCH.

Screen idols and sex symbols flood the front terrace of this place during the film festival. Almost every chair is emblazoned with the names of movie stars (who may or may not have graced it with their bottoms), and tables here are among the most sought-after entity in town. You can choose from the Restaurant or the less formal Grill Room. Meals in the Restaurant may include bourride Provençale; *soupe des poissons* (fish soup) with *rouille;* simply grilled fresh fish (perhaps with aïoli); bouillabaisse with lobster; pepper steak; and sea bass flambéed with fennel. Items in the Grill are more in the style of an elegant brasserie, served a bit more rapidly and without as much fuss but at more or less the same prices. An appropriate finish in either section might be a smoothly textured peach Melba.

MODERATE

La Villa. 7 rue Marceau. ☎ **04-93-38-79-73.** Reservations recommended. Main courses 105–165 F ($16.80–$26.40); fixed-price menus 190–275 F ($30.40–$44). AE, DC, MC, V. Daily 8pm–4am (till 5am during the Film Festival). FRENCH.

Sophisticated, urbane, and permissive, this restaurant also features a bar and a dance floor where patrons can dance and drink till long, long after the usual dinner hour, and even arrive for a meal long after everything else in Cannes is closed. The interior has trompe l'oeil and ornate plaster ceilings, and an outdoor terrace that's accented with the decorative columns and the smell of night-flowering vines. The menu is not terribly long, but it's well-chosen and filled with the kind of food that stars, starlets, movie-industry wanna-bes, and the merely rich can nibble and never feel guilty. Examples include a diet-conscious array of grilled fish, such as sea bass; a platter with shrimp and scallops; and fillets of beef garnished either with morels or foie gras. Live music sometimes supplements a regime of recorded music. If you opt to come in here just for a drink, expect to pay from around 50 F ($8) for a beer, and from around 70 F ($11.20) for a whiskey with soda.

Le Marais. 9 rue du Suquet. ☎ **04-93-38-39-19.** Reservations recommended. Main courses 80–130 F ($12.80–$20.80); fixed-price menu 135–190 F ($21.60–$30.40). CB, V. Tues–Sun 7:30–11pm. FRENCH.

This is the most successful gay restaurant in Cannes, with a crowd of mostly gay men, sometimes with their entourages from the worlds of fashion and entertainment. The setting is a warm and appealing mix of Parisian and Provençal, with paneled walls and a bustling terrace that in its way is one of the most sought-after outdoor venues in town. Menu items are conservative and not particularly experimental, like ravioli of duck meat, a mixed fish platter, and jumbo shrimp fried with garlic.

INEXPENSIVE

Au Bec Fin. 12 rue du 24-Août. ☎ **04-93-38-35-86.** Reservations required. Main courses 55–70 F ($8.80–$11.20); fixed-price menus 105–125 F ($16.80–$20). AE, DC, MC, V. Mon–Sat noon–2:30pm and 6–10:30pm. Closed Dec 15–Jan 15. FRENCH.

On a street halfway between the train station and the beach, this 1880s bistro has little decor but offers especially good meals. Sometimes red carnations are brought in from the fields to brighten the tables. A typical meal might include salade Niçoise, the house specialty; then *caneton* (duckling) with *cèpes* (flap mushrooms); and finally a choice of cheese and dessert.

✪ **Le Monaco.** 15 rue du 24-Août. ☎ **04-93-38-37-76.** Reservations required. Main courses 55–90 F ($8.80–$14.40); fixed-price menus 70–125 F ($11.20–$20). MC, V. Mon–Sat noon–2:30pm and 7–10:30pm. Closed Nov 10–Dec 10. FRENCH/ITALIAN/PROVENÇAL.

Restaurant tabs on La Croisette often resemble the annual budget of an Ivory Coast country. But believe it or not, pricey Cannes has working people who have to eat, and they often go to Le Monaco, a blue-collar eatery with great food served bistro style.

Menu choices include osso buco with sauerkraut, spaghetti bolognese, paella, couscous, roast rabbit with mustard sauce, mussels, trout with almonds, and minestrone with basil. Another specialty is grilled sardines, which many restaurants won't serve anymore, considering them too messy and old-fashioned.

CANNES AFTER DARK

On the eighth floor (seventh in France) of the Hôtel Carlton Intercontinental, 58 bd. de la Croisette, is **Le Carlton Casino Club** (☎ 04-92-99-51-00). Considerably smaller than its major competitor (the Casino Croisette), its modern decor nonetheless draws many devotees. Jackets are required for men, and a passport or government-issued identity card is required for admission. It's open daily from 7:30pm to 4am; however, access to the slot machines is from noon daily. Admission is 70 F ($11.20).

The largest and most legendary casino in Cannes is the **Casino Croisette,** in the Palais des Festivals, 1 jetée Albert-Edouard, near promenade de la Croisette (☎ 04-92-98-78-00). Within its glittering confines you'll find all the roulette and blackjack you'd expect. Entrance into the more glamorous gaming rooms incurs a fee of 70 F ($11.20). Men are required to wear a jacket and all guests must present their passport or identity card. The gaming room is open from 7:30pm till 4 or 5am. For a more casual spot of gambling, there are also slot machines available from 11am until closing. Entrance is free and the dress code is far more relaxed. The casino also has one of the best nightclubs in town, **Jimmy's de Régine** (☎ 04-93-68-00-07). Jimmy's is open Thursday to Sunday from 11pm to dawn. Admission, 100 F ($16), includes a drink.

Less formal less rigidly stylish discos include **Jane's Club,** in the cellar of the Hôtel Gray-d'Albion, 38 rue des Serbes (☎ 04-92-99-79-79), where male clients tend to wear jackets and ties and come in a wide range of ages. At this writing, the hippest and most consistently in demand is **Le Cat-Corner,** 22 rue Macé (☎ 04-93-39-31-31), where a multicultural blend of very hip night owls, most under 35, come to dance, drink, talk, and flirt.

Gays and lesbians will feel especially comfortable in **Le Vogue,** 20 rue du Suquet (☎ 04-93-39-99-18), a mixed bar that's open Tuesday to Sunday from around 9pm till 2:30am. Another gay option is **Disco Le Sept,** 7 rue Rouguière (☎ 04-93-39-10-36), with two shows, each lasting 2 hours, that begin every night at 11:30pm and at 2am. Entrance is free, but drinks begin at 70 F ($11.20) each. Attracting an older, somewhat more conservative crowd of mostly gay men, you'll find the **Zanzi-Bar Pub,** La Pantiéro, rue Félix Faure (no phone), opposite Vieux Port.

4 Mougins

561 miles S of Paris, 7 miles S of Grasse, 5 miles N of Cannes

This once-fortified town on the crest of a hill provides an alternative for those who want to be near the excitement of Cannes but not in the midst of it. Picasso and other artists appreciated the rugged, sun-drenched hills covered with gnarled olive trees. The artist arrived in 1936 and in time was followed by Jean Cocteau, Paul Eluard, and Man Ray. Picasso decided to move here permanently, choosing as his refuge an ideal site overlooking the Bay of Cannes, near the Chapelle Notre-Dame de Vie, which Winston Churchill once painted. Here Picasso continued to work and spend the latter part of his life with his wife, Jacqueline. Fernand Léger, René Clair, Isadora Duncan, and even Christian Dior have lived at Mougins.

Mougins is the perfect haven for those who feel that the Riviera is overrun, spoiled, and overbuilt. It preserves the quiet life even though it's a stone's throw from Cannes. The wealthy come from Cannes to golf here. Though Mougins looks serene and tranquil, it's actually part of the industrial park of Sophia Antipolis, a technological center where more than 1,000 national and international companies have offices.

ESSENTIALS

GETTING THERE   The best way to get to Mougins is to **drive.** From Nice, follow E80/A8 west, then cut north on Route 85 into Mougins. From Cannes, head north of the city along N85. From La Napoule-Plage, head east toward Cannes on N7, then north at the signposted turnoff to Mougins up in the hills.

There's no railway station in Mougins, but there's limited daily **bus** service into Mougins from Cannes aboard the bus that travels from Cannes to Grasse. En route to Grasse, it stops in Mougins at Val de Mougins, about a 10-minute walk from the center. Fares from Cannes to Mougins are about 22 F ($3.50) each way. For information about departure times and schedules, call Rapides-Côte-d'Azur (☎ **04-93-39-11-39**). Given the complexities of a bus transfer from Cannes, it will invariably be a lot easier just to pay about 125 F ($20) for a **taxi** to haul you and your possessions northward from Cannes.

VISITOR INFORMATION   The **Office de Tourisme** is at 15 av. Jean-Charles-Mallet (☎ **04-93-75-87-67**).

SEEING THE SIGHTS

For a look at the history of the area, head to **Musée Municipal,** place du Village (☎ **04-92-92-50-42**), which is in the Saint Bernardin Chapel. It was built in 1618 and traces the local history of life in the area from 1553 to the 1950s. It's open December to October, Monday to Friday from 10am to noon and 2 to 6pm; free admission.

You can also visit the **Chapelle Notre-Dame de Vie,** Chemin de la Chapelle, a mile southeast of Mougins. The chapel, once painted by Churchill, is more famous for the priory next door where Picasso spent the last 12 years of his life. It was built in the 12th century and then reconstructed in 1646. The priory is still a private home occupied intermittently by the Picasso heirs. It was an old custom to bring stillborn babies to the chapel to have them baptized. Unfortunately, because of a series of break-ins, the chapel is only open during Sunday mass between 9 and 10am.

Musée de l'Automobiliste. Aire des Bréguières. ☎ **04-93-69-27-80.** Admission 40 F ($6.40) adults, 25 F ($4) children 11 and under. Oct–Mar, daily 10am–6pm; Apr–Sept, daily 10am–7pm. Closed Nov.

This is one of the top attractions on the Riviera. Founded in 1984 by Adrien Maeght, this ultramodern concrete-and-glass structure rises out of a green clearing. It houses temporary exhibitions but also owns one of Europe's most magnificent collections of original and prestigious automobiles. In all, there are more than 100 vehicles from 1908 until the present.

ACCOMMODATIONS
EXPENSIVE

Le Moulin de Mougins (see "Dining," below) also offers charming rooms and suites.

Mas Candille. Bd. Rebuffel, 06250 Mougins. ☎ **04-92-28-43-43.** Fax 04-92-92-85-56. 24 units. A/C MINIBAR TV TEL. 980–1,500 F ($156.80–$240) double; from 1,800 F ($288) suite. AE, DC, MC, V. Closed Nov to mid-Mar.

This 200-year-old Provençal farmhouse was skillfully converted. The public rooms contain many 19th-century furnishings, and some open onto the gardens. The renovated guest rooms are cozy and tranquil, with traditional Provençal furnishings. The family managers are always willing to provide you with whatever you need to make your room more comfortable.

The **dining room** has elegant stone detailing and a massive fireplace with a timbered mantel. The food is exceptional, with menus costing 195 F to 280 F ($31.20 to $44.80). Typical dishes are *soupe de poissons* (fish soup), stuffed zucchini flowers, and braised sweetbreads with mushrooms. Fresh salads and light meals are available throughout the day. In good weather lunch is served on the terrace; dinner is served on the terrace in summer only.

MODERATE

Manoir de l'Etang. Aux Bois de Font-Merle, allée du Manoir, 06250 Mougins. ☎ **04-92-28-36-00.** Fax 04-92-28-36-10. E-mail: manoiretang@wanadoo.fr. 16 units. TV TEL. 600–1,000 F ($96–$160) double; 1,350–1,600 F ($216–$256) apt. AE, MC, V. Closed Nov–Feb.

This 19th-century Provençal building in the midst of olive trees and cypresses is one of the choice places to stay on the Riviera. It boasts all the romantic extras associated with some Riviera properties, including "love goddess" statuary in the garden and candlelit dinners around a pool, but it charges reasonable rates. The rooms are bright and modern—you'll feel almost as if you're staying in a private home, which this place virtually is. Some rooms are extremely spacious. Each is exceedingly comfortable, with quality mattresses and fine linen. In winter, **meals** are served around a wood-burning fireplace. The chef bases his menu on the freshest ingredients available in any season. Fixed-price lunches, with wine included, cost from 190 F to 250 F ($30.40 to $40). Fixed-price dinners, without wine, cost from 150 F to 190 F ($24 to $30.40).

DINING

L'Amandier de Mougins Café-Restaurant. Place du Commandant-Lamy. ☎ **04-93-90-00-91.** Reservations recommended. Main courses 75–135 F ($12–$21.60); fixed-price menus 155–190 F ($24.80–$30.40). AE, DC, MC, V. Daily noon–2:15pm and 8–10pm. NIÇOISE/PROVENÇAL.

The illustrious founder of this relatively inexpensive bistro is the world-famous Roger Vergé, whose much more expensive Moulin de Mougins is described below. Conceived as a mass-market satellite to its exclusive neighbor, this restaurant serves relatively simple platters in an airy stone house. The specialties are usually based on traditional recipes and may include a terrine of the elusive Mediterranean hogfish with lemon; a tartare of fresh salmon and a céviche of tuna with hot spices; magrêt of grilled duckling with honey sauce and lemons, served with deliberately undercooked polenta; and fillets of farm-raised sea bass on a Moroccan-inspired ragoût of vegetables and saffron-flavored potatoes.

✪ **Le Moulin de Mougins.** Notre-Dame de Vie, 06250 Mougins. ☎ **04-93-75-78-24.** Fax 04-93-90-18-55. Reservations required. Main courses 190–450 F ($30.40–$72); fixed-price menus 270–740 F ($43.20–$118.40) at lunch, 550–740 F ($88–$118.40) at dinner. AE, DC, MC, V. Tues–Sun noon–2:15pm and 8–10pm. Closed Feb 12–Mar 12. FRENCH.

This place is among France's top 20 restaurants. A 10-foot-wide stone oil vat, with a wooden turnscrew and a grinding wheel, is near the entrance. This is the kingdom of Roger Vergé, the *maître cuisinier de France.* His specialties include *fillets de rougets* (red mullet) with artichokes; *noisettes d'agneau* (lamb) de Sisteron with an eggplant cake in thyme-flavored sauce and *poupeton* (zucchini flowers) stuffed with a mixture of truffles and pulverized mushrooms, served with truffle-flavored butter sauce; fricassée of lobster with sweet wine, cream sauce, and sweet peppers; and pepper steak "à la Mathurin," with grapes, pepper, and brandy. His forte is fish from the Mediterranean, bought fresh each morning. Dessert might be a lemon soufflé. Monsieur Vergé offers a lot of fantastic, even historic wines but also has a good selection of local vintages.

The old mill offers **four beautiful suites and three rooms,** with air-conditioning, minibars, TVs, phones, and fax machines. The rooms are decorated with French antiques. These rent for 850 F to 1,800 F ($136 to $288).

5 Grasse

563 miles S of Paris, 11 miles N of Cannes, 6 miles N of Mougins, 14 miles NW of Antibes

Grasse, a 20-minute drive from Cannes, is the most fragrant town on the Riviera, though it looks tacky and modern. Surrounded by jasmine and roses, it has been the capital of the perfume industry since the days of the Renaissance. It was once a famous resort, attracting such royalty as Queen Victoria and Princess Pauline Borghese, Napoléon's lascivious sister.

Today some three-quarters of the world's essences are produced here from foliage that includes violets, daffodils, wild lavender, and jasmine. It takes 10,000 flowers to produce 2.2 pounds of jasmine petals. Another statistic: Almost a ton of petals is needed to distill 1$\frac{1}{2}$ quarts of essence. These figures are important to keep in mind when looking at that high price tag on a bottle of perfume.

ESSENTIALS

GETTING THERE **Buses** pull into town at intervals of between 30 and 60 minutes every day from Cannes (trip time: 45 min). The one-way fare is 20 F ($3.20). There are also about 30 buses every day arriving from Nice, a trip time of around 60 minutes. The one-way fare costs around 38 F ($6.10). The buses disembark at the Gare Routière, Av. Thiers (☎ **04-93-36-37-37**), a 10-minute walk north of the town center. Visitors arriving by **car** usually take the A8 superhighway, which funnels in traffic from Monaco, Aix-en-Provence, and Marseilles.

VISITOR INFORMATION The **Office de Tourisme** is in the Palais des Congrès on place du Cours (☎ **04-93-36-66-66**).

SEEING THE SIGHTS

✪ Parfumerie Fragonard. 20 bd. Fragonard. ☎ **04-93-36-44-65.** Daily 9am–6pm. Nov–Jan, closed noon–2pm.

One of the best-known perfume factories is named after an 18th-century French painter. This factory has the best villa, the best museum, and the best tour. An English-speaking guide will show you how "the soul of the flower" is extracted. After the tour, you can explore the museum of perfumery, which displays bottles and vases that trace the industry back to ancient times. Of course, if you're shopping for perfume and want to skip the tour, that's okay with the factories.

Musée International de la Parfumerie. 8 place de Cours. ☎ **04-93-36-80-20.** Admission 20 F ($3.20) adults, 10 F ($1.60) children. Oct–May, Wed–Mon 10am–12:30pm and 2–5:30pm; June–Sept, Wed–Mon 10am–7pm.

This museum will teach everything about perfume. You learn that it takes a metric ton of flowers to make one liter of fragrance; you'll also see interesting, often bizarre, exhibits relating to the perfume industry. One of the most fascinating on the second floor displays a 3,000-year-old mummy's perfumed hand and foot. Apparently the flesh stayed preserved over the centuries because of some perfuming process. In the fourth floor greenery, you can smell some of the base elements that go into the creation of celebrated perfumes.

Villa Fragonard. 23 bd. Fragonard. ☎ **04-93-36-01-61.** Admission 20 F ($3.20) adults, 10 F ($1.60) children. June–Sept, Wed–Mon 10am–7am; Oct–May, Wed–Mon 10am–12:30pm and 2–5:30pm.

The collection displayed here includes the paintings of Jean-Honoré Fragonard; his sister-in-law, Marguerite Gérard; his son, Alexandre; and his grandson, Théophile. Fragonard was born in Grasse in 1732. The grand staircase was decorated by Alexandre.

Parfumerie Molinard. 60 bd. Victor-Hugo. ☎ **04-93-36-01-62.** Free admission. May–Sept, daily 9am–6:30pm; Oct–Apr, daily 9am–12:30pm and 2–6pm.

The firm is well known in the United States, and its products are sold at Saks, Neiman Marcus, and Bloomingdale's. In the factory you can witness the extraction of the essence of the flowers. You'll also learn all the details of the process of converting flowers into essential oils. You can admire a collection of antique perfume-bottle labels as well as see a rare collection of perfume *flacons* (bottles) by Baccarat and Lalique.

Musée d'Art et d'Histoire de Provence. 2 rue Mirabeau. ☎ **04-93-36-01-61.** Admission 20 F ($3.20) adults, 10 F ($1.60) children 8–16, free for children 7 and under. June–Sept, daily 10am–7pm; Oct–May, Wed–Mon 10am–12:30pm and 2–5:30pm.

This museum is in the Hôtel de Clapiers-Cabris, built in 1771 by Louise de Mirabeau, the marquise de Cabris and sister of Mirabeau. The collection includes paintings, four-poster beds, marquetry, ceramics, brasses, kitchenware, pottery, urns, and even archaeological finds.

ACCOMMODATIONS

La Bastide St-Antoine (Restaurant Chibois; see "Dining," below) also rents rooms.

Hôtel La Bellaudière. 78 rte. de Nice, 06130 Grasse. ☎ **04-93-36-02-57.** Fax 04-93-36-40-03. 17 units. TEL. 305–395 F ($48.80–$63.20) double. AE, DC, MC, V. Closed Nov 15–Feb 1. Free parking.

Here you'll find a cost-conscious, completely unpretentious family-run hotel. It's located 2 miles north of the town center, in a stone-sided farmhouse built in stages beginning 400 years ago. Bedrooms are simple but severely dignified, and outfitted with as many Provençal motifs and accessories as possible. The hotel benefits from an establishment of minimum standards from the well-respected Logis de France chain. There's a view of the sea from many of the bedrooms, a garden terrace lined with flowering shrubs, and a sense of friendly cooperation from the hosts.

DINING

✪ **La Bastide St-Antoine (Restaurant Chibois).** 48 av. Henri-Dunant. ☎ **04-93-70-94-94.** Reservations recommended. Main courses 170–280 F ($27.20–$44.80); fixed-price menus 230 F ($36.80) at lunch Mon–Sat, 550–700 F ($88–$112) at dinner. AE, DC, MC, V. Daily noon–2pm and 8–10:30pm. FRENCH/PROVENÇAL.

The fame that this restaurant has attracted since it opened in 1996 is viewed with amazement and envy by every restaurateur in France. It occupies a 200-year-old Provençal farmhouse surrounded by 7 acres of stately trees and verdant shrubberies. Jacques Chibois has set the French press on fire; his elevation to superstardom came in 1997 through awards lavished on him by the controversial Gault-Millau group.

The restaurant serves a sophisticated array of dishes. How's this for your salad choices: foie gras with green beans flavored with beetroot; or red snapper with parsley, Provençal vegetables, and olive oil. Delight your palate with such main courses as scallops with a fricassée of artichokes with truffles, or rabbit with a vegetable fricassée Provençal-style. The chef also does wonders with wild duck.

In 1998, the owners added **eight rooms and three suites,** each outfitted in a whimsical and idiosyncratic Provençal style. Each has air-conditioning, minibar, TV, telephone, upscale furnishings, and exceptionally comfortable beds. Doubles cost from 1,080 F to 1,440 F ($172.80 to $230.40); suites from 1,620 F to 2,160 F ($259.20 to $345.60). Free parking is available.

Restaurant Amphitryon. 16 bd. Victor-Hugo. ☎ **04-93-36-58-73.** Reservations recommended. Main courses 105–175 F ($16.80–$28); fixed-price menus 127–254 F ($20.30–$40.65). AE, DC, MC, V. Mon–Sat noon–1:30pm and 7:30–9:30pm. Closed Aug 1–Sept 1 and Dec 23–31. FRENCH.

Many of the buildings that line this street, including the one that houses this restaurant, functioned as stables in the 19th century. Today, amid fabric-covered walls and soothing grays and off-whites, you can enjoy the flavorful cuisine of Michel André. The food is inspired by southwestern France, with plenty of foie gras and duckling, as well as lamb roasted with thyme and a ragoût of fish in red wine that in recent years has become one of the chef's most popular dishes. Also recommendable are the Mediterranean fish soup with Provençal rouille and virtually any of the autumn dishes enhanced with seasonal fresh mushrooms.

6 Biot

570 miles S of Paris, 6 miles E of Cagnes-sur-Mer, 4 miles NW of Antibes

Biot has been famous for its pottery ever since merchants began to ship earthenware jars to Phoenicia and destinations throughout the Mediterranean. Biot was first settled by Gallo-Romans and has had a long, war-torn history. Somehow the potters still manage to work at their ancient craft. Biot is also the place Fernand Léger chose to paint until the day he died. A magnificent collection of his work is on display at a museum here.

ESSENTIALS

GETTING THERE   Biot's **train station** is 2 miles east of the town center. There's frequent service from Nice and Antibes. For rail information and schedules, call ☎ **08-36-35-35-35.** The **bus** from Antibes is even more convenient than the train. For bus information and schedules, call ☎ **04-93-34-37-60** in Antibes. In Biot, buses pull into, and depart from, the Place Guynemer.

To **drive** to Biot from Nice, take N7 west. From Antibes, follow N7 east.

VISITOR INFORMATION   The **Office de Tourisme** is on rue St-Sebastien (☎ **04-93-65-78-00**).

EXPLORING THE TOWN

If you have time, you might explore the village. Begin at the much-photographed **place des Arcades,** where you can see the 16th-century gates and the remains of the town's former ramparts. The town also is known for its carnations and roses, which are sold on this lovely square. **Église de Biot,** place des Arcades (☎ **04-93-65-00-85**), dates from the 15th century, when it was built by Italian immigrants who came here to resettle the town after it was decimated by the Black Death. The church is known for two stunning 15th-century *retables:* the red-and-gold *Retable du Rosaire* by Ludovico Bréa and the recently restored *Christ aux Plaies* by Canavesio.

In the late 1940s, glassmakers created a bubble-flecked glass known as *verre rustique.* It comes in brilliant colors like cobalt and emerald and is displayed in many store windows on the main shopping street, **rue St-Sebastien.** The best place to watch the glassblowers and buy glass, aside from the shops along rue St-Sebastien, is **Verrerie de Biot,** 5 chemin des Combes (☎ **04-93-65-03-00**), at the edge of town. Prices are about the same as in town. Hours are Monday to Saturday from 9:30am to 6:30pm. You can also visit the showroom on Sunday from 10:30am to 1pm and 2:30 to 6:30pm. While you're here, you can call at **Galerie International du Verre,** where beautifully displayed glass works are for sale, often at exorbitant prices. Even if you don't buy, you can admire these one-of-a-kind collector pieces.

There's also the **Galerie Jean-Claude Novaro** (also known as Galerie de la Patrimoine), place des Arcades (☎ **04-93-65-60-23**). Its namesake is known as the Picasso of glass artists. His works are pretty and colorful though they sometimes lack the diversity and intellectual flair of works by some of the artists displayed at the Galerie International du Verre. Most of his glass art, except for some exhibition pieces, is for sale.

You may also want to shop at **La Poterie Provençale,** 1689 Rte. de la Mer (☎ **04-93-65-63-30**). Set nearly adjacent to the Musée Fernand-Léger, about 2 miles southeast of town, it's one of the last potteries in Provence to specialize in the tall amphoralike containers known as *jarres.*

Musée d'Histoire Locale et de Céramique Biotoise, 9 rue St-Sebastien (☎ **04-93-65-54-54**), has assembled the best work of local glassblowing artists, potters, ceramists, painters, and silver- and goldsmiths. It's open Wednesday to Sunday from 2 to 6pm, charging 10 F ($1.60) for adults, 5 F (80¢) for ages 6 to 16, and free for children under 6.

✪ **Musée National Fernand-Léger.** Chemin du Val-de-Pome (on the eastern edge of town, beside the road leading to Biot's rail station). ☎ **04-92-91-50-30.** Admission 30–38 F ($4.80–$6.10) adults, 20–28 F ($3.20–$4.50) ages 18–24 and seniors over 60, free for children 17 and under. (Prices vary depending on the exhibition.) Oct–June, Wed–Mon 10am–12:30pm and 2–5:30pm; July–Sept, Wed–Mon 11am–6pm.

This collection was assembled by the artist's widow, Nadia Léger, who donated its contents to the French government after the artist's death. The stone-and-marble facade is enhanced by Léger's mosaic-and-ceramic mural. On the grounds is a polychrome ceramic sculpture, *Le Jardin d'enfant.* Inside are two floors of geometrical forms in pure flat colors. The collection includes paintings, ceramics, tapestries, and sculptures showing the development of the artist from 1905 until his death. His paintings abound with cranes, acrobats, scaffolding, railroad signals, buxom nudes, casings, and crankshafts. The most unusual work depicts a Léger Mona Lisa (*La Giaconde aux Clés*) contemplating a set of keys, a wide-mouthed fish dangling over her head.

DINING

✪ **Les Terraillers.** 11 rte. du Chemin-Neuf. ☎ **04-93-65-01-59.** Reservations required, as far in advance as possible. Main courses 170–190 F ($27.20–$30.40); fixed-price menus 220–380 F ($35.20–$60.80) at lunch, 250–380 F ($40–$60.80) at dinner. AE, MC, V. Thurs–Tues noon–2pm and 7–10pm. Take rte. du Chemin-Neuf, following the signs to Antibes. MEDITERRANEAN.

Stone-sided and deeply evocative of Provence, this restaurant is about half a mile south of Biot, in what was built in the 1500s as a studio for the production of clay pots and ceramics. Today, under the guidance of chef Claude Jacques, it functions as a well-respected restaurant. The cuisine produced by this young and effervescent staff changes with the seasons, and is much, much more sophisticated and appetizing than that served by many equivalently priced competitors. Examples include roasted scallops with a saffron and mussel-flavored cream sauce and a confit of leeks; a tart with artichoke hearts and tomatoes en confit with a lobster salad; and ravioli filled with panfried foie gras served with essence of morels and a duxelle of mushrooms. Main courses include a platter containing two distinctly different preparations of pigeon (thigh and breast cooked in different ways) served with a corn galette and the pigeon's own drippings; or a simply braised John Dory Provençal style, with olive oil and a fricassée of zucchini, artichokes, tomatoes, and olives.

7 Golfe-Juan & Vallauris

Golfe-Juan: 567 miles S of Paris, 4 miles E of Cannes; Vallauris: 565 miles S of Paris, 4 miles E of Cannes

Napoléon and 800 men landed at Golfe-Juan in 1815 to begin his Hundred Days. Protected by hills, this spot beside the coast was also the favored port for the American navy. Today it's primarily a family resort known for its beaches and a noteworthy restaurant (Chez Tétou).

The 1¼-mile-long RN135 leads inland from Golfe-Juan to Vallauris. Once merely a stopover along the Riviera, Vallauris (noted for its pottery) owes its reputation to Picasso, who "discovered" it. The master came to Vallauris after World War II and occupied a villa known as "The Woman from Wales."

ESSENTIALS

GETTING THERE   You can **drive** to Golfe-Juan or Vallauris along any of the three east-west highways along the Riviera. Although route numbers are not always indicated, city names are abundantly clear once you're on the highway. From Cannes or Antibes, N7 east is the fastest route. From Nice or Biot, take A8/E80 west.

There's a sleepy-looking railway station in Golfe-Juan, on Avenue de la Gare. To get here, you'll have to transfer from a **train** in Cannes. The train from Cannes costs around 10 F ($1.70) each way. For railway information and schedules, call ☎ 08-36-35-35-35. Alternatively, a flotilla of **buses,** operated by RCA (Rapides Côte-d'Azur; ☎ 04-93-39-11-39 for information), makes frequent transits from Cannes; the 20-minute trips cost 10 F ($1.60) each way; and from Nice, the 60-minute trip costs 25 F ($4) each way.

VISITOR INFORMATION   There's an **Office de Tourisme** at 84 av. de la Liberté in Golfe-Juan (☎ 04-93-63-73-12) and another on square 8-Mai in Vallauris (☎ 04-93-63-82-58).

EXPLORING THE AREA

BEACHES   Because of its position beside the sea, Golfe-Juan developed long ago into a warm-weather resort. The town's twin strips of beach are **Plages du Soleil** (east of the Vieux Port and the newer Port Camille-Rayon) and **Plages du Midi** (west of those two). Each stretches half a mile and charges no entry fee, with the exception of small areas administered by concessions that rent mattresses and chaises and offer access to kiosks dispensing snacks and cold drinks. Regardless of which concession you select (on Plage du Midi they sport names like Au Vieux Rocher, Palma Beach, and Corail Plage; on Plage du Soleil, Plage Nounou and Plage Tétou), you'll pay around 90 F ($14.40) for a day's use of a mattress. Plage Tétou is associated with the upscale Chez Tétou (see "Dining," below). If you don't want to rent a mattress, you can cavort unhindered anywhere along the sands, moving freely from one area to another. Golfe-Juan indulges bathers who remove their bikini tops, but in theory it forbids nude sunbathing.

ATTRACTIONS   Picasso's *Homme et Mouton* (Man and Sheep) is the outdoor statue at which Aly Kahn and Rita Hayworth were married. The council of Vallauris had intended to ensconce this statue in a museum, but Picasso insisted that it remain on the square "where the children could climb over it and the dogs water it unhindered."

Musée Magnelli/Musée de la Céramique/Musée National Picasso La Guerre et La Paix. Place de la Libération. ☎ **04-93-64-16-05.** Admission 17 F ($2.70) adults, 8.50 F ($1.35) students, free for children 15 and under. Oct–Mar, Wed–Mon 10am–noon and 2–6pm; Apr–Sept, Wed–Mon 9am–6pm.

A chapel of rough stone shaped like a Quonset hut is the focal point of a three-in-one sightseeing highlight. The museum grew from the site of a chapel that Picasso decorated with two paintings: *La Paix* (Peace) and *La Guerre* (War). The paintings offer contrasting images of love and peace on the one hand and violence and conflict on the other. In 1970 a house painter gained illegal entrance to the museum one night and substituted one of his own designs, after whitewashing a portion of the original. When the aging master inspected the damage, he said, "Not bad at all." In July 1996 the site was enhanced with a permanent exposition devoted to the works of the Florentine-born Alberto Magnelli, a pioneer of abstract art whose first successes were acclaimed in 1915 and who died in 1971, 2 years before Picasso. A third section showcases ceramics, both traditional and innovative, from potters throughout the region.

SHOPPING

One shop that rises far above its neighbors is the **Galerie Madoura,** avenue de Georges et Suzanne Ramié, in Vallauris (☎ **04-93-64-66-39**); it's the only shop licensed to sell Picasso reproductions. The master knew and admired the work of the Ramie family, who founded Madoura, open Monday to Friday from 10am to 12:30pm and 2:30 to 7pm (to 6pm October to March). Some of the reproductions are limited to 25 to 500 copies.

Other galleries to seek out are **Galerie Jean Marais,** avenue des Martyrs-de-la-Résistance (☎ **04-93-63-85-74**); and **Galerie Sassi-Milici,** 65 bis av. Georges-Clemenceau (☎ **04-93-64-65-71**), displaying works by contemporary artists.

Market day at Vallauris takes place every day except Monday, from 7am to 12:30pm, at the **place de l'Homme au Mouton,** with its flower stalls and local produce. For a souvenir, you may want to visit a farming cooperative, **Cooperative Nérolium,** 12 av. Georges-Clemenceau (☎ **04-93-64-27-54**). The cooperative produces such foods as bitter orange marmalade and quince jam, and such scented products as orange flower water. Another unusual outlet for local products is **Parfumerie Bouis,** 50 av. Georges-Clemenceau (☎ **04-93-64-38-27**). Local glass, blown by artisans in and around the town, is available from **Creations GR,** 69 av. Georges Clemenceau (☎ **04-93-63-19-20**).

La Boutique de l'Olivier, 46 av. Georges-Clemenceau (☎ **04-93-64-66-45**), is a specialist in objects made of olive wood. These include pepper mills, salad servers, cheese boards, free-form bowls, and slatted bread-slicing boxes. A final place, **Terres à Terre,** 58 av. Georges-Clemenceau (☎ **04-93-63-16-80**), is known for its culinary pottery, made of local clay. This is an excellent outlet for picking up earthenware terracotta pottery. Gratin dishes and casseroles have long been big sellers here.

DINING

✪ **Chez Tétou.** Av. des Frères-Roustand, sur la Plage, Golfe-Juan. ☎ **04-93-63-71-16.** Reservations required. Fixed-price menus 500–700 F ($80–$112); bouillabaisse 400–480 F ($64–$76.80). No credit cards. Daily noon–2:30pm and 8–10pm. Closed Nov–Mar 10. SEAFOOD.

In its own amusing way, this is one of the Côte d'Azur's most famous restaurants, capitalizing richly on the glittering beau monde who frequented it during the 1950s and 1960s. Retaining its Provençal earthiness despite its incredibly high prices, it has thrived in a white-sided beach cottage for more than 65 years. It still serves a bouillabaisse often remembered years later by diners. The list of appetizers is limited to platters of charcuterie (cold cuts) or several almost-perfect slices of fresh melon, as most diners order the house specialty, bouillabaisse. Other items on the deliberately limited menu are grilled sea bass with tomatoes Provençal, sole meunière, and several preparations of lobster—the most famous of which is grilled and served with lemon-butter sauce, fresh parsley, and a bed of Basmati rice. Your dessert might be a special powdered croissant with grandmother's jams (winter) or a homemade raspberry and strawberry tart (summer).

8 Juan-les-Pins

567 miles S of Paris, 6 miles S of Cannes

This suburb of Antibes is a resort developed in the 1920s by Frank Jay Gould. At that time people flocked to "John of the Pines" to escape the "crassness" of nearby Cannes. In the '30s Juan-les-Pins drew a chic winter crowd. Today it attracts young Europeans from many economic backgrounds, in pursuit of sex, sun, and sea, in that order.

Juan-les-Pins is often called a honky-tonk town or the "Coney Island of the Riviera," but anyone who calls it that hasn't seen Coney Island in a long time. One newspaper writer called it "a pop-art Monte Carlo, with burlesque shows and nude beaches," a description much too provocative for such a middle-class resort. Another newspaper writer said that Juan-les-Pins is "for the young and noisy." Even F. Scott Fitzgerald decried it as a "constant carnival." If he could see it now, he'd know he was a prophet.

ESSENTIALS

GETTING THERE   Juan-les-Pins is connected by rail and bus to most other Mediterranean coastal resorts, especially Nice (trip time: 30 minutes). For rail information and schedules, call ☎ **08-36-35-35-35.** There are also **buses** that arrive from Nice and its airport at 40-minute intervals throughout the day. To **drive** to Juan-les-Pins from Nice, travel along N7 south; from Cannes, follow the signposted roads. Juan-les-Pins is just outside of Cannes.

VISITOR INFORMATION   The **Office de Tourisme** is at 51 bd. Charles-Guillaumont (☎ **04-92-90-53-05**).

SPECIAL EVENTS   The town offers some of the best nightlife on the Riviera, and the action reaches its frenzied height during the annual jazz festival. The **Festival International de Jazz** descends at the end of July for 10 days, attracting stellar jazz masters and their devoted fans. Concerts are presented within a temporary stadium, custom built for the event within Le Parc de la Pinède, and which is dismantled at the end of the festival. Tickets range from 110 F to 200 F ($17.60 to $32) and can be purchased at the Office de Tourisme.

EXPLORING THE TOWN

Part of the reason people flock here is that the town's beaches actually have sand, unlike many of the other resorts along this coast, which have pebbly beaches. **Plage de Juan-les-Pins** is the town's most central beach. Its subdivisions, all public, include **Plage de la Salis** and **Plage de la Garoupe.** If you don't have your own beach chair, go to the concessions operated by each of the major beachfront hotels. Even if you're not a guest, you can rent a chaise and mattress for 80 F to 120 F ($12.80 to $19.20). The most chic of the lot is the area maintained by the Hôtel des Belles-Rives. Competitors more or less in the same category are La Jetée and La Voile Blanche, both opposite the tourist information office. Topless sunbathing is permitted, but total nudity isn't.

WATER SPORTS If you're interested in scuba diving, check with your hotel concierge or one of these companies: **Club de la Mer,** Port Gallice (☎ **04-93-61-26-07**); or **EPAJ,** embarcadère Courbet (☎ **04-93-67-52-59**). **Waterskiing** is available at virtually every beach in Juan-les-Pins, including one outfit that's more or less permanently located on the beach of the Hôtel des Belles-Rives. Ask any beach attendant or bartender and he or she will guide you to the waterskiing representatives who station themselves on the sands. A 10-minute session costs about 150 F ($24).

ACCOMMODATIONS
VERY EXPENSIVE

Hôtel des Belles-Rives. 33 bd. Baudoin, 06160 Juan-les-Pins. ☎ **04-93-61-02-79.** Fax 04-93-67-43-51. www.bellesrives.com. E-mail: info@belles-rives.com. 45 units. A/C MINIBAR TV TEL. 1,150–2,900 F ($184–$464) double; from 3,200 F ($512) suite. Half board 390 F ($62.40) per person extra. AE, DC, DISC, MC, V. Closed Oct–Mar. Free parking.

This is one of the Riviera's fabled addresses, on a par with the equally famous Juana (see below), though the Juana boasts a somewhat superior cuisine. Once it was a holiday villa occupied by Zelda and F. Scott Fitzgerald, so it was the scene of many a drunken brawl. In the following years it hosted the illustrious, like the duke and duchess of Windsor, Josephine Baker, and even Edith Piaf. A certain 1930s aura still lingers through recent renovations. Double-glazing and a new air-conditioning system help a lot. As befits a hotel of this age, rooms come in a variety of shapes and sizes, ranging from small to spacious, but each is fitted with a luxurious mattress.

Dining: The lower terraces are devoted to garden dining rooms and a waterside aquatic club with a snack bar/lounge and a jetty extending into the water. Dinners are served in the romantic setting at "La Terrasse" with a panoramic bay view. Fixed-price menus cost from 290 F ($46.40) each. Lunches are stylish but somewhat less formal and offered in a setting overlooking the beach.

Amenities: Landing dock, car-rental desk, concierge, room service, dry cleaning/laundry, baby-sitting, courtesy car, private beach.

✪ **Hôtel Juana.** La Pinède, av. Gallice, 06160 Juan-les-Pins. ☎ **04-93-61-08-70.** Fax 04-93-61-76-60. www.hotel-juana.com. E-mail: info@hotel-juana.com. 50 units. A/C TV TEL. 750–1,350 F ($120–$216) double; 1,800–3,800 F ($288–$608) suite. MC, V. Closed Nov–Mar. Parking 50 F ($8).

This balconied Art Deco four-star hotel, owned by the Barache family since 1929, is separated from the sea by the park of pines that gave Juan-les-Pins its name and that was so beloved by F. Scott Fitzgerald. The hotel has a private swimming club where you can rent a "parasol and pad" on the sandy beach at reduced rates. Nearby is a park with umbrella tables and shady palms. The hotel is constantly being refurbished, as reflected in the attractive rooms with mahogany pieces, well-chosen fabrics, tasteful carpets, and large baths in marble or tile imported from Italy. The rooms also have such extras as safes and (in some) balconies.

Dining: We review La Terrasse restaurant below. There's a bar in the poolhouse.

Amenities: Private beach club and a heated marble outdoor pool with a solarium, concierge, room service, dry cleaning and laundry service, massage, bicycle rentals, baby-sitting, secretarial services.

MODERATE

Hôtel des Mimosas. Rue Pauline, 06160 Juan-les-Pins. ☎ **04-93-61-04-16.** Fax 04-92-93-06-46. 34 units. MINIBAR TV TEL. 470–680 F ($75.20–$108.80) double. AE, MC, V. Closed Sept 30–Apr 30. From the town center, drive a quarter mile west, following N7 toward Cannes.

This elegant 1870s-style villa sprawls in a tropical garden on a hilltop. The decor is a mix of high-tech and Italian-style comfort, with antique and modern furniture. There's a bar but no restaurant. The rooms have balconies. A pool is set amid huge palm trees. The hotel is fully booked in summer, so reserve far in advance.

INEXPENSIVE

Hôtel Cecil. Rue Jonnard, 06160 Juan-les-Pins. ☎ **04-93-61-05-12.** Fax 04-93-67-09-14. www.sites.netscape.net/hotelcecilfrance. E-mail: hotelcecil@yahoo.com. 21 units. TV TEL. Apr–Sept, 600 F ($96) double. AE, DC, MC, V. Closed Nov to mid-Jan. Parking 50 F ($8).

Located 50 yards from the beach, this small, well-kept hotel is one of the best bargains in Juan-les-Pins. The rooms are well worn yet clean. The owner/chef Michel Courtois provides a courteous welcome and good **meals** beginning at 80 F ($12.80). In summer you can enjoy his food on a patio.

Hôtel Le Pré Catelan. 22 av. des Palmiers, 06160 Juan-les-Pins. ☎ **04-93-61-05-11.** Fax 04-93-67-83-11. E-mail: trevoux@club-internet.fr. 24 units. MINIBAR TV TEL. 450–600 F ($72–$96) double. AE, DC, MC, V. Closed Nov–Mar.

In a residential area near the town park, this circa-1900 Provençal villa has a garden with rock terraces, towering palms, lemon and orange trees, large pots of pink geraniums, trimmed hedges, and outdoor furniture. The atmosphere is casual, the setting uncomplicated and unstuffy. The more expensive rooms have terraces, but the furnishings are durable and rather basic. Despite the setting in the heart of town, the garden here manages to provide a sense of isolation. Breakfast is the only meal served.

DINING

La Romana. 21 av. Dautheville. ☎ **04-93-61-05-66.** Pizzas 35–55 F ($5.60–$8.80); main-course salads and platters 50–100 F ($8–$16). DC, V. Daily noon–2:30pm and 7pm–midnight. Winter, noon–2:30pm only. FRENCH/INTERNATIONAL.

Behind the casino, this aggressively unpretentious restaurant successfully caters its trade to the thousands of budget-conscious holiday makers who flood the town every season. Don't expect grande cuisine, as the venue is too simple, too informal. What you'll get—amid a generic 1930s-style decor accented with touches of wrought iron—is pizzas, meal-size salads, fried fish and fried scampi, grilled steaks with French fries, and *plats du jour* whose composition changes every day.

✪ **La Terrasse.** In the Hôtel Juana, La Pinède, av. Gallice. ☎ **04-93-61-20-37.** Reservations required. Main courses 295–425 F ($47.20–$68); fixed-price menus 290 F ($46.40) at lunch, 490–680 F ($78.40–$108.80) at dinner. AE, MC, V. July–Aug, daily 12:30–2pm and 7:30–10:30pm; Apr–June and Sept–Oct, Thurs–Tues 12:30–2pm and 7:30–10:30pm. Closed Nov–Mar. FRENCH/MEDITERRANEAN.

Bill Cosby loves this gourmet restaurant so much that he's been known to fly chef Christian Morisset to New York to prepare dinner for him. Morisset, who trained with Vergé and Lenôtre, cooks with a light, precise, and creative hand. His cuisine is the best in Juan-les-Pins. The chic, airy setting is lively and sophisticated, with a conservatively modern decor overlooking the verdant garden, and a glassed-in terrace whose roof opens for midsummer ventilation and a view of the stars. Menu items are steeped in the flavors and preoccupations of Provence. Examples include giant raviolis stuffed with fresh crayfish and an olive-flavored essence of shellfish; and a rack of lamb from the salt marshes of Pauillac cooked in a clay pot from nearby Vallauris, served with stuffed zucchini flowers and Provençal herbs. Dessert might include a Napoléon (*mille feuille*) of wild strawberries with a mascarpone cream sauce.

✪ **Le Bijou.** Bd. Charles-Guillaumont. ☎ **04-93-61-39-07.** Reservations recommended. Main courses 175–450 F ($28–$72); fixed-price menus 175–290 F ($28–$46.40); shellfish platters 280 F ($44.80); bouillabaisse 350 F ($56). AE, DC, MC, V. Daily noon–2:30pm and 7:30–10:30pm (to 11:30pm June to mid-Sept). FRENCH/PROVENÇAL.

This upscale brasserie has flourished beside the seafront promenade for almost 80 years. The marine-style decor includes lots of varnished wood and bouquets of blue and white flowers in a mostly blue-and-white interior. Windows overlook a private beach whose sands are much less crowded than those of the public beaches nearby. Menu items are succulent, sophisticated, and less expensive than you'd expect. Examples are a version of bouillabaisse that might make you clamor for more, platters of grilled sardines, steamed mussels with *sauce poulette* (frothy cream sauce with herbs and butter), grilled John Dory with a vinaigrette enriched with a tapenade of olives and fresh basil, and a super-size *plateau des coquillages et fruits de mer* (shellfish). Don't confuse this informally elegant place with its beachfront terrace, open only from April to September every day from noon to 4pm. Here a lunch buffet—served to diners in swimsuits, which are strictly forbidden in the main restaurant several paces uphill—is 70 F ($11.20) per person.

JUAN-LES-PINS AFTER DARK

For starters, visit the **Eden Casino,** boulevard Baudoin in the heart of Juan-les-Pins (☎ **04-92-93-71-71**), and try your luck at the roulette wheel or at one of the slot machines. The area containing slot machines doesn't charge admission. It's open every day from 10am to 5pm. The area containing *les grands jeux* (blackjack, roulette, and chemin de fer) is open daily from 9:30pm to 5am, and charges an entrance fee of 70 F ($11.20) per person.

For a more tropical experience, head to **Le Pam Pam,** route Wilson (☎ **04-93-61-11-05**), where you can sip rum drinks in an exotic ambience created and celebrated by live reggae, Brazilian, and African performances of music and dance.

If you prefer some high-energy reveling, check out the town's many discos, the best of which are **Whisky à Gogo,** boulevard de la Pinède (☎ **04-93-61-26-40**), with its young trendsetters and pounding rock beat; the richly dramatic **Le J's,** avenue Georges-Gallice (☎ **04-93-67-22-74**), offering the latest music; and **Le Village,** 1 bd. de la Pinède (☎ **04-93-61-18-71**), which boasts an action-packed dance floor and hip DJs spinning the latest from the international music scene. The cover charge at these clubs is a stiff 100 F ($16).

For a more relaxed evening, go to the British pub **Le Ten's Bar,** 25 av. du Dr.-Hochet (☎ **04-93-67-20-67**), where you'll find 56 brands of beer and a sociable crowd of young and old merrymakers. You could even choose the tranquil piano bar **Le Cambridge,** 25 rue du Dr.-Hochet (☎ **04-93-67-49-89**), with its older, more sophisticated crowd; or **Le Madison,** 1 av. Alexandre-III (☎ **04-93-67-83-80**), with the town's best jazz and blues.

9 Antibes & Cap d'Antibes

567 miles S of Paris, 13 miles SW of Nice, 7 miles NE of Cannes

On the other side of the Baie des Anges (Bay of Angels), across from Nice, is the port of Antibes. This old Mediterranean town has a quiet charm unique on the Côte d'Azur. Its little harbor is filled with fishing boats and pleasure yachts, and in recent years it has emerged as a new hot spot. The marketplaces are full of flowers, mostly roses and carnations. If you're in Antibes in the evening, you can watch fishers playing the popular Riviera game of boule.

Spiritually, Antibes is totally divorced from Cap d'Antibes, a peninsula studded with the villas and pools of the super-rich. In *Tender Is the Night,* F. Scott Fitzgerald described it as a place where "old villas rotted like water lilies among the massed pines." Photos of film and rock stars lounging at the Eden Roc have appeared in countless magazines.

ESSENTIALS

GETTING THERE   **Trains** from Cannes arrive at the railway station, in the place Pierre Semard, every 20 minutes (trip time: 10 minutes), at a one-way fare of around 14 F ($2.25). Trains from Nice arrive every 30 minutes (trip time: 18 minutes), charging a one-way fare of around 20 F ($3.20). There's also a **bus** station, La Gare Routière, on the place Guynemer (☎ **04-93-34-37-60**), that receives buses from throughout Provence.

If you're **driving,** take E1 east from Cannes, taking the turn-off signposted to the south for Antibes, which will lead to the historic core of the old city. From Nice, take E1 west until you come to the signposted turnoff for Antibes. From the center of Antibes, follow the coastal road, boulevard Leclerc, south until you come to Cap d'Antibes.

VISITOR INFORMATION   The **Office de Tourisme** is at 11 place du Général-de-Gaulle (☎ **04-92-90-53-00**).

SEEING THE SIGHTS

✪ **Musée Picasso.** Place du Château. ☎ **04-92-90-54-26** for recorded message or 04-92-90-54-20 for an attendant. Admission 30 F ($4.80) adults, 18 F ($2.90) students and ages 15–24 and over 60, free for children 14 and under. Tues–Sun 10–11:50am and 2–4:50pm (until 5:50pm July–Sept).

On the ramparts above the port is the Château Grimaldi, once the home of the princes of Antibes of the Grimaldi family, who ruled the city from 1385 to 1608. Today it houses one of the world's greatest Picasso collections. Picasso came to the small town after his bitter war years in Paris and stayed in a small hotel at Golfe-Juan until the museum director at Antibes invited him to work and live at the museum. Picasso then spent 1946 painting here. When he departed, he gave the museum all the work he'd done: 24 paintings, 80 pieces of ceramics, 44 drawings, 32 lithographs, 11 oils on paper, 2 sculptures, and 5 tapestries. In addition, there's a gallery of contemporary art, which exhibits Léger, Miró, Ernst, and Calder, among others. Some of the works by these other artists might be in storage at the time of your visit, based on whatever temporary exhibition is being displayed.

Musée Naval et Napoléonien. Batterie du Grillon, bd. J.-F.-Kennedy. ☎ **04-93-61-45-32.** Admission 20 F ($3.20). Mon–Fri 9:30am–noon and 2:15–6pm, Sat 9:30am–noon.

In a stone-sided fort and tower that was built in stages between the 17th and 18th centuries, there's an interesting collection of Napoleonic memorabilia, naval models, paintings, and mementos, many of which were donated to the museum by at least two world-class collectors. A toy soldier collection depicts various uniforms, including one used by Napoléon in the Marengo campaign. A wall painting on wood shows Napoléon's entrance into Grenoble; another tableau shows him disembarking at Golfe-Juan on March 1, 1815. In contrast to Canova's Greek-god image of Napoléon, a miniature pendant by Barrault reveals the Corsican general as he really looked, with pudgy cheeks and a receding hairline. In the rear rotunda is one of the many hats worn by the emperor. You can climb to the top of the tower for a view of the coast that's worth the admission price.

ACCOMMODATIONS
VERY EXPENSIVE

✪ **Hôtel du Cap-Eden Roc.** Bd. J.-F.-Kennedy, 06600 Cap d'Antibes. ☎ **04-93-61-39-01.** Fax 04-93-67-76-04. www.edenroc-hotel.fr. E-mail: edenroc-hotel@wanadoo.fr. 130 units. A/C TEL. 2,500–3,000 F ($400–$480) double; 5,500–9,500 F ($880–$1,520) suite. No credit cards. Closed mid-Oct to Mar. Bus: A2.

Legendary for the glamour of both its setting and its clientele, this Second Empire hotel, opened in 1870, is surrounded by 22 splendid acres of gardens. It's like a great country estate, with spacious public rooms, marble fireplaces, scenic paneling, chandeliers, and richly upholstered armchairs. Some guest rooms and suites have regal period furnishings. The rooms here are among the most sumptuous on the Riviera, each a statement to the deluxe tastes of another era. Beds are lush and plush with deluxe mattresses and elegant appointments. Even though the guests snoozing by the pool, which was blasted out of the cliffside at enormous expense, might appear artfully undraped during daylight hours, evenings here are intensely upscale, with lots of emphasis on clothing and style. The staff is well rehearsed, but regardless of how important you are, they can always say they've dealt with bigger, more famous names.

Dining: The world-famous Pavillon Eden Roc, near a rock garden apart from the hotel, has a panoramic Mediterranean view. Venetian chandeliers, Louis XV chairs, and elegant draperies add to the drama. Lunch is served on an outer terrace, under umbrellas and an arbor. Dinner specialties include bouillabaisse, lobster Thermidor, and sea bass with fennel. Lunches cost from around 400 F ($64) each; and dinners from around 500 F ($80).

Amenities: Concierge, 24-hour room service, dry cleaning and laundry service, massage, secretarial services, baby-sitting.

✪ **Hôtel Imperial Garoupe.** 770 Chemin de la Garoupe, 06600 Antibes. ☎ **800/ 525-4800** or 04-92-93-31-61. Fax 04-92-93-31-62. www.imperial-garoupe.com. E-mail: hotel-imp@webstore.fr. 34 units. A/C MINIBAR TV TEL. 1,250–2,900 F ($200–$464) double; 2,300–5,100 F ($368–$816) suite. AE, DC, MC, V. Free parking. Bus: A2.

This hotel was built in 1993 by the heiress to the Moulinex housewares fortune. After an unprofitable first season, Gilbert Irondelle, son of the director of Antibes's hyper-chic, hyper-expensive Hôtel du Cap, bought it and transformed it into a low-key and very charming pocket of posh that's a bit less intimidating than the more monumental hotel run by his father. The hotel offers luxurious and comfortable bedrooms filled with oversized contemporary furnishings, lots of padded upholsteries, and pastel-inspired color schemes. Bedrooms are generous in size and fitted with luxury mattresses on the plush beds. Set within 50 yards of the beach, the hotel is the centerpiece of a 3^{1}/$_{2}$-acre park whose rows of pines block some of the views of the sea.

Dining/Diversions: You can always get a drink at this hotel, served virtually wherever you want it, although none of the interiors are specifically designated as a bar per se. The in-house restaurant serves a French and international cuisine.

Amenities: Heated pool, 24-hour room service, concierge.

MODERATE

Castel Garoupe. 959 bd. de la Garoupe, 06160 Cap d'Antibes. ☎ **04-93-61-36-51.** Fax 04-93-67-74-88. www.castelgaroupe.com. 27 units. TV TEL. 695–870 F ($111.20–$139.20) double; 865–1,105 F ($138.40–$176.80) studio apt with kitchenette. Closed Nov to mid-Mar. Bus A2.

We highly recommend this Mediterranean villa, which was built in 1968 on a private lane in the center of the cape, because it offers spacious, tastefully furnished rooms, some equipped with kitchenettes. Accommodations are comfortable, with fine mattresses, quality linens, and well-maintained, compact bathrooms. Many of the rooms have private balconies, and each has shuttered windows. There's a tranquil garden on the premises, as well as a freshwater pool and a tennis court.

INEXPENSIVE

Auberge de la Gardiole. Chemin de la Garoupe, 06160 Cap d'Antibes. ☎ **04-93-61-35-03.** Fax 04-93-67-61-87. 20 units. MINIBAR TV TEL. 490–590 F ($78.40–$94.40) double; from 790 F ($126.40) suite. AE, MC, V. Closed Nov–Feb. Bus: A2.

Monsieur and Mme Courtot run this country inn with a delightful personal touch. The large villa, surrounded by gardens, is in an area of private estates. The charming rooms, on the upper floors of the inn and in the little buildings in the garden, contain personal safes; 15 are air-conditioned. Rooms come in a variety of shapes and sizes, each furnished with a certain charm and an eye on comfort, especially when it comes to the fine mattresses and good linens on the French beds. The owners buy the food and supervise its preparation; the cuisine is French/Provençal with fixed-price menus at 150 F ($24). The cheerful **dining room** has a fireplace and hanging pots and pans; in good weather you can dine under a wisteria-covered trellis.

DINING

La Bonne Auberge. Quartier de Brague, rte. N7. ☎ **04-93-33-36-65.** Reservations required. Main courses 130–195 F ($20.80–$31.20); fixed-price menu 220–380 F ($35.20–$60.80). MC, V. Tues–Sun noon–2pm; Tues–Sat 7–10pm. Closed mid-Nov to mid-Dec. Take coastal highway N7 east 2¹/₂ miles from Antibes. FRENCH.

For many years following its 1975 opening, this was one of the most famous restaurants on the French Riviera. In 1992, in the wake of the death of its famous founder, Jo Rostang, his culinary heir, Philippe Rostang, wisely limited its scope and transformed it into a worthwhile but less ambitious restaurant. The fixed-price menu offers a wide selection. Choices vary every 3 weeks but may include a Basque-inspired pipérade with poached eggs, sea wolf with soya sauce, savory swordfish tart, and chicken with vinegar and garlic. Dessert might be an enchanting peach soufflé.

La Taverne du Saffranier. Place du Saffranier. ☎ **04-93-34-80-50.** Reservations recommended. Main courses 50–120 F ($8–$19.20); fixed-price menu 62 F ($9.90). No credit cards. Tues–Sun noon–12:30pm; Tues–Sat 7–10:30pm. PROVENÇAL.

Earthy, irreverent, and firmly entrenched in a century-old building in the Provençal motif, this cost-conscious brasserie trots out a changing medley of local specialties for a local clientele. Portions are savory and generous, and replete with the associations everyone in town retains of his real or imagined childhood in Provence. Examples include a platter of stuffed vegetables (*petits farcis*); *céviche,* the cold raw fish in hot sauce that's particularly refreshing on a hot day; a savory version of fish soup; and a medley of grilled fish that's invariably served only with a dash of fresh lemon. The kitchens can also prepare their own version of bouillabaisse, but only if you give them a day's advance notice. Lunch hours are very limited.

✪ **Restaurant de Bacon.** Bd. de Bacon. ☎ **04-93-61-50-02.** Reservations required. Fixed-price menus 280–450 F ($44.80–$72). AE, DC, MC, V. Tues–Sun 12:30–2pm and 8–10pm. Closed Nov–Jan. SEAFOOD

Set among ultra-expensive residences, this restaurant on a rocky peninsula has a panoramic coast view. Bouillabaisse aficionados claim that Bacon offers the best version in France. This fish stew, conceived centuries ago as a simple fisher's supper, is now one of the world's great dishes. In its deluxe version, saltwater crayfish float atop the savory brew; we prefer the simple version—a waiter adds the finishing touches at your table. If bouillabaisse isn't to your liking, try fish soup with the traditional garlic-laden rouille sauce, fish terrine, sea bass, John Dory, or something from an exotic collection of fish unknown in North America. These include sar, pageot, and denti, prepared in several ways. Many visitors are confused by the way fish dishes are priced by the gram: A guideline is that light lunches cost around 250 F to 400 F ($40 to $64); substantial dinners go for 550 F to 800 F ($88 to $128).

10 Cagnes-sur-Mer

570 miles S of Paris, 13 miles NE of Cannes

Cagnes-sur-Mer, like the Roman god Janus, has two faces. Perched on a hill in the "hinterlands" of Nice, **Le Haut-de-Cagnes** is one of the most charming spots on the Riviera. At the foot of the hill is an old fishing port and rapidly developing beach resort called **Cros-de-Cagnes,** between Nice and Antibes.

For years Le Haut-de-Cagnes attracted the French literati, including Simone de Beauvoir, who wrote *Les Mandarins* here. A colony of painters also settled here; Renoir said the village was "the place where I want to paint until the last day of my life." Today the racecourse is one of the finest in France.

ESSENTIALS

GETTING THERE   **Buses** from Nice and Cannes stop at Cagnes-Ville and at Béal/Les Collettes, within walking distance of Cros-de-Cagnes. For bus information, call ☎ **04-93-45-20-08** in Cannes or **04-93-85-61-81** in Nice. The climb from Cagnes-Ville to Le Haut-de-Cagnes is very strenuous, so in summer, between June and September, there's a minibus running about every 30 minutes from place du Général-de-Gaulle in the center of Cagnes-Ville to Le Haut-de-Cagnes at a cost of 8 F ($1.30) per person. By **car,** from any of the coastal cities of Provence, follow the A8 coastal highway, exiting at "Cagnes-sur-Mer/Cros-de-Cagnes."

VISITOR INFORMATION   The **Office de Tourisme** is at 6 bd. Maréchal-Juin, Cagnes-Ville (☎ **04-93-20-61-64**).

SPECIAL EVENTS   The **Festival International de Peinture** (International Festival of Painting) is presented in cooperation with Cagnes's Town Hall and the Musée d'Art Moderne Méditerranéen, and takes place from mid-November to mid-January in the Château-Musée, 7 place Grimaldi. Painters from about 40 nations participate in the exposition and promotion of their works. For information, call ☎ **04-93-20-87-29.**

EXPLORING THE TOWN

Cros-de-Cagnes is known for 2¼ miles of seafront evenly covered with light-gray pebbles that've been worn smooth by centuries of wave action. These beaches are collectively identified as **Plages de Cros-de-Cagnes.** The expanse is punctuated by five concessions that rent beach mattresses and chaises for around 85 F ($14.45). The best, or at least the most centrally located, are **Tiercé Plage** (☎ 04-93-20-13-89), **Le Cigalon** (☎ 04-93-07-74-82), and **La Gougouline** (☎ 04-93-31-08-72). As usual, toplessness is accepted but full nudity isn't.

The orange groves and fields of carnations of the upper village provide a beautiful setting for the narrow cobblestone streets and 17th- and 18th-century homes. Drive your car to the top, where you can enjoy the view from **place du Château** and have lunch or a drink at a sidewalk cafe.

Musée de l'Olivier/Musée d'Art Moderne Méditerranéen. 7 place Grimaldi. ☎ **04-93-20-87-29.** Admission to both museums 20 F ($3.20) adults, 10 F ($1.60) students. May–Sept, Wed–Mon 10am–noon and 2–6pm; Oct–Apr, Wed–Mon 10am–noon and 2–5pm.

This structure was originally a fortress built in 1301 by Rainier Grimaldi I, a lord of Monaco and a French admiral (see the portrait inside). Charts reveal how the defenses were organized. In the early 17th century, the dank castle was converted into a more gracious Louis XIII château, which now contains two museums; you won't have any trouble telling them apart. The Museum of the Olive Tree shows the steps in cultivating and processing the olive. The Museum of Mediterranean Modern Art displays works by Kisling, Carzou, Dufy, Cocteau, and Seyssaud, among others, with temporary exhibitions. In one salon is an interesting trompe-l'oeil fresco, *La Chute de Phaeton*. From the tower you get a panoramic view of the Côte d'Azur. The International Festival of Painting (see "Special Events," above) takes place here.

Musée Renoir/Les Collettes. 19 chemin des Collettes. ☎ **04-93-20-61-07.** Admission 20 F ($3.20) adults, 10 F ($1.60) children. May–Sept, Wed–Mon 10am–noon and 2–6pm; Oct–Apr, Wed–Mon 10am–noon and 2–5pm. Ticket sales end 30 min. before the lunch and evening closing hour.

Les Collettes has been restored to what it looked like when Renoir lived here from 1908 until his death in 1919. He continued to sculpt here, even though he was crippled by arthritis and had to be helped in and out of a wheelchair. He also continued to paint, with a brush tied to his hand and with the help of assistants.

The house was built in 1907 in an olive and orange grove. There's a bust of Mme Renoir in the entrance room. You can explore the drawing room and dining room on your own before going up to the artist's bedroom. In his atelier are his wheelchair, easel, and brushes. From the terrace of Mme Renoir's bedroom is a stunning view of Cap d'Antibes and Le Haut-de-Cagnes. On a wall hangs a photograph of one of Renoir's sons, Pierre, as he appeared in the 1932 film *Madame Bovary.*

Although Renoir is best remembered for his paintings, it was in Cagnes that he began experimenting with sculpture. The museum has 20 portrait busts and portrait medallions, most of which depict his wife and children. The curators say they represent the largest collection of Renoir sculpture in the world.

SHOPPING

Terraïo (12 place du Docteur Maurel, ☎ **04-93-20-86-83**) is a tiny gem. Art critics claim the stoneware sold in this charming shop perfectly captures the blue-green celadon tones of the nearby Mediterranean. Part of that derives from artist/owner and native son Claude Barnoin, who has spent nearly 25 years perfecting the mixture of copper-based glazes that produce these heavenly tones. The ashtrays, dinner services, and enormous showcase pieces produced in the artist's studio (which, alas, cannot be visited) are the pride of many private French and U.S.-based collections. Prices begin at around 100 F ($16) for a simple ashtray, stretching upwards to as much as 3,500 F ($560) for something truly spectacular. The shop, which lies just across the square from the château-museum of Haut-de-Cagnes, is open every afternoon from 2 till around 6pm, except in midsummer, when it might close for an occasional day, based on the production schedule of the owner.

ACCOMMODATIONS
IN CAGNES-SUR-MER

Hôtel Le Chantilly. 31 chemin de la Minoerie, 06800 Cagnes-sur-Mer. ☎ **04-93-20-25-50.** Fax 04-92-02-82-63. 20 units. MINIBAR TV TEL. 320 F ($51.20) double. MC, V. Free parking.

This is the best bargain for those who prefer to stay at a hotel near the beach. It won't win any architectural awards, but the owners have landscaped the property and made the interior as homey and inviting as possible, with Oriental rugs and potted plants. The rooms, for the most part, are small but cozily furnished and well kept, often opening onto balconies. In fair weather you can enjoy breakfast, the only meal served, on an outdoor terrace.

IN LE HAUT-DE-CAGNES

✪ **Le Cagnard.** Rue du Pontis-Long, Le Haut-de-Cagnes, 06800 Cagnes-sur-Mer. ☎ **04-93-20-73-21.** Fax 04-93-22-06-39. www.le-cagnard.com. E-mail: lecagnard@csi.com. 25 units. A/C MINIBAR TV TEL. 900–1,300 F ($144–$208) double; 1,500–2,600 F ($240–$416) suite. AE, DC, MC, V. Parking 50 F ($8).

Several village houses have been joined to form this handsome hostelry. The dining room is covered with frescoes, and there's a vine-draped terrace. The rooms and salons are furnished with family antiques, such as provincial chests, armoires, and Louis XV chairs. Each room has its own style: Some are duplexes; others have terraces and views of the countryside.

The **cuisine** of chef Jean-Yves Johany is reason enough to make the trip here. Fresh ingredients are used in the delectable dishes placed on one of the finest tables set in Provence. This talented chef features Sisteron lamb (*carré d'agneau*) spit-roasted with Provençal herbs for two, as well as tender côte de boeuf. The pièce de résistance dessert is the extravagant mousseline of ice cream.

DINING

In Le Haut-de-Cagnes, the hotel **Le Cagnard** (see "Accommodations," above) has a remarkable restaurant.

IN LE HAUT-DE-CAGNES

À la Table d'Yves. 85 Montée de la Bourgade. ☎ **04-93-20-33-33.** Reservations recommended. Main courses 70–120 F ($11.20–$19.20); fixed-price menus 125–230 F ($20–$36.80). MC, V. Fri–Mon noon–2pm and 7:30–10pm, Tues 7:30–10pm, Thurs 7:30–10pm. FRENCH/PROVENÇAL.

Part of the charm of a meal at this well-recommended culinary institution involves its setting within a 200-year-old village house. Menu items are reasonably priced and savory, usually reflecting the sophisticated training of chef and owner Yves Merville. Menu choices change virtually every day according to whatever's fresh in the local markets, but they make ample use of fish, vegetables, cheeses, and herbs. Panfried foie gras is an ongoing favorite here, as well as the chef's idiosyncratic version of a dessert favorite, *pain perdu*. Other than that, take your pick from the day's assortment of bourrides, stews, blanquettes, fresh-grilled fish, soups, and roasts.

Josy-Jo. 8 place du Planastel. ☎ **04-93-20-68-76.** Reservations required. Main courses 145–210 F ($23.20–$33.60). AE, MC, V. Mon–Fri noon–2pm and 7:30–10pm, Sat 7:30–10pm. Closed Aug 1–15. FRENCH.

Sheltered behind a 200-year-old facade covered with vines and flowers, this restaurant on the main road to the château used to be the home and studio of Modigliani and Soutine, when they borrowed it from a friend during their hungriest years. Today it functions as a cheerful and often bustling dining enclave. The walls of the restaurant are covered with paintings and everything is kept running smoothly by the good-natured Bandecchi family. Their cuisine is simple, fresh, and excellent, featuring grilled meats and a roster of fish. You can enjoy brochette of gigot of lamb with kidneys, four succulent varieties of steak, calves' liver, a homemade terrine of foie gras of duckling, and an array of salads.

IN CROS-DE-CAGNES

✪ **Loulou (La Réserve).** 91 bd. de la Plage. ☎ **04-93-31-00-17.** Reservations recommended. Main courses 150–325 F ($24–$52); fixed-price menu 225 F ($35.70). AE, MC, V. Mon–Fri noon–2:30pm and 7–9:45pm, Sat 7–9:45pm. July 14–Aug 31, closed for lunch. FRENCH.

This restaurant across from the sea is named for a famous long-departed chef. Of particular note are brothers Eric and Joseph Campo, who prepare dishes that include spectacular versions of calamari and octopus salad; fish soup; shrimp that's steamed and then served with fresh ginger and cinnamon; and grilled, very fresh versions of whatever catch the local suppliers might have brought in that day. These are served as simply as possible, usually with just a drizzling of olive oil and balsamic vinegar. Meat dishes include a flavorful version of veal kidneys with port sauce, usually featured in autumn and winter, and delectable grilled steaks, chops, and cutlets. Everything here is solid and reliable. In front is a glassed-in veranda that's a prime people-watching spot.

11 St-Paul-de-Vence

575 miles S of Paris, 14 miles E of Grasse, 17 miles E of Cannes, 19 miles N of Nice

Of all the perched villages of the Riviera, St-Paul-de-Vence is the best known. It was popularized in the 1920s when many noted artists lived here, occupying the 16th-century houses flanking the narrow cobblestone streets. The feudal hamlet grew up on a bastion of rock, almost blending into it. Its ramparts (allow about 30 minutes to circle them) overlook a peaceful setting of flowers and olive and orange trees. They haven't changed much since they were constructed from 1537 to 1547 by order of François I. From the ramparts to the north you can look out on Baou de St-Jeannet, a sphinx-shaped rock that was painted into the landscape of Poussin's *Polyphème*.

ESSENTIALS

GETTING THERE   The nearest **railway** station is in Cagnes-sur-Mer. **Buses** depart from the station every 45 minutes for St-Paul-de-Vence. If you're coming from Nice, about 20 daily buses head to Gare Routière, near the railway station. For bus information, call Cie SAP (☎ **04-93-58-37-60**). Buses stop in St-Paul near the post office, on the Route de Vence, about a quarter mile from the town center. If you're **driving** from Nice, take the coastal A8 highway east, turning inland at Cagnes-sur-Mer; then follow the signs northward to St-Paul-de-Vence.

VISITOR INFORMATION   The **Office de Tourisme** is at Maison Tour, 2 rue Grande (☎ **04-93-32-86-95**).

EXPLORING THE TOWN

Note: Driving a car within the center of St-Paul's old town is prohibited, except to drop off your luggage at your hotel. The pedestrian-only **rue Grande** is the most interesting street, running the entire length of St-Paul. Most of the stone houses along it are from the 16th and 17th centuries, many still bearing the coats-of-arms placed here by the original builders. Today most of the houses are antiques shops, art-and-craft galleries, and souvenir and gift shops; some are still artists' studios.

The village's chief sight is **La Collégiale de la Conversion de St-Paul,** constructed in the 12th and 13th centuries though much altered over the years. The Romanesque choir is the oldest part, containing some remarkable stalls carved in walnut in the 17th century. The bell tower was built in 1740. Once inside, look to the left as you enter. You'll see the painting *Ste-Cathérine d'Alexandrie,* which has been attributed to Tintoretto. The Trésor de l'Église is one of the most beautiful in the Alpes-Maritimes, with a spectacular ciborium. Look also for a low relief of the Martyrdom of St-Clément on the last altar on the right. In the baptismal chapter is a 15th-century alabaster Madonna. It's open daily 9am to 6pm (7pm during July and August). Admission is free.

Near the church is the **Musée d'Histoire de St-Paul,** place de Castre (☎ **04-93-32-53-09**), a minor museum in a 16th-century village house. It was restored and refurnished in a 1500s style, with many artifacts illustrating the history of the village. It's open daily from 10am to noon and 1:30 to 5:30pm. Admission is 20 F ($3.20) adults, 12 F ($1.90) students and children under 12.

✪ **Fondation Maeght.** Outside the town walls. ☎ **04-93-32-81-63.** Admission 50 F ($8) adults, 40 F ($6.40) students and ages 12–18, free for children 9 and under. July–Sept, daily 10am–7pm; Oct–June, daily 10am–12:30pm and 2:30–6pm.

This is one of the most modern art museums in Europe. On a hill in pine-studded woods, the Maeght Foundation is like a Shangri-La. This avant-garde building houses one of the finest collections of contemporary art along the Riviera. Nature and the creations of men and women blend harmoniously in this unique achievement of the architect José Luis Sert. Its white concrete arcs give the impression of a giant pagoda.

A stark Calder rises like some futuristic monster on the grassy lawns. In a courtyard, the elongated bronze works of Giacometti form a surrealistic garden, creating a hallucinatory mood. Sculpture is also displayed inside, but the museum is at its best in a natural setting of surrounding terraces and gardens. It's built on several levels, its many glass walls providing an indoor-outdoor vista. The foundation, a gift "to the people" from Aimé and Marguerite Maeght, also provides a showcase for new talent. Exhibitions are always changing. Everywhere you look, you see 20th-century art: mosaics by Chagall and Braque, Miró ceramics in the "labyrinth," and Ubac and Braque stained glass in the chapel. Bonnard, Kandinsky, Léger, Matisse, Barbara Hepworth, and many other artists are well represented.

There are a library, a cinema, and a cafeteria here. In one showroom you can buy original lithographs by artists like Chagall and Giacometti and limited-edition prints.

ACCOMMODATIONS

La Colombe d'Or also rents deluxe rooms (see below).

VERY EXPENSIVE

Le Mas d'Artigny. Rte. de la Colle et des Hauts de St-Paul, 06570 St-Paul-de-Vence. ☎ **04-93-32-84-54.** Fax 04-93-32-95-36. www.mas-artigny.com. E-mail: contact@mas-artigny.com. 83 units. A/C MINIBAR TV TEL. 1,000–2,300 F ($160–$368) double; 3,400 F ($544) suite. Rates about 30% lower in the off-season. AE, DC, MC, V. Parking 60 F ($9.60) in a garage. From the town center, follow signs west about 1^1/$_4$ miles.

This hotel, one of the Riviera's grandest, evokes a sprawling Provençal homestead set in an acre of pine forests. In the lobby is a constantly changing exhibition of art. Each of the comfortably large rooms has its own terrace or balcony. Suites have a private pool with hedges.

Dining: For such an elegant hotel, the restaurant is a bit lackluster in decor and the staff isn't always too alert. But it does have great views of the garden. Chef Francis Scordel regales you with his flavors of Provence. Only quality ingredients are used to shape this harmonious and rarely complicated cuisine. The wine cellar deserves a star for its vintage collection, but watch those prices!

Amenities: Pool, tennis courts.

EXPENSIVE

Hôtel Le St Paul. 86 rue Grande, 06570 St-Paul-de-Vence. ☎ **04-93-32-65-25.** Fax 04-93-32-52-94. www.relaischateaux.fr. E-mail: stpaul@relaischateaux.fr. 19 units. A/C MINIBAR TV TEL. 1,150–1,900 F ($183–$302) double; 1,650–3,700 F ($262–$587) suite. Half board 385 F ($61.60) per person extra. AE, CB, DC, MC, V.

Converted from a 16th-century Renaissance residence and retaining many original features, this four-star Relais & Châteaux is in the heart of the medieval village. The rooms are decorated in a sophisticated Provençal style. Beds are quite sumptuous, with elegant fabrics, deluxe mattresses, and quality linen. One woman wrote us that while sitting on the balcony of room 30 she understood why Renoir, Léger, Matisse, and even Picasso were inspired by Provence. Many rooms enjoy a view of the valley with the Mediterranean in the distance.

Dining: The restaurant has a flower-bedecked terrace sheltered by the 16th-century ramparts as well as a superb dining room with vaulted ceilings. Menus may include locally inspired dishes like cream of salt cod with a thin slice of grilled pancetta, risotto of crayfish and broad beans, roast veal chop with morels and barley, and a delightful crème brûlée with a hint of rosemary.

MODERATE

Auberge Le Hameau. 528 rte. de la Colle (D107), 06570 St-Paul-de-Vence. ☎ **04-93-32-80-24.** Fax 04-93-32-55-75. 17 units. A/C MINIBAR TEL. 550–830 F ($88–$132.80) double; from 950 F ($152) suite. AE, MC, V. Closed Jan 6–Feb 15 and Nov 16–Dec 22. From the town, take D107 about a half mile, following the signs south of town toward Colle.

This romantic Mediterranean villa is on a hilltop on the outskirts of St-Paul-de-Vence, on the road to Colle at Hauts-de-St-Paul. Originally built as a farmhouse in the 1920s, and enlarged and transformed into a hotel in 1967, it contains high-ceilinged, comfortable bedrooms. You get a remarkable view of the surrounding hills and valleys. There's also a vineyard and a sunny terrace with fruit trees, flowers, and a pool.

Les Bastides St-Paul. 880 rte. des Blaquières (rte. Cagnes-Vence), 06570 St-Paul-de-Vence. ☎ **04-92-02-08-07.** Fax 04-93-20-50-41. E-mail: bastides.sf.paul@worldonline.fr. 19 units. MINIBAR TV TEL. 450–750 F ($72–$120) double. AE, DC, MC, V. From the town center, follow the signs toward Cagnes-sur-Mer for 1 mile south.

This hotel is in the hills outside town, a mile south of St-Paul and 2^1/$_2$ miles south of Vence. Divided into three buildings, it offers clean and comfortably carpeted rooms, each accented with regional artifacts and a terrace and garden. If you want a room with a hair dryer, you'll have to request it. On the premises is a pool shaped like a clover leaf, a cozy breakfast area, and a sensitive management staff headed by the long-time hoteliers Marie José and Maurice Giraudet. Breakfast is served anytime you want it.

Les Orangers. Chemin des Fumerates, rte. de la Colle (D107), 06570 St-Paul-de-Vence. ☎ **04-93-32-80-95.** Fax 04-93-32-00-32. 5 units. TEL. 760–1,200 F ($121.60–$192) double; 1,200 F ($192) suite. Rates include breakfast. MC, V. Free parking. From the town center, follow the signs to Cagnes-sur-Mer for ¹/₂ mile south.

Monsieur Franklin has created a beautiful "living oasis" in his villa. The scents of roses, oranges, and lemons waft through the air. The main lounge is impeccably decorated with original oils and furnished in a provincial style. Expect to be treated like a guest in a private home. The rooms, with antiques and Oriental carpets, have panoramic views. Banana trees and climbing geraniums will accompany you while you relax on the sun terrace.

DINING

La Colombe d'Or. 1 place du Général-de-Gaulle, 06570 St-Paul-de-Vence. ☎ **04-93-32-80-02.** Fax 04-93-32-77-78. Reservations required. Main courses 110–250 F ($17.60–$40). AE, DC, MC, V. Daily noon–2pm and 7–10pm. Closed Feb 21–Mar 3 and Nov–Dec 20. FRENCH.

For a decade, "The Golden Dove" has been St-Paul's most celebrated restaurant, not for cutting-edge cuisine or wildly exotic experiments, but for its remarkable art collection. You can dine amid Mirós, Picassos, Klees, Dufys, Utrillos, and Calders. In fair weather everyone tries for a seat on the terrace. You may begin with smoked salmon or foie gras from Landes if you've recently won at the casino. Otherwise, you can count on a soup made with fresh seasonal vegetables. The best fish dishes are poached sea bass with mousseline sauce, and sea wolf baked with fennel. Tender beef comes with *gratin dauphinois* (potatoes), or you may prefer lamb from Sisteron. A classic finish to any meal is a *soufflé flambé au Grand-Marnier.*

The **guest rooms** (16 doubles, 10 suites) in this three-star hotel contain French antiques and fabrics and accessories inspired by the traditions of Provence. They're scattered among three areas: the original 16th-century stone house, a more recent wing that stretches into the garden adjacent to the pool, and an even more modern annex, built in the 1950s and upgraded several times since. Some have exposed stone and heavy ceiling beams; all are comfortable and clean, with air-conditioning, minibars, TVs, and phones. Prices are 1,350 F ($216) for a double and 1,550 F ($248) for a suite.

12 Vence

575 miles S of Paris, 19 miles N of Cannes, 15 miles NW of Nice

Travel up into the hills northwest of Nice—across country studded with cypresses, olive trees, and pines, where bright flowers, especially carnations, roses, and oleanders, grow in profusion—and Vence comes into view. Outside the town, along boulevard Paul-André, two olive presses carry on with their age-old duties. But the charm lies in the **Vieille Ville** (Old Town). Visitors invariably have themselves photographed on place du Peyra in front of the **Vieille Fontaine** (Old Fountain), a background shot in several motion pictures. The 15th-century square tower is also a curiosity.

If you're wearing sturdy shoes, the narrow, steep streets of the Old Town are worth exploring. Dating from the 10th century, the cathedral on place Godeau is unremarkable except for some 15th-century Gothic choir stalls. But if it's the right day of the week, most visitors quickly pass through the narrow gates of this once-fortified walled town to where the sun shines more brightly—to see one of Matisse's most remarkable achievements, the Chapelle du Rosaire.

ESSENTIALS

GETTING THERE   Frequent **buses** (no. 400 or 410) originating in Nice take about an hour to reach Vence, and cost 22 F ($3.50) each way. For bus information, contact Compagnie SAP (☎ **04-93-58-37-60**) for schedules. The nearest **railway station** is in Cagnes-sur-Mer, about 4¹/₂ miles from Vence. From here, about 20 buses per day make the trip to Vence. For train information, call ☎ **08-36-35-35-35.**

To **drive** to Vence from Nice, travel along N7 west to Cagnes-sur-Mer and then connect to D236 north to Vence.

VISITOR INFORMATION   The **Office de Tourisme** is on place Grand-Jardin (☎ **04-93-58-06-38**).

A MATISSE MASTERPIECE

Chapelle du Rosaire. Av. Henri-Matisse. ☎ **04-93-58-03-26.** Admission 15 F ($2.40) adults, 5 F (80¢) children; contributions to maintain the chapel are welcomed. Unless special arrangements are made, the chapel is open only Tues and Thurs 10–11:30am and 2–5:30pm.

It was a beautiful golden autumn along the Côte d'Azur. The great Henri Matisse was 77, and after a turbulent introspective time he set out to design and decorate his masterpiece—"the culmination of a whole life dedicated to the search for truth," as he said. Just outside Vence, Matisse created the Chapelle du Rosaire for the Dominican nuns of Monteils. (Part of his action was a gesture of thanks for Sister Jacques-Marie, a member of the order who nursed him back to health after a debilitating illness.) From the front you might find it unremarkable and pass it by—until you spot a 40-foot crescent-adorned cross rising from a blue-tile roof.

Matisse wrote: "What I have done in the chapel is to create a religious space . . . in an enclosed area of very reduced proportions and to give it, solely by the play of colors and lines, the dimensions of infinity." The light picks up the subtle coloring in the simply rendered leaf forms and abstract patterns: sapphire blue, aquamarine, and lemon yellow. In black-and-white ceramics, St. Dominic is depicted in only a few lines. The most remarkable design is in the black-and-white tile Stations of the Cross, with Matisse's self-styled "tormented and passionate" figures. The bishop of Nice came to bless the chapel in the late spring of 1951 when the artist's work was completed. Matisse died 3 years later.

The price of admission includes entrance to **L'Espace Matisse,** a gallery devoted to the documentation of the way Matisse handled the design and construction of the chapel during its construction (1949–51). It also contains lithographs and religious artifacts that concerned Matisse in one way or another.

ACCOMMODATIONS
VERY EXPENSIVE

Le Château du Domaine St-Martin. Av. des Templiers BP102, 06142 Vence. ☎ **04-93-58-02-02.** Fax 04-93-24-08-91. www.chateau-st-martin.com. E-mail: st-martin@webstore.fr. 34 units, 6 cottages. A/C TV TEL. 1,500–3,000 F ($240–$480) double; 2,800–3,200 F ($448–$512) suite; 3,200 F ($512) cottage. AE, DC, MC, V. Closed Nov–Mar. From the town center, follow the signs toward Coursegoules and Col-de-Vence for 1 mile north.

This château, in a 35-acre park, was built in 1936 on the grounds where the Golden Goat treasure was reputedly buried. A complex of tile-roofed villas with suites was built in the terraced gardens. You can walk through the gardens on winding paths lined with tall cypresses, past the ruined chapel and olive trees. The guest rooms are furnished in elegant taste. Rooms are exceedingly spacious.

Dining: The restaurant has a view of the coast and offers superb French cuisine. In summer, many guests prefer the poolside grill.

Amenities: Room service, pool, two championship tennis courts.

MODERATE

✪ **Hôtel Villa Roseraie.** Av. Henri-Giraud, rte. de Coursegoules, 06140 Vence. ☎ **04-93-58-02-20.** Fax 04-93-58-99-31. 14 units. TV TEL. 590–750 F ($94.40–$120) double. AE, MC, V. From the town center, drive for less than ¹/₄ mile, following the signs toward Col-de-Vence.

This charming small hotel, lying a 5-minute walk from the historic center of Vence, is in a renovated 19th-century manor house. Marc Chagall lived for many years on a hill across from the hotel, which is within an easy walk of the Matisse chapel. Monica and Maurice Garnier are among the most gracious hosts at Vence, and they've furnished their home with old-fashioned pieces, often antiques. The garden offers perfect southern exposure and contains a moon-shaped swimming pool. The "Rose Garden" (English for Villa Roseraie) is studded with magnolias, yucca, eucalyptus, banana trees, palms, and, of course, roses. Rooms 4, 5, and 8 have balconies, while rooms 12, 14, 15, and 16 have ground-floor patios. Mattresses are comfortable and recently changed. There's no better way to start the day than with one of the fresh house-baked croissants.

Relais Cantemerle. 258 chemin Cantemerle, 06140 Vence. ☎ **04-93-58-08-18.** Fax 04-93-58-32-89. www.relais-cantemerle.com. E-mail: info@relais-cantemerle.com. 19 units. A/C MINIBAR TV TEL. 680 F ($108.80) double; 1,030 F ($164.80) 1-bedroom duplex for 2; 1,230 F ($196.80) 1-bedroom duplex for 3. 200 F ($32) additional bed for 4th occupant. 270 F ($43.20) supplement for half board. AE, MC, V. Closed mid-Oct to mid-Apr.

One of the most appealing places in Vence is this artfully designed cluster of accommodations that resembles an old-fashioned compound of Provençal buildings. Capped with rounded terra-cotta roof tiles, they surround a verdant lawn dotted with old trees, in the center of which is a swimming pool. Public areas are stylishly outfitted with Art Deco furniture and accessories, and include a richly paneled bar area and a flagstone terrace that's the site of sun-flooded meals. Rooms aren't overly large but contain unusual reproductions of overscaled Art Deco armchairs, louvered wooden closet doors, and balcony-style sleeping lofts with low-profile, comfortable beds. An on-site restaurant serves worthwhile versions of regional and mainstream French cuisine.

INEXPENSIVE

Auberge des Seigneurs. Place du Friene, 06140 Vence. ☎ **04-93-58-04-24.** Fax 04-93-24-08-01. 6 units. TEL. 374–394 F ($59.85–$63.05) double. AE, DC, MC, V. Closed Nov 15–Mar 15.

This 400-year-old stone hotel gives you a taste of Old Provence. Fascinating decorative objects and antiques are everywhere. The guest rooms are well maintained and comfortable, but the management dedicates its precious energy to the restaurant. Nevertheless, bedrooms have lots of exposed paneling and beams.

Inside the dining room, there's a long wooden dining table, in view of an open fireplace with a row of hanging copper pots and pans. The cuisine of François I is served in an antique atmosphere with wooden casks of flowers and an open spit for roasting and grilling. Fixed-price menus range from 175 F to 250 F ($28 to $40).

DINING

Auberge des Seigneurs (see above) is an excellent place to dine at reasonable prices.

✪ **Jacques Maximin.** 689 chemin de la Gaude. ☎ **04-93-58-90-75.** Reservations required. Main courses 240–500 F ($38.40–$80); fixed-price menus 240–500 F ($38.40–$80) at lunch, 350–500 F ($56–$80) at dinner. AE, AC, MC, V. Tues–Sun 12:30–2pm; Tues–Sat 7:30–10pm. From the historic core of Vence, drive SW for 2¹/₂ miles, following the signs to Cagnes-sur-Mer. FRENCH

The setting for this sought-after restaurant is an artfully rustic 19th-century manor house that was transformed in the mid-1980s into the private home of culinary superstar Jacques Maximin. Today, it's the target of pilgrimages by foodies and movie stars venturing north from the Cannes Film Festival, including Hugh Grant, Elizabeth Hurley, and Robert DeNiro. You can sample a menu firmly entrenched in the seasonal produce of the surrounding countryside. Stellar examples include salads made with asparagus and truffles, Canadian lobster, or fresh scallops; seawolf *à la Niçoise;* peppered duck; and some of the best beef dishes in the region. Expect surprises from the capricious chef, whose menu changes virtually every day.

La Farigoule. 15 rue Henri-Isnard. ☎ **04-93-58-01-27.** Reservations recommended. Main courses 90–150 F ($14.40–$24); fixed-price menus 160–220 F ($25.60–$35.20). Wed 7:30–10:30pm, Thurs–Mon noon–2:30pm and 7:30–10:30pm. PROVENÇAL.

Set within a century-old house that opens onto a rose garden, where tables are set out during summer, this restaurant specializes in Provençal cuisine. Menu items include a conservative but flavorful array of dishes that feature a *bourride Provençal* (a bouillabaisse with a dollop of cream and lots of garlic); shoulder of roasted lamb with a ragoût of fresh vegetables, served with fresh thyme; aïoli; and such fish dishes as dorado with a confit of lemons and fresh aromatic coriander.

13 Nice

577 miles S of Paris, 20 miles NE of Cannes

Nice is the capital of the Riviera, the largest city between Genoa and Marseille. It's also one of the most ancient, having been founded by the Greeks, who called it Nike, or Victory. By the 19th century, the Victorian upper class and tsarist aristocrats were flocking here. But these days it's not as chichi and astronomically expensive, especially compared to Cannes. In fact, of all the major resorts of France, from Deauville to Biarritz to Cannes, Nice is the most affordable. It's also the best place to base yourself on the Riviera, especially if you're dependent on public transportation. For example, you can go to San Remo, "the queen of the Italian Riviera," and return to Nice by nightfall. From the Nice airport, the second largest in France, you can travel by train or bus along the entire coast to resorts like Juan-les-Pins and Cannes.

Because of its brilliant sunshine and relaxed living, artists and writers have been attracted to Nice for years. Among them were Dumas, Nietzsche, Flaubert, Hugo, Sand, and Stendhal. Henri Matisse, who made his home in Nice, said, "Though the light is intense, it's also soft and tender." The city has, on average, 300 days of sunshine a year.

ESSENTIALS

GETTING THERE   Trains arrive at Gare Nice-Ville, avenue Thiers (☎ **08-36-35-35-35**). From here you can take frequent trains to Cannes, Monaco, and Antibes, with easy connections to virtually anywhere else along the Mediterranean coast. There's a small-scale tourist information center at the train station. It's open Monday to Saturday from 8am to 6:30pm and Sunday from 8am to noon and 2 to 5:30pm. If you face a long delay, you can eat at the cafeteria and even take showers at the station.

<table>
<tr><td>Nice Bus Tip</td></tr>
</table>

If you plan on traveling a lot via the city's municipal buses, consider buying a **Carte-Passe Niçoise,** available from the local tourist office or on any bus. It allows unlimited transit on any city bus. The price is 25 F ($4) for 1 day, 85 F ($13.60) for 5 days, and 110 F ($17.60) for a week.

Visitors who arrive at **Aéroport Nice-Côte d'Azur** (☎ 04-93-21-30-30) can board a yellow-sided **bus,** known as the *navette Nice-Aéroport,* which travels several times a day between the railway station and the airport for 21 F ($3.35) each way. They operate every day from 6am to 10:30pm or until the last incoming flight arrives, no matter how delayed. A **taxi** ride from the airport into the city center will cost at least 140 F ($22.40) each way. Trip time is about 30 minutes.

VISITOR INFORMATION   The hysterically overworked **Office de Tourisme** is at 5 promenade des Anglais (☎ 04-92-14-48-00), near place Masséna. This office will make you a hotel reservation without charging a fee, but only if you show up in person. The office doesn't have enough staff members, so there's an intense emphasis on quickly getting you in and out.

GETTING AROUND   Most of the local buses in Nice create connections with one another at their central hub, the **Station Central,** 10 av. Felix Faure (☎ 04-93-16-52-10), which lies a very short walk from the place Masséna. Municipal buses each charge 8.50 F ($1.35) for a ride within Greater Nice. To save money, consider the purchase of a five-ticket carnet for 34 F ($5.45). Bus nos. 2 and 12 make frequent trips to the beach. Long-distance buses making the trek, say, between Nice and such long-haul destinations as Monaco, Cannes, St-Tropez, and other parts of France and Europe depart from the **Gare Routière,** 5 bd. Jean-Jaurès (☎ 04-93-85-61-81).

You can rent bicycles and mopeds at **Nicea Rent,** 9 av. Thiers (☎ 04-93-82-42-71), near the Station Centrale. From March through October, it's open daily from 9am to noon and 2 to 6pm (closed Sunday November to April). The cost begins at 120 F ($19.20) per day, plus a 1,500 F ($240) deposit. Credit cards are accepted.

SPECIAL EVENTS   The **Nice Carnaval** draws visitors from all over Europe and North America to this ancient spectacle. This "Mardi Gras of the Riviera" begins sometime in February, usually 12 days before Shrove Tuesday, celebrating the return of spring with parades, floats (*corsi*), masked balls (*veglioni*), confetti, and battles in which young women toss flowers. Only the most wicked throw rotten eggs instead of carnations. Climaxing the event is a fireworks display on Shrove Tuesday, lighting up the Baie des Anges (Bay of Angels). King Carnival goes up in flames on his pyre but rises from the ashes the following spring.

Also important is the **Nice Festival du Jazz,** from July 10 to 17, when a roster of jazz artists perform in the ancient Arène de Cimiez. For information and tickets, contact the **Comité des Fêtes,** Mairie (town hall) de Nice, 5 rue de l'Hôtel-de-Ville, 06000 Nice (☎ 04-97-13-20-00).

EXPLORING THE CITY

There's a higher density of museums in Nice than in many comparable French cities. If you decide to forgo the beach and devote your time to visiting some of the best-respected museums in the south of France, you can buy a **Carte Passe-Musée** from the local tourist office for 70 F ($11.20) for a 3-day pass, or 140 F ($22.40) for a 4-day pass. There are no reductions for students or children. It will allow you admission into seven of the city's largest museums.

Nice

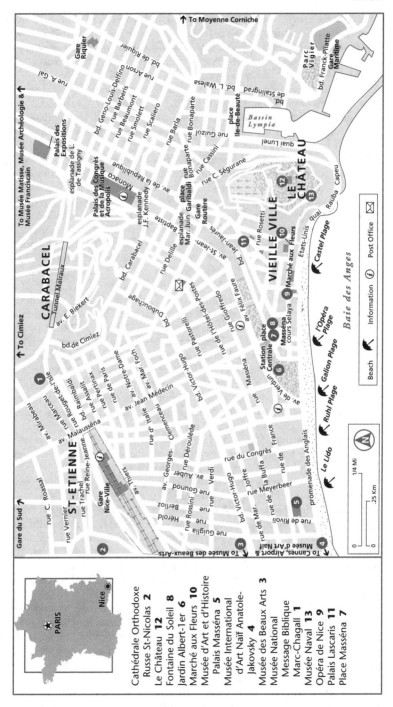

↑ To Moyenne Corniche

To Cimiez ↑

← Gare du Sud ↑

To Musée Matisse, Musée Archéologie & ↑↑
Musée Franciscain

Gare
Riquier

Palais des
Expositions

Monaco

Palais des Congrès
et de la Musique
Acropolis

CARABACEL

Tunnel Malraux

bd. de Cimiez

bd. Carabacel

bd. Dubouchage

ST-ETIENNE

Gare
Nice-Ville

Gare
Routière

Station
Centrale

VIEILLE
VILLE

LE
CHÂTEAU

Bassin
Lympia

quai Lunel

place
Ile-de-Beauté

place
Garibaldi

place
Masséna
cours Saleya

Marché aux Fleurs

Parc
Vigier

Gare
Franck-Pilatte
Gare
Maritime

Baie des Anges

l'Opéra Plage

Castel Plage

Galion Plage

Ruhl Plage

Le Lido

promenade des Anglais

To Musée des Beaux-Arts →
To Cannes, Airport & →
Musée d'Art Naïf

Beach ⚓   Information ⓘ   Post Office ✉

N

0   ¼ Mi
0   .25 Km

PARIS ★

Nice ●

Cathédrale Orthodoxe
Russe St-Nicolas **2**
Le Château **12**
Fontaine du Soleil **8**
Jardin Albert-1er **6**
Marché aux Fleurs **10**
Musée d'Art et d'Histoire
Palais Masséna **5**
Musée International
d'Art Naïf Anatole-
Jakovsky **4**
Musée des Beaux Arts **3**
Musée National
Message Biblique
Marc-Chagall **1**
Musée Naval **13**
Opéra de Nice **9**
Palais Lascaris **11**
Place Masséna **7**

In 1822 the orange crop at Nice was bad and the workers faced a lean time. So the English residents put them to work building the **promenade des Anglais,** a wide boulevard fronting the bay, split by "islands" of palms and flowers and stretching for about 4 miles. Fronting the beach are rows of grand cafes, the Musée Masséna, villas, and hotels—some good, others decaying.

Crossing this boulevard in the briefest of bikinis or thongs are some of the world's most attractive, bronzed bodies. They're heading for the **beach**—"on the rocks," as it's called here. Tough on tender feet, the beach is made not of sand, but of pebbles (and not too small ones). It's one of the least attractive aspects of the cosmopolitan resort city. Many bathhouses provide mattresses for a fee.

In the east, the promenade becomes **quai des États-Unis,** the original boulevard, lined with some of the best restaurants in Nice, all specializing in bouillabaisse. Rising sharply on a rock is the site known as **Le Château,** the spot where the ducs de Savoie built their castle, which was torn down in 1706. All that remains are two or three stones—even the foundations have disappeared in the wake of Louis XIV's deliberate destruction of what was viewed as a bulwark of Provençal resistance to his regime. The steep hill has been turned into a garden of pines and exotic flowers. To reach the panoramic site, you can take an elevator; indeed, many prefer to take the elevator up, then walk down. The park is open daily from 8am to dusk.

At the north end of Le Château is the famous old **graveyard** of Nice, visited primarily for its lavishly sculpted monuments that form their own enduring art statement. It's the largest one in France and the fourth largest in Europe. To reach it, you can take a small canopied **Train Touristique de Nice** (☎ 04-93-92-45-59), which departs from the Jardin Albert-1er. It makes a 40-minute sightseeing transit past many of Nice's most heralded sites, including place Masséna, promenade des Anglais, and quai des États-Unis. The train operates daily, with departures every 30 to 60 minutes, depending on the season. It operates from 10am to 5pm (until 6pm in April, May, and September; until 7pm from June to August). There's no service between mid-November and mid-December, and during most of January. Train rides last about 45 minutes each. The price is 35 F ($5.60) per person.

Continuing east from "the Rock" (the ruined site of Le Château), you reach the **harbor,** where the restaurants are even cheaper and the bouillabaisse is just as good. While sitting here lingering over a drink at a sidewalk cafe, you can watch the boats depart for Corsica. The port was excavated between 1750 and 1830. Since then an outer harbor, protected by two jetties, has been created.

The "authentic" Niçoise live in **Vieille Ville,** the Old Town, beginning at the foot of "the Rock" and stretching out to place Masséna. Sheltered by sienna-tiled roofs, many of the Italianate facades suggest 17th-century Genoese palaces. The old town is a maze of narrow streets, teeming with local life and studded with the least expensive restaurants in Nice. Buy an onion pizza (*la pissaladière*) from one of the local vendors. Many of the old buildings are painted a faded Roman gold, and their banners are multicolored laundry flapping in the sea breezes.

While here, try to visit the **Marché aux Fleurs,** the flower market at cours Saleya. The vendors start setting up their stalls Tuesday to Sunday from 8am to 6pm in summer, and from 8am till between 2 and 4pm in winter, depending on the vendor's remaining inventory and energy level. A flamboyant array of carnations, violets, jonquils, roses, and birds of paradise is hauled in by vans or trucks, then displayed in the most fragrant, regularly scheduled market in town.

Nice's commercial centerpiece is **place Masséna,** with pink buildings in the 17th-century Genoese style and the **Fontaine du Soleil** (Fountain of the Sun) by Janoit, from 1956. Stretching from the main square to the promenade is the **Jardin Albert-1er,** with an open-air terrace and a Triton Fountain. With palms and exotic flowers, it's the most relaxing oasis in town.

⭘ **Cathédrale Orthodoxe Russe St-Nicolas à Nice.** Av. Nicolas-II (off bd. du Tzaréwitch). ☎ **04-93-96-88-02.** Admission 15 F ($2.40). May–Sept, daily 9am–noon and 2:30–6pm; Oct–Apr, daily 9:30am–noon and 2:30–5pm. From the central rail station, head west along av. Thiers to bd. Gambetta; then go north to av. Nicolas-II.

Ordered built by none other than Tsar Nicholas II, this is the most beautiful religious edifice of the Orthodoxy outside Russia and is the perfect expression of Russian religious art abroad. It dates from the belle époque, when some of the Romanovs and their entourage turned the Riviera into a stomping ground (everyone from grand dukes to ballerinas walked the promenade). The cathedral is richly ornamented and decorated with lots of icons. You'll easily spot the building from afar because of its collection of ornate onion-shaped domes. Church services are held on Sunday morning.

✪ **Musée des Beaux-Arts.** 33 av. des Baumettes. ☎ **04-92-15-28-28.** Admission (includes entry to the Galerie-Musée Raoul-Dufy) 25 F ($4) adults, 15 F ($2.40) children under 16. Tues–Sun 10am–noon and 2–6pm. Bus: 3, 9, 12, 22, 23, or 38.

The collection is housed in the former residence of the Ukrainian Princess Kotchubey. There's an important gallery devoted to the masters of the Second Empire and belle époque, with an extensive collection of the 19th-century French experts. The gallery of sculptures includes works by J. B. Carpeaux, Rude, and Rodin. Note the important collection by a dynasty of painters, the Dutch Vanloo family. One of its best-known members, Carle Vanloo, born in Nice in 1705, was Louis XV's premier *peintre.* A fine collection of 19th- and 20th-century art is displayed, including works by Ziem, Raffaelli, Boudin, Renoir, Monet, Guillaumin, and Sisley.

Musée d'Art et d'Histoire Palais Masséna. 65 rue de France. ☎ **04-93-88-11-34.** Admission 25 F ($4) adults, 15 F ($2.40) children; free for everyone 1 Sun per month. Tues–Sun 10am–noon and 2–6pm. Bus: 3, 7, 8, 9, 10, 12, 14, or 22. Closed for renovations; call first.

The fabulous villa housing this collection was built in 1900 in the style of the First Empire as a residence for Victor Masséna, the prince of Essling and grandson of Napoléon's marshal. The city of Nice has converted the villa, next door to the Hôtel Négresco, into a museum of local history and decorative art. A remarkable First Empire drawing room furnished in the opulent taste of that era, with mahogany-veneer pieces and ormolu mounts, is on the ground floor. Of course there's the representation of Napoléon as a Roman Caesar and a bust by Canova of Maréchal Masséna. The large first-floor gallery exhibits a collection of Niçoise primitives and also has a display of 14th- and 15th-century painters, as well as a collection of 16th- to 19th-century masterpieces of plates and jewelry decorated with enamel (Limoges). There are art galleries devoted to the history of Nice and the memories of Masséna and Garibaldi. Yet another gallery is reserved for a display of views of Nice during the 18th and 19th centuries. *Warning:* Check with the tourist office before going here, as the museum will be closed for part of 2000 for renovations.

Musée International d'Art Naïf Anatole-Jakovsky (Museum of Naïve Art). Av. Val-Marie. ☎ **04-93-71-78-33.** Admission 25 F ($4) adults, 15 F ($2.40) students and seniors, free for children 17 and under. Wed–Mon 10am–noon and 2–6pm. Bus: 9, 10, or 12; the walk from the bus stop takes 10 min.

This museum is housed in the beautifully restored Château Ste-Hélène in the Fabron district. The collection was once owned by the museum's namesake, for years one of the world's leading art critics. His 600 drawings and canvases were turned over to the institution and made accessible to the public. Artists from more than two dozen countries are represented here—from primitive painting to contemporary 20th-century works.

Musée Naval (Naval Museum). Parc du Château. ☎ **04-93-80-47-61.** Admission 15 F ($2.40) adults, free for students and children under 16. June–Sept, Wed–Sun 10am–noon and 2–7pm.

In the Tour Bellanda is the Naval Museum, sitting on "the Rock." The tower stands on a precariously perched belvedere overlooking the beach, the bay, the old town, and even the terraces of some of the nearby villas. Of the museum's old battle prints, one depicts the exploits of Caterina Segurana, the Joan of Arc of the Niçoise. During the 1543 siege by Barbarossa, she ran along the ramparts, raising her skirt to show her shapely bottom to the Turks as a sign of contempt, though the soldiers were reported to have been more excited than insulted.

Palais Lascaris. 15 rue Droite. ☎ **04-93-62-72-40.** Free admission. Tues–Sun 10am–noon and 2–6pm. Bus: 1, 2, 3, 5, 6, 14, 16, or 17.

The baroque Palais Lascaris in the city's historic core is intimately linked to the Lascaris-Vintimille family, whose recorded history predates the year 1261. Built in the 17th century, it contains elaborately detailed ornaments. An intensive restoration undertaken by the city of Nice in 1946 brought back its original beauty, and the palace is now classified as a historic monument. The most elaborate floor is the *étage noble*, retaining many of its 18th-century panels and plaster embellishments. A circa-1738 pharmacy, complete with many of the original Delftware accessories, is on the premises. Every Wednesday between 2 and 4pm, the museum appeals to children, inviting craftspeople to show the details of how they accomplish their art forms through live demonstrations.

Nearby Attractions in Cimiez

In the once-aristocratic hilltop quarter of Cimiez, Queen Victoria wintered at the Hôtel Excelsior and brought half the English court with her. Founded by the Romans, who called it Cemenelum, Cimiez was the capital of the Maritime Alps province. Recent excavations have uncovered the ruins of a Roman town, and you can wander among the diggings. The arena was big enough to hold at least 5,000 spectators, who watched contests between gladiators and wild beasts shipped in from Africa. To reach this suburb, take bus no. 15 or 17 from place Masséna.

Monastère de Cimiez (Cimiez Convent). Place du Monastère. ☎ **04-93-81-00-04.** Free admission. Museum, Mon–Sat 10am–noon and 3–6pm; church, daily 8:30am–12:30pm and 2–7pm.

The convent embraces a church that owns three of the most important works from the primitive painting school of Nice by the Bréa brothers. See the carved and gilded wooden main altarpiece. In a restored part of the convent where some Franciscan friars still live, the Musée Franciscain is decorated with 17th-century frescoes. Some 350 documents and works of art from the 15th to the 18th century are displayed, and a monk's cell has been re-created in all its severe simplicity. See also the 17th-century chapel. In the gardens you can get a panoramic view of Nice and the Baie des Anges. Matisse and Dufy are buried in the cemetery.

Musée Matisse. In the Villa des Arènes-de-Cimiez, 164 av. des Arènes-de-Cimiez. ☎ **04-93-81-08-08.** Admission 25 F ($4) adults, free for children 17 and under. Wed–Mon 10am–6pm (5pm off-season).

This museum honors the artist, who died in Nice in 1954. Seeing his nude sketches today, you'll wonder how early critics could have denounced them as "the female animal in all her shame and horror." The museum has several permanent collections, most painted in Nice and many donated by Matisse and his heirs. These include *Nude in an Armchair with a Green Plant* (1937), *Nymph in the Forest* (1935/1942), and a chronologically arranged series of paintings from 1890 to 1919. The most famous of these is *Portrait of Madame Matisse* (1905), usually displayed near a portrait of the artist's wife by Marquet, painted in 1900. There's also an ensemble of drawings and designs (*Flowers and Fruits*) he prepared as practice sketches for the Matisse Chapel at Vence. The most famous are *The Créole Dancer* (1951), *Blue Nude IV* (1952), and around 50 dance-related sketches he did between 1930 and 1931.

✪ **Musée National Message Biblique Marc-Chagall.** Av. du Dr.-Ménard. ☎ **04-93-53-87-20.** Admission 30 F ($4.80) adults, 20 F ($3.20) ages 18–24, free for children 17 and under. Fees may be higher for special exhibits. Wed–Mon 10am–5pm (until 6pm July–Sept).

In the hills of Cimiez above Nice, this handsome museum, surrounded by shallow pools and a garden, is devoted to Marc Chagall's treatment of biblical themes. Born in Russia in 1887, Chagall became a French citizen in 1937. The artist and his wife donated the works—the most important collection of Chagall ever assembled—to France in 1966 and 1972. Displayed are 450 of his oils, gouaches, drawings, pastels, lithographs, sculptures, and ceramics; a mosaic; three stained-glass windows; and a tapestry. A splendid concert room was especially decorated by Chagall with brilliantly hued stained-glass windows. Temporary exhibitions are organized each summer featuring great periods and artists of all times.

OUTDOOR PURSUITS

BEACHES   Nice's seafront is home to at least seven different public beaches. None of them has sand; they're covered with gravel (often the size of golf balls). The rocks are smooth, but can still be nettlesome to people with poor balance or tender feet. Tucked in between the public beaches are the private beaches of hotels such as the Beau Rivage. Most of the public beaches are neatly divided into two sections: a free area and an area where you can avail yourself of the chaise longues, mattresses, parasols, changing cabanas, and freshwater showers. For the privilege, you'll pay between 50 F and 60 F ($8 to $9.60) for a half-day, and between 75 F and 90 F ($12 to $14.40) for a full day. Nude sunbathing is prohibited, but toplessness is common. Take bus nos. 9, 10, 12, and 23 from the center of town to get to the beach.

GOLF   The oldest golf course on the Riviera is about 10 miles from Nice: **Golf Bastide du Roi** (also known as the Golf de Biot), is at av. Jules-Grec, Biot (☎ **04-93-65-08-48**). Open daily throughout the year, this is a flat, not particularly challenging sea-fronting course. (Regrettably, it's necessary to cross over a highway midway through the course to complete the full 18 holes.) Tee times are 8am to 6pm; you can play until the sun sets. Reservations aren't necessary, though on weekends you should probably expect a delay. Greens fees are 240 F ($38.40) for 18 holes; club rental is 50 F ($8).

SCUBA DIVING   The best outfit is the **Centre International de Plongée de Nice,** 2 ruelle des Moulins (☎ **04-93-55-59-50**), adjacent to the city's old port, midway between quai des Docks and boulevard Stalingrad. A baptême (initiatory dive for first-timers) costs 150 F ($24) and a one-tank dive for experienced divers, with all equipment included, is 190 F ($30.40).

TENNIS   The oldest tennis club in Nice is the **Nice Lawn Tennis Club,** Parc Impérial, 5 av. Suzanne-Lenglen (☎ **04-92-15-58-00**), near the train station. It's open daily from 7:30am to 8pm and charges 120 F ($19.20) per person for 2 hours of court time, or a reduced rate of 300 F ($48) per person for unlimited access to the courts for 1 week. The club contains a cooperative staff, a loyal clientele, 13 clay courts, and six hard-surfaced courts. Reserve a court the night before.

SHOPPING

You might want to begin with a stroll through the streets and alleys of Nice's historic core. The densest concentrations of boutiques are along **rue Masséna, place Magenta, l'avenue Jean-Médecin, rue de Verdun,** and the **rue Paradis,** as well as on the streets funneling into and around them. Individual shops of note include **Gigi,** 7 rue de la Liberté (☎ **04-93-87-81-78**), and **Carroll,** 9 rue de la Liberté (☎ **04-93-87-98-07**), both of which sell sophisticated-looking clothing for women; and **Trabaud,** 10 rue de la Liberté (☎ **04-93-87-53-96**), an emporium for menswear. Timeless and endlessly alluring, despite the passage of time, are the products sold at **Yves Saint-Laurent Rive Gauche,** 4 av. de Suède (☎ **04-93-87-70-79**), where the most upscale of the ready-to-wear St-Laurent line is sold, as well as the less expensive garments from the company's cost-conscious *Variations* line.

Opened in 1949 by Joseph Fuchs, the grandfather of the present English-speaking owners, the **Confiserie Florian du Vieux-Nice,** 14 quai Papacino (☎ **04-93-55-43-50**), is near the Old Port. The specialty here is glazed fruits crystallized in sugar or artfully arranged into chocolates. Look for exotic jams (rose-petal preserves or mandarin marmalade) and the free recipe leaflet as well as candied violets, verbena leaves, and rosebuds. Prices for the sugary candied fruit range from 150 F to 215 F ($24 to $34.40) per kilo, depending on the fruits you select.

Façonnable, 7–9 rue Paradis (☎ **04-93-87-88-80**), is the original site that sparked the creation of several hundred branches around the world. This is one of the largest, with a wide range of men's suits, raincoats, overcoats, sportswear, and jeans. The look is youthful and conservatively stylish, for relatively slim (French) bodies.

If you're thinking of indulging in a Provençale *pique-nique,* **Nicola Alziari,** 14 rue St-François-de-Paule (☎ **04-93-85-76-92**), will provide everything you'll need: from olives, anchovies, and pistous to aïolis and tapenades. It's one of Nice's oldest purveyors of olive oil, with a house brand that comes in two strengths: a light version that aficionados claim is vaguely perfumed with Provence, and a stronger version suited to the earthy flavors and robust ingredients of a Provençal winter. Also look for a range of objects crafted from olive wood.

Other shopping recommendations are **La Couquetou,** 8 rue St-François-de-Paule (☎ **04-93-80-90-30**), selling *santons,* the traditional Provençal figurines. The best selection of Provençal fabrics is found at **Le Chandelier,** 7 rue de la Boucherie (☎ **04-93-85-85-19**), where the designs of two of the region's best-known producers of cloth, Les Olivades and Valdrôme, are modeled on the burnt yellows and cerulean tones of Provence.

Nice is also known for its colorful street markets. In addition to the flower market, **Marché aux Fleurs** (see "Exploring the City," above) there's the main Nice flea market, **Marché à la Brocante,** also at cours Saleya, which takes place every Monday from 8am to 5pm. There's another flea market on the port, **Les Puces de Nice,** place Robilante, open Tuesday to Saturday from 9am to 6pm.

ACCOMMODATIONS
VERY EXPENSIVE

✪ **Hôtel Négresco.** 37 promenade des Anglais, 06007 Nice CEDEX. ☎ **04-93-16-64-00.** Fax 04-93-88-35-68. E-mail: negresco@nicematin.fr. 150 units. A/C MINIBAR TV TEL. 1,400–2,750 F ($224–$440) double; 3,400–8,600 F ($544–$1,376) suite. AE, DC, MC, V. Free parking in garage.

The Négresco is one of the Riviera's many super-glamorous hotels, right in the heart of noisy Nice. Jeanne Augier has taken over the place and has triumphed. This Victorian wedding-cake hotel is named after its founder, Henry Négresco, a Romanian who died franc-less in Paris in 1920. It was built on the seafront, in the French château style, with a mansard roof and domed tower; its interior design was inspired by the country's châteaux, and the decorators scoured Europe to gather antiques, tapestries, paintings, and art. Some of the guest rooms are outfitted in homage to the personalities who have stayed here during the hotel's long and illustrious history: The Coco Chanel Room, for example. Others are fancifully modeled after literary or musical themes, such as La Traviata. Each has been recently renovated, and in 1998, most of the bathrooms were upgraded into well-engineered, state-of-the art affairs. Suites and public areas are even grander, as is the case with the Louis XIV salon, reminiscent of the Sun King himself, or the Napoléon III suite, where swagged walls, a leopard-skin carpet, and a half-crowned canopy in pink create an undeniable sense of majesty. The most expensive rooms with balconies face the Mediterranean. The staff wears 18th-century costumes.

Dining: Reasonably priced meals are served in La Rotonde, but the featured restaurant—one of the Riviera's greatest—is Chantecler (see below).

Amenities: Room service, maid service, massage, baby-sitting, secretarial services.

✪ **Palais Maeterlinck.** Basse Corniche, 06300 Nice. ☎ **04-92-00-72-00.** Fax 04-92-04-18-10. www.palais-maeterlinck.com. E-mail: info@palaismaeterlinck.com. 40 units. A/C MINIBAR TV TEL. 1,450–2,900 F ($232–$464) double; 2,500–15,000 F ($400–$2,400) suite. AE, DC, MC, V. Closed Jan 4 to mid-Mar. Drive 4 miles east of Nice along the Basse Corniche.

On 9 landscaped acres east of Nice, this deluxe hotel—"the jewel of the Côte d'Azur"—occupies a fin-de-siècle villa that was inhabited between the World Wars by the Belgian-born writer Maurice Maeterlinck, winner of the Nobel Prize for Literature. While many visitors find the setting sumptuous, the service and experience of the staff pale in comparison to the staff at similarly priced hotels. But on the plus side, since it's calmer and more tranquil than the hotels in more central locations, it enjoys the allure of verdant terraces and a large outdoor pool, set amid banana trees, gnarled olive trees, and soaring cypresses. A funicular will carry you down to the rock-strewn beach and nearby marina. Each of the elegant guest rooms is outfitted in a different monochromatic color scheme and neoclassical Florentine styling, each with a terrace opening onto views of Cap d'Antibes and Cap-Ferrat.

Dining: The hotel's two restaurants include Mélisande, a gastronomic hideaway whose neo-Renaissance decor was upgraded and richly renovated in 1998. Fixed-price meals here cost 290 F ($46.40). Less formal, and slightly less expensive, is the Club Nautique, a *salle de banquet* with a nautical theme and a series of Provençal and international specialties.

Amenities: Outdoor pool, concierge, room service, baby-sitting, laundry service. A funicular will carry you down to the rock-strewn beach and nearby marina.

EXPENSIVE

Grand Hôtel Aston. 12 av. Félix-Faure, 06000 Nice. ☎ **04-92-17-53-00.** Fax 04-93-80-40-02. www.hotel-aston.com. E-mail: hotel-aston@hotel-aston.com. 155 units. 900–1,500 F ($144–$240) double. AE, DC, MC, V. Parking 100 F ($16). Bus: 12.

This elegantly detailed 19th-century hotel is one of the most alluring in its price bracket. After undergoing radical renovations, bedrooms are now outfitted with comfortable mattresses. The prices of the rooms vary according to their views over the street, the splashing fountains of the Place Masséna, or the coastline panorama from the uppermost floor. On summer evenings, an outdoor, garden-style bar, sometimes with dance music, provides diversions from a spot on the hotel's uppermost floor. The hotel is associated with Holland's Golden Tulip chain.

❂ **La Pérouse.** 11 quai Rauba-Capéu, 06300 Nice. ☎ **04-93-62-34-63.** Fax 04-93-62-59-41. 63 units. A/C MINIBAR TV TEL. 745–1,305 F ($119.20–$208.80) double; 2,350–3,000 F ($376–$480) suite. AE, DC, MC, V. Parking 80 F ($12.80).

Once a prison, La Pérouse has been reconstructed and is now a unique Riviera hotel. Set on a cliff, it's built right into the gardens of an ancient château-fort. There's no hotel in Nice with a better view over both the old city and the Baie des Anges. In fact, many people stay here just for the view alone. Inside, the hotel is like an old Provençal home, with low ceilings, white walls, and antiques. Most of the lovely rooms have loggias overlooking the bay. Guest rooms are fairly standardized but evoke the tropics in their use of rattan and bamboo furnishings along with floral fabrics.

Dining: The restaurant, with a different menu every day, specializes in a Niçoise cuisine and is open only for dinner in summer (there's room service in winter).

Amenities: Outdoor pool, Jacuzzi, room service, dry cleaning, concierge, sauna, fitness center.

Westminster Concorde. 27 promenade des Anglais, 06000 Nice. ☎ **04-92-14-86-86.** Fax 04-93-82-45-35. www.westminster-nice.com. 100 units. A/C MINIBAR TV TEL. 750–1,360 F ($120–$217.60) double; from 2,000 F ($320) junior suite. AE, DC, MC, V. Parking 120 F ($19.20). Bus: 9, 10, or 11.

This 1860 hotel stands prominently along the famous promenade. Its elaborate facade was restored in 1986 to its former grandeur, and many renovations were made, including the installation of air-conditioning. The contemporary rooms are comfortable and have soundproof windows; a few open onto balconies. Most rooms have high ceilings, antique mirrors, French windows, and brass beds.

Dining: The dining and drinking facilities include plant-ringed terraces with a view of the water and a simple in-house restaurant.

MODERATE

Château des Ollières. 39 av. des Baumettes, 06000 Nice. ☎ **04-92-15-77-99.** Fax 04-92-15-77-98. www.chateaudesollieres.com. 8 units. A/C MINIBAR TV TEL. 750–950 F ($120–$152) double; 1,750–3,000 F ($280–$480) suite. AE, MC, V. Bus: 38.

The most appealing and unusual hotel to open in Nice in many years made its debut as a hotel in 1996, and as a restaurant a year later. It's conveniently located within a 5-minute walk of the Négresco and the Promenade des Anglais. The setting is one of the largest tracts of privately owned land in Nice—a 20-acre park loaded with exotic trees and shrubs. The centerpiece is a Beaux-Arts villa that was built in the 1870s by a Russian prince who had fallen in love with the wife of the French ambassador to Turkey. Inside, you'll find a noteworthy collection of oil paintings and "neo-Napoléonienne" and Empire-inspired antiques. One of the highlights is a set that was custom-made for the villa's dining room, when the villa was being constructed. Bedrooms are outfitted in the same high-ceilinged, ornate style as the public areas.

Dining: The hotel restaurant occupies both the villa's original dining room as well as a garden wing whose big windows give the impression of dining directly within the garden. Menus change weekly, according to the inspiration of the chef and the availability of fresh ingredients. Fixed-price lunches cost around 220 F ($35.20); fixed-price dinners cost around 259 F ($41.45). Advance reservations are important.

✪ **Hôtel Gounod.** 3 rue Gounod, 06000 Nice. ☎ **04-93-16-42-00.** Fax 04-93-88-23-84. www.info@gounod-nice.com. 46 units. A/C MINIBAR TV TEL. 510–730 F ($81.60–$116.80) double; 665–1,005 F ($106.40–$160.80) suite. AE, DC, MC, V. Closed Nov 20–Dec 20. Parking 65 F ($10.40). Bus: 8.

This is our favorite three-star hotel in Nice. It was built around 1910 in a neighborhood where the street names honor composers. The Gounod boasts ornate balconies, a domed roof, and an elaborate canopy of wrought iron and glass. The attractive lobby and adjoining lounge are festive and stylish, with old prints, copper pots with flowers, and antiques. The high-ceilinged guest rooms are quiet and usually overlook the gardens of private homes. There aren't many amenities to speak of here, but guests have free unlimited use of the pool, cafe-bar, and heated Jacuzzi at the Hotel Splendid next door.

Hotel Windsor. 11 rue Dalpozzo, 06000 Nice. ☎ **04-93-88-59-35.** Fax 04-93-88-94-57. www.webstore.fr/windsor or www.rom.fr/hotelwindsor. E-mail: windsor@webstore.fr. 420–750 F ($67.20–$120) double. AE, DC, MC, V. Parking 60 F ($9.60). Bus: 8

One of the most arts-conscious hotels in Provence is set within a *maison bourgeoise* (near the Hotel Négresco and the Promenade des Anglais), built by disciples of Gustav Eiffel in 1895. Inside, you'll find an artful, artsy, somewhat claustrophobic environment. High points include a complicated fifth-floor superstructure, site of a health club, steamroom and sauna that's considered highly unusual by local architects; and a one-of-a-kind series of frescoes that adorn each of the bedrooms. Attribute this to the heir and scion of the Redolfi family—the long-time owners of the place—who commissioned manifestations of his mystical and mythical visions after his years of traveling through Asia, Africa, and South America. Public areas include all the artfully mythical frescoes you'd expect, a somewhat dilettantish sense of Zen-inspired well-being, and a dining room that's open only to residents of the hotel. The garden contains scores of tropical and exotic plants, and the recorded sounds of birds singing in the jungles of the Amazon. There's also a swimming pool.

Le Petit Palais. 10 av. Emile-Bieckert, 06000 Nice. ☎ **04-93-62-19-11.** Fax 04-93-62-53-60. www.guide-gerard.com. E-mail: petitpalais@provence.riviera.com. 25 units. TV TEL. 430–810 F ($68.80–$129.60) double. AE, DC, MC, V. Parking 50 F ($8).

This whimsical hotel occupies a mansion built around 1890; in the 1970s it was the home of the actor/writer Sacha Guitry, a name that's instantly recognized in millions of French households. It lies about a 10-minute drive from the city center in the Carabacel residential district. Much of its architectural grace remains, as evoked by the Art Deco/Italianate furnishings and Florentine moldings and friezes. The preferred rooms, and the most expensive, have balconies for sea views during the day and sunset watching at dusk. You can order light food from room service until midnight, and breakfast is served in a small but pretty salon.

INEXPENSIVE

Flots d'Azur. 101 promenade des Anglais, 06000 Nice. ☎ **04-93-86-51-25.** Fax 04-93-97-22-07. E-mail: flotsazur@wanadoo.fr. 21 units. A/C TEL. 250–550 F ($40–$88) double. MC, V. Bus: 8.

This three-story villa-hotel is next to the sea and a short walk from the more elaborate and costlier promenade hotels. While the rooms vary in size and decor, all have good views and sea breezes. Twelve of the rooms have TVs and minibars. Double-glazed windows were recently added to cut down on the noise. There's a small sitting room and sun terrace in front, where a continental breakfast is served.

Hôtel de la Mer. 4 place Masséna, 06000 Nice. ☎ **04-93-92-09-10.** Fax 04-93-85-00-64. 12 units. TV TEL. 280–630 F ($44.80–$100.80) double. AE, MC, V. Bus: 1, 2, 5, 15, or 17.

In the center of Old Nice, this place was built around 1910, transformed into a hotel in 1947, and renovated in 1993. Despite that, it manages to keep its prices low. Ms. Feri Forouzan, the owner, welcomes you with personalized charm. Most guest rooms are of good size and have such items as a minibar and TV, not often found in inexpensive Nice hotels. From the hotel it's a 2-minute walk to promenade des Anglais and the seafront. Breakfast is served in one of the public salons or your room.

Hôtel du Centre. 2 rue de Suisse, 06000 Nice. ☎ **04-93-88-83-85.** Fax 04-93-82-29-80. www.webstore.fr/hotel-centre. E-mail: hotel-centre@webstore.fr. 28 units. TV TEL. 257–297 F ($41.10–$47.50) double. AE, MC, V. Parking 8 F ($1.30). Bus: 23.

Near the train station, this simple but clean hotel was built in 1947. Today it welcomes an almost entirely gay clientele. The simple, clean, uncomplicated rooms are very close to the attractions and charms of downtown Nice with its bars. The staff is well versed in the many diversions of the city.

Hôtel Excelsior. 190 av. Durante, 06000 Nice. ☎ **04-93-88-18-05.** Fax 04-93-88-38-69. 45 units. TV TEL. 337–577 F ($53.90–$92.30) double. AE, CB, V. Parking 65 F ($10.40). Bus: 1, 2, 5, 12, 18, 23, or 24.

The Excelsior's ornate corbels and chiseled stone pediments rise grandly a few steps from the railway station. This much renovated 19th-century hotel has a pleasantly modern decor with durable rooms that have seen a lot of wear but are still comfortable and serviceable. Furnishings, for the most part, are functional and conservative. There's a reflecting pool in the lobby; the beach is a 20-minute walk through the residential and commercial heart of Nice.

Hôtel Magnan. Square du Général-Ferrié, 06200 Nice. ☎ **04-93-86-76-00.** Fax 04-93-44-48-31. E-mail: hotelmagnan@wanadoo.fr. 25 units. TV TEL. 280–380 F ($44.80–$60.80) double. AE, MC, V. Parking 35 F ($5.60). Bus: 12, 23, or 24.

This well-run modern hotel was built around 1945 and has been renovated frequently since then. It's a 10-minute bus ride from the heart of town but only a minute or so from promenade des Anglais and the bay. Many of the simply furnished rooms have balconies facing the sea, and some contain minibars. The look is a bit functional, but for Nice this is a good price, especially considering how comfortable the beds are. The owner, Daniel Thérouin, occupies the apartment on the top floor, guaranteeing a closely supervised set-up. Breakfast can be served in your room.

✪ Hôtel Villa Eden. 99 bis promenade des Anglais, 06000 Nice. ☎ **04-93-86-53-70.** Fax 04-93-97-67-97. E-mail: hotelvillaeden@caramail/.com. 14 units. A/C TV TEL. 200–390 F ($32–$62.40) double. AE, DC, MC, V. Bus: 3, 9, 10, 22, 23, or 24 from the center, or 12 from the train station.

In 1925 an exiled Russian countess built this Art Deco villa on the seafront, surrounded it with a wall, and planted a tiny garden. The pastel-pink villa still remains, despite the construction of much-taller modern buildings on both sides. You can enjoy the ivy and roses in the garden and stay in old-fashioned partly modernized rooms whose sizes vary greatly. The owner maintains a wry sense of humor and greets you at breakfast, the only meal served.

DINING
VERY EXPENSIVE

✪ **Chantecler.** In the Hôtel Négresco, 37 promenade des Anglais. ☎ **04-93-16-64-00.** Reservations required. Main courses 240–350 F ($38.40–$56); fixed-price menus 430–580 F ($68.80–$92.80). AE, DC, MC, V. Daily 12:30–2pm and 7:30–10pm. Closed mid-Nov to mid-Dec. Bus: 9, 17, or 22. FRENCH.

This is Nice's most prestigious restaurant. In 1989 a massive redecoration sheathed its walls with panels removed from a château in Puilly-Fussé; a Regency-style salon was installed for before- or after-dinner drinks; and a collection of 16th-century paintings, executed on leather backgrounds in the Belgian town of Malines, was imported. A much-respected chef, Alain Llorca, revised the menu to include the most sophisticated and creative dishes in Nice. They change almost weekly but may include fillet of turbot served with a purée of broad beans, sun-dried tomatoes, and fresh asparagus; roasted suckling lamb served with beignets of fresh vegetables and ricotta-stuffed ravioli; and a melt-in-your-mouth fantasy of marbled hot chocolate drenched in an almond-flavored cream sauce.

EXPENSIVE

Chez Michel (Le Grand Pavois). 11 rue Meyerbeer. ☎ **04-93-88-77-42.** Reservations required. Main courses 125–210 F ($20–$33.60); fixed-price menus 195–300 F ($31.20–$48); bouillabaisse 330–450 F ($52.80–$72). MC, V. Daily noon–2:30pm and 7–11pm. Bus: 8. SEAFOOD.

This seafood brasserie behind the Négresco Hotel was established by members of the family that own Chez Tétou, the fabulously stylish, fabulously relaxed seafood restaurant in Golfe Juan that's beloved by movie stars, glitterati, and the merely rich. Jacques Marquise, one of the patriarchs of the Chez Tétou success story, is the creative force here; he's committed to maintaining prices that are between 30% and 40% less than those charged by Chez Tétou. Bouillabaisse is the specialty here, priced at 330 F ($52.80) for a succulent and authentic version, and at 450 F ($72) for a royal version garnished with lobster and crayfish. Other delectable choices include sea bass in white wine, herbs, and lemon sauce; and fish (snapper, hogfish, sea bass, and John Dory) that's grilled and then flambéed with a combination of fennel and fennel-flavored brandy. The wine list has a number of reasonably priced bottles.

✪ **La Merenda.** 4 rue Terrasse. No phone. Reservations required. Main courses 150–210 F ($24–$33.60). No credit cards. Mon–Fri noon–2pm and 7–9:30pm. Closed Aug 4–18, Dec 24–Jan 4, and Feb 16–22. Bus: 8. NIÇOISE.

Since there's no phone, you have to go by this place twice: once to make a reservation and once to dine. However, it's worth the extra effort, as this is the best bistro in Nice. Forsaking his two-star chef crown at the renowned Chantecler (see above), Dominique Le Stanc opened this tiny bistro serving a sublime cuisine. "A no-star hole in the wall," the press screamed. But that's what Le Stanc wanted. Born in Alsace, his heart and soul belong to the Mediterranean, the land of black truffles, seasonal wild morels, fat sea bass, and plump asparagus. His food is rightly called a lullaby of gastronomic unity, with texture, crunch, richness, and balance. "I've known my days of glory in the gastronomic world. Now I'm doing family cooking, which is what I always like to eat." Le Stanc never knows what he's going to serve until he goes to the market. Look for his specials on a chalkboard. Perhaps you'll find stuffed cabbage, fried zucchini flowers, or oxtail flavored with fresh oranges. Lamb from the Sisteron is cooked until it practically falls from the bone. Raw artichokes are paired with a salad of mâche. Service is discreet and personable. We wish we could dine here every day.

MODERATE

Ane Rouge. 7 quai des Deux-Emmanuels. ☎ **04-93-89-49-63.** Reservations required. Main courses 95–210 F ($15.20–$33.60); fixed-price menus 158–258 F ($25.30–$41.30); bouillabaisse 265 F ($42.40). AE, DC, MC, V. Thurs–Tues noon–2pm and 7:30–10:30pm. Closed 2 weeks in Feb. Bus: 30. PROVENÇAL.

Facing the old port and occupying an antique building whose owners have carefully retained its ceiling beams and stone walls, this is one of the city's best-known seafood restaurants. In the two modern dining rooms noteworthy for their coziness, you can enjoy traditional and time-tested specialties like bouillabaisse; bourrides; fillet of John Dory with roulades of stuffed lettuce leaves; mussels stuffed with breadcrumbs and herbs; and salmon in wine sauce with spinach. Service is correct and commendable.

Brasserie Flo. 2–4 rue Sacha-Guitry. ☎ **04-93-13-38-38.** Reservations recommended. Main courses 85–120 F ($13.60–$19.20); fixed-price menus 119–169 F ($19.05–$27.05) at lunch, 159 F ($25.45) all day, 119 F ($19.05) after 10:30pm. AE, DC, MC, V. Daily noon–3pm and 7pm–midnight. Bus: 1, 2, or 5. FRENCH.

In 1991, the Jean-Paul Bucher group, a French chain noted for its skill at restoring historic brasseries, bought the premises of a faded turn-of-the-century restaurant near place Masséna and injected it with new life. Its high ceilings are covered with their original frescoes. The place is brisk, stylish, reasonably priced, and fun. Menu items include an array of grilled fish, *choucroute* (sauerkraut) Alsatian style, steak with brandied pepper sauce, and fresh oysters and shellfish.

La Nissarda. 17 rue Gubernatis. ☎ **04-93-85-26-29.** Reservations recommended. Main courses 98–138 F ($15.70–$22.10). MC, V. Mon–Sat noon–2pm and 7–10pm. Closed Aug. NIÇOISE.

Set in the heart of town, about a 10-minute walk from place Masséna, this restaurant is maintained by a Normandy-born family who work hard to maintain the aura and the culinary traditions of Nice. In an intimate (40-seat) setting lined with old engravings and photographs of the city, the place serves local versions of ravioli, spaghetti, carbonara, lasagne, and fresh-grilled salmon with herbs. A handful of Norman-based specialties also manage to creep into the menu, much to the appreciation of diners longing for northern France, including escalopes of veal with cream sauce and apples.

✪ **Le Safari.** 1 cours Saleya. ☎ **04-93-80-18-44.** Reservations recommended. Main courses 80–130 F ($12.80–$20.80); fixed-price menus 150–200 F ($24–$32). AE, DC, MC, V. Daily noon–2:30pm and 7–11:30pm. Closed Mon Nov–Mar. Bus: 1. PROVENÇAL/NIÇOISE.

The decor couldn't be simpler: a black ceiling, white walls, and an old-fashioned terracotta floor. The youthful staff is relaxed, sometimes in jeans, and always alert to the waves of fashion. Look for mobs here, many of whom prefer the outdoor terrace overlooking the Marché aux Fleurs and all of whom appreciate the earthy, reasonably priced meals that appear in generous portions. Menu items include a pungent *bagna cauda,* in which vegetables are immersed in a sizzling brew of hot oil and anchovy paste; grilled peppers bathed in olive oil; *daube* (stew) of beef; fresh pasta with basil; and an omelet with *blettes* (tough but flavorful greens). The unfortunately named *merda de can* (dog shit) is gnocchi stuffed with spinach, and is a lot more appetizing than it sounds. Wouldn't it have to be?

INEXPENSIVE

L'Olivier. 3 place Garibaldi. ☎ **04-93-26-89-09.** Reservations recommended. Main courses 60–90 F ($9.60–$14.40). AE, DC, MC, V. Daily noon–2:30pm; Thurs–Tues 7:45–10pm. Closed 1 week in Aug. PROVENÇAL/SICILIAN.

Established in 1989, this charming restaurant lies beneath the arcades of place Garibaldi, in the heart of Old Nice, just in back of the Museum of Modern Art. Named in honor of the premises' former occupant, an old-style shop selling olives, olive oil, and anchovies, the restaurant serves an original and sometimes unique cuisine based on modern versions of local culinary traditions. Flavorful and well-prepared items include smoked slices of foie gras; deboned sea bass stuffed with shellfish and herbs and served with a crabmeat sauce; and a Sicilian-inspired medley of eggplant, olives, olive oil, and herbs combined into a southern Italian ratatouille. Dessert might be a gratin of frozen and caramelized lemons, or black-chocolate truffles.

Restaurant L'Estocaficada. 2 rue de l'Hôtel-de-Ville. ☎ **04-93-80-21-64.** Reservations recommended. Main courses 55–95 F ($8.80–$15.20); fixed-price menus 68–125 F ($10.90–$20). AE, MC, V. Tues–Sun noon–2pm and 7–9:30pm. Bus: 1, 2, or 5. NIÇOISE.

Estocaficada is the Provençal word for stockfish, the ugliest fish in Europe. There might be a dried-out, balloon-shaped version on display in the cozy dining room. Brigitte Autier is the owner/chef, and her busy kitchens are visible from everywhere in the dining room. Descended from a matriarchal line (since 1958) of mother-daughter teams who have managed this place, she's devoted to the preservation of recipes prepared by her Niçoise grandmother. Examples are gnocchis, beignets, several types of *farcies* (tomatoes, peppers, or onions stuffed with herbed fillings), grilled sardines, or bouillabaisse served as a main course or in a mini-version. As a concession to popular demand, the place also serves pastas.

NICE AFTER DARK

Nice has some of the most active nightlife along the Riviera, with evenings usually beginning at a cafe. You can pick up a copy of *La Semaine des Spectacles,* available at kiosks around town, that outlines the week's diversions.

The major cultural center along the Riviera is the **Opéra de Nice,** 4 rue St-François-de-Paule (☎ **04-92-17-40-44**), which was built in 1885 by Charles Garnier, fabled architect of the Paris Opera House. A full repertoire is presented, with special emphasis on serious, often large-scale operas. In one season you might see *Tosca, Tristan und Isolde,* Verdi's *MacBeth,* Beethoven's *Fidelio,* and *Carmen,* as well as a *saison symphonique,* dominated by the Orchestre Philharmonique de Nice. The opera hall is also the major venue for concerts and recitals. Tickets are available, both to concerts, recitals, and full-blown operas, up to about a day or two prior to any performance. You can show up at the box office (Tuesday to Friday 10am to 5:30 pm), or buy tickets in advance with a major credit card by phoning ☎ **04-92-17-40-40.** Tickets range from 40 F ($6.40) for a nose-bleed (and we mean it) seat to 450 F ($72) for front-and-center seats.

Near the Hotel Ambassador, *L'Ambassade,* 18 rue des Congrès (☎ **04-93-88-88-87**), was deliberately designed in a mock-Gothic style that includes the wrought-iron accents you'd expect to find in a château, two bars, and a dance floor. At least 90% of its clients are straight, and come in all physical types and age ranges. The cover is 100 F ($16) and includes the first drink. **Piano Bar Louis XV/Disco Inferno,** 10 rue Cité-du-Parc (☎ **04-93-80-49-84**), is a double-tiered nightclub with a piano bar in its 200-year-old vaulted cellar and a modern disco on its street level. There's a cover of 80 F ($12.80), including the first drink. Newer contenders include **Disco Butterfly,** 67 rue des États-Unis (☎ **04-93-92-27-31**), a site where hip recorded music (including house, garage, techno, and whatever strikes the fancy of the DJ) attracts a high-energy, highly sociable crowd under 35 to dance and boogie the night away.

Le Cabaret du Casino Ruhl, in the Casino Ruhl, 1 promenade des Anglais (☎ **04-97-03-12-22**), is Nice's answer to the cabaret glitter that appears in more ostentatious forms in Monte Carlo and Las Vegas. It includes just enough flesh to titillate; lots of spangles, feathers, and sequins; a medley of cross-cultural jokes and nostalgia for the good old days of French chanson; and an acrobat or juggler. The cover of 130 F ($20.80) includes the first drink; dinner and the show, complete with a bottle of wine per person, costs 300 F ($48). Shows are presented every Friday and Saturday at 10:30pm. No jeans or sneakers.

The casino contains an area devoted exclusively to slot machines, open daily from 10am to 4 or 5am, entrance to which is free. A more formal gaming room (a jacket is required, but not a tie), replete with blackjack, baccarat, chemin de fer, and 21 tables, is open nightly, at a fee of 75 F ($12) per person, every Monday to Friday from 8pm to 4am, and every Saturday and Sunday from 5pm to 5am.

Le Relais American Bar, in the Hotel Négresco, 37 promenade des Anglais (☎ **04-93-16-64-00**), is the most beautiful bar in Nice, filled with white columns, an oxblood-red ceiling, Oriental carpets, English paneling, Italianate chairs, and tapestries. It was once a haunt of the actress Lillie Langtry. With its piano music and white-jacketed waiters, the bar still attracts a chic crowd.

GAY NIGHTLIFE

Increasingly, Nice remains the gay capital of southern France. You can make a night of it (or several nights of it) at the following establishments: **Le Santiago,** 28 rue Lepante (☎ **04-93-13-83-01**), with its hotel bar and restaurant; **Latinos,** 6 rue Chauvain (☎ **04-93-85-01-10**), for "gay tapas"; **La Table Coquine,** 44 av. de la République (☎ **04-93-55-39-99**), a gay restaurant; **Café Chris,** 3 rue Smolett (☎ **04-93-26-75-85**), a gay cafe; and **Le C.D. Restaurant and Salad Bar,** 22 rue Benoit Bunico (☎ **04-93-92-47-65**), where you can cruise while you munch.

Near the Hôtel Négresco and promenade des Anglais, **Le Blue Boy,** 9 rue Spinetta (☎ **04-93-44-68-24**), is the oldest gay disco on the Riviera. With two bars and two floors, it's a vital nocturnal stopover for passengers aboard the dozens of all-gay cruises that make regular calls at Nice. The cover varies from free to 50 F ($8).

L'Ascenseur, 18 bis rue Emmanuel Philibert (☎ **04-93-26-35-30**), is one of the most popular of the several new crops of gay bars in and around Nice. This is a bustling, friendly gay bar loaded with wood paneling, billiard tables, metallic accents, and some of the more appealing gay men in all of Europe. It's open Tuesday through Saturday from 9pm till at least 3am. There's no dance floor, but disco music plays as men, and to a lesser degree, gay women, laugh, converse, and flirt.

14 Villefranche-sur-Mer

581 miles S of Paris, 4 miles E of Nice

According to legend, Hercules opened his arms and Villefranche was born. It sits on a big blue bay that looks like a gigantic bowl, large enough to attract U.S. Sixth Fleet cruisers and destroyers. Quietly slumbering otherwise, Villefranche takes on the appearance of an exciting Mediterranean port when the fleet's in. Four miles east of Nice, it's the first town you reach along the Lower Corniche.

ESSENTIALS

GETTING THERE   Trains arrive from most towns on the Côte d'Azur, especially Nice (every 30 minutes), but most visitors **drive** via the Corniche Inférieure (Lower

Corniche). For more rail information and schedules, call ☎ **08-36-35-35-35.** There's no formalized **bus** station in Villefranche.

VISITOR INFORMATION   The **Office de Tourisme** is on Jardin François-Binon (☎ **04-93-01-73-68**).

EXPLORING THE TOWN

The vaulted rue Obscure is one of the strangest streets in France (to get to it, take rue de l'Église). In spirit it belongs more to a North African casbah. People live in tiny houses on this street, but occasionally there's an open space, allowing for a tiny court-yard.

Once popular with such writers as Katherine Mansfield and Aldous Huxley, the town is still a haven for artists, many of whom take over the little houses that climb the hillside. Two of the more recent arrivals who've bought homes in the area are Tina Turner and Bono (not together).

One artist who came to Villefranche left a memorial: Jean Cocteau, the legendary painter, writer, filmmaker, and well-respected dilettante, spent a year (1956 to 1957) painting frescoes on the 14th-century walls of the **Romanesque Chapelle St-Pierre,** quai de la Douane/rue des Marinières (☎ **04-93-76-90-70**). He eventually presented it to "the fishermen of Villefranche in homage to the Prince of Apostles, the patron of fishermen." One panel pays homage to the gypsies of the Stes-Maries-de-la-Mer. In the apse is a depiction of the miracle of St. Peter walking on the water, not knowing that he's supported by an angel. Villefranche's young women in their regional cos-tumes are honored on the left side of the narthex Cocteau. The chapel, which charges 12 F ($1.90) admission, is open Tuesday to Sunday: July to September from 10am to noon and 4 to 8:30pm, October to March from 9:30am to noon and 2 to 5pm, and April to June from 9:30am to noon and 2:30 to 7:30pm (closed mid-November to mid-December).

ACCOMMODATIONS

Hôtel Versailles. Av. Princesse-Grace-de-Monaco, 06230 Villefranche-sur-Mer. ☎ **04-93-76-52-52.** Fax 04-93-01-97-48. www.hotelversailles.com. E-mail: hotel.le.versailles@ wanadoo.fr. 49 units. A/C TV TEL. 550–700 F ($88–$112) double; 750–1,050 F ($120–$168) suite. AE, DC, MC, V. Closed late Oct–late Dec. Free parking.

Several blocks from the harbor and outside the main part of town, this three-story hotel gives you a perspective of the entire coast. The hotel offers comfortably furnished rooms and suites (suitable for up to three) with big windows and panoramas. Guests congregate on the roof terrace, for breakfast or lunch under an umbrella. The pool is on another terrace, surrounded by palms and bright flowers.

Hôtel Welcome. 1 quai Courbet, 06230 Villefranche-sur-Mer. ☎ **04-93-76-27-62.** Fax 04-93-76-27-66. www.welcomehotel.com. 32 units. A/C MINIBAR TV TEL. 570–950 F ($91.20–$152) double. Half board 160 F ($25.60) per person extra. AE, DC, MC, V. Closed Nov 15–Dec 20.

The Welcome was a favorite of Jean Cocteau. In this six-floor villa hotel, with shut-ters and balconies, everything has recently been modernized and extensively renovated. Try for a fifth-floor room overlooking the water. Pope Paul III once embarked from this site with Charles V, but nowadays the departures are more casual—usually for fishing expeditions. The sidewalk cafe is the focal point of town life. The lounge and the restaurant, St-Pierre, have open fireplaces and fruitwood furniture.

DINING

La Mère Germaine. Quai Courbet. ☎ **04-93-01-71-39.** Reservations recommended. Main courses 140–505 F ($22.40–$80.80); fixed-price menu 223–255 F ($35.70–$40.80). AE, MC, V. Daily noon–2:30pm and 7–10pm. Closed Nov 15–Dec 25. FRENCH/SEAFOOD.

This is the very best of a string of restaurants on the port. Plan to relax here over lunch while watching fishermen repair their nets. Mère Germaine opened the place in the 1930s, and her grandson, the likable Thierry Blouin, deftly handles the cuisine these days. It's popular with U.S. Navy officers, who've discovered the bouillabaisse made with tasty morsels of fresh fish and mixed in a cauldron with savory spices. We recommend the grilled *loup* (sea bass) with fennel, salade Niçoise, sole Tante Marie (stuffed with mushroom purée), and beef fillet with three peppers. The perfectly roasted *carré d'agneau* (lamb) is for two. Most dishes are at the lower end of the price scale.

✪ **La Trinquette.** Port de la Darse. ☎ **04-93-01-71-41.** Reservations recommended. Main courses 55–140 F ($8.80–$22.40); fixed-price menus 115–190 F ($18.40–$30.40); bouillabaisse 240 F ($38.40). No credit cards. Thurs–Tues noon–2:15pm and 7–10pm. Closed Dec–Jan. PROVENÇAL/SEAFOOD.

Charming and traditional, in a pre-Napoleonic building that rises a few steps from the harborfront, this restaurant prides itself on the excellence of its fish and bouillabaisse. The fish is hauled out of a backroom, on platters, for anyone skeptical enough to ask to see the actual fish before it's cooked. You can choose from among 15 to 20 kinds, prepared any way you specify, with a wide variety of well-flavored sauces. Bouillabaisse is an enduring favorite that's much cheaper here than at many other places. There's even a roasted version of *chapon de mer,* served with a Provençal sauce. How do the hardworking owners, Paul and Monique Osiel, recommend their John Dory? Roasted in as simple and fresh a means as possible, served only with a hint of beurre blanc.

15 St-Jean-Cap-Ferrat

583 miles S of Paris, 6 miles E of Nice

Of all the oases along the Côte d'Azur, no place has the snob appeal of Cap-Ferrat. It's a 9-mile promontory sprinkled with luxurious villas, outlined by sheltered bays, beaches, and coves. The vegetation is lush. In the port of St-Jean, the harbor accommodates yachts and fishing boats.

ESSENTIALS

GETTING THERE   Most visitors drive or take a **bus** or **taxi** from the rail station at nearby Beaulieu. Buses from the station at Beaulieu depart at hourly intervals for Cap-Ferrat. There's also bus service from Nice. For bus information and schedules, call ☎ **04-93-85-61-81.** By **car,** St-Jean-Cap-Ferrat is best reached from Nice by **driving** along N7 east.

VISITOR INFORMATION   The **Office de Tourisme** is on av. Denis-Séméria (☎ **04-93-76-08-90**).

SEEING THE SIGHTS

One of the ways to enjoy the scenery here is to wander on some of the public paths. The most scenic goes from **Plage de Paloma** to **Pointe St-Hospice,** at which point a panoramic view of the Riviera landscape unfolds.

You can also spend time wandering around St-Jean, a colorful fishing village with bars, bistros, and simple inns. The beaches, although popular, are pebbly, not sandy.

The best and most luxurious one belongs to the Grand Hôtel du Cap-Ferrat (see below), and it is open to nonguests who pay 100 F ($16) to rent a mattress and an umbrella.

Everyone tries to visit the **Villa Mauresque,** avenue Somerset-Maugham, but it's closed to the public. Near the cape, it's where Maugham spent his final years, almost begging for death. When tourists tried to visit him, he proclaimed that he wasn't one of the local sights. One man did manage to crash through the gate, and when he encountered the author, Maugham snarled, "What do you think I am, a monkey in a cage?"

Once the property of King Leopold II, of Belgium, the **Villa Les Cèred** lies directly west of the port of St-Jean. Although the villa is in private hands and can't be visited, you can go to the **Parc Zoologique,** boulevard du Général-de-Gaulle, northwest of the peninsula, near Villa Les Cèdres (☎ 04-93-76-04-98). It's open daily: April to October from 9:30am to 7pm, to 6pm in winter. Admission is 58 F ($9.30). This private zoo is set in the basin of a now-drained lake and was Leopold's private domain. It houses a wide variety of reptiles, birds, and animals in outdoor cages. Six times a day there's a chimps' tea party, which explains Maugham's remark.

✪ **Musée Île-de-France.** Av. Denis-Séméria. ☎ **04-93-01-33-09.** Admission 69 F ($11.05) adults, 37 F ($5.90) ages 9–24, free for children 8 and under. July–Aug, daily 10am–7pm; Sept–June, daily 10am–6pm.

Built by Baronne Ephrussi, this is one of the Côte d'Azur's most legendary villas. Born a Rothschild, she married a Hungarian banker and friend of her father, M. Ephrussi, about whom even the museum's curator knows little. She died in 1934, leaving the stately Italianate building and its magnificent gardens to the Institut de France on behalf of the Académie des Beaux-Arts. The wealth of her collection is preserved: 18th-century furniture; Tiepolo ceilings; Savonnerie carpets; screens and panels from the Far East; tapestries from Gobelin, Aubusson, and Beauvais; drawings by Fragonard; canvases by Boucher; rare Sèvres porcelain; and more. Covering 12 acres, the gardens contain fragments of statuary from churches, monasteries, and torn-down palaces. One entire section is planted with cacti.

HITTING THE BEACH

The town's most visible and popular beaches include **Plage Passable,** on the northeastern "neck" of the Cap Ferrat peninsula, close to where it's connected to the French mainland; and **Plage Paloma,** near the peninsula's southernmost tip, and overlooked by the Chapelle St-Hospice. Neither have sandy surfaces (they're composed of pebbles and gravel), but they do have snack bars, souvenir stands, and beachfront restaurants. Most hotel clients opt to remain around the swimming pools of their hotels, and indeed, many hotels do not even have beaches of their own. A noteworthy exception is the Grand Hotel du Cap Ferrat, which acquired a beach around the turn of the century (the 20th century, not the 21st).

ACCOMMODATIONS
EXPENSIVE

✪ **Grand Hôtel du Cap-Ferrat.** Bd. du Général-de-Gaulle, 06230 St-Jean-Cap-Ferrat. ☎ **04-93-76-50-50.** Fax 04-93-76-04-52. www.grand-hotel-cap-ferrat.com. 53 units. A/C MINIBAR TV TEL. 1,200–7,100 F ($192–$1,136) double; 4,000–15,000 F ($640–$2,400) suite. AE, DC, MC, V.

One of the best features of this turn-of-the-century palace is its location: at the tip of the peninsula in the midst of a 14-acre garden of semitropical trees and manicured lawns. It has been the retreat of the international elite since 1908, and it occupies the same celestial status as the Réserve and Métropole in Beaulieu. Its cuisine even equals the Métropole's. Parts of the exterior have open loggias and big arched windows; you can also enjoy the views from the elaborately flowering terrace over the sea. Accommodations look as if the late Princess Grace might settle in comfortably at any minute. They are generally spacious and open to sea views. Rates include admission to the pool, Club Dauphin. The beach is accessible via funicular from the main building. The hotel is open year-round.

Dining/Diversions: The hotel's indoor/outdoor restaurant serves *cuisine du marché*, which might include salad of warm foie gras and chanterelle mushrooms, nage of crayfish and lobster, or breast of duckling with honey and cider vinegar. The dining room is one of the last of the great belle époque palaces on the Côte d'Azur. The meals and service are flawless but come at a very high price. The American-style bar opens onto the garden.

Amenities: 24-hour room service, same-day laundry, Olympic-size heated pool, tennis courts, hotel bicycles.

✪ **La Voile d'Or.** 31 av. Jean-Mermoz, St-Jean-Cap-Ferrat, 06230 Villefranche-sur-Mer. ☎ **04-93-01-13-13.** Fax 04-93-76-11-17. E-mail: voiledor@calva.net. 45 units. A/C MINI-BAR TV TEL. 1,150–3,800 F ($184–$608) double; 2,750–4,400 F ($440–$704) suite. Rates include continental breakfast. AE, MC, V. Closed Nov–Apr. Parking 100 F ($16).

The "Golden Sail" is a tour de force, offering intimate luxury in a converted villa. It's set at the edge of the little fishing port and yacht harbor, with a panoramic view of the coast. It's equal in every way to the Grand Hôtel except for its cuisine, which is just a notch below. The guest rooms, lounges, and restaurant all open onto terraces. The rooms are individually decorated with hand-painted reproductions, carved gilt headboards, baroque paneled doors, parquet floors, antique clocks, and paintings.

Dining/Diversions: Guests gather on the canopied outer terrace for lunch and in the evening dine in a stately room with Spanish armchairs and white wrought-iron chandeliers. The sophisticated menu offers regional specialties and international dishes, as well as classic French cuisine. Fixed-price menus cost from 350 F to 500 F ($56 to $80). The drawing room is richly decorated. Most intimate is a little bar, with Wedgwood-blue paneling and antique mirroring.

Amenities: Two pools, private beach.

MODERATE

Hôtel Brise Marine. Av. Jean-Mermoz, St-Jean-Cap-Ferrat, 06230 Villefranche-sur-Mer. ☎ **04-93-76-04-36.** Fax 04-93-76-11-49. www.hotel-brisemarine.com. E-mail: bmarine@nicematin.fr. 16 units. A/C TV TEL. 730–790 F ($116.80–$126.40) double. AE, DC, MC, V. Closed Nov–Jan.

This circa-1878 villa with a front and rear terrace is on a hillside. A long rose arbor, beds of subtropical flowers, palms, and pines provide an attractive setting. The atmosphere is casual and informal, and the rooms are comfortably but simply furnished. You can have breakfast either in the beamed lounge or under the rose trellis. The little corner bar is for afternoon drinks.

✪ **Hôtel Clair Logis.** 12 av. Centrale, 06230 St-Jean-Cap-Ferrat. ☎ **04-93-76-04-57.** Fax 04-93-76-11-85. www.hotel-clair-logis.fr. 18 units. TEL. 650–750 F ($104–$120) double. AE, DC, MC, V. Closed Nov to mid-Mar.

This rare find occupies what was a 19th-century villa surrounded by 2 acres of semi-tropical gardens. The hotel's most famous guest was de Gaulle, who lived in a room called *Strelitzias* (Bird of Paradise) during many of his retreats from Paris. The pleasant rooms, each individually named after a flower, are scattered over three buildings in the confines of the garden. The most romantic and spacious accommodations are in the main building; the seven rooms in the annex are the most modern but have the least character, and tend to be smaller and cheaper.

DINING

✪ **Le Provençal.** 2 av. Denis-Séméria. ☎ **04-93-76-03-97.** Reservations required. Main courses 230–360 F ($36.80–$57.60); fixed-price menus 280–350 F ($44.80–$56). AE, MC, V. Mid-May to mid-Oct, Fri–Sun noon–2:30pm, daily 7:30pm–midnight; Nov–Apr, Fri–Sun noon–3pm and 7:30–midnight. FRENCH.

With the possible exception of the Grand Hôtel's dining room, this is the grandest restaurant of this very grand resort. Near the top of Nice's highest peak, it has the most panoramic view, with sightlines that sweep, on good days, as far away as Menton and the Italian border. Many of the menu items are credited directly to the inspiration of "the Provençal" in the kitchens. Menu items include marinated artichoke hearts presented beside half a lobster, a tarte fine of potatoes with deliberately undercooked foie gras, rack of lamb with local herbs and tarragon sauce, and crayfish with asparagus and black-olive tapenade. The best way to appreciate the desserts is to order the house sampler, *les cinq desserts du Provençal*—a potpourri of five petite desserts that usually includes macaroons with chocolate and crème brûlée. With the passage of years here, the cooking seems more inspired than ever.

Le Sloop. Au Nouveau Port. ☎ **04-93-01-48-63.** Reservations recommended. Main courses 140–160 F ($22.40–$25.60); fixed-price menu 160 F ($25.60). AE, MC, V. June–Sept, Wed 7–9:30pm, Thurs–Tues noon–2pm and 7–11pm; Oct–Nov 15 and Dec 18–May, Thurs–Mon noon–2pm and 7–11pm. Closed Nov 15–Dec 20. FRENCH.

This is the most popular and most reasonably priced bistro in this very expensive area. Outfitted in blue and white inside and out, it sits directly at the edge of the port, overlooking the yachts in the harbor. A meal here might begin with a salad of flap mushrooms steeped "en cappuccino" with liquefied foie gras; or perhaps a sautéed panful of flap mushrooms served with grated parmesan cheese. This might be followed with a fillet of deboned sea bass served with a red wine sauce; or a mixed fish fry of three kinds of Mediterranean fish, bound together with olive oil and truffles. Dessert might include a custom-baked tarte with red plums, or any of about seven other desserts, each based on "the red fruits of the region." The regional wines are reasonably priced.

16 Beaulieu-sur-Mer

583 miles S of Paris, 6 miles E of Nice, 7 miles W of Monte Carlo

Protected from the cold north winds blowing down from the Alps, Beaulieu-sur-Mer is often referred to as "La Petite Afrique" (Little Africa). Like Menton, it has the mildest climate along the Côte d'Azur and is especially popular with wintering wealthy. Originally, English visitors staked it out, after an English industrialist founded a hotel here between the rock-studded slopes and the sea. Beaulieu is graced with lush vegetation, including oranges, lemons, and bananas, as well as palms.

ESSENTIALS

GETTING THERE   Most visitors **drive** from Nice via the Moyenne Corniche or the coastal highway. **Train** service connects Beaulieu with Nice, Monaco, and the rest of the Côte d'Azur. For rail information and schedules, call ☎ **08-36-35-35-35.**

VISITOR INFORMATION The **Office de Tourisme** is on place Georges-Clemenceau (☎ 04-93-01-02-21).

FUN ON & OFF THE BEACH

Beaulieu does have a beach, but don't expect soft sands. The beaches aren't as rocky as those in Nice or other nearby resorts, but they're still closer to gravel than to sand. The longer of the town's two free public beaches is **Petite Afrique**, adjacent to the yacht basin; the shorter is **Baie des Fourmis**, beneath the casino. **Africa Plage** (☎ 04-93-01-11-00) rents mattresses for 90 F ($14.40) per day. They also sell snacks and drinks.

The town boasts an important church, the late 19th-century **Église de Sacré-Coeur**, a quasi-Byzantine, quasi-Gothic mishmash at 13 bd. du Maréchal-Leclerc (☎ 04-93-01-18-24). With the same address and phone is the 12th-century Romanesque chapel of Santa Maria de Olivo, used mostly for temporary exhibits of painting, sculpture, and civic lore. Both sites are open daily from 8am to 7pm.

As you walk along the seafront promenade, you can see many stately belle époque villas that evoke the days when Beaulieu was the very height of fashion. Although you can't go inside, you'll see signs indicating **Villa Namouna**, which once belonged to Gordon Bennett, the owner of the *New York Herald*, and **Villa Léonine**, former home of the marquess of Salisbury.

For a memorable 2-hour walk, start directly north of boulevard Edouard-VII, where a path leads up the Riviera escarpment to **Sentier du Plateau St-Michel.** A belvedere here offers panoramic views from Cap d'Ail to the Estérel. A 1-hour alternative is the stroll along **promenade Maurice-Rouvier.** The promenade runs parallel to the water, stretching from Beaulieu to St-Jean. On one side you'll see the most elegant of mansions set in well-landscaped gardens; on the other you'll get views of the distant Riviera landscape and the peninsular point of St-Hospice.

Casino de Beaulieu, av. Fernand-Dunan (☎ 04-93-76-48-00), built in the Art Nouveau style in 1903, was revitalized with new management in 1997. The main part of the casino where the blackjack, roulette, and chemin de fer tables are housed is open every night from 8pm to dawn. The ambience is glamorous and men are required to wear jacket and tie. Entrance is 70 F ($11.20). For a more casual spot of gambling, the casino has a separate area reserved for slot machines only. Entrance is free and there is no dress code. This area is open every day from 11am to dawn. There are also a bar and a disco on the premises.

Villa Kérylos. Rue Gustave-Eiffel. ☎ **04-93-01-01-44.** Admission 40 F ($6.40) adults, 20 F ($3.20) children and seniors. Daily 10:30am–6pm.

This is a replica of an ancient Greek residence, painstakingly designed and built by the archaeologist Theodore Reinach. Inside, the cabinets are filled with a collection of Greek figurines and ceramics. But most interesting is the reconstructed Greek furniture, much of which would be fashionable today. One curious mosaic depicts the slaying of the minotaur and provides its own labyrinth (if you try to trace the path, expect to stay for weeks).

ACCOMMODATIONS
VERY EXPENSIVE

✪ **La Réserve de Beaulieu.** 5 bd. du Maréchal-Leclerc, 06310 Beaulieu-sur-Mer. ☎ **04-93-01-00-01.** Fax 04-93-01-28-99. www.reservebeaulieu.com. E-mail: reservebeaulieu@relaischateau.fr. 38 units. A/C MINIBAR TV TEL. High season 2,950–4,150 F ($472–$664) double, 6,160–9,450 F ($985.60–$1,512) suite; low season 980–2,180 F ($156.80–348.80) double, 3,150–5,690 F ($504–$910.40) suite. Rates even more astronomical during the Grand Prix of Monaco (June 1–4). AE, DC, MC, V. Closed Nov 20–Dec 20 and Jan–Mar. Parking 100 F ($16).

This pink-and-white fin-de-siècle palace on the Mediterranean is one of the Riviera's most famous hotels. Here you can sit having an apéritif watching the sun set over the Riviera while a pianist treats you to Mozart. A number of the public lounges open onto a courtyard with bamboo chairs, grass borders, and urns of flowers. The social life revolves around the main drawing room, much like the grand living room of a country estate. The rooms range widely in size and design; however, all are deluxe and individually decorated, with a beautiful view of either the mountains or the sea. Accommodations are sumptuous. They come with private safes, generous closets, rich carpeting, elegant fabrics, and deluxe mattresses. Most of them overlook the Mediterranean, and some even have their own private balconies. In 1998, the hotel joined the ranks of Europe's Relais & Châteaux.

Dining/Diversions: The dining room has a covered frescoed ceiling, parquet floors, crystal chandeliers, and picture windows facing the Mediterranean. Specialties are sea bass with thin slices of potatoes in savory tomato sauce, sea bream stuffed with local vegetables, and roast rack of lamb.

Amenities: Private harbor for yachts, submarine fishing gear, sauna, thalassotherapy, seawater pool.

✪ **Le Métropole.** 15 bd. du Maréchal-Leclerc, 06310 Beaulieu-sur-Mer. ☎ **04-93- 01-00-08.** Fax 04-93-01-18-51. www.le-metropole.com/. E-mail: metropole@relaischateaux.fr. 42 units. A/C MINIBAR TV TEL. July–Aug, 1,500–3,100 F ($240–$496) double, 3,700–4,400 F ($592–$704) suite; Sept–June, 1,000–2,100 F ($160–$336) double, 2,500–2,600 F ($400–$416) suite. Half board 450 F ($72) per person extra. AE, CB, DC, MC, V. Closed Oct 20–Dec 20.

This Italianate villa is as good as it gets, offering some of the most luxurious accommodations along the Côte d'Azur. It's classified as a Relais & Châteaux and set on 2 acres of grounds discreetly shut off from the traffic of the resort. Here you'll enter a world of polished French elegance, with lots of balconies opening onto sea views. The marble, Oriental carpets, and polite staff members set a pervasive tone. The guest rooms are furnished in tasteful fabrics and flowery wallpapers. The comfortable beds feature deluxe mattresses and quality linens.

Dining/Diversions: Though the in-house restaurant lost a star from the Michelin judges in 1997, the food is nonetheless superb. The restaurant has a seaside terrace/bar.

Amenities: 24-hour room service, concrete jetty for sunning, heated pool; tennis and golf nearby.

INEXPENSIVE

Hôtel Frisia. Bd. Eugène-Gauthier, 06310 Beaulieu-sur-Mer. ☎ **04-93-01-01-04.** Fax 04-93-01-31-92. E-mail: info@hotel-frisia.com. 32 units. A/C MINIBAR TV. 350–620 F ($56–$99.20) double. AE, MC, V. Closed Nov 12–Dec 14.

Most of the Frisia's rooms, decorated in a modern style, open onto views of the harbor. Expectedly, sea-view rooms are the most expensive. Public areas include a sunny garden and inviting lounges. English is widely spoken here, and the American ownership makes foreign guests feel especially welcome. Breakfast is the only meal served, but many reasonably priced dining places are nearby.

Hôtel Le Havre Bleu. 29 bd. du Maréchal-Joffre, 06310 Beaulieu-sur-Mer. ☎ **04-93- 01-01-40.** Fax 04-93-01-29-92. www.perso.wanadoo.fr/hotel.havrebleu. E-mail: tascal.cherny@ wanadoo.fr. 22 units. TEL. 330–350 F ($52.80–$56) double. AE, DC, MC, V.

Le Havre Bleu has one of the prettiest facades of any inexpensive hotel in town. Housed in a former Victorian villa, the hotel has a front garden dotted with flowering urns and arched ornate windows. The comfortable guest rooms are impeccable and functional. Breakfast is the only meal served.

Hôtel Marcellin. 18 av. Albert-1er, 06310 Beaulieu-sur-Mer. ☎ **04-93-01-01-69.** Fax 04-93-01-37-43. 21 units, 14 with bathroom. TEL. 180 F ($28.80) double without bathroom, 250–360 F ($40–$57.60) double with bathroom; 500–700 F ($80–$112) suite. MC, V. Closed Nov–Dec 15 and Feb.

The turn-of-the-century Marcellin is a good budget selection in an otherwise high-priced resort. The restored rooms come with homelike amenities and a southern exposure. The location isn't bad either: amid the town's congestion, near its western periphery, but only a 5-minute walk to the beach. Overall, this is a pleasant and well-maintained place to stay. Its two-star status granted by the government is well-deserved. Breakfast is the only meal served, but many restaurants are nearby.

DINING

La Pignatelle. 10 rue de Quincenet. ☎ **04-93-01-03-37.** Reservations recommended. Main courses 60–150 F ($9.60–$24); fixed-price menus 85–195 F ($13.60–$31.20). AE, MC, V. Thurs–Tues noon–2pm and 7–9:30pm. Closed mid-Nov to mid-Dec. FRENCH.

Even in this super-expensive resort town, you can find an excellent and affordable Provençal bistro. After all, the locals have to eat somewhere and not every visitor can afford the higher-priced palaces. Despite its relatively low prices, La Pignatelle prides itself on the fact that all the products that go into its robust cuisine are fresh. As a result, it's usually crowded. Specialties are salade Niçoise, a succulent version of *soupe de poissons* from which someone has labored to remove the bones, cassolette of mussels, monkfish steak garnished only with olive oil and herbs, scampi Provençal, tripe Niçoise, scallops, and a *"petite friture du pays"* that incorporates very small fish with Provençal traditions that are hundreds of years old.

Les Agaves. 4 av. Maréchal Foch. ☎ **04-93-01-13-12.** Reservations recommended. Main courses 55–190 F ($8.80–$30.40); bouillabaisse 250 F ($40) per person; fixed-price menu 175 F ($28). AE, MC, V. Tues–Sun noon–3pm; Tues–Sat 7:15–10:30pm. Closed Nov. FRENCH.

One of the most stylish and artfully managed restaurants in Beaulieu is housed within a turn-of-the-century villa across the street from the Beaulieu's railway station. U.S.-based publications such as *Bon Appétit* have praised the cuisine as delectable. Of particular note are a form of curry-enhanced scallops served with garlic-flavored tomatoes and parsley, lobster salad with mango, chopped shrimp with Provençal herbs, and several different preparations of foie gras. Fillet of sea bass with truffles and champagne sauce is particularly delectable.

17 Eze & La Turbie

585 miles S of Paris, 7 miles NE of Nice

The hamlets of Eze and La Turbie, though 4 miles apart, have so many similarities that most of France's tourist officials speak of them as if they're one. Both boast fortified feudal cores high in the hills overlooking the Provençal coast, and both were built during the early Middle Ages to stave off raids from corsairs who wanted to capture harem slaves and laborers. Clinging to the rocky hillsides around these hamlets are upscale villas, many of which have been built since the 1950s by retirees from colder climes. Closely linked, culturally and fiscally, to nearby Monaco, Eze and La Turbie have full-time populations of fewer than 3,000. The medieval cores of both contain art galleries, boutiques, and artisans' shops that have been restored.

Eze is accessible via the Moyenne (Middle) Corniche, La Turbie via the Grande (Upper) Corniche. Signs are positioned along the coastal road indicating the direction motorists should take to reach either of the hamlets.

The leading attraction in Eze is the **Jardin Exotique,** bd. du Jardin-Exotique (☎ **04-93-41-10-30**), a lushly landscaped showcase of exotic plants set in Eze-Village, at the pinnacle of the town's highest hill. Admission is 15 F ($2.40), free for children 11 and under. In July and August, it's open daily from 9am to 8pm; the rest of the year, it opens at 9am and closes between 5 and 7:30pm, depending on sunset.

La Turbie boasts a ruined monument erected by the ancient Roman emperor Augustus in 6 B.C., the **Trophée des Alps** (Trophy of the Alps). (Many locals call it La Trophée d'Auguste.) It rises near a rock formation known as La Tête de Chien, at the highest point along the Grand Corniche, 1,500 feet above sea level. The monument, restored with funds donated by Edward Tuck, was erected by the Roman Senate to celebrate the subjugation of the people of the French Alps by the Roman armies.

A short distance from the monument is the **Musée du Trophée des Alps,** rue Albert-1er, La Turbie (☎ **04-93-41-20-84**), a mini-museum containing finds from archaeological digs nearby and information about the monument's restoration. It's open daily from 9:30am to 5pm (until 6pm April to June, and until 7pm July to September). Admission is 25 F ($4) for adults, 15 F ($2.40) for students and ages 12 to 25, and free for children 11 and under. It's closed January 1, May 1, November, and December 25.

The **Office de Tourisme** is on place du Général-de-Gaulle, Eze-Village (☎ **04-93-41-26-00**).

ACCOMMODATIONS & DINING

Auberge Eric Rivot. 44 av. de la Liberté, 06360 Eze-Bord-de-Mer. ☎ **04-93-01-51-46.** Fax 04-93-01-58-40. E-mail: rivot.eric.@wanadoo.fr. 10 units. TV TEL. 420 F ($67.20) double. Half board 420 F ($67.20) per person extra. AE, V. Closed mid-Nov to Dec 1.

This straw-yellow stucco villa is a few steps from the Basse Corniche. The interior and the quiet rear terrace are filled with rattan chairs, exposed brick, and lots of brass. The simply furnished doubles draw mainly a summer crowd, though the inn is open most of the year. Half board is a good deal here. The meals are satisfying, with wine included.

✪ **Hostellerie du Château de la Chèvre d'Or.** Rue du Barri, 06360 Eze-Village. ☎ **04-92-10-66-66.** Fax 04-93-41-06-72. www.chevredor.com. E-mail: chevredor@ relaischateau.fr. 33 units. A/C MINIBAR TV TEL. 1,600–3,200 F ($256–$512) double; 3,200–15,000 F ($512–$2,400) suite. AE, MC, DC, V. Closed mid-Nov to Mar.

This miniature-village retreat was built in the 1920s in neo-Gothic style. It's a Relais & Châteaux in a complex of village houses, all with views of the coastline. But unlike most villages in the area, this mini-village doesn't have a beach. It's located on the side of a stone village off the Moyenne Corniche. The owner has had the interior of the "Golden Goat" flawlessly decorated to maintain its old character while adding modern comfort. Even if you don't stop in for a meal or a room, try to visit for a drink in the lounge, which has a panoramic view.

Dining/Diversions: This hotel maintains three restaurants, the most expensive and prestigious of which is the Restaurant de la Chèvre d'Or. It charges from 320 F to 490 F ($51.20 to $78.40) for a fixed-price lunch, and 690 F ($110.40) for a fixed-price dinner. Their middle-bracket choice is an Italian trattoria, Olivetto, and their least formal, least expensive choice is Le Grill du Château. All three enterprises are open daily, except during the hotel's annual closing noted above, for both lunch and dinner.

Amenities: Heated outdoor pool, tennis courts within a short walk, room service, concierge, laundry/dry cleaning.

18 Monaco

593 miles S of Paris, 11 miles E of Nice

Monaco, according to a famous quote from Somerset Maugham, is defined as 370 sunny acres peopled with shady characters. The outspoken Katharine Hepburn once called it "a pimple on the chin of the south of France." She wasn't referring to the principality's lack of beauty but rather to the preposterous idea of having a little country, a feudal anomaly, taking up some of the choicest coastline along the Riviera. Monaco became a property of the Grimaldi clan, a Genoese family, as early as 1297. With shifting loyalties, it has maintained something resembling independence ever since. In a fit of impatience the French annexed it in 1793, but the ruling family recovered it in 1814.

Hemmed in by France on three sides and the Mediterranean on the fourth, tiny Monaco staunchly maintains its independence. Even Charles de Gaulle couldn't force Prince Rainier to do away with his tax-free policy. As almost everybody in an overburdened world knows by now, the Monégasques do not pay taxes. Nearly all their country's revenue comes from tourism and gambling.

Monaco, or more precisely its capital of Monte Carlo, has for a century been a symbol of glamour. Its legend was enhanced by the 1956 marriage of the world's most eligible bachelor, Prince Rainier III, to the American actress Grace Kelly. She had met the prince when she was in Cannes for the film festival to promote *To Catch a Thief,* the Hitchcock movie she made with Cary Grant. A journalist friend arranged a *Paris Match* photo shoot with the prince, and the rest is history. A daughter, Caroline, was born to the royal couple in 1957; a son, Albert, in 1958; and a second daughter, Stephanie, in 1965. The Monégasques welcomed the birth of Caroline but went wild at the birth of Albert, a male heir. According to a 1918 treaty, Monaco would become an autonomous state under French protection should the ruling dynasty become extinct. However, the fact that Albert is still a bachelor has the entire principality concerned.

Though not always happy in her role, Princess Grace soon won the respect and adoration of her people. In 1982 she accidentally drove her sports car over a cliff. The Monégasques still mourn her death.

The second-smallest state in Europe (Vatican City is the tiniest), Monaco consists of four parts. The old town, **Monaco-Ville,** on a promontory, "the Rock," 200 feet high, is the seat of the royal palace and the government building, as well as the Oceanographic Museum. To the west of the bay, **La Condamine,** the home of the Monégasques, is at the foot of the old town, forming its harbor and port sector. Up from the port (walking is steep in Monaco) is **Monte Carlo,** once the playground of European royalty and still the center for wintering wealthy, the setting for the casino and its gardens and the deluxe hotels. The fourth part, **Fontvieille,** is a neat industrial suburb. Ironically, **Monte-Carlo Beach,** at the far frontier, is on French soil. It attracts a chic crowd, including movie stars in the skimpiest bikinis and thongs.

No one used to go to Monaco in summer, but now July and August tend to be so crowded it's hard to get a room. The Monégasques very frankly court an affluent crowd. But with the decline of royalty, Monaco has had to develop a broader base of tourism. You can now stay here moderately, though still not cheaply. As always, you can lose your shirt at the casinos. "Suicide Terrace" at the casino, though not used as frequently as in the old days, is still a real temptation to many who have gambled away family fortunes.

Monaco

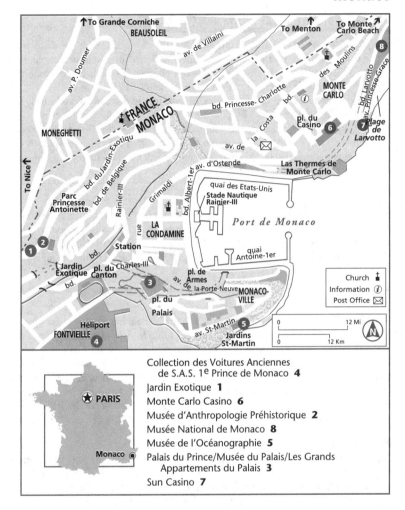

To Grande Corniche
BEAUSOLEIL
To Menton
To Monte Carlo Beach

av. de Villaini

av. P. Doumer

des Moulins

MONTE CARLO

bd. Princesse-Charlotte

la Costa

bd.

av. Larvotto
av. Princesse-Grace

FRANCE
MONACO

MONEGHETTI

pl. du Casino

To Nice

bd. duJardin-Exotiqu

bd. de Belgique

av. de

Plage de Larvotto

Parc Princesse Antoinette

Rainier-III

Grimaldi

bd. Albert-1er

av. d'Ostende

Las Thermes de Monte Carlo

quai des Etats-Unis
Stade Nautique Rainier-III

Port de Monaco

rue

LA CONDAMINE

Station

bd.

quai Antoine-1er

Jardin Exotique

pl. du Canton

pl. du Charles-III

pl. de Armes

av. de la Porte-Neuve

MONACO-VILLE

bd.

pl. du Palais

Héliport
FONTVIEILLE

av. St-Martin

Jardins St-Martin

Church ✝
Information ⓘ
Post Office ✉

0   12 Mi
0   12 Km

PARIS

Monaco

Collection des Voitures Anciennes
    de S.A.S. 1e Prince de Monaco 4
Jardin Exotique 1
Monte Carlo Casino 6
Musée d'Anthropologie Préhistorique 2
Musée National de Monaco 8
Musée de l'Océanographie 5
Palais du Prince/Musée du Palais/Les Grands
    Appartements du Palais 3
Sun Casino 7

Even when family fortunes aren't slipping through the fingers of gamblers, the casino has been the subject of countless legends and the setting for many films (Richard Burton presented Elizabeth Taylor with the obscenely huge Koh-i-noor diamond here). Because Monaco is a tax haven, many celebrities have in recent years become residents, including Plácido Domingo, Claudia Schiffer, Boris Becker, and Ringo Starr.

ESSENTIALS

GETTING THERE Monaco has rail, bus, and highway connections from other coastal cities, especially Nice. **Trains** arrive every 30 minutes from Cannes, Nice, Menton, and Antibes. For more rail information and schedules, call ☎ 08-36-35-35-35. Monaco's railway station (Gare SNCF) is on the avenue Prince Pierre. It's a long steep walk uphill from the train station to Monte Carlo. If you'd rather take a taxi but can't find one at the station, call ☎ 93-50-56-28 or 93-15-01-01. There are

---

Reach Out & Touch Someone in Monaco

To call Monaco from within France, dial 00 (the new access code for all international long-distance calls placed from France), followed by Monaco's new country code, 377, and then the eight-digit local phone number. (Don't dial the 33 code; this is the country code for France, which no longer applies to Monaco.)

To call Monaco from North America, dial the international access code, 011, followed by the country code, 377, plus the local eight-digit Monaco number.

To call any other country from within Monaco, dial 00 (the international access code), then the applicable country code, and the number. For example, to call Cannes, you would dial 00, 33 (France's country code), 4 (the city code, without the zero), and the eight-digit number.

---

no border formalities for anyone entering Monaco from mainland France. Monaco is a rather lengthy **drive** from Paris. Take A6 south to Lyon. At Lyon, connect with A7 south to Aix-en-Provence; from here, take A6 south directly to Monaco. If you're already on the Riviera, drive from Nice along N7 northeast. It's only 12 miles, but with traffic, the drive can take 30 minutes.

VISITOR INFORMATION   The **Direction du Tourisme** office is at 2A bd. des Moulins (☎ 92-16-61-16).

SPECIAL EVENTS   Some of the most-watched **car-racing events** in Europe are held in January (Le Rallye) and May (the Grand Prix). Mid-April witnesses one of the Riviera's most famous **tennis tournaments.** Every February, Monte Carlo is home to a week-long convention that attracts media moguls from virtually everywhere: **Le Festival International de la Télévision,** wherein the winning shows from all over the world are broadcast and judged on their individual merits. For information and further details, write or call Festival International de la Télévision, 4 bd. des Jardins Exotiques (☎ 93-10-40-60).

FUN ON & OFF THE BEACH

BEACHES   Just outside the border, on French (not Monacan) soil, the **Monte-Carlo Beach Club** adjoins the Monte-Carlo Beach Hotel, 22 av. Princesse-Grace (☎ 04-93-28-66-66). Permeated with intricate social rituals that might not be immediately visible to first-timers, the beach club has thrived for years as an integral part of Monaco's social life. Princess Grace used to come here in flowery swimsuits, greeting her friends and subjects with humor and style. The sand is replenished at regular intervals, and you'll find two large pools (one for children), beach cabanas, a restaurant, a cafe, and a bar. As the temperature drops in late August, expect the beach to close for the winter. The admission charge, depending on the season, varies from 150 F to 200 F ($24 to $32) for the day, which grants you access to the public changing rooms, toilets, restaurants, and bar. A day's use of a private cubicle, where you can lock up your street clothes, costs an additional 65 F ($10.40). And a full day's rental of a mattress for sunbathing costs 75 F ($12). As usual, topless is *de rigeur,* but bottomless isn't.

Monaco itself, the quintessential kingdom by the sea, also offers swimming and sunbathing at the popular **Plage de Larvotto,** off av. Princesse-Grace (☎ 93-30-63-84). There's no charge for entering this strip of beach, whose sands are frequently replenished with sand hauled in by barge. The beach is open to the public at all hours.

GOLF   The prestigious **Monte Carlo Golf Club,** Route N7, La Turbie (☎ **04-93-41-09-11**), on French soil, is a par-72 golf course with scenic panoramas. Certain perks (including use of electric golf buggies) are reserved for members. Before they're allowed to play, nonmembers are asked to show proof of membership in another golf club and provide evidence of their handicap ratings. Greens fees for 18 holes are 400 F ($64) Monday through Friday and 500 F ($80) Saturday and Sunday. Clubs can be rented for 80 F ($12.80). The course is open daily from 8am to sunset.

SPA TREATMENTS   In 1908 the Société des Bains de Mer launched a seawater (thalassotherapy) spa in Monte Carlo. It was inaugurated by Prince Albert I himself. However, it was bombed during World War II and didn't reopen until 1996. **Les Thermes Marins de Monte-Carlo,** 2 av. de Monte-Carlo (☎ **92-16-40-40**), is one of the largest spas in Europe. Spread over four floors are a gigantic pool, a Turkish *haman,* a diet restaurant, a juice bar, two tanning booths, a fitness center, a beauty center, and private treatment rooms. A day pass, giving access to the sauna, steam rooms, fitness facilities, and swimming pools costs 730 F ($116.80). Hour-long massages cost an additional fee, ranging from 400 F to 700 F ($64 to $112), depending on what type of massage you want.

SWIMMING   Of course, you can try the beaches mentioned above. But if you're looking for a pool instead, you might want to try these two. Built to overlook the yacht-clogged harbor, the stupendous **Stade Nautique Rainier-III,** quai Albert-1er, at La Condamine (☎ **93-30-64-83**), a pool frequented by the Monégasques, was a gift from the prince to his loyal subjects. It's open May to October daily from 9am to 6pm (open till midnight in July and August); closed November to April. Admission is 25 F ($4).

In cooler weather, try the indoor **Piscine du Prince Héréditaire Albert,** in the Stade Louis II, at 7 av. de Castellane (☎ **92-05-42-13**). It's open Monday, Tuesday, Thursday, and Friday from 7:30am to 2:30pm; Saturday from 2 to 6pm; and Sunday from 9am to 1pm. Admission is 15 F ($2.40).

TENNIS & SQUASH   The **Monte Carlo Country Club,** in France on av. Princesse-Grace, Roquebrune-St-Roman (☎ **04-93-41-30-15**), includes 21 clay and two concrete courts. The 220 F ($35.20) entrance fee provides access to a restaurant, a health club with Jacuzzi and sauna, a putting green, a beach, squash courts, and the well-maintained tennis courts. Plan to spend at least half a day, ending a round of tennis with use of any of the other facilities. It's open daily from 8am to 8pm or 9pm, depending on the season.

SHOPPING

Bijoux Cassio, 10 bd. des Moulins (☎ **93-25-55-10**), sells only imitation gemstones. They're rather shamelessly copied from the real McCoys sold by Cartier and Van Cleef & Arpels. Made in Italy of gold-plated silver, the fake jewelry costs between 200 and 2,000 F ($32 and $320) per piece, many thousands of francs less than what you might have paid for the authentic gems.

The **Boutique du Rocher,** 1 av. de la Madone (☎ **93-30-91-17**), is the largest of two roughly equivalent boutiques opened in 1966 by Princesse Grace as the official retail outlets of her charitable foundation. The organization merchandizes Monégasque and Provençal handcrafts. A short walk from place du Casino, the shop sells carved frames for pictures or mirrors; housewares; gift items crafted from porcelain, textiles, and wood; toys; and dolls. On the premises are workshops where local artisans produce the goods you'll find for sale. The organization also maintains a second branch at 25 rue Émile de Loth, in Monaco-Ville (☎ **93-30-33-99**).

Brett Merrill, 17 bd. des Moulins (☎ **93-50-33-85**), is a menswear store aiming at a solid middle-bracket man who simply wants to dress appropriately and look good. You can pick up a swimsuit, shorts, slacks, a blazer, and a pair of socks to replace the ones you ruined by too many walking tours, at prices that won't require that you remortgage your house.

You don't have to be Princess Caroline to be able to afford to shop in Monaco, especially now that **FNAC** (☎ **93-10-81-81**), a member of the big French chain that sells records, CDs, tapes, and books, has opened in the heart of town at the **Centre Commercial Le Métropole,** 17 av. des Spélugues in the Jardins du Casino, alongside the Hôtel Métropole and across from the casino.

If you insist on ultra-fancy stores, you'll find them cheek by jowl with the Hôtel de Paris and the casino, lining the streets leading to the Hôtel Hermitage, or across from the gardens at the mini-mall Park Palace. Allée Serge-Diaghilev is just that, an alley, but a very tiny one filled with designer shops.

To get a better perspective on upper-middle-class shopping, visit the **Galaxie de Metropole,** 17 av. des Spélugues. It has a few specialty shops worth visiting (especially if you aren't going into France). Check out **Geneviève Lethu** (☎ **93-50-09-41**) for colorful and country tabletop design; or **Manufacture de Monaco** (☎ **93-50-64-63**) for glorious bone china and elegant tabletop design. If the prices send you to bed, two doors away is a branch of the chic but often affordable French linen house **Yves Delorme** (☎ **93-50-08-70**). **Royal Food** (☎ **93-15-05-04**) is a tiny gourmet grocery store down a set of curving stairs hidden in the side entrance of the mall; here you can buy food items from France, Lebanon, and the U.S.A., or stock up for *le pique-nique* or for your day trips. This market is open Monday to Saturday from 9:30am to 8pm.

For real-people shopping, stroll **rue Grimaldi,** the principality's most commercially minded street, near the fruit, flower, and food market (see below) and **boulevard des Moulins,** closer to the casino, where glamorous boutiques specialize in international chicness. There's also an all-pedestrian thoroughfare with shops less forbiddingly chic than those along boulevard des Moulins: **rue Princesse-Caroline** is loaded with bakeries, flower shops, and the closest thing you'll find to funkiness in Monaco. Also check out the **Formule 1** shop, 15 rue Grimaldi (☎ **93-15-92-44**), where everything from racing helmets to specialty keychains and T-shirts celebrates the roar of high-octane racing machines.

MARKETS   Should you be looking for the heart and soul of the real Monaco, get away from the glitz and head to place des Armes for the **fruit, flower, and food market** held daily from 7:30am to 1pm. It has an indoor and an outdoor market complete with a fountain, cafes, and hand-painted vegetable tiles set beneath your feet. While the outdoor market packs up promptly at noon, some dealers at the indoor market stay open to 2pm. If you prefer bric-a-brac, there's a small but very funky (especially for Monaco) flea market, **Les Puces de Fontvieille,** held Saturday from 10am to 5:30pm at the Espace Fontvieille, a panoramic open-air site near the heliport in Monaco's Fontvieille district.

SEEING THE SIGHTS

Les Grands Appartements du Palais. Place du Palais. ☎ **93-25-18-31.** Combination ticket 40 F ($6.40) adults, 20 F ($3.20) children 8–14, free for children 7 and under. Palace, June–Sept, daily 9:30am–6:30pm; Oct, daily 10am–5pm. Closed Nov–May. Museum, June–Sept, daily 9:30am–6:30pm; Oct–Nov 11, daily 10am–5pm; Dec 17–May, Tues–Sun 10:30am–12:30pm and 2–5pm. Closed Nov 12–Dec 16.

During summer, most daytrippers from Nice want to see the Italianate home of Monaco's royal family, the Palais du Prince, dominating the principality from "the Rock." A tour of Les Grands Appartements allows you a glimpse of the Throne Room and some of the art collection (including works by Brueghel and Holbein) as well as Princess Grace's stunning state portrait. The palace was built in the 13th century, and part dates from the Renaissance. You also see the chamber where England's George III died. The ideal time to arrive is 11:55am to watch the 10-minute **Relève de la Garde** (changing of the guard).

In a wing of the palace, the **Musée du Palais du Prince (Souvenirs Napoléoniens et Collection d'Archives),** place du Palais (☎ **93-25-18-31**), contains a collection of mementos of Napoléon and Monaco itself. When the royal residence is closed, this museum is the only part of the palace the public can visit.

Jardin Exotique. Bd. du Jardin-Exotique. ☎ **93-15-29-80.** Admission to garden 40 F ($6.40) adults, 19 F ($3.05) children 6–18, free for children 5 and under. June–Sept, daily 9am–7pm; Oct–May, daily 9am–6pm.

Built on the side of a rock, the gardens are known for their cactus collection. They were begun by Prince Albert I, who was a naturalist and a scientist. He spotted some succulents growing in the palace gardens and created this garden from them. You can also explore the grottoes here, as well as the **Musée d'Anthropologie Préhistorique** (☎ **93-15-80-06**). The view of the principality is splendid.

Musée de l'Océanographie. Av. St-Martin. ☎ **93-15-36-00.** Admission 60 F ($9.60) adults, 30 F ($4.80) children 6–18, free for children 5 and under. Apr–June and Sept, daily 9am–7pm; July–Aug, daily 9am–8pm; Mar and Oct, daily 9:30am–7pm; Nov–Feb, daily 10am–6pm.

This museum was founded in 1910 by Albert I, great-grandfather of the present prince. In the main rotunda is a statue of Albert in his favorite costume: that of a sea captain. Displayed are specimens he collected during 30 years of expeditions. The aquarium, one of the finest in Europe, contains more than 90 tanks.

Prince Albert's collection is exhibited in the zoology room. Some of the exotic creatures here were unknown before he captured them. You'll see models of the oceanographic ships aboard which he directed his scientific cruises from 1885 to 1914. The most important part of the laboratory has been preserved and reconstituted as closely as possible. Skeletons of specimens are on the main floor, including a giant whale that drifted ashore at Pietra Ligure in 1896. The skeleton is remarkable for its healed fractures sustained when a vessel struck the animal as it was drifting asleep on the surface. An exhibition devoted to the discovery of the ocean is in the physical-oceanography room on the first floor. Underwater movies are shown continuously in the lecture room.

Collection des Voitures Anciennes de S.A.S. le Prince de Monaco. Les Terrasses de Fontvieille. ☎ **92-05-28-56.** Admission 30 F ($4.80) adults, 15 F ($2.40) students and children 8–14, free for children 7 and under. Daily 10am–6pm. Closed Nov.

Prince Rainier III has opened a showcase of his private collection of more than 100 exquisitely restored vintage autos, including the 1956 Rolls-Royce Silver Cloud that carried the prince and princess on their wedding day. It was given to the royal couple by Monaco shopkeepers as a wedding present. A 1952 Austin Taxi on display was once used as the royal "family car." Other exhibits are a Woodie, a 1937 Ford station wagon once used by Prince Louis II when on hunting trips, and a 1925 Bugatti 35B, winner of the Monaco Grand Prix in 1929. Other outstanding autos are a 1903 De Dion Bouton and a 1986 Lamborghini Countach.

Musée National de Monaco. 17 av. Princesse-Grace. ☎ **93-30-91-26.** Admission 30 F ($4.80) adults, 20 F ($3.20) children 6–14, free for children 5 and under. Easter–Sept, daily 10am–6:30pm; Oct–Easter, daily 10am–12:15pm and 2:30–6:30pm.

In a villa designed by Charles Garnier (architect of Paris's Opéra Garnier), this museum houses one of the world's greatest collections of mechanical toys and dolls. See especially the 18th-century Neapolitan crib, which contains some 200 figures. This collection, assembled by Mme de Galea, was presented to the principality in 1972; it stemmed from the 18th- and 19th-century trend of displaying new fashions on doll models.

ACCOMMODATIONS
VERY EXPENSIVE

✪ **Hôtel de Paris.** Place du Casino, 98000 Monaco. ☎ **92-16-30-00.** Fax 93-16-38-50. www.montecarloresort.com. E-mail: hp@sbm.mc. 200 units. A/C MINIBAR TV TEL. 2,240–3,710 F ($358.40–$593.60) double; from 6,200 F ($992) suite. AE, DC, MC, V. Parking 130 F ($20.80).

On the resort's ornate main plaza, opposite the casino, this is one of the world's most famous hotels and most spectacular beaux-arts monuments. Linked with the sybaritic, high-spending image of Monte Carlo, it's the principality's choice address, more famous and legendary even than the Hermitage (see below). At least two dozen movie companies have used its lobby as a background. The ornate facade has marble pillars, and the impressive lounge has an Art Nouveau rose window at the peak of the dome. The hotel is furnished with a dazzling decor that includes marble pillars, statues, crystal chandeliers, sumptuous carpets, Louis XVI chairs, and a wall-size fin-de-siècle mural. The guest rooms are fashionable and, in many cases, sumptuous. They come in a variety of styles, either with an elaborate period decor or a fashionably contemporary one. Some of the rooms are so large that Edward VII would find plenty of living space for his corpulent body (were he still alive). Elegant tasteful fabrics, rich carpeting, and classic accessories make this a continuing favorite among the world's most discerning guests. Note that the rooms opening onto the sea aren't as spacious as those in the rear.

Dining: The evening usually begins in the bar. The hotel's most famous dining options are Le Louis XV (see "Dining," below) and Le Grill. Both restaurants benefit from a collection of rare fine wines kept in a dungeon chiseled out of the rocks. The less formal Restaurant Côté Jardin offers a daily lunch buffet whose rich offerings are inspired by the Mediterranean.

Amenities: Thermes Marins spa, directly connected to both the Hôtel de Paris and the Hôtel Hermitage, offers complete cures of thalassotherapy under medical supervision (including "antismoking," "anticellulite thighs," and "postnatal" cures); large indoor pool; two saunas; fitness center; beauty center; room service; concierge; babysitting; valet parking.

✪ **Hôtel Hermitage.** Square Beaumarchais, 98005 Monaco CEDEX. ☎ **92-16-40-00.** Fax 92-16-38-52. www.montecarloresort.com. E-mail: HH@SBM.MC. 247 units. A/C MINIBAR TV TEL. 1,910–3,020 F ($305.60–$483.20) double; 3,020–11,030 F ($483.20–$1,764.80) suite. AE, MC, V. Parking 120 F ($19.20).

Picture yourself sitting in a wicker armchair, being served drinks under an ornate stained-glass dome with an encircling wrought-iron balcony. You can do this at the clifftop Hermitage, with its wedding cake facade. The "palace" was the creation of Jean Marquet (who also created marquetry). Large brass beds anchor every room, wherein decoratively framed doors open onto balconies. Even the smallest rooms are medium in size, the largest one fit for the arrival of the biggest movie star with the most trunks. Luxury is the watchword here. Large mirrors, spacious lighted closets, private safes, elegant fabrics and upholstery, and sumptuous beds with luxurious mattresses make living here idyllic. The newest rooms are in the Coasta and Excelsior wings. They lack tradition, but they equal the accommodations in the main building, which many guests still prefer because of its old-fashioned French decor and streetfront exposures. High-season rates are charged during Christmas, New Year's, Easter, and July and August.

Dining/Diversions: A stylish restaurant with a refined cuisine, Vista Mare, specializes in fresh seafood. The Bar Terrasse is a chic piano bar at night.

Amenities: Concierge, room service, massage, maid service, gym, Jacuzzi, sauna, tennis courts, 18-hole golf course.

Le Monte Carlo Grand Hotel. 12 av. des Spélugues, 98007 Monaco CEDEX. ☎ **93-50-65-00.** Fax 93-30-01-57. www.monaco.mc. E-mail: grandhotel@monaco.mc. 619 units. A/C MINIBAR TV TEL. 1,950–2,400 F ($312–$384) double; 3,000–8,400 F ($480–$1,344) suite. AE, DC, MC, V. Parking 120 F ($19.20).

Originally conceived and built by the Loews Corporation, this glittering modern palace hotel was bought in late 1998 by a consortium of local investors, and renamed. It hugs the sea coast from a position below the terraces that support the famous casino, on one of the most valuable pieces of real estate along the Côte d'Azur. Architecturally daring when it was completed in 1975 (some of its foundations were sunk directly into the seabed, and some of the principality's busiest highways roar beneath it), the resort is now viewed as an integral and much-appreciated enhancement of Monégasque life. It contains Monaco's highest concentration of restaurants, bars, and nightclubs—think of it as Las Vegas with a Gallic accent. Guest rooms are tastefully, even conservatively, furnished in a style somewhere between Los Angeles and Miami. Each has a summery, pastel-colored decor that's flooded with light from big windows, and views over the town or the sea.

Dining/Diversions: There's a sprawling lobby bar festooned with potted palms and a view of the sea. L'Argentin serves South American-style grilled meats and succulent, very fresh fish. Near the rooftop, Le Pistou re-creates the flavors of Provence. There's also the cavernous Sun Casino in the lobby, combining aspects of Atlantic City with *La Belle France,* and a separate area with slot machines on the seventh floor. Le Café Viennois is the place for elaborate pastries, teas, snacks, and coffee. La Truffe is open only for dinner.

Amenities: Easy access to tennis, golf, deep-sea fishing, sailing, and scuba diving; and a radically upgraded, state-of-the-arts fitness center that was redesigned and reconfigured in 1999.

Monte-Carlo Beach Hotel. Av. Princesse-Grace, Monte-Carlo Beach, 06190 Roquebrune/Cap-Martin. ☎ **04-93-28-66-66.** Fax 04-93-78-14-18. 45 units. A/C MINIBAR TV TEL. 1,800–2,700 F ($288–$432) double; 2,700–4,500 F ($432–$720) suite. AE, DC, MC, V. Closed Jan–Feb. Free parking. The hotel is located on the France/Monaco border.

Despite its name, this hotel is in France, not Monaco. Built in 1928, it was known for years as the "Old Beach Hotel" until the Société des Bains de Mer decided that that was too unglamorous a title for such a luxury retreat. Tons of money later—most recently in 1995—it emerged with a new name and vastly improved rooms and facilities. The most pampered guest always asks for the most beautiful accommodation in the house, the spacious circular unit above the lobby. Eva Peron stayed here in 1947 during her infamous Rainbow Tour of Europe. Princess Grace came here almost every day in summer to paddle around the pool, a rendezvous for the rich and beautiful. All of the rooms are identical, right down to the sea view.

Dining/Diversions: The greatest choice of dining venues is available between June and September, when "Le Restaurant," the hotel's best, serves gourmet meals at both lunch and dinner. The reliable and consistent "Le Rivage" offers brasserie-style lunches and dinners from a point near the pool, and is the only restaurant open year-round. Le Potinière features gastronomic lunches, but isn't open for dinner in any season. La Vigie, a short walk from the hotel, and accessible to several piers where yacht-owners can tie up their boats, presents a series of buffets inspired by the cuisine of Provence.

Amenities: The most famous pool in the area; a beachfront kiosk arranging water-skiing and water scooters; tennis courts within a 10-minute walk.

MODERATE

Hôtel Alexandra. 33 bd. Princesse-Charlotte, 98000 Monaco. ☎ **93-50-63-13.** Fax 92-16-06-48. 56 units. A/C TV TEL. 650–880 F ($104–$140.80) double. AE, DC, MC, V. Parking 45 F ($7.20).

This hotel is on a busy and often-noisy street corner in the center of the business district above the Casino Gardens. Its comfortably furnished guest rooms don't generate much excitement, but they're reliable and respectable. The Alexandra knows it can't compete with the giants of Monaco and doesn't even try. But it attracts those who'd like to visit the principality without spending a fortune.

Hôtel du Louvre. 16 bd. des Moulins, 98000 Monaco. ☎ **93-50-65-25.** Fax 04-93-30-23-68. E-mail: hotel-louvre@monte-carlo.mc. 33 units. A/C MINIBAR TV TEL. 780–980 F ($124.80–$156.80) double. AE, DC, MC, V. Parking 42 F ($6.70).

Built like a traditional century-old mansion, this hotel is filled with antique furniture. The guest rooms are comfortable, carpeted, and come in a variety of shapes and sizes. Expect to pay higher prices for rooms facing the sea. Breakfast is the only meal served.

INEXPENSIVE

Hôtel Cosmopolite. 4 rue de la Turbie, 98000 Monaco. ☎ **93-30-16-95.** Fax 93-30-23-05. 24 units, none with toilet, all with sink, some with shower. 250 F ($40) double without shower or toilet, 320–370 F ($51.20–$59.20) with shower but without toilet. No credit cards. Free parking on street.

When it was built in the 1930s, this hotel was sited in the then-fashionable neighborhood a few steps downhill from the railway station. Today it's an appealingly dowdy Art Deco monument with three floors, no elevator, and comfortable but anonymous-looking rooms. Madame Gay Angèle, the English-speaking owner, is proud of her "Old Monaco" establishment. Her more expensive rooms have showers, but the cheapest way to stay here is to request a room without a shower—there are adequate facilities in the hallway. Mattresses and towels are a bit thin, but there is still reasonable comfort here, especially at these prices.

Hôtel de France. 6 rue de la Turbie, 98000 Monaco. ☎ **93-30-24-64.** Fax 92-16-13-34. www.monte-carlo.MC/france. E-mail: hotel-france@monte-carlo.mc. 26 units. TV TEL. 490 F ($78.40) double; 610 F ($97.60) triple. Rates include breakfast. MC, V. Parking 45 F ($7.20).

Not all Monégasques are rich, as a stroll along this street will convince you. Here you'll find some of the cheapest living and eating places in the high-priced principality. This 19th-century hotel, 3 minutes from the rail station, has modest furnishings but is clean and comfortable.

DINING

VERY EXPENSIVE

✪ **Le Louis XV.** In the Hôtel de Paris, place du Casino. ☎ **92-16-30-01.** Reservations recommended. Jacket and tie required for men. Main courses 310–590 F ($49.60–$94.40); fixed-price menus 500–980 F ($80–$156.80) at lunch, 860–980 F ($137.60–$156.80) at dinner. AE, DC, MC. July–Aug, Wed 8–10pm, Thurs–Mon noon–2pm and 8–10pm; Sept–June, Thurs–Mon noon–2pm and 8–10pm. Closed Nov 28–Dec 28 and Feb 20–Mar 7. FRENCH/ITALIAN.

On the lobby level of the five-star Hôtel de Paris, the three-star Louis XV offers what one critic called "down-home Riviera cooking within a Fabergé egg." Despite the place's regal trappings, the culinary star chef Alain Ducasse creates a refined but not overly adorned cuisine, served by the finest staff in Monaco. Everything is light, attuned to the seasons, with an intelligent and modern interpretation of both Provençal and northern Italian dishes. Ducasse is now dividing his time between this glittering enclave and his new restaurant in Paris, but his name still commands the finest ingredients in Europe wherever he goes.

EXPENSIVE

Le Café de Paris. Place du Casino. ☎ **92-16-20-20.** Reservations recommended. Main courses 100–210 F ($16–$33.60). AE, DC, MC, V. Daily 8am–4am. FRENCH.

Its *plats du jour* are well-prepared, and its location, the plaza adjacent to both the casino and the Hôtel de Paris, provides you with a front-row view of the comings and goings on the nerve center of Monte Carlo. But to our tastes, this 1985 re-creation of old-time Monaco is a bit too theme-ish, a bit too enraptured with the devil-may-care casino-conscious glamour of turn-of-the-century Monte Carlo, and a bit too claustro-phobic to be really comfortable. Despite that, the Café de Paris continues to draw an active crowd of patrons who appreciate the materialistic razzmatazz, the glass and chrome, and the casually upscale format. Menu items change frequently, and platters, especially at lunchtime, are appreciated by local office workers because they can be served and consumed relatively quickly. Adjacent to the restaurant, you'll find (and hear) a jangling collection of slot machines and a cliché-riddled cluster of boutiques selling expensively casual resort wear and souvenirs.

Rampoldi. 3 av. des Spélugues. ☎ **93-30-70-65.** Reservations required. Main courses 120–240 F ($19.20–$38.40). AE, MC, V. Daily 12:15–2:30pm and 7:30–11:30pm. FRENCH/ITALIAN.

More than any other restaurant in Monte Carlo, Rampoldi is inextricably linked to the charming but somewhat dated interpretation of *La Dolce Vita*. Established in the 1950s, and staffed with a complementary mix of old and new, it has a spirit that's more Italian than French. It also serves some of the best cuisine in Monte Carlo from an agreeable location at the edge of the Casino Gardens. Menu items include a suc-culent array of such pastas as tortelloni with cream and white truffle sauce; sea bass roasted in a salt crust; ravioli stuffed with crayfish; chateaubriand with béarnaise sauce; and veal kidneys in Madeira sauce. Crêpes Suzette makes a spectacular finish.

MODERATE

Le Texan. 4 rue Suffren-Reymond. ☎ **93-30-34-54.** Reservations recommended. Main courses 68–148 F ($10.90–$23.70). AE, DC, MC, V. Daily noon–midnight. TEX-MEX.

These Tex-Mex specialties have entertained even the most discriminating French taste buds. There's a handful of outdoor tables, a long bar, a roughly plastered dining room draped with the flag of the Lone Star State, and a scattering of Mexican artifacts. You'll find Le Texan on a sloping residential street leading down to the old harbor—a world away from the glittering casinos and nightlife of the upper reaches. Menu items include T-bone steak, barbecued ribs, pizzas, nachos, tacos, a Dallasburger (*avec* guacamole), and the best margaritas in town.

INEXPENSIVE

Stars 'n Bars. 6 quai Antoine-1er. ☎ **93-97-95-95.** Reservations recommended. Dinner salads and platters 60–140 F ($9.60–$22.40); sandwiches 45–80 F ($7.20–$12.80). AE, DC, MC, V. Tues–Sun 11am–midnight. AMERICAN.

This place deliberately revels in the cross-cultural differences that have contributed so much to Monaco's recent history. Modeled on the sports bars popular in the States, it features two distinct dining and drinking areas devoted to American-style food, as well as a third-floor space, The Club, which is a sports bar with memorabilia donated by many athletes of note. There's even a disco every night after midnight (sometimes with live performances). No one will mind if you drop in just for a drink—they cost 45 F to 90 F ($7.20 to $14.40) each—but if you're hungry, menu items read like an homage to the macho American experience. Try an Indy 500, a Triathlon salad, a Slam Dunk sandwich, or the Breakfast of Champions (eggs and bacon and all the fixings). If you've got kids under 12, order the Little Leaguer's Platter. Unless an artist of international note appears, there's never a cover charge.

MONACO AFTER DARK
CASINOS

Sun Casino, in the Monte Carlo Grand Hotel, 12 av. des Spélugues (☎ 93-50-65-00), is a huge room filled with one-armed bandits. It also features blackjack, craps, and American roulette. Additional slot machines are available on the roof starting at 11am—for those who want to gamble with a wider view of the sea. It's open daily from 5pm to 4am (to 5am for slot machines). Admission is free.

A speculator, François Blanc, developed the ✪ **Monte Carlo Casino,** place du Casino (☎ 92-16-21-21), into the most famous in the world, attracting the exiled aristocracy of Russia, Sarah Bernhardt, Mata Hari, King Farouk, and Aly Khan. The architect of Paris's Opéra Garnier, Charles Garnier, built the oldest part of the casino, and it remains an extravagant example of the 19th century's most opulent architecture. It's rather schizophrenically divided into an area devoted to the casino and others for different kinds of nighttime entertainment, including a theater (see below) presenting opera and ballet.

Unlike the jaded roués whose presence here became a cliché during the belle époque, the new grand dukes are likely to include fast-moving international business-people on short-term vacations and a crowd that's infinitely more democratized than in days of yore. Baccarat, roulette, and chemin-de-fer are the most popular games, though you can play *le craps* and blackjack as well.

Salle Américaine, containing only slot machines, opens at noon, as do doors for roulette and *trente-quarente*. A section for roulette and chemin-de-fer opens at 3pm. Most of the facilities inside are operational by 4pm, when additional rooms open with more roulette, craps, and blackjack. The gambling continues until very late/early, the closing depending on the crowd. The casino classifies its "private rooms" as the more demure, nonelectronic areas devoid of slot machines. To enter the casino, you must carry a passport, be at least 21, and pay an admission of between 50 F and 100 F ($8 and $16), depending on where you want to go. In lieu of a passport, an identity card or driver's license will suffice. After 9pm, the staff will insist that gentlemen wear jackets and neckties for entrance into the private rooms.

8

The premises also contains a **Cabaret** in the Casino Gardens, where the show is usually preceded by the music of a well-rehearsed orchestra. A sexy cabaret featuring lots of feathers, glitter, jazz dance, ballet, and Riviera-style seminudity is presented at 10pm Wednesday to Monday from mid-September to the end of June. If you want dinner as part of the show, service begins at 9pm and costs 450 F ($72) per person (show included). If you want to see just the show, your drinks will cost from 150 F ($24) each. For reservations, call ☎ **92-16-36-36.**

In the casino's **Salle Garnier,** where lots of gilt and belle époque accents evoke the l9th-century opera house of Paris, concerts are held periodically; for information, contact the tourist office (see "Essentials," above) or the Atrium du Casino (see below). The music is usually classical, featuring the Orchestre Philharmonique de Monte Carlo.

The casino also contains the **Opéra de Monte-Carlo,** whose patron is Prince Rainier. This world-famous house, opened in 1879 by Sarah Bernhardt, presents a winter and spring repertoire that traditionally includes Puccini, Mozart, and Verdi. The famed Ballets Russes de Monte-Carlo, starring Nijinsky and Karsavina, was created in 1918 by Sergei Diaghilev. The national orchestra and ballet company of Monaco appear here. Tickets may be hard to come by; your best bet is to ask your hotel concierge. You can make inquiries about tickets on your own at the **Atrium du Casino** (☎ **92-16-22-99**), open Tuesday to Saturday from 10am to 5:30pm. Standard tickets are 150 F to 800 F ($24 to $128).

DANCING & DRINKING

Tiffany, avenue des Spélugues (☎ **93-50-53-13**), is a favorite of the 25- to 40-year-old crowd who like a glamorous modern setting. Come on Sundays to catch some showgirls. **Le Symbole,** rue du Portier (☎ **93-25-09-25**), is a hot spot for those over 30. The decor glitters in a high-tech gloss, and the music is disco.

19 Roquebrune & Cap-Martin

Roquebrune: 592 miles S of Paris, 3 miles W of Menton, 36 miles NE of Cannes, 2 miles E of Monaco; Cap-Martin: 3 miles W of Menton, 1¹/₂ miles W of Roquebrune

Roquebrune, along the Grande Corniche, is a charming mountain village with vaulted streets. It has been restored, though some critics have found the restoration artificial. Today its rue Moncollet is lined with artists' workshops and boutiques with inflated merchandise.

Three miles west of Menton, Cap-Martin is a satellite of the larger resort that's been associated with the rich and famous since the empress Eugénie wintered there in the 19th century. In time the resort was honored by the presence of Sir Winston Churchill, who came here often in his final years. Two famous men died here—William Butler Yeats in 1939 and Le Corbusier, who drowned while swimming off the cape in 1965. Don't expect to find a wide sandy beach—you'll encounter plenty of rocks, against a backdrop of pine and olive trees.

ESSENTIALS

GETTING THERE   To **drive** to Roquebrune and Cap-Martin, follow N7 east for 16 miles from Nice. Cap-Martin has **train** and bus connections from the other cities of the Mediterranean coast, including Nice and Menton. For more **railway** information and schedules, call ☎ **08-36-35-35-35.** To reach Roquebrune, you'll have to take a **taxi.** You can take a bus, but there's no formal bus station in Roquebrune; you just get off on the side of the highway. For more information about **bus** routes, contact the Gare Routière in Menton (☎ **04-93-85-64-44**).

VISITOR INFORMATION　The **Office de Tourisme** is at 218 av. Aristode Briand in Roquebrune (☎ **04-93-35-62-87**).

SEEING THE SIGHTS
IN ROQUEBRUNE

It'll take you about an hour to explore Roquebrune. You can stroll through its color-ful covered streets, which retain their authentic look even though the buildings are now devoted to handcrafts, gift and souvenir shops, or art galleries. From the parking lot at place de la République, you can head for place des Deux-Frères, turning left into rue Grimaldi. Then head left to **rue Moncollet.** This long, narrow street is covered with stepped passageways and filled with houses that date from the Middle Ages, most often with barred windows. Rue Moncollet leads into **rue du Château,** where you may want to explore the château.

The only one of its kind, **Château de Roquebrune** (☎ 04-93-35-07-22) was originally a 10th-century Carolingian castle; the present structure dates in part from the 13th century. Dominated by two square towers, it houses a historic museum. From the towers there's a panoramic view along the coast to Monaco. The castle gates are open daily from 10am to 12:30pm and 2 to 6pm. Admission is 20 F ($3.20) for adults, 15 F ($2.40) for seniors, and 10 F ($1.60) for students and children 7 to 11. From February through May, it's open daily 10am to 12:30pm and 2 to 6pm; from June through September 10am to 12:30pm and 3 to 7:30pm; and October through January 10am to 12:30pm and 2 to 5pm.

Rue du Château leads to place William-Ingram. After crossing this square, you reach rue de la Fontaine. Take a left. This will lead you to the **Olivier millénaire** (mil-lennary olive tree), one of the oldest in the world, having survived for at least 1,000 years.

Back on rue du Château you can reach **Église Ste-Marguerite,** which hides behind a relatively common baroque facade. But this exterior merely masks the church from the 12th century. It's not entirely from that time, however, having seen many alter-ations over the years. The interior is of polychrome plaster. Look for two paintings by a local artist, Marc-Antoine Otto, who in the 17th century painted a Crucifixion (in the second altar) and a Pietà (above the entrance door).

IN CAP-MARTIN

Cap-Martin is a rich town. At the center of the cape is a feudal tower that's today a telecommunications relay station. At its base you can still see the ruins of the **Basilique St-Martin,** the only evidence remaining of a priory constructed here by the monks of the Lérins Islands in the 11th century. After repeated pirate raids in the cen-turies to come, notably around the 15th century, it was destroyed and abandoned. If you follow the road (by car) along the eastern shoreline of the cape, you'll be rewarded with a view of Menton set against a backdrop of mountains. In the far distance looms the coastline of the Italian Riviera, and you can see as far as the resort of Bordighera.

Although it takes about 3 hours, you can take one of the most interesting walks along the Riviera here. The coastal path, called **Sentier Touristique,** leads from Cap-Martin to Monte Carlo Beach. If you have a car, you can park it in the lot at av. Winston-Churchill and begin your stroll. The path is marked by a sign labeled PROMENADE LE CORBUSIER. As you go along you'll be able to take in a view of Monaco set in a natural amphitheater. In the far distance, you'll view Cap-Ferrat and even Roquebrune with its château. The scenic path comes to an end at Monte Carlo Beach.

If you have a car, you can also take a **scenic 6-mile drive,** taking about an hour. Leave by D23, following the signs to Gorbio, a village perched on a hill and reached by this narrow, winding road. Along the way you'll pass homes of the wealthy and view a verdant setting with pines and silvery olives. The site is wild and rocky, the buildings having been constructed as a safe haven from pirate attacks. The most interesting street is rue Garibaldi, which leads past an old church to a panoramic belvedere.

ACCOMMODATIONS

Hôtel Victoria. 7 promenade du Cap, 06190 Roquebrune/Cap-Martin. ☎ **04-93-35-65-90.** Fax 04-93-28-27-02. 32 units. A/C MINIBAR TV TEL. 410–560 F ($65.60–$89.60) double. AE, DC, MC, V. Closed Jan 5–Feb 5. Parking 40 F ($6.40).

This rectangular low-rise building is set behind a garden in front of the beach. Built in the 1970s, it was renovated in the mid-1990s in a neoclassical style that weds tradition and modernity. It's the "second choice" in town for those who can't afford the lofty prices of the more spectacular Vista Palace. Rooms open onto balconies fronting the sea. The casual bar/lounge near the entrance sets a stylishly relaxed tone. Breakfast is the only meal served.

✪ **Hôtel Vista Palace.** Grande Corniche, 06190 Roquebrune/Cap-Martin. ☎ **04-92-10-40-00.** Fax 04-92-10-40-40. www.webstore.fr/vistapalace. E-mail: vistapalace@ webstore.fr. 68 units. A/C MINIBAR TV TEL. 1,200–2,300 F ($192–$368) double; 2,300–7,000 F ($368–$1,120) suite. AE, DC, MC, V. Parking 130 F ($20.80) in garage.

This extraordinary hotel/restaurant stands on the outer ridge of the mountains running parallel to the coast, giving an "airplane view" of Monaco that's spectacular. And the design of the Vista Palace is just as fantastic: Three levels are cantilevered out into space so every room seems to float. Nearly all the rooms have balconies facing the Mediterranean.

Dining: If you don't want to stay here, at least consider stopping by for a meal— it's expensive but worth it. Le Vistaero is open daily from noon to 2pm and 7:30 to 10pm; three fixed-price menus are available featuring Mediterranean cuisine envied by the region's other restaurateurs. The restaurant is closed for lunch July and August.

Amenities: Pool, sauna, masseuse, indoor squash court, fitness center, boutique, helipad, and 9-acre landscaped Mediterranean garden.

DINING

You might also like to try **Le Vistaero** at the Hôtel Vista Palace (see above).

Au Grand Inquisiteur. 18 rue du Château. ☎ **04-93-35-05-37.** Reservations required. Main courses 77–140 F ($12.30–$22.40); fixed-price menus 150–222 F ($24–$35.50). MC, V. Wed–Sun noon–1:30pm and Tues–Sun 7:30–10pm. Closed Nov–Dec 26. FRENCH.

This culinary find is a 28-seat restaurant in a two-room cellar near the top of the medieval mountaintop village of Roquebrune. On the steep, winding road to the château, this climate-controlled building is made of rough-cut stone, with large oak beams. The cuisine, though not the area's most distinguished, is quite good, especially the chef's duck special or scallops meunière. Most diners opt for one of the fresh fish choices. The wine list is exceptional—some 150 selections, most at reasonable prices.

20 Menton

596 miles S of Paris, 39 miles NE of Cannes, 5 miles E of Monaco

Menton is more Italian than French. Right at the border of Italy, Menton marks the eastern frontier of the Côte d'Azur. Its climate, incidentally, is the warmest on the

Mediterranean coast, attracting a large, rather elderly British colony throughout the winter. Because these senior citizens form a large part of the population of 130,000, Menton today is called "the Fort Lauderdale of France." Menton experiences a foggy day every 10 years—or so they say.

According to a local legend, Eve was the first to experience Menton's glorious climate. Expelled from the Garden of Eden along with Adam, she tucked a lemon in her bosom, planting it at Menton because it reminded her of her former stomping grounds. The lemons still grow in profusion here, and the fruit of that tree is given a position of honor at the Lemon Festival in February. Actually, the oldest Menton visitor may have arrived 30,000 years ago. He's still around—or at least his skull is—in the Municipal Museum.

Don't be misled by all those "palace-hotels" studding the hills. No longer open to the public, they've been divided up and sold as private apartments. Many of these turn-of-the-century structures were erected to accommodate elderly Europeans, mainly English and German, who arrived carrying a book written by one Dr. Bennett in which he extolled the joys of living at Menton.

ESSENTIALS
GETTING THERE Many visitors arrive by **car** along one of the corniche roads. More specifically, you can follow N7 east from Nice and arrive within 45 minutes.

There are good **bus and rail connections** that make stops at each resort along the Mediterranean coast, including Menton. Two trains per hour pull in from Nice (trip time: 35 minutes), and two trains per hour from Monte Carlo (trip time: 10 minutes). For rail information and schedules, call ☎ **08-36-35-35-35.** Two local bus companies, **Autocars Broch** (☎ **04-93-31-10-52**) and **RCA** (☎ **04-93-85-64-44**), run buses between Nice, Monte Carlo, and Menton, usually around two per hour, for a round-trip fee of 28 F ($4.50) from Nice.

VISITOR INFORMATION The **Office de Tourisme** is in the Palais de l'Europe, 8 av. Boyer (☎ **04-92-41-76-76**).

EXPLORING THE TOWN
On the Golfe de la Paix (Gulf of Peace), Menton, which used to belong to Monaco, is on a rocky promontory, dividing the bay in two. The fishing town, the older part with narrow streets, is in the east; the tourist zone and residential area are in the west.

Menton's beaches stretch for 2 miles between the Italian border and the city limits of Roquebrune and are interrupted only by the town's old and new ports. Collectively, they're known as **La Plage de la Promenade du Soleil** and with rare exceptions are public and free. Don't expect soft sand; the beaches are narrow, covered with gravel (or more charitably, big pebbles), and notoriously uncomfortable to lie on. Don't expect big waves or tides either.

So with no waves and no sand, who goes to the beach here? In the words of one nonswimming resident, mostly Parisians or residents of northern France, who are grateful for any escape from their urban milieux. Topless bathing is widespread, but complete nudity is forbidden.

Unlike in Cannes, where tens of thousands of chaises pepper the beaches, there aren't many options in Menton for renting mattresses and parasols; most people bring their own. Two exceptions are **Le Splendid Plage** (☎ **04-93-35-60-97**) and **Les Sablettes** (☎ **04-93-35-44-77**), both charging around 85 F ($13.60) for use of a mattress. They're immediately to the east of the Vieux Port.

Musée Jean-Cocteau. Bastion du Port, quai Napoléon-III. ☎ **04-93-57-72-30.** Admission 20 F ($3.20) adult, 15 F ($2.40) children under 18. Wed–Mon 10am–noon and 2–6pm.

The writer/artist/filmmaker Jean Cocteau liked Menton, and this museum, in a 17th-century fort, contains two MacAvoy portraits of Cocteau: one while he was alive and another at his death. Some of the artist's memorabilia is here—stunning charcoals and watercolors, ceramics, signed letters, and 21 brightly colored pastels.

La Salle des Mariages. In the Hôtel de Ville (town hall), rue de la République. ☎ **04-92-10-50-00.** Admission 10 F ($1.60). Mon–Fri 8:30am–12:30pm and 1:30–5pm.

Here Cocteau painted frescoes depicting the legend of Orpheus and Eurydice, among other things. A tape in English helps explain them. The room contains red-leather seats and leopard-skin rugs and is used for civil marriage ceremonies.

Musée de Préhistoire Régionale. Rue Lorédan-Larchey. ☎ **04-93-35-84-64.** Free admission. Wed–Mon 10am–noon and 2–6pm.

This collection presents human evolution on the Côte d'Azur for the past million years. It emphasizes the prehistoric era, including the 25,000-year-old head of the Nouvel Homme de Menton (sometimes known as "Grimaldi Man") found in 1884 in the Baousse-Rousse caves. Audiovisual aids, dioramas, and videos enhance the exhibition.

Musée des Beaux-Arts. Palais Carnoles, 3 av. de la Madone. ☎ **04-93-35-49-71.** Free admission. Wed–Mon 10am–noon and 2–6pm.

Here you'll find 14th-, 16th-, and 17th-century paintings from Italy, Flanders, Holland, and the French schools. You'll also find modern paintings, including works by Dufy, Valadon, Derain, and Leprin.

ACCOMMODATIONS

Hôtel Aiglon. 7 av. de la Madone, 06500 Menton. ☎ **04-93-57-55-55.** Fax 04-93-35-92-39. www.perso.wanadoo.fr/aiglon. E-mail: Aiglon.Hotel@wanadoo.fr. 30 units. A/C MINIBAR TV TEL. 440–800 F ($70.40–$128) double; 770–1,040 F ($123.20–$166.40) suite. Half board 400–700 F ($64–$112) per person extra. AE, DC, MC, V. Closed Nov 6–Dec 18. Free parking.

A nugget along the coast, this three-star hotel was converted from a stately Riviera villa. In a large park filled with Mediterranean vegetation, it offers a more intimate and homelike environment than any other hotel in Menton in its league. The former private residence has been skillfully converted to receive guests, and each room is tastefully furnished. Bedrooms come in various shapes and sizes, each well upholstered and containing quality mattresses on the elegant beds. The magnet of the hotel is a heated pool surrounded by a veranda. The garden setting is beautifully maintained, and other facilities include a solarium and a children's game area. An excellent Provençal-and-international **cuisine** is offered with view windows opening onto the pool and garden.

Hôtel Princesse et Richmond. 617 promenade du Soleil, 06500 Menton. ☎ **04-93-35-80-20.** Fax 04-93-57-40-20. www.princess-richmond.com. E-mail: princess.hotel@wanadoo.fr. 46 units. A/C MINIBAR TV TEL. 360–650 F ($57.60–$104) double; 700–1,000 F ($112–$160) suite. AE, CB, DC, V. Closed Nov 4–Dec 18. Parking 45 F ($7.20).

At the edge of the sea near the commercial district, this hotel boasts a facade of warm Mediterranean colors, with a sunny garden terrace. The owner rents comfortable soundproof rooms with modern and French traditional furnishings and balconies. Drinks are served on the roof terrace, where you can enjoy a view of the curving shoreline. A restaurant in the garden of the nearby Hôtel Aiglon, under the same own-ership, offers lunch and dinner beside a heated pool you may use as well. There's also an open-air Jacuzzi, plus a small fitness room in the solarium. The staff organizes sightseeing excursions.

DINING

✪ **La Calanque.** 13 square Victoria. ☎ **04-93-35-83-15.** Main courses 60–100 F ($9.60–$16); fixed-price menus 98–145 F ($15.70–$23.20). MC, V. Tues–Sat noon–2pm and 7:15–9:30pm, Sun noon–2pm. FRENCH/SEAFOOD.

Informal and earthy in a charming, rustic Provençal way, this restaurant provides a waterside view and well-prepared food. In fair weather, tables are set under shade trees in full view of the harbor. We recommend the *soupe de poissons* (fish soup), and fresh sardines (grilled over charcoal and very savory). Another specialty is bouillabaisse. You can always count on an array of fresh fish and shellfish dishes prepared to perfection.

L'Albatros. 31 quai Bonaparte. ☎ **04-93-35-94-64.** Reservations recommended. Main courses 50–200 F ($8–$32); fixed-price menu 130 F ($20.80). MC, V. Tues–Sun noon–3pm and 7pm–midnight. FRENCH/PROVENÇAL.

This charming little bistro along the port specializes in fish dishes from the Mediter-ranean. On the second floor and on the terrace you can enjoy a view over the old har-bor and bay while sampling fresh fish purchased directly from Menton fishers. Menu items are conservative but savory, with lots of emphasis on Provençal interpretations of fish and seafood. Examples include a succulent bouillabaisse, prepared only for a minimum of two diners, and priced at 200 F ($32) per person. There's also a *cassoulet des pêcheurs*, a stewpot brimming with herbs, saffron, and fish; and a thick and juicy charolais of beef with béarnaise sauce. Everything here is fresh, unpretentious, and low-key.

Rocamadour. 1 square Victoria. ☎ **04-93-35-76-04.** Reservations recommended. Main courses 45–145 F ($7.20–$23.20); fixed-price menus 85–190 F ($13.60–$30.40). MC, V. Sept–June, Fri–Tues noon–2:30pm and 7:30–10pm; July–Aug, daily noon–2:30pm and 7:30–10pm. FRENCH.

This pleasant restaurant overlooks the port. You dine at tables set under a canopy. Some specialties are from the Périgord region, including foie gras. *Magrêt de canard* (duckling) is another specialty. But basically the cookery is grounded in the rich tra-dition of the Côte d'Azur, with an emphasis on very fresh fish. The restaurant was founded almost a century ago by a chef from Rocamadour, and the name of that town has stayed with the place.

Languedoc-Roussillon

Languedoc, one of southern France's great old provinces, is a loosely defined area encompassing such cities as Nîmes, Toulouse, and Carcassonne. It's one of the leading wine-producing areas and is fabled for its art treasures.

The coast of Languedoc, from Montpellier to the Spanish frontier, might be called France's "second Mediterranean" (first place naturally goes to the Côte d'Azur). A land of ancient cities and a generous sea, it's less spoiled than the Côte d'Azur, with an almost-continuous strip of sand stretching west from the Rhône and curving toward the Pyrénées. Back in the days of de Gaulle, the government began an ambitious project to develop the Languedoc-Roussillon coastline, and it has been a booming success. In July and August, the miles of sun-baking bodies along the coast attest to this success.

Ancient Roussillon is a small region of greater Languedoc, forming the Pyrénées Orientales *département.* This is the French Catalonia, inspired more by Barcelona in neighboring Spain than by remote Paris. Over its long and colorful history it has known many rulers. Legally part of the French kingdom until 1258, it was surrendered to James I of Aragón. Until 1344, it was part of the ephemeral kingdom of Majorca, with Perpignan as the capital. By 1463, Roussillon was annexed to France again. Then Ferdinand of Aragón won it back, but by 1659 France had it again. In spite of local sentiment for reunion with the Cataláns of Spain, France still firmly controls the land.

The Camargue is a marshy delta between two arms of the Rhône. South of Arles is cattle country. Strong, wild black bulls are bred here for the arenas of Arles and Nîmes. The small white horses, amazingly graceful, were said to have been brought here by the Saracens. They're ridden by *gardiens,* French cowboys, who can usually be seen in wide-brimmed black hats. The whitewashed houses, plaited-straw roofs, pink flamingos that inhabit the muddy marshes, vast plains, endless stretches of sandbars—all this qualifies as Exotic France.

REGIONAL CUISINE   The cuisine of Languedoc-Roussillon is heavily influenced by garlic, olive oil, and strong flavors. The region has plentiful game, trout, succulent lamb, and seafood, usually prepared with local herbs, wine, and garlic.

One of the region's legendary dishes is usually prepared on a brazier in a boat on the open sea: the tripe (intestines) of tuna mixed with white wine and herbs, accompanied by a glass of seawater, whose salt

Languedoc-Roussillon

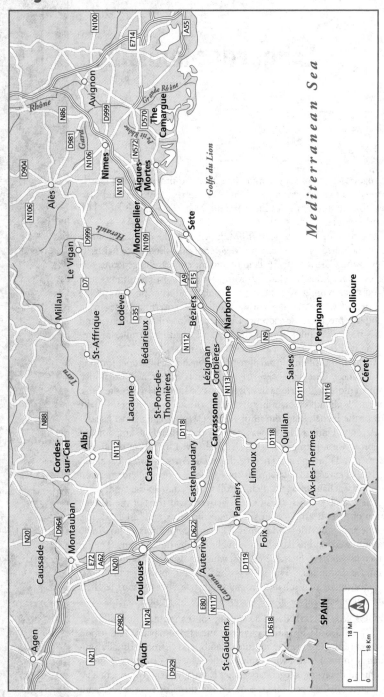

alleviates some of the unpleasantness. A vastly more palatable dish is *pouillade,* which requires the simultaneous preparation of two pots of soup (one made with cabbage, the other with white beans). Just before serving, the contents are mixed together in a serving bowl.

Other regional specialties include excellent fish stews, foie gras, truffles, escargots, exotic mushrooms from the north-central areas, pâté of thrush from Rodez, cherries from Lodève, *aigo bouillido* (a soup made with garlic, eggs, aromatic herbs, and croûtons), *aligot* (a dish with garlic-laced cream, butter, potatoes, and cheese), and cassoulet of white beans and various meats. The region's most famous cheese is pélardon, made from goat's milk. The best known pastry is the Alleluia.

As for wine, Hérault, Aude, and Garde rank first, second, and third, respectively, in total wine production in France. Most of this is ordinary table wine. A few, however, have been granted an Appellation d'Origine Contrôlée. Some of the best are Fitou, produced in the Hautes-Corbières district near Narbonne, and Minervois, from west and northwest of Narbonne.

1 Nîmes

440 miles S of Paris, 27 miles W of Avignon

Nîmes, the ancient Nemausus, is one of the finest places in the world for wandering among Roman relics. The city grew to prominence during the reign of Caesar Augustus (27 B.C. to A.D. 14). Today it possesses one of the best-preserved Roman amphitheaters in the world and a near-perfect Roman temple. The city of 135,000 is more like Provence than Languedoc, in which it lies. There's a touch of Pamplona, Spain, here in the festivals of the *corridas* (bullfights) at the arena. The Spanish image is even stronger at night, when the bodegas fill, usually with students, drinking sangria and listening to the sounds of flamenco.

By 1860, the togas of Nîmes's citizenry had long given way to denim, the cloth de Nîmes. An Austrian immigrant, Leví-Strauss, exported this heavy fabric to California for use as work-pants material for gold diggers in those boomtown years. The rest, as they say, is history.

ESSENTIALS

GETTING THERE   Nîmes has bus and train service from the rest of France and is near several autoroutes. It lies on the main rail line between Marseille and Bordeaux. Six **trains** a day arrive from Paris (trip time: 4¹/₂ hours). For train information and schedules, call ☎ **08-36-35-35-35.** If you're **driving,** take A7 south from Lyon to the town of Orange, connecting here to A9 into Nîmes.

VISITOR INFORMATION   The **Office de Tourisme** is at 6 rue Auguste (☎ **04-66-67-29-11**).

SPECIAL EVENTS   Festivals, parties, and cultural events rule the summer nightlife scene in Nîmes. Once the warm weather hits, all sorts of activities take place at the arena, including concerts and theater under the stars. The Office de Tourisme has a complete listing of events and schedules, or you can contact the **Bureau de Location des Arènes,** 1 rue Alexandre-Ducros (☎ **04-66-67-28-02**).

During the heat of midsummer, many of Nîmes's central squares burst forth with music, crowds of pedestrians, and one of the richest troves of used objects, paintings, crafts, and sculpture, every Thursday night during July and August. Artists, musicians, and local residents gather in observance of the city's **Les Jeudis de Nîmes.** Of special interest are the place de l'Horloge, the place du Marché, and the place aux Herbes.

EXPLORING THE CITY

If you really want to see all of the city's monuments and museums, consider buying a **billet global,** sold at the ticket counter of any of the local attractions. It provides access to all the cultural sites described below over a 3-day period, for an all-inclusive fee of 60 F ($9.60) for adults and 30 F ($4.80) for students and children 15 and under. Entrance is free for children under 10.

The pride of Nîmes is the ✪ **Maison Carrée,** place de la Comédie (☎ 04-66-36-26-76), built during the reign of Caesar Augustus. On a raised platform with tall Corinthian columns, it's one of the most beautiful, and certainly one of the best-preserved, Roman temples of Europe. It inspired the builders of La Madeleine in Paris as well as Thomas Jefferson. A changing roster of cultural and art exhibits is presented here, beneath an authentically preserved roof that the city of Nîmes repaired, at great expense, in 1996. It's open October to May daily from 9am to 12:30pm and 2 to 6pm, June to September daily from 9am to noon and 2:30 to 7pm. Admission is free.

Across the square stands its modern-day twin, the **Carrée d'Art,** a sophisticated research center and exhibition space that contains a library, a newspaper kiosk, and an art museum. Its understated design was inspired by (but doesn't overpower) the ancient monument nearby. The most visible component here is the **Musée d'Art Contemporain,** place de la Maison Carré (☎ 04-66-76-35-35), whose permanent expositions are often supplemented with temporary exhibits of contemporary art. It's open Tuesday through Sunday from 10am to 6pm, charging 28 F ($4.50) for adults and 20 F ($3.20) for students and children 14 and under. *Note:* This modern building's terrace provides a panorama of most of the ancient monuments and medieval churches of Nîmes, above all of the neighborhood's roaring traffic.

The elliptically shaped ✪ **AmphiThéâtre Romain,** place des Arènes (☎ 04-66-76-72-77), a better-preserved twin to the one at Arles, is far more complete than the Colosseum of Rome. It's two stories high—each floor has 60 arches—and was built of huge stones painstakingly fitted together without mortar. One of the best preserved of the arenas from ancient times, it once held more than 20,000 spectators who came to see gladiatorial combats and wolf or boar hunts. Today it's used for everything from ballet recitals to bullfights and is open daily from 9am to 6pm. Admission is 28 F ($4.50) for adults and 20 F ($3.20) for students and children 15 and under.

Jardin de la Fontaine, at the end of quai de la Fontaine, was laid out in the 18th century, using the ruins of a Roman shrine as an ornamental centerpiece. It was planted with rows of chestnuts and elms, adorned with statuary and urns, and intersected by grottoes and canals—making it one of the most beautiful gardens in France. Adjoining it is the ruined **Temple of Diana** and the remains of some Roman baths. Over the park, within a 10-minute walk north of the town center, rises **Mont Cavalier,** a low but rocky hill on top of which rises the sturdy bulk of the **Tour Magne,** the city's oldest Roman monument. You can climb it for 15 F ($2.40) for adults and 12 F ($1.90) for students and children 14 and under; it offers a panoramic view over Nîmes and its environs. It's open daily from 9am to 5pm (until 7pm May to September).

Nîmes is home to a great many museums. The largest and best respected, **Musée des Beaux-Arts,** rue Cité-Foulc (☎ 04-66-67-38-21), contains French paintings and sculptures from the 17th to the 20th centuries as well as Flemish, Dutch, and Italian works from the 15th to the 18th centuries. Seek out in particular one of G. B. Moroni's masterpieces, *La Calomnie d'Apelle,* and a well-preserved Gallo-Roman mosaic. The museum is open Tuesday through Sunday from 11am to 6pm. Admission is 28 F ($4.50) for adults and 20 F ($3.20) for students and children 14 and under.

Nîmes

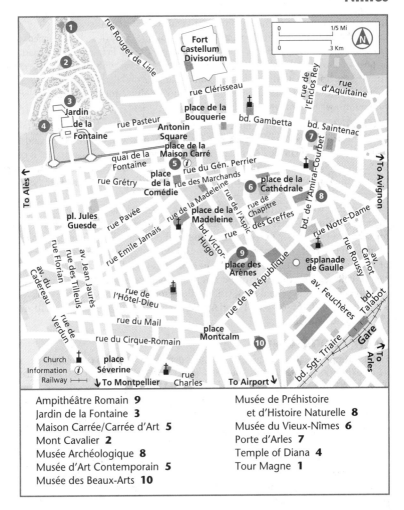

Amphithéâtre Romain **9**	Musée de Préhistoire
Jardin de la Fontaine **3**	et d'Histoire Naturelle **8**
Maison Carrée/Carrée d'Art **5**	Musée du Vieux-Nîmes **6**
Mont Cavalier **2**	Porte d'Arles **7**
Musée Archéologique **8**	Temple of Diana **4**
Musée d'Art Contemporain **5**	Tour Magne **1**
Musée des Beaux-Arts **10**	

If time allows, visit the **Musée du Vieux-Nîmes,** place de la Cathédrale (☎ **04-66-76-73-70**), housed in an episcopal palace from the 1700s. It's rich in antiques, including pieces from the 17th century. The museum is open Tuesday through Sunday from 11am to 6pm, charging 28 F ($4.50) for adults and 20 F ($3.20) for children.

One of the city's busiest thoroughfares, boulevard de l'Amiral-Courbet, leads to the **Porte d'Arles**—the remains of a monumental gate built by the Romans during the reign of Augustus. Farther south, contained in the same stately building at 13 bis bd. l'Amiral-Courbet, are the **Musée de Préhistoire et d'Histoire Naturelle** (☎ **04-66-67-39-14**) and the **Musée Archéologique** (☎ **04-66-67-25-57**). Both are open Tuesday through Sunday from 11am to 6pm; a fee of 28 F ($4.50) for adults and 20 F ($3.20) for children admits you to both museums.

Outside the city, 14 miles to the northeast, the well-preserved, much-photographed **pont du Gard** spans the Gard River and was built without mortar; its huge stones have evolved into one of the region's most vivid reminders of the ancient glory and technical competence of the Romans. Consisting of three tiers of arches arranged into gracefully symmetrical patterns, it dates from about 19 B.C. Frédéric Mistral, national poet of Provence and Languedoc, recorded a legend alleging that the devil constructed the bridge with the promise he could claim the soul of the first person to cross it. To visit it, take highway N86 from Nîmes to a point 2 miles from the village of Remoulins, where signs are posted.

SHOPPING   If you'd rather concentrate on serious shopping, head to the center of town and **rue du Général-Perrier, rue des Marchands, rue du Chapître,** and the pedestrian streets of **rue de l'Aspic** and **rue de la Madeleine.** A Sunday market is conducted from 8am to around 1pm in the parking lot of the **Stade des Castières,** site of most of the town's football (soccer) matches, adjacent to the boulevard Périphérique that encircles Nîmes.

To appease your sweet tooth, go to just about any pastry shop in town and ask for the regional almond-based cookies called *croquants villaret* and *caladons.* They're great for a burst of energy or for souvenirs. One of the best purchases you can make in Nîmes, especially if you're not continuing east into Provence, is a *santon.* These wood or clay figurines are sculpted into a cast of characters from Provençal country life and can be collected together to create a uniquely country-French nativity scene. For a selection of *santons* in various sizes, visit the **Boutique Provençale,** 10 place de la Maison Carré (☎ **04-66-67-81-71**), or **Au Papillon Bleu,** 15 rue du Général-Perrier (☎ **04-66-67-48-58**).

ACCOMMODATIONS

Hôtel l'Amphithéâtre. 4 rue des Arènes, 30000 Nîmes. ☎ **04-66-67-28-51.** Fax 04-66-67-07-79. 17 units. TV TEL. 240–270 F ($38.40–$43.20) double; 300 F ($48) triple or quad. AE, MC, V. Closed Dec 20–Jan 25. Parking 50 F ($8).

The core of this small-scale, old-fashioned hotel dates from the 18th century, when it was built as a private home. It has functioned as a hotel for longer than anyone remembers. A stay here involves trekking to your room up steep flights of creaking stairs, and navigating your way through a labyrinth of upper corridors. Small bedrooms are deliberately old-fashioned, usually containing antiques or antique reproductions, wall-to-wall carpeting, and creaky albeit comfortable mattresses. The staff here grew jaded long ago to the fact that their hotel is less than perfect, but at these prices, who's complaining?

Hôtel Vatel. 140 rue Vatel, B.P. 7128, 30913 Nîmes CEDEX. ☎ **04-66-62-57-57.** Fax 04-66-57-50. 46 units. A/C MINIBAR TV TEL. 600 F ($96) double; 1,200 F ($192) suite. AE, DC, MC, V. From the A4 autoroute, exit at "Nîmes Ouest."

This seven-story, circa 1990 hotel lies 2 miles north of the town center, within a cluster of other buildings that include a technological university and a large hospital. It's efficiently staffed with students from the local hotel school, who work on-site as part of their on-the-job training. Rooms are streamlined, tasteful, and modern, with terraces. In all, the modern format of this hotel manages to provide a level of comfort that older hotels, in more historic but restricted settings, simply can't provide.

Dining: Les Palmiers is the more formal and expensive of the hotel's two restaurants. More casual is Le Restaurant Provençal, which occupies something akin to a greenhouse, and which specializes in regional cuisine.

Amenities: Swimming pool and health club, exercise room, solarium, sauna, tennis court, conference and convention facilities.

Imperator Concorde. Quai de la Fontaine, 30900 Nîmes. ☎ **04-66-21-90-30.** Fax 04-66-67-70-25. www.concorde-hotels.com. E-mail: hotel.imperator@wanadoo.fr. 63 units. A/C MINIBAR TV TEL. 550–1,000 F ($88–$160) double; 1,200 F ($192) suite. AE, DC, MC, V. Parking 70 F ($11.20).

This is the largest hotel in town, a member of the well-managed Concorde chain, and one of only two four-star properties within the city limits. (The other is the also-recommended Hotel Vatel, which doubles as a training school for the hotel and restaurant industry.) It's set behind the town's ancient Roman monuments—it's the one with the pale pink Italianate facade. With a recent major renovation, it's been much improved. The artful and cozy bedrooms have traditional or French furniture, either with fluted or cambriole-shaped legs, adhering to one or another of the Louis styles. You can order a meal in the hotel's verdant rear gardens, or within a sun-flooded, high-ceilinged **dining room, L'Enclos de la Fontaine.** Fixed-price menus are priced from 145 F to 380 F ($23.20 to $60.80) each.

New Hôtel La Baume. 21 rue Nationale, 30000 Nîmes. ☎ **04-66-76-28-42.** Fax 04-66-76-28-45. 34 units. A/C MINIBAR TV TEL. 510 F ($81.60) double. AE, DC, MC, V. Parking 50 F ($8).

Our favorite nest in Nîmes sits in a 17th-century mansion. The designers were careful to preserve the original architectural heritage during its creation, and the result is a winning combination of modern and traditional. The 24 rooms are fitted with exceptional charm, always in warm Provençal colors of ocher, burnt orange, and yellow. The hotel **restaurant** is also worth a visit, turning out such dishes as fresh salmon flavored with anise, and chicken saltimbocca with ham. Fixed-price menus are reasonably priced at 80 F to 105 F ($12.80 to $16.80) each.

DINING

The dining room at the **New Hôtel La Baume** (see "Accommodations," above) is also a good choice.

Alexandre. Rte. de l'Aéroport de Garons. ☎ **04-66-70-08-99.** Reservations required. Main courses 140–200 F ($22.40–$32); fixed-price menus 195–450 F ($31.20–$72) at lunch, 285–450 F ($45.60–$72) at dinner. AE, MC, V. July–Aug, Tues–Sat noon–1:45pm and 8–9:45pm; Sept–June, Tues–Sun noon–1:45pm and Tues and Thurs–Sat 8–9:45pm. Closed 2 weeks in Feb. From the town center, take rue de la République southwest to av. Jean-Jaurès; then head south and follow the signs to the airport in the direction of Garons. FRENCH.

The most charming, amusing, and competent restaurant around is on the outskirts of Nîmes, 5 miles south of the center. Its verdant setting is the elegant and rustic domain of Michel Kayser, who adheres to classic tradition, with subtle improvements. He's assisted in the dining room by his charming wife, Monique. Menu items are designed to amuse as well as delight the palate. Examples are *île flottante* with truffles and *velouté* of cèpe mushrooms, roasted pigeon stuffed with purée of vegetables and foie gras, and the region's most sophisticated version of an old country recipe, *pieds et paquets.* Especially appealing is the cheese trolley loaded with esoteric goat cheeses from the region and worthy cheeses from other parts of France. The dessert trolley is incredibly hard to resist.

Restaurant au Chapon Fin. 3 rue du Château-Fadaise. ☎ **04-66-67-34-73.** Reservations required. Main courses 70–115 F ($11.20–$18.40); fixed-price menu 75 F ($12) at lunch, 120 F ($19.20) at dinner. AE, DC, MC, V. Mon–Fri noon–2pm and 7:30–10pm, Sat 7:30–10pm. Closed 2 weeks in Aug. FRENCH.

This tavern/restaurant, on a little square behind St-Paul's, is run by M. and Mme Grangier. It has beamed ceilings, small lamps, and a black-and-white stone floor.

Madame Grangier is from Alsace, so you'll find both Alsatian and Languedocienne specialties here. From the à la carte menu you can order foie gras with truffles, *coq au vin* (chicken with wine), and entrecôte flambéed with morels. The proprietor makes his own *confit d'oie* (goose preserved in its own fat) from birds shipped in from Alsace.

San Francisco Steak House. 33 rue Roussy. ☎ **04-66-21-00-80.** Reservations required. Main courses 60–150 F ($9.60–$24). AE, DC, MC, V. Mon–Fri noon–2pm; Mon–Sat 7:30pm–midnight. Bus: 3 or 5. STEAK/FRENCH.

After traveling through the U.S., the founders of this restaurant transported some ideas from California and created the most popular theme restaurant in Nîmes. It's located near place de la Couronne. You'll find the best steaks and seafood in Nîmes here, always in generous portions with plenty of flavor. In addition to the juicy steaks, you can order succulent veal or lamb chops. The most trendy dishes are grilled ostrich or bison steaks. The full range of traditional beef dishes includes steak tartare. Begin your meal with a shrimp-stuffed avocado or a salad of grapefruit and crayfish segments.

Wine Bar Chez Michel. 11 place de la Couronne. ☎ **04-66-76-19-59.** Main courses 60–130 F ($9.60–$20.80); fixed-price menus 80 F ($12.80) at lunch, 85–130 F ($13.60–$20.80) at dinner. AE, DC, MC, V. Tues–Sat noon–2pm; Mon–Sat 7pm–midnight. FRENCH.

This place is paneled with mahogany and has leather banquettes evocative of a turn-of-the-century California saloon. Choices include an array of salads and platters. At lunch you can order a quick menu, including an appetizer, a garnished main course, and two glasses of wine. Typical dishes are magrêt of duckling and contrefillet of steak with Roquefort sauce. You can now enjoy lunch on the terrace in the newly renovated courtyard. A restaurateur extraordinaire, Michel Hermet also makes his own wine within vineyards that have been associated with his family for many generations. There are more than 300 other varieties of wine to choose from, by the glass or the pitcher.

NÎMES AFTER DARK

Once the warm weather hits, all sorts of activities take place at the arena, including concerts and theater under the stars. The Office de Tourisme has a complete listing of events and schedules. Otherwise, for popular events like football (i.e., soccer), bull-fights, and rock-and-roll concerts, you can contact the **Bureau de Location des Arènes,** 1 rue Alexandre-Ducros (☎ **04-66-67-28-02**). Tickets for more highbrow events such as symphonic or chamber-music concerts, theater, and opera performances are sold through **Hall du Théâtre,** 1 place de la Calade (☎ **04-66-36-65-00**).

If you like hanging out with a mix of French students and French soldiers, head to **Café Le Napoléon,** 46 bd. Victor-Hugo (☎ **04-66-67-20-23**). Popular with the intelligentsia is the **Haddock Cafe,** 13 rue de l'Agau (☎ **04-66-67-86-57**), with its weekly live rock concerts.

All the town's jazz aficionados know that **Le Diagonal,** 41 bis rue Emile-Jamais (☎ **04-66-21-70-01**), hosts the area's best jazz and blues concerts every Saturday. The flashy, sexy, and hip **La Comédie,** 28 rue Jean-Reboul (☎ **04-66-76-13-66**), is the hands-down best for dancing and attracts a pretty crowd of youthful danceaholics. A little less flashy, but a lot more fun, **Lulu Club,** 10 impasse de la Curaterie (☎ **04-66-36-28-20**), is the gay and lesbian stronghold in Nîmes.

A newer contender for the nightlife attentions of the city's young and restless is **Le C.K.F.,** 20 rue de l'Étoile (☎ **04-66-21-59-22**). Open every Wednesday to Saturday, beginning after 11pm, it rocks and rolls to music from Los Angeles and London, as clients dance, dance, dance. Clubs with dancing and/or entertainment generally impose a cover of 50 F to 70 F ($8 to $11.20), depending on the night.

Other streets to explore for a healthy dose of nocturnal good times on virtually any night of the week include **impasse Porte-de-France** and **boulevard Victor-Hugo.**

2 Aigues-Mortes

466 miles SW of Paris, 39 miles NE of Sëte, 25 miles E of Nîmes, 30 miles SW of Arles

South of Nîmes, you can explore much of the Camargue by car. The most rewarding place to focus on is Aigues-Mortes, the city of the "dead waters." In the middle of dismal swamps and melancholy lagoons, Aigues-Mortes is France's most perfectly preserved walled town. Now 4 miles from the sea, it stands on four navigable canals. Louis IX and his crusaders once set forth from Aigues-Mortes, then a thriving port, the first in France on the Mediterranean. The walls, which still enclose the town, were constructed between 1272 and 1300. The **Tour de Constance** (☎ 04-66-53-61-55) is a model castle of the Middle Ages, its stones looking out on the marshes. At the top, which you can reach by elevator, a panoramic view unfolds. Admission is 32 F ($5.10) for adults, 21 F ($3.35) for ages 18 to 25, and free for children 17 and under. The monument is open May to August daily from 9:30am to 8pm; September 9:30am to 7pm; October to January 10am to 5pm; and February to April 10am to 6pm.

Frankly, the main allure in Aigues-Mortes involves the city itself, and the way a sense of medievalism still permeates virtually every building, every rampart, and every cobble-covered street in town. The city's religious centerpiece is the **Église Notre Dame des Sablons,** rue Jean-Jaurès (☎ 04-66-53-86-73). Originally constructed of wood in 1183, it was rebuilt in stone in 1246 in the ogival style. Its stained-glass windows are modern, having been installed in 1980 as replacements for the badly damaged and weather-beaten originals. The church is open daily from 8:30am to 6pm.

ESSENTIALS

GETTING THERE   Five **trains** and four **buses** per day connect Aigues-Mortes and Nîmes. Trip time is about an hour. For information and schedules, call ☎ 08-36-35-35-35. If you're **driving** to Aigues-Mortes, take D979 south from Gallargues, or A9 from Montpellier or Nîmes.

VISITOR INFORMATION   There's an **Office de Tourisme** at Porte de la Gardette (☎ 04-66-53-73-00).

ACCOMMODATIONS

The **Restaurant Les Arcades** (see "Dining," below) also rents rooms.

Hostellerie des Remparts. 6 place Anatole-France, 30220 Aigues-Mortes. ☎ **04-66-53-82-77.** Fax 04-66-53-73-77. 19 units. TEL. 280–390 F ($44.80–$62.40) double. AE, DC, V.

Established about 300 years ago, this weather-worn inn lies at the foot of the Tour de Constance, adjacent to the medieval fortifications. Popular and often fully booked (especially in summer), it evokes the defensive atmosphere of the Middle Ages, albeit with charm and a sense of nostalgia. The rooms with simple furniture are accessible via narrow stone staircases; 13 contain TVs. Breakfast is the only meal served.

Hôtel Les Templiers. 23 rue de la République, 30220 Aigues-Mortes. ☎ **04-66-53-66-56.** Fax 04-66-53-69-61. 10 units. A/C TV TEL. 570–800 F ($91.20–$128) double. AE, DC, V. Closed Nov–Feb.

At the leading inn in town, you'll find a gem of peace and tranquillity, along with luxurious comfort. Protected by the ramparts built by St. Louis, king of France, this 17th-century residence has been tastefully converted to receive guests. Your stay includes all the comforts of a private home. The small- to medium-size guest rooms are decorated in a Provençal style, with color coordination and just enough decorative objects to lend a homelike aura. You can relax in the courtyard, where you can also enjoy breakfast. An on-site **restaurant** is open only for dinner costing around 200 F ($32). The cuisine is regional, using fresh products from the surrounding region.

Hôtel St-Louis. 10 rue de l'Amiral-Courbet, 30220 Aigues-Mortes. ☎ **04-66-53-72-68.** Fax 04-66-53-75-92. 22 units. MINIBAR TV TEL. 335–510 F ($53.60–$81.60) double. AE, DC, MC, V. Closed Jan–Mar 10. Parking 45 F ($7.20).

This small inn near place St-Louis offers attractively furnished but somewhat basic rooms. Nevertheless, it's one of the most desirable addresses in town. The **restaurant** offers good regional cuisine that justifies its reputation among local foodies. A fixed-price menu ranges from 105 F to 195 F ($16.80 to $31.20).

DINING

Note that **Hôtel St-Louis** and **Hôtel Les Templiers** (see "Accommodations," above) also have good restaurants.

Restaurant Les Arcades. 23 bd. Gambetta, 30220 Aigues-Mortes. ☎ **04-66-53-81-13.** Fax 04-66-53-75-46. Reservations recommended. Main courses 75–165 F ($12–$26.40); fixed-price menus 130–275 F ($20.80–$44). AE, DC, MC, V. Tues 7:30–9:30pm, Wed–Sun noon–2pm and 7:30–9:45pm (also open Mon night July–Aug). Closed 2 weeks in Mar and 2 weeks in Nov. FRENCH.

This restaurant has several formal sections with ancient beamed ceilings or intricately fitted stone vaults. Almost as old as the nearby fortifications, the place is especially charming on sultry days, when the thick masonry keeps the interior cool. Good food is served at reasonable prices and is likely to include warm oysters, fish soup, pot-au-feu with three different meats, roasted monkfish in red-wine sauce, lobster fricassée, grilled fillet of bull from the Camargue, and grilled duckling. Especially charming is a platter piled high with stuffed zucettini flowers served with pesto sauce.

The owner also rents 10 large, comfortable **rooms,** each with air-conditioning, TV, and phone. A double is 480 F to 700 F ($76.80 to $112), breakfast included.

3 Montpellier

471 miles SW of Paris, 100 miles NW of Marseille, 31 miles SW of Nîmes

The capital of Mediterranean (or Lower) Languedoc, this ancient university city is still renowned for its medical school, founded in the 13th century. Nostradamus qualified as a doctor here, and even Rabelais studied at the school. Petrarch came to Montpellier in 1317, staying for 7 years.

Today Montpellier is a bustling metropolis, one of southern France's fastest-growing cities thanks to an influx of new immigrants. Except for some dreary suburbs, the city has a handsomely laid out core, with tree-flanked promenades, broad avenues, and historic monuments. Students make up a quarter of the population, giving the city a lively, animated feel. In recent years many high-tech corporations, including IBM, have settled in Montpellier.

ESSENTIALS

GETTING THERE Some 20 **trains** per day arrive from Avignon (trip time: 1 hour), eight from Marseille (trip time: 45 minutes), one every 2 hours from Toulouse (trip time: 2 hours), and 10 per day from Perpignan (trip time: 1¹/₂ hours). Eight trains per day arrive from Paris, calling for a change in Lyon (trip time: 4¹/₂ hours). For rail information and schedules, call ☎ 08-36-35-35-35. Two **buses** a day arrive from Nîmes (trip time: 1³/₄ hours).

If you're **driving,** Montpellier lies off A9 heading west.

VISITOR INFORMATION   The **Office de Tourisme** is at 30 av. Jean de Lattre de Tassigny (☎ 04-67-60-60-60).

SPECIAL EVENTS   From late June to early July, an array of classical and modern dance performances cascade into town for the **Festival International Montpellier Danse.** Tickets sell for 35 F to 260 F ($5.60 to $41.60) and can be purchased through the **Hôtel d'Assas,** 6 rue de la Vieille Aiguillerie (☎ 04-67-60-83-60). In late July, the **Festival de Radio France et de Montpellier** presents a variety of orchestral music, jazz, and opera. Tickets range from 50 F to 150 F ($8 to $24); call ☎ 04-67-02-02-01, or contact the Corum Theater (☎ 04-67-61-67-61).

EXPLORING THE TOWN

Called the Oxford of France because of its burgeoning academic community, Montpellier is a city of young people, as you'll notice if you sit at a cafe opening onto the heartbeat **place de la Comédie,** admiring the Théâtre, the 18th-century Fountain of the Three Graces, or whatever else amuses you. It's the living room of Montpellier, the ideal place to flirt, chat, people-watch, cruise, or just hang out.

Before leaving town, take a stroll along the 17th-century **promenade du Peyrou,** a terraced park with views of the Cévennes and the Mediterranean. This is a broad esplanade constructed at the loftiest point of Montpellier. Opposite the entrance is an **Arc de Triomphe,** erected in 1691 to celebrate the victories of Louis XIV. In the center of the promenade is an equestrian statue of Louis XIV, and at the end, the **Château d'Eau,** a pavilion with Corinthian columns that serves as a monument to 18th-century classicism. Water travels here via a 9-mile-long conduit and an aqueduct.

Cathédrale St-Pierre. Place St-Pierre. ☎ 04-67-66-04-12. Free admission. Daily 9am–noon and 2:30–7pm.

The town's spiritual centerpiece was founded in 1364. Once associated with a Benedictine monastery, the cathedral suffered badly in religious wars. (After 1795 the monastery was occupied by the medical school.) Today it has a somewhat bleak western front with two towers and a canopied porch.

Jardin des Plantes. 163 rue Auguste-Broussonnet (reached from bd. Henri-IV). ☎ 04-67-63-43-22. Free admission. Tues–Sun 10am–5pm (Apr–Sept, until 7pm).

Paul Valéry met André Gide in the Jardin des Plantes, the oldest such garden in France. This botanical garden, filled with exotic plants and a handful of greenhouses, was opened in 1593.

✪ **Musée Fabre.** 39 bd. Bonne-Nouvelle. ☎ 04-67-14-83-00. Admission 20 F ($3.20) adults, 10 F ($1.60) students and persons 20 and under. Tues–Fri 9am–5:30pm, Sat–Sun 9:30am–5pm.

One of France's great provincial art galleries occupies the former Hôtel de Massilian, where Molière once played for a season. The collection originated with an exhibition of the Royal Academy that was sent to Montpellier by Napoléon in 1803. Its most important works, however, were given by François Fabre, a Montpellier painter, in 1825. After Fabre's death, many other paintings from his collection were donated to the gallery. Several of these were of his own creation, but the more significant works were ones he had acquired—including Poussin's *Venus and Adonis* and Italian paintings like

The Mystical Marriage of Saint Catherine. This generosity was followed by donations from other parties, notably Valedau, who in 1836 left his collection of Rubens, Gérard Dou, and Téniers.

ACCOMMODATIONS

The **Jardin des Sens** (see "Dining" below) also rents rooms.

Hôtel du Palais. 3 rue du Palais, 34000 Montpellier. ☎ **04-67-60-47-38.** Fax 04-67-60-40-23. 26 units. A/C MINIBAR TV TEL. 340–420 F ($54.40–$67.20) double. AE, DC, MC, V. Parking 25 F ($4).

This hotel, built in the late 18th century, is set in the town center, amid a labyrinth of narrow streets and monumental plazas and parks. As such, it's one of the most historic in town, with a design that evokes the kind of grandly symmetrical architecture that you might have associated with the *ancien régime.* Much of the decor you'll see today dates from around 1983, when the hotel was richly restored to a motif that uses lots of fabrics, big curtains, and walls of public areas that are painted to resemble marble. Bedrooms are relatively large, cozy, and appealing, thanks to thoughtful placements of antique reproductions and good maintenance. Breakfast is the only meal served.

La Maison Blanche. 1796 av. de la Prompignane, 34000 Montpellier. ☎ **04-99-58-20-70.** Fax 04-67-79-53-39. 38 units. A/C TV TEL. 500 F ($80) double; 780 F ($124.80) suite. AE, DC, MC, V. Free parking. A 5-minute drive northeast of Montpellier's center: Take bd. d'Antigone east until you reach the intersection with av. de la Pompignane and head north until you come to the hotel, on your right.

Few other hotels in the south of France have worked so hard to emulate the gingerbread and French Créole ambience of this hotel. The rooms are stylishly furnished in rattan and wicker. Parts of the interior, especially the dining room, might remind you of Louis XIII France more than Old Louisiana, but overall the setting is as charming and unusual as anything else in town. The in-house **restaurant,** open daily for lunch and Tuesday to Saturday for dinner, serves fixed-price menus at 110 F to 160 F ($17.60 to $25.60).

Les Arceaux. 33–35 bd. des Arceaux, 34000 Montpellier. ☎ **04-67-92-03-03.** Fax 04-67-92-05-09. 18 units. TV TEL. 300–335 F ($48–$53.60) double. MC, V.

A hotel has stood at this prime location, right off the renowned promenade du Peyrou, since the turn of the century. The smallish rooms are pleasantly but simply furnished, and a shaded terrace adjoins the hotel. Breakfast is the only meal served.

Sofitel Antigone. 1 rue Pertuisanes, 34000 Montpellier. ☎ **04-67-99-72-72.** Fax 04-67-65-17-50. www.sofitel-montpellier.com. E-mail: sofitel.mpl.sales@wanadoo.fr. 90 units. A/C TV TEL. 870–970 F ($139.20–$155.20) double; 1,500 F ($240) suite. AE, DC, MC, V. Parking 70 F ($11.20).

In the heart of Montpellier, this modern hotel is a favorite with businesspeople. However, in summer it does quite a trade with visitors. It's particularly distinguished for its pool, which, along with a bar and breakfast room, occupies most of the top floor. The rooms are chain format but first class. The best accommodations are on a floor known as Privilège, where you get such extras as an all-marble bath with generous towels and a hair dryer. Some rooms are suitable for those with disabilities. It's a winning choice, with the most efficient staff in the city. In 1998, management added a new bar, the Botanica, one of the coziest hideaways in town.

Ulysse. 338 av. de St-Maur, 34000 Montpellier. ☎ **04-67-02-02-30.** Fax 04-67-02-16-50. 27 units. MINIBAR TV TEL. 320–350 F ($51.20–$56) double. AE, DC, V. From bd. d'Antigone, head north along av. Jean-Mermoz to rue de la Pépinière; continue right for a short distance, then take a sharp left at the first intersection, which leads to av. de St-Maur.

One of the city's better bargains, Ulysse delivers a lot of bang for your buck. There's a simplicity here, though the owners have worked hard—on a budget—to make the hotel as stylish as possible. Each room is unique in its composition of colors and decorations. The furnishings are made with an original wrought-iron design, functional but with a certain flair. Much in-room comfort is found here, including fully equipped baths and extra features like a minibar, unusual for a budget hotel.

DINING

La Réserve Rimbaud. 820 av. de St-Maur. ☎ **04-67-72-52-53.** Reservations recommended. Main courses 90–160 F ($14.40–$25.60); fixed-price menus 180–380 F ($28.80–$60.80). AE, DC, MC, V. Tues–Sat noon–2pm and 8–10pm, Sun noon–2pm. Closed Jan–Mar 20. Take N113 (av. de Nîmes) northeast toward Nîmes and follow it to the intersection with av. St-Lazare, then turn left; the restaurant is on the right. FRENCH.

The most memorable restaurant in town is located in a bulky, rectangular manor house, built in 1875 by a prosperous local family, the Rimbauds. It offers only about 30 seats in a setting that might've been plucked from the early 1900s. Menu items, prepared and presented by English-speaking members of the Tarrit family, change with the season but are likely to include monkfish with local herbs; curried crayfish; stuffed calamari; warm foie gras with apples; fricassée of sole with baby vegetables; and a thin-crusted *croustillant aux pommes* served with English cream.

Le Chandelier. Immeuble La Coupole Antigone, 267 rue Léon-Blum. ☎ **04-67-15-34-38.** Reservations recommended. Main courses 120–220 F ($19.20–$35.20); fixed-price menus 220 F ($35.20) Mon–Fri and Sat lunch, 290–400 F ($46.40–$64) Sat night. AE, DC, MC, V. Tues–Sat noon–1:30pm; Mon–Sat 8–10pm. FRENCH.

This is the most dramatic modern restaurant in Montpellier, with superb food prepared by Gilbert Furland, superb service choreographed by Jean-Marc Forest, and a sweeping view over an upscale residential neighborhood (l'Antigone). You'll find it on the 7th floor of a modern office building, with access to a large terrace. The staff searches for "temptations of the palate," which means that you'll be presented with some unusual flavor combinations. Examples include a sophisticated version of calamari fried with fresh thyme; an escalope of foie gras in orange sauce; an award-winning ragoût of lobster; and sautéed pigeon in a Provençal pistou. A particularly scrumptious dessert is a crispy tarte with caramelized mango.

☼ Le Jardin des Sens. 11 av. St-Lazare. ☎ **04-67-79-63-38.** Fax 04-67-72-13-05. E-mail: jardinsens@relaischateaux.fr. Reservations required. Main courses 160–280 F ($25.60–$44.80); fixed-price menus 240 F ($38.40) at lunch (Mon–Fri), 240–660 F ($38.40–$105.60) at dinner. AE, MC, V. Mon–Sat noon–2pm and 7:30–10pm. FRENCH.

If we could award more than one star, we'd grant three to this citadel of fine cuisine. The chefs, twins Laurent and Jacques Pourcel, have taken Montpellier by storm. The cuisine could be almost anything, depending on where the chefs' imaginations roam. Michelin has awarded them three stars, its highest praise. The rich bounty of Languedoc is served, but only after going through a process designed to enhance its natural flavor. The meals often seem flawless, so it's no wonder the restaurateurs of Montpellier are wishing these twins had settled in some other city. An appropriate starter might be ravioli stuffed with foie gras of duckling and flap mushrooms, floating in chicken bouillon fortified with truffles, broad beans, and crispy potatoes. A main course of note involves crisp-fried crayfish tails, served with a confit of pigeon and a fricassée of green peas with slices of Bayonne ham. A *tarte fine* with tomatoes, roasted monkfish, and essence of thyme is memorable, as is a fillet of pigeon stuffed with pistachios. A dessert specialty is a gratin of limes with slices of pineapple *en confit*.

The Jardin des Sens also rents 12 deluxe **guest rooms** and two suites, each designed in cutting-edge modernism by Bruno Borrione, a colleague of Philippe Starck. They cost 980 F to 1,380 F ($156.80 to $220.80) for a double and 1,680 F to 2,500 F ($268.80 to $400) for a suite.

✪ **L'Olivier.** 12 rue Aristide-Olivier. ☎ **04-67-92-86-28.** Reservations required. Main courses 90–160 F ($14.40–$25.60); fixed-price menus 198–218 F ($31.70–$34.90). AE, DC. Tues–Sat noon–1:30pm and 7:30–9:30pm. Closed Aug and holidays. FRENCH.

No restaurant, with the exception of Le Jardin des Sens, has improved more than this. Chef Michel Breton, assisted by his wife Yvette, is becoming a name in the restaurant guides to the south of France. Don't even dream of showing up here without a reservation: The establishment holds places for only 20 diners at a time, within a subdued, and rather bland-looking modern space accented only by a collection of contemporary paintings. But you don't come to L'Olivier to look at the walls. You come for Breton's salmon with oysters, warm monkfish terrine, frogs' legs with wild mushrooms, haunch of rabbit stuffed with wild mushrooms, and salad of lamb sweetbreads with extract of truffles. The welcome is warm-hearted and sincere.

MONTPELLIER AFTER DARK

After the sun sets, head for **place Jean-Jaurès, rue de Verdun,** and **rue des Écoles Laïques,** or take a walk down **rue de la Loge** for its carnival atmosphere of talented jugglers, mimes, and musical artists.

Rockstore, 20 rue de Verdun (☎ **04-67-06-80-00**), with its 1950s rock memorabilia and live concerts, draws lots of students. Then walk up a flight of stairs to its disco, which pounds out techno and rock. The cover for the disco is 50 F ($8).

An exotic cocktail bar is **Viva Brazil,** 7 rue de Verdun (☎ **04-67-58-63-33**), where you chop your way through the lush rain-forest vegetation and friendly natives to reach the mirrored sanctuary of the dance floor. For the best jazz and blues in town, check out **JAM,** 100 rue Ferdinand-de-Lesseps (☎ **04-67-58-30-30**). In a noisy, smoky, and even gritty space, its regular concerts attract jazz enthusiasts from miles around. Concert tickets average 50 F ($8).

A more recently inaugurated disco is **La Tipola,** route de Palavas (☎ **04-67-65-62-95**), a modern, sparsely decorated bar and dance hall with enough bars to ensure that everyone can get a drink at any time, and a clientele that tends to be between 20 and 38 years old. Open every Wednesday to Sunday beginning around 10pm, it charges a 50 F ($8) cover, a price that includes the first drink.

Gays and lesbians gather at the town's most animated gay bar and disco, **La Villa Rouge,** route de Palavas (☎ **04-67-06-52-15**), a short distance from La Tipola (see above). Both of them lie about 3 miles south of the town center.

Le Corum (☎ **04-67-61-67-61**), the most up-to-date theater in town, is the site of many different plays, dance recitals, operas, and symphonic presentations. It lies within the Palais des Congrès, esplanade Charles-de-Gaulle, in the heart of town. For complete ticket information and schedules, contact either the Corum directly, or an organization that's instrumental in its management, the **Opéra Comédie,** place de la Comédie (☎ **04-67-60-19-99**).

4 Narbonne

525 miles SW of Paris, 38 miles E of Carcassonne, 58 miles S of Montpellier

Medieval Narbonne was a port to rival Marseille in Roman times, its "galleys laden with riches." Since then, the Mediterranean has receded from Narbonne, and the town is now 5 miles inland.

Narbonne was the first town outside Italy to be colonized by the Romans. For that reason it's an intriguing place, steeped with antiquity. After Lyon, Narbonne was the largest town in Gaul. Even today you can still see evidence of the town's former wealth. Too far from the sea to be a beach town, it attracts history buffs and others aware of the memories of its glorious past. Some 50,000 Narbonnais live here, in what is really a sleepy backwater. However, many locals are trying to make a go with their vineyards. Caves are open to visitors in the surrounding area (the tourist office will advise). If you want to go to the beach, you'll have to head to the nearby sands at the village of **Gruisson** and the beach (Gruisson-Plage) that adjoins it, or the suburb of **St-Pierre la Mer** and the adjoining beach (Narbonne-Plage). Both lie 9 miles south from Narbonne. Buses from the town center are frequent, each marked with its destination.

ESSENTIALS

GETTING THERE   Narbonne has rail, bus, and highway connections with other cities on the Mediterranean coast and with Toulouse. Rail travel is the most popular way to get here, with 14 **trains** per day arriving from Perpignan (trip time: 50 minutes), 13 per day from Toulouse (trip time: $1^1/2$ hours), and 12 per day from Montpellier (trip time: 1 hour). For rail information and schedules, call ☎ **08-36-35-35-35.** If you're **driving,** Narbonne is located at the junction of A61 and A9, making it easily accessible from either Toulouse or the Riviera.

VISITOR INFORMATION   The **Office de Tourisme** is on place Roger-Salengro (☎ **04-68-65-15-60**).

SEEING THE SIGHTS

Few other cities in France contain such a massive medieval architectural block in their centers. Foremost among Narbonne's labyrinth of religious and civic buildings is the **Cathédrale St-Just,** place de l'Hôtel-de-Ville, entrance on rue Gauthier (☎ **04-68-32-09-52**). Its construction began in 1272 but was never finished. Only the transept and a choir were completed; the choir is 130 feet high, built in the bold Gothic style of northern France. At each end of the transept are 194-foot towers from 1480. Inside is an impressive collection of Flemish tapestries. The cloisters are from the 14th and 15th centuries and connect the cathedral with the Archbishops' Palace. It's open daily, May to September from 10am to 7pm and October to March from 9am to noon and 2 to 6pm. Entrance is free.

The cathedral is attached to the **Palais des Archevêques** (Archbishops' Palace, sometimes referred to as the Vieux-Palais), place de l'Hôtel-de-Ville (☎ **04-68-90-30-30**). It was conceived as part fortress, part pleasure palace, with three military-style towers from the 13th and 14th centuries. The Old Palace on the right is from the 12th century and the so-called New Palace on the left is from the 14th. It's said that the old, arthritic, and sometimes very overweight archbishops used to be hauled up the interior's monumental Louis XIII-style stairs on mules.

Part of the complex is devoted to the neo-Gothic **Hôtel de Ville (town hall),** which was reconstructed by Viollet-le-Duc, a 19th-century architect involved with the refurbishment of such sites as the cathedral at Paris, between 1845 and 1850.

Today the once-private apartments of the former archbishops contain three museums. Admission is 10 F ($1.60) to each museum (you can buy a global ticket that gets you into all three, plus the **Musée Lapidaire,** but it's no cheaper that way). Hours are the same at all three: April to September daily from 9:30am to 12:15pm and 2 to 6pm, October to March Tuesday to Sunday from 10am to noon and 2 to 5pm. For more information, call ☎ **04-68-90-30-54.**

Musée Archéologique contains prehistoric artifacts, Bronze Age tools, 14th-century frescoes, and Greco-Roman amphorae. Several of the sarcophagi date from the 3rd century and some of the mosaics are of pagan origin. **Musée d'Art et d'Histoire de Narbonne** is located three floors above street level in the archbishop's once-private apartments, the rooms in which Louis XII stayed during his siege of Perpignan. Their coffered ceilings are enhanced with panels depicting the nine Muses. A Roman mosaic floor and 17th-century portraits are on display. There's also a collection of antique porcelain, enamels, and a portrait bust of Louis XIV. In the **Horreum Romain,** you'll find a labyrinth of underground passageways, similar to catacombs but with none of the burial functions, dug by the Gallo-Romans and their successors for storage of food and supplies during times of siege.

If you visit between mid-June and mid-September, you might want to participate in one of the occasional hikes up the steep steps of the **Donjon Gilles-Aycelin,** place de l'Hôtel-de-Ville. Originally a watchtower and prison in the late 13th century, it has a lofty observation platform with a view of the cathedral, the surrounding plain, and the Pyrénées. Entrance costs 10 F ($1.60) for adults and 5 F (80¢) for students and children 11 to 18. The watchtower is open daily April to September from 11am to 7pm. October to March, it's open daily from 10am to noon, and from 2 to 5pm.

You can see Roman artifacts at the **Musée Lapidaire,** place Lamourguier (☎ **04-68-65-53-58**), in the 13th-century Notre Dame de Lamourguier. The broken sculptures, Roman inscriptions, and relics of medieval buildings make up one of the largest (and most important) exhibits of its kind in France. Although it maintains regular hours only in July and August (daily from 9:30am to 12:15pm and 2 to 6pm), you can visit it as part of the global museum ticket described above; outside those dates, you can visit only by making special arrangements with the tour operator (☎ **04-68-90-30-66**).

A final site worth visiting is the early Gothic **Basilique St-Paul-Serge,** rue de l'Hôtel-Dieu (☎ **04-68-32-68-98**), which was built on the site of a 4th-century necropolis. It has an elegant choir with fine Renaissance wood carvings and some ancient Christian sarcophagi. The chancel, from 1229, is admirable. The north door leads to the Paleo-Christian Cemetery, part of an early Christian burial ground. From April to September, it's open daily from 9am to 7pm. From October to March, it's open daily from 9am to noon, and from 2 to 6pm.

ACCOMMODATIONS

Hôtel Languedoc. 22 bd. Gambetta, 11100 Narbonne. ☎ **04-68-65-14-74.** Fax 04-68-65-81-48. E-mail: languedoc@wanadoo.fr. 40 units. TV TEL. 290–400 F ($46.40–$64) double; 480 F ($76.80) suite. AE, DC, MC, V. Parking 35 F ($5.60).

This oft-modernized turn-of-the-century hotel is near the canal de la Rhône. Rooms come in various shapes and sizes. The on-site **restaurant** specializes in regional dishes. The hotel's wine bar, Le Bacchus, is open daily from 7:30am (yes, in the morning) to 7pm. Specializing in the many esoteric vintages grown nearby, it sells wine by the glass and serves simple but flavorful accompaniments to those wines. Examples are grilled salmon with anchovy butter, tender lamb cooked with beans, sautéed chicken *chasseur,* fresh oysters, and *marmites* of fish. Fixed-price menus cost from 120 F to 360 F ($19.20 to $57.60).

La Résidence. 6 rue du 1er-Mai, 11100 Narbonne. ☎ **04-68-32-19-41.** Fax 04-68-65-51-82. 25 units. A/C MINIBAR TV TEL. 436–457 F ($69.75–$73.10) double. AE, DC, MC, V. Parking 40 F ($6.40). Closed Jan 16–Feb 14.

Our favorite hotel in Narbonne is near the Cathédrale St-Just. The 19th-century La Résidence, converted from a once-stately villa, is comfortable and decorated with antiques. It doesn't have a restaurant but offers breakfast and a gracious welcome.

DINING

✪ **La Table St-Crescent.** In the Palais des Vins, rte. de Perpignan. ☎ **04-68-41-37-37.**
Reservations recommended. Main courses 50–150 F ($8–$24); fixed-price menus 158–258 F
($25.30–$41.30), 100 F ($16) Mon–Fri only. AE, DC, MC, V. Tues–Fri and Sun noon–2pm;
Mon–Sat 7–9:30pm. FRENCH/LANGUEDOCIENNE.

This is one of the most well-respected restaurants in this region of France. It's less than
a mile east of town, beside the road leading to Perpignan, in a complex of wine-
tasting boutiques established by a local syndicate of wine growers. Understandably, it
attracts some of the most sophisticated oenophiles around. The foundations of this
place date, it's said, from the 8th century, when it functioned as an oratory (small
chapel) and prayer site. Today, it's outfitted with nondescript modern furniture that's
obviously little more than a foil for the inspired cuisine of master chef Claude Giraud.
The chef delivers a refined, brilliantly realized repertoire. Expect sublime sauces and
sophisticated herbs and seasonings. Menu items change four times a year based on sea-
sonality of ingredients and the inspiration of the owners. Main courses include sea bass
marinated with olives, and a lasagne of grilled eggplant with a confit of tomatoes and
oil of pistou. Especially succulent is roasted shoulder of lamb with crispy noodles and
a sweet garlic and sage sauce. Wine steward Sabrine Giraud (the chef's wife) will help
you select a wine to accompany your fixed-price menu for a mere 40 F ($6.40) per
person. Be assured that the wine will be well-selected, usually local, and sometimes
rather obscure vintages.

5 Collioure

577 miles SW of Paris, 17 miles SE of Perpignan

You may recognize this port and its sailboats from the Fauve paintings of Lhote and
Derain. It's said to resemble St-Tropez before it was overrun, attracting, in days past,
Matisse, Picasso, and Dalí. Collioure is the most authentically alluring port of Roussillon, a gem with a vivid Spanish and Catalan image and flavor. Some visitors believe
it's the most charming village on the Côte Vermeille. The town's sloping narrow
streets, charming semi-fortified church, antique lighthouse, and eerily introverted culture make it worth an afternoon stopover. This is the ideal small-town antidote to the
condo-choked Riviera.

The two curving ports are separated from each other by the heavy masonry of the
13th-century **Château Royal,** place du 8-Mai-1945 (☎ **04-68-82-06-43**). The
château, now a museum of painting and folkloric artifacts, is open daily, June to September from 10am to 6pm and October to May from 9am to 5pm; closed January 1,
May 1, and December 25. Admission is 20 F ($3.20) for adults and 10 F ($1.60)
for children. Free for children under 7. Also try to visit the **Musée Jean-Peské,**
route de Port-Vendres (☎ **04-68-82-10-19**), with its collection of works by artists
who migrated here to paint. It's open in July and August daily from 10am to noon and
3 to 7pm, September to June Wednesday through Monday from 10am to noon and
2 to 6pm. Admission is 12 F ($1.90) for adults, 8 F ($1.30) for children 12 to 16,
and free for children under 12.

ESSENTIALS

GETTING THERE   Collioure is serviced by frequent **train** and bus connections,
especially from Perpignan. For train information and schedules, call ☎ **08-36-
35-35-35.** Many visitors **drive** along the coastal road (RN 114) leading to the Spanish border.

VISITOR INFORMATION   The **Office de Tourisme** is on place du 18-Juin (☎ **04-68-82-15-47**).

ACCOMMODATIONS

Casa Pairal. Impasse des Palmiers, 66190 Collioure. ☎ **04-68-82-05-81.** Fax 04-68-82-52-10. 28 units. MINIBAR TV TEL. Summer, 440–640 F ($70.40–$102.40) double, 790–990 F ($126.40–$158.40) junior suite. Winter, all rooms $10–$15 less. AE, MC, V. Closed Nov–Mar. Parking 40 F ($6.40).

This small-scale, family-operated place in a 150-year-old house has a certain charm. On sunny days, guests can take a dip in the outdoor swimming pool, which sits in the shadow of century-old trees. The bedrooms are filled with charming old antiques blended with more modern pieces. The best doubles have a petit salon plus a small balcony. Only breakfast is served, but there are many restaurants nearby. The hotel lies 150 meters from the port and the beach.

Les Caranques. Rte. de Port-Vendres, 66190 Collioure. ☎ **04-68-82-06-68.** Fax 04-68-82-00-92. E-mail: les-caranques@little.france.com. 22 units. TEL. 380–420 F ($60.80–$67.20) double. AE, MC, V. Closed Oct 15–Mar.

Constructed around the core of a private villa built after World War II and enlarged twice since then, this hotel is well scrubbed, comfortably furnished, personalized, and one of the best bargains in town. Set on the perimeter of Collioure, away from the crush (and the charm) of the center, it features a terrace that opens onto a view of the old port.

✪ **Relais des Trois Mas et Restaurant La Balette.** Rte. de Port-Vendres, 66190 Collioure. ☎ **04-68-82-05-07.** Fax 04-68-82-38-08. 23 units. A/C MINIBAR TV TEL. 540–1,560 F ($86.40–$249.60) double; 1,300–2,580 F ($208–$412.80) suite. MC, V. Closed Nov 15–Dec 15. Parking 88 F ($14.10).

This is not only the town's premier hotel but also the restaurant of choice. The hotel honors the famous artists who've lived at Collioure in the decor of its beautiful rooms, which lead to spacious baths with Jacuzzis. The rooms open onto views of the water. Even if you aren't a guest, you may want to take a meal in the **dining room,** with its vistas of the harbor. Christian Peyre is unchallenged as the best chef in town. His cooking is inventive—often simple but always refined. There's an outdoor heated pool.

DINING

The **Restaurant La Balette** at the Relais des Trois Mas (see "Accommodations," above) is the best dining room in town.

L'Andalou. 10 rue de la République. ☎ **04-68-82-32-78.** Reservations recommended. Main courses 89–109 F ($14.25–$17.45). AE, MC, V. Thurs–Tues noon–2:30pm and 7pm–midnight. FRENCH/SPANISH.

This cozy bistro and tavern are at the edge of Collioure's historic core. Your hosts are Manuel Fernandez, his wife Caroline, and extended members of their family. The place is decorated with a hanging collection of flamenco dresses and depictions of the surrounding landscapes. Look for succulent, well-prepared Spanish-style dishes like a parillade of seafood, a spicy, garlic-laced soupe de poissons, or perhaps yellow Manchego cheese in a style you might have expected in Madrid. A particularly attractive bargain is the house paella, priced at 59 F ($9.45) for one, or 175 F ($28) for enough to feed the whole table. Snails are usually drenched in butter and roasted garlic, while a brochette andaluz brings grilled and herbed beef to succulent new heights. Also look for thin-sliced Serrano ham, tortilla (the omelet, not the burrito wrapper), and several different preparations of mussels, including a grilled form (*à la plancha*) that's particularly delectable. A roster of French and Spanish wines (especially riojas) can accompany your meal.

6 Perpignan

562 miles SW of Paris, 229 miles NW of Marseille, 40 miles S of Narbonne

At Perpignan you may think you've crossed the border into Spain, for this was once Catalonia's second city, after Barcelona. Even earlier, it was the capital of the kingdom of Majorca. But when the Roussillon—the French part of Catalonia—was finally partitioned off, Perpignan became French forever, authenticated by the Treaty of the Pyrénées in 1659. However, Catalan is still spoken here, especially among country folk.

Today Perpignan is content to rest on its former glory. Its residents—some 110,000 in all—enjoy the closeness of the Côte Catalane and the mountains to their north. The pace is decidedly relaxed. You'll even have time to smell the flowers that grow here in great abundance.

This is one of the sunniest places in France, but summer afternoons in July and August are a cauldron. That's when many of the locals take the 6-mile ride to the beach to cool off. There's a young scene here that brings vibrance to Perpignan, especially along the quays of the Basse River, site of impromptu nighttime concerts, beer drinking, and the devouring of tapas, a tradition inherited from nearby Barcelona.

ESSENTIALS

GETTING THERE   Four **trains** per day arrive from Paris (trip time: 6 to 10 hours); the high-speed TGV goes on to Montpellier. There are also at least 15 trains that pull into Perpignan from Nice (trip time: 6 hours). For rail information and schedules, call ☎ 08-36-35-35-35. If you're **driving** from the French Riviera, drive west along A9 to Perpignan.

VISITOR INFORMATION   The **Office Municipal du Tourisme** is within the Palais des Congrès, place Armand-Lanoux (☎ 04-68-66-30-30).

SPECIAL EVENTS   During a terribly hot 3-week period of July, **Les Estivales** causes the city to explode with a medley of music, expositions, and theater. For information, call ☎ 04-68-35-01-77. Our favorite time to visit this area is during the grape harvest in September. If you visit at this time, you may want to drive through the Rivesaltes district bordering the city to the west and north. Temperatures have usually dropped by then.

Perpignan is host to one of the most widely discussed celebrations of photojournalism in the industry. Established in the late 1980s, it's the **Festivale Internationale de Photo-Journalisme,** also referred to as **Le Visa pour l'Image.** During a 2-week period, from the 28th of August to the 12th of September, at least 10 sites of historic, usually medieval, interest are devoted to the exposition of photo-journalistic expositions from around the world. Entrance to all the expositions is free, and prizes are awarded by an international committee.

SEEING THE SIGHTS

With its inviting pedestrian streets, Perpignan is a good town for shopping. Catalan is the style indigenous to the area, and it's in evidence in the textiles, pottery, and furniture. For one of the best selections of Catalan pieces, including pottery, furniture, carpets, and even antiques, visit the **Centre Sant-Vicens,** rue Sant-Vicens (☎ 04-68-50-02-18), site of about a dozen independent merchants, each operating as an independent entity. You'll find it 2¹/₂ miles south of the town center, following the signs pointing to Enne and Collioures. A competitor, located within the town center, whose inventories contain mostly Catalan-inspired items for home decorating, is **La Maison Quinta,** 3 rue des Grands-des-Fabriques (☎ **04-68-34-41-62**).

There's a 3-hour guided walking tour that has proved to be a worthwhile way to see the main attractions within the town's historic core. Some tour leaders even lace their commentary with English. These tours are conducted only between mid-June and mid-September, at hours that change every day according to demand. They depart from the sidewalk in front of the tourist office, and are priced at 25 F ($4) per participant, regardless of age. For more information, contact the tourist office (see above).

Castillet. Place de Verdun. ☎ **04-68-35-42-05.** Admission 25 F ($4) adults, 15 F ($2.40) students and children 17 and under. Mid-June to mid-Sept, Wed–Mon 9:30am–7pm; mid-Sept to mid-June, 9am–6pm.

This crenellated redbrick building is a combination gateway and fortress from the 14th century. You can climb its bulky-looking tower for a good view of the town. Also housed here is the **Musée des Arts et Traditions Populaires Catalans** (also known as La Casa Païral), which contains exhibitions of Catalan regional artifacts and folkloric items, including typical dress.

Cathédrale St-Jean. Place Gambetta/rue de l'Horloge. ☎ **04-68-51-33-72.** Free admission. Daily 7:30am–noon and 3–7pm.

The cathedral dates from the 14th and 15th centuries and has an admirable nave and interesting 17th-century retables. Leaving via the south door, you'll find on the left a chapel with the Devout Christ, a magnificent wood carving depicting Jesus contorted with pain and suffering—his head, crowned with thorns, drooping on his chest.

Palais des Rois de Majorque (Palace of the Kings of Majorca). Rue des Archers. ☎ **04-68-34-48-29.** Admission 25 F ($4) adults, 10 F ($1.60) students, free for children 7 and under. June–Sept, daily 10am–6pm; Oct–May, daily 9am–5pm.

Situated at the top of the town, the Spanish citadel encloses the Palace of the Kings of Majorca. This structure from the 13th and 14th centuries, built around a court encircled by arcades, has been restored by the government. You can see the old throne room with its large fireplaces and a square tower with a double gallery; from the tower there's a fine view of the Pyrénées. A free guided tour, in French only, departs four times a day if demand warrants it. The tour cost is 20 F ($3.20).

Château de Salses. In the town of Salses, 15¹/₂ miles north of the city center. ☎ **04-68-38-60-13.** Admission 32 F ($5.10) adults, 21 F ($3.35) under 25, free under 17. Apr–May and Oct, daily 9:30am–12:30pm and 2–6pm; June and Sept, daily 9:30am–6:30pm; July–Aug, daily 9:30am–7pm; Nov–Mar, daily 10am–noon and 2–5pm.

This fort has guarded the main road linking Spain and France since the days of the Romans. Ferdinand of Aragón erected a fort here in 1497 hoping to protect the northern frontier of his kingdom. Even today, Salses marks the language-barrier point between Catalonia in Spain and Languedoc in France. This Spanish-style fort designed by Ferdinand is a curious example of an Iberian structure in France, but in the 17th century it was modified by Vauban to look more like a château. After many changes of ownership, Salses fell to the forces of Louis XIII in September 1642; its Spanish garrison left forever. Some 2 decades later, Roussillon was incorporated into France.

ACCOMMODATIONS

La Villa Duflot. 109 av. Victor-Dalbiez, 66000 Perpignan. ☎ **04-68-56-67-67.** Fax 04-68-56-54-05. www.little-france.com/villa.duflot. 24 units. A/C MINIBAR TV TEL.

640–1,100 F ($102.40–$176) double. Half board 560–790 F ($89.60–$126.40) per person double occupancy. AE, DC, MC, V.

This is the area's greatest hotel, yet its prices are reasonable for the luxury offered. Tranquillity, style, and refinement reign supreme. When this hotel opened, the mayor proclaimed, "Now we have some class in Perpignan." Located in a suburb, La Villa Duflot is a Mediterranean-style dwelling surrounded by a 3-acre park of pine, palm, and eucalyptus. The hotel has an appealing, almost family touch to it and isn't the least bit intimidating. You can sunbathe in the gardens surrounding the pool and order drinks at any hour at the outside bar. The good-size guest rooms are situated around a patio planted with century-old olive trees. All are spacious and soundproof, with solid marble baths and Art Deco interiors. To get here from the center of town, follow the signs to Perthus-Le Belou and the A9 autoroute, and travel 2 miles south of Perpignan's center. Just before you reach A9, you'll see the hotel. The **restaurant** (see "Dining," below) is reason enough to stay here.

Park Hotel. 18 bd. Jean-Bourrat, 66000 Perpignan. ☎ **04-68-35-14-14.** Fax 04-68-35-48-18. 67 units. A/C MINIBAR TV TEL. 300–480 F ($48–$76.80) double. AE, DC, MC, V. Parking 45 F ($7.20).

This four-story hotel, facing the Jardins de la Ville, offers well-furnished, soundproofed rooms. The restaurant, Le Chapon Fin, serves up first-class cuisine. The food, made from prime regional produce, is some of the finest in the area. Post-nouvelle choices include roast sea scallops flavored with succulent sea urchin velouté, various lobster dishes, and penne with truffles. As an accompaniment, try one of the local wines—perhaps a Collioure or Côtes du Roussillon. The restaurant is open for lunch Monday to Saturday and for dinner Monday to Friday. The hotel also houses **Le Bistrot du Park,** a less expensive eatery specializing in seafood.

DINING

There is also a wonderful restaurant in the **Park Hotel** (see above).

✪ **Côté Théâtre.** 7 rue du Théâtre. ☎ **04-68-34-60-00.** Reservations recommended. Main courses 75–120 F ($12–$19.20); fixed-price menus 148 F ($23.70) at lunch Mon–Fri, 230–330 F ($36.80–$52.80) dinner and Sat lunch. AE, DC, MC, V. Tues–Sat noon–2pm; Mon–Sat 7:30–10:30pm. Closed 2 weeks in late July–early Aug. MEDITERRANEAN.

Here's your once-in-a-lifetime chance to dine in a 15th-century, dignified stone building that was the former home of a grand inquisitor for the Catholic church. The elaborately crafted wooden ceiling has been designated as a historic monument in its own right. The restaurant attracts a quietly conservative crowd who dine under no pretenses. The cuisine is traditional, earthy, and completely unafraid of strong, even gutsy, flavors and old-fashioned traditions. Menu items include calamari or octopus salad with herbs and vinaigrette; braised sea scallops with shallots; a variety of different fish hauled from local waters, sometimes prepared with flap mushrooms; and deboned and stuffed pig's foot.

✪ **La Villa Duflot.** 109 ave. Victor Dalbiez, 66000 Perpignan. ☎ **04-68-56-67-67.** Fax 04-68-56-54-05. Reservations required. Main courses 200–250 F ($32–$40); fixed-price menu 200 F ($32) Sat–Sun only. Daily noon–2:30pm and 8–11pm. AE, MC, V. Take N9 from the town center leading to autoroute, exiting at Perpignan Sud (South) heading toward Argeles. FRENCH.

Slightly removed from the city center, this *restaurant avec chambres* (see also "Accommodations," above) is the most tranquil oasis in the area. Owner André Duflot employs top-notch chefs who turn out dish after dish with remarkable skill and professionalism. Try, for example, a salad of warm squid or a platter of fresh anchovies marinated in vinegar. Sample the excellent foie gras of duckling. Two new specialties include gratin of lobster and a succulent magrêt of duckling with figs. The dessert sensation is fresh peaches in Banyuls wine. On the premises is an American bar.

✪ **Le Bistrot Gourmand.** 40 rue de la Fusterie. ☎ **04-68-51-21-14.** Reservations recommended. Main courses 60–95 F ($9.60–$15.20); fixed-price menu 65 F ($10.40) at lunch, 85–115 F ($13.60–$18.40) at dinner. V. Mon–Sat noon–2pm and 7–10pm. July–Aug, closed for dinner. FRENCH/CATALONIAN.

Set in the heart of Perpignan's oldest neighborhood, this informal and charming bistro serves excellent food. It's usually busier at lunch than at dinner. Menu items include mussels in cream sauce; salmon steak with a leek-flavored cream sauce; medaillons of sea bass with a sweet white wine sauce; and fillet of beef drenched in a heady Banyuls wine. One particular dish that's not to be missed if you crave strong Mediterranean flavors is an *anchoiade* (a paste of grilled anchovies) that's served with a medley of grilled Languedocien red peppers.

PERPIGNAN AFTER DARK

Unlike the towns farther up north in France, Spanish and Catalan influences permeate Perpignan. At night, especially, there's an influence on tapas and late-night promenades. The streets that radiate outward from **place de la Loge** contain a higher concentration of bars and nightclubs than any other part of town. For a traditional Catalan-style bar with a hip staff, visit **Le Festival,** 40 place Rigaud (☎ **04-68-34-31-60**), a hot spot for tantalizing tapas and heady sangréa. But the bars in the center of town, including the **Républic Café,** 2 place de la République (☎ **04-68-51-11-64**), can be stimulating alternatives with their vivacious student scene and live music. The most visible and oft-visited gay and lesbian hangout, featuring both a bar and a disco, is **Le Tapis Volé,** 3 rue Honoré Daumier (☎ **04-68-63-90-79**), about a half-mile north of the town center. During summer, the nearby resort complex of **Canet-Plage,** 7^1/$_2$ miles east of Perpignan's historic core, contains a beachfront strip of seasonal bars and dance clubs that come and go with the tides and with midsummer tourism.

7 Carcassonne

495 miles SW of Paris, 57 miles SE of Toulouse, 65 miles S of Albi

Evoking bold knights, fair damsels, and troubadours, the greatest fortress city of Europe rises against a background of the snowcapped Pyrénées. Floodlit at night, it suggests fairy-tale magic, but back in its heyday in the Middle Ages, all wasn't so romantic. Shattering the peace and quiet were battering rams, grapnels, a mobile tower (inspired by the Trojan horse), catapults, flaming arrows, and the mangonel.

Today, the city that served as a backdrop for the 1991 movie *Robin Hood, Prince of Thieves,* is overrun with hordes of visitors and tacky gift shops. But the elusive charm of Carcassone still emerges in the evening, when thousands of day-trippers have departed and floodlights bathe the ancient monuments.

ESSENTIALS

GETTING THERE   Carcassonne is a major stop for **trains** between Toulouse and destinations south and east. There are 24 trains per day from Toulouse (trip time: 50 minutes), 14 trains per day from Montpellier (trip time: 2 hours), and 12 trains per day from Nîmes (trip time: 2^1/$_2$ hours). For rail information and schedules, call ☎ **08-36-35-35-35.** If you're **driving,** Carcassonne lies on A61 south of Toulouse.

VISITOR INFORMATION   The **Office de Tourisme** is at 15 bd. Camille-Pelletan (☎ **04-68-10-24-30**) and in the medieval town at Porte Narbonnaise (☎ **04-68-10-24-36**).

SPECIAL EVENTS   The town's nightlife sparkles with real pizzazz during its major summer festivals. The whole month of July is devoted to **Festival de Carcassonne,** when instrumental concerts, modern and classical dance, operas, and original theater shower the city. Tickets range from 140 F to 300 F ($22.40 to $48) for adults or 60 F ($9.60) for children under 15 and can be purchased by calling ☎ **04-68-77-71-05.** For more information, contact the **Théâtre Municipal** at ☎ **04-68-25-33-13.** On the night of July 14, **Bastille Day,** one of the best fireworks spectacles in all of France lights up the skies. In early August, the unadulterated merriment and good times of the Middle Ages overtake the city during the **Cité en Scènes.** For information, contact the Office de Tourisme or **Carcassone Terre d'Histoire,** chemin de Serres (☎ **04-68-47-97-97**).

EXPLORING THE TOWN

Carcassonne consists of two towns: the **Ville Basse** (Lower City) and the medieval **Cité.** The former has little interest, but the latter is among the major attractions in France and the goal of many a pilgrim. The fortifications consist of the inner and outer walls, a double line of ramparts. The inner rampart was built by the Visigoths in the 5th century. Clovis, king of the Franks, attacked in 506 but failed. The Saracens overcame the city in 728, until Pepin the Short (father of Charlemagne) drove them out in 752. During a long siege by Charlemagne, the populace of the walled city was starving and near surrender until Dame Carcas came up with an idea. According to legend, she gathered up the last remaining bit of grain, fed it to a sow, then tossed the pig over the ramparts. It's said to have burst, scattering the grain. The Franks concluded that Carcassonne must have unlimited food supplies and ended their siege.

Carcassone's walls were further fortified by the vicomtes de Trencavel in the 12th century and by Louis IX and Philip the Bold in the following century. However, by the mid–17th century its position as a strategic frontier fort was over, and the ramparts were left to decay. In the 19th century the builders of the Lower Town began to remove the stone for use in new construction. But interest in the Middle Ages revived, and the government ordered Viollet-le-Duc (who restored Notre-Dame in Paris) to repair and, where necessary, rebuild the walls. Reconstruction continued until very recently. Within the walls resides a small populace.

The **Basillique St-Nazaire,** La Cité (☎ **04-68-25-27-65**), dating from the 11th to 14th centuries, contains some beautiful stained-glass windows and a pair of rose medallions. The nave is in the Romanesque style, but the choir and transept are Gothic. The organ, one of the oldest in southwestern France, is from the 16th century. The tomb of Bishop Radulph, from 1266, is well preserved. The cathedral is open daily, in July and August from 9am to 7:30pm and off-season from 9:30am to noon and 2 to 5:30pm. Mass is celebrated on Sunday at 11am. Admission is free.

SHOPPING   Carcassone, more than other French cities, is really two distinct shopping towns in one. In the modern lower city, the major streets for shopping are **rue Clemenceau** and **rue de Verdun,** particularly if you're in the market for clothing. In the walled medieval city, the streets are chock-full of tiny stores and boutiques selling mostly gift items like antiques and local arts and crafts. On the third Saturday of every month at the portail Jacobin, in the center of the modern town, a **flea market** is set up from 8am to 6pm.

Stores worth visiting are the **Caveau des Vins,** tour du Tréseau (☎ **04-68-25-31-00**), where you'll find a wide selection of regional wines ranging from simple table wines to those awarded the distinction of Appellation d'Origine Contrôlée; **Antiquités "Le St-Georges,"** 36 rue Victor-Hugo (☎ **04-61-23-33-97**), which specializes in antique scientific instruments and furniture from the 17th to the 19th centuries; and **Dominique Sarraute,** 15 rue Porte d'Aude (☎ **04-68-72-42-90**), for antique firearms.

ACCOMMODATIONS
IN THE CITÉ

Cité. Place de l'Église, 11000 Carcassonne. ☎ **04-68-71-98-71.** Fax 04-68-71-50-15. www.hoteldelacite.com. E-mail: reservations@hoteldelacite.com. 61 units. A/C MINIBAR TV TEL. 1,200–2,050 F ($192–$328) double; 2,700–3,200 F ($432–$512) suite. AE, DC, MC, V. Parking 90 F ($14.40).

Originally a palace for whatever bishop or well-placed prelate happened to be in control at the time, this historically important site has thrived as the most desirable hotel in town since it was built in 1909. Massively and luxuriously renovated, it's constructed into the actual walls of the city, adjoining the cathedral. The hotel has been acquired by the luxury-minded Orient-Express Hotel group and grandly fluffed up to the tune of $3 million. You enter into a long Gothic corridor/gallery leading to the lounge. Many rooms open onto the ramparts and a garden and feature antiques or reproductions. A few rooms boast brass beds and four-posters, but unit 33 is the only one with a balcony, opening onto views of Carcassonne. Modern equipment has been discreetly installed, as well as a heated pool.

The hotel is renowned for its restaurant, **La Barbacane** (see "Dining," below).

AT THE ENTRANCE TO THE CITÉ

Hôtel du Donjon. 2 rue du Comte-Roger, 11000 Carcassonne. ☎ **800/528-1234** in the U.S. and Canada, or 04-68-11-23-80. Fax 04-68-25-06-60. www.hotel-donjon.fr. E-mail: hotel.donjon.best.western@wanadoo.fr. 63 units. A/C MINIBAR TV TEL. 420–550 F ($67.20–$88) double; 770–1,000 F ($123.20–$160) suite. AE, DC, MC, V. Parking 26 F ($4.15).

This little hotel is big on charm and the best value in the moderate range. Built in the style of the old Cité, it has a honey-colored stone exterior with iron bars on the windows. The interior is a jewel, reflecting the sophistication of the owner, Christine Pujol. Elaborate Louis XIII–style furniture graces the reception lounges. A newer wing contains additional rooms in a medieval architectural style, and the older rooms have been renewed. Their furnishings are in a severe style that's consistent with the artfully medieval look of the nearby ramparts. The hotel also runs a restaurant nearby, the Brasserie Le Donjon. In summer the garden is the perfect breakfast spot.

IN VILLE-BASSE

Hôtel du Pont-Vieux. 32 rue Trivalle, 11000 Carcassonne. ☎ **04-68-25-24-99.** Fax 04-68-47-62-71. E-mail: hoteldupontvieux@minitel.net. 19 units. TV TEL. 400–450 F ($64–$72) double. Rates include breakfast. AE, DC, V. Parking 30 F ($4.80).

One of the best and most reasonably priced hotels in Carcassonne, this rustic boardinghouse lies at the foot of the medieval city. It has been completely restored without losing its provincial French charm. From the elegantly furnished lounge to the quiet reading room, it's cozy and inviting. The medium-size rooms have traditional furnishings and double-glazed windows to cut down on the noise. An indoor garden provides a retreat from the crowds.

Hôtel Montségur. 27 Allée d'Iéna, 11000 Carcassonne. ☎ **04-68-25-31-41.** Fax 04-68-47-13-22. http://perso.wanadoo.fr/hotel.montsegur/. E-mail: hotelmontsegur@ wanadoo.fr. 21 units. A/C TV TEL. 390–490 F ($62.40–$78.40) double. AE, DC, MC, V. Free parking.

This circa 1887 stately town house with a mansard roof and dormers has a front garden that's screened from the street by trees and a high wrought-iron fence. Didier and Isabelle Faugeras have furnished the hotel with antiques, avoiding that institutional look. Modern amenities include an elevator. The rooms, furnished with antiques, are cheaper than you'd imagine from the looks of the place. A continental breakfast is available; Didier is the chef at the highly recommended Le Languedoc across the street (See "Dining," below).

DINING

Au Jardin de la Tour. 11 rue Porte-d'Aude. ☎ **04-68-25-71-24.** Reservations recommended in summer. Main courses 65–140 F ($10.40–$22.40), 80–100 F ($12.80–$16) at dinner. MC, V. Daily noon–2pm and 8–10pm. Nov–Easter, closed Mon. FRENCH.

This restaurant with a verdant garden infuses greenery and charm into the city's tightly organized medieval core. It's housed in a building that dates from the early 1800s. Today, within an environment bristling with rustic finds from local antique fairs, you can order from a large selection of salads, fillet of beef with morels, cassoulet, terrines of foie gras, and all kinds of grilled fish. The cookery is consistently good, relying on fresh ingredients deftly handled by a talented kitchen staff.

La Barbacane. In the Hôtel de la Cité, place de l'Église. ☎ **04-68-71-98-71.** Reservations recommended. Main courses 150–350 F ($24–$56); fixed-price menus 380–550 F ($60.80–$88). AE, DC, MC, V. Daily 7:30–10pm. Nov, Dec, and Mar, closed Sun. FRENCH.

Named after the medieval neighborhood (La Barbacane) in which it sits, this restaurant enjoys equal billing with the celebrated hotel that contains it. Its soothing-looking dining room, whose walls are upholstered in fabric with gold fleur-de-lis on a cerulean blue background, features the cuisine of the noted chef Franck Putelat. Menu items are based on seasonal ingredients, with just enough zest. Examples are green ravioli perfumed with *seiche* (a species of octopus) and its own ink, crisp-fried cod with black olives, saltwater crayfish with strips of Bayonne ham, Breton lobster with artichoke hearts and caviar, and organically fed free-range chicken stuffed with truffles. A particularly succulent dessert is a chestnut parfait with malt-flavored cream sauce and date-flavored ice cream.

Le Languedoc. 32 allée d'Iéna. ☎ **04-68-25-22-17.** Reservations recommended. Main courses 95–140 F ($15.20–$22.40); fixed-price menus 135–245 F ($21.60–$39.20). AE, DC, V. Tues–Sat noon–2pm and 7:30–9:30pm (June–Sept, until 10pm), Sun noon–2pm. Closed Dec 20–Jan 20. FRENCH.

Acclaimed chef Didier Faugeras is the creative force behind the inspired cuisine here. The high-ceilinged, century-old dining room is filled with antiques; a brick fireplace contributes to the warm Languedoc atmosphere. The specialty is *cassoulet au confit de canard* (the famous stew made with duck cooked in its own fat). It has been celebrated as a much-perfected staple here since the early 1960s. The *pièce de résistance* is tournedos Rossini, with foie-gras truffles and madeira sauce. A smooth dessert is flambéed crêpes Languedoc. In summer you can dine on a pleasant patio or in the air-conditioned restaurant. (Faugeras and his wife, Isabelle, are the owners of the worthy **Hotel Montségur,** just across the street.)

NEARBY ACCOMMODATIONS & DINING

Château Saint-Martin. Montredon. ☎ **04-68-71-09-53.** Reservations required. Main courses 95–165 F ($15.20–$26.40); fixed-price menus 165–305 F ($26.40–$48.80). AE, DC, MC, V. Thurs–Tues noon–1:45pm and 7:30–9:45pm. Lies 2^1/$_2$ miles northeast of La Cité. Follow the signs pointing to Stade Albert Domec.

One of the most successful chefs of Languedoc operates out of this historic 16th-century château at Amontredon, 2^1/$_2$ miles northeast of Carcassonne. Ringed by a wooded park, the restaurant is graced with the superb cuisine of co-owners Jean-Claude and Jacqueline Rodriguez. Dine inside or on the outdoor terrace. Menu items that have proven successful include turbot with a fondue of baby vegetables, sea bass with a mousseline of scallops, sole in tarragon, and a richly flavored *confit d'oie carcassonnaise*, which is goose meat delicately cooked in its own fat and kept in earthen-ware pots. Two other specialties include a *cassoulet languedocienne* and a *boullinade nouvelloise*, which is a bouillabaisse but made with different sorts of fish that include scallops, sole, turbot, and most definitely not a rascasse or hogfish. The site consists of a 12th-century tower and entrance, and a 16th-century main core, which contains the original ceiling beams, the grand dignity of a château, and pale yellow walls.

✪ **Domaine d'Auriac.** Rte. St-Hilaire, 11000 Carcassonne. ☎ **04-68-25-72-22.** Fax 04-68-47-35-54. www.relaischateaux.fr. E-mail: auriac@relaischateaux.fr. 26 units. A/C MINI-BAR TV TEL. 650–2,000 F ($104–$320) double. AE, DC, MC, V. Closed Feb 15–Mar 2 and Nov 15–Dec 7. Free parking. Take D104 west 1^1/$_2$ miles from Carcassonne.

The premier place for food and lodging is this moss-covered 19th-century manor house, boasting gardens with reflecting pools and flowered terraces. The uniquely dec-orated rooms in this Relais & Châteaux have a certain photo-magazine glamour; some are in an older building with high ceilings, whereas others have a more modern decor.

Dining: Bernard Rigaudis sets a grand table in his lovely dining room. In summer, meals are served beside the pool on the terraces. Afterward you might work off lunch on the tennis courts or golf course. The menu changes about five or six times yearly but might include truffles and purple artichokes with essences of pears and olives. Meals cost around 250 F ($40) for the minimalist and around 450 F ($72) for the gourmand. The restaurant is open daily from 12:30 to 2pm and 7:30 to 9:15pm, and reservations are required.

CARCASSONE AFTER DARK

Carcassonne nightlife is centered along the rue **Omer-Sarraut** (in La Bastide) and the **place Marcou** (in La Cité). **La Bulle,** 115 rue Barbacane (☎ **04-68-72-47-70**), explodes with techno and rock dance tunes for an under-30 crowd that keeps the ener-gy pumping and the place hopping till 4am. The cover charge, depending on the night of the week, begins at 60 F ($9.60) per person. Another enduringly popular disco, 2^1/$_2$ miles southwest of town, is **Le Black Bottom,** route de Limoux (☎ **04-68-47-37-11**), which rocks and rolls to every conceivable kind of dance music every Thursday to Saturday beginning at 11pm. Entrance costs 60 F ($9.60) per person.

8 Castres

452 miles SW of Paris, 26 miles S of Albi

Built on the bank of the Agout River, Castres is the gateway for trips to the Sidobre, the mountains of Lacaune, and the Black Mountains. Today the wool industry, whose origins go back to the 14th century, has made Castres one of France's two most impor-tant wool-producing areas. The town was formerly a Roman military installation.

A Benedictine monastery was founded here in the 9th century, and the town fell under the comtes d'Albi in the 10th century. During the wars of religion, it was Protestant.

ESSENTIALS

GETTING THERE   From Toulouse, there are eight **trains** per day (trip time: 1 hour). For rail information and schedules, call ☎ **08-36-35-35-35.** If you're **driving,** Castres is located on N126 east from Toulouse and along N112 south from Albi.

VISITOR INFORMATION   The **Office de Tourisme** is at 3 rue Milhau Ducommun (☎ **05-63-62-63-62**).

SEEING THE SIGHTS

Église St-Benoît. Place du 8-Mai-1945. ☎ **05-63-59-05-19.** Free admission. Mon–Sat 9am–noon and 1:30–6:30pm, Sun 8:30am–12:30pm. Oct–May, except for religious services, the church is closed to casual visitors every Sun.

The town's most prominent and important church is an outstanding example of French baroque architecture. The architect Caillau began construction in 1677 on the site of a 9th-century Benedictine abbey, but the structure was never completed according to its original plans. The painting at the church's far end, above the altar, was executed by Gabriel Briard in the 18th century.

Le Centre National et Musée Jean-Jaurès. 2 place Pélisson. ☎ **05-63-72-01-01.** Admission 10 F ($1.60) adults, 5 F (80¢) children under 14. Tues–Sun 9am–noon and 2–5pm (Apr–Sept, opens at 10am Sun; July–Aug, open Mon).

Dedicated to the workers' movements of the late 19th and early 20th centuries, this collection includes printed material issued by various Socialist factions in France during this era. See, in particular, an issue of *L'Aurore* containing Zola's famous "J'accuse" article from the Dreyfus case. Paintings, sculptures, films, and slides round out the collection.

✪ **Musée Goya.** In the Jardin de l'Evêché. ☎ **05-63-71-59-28.** Admission 15 F ($2.40) adults, 8 F ($1.30) children. Apr–Sept, Tues–Sat 9am–noon and 2–5pm, Sun 10am–noon and 2–6pm; Oct–Mar, Tues–Sun 9am–noon and 2–5pm (July–Aug, open Mon).

The museum is located in the town hall, an archbishop's palace designed by Mansart in 1669. Some of the spacious public rooms have ceilings supported by a frieze of the archbishop's coats-of-arms. The collection includes 16th-century tapestries and the works of Spanish painters from the 15th to the 20th centuries.

Most notable, of course, are the paintings of Francisco Goya y Lucientes, all donated to the town in 1894 by Pierre Briguiboul, son of the Castres-born artist Marcel Briguiboul. *Les Caprices* is a study of figures created in 1799, after the illness that left Goya deaf. Filling much of an entire room, the work is composed of symbolic images of demons and monsters, a satire of Spanish society.

ACCOMMODATIONS

✪ **Hôtel de l'Europe.** 5 rue Victor-Hugo, 81100 Castres. ☎ **05-63-59-00-33.** Fax 05-63-59-21-38. 35 units. MINIBAR TV TEL. 335–375 F ($53.60–$60) double. AE, DC, MC, V. Free parking on street.

This hotel exudes charm, especially in the bedrooms capped with ceiling beams, where the pinkish-gray masonry from the building's original construction during the 18th century still remains. Plus, each room has a view over the oldest part of the historic town.

There's an in-house **restaurant** that serves a cold buffet every day at lunch, priced at 49 F ($7.85) per person; for dinner, the fixed-price menus range from 90 F to 110 F ($14.40 to $17.60). The food may not be glamorous, but it's solid and affordable.

Hôtel Renaissance. 17 rue Victor-Hugo, 81100 Castres. ☎ **05-63-59-30-42.** Fax 05-63-72-11-57. 20 units. TV TEL. 350–450 F ($56–$72) double; 540–710 F ($86.40–$113.60) suite. AE, DC, MC, V.

The Renaissance is the best hotel in Castres. It was built in the 17th century as the courthouse, then functioned as a colorful but run-down hotel throughout most of the 20th century—until 1993, when it was discreetly restored. Today you'll see a severely dignified building composed of *colombages*-style half-timbering, with a mixture of chiseled stone blocks and bricks. Some rooms have exposed timbers; all are clean and comfortable, evoking the crafts of yesteryear. Simple platters can be prepared if you wish to eat in your room, but a recently completed **restaurant** and bar, Le Montaigne, provides other options. Fixed-price menus run from 95 F to 250 F ($15.20 to $40).

DINING

○ **Brasserie des Jacobins.** 1 place Jean-Jaurès. ☎ **05-63-59-01-44.** Reservations recommended. Main courses 40–90 F ($6.40–$14.40). AE, MC, V. Daily noon–2:15pm and 7–10:30pm. FRENCH/PROVENÇAL.

This simple, modern brasserie is a good bet for solid, well-seasoned, and conservative French and Provençal cuisine. So solid in fact, that the menu hasn't changed in years, and most of the patrons are local. Menu items include blanquettes of veal, cassoulets, and caramelized fillets of pork with Provençal herbs. Decor is rustic, service is cordial, and many visitors find it especially suitable for a simple noontime meal.

La Mandragore. 1 rue Malpas. ☎ **05-63-59-51-27.** Reservations recommended. Main courses 75–190 F ($12–$30.40); fixed-price menu 75 F ($12) at lunch and dinner (including wine), 90–240 F ($14.40–$38.40) at dinner. AE, DC, V. Mon 7–10pm, Tues–Sat noon–2pm and 7–10pm. LANGUEDOCIENNE.

On an easily overlooked narrow street, this restaurant occupies a small section of one of the many wings of the medieval château-fort of Castres. The decor is consciously simple, perhaps as an appropriate foil for the stone walls and overhead beams. Sophie (in the dining room) and Jean-Claude (in the kitchen) Belaut prepare a regional cuisine that's among the best in town. Served with charm and tact, it might include artichokes with foie gras and truffle-flavored vinaigrette, roast pigeon stuffed with foie gras and served with gâteau of potatoes and flap mushrooms, fillet of tuna with sweet peppers and cured ham, and magrêt of duckling with truffle oil and braised leeks.

9 Albi

433 miles SW of Paris, 47 miles NE of Toulouse

The "red city" (for the color of its bricks) of Albi straddles both banks of the Tarn River and is dominated by its brooding 13th-century cathedral. Toulouse-Lautrec was born in the Hôtel Bosc in Albi; it's still a private home and cannot be toured, but there's a plaque on the wall of the building, on rue Toulouse-Lautrec (no number) in the historic town center. The town's major attraction is a museum with a world-class collection of the artist's work.

ESSENTIALS

GETTING THERE   Fifteen **trains** per day link Toulouse with Albi (trip time: 1 hour); there's also a direct Paris-Albi night train. For rail information and schedules, call ☎ **08-36-35-35-35.** If you're **driving** from Toulouse, take N88 northeast.

Toulouse-Lautrec: Little Big Man

Painter Henri de Toulouse-Lautrec spent his most creative years in Paris, but the pink-walled city of Albi in southwestern France, where the artist was born, clings tenaciously to his legacy. Only 5 feet tall, Toulouse-Lautrec was famous for his unfettered portraits of prostitutes and cabaret entertainers and for his brilliantly vicious caricatures of belle époque pretensions.

Born into an intermarried family of aristocrats whose ancestors could be traced back to Charlemagne, he was the only surviving child of his parents' union and the cousin of several children with epilepsy, dwarfism, neurological disorders, and alarming skeletal malformations. Toulouse-Lautrec grew into a short but relatively normal-looking young man, but his later years were marred by changes in his appearance that included violent toothaches, repeated fractures in the bones of his legs, and a growth in the side of his nose and lips that led to frequent drooling.

Scientists blame some of the artist's problems on his genetic makeup. But no one will ever know for sure. His descendents have repeatedly refused to be genetically tested or to have the artist's corpse exhumed. (Ironically, Toulouse-Lautrec's death in 1901, at age 36, had little to do with his dwarfism: The cause was acute alcoholism.)

Despite his physical stature, no one can debate the titanic dimensions of Toulouse-Lautrec's art. In a span of less than 20 years he executed 737 canvases, 275 watercolors, 363 prints and posters, more than 5,000 drawings, some ceramics and stained-glass windows, and more than 300 artworks classified as "pornography." Many believe that he depicted his characters in a ruthless and cruel light to get even with the world for the way those around him treated him because of his size and deformities. Yet he was brilliant in his ability to capture images, whether real or imagined, and in his ability to free colors from reality (and lines from form) to create his caricaturelike figures.

The family's **Château du Bosc,** also known as the Fortresse Berenger-Bosc, owned during his life by the artist's grandmother, is reached from Albi by N88 (☎ **05-65-69-20-83**). Built in 1180 and renovated in the 1400s, the château is midway between Albi and Rodez (also spelled Rodes) and is open to visitors daily from 9am to 6pm. Admission is 30 F ($4.80) for adults, 20 F ($3.20) for children 8 to 14, and free for children 7 and under. The present owner, Mlle de Céleran, is most gracious to those interested in Toulouse-Lautrec's life. Call before you go, since visitors must be accompanied by a guide.

VISITOR INFORMATION   The **Office de Tourisme** is in the Palais de la Serbie, place Ste-Cécile (☎ **05-63-49-48-80**).

THE TOP ATTRACTIONS

Cathédrale Ste-Cécile. Near place du Vigan, in the medieval center of town. ☎ **05-63-43-23-43.** Cathédrale, 5 F (80¢); treasury, 20 F ($3.20). June–Oct, daily 9am–7pm; Nov–May, daily 9am–noon and 2:30–6:30pm.

Fortified with ramparts and parapets and containing frescoes and paintings, this 13th-century cathedral was built by a local lord-bishop after a religious struggle with the comte de Toulouse (the crusade against Cathars). Note the exceptional 16th-century rood screen with a unique suit of polychromatic statues from the Old and New Testaments.

✪ **Musée Toulouse-Lautrec.** Opposite the north side of the cathedral. ☎ **05-63-49-48-70.** Admission 24 F ($3.85) adults, 12 F ($1.90) ages 12–18, free for children under 12. Apr–Sept, daily 9am–noon and 2–6pm; Oct–Mar, Wed–Mon 10am–noon and 2–5pm. Closed Dec 25 and Jan 1.

The Palais de la Berbie (Archbishop's Palace) is a fortified structure dating from the late 13th century. Inside, the Musée Toulouse-Lautrec contains the world's most important collection of the artist's paintings, more than 600 in all. His family bequeathed the works remaining in his studio. The museum also owns paintings by Degas, Bonnard, Matisse, Utrillo, and Rouault.

ACCOMMODATIONS

Hostellerie St-Antoine. 17 rue St-Antoine, 81000 Albi. ☎ **05-63-54-04-04.** Fax 05-63-47-10-47. www.chateauxethotels.com. E-mail: stantoine@ilink.fr. 44 units. A/C MINI-BAR TV TEL. 780–984 F ($124.80–$157.45) double; 984–1,082 F ($157.45–$173.10) suite. AE, DC, MC, V. Parking 40 F ($6.40).

This 250-year-old hotel has been owned by the same family for five generations; today it's managed by Jacques and Jean-François Rieux. Their mother focused on Toulouse-Lautrec when designing the hotel, since her grandfather was a friend of the painter and was given a few of his paintings, sketches, and prints. Several are in the lounge, which opens onto a rear garden. The rooms have been delightfully decorated, with a sophisticated use of color, good reproductions, and occasional antiques. Bedrooms are generally spacious, furnished with French provincial pieces.

Even if you're not staying at the hotel, the **dining room** is definitely worth a visit. The Rieux culinary tradition as manifested by chef Laurent Dodé is revealed in their traditional yet creative cuisine, and everything tastes better washed down with Gaillac wines. Specific menu items include breast of chicken prepared with sherry sauce; fried lamb chops served with a confit of garlic; and dessert crêpes flambéed with Grand Marnier.

Hôtel Chiffre. 50 rue Séré-de-Riviéres, 81000 Albi. ☎ **05-63-48-58-48.** Fax 05-63-47-20-61. 36 units. TV TEL. 360–420 F ($57.60–$67.20) double. AE, DC, MC, V. Parking 25 F ($4).

This well-managed hotel in the city center was originally built as lodgings for passengers on the mail coaches that hauled letters and people across the landscapes of southern France. Today, despite frequent renovations, it maintains the original porch that used to shelter carriages from the rain and sun as they pulled up to unload their passengers after a long day on the road. Bedrooms are outfitted with an artful kind of coziness, usually with upholstered walls in floral patterns, sometimes with views of the quiet inner courtyard. About half contain air-conditioning.

The hotel **restaurant, Bateau Ivre,** is popular among locals because of the good value represented by fixed-price menus that range in price from 135 F to 380 F ($21.60 to $60.80). One of these, priced at 190 F ($30.40), is named after Toulouse-Lautrec. It consists of a series of dishes that were compiled after his death by his friends, who remembered the way he'd often prepare the dishes himself during his dinner parties. It includes radishes stuffed with braised foie gras; supreme of sandre; and ducklings that are roasted with garlic produced in the nearby town of Lautrec.

La Réserve. Rte. de Cordes à Fonvialane, 81000 Albi. ☎ **05-63-60-80-80.** Fax 05-63-47-63-60. www.relaischateaux.fr/reservealbi. E-mail: lareserve@ilink.fr. 28 units. MINI-BAR TV TEL. 790–1,450 F ($126.40–$232) double; 1,450–1,950 F ($232–$312) suite. AE, DC, MC, V. Closed Nov–Apr. From the center of town, follow the signs to Carmaux-Rodez until you cross the Tarn, then follow the signs to Cordes; the hotel is adjacent to the main road leading to Cordes, 1¹/₄ miles from Albi.

This country-club villa set in a 4-acre park on the northern outskirts of Albi is managed by the Rieux family, who also run the Hostellerie St-Antoine. It was built in the Mediterranean style, with tennis courts, a pool, and a fine garden in which you can dine. The rooms, well furnished and color coordinated, contain imaginative decorations (but avoid those rooms over the kitchen); the upper-story rooms have sun terraces and French doors. Bedrooms are pockets of charm and style, with comfortable mattresses and fine linens.

In the **restaurant,** specialties are *pâté de grives* (thrush), lamb with flap mushrooms, and fillet of beef with béarnaise sauce. Even if you're not a guest, consider a visit. The wine list is rich in Bordeaux, and the prices per bottle are reasonable. Meals cost from 160 F to 300 F ($25.60 to $48).

DINING

La Réserve boasts a wonderful restaurant, as does **Hostellerie St-Antoine** (see "Accommodations," above).

Jardin des Quatre Saisons. 19 bd. de Strasbourg. ☎ **05-63-60-77-76.** Reservations recommended. Main courses 95–120 F ($15.20–$19.20); fixed-price menus 130–185 F ($20.80–$29.60). AE, DC, MC, V. Tues–Sun noon–2:30pm; Tues–Sat 7–10pm. FRENCH.

The best food in Albi is served by Georges Bermond, who believes that menus, like life, should change with the seasons. That's how the restaurant got its name. The setting is a modern, deceptively simple pair of dining rooms; the service is always competent and polite. Menu items have been fine-tuned to an artful science and include delicious versions of a fricassée of snails garnished with strips of the famous hams produced in the nearby hamlet of Lacaune; and ravioli stuffed with pulverized shrimp and served with a truffled cream sauce. Most delectable of all—an excuse for returning a second time to this restaurant—is a pot-au-feu of the sea with three or four species of fish garnished with a crayfish-flavored cream sauce. The wine list is the finest in Albi.

✪ **Le Moulin de la Mothe.** Rue de Lamothe. ☎ **05-63-60-38-15.** Reservations recommended. Fixed-price menus 145–170 F ($23.20–$27.20). Main courses 110–135 F ($17.60–$21.60). Thurs–Tues noon–2pm; Thurs–Sat and Mon–Tues 7:45–9:15pm. Closed 1 week in Feb and 1 week in Mar. AE, DC, MC, V. FRENCH.

One of the best aspects of this well-respected, long-term culinary staple is its location within a verdant park on the western bank of the Tarn, with views that sweep out over the river, the cathedral, and most of the monuments of historic Albi. Michel and Marie-Claude Pellaprat celebrate local culinary traditions with verve. Within dining rooms flooded with sunlight from big bay windows, and surrounded by white brick walls and gleaming paneling, you can order dishes such as fried foie gras garnished with local grapes, scallops with exotic mushrooms, pigeon cooked *en papillote* (in a paper bag) and garnished with slices of blood sausage, and lobster salad garnished with red "Chinese" apples. Dessert might include a thin tart made with local species of apple (*les reinettes*) and garnished with cinnamon-flavored *crème fraîche.*

10 Cordes-sur-Ciel

421 miles SW of Paris, 15¹/₂ miles NW of Albi

This remarkable site is like an eagle's nest on a hilltop, opening onto the Cérou valley. In days gone by, celebrities like Jean-Paul Sartre and Albert Camus considered this town a favorite hideaway.

Throughout the centuries, Cordes has been known for its textile, leather, and silk industries. Even today, it's an arts-and-crafts city, and many of the old houses on the narrow streets contain artisans—blacksmiths, enamelers, graphic artists, weavers, engravers, sculptors, and painters—plying their trades. Park outside, then go under an arch leading to the old town.

ESSENTIALS

GETTING THERE   If you're **driving,** take N88 northwest from Toulouse to Gaillac, turning north on D922 into Cordes-sur-Ciel. If you're coming by **train,** you'll have to get off in nearby Vindrac and walk, rent a bicycle, or take a taxi the remaining 2 miles to Cordes. For train information and schedules, call ☎ 08-36-35-35-35.

VISITOR INFORMATION   The **Office de Tourisme** is in the Maison Fonpeyrouse, Grand Rue Raymond VII (☎ **05-63-56-00-52**).

SEEING THE SIGHTS

Often called "the city of a hundred Gothic arches," Cordes contains numerous old houses built of pink sandstone. Many of the doors and windows are fashioned of pointed (broken) arches that still retain their 13th- and 14th-century grace. Some of the best-preserved ones line **Grande-Rue,** also called **rue Droite.**

Musée d'Art et d'Histoire le Portail-Peint (Musée Charles-Portal). Grande Rue Haute. ☎ **05-63-56-00-52** for information. Admission 15 F ($2.40) adults, 7 F ($1.10) for children. Apr–June and Sept–Oct, Sun and holidays 3–6pm; July–Aug, daily 11am–noon and 3–6pm. Closed Nov–Mar.

Small, quirky, and relatively unvisited even by residents of Cordes, this dusty and somewhat sleepy museum is named after a nearby gateway (the Painted Gate) that pierces the fortifications surrounding the city's medieval center. It's also named for Charles-Portal, an archivist of the Tarn region and a local historian. Set in a medieval house whose foundations date from the Gallo-Roman era, it contains artifacts of the textile industry, farming implements, samples of local embroideries, a reconstruction of an old peasant home, and a scattering of medieval pieces. Part of the museum's charm derives from its status as a holdover from small-time, bureaucratic France of long ago. If you happen to arrive when the museum is closed (which is frequently), ask someone at the tourist office to arrange a private visit at a convenient time.

Musée Yves-Brayer. Grande-Rue. ☎ **05-63-56-00-40.** Admission 15 F ($2.40) adults, 7 F ($1.10) children 11 and under. July–Aug, daily 10:30am–12:30pm and 1–6pm; Sept–June, Sat–Sun 10am–noon and 2–6pm.

Maison du Grand-Fauconnier (House of the Falcon Master), named for the falcons carved into the stonework of the wall, contains a grand staircase that leads to the Musée Yves-Brayer. Brayer came to Cordes in 1940 and became one of its most ardent civic boosters. After watching Cordes fall gradually into decay, he renewed interest in its restoration. The museum contains minor artifacts relating to the town's history; the most interesting exhibits are rather fanciful scale models of the town itself.

Église St-Michel. Grande-Rue. Visiting hours are erratic. If the church is closed, ask at the *tabac* (tobacco shop) across from the front entrance or call the tourist office to make an appointment.

The church dates from the 13th century, but many alterations have been made since. The view from the top of the tower encompasses much of the surrounding area. Most of the lateral design of the side chapels probably comes from the cathedral at Albi. Before being shipped here, the organ (dating from 1830) was in Notre-Dame de Paris.

ACCOMMODATIONS & DINING

Hostellerie du Parc. Les Cabannes, 81170 Cordes. ☎ **05-63-56-02-59.** Fax 05-63-56-18-03. Reservations recommended. Main courses 75–110 F ($12–$17.60); fixed-price menus 98–320 F ($15.70–$51.20) at lunch, 98–320 F ($15.70–$51.20) at dinner. AE, DC, MC, V. Mon–Sat noon–2pm and 7–10pm, Sun noon–2pm. Nov–Mar, closed Mon. Take rte. de St-Antonin (D600) for about 1 mile west from the town center. FRENCH.

This century-old stone house offers generous meals in a wooded garden or paneled dining room. The specialties include homemade foie gras, duckling, *poularde* (chicken) *occitaine*, rabbit with cabbage leaves, and calf's sweetbreads with morels. Specialties of the house are unusual and, in many cases, charming, featuring a ballotine of guinea fowl served with sweetbreads; and a confit of roasted rabbit with pink garlic from the nearby town of Lautrec.

The **hotel** offers 17 simply furnished rooms; a double costs 300 F to 400 F ($48 to $64). There's an outdoor pool. The chef even offers French cooking lessons (in English).

Maison du Grand Ecuyer. Rue Voltaire, 81170 Cordes. ☎ **05-63-53-79-50.** Fax 05-63-53-79-51. E-mail: grand-ecuyer@thuries.fr. Reservations required. Main courses 150–210 F ($24–$33.60); fixed-price menus 170–470 F ($27.20–$75.20). AE, DC, MC, V. Easter–June, Tues–Sun 7–9:30pm; July–Oct, Wed–Sun noon–2pm and 7–9:30pm. Closed Oct 15–Easter. FRENCH.

The medieval monument that contains this restaurant (the 15th-century hunting lodge of Raymond VII, comte de Toulouse) is classified as a national historic treasure. It's perched near the top of the steep rock that's the site of the village of Cordes. But despite its glamour and undeniable charm, the restaurant remains intimate and unstuffy. Chef Yves Thuriès prepares platters that have made his dining room an almost mandatory stop. Specialties include three confits of lobster, red mullet salad with fondue of vegetables, and noisette of lamb in chicory sauce. The dessert selection is about the grandest and most overwhelming in this part of France.

The **hotel** contains 12 rooms and one suite, all with antiques and an undeniable sense of the Middle Ages blended discreetly with modern comforts. Doubles cost 750 F to 850 F ($120 to $136); the suite is 1,300 F ($208). The most-desired room, honoring a former guest, Albert Camus, has a four-poster bed and a fireplace.

11 Toulouse

438 miles SW of Paris, 152 miles SE of Bordeaux, 60 miles W of Carcassonne

The old capital of Languedoc and France's fourth-largest city, Toulouse (known as *La Ville Rose*) is cosmopolitan in flavor. The major city of the southwest, filled with gardens and squares, it's the gateway to the Pyrénées. Toulouse has a number of fine old mansions, most of them dating from the Renaissance, when this was one of the richest cities in Europe. Today Toulouse is an artistic and cultural center, but also a high-tech center, home to two huge aircraft makers—Airbus and Aerospatiale. Also making the city tick is its extraordinarily high population of students: some 100,000 in all, out of a total population of 600,000.

Toulouse may be a city with a distinguished historical past, but it is also a city of the future and the center of the aerospace industry in France. The National Center for Space Research has been headquartered here for more than 3 decades. The first regularly scheduled airline flights from France took off from the local airport in the 1920s. Today long-range passenger planes of the Airbus consortium, the most important rivals in the world to Boeing, are assembled in a gargantuan hangar in the suburb of Colombiers.

ESSENTIALS

GETTING THERE   The Toulouse-Blagnac international **airport** lies in the city's northwestern suburbs, 7 miles from the center; for flight information, call ☎ **05-61-42-44-00.**

Air France (☎ **08-02-80-28-02**) has about 25 flights a day from Paris and two per day from London. **Air Liberté** (☎ **08-03-80-58-05**) also flies from Paris about a dozen times each day.

Some nine high-speed TGV **trains** per day arrive from Paris (trip time: 5 hours), eight from Bordeaux (trip time: $2^1/4$ hours), and 11 from Marseille (trip time: $4^1/2$ hours). For rail information and schedules, call ☎ **08-36-35-35-35.**

The **drive** to Toulouse from Paris takes 6 to 7 hours. Take A10 south to Bordeaux, connecting to A62 to Toulouse.

The Canal du Midi links many of the region's cities with Toulouse by waterway.

VISITOR INFORMATION   The **Office de Tourisme** is in the Donjon du Capitole, rue Lafayette (☎ **05-61-11-02-22**).

EXPLORING THE CITY

In addition to the sights listed below, the architectural highlights include the Gothic brick **Église des Jacobins,** parvis des Jacobins, in Old Toulouse, west of place du Capitole along rue Lakanal (☎ **05-61-22-21-92**). The convent, daring in its architecture, has been restored and forms the largest extant monastery complex in France. It's open year-round, daily from 10am to 7pm. Admission to most of the complex is free, but a visit to the cloisters is 10 F ($1.60) per person. Small, charming, and dating mostly from the 18th century, **Basilique Notre-Dame La Daurade** is at 7 quai de la Daurade (☎ **05-61-21-38-32**); its name derives from the gilding that covers its partially baroque exterior. It's open daily from 8am to 7pm. Admission is free.

In civic architecture, **Capitole,** place du Capitole (☎ **05-61-22-29-22**), is an outstanding achievement and one of the most potent symbols of Toulouse itself. Built in 1753, it houses the **Hôtel de Ville** (city hall), plus the **Théâtre du Capitole** (☎ **05-61-63-13-13**), which is devoted to concerts, ballets, and operas. Renovated in 1996, it's outfitted in an Italian-inspired 18th-century style with shades of scarlet and gold. Admission, which usually includes a view of the theater, is free. The Capitole complex is open Monday through Saturday from 9am to noon and 2 to 6pm (no afternoon hours on Saturday).

After all that sightseeing, head for place Wilson, a showcase 19th-century square (it's actually an oval) lined with fashionable cafes.

When you're in the mood to shop, head for **rue St-Rome** and **rue d'Alsace-Lorraine,** both of which are especially rich in clothing and housewares. This town has a great shopping mall, **Centre Commercial St-Georges,** rue du Rempart St-Etienne, where you can fill your suitcases with all kinds of glittery loot. But for upscale clothing boutiques, head for **rue Croix-Baragnon** and **rue des Arts,** and the **rue St-Antoine du T.** The pearly gates of antiques heaven can be found on **rue Fermat.** More downmarket antiques are sprawled out each Sunday from 8am to noon during the weekly **flea market** that's conducted adjacent to the Basilique St-Sernin. In addition to that, there's a once-a-month sale of knickknacks (*brocante*) on the first weekend (Friday, Saturday, and Sunday from 8am to 1pm) of every month. Here, the contents of attics that have been undisturbed since the invasion of Normandy are disgorged, with trash and possible treasures as well, into the light of day.

In addition, **Olivier Desforges,** 3 place St-Georges (☎ **05-61-12-07-00**), sells the most exotic and luxurious linens; and **Violettes & Pastels,** 10 rue St-Pantaléon

Toulouse

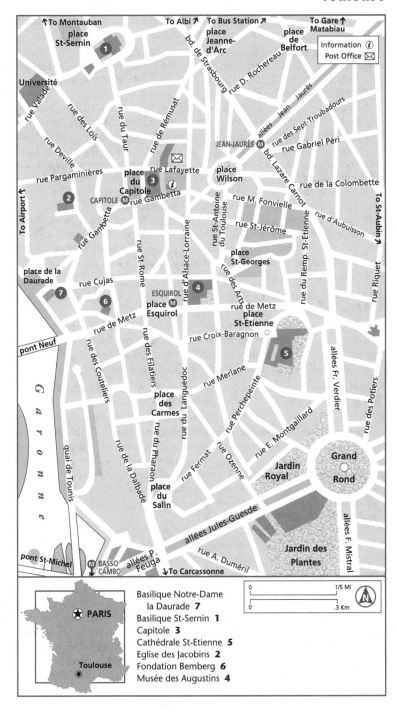

↑To Montauban   **To Albi ↗**   **To Bus Station ↗**   **To Gare ↑ Matabiau**

place St-Sernin

place Jeanne-d'Arc

place de Belfort

Information ⓘ
Post Office ✉

Université

rue Valade

rue des Lois

rue du Taur

rue de Remusat

bd. de Strasbourg

rue D. Rochereau

rue Deville

allées Jean Jaurès

rue des Sept-Troubadours

JEAN-JAURÈS Ⓜ

rue Gabriel Péri

rue Pargaminières

✉

rue Lafayette

place du Capitole ③ ⓘ

place Wilson

bd. Lazare Carnot

rue de la Colombette

To Airport ↑

rue Gambetta

② **CAPITOLE** Ⓜ rue Gambetta

rue M. Fonvielle

To St-Aubin ↗

rue Riquet

rue St-Antoine du Toulouse

rue St-Jérôme

rue d'Aubuisson

place de la Daurade

rue Cujas

rue St-Rome

rue d'Alsace-Lorraine

place St-Georges

rue du Remp. St-Etienne

⑦

⑥

ESQUIROL
place Ⓜ
Esquirol ④

rue des Arts

rue de Metz

place St-Etienne

rue de Metz

rue des Couteliers

rue des Filatiers

rue Croix-Baragnon

⑤

allées Fr. Verdier

rue des Potiers

pont Neuf

rue du Languedoc

rue Merlane

place des Carmes

rue du Pharaon

rue de la Dalbade

rue Perchepeinte

rue Fermat

rue Ozenne

rue E. Montgaillard

Jardin Royal

Grand Rond

quai de Tounis

place du Salin

allées Jules-Guesde

rue A. Duméril

Jardin des Plantes

allées F. Mistral

pont St-Michel

Ⓜ **BASSO CAMBO** ↓

allées P. Feuga

↓To Carcassonne

G a r o n n e

Map Legend

★ **PARIS**

Toulouse

	0	1/5 Mi
	0	.3 Km

🧭 N

Basilique Notre-Dame la Daurade **7**
Basilique St-Sernin **1**
Capitole **3**
Cathédrale St-Etienne **5**
Eglise des Jacobins **2**
Fondation Bemberg **6**
Musée des Augustins **4**

(☎ **05-61-22-14-22**), offers everything imaginable connected with violets, from violet-scented perfume to silk scarves patterned with the dainty purple flower.

○ **Basilique St-Sernin.** 13 place St-Sernin. ☎ **05-61-21-80-45.** Church, free admission; crypt, 10 F ($1.60). Church, daily 10am–11:30am and 2:30–5pm, though please refrain from sightseeing during Sun morning masses; crypt, Mon–Sat 9am–noon and 2–6pm, Sun noon– 6pm.

Consecrated in 1096, this is the largest and finest Romanesque church extant in the Old World. One of its most outstanding features is the Porte Miègeville, opening onto the south aisle and decorated with 12th-century sculptures. The door opening into the south transept is the Porte des Comtes, its capitals depicting the story of Lazarus. Nearby are the tombs of the comtes de Toulouse. Entering by the main west door, you can see the double side aisles that give the church five naves, an unusual feature in Romanesque architecture. An upper cloister forms a passageway around the interior. Look for the Romanesque capitals surmounting the columns.

In the axis of the basilica, 11th-century bas-reliefs depict *Christ in His Majesty.* The ambulatory leads to the crypt (ask the custodian for permission to enter), containing the relics of 128 saints, plus a thorn said to be from the Crown of Thorns. The old baroque retables and shrine in the ambulatory have been reset; the relics here are those of the Apostles and the first bishops of Toulouse.

Cathédrale St-Etienne. Place St-Etienne, at the eastern end of rue de Metz. ☎ **05-61-52-03-82.** Daily 7:30am–7pm.

Because of the eons required to build it (it was designed and constructed between the 11th and the 17th centuries), some critics scorn this cathedral for its mishmash of styles; nonetheless, it successfully conveys a solemn dignity. The rectangular bell tower is from the 16th century. A Gothic choir has been added to its unique ogival nave.

Fondation Bemberg. Place d'Assézat, rue de Metz. ☎ **05-61-12-06-89.** Admission 30 F ($4.80). Tues–Wed and Fri–Sun 10am–6pm, Thurs 10am–9pm.

Opened in 1995, this quickly became one of the city's most important museums. Housed in the Assézat mansion, a magnificent structure that's a sightseeing attraction in its own right, the museum offers an overview of 5 centuries of European art. The nucleus of the collection represents the lifelong work of collector extraordinaire George Bemberg, who donated 331 works. The largest bequest was 28 paintings by Pierre Bonnard, including his *Moulin Rouge.* Bemberg also donated works by Pissarro, Matisse (*Vue d'Antibes*), and Monet, plus the Fauves. The foundation also owns Canaletto's much-reproduced *Vue de Mestre.*

The mansion housing the foundation, the Hôtel d'Assézat, was built in 1555 and still has an unaltered 16th-century courtyard. It also houses the Académie des Jeux-Floraux, which since 1323 has presented flowers made of wrought metal to poets.

La Cité de Espace. Av. Jean Gonord. ☎ **05-62-71-48-71.** Admission 69.40 F ($11.10) adults, 59 F ($9.45) senior citizens over 60, 48.20 F ($7.70) children 6–17, free for children 6 and under, family tickets (2 adults, 2 children) 193 F ($30.90). Tues–Fri 9:30am–6pm, Sat–Sun 9:30am–7pm. Exit 17 of the East Peripheral Route. Bus: 19 (only Sat–Sun).

This is the place to go to learn what space exploration is all about, and how it's done. Some half a million visitors a year come here to learn what it's like to program the launch of a satellite into orbit or how satellites are maneuvered in space. You learn, for example, how easy it is to lose a satellite in space by putting on a burst of speed at the wrong point during a launch. Life-size structural models abound, including a model of an astronaut riding an exercise bike in zero gravity. On the grounds outside you can walk through a replica of Russia's *Mir* space station. The place is both a teaching tool and a lot of fun to visit. The top floor focuses on exploration of the universe, with close-ups from fly-bys of the moons of Jupiter.

Musée des Augustins. 21 rue de Metz. ☎ **05-61-22-21-82.** Admission 12 F ($1.90), free for children 11 and under. Wed 10am–9pm, Thurs–Mon 10am–6pm. Closed May 1, Dec 25, and Jan 1.

Originally conceived as a convent, this museum's 14th-century cloisters contain the world's largest and most valuable collection of Romanesque capitals. The sculptures and carvings are magnificent, and there are some fine examples of early Christian sarcophagi. On the upper floors is a large painting collection, with works by Toulouse-Lautrec, Gérard, Delacroix, and Ingres. The museum also contains several portraits by Antoine Rivalz, a local artist of major talent.

ACCOMMODATIONS
EXPENSIVE

Sofitel Toulouse Centre. 84 Allée Jean-Jaurès, 31000 Toulouse. ☎ **05-61-10-23-10.** Fax 05-61-10-23-20. www.sofitel.com. E-mail: sofitel@cadrus.fr. 119 units. A/C MINIBAR TV TEL. 1,000 F ($160) double; 1,350–1,850 F ($216–$296) suite. AE, DC, MC, V. Parking 75 F ($12). Métro: Jean-Jaurès.

Business travelers deem this eight-story hotel the best in town (though we still prefer the Grand Hôtel de l'Opéra as the choicest, most tranquil retreat). Adjacent to place Wilson, this Sofitel employs a charming bilingual staff and offers rooms for travelers with disabilities and suites big enough to fit an entire family or serve as an office away from the office. Rooms are furnished in an international chain format. The hotel has 24-hour room service, an in-house parking garage (much needed in this congested neighborhood), a bar, and a bustling brasserie.

MODERATE

✪ **Grand Hôtel de l'Opéra.** 1 place du Capitole, 31000 Toulouse. ☎ **05-61-21-82-66.** Fax 05-61-23-41-04. E-mail: toulousy@wanadoo.fr. 54 units. A/C TV TEL. 720–1,050 F ($115.20–$168) double; 1,500 F ($240) suite. AE, DC, MC, V. Parking 80 F ($12.80). Métro: Capitole.

The owners have won several prestigious awards for transforming this 17th-century convent into a sophisticated and opulent hotel. The public rooms contain early 19th–century antiques and Napoleonic-inspired tenting over the bars. Some guest rooms have urn-shaped balustrades overlooking formal squares, and all have high ceilings and modern amenities. Bedrooms are spacious and stylish with private safes, usually with ample sitting areas and good desk space. The beds are elegantly attired in tasteful fabrics, fine mattresses, and soft pillows. Upper-floor rooms damaged by a 1996 fire were recently renovated. The hotel also runs a brasserie and the town's most prestigious **restaurant** (see "Dining," below).

Hôtel des Beaux-Arts. 1 place du pont-Neuf, 31000 Toulouse. ☎ **05-34-45-42-42.** Fax 05-34-45-42-43. www.hoteldesbeauxarts.com. E-mail: contact@hoteldesbeauxarts.com. 20 units. A/C MINIBAR TV TEL. 600–980 F ($96–$156.80) double; 1,000 F ($160) junior suite. AE, DC, MC, V. Parking 40 F ($6.40).

This charming hotel occupies a richly dignified 250-year-old villa in the heart of town, on the banks of the Garonne. Despite the historic facade, the well-equipped, sound-proof rooms are modern, refined, and comfortable. Each contains a quality mattress and some form of original modern art. Breakfast is the only meal served; diners often head for the Brasserie des Beaux-Arts (see "Dining," below), in the same building but with an entrance around the corner.

INEXPENSIVE

Hôtel Raymond-IV. 16 rue Raymond-IV, 31000 Toulouse. ☎ **05-61-62-89-41.** Fax 05-61-62-38-01. 38 units. MINIBAR TV TEL. 210–600 F ($33.60–$96) double. AE, DC, MC, V. Parking 25 F ($4). Métro: Jean-Jaurès or Capitole.

On a quiet street close to the town center and the train station, this antique building contains pleasantly decorated rooms, each with bland but comfortable furniture and restful mattresses. The location means that you're within walking distance of the historic quarter with its theaters, shops, and nightclubs. Although breakfast is the only meal served, the English-speaking staff will direct you to nearby restaurants.

DINING
EXPENSIVE

✪ **Chez Michel Sarran.** 21 bd. Armand du Portal. ☎ **05-61-12-32-32.** Reservations recommended. Main courses 120–300 F ($19.20–$48); fixed-price menus 240 F ($38.40). AE, MC, V. Mon–Fri noon–2pm and 7:30–10pm. Métro: Capitole. FRENCH.

At the most stylish and consistently praised restaurant in Toulouse, you can enjoy the well-cultivated cuisine of rising star Michel Sarran. The two beige-and-salmon colored dining rooms are in the heart of town, on two separate floors of a building near the Novotel Centre. The walls are upholstered with beige-toned linen from the Provençal upholsterer Soleiado. Sarran's wife, Françoise, oversees the dining rooms.

The very fresh, very creative array of dishes have attracted diners as diverse as the Prime Minister of France and such show-biz types as Sophie Marceau and Gilbert Becaud. The food seems designed to bring out the flavors of southern and southwestern France. Examples include a platter of stuffed seasonal vegetables served with an anchovy-flavored mayonnaise and ratatouille; a *salade* of braised crayfish with crabmeat and a tapenade of olives; a creamy soup of white beans, lard, and foie gras; grilled snapper with caramelized tomatoes and sweet Basque tomatoes stuffed with anchovies; and grilled foie gras in a duckmeat bouillon with sage and Parmesan. Dessert might include ravioli stuffed with creamed oranges and served with an aspic of sweet white Gaillac wine.

Le Pastel. 237 rte. de St-Simon. ☎ **05-62-87-84-30.** Reservations required. Main courses 160–250 F ($25.60–$40); fixed-price menus 170–230 F ($27.20–$36.80) at lunch, 370 F ($59.20) at dinner. MC, V. Tues–Sat noon–2pm and 8–9:30pm. Métro: Basso-Cambo. FRENCH.

One of the most luxurious and appealing restaurants around Toulouse occupies a stone-sided manor house that was originally built around 1850. Today it's the domain of Paris-trained chef and entrepreneur Gérard Garrigues. The setting is as restful as the cuisine is superb: Terraces ringed with flowers, and dining rooms accented with paintings by local artists contribute to the placidity. Menu items change about every 2 weeks. During our visit, the menu featured such game dishes as partridge and foie gras cooked in puffy pastry that seals in the juices; fillet of sea bass prepared in a minestrone of shellfish; caramelized turnips served as a *"tarte tatin"* and topped with pan-seared foie gras; and pigeon stuffed with pine nuts and dried fruit, served on a bed of braised cabbage. Wine choices are as comprehensive and sophisticated as anything else you're likely to find in Toulouse.

✪ **Les Jardins de l'Opéra.** In the Grand Hôtel de l'Opéra, 1 place du Capitole. ☎ **05-61-23-07-76.** Reservations required. Main courses 165–280 F ($26.40–$44.80); fixed-price menus 200 F ($32) at lunch, 295–540 F ($47.20–$86.40) at dinner. AE, DC, MC, V. Mon–Sat noon–2pm and 8–10pm. Closed Jan 1–4 and Aug 3–26. Métro: Capitole. FRENCH.

The entrance to the city's best restaurant is in the 18th-century Florentine courtyard of the Grand Hôtel. The dining area is a series of intimate salons, several of which face a winter garden and a reflecting pool. You'll be greeted by the gracious Maryse Toulousy, whose husband, Dominique, prepares what critics have called the perfect combination of modern and old-fashioned French cuisine. The outstanding menu listings are likely to include a salad of scallops and purple artichokes; tournedos of rabbit and fresh foie gras with a pepper sauce; strips of duckling with tarragon-flavored butter sauce; crayfish served in a mushroom-enriched puff pastry; and leg of lamb stuffed with exotic mushrooms, braised in saffron. The vice versa de *poivron rouge et calmar* (calamari stuffed with roasted red pepper and flavored with squid ink) is a tour de force. Desserts feature a sophisticated array of soufflés and tarts, some of which must be ordered at the beginning of the meal. If you forget, console yourself with the luscious roasted figs stuffed with vanilla ice cream, drenched with Banyuls wine, which can be whipped up in an instant.

MODERATE

Brasserie des Beaux-Arts. 1 quai de la Daurade. ☎ **05-61-21-12-12.** Reservations recommended. Main courses 70–160 F ($11.20–$25.60); fixed-price menus 119 and 169 F ($19.05 and $27.05). AE, DC, MC, V. Daily noon–3:30pm and 7pm–1am. Métro: Esquirol. FRENCH.

This turn-of-the-century brasserie offers a pure and authentic Art Nouveau decor that's been enhanced because of its connection with the Jean Bucher chain. (They're the most successful directors of Art Nouveau French brasseries in the world, with at least a dozen similar places, some of which are classified as national historic monuments.) The carefully restored decor includes walnut paneling and many mirrors, and the cuisine emphasizes well-prepared seafood and all the predictable local dishes, including cassoulet, magrêt of duckling, and confit of duckling. Try the foie gras or country-style sauerkraut, accompanied by the house Riesling, served in an earthenware pitcher. During warm weather, eat on the terrace. The staff here is likely to be hysterical during peak times, and when that happens, they tend to become less than suave.

Chez Émile/La Terrasse D'Émile. 13 place St-Georges. ☎ **05-61-21-05-56.** Reservations recommended. Main courses 88–139 F ($14.10–$22.25); fixed-price menus 110–148 F ($17.60–$23.70) at lunch, 220–295 F ($35.20–$47.20) at dinner. AE, DC, MC, V. Tues–Sat noon–2pm and 7–10:30pm (summer, also Mon 7–10:30pm). Métro: Capitole or Esquirol. TOULOUSIEN.

In an old-fashioned house on one of the most beautiful squares of Toulouse, this restaurant offers the specialties of chef François Ferrier. In winter, meals are served upstairs in a cozy enclave overlooking the square; in summer, the venue moves to the street-level dining room and the flower-filled terrace. Menu choices include cassoulet toulousain, magrêt of duckling traditional style, a medley of Catalonian fish, and parillade of grilled fish with a pungently aromatic cold sauce of sweet peppers and olive oil. The wine list is filled with intriguing surprises.

INEXPENSIVE

Eau de Folles. 14 Allée du President Roosevelt. ☎ **05-61-23-45-50.** Reservations recommended. Fixed-price menu 140 F ($22.40). No credit cards. Mon–Sat 11:45am–2pm and 7:30pm–1am. Métro: Capitole. FRENCH.

This is a relative newcomer to the restaurant scene in Toulouse, but its low prices and the variety of its menu promise to make it a long-term contender. In a room filled with mirrors, you can choose from 10 starters, 10 main courses, and 10 desserts on the fixed-price menu. Menu items vary according to the inspiration of the chef and the availability of fresh ingredients. A typical meal might include a marinade of fish, followed by strips of duck meat with green pepper sauce, and a homemade pastry such as a *tarte tatin*. Everything is very simple, served in a cramped but convivial setting.

NEARBY ACCOMMODATIONS & DINING

Hôtel de Diane. 3 rte. de St-Simon, 31100 St-Simon. ☎ **05-61-07-59-52.** Fax 05-61-86-38-94. 22 units, 13 bungalows. MINIBAR TV TEL. 450 F ($72) double; 510 F ($81.60) bungalow. AE, DC, MC, V. Free parking. Take D23 to exit 27, 5 miles east from Toulouse.

This hotel/restaurant surrounded by a 5-acre park is the most tranquil retreat near Toulouse. It occupies a turn-of-the-century villa with comfortable but not particularly opulent rooms that appeal to people who want to be away from the traffic and congestion of the inner city. Bedrooms are of a standard motel size. The bungalow-style units are built in a row facing the park. None have kitchens, but each has a private terrace and private parking. The rustic atmosphere befits this getaway, where there's a private pool and groves of pines and venerable hardwoods.

Dining: The restaurant, Saint-Simon, offers a choice of meals in the garden or the Louis XV-style dining room. The fixed-price menus at 105 F to 190 F ($16.80 to $30.40) offer the best value. The restaurant serves lunch Monday to Friday and dinner Monday to Saturday until 9:30pm. In spite of the attentive service and gracious welcome, the food is somewhat uneven—sometimes delicious, other times less so. The Bordeaux, however, is divine.

La Flanerie. Route de Lacroix-Falgarde, 31320 Vieille-Toulouse. ☎ **05-61-73-39-12.** Fax 05-61-73-18-56. 12 units. MINIBAR TV TEL. 400–600 F ($64–$96) double. AE, DC, MC, V. Free parking. Bus: R. Take the D4 south of Toulouse for 5 miles.

Set within a verdant, 6-acre garden that slopes down to the edge of the Garonne, this establishment was built in the 1850s as the centerpiece of a large farm. Bedroom furnishings have been carefully selected, and include a high level of style, and, in some cases, canopied beds and some genuine antiques. These include fine marquetry desks, bronze lighting fixtures, and other remnants of turn-of-the-century France. The hotel has a swimming pool and is permeated throughout with a sense of respectable virtue.

TOULOUSE AFTER DARK

Toulouse has theater, dance, and opera that's often on a par with that found in Paris. The best way to stay on top of the city's arts scene is to pick up a copy of the monthly magazine *Toulouse Culture* from the Office de Tourisme. It's free.

The city's most notable theaters are the **Théâtre du Capitole,** place du Capitole (☎ 05-61-22-31-31), which specializes in operas, operettas, and often works from the classical French repertoire; the **Théâtre de la Digue,** 3 rue de la Digue (☎ 05-61-42-97-79), site of ballets and works by local theater companies; and the **Halle aux Grains,** place Dupuy (☎ 05-61-62-02-70), the venue for many pop and classical concerts. Another contender is the **Théâtre Garonne,** 1 av. du Château d'Eau (☎ 05-61-48-56-56), site of everything from works by Molière to 20th-century existentialist dramas.

The liveliest squares to wander after dark are place du Capitole, place St-Georges, place St-Pierre, and just off rue St-Rome and rue des Filatiers.

For bars and pubs, check out the Latin flair of **La Tantina de Bourgos,** 27 rue de la Garonette (☎ 05-61-55-59-29), which is always popular with the student scene, and the rowdier **Chez Tonton,** 16 place St-Pierre (☎ 05-61-21-89-54), with its *après-match* frolicking atmosphere complete with the winning teams boozing it up. To keep the party going, try out the rock club **Le Bikini,** route de Lacroix-Falgarde (☎ 05-61-55-00-29), with its occasional live concerts and endless supply of hot bods and a clientele that doesn't usually exceed age 25.

A couple of out-of-the-ordinary entertainment venues are the **Cave Poésie,** 71 rue du Taur (☎ 05-61-23-62-00), where you can see a full range of stand-up comics, poetry readings, small concerts, you name it; and the disco/restaurant **L'Ubu,** 16 rue St-Rome (☎ 05-61-23-26-75), where the stars come out to eat, dance, and be seen.

Mostly heterosexual audiences migrate to **Disco La Strada,** 4 rue Gabrielle Peri (☎ 05-34-41-15-65), which begins to get animated every Wednesday to Saturday after 11pm; and a vaguely Iberian-looking establishment, **Bar La Bodega Bodega,** 1 rue Gabrielle Peri (☎ 05-61-63-03-63). Site of recorded music and a scene that's more hip and fashionable than at many of its competitors, it features recorded music and a venue where many friends seem to meet spontaneously over drinks.

As you first enter **Le New Shanghai,** 12 rue de la Pomme (☎ 05-61-23-37-80), you notice that this is a man's dance domain playing the latest in techno; then, venturing farther inside, you'll discover that it gives way to a darker, sexy cruise-bar environment with lots of hot men on the prowl. Plan on paying 40 F ($6.40) to get in. Gay women appreciate **Le B. Machine,** 37 place des Carmes (☎ 05-61-55-57-59), the most popular women's bar in town, which plays recorded music but doesn't have a dance floor.

12 Auch

451 miles SW of Paris, 126 miles SE of Bordeaux, 40 miles W of Toulouse

On the west bank of the Gers, in the heart of the ancient Duchy of Gascony, of which it was the capital, the lively market town of Auch is divided into upper and lower quarters, connected by several flights of steps. In the old part of town the narrow streets, called *pousterles,* center on place Salinis, from which there's a good view of the Pyrénées. Branching off from here, the **Escalier Monumental** leads down to the river, a descent of 232 steps.

North of the square is the **Cathédrale Ste-Marie,** at place de la Cathédrale (☎ 05-62-05-72-71). Built from the 15th to the 17th centuries, this is one of the most handsome Gothic churches in the south of France. It has 113 Renaissance choir stalls made of carved oak and impressive stained-glass windows, also from the Renaissance. Its 17th-century organ was one of the finest in the world at the time of Louis XIV. The cathedral is open daily from 8:30am to noon and 2 to 5pm (from 9:30am to noon and 2 to 5pm in winter).

Next to the cathedral stands an 18th-century **archbishop's palace** with a 14th-century bell tower, the **Tour d'Armagnac,** which was once a prison.

For shops and boutiques, walk down **rue Dessoles** and **avenue de l'Alsace.** Here you'll find everything from confectionery shops to clothing stores. Also consider visiting the **Caves de l'Hôtel de France,** rue d'Etigny (☎ 05-62-61-71-71), for a bottle or two of Armagnac. It has the best selection of this firewater, with more than 100 distilleries represented.

ESSENTIALS

GETTING THERE   Five to 10 SNCF **trains** or **buses** per day run between Toulouse and Auch (trip time: 1¹/₂ hours); six to 13 SNCF buses arrive in Auch daily from Agen (trip time: 1¹/₂ hours). For more information and schedules, call ☎ 08-36-35-35-35. If you're **driving** to Auch, take N124 west from Toulouse.

VISITOR INFORMATION   The **Office de Tourisme** is at place de la Cathédrale (☎ 05-62-05-22-89).

ACCOMMODATIONS & DINING

Hôtel de France (Restaurant Gourmand du Terroir/Brasserie Le Neuvième). Place de la Libération, 32003 Auch CEDEX. ☎ **05-62-61-71-84.** Fax 05-62-61-71-81. 29 units. A/C MINIBAR TV TEL. 385–750 F ($61.60–$120) double; 900–1,850 F ($144–$296) suite. AE, DC, MC, V. Parking 40 F ($6.40).

A lot has changed here since the 1970s, when the Hôtel de France was celebrated throughout France. It was built around the much-modernized 16th-century core of an old inn. The rooms are comfortable, conservative, and furnished with French provincial pieces. Some, however, are a bit dowdy.

Dining: The cuisine here somewhat slavishly follows many of the culinary trends established by the since-departed founder, André Daguin. Today, with kitchens directed by Roland Garreau, the cuisine is "innovative within traditional boundaries." The more glamorous of the hotel's two restaurants is the **Restaurant Gourmand Côte Jardin,** where fixed-price menus cost from 100 to 480 F ($16 to $76.80), and where main courses cost from 150 F to 220 F ($24 to $35.20). Menu choices include an assortment of preparations of foie gras from Gascony, brochette of oysters with foie gras, a duo of *magrêt de canard* (duck) cooked in a rock-salt shell and served with a medley of vegetables, and stuffed pigeon roasted with spiced honey. The desserts include a platter of four chocolate dishes and café au café, a presentation of mousses and pastries unified by their coffee content. Over the years we've had some of our most memorable meals here, yet there have also been disappointments, particularly since the staff here is simply not as hip or as alert as is needed to sustain the high expectations.

You might actually be happier within the hotel's less pretentious and much less expensive **Brasserie Le Neuvième,** where set meals costing 85 F to 100 F ($13.60 to $16) are a good deal. Both sites are open for business daily from noon to 2pm and from 7:30 to 10pm.

The Basque Country 17

The chief interest in the Basque country, a land rich in folklore and old customs, is confined to a small corner of southwestern France, near the Spanish border. Here you can visit the Basque capital, Bayonne, and explore the coastal resorts, chic Biarritz and St-Jean-de-Luz. In Bayonne's Roman arena, you can see a real Spanish-style bullfight. The typical costume of the Basque men—beret and cummerbund—isn't as evident as it once was, but you can still spot it here and there.

The vast Pyrénéan region is a land of glaciers, summits, thermal baths, subterranean grottoes and caverns, winter-sports centers, and trout-filled mountain streams. **Pau** is a good base for excursions to the western Pyrénées. **Lourdes** is the major religious pilgrimage center in France.

REGIONAL CUISINE Several distinct culinary traditions have flourished in and around the Pyrénées: those of the Basque, the Béarn, the Catalán, and the Landes region.

The food here is simple, hearty, and fresh, traditionally served on a table draped with the roughly woven, brightly striped cloths that have always been associated with the region. Basque cuisine transforms ordinary ingredients into aromatically tantalizing concoctions, usually with the liberal addition of pepper.

One savory delicacy is tuna grilled with local herbs over a wood fire and served with chopped garlic, parsley, vinaigrette sauce, and freshly pounded pepper. Other regional specialties include *bigorneaux* (periwinkles), which diners skewer from their shells with toothpicks; *cèpes,* meaty flap mushrooms braised with garlic and sprinkled with parsley; and lamb chops, pork chops, and Basque *bourrides* (fish stews), all with dollops of garlic. Basque bouillabaisse is called *ttoro,* and *chipirones* are cuttlefish, which the Basques stuff or stew after beating the flesh to break apart its toughness.

Basque country also produces *pipérade Basque,* scrambled eggs with tomatoes, onions, green peppers, and black pepper. Sausages popular here include *tripoxa,* made from calves' blood and hot peppers; *tripotcha,* from tripe of baby veal; and *loukinkas,* small garlic-laden sausages. A local sour cider is *pittara,* and the region's best wine is Irouléguy. Bayonne's chocolate is famous throughout France.

In the Béarn, centered around Pau, the wines are excellent and liberally consumed with the contents of the family *toupi* (soup pot). Many kinds of onion, beet, sorrel, chicory, bacon/cabbage, and garlic/tomato soup are prepared in this pot. Thick and aromatic stews are

The Basque Country

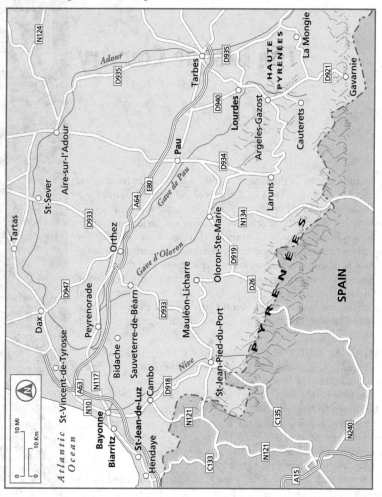

called *garbure,* and they're not considered suitable unless the ladle can stand upright in the pot. With bread and wine, the garbure is a full meal. The wines of the Béarn are better than those of the Basque country and include its most famous vintage, Jurançon. Sadly for its regional pride, however, sauce béarnaise wasn't created here—it was invented by a Basque chef in Paris.

The Pyrénées are also inhabited by the Cataláns, who do much of their cooking in olive oil with generous amounts of garlic. The Catalán national dish is *ouillade,* a constantly replenished pair of stewpots that are never emptied, washed, or cleaned. Catalán bouillabaisse is called *bouillinade* and is prepared with crayfish (among other fish) boiled in dry Banyuls wine.

Finally, in the northwestern Pyrénées, the traditional cooking medium is goose fat, which occasionally flavors the aromatic and delicious *cassoulet.* A cassoulet must always be cooked in a *cassoule* (earthenware pot), simmered in an oven for hours, and contains white beans and either goose meat, pork, lamb, partridge, or a combination of any of the above.

1 Lourdes

497 miles SW of Paris, 25 miles SE of Pau

Muslims turn to Mecca, Hindus to the Ganges, but for Catholics Lourdes is the world's most beloved shrine. Nestled in a valley in the southwestern part of the Hautes-Pyrénées, it's the scene of pilgrims gathering from all over the world. If you're coming in August, be sure to book your hotel as early as possible.

The Roman Catholic world believes that on February 11, 1858, the Virgin revealed herself to a poor shepherd girl, Bernadette Soubirous. Eighteen such apparitions were reported. Bernadette, subject of the film *Song of Bernadette* starring Jennifer Jones, died in a convent in 1879. She was beatified in 1925, then canonized in 1933.

Her apparitions put Lourdes on the map. The town has subsequently attracted millions of visitors, from the illustrious to the poverty-stricken. The truly devout are often disheartened at the tawdry commercialism of Lourdes today. And some vacationers are acutely disturbed by the human desperation of victims of various afflictions spending their hard-earned savings seeking a "miracle," then having to return home without a cure. However, the church has recognized many "cures" that took place after patients bathed in the springs, labeling them "true miracles."

ESSENTIALS

GETTING THERE   Six **trains** run from Pau (see section 2 in this chapter) daily (trip time: 30 minutes); there are also five trains from Bayonne (trip time: 2 hours) and Paris (trip time 5$^{1}/_{2}$ to 9$^{1}/_{2}$ hours, depending on the train). For train information and schedules, call ☎ **08-36-35-35-35.**

If you're **driving** from Toulouse, take N117 west until you reach Tarbes. From here take N21 south to Lourdes. From Paris, follow A10 south to Vierzon, changing to N20 south to Limoges, continuing on N21 south to Lourdes.

VISITOR INFORMATION   The **Office de Tourisme** is on place Peyramale (☎ **05-62-42-77-40**).

SPECIAL EVENTS   From July 1 to September 20, tourists and pilgrims can join the ✪ **Day Pilgrims** (*Pélerin d'un Jour*) (☎ **05-62-42-78-78**), a pilgrimage (in English) that gathers at 9am at the statue of the Crowned Virgin for a prayer meeting in the meadow facing the Grotto. The services include a 9:30am Stations of the Cross and an 11am mass. At 2:30pm, assembling at the same spot, pilgrims are taken on a guided visit to the Sanctuaries, or places associated with Bernadette. In the Sanctuaries you'll hear the story of Lourdes and of Bernadette, complete with a free 30-minute slide show (also in English). At 4:30pm there's a Procession of the Blessed Eucharist, starting from the Grotto. The 8:45pm Marian celebration, rosary, and torchlight procession all start from the Grotto as well.

EXPLORING THE TOWN & ITS ENVIRONS

At the **Grotto of Massabielle** the Virgin is said to have appeared 18 times to Bernadette between February 11 and July 16, 1858. This venerated site is accessible to pilgrims both day and night, and mass is celebrated here every day. The Statue of Our Lady depicts the Virgin in the posture she is said to have taken in the place she reputedly appeared, saying to Bernadette in Pyrénéan dialect, "I am the Immaculate Conception."

At the back of the Grotto, on the left of the altar, is the **Miraculous Spring** that reportedly spouted on February 25, 1858, during the ninth apparition, when Bernadette scraped the earth as instructed. The Virgin is said to have commanded her,

"Go and drink at the spring and wash there." The water from this spring is collected in several reservoirs, from which you can drink.

The **Upper Basilica,** at place du Rosaire, was built in the 13th-century ogival style but wasn't consecrated until 1876. It contains one nave split into five equal bays. Lining its interior are votive tablets. On the west side of the square is the Rosary Basilica, with two small towers. It was built in 1889 in the Roman-Byzantine style and holds up to 4,000. Inside, 15 chapels are dedicated to the "mysteries of the rosary."

The oval **Basilica of Pius X,** 1 ave. Monseigneur Théas, was consecrated in 1958. An enormous underground chamber covered by a concrete roof, it's 660 feet long and 270 feet wide, holding as many as 20,000. It's one of the world's largest churches. It's open daily from 7am to 7pm. International masses are conducted in six languages, including English, every Wednesday and Sunday at 3:30am from Easter to October.

Nearby, the **Musée Ste-Bernadette** (☎ 05-62-42-78-78) contains scenes representing the life of the saint; it's open daily from 10am to noon and 2:30 to 5pm (call ahead during winter). True Bernadette devotees will also seek out the **Maison Natale de Bernadette,** rue Bernadette-Soubirous (☎ 05-62-42-16-36), where the saint was born on January 7, 1844, the daughter of a miller. Her former home is open November to March daily from 3 to 5pm and from April to October daily from 9am to noon and 2 to 6:30pm. This was actually her mother's house. Bernadette's father, François Soubirous, had his family home in another mill, **Moulin Lacadé,** at 2 rue Bernadette-Soubirous. You can visit daily from 9am to noon and 2 to 7pm in summer; in winter daily 2:15 to 5:45pm. None of these sites charges admission. For more information contact the Office de Tourisme (see above).

You can visit the privately owned and overly commercialized wax museum, **Musée Grévin,** 87 rue de la Grotte (☎ 05-62-94-33-74), where displays retrace not only Bernadette's life but also the life of Christ, with a bad reproduction of Leonardo da Vinci's *Last Supper.* In February and March and November and December, it is open daily from 2 to 6pm. From April to October, hours are daily from 9 to 11:30am and 1:30 to 6pm. Closed in January. Admission is 35 F ($5.60) for adults, 17 F ($2.70) for children ages 6 to 12, and free for children 5 and under.

If you want a panoramic view, take an elevator to the terrace of the **Château-Fort de Lourdes,** an excellent example of medieval military architecture. The castle contains the **Musée Pyrénéen,** 25 rue du Fort (☎ 05-62-42-37-37), with regional handcrafts and costumes, including a collection of dolls in nuns' habits. In the courtyard are scale models of different styles of regional architecture. Both the château and the museum can be visited April to September, daily from 9am to noon and 1:30 to 6:30pm; off-season it closes at 6pm and is closed Tuesday. Admission is 32 F ($5.10) for adults, 16 F ($2.55) for children 6 to 12, and free for children 5 and under.

OUTDOOR PURSUITS   Lourdes is a good base for exploring the Pyrénées. You can take tours into the snowcapped mountains across the border to Spain or go horseback riding near **Lac de Lourdes,** 2 miles northwest of town. Outstanding sites are **Bagnères-de-Bigorre** (14 miles east of Lourdes via D935), a renowned thermal spa; **Pic du Jer,** for a panoramic vista of the countryside—to get here you can board the funicular in Lourdes south of Esplanade des processions (one-way fare 22 F/$3.50); **Béout,** for a view and an underground cave where prehistoric implements have been found (reached by funicular along Avenue Foch, cost 22 F/$3.50); the **Caves of Medous,** an underground river with stalactites (located southeast of Lourdes via D26, open April to October); and for a full-day tour, the **Heights of Gavarnie** (*Cirque de Gavarnie*), at 4,500 feet one of France's great natural wonders—to get here go south of Lourdes along D921.

ACCOMMODATIONS

The two restaurants reviewed below also offer rooms.

Grand Hôtel de la Grotte. 66–68 rue de la Grotte, 65000 Lourdes. ☎ **05-62-94-58-87.** Fax 05-62-94-20-50. www.hotel-grotte.com. E-mail: grotte@sudfr.com. 83 units. A/C MINI-BAR TV TEL. 420–620 F ($67.20–$99.20) double. AE, DC, MC, V. Closed Oct 30–May. Bus: 2.

Grand Hôtel is an old favorite, having catered to Catholic pilgrims (and to an increasing degree, tourists) since 1870. It's furnished in a staid but comfortable upper-bourgeois French decor that's slowly being updated. Some of the rooms on the upper floor open onto one of the most panoramic views in town, not only of the sanctuaries and the river but also the mountains. Rooms on the basilica side tend to be noisy. The hotel has a garden set beside the banks of the river Gave de Pau. Its restaurant, open to the public, offers straightforward meals inspired by French and regional cuisine. Fixed-price menus range from 110 F to 135 F ($17.60 to $21.60).

Hôtel Adriatic. 4 rue Baron-Duprat, 65100 Lourdes. ☎ **05-62-94-31-34.** Fax 05-62-42-14-70. 87 units. TEL. 260–395 F ($41.60–$63.20) double. AE, MC, V. Closed Oct–Easter. Bus: 2.

With a bright English-speaking staff, this hotel offers clean and traditional rooms; about 23 contain TVs and minibars. The in-house **restaurant** serves fine regional cuisine. The hotel is close to the shrines, the home of St. Bernadette, the parish church, and the town's fortified castle.

Hôtel Galilée et Windsor. 10 av. Peyramale, 65100 Lourdes. ☎ **05-62-94-21-55.** Fax 05-62-94-53-66. www.galileewindsor.fr. 163 units. TV TEL. 450 F ($72) double. Half board 630 F ($100.80) double. Rates include breakfast. AE, DC, MC, V. Closed Nov 15–Easter.

This three-star hotel, often confused with the more comfortable, more expensive Gallia et Londres, was built after World War II. The rooms are pleasant, if rather dull and anonymous-looking. Since this is the largest hotel in Lourdes, it's a magnet for religious groups. The **restaurant** serves regional and continental meals but offers nothing to challenge the taste buds.

Hôtel Gallia et Londres. 26 av. Bernadette-Soubirous, 65100 Lourdes. ☎ **05-62-94-35-44.** Fax 05-62-42-24-64. 90 units. A/C TV TEL. 420–460 F ($67.20–$73.60) double. Rate includes breakfast. AE, V. Closed Apr–Oct 30.

This old-fashioned hotel with a provincial flavor is among the most popular in Lourdes. In 1998, it underwent major refurbishment and renovations. There was a complete overhaul of the bedrooms, including a change in decor to a more modern conservative style, and an upgrade in the quality of the mattresses. There's a pub, a bar, and a **restaurant** with a 125 F ($21.25) fixed-price menu. Most guests here are part of religious groups that tend to book *en masse.*

Hôtel Notre-Dame de France. 8 av. Peyramale, 65100 Lourdes. ☎ **05-62-94-91-45.** Fax 05-62-94-57-21. E-mail: jean-michel.imbert@wanadoo.fr. 76 units. TEL. 330–340 F ($52.80–$54.40) double. Half board 290 F ($46.40) per person extra. AE, MC, V. Closed Oct 15–Mar 15. Free parking. Bus: 2.

Next to the Galilée et Windsor, this hotel is less than 100 yards from the main religious monument (the sanctuaries associated with the visions of Bernadette). Originally built around 1928, it underwent radical rebuilding in the late 1980s that eliminated virtually every vestige of its Art Deco detailing. It offers clean, simple, no-frills rooms with almost monastic furnishings. Some pilgrims appreciate the emphasis here on religious activities. Overall, it's a worthy budget choice. Fixed-price menus in the **dining room** focus on regional cuisine, and cost 90 F ($14.40).

DINING

Relais de Saux. Rte. de Tarbes (N21), 65100 Lourdes. ☎ **05-62-94-29-61.** Fax 05-62-42-12-64. Reservations recommended. Fixed-price menus 140–310 F ($22.40–$49.60) at lunch, 180–310 F ($28.80–$49.60) at dinner. AE, DC, MC, V. Daily noon–2pm and 7:15–9:30pm. Take N117 2 miles northeast of Lourdes to the village of Saux. From there follow the signs to Tarbes. BIGORRE.

This is the area's best restaurant, housed in an ivy-covered manor. It specializes in the regional mountain cuisine of the Pyrénées. The carved-wood fireplaces complement the beamed ceilings, silk-upholstered walls, and rustic artifacts. Meals are supervised by innkeepers Madeleine and Bernard Heres. Begin with a selection of hot or cold hors d'oeuvres, ranging from beet flan with cheese fondue to smoked swordfish. The boneless quail and the escalope of warm duck liver are especially delectable.

Upstairs are six **guest rooms,** some with large windows overlooking the garden. A double costs 500 F to 580 F ($80 to $92.80).

Taverne de Bigorre et Hôtel d'Albret. 21 place du Champs-Commun, 65100 Lourdes. ☎ **05-62-94-75-00.** Fax 05-62-94-78-45. Reservations recommended. Main courses 60–130 F ($9.60–$20.80); fixed-price menus 70–148 F ($11.20–$23.70). AE, DC, MC, V. Daily noon–1:30pm and 7–9pm. Closed Jan 6–Feb 6 and Nov 13–Dec 23. BIGORRE.

This restaurant has some of the best food in town; tournedos with flap mushrooms is a specialty. You can also order such country dishes as escalope of hot duck foie gras with apples, and duck steak kebab with green-pepper sauce. The mountain trout is especially good here.

Hôtel d'Albret is one of the best **budget hotels** in Lourdes, with 27 comfortable rooms. A double costs 212 F to 238 F ($33.90 to $38.10), with half board at 208 F ($33.30) per person extra.

2 Pau

477 miles SW of Paris, 122 miles SW of Toulouse

High above the banks of the Gave de Pau River, this year-round resort is a good place to pause in your trek through the Pyrénées. The British discovered Pau in the early 19th century, launching such innovative practices here as fox hunting, a custom that's lingered. Even if you're just passing through, go along boulevard des Pyrénées, an esplanade erected on Napoléon's orders, for the most famous panoramic view in the Pyrénées.

Today Pau is the most cosmopolitan city in the western Pyrénées, the capital of the Pyrénées-Atlantiques *département.* It was once the capital of the Béarn region, the land of the kings of Navarre, the most famous and beloved of whom was Henri IV. Its population of approximately 90,000 still observes some English traditions, such as afternoon tea. At one time the English formed 15% of the population, but with the arrival of two world wars, many of them left.

ESSENTIALS

GETTING THERE   Pau-Uzein airport is 7½ miles north of town; call ☎ **05-59-33-33-00** for flight information. There are good **train** connections from Biarritz (six per day taking 1½ hours); for train information and schedules, call ☎ **08-36-35-35-35. Driving** to Pau is relatively easy because of its location along the N117 roadway, which is directly accessible from Toulouse. From Paris, take A10 south to Vierzon, changing to N20 south to Limoges, continuing on N21 south to Tarbes, and finally turning west along N117 to Pau.

VISITOR INFORMATION   The **Office de Tourisme** is on place Royale (☎ 05-59-27-27-08).

SPECIAL EVENTS   For 2 days in May, there's the **Grand Prix de Pau,** where race cars from around France compete for speed records in what might remind you of a small-scale replica of the Grand Prix in Monaco. During June and early July, as part of the **Festival de Pau,** the municipality arranges for frequent theatrical, musical, and dance performances, either in public squares, in the streets, or in the courtyard of the château. Many of the events within the festival are presented in public venues for free; if there is a charge, it usually ranges from 80 F to 200 F ($12.80 to $32) for the various events. The local tourist office has complete details.

EXPLORING THE CITY

The heart of the commercial district is busy **place Clémenceau,** out of which radiate at least five boulevards. At the western end of town stands the **Château de Pau,** 2 rue du Château (☎ 05-59-82-38-00), dating from the 12th century and still steeped in the Renaissance spirit of the bold Marguerite de Navarre, who wrote the bawdy *Heptaméron* at 60. The castle has seen many builders and tenants. Louis XV ordered the bridge that connects the castle to the town, whereas the great staircase hall was commissioned by Marguerite herself. Louis-Philippe had all the apartments redecorated around 1840. Inside are many souvenirs, including a crib made of a single tortoise shell for Henri de Navarre, who was born here. There's also a splendid array of Flemish and Gobelin tapestries. The great rectangular tower, **Tour de Gaston Phoebus,** is from the 14th century.

Another intriguing area within the château is *La Salle aux 100 Couverts,* site of some of the enormous receptions that were held here during the building's medieval heyday. The château is open daily from 9:30 to 11:45am and from 2 to 5:15pm. Admission costs 25 F ($4) for adults and 17 F ($2.70) for students 18 to 25. It's free for children 17 and under. **Musée des Beaux-Arts,** rue Mathieu-Lalanne (☎ 05-59-27-33-02), displays a collection of European paintings, including Spanish, Flemish, Dutch, English, and French masters, such as El Greco, Zurbarán, Degas, and Boudin. It's open Wednesday to Monday from 10am to noon and 2 to 6pm. Admission is 10 F ($1.60) for adults and 5 F (80¢) for children.

SHOPPING

Pau affords ample opportunities for you to buy some authentic regional specialties, such as mouthwatering chocolates, sweet jams, and Basque antiques. The pedestrian **rue Serviez** and **rue des Cordelières** harbor an array of petit boutiques and shops that carry many of these items, as do **rue Louis-Barthou, rue Henry-IV,** and **rue du Maréchal-Foch.**

Pau is home to some of the best antiques shops in the region, such as **Champeau Paul,** 14 rue Castetnau (☎ 05-59-02-40-03), with its mélange of 18th- to 20th-century treasures for the home. The area around the château is well known as the antiques center of town. On Saturday, Sunday, and Monday from 10am to 6pm, you'll find a large **flea market** on place du Forail, selling everything from antiques to modern-day gadgets.

Local confectionery specialties include **armes de Pau,** the small squares of secret-recipe medium-dark chocolate with the town's coat of arms emblazoned on top. Some of the best of these decadent morsels can be found at **Chadeuf Bouzon,** 6 rue Henri-IV (☎ 05-59-27-70-88). The **Musée de la Confiture,** 48 rue du Maréchal-Joffre (☎ 05-59-27-69-51), not only traces the rich history of jam making in this region but also has fabulously fruity jams for sale.

ACCOMMODATIONS

Hôtel Continental. 2 rue du Maréchal-Foch, 64000 Pau. ☎ **05-59-27-69-31** or 800/528-1234 in the U.S. Fax 05-59-27-99-84. www.bestwestern.com. E-mail: hotel.continental@libertysurf.fr. 80 units. MINIBAR TV TEL. 500–580 F ($80–$92.80) double. AE, DC, DISC, MC, V. Free parking in garage.

The centrally located, three-star Continental is the largest, most prominent hotel in Pau. Renovated several times since its original construction around 1900, it's the best of a lackluster lot in town. Even so, don't expect grand theatricality or even a particularly well-trained staff. Rooms are functionally decorated, modernized, and soundproofed.

Hôtel de Gramont. 3 place Gramont, 64000 Pau. ☎ **05-59-27-84-04.** Fax 05-59-27-62-23. www.hotel-gramont.fr. E-mail: gramont@club.internet.fr. 36 units. TV TEL. 280–400 F ($44.80–$64) double; 495 F ($79.20) suite. AE, DC, DISC, MC, V.

Within walking distance of the château and the rail station, this hotel is a truly impressive building. The four-story château-like structure has street-level arcades and high-ceilinged soundproofed rooms, 10 of which are air-conditioned. Some are suitable for persons with disabilities. Although not as impressive as the exterior, the rooms are simply furnished with standard amenities and reasonably comfortable mattresses.

Hôtel Le Postillon. Place de Verdun, 10 cours Camou, 64000 Pau. ☎ **05-59-72-83-00.** Fax 05-59-72-83-13. 25 units. TV TEL. 235–330 F ($37.60–$52.80) double. DC, V. Bus: 1.

This is a cozy hotel, with French provincial decor and a flower-filled courtyard. The rooms are comfortably furnished, each individually decorated. Some rooms have a balcony overlooking the garden. The reasonable price keeps the place consistently full. Breakfast is the only meal served, but there's a choice of restaurants nearby.

Hôtel-Restaurant Corona. 71 av. du Général-Leclerc, 64000 Pau. ☎ **05-59-30-64-77.** Fax 05-59-02-62-64. 20 units. MINIBAR TV TEL. 230–290 F ($36.80–$46.40) double. AE, DC, MC, V.

The French architect who designed this hotel had completed many commissions in Montréal. In honor of them, he added what were considered at the time many Canada-inspired touches, including the ample use of exposed pinewood. About a mile east of the center of Pau, this hotel offers comfortable accommodations. There are two dining rooms, where you can enjoy hearty portions of food. The **restaurant** (but not the brasserie) is closed on Saturday and from December 23 to January 10. It is also closed for dinner on Friday and Sunday evening.

DINING

Au Fin Gourmet. 24 av. Gaston-Lacoste. ☎ **05-59-27-47-71.** Reservations recommended. Main courses 80–130 F ($12.80–$20.80); fixed-price menus 95–170 F ($15.20–$27.20). AE, DC, MC, V. Tues–Sun noon–2:15pm; Tues–Sat 7–10pm. BASQUE.

This restaurant is maintained by Christian, Laurent, and Patrick, sons of the retired founder, Clément Ithurriague. It offers an outdoor terrace for warm-weather dining and a cuisine based almost exclusively on regional ingredients. Menu items include marinated codfish with herbs from the kitchen garden and bouillon-flavored potatoes, rack of lamb flavored with herbs from the Pyrénées in a parsley-enriched crust, sliced and sautéed foie gras, and braised stuffed trout. The 95 F ($15.20) fixed-price menu is a crowd pleaser and one of Pau's best dining values.

✪ **Chez Pierre.** Rue Louis-Barthour. ☎ **05-59-27-76-86.** Reservations required. Main courses 115–200 F ($18.40–$32); fixed-price menu 200 F ($32). AE, DC, MC, V. Mon–Fri noon–2:30pm; Mon–Sat 7–10pm. BÉARNAISE/FRENCH.

Year after year, we always have our finest meal in Pau at Chez Pierre, where regional products are spun into extraordinarily creative dishes. In air-conditioned comfort, you can sit downstairs at one of the eight tables or upstairs in one of three tiny salons. Chef Raymond Casau, who spent years apprenticing with some of the most successful chefs in France, is among the finest around, and his specialties are sole braised with wine, fresh salmon braised with Jurançon (a sweet, golden Pyrénéan wine), and a Béarnais version of cassoulet. (It employs different sausages than the version found in Toulouse, and places a greater emphasis on confit of goose.) One of the most attractive **bars** in town, outfitted like an English golf course's club room, is adjacent to the dining rooms.

La Gousse d'Ail. 12 rue du Hédas. ☎ **05-59-27-31-55.** Fixed-price menus 98–198 F ($15.70–$31.70). MC, V. Sun–Fri noon–1:30pml; Mon–Sat 7–10:30pm. BASQUE.

A few blocks from the château, this restaurant has a stone, brick, and stucco interior with ceiling beams and a fireplace. The place is small-scale, medieval-looking, and permeated with a respect for the culinary techniques and ingredients of the Basque country. Fixed-price menus might include a version scallops and shrimp cooked with Jurançon, or a confit of duck thighs with French fries that are cooked in the duck's own juices. Desserts and breads are homemade, and the menu changes with the season.

NEARBY ACCOMMODATIONS & DINING
Some of the world's most discerning people head to the town of Eugénie-les-Bains, about 33 miles north of Pau, in search of the marvelous domain of Michel Guérard. The town has no rail station, so most people drive from Pau. To get there, take N134 north to the town of Garlin, then follow the unmarked road west to the town of Geaune and then follow signs to Eugénie-les-Bains.

✪ **Les Prés d'Eugénie (Michel Guérard).** Eugénie-les-Bains, 40320 Beaune. ☎ **05-58-05-06-07.** Fax 05-58-51-10-10. Reservations recommended. Main courses 190–310 F ($30.40–$49.60); fixed-price menus 600–780 F ($96–$124.80). AE, DC, MC, V. Fri–Tues 12:30–2pm; Thurs–Tues 7:30–10pm (July–Aug, open daily). BASQUE.

This Relais & Châteaux is the creation of Michel Guérard, the innovative chef whose *cuisine minceur* started a culinary revolution in the early 1970s. Built during the 19th century as a spa where the Empress Eugénie could take a rest cure, it attracts a stream of diners who appreciate the calm, the much-publicized cooking, and the endless business expansions of its owner. Offered here are both *cuisine minceur,* so calorie counters can still enjoy well-seasoned flavors and fresh ingredients, and the heartier *cuisine gourmand,* whose traditions are influenced by Basque and classic French recipes. Dishes are constantly evolving here, usually tapping into a sense of regional sentimentality, as in the case of "bourgeois-style" veal chops fried "over low flame in a corner of the fireplace." Specialties include cream of crayfish soup, whiting in white-wine sauce, mullet steamed with seaweed and oysters, lamb steamed with fennel, and a wide variety of simply steamed fish with fresh vegetables.

Those unwilling to pay the stratospheric prices in the main restaurant sometimes select a table in a satellite restaurant operated by M. Guérard called **La Ferme aux Grives.** The cuisine here focuses on more rural specialties of the region, offering a single fixed-price menu costing 205 F ($32.80). Comfortable and rustically elegant, it's open for lunch Wednesday to Monday and dinner Wednesday to Sunday.

In addition to the restaurants, there is a variety of **accommodations.** The most comfortable, and expensive, are the eight high-ceilinged units within an outlying annex, **Le Couvent des Herbes.** They cost 1,150 F to 1,900 F ($184 to $304) for a double and from 2,000 F to 2,400 F ($320 to $384) for a suite. Only slightly less glamorous are the 35 units within the establishment's main building, renting for 1,100 F to 1,950 F ($176 to $312) each, and from 1,500 F to 2,200 F ($240 to $352) for a suite. Rooms are decorated in the style of a private manor house in the French countryside. Less expensive, and deliberately geared to the family-with-children trade, are the 32 units within **La Maison Rose,** where double occupancy costs from 500 F to 800 F ($80 to $128). Some of the units contain kitchenettes.

PAU AFTER DARK

The highest concentration of nightlife in Pau occurs within **Le Triangle,** an area in the town center flanked by the rue Emile Garet, rue Lespy, and rue Castetnau. Within those confines, you'll find one of our favorite bars, **Le Garage,** 49 rue Emile Garet (☎ 05-59-83-75-17), as well as the rough but congenial **Le Béarnais,** 3 rue Lespy (☎ 05-59-83-72-11), with its fun staff and convivial atmosphere; and **Le Caveau,** 18 rue Castetnau (☎ 05-59-27-35-37), more laid-back and not quite so loud. But if you need a more diverse and older crowd, check out the streets around the château. At **Le Paradis,** 11 place du Forail (☎ 05-59-84-06-73), all ages mix, mingle, and bop the night away on the immense dance floor to the beat of popular Top-40 tunes. Covers range between 40 F and 60 F ($6.40 and $9.60).

3 Bayonne

478 miles SW of Paris, 114 miles SW of Bordeaux

Bayonne is not only the leading port/pleasure-yacht basin of the Côte Basque, divided by the Nive and Adour rivers, it's also a cathedral city and capital of the Pays Basque. It's characterized by narrow streets, quays, and ramparts. Enlivening the scene are bullfights, *pelote* games (jai alai), and street dancing at annual fiestas. While here you may want to buy some of Bayonne's chocolate at one of the arcaded shops along rue du Port-Neuf, then enjoy coffee at a cafe along place de la Liberté, the hub of town.

ESSENTIALS

GETTING THERE   Bayonne is linked to Paris by 10 **trains** per day (regular trains make the trip in 8 hours, TGV trains do it in 5¹/₂). Nine trains per day arrive from Bordeaux (trip time: 2¹/₂ hours). For train information and schedules, call ☎ 08-36-35-35-35.

There's **bus** service from Biarritz. (Bus no. 1 departs from Biarritz at 12-minute intervals throughout the daylight hours, depositing passengers on place de la Mairie in Bayonne.) There's also bus service between Bayonne and outlying towns and villages not serviced by train.

If you're **driving,** note that Bayonne is located near the end of the N117 roadway, easily accessible from Toulouse and other cities in the south of France. From Paris, take A10 south to Vierzon, changing to N20 south to Limoges, continuing on N21 south to Tarbes, finally turning west along N117 to Bayonne.

VISITOR INFORMATION   The **Office de Tourisme** is on place des Basques (☎ 05-59-46-01-46).

SPECIAL EVENTS   The days around July 17 to 21 are the traditional start of the town's jazz festival called **Jazz aux Remparts.** Great jazz musicians from as far away as the United States come here for a week of superb high-energy concerts. Tickets to most concerts range between 120 F and 200 F ($19.20 and $32) and are available along with complete details from the Théâtre Municipal (☎ 05-59-59-07-27). During **Fête de Bayonne,** held the first weeks in August, a frenzy of music concerts and dancing fill the streets. The celebration is intense. For **free concerts** on fair-weathered Thursday evenings in July and August, head over to the gazebo on place de Gaulle, where musical styles range from jazz to traditional Basque.

EXPLORING THE TOWN

The old town, **Grand Bayonne,** is inside the ramparts of Vauban's fortifications, on the left bank of the Nive. This part of town is dominated by the early 13th-century ✪ **Cathédrale Ste-Marie,** rue d'Espagne/rue des Gouverneurs (☎ 05-59-59-17-82). This outstanding Gothic building is distinguished by its nave's stained-glass windows and many niches containing elaborate sarcophagi. From the 13th-century cloister you have a view of the cathedral's remarkable architecture. It's open daily from 10am to noon and 3 to 6pm.

The **Musée Bonnat,** 5 rue Jacques-Lafitte (☎ 05-59-59-08-52), contains a collection of artwork that the painter Léon Bonnat donated to the city, including his own. Bonnat was especially fond of portraits, often of ladies in elegant 1890s gowns. Also on display are works by Degas, David, Goya, Ingres, Rubens, van Dyck, Rembrandt, Tiepolo, El Greco, and even Leonardo. The museum is open Wednesday to Monday from 10am to noon and 2 to 6pm. Admission is 20 F ($3.20) for adults and 10 F ($1.60) for students and children 11 and under.

SHOPPING

Most of its specialty shops and boutiques lie inside the ramparts of the old town, Grand Bayonne. The pedestrian streets of **rue Port-Neuf** (aptly nicknamed the "street of chocolate shops"), **rue Victor-Hugo,** and **rue Salie** are the major venues. For antiques, walk over to **place Montaut,** just behind the cathedral. Most of the modern, everyday shops and French chain stores are on **rue Thiers** and **quai de la Nive,** outside the old town. In particular, visit **Maison de Blanc Berrogain,** place de 5 Cantons (☎ 05-59-59-16-18), to meet your quota of Basque bath, kitchen, and bed linens. **Cazenave,** 19 rue Port-Neuf (☎ 05-59-59-03-16), specializes in chocolats de Bayonne that include rich, dark, strong chocolate nougats; stop in the tearoom here for warm chocolate mousses.

You can also head for a 150-year-old shop in the shadow of Bayonne's cathedral, **La Maison Tajan,** 62–64 rue d'Espagne (☎ 05-59-59-00-39), where you'll find the region's widest selection of glazed terra-cotta platters and pots, all of them safe for the oven and the microwave. Imported from nearby Spain and decorated only with a translucent earth-toned glaze, they're among the best accessories for the slow-cooking processes necessary in preparing Basque cuisine.

The accessories of one Basque tradition have become something of a fine art. They are called *makilas,* which in olden days were used as either a walking stick, a cudgel, or—when equipped with a hidden blade—a knife. Today, carved makilas are sold in gentrified formats as collectors' items and souvenirs. For safety's sake, they almost never come with a blade. One of the best outlets for these objects in town is **Fabrication de Makilas,** 37 rue Vieille Boucherie (☎ 05-59-59-18-20). Another famous product of the Basque country is its cured hams, which seem to taste best when shaved into paper-thin slices and consumed with one of the region's heady red wines. A site that both manufactures and sells them is **Conserverie Artisanale de Jambon de Bayonne,** 41 rue des Cordeliers (☎ 05-59-25-65-30), where the famous hams (sold in their entirety or sliced and sold by the pound) are available along with various pâtés, sausages, and terrines.

ACCOMMODATIONS

Best Western Grand Hôtel. 21 rue Thiers, 64100 Bayonne. ☎ **800/528-1234** in the U.S. and Canada, or 05-59-59-62-00. Fax 05-59-59-62-01. www.bestwestern.fr. 54 units. MINIBAR TV TEL. 420–680 F ($67.20–$108.80) double. AE, DC, MC, V. Parking 55 F ($8.80).

This hotel, the best in town, was built in 1835 amid the ruins of a medieval Carmelite convent. In 1991, after a total renovation, it attained three-star status. The rooms are appointed with modern fittings and cable TV, yet maintain an antique, period feel. The refurbishment also managed to preserve the medieval feel in the **restaurant, Les Carmes.** Here the original convent's bulky, carefully chiseled arcades are sheltered with a glass, greenhouse-style roof that can be opened for ventilation during warm weather. Fixed-price meals cost 90 F to 140 F ($14.40 to $22.40).

Mercure Agora Bayonne. Av. Jean-Rostand, 64100 Bayonne. ☎ **05-59-52-84-44.** Fax 05-59-52-84-20. E-mail: h0953@accord-hotels.com. 109 units. A/C MINIBAR TV TEL. 465–560 F ($74.40–$89.60) double. AE, DC, MC, V.

Widely considered the second best choice in Bayonne, the Mercure provides well-furnished rooms with views over the river Nive, which flows nearby. Drinks are served on the terrace, which was carved out of an otherwise wooded setting beside the river. Bedrooms are typical, chain hotel style. The **restaurant's** fixed-price menus begin at 150 F ($24), but the cuisine isn't the reason to stay here.

DINING

Cheval Blanc. 68 rue Bourgneuf. ☎ **05-59-59-01-33.** Reservations recommended. Main courses 95–160 F ($15.20–$25.60); fixed-price menus 128–290 F ($20.50–$46.40). AE, DC, V. Tues–Sat noon–2pm; Mon–Sun 7:30–10pm. Closed Feb 2–Mar 2 and Aug 4–8. BASQUE.

The finest restaurant in Bayonne occupies a half-timbered Basque-style house that was built in 1715 in the heart of the historic center. In a rustically elegant dining room you can enjoy the cuisine of Jean-Claude Tellechea, served by one of the most skilled maîtres d' in the Basque country, Robert Hualte. Menu items vary with the season but may include slices of foie gras with caramelized endive and pine nuts, ravioli stuffed with wild boar and flavored with local red wine and a confit of baby onions, and corn blinis with flap mushrooms. Dorado might be simmered in garlic and served with *crépinette de marmitako* (diced tuna with red and green peppers, bound in a pig's stomach). One of the best desserts is an *amandine bayonnais* with chocolate sauce.

François Miura. 24 rue Marengo. ☎ **05-59-59-49-89.** Reservations recommended. Main courses 100–120 F ($16–$19.20); fixed-price menus 115–185 F ($18.40–$29.60). AE, DC, MC, V. Thurs–Tues noon–2pm; Mon–Tues and Thurs–Sat 8–10pm. FRENCH.

The cuisine here is the most eclectic and personalized in town. Chef François Miura makes creative use of fresh ingredients, and his wife, Nadine, serves the dishes with humor and style. A few steps from the Église St-André, the restaurant occupies a late-19th-century cloister originally built for Visitandine nuns, which has been renovated into an appealing combination of old masonry and angular postmodern design. Menu items are sophisticated and composed with intelligence, including flavorful but complicated dishes such as stuffed squid served with a confit of pig's foot flavored with squid ink and an essence of crayfish. Less daring examples include crayfish tails with leeks, mushrooms, and coriander sauce; warm calamari salad with two kinds of peppers; and rack of lamb with basil, baby vegetables, and toast drenched in local ewes' cheese. Dessert may include a soufflé with pear liqueur.

BAYONNE AFTER DARK

Rue des Tonneliers, rue Pannecau, and **rue des Cordeliers** are the liveliest areas after dark. The only pub in town is the **Killarney Pub,** rue des Cordeliers (☎ **05-59-25-75-51**), where you'll find plenty of music and hearty laughter from a carefree group of rowdies. For a taste of local color, try **Le Cabaret La Luna Negra,** rue des Augustins (☎ **05-59-25-78-05**), where the cover charge of 30 F to 60 F ($4.80 to $9.60) includes cabaret, jazz or blues performances, and French popular song. Danceaholics appreciate **Disco La Pompe,** 7 rue des Augustins (☎ **05-59-25-48-12**), where the action starts around 11:30pm.

4 Biarritz

484 miles SW of Paris, 120 miles SW of Bordeaux

One of the most famous seaside resorts in the world, Biarritz was once a simple fishing village near the Spanish border. Favored by Empress Eugénie, the Atlantic village soon attracted her husband, Napoléon III, who truly put it on the map. Later, Queen Victoria showed up often, and her son, Edward VII, visited more than once.

In the 1930s the prince of Wales (before he became, and then unbecame, Edward VIII) and the American divorcee he loved, Wallis Simpson, did much to make Biarritz even more fashionable, as they headed south with these instructions: "Chill the champagne, pack the pearls, and tune up the Bugatti." Biarritz became the pre-jet set's favorite sun spot, though those legendary days are long gone and aren't coming back. The resort is still fashionable, but the unthinkable has happened: It now offers surf shops, snack bars, and even some reasonably priced hotels.

ESSENTIALS

GETTING THERE Ten **trains** arrive daily from Bayonne (trip time: 10 minutes), which has rail links with Paris and other major cities in the south of France. The rail station is 2 miles south of the town center, in La Négresse. For train information and schedules, call ☎ **08-36-35-35-35.** Bus no. 2 carries passengers at frequent intervals from the station to the center of Biarritz for a fee of 9 F ($1.45) per person, or you can take a cab for not much more. If you're **driving,** Biarritz is located at the end of the N117 roadway, which is the major thoroughfare for the Basque Country. From Paris, take A10 south to Vierzon, changing to N20 south to Limoges, continuing on N21 south to Tarbes, and finally turning west along N117 to Biarritz.

VISITOR INFORMATION The **Office de Tourisme** is on Square d'Ixelles (☎ **05-59-22-37-10**).

SPECIAL EVENTS If you're in town in September, check out some of the concerts and ballet performances that make up the 3-week festival of **Le Temps d'Aimer.** Cultural presentations are presented in parks, churches, and auditoriums throughout town, with tickets to the various events ranging from 60 F to 200 F ($9.60 to $32) each. Other music is showcased at the **Musique d'Été** festival for a 10-day period in late June and early July, usually within the Théâtre Gare du Midi, which was originally built as a railway station and later transformed into a concert space. For reservations and ticket sales to either of the above-mentioned festivals, or for tickets to any of the cultural events within the Théâtre Gare du Midi, contact **Biarritz Reservations** at ☎ **05-59-22-12-21.**

Biarritz is known as the surf capital of France. Every July, cadres of skilled surfboard enthusiasts descend on the town for a week for the annual **Biarritz Surf Festival.** You don't need to buy a ticket or even show up at any particular time. The festival utilizes all the beachfronts in town, and a Hawaiian spirit permeates the old Basque town as surfers from everywhere re-create the California Dream and the search for the Endless Summer. And if golf is your passion, consider visiting during a week in late July during the **Biarritz Cup,** a nationwide competition attended by mostly French golfers. This series of playoffs is held at the Golf du Phare (☎ **05-59-03-71-80**); it's usually televised. More information on all of the above-mentioned festivals is available from the tourist office.

A DAY AT THE BEACH

Along the seafront is the **Grande Plage.** During the belle époque, this was where Victorian ladies under parasols and wide-brimmed veiled hats would promenade. Today's women bathers don't dress up in such billowing skirts. Sometimes they don't even wear tops. The beach is also popular with surfers.

Promenade du bord de mer, stretching 9 miles along the coast, is still a major attraction. The paths along this walk are often carved into cliffs. Sections have been planted with flowers growing in these rock gardens, turning the area into a well-manicured public park. From here, you can head north to **Pointe St-Martin,** where you'll find more gardens and a staircase (look for the sign DESCENTE DE L'OCEAN) leading you to allée Winston-Churchill, a paved path going along **Plage Miramar.**

La Perspective de la Côte des Basques, a walk that goes up to another plateau, leads eventually to a beach that's one of the wildest and most exposed in France: **Plage de la Côte des Basques,** with breakers crashing at the base of the cliffs. This is where surfers head. For surfing rentals, contact **Ripcurl,** 2 av. de la Reine-Victoria (☎ **05-59-24-38-40**), or **Moraiz Surf Shop,** avenue Bidart (☎ **05-53-41-22-09**).

If you like your beaches calmer, head for the safest beach, the small horseshoe-shaped **Plage du Port-Vieux,** lining the path from plateau de l'Atalaye. Its tranquil waters, protected by rocks, make it a favorite with families.

SEEING THE SIGHTS

Église St-Martin, rue St-Martin (☎ **05-59-23-05-19**), is one of the few vestiges of the port's early boom days. In the 12th century Biarritz grew prosperous as a whaling center until the animals left the Bay of Biscay, marking a decline in the port's fortune. The church dates from the 1100s and was restored in 1541 with a Flamboyant Gothic chancel. It's away from the center of the resort and the town's beaches. Admission is free, and it's open daily from 8am to 7:30pm.

Biarritz's turning point came with the arrival of the comtesse de Montijo, who spent lazy summers here with her two daughters. One of these, Eugénie, married Napoléon III in 1853 and prevailed on him to visit Biarritz the next year. The emperor fell under its spell and ordered the construction of the **Hôtel du Palais** (see below). The hotel remains the town's most enduring landmark, though it was originally dubbed "Eugénie's Basque folly." Edward VII stayed there in 1906 and again in 1910, only days before his death. Set in a commanding spot on Grande Plage, the hotel is worth a visit even if you're not a guest. You can view the palatial trappings of its public rooms.

Before the Russian Revolution of 1917, great numbers of Russian nobility arrived, so many, in fact, that they erected the **Église Orthodoxe Russe,** 8 av. de l'Impératrice (☎ **05-59-24-16-74**). Across from the Hôtel du Palais, this Byzantine-Russian landmark was built in 1892 so the wintering Russian aristocrats could worship when they weren't enjoying champagne, caviar, and Basque prostitutes. It's noted for its striking dome, the color of a blue sky on a sunny day.

After you pass the Hôtel du Palais, the walkway widens into **quai de la Grande Plage,** Biarritz's principal promenade. This walkway continues to the opposite end of the resort, where there's a final belvedere opening onto the southernmost stretch of beach. This whole walk would take about 3 hours.

At the southern edge of Grande Plage, steps will take you to **place Ste-Eugénie,** Biarritz's most gracious old square. Lined with terraced restaurants, it's the rendezvous point. Right below place Ste-Eugénie is the colorful **Port des Pêcheurs** (fishers' port). Crowded with fishing boats, it has old wooden houses and shacks backed up against a cliff. Here you'll find driftwood, rope, and plenty of lobster traps along with small harborfront restaurants and cafes.

The rocky **plateau de l'Atalaye** forms one side of the Port des Pêcheurs. Ordered carved by Napoléon III, a tunnel leads through the plateau to an esplanade. Here a metal footbridge stretches out into the sea to a rocky islet that takes its name **Rocher de la Vierge** (Rock of the Virgin) from the statue crowning it. Since 1865 this statue is said to have protected the sailors and fishers in the Bay of Biscay. Alexandre-Gustave Eiffel (he of the tower of the same name) directed the construction of the footbridge. This walk out into the terraced edge of the rock, with crashing surf on both sides, is the most dramatic in Biarritz. From this rock you can see far to the south on a clear day, all the way to the mountains of the Spanish Basque country.

Once here, you can visit the **Musée de la Mer,** 14 plateau de l'Atalaye (☎ 05-59-24-02-59), which houses 24 aquariums of fish native to the bay. The seals steal the show at their daily 10:30am and 5pm feedings. The museum also houses *requins* (sharks) that are fed on Tuesday and Friday at 11am and Wednesday and Sunday at 4:30pm. The museum is open May to June, Monday to Friday from 9:30am to 12:30pm and 2 to 6pm, and Saturday and Sunday from 9:30am to 7pm; July 1 to 13, daily from 9:30am to 8pm; July 14 to August 30, daily from 9:30am to midnight; and August 16 to September, Monday to Friday from 9:30am to 6pm and Saturday and Sunday from 9:30am to 7pm. Admission is 45 F ($7.20) for adults, 30 F ($4.80) for students and children 5 to 16, and free for children 4 and under.

SHOPPING

The major fashion boutiques, with all the big designer names from Paris, are centered on **place Clemenceau** in the heart of Biarritz. From this square, fan out to **rue Gambetta, rue Mazagran, avenue Victor-Hugo, avenue Edouard-VII, avenue du Maréchal-Foch,** and **avenue de Verdun.** Of particular interest are the exceptional Biarritz chocolates and confections and the select textiles that filter in from the Basque country.

The finest chocolatiers are **Pariès,** 27 place Clemenceau (☎ 05-59-22-07-52), where you can choose from among seven varieties of *tournons,* ranging from raspberry to coffee; **Daranatz,** 12 av. du Maréchal-Foch (☎ 05-59-24-21-91); and **Henriet,** place Clemenceau (☎ 05-59-24-24-15), with its house specialty of *rochers de Biarritz:* morsels of candied orange peel and roasted almonds covered in creamy dark chocolate. At the other end of the gastronomic spectrum, try **Mille et Un Fromages,** 8 rue Victor Hugo (☎ 05-59-24-67-88), specializing in, as the name suggests, a myriad of tasty French cheeses as well as a host of hearty wines to accompany them.

Among antiques stores, your best bet is **Bakara,** 23 rue Mazagran (☎ 05-59-22-08-95), with its special porcelain dolls. For the finest in Basque tablecloths, sheets, and other household linens, visit **St-Léon,** 18 av. Victor-Hugo (☎ 05-59-24-19-81).

If a bottle of souvenir spirits appeals to you, join the stream of artists, actors, and gourmands who value **Arosteguy,** 5 av. Victor-Hugo (☎ 05-59-24-00-52). You can procure an affordable wine or bottle of deceptively potent spirits distilled from pears, plums, or raspberries.

Incidentally, **espadrilles,** the canvas-topped, rope-bottomed slippers, are sold at virtually every souvenir shop and department store in the region. A simple off-the-shelf model begins at a mere 52 F ($8.30), and made-to-order versions (special sizes, special colors) rarely rise above 400 F ($64) per pair. Upscale espadrilles are made to order at **Maison Garcia,** pont de Baskutenea, in Bidart, a hamlet midway between Biarritz and St-Jean-de-Luz (☎ **05-59-26-51-27**). Opened in 1937, this is one of the last manufacturers to finish its product the old-fashioned way—by hand.

ACCOMMODATIONS

Café de Paris (see below) also rents rooms.

Carlina Lodge. Bd. du Prince-de-Galles, 64200 Biarritz. ☎ **05-59-24-42-14.** Fax 05-59-24-95-32. 18 units, 5 apts with kitchenettes. MINIBAR TV TEL. 380–490 F ($60.80–$78.40) double; 600–1,300 F ($96–$208) apt. AE, DC, MC, V. Parking 30 F ($4.80).

This hotel manages to keep its prices low by providing almost no amenities other than daily maid service. There's no night watchman, no restaurant, and a staff that seems to highlight the site's disadvantages rather than its advantages. But if you're looking for a bargain and you don't mind a no-frills setting, consider emulating the French, who often check into one of the rooms or apartments for a week or more. Built in 1972, it offers an exceptional view of the Pyrénées and the Atlantic. Don't expect much style in the rooms. There's a security code you'll punch into a keypad at night to regain admission to the lobby, since the staff goes home around nightfall. But many French clients consider this place roughly equivalent to their private apartments back in Paris, and the low prices justify the relative lack of comforts.

✪ **Château de Brindos.** Lac de Brindos, 64600 Anglet. ☎ **05-59-23-17-68.** Fax 05-59-23-48-47. www.chateau-de-brindos.com. E-mail:chateau.de.brindos@wanadoo.fr. 13 units. TV TEL. 650–950 F ($104–$152) double; 950–1,250 F ($152–$200) suite. AE, DC, MC, V. From the town center, follow the AEROPORT signs; after the second roundabout (*rond-point*), follow the signs to the château; it's about 1$^1/_2$ miles north of Biarritz.

This is one of the most architecturally and culturally unusual homes in the southwest of France, with a history firmly entrenched in the Jazz Age. Built by the American railway heiress Virginia Gould in 1920, it occupies 27 acres of park and garden set inland from the sea. With a facade inspired vaguely by the architecture of Spain, and an interior loaded with architectural remnants such as fireplaces and staircases from the Gothic age, this is the most romantic stopover on the Côte Basque. The rooms are spacious with antique furnishings and modern fittings. Amenities include a private lake (where fishing can be arranged), tennis courts, and heated pool.

Set overlooking the lake, the **restaurant** serves a Franco-Basque cuisine. The food is superb, with a menu changing four times a year, which usually includes lobster salad, ravioli stuffed with a combination of scallops and fresh lobster, sautéed duck liver garnished with white grapes, sea bass grilled with fennel, and a mousseline of turbot in caviar sauce. The service is flawless but never intimidating.

Hôtel Atalaye. Plateau de l'Atalaye, 64200 Biarritz. ☎ **05-59-24-06-76.** Fax 05-59-22-33-51. 24 units. TV TEL. 250–350 F ($40–$56) double; 330–420 F ($52.80–$67.20) triple or quad. MC, V.

For economy with a bit of style, head here. In the heart of town on a tranquil spot overlooking the ocean, this circa 1900 hotel is open year-round, although it gets rather sleepy in winter. Each guest room is well maintained and traditionally furnished, though not a decorator's showcase. An elevator services all rooms. Breakfast is provided anytime you request it. The location is right off place Ste-Eugénie near the beaches, lighthouse, and casino.

✪ **Hôtel du Palais.** Av. de l'Impératrice, 64200 Biarritz. ☎ **800/223-6800** in the U.S. and Canada, or 05-59-41-64-00. Fax 05-59-41-67-99. www.hotel-du-palais.com. E-mail: manager@ hotel-du-palais.com. 165 units. A/C MINIBAR TV TEL. 1,600–2,950 F ($256–$472) double; 2,750–6,350 F ($440–$1,016) suite. AE, DC, MC, V.

This has been the grand playground for the international elite for the past century. It was built in 1854 by Napoléon III as a private villa for Eugénie so she wouldn't get homesick for Spain. He picked the most ideal beachfront, in view of the rocks and rugged shoreline. Of course there are elaborately furnished suites here, but even the average rooms have period furniture, silk draperies, marquetry, and bronze hardware. In 1998 the final touches were added to an air-conditioning system that reaches every area of the hotel. Try to get a room facing west to enjoy the sunsets over the Basque coast.

Villa Eugénie, a gourmet **restaurant** with classic columns and chandeliers, serves excellent meals. You can also dine at La Rotonde, enjoying typical Basque as well as international cuisine, and at lunch-only L'Hippocampe, a buffet restaurant around the heated seawater pool.

Hôtel Plaza. 10 av. Edouard-VII, 64200 Biarritz. ☎ **05-59-24-74-00.** Fax 05-59-22-22-01. E-mail: hotel.plazabiarritz@wanadoo.fr. 60 units. A/C MINIBAR TV TEL. 320–620 F ($51.20–$99.20) double. AE, DC, MC, V. Free parking.

Near the casino and beach, this hotel is a gorgeous Art Deco monument. Built in 1928, it has remained virtually unchanged, except for discreet renovations, so it's classified as a historic monument and a civic treasure. The rooms contain their original Art Deco furnishings and doors; they tend to be large and high ceilinged, and some have a private terrace. Those overlooking the back and side cost less than those with frontal sea views.

Meals are served in a formal dining room that's open for lunch and dinner daily except Monday at lunch and all day Sunday. The only inauthentic decor in the hotel is the bar, which, despite its relative newness, was designed in a—you guessed it— modernized Art Deco style. Fixed-price menus in the restaurant begin at 85 F ($13.60).

DINING

The restaurant at **Château de Brindos** (see "Accommodations" above) also serves excellent Franco-Basque cuisine.

Auberge de la Négresse. 10 bd. Marcel Dassault. ☎ **05-59-23-15-83.** Reservations required. Main courses 40–76 F ($6.40–$12.15); fixed-price menus 60–178 F ($9.60–$28.50). CB, V. Daily noon–2:15pm; Tues–Sun 7–10:15pm. BASQUE.

Just 1¹/₂ miles south of Biarritz, this restaurant was named for a 19th-century slave who escaped from an American plantation by hiding in the bottom of a French ship. The inn she established on this site was used by Napoléon's army on its passage to Spain. The inn doubles as a delicatessen, but the two dining rooms also serve flavorful meals. Typical dishes include salmon cooked in parchment, an array of homemade terrines, and fresh fish.

✪ **Café de Paris.** 5 place Bellevue, 64200 Biarritz. ☎ **05-59-24-19-53.** Fax 05-59-24-18-20. Reservations required. Restaurant, main courses 140–190 F ($22.40–$30.40); fixed-price menus 200–420 F ($32–$67.20). Bistro, main courses 80–120 F ($12.80–$19.20); fixed-price menu 195 F ($31.20). AE, DC, MC, V. Daily noon–2:30pm and 7–10pm. Closed Nov to mid-Mar. BASQUE.

The supercharged chef here, Didier Oudill, and his colleague Edgar Duhr, is the hottest in town and has rescued the Café de Paris from its long decline. Although Oudill was the protégé of Michel Guérard, he has also come up with many interesting creations of his own. He's not afraid to use Bayonne ham, Spanish merluza (hake), or even earthy fava beans. The setting is naturally elegant, from the mirrors for looking at how glamorous you are to the inevitable palm trees. If you'd like to spend less, you can go to the bistro, where the menu changes often, though fish is always a feature.

The restaurant offers 18 comfortable **guest rooms,** each with a sea view. Decorated in a conservatively traditional style, each has a TV and telephone, and accessories that evoke the Basque Country. They cost 950 F to 1,300 F ($152 to $208) for a double.

BIARRITZ AFTER DARK

Start the night by taking a stroll around **Port des Pécheurs,** an ideal spot for people-watching, with its stable of sport fishers, restaurants, and fascinating crowds.

Fortunes have been made and lost at the town's own municipal **Casino,** boulevard du Général-de-Gaulle (☎ **05-59-22-77-77**), where you can easily catch gambling fever. While at the casino, check out its disco **Le Flamingo** (☎ **05-59-22-77-59**), with its stylish crowd of movers and shakers. Usually there is no cover.

The most hip and desirable nightclub in town is **Le Copacabana,** 24 ave. Edouard-VII (☎ **05-59-24-65-39**), where Latin (especially Cuban) salsa is played along with virtually every other kind of danceable music. **Le Play Boy,** 15 place Clemenceau (☎ **05-59-24-38-46**), appeals to a diversified crowd ranging from 20 to 40. More appealing is **Disco Le Caveau,** 4 place Gambetta (☎ **05-59-24-16-17**), where a well-dressed and attractive combination of gay and straight people mingle together with ease. And for a site that's patronized almost exclusively by **gay men,** check out the pub-style **L'Opéra Café,** 31 av. de Verdun (☎ **05-59-24-27-85**).

5 St-Jean-de-Luz

491 miles SW of Paris, 9 miles S of Biarritz

This Basque country tuna-fishing port and beach resort is ideal for a seaside vacation. St-Jean-de-Luz lies at the mouth of the Nivelle opening onto the Bay of Biscay, with the Pyrénées in the background. Tourists have been flocking here ever since the 19th century, when the town was "discovered" by H. G. Wells.

ESSENTIALS

GETTING THERE   Some eight to 10 **trains** per day arrive from Biarritz (trip time: 15 minutes), and there are also 10 trains per day from Paris (regular trains make the trip in 10 hours, TGV trains in 5). For train information and schedules, call ☎ **08-36-35-35-35. Buses** pulling into town from other parts of the Basque Country arrive at the Gare Routière (☎ **05-59-26-06-99**), in front of the railway station. St-Jean-de-Luz is a short **drive** from Biarritz along N10 south on the west coast of the Basque Country.

VISITOR INFORMATION   The **Office de Tourisme** is on place du Maréchal-Foch (☎ **05-59-26-03-16**).

SPECIAL EVENTS   On Wednesday and Sunday nights during July and August, people pile into place Louis-XIV to take part in **Toro de Fuego,** a celebration of the bull, when revelers take to the streets, dance, and watch fireworks. The highlight of the festivities is when a snorting papier-mâché bull is carried through town. For a line-up of festivals, check with the Office de Tourisme (see above).

FUN ON & OFF THE BEACH

THE BEACH   The major draw here is the wide, gracefully curving stretch of the white-sand **Plage St-Jean-de-Luz;** it's one of the best beaches in all of France, and consequently very crowded in July and August. The beach lies in a half-moon-shaped bay between the ocean and the source of the Nivelle River.

THE PORT TOWN   Though tourism accounts for most of the revenue around here, fishing is still important. In fact, the town is the major fishing port along the Basque coast. Eating seafood only recently plucked from the sea is one of the reasons to visit, especially when Basque chefs prepare the big catch into intriguing platters. This port's many narrow streets flanked by old houses are great for strolling.

ATTRACTIONS

In the town's principal church, the 13th-century **Église St-Jean-Baptiste,** at the corner of rue Gambetta and rue Garat (☎ **05-59-26-08-81**), Louis XIV and the Spanish infanta, Marie-Thérèse, were married in 1660, as a celebration of the cessation of fighting between France and Spain over Hapsburg possessions in Holland and Flanders. The interior is among the most handsome of all Basque churches. Surmounting the altar is a statue-studded gilded retable. The interior can be visited daily from 8am to noon and 2 to 6pm. At the harbor, the brick-and-stone **Maison de l'Infante,** in Louis XIII style, sheltered the Spanish princess. Entrance costs 25 F ($4) per adult, and 13 F ($2.10) for students and children under 12.

The Sun King, meanwhile, dreamed of another woman at **La Maison de Louis XIV** (also known as the Château Lohobiague), on place Louis-XIV, the center of the old port (☎ **05-59-26-01-56**). Built in 1643 by a rich ship owner, Johannis of Lohobiague, the Maison de Louis XIV received its young namesake in 1660 for more than a month. The noble facade is distinguished by small towers built into each corner. The interior is in old Basque style, with beams and iron nails still visible. The second-floor stairwell leads to the apartments where Louis XIV stayed when he came to sign the Treaty of the Pyrénées and get married in the church of St-Jean-de-Luz to Maria-Thérèse. It's open June to October, daily from 10:30am to noon and 2:30 to 6:30pm. Admission is 25 F ($4) for adults and 20 F ($3.20) for children.

SHOPPING

You'll find the best shopping along the pedestrian **rue Gambetta** as well as around the Église St-Jean-de-Luz. These are the spots where you can find just about anything, from clothes and leather handbags to books, chocolates, dishes, and linens.

You can also ramble around the port, sip pastis in a harborfront cafe, and debate the virtues of the beret. Then scout out **Maison Adam,** which has sold almond-based confections since 1660 from a boutique at 6 place Louis-XIV (☎ **05-59-26-03-54**). Specialties include sugared macaroons, *tournons* (an almond-paste confection flavored with everything from chocolate to confit of berries), and *canougat* (soft caramels). Closed between January and March.

ACCOMMODATIONS

✪ **Hotel de Chantaco.** Gulf de Chantaco, 64500 Chantaco, 64500 St-Jean-de-Luz. ☎ **05-59-26-14-76.** Fax 05-59-26-35-97. E-mail: resa@hotel-chantaco.com. 23 units. A/C MINIBAR TV TEL. 950–1,600 F ($152–$256) double; 1,800–1,900 F ($288–$304) suite. AE, DC, MC, V. Closed Nov 15–Dec 20 and Jan 5–Mar 30. Free parking. Take D918 1 mile from the town center.

There's enough memorabilia from this mansion's heyday to remind you of the days when aristocrats from around Europe made it one of their preferred hotels. Surrounded by an 18-hole golf course and verdant parklands, within an hour from the beach, it resembles an eclectically designed country château that belonged to an erudite and somewhat eccentric industrialist. Inside, you'll find Moorish arches, a patio garden, a reception hall graced with two stone fireplaces, a salon with refectory tables and severely dignified chairs, and an upper gallery flanked with wrought-iron balustrades. Bedrooms are luxurious, with lots of personalized touches and memorabilia from the gilded age. Breakfast is served beneath the wisteria-covered arches of an outdoor patio; dinners are at El Patio, a **restaurant** well recommended for its international and regional cuisine. Fixed-price menus range from 265 F ($42.40).

Hôtel Hélianthal. Place Maurice-Ravel, 64540 St-Jean-de-luz. ☎ **05-59-51-51-51.** Fax 05-59-51-51-54. E-mail: Helianthalinfouie@infouie.fr. 100 units. A/C MINIBAR TV TEL. 720–935 F ($115.20–$149.60) double; 1,230 F ($196.80) 2-bedroom suite. AE, DC, MC, V. Parking 50 F ($8).

Efficient, well designed, and comfortable, this three-star contemporary hotel boasts a good restaurant and lies in the commercial heart of town, near the beach. Unfortunately, none of the Art Deco-style rooms overlooks the sea, but many have terraces, bay windows, or balconies. The hotel's big-windowed **restaurant, L'Atlantique,** offers a terrace overlooking the sea and a fixed-price menu at 270 F ($43.20). The fare includes a spa-style light cuisine, lots of fish, and traditional dishes inspired by age-old Basque cuisine. Lunch and dinner are served daily.

Hôtel/Restaurant Lafayette. 18–20 rue de la République, 64500 St-Jean-de-Luz. ☎ **05-59-26-17-74.** Fax 05-59-51-11-78. 17 units, 16 with bathroom. TV TEL. 230–550 F ($36.80–$88) double with bathroom. AE, DC, MC, V.

This utterly unpretentious hotel and **restaurant** occupy a central location near place Louis-XIV and the town's beaches. Its rooms evoke a dignified (albeit slightly battered) age. The Basque cuisine prepared by the experienced matriarch Mayie Colombet is one of the most solidly reliable in town. Tried-and-true dishes include seafood casseroles, grilled duck, sea bass with thyme and lemon-butter sauce, and roast rack of lamb. The restaurant is closed on Monday from mid-November to mid-March, but during many school holidays business is so good that Ms. Colombet usually decides to remain open anyway. Fixed-price menus, served at both lunch and dinner, range from 92 F to 170 F ($14.70 to $27.20).

La Devinière. 5 rue Loquin, 64500 St-Jean-de-Luz. ☎ **05-59-26-05-51.** Fax 05-59-51-26-38. 11 units. TEL. 600–850 F ($96–$136) double. AE, DC, MC, V. Parking 40 F ($6.40).

Perhaps because of its small size, this is the best-furnished moderately priced hotel in St-Jean-de-Luz. It occupies the premises of what was originally a private town house and was brought to its present level of 18th-century elegance thanks to the unsold inventories of its antiques-dealer owner. The rooms are comfortable, well maintained, and filled, like the rest of the hotel, with attractive antiques. Although breakfast is the only meal served, the hotel contains a tea salon (L'Heure du Thé; same phone). It's open Tuesday to Saturday only from 4 to 6:30pm and seems to do a rollicking business every afternoon.

DINING

The only really grand cuisine in town is served at the **Hôtel Grand,** but you might also like to check out the restaurant at the **Hôtel Hélianthal** or the reliable Basque food prepared at the **Hôtel/Restaurant Lafayette** (see "Accommodations" above).

Auberge Kaïku. 17 rue de la République. ☎ **05-59-26-13-20.** Reservations recommended. Main courses 85–145 F ($13.60–$23.20); fixed-price menus 145–220 F ($23.20–$35.20). AE, MC, V. Mid-Sept to mid-June, Tues and Thurs–Sun 12:15–2:15pm and Thurs–Tues 7:15–10:30pm; mid-June to mid-Sept, Tues–Sun 12:15–2:15pm; daily 7:15–10:30pm. Closed mid-Nov to Dec 22. BASQUE.

On a narrow street off place Louis-XIV, Auberge Kaïku is the best restaurant in town outside the hotels. The structure, with hand-hewn beams and chiseled masonry, dates from 1540 and is said to be the oldest in town. The auberge is run by Emile and Jeanne Ourdanabia, who serve Basque cuisine that's been enhanced with modern touches. Examples are roast suckling Pyrénéan lamb, a parillade of shellfish, John Dory with fresh mint, grilled shrimp, fillet of beef with essence of truffles, and duckling in honey. A particularly succulent starter is the salade Kaïku, garnished with panfried strips of foie gras and raspberry vinegar.

Chez Maya (Petit Grill Basque). 4 rue St-Jacques. ☎ **05-59-26-80-76.** Reservations recommended. Main courses 60–100 F ($9.60–$16); fixed-price menus 110–155 F ($17.60–$24.80). AE, DC, MC, V. Thurs–Tues noon–2pm; Thurs–Mon 7–10pm. Closed Dec 20–Jan 20. BASQUE.

This small auberge is highly acclaimed for quality and value, with specialties that include a delectable fish soup and paella. Don't expect urban glitter. Things are too conservative and old-fashioned for that. The fixed-price menu is the best value in town. The chefs cook as their grandparents did, including all the old favorites, such as squid cooked in its own ink.

La Vieille Auberge. 22 rue Tourasse. ☎ **05-59-26-19-61.** Reservations required. Main courses 60–125 F ($9.60–$20); fixed-price menus 82–129 F ($13.10–$20.65). MC, V. July–Aug, Wed–Mon noon–2pm, daily 7–10:30pm; Apr 2–June and Sept–Nov 11, daily noon–2pm, Thurs–Mon 7–10pm. Closed Nov 12–Apr 1. BASQUE/LANDAISE.

This Basque tavern specializes in seafood, and the owners claim that the fish soup is second to none. They offer good-value fixed-price menus, the most expensive of which is enormous. Generally, the recipes are part-Basque/part-Landaise, and each dish goes well with the *vin du pays*, especially mussels *à la crème*. A parillade of fish (mixed seafood grill) is particularly appealing.

ST-JEAN-DE-LUZ AFTER DARK

You can start by taking a walk along the promenade to watch the sunset. If you check out **place Louis-XIV,** you'll find a hotbed of activity at the surrounding cafes and bars.

A fun spot worth a visit is **Pub du Corsaire,** 16 rue de la République (☎ **05-59-26-10-74**), one of the main places in town for simple, unpretentious merrymaking, good times, and revelry. It's all accompanied, of course, by copious amounts of drinking and old-fashioned rock-and-roll. For dancing, virtually everyone heads north of town to the string of nightclubs and discos that stretch beside the R.N.10. (Follow the signs from the town center for Biarritz.) The best of the lot include **Le Paseo,** R.N. 10 (☎ **05-59-26-04-28**), about a half-mile north of town, which seems to be packed with nightlife maniacs under 25; and **Disco La Tupina,** R.N. 10 (☎ **05-59-54-73-23**), about 2 miles north of town.

18 Bordeaux & the Atlantic Coast

From historic La Rochelle to the Bordeaux Wine District, the south-west of France is often a quick glimpse for visitors driving from Paris to Spain. However, this area is noted for its Atlantic beaches, medieval and Renaissance ruins, Romanesque and Gothic churches, vineyards, and charming old inns serving up splendid regional cuisine.

In our journey through this intriguing region, we detour inland for a snifter of cognac in Cognac and for trips to nearby art cities like Poitiers and Angoulême. If you can manage it, it's great to allow a week in this region—just enough time to sample the wine, savor the cuisine, and see at least some of the major sights.

REGIONAL CUISINE   Major specialties from this region are the *huîtres* (oysters) from Arcachon or Marennes, *jambon* (ham) from Poitou, *esturgeon* (sturgeon) or *saumon* (salmon) from the Gironde, *canard* (duck) from Challans, *chapon* (capon) or *poularde* (chicken) from Barbezieux, and *agneau* (lamb) from Pauillac.

Other specialties include *mouclade* (a mussel stew prepared with cream or white wine and shallots), *lamproie* or *l'anguille à la bordelaise* (lamprey eels from local rivers, served with a blood-enriched red-wine sauce), *entrecôte à la bordelaise* (steak in a wine-laced brown sauce with shallots, tarragon, and bone marrow), *cèpes à la bordelaise* (flap mushrooms sautéed in oil and seasoned with chopped shallots and garlic), *escargots à la vigneronne* (snails simmered in a sauce of wine, garlic, and onions), and *chaudrée* (a local fish soup). The region's most famous cheese is chabichou, a variety of goat cheese, from Poitou; its best chocolate is les duchesses d'Angoulême.

Bordeaux wines include everything from the finest French vintages to ordinary table wines found on supermarket shelves. Among the best are the incomparable wines from the Médoc and Graves. Other reds include St-Emilion and Pomerol.

1 Poitiers

207 miles SW of Paris, 110 miles SE of Nantes

This city, the ancient capital of Poitou, the northern part of Aquitaine, is filled with history. Everybody has passed through here—from England's Black Prince to Joan of Arc to Richard the Lion-Hearted.

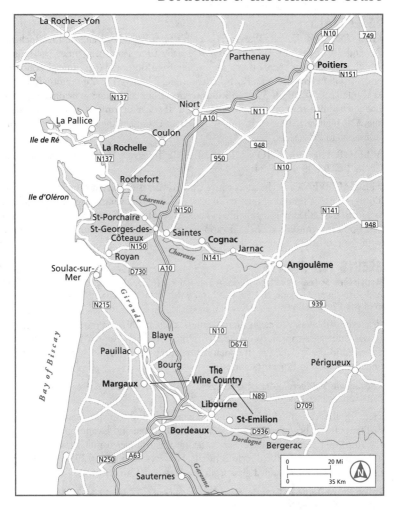

Poitiers stands on a hill overlooking the Clain and Boivre rivers. It was this very strategic location that tempted so many conquerors. Charles Martel proved the savior of Christendom by chasing out the Muslims in 732 and altering the course of European civilization. Poitiers was the chief city of Eleanor of Aquitaine, who had her marriage to pious Louis VII annulled so she could wed England's Henry II.

For those interested in antiquity, this is one of the most fascinating towns in France. That battle we learned about in history books was fought on September 19, 1356, between the armies of Edward the Black Prince and those of King John of France. It was one of the three great English victories of the Hundred Years' War, distinguished by the use of the longbow in the skilled hands of English archers.

After decades of slumber, the town has really come alive, with the opening of **Futuroscope,** a futuristic cinema theme park. The thriving student population (a third of the 85,000 residents here are students) adds a slice of vitality as well.

ESSENTIALS

GETTING THERE   Rail service is available from Paris, Bordeaux, and La Rochelle. Around 18 of the fast TGV **trains** arrive daily from Paris (trip time: 1^1/$_2$ hours). Another 18 (regular speed) trains arrive daily from Bordeaux (trip time: 1^3/$_4$ hours), and 11 pull in daily from La Rochelle (trip time: 2 hours). For train information and schedules, call ☎ **08-36-35-35-35.** Bus services from Poitiers are so inconvenient and badly scheduled as to be virtually nonexistent. If you're **driving,** Poitiers is located on the A10 highway; from Paris, follow A10 south through the cities of Orléans and Tours, on to Poitiers.

VISITOR INFORMATION   The **Office de Tourisme** is at 8 rue des Grandes-Écoles (☎ **05-49-41-21-24**).

SPECIAL EVENTS   The most active time to visit is in July and August during the **Poitiers l'Été,** a festival of live jazz, opera, rock, and fireworks. Over that period the facade of the cathedral is highlighted in colored lights for 15 minutes every evening at 10:30pm; free concerts are held at various parks and churches around the city. Check with the tourist office for schedules.

SEEING THE SIGHTS

Baptistère St-Jean. Rue Jean-Jaurès. Admission 4 F (65¢). July–Aug, daily 10am–12:30pm and 2:30–6pm; Apr–June and Sept–Oct, daily 10:30am–12:30pm and 3–6pm; Nov–Mar, Wed–Mon 2:30–4:30pm.

From the cathedral, you can walk to the most ancient Christian monument in France. It was built as a baptistery in the early 4th century on Roman foundations, then extended in the 7th century. It contains frescoes from the 11th to the 14th centuries and a collection of funerary sculpture.

Cathédrale St-Pierre. Place de la Cathédrale. ☎ **05-49-41-23-76.** Free admission. Daily 8am–7pm (winter, until 6pm).

Here in the eastern sector of Poitiers, you'll find the twin-towered Cathédrale St-Pierre. It was begun in 1162 by Henry II of England and Eleanor of Aquitaine on the ruins of a Roman basilica. The cathedral was completed much later, but it has always been undistinguished architecturally. However, the interior, 295 feet long, contains some admirable stained glass from the 12th and 13th centuries.

Église Notre-Dame-la-Grande. Place Charles-de-Gaulle. ☎ **05-49-41-22-56.** Free admission. Daily 8:15am–7pm.

This church, built in the Romanesque-Byzantine style and richly decorated, is from the late 11th century. See in particular its western front, dating from the mid-12th century. Surrounded by an open-air market, the facade, carved like an ivory casket, is characterized by pine cone–shaped towers. It was thoroughly cleaned and restored in 1996. Carvings on the doorway represent biblical scenes.

Église Ste-Radegonde. Place St-Radegonde. ☎ **05-49-41-23-76.** Free admission. Apr–Sept, daily 8am–7:30pm; Oct–Mar, 8am–6pm.

A favorite place of pilgrimage in times gone by, this 11th-century structure in the eastern section of Poitiers commemorates the patroness of Poitiers, Radegonde. Her black marble sarcophagus is in the crypt. Radegonde, who died in 587, was the consort of Clotaire, king of the Franks.

Futuroscope. About 5^1/$_2$ miles north of Poitiers in Jaunay-Clan. ☎ **05-49-49-30-00.** Admission 145–210 F ($23.20–$33.60) adults, 100–145 F ($16–$23.20) children 5–12, free for children 4 and under. Daily 9am–6pm (Apr–Sept, until 11pm). From Poitiers, bus no. 16 or 17 runs to the park; if you're driving, take N10.

Drawing some three million visitors annually, this science amusement park is a wonderland of technology that lets you experience new sounds, images, and sensations with the world's most advanced film-projection techniques and largest screens. Exhibitions include **Kinemax** (a rock crystal covered with mirrors with a 400-seat cinema); **Omnimax** (films projected onto a gigantic dome via a special fish-eye lens, putting you into the heart of the action); **Le Tapis Magique** (a film that shows you what it's like to fly above a continent with a monarch butterfly); and a 3-D cinema that takes you on a journey through the area's most impressive monuments and sites of natural beauty. **L'IMAX 3D** features films presented on a 600mm flat screen. The 40-minute film, *Guillaumet: Wings of Courage*, follows a heroic (fictional) episode in the history of airmail.

Musée St-Croix. Accessible from 3 bis, rue Jean Jaurès, 8600 Poitiers. ☎ **05-49-41-07-53.** Admission 20 F ($3.20) adult, free for children 18 and under. Oct–May, Mon and Wed–Fri 1–5pm, Tues 10am–5pm, Sat–Sun 2–6pm; June–Sept, Mon 1:15–6pm, Tues–Fri 10am–noon and 1:15–6pm, Sat–Sun 10am–noon and 2–6pm.

This museum, built on the site of the old abbey of St-Croix, has a fine-arts section devoted mainly to painting—especially Flemish art from the 16th and 17th centuries and Dutch paintings from the 16th to the 18th centuries. Several works by Bonnard, Sisley, and Oudot are displayed, along with a bronze, *The Three Graces*, by Maillol. A separate archaeological section documents the history of Poitou, from prehistoric times to the Gallo-Roman era, the Renaissance, and up to the end of the 19th century.

Palais de Justice. Place Lepetit. ☎ **05-49-50-22-00.** Free admission. Mon–Fri 9am–noon and 1–5pm.

This structure incorporates the 14th-century keep and some other parts of a ducal palace dating from the Gallo-Roman era. It was here that Joan of Arc was questioned by the doctors of the university who composed the French Court of Parliament, and also here that Richard the Lion-Hearted was proclaimed comte de Poitou and duc d'Anjou in 1170. Unfortunately, only one room within the stately municipal building can be visited, the **Salle des Pas Perdus.** Here, vaulted ceilings, majestic-looking columns, and an enormous fireplace mark the site where Eleanor d'Aquitaine conducted some of her receptions.

ACCOMMODATIONS

Grand Hôtel de l'Europe. 39 rue Carnot, 86000 Poitiers. ☎ **05-49-88-12-00.** Fax 05-49-88-97-30. 88 units. TV TEL. 330–480 F ($52.80–$76.80) double. AE, DC, MC, V. Parking 20 F ($3.20).

Some 200 years ago this was a coaching inn; later the stables were transformed into additional rooms. The field where the horses were watered is now a quiet courtyard with trees and shrubbery. The isolation of this place enhances its sense of 1930s civility. The bedrooms are more modern and streamlined than the gracefully antique public rooms would suggest. About 50 of the rooms contain minibars. Breakfast is the only meal served, in an old-fashioned dining room with tall windows and an elaborate fireplace.

Hôtel du Plat d'Etain. 7 rue du Plat-d'Etain, 86000 Poitiers. ☎ **05-49-41-04-80.** Fax 05-49-52-25-84. 24 units, 21 with bathroom. MINIBAR TV TEL. 150 F ($24) double without bathroom, 260–300 F ($41.60–$48) double with bathroom. AE, DC, MC, V. Parking 20 F ($3.20). Bus: 2A.

One of the best bargains in Poitiers, this renovated hotel is on a narrow alley, a few steps from place du Maréchal-Leclerc. Many restaurants and sights are nearby. Several readers have commented on the warmth of the staff. There's a guarded parking area.

Le Chalet de Venise. 6 rue du Square (B.P. 4), 86280 St-Benoît-Bourg. ☎ **05-49-88-45-07.** Fax 05-49-52-95-44. 12 units. MINIBAR TV TEL. 350 F ($56) double. AE, DC, MC, V. Take D88 south 2$^1/_2$ miles from Poitiers to St-Benoît or A10 to exit 20, "Poitiers Sud."

Those who don't want to stay in the town center will enjoy this reasonably priced inn. It's surrounded by trees and shrubbery, and its chalet opens onto the water. The rooms are simply furnished, clean, and comfortable, each with a distinct personality. Drinks are served on a flagstone terrace overlooking one of the many tributaries of the region. The food is among the best in the Poitiers area, and portions are generous. Fixed-price menus are offered at 175 F to 295 F ($28 to $47.20), but you have to order à la carte for many of the specialties. Breakfast is served in a room overlooking a garden. The **restaurant** is open Tuesday through Saturday for lunch and dinner (closed 2 weeks in February and 1 week in late August).

DINING

Le Chalet de Venise (see "Accommodations," above), serves some of the best food in the area.

Le Saint Hilaire. 65 rue Théophraste-Renaudot. ☎ **05-49-41-15-45.** Reservations recommended. Main courses 80–125 F ($12.80–$20); fixed-price menus 99–290 F ($15.85–$46.40). AE, DC, MC, V. Tues–Sat noon–2pm; Mon–Sat 7:30–9:45pm. Closed Jan 1–15; July–Aug, closed Sun–Mon. FRENCH/POITOU.

This is the most historic and unusual restaurant in Poitiers and would be popular with foreigners if it were more centrally located. It's on a quiet street in the southern periphery of the medieval center. During the 12th century, this building served as lodging for the plainsong singers at the nearby Église St-Hilaire. You can look into the exposed kitchen (and perhaps chat with the staff) on your way into a dining room, whose medieval vaults are supported on four massive columns with Romanesque capitals. The fixed-price menus offer three distinct types of cuisine: medieval, regional, and seasonal. The fare of André Point and his wife, Danielle, is superb, based on fresh seasonal ingredients. Examples include scallops marinated in lime juice; strips of pork braised with cabbage; and a beautiful slice of fresh, home-style foie gras prepared with cardamon. Especially succulent is a stew made from locally raised lamb, served with a mushroom-flavored cream sauce. A light-textured dessert is a sorbet of fresh pears, flavored with pear-derived *eaux-de-vie*.

Maxime. 4 rue St-Nicolas. ☎ **05-49-41-09-55.** Reservations recommended. Main courses 90–165 F ($14.40–$26.40); fixed-price menus 105–260 F ($16.80–$41.60). AE, DC, MC, V. Mon–Fri noon–2pm and 7:30–10pm. Closed 4 weeks over July–Aug. FRENCH.

Maxime is the most sophisticated restaurant in town, and for some lucky reason it's completely ignored by the weekend crowds descending to visit Futuroscope. Start with a drink in the salon before heading to the twin upstairs dining rooms, filled with bourgeois warmth. Christian Rougier, the hardworking chef, offers a menu that varies with the seasons but always includes ravioli with hot oysters and sometimes features baked back of rabbit stuffed with eggplant, mushrooms, and *fines herbes,* served with chardonnay sauce; fried foie gras served with asparagus; and an herb-laden roast rack of lamb from nearby Montmorillon, a site famous for the quality of its lamb.

POITIERS AFTER DARK

Some of the town's most popular techno and electronic-music concerts occur at **Le Confort Moderne,** 185 rue du Faubourg du Pont-Neuf (☎ **05-49-46-08-08**), details for which are prominently posted on virtually every billboard in town. A high-profile disco is **La Grand' Goule,** 46 rue du Pigeon-Blanc (☎ **05-49-50-41-36**), which doesn't get going until after 11pm. Two other nightclubs playing the latest music trends from Paris include **Le Loft,** 85 promenade des Courts (☎ **05-49-41-04-37**), and within a few steps, **L'Eclipse,** 55 promenade des Courts (☎ **05-49-88-34-21**). Both cater to a youthful, high-energy crowd who all seem to know each other. A final, somewhat more worldly looking alternative, is a two-in-one disco at 195 Avenue du 8 mai 1945 (☎ **05-49-57-08-21**). Inside, you'll find **Le Black House,** a bar and disco that attracts a higher-than-usual percentage of gay men and women, and its heterosexual alternative, **Le Privilège.** The most frequented exclusively gay bar and disco in town is **Le George-Sand,** 25 rue St-Pierre-le-Puellier (☎ **05-49-55-91-58**). Many gay students, often from countries other than France, hang out at cozy **Le Café Sixties,** 1 rue des Quatre Voûtes (☎ **05-49-52-19-44**).

2 La Rochelle

290 miles SW of Paris, 90 miles SE of Nantes, 100 miles S of Bordeaux, 88 miles NW of Angoulême

Once known as the French Geneva, La Rochelle is a historic Atlantic port and ancient sailors' city, formerly the stronghold of the Huguenots. It was founded as a fishing village in the 10th century on a rocky platform in the center of a huge marshland. Eleanor of Aquitaine gave La Rochelle a charter in 1199, thereby freeing it from feudal dues. After becoming an independent city-state, the port capitalized on the wars between France and England. It was the departure point for the founders of Montréal and others who helped colonize Canada. From the 14th to the 16th centuries, La Rochelle enjoyed its heyday as one of France's great maritime cities. It became the principal port between France and the colony of Canada, but France's loss of Canada ruined its Atlantic trade.

As a hotbed of Protestant factions, it armed privateers to prey on Catholic vessels but was eventually besieged by Catholic troops. Two strong men led the fight: Cardinal Richelieu (with, of course, his Musketeers) and Jean Guiton, formerly an admiral and then mayor of the city. Richelieu proceeded to blockade the port. Although La Rochelle bravely resisted, on October 30, 1628, Richelieu entered the city. Among the almost 30,000 citizens of the proud city, he found only 5,000 survivors.

Today La Rochelle, with its population of 120,000, is the cultural and administrative center of the Charente-Maritime *département.* Its famous city lights have earned it the title "City of Light," like its grander sibling, Paris. Although much of La Rochelle's sights are very old, the city is also riddled with high-rise condos and the largest pleasure-boat basin in Europe. In summer, the city is overrun with visitors.

ESSENTIALS

GETTING THERE   The La Rochelle-Laleu **airport** (☎ **05-46-42-30-26**) is on the coast, 3 miles north of the city. Rail connections from Bordeaux and Nantes are frequent. Six to eight **trains** from Bordeaux and Nantes arrive daily (trip time: 2 hours), and there are five to seven daily fast TGV trains from Paris (Gare Montparnasse). The trip from Paris takes about 3 hours. For train information and schedules, call ☎ **08-36-35-35-35.** Buses pull into La Rochelle at the Gare Routière, on the Place de Verdun (☎ **05-46-34-02-22** for information). If you're **driving** from La Rochelle, it's best to stay near the A10 highway. Follow A10 south from Poitiers to exit Niort/St-Maixent, then take N11 east to the coast and La Rochelle.

VISITOR INFORMATION   The **Office de Tourisme** is on place de la Petite-Sirène, Le Gabut (☎ **05-46-41-14-68**).

SPECIAL EVENTS   The busiest month is July, when the **Festival International du Film de La Rochelle** rolls in during the beginning of the month. It attracts a huge following of fans, press, actors, directors, and, of course, paparazzi. Screenings are held around town; tickets cost from 40 F to 55 F ($6.40 to $8.80) each, depending on the movie. For information, contact the festival's organizing office in the Maison de la Culture, rue St-Jean de Perot (☎ **05-46-51-54-00**). Right on the heels of this festival, during a 3-day period in mid-July, comes **Les Francofolies,** a music festival with big names as well as not-so-famous groups, most of them pop musicians, from the world over. The town is overrun with groupies and fans, and a festive party atmosphere prevails. Tickets range from 50 F to 175 F ($8 to $28). Call ☎ **05-46-28-28-28** for details. The Office de Tourisme can also provide details on both festivals.

La Rochelle is also the site of the biggest showcasing of boats and yachts in Europe, **Le Grand Pavois Salon Nautique.** It's a 5-day extravaganza that takes place yearly in mid-September. The action is based in and around La Rochelle's Port de Plaisance (Yacht Basin). Sellers and buyers of boats and marine hardware, as well as weekend sailors from everywhere, usually attend. For information about dates and venues, call ☎ **05-46-44-46-39.**

EXPLORING THE CITY

There are two sides to La Rochelle: the old and unspoiled town inside the Vauban defenses, and the tacky modern and industrial suburbs. Its **fortifications** have a circuit of 3^1/$_2$ miles with a total of seven gates.

STROLLING   The town, with its arch-covered streets, is great for strolling. The port is still a bustling fishing harbor and one of the major sailing centers in Western Europe. Try to schedule a visit in time to attend a fish auction at the harbor. The best streets for strolling are **rue du Palais, rue Chaudrier,** and **rue des Merciers** with its ancient wooden houses. On the last street, seek out the houses at nos. 17, 8, 5, and 3.

SHOPPING   The main shopping streets are **rue du Palais, rue du Temple, rue de Merciers,** and **rue St-Yon,** where name-brand department stores as well as smaller shops sell everything from clothing to canned goods. If you want to explore antiques shops, art galleries, jewelry studios, and more high-end gift shops, enter the **old town.** On Saturday mornings, an **antiques market** sets up along rue St-Nicholas with a multitude of dealers carrying mainly bric-a-brac and flea market items. For one of the largest selections of beachwear, parkas, windbreakers, and great wool pullover sweaters, stop in at the **Cooperative Maritime,** Port de Pêche, chef de Baie (☎ **05-46-41-31-66**).

ATTRACTIONS

Hôtel de Ville (City Hall). Place de la Mairie, in the city center. ☎ **05-46-41-14-68.** You must visit on a guided tour by reserving in advance. Tours 20 F ($3.20) adults, 10 F ($1.60) children, free for children 3 and under. Tours daily 3pm.

The town's 14th-century showcase is constructed in Flamboyant Gothic style, with battlements. Inside you can admire the Henry II staircase with canopies and the marble desk of the heroic Jean Guiton. In 1996, major restoration work was needed after Corsican separatists bombed the building, causing heavy damage. Prime Minister Alain Juppé had left the building not long before the explosion occurred.

Tour de la Chaîne. Quai du Gabut. ☎ **05-46-34-11-81.** Admission 25 F ($4) adults, free for children under 18. Apr–Sept, daily 10am–1pm and 2–7pm; Oct–Mar, 9:30am–12:30pm and 2–5:30pm.

During the 1300s, this tower was built as an anchor piece for the large forged-iron chain that stretched across the harbor, as a means of closing it against hostile warships. Today, it's a sightseeing attraction in its own right, with unusual exhibits on the history of medieval naval warfare.

Tour St-Nicolas. Quai du Gabut. ☎ **05-46-41-74-13.** Admission 25 F ($4) adults, 15 F ($2.40) for ages 18–25, free for children 17 and under. Apr–Sept, daily 10am–7pm; Oct–Mar, daily 9:30am–12:30pm and 2–5:30pm.

The oldest tower in La Rochelle was built between 1371 and 1382. From its second floor you can enjoy a panoramic view of the town and harbor; from the top, however, you can see only the old town and Île d'Oléron.

Tour de la Lanterne. Opposite Tour St-Nicolas. Admission 25 F ($4) adults, 15 F ($2.40) ages 18–25, free for children 17 and under. Apr–Sept, daily 10am–5:30pm; Oct–Mar, daily 9:30am–12:30pm and 2–5:30pm.

Built between 1445 and 1476, this was once a lighthouse but was used mainly as a jail as late as the 19th century.

Musée des Beaux-Arts. 28 rue Gargolleau. ☎ **05-46-41-64-65.** Admission 22 F ($3.50) adults, 16 F ($2.55) students, free for children 18 and under. Wed–Mon 2–5pm.

The museum is housed in an Episcopal palace built in the mid-18th century. The art spans the 17th to the 19th centuries, with works by Eustache Le Sueur, Brossard de Beaulieu, Corot, and Fromentin. Some 20th-century pieces include works by Maillol and Léger.

Musée d'Obigny-Bernon. 2 rue St-Côme. ☎ **05-46-41-18-83.** Admission 22 F ($3.50) adults, free for children 18 and under. Mon and Wed–Sat 10am–noon and 2–6pm, Sun 2–6pm.

The most important artifacts pertaining to the history of ceramics and of La Rochelle are in this collection, which includes painted porcelain. Established in 1917, the museum also houses a superb collection of Far Eastern art.

Musée du Nouveau-Monde. In the Hôtel Fleuriau, 10 rue Fleuriau. ☎ **05-46-41-46-50.** Admission 22 F ($3.50) adults, free for children 18 and under. Wed–Mon 10:30am–12:30pm and 1:30–6pm, Sun 3–6pm.

The displays here trace the port's 300-year history with the New World. Exhibits start with the discovery of the Mississippi Delta in 1682 by LaSalle and end with the settling of the Louisiana territory. Other exhibits depict French settlements in the French West Indies, including Guadeloupe and Martinique.

Musée d'Histoire Naturelle. 28 rue Albert-1er. ☎ **05-46-41-18-25.** Admission 22 F ($3.50), free for children 18 and under. Tues–Fri 10am–12:30pm and 1:30–5:30pm, Sat–Sun 2–6pm.

This ethnography/zoology museum is housed in a handsome 18th-century building surrounded by a garden; the original paneling has been preserved. Clement de Lafaille, a former comptroller of war, assembled much of the collection, which has been enlarged since he donated it to the city. Displays include rare shellfish, an idol from Easter Island, an embalmed giraffe given to Charles X (the first of the species to be seen in France), and a parade boat encrusted with gems that was presented to Napoléon III by the king of Siam.

ACCOMMODATIONS

✪ **Hotel de France et d'Angleterre et de Champlain.** 20 rue Rambaud, 17000 La Rochelle. ☎ **800/528-1234** in the U.S., or 05-46-41-23-99. Fax 05-46-41-15-19. E-mail: hotel@bw.fr.champlain.com. 36 units. A/C MINIBAR TV TEL. 400–580 F ($64–$92.80) double; 700 F ($112) suite. AE, DC, MC, V. Parking 48 F ($7.70).

Close to the major parks and the old port, this is the most gracious choice in La Rochelle. It was created in 1990 when a 16th-century town house was combined with a late 19th–century hotel. It's furnished with a winning combination of antiques and art objects. This is complemented with a genial staff. Bedrooms are tasteful and dignified. One of the best aspects of the hotel is its romantic garden brimming with flowers, shrubbery, and shade trees. Breakfast is the only meal served.

Hôtel Les Brises. Chemin de la Digue de Richelieu, 17000 La Rochelle. ☎ **05-46-43-89-37.** Fax 05-46-43-27-97. 48 units. TV TEL. 450–645 F ($72–$103) double; 985 F ($157.60) suite. AE, DC, MC, V.

This tranquil, seaside hotel opposite the new Port des Minimes offers a view of the soaring 19th-century column dedicated to the Virgin. You can enjoy the view from the front balconies as well as the parasol-shaded patio. The immaculate rooms have cherrywood furniture. Breakfast is the only meal served.

Novotel La Rochelle Centre. 1 av. de la Porte-Neuve, 17000 La Rochelle. ☎ **05-46-34-24-24.** Fax 05-46-34-58-32. E-mail: hog65@accor-hotels.com. 94 units. MINIBAR TV TEL. 530–680 F ($84.80–$108.80) double. Children 15 and under stay free in parents' room. AE, DC, MC, V.

This hotel, one of the best in town, occupies a desirable verdant location in the Parc Charruyer, a greenbelt about a 5-minute walk from the town center. The rooms are monochromatic, standardized, and well maintained, with generous writing desks and big windows overlooking the park. There's also an outdoor pool. A charmless in-house **restaurant** serves drinks and platters throughout the day, with both regional and continental dishes.

DINING

Le Relais. 14 rue St-Jean-du-Perot. ☎ **05-46-41-17-03.** Reservations required in summer. Main courses 60–110 F ($9.60–$17.60); fixed-price menus 78–159 F ($12.50–$25.45). AE, DC, MC, V. Daily noon–midnight. FRENCH.

In 1998 an upscale temple of gastronomy within an old stone-sided house near the port was reorganized into this less expensive but well-qualified newcomer. Since then, its well-prepared food and hardworking staff have gained the respect of other restaurants nearby, especially since the prices they charge are reasonable. The decor includes nautical-looking wooden paneling, a bubbling aquarium, and the kinds of accessories you'd expect in an Alsatian tavern. Menu items are savory and surprisingly sophisticated: Examples include warm pâté of scallops served with a cup of lobster bisque; a salad of mâche, grilled scallops, and vinaigrette; fresh codfish with a purée of garlic; and a filet of sea bass with asparagus.

Les Quatre Sergents. 49 rue St-Jean-du-Pérot. ☎ **05-46-41-35-80.** Reservations required. Main courses 65–100 F ($10.40–$16); fixed-price menus 82–188 F ($13.10–$30.10). AE, DC, MC, V. Tues–Sun noon–2pm; Tues–Sat 7:30–10pm. FRENCH.

This restaurant is housed in a fanciful Art Nouveau greenhouse some visitors compare to the framework of the Eiffel Tower. Specialties include seafood ragoût, duxelles of turbot, mussels in curry sauce, and several regional favorites that have been going strong for the better part of 100 years.

⊛ **Relais Gourmand-Richard Coutanceau.** Plage de la Concurrence. ☎ **05-46-41-48-19.** Reservations required. Main courses 135–195 F ($21.60–$31.20); fixed-price menus 235–450 F ($37.60–$72). AE, DC, MC, V. Mon–Sat noon–2pm and 7:30–9:30pm. FRENCH.

Delectable cuisine is served in this circular concrete pavilion in a pine-filled park. Half of the space is devoted to a tearoom, the rest to an elegant and informal dining room. This is not only the most glamorous restaurant in La Rochelle but also one of the finest along the Atlantic coast, vastly superior to the highly touted La Marmite at 14 rue St-Jean-du-Pérot. Clearly an artist, Richard Coutanceau is both the owner and the genius chef; his "modernized" cuisine often includes fresh shellfish from nearby waters, lobster-filled ravioli with zucchini flowers, roast bass, and Brittany lobster.

LA ROCHELLE AFTER DARK

To find the heart of La Rochelle's vibrant nightlife from July to September, head for **quai Duperré** and **cours des Dames.** Once the sun starts to set, cars are cleared away and the area becomes one big pedestrian zone peppered with street performers. It's a fun, almost magical area that sets the tone for the rest of the night.

Later you might find yourself at **Bar Le Garibaldi,** rue St-Nicholas (☎ **05-46-41-05-49**), with its friendly mixed-age crowd. Good live blues, jazz, and folk concerts regularly fill both houses. For a beer in a relaxed, laid-back atmosphere, head over to **MacEwan's,** 7 rue de la Chaîne (☎ **05-46-41-18-94**). At cour du Temple, you'll find two little hotbeds of fun. The proudly French-style **Le Piano Pub,** 12 cour du Temple (☎ **05-46-41-03-42**), hosts regular rock concerts that keep the 18- to 35-year-old crowd coming back for more. With its staunchly English decor of wood and leather, **Le Mayflower,** 14 bis cour du Temple (☎ **05-46-50-51-39**), is just as popular with the same age group. Both places are loud, boisterous, and very friendly.

Gays are often attracted to the mixed crowds at **Le Tuxedo Café,** 21 Place du Maréchal Foch (☎ **05-46-50-01-22**).

3 Cognac

297 miles SW of Paris, 23 miles NW of Angoulême, 70 miles SE of La Rochelle

The world enjoys 100 million bottles a year of the nectar known as cognac, which Victor Hugo called "the drink of the gods." Sir Winston Churchill required a bottle a day. It's worth a detour to visit one of the château warehouses of the great cognac bottlers. Martell, Hennessy, and Otard welcome visits from the public and even give you a free drink at the end of the tour.

ESSENTIALS

GETTING THERE   Cognac's rail station is south of the town center. Seven **trains** per day arrive from Angoulême (trip time: 1 hour), and seven trains pull in from Saintes (trip time: 20 minutes). For train information and schedules, call ☎ **08-36-35-35-35. Bus** travel is scarce in this part of France. For information contact La Gare Routière (☎ **05-45-82-01-99**), which is located next to the railway station.

If you're **driving** to Cognac, the best route is from Saintes (which lies along the major route A10); follow N141 west.

VISITOR INFORMATION   The **Office de Tourisme** is at 16 rue du 14-Juillet (☎ **05-45-82-10-71**).

SPECIAL EVENTS   Cognac grapes are among the last to be picked in France. Harvest time usually begins in mid-October.

For the ultimate in the newest whodunit movies, come to town during the first week in April for the **Festival du Film Policier.** Screenings of crime films by each year's new wave of directors are held in various theaters around town. Contact the **Bureau National de Cognac** at ☎ **05-45-35-60-89** for complete information.

ALL ABOUT COGNAC

Many visitors don't realize that this unassuming town of some 22,000 people is actually a town, and not just a drink. Cognac may be beautiful to drink, but it's not beautiful to make. A black fungus that lives on the vapors released by the cognac factories has turned the town's buildings an ugly gray. But while the fumes may blacken the houses, they also fill the air here with a kind of sweetness.

If you'd like to visit a distillery, go to its main office during regular business hours and request a tour. The staffs are generally receptive, and you'll see some brandies that have aged for as long as 50 or even 100 years. You can ask about guided tours at the tourist office. The best distillery tour is offered by ✪ **Hennessy,** 1 rue de la Richonne (☎ **05-45-35-72-68**). It's open daily from 10am to 6pm (closed January 1, May 1, and December 25). Guided tours cost 30 F ($4.80) and last 75 minutes.

To buy bottles of cognac, you can visit one of the distilleries, take the tour, have a free taste, and then purchase a bottle or two. In addition to Hennessy, you can try **Camus,** 29 rue Marguerite-de-Navarre (☎ **05-45-32-28-28**); **Martell,** place Edouard-Martell (☎ **05-45-36-33-33**); and **Rémy-Martin,** domaine de Merpins, route de Pons (☎ **05-45-35-76-66**). If you're short on time, opt for **La Cognathèque,** 10 place Jean-Monnet (☎ **05-45-82-43-31**), which prides itself on having the widest selection of cognac from all the distilleries, though you'll pay extra for the convenience of having everything under one roof.

At the **Musée de Cognac,** 48 bd. Denfert-Rochereau (☎ **05-45-32-07-25**), you can see a collection including exhibits on popular arts and traditions (local artifacts and the cognac industry) as well as archaeological exhibits, plus a fine-arts collection (painting, sculpture, decorative arts, and furniture). It's open Wednesday through Monday, June to September from 10am to noon and 2 to 6pm and October to May from 2 to 5:30pm. Admission is 13 F ($2.10), 6.50 F ($1.05) for students, free for children 17 and under.

Cognac has two beautiful parks: the **Parc François-1er** and the **Parc de l'Hôtel-de-Ville.** The Romanesque-Gothic **Église St-Léger,** rue d'Angoulême (☎ **05-45-82-05-71**), is from the 12th century, and its bell tower is from the 15th. The town is imbued with memories of François I, who was born in the **Château de Cognac** (☎ **05-45-36-88-86**), which today belongs to the Otard cognac firm.

ACCOMMODATIONS

Domaine du Breuil. 104 rue Robert-Daugas, 16100 Cognac. ☎ **05-45-35-32-06.** Fax 05-45-35-48-06. 24 units. TV TEL. 300–400 F ($48–$64) double. AE, MC, V.

This 18th-century manor house, studded with magnificent windows, is set in an 18-acre landscaped park 2 minutes from the center of Cognac. Cognac aficionados and those in town to do business with the factories head here for the traditional hospitality; the comfortable, well-appointed rooms; and the excellent **cuisine** from the southwest of France. The bedrooms have a pristine simplicity but are well furnished and well maintained. The food is reason enough to visit even if you aren't staying here, and, naturally, you finish off with a cognac in the bar to aid digestion. Fixed-price menus cost 90 F, 120 F, and 165 F ($14.40, $19.20, and $26.40).

✪ **Hostellerie Les Pigeons Blancs.** 110 rue Jules-Brisson, 16100 Cognac. ☎ **05-45-82-16-36.** Fax 05-45-82-29-29. 6 units. TV TEL. 400–600 F ($64–$96) double. AE, DC, V. Closed Jan 1–15.

This stylish hotel is named after the white pigeons that nest in its moss-covered stone walls. The angular farmhouse with sloping tile roofs was built in the 17th century as a coaching inn. For many years, it was the home of the Tachet family, until three of the siblings transformed it into a hotel/restaurant in 1973. It's a mile northwest of the town center and offers elegant guest rooms. There's also a **restaurant** (see "Dining," below).

Hôtel Ibis. 24 rue Elisée-Mousnier, 16100 Cognac. ☎ **05-45-82-19-53.** Fax 05-45-82-86-71. 40 units. A/C MINIBAR TV TEL. 370 F ($59.20) double. AE, DC, MC, V. Parking 20 F ($3.20).

Clean, comfortable, and unpretentious, this hotel is identified by townspeople as either the Ibis or the Urbis, though management suggests the name Ibis will stick. There's a relaxed ambience in the public rooms, and the pleasant guest rooms are outfitted in a standardized modern style with comfortable bedding and fresh linen. Some overlook a garden. Breakfast is the only meal served, but sometimes the management will prepare you a simple platter if you prefer to dine in.

DINING

The restaurant at **Domaine du Breuil** (see "Accommodations," above) also offers worthwhile meals.

Hostellerie Les Pigeons Blancs. 110 rue Jules-Brisson. ☎ **05-45-82-16-36.** Reservations recommended. Main courses 75–120 F ($12–$19.20); fixed-price menus 120–280 F ($19.20–$44.80). AE, DC. Daily noon–2pm; Mon–Sat 7–10pm. Closed Jan 1–15. FRENCH.

This restaurant, run by the Tachet family, has two elegant dining rooms with exposed ceiling beams and limestone fireplaces. Jacques is the chef, Jean-Michel the maître d', and Catherine the hostess. Menu offerings depend on the availability of ingredients but might include warm oysters with mushrooms and a champagne-flavored cream sauce; a stewpot of lobster with croutons; roasted sea bass served with spice-flavored butter sauce; slices of warm goose liver with pears and white wine; and a particularly succulent version of duck steak with warm mandarin oranges flambéed with cognac. The flavor combinations always seem successful here.

NEARBY ACCOMMODATIONS & DINING

✪ **Moulin de Cierzac.** Rte. de Barbezieux, 16130 St-Fort-sur-le-Né. ☎ **05-45-83-01-32.** Fax 05-45-83-03-59. www.moulindecierzac.com. E-mail: moulin-cierzac@wanadoo.fr. 10 units. TV TEL. 295–480 F ($47.20–$76.80) double. AE, DC, MC, V. Closed Jan. From Cognac, drive 8 miles south of town, following the signs for Bordeaux and Barbezieux.

The site of this restaurant and hotel has been around for 150 years. This former mill house is set beside a flowing stream at the southern periphery of a village (St-Fort-sur-le-Né), 8 miles south of Cognac. Loaded with character, and under the dedicated management of the well-respected team of Georges Renault and his wife Evelyne, it's best known as the site of a superb restaurant, more so than a hotel. Many diners, however, do opt to spend the night here in one of the quaint, charmingly decorated bedrooms.

Cuisine is crafted by Laurent Pichaureaux, a gifted chef whose reputation is already of the highest caliber in the region. He makes abundant use of local products, especially the foie gras, vegetables, nuts, and berries of the region. Fixed-price menus cost from 138 F to 258 F ($22.10 to $41.30); main courses from 85 F to 135 F ($13.60 to $21.60), and are served at lunch and dinner every day except Monday. Advance reservations are highly recommended. Come for the crust-covered version of warm foie gras of duckling, served with sesame, pineapple, and essence of morels; strips of veal braised in local wine, served with mashed potatoes; and desserts such as a grapefruit-flavored "cappuccino" served with Szechuan pepper.

4 Angoulême

275 miles SW of Paris, 72 miles NE of Bordeaux

The old town of Angoulême, population 46,000, hugs a hilltop between the Charente and Aguienne rivers. You can easily visit it on the same day you visit Cognac. The town was the center of the French paper industry in the 17th century, a tradition that is still carried on today: Angoulême remains the center of French comic-strip production. Rolling off the presses are the latest adventures of Tintin, Astérix, and Lucky Luke.

ESSENTIALS

GETTING THERE   There are 12 regular **trains** and eight to 10 TGV trains every day from Bordeaux. Trip time is 1¹/₂ hours by regular train or 55 minutes by TGV. There are also four to five trains daily from Saintes and another five from Poitiers (trip time from either city is 1 hour). From Paris, there are seven trains daily; travel time is 3 hours. For train information and schedules, call ☎ **08-36-35-35-35.** If you're **driving,** take N10 northeast to Angoulême.

VISITOR INFORMATION   The **Office de Tourisme** is at 7 bis rue du Chat (☎ **05-45-95-16-84**).

EXPLORING THE TOWN

The hub of the town is **place de l'Hôtel-de-Ville.** The town hall was erected from 1858 to 1866 on the site of the old palace of the ducs d'Angoulême, where Marguerite de Navarre, sister of François I, was born. All that remains of the ducal palace are the 15th-century Tour de Valois and the 13th-century Tour de Lusignan.

   Cathédrale St-Pierre, place St-Pierre (☎ **05-45-95-20-38**), was begun in 1128 and greatly restored in the 19th century. Flanked by towers, its facade boasts 75 statues, each in a separate niche, representing the Last Judgment. This is one of France's most startling examples of Romanesque-Byzantine style. Some of its restoration was questionable, however. The architect, Abadie (designer of Sacré-Coeur in Paris), tore down the north tower, then rebuilt it with the original materials in the same style. In the interior you can wander under a four-domed ceiling. It's open Monday through Saturday from 8am to 7pm and Sunday from 9am to 6:30pm.

   Adjoining is the former bishops' palace, which has been turned into the **Musée Municipal,** 1 rue Friedland (☎ **05-45-95-07-69**), with a collection of European paintings, mainly from the 17th to the 19th centuries. The most interesting exhibits are the African art, ethnological, and archaeological collections. It's open Monday through Friday from noon to 6pm and Saturday and Sunday from 2 to 6pm. Admission is 15 F ($2.40), free for children 18 and under and students.

   Finally, you can take the **promenade des Remparts,** a boulevard laid on the site of the virtually demolished walls that once surrounded the city. From certain points along the way, you'll have superb views of the valley almost 250 feet below.

ACCOMMODATIONS

Mercure Hôtel de France. 1 place des Halles, 16000 Angoulême. ☎ **05-45-95-47-95.**
Fax 05-45-92-02-70. 89 units. A/C MINIBAR TV TEL. 525 F ($84) double; 625 F ($100) suite.
AE, DC, MC, V. Parking 42 F ($6.70).

This grand hotel stands in the center of the old town on extensive grounds. Rooms are
generally spacious, with high ceilings and French provincial furnishings. The beds are
comfortable with fresh linen and firm mattresses. On the lobby level, a formal **restaurant** offers excellent food and polite service. Specialties include foie gras, sole meunière, and trout with almonds. Lunch is served Monday through Friday; dinner is
offered nightly.

Relais Mercure Angoulême Nord. Rte. de Poitiers, 16430 Champniers. ☎ **05-45-68-53-22.** Fax 05-45-68-33-83. E-mail: ho397@accor-hotels.com. 103 units. A/C TV TEL. 420 F
($67.20) double. AE, DC, MC, V. Take N10 from Angoulême about 4 miles toward Poitiers.

This dependable hotel is the area's family-friendly choice. The grounds are filled with
evergreens and well-maintained lawns. Inside, the rooms are simple and chain-hotel
uniform, each featuring a double bed with a comfortable mattress, and a couch that
transforms into a twin. The sunny modern **restaurant** serves a variety of local and
international specialties, but the cuisine is no reason to stay here.

DINING

La Ruelle. 6 rue Trois-Notre-Dame. ☎ **05-45-92-94-64.** Reservations recommended. Main
courses 95–190 F ($15.20–$30.40); fixed-price menus 150 F ($24) at lunch, 180–300 F
($28.80–$48) at dinner. AE, DC, MC, V. Tues–Fri noon–2pm; Mon–Sat 7:30–10pm. Closed Jan
1–14, Apr 8–14, and Aug 5–23. FRENCH.

This first-class restaurant, in the center of the oldest part of town, was once a pair of
medieval houses separated by a narrow alley (*ruelle*) that was covered over. Jean-
François Dauphin is the proprietor, and his wife, Véronique, is the cook, and they're
the only shining lights in Angoulême's dim culinary scene. The menus change with
the chef's mood and the availability of ingredients, but you can count on classic
French recipes with a modern twist. Specialties are smoked haddock with exotic mushrooms, saffron-laced seafood stew, and game cock stuffed with grapes and mushrooms.
We especially recommend the fixed-price menus.

NEARBY ACCOMMODATIONS & DINING

✪ **Le Moulin du Maine-Brun.** R.N. 141, Lieu-Dit la Vigerie, 16290 Asnières-sur-Nouère.
☎ **05-45-90-83-00.** Fax 05-45-96-91-14. 20 units. MINIBAR TV TEL. 590–750 F
($94.40–$120) double; 950–1,300 F ($152–$208) suite. AE, DC, MC, V. Hotel and restaurant
closed Oct 15–Apr 15. Take R.N. 141 4$^{1}/_{2}$ miles west of Angoulême and turn right at Vigerie.

Before becoming the premier place to stay and dine in this area, this Relais du Silence
(part of a chain of hotels noted for their tranquility) was originally a flour mill. It's surrounded by 80 acres of lowlands, about half of which are now devoted to the production of cognac. The maître d'hôtel's preferred brand is the one made in the hotel's
distillery: Moulin du Domaine de Maine-Brun. These are the most luxurious accommodations around. The rooms are individually decorated with French period furniture
from the 18th and 19th century but with new, comfortable mattresses.

Dining: The restaurant serves splendid fare; specialties include a tartare of raw
salmon with a lime-flavored chive sauce, and a ragoût of four kinds of fish and shellfish cooked with leeks and local white wine. Fixed-price menus cost 105 F to 205 F
($16.80 to $32.80). The restaurant is open daily for lunch and dinner (closed Monday to nonguests).

5 Bordeaux

359 miles SW of Paris, 341 miles W of Lyon

Situated on the Garonne River, the great port of Bordeaux, the capital of Aquitaine, is the center of the world's most important wine-producing area. It attracts many visitors to the offices of wine exporters here, most of whom welcome guests. (For a trip through the surrounding Bordeaux Wine Country, refer to the next section.)

Bordeaux is a city of warehouses, factories, mansions, and exploding suburbs, as well as wide quays 5 miles long. Now the fifth-largest French city, Bordeaux belonged to the British for 300 years, and even today is considered the most un-French of French cities.

It may not exude the joie de vivre of Paris, but Bordeaux is a major cultural center and a transportation hub between southern France and Spain. With a population of some 650,000, much of Bordeaux is looking seedy, but the worn-out docklands to the south of the center are slated for urban renewal.

ESSENTIALS

GETTING THERE   The local **airport,** Bordeaux-Mérignac (☎ **05-56-34-50-50** for flight information), is served by flights from as far away as London and New York. It's 6³/₄ miles west of Bordeaux in Mérignac. A **shuttle bus** connects the airport with the train station, departing every 30 minutes from 6am to 10:30pm (trip time: 40 minutes), and costing 37 F ($5.90) one-way for adults and 29 F ($4.65) for students. The railway station, Gare St-Jean, is on the west bank of the river, within a 30-minute walk (or 5-minute taxi ride) of the center of the old town. Some 12 to 15 **trains** from Paris arrive per day (trip time: 3 hours by TGV). For train information and schedules, call ☎ **08-36-35-35-35.**

Bordeaux is easily reached **by car.** From Paris, follow A10 south through the cities of Orléans, Tours, and Poitiers into Bordeaux (trip time: about 5 hours). Be aware that navigating the city streets of Bordeaux is fraught with almost as many hazards as you'd face in Paris: narrow 18th-century alleys, massive traffic jams on the quays beside the Garonne, and simply too many cars and people. Consequently, expect a lack of easily available parking within the city's historic core, and head, whenever possible, for any of the blue-and-white "P" signs that indicate public garages.

VISITOR INFORMATION   The **Office de Tourisme** is at 12 cours du 30-Juillet (☎ **05-56-00-66-00**).

EXPLORING THE TOWN

Wine exporters welcome guests who come to sample wines and learn about the industry. In the next section of this chapter we take a tour of the Bordeaux Wine Country. Plan your trip with maps and guides that are available free from the **Maison du Vin (House of Wine),** 3 cours du 30-Juillet (☎ **05-56-00-22-88**), opposite the tourist office. To make the rounds of the vineyards, consider alternative forms of transportation: bus, bicycle, or even walking.

STROLLS THROUGH TOWN   You can traipse around the **old town** on your own, since it's a fairly compact neighborhood, or you can take advantage of the 2-hour **walking tour** that the tourist office (see above) arranges daily at 10am. Conducted in both French and English, it begins at the tourist office, costs 40 F ($6.40) per adult and 35 F ($5.60) for students and children 17 and under, and takes in all the most important sites. We strongly recommend it, as it corresponds to the opening hours of

Bordeaux

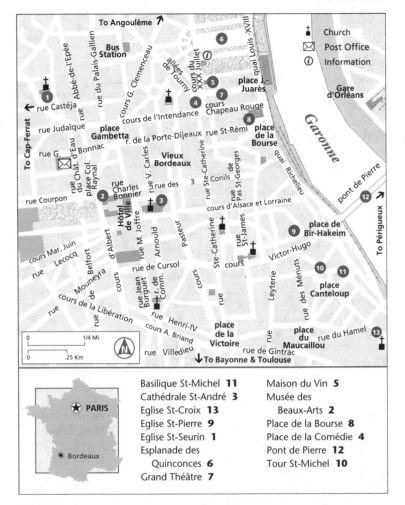

Church
Post Office
Information

To Angoulême ↗

Bus Station

6

To Cap-Ferrat

1 rue Castéja

rue Judaïque

place Gambetta

rue G.

rue Courpon

Abbé-de-l'Épée

rue du Palais-Gallien

allées de Tourny

cours G. Clemenceau

cours du XXX Juillet

cours de l'Intendance

cours Chapeau Rouge

rue St-Rémi

r. de la Porte-Dijeaux

du Chât. d'Eau

Bonnac

place Col. Raynal

rue Charles Bonnier

rue V. Carles

rue des

2 **3**

Hôtel de Ville

rue M. Joffre

d'Albert

5 **7**

place J.-Juarès

4

place de la Bourse

8

Vieux Bordeaux

rue Ste-Catherine

3 rue de Conils

rue Pas St-Georges

cours d'Alsace et Lorraine

Pasteur

rue Arnould

cours Mar. Juin

Lecocq

rue

Belfort

Mouneyra

cours de

cours

rue Jean Burguet

r. de Comm.

rue de Cursol

cours de la Libération

rue Henri-IV

cours A. Briand

rue Villedieu

place de la Victoire

To Bayonne & Toulouse

Ste-Catherine

rue St-James

cours

place de Bir-Hakeim

9

Victor-Hugo

Leyterie

rue des Menuts

10 **11**

place Canteloup

rue

place du Maucaillou

rue de Gintrac

rue du Hamel

13

Gare d'Orléans

Garonne

quai Richelieu

Quai Louis XVIII

pont de Pierre

12

To Périgueux ↗

0 — 1/4 Mi
0 — .25 Km

★ PARIS

● Bordeaux

Basilique St-Michel **11**
Cathédrale St-André **3**
Eglise St-Croix **13**
Eglise St-Pierre **9**
Eglise St-Seurin **1**
Esplanade des Quinconces **6**
Grand Théâtre **7**

Maison du Vin **5**
Musée des Beaux-Arts **2**
Place de la Bourse **8**
Place de la Comédie **4**
Pont de Pierre **12**
Tour St-Michel **10**

each of the monuments listed separately below. Reserve in advance, or at least call to confirm that the tour is on for the day of your arrival.

If you go it alone, your tour of Old Bordeaux can begin at **place de la Comédie,** at the very heart of this venerated old city, a busy traffic hub that was once the site of a Roman temple. On this square one of the great theaters of France, the **Grand Théâtre,** was built between 1773 and 1780 as testimony to the burgeoning prosperity of Bordeaux's emerging bourgeoisie. A colonnade of 12 columns graces its facade. Surmounted on these are statues of goddesses and the Muses. If you'd like to visit the richly decorated interior, ask the porter; you can also phone the tourist office about the schedule for one of the weekly guided tours of the site. They cost 30 F ($4.80) per person and are scheduled to coincide with French school holidays.

From here you can walk north to **esplanade des Quinconces,** the largest square of its kind in Europe. It was laid out between 1818 and 1828, and covers nearly 30 acres. A smaller but lovelier square is **place de la Bourse,** bounded by quays opening onto the Garonne. It was laid out between 1728 and 1755; the fountain of the Three Graces is at its center. Flanking the square are the Custom House and the Stock Exchange.

CHURCHES   The largest and most ostentatious church in Bordeaux, and the city's official religious centerpiece, is the **Cathédrale St-André,** place Pey-Berland (☎ 05-56-81-64-36), standing near the southern perimeter of the old town. The sculptures on the 13th-century Porte Royale (Royal Door) are admirable; see also the 14th-century sculptures on the North Door. Separate from the rest of the church is the 155-foot **Tour Pey-Berland,** a belfry begun in the 15th century. Foundations date from 900 years ago. The church is open July to September, daily from 7:30 to 11:30am and 2 to 6:30pm. Off-season, it's closed on Sunday afternoons. The tower is open daily from 10am to 5pm (until 6pm in April, May, June, and September, and until 7pm in July and August). Tower admission is 25 F ($4) for adults and 15 F ($2.40) for those 25 and under. Organ recitals are held every Tuesday in summer from 6:30 to 7:30pm. Admission is free.

Bordeaux, always a magnet for power, money, and ecclesiastical zeal, has four other important churches, each smaller than the cathedral but each with an unusual charm. Foremost among these is the **Basilique St-Michel,** place St-Michel (place Canteloup). The church itself is incredibly charming, but more impressive is the **Tour St-Michel** across the street. The belfry, erected in 1472, is the tallest stone tower in France, rising 374 feet. The belfry (and the 228 steps you'll have to climb to reach its summit) is open for visits only between mid-June and mid-September, daily from 3 to 7pm, for a fee of 10 F ($1.60) per person. From the top, you are confronted with sweeping views out over the port. The rest of the year, unless you receive special permission from the tourist office, you'll have to appreciate the architecture of the tower from the ground.

Another interesting church is **Église St-Seurin,** place des Martyrs de la Résistance (☎ 05-56-48-22-08), whose most ancient sections, like its crypt, date from the 5th century. See the porch left over from an earlier church; it has some capitals from the Romanesque era. It's open daily from 8am to noon and 2 to 7:30pm. Equally appealing is **Église St-Pierre,** place du Parlement, dating from the 14th and 15th centuries.

Église Ste-Croix, place Pierre-Renaudel, gained attention in musical circles around the world when its organ, a musical marvel built by a monk, Dom Bedos, was restored to its original working order in 1996. The church itself, a severe Romanesque structure from the 11th and 12th centuries, is revered for its stately dignity.

For information about any of the four "secondary" churches above, you can call the **Presbytère de l'Église St-Michel** (☎ 05-56-94-30-50), but the kindly prelates who answer are likely to speak only French. Opening hours of each vary slightly, according to the day's schedule for masses and celebrations, but are usually Monday through Saturday from 8am to 6pm and Sunday from 9am to noon.

A MUSEUM   **Musée des Beaux-Arts,** 20 cours d'Albret (Jardin du Palais-Rohan) (☎ 05-56-10-20-30), has an outstanding collection ranging from the 15th to the 20th centuries. Works by Perugina, Titian, Rubens, Veronese, Delacroix, Marquet, and Lhote are displayed. The museum is open Wednesday to Monday from 11am to 6pm. Admission is 25 F ($4) for adults; free for children and students.

BOAT RIDES   **Pont de Pierre,** with 17 arches, stretches 1,594 feet across the Garonne and is one of the most beautiful bridges in France. Ordered built by Napoléon I in 1813, the bridge can be crossed on foot for a fine view of the quays and the port. But for an even better view we suggest a **tour of the port,** which lasts about 1¹/₂ hours and encompasses a float up the river and all around the harbor. It departs from the Embarcadères des Quinconces, on quai Louis-XVIII in the center of town. It's open year-round. The cost is 50 F ($8) for adults and 45 F ($7.20) for children 9 and under. For exact times, call the tourism office (see "Essentials," above) or the **boat captains' office** near the quai (☎ **05-56-52-88-88**). Ask about the occasional floating concerts at night. Note that tours may be canceled without warning.

You may enjoy a **cruise** on one of France's mightiest (and least-visited) rivers, the Garonne. In July and August, **Alienor Loisirs,** Hangar 7, quai Louis-XVIII (☎ **05-56-51-27-90**), offers a Sunday-afternoon ride downriver from Bordeaux to the château town of Blaye. Boarding at the company's dock begins at around 11am for an 11:30am departure. Lunch is served on board, and between 2 and 4pm you enjoy a shore excursion in Blaye. The return to Bordeaux is usually scheduled for around 6:30pm the same day. The cost, lunch included, is 270 F ($43.20). The rest of the year, roughly equivalent excursions are offered, depending on the number of prepaid advance reservations. Closed each February. For more information, call the Bordeaux tourist office or Alienor Loisirs.

SHOPPING

If you want antiques, concentrate your search around **rue Bouffard, rue des Remparts,** and **rue Notre-Dame,** where you'll find a market area known as **Village Notre-Dame,** housing all sorts and sizes of antiques shops. Another haven is the neighborhood around **Église St-Michel.**

If you need to fill up some empty suitcases with new clothes, go to the couture quarter around **place des Grands Hommes** with its many upscale, trendy, and classic clothing emporiums. If you're out for a younger, more casual style, try the shops (and also the many restaurants) around **place du Parlement.** And for the highest concentration of shops in town, head for the **Centre Commercial Meriadeck,** in the rue du Château d'Eau (☎ **05-56-99-59-00**), the site of more than 100 boutiques selling everything from sportswear to housewares.

The better-known choices include the haute couture boutique of the Bordeaux fashion designer **Jacqueline Dourthe,** 18 rue Lafaurie-de-Monbadon (☎ **05-56-52-35-78**), where you can find everything from cocktail and evening dresses to the most luxurious wedding gowns; and **La Soierie,** 54 cours George Clemenceaux (☎ **05-56-51-23-75**), which carries a complete line of chic women's silk garments.

Galerie Condillac, 24 rue Condillac (☎ **05-56-79-04-31**), is one of the classier art houses that specializes in mostly local artists who paint with strong, vibrant colors. A relatively cramped but choice emporium for French crystal and antique engravings is **Maurice Mazuque,** 6 rue du Parlement Ste-Catherine. For a sugar rush, head over to **Cadiot Badie,** 26 allées de Tourny (☎ **05-56-44-24-22**), where you'll find everything from sinfully good pralines to creamy and decadent Bordeaux truffles.

ACCOMMODATIONS

Hôtel Continental. 10 rue Montesquieu, 33000 Bordeaux. ☎ **05-56-52-66-00.** Fax 05-56-52-77-97. www.hotel-le-continental.com. E-mail: continental@hotel-le-continental. com. 50 units. A/C MINIBAR TV TEL. 360–570 F ($57.60–$91.20) double; 1,200 F ($192) suite. AE, DC, MC, V.

To get a certain class, charm, and elegance in Bordeaux at this affordable price is a rarity. In the center of the golden triangle, on a semi-pedestrian mall dotted with boutiques, this restored 18th-century town house wins new converts every year. You'll get a warm welcome and a fine dose of Bordelaise hospitality; the rooms, although a bit

Buying Wine in Bordeaux

Of course, many visitors come to Bordeaux to buy wine. There are many inexpensive wines, but it doesn't make sense to blow your one-bottle-per-adult liquor allowance on a 15F bottle. Try to pick a wine that carries personal significance because you've visited the vineyard, or chat up the experts at some of the most famous wine shops. We recommend **La Vinothèque,** 8 cours du 30-Juillet (☎ **05-56-52-32-05**); and **Badie,** 62 allées de Tourny (☎ **05-56-52-23-72**). The best spots for red Bordeaux wines from small houses are **Château Lespare,** Beychac-et-Caillau, 24 miles north of Bordeaux (☎ **05-57-24-51-23**); **Château Bel Air,** Naujan-et-Postiac, 9 miles east of Bordeaux (☎ **05-57-84-55-08**); and **Château Les Bouzigues,** Saintes Gemmes, 47 miles south of Bordeaux (☎ **05-56-61-65-92**).

small (especially the singles), are warmly decorated and comfortably furnished. A few have balconies, but space is at an absolute minimum. Public areas are richly accessorized and furnished, and breakfasts are brunch style.

Hôtel de Sèze. 23 allées de Tourny, 33000 Bordeaux. ☎ **05-56-52-65-54.** Fax 05-56-44-31-83. 24 units. MINIBAR TV TEL. 300–420 F ($48–$67.20) double. AE, DC, MC, V. Parking 40 F ($6.40).

This three-star hostelry occupies an 18th-century building that's an antique in its own right, roughly equivalent to many others in its historic neighborhood. The hotel is such a well-known value that you should make reservations as early as possible. The rooms, which are scattered over four floors, are comfortable and well furnished; the cheapest has only a bed and bathroom (with shower only).

Hôtel Majestic. 2 rue de Condé, 33000 Bordeaux. ☎ **05-56-52-60-44.** Fax 05-56-79-26-70. www.hotel-majestic.com. E-mail: majestic@hotel-majestic.com. 50 units. A/C MINIBAR TV TEL. 390–600 F ($62.40–$96) double. AE, DC, V. Parking 60 F ($9.60).

Set back from quai Louis-XVIII, which opens onto the Garonne, this three-star choice is sheltered in a sturdy 18th-century town house, which has been carefully restored and renovated to offer modern comforts. In the historic and commercial heart of Bordeaux, it lies on a tranquil street near the Grand Theater. Each of its bedrooms is decorated in a traditional French provincial style and contains soundproofing and air-conditioning. A carefully prepared continental breakfast is the only meal served, but room service is always available. The street outside is one of the most bustling in Bordeaux, with boutiques, museums, cafes, and restaurants.

Mercure Bordeaux Mériadeck. 5 rue Robert-Lateulade, 33000 Bordeaux. ☎ **05-56-56-43-43.** Fax 05-56-96-50-59. www.mercure.com. E-mail: h128@accor-hotels.com. 194 units. A/C MINIBAR TV TEL. 580 F ($92.80) double; 950 F ($152) suite. AE, DC, MC, V. Bus: 7 or 8.

This hotel, in a sleek building facing a shopping mall in the Mériadeck business district, and only a 5-minute walk from the town center, offers modern comforts that are popular with business travelers and groups. The well-furnished rooms with modern amenities and comfortable mattresses attract vine growers and wine merchants from abroad. The best rooms are on the sixth floor (some are showing signs of wear and tear). La Brasserie du Festival, the main **restaurant,** is one of the finest hotel grills.

Mercure Château Chartrons. 81 cours St-Louis, 33300 Bordeaux. ☎ **05-56-43-15-00.** Fax 05-56-69-15-21. www.mercure.com. E-mail: h1810@accor-hotels.com. 144 units. A/C

MINIBAR TV TEL. 570–640 F ($91.20–$102.40) double; 780 F ($124.80) suite. AE, DC, MC, V. Parking 45 F ($7.20).

Operated by a prestigious wine exporter, La Maison Ginneste, this is one of Bordeaux's leading hotels. Near the landmark place Tourny, it opened in 1991 behind the grace-fully restored facade of an 18th-century mansion. The rooms are decorated with mem-orabilia of the wine trade. The bar here has an impressive array of local vintages sold by the glass. The **restaurant, Le Cabernet,** serves regional specialties. Try the seven o'clock roast leg of lamb, the veal kidneys and sweetbreads in a ramekin with a pota-to crust, or the Graves-style duck with peaches. At 115 F ($18.40), the fixed-price menu is a good value.

Novotel Bordeaux Centre. 45 cours du Maréchal-Juin, 33000 Bordeaux. ☎ **05-56-51-46-46.** Fax 05-56-98-25-56. www.novotel.com. E-mail: H1023@accor-hotels.com. 140 units. A/C MINIBAR TV TEL. 560 F ($89.60) double; 820 F ($131.20) suite. Children 15 and under stay free in parents' room. AE, DC, MC, V. Free parking.

Built in 1989, this first-class hotel is in the heart of the city near the railway station, a short walk from the busy rue Sainte Catherine, quai des Chartrons, and the cathe-dral. The rooms are comfortably furnished, with good quality mattresses and pillows. Some rooms are suitable for individuals with disabilities. The hotel also offers laundry and room service.

✪ **Tulip Inn Le Bayonne Etche-Ona.** 15 cours de l'Intendance (with entrances at 4 rue Martignac and 11 rue Mautrec), 33000 Bordeaux. ☎ **05-56-48-00-88.** Fax 05-56-48-41-60. www.bordeaux-hotel.com. E-mail: bayetche@bordeaux-hotel.com. 63 units. A/C MINIBAR TV TEL. 450–610 F ($72–$97.60) double; 1,200 F ($192) suite. AE, DC, MC, V. Parking 70 F ($11.20).

In 1997, two antique stone-fronted town houses, Le Bayonne Hotel and its equally antique but less elegant neighbor, Hotel Etche-Ona, were radically upgraded and joined together to form this all-new, three-star entity. Today they compose part of the grand infrastructure of Bordeaux's cours de l'Intendance (grand arcade), and they're a great example of an intelligent use of historically important buildings. The aura of the 1930s has been retained, and many features have been added, most notably air-conditioning, soundproofing, and comfortable furnishings. Many attractions, includ-ing several good restaurants, the cathedral, place de la Bourse, the quays, and the Grand Théâtre, are nearby. Breakfast is the only meal served.

DINING

You can also try the restaurant at **Mercure Château Chartrons** (see "Accommoda-tions," above).

La Chamade. 20 rue des Piliers-de-Tutelle. ☎ **05-56-48-13-74.** Reservations required. Main courses 100–250 F ($16–$40); fixed-price menus 100–350 F ($16–$56). AE, DC, MC, V. Daily noon–2:30pm and 7:30–10:30pm. Closed last week July and first week Aug. FRENCH.

You'll have a delightful time at La Chamade, in a vaulted 18th-century cellar of honey-colored stone. Specialties include roasted foie gras with confit of leeks and scallops with truffles. The fish is steamed to perfection and served simply, often with warm vinaigrette of tomatoes and basil. The owner, M. Lasserre, has an impressive collection of bordeaux.

La Forge. 8 rue du Chai-des-Farines. ☎ **05-56-81-40-96.** Reservations recommended. Main courses 60–100 F ($9.60–$16); fixed-price menus 88–150 F ($14.10–$24). AE, DC, MC, V. Tues–Sat noon–1:30pm and 7:30–10pm. Closed mid-Aug to mid-Sept. FRENCH.

Jean-Michel Pouts, a former chef on the ocean liner *France,* owns this bistro. The well-prepared specialties include brochette of pork with Gruyère, savory grilled meats, and an excellent cassoulet. The fixed-price menus are among the best value in town. The restaurant's devotion to a regional repertoire and attempts to keep prices down are most admirable. Everything is homemade.

✪ **La Tupina.** 6 rue de la Porte de la Monnaie. ☎ **05-56-91-56-37.** Reservations recommended. Main courses 85–295 F ($13.60–$47.20); fixed-price menus 100 F ($16) at lunch, 200–300 F ($32–$48) at dinner. AE, DC, MC, V. Daily noon–2pm and 7–11pm. FRENCH.

One of Bordeaux's most talented chefs runs this cozy restaurant with a summer terrace near quai de la Monnaie. It's been called "a tribute to country kitchens and the grandmothers who cooked in them," and its entryway looks like a farmhouse larder. Jean-Pierre Xiradakis's specialty is duck, so your meal might begin with croûtons spread with duck rillettes, and his salads often use duck giblets, skin, and livers. Regional specialties include truffles and foie gras; a recently sampled potato salad contained slices of black truffles from Périgord, and the foie gras often comes steamed in parchment. Sample one of the fine wines from the cellar, and definitely ask for the *assiette grand-mère,* an assortment of classic homespun desserts.

✪ **Le Chapon-Fin.** 5 rue Montesquieu. ☎ **05-56-79-10-10.** Reservations required. Main courses 180–250 F ($28.80–$40); fixed-price menus 160–425 F ($25.60–$68) at lunch, 275–425 F ($44–$68) at dinner. AE, DC, MC, V. Tues–Sat noon–2pm and 7:30–10pm. FRENCH.

Under the guidance of Francis Garcia from Barcelona, this is the leading restaurant in Bordeaux, serving an even more refined cuisine than that found at the also-highly rated La Chamade (see above). The dining room boasts elaborate latticework and several banquettes in artificial stone grottoes; a pivoting skylight lets in summer breezes. The wines are usually selected from the most respected and expensive French vintages, and menu specialties are among the best of the southwest. A meal might include truffle flan with essence of morels, gratin of oysters with foie gras, salmon steak grilled in its skin with pepper-flavored sabayon, and superb cheeses and desserts.

✪ **Le Vieux Bordeaux.** 27 rue Buhan. ☎ **05-56-52-94-36.** Reservations recommended. Main courses 80–165 F ($12.80–$26); fixed-price menus 165–300 F ($26.40–$48). AE, DC, MC, V. Mon–Fri noon–2pm and 8–10:30pm, Sat 8–10:30pm. Closed 2 weeks in Feb and 3 weeks in Aug. FRENCH.

Nearly a neighborhood institution, this restaurant ranks among the top five in highly competitive Bordeaux, one of the culinary capitals of France. The decor is an almost-incongruous mix of exposed wood and modern accents, with a summer terrace. Specialties include pavé of fresh salmon with warm oysters, roasted sweetbreads, and turbot with Basque pepper and strips of Basque ham. Dessert might be chocolate ice cream flavored with Izarra, the Basque liqueur.

NEARBY ACCOMMODATIONS & DINING

✪ **Restaurant St-James/Hôtel Hautrive.** 3 place Camille-Hostein, 33270 Bouliac. ☎ **05-57-97-06-00.** Fax 05-56-20-92-58. Reservations required. Main courses 140–300 F ($22.40–$48); fixed-price menu 400 F ($64). AE, DC, MC, V. Apr–Nov, daily noon–2pm and 8–10pm; Dec–Mar, daily 8–10pm. From Bordeaux, follow the signs south to Toulouse/Bayonne. At the périphérique encircling Bordeaux, follow the signs toward Paris; take exit 23 and follow the signs to Bouliac. FRENCH.

This is the domain of Jean-Marie Amat, whose specialties are based on local seasonal ingredients. These may revolve around the abundance of *cèpes* (the district's meaty flap mushrooms), game (venison and pheasant), *girolles* (another kind of mushroom), and fruit. In an ultramodern dining room whose windows offer a view of some of the most famous vineyards in Europe, you can enjoy such dishes as terrine of mixed wild game and foie gras served with a chanterelle salad and stewed rhubarb; a salad of raw scallops with balsamic vinegar; stuffed octopus served with risotto flavored with squid ink; escalope of fresh foie gras fried with apples; and fillet of venison, served rare, and cooked with a sauce made from strong red Banyuls wine, winter berries, and root vegetables. Dessert might include a confit of figs, cooked with a crusty-crispy top and served with mandarin sorbet. You can dine less expensively in the brasserie, Le Bistroy, where meals average 160 F ($25.60) without beverage.

Adjacent is the Hôtel Hautrive, whose 15 elegant rooms and three suites are scattered among four modern pavilions. Doubles go for 900 F to 1,100 F ($144 to $176); suites cost 1,400 F to 1,700 F ($224 to $272).

BORDEAUX AFTER DARK

Pick up a copy of *Clubs et Concerts* at the Office de Tourisme or *Bordeaux Plus* at one of the newsstands; both publications detail the goings-on in and around town.

Taking in a play or an opera could make for a good start to your evening. **Grand Théâtre,** place de la Comédie (☎ **05-56-00-85-20**), has a very busy and diverse performance schedule.

To pick up the pace, head for **place de la Victoire** and **place Gambetta,** alive and pulsating with hordes of students. For some of the best pubbing around, hit the **Connemara Irish Pub,** 18 cours d'Albret (☎ **05-56-52-82-57**), where the Guinness flows freely and a noisy crowd gathers to hear traditional Irish music; or **Dick Turpin's Bar,** 72 rue du Loup (☎ **05-56-48-07-52**), which specializes in just about every brand of whiskey imaginable. With its white piano and live jazz, the piano/jazz club **Black Jack,** 35 place Gambetta (☎ **05-56-81-71-38**), creates a soft, stylish ambience that pulls in a sophisticated middle-aged crowd.

More raucous partyers of all ages head for the immense **L'Ane Qui Tousse,** 57 rue de Bègles (☎ **05-56-92-52-98**), with its two dance floors and tropical motifs. Frat types congregate at **Le Plana,** 22 place de la Victoire (☎ **05-56-91-73-23**), where the space around the bar turns into a makeshift dance floor once the party gets going. An even better choice for dancing is **Sénéchal,** 57 bis quai de Paludate (☎ **05-56-85-54-80**), with its classic 1970s decor and just as classic 25- to 45-year-old crowd. An increasingly popular, and very hip, disco favorite that's spiced up with the occasional live cabaret or musical act is **Le Caesar's,** Quai Louis XVIII (☎ **05-56-51-99-41**). At **Bar Le Moyen-Age,** 8 rue des Remparts (☎ **05-56-44-12-87**), a mostly **gay male** crowd congregates in a medieval-looking cellar.

6 The Wine Country

The major Bordeaux wine districts are Graves, Médoc, Sauternes, Entre-deux-Mers, Libourne, Blaye, and Bourg. North of the city of Bordeaux, the Garonne River joins the Dordogne. This forms the Gironde, a broad estuary at the heart of the wine country. More than 100,000 vineyards produce some 70 million gallons of wine a year, some of which are among the greatest reds in the world. (The white wines are lesser known.)

Some of the famous vineyards are pleased to welcome visitors, providing you don't arrive at the busy harvest time. However, most vineyards aren't likely to have a permanent staff to welcome you. Don't just show up. Call first or check with local tourist offices about appropriate times to visit.

VISITOR INFORMATION   The best-respected source of information about the wines of Bordeaux (and French wines in general) is the **Centre d'Information, de**

Documentation, et de Dégustation (CIDD), 30 rue de la Sablière, 75014 Paris (☎ 01-45-45-44-20; fax 01-45-42-78-20). This self-funded school presents about a dozen courses throughout the year addressing all aspects of wine tasting, producing, buying, and merchandising. They will also send information to anyone anticipating a tour of the vineyards of France, either in the region around Bordeaux, or elsewhere.

Before heading out on this wine road, make sure you get a detailed map from the Bordeaux tourist office (see "Essentials" in the Bordeaux section of this chapter), since the "trail" isn't well marked. From Bordeaux, head north toward Pauillac on D2, the wine road, called the Route des Grands-Crus.

MÉDOC

The Médoc, an undulating plain covered with vineyards, is one of the most visited regions in southwestern France. Its borders are marked by Bordeaux and the Pointe de Grave. Throughout the region are many isolated châteaux producing grapes; only a handful of these, however, are worthy of your attention. The most visited château is that of Mouton-Rothschild, said to be second only to Lourdes among attractions in southwestern France, in spite of the red tape involved in visiting.

In Haut-Médoc, the soil isn't especially fertile but absorbs much heat during the day. To benefit from this, the vines are clipped close to the ground. The French zealously regulate the cultivation of the vineyards and the making of the wine. Less than 10% of the wines from the region are called Bordeaux. These are invariably red, including famous labels like Château Margaux, Château Latour, Château Mouton, and Château Lafite. Most of these are from grapes grown some 3,000 feet from the Gironde River.

EXPLORING THE AREA

Château Lafite. On D2. ☎ **05-56-73-18-18**, or 01-53-89-78-00 for appointments. Free admission. Tours by appointment only. Mon–Fri 9–11am and 2–5pm. Closed Aug–Oct.

This site is second only to the nearby Château Mouton-Rothschild. Count on spending at least an hour here. The vinothèque contains many vintage bottles, several dating from 1797. The château was purchased in 1868 by the Rothschilds.

Château Margaux. On D2, 33460 Margaux. ☎ **05-57-88-83-83**. Vat rooms and wine cellars open by appointment only. Mon–Fri 10am–noon and 2–4pm. Closed Aug–Oct.

Known as the Versailles of the Médoc, this Empire-style château was built in the 19th century near the village of Margaux. The estate covers more than 650 acres, of which 193 produce Château Margaux and Pavillon Rouge du Château Margaux; almost 30 acres are devoted to producing Pavillon Blanc du Château Margaux. There are no tours of the chateau; you can only admire it from the outside. To see the vat rooms and wine cellars, make an appointment by letter or phone. You can also contact them by E-mail: chateau-margot@chateaux-margaux.com.

✪ **Château Mouton-Rothschild.** Le Pouyalet, 33250 Pauillac. ☎ **05-56-73-21-29**. Tours 30 F ($4.80) per person without a tasting, 80–150 F ($12.80–$24) per person with a tasting. Tours by appointment only. Apr–Oct, Sat–Thurs 9am–4pm, Fri 9am–3:30pm; Nov–Mar, Mon–Fri 9am–4pm. Call to make an appointment well in advance to see the cellars.

Thousands of tourists visit this outstanding château, one of the many former homes of the baron Philippe de Rothschild and his American-born wife, Pauline. Today their only daughter, Philippine de Rothschild, carries on their work. The welcoming room is beautifully furnished with a collection of sculptures and paintings that portray wine as art, plus a 16th-century tapestry depicting the grape harvest. An adjoining museum, in former wine cellars, has art from many eras, much of it related to the cultivation of the vineyards. Note the collection of modern art, including a statue by the American sculptor Lippold.

✪ **Société Duboscq.** Château Haut-Marbuzet, 33180 St-Estephe ☎ **05-56-59-30-54.** Free admission. Mon–Sat 8am–noon and 2–5pm. Tours in English on Tues.

Your free visit to the cellars here will be followed by a complimentary *dégustation des vins* of whichever product you request. A relative newcomer whose prestige has grown rapidly, Duboscq offers excellent opportunities for studying the ancient fermentation process in its modern forms and the maturation process in new oak casks.

DINING

Auberge André. Le Grand Port, 33880 Cambes. ☎ **05-56-21-34-69.** Reservations recommended. Main courses 75–118 F ($12–$18.90); fixed-price menu 135–245 F ($21.60–$39.20). AE, MC, V. June–Sept, Tues–Sun noon–2pm, Mon–Sat 8–10:30pm; Oct–May, Wed–Sun noon–2pm, Wed–Sat 8:30–10:30pm. FRENCH.

This charming hideaway is located at the edge of Cambes, a village with no more than 100 residents, in a century-old farmhouse whose awning-covered terrace offers a sweeping view of the Garonne. Menu items might include fillet of eel with parsley-butter sauce, lamprey eels in bordelaise-wine sauce, *confit de canard,* fillet of sea bass infused with essence of laurel, salmon cooked with port and, over autumn and winter, an impressive collection of game.

LIBOURNE

This is a sizable market town with a railway connection. At the junction of the Dordogne and Isle rivers, Libourne is roughly the center of the St-Emilion, Pomerol, and Fronsac wine districts. In the town, a large colonnaded square still contains some houses from the 16th century, including the **Hôtel-de-Ville** (town hall). You can also explore the remains of 13th-century ramparts. In the town center is the **Office de Tourisme,** 40 place Abel-Surchamp (☎ **05-57-51-15-04**), where you can get details on visiting the Bordeaux vineyards.

NEARBY ACCOMMODATIONS & DINING

La Bonne Auberge. Rue du 8-Mai-1945 et av. John-Talbot, 33350 Castillon-la-Bataille. ☎ **05-57-40-11-56.** Fax 05-57-40-21-66. 10 units. TV TEL. 150–330 F ($24–$52.80) double. AE, MC, V. From Libourne, follow the signs to Bergerac; take the highway for 18 miles to Castillon-la-Bataille, then continue to the far end of the village.

This family hotel is located near an intersection of two busy highways. Although basic, the rooms are comfortable and welcoming. This still feels more like a *restaurant avec chambres* than a full-fledged hotel. Closed last 2 weeks in November.

Dining: The food served here is good and plentiful. Serious diners go to the restaurant at the top of the exterior stairs; there's also a brasserie on the ground level. A fixed-price menu in the brasserie is only 59 F to 70 F ($9.45 to $11.20), whereas the fixed-price menu in the restaurant goes for 74 F to 207 F ($11.85 to $33.10). Specialties are grilled salmon with shallot-flavored butter, omelets, lamb with parsley, snails in a red wine sauce, sweetbreads with mushrooms, and entrecôte in bordelaise-wine sauce. The restaurant is open daily for lunch and dinner; from November to March, it's closed Saturday for lunch and Monday for dinner.

ST-EMILION

Surrounded by vineyards, St-Emilion is on a limestone plateau overlooking the Valley of the Dordogne; a maze of wine cellars has been dug from the limestone beneath the town. The wine made in this world-famous district has been called "Wine of Honor," and British sovereigns nicknamed it "King of Wines." The town, constructed mostly of golden stone and dating from the Middle Ages, is also known for its macaroons.

St-Emilion still maintains the ancient tradition of La Jurade. Members of this society wear silk hats and scarlet robes edged with ermine, and the Syndicat Viticole, which watches over the quality of wine, have all been around the world to promote the wines with this appellation.

GETTING THERE   St-Emilion lies 22 miles northeast of Bordeaux between Libourne (5 miles away) and Castillon-la-Bataille (7 miles away). **Trains** from Bordeaux make the 45-minute trip to St-Emilion three times per day. Trains from other parts of France usually require transfers in either Bordeaux or Libourne, a 10-minute train ride from St. Emilion.

EXPLORING THE TOWN

The **Office de Tourisme** is on place des Créneaux (☎ **05-57-55-28-28**).

At the heart of St-Emilion is **place du Marché,** between two hills. An old acacia tree marks the center. St-Emilion is loaded with unusual monuments, some of which were dug, for defensive reasons, into the soft limestone bedrock that adds such verve to the vineyards. Foremost of these is the **Église Monolithe,** place du Marché (☎ **05-57-55-28-28**), the largest underground church in Europe, carved by Benedictine monks during the 9th to 12th centuries. Its facade is marked by three 14th-century bay windows. A 14th-century sculpted portal depicts the Last Judgment and resurrection of the dead. The church is about 37 feet high, 67 feet wide, and 125 feet long. It can be visited only as part of organized tours, in English and French, which leave from the tourist office. Tours depart at 10, 10:45, and 11:30am and 2, 2:45, 3:30, 4:15, and 5pm. Between April and October, an additional tour is offered at 5:45pm; and during July and August, another additional tour is at 6:30pm. They include a visit to the above-mentioned Église Monolithe, as well as the Benedictine catacombs and the 13th-century **Chapelle de la Trinité** and its underground grotto (the Hermitage, the site where St-Emilion sequestered himself for the latter part of his life). The entire complex was kept alive during the heyday of its use by underground springs, which were surrounded in the 1500s by ornate balustrades. The tour, which lasts 45 minutes, costs 33 F ($5.30) for adults, 20 F ($3.20) for students, 16 F ($2.55) for children 13 to 18, and free for children 12 and under.

The city contains two additional monuments that can be visited without an organized tour. The first is the **Bell Tower** (*clocher*) of the above-mentioned Église Monolithe. It rises from a position on place des Créneaux, near place du Marché. Built between the 1100s and the 1400s, it's the second-highest tower in La Gironde and for years after its construction was the only above-ground landmark that indicated the position of the underground church. You can climb the bell tower during daylight hours every day except Christmas and New Year's Day for a fee of 6 F ($1) per person. Naturally, views from the top are panoramic.

Finally, you may want to visit the **Château du Roi** (☎ **05-57-24-61-07**), founded by Henry III of the Plantagenet line during the 13th century. Don't expect a full-fledged castle. The tower was the first section built, and the limited construction that followed was either demolished later or never completed. Until 1608 it functioned as the local Town Hall. From its summit, on a clear day, you can see as far away as the Dordogne. You can climb the tower during daylight hours every day except Christmas and New Year's Day, from 9:30am to noon and 1:45 to 6pm (till 6:30pm from April to September) for a fee of 6 F (95¢) per person.

ACCOMMODATIONS & DINING

✪ **Hostellerie de Plaisance.** Place du Clocher, 33330 St-Emilion. ☎ **05-57-55-07-55.**
Fax 05-57-74-41-11. www.hostellerie.plaisance@wanadoo.fr. E-mail: hostelleriedeplaisance@
saint-emilion.org. 16 units. A/C TEL. 590–1,100 F ($94.40–$176) double; 1,400–1,800 F
($224–$288) suite. AE, DC, MC, V. Closed Jan.

This 200-year-old stone building, set on 14th-century foundations, is the best choice
in this medieval town. The well-styled rooms, some with views of stone monuments
and towers, welcome sophisticated wine tasters and buyers from all over the world.
Some rooms are quite small, but the best doubles have terraces where you can enjoy
breakfast. Artifacts in the rooms reflect the age of the building and the importance of
the local wine trade.

Dining: The cuisine of Louis Quilain is the best known and most praised in the
area. He's at his best when working with the region's bountiful seasonal ingredients,
especially game dishes, which are rich, well-seasoned, and usually available between
October and February. Otherwise, menu items include a salad of grilled quail served
with avocados; a civet of sturgeon cooked with local red wine; a *timbale* of filets of sole
with crayfish tails; a ballotine of foie gras with shallots and grilled toast; turbot with
fresh duck liver, served with raisins; and fillet mignon of veal with wild mushrooms.
Top it all off with a warm soufflé flavored with pear liqueur and served with nougat
ice cream and chocolate sauce.

19

The Dordogne & Périgord: Land of Prehistoric Caves, Truffles & Fine Wine

Lovers of foie gras and truffles, not to mention nature-lovers, have always sought out the Dordogne and Périgord regions of France. Our first stop, Périgueux, was the capital of the old province of Périgord. After following the trail of the Cro-Magnon people to prehistoric caves, we'll visit Cahors, the ancient capital of Quercy, then Montauban, where the great painter Ingres was born. But the towns themselves aren't the stars—it's the unspoiled fertile countryside, of much hidden charm and antique character, that holds the fascination. In some villages the Middle Ages seem to live on. It's said that there are no discoveries to be made in France, but you can defy the experts and make many discoveries if you give yourself adequate time to visit a region too often neglected by North Americans.

REGIONAL CUISINE   Ask gastronomes about the cuisine of the Dordogne and Périgord, and the first thing to come to mind will be truffles, one of the most sought-after delicacies in France. The region produces more than 30 types. They all grow underground, without a root or stem, at the base of one type of oak tree in light soil of a certain degree of acidity. It gives off a distinctive odor, said by one 19th-century gastronome "to epitomize the perfumed soul of the Périgord." Because truffles grow underground (they're technically classified as a "subterranean fungus"), truffle hunters have traditionally used carefully trained dogs to smell out their location. Trained pigs have also been used to find them, but unlike dogs, who turn up their noses when they turn up a truffle, pigs tend to eat the morsel before it can be retrieved by the hunter.

Equally famous are the region's pâtés, which, when studded with "black diamonds" (truffles), have conquered many a resistant appetite. These are made from the enlarged livers of geese that have been force-fed a diet of rich corn. Some pâtés are still made of unadulterated goose liver, but the more frequently seen version is a ballotine of foie gras. This will usually have been prepared in a factory, where the goose liver is mixed with white turkey meat and then covered with meat gelatin.

One characteristic of the region's cuisine is the stuffing of many roasts and joints. It usually includes bread crumbs, truffles, and segments of goose liver. The most famous sauce here is a sauce Périgueux, made from sweet madeira wine and truffles. Anything prepared *à la périgourdine* includes a garnish of truffles to which foie gras has been

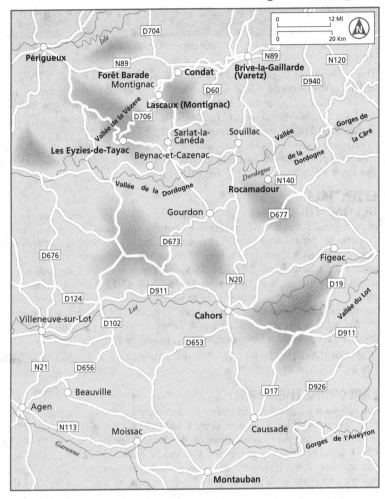

added. Another staple of the cuisine is *cèpes* (flap mushrooms). Other regional specialties are *bréjaude* (a cabbage/bacon soup served with rye bread) and *lièvre en chabessal* (freshly killed rabbit stuffed with highly seasoned pork, ham, and veal).

Rich in nutrients, the soil here produces huge quantities of walnuts, vegetables, and fruits. In this region, you'll also find succulent beef and veal. The Limousin breed of cows has been exported to Australia and South America, where it has thrived.

The most famous wines here are the red and white Bergerac, the red Pécharmant, and the deep-red Cahors. Cahors is best aged for a dozen years (some of them in an oak cask) before reaching a suitable sophistication. The Montbazillac is a sweet, tawny dessert wine whose grapes have been deliberately permeated with a whitish-green mold known as noble rot (*pourriture noble*). When it's fermented, this improves the flavor of the wine, partly by reducing its acidity and partly because of a mystery that only Dionysius could fully understand.

1 Périgueux

301 miles SW of Paris, 53 miles SE of Angoulème, 70 miles NE of Bordeaux, 63 miles SW of Limoges

This is the city of foie gras and truffles. Capital of the old province of Périgord, Périgueux stands on the Isle River. In addition to its food products, the region is known for its Roman ruins and medieval churches. The city is divided into three sections: the Cité (old Roman town), Le Puy St-Front (the medieval town) on the slope of the hill, and to the west, the modern town.

Périgueux today is a sleepy provincial backwater, with a population of 35,000. Its attractions probably won't hold your interest more than a day, but it's a gateway to the Dordogne Valley and the cave paintings at Les Eyzies.

ESSENTIALS

GETTING THERE   **Trains** run frequently from Paris, Lyon, and Toulouse, plus many regional towns and villages. Six trains per day arrive from Paris (trip time: 6 to 7 hours), four trains from Lyon (trip time: 7 hours), 10 trains from Bordeaux (trip time: 2¹/₂ hours), and seven trains from Toulouse (trip time: 4 hours). For train information and schedules, call ☎ **08-36-35-35-35.** For the most part, the local bus station (Gare Routière; place Francheville; ☎ **05-53-08-43-13**), adjacent to the tourist office, only provides infrequent services to villages in the surrounding district. When **driving** from Bordeaux, drive along N89 east. From Paris it's a much longer drive, taking A10 south to Orléans, connecting to A71 south to Vierzon, continuing along N20 south to Limoges, and then connecting to N21 south to Périgueux.

VISITOR INFORMATION   The **Office du Tourisme** is at 26 place Francheville (☎ **05-53-53-10-63**).

EXPLORING THE TOWN

You may want to rent a bike and explore the surrounding countryside; a map is available from the tourist office. Rent from **Cycle-Cum's,** 41 bis cour St-Georges (☎ **05-53-53-31-56**), or **Cycle Evasion Peugeot,** 46 Rond-Point de Chanzy (☎ **05-53-05-21-80**). They both charge between 50 F and 80 F ($8 and $12.80) per day for the first and second day. If you rent for 3 days or more, inquire about a 20% discount.

Périgueux is a treasure trove of Gallo-Roman antiquities. The most visible of these is the **Tour de Vésone,** a partially ruined site that stands 85 feet tall beyond the railway station, half a mile southwest of town. There, you'll find the remains of a Roman temple dedicated to the goddess Vesuna.

Jardin des Arènes, a vast elliptical amphitheater that once held as many as 22,000 spectators, is another reminder of Roman days. Now in ruins, the amphitheater, with a diameter of 1,312 feet, dates from the 2nd or 3rd century. The site is open daily May to August from 7:30am to 9pm and September to April from 8am to 6pm (no admission charge). Near the arena are the crumbling remains of the **Château Barrière,** rue Turenne, built in the 11th or 12th century on Roman foundations. Between June and August, Périgueux's tourist office offers organized walking tours of the city that incorporate both its ancient Roman and its medieval attractions. During that period, the tours depart Monday to Saturday at 10am and 2:30pm, last for 90 minutes each, and cost 25 F ($4) per person.

Above all, gastronomy reigns supreme in Périgueux, especially when it comes to smooth, melt-in-your-mouth foie gras. Stores that sell this regional delicacy abound. The best foie gras emporiums include **La Maison Léon,** 9 place de la Clautre

(☎ **05-53-53-29-96**), and **A la Cathédrale,** 9 rue des Chaînes (☎ **05-53-53-47-04**). But if you want an adventure while shopping for great goose liver, then head for a real goose farm by the name of **A la Ferme de Puy Gauthier,** about 15 minutes south of town in the village of Marsaneix (☎ **05-53-08-87-07**), where they make their own foie gras home-style. To get there, follow the signs to Brive. For those who enjoy the stimuli of an outdoor marketplace, head for the open-air food market at **place St-Louis** every Saturday from 8am to around 5pm. Fresh foie gras, sold either in its natural state or factored into terrines and pâtés, is available from many different vendors between November and March. A different series of food markets are held every Wednesday morning, between 8am and around 1pm, in the **place Francheville,** the **place Bugeaud,** and the above-mentioned place St-Louis.

Cathédrale St-Front. Place de la Clautre. ☎ **05-53-53-23-62.** Free admission. Daily 8am–noon and 2:30–7:30pm (winter, closes at dusk).

In Le Puy St-Front (the medieval quarter) rises the Cathédrale St-Front, the last of the Aquitanian domed churches. Built from 1125 to 1150, it was dedicated to St. Front, a local bishop. It's one of the largest churches in southwestern France. The cathedral's four-story bell tower rises nearly 200 feet, overlooking the marketplace; it's surmounted by a cone-shaped spire. With its five white domes and colonnaded turrets, St-Front evokes memories of Constantinople. The interior, somewhat bare, is built on the plan of a Greek cross, unusual for a French cathedral. On this tour, you can walk between the domes and turrets, looking out over Vieux Périgueux with its old houses running down to the Isle. In rare cases, qualified students of art history or architecture are admitted to the crypt and cloisters, which date from the 9th century, although those are otherwise closed to the public. Mass is celebrated every Monday to Thursday and Saturday at 9am; Fridays at 6:30pm; and Sundays at 11am.

Église St-Etienne-de-la-Cité. 10 av. Cavaignac. ☎ **05-53-53-21-35.** Free admission. Daily 8am–7pm.

Périgueux's other remarkable church—this one in the Cité area on rue de la Cité—was a cathedral until 1669, when it lost its position to St-Front. The church was built in the 12th century but has been much damaged since. It contains a 12th-century bishop's tomb and a carved 17th-century wooden reredos depicting the Assumption of the Madonna.

Musée de Périgord. 22 cours Tourny. ☎ **05-53-06-40-70.** Admission 20 F ($3.20) adults, 10 F ($1.60) students, free for children 17 and under. Mon–Fri 10am–5pm, Sat–Sun 1–6pm.

Built on the site of an Augustinian monastery, this museum has an exceptional collection of prehistoric relics, sculptures, and Gallo-Roman mosaics. Many of the artifacts were recovered from digs in the Périgord region, which is rich in prehistoric remains.

ACCOMMODATIONS & DINING

Hôtel Bristol. 39 rue Antoine-Gadaud, 24000 Périgueux. ☎ **05-53-08-75-90.** Fax 05-53-07-00-49. E-mail: bristol.hotel@wanadoo.fr. 29 units. A/C MINIBAR TV TEL. 365–385 F ($58.40–$61.60) double. AE, MC, V. Closed Dec 23–Jan 4.

This modern three-star hotel is centrally located behind a small parking lot and offers comfortable, serviceable rooms, often with sleek styling. It's your best bet among a limited, lackluster selection. Breakfast is the only meal served, but it's only a 5-minute walk to the town's best restaurants and major points of interest. The owners have spent much of their lives in North America and offer both a French and an English welcome to all international travelers.

Biking Through the Dordogne

The Dordogne's rivers meander through countryside that's among the most verdant and historic in France. This area is relatively underpopulated, but it's dotted with monuments, feudal châteaux, 12th-century villages, and charming churches.

As you bike around, the rural character of the area will unfold before you. Unlike in more pretentious regions of France, no château-hotel or inn will treat you disdainfully if you show up on two rather than four wheels. (*Au contraire,* the staff will probably offer advice on suitable bike routes for your departure.) If you're ever in doubt about where your handlebars should lead you, know that you'll rarely go wrong if your route parallels the meandering riverbanks of the Lot, the Vézère, the Dordogne, or any of their tributaries. Architects and builders since the 11th century have appreciated their charm and added greatly to the visual allure of their watersides.

The SNCF makes it easy to transport a bike on the nation's railways and if you don't want to bring your own wheels on the train, there are plenty of rental shops throughout the region. (We recommend rentals in this chapter's sections on Périgueux, Les Eyzies-de-Tayac, and Montauban.)

Locally there are many organizations through the Dordogne that can help you with organizing bike trips. An authority on bike tours through the region is **Animation Vézère,** Base des Eyzies, Les Eyzies (☎ **05-53-06-92-92**). Two worthy competitors, each of which also arrange canoe and kayak expeditions, are **Canoé Loisin,** in the hamlet of Sailat (☎ **05-53-28-23-43**), and **Canoé Dordogne,** in the hamlet of La Roque Gageac (☎ **05-53-29-58-50**). The ultimate authority on the many bike, canoeing, and hiking expeditions throughout the region is **Le Comité Départemental du Tourism,** 25 rue du Président Wilson, 24000 Périgueux (☎ **05-53-35-50-24**), which provides information about the attractions and allure of all the towns within the *département.*

✪ **L'Oison.** In the Château des Reynats, at Chancelade, 24650 Périgueux. ☎ **05-53-03-53-59.** Fax 05-53-03-44-84. Reservations recommended. Main courses 95–200 F ($15.20–$32); fixed-price menus 140 F ($22.40) at lunch, 190–350 F ($30.40–$56) at dinner. AE, DC, MC, V. Tues–Fri noon–2pm; Tues–Sat 7:30–10pm. Closed Jan–Mar 6. FRENCH.

In 1995, the most acclaimed restaurant in Périgueux moved to the finest hotel, the 19th-century Château des Reynats. It's encircled by a manicured park. This slate-roofed manor offers an Empire dining room in which you can enjoy the cuisine du marché of the talented chef Régis Chiorozas, who can do more with fresh ingredients than anyone else in the area. In landlocked Périgueux he concentrates on seafood—and does it taste fresh! But his menu also includes traditional regional dishes, even a salad of fresh truffles that's among the most delectable we've ever sampled. In season, young partridge, roebuck, and hare are available. The desserts are sublime.

The château also rents 37 beautiful **rooms,** costing 640 F to 690 F ($102.40 to $110.40) for a double, or 800 F to 1,050 F ($128 to $168) for a suite.

PÉRIGUEUX AFTER DARK

If the weather is good, start your evening with a walk over to **place St-Silain, place St-Louis,** and **place du Marché,** where you'll most likely stumble onto a great little bar or even a bit of live impromptu music.

If you're in the mood for a beer and a *Cheers* type of atmosphere, go to the **Gordon Pub,** 12 rue Condé (☎ **05-53-35-03-74**). A regular stop for the dance-crazed youth of town is **La Régence,** 16 rue des Chancelier-de-l'Hôpital (☎ **05-53-53-10-55**), with its booming techno-rock beat and more than ample supply of pheromones. If you prefer to while the night away over drinks and good conversation, stop by **Café Le St-Louis,** place St-Louis (☎ **05-53-53-53-90**), or **Café La Rotonde,** 9 cours Montaigne (☎ **05-53-08-30-31**), or **Café de Paris,** 19 cours Montaigne (☎ **05-53-08-29-15**). You can always find a full house at **L'An des Rois,** 51 rue Aubarède (☎ **05-53-53-01-58**), the only gay and lesbian disco/bar in town. There are separate areas for men and women. The cover is 60 F ($9.60).

2 Lascaux (Montignac)

308 miles SW of Paris, 29 miles SE of Périgueux

The **Caves at Lascaux,** near the Vézère River town of Montignac in the Dordogne region, contain the most beautiful and most famous cave paintings in the world. But unless you were among the fortunate thousands who got to view the actual paintings by 1964, you're out of luck. The drawings have been closed to the general public to prevent deterioration, but a replica gives you a clear picture of the remarkable works.

They were discovered in 1940 by four boys looking for a dog and were opened to the public in 1948, quickly becoming one of France's major attractions, drawing 125,000 visitors annually. However, it became evident that the hordes of tourists had caused atmospheric changes in the caves, endangering the paintings. Scientists went to work to halt the deterioration, known as "the green sickness."

ESSENTIALS

GETTING THERE   Because of infrequent use, Montignac no longer maintains its own railway station. Rail passengers must get off at the neighboring hamlet of Condat-Le-Lardin, 6 miles to the northeast. From here, taxis (☎ **05-53-51-27-62**), which usually wait at the railway station, take visitors the remaining distance to Montignac (fare: 150 F ($24). If there are no taxis waiting, a railway station employee will call one for you. For **train information** about rail travel to Condat or anywhere else in France, call ☎ **08-36-35-35-35.**

There are no **bus connections** from Condat to Montignac. There are bus connections from Sarlat, but because they're relatively infrequent, the easiest way to reach Montignac is **driving** northeast from Eyzies on N704 for 12 miles.

VISITOR INFORMATION   The **Office de Tourisme** is on place Bertrand-de-Born (☎ **05-53-51-82-60**), in Montignac.

EXPLORING THE CAVES

Public visits to Lascaux I ceased in 1964. Permission to visit for research purposes is given only to qualified archaeologists: Apply for permission to **Direction Régionale des Affaires Culturelles (D.R.A.C.),** Service Régional de l'Archéologie, 54 cours Magendie, 33074 Bordeaux CEDEX (☎ **05-57-95-02-02**). If you want to contact the staff at the famous cave, call ☎ **05-53-51-90-29.** *Be warned:* It's not easy to get around the rigid protocol regarding visits to the interior.

Lascaux II. ☎ **05-53-51-95-03.** Admission 50 F ($8) adults, 25 F ($4) children 6–12, free for children under 6. Apr–June and Sept–Oct, daily 9am–6pm; July–Aug, daily 9am–7pm; Nov–Mar, Tues–Sun 10am–12:30pm and 1:30–5:30pm. Closed Jan 2–Feb 8.

A short walk downhill from the real caves leads to Lascaux II, an impressive reproduction of the originals, duplicated in concrete, molded above ground. The 131-foot-long reproduction displays some 200 paintings so that you'll at least have some idea of what the "Sistine Chapel of Prehistory" looks like. Here you can see majestic bulls, wild boars, stags, "Chinese horses," and lifelike deer, the originals of which were painted by Stone Age hunters 15,000 to 20,000 years ago.

Try to show up as close to opening time as possible—the number of visitors per day is limited to 2,000, and tickets are usually sold out by 2pm. During most of the year you can buy tickets directly at Lascaux II, but from April through October you must purchase them from a kiosk adjacent to the tourist office, place Bertran de Born, in Montignac. For information, call the number above.

Le Thot. 4¹/₂ miles southwest of Montignac along D706 (follow the signs pointing to the hamlet of Les Eyzies). ☎ **05-53-50-70-44.** Admission 28 F ($4.50) adults, 14 F ($2.25) children 6–12. You'll save some money by buying a combination ticket that grants access to both Lascaux II and Le Thot for 57 F ($9.10) for adults and 30 F ($4.80) for children 6–12. July–Aug, daily 9am–7pm; Sept–June, Tues–Sun 10am–12:30pm and 1:30–5:30pm. Closed Jan 2–Feb 8.

On the premises is a zoo with live animals, two projection rooms showing short films on the discovery of cave art at Lascaux, and exhibitions relating to prehistoric communities in the Dordogne. After your visit to Le Thot, walk out on the terrace for a view of the Vézère Valley and the Lascaux hills.

Site Préhistorique de Regourdou. ☎ **05-53-51-81-23.** Admission 25 F ($4) adults, 15 F ($2.40) children 8–15, free for children 7 and under. June–Aug, daily 10am–7pm; Sept–May, Sun–Thurs 10am–5pm, Sat 2–5pm.

About 500 yards uphill from the barricaded grotto of Lascaux, a narrow road branches off through a forest until it reaches this site, discovered in 1954, where a humanoid jawbone and other artifacts were found.

ACCOMMODATIONS & DINING

Château de Puy Robert. Rte. 65, 24290 Montignac Lascaux. ☎ **05-53-51-92-13.** Fax 05-53-51-80-11. www.perso.wanadoo.fr/chateau.puy.robert. E-mail: chateaupuyrobert@ wanadoo.fr. 38 units. MINIBAR TV TEL. 710–1,440 F ($113.60–$230.40) double; 1,860 F ($297.60) suite. AE, DC, MC, V. Closed Oct 25–May 1.

This mansion, set on 16 acres (about a 15-minute walk from the grottoes), was built in 1860 as a country home. It was later enlarged to include a separate house ("*le gentihommière*") that functions today as a comfortable annex. Bedrooms are handsomely furnished and comfortable. Those in the annex are more modern and contemporary-looking, whereas the 15 rooms in the original manor house have higher ceilings, thicker walls, and a more pronounced sense of nostalgia. Many offer views over the Vézère Valley. On the premises is an outdoor pool. The owners and most of the staff of this place migrate to Courchevel to operate a ski hotel in the Alps during the winter, so they're not always on their toes are at the beginning and end of this hotel's season. Expect glitches, confusion, and some absent-mindedness

Dining: The owner, Laurent Dufour, plays a active role in configuring the cuisine at the in-house restaurant, treading a delicate line between traditional and postnouvelle cuisine. Meals cost 215 F to 455 F ($34.40 to $72.80) each, depending on how elaborate they are.

Hôtel Le Relais du Soleil d'Or. 16 rue du 4-Septembre, 24290 Montignac Lascaux. ☎ **05-53-51-80-22.** Fax 05-53-50-27-54. www.soleil-dor-com. E-mail: le.relais.du.soleil. dor@wanadoo.fr. 32 units. MINIBAR TV TEL. 400–500 F ($64–$80) double; 550–800 F ($88–$128) suite. AE, DC, MC, V. Closed Jan–Feb 10.

In the heart of Montignac, this place functioned during the 1800s as a postal relay station, providing food and lodging to travelers and horses. Today, much improved, it offers traditionally furnished rooms, an outdoor pool, and a landscaped garden. Bedrooms range in size from small to medium, each fitted with a first-rate mattress.

Dining: There are two restaurants, the less formal of which, Le Bistrot, offers salads, snacks, and simple platters at around 50 F to 90 F ($8 to $14.40). The restaurant serves traditional Dordogne fare like stewed snails with garlic, and a confit of duck with a fricassée of flap mushrooms, as part of fixed-price meals costing 110 F to 275 F ($17.60 to $44). There's also a pub.

3 Les Eyzies-de-Tayac

331 miles SW of Paris, 28 miles SE of Périgueux

When prehistoric skeletons were unearthed here in 1868, the market town of Les Eyzies suddenly became an archaeologist's dream. This area in the Dordogne Valley was found to be one of the richest in the world in ancient sites and deposits. Little by little, more caves were discovered here. In some of these caves, our early ancestors made primitive drawings 30,000 years ago,. The most beautiful and most famous, of course, are at Lascaux (see above). Many caves around Les Eyzies are open to the public.

ESSENTIALS

GETTING THERE   Local **trains** run from nearby Le Buisson, 12 miles away, which has direct connections from larger cities like Bordeaux. The several daily trains from Périgueux are more direct. For train information and schedules, call ☎ 08-36-35-35-35. A **drive** to Les Eyzies-de-Tayac will be a rural route from Périgueux, starting along D710 southeast to the town of le Bugue, then following the rural road east for a short drive. Look out for the road sign leading into Les Eyzies-de-Tayac.

VISITOR INFORMATION   The **Office de Tourisme,** place de la Mairie (☎ 05-53-06-97-05), is open year-round.

EXPLORING THE AREA

If you want to pedal around the countryside, you can rent bicycles at the tourist office, beginning at 40 F ($6.40) per half day or 60 F ($9.60) per full day. A 200 F ($32) deposit is required.

Whether you're driving or biking, some of the loveliest villages to visit include towns like **Beynac-et-Cazenac** (9 miles southeast of Les Eyzies) and **Sarlat-la-Canéda** (4¹/₂ miles northeast of Beynac). Both routes follow country roads marked only with signs leading to the above-mentioned destinations.

Make a special effort to relax within the shadow of the severely foreboding **Château de Beynac,** 24220 Beynac (☎ 05-53-29-50-40), a 13th-century curiosity that opened its doors to visitors in 1998 after almost 40 years of renovation by the Grosso family. (By their own calculations, at their present pace, they estimate that renovations on their monument won't be complete until 2020.) Once it was the gathering place for the aristocracy of Périgord; today its view over the valley, coupled with its evocative sense of history, make a visit here especially worthwhile. It's open daily year-round from 10am to 6pm, with guided tours (in French and broken English) conducted at 30-minute intervals from 10am to noon and 2 to 6pm. (There are no guided tours between December and February.) Whether you participate in a guided tour or wander around alone, the visit costs 40 F ($6.80) per person. There's a worthy restaurant nearby, within the **Hôtel Bonnet** (☎ 05-53-29-50-01), which occupies the site of a converted forge and blacksmith's shop in the center of town.

Sarlat-la-Canéda, 6 miles northeast, is home of the unusual **Cathédrale St-Sacerdos** as well as the **Maison de la Boétie,** located at place André-Malraux, which belonged

---

A Tip About Cave Tickets

To prevent deterioration of the art, only a limited number of visitors are allowed into the caves of Les Eyzies-de-Tayac each day. But tickets are available up to a year in advance. If you plan on visiting these caves, call and reserve tickets as far in advance as possible.

---

to one of France's most famous Renaissance writers, Etienne de la Boétie. You might be tempted to enjoy a meal at one of the town's most endearing restaurants, the **Hostellerie Marcel,** 50 av. de Selves (☎ **05-53-59-21-98**).

Grotte de Font-de-Gaume. Less than a mile outside Les Eyzies on D47. ☎ **05-53-06-90-80.** Admission 35 F ($5.60) adults, 23 F ($3.70) ages 18–25 and over 60, free for children 17 and under. Apr–Sept, Thurs–Tues 9am–noon and 2–6pm; Oct–Mar, Thurs–Tues 10am–noon and 2–5pm. Closed holidays.

This is one of the few authentic caves still open to visitors, though access is very limited in summer. Unfortunately, some of the markings you see aren't from the Magdalenian ages, but from British students on a holiday back in the 18th century. Here depictions of bison, reindeer, and horses, along with other animals, reveal the skill of the prehistoric artists. Note that only 200 visitors per day are permitted in the caves. In midsummer, demand far exceeds the supply of tickets, and many people are shut out. Call and reserve tickets far in advance if you're coming between April and September.

Grotte des Combarelles. On D47, 10^1/$_2$ miles north of Bergerac. ☎ **05-53-06-90-80.** Admission 35 F ($5.60) adults, 23 F ($3.70) ages 18–25, free for children 17 and under. Apr–Sept, Thurs–Tues 9am–noon and 2–6pm; Oct–Mar, Thurs–Tues 10am–noon and 2–6pm. Closed holidays.

Discovered at the turn of the century, the Grotte des Combarelles has many drawings of animals, including musk oxen, horses, bison, and aurochs. Think of it as a gallery of Magdalenian art. Tickets are limited to 70 per day, but you can make reservations up to a year in advance by calling the number above.

Grotte du Grand-Roc (Cave of the Big Rock). On D47. ☎ **05-53-06-92-70.** Admission 38 F ($6.10) adults, 20 F ($3.20) children. June–Sept, daily 9:30am–7pm; Oct–May, Sun–Fri 10am–5pm. Closed Jan.

This is one of most interesting caves. Upon entering you'll come on a tunnel of stalagmites and stalactites. The cave is about a mile northwest of Les Eyzies on the left bank of the Vézère (signs point the way on D47).

Musée National de Préhistoire. ☎ **05-53-06-45-45.** Admission 22 F ($3.50) adults, 15 F ($2.40) ages 18–25, free for children 17 and under. Dec–Mar, Wed–Mon 9:30am–noon and 2–5pm; Apr–June and Sept–Nov, Wed–Mon 9:30am–noon and 2–6pm; July–Aug, daily 9:30am–7pm.

Prehistoric artifacts from local excavations are on display in this late-16th-century fortress-castle on a cliff overlooking Les Eyzies. On the terrace is a statue of a Neanderthal man. One building displays a reconstructed Magdalenian tomb containing a woman's skeleton.

ACCOMMODATIONS & DINING

Hôtel du Centre. Place de la Mairie, 24620 Les Eyzies-de-Tayac. ☎ **05-53-06-97-13.** Fax 05-53-06-91-63. 20 units. TV TEL. 280–450 F ($44.80–$72) double. CB, MC, V. Closed Nov–Jan.

Adapted during the 1980s from the premises of a very old building on the banks of the Vézère, this well-maintained hotel contains simple but cozy bedrooms. On-site there is also a family-run **restaurant** with a well-crafted cuisine. The fixed-price menus represent some of the best values in town. Priced at 120 F to 225 F ($19.20 to $36) each, they contain such dishes as an escalope of sweetbreads with *cèpes* (flap mushrooms), an *assiette gourmande* with three different preparations of foie gras, and roasted pigeon with mushrooms. During good weather, you can enjoy your meal on a shaded terrace.

✪ **Hôtel Le Centenaire.** Rocher de la Penne, 24620 Les Eyzies-Tayac-Sireuil. ☎ **05-53-06-68-68.** Fax 05-53-06-92-41. www.hotelducentenaire.fr. E-mail: hotel.centenaire@wanadoo.fr. 24 units. MINIBAR TV TEL. 700–1,050 F ($112–$168) double; 1,300–1,700 F ($208–$272) suite. AE, DC, MC, V. Closed Nov–Apr 1.

Opened in 1964, this hotel's name recognizes the 100th anniversary of the discovery of the first prehistoric cave painting in the nearby grottoes. Part of the Relais & Châteaux chain, it has undergone extensive renovations. The very comfortable bedrooms are conservatively modern, with few frills. It offers a heated pool, health club, and shopping gallery.

Dining: The talented chef, Roland Mazère, creates a light, modern French cuisine, the finest of any restaurant mentioned in this chapter. His menu might include terrine of fresh foie gras, brochette of salmon (May to September only), *noisettes d'agneau* (lamb), young hare with onion purée, and lobster with truffles. The restaurant is closed Tuesday and Wednesday at lunch. Fixed-price dinners cost 325 F to 600 F ($96), with a fixed-price lunch costing 180 F ($28.80).

Hôtel Les Glycines. Rte. de Périgueux (D47), 24620 Les Eyzies-Tayac-Sireuil. ☎ **05-53-06-97-07.** Fax 05-53-06-92-19. www.les-glycines-dordogne.com. 23 units. TEL. 398–620 F ($63.70–$99.20) double. DC, MC, V. Closed Nov to mid-Mar.

Since 1862, this establishment has offered substantial regional cuisine, comfortable accommodations, and dozens of charming touches, such as drinks served on a veranda with a grape arbor. The rooms are quaint with a regional charm. The Lombard family are the hardworking owners of this 4-acre garden inn. **Restaurant** specialties include confit de canard with truffle juice, and escalope of duck liver with lime juice. Fixed-price menus are 138 F to 280 F ($22.10 to $44.80).

4 Rocamadour

336 miles SW of Paris, 41 miles SE of Sarlat-la-Canéda, 34 miles S of Brive, 39 miles NE of Cahors

The Middle Ages seem to live on here. After all, ✪ **Rocamadour** reached the zenith of its fame and prosperity in the 13th century. Make an effort to see it even if it's out of your way. The setting is striking, one of the most unusual in Europe: Towers, old buildings, and oratories rise in stages up the side of a cliff on the right slope of the usually dry gorge of Alzou. The population has held steady at around 5,000 for many years.

The faithful continue to arrive today as they did more than 8 centuries ago. As a pilgrimage site, Rocamadour is billed as "the second site of France," with Mont-St-Michel ranking first, of course. Summer visitors descend in droves, and vehicles are prohibited. Park in one of the big lots and make your way on foot.

ESSENTIALS
GETTING THERE   The best way to reach Rocamadour is **by car.** From Bordeaux, travel east along N89 to Brive-la-Gaillarde, connecting to N205 east into Cressensac, continuing along N140 south into Rocamadour.

Rocamadour and neighboring Padirac share a **train** station that isn't really convenient to either—it's 3 miles east of Rocamadour on N140, serviced by infrequent trains from Brive in the north and Capdenac in the south. Most visitors avoid the inconvenience and drive. For train information and schedules, call ☎ **08-36-35-35-35.** The bus service in and out of town is so infrequent as to be almost nonexistent.

VISITOR INFORMATION　　The **Office de Tourisme,** in the Hôtel de Ville, rue Roland-le-Preux (☎ **05-65-33-62-59**), is open year-round except Christmas and New Year's Day.

SEEING THE TOWN

This gravity-defying village, with its single street (lined with souvenir shops), rises abruptly along the side of a steep hill. It's best seen when approached from the road coming in from the tiny village of L'Hospitalet. Once in Rocamadour, you can take a flight of steps from the lower town (Basse Ville) to the town's **Cité Religieuse,** a cluster of chapels and churches halfway up the cliff. The less agile are advised to take the elevator instead.

There's a fee of 26 F ($4.15) one-way or 38 F ($6.10) round-trip to ride both of the town's two elevators. One goes from the Basse Ville to the Cité Religieuse; the other goes from the Cité Religieuse to the panoramic medieval ramparts (*"le château"*) high above the town.

Château de Rocamadour (*"le château"*) is perched on a rock spur above the town center. You can reach it via the curvy *"chemin de la Croix."* It was originally built in the 14th century, and was restored by the local bishops in the 19th century. Today, its interior is strictly off-limits except for invited guests of the church officials who live and work here. You can, however, walk along its panoramic ramparts, which are open daily year round, from 9am to 7pm. Admission to the ramparts costs 15 F ($2.40).

The most photogenic entrance to the Basse Ville is through the **Porte de Figuier** (Fig Tree Gate), through which many of the most illustrious Europeans of the 13th century passed.

One of the oldest places of pilgrimage in France, Rocamadour became famous as a cult center of the black Madonna. It was supposedly founded by Zacchaeus, who entertained Christ at Jericho. He's claimed to have come here with a black wooden statue of the Virgin, although some authorities have suggested that this statue was carved in the 9th century.

Basilique St-Sauveur. Place St-Amadour. ☎ **05-65-33-23-23.** Daily 9am–5pm.

Against the cliff, this basilica was built in the Romanesque-Gothic style from the 11th to the 13th centuries. It's decorated with paintings and inscriptions, recalling visits of celebrated persons, including Philippe the Handsome. In the Chapelle Miraculeuse, the "holy of holies," the mysterious St. Amadour is said to have carved out an oratory in the rock. Hanging from the roof of this chapel is one of the oldest clocks known, dating back to the 8th century. Above the altar is the venerated statue of the Madonna, which Zacchaeus reportedly brought here. The Romanesque Chapelle St-Michel is sheltered by an overhanging rock; inside are two frescoes rich in coloring, dating from the 12th century. Above the door leading to the Chapelle Notre-Dame is a large iron sword that, according to legend, belonged to Roland.

Cité Religieuse. Place de la Carreta. Free admission, but donation to churches and guides appreciated. Guided tours of the chapels June–Sept 15, Mon–Sat 9am–6pm.

The entrance to the **Grand Escalier** (a stairway of 216 steps) leads up to the town's religious centerpiece. Even today, devout pilgrims make this difficult journey on their knees in penance: A recent devotee was the French composer Francis Poulenc, who remained in Rocamadour after a religious conversion he experienced here, and in honor of which he composed his *Litanies à la Vierge Noire.* Climbing its weathered steps will lead to the **Parvis des Églises,** place St-Amadour, with seven chapels.

Musée d'Art Sacré/Trésor Francis Poulenc. Parvis du Sanctuaire. ☎ **05-65-33-23-30.** Admission 28 F ($4.50) adults, 15 F ($2.40) children 10–18, free for children under 10. Jan–June and Sept–Dec, Mon–Fri 10am–noon and 2–6pm; July–Aug, daily 10am–7pm. Closed Nov–Apr.

This artistic highlight of the religious complex, which was radically enlarged and renovated in 1996, contains a gold chalice presented by the 19th-century pope, Pius II, among other treasures. There is a panoramic elevator between the different floors.

ACCOMMODATIONS & DINING

Hôtel Beau-Site et Le Jehan de Valon. Cité Médiévale, 46500 Rocamadour. ☎ **800/ 528-1234** in the U.S., or 05-65-33-63-08. Fax 05-65-33-65-23. www.bw-beausite.com. E-mail: beausite.rocamadour@wanadoo.fr. 43 units. TV TEL. 385–495 F ($61.60–$79.20) double; 555–695 F ($88.80–$111.20) suite. AE, DC, MC, V. Closed Nov 12–Feb 12.

The stone walls here were built in the 15th century by an Order of Malta commander. Today the rear terrace provides a sweeping view of the Val d'Alzou. The reception area has heavy beams and a cavernous fireplace big enough to roast an ox. The rooms (in the main building and a less desirable annex) are comfortable; 23 are air-conditioned.

Dining: The restaurant serves flavorful regional cuisine prepared by the Menot family, who've owned the place for generations. Specialties include foie gras of duck with dark truffles, duckmeat salad, raw marinated salmon with green peppercorns, and a cake of caramelized walnuts. Fixed-price menus run 115 F to 290 F ($18.40 to $46.40).

Hôtel Domaine de La Rhue. 46500 Rocamadour. ☎ **05-65-33-71-50.** Fax 05-65-33-72-48. www.rocamadour.com/us/hotels/LaRhue/index.htm. E-mail: domainedelarhue@ rocamadour.com. 14 units. TEL. 380–580 F ($60.80–$92.80) double. DC, MC, V. Closed Nov–Easter. Follow route D673, then N140 signposted Rhue for a total of $3^1/_4$ miles from town.

The three-star Domaine de La Rhue, a renovated 19th-century stable, is between the Dordogne and Quercy. The charming owners, Christine and Eric Jooris, gutted the old stable and turned it into a series of handsome and spacious bedrooms, each individually decorated in superb taste. Some even have TVs, minibars, and terraces. On the lower level there's an inviting reception and breakfast with a huge, very warm and welcoming fireplace. There is also a swimming pool outside. The Joorises, who speak English, are most helpful in directing you to the best places for dinner in the center of Rocamadour, which is only a few minutes' drive away. Christine enjoys mapping out perfect tours of the nearby villages and plotting the best direction from which to approach each town and/or castle so as to have a commanding view from the distance and to take advantage of afternoon sun for photographs. Eric is a pilot and takes clients for a 45-minute-long hot air balloon ride over the canyon of Rocamadour for 800 F ($128).

NEARBY ACCOMMODATIONS & DINING

Château de Roumégouse. N140, Rignac, 46500 Gramat. ☎ **05-65-33-63-81.** Fax 05-65-33-71-18. www.integra.fr/relaischateaux.fr/roumegouse. E-mail: roumegouse@ relaischateaux.fr. 15 units. A/C MINIBAR TV TEL. 690–1,060 F ($110.40–$169.60) double; 1,220–1,420 F ($195.20–$227.20) suite. AE, DC, MC, V. Closed Nov–Apr 20. Take N140 to Roumégouse, 4 miles southeast of Rocamadour.

If you prefer to be away from the tourist bustle, try this Relais & Châteaux in Roumégouse. The 15th-century château overlooking the Causse is surrounded by 12 acres of parkland. Each room is unique in both decor and architecture and is fitted with antique furniture and paintings.

Dining: In the lovely dining room, fixed-price menus cost 190 F to 360 F ($30.40 to $57.60). Even the scrambled eggs come with truffles! It's closed Tuesday at dinner except in July and August, and it's closed altogether from December to Easter.

5 Cahors

336 miles SW of Paris, 135 miles SE of Bordeaux, 55 miles N of Toulouse

The ancient capital of Quercy, Cahors was a thriving university city in the Middle Ages, and many antiquities from its illustrious past life remain. However, Cahors is best known today for the almost-legendary red wine that's made principally from the Malbec grapes grown in vineyards around this old city in central France. Firm but not harsh, Cahors is one of the most deeply colored fine French wines.

ESSENTIALS
GETTING THERE   The **drive** to Cahors is a simple one from Toulouse. Follow A62 north to its junction with N20, continuing along N20 north into Cahors.

Cahors is serviced by **train** from Toulouse, Brive, and Montauban. You may have to transfer in neighboring towns. For train information and schedules, call ☎ **08-36-35-35-35.** There's infrequent bus service from some of the outlying villages, several of which are of historic interest, but it's vastly easier to drive.

VISITOR INFORMATION   The **Office de Tourisme** is on place François-Mitterrand (☎ **05-65-53-20-65**).

SPECIAL EVENTS   The **Festival de Blues** turns this town upside down for 3 days in mid-July when famous blues groups, including some from the United States, descend on different venues around Cahors. Tickets range from 80 F to 200 F ($12.80 to $32), and exact dates and performing artists can be obtained from the Office de Tourisme (see above). For tickets, contact **Mme Nicola Tertre,** 349 rue Wilson, 46000 Cahors (☎ **05-65-35-22-29**).

EXPLORING THE AREA
The town is on a rocky peninsula almost entirely surrounded by a loop of the Lot River. It grew up near a sacred spring that still supplies the city with water. At the source of the spring, the **Fontaine des Chartreux** stands by the side of the **pont Valentré** (also called the pont du Diable), a bridge with a trio of towers. It's a magnificent example of medieval defensive design erected between 1308 and 1380. It was restored in the 19th century. The pont, the first medieval fortified bridge in France, is the most colorful site in Cahors, with crenellated parapets, battlements, and seven pointed arches.

Dominating the old town, the **Cathédrale St-Etienne,** 30 rue de la Chanterie (☎ **05-65-35-27-80**), was begun in 1119 and reconstructed between 1285 and 1500. It was the first cathedral in the country to have cupolas, giving it a Romanesque-Byzantine look. One remarkable feature is its finely sculptured Romanesque north portal, carved about 1135 in the Languedoc style. It's open daily from 8am (scheduled hour for daily mass) to 6 or 7pm, depending on the season. Adjoining the cathedral are the remains of a Gothic cloister from the late 15th century.

Cahors for Wine Lovers

Woven into the fabric of Cahors's heritage is a rich tradition of wine making. The wines of Cahors are characterized by a heady robustness that mellows over time. Two wineries of exceptional merit are Jean Jouffreau's **Clos de Gamot** in Prayssac, about 20 minutes west of Cahors (☎ **05-65-22-40-26**), and **Château de Gaudou** in Vire-sur-Lot (☎ **05-65-36-52-93**). Their dark wines are of consistently high quality and easily hold their own with any of the region's rich, hearty dishes. The Office de Tourisme (see above) provides detailed information and maps to these wineries.

SIDE TRIPS Cahors is a starting point for an excursion to the **Célé and Lot valleys,** a long journey that many French are fond of taking in summer, a round-trip of about 125 miles. If you have time for sightseeing, the trip should last 2 days. The Office de Tourisme (see above) provides maps that offer itineraries.

The **Grotte du Pech-Merle** (☎ **05-65-31-27-05**), a prehistoric cave near Cabrerets, 21 miles east of Cahors (take D653), was once used for ancient religious rites. The wall paintings, footprints, and carvings were discovered in 1922 and are approximately 20,000 years old. The cave may be explored only from April to October, daily from 9:30am to noon and 1:30 to 5pm. Admission is 44 F ($7.05) for adults and 30 F ($4.80) for children. There are 2 miles of chambers and galleries open to the public, especially interesting for those familiar with geology. The Aurignacian- and Magdalenian-age art includes drawings of mammoths, bison, aurochs, horses, deer, mountain goats, and women.

ACCOMMODATIONS

Hôtel de France. 252 av. Jean-Jaurès, 46000 Cahors. ☎ **05-65-35-16-76.** Fax 05-65-22-01-08. E-mail: hdf46@crdi.fr. 79 units. MINIBAR TV TEL. 365 F ($58.40) double. AE, DC, MC, V. Closed Dec 20–Jan 5. Parking 40 F ($6.40).

This hotel, between pont Valentré and the train station, provides the best rooms in the town center. They're well furnished and modern in design; 40 of them have air-conditioning. The room service is efficient, but breakfast is the only meal served.

Hôtel Terminus. 5 av. Charles-de-Freycinet, 46000 Cahors. ☎ **05-65-53-32-00.** Fax 05-65-53-32-26. E-mail: terminus.bouandie@wanadoo.fr. 22 units. MINIBAR TV TEL. 550–1,100 F ($88–$176) double. AE, DC, MC, V. Free parking in open courtyard, 45 F ($7.20) in covered garage.

On the avenue leading from the railway station into the heart of town, this hotel still oozes with the turn-of-the-century character of its original stone construction. The rooms are conservative, yet tastefully decorated with lots of floral prints, fresh flowers, and firm comfortable mattresses. The staff is extraordinarily warm and helpful.

On the premises is **Le Balandre,** which was awarded a Michelin star last year. Even if you don't opt for a meal in its art deco dining room or on its outdoor terrace, you might want to step into its 1920s-style bar for a drink.

DINING

The **Hôtel Terminus** restaurant, Le Balandre (see "Accommodations," above), has won a Michelin star. Popular with a young crowd is **Les Terrasses Valentré** (☎ **05-65-35-95-88**), a block to the left of pont Valentré. Here you can order a beer, meet some locals, and take in one of the best river views in town, especially of the flamboyant bridge.

La Taverne. Place Escorbiac. ☎ **05-65-35-28-66.** Reservations recommended. Main courses 70–110 F ($11.20–$17.60); fixed-price menus 75–149 F ($12–$23.85). V. Daily noon–2pm and 7–9:30pm. Closed Feb; winter, closed Sat–Sun. FRENCH.

This restaurant serves outstanding local cuisine in a rustic atmosphere. The finely crafted cuisine of Quercy is featured here, along with other regional specialties. Typical dishes are truffles in puff pastry, tournedos with foie gras and truffles, duck fillet, breast of chicken with morels, and fresh fish.

6 Montauban

404 miles SW of Paris, 45 miles NW of Albi, 31 miles N of Toulouse

This pink-brick capital of the Tarn-et-Garonne is the city of the painter Ingres and the sculptor Bourdelle. Montauban, on the right bank of the Tarn, is one of the most ancient of southwest France's towns, still dominated by the fortified Église St-Jacques. The most scenic view of Montauban is at the 14th-century brick bridge, pont Vieux, which connects the town to its satellite of Villebourbon.

Jean-Auguste-Dominique Ingres, an admirer of Raphael and a student of David, was born in 1780 in Montauban. His father, an ornamental sculptor/painter, recognized his son's artistic abilities early and encouraged him. He was noted for his nudes and historical paintings, now fine examples of neoclassicism. One of his first exhibitions of portraits in 1806 met with ridicule, but later generations have been more appreciative. His work is displayed in town at the **Cathédrale Notre-Dame** and the **Musée Ingres** (see below).

ESSENTIALS

GETTING THERE   If you're **driving,** R.N. 20 (Paris-Toulouse-Andorra, Spain), R.N. 113 (Bordeaux-Marseille), and the A61 motorway run through the Tarn-et-Garonne.

Seven **trains** arrive here daily from Paris (trip time: 4½ to 6 hours); trains arrive every hour from Toulouse (trip time: 25 minutes). For train information and schedules, call ☎ **08-36-35-35-35.** For **bus** information contact the Gare Routière (☎ **05-63-93-34-34**).

VISITOR INFORMATION   The **Office de Tourisme** is on 4 rue du Collège (☎ **05-63-63-60-60**).

SPECIAL EVENTS   The two major festivals that take place in Montauban occur in June and the end of July. The Festival Alors Chante in June showcases French music and song and offers performances by some of the biggest French stars. From July 17 to 26 the Festival de Jazz fills the outdoor venues with blues and jazz concerts, including the wildly popular Baltimore Baptist Church Choir. The Office de Tourisme has information on both events, or contact Synergie (☎ **05-63-20-46-72**) for specifics on the Festival de Jazz.

EXPLORING THE AREA

You can rent bicycles at **Denayrolles,** 878 av. Jean-Moulin (☎ **05-63-03-62-02**), open Monday from 2 to 7pm and Tuesday to Saturday from 8:15am to noon and 2 to 7pm. A credit card or cash deposit of 1,500 F ($240) is required.

Shoppers may want to pick up some foie gras and other goose products at the **Conserverie Artisanale Larroque,** 1300 av. de Falguières (☎ **05-63-63-45-40**). Or visit a pâtisserie for a supply of Montauriol (a chocolate-covered cherry with a shot of Armagnac) and Boulet de Montauban (a chocolate-covered roasted hazelnut). For a collectible specialty of the town, go to the **Librairie Deloche,** 21 rue de la Résistance (☎ 05-63-63-22-66), where you can buy a *pigeonnier miniature*—miniature models of pigeon coops that were built on local farms to attract pigeons for their "fertilizer." Deloche carries 30 models of various architectural styles and a selection of books on pigeonniers.

In addition to taking in the Ingres masterpieces in the museum listed below, head for the **Cathédrale Notre-Dame,** place Roosevelt, a classical building framed by two square towers. In the north transept is the painting the church commissioned from Ingres, *Vow of Louis XIII.* It's open daily from 9am to noon and 2 to 6pm.

✪ **Musée Ingres.** 19 rue de l'Hôtel-de-Ville. ☎ 05-63-22-12-91. Admission 20 F ($3.20) adults, free children under 18. July–Aug, daily 9:30am–noon and 1:30–6pm; Sept–June, Tues–Sun 10am–noon and 2–6pm.

Upon his 1867 death the artist bequeathed to Montauban more than two dozen paintings and some 4,000 drawings (more than any other museum except the Louvre in Paris). They're displayed at this 17th-century bishops' palace. One painting in the collection is *Christ and the Doctors,* a work Ingres completed at 82. The *Dream of Ossian* was intended for Napoléon's bedroom in Rome. On the ground floor are works by Antoine Bourdelle, who was heavily influenced by Rodin. The two busts Bourdelle sculpted of Ingres and of Rodin are particularly outstanding.

ACCOMMODATIONS

The **Hôtel Orsay** (see below) also rents rooms.

Hostellerie Les Coulandrières. Rte. de Castelsarrasin, 82290 Montbeton, near Montauban. ☎ 05-63-67-47-47. Fax 05-63-67-46-45. 22 units. TV TEL. 460–490 F ($73.60–$78.40) double. Half board 370–400 F ($59.20–$64) per person extra. AE, DC, MC, V. Free parking.

This inn, 2 miles northwest of Montauban's center in the village of Montbeton, occupies the site of an old farm. The original buildings house the reception area, bar, and restaurant. Set in a 10-acre park, it offers pleasant, traditionally furnished bedrooms in a nearby annex built around 1975. Facilities include a pool and miniature-golf course. The inn also makes an excellent **dining** choice, as first-class ingredients are deftly handled by the chefs. In summer, grills are a specialty.

✪ **Hôtel Mercure Montauban.** 12 rue Notre-Dame, 82000 Montauban. ☎ 05-63-63-17-23. Fax 05-63-66-43-66. 44 units. A/C TV TEL. 530 F ($84.80) double. AE, DC, MC, V. Parking 25 F ($4).

One of the most dramatic hotel renovations in the district occurred in 1999, when the Mercure chain gutted and rebuilt this formerly decrepit two-star hotel near the cathedral—at a cost of more than $3.5 million. Today, it's the most appealing modern hotel in town, with four floors of relatively large bedrooms, each with comfortable mattresses, streamlined furniture, and a color scheme of terra-cotta and ochre that's inspired by the landscapes around Montauban. The restaurant, **La Brasserie Bourdelle,** named after a local sculptor, serves fixed-price menus that range in price from 85 F to 210 F ($13.60 to $33.60). It's open daily for both lunch and dinner.

DINING

The two accommodations recommended above also have decent restaurants.

Hôtel Orsay et Restaurant La Cuisine d'Alain. Face Gare (across from the train station). ☎ 05-63-66-06-66. Fax 05-63-66-19-39. Reservations recommended. Main courses 95–140 F ($15.20–$22.40); fixed-price menus 130–280 F ($20.80–$44.80). AE, DC, MC, V. Tues–Sat 12:30–2pm; Mon–Sat 7:30–9:30pm. Closed Dec 23–Jan 6, a week in May, and the 2nd and 3rd weeks in Aug. FRENCH.

This is the best restaurant in town, as chef Alain Blanc is talented and inventive. Try his terrine of lentils flavored with the neck of a fattened goose en confit, filet of beef with liver and apple flan, or escalope of foie gras *poêlée*. The amazing dessert trolley offers plenty of choices.

Twenty reasonably priced **rooms** also are available in the Hôtel Orsay. Built a century ago, and renovated in frequent stages by the hardworking staff ever since, the Hôtel Orsay has well-decorated but unpretentious bedrooms. Doubles run from 250 F to 350 F ($40 to $56).

MONTAUBAN AFTER DARK

Our favorite nightspot here is **La Santa Maria,** quai Montmurat (☎ **05-63-91-99-09**), close to the Musée d'Ingres. It's a bar loaded with ambience. Theme nights include salsa, merengue, rock, and retro disco. The place gets lively after 9:30pm. Less stylish is **Bar Le Flamand,** 8 rue de la République, near the cathedral (☎ **05-63-66-12-20**), with an easygoing crowd and a broad roster of Belgian beers. If you're under 25 and want to party with your contemporaries, head for **Le Doppler,** 13 av. Jean-Jaurès, adjacent to the rail station (☎ **05-63-03-07-45**).

The Massif Central 20

In your race south to Biarritz or through the Rhône Valley to the Riviera, you'll pass through the Massif Central, the rugged agricultural heartland of France. Here you'll find ancient cities, lovely valleys, and a wonderful provincial cuisine. With its rolling farmland, isolated countryside, and châteaux and manor houses (in many of which you can stay and dine), this is one of the most unspoiled parts of France—your chance to see a life all too rapidly fading.

From the spa at Vichy to the volcanic *puys* of the Auvergne, there's much of interest here and much to learn about the art of good living. We begin in George Sand country in the old province of Berry, then proceed to the Auvergne and west to Limousin.

REGIONAL CUISINE   Fans of this region's cuisine often praise it for its simple honesty and adherence to tradition; its critics claim that it lacks finesse and creativity. Everyone, however, agrees that this is a rural, family-inspired cuisine, based on generous quantities of fresh ingredients and few pretensions.

Characteristic dishes include soup (*une potée*) made with cabbage and about a dozen other ingredients (usually including both fresh and salted pork), and stuffed sheep's foot cooked inside a sheep's stomach. The region's cheeses include enormous wheels known as Cantal, bleu d'Auvergne, St-Nectaire, and a goats'-milk cheese called *le cabecou,* which appears on cheese trays in grand restaurants throughout France. The Massif Central is famous for its desserts, including cherry tarts (sometimes with the cherry pits still in place) and many exceptional pastries.

The climate and soil aren't conducive to grape growing, so most regional wines just pass as straightforward table wine. The best local spirits are several types of distilled alcohol traditionally served after meals. These are usually distilled from the fermented essence of flowers and herbs that include strawberries, raspberries, blossoms from the linden tree, myrtle, and a mountain flower called *gentiane.*

1 Bourges

148 miles S of Paris, 43 miles NW of Nevers, 95 miles NW of Vichy, 175 miles NW of Lyon

Once the capital of Aquitaine, Bourges lies in the heart of France; you can easily tie in a visit here from Orléans at the eastern end of the Loire

Valley. The commercial/industrial center of Berry, this regional capital is still off the beaten path for most tourists, even though it boasts a rich medieval past still in evidence today. Its history goes back far beyond the Middle Ages: In 52 B.C. Caesar called it the finest city in Gaul. Today Bourges remains a rather sleepy provincial town, awakened only by the life surrounding the Institut Universitaire de Technologie.

ESSENTIALS

GETTING THERE   There are good road and rail connections from Tours and other regional cities. Four **trains** arrive daily from Paris (trip time: 2¹/₂ hours); sometimes a transfer is required at nearby Vierzon. Eight trains a day arrive from Tours, taking 1¹/₂ hours. For information and schedules, call ☎ **08-36-35-35-39.**

If you're **driving,** from Paris, take A10 south to Orléans, then route 20 to Vierzon, where you pick up Route 76 east into Bourges. From Tours, head east along Route 76.

VISITOR INFORMATION   The **Office de Tourisme** is at 21 rue Victor-Hugo (☎ **02-48-23-02-60**).

SPECIAL EVENTS   The energy level really picks up between April and August, thanks to several colorful music festivals. The **Festival Printemps de Bourges** jumpstarts the season for a week in April with its dozens of concerts ranging from traditional French to international rock. Most events cost between 30 F and 170 F ($5.10 and $28.90), though any number of seemingly spontaneous performances always pop up along the sidewalks for everyone to enjoy at no charge. For tickets and more information, contact the **Association Printemps de Bourges,** 22 rue Henri-Sellier (☎ **02-48-70-61-11**). At the beginning of June, a younger, more free-form and high-impact music scene explodes during the **Festival International des Groupes de Musique Experimentale de Bourges,** during which groups such as U2 have appeared. For information, call ☎ **02-48-20-41-87. Un Été à Bourges** kicks off yearly in late June, and runs until mid-September. During this time, the streets are once again filled with musical performers and actors. More structured performances also take place, with tickets ranging from 30 F to 200 F ($4.80 to $32). The Office de Tourisme (see above) has complete details on all festivals.

SEEING THE SIGHTS

✪ Cathédrale St-Etienne. Place Etienne-Dolet. ☎ **02-48-65-72-89.** Cathedral, free admission; tower and crypt, 32 F ($5.10) adults, 21 F ($3.35) ages 18–25, free for children under 17. Combination ticket to both cathedral and Palais Jacques-Coeur 50 F ($8) for everyone. Cathedral, Apr–Sept, daily 9am–6pm, Oct–Mar, daily 9am–4pm; crypt cannot be visited Sun 8am–1pm during mass.

On the summit of a hill dominating the town, this is one of the largest and most beautiful Gothic cathedrals in France. Its construction began at the end of the 12th century and wasn't completed until a century and a half later; subsequent additions have been made. Flanked by asymmetrical towers, it has five magnificent doorways, including one depicting episodes in the life of St. Stephen. The cathedral has a high vaulted roof and five aisles and is remarkably long (407 feet deep); it's distinguished for its stained-glass windows, best viewed with binoculars. Many of these rich blue and deep ruby red windows were made between 1215 and 1225. One particularly impressive scene, *A Meal in the House of Simon,* is vividly colored, showing Jesus lecturing Simon on the forgiveness of sins as Mary Magdalene repents at his feet.

To climb the north tower for a view of the cathedral and Bourges, you must buy a ticket from the custodian. The same ticket allows you to explore the church's 12th-century crypt, the largest in France. In the crypt rests the tomb (built between 1422

The Massif Central

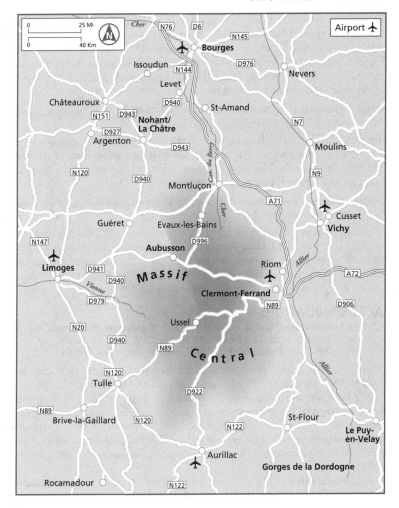

and 1438) of Jean de Berry, who ruled this duchy in the 14th century. Fanatically dedicated to art, he directed a "small army" of artisans, painters, and sculptors. The recumbent figure is the only part of the original tomb that has survived.

After your visit, you may want to wander through the **Jardins de l'Archevêché,** the archbishop's gardens, credited to Le Nôtre. From these gardens you'll have a good view of the eastern side of the cathedral.

Palais Jacques-Coeur. Rue Jacques-Coeur. ☎ **02-48-24-06-87.** Admission 32 F ($5.10) adults, 21 F ($3.35) ages 18–24 and over 60, free for children 17 and under. Combination ticket to cathedral and Palais Jacques-Coeur 50 F ($8) for everyone. The palace can be seen only on a 60-min. guided tour in French (English-speakers receive a printed English-language text of the commentary). Tours daily at 9, 10, and 11am and 2, 3, and 4pm; Apr–Oct, additional tour 5pm; July–Aug, additional tour 6pm.

This is one of the country's greatest secular Gothic structures. Take a guided tour through the four buildings around a central court, constructed around 1450 by the finance minister/banker Jacques Coeur, who had amassed a fortune. Monsieur Coeur never got to enjoy the palace, however. After a trial by a jury of his creditors, he was tossed into prison by Charles VII and died there in 1456. His original furnishings no longer remain, but the decor and wealth of detail inside the palace form a remarkable view of 15th-century opulence. In the dining hall is a monumental chimneypiece, and in the great hall are sculptures from the 15th and 16th centuries.

Hôtel Lallemant. 6 rue Bourbonnoux. ☎ **02-48-57-81-17.** Free admission. Tues–Sat 10am–noon and 2–6pm, Sun 2–6pm.

The Renaissance Hôtel Lallemant, north of the cathedral, has been transformed into a museum of decorative art. The mansion was built for a textile merchant; today its galleries display a colorful history of Bourges. Exhibits include china, objets d'art, ceramics, and a large display of antique furniture.

Musée du Berry. 4 rue des Arènes. ☎ **02-48-70-41-92.** Free admission. Mon and Wed–Sat 10am–noon and 2–6pm, Sun 2–6pm.

The museum is inside the elegant Hôtel Cujas, built about 1515. On display is a large collection of Celtic and Gallo-Roman artifacts; especially impressive are the 280 funerary sculptures. Some rooms are devoted to finds from Egyptian archaeological digs, along with medieval masterpieces of sculpture dating from around 1400, and some rooms on the second floor have ethnological exhibitions.

ACCOMMODATIONS

✪ **Hôtel de Bourbon/Grand Hôtel Mercure et Restaurant St-Ambroix.** Bd. de la République, 18000 Bourges. ☎ **02-48-70-70-00.** Fax 02-48-70-21-22. 59 units. A/C TV TEL. 550–750 F ($88–$120) double; 990 F ($158.40) suite. AE, DC, V. Free parking.

This is the finest hotel in Bourges, and its cuisine is the best in the entire area. In the early 1990s the Mercure chain (a budget-conscious outfit not normally known for salvaging historic properties) converted a ruined 17th-century abbey into this first-class hotel. The cheerful rooms are comfortable (except for the half-timbered sloping rooms beneath the mansard roof on the third floor, which are short on style). Despite this, the venerable stonework of the exterior and the dignified public areas are quite beautiful. The setting is convenient for train travelers, as it lies almost adjacent to the town's railway station.

The refined **cuisine** of Pascal Auger is a draw even for locals. Under a vaulted ceiling of a former Renaissance chapel, you can select delectable main courses—perhaps baked saddle of lamb (pink and juicy) or *escalope de foie gras de canard* (duckling). The *noix de ris de veau braisée* (sweetbreads) is among the finest you're likely to sample anywhere. The menu changes four times a year but invariably offers a *crottin de chavignol* made from local goat cheese, and a local almond-flavored bonbon, *des forestines*. Fixed-price menus range from 150 F to 380 F ($24 to $60.80), and are served daily at lunch and dinner.

Le Christina. 5 rue de la Halle, 18000 Bourges. ☎ **02-48-70-56-50.** Fax 02-48-70-58-13. 71 units. TV TEL. 259–399 F ($41.45–$63.85) double. AE, DC, MC, V. Parking 30 F ($4.80).

This is a simple but comfortable two-star inn, built in the 1930s and renovated many times since. It rises three and five stories (depending on which part of the hotel you're in). The location, a few steps from the cathedral and the Palais Jacques-Coeur, is especially convenient. Breakfast is the only meal served, but there are several simple brasseries within walking distance.

DINING

Jacques-Coeur. 3 place Jacques-Coeur. ☎ **02-48-70-12-72.** Reservations required. Main courses 65–135 F ($10.40–$21.60); fixed-price menus 145–180 F ($23.20–$28.80). AE, DC, MC, V. Sun–Fri noon–2:15pm; Mon–Fri 7:15–9:15pm. Closed July 23–Aug 23 and Dec 24–Jan 2. FRENCH.

François Bernard serves tasty traditional bourgeois cuisine amid a medieval Gothic decor, though the food at Bourbon et Restaurant St-Ambroix (see "Accommodations," above) is better. Specialties here include veal kidneys *berrichonne,* frogs' legs sautéed with herbs, *scallops à la façon* (with a *concasse* of tomatoes, snail-flavored butter, and *beignets* of onion), and chicken *en barbouille* (with a sauce made of wine and blood). The desserts are all homemade and tempting, and service is politely efficient. The featured wines from a balanced list include Quincy and Menetou-Salon, two excellent but not very well-known vintages from the region. And while the competition for the dining franc in this town has heated up considerably in recent years, this place continues rather smugly doing what it's always done: Serve fresh, classical cuisine. Of the two dining rooms, the one on the upper floor is more interesting, with exposed beams and plaster impressions of scallop shells on its circa 1947 ceiling.

BOURGES AFTER DARK

In general, most of the best clubs are in Bourges's old town. For the crème de la crème of your good old-fashioned drinking establishments, try **Le Pub Birdland,** 4 av. Jean-Jaurès (☎ **02-48-70-66-77**), with its wood interior, young crowd of heavy-duty beer drinkers, and jazz and rock. **Beau Bar,** rue des Beaux-Arts (☎ **02-48-24-40-49**), pulls in a very bohemian crowd—artists, poets, songwriters, and the like—whereas the most popular bar in town, **La Comédie,** 10 place Mirepied (☎ **02-48-65-95-85**), has no problem packing its below-street-level vaulted dance floor with young hot bodies. A 50 F ($8) cover charge is sometimes imposed.

For something a little different, head over to **La Soupe aux Choux,** which is part of the restaurant "Le Guillotin," place Gordaine (☎ **02-48-65-43-66**), where you can take in an evening of cafe-théâtre. Shows can be anything from musical performances to stand-up comics; ticket prices run around 70 F ($11.20).

2 Nohant/La Châtre

180 miles S of Paris, 19 miles S of Châteauroux

George Sand was the pen name of Amandine Lucile Aurore Dupin, baronne Dudevant, the French novelist born in 1804. Her memory is forever connected to this little Berry hamlet near the Indre Valley.

In her early life she wrote bucolic tales of peasants, but she also penned romantic novels in which she maintained that women were entitled to as much freedom as men. Among her 80 novels, some of the best known were *François le Champi* and *La Mare au Diable.* She was also known for her love affairs, of which her two most notorious were with the poet Alfred de Musset, who journeyed with her to Venice, and with the composer Frédéric Chopin, with whom she traveled to Majorca. By the time of her death in Nohant in 1876, George Sand had become a legend.

ESSENTIALS

GETTING THERE   If you're **driving,** it's a 1-hour trip from Bourges to La Châtre via D940 south. The closest **train** station is in Châteauroux, with a connecting bus to Nohant/La Châtre. From Bourges, you can buy a combination train/bus ticket to

La Châtre via Châteauroux. Five daily trains make the run to Châteauroux, where you'll then transfer to a bus to complete the 2¹/₂-hour trip. For complete train information, call ☎ **08-36-35-35-35.**

VISITOR INFORMATION The nearest **Office de Tourisme** is on square George-Sand (☎ **02-54-48-22-64**) in La Châtre, open daily year-round.

IN THE FOOTSTEPS OF GEORGE SAND

La Maison de George Sand. 36400 Nohant-Vic. ☎ **02-54-31-06-04.** Visits only with a 45-minute guided tour in French (non-French speakers can follow the lecture with a printed text) for 32 F ($5.10) adults, free for children 17 and under. Tours depart at regular intervals according to the number of people waiting and/or the day's schedule, every day 10:30–11:15am and 2:30–3:30pm.

It was at the Château de Nohant, known today as La Maison de George Sand, that the famous novelist learned the ways and thoughts of the peasants. During her time here, she entertained some of the intellectual and artistic elite of Europe—Flaubert, Balzac, Delacroix, Liszt, and Gautier. The building, which its guides prefer to define as a large but not imperial-looking *maison bourgeoise,* set in its own 7-acre park, was constructed of stone in 1763 and purchased in 1793 by the family of George Sand. Today it houses the mementos of Sand and her admirers and friends, with ample testimonials to the literary conceits and eccentricities of one of France's most enduringly famous female writers. You can see the boudoir where she wrote *Indiana,* the popular novel published when she was 28. You can also visit her private bedchamber/study. At Nohant, George Sand staged theatricals, dramatizing several of her novels—not very successfully, according to reports. Today, *fêtes romantiques de Nohant* are sometimes staged, with an impressive list of musical performers.

ACCOMMODATIONS & DINING

Auberge de la Petite Fadette. Nohant-Vic, 36400 La Châtre. ☎ **02-54-31-01-48.** Fax 02-54-31-10-19. 10 units. TV TEL. 300–600 F ($48–$96) double. AE, MC, V.

This compound of 19th-century ivy-covered buildings abuts a château and is the focal point for one of the smallest villages in the region. Since 1890, the compound has been owned by four generations of the Chapleau family; it was renovated in 1995. A scattering of antiques decorates the interior. Bedrooms are cozy and comfortable, although a bit small.

Dining: The dining room serves fixed-price menus, ranging in price from 85 F to 230 F ($13.60 to $36.80), throughout the year.

✪ **Château de la Vallée Bleue.** Rte. de Verneuil, St-Chartier, 36400 La Châtre. ☎ **02-54-31-01-91.** Fax 02-54-31-04-48. 15 units. MINIBAR TV TEL. 390–645 F ($62.40–$103.20) double. MC, V.

This small and charming château was built in 1840 by Dr. Pestel so that he could be close to his patient, George Sand. It's now a hotel/restaurant owned by Gérard Gasquet. The rooms have been named after the doctor's former guests, including Musset, Delacroix, Flaubert, Chopin, and Liszt. Each has dignified, sometimes antique furniture. There's also a 10-acre wooded park and a pool.

Dining: The excellent regional specialties are characterized as cuisine *actuelle,* with an accent on presentation; they include goat cheese and carp with lentils, and chicken à la George Sand (with crayfish sauce). For dessert, try a delectable pear baked in pastry. Fixed-price menus cost 100 F to 295 F ($16 to $47.20) at lunch, and 150 F to 295 F ($24 to $47.20) at dinner; nonguests should call for a reservation. The restaurant is open Wednesday to Sunday from early March to mid-November; it's closed completely from mid-November to early March.

3 Vichy

216 miles S of Paris, 33 miles NE of Clermont-Ferrand, 108 miles NW of Lyon

This world-renowned spa on the northern edge of the Auvergne, in the heart of Bourbon country, is noted for its sparkling waters (said to alleviate liver and stomach ailments). It looks much as it did a century ago, when princes and industrial barons filled its rococo casino. (The casino you'll visit today isn't the one that thrived during the spa's 19th-century heyday. That edifice, at 5 rue du Casino, now functions as a convention hall. Within its premises, Diaghilev produced his first ballet and Strauss directed *Salomé*.)

Since 1861, when Napoléon III was a frequent visitor, much has been done to add to the spa's fame. During the 1980s, the hotels and baths of Vichy underwent a modernization program to keep up with the times and other baths of France, much to the pleasure of their clients and their ever-changing tastes.

The city's current reputation for health and relaxation has been aided greatly by the Perrier craze that has swept most of the world. The Perrier Company has a contract to bottle Vichy water for sale elsewhere and also runs the city's major attractions. Vichy is a sports and recreation center, boasting a casino, theaters, regattas, horse racing, and golf. A promenade with covered walks, the **Parc des Sources** is the center of Vichy's fashionable life, which is at its peak from May to the end of September.

ESSENTIALS

GETTING THERE   Vichy lies on the heavily traveled Paris-Clermont-Ferrand rail line. Some 20 **trains** per day arrive from Clermont-Ferrand (trip time: 30 minutes); 10 trains per day arrive from Paris (trip time: 3 hours). For train information and schedules, call ☎ **08-36-35-35-35. Bus** service into town is possible, although it's usually not as convenient or well-orchestrated as the train. Gare Routière (☎ **04-70-98-41-33**) lies adjacent to the railway station.

If you're **driving** to Vichy from Paris, take A10 south to Orléans, then connect to A71 south. At the Gannat/Vichy exit, follow N209 east to Vichy.

VISITOR INFORMATION   The **Office de Tourisme** is at 19 rue du Parc (☎ **04-70-98-71-94**).

ACCOMMODATIONS

Aletti Palace Hôtel. 3 place Joseph-Aletti, 03200 Vichy. ☎ **800/528-1234** in the U.S., or 04-70-31-78-77. Fax 04-70-98-13-82. 133 units. TV TEL. 650–840 F ($104 to $134.40) double; 950–1,100 F ($152–$176) suite. AE, DC, MC, V.

This turn-of-the-century hotel, the largest and, in some ways, most stately in town, contains all the grand vistas and elegant accessories of the belle époque. The rooms are high-ceilinged and comfortably furnished. Many have balconies overlooking the wooded park and casino. If you ask, the staff will tell you about the role of this monument (under a different name, the Thermal Palace) during the tenure of the collaborationist Vichy government: It housed the headquarters of Vichy France's Ministry of War. These days, the hotel has a good restaurant and offers a bar and a terrace with a view of Vichy.

Hôtel Chambord. 82–84 rue de Paris, 03200 Vichy. ☎ **04-70-31-22-88.** Fax 04-70-31-54-92. 28 units. TV TEL. 200–300 F ($32–$48) double. AE, DC, MC, V.

This pleasant four-story hotel was built near the railway station in the 1930s, with high ceilings and a bit more space than you might find within newer buildings. Its bedrooms were renovated in 1998.

The Escargot Qui Tette **restaurant** offers well-prepared meals in a sunny setting with reasonable prices. It's open Tuesday through Sunday (closed Sunday night); in July and August, it's open daily. Many visitors find the restaurant better than the hotel.

DINING

Brasserie du Casino. 4 rue du Casino. ☎ **04-70-98-23-06.** Reservations recommended at lunch. Main courses 80–100 F ($12.80–$16); fixed-price menus 85 F ($13.60) at lunch (Mon–Tues and Thurs–Sat), 145 F ($23.20) at dinner. MC, V. Mon–Tues and Thurs–Sat noon–1:30pm and 7–10pm. Closed Nov. FRENCH.

This has been a thriving brasserie since the 1920s, and it's a preferred stopover for actors and musicians visiting from Paris to perform at the casino. The de Chassat family is charming and especially solicitous to foreigners. Their restaurant, known for its sheathing of copper and Art Deco mahogany, is busy at lunch, but the real charm comes out at night, when a pianist entertains. Specialties are duck breast with a confit of figs, paupiette of rabbit with shallots, and veal liver with fondue of onions.

✪ **L'Alambic.** 8 rue Nicolas-Larbaud. ☎ **04-70-59-12-71.** Reservations required for certain seatings. Main courses 95–180 F ($15.20–$28.80); fixed-price menus 160–280 F ($25.60–$44.80). MC, V. Wed–Sun noon–1:30pm and 7:30–9:30pm. Closed Feb 20–Mar 13 and Aug 20–Sept 15. FRENCH.

There are only 18 seats at this small restaurant. And since this is the best food in Vichy, they fill up quickly. Since 1989, Jean-Jacques Barbot has run a busy place, appealing to what one food critic called "the jaded palates of Vichy." If you're in the mood for vichyssoise—the soup that bears this town's name, but which was invented elsewhere—the version concocted here is particularly delicious, studded as it is with mussels and crayfish tails. Other choices include ravioli stuffed with a mousse of red snapper and crayfish tails; a casserole with crayfish, pork leg with truffles and lentils, and an unusual ravioli stuffed with confit of duckling and snails.

VICHY AFTER DARK

Head straight for the **Casino Elysée Palace,** passage Clémenceau (☎ **04-70-98-50-41**). What was built around 1900 as the Elysée Palace Hotel was converted into the more glamorous of the town's two casinos in the early 1990s. But don't expect the imperial grandeur that Napoléon III would have met. Today, it's a lot more modern and informal. An area devoted to slot machines, where entrance is free, is open Sunday through Thursday from 11am to 3am, to 4am on Friday and Saturday. A separate area featuring roulette and blackjack is open Monday, Tuesday, and Friday from 8pm to 4am and Saturday and Sunday from 4pm to 4am. Entrance is 70 F ($11.20) per person. Men must wear jackets in this area.

A less impressive place to gamble, with only whirring slot machines and roulette (no blackjack), is an annex of the old-casino-turned-convention-center, **Le Grand Café,** 5 rue du Casino (☎ **04-70-97-16-45**). It shares its space with, as you guessed, a cafe and restaurant. Entrance is free.

4 Clermont-Ferrand

248 miles S of Paris, 110 miles W of Lyon

This old city in south-central France was the ancient capital of the Auvergne. Ever since then, it's seen a long parade of history. It was created in 1731 by a merger of two towns, Clermont and Montferrand. It's surrounded by hills. One of the great attractions of Auvergne, the volcanic mountain, **Puy-de-Dôme,** stands in the distance.

The city today is hardly celebrated for its ancient appearance and medieval streets. Much of the town looks as if it were created in the stark 1960s and 1970s, with unimpressive buildings, car dealerships, and plenty of shopping malls. With a population hovering around 150,000, it's an important rail hub in this region. Clermont-Ferrand, with its smoke-spitting factories, is not a town in which we'd choose to linger, although it has a number of attractions that do bring in visitors.

ESSENTIALS

GETTING THERE   Rail lines converge on Clermont-Ferrand from all parts of France, including Paris's Gare de Lyon, Marseille, and Toulouse. **Trains** from small towns in the Auvergne usually require a connection. For train information and schedules, call ☎ **08-36-35-35-35.**

Clermont-Ferrand is best approached by **car** from two cities. A lengthy drive from Paris begins along A10 south to Orléans, continuing south along A71 to Clermont-Ferrand. From Lyon, take A47 west to St-Etienne, traveling northwest on A89 to Clermont-Ferrand.

Clermont-Ferrand is the biggest hub of **Regional Airlines** (☎ **04-73-62-71-76**). Consequently, *L'Aéroport de Clermont-Aulnat* (☎ **04-73-62-71-00**), about 3 miles southwest of the town center, receives about 130 flights a day from all over France as well as parts of Italy and Germany. **Air France** (☎ **08-02-80-28-02**) flies here from Paris at a price of around 2,000 F ($320) round-trip. Buses meet every flight and take passengers to town, the bus station, or the railway station. Cost is 25 F ($4) per person each way. Service to Paris is provided by Air France Service to about a dozen other points within France, as well as to some of the airports of Germany and Italy.

Passengers arriving in town by bus pull into the **Gare Routière,** bd. François Mitterand (☎ **04-73-93-13-61** for information), on the southern periphery of town. Overall, train travel into Clermont-Ferrand is, in virtually every case, more convenient and efficient than bus service.

VISITOR INFORMATION   The **Office de Tourisme et des Congrès** is on place de la Victoire (☎ **04-73-98-65-00**). This tourist office is unique in France in that it also houses an interesting museum called **Espace Art Romain.** Here, an interactive presentation combines a slide show with captioned photographs and archaeological remnants depicting Auvergne as a rich repository of ancient Roman, Gallo-Roman, and Romanesque architecture and artifacts. The slide show takes 30 minutes and it is worth spending another hour digesting all the additional information. Admission is free. Between May and September, it's open daily 8:30am to 7pm; from October to April, daily 8:45am to 6:30pm.

SPECIAL EVENTS   If you're in town at the end of January, check out one of the 40 screenings during the week-long **Festival du Court Métrage.** The works, by up-and-coming directors, are shown in seven theaters, mainly concentrated on boulevard François-Mitterrand. Tickets are 20 F ($3.20) per showing, with discounts for packages of 20 showings, and can be purchased through Sauve Qui Peut le Court Métrage, 26 rue des Jacobins (☎ **04-73-91-65-73**).

EXPLORING THE ENVIRONS: A SPECTACULAR VOLCANIC LANDSCAPE

The region surrounding Clermont-Ferrand is one of France's most geologically distinctive. In 1977, the government designated 946,000 acres of its undulating, dark-stoned terrain as the **Parc Naturel Régional des Volcans d'Auvergne.** The park contains 186 villages as well as farms with herds of cows and goats that produce the

Auvergne's cheeses and charcuteries. Scattered among them are at least 90 extinct volcanic cones (*puys*), which rise dramatically and eerily above the pine forests.

The highest and oldest of these is **Puy-de-Dôme** (4,800 feet above sea level), a site used for worship since prehistoric times by the Gauls and the Romans. In 1648, Pascal used this mountaintop for his experiments that proved Torricelli's hypothesis about how altitudes affect atmospheric pressure. And in 1911, one of the most dramatic events in French aviation occurred at Puy-de-Dôme when Eugène Renaux, with a passenger, flew nonstop from Paris in just over 5 hours, to land precariously on its summit and collect a 100,000-franc prize. From the summit you'll have a panoramic view—on a clear day you can see as far east as Mont Blanc. Shuttle buses run daily from the base to the summit in July and August and Sundays in September from 11am to 6pm, costing 21 F ($3.35) round-trip. You can drive your car to the summit daily, before 11am only, for 22 F ($3.50).

The different areas of the park contain radically dissimilar features. **Les Puys** (also known as Monts Dômes) are a minichain of 112 extinct volcanoes (some capped with craters, some with rounded peaks) packed densely into an area 3 miles wide by 19 miles long. Each dome is unique: Some were built up by slow extrusions of rock; others were the source of vast lava flows. Those with craters at their summits were the site of violent explosions whose power stands in direct contrast to the region's peace and quiet today. The geological fury that created these hills ended between 5,000 and 6,000 years ago, but the rectangle of extinct volcanoes is aligned along one of the most potentially unstable fault lines in France, the San Andreas fault of the French mainland.

This region is relatively underpopulated, so you may not be aware of the park's boundaries during your explorations. Details about trekking and camping are available from the Parc Naturel Régional des Volcans d'Auvergne, Montlosier, 63970 Aydat (☎ **04-73-65-64-00**), 12¹/₂ miles southwest of Clermont-Ferrand. A branch office is at Château St-Etienne, 15000 Aurillac (☎ **04-71-48-68-68**). You can buy at least half a dozen guidebooks (priced from 60 F to 95 F [$9.60 to $15.20]) covering specific hikes and walks (from 2 to 6 hours in duration) at either branch.

SEEING THE SIGHTS IN TOWN

Begin your tour in the center of Clermont, the bustling **place de Jaude,** where you can sample a glass of regional wine at a cafe under the shade of a catalpa tree. Later, walk north on rue du 11-Novembre, which branches off from the main plaza. This street leads to **rue des Gras,** the most interesting artery of Clermont.

Most of the interesting old buildings are in **Vieux-Clermont,** whose focal point is **place de la Victoire,** site of the black-lava ✪ **Cathédrale Notre-Dame** (☎ 04-73-92-46-61). One of the great churches of central France, it dates back to the 13th and 14th centuries. Structural additions were made in the 19th century. Its most outstanding feature is the series of stained-glass windows from the 13th and 14th centuries. Admission is free; it's open Monday through Saturday from 9:30am to noon and 2 to 6:30pm, and Sunday from 9am to noon and 2 to 5pm.

After leaving the cathedral, explore the buildings in this historic neighborhood. In particular, look for the **Maison de Savaron,** at 3 rue des Chaussetiers, constructed in 1513. It's noted for the exceptional beauty of its courtyard and its Renaissance vaulting. The site is occupied today by a crêperie, **Le Quinze-Treize** (☎ 04-73-84-87-33), where you can enjoy either a meal-sized (i.e., salted) or dessert-style (i.e., sugared) crêpe beneath the artfully crafted vaulting. It's open daily for lunch and dinner.

Several blocks northeast of the cathedral is the finest example of Auvergnat Romanesque architecture, made of lava from volcanic deposits in the region: the **Église Notre-Dame-du-Port,** rue du Port (☎ **04-73-91-32-94**). Dating from the 11th and 12th centuries, the church has four radiating chapels and a transept surmounted by an octagonal tower. The crypt holds a 17th-century "black Madonna." The entire complex is listed as a World Heritage Site by UNESCO. Admission is free; it's open daily from 8am to 7pm (to 8pm from June to mid-October).

Between the two churches stands the Renaissance **Fontaine d'Amboise,** on place de la Poterne, its pyramid supporting a statue of Hercules. Nearby is square Pascal, commemorating the birth of mathematician Blaise Pascal in 1623 in a house on rue des Gras. Regrettably, the house was demolished in 1958, but a statue was erected in honor of the native son.

Musée Bargoin. 45 rue de Ballainvilliers. ☎ **04-73-91-37-31.** Admission 25 F ($4) adults, 13 F ($2.10) children 12–16 and students, free for children 11 and under. Tues–Sun 10am–6pm.

The collection here consists of objects excavated from Auvergnat sites founded by the Gallo-Romans and their predecessors: pottery shards, bronzes, wood carvings, and an array of works noteworthy for anyone interested in France's prehistoric and pre-Roman origins. There's also an unusual collection of antique Oriental carpets.

In the same building, maintaining the same hours and prices, is the **Musée des Tapis d'Art** (☎ **04-73-90-57-48**), with a collection of around 80 rare and very rare Middle Eastern and east Asian carpets. Each is artfully lit and suspended from walls and ceilings, and together represent the evolution of the carpet as a prayer aid and a decorative work of art. Don't expect anything French within the confines of this place, as the carpets produced in nearby Aubusson are, ironically, completely omitted.

Musée des Beaux-Arts. Place Louis-Deteix. ☎ **06-73-16-11-30.** Admission 27 F ($4.30) adults, 13 F ($2.10) children 13–16 and students, free for children 12 and under. Tues–Sun 10am–6pm.

This museum is set 2 miles north of Clermont's center in an award-winning building erected in 1992. This is the cultural showcase of the Auvergne. When it was created, multiple works of art were culled from other museums throughout the Auvergne, then reassembled into a format that displays European art and culture in chronological order. Visitors navigate their way in a circular pattern through rooms devoted to French, Italian, and Flemish works progressing from the 7th to the 20th centuries.

ACCOMMODATIONS

Hôtel Gallieni. 51 rue Bonnabaud, 63000 Clermont-Ferrand. ☎ **04-73-93-59-69.** Fax 04-73-34-89-29. 80 units. MINIBAR TV TEL. 305–345 F ($48.80–$55.20) double. AE, MC, V. Parking 25 F ($4).

This is not the best hotel in town, but it's still a good value. The Gallieni has a completely unassuming 1960s style, with rooms that, for the most part, have been recently renovated and are comfortably furnished though somewhat uninspired. Much emphasis here is placed on its role as an overnight stop for farmers and sales representatives of companies selling farm equipment, so as a casual visitor, you might feel somewhat in the minority. A simple **bistro, Le Clos Maréchal,** offers affordable meals; fixed-price menus begin at 89 F ($15.15); plats du jour start at 59 F ($9.45).

Mercure Gergovie. 82 bd. François-Mitterrand, 63000 Clermont-Ferrand. ☎ **04-73-34-46-46.** Fax 04-73-34-46-36. 123 units. A/C MINIBAR TV TEL. 595 F ($95.20) double. AE, DC, MC, V. Parking 42 F ($6.70).

This modern hotel—the best in town—was built in the early 1970s by another chain (Altea), then switched its affiliation to Mercure and was radically renovated in 1997. Its location near the lovely Jardin Lecoq is great for jogging and taking strolls. The rooms are well furnished and very clean; most are rather spacious. Everything about the hotel is functional and businesslike, but not necessarily exciting. Corporate types in town doing business with the Michelin company often stay here. The on-site **restaurant, La Retirade,** is a worthwhile choice.

DINING

Daniele Bath. Place du Marché-St-Pierre. ☎ **04-73-31-23-22.** Reservations required. Main courses 140–190 F ($22.40–$30.40); fixed-price menus 150–320 F ($24–$51.20). V. Tues–Sat noon–1:30pm and 7:30–10:30pm. Closed 2 weeks in Feb and 3 weeks in Sept. FRENCH.

For years Jean-Yves Bath reigned supreme as the leading chef of the city and became a local culinary legend. Gourmets in the area lamented when he sold the restaurant to his sous chef and departed for Paris. Their concern is groundless. Not only has the new owner/chef retained all the recipes from his previous employer, he's added many imaginative dishes of his own. Lots of superb flavors go into the locally inspired, yet grandly creative cuisine.

Begin with such delights as a tarte of scallops with black truffles or perhaps a small lasagne of salmon with black olives. The fish is truly excellent and changes seasonally, and you can also count on any number of savory meat dishes, including roast lamb which is very tender and flavorful and served with glazed turnips. Pigeon is another specialty, served with roasted foie gras.

Le Clavé. 10–12 rue St-Adjutor. ☎ **04-73-36-46-30.** Reservations required. Main courses 120–190 F ($19.20–$30.40); fixed-price menus 160–430 F ($25.60–$68.80) at lunch, 210–430 F ($33.60–$68.80) at dinner. MC, V. Daily noon–2pm and 7:30–10:30pm. FRENCH.

This well-known restaurant inside a 19th-century stone house brings big-city style and some of the most creative and intelligent food in the region to the heart of Clermont-Ferrand. Attentive staff serve you in the monochromatic dining rooms. Menu items are both classic and contemporary. They are invariably well-prepared. Main course choices include foie gras with garnishes tailored to the seasons (fresh fruit in summer, asparagus tips in spring); warm chiffonnade of shellfish; roasted lobster served with a creamy, truffle-studded risotto; roasted rabbit with a galette of sweet polenta and tarragon sauce; and fillet of Salers beef with sauce Périgueux (foie gras and truffles), accompanied with roasted potatoes drizzled with a local cheese.

CLERMONT-FERRAND AFTER DARK

A very hip crowd gathers all year at **Le Blue Sport Café,** 68 place de l'Étoile (☎ **04-73-36-08-92**), where jazz and rock blend with a lively pub atmosphere to create one of the most popular meeting places around.

For the best cafe/bar in town, complete with regular jazz and rock concerts, go to **Le 15e Avenue,** rue des Petits Gras (no phone). Always in danger of closing down for lack of funds, it's informal, with a schedule of events that's usually planned at the last minute. Two discos that are a lot more certain to survive deep into the millennium include **Le Frog,** 12 rue des Petits Gras (☎ **04-73-37-99-73**), and **Le Symbol,** 11 rue de Serbie (☎ **04-73-31-01-01**). Both attract a clientele over 25, including lots of single, divorced, or nominally married clients looking for a dance and perhaps a fling. If you're gay and looking for a night on the town, consider the most visible gay disco in Clermont, **Le Zyzy Folies,** 31 rue Anatole France (☎ **04-73-90-21-21**). You might also consider dropping into the previously recommended **Le Frog.** It's not altogether gay, but its trendiness and hipness make it an agreeable place for lots of outwardly gay clients (along with everyone else).

5 Aubusson

236 miles S of Paris, 55 miles E of Limoges, 59 miles NW of Clermont-Ferrand

In the Creuse Valley, the little market town of Aubusson enjoys world renown for its carpets and tapestries. Aubusson is characterized by clock towers, bridges, peaked roofs, and turrets—all of which inspired the painter Gromaire's widely reproduced cartoon *View of Aubusson.*

Against the gray granite, rainbow-hued skeins of wool hang from windows. The workshops of the craftspeople are spread throughout the town; many are open to the public (just ask). The origin of the industry is unknown. Some credit the Arabs who settled here in 732. Others think the craft came from Flanders in the Middle Ages. For years the favorite subject was *The Lady and the Unicorn,* the original of which was discovered in the nearby Château de Boussac. Many tapestry reproductions of the works of 18th-century painters like Boucher and Watteau have been made. Since World War II, designs by painters like Picasso, Matisse, and Braque have been stressed.

Musée Départemental de la Tapisserie, avenue des Lissiers (☎ 05-55-66-33-06), has exhibits related to the 6-century-long tradition of the Aubusson carpet- and tapestry-weaving industry. The displays also highlight the 20th-century rebirth of the Aubusson carpet and the art of tapestry weaving. It's open Wednesday through Monday from 9:30am to noon and 2 to 6pm (in summer from 9am to 6pm). Admission is 20 F ($3.20) for adults, 75 F ($12) for children 12 to 16, and free for children 11 and under.

La Maison du Tapissier, rue Vieille (☎ 05-55-66-32-12), exhibits old carpets and displays a reconstruction of an old carpet-weaving studio. It's open from 9:30am to noon and 1:30 to 6pm, daily from mid-June to September, and Tuesday through Saturday off-season. Admission is 17 F ($2.70).

ESSENTIALS

GETTING THERE   Aubusson does have rail service, much of it indirect, from Clermont-Ferrand and Paris, among other cities. Ten **trains** leave from Paris's Gare d'Austerlitz for Aubusson with a change in Limoges. From Clermont-Ferrand to Aubusson, four trains depart daily for a nearly 4-hour trip (with a minimum of two stops). For complete train information, call ☎ 08-36-35-35-35. Passengers interested in **bus** transit usually find that the routes leading into town only service the towns and communities in the neighborhood, with inconvenient connections from other parts of France. For information, call La Gare Routière (☎ 05-55-10-31-00).

If you're **driving** from Clermont-Ferrand, take D941 west to Aubusson. The trip takes between 1 and 1 1/2 hours.

VISITOR INFORMATION   The **Office de Tourisme** is on rue Vieille (☎ 05-55-66-32-12).

ACCOMMODATIONS & DINING

Le Lion d'Or. Place du Général-Espagne, 23200 Aubusson. ☎ 05-55-66-13-88. Fax 05-55-66-84-73. 11 units. TV TEL. 270–300 F ($43.20–$48) double. AE, MC, V.

This two-star hotel occupies a building erected around 1800 on the town's main square. It's unpretentious but still one of the town's best choices, with polite but no-nonsense management by the Chaussoy family. The rooms are simple yet comfortable.

Dining: The street level contains a restaurant that serves the town's best food. In summer, lunch and dinner are offered daily, but between October 15 and April 15 no meals are served on Sunday nights. Fixed-price menus cost from 85 F to 145 F ($13.60 to $23.20), and might feature such dishes as stingray with butter-flavored cabbage, and a local specialty, a *fondue Creusoise,* which is something you might have more readily expected in the French Alps. It consists of a pot of melted local cheese (Le Creusois) served with strips of locally cured ham, French fries, and salad.

6 Limoges

246 miles S of Paris, 193 miles N of Toulouse, 58 miles NE of Périgueux

Limoges, the ancient capital of Limousin in west-central France, is world famous for its exquisite porcelain and enamel works, the latter a medieval industry revived in the 19th century. The industry is still going strong today. In fact, Limoges is the economic capital of western France. On the Vienne's right bank, the town has historically consisted of two parts: the Cité, its narrow streets and old *maisons* on the lower slope, and the town proper at the summit.

ESSENTIALS

GETTING THERE   Limoges has good **train** service from most regional cities, with direct trains from Toulouse, Poitiers, and Paris. Ten trains depart daily from Paris's Gare d'Austerlitz for Limoges (trip time: 3 hours). For complete train information, call ☎ 08-36-35-35-35. **Bus** transit in and out of the small towns and villages nearby can be arranged through the Gare Routière, place des Charentes (☎ 05-55-10-31-00).

If you're **driving** from Aubusson, take D941 west for the 1-hour trip.

VISITOR INFORMATION   The **Office de Tourisme** is on boulevard de Fleurus (☎ 05-55-34-46-87).

EXPLORING THE TOWN

If you'd like to see an enameler or a porcelain factory producing its wares, ask at the tourist office (see above) for a list of workshops, or go directly to the famous Pavillon de la Porcelaine.

To stock up on local porcelain, try these three **Prestige de Limoges** shops owned by the same company: At 2 bd. Louis-Blanc (☎ 05-55-34-44-15) you'll find Limoges's own "unblemished crystal" as well as crystal from Lalique, St. Louis, and Baccarat, and silverware from Christofle and Puiforcat. At 13 and 27 bd. Louis-Blanc (☎ 05-55-34-58-61), you can buy porcelain from Haviland, Bernardaud, Raynaud, and Lafarge, as well as slightly imperfect seconds.

For a sales-oriented overview of the abundance of locally made porcelain that's available, visit any of three branches of the **Société Lachaniette,** which lie, respectively, at nos. 2, 13, and 27 bd. Louis-Blanc. They share a communal switchboard at ☎ 05-55-34-58-61. At nos. 13 and 27, you'll find examples of porcelain from each of the manufacturers in Limoges, including Haviland, Bernardaud, Raynaud, and Laure Japy (formerly known as Laforge). At no. 2, you'll find mostly crystal from Lalique, St. Louis, and Baccarat, and silverware from Christofle and Puiforcat. Specific inventories are shifted between the three branches as new collections are released, but overall, by wandering among all three, you'll get a fast overview of what's available.

Thanks to the rich deposits of kaolin (known locally as "white gold") that were found near Limoges in the 18th century, more than 30 manufacturers of delicate porcelain have set up operations through the years in and around the town. Many of them maintain factory outlets, sometimes offering good-quality seconds at reduced prices. Some of the best outlets, with the widest inventories, are as follows: For a thoroughly antique style of porcelain, visit the **Ancienne Manufacture Royale,** 7 Place Horteils, in Limoges' suburb of Aixe-sur-Vienne (☎ **05-55-70-44-82**), 3¹/₂ miles west of Limoges. Within the center of town, you'll find **Raynaud,** 14 ancienne route d'Aixe (☎ **05-55-01-77-65**), and **Chastigner,** 20 av. des Casseaux (☎ **05-55-33-45-74**). Largest of all, with the most evolved sense of public relations and marketing, is **Bernardaud,** 27 rue Albert-Thomas (☎ **05-55-10-55-91**), where a small-scale museum (focusing on past porcelain-related triumphs) and a tearoom adjoin the showroom.

Pavillon de la Porcelaine. Av. John-Kennedy. ☎ **05-55-30-21-86.** Free admission. Apr–Oct, daily 8:30am–7:30pm; Nov–Mar, daily 9:30am–7pm.

Haviland has been exporting its porcelain to the U.S. and other countries since 1842, when a group of American entrepreneurs emigrated to France from Boston to found the first American-owned company ever established in Europe. Over the years, it has used the designs of artists like Gauguin and Dalí. In the museum, you can see the masterpieces as well as original pieces for the U.S. White House. Later, visit an air-conditioned room where you can learn the history of this unusual company as well as follow the manufacturing process with the help of a video on a giant screen. A large shop also sells the porcelain at factory prices.

Musée National de la Porcelaine Adrien-Dubouché. Place Winston Churchill, 87000 Limoges. ☎ **05-55-33-08-50.** Admission 22 F ($3.50) adults, 15 F ($2.40) ages 18–25, free for children 17 and under. July–Aug, Wed–Mon 10am–5:45pm; Sept–June, Wed–Mon 10am–12:30pm and 2–5:45pm.

This museum, housed in a 19th-century building, boasts the largest public collection of Limoges porcelain. Its 12,000 pieces illustrate the history of glassmaking and ceramics (porcelain, glazed earthenware, stoneware, and terra-cotta) throughout the ages. In France, its porcelain collection is second only to that of Sèvres. One room is devoted to the various stages of ceramics manufacturing. The main gallery contains whole dinner sets of noted figures and some contemporary Limoges ware.

Cathédrale St-Etienne. Place de la Cathédrale. ☎ **05-55-34-53-81.** Free admission. Summer, daily 10am–6pm; winter, daily 10am–5pm.

The cathedral was begun in 1273 but took many years to complete. The choir, for example, was finished in 1327, but work continued in the nave until almost 1890. The cathedral is the only one in the old province of Limousin to be built entirely in the Gothic style. The main entrance is through Porte St-Jean, which has beautifully carved wooden doors from the 16th century (constructed at the peak of the Flamboyant Gothic style). Inside, the nave appears so harmonious it's hard to imagine that its construction took 6 centuries. The rood screen is of particular interest, built in 1533 in the ornate style of the Italian Renaissance. The cathedral also contains some admirable bishops' tombs from the 14th to the 16th centuries.

Musée Municipal. Place de la Cathédrale. ☎ **05-55-45-61-75.** Free admission. June–Sept, daily 10–11:45am and 2–6pm; Oct–May, Wed–Mon 10am–11:45 and 2–5pm.

Adjoining the cathedral in the Jardins de l'Evêché—which offer a view of the Vienne and the pont St-Etienne from the 13th century—the old archbishops' palace has been turned into the Musée Municipal. The 18th-century building, elegant in line, has an outstanding collection of Limoges enamels from the 12th century, as well as some enamel paintings by Leonard Limousin, who was born in 1505 in Limoges and went on to win world acclaim and the favor of four monarchs. Limoges was also the birthplace of Renoir, and the museum displays several works by this world-class artist.

Église St-Michel-des-Lions. Place St-Michel. ☎ **05-55-34-18-13.** Free admission. Mon–Sat 8am–noon and 2–6pm, Sun 8am–11:45 and 4–6pm.

Construction of this church was launched in the 14th century, and work continued into the 15th and 16th centuries. Although the church is not as interesting as older, Romanesque churches scattered in other parts of the Auvergne, it's the headquarters of the cult of St-Martial, a Limoges hometown bishop (and saint) who died in the 3rd century. The church is the home of what's reputed to be his skull, which is stored in an elaborately enamelled reliquary. "Les Ostensions" is a religious procession, established in 994, which occurs every 7 years, when the skull—which some adherents credit with mystical powers—is removed from storage and exhibited as part of religious ceremonies that attract as many as 100,000 devout adherents. The next such procession is scheduled for the year 2002.

ACCOMMODATIONS

Hôtel La Caravelle. 21 rue Armand-Barbès, 87000 Limoges. ☎ **05-55-77-75-29.** Fax 05-55-79-27-60. 30 units. TV TEL. 350–380 F ($56–$60.80) double. AE, V. Parking 40 F ($6.40).

Just north of the city center, this modern hotel is the most recent manifestation of a building erected around 1900, but frequent renovations have kept the four-story site looking fresh. The calm, quiet rooms are simply but comfortably furnished in a modern style. Breakfast is the only meal served, but the management can direct you to the half dozen or so restaurants on rue Garibaldi, a short walk away.

Hôtel Royal Limousin. Place de la République, 87000 Limoges. ☎ **05-55-34-65-30.** Fax 05-55-34-55-21. 77 units. MINIBAR TV TEL. 485–590 F ($77.60–$94.40) double; 680–1,200 F ($108.80–$192) suite. AE, DC, MC, V.

This modern, six-story oasis was built in the 1960s adjacent to a municipal parking lot in the center of Limoges. It's the town's best address and welcomes virtually every large-scale buyer of Limoges's famous product. The rooms are outfitted in a neutrally modern, chain-hotel style but are generally large and sunny. Accommodations on the noisier avenue Carnot side rent for less than those on the quieter place de la République side. The only drawback is that the hotel is often booked by summer group tours. There's no restaurant, but the staff refers hotel guests to the restaurant next door, which is under separate management.

DINING

Philippe Redon. 3 rue Aguesseau. ☎ **05-55-34-66-22.** Reservations recommended. Fixed-price menus 160–260 F ($25.60–$41.60). AE, DC, V. Tues–Fri noon–2:30pm; Tues–Sat 7–10pm. Closed Aug 1–15. FRENCH.

In a 19th-century house a few steps from the produce market, this restaurant is maintained by a youthful team of waiters headed by the owner/chef, Philippe Redon, the finest cook in Limoges. It contains a 1930s Art Deco–style interior accented with exposed stone and flowers. Menu items vary with the availability of local ingredients. Examples include a lobster casserole with delectable fresh seasonings, slices of foie gras and duckling, or sea bass grilled or roasted to perfection.

NEARBY ACCOMMODATIONS & DINING
IN ST-MARTIN-DU-FAULT

✪ **La Chapelle St-Martin.** 87510 Nieul. ☎ **05-55-75-80-17.** Fax 05-55-75-89-50. www.chapellesaintmartin.com. E-mail: chapelle@relaischateaux.fr. 13 units. TV TEL. 590–980 F ($94.40–$156.80) double; 1,500 F ($240) suite. AE, MC, V, DC. Closed Jan–Feb 18; year-round, restaurant closed Mon. Free parking. Take N147 and D35 7 miles northeast from Limoges.

This is the best place in the environs if you enjoy turn-of-the-century-style living and superb food in the tradition of the Relais & Châteaux group. The hotel is graciously situated in a private park with two ponds. Your host, Gilles Dudognon, requests that you reserve well in advance. The rooms are individually decorated and tasteful, and some are suitable for those with disabilities. Each has a 19th-century theme (usually Directoire or Empire). The restaurant offers excellent food, using raw materials selected and handled with care and deftness by the chefs. Fixed-price menus cost from around 350 F ($56) each.

IN NIEUIL

To get to Nieuil from Limoges, take N141 west of the town center (signposted Angoulême). The town of Nieuil is signposted at the town of Suaux. Follow the signs for about a mile east of the village toward Fontafie. Nieuil lies $7^1/_2$ miles northwest of Limoges. *Note:* Don't confuse Nieuil with La Chapelle St-Martin at Nieul (with a slightly different spelling).

✪ **Château de Nieuil.** 16270 Nieuil. ☎ **05-45-71-36-38.** Fax 05-45-71-46-45. www. relaischateaux.fr/nieuil. E-mail: nieuil@relaischateaux.fr. 14 units. A/C MINIBAR TV TEL. 900–1,600 F ($144–$256) double; 1,800–2,400 F ($288–$384) suite. AE, DC, MC, V. Closed Nov–Apr.

This château, built in the 16th century as a hunting lodge for François I, was transformed in 1937 into the first château-hotel in France. Restored by the comte de Dampierre early in the 1800s after its destruction in the Revolution, it has remained in the antique-collecting family of Jean-Michel Bodinaud since around 1900. Today 400 acres of park and forest lead up to a series of beautifully maintained gardens, the pride of the owners.

Dining: The cuisine, crafted and supervised by Mme Luce Bodinaud, is superb, focusing on classic traditions and regional recipes. A typical dish is stuffed cabbage (*farci Charentais*), though you may prefer the fillet of beef du Limousine or a selection of fish that includes fillet of sole in the style *"pêcheurs d'Oléron,"* prepared with a compôte of leeks and crayfish. Fixed-price menus cost 280 F to 350 F ($44.80 to $56). Nonguests can dine here if they call ahead.

Amenities: Tennis courts, pool, art and antiques gallery that specializes in Art Deco furniture and old posters.

7 Le Puy-en-Velay

325 miles S of Paris, 80 miles SE of Clermont-Ferrand

Le Puy-en-Velay (usually shortened to Le Puy) is one of the most extraordinary sights of France. Steep volcanic spires, left from geological activity that ended millennia ago, were capped with Romanesque churches, a cathedral, and medieval houses that rise sinuously from the plain below. The history of Le Puy is centered around the cult of the Virgin Mary, which prompted the construction of many of the city's churches.

Le Puy today is a provincial French city of steep cobblestone streets with lots of rather shabby buildings (many of which are now being restored). Many of the population of approximately 22,000 live off the tourist trade; today's visitors follow in the footsteps of Charlemagne, "the first tourist" here. Le Puy remains a major pilgrimage destination of France, although it is not as famous as Lourdes.

ESSENTIALS

GETTING THERE   Passengers arriving in Le Puy from anywhere in Europe must change **trains** at the railway junction of St-Georges d'Aurac. From here, small trains, timed for convenient connections, travel along the 17-mile spur route that connects Le Puy's small railway station to the rest of the lines of the SNCF. For train information and schedules, call ☎ **08-36-35-35-35. Bus service** in and out of Puy-en-Velay is relatively inefficient, and of use only to passengers coming in and out of the small-scale villages within the Auvergne. Even buses from Clermont-Ferrand take at least 3 hours for the relatively short distance. For **bus** information, contact La Gare Routière at ☎ **04-71-09-25-60.**

If you're **driving,** the best way to reach Le Puy is from St-Etienne, traveling southwest along N88. From Clermont-Ferrand, drive south along N88 to Lempdes, continuing southeast along N102 to Le Puy.

VISITOR INFORMATION   The **Office de Tourisme** is on place du Breuil (☎ **04-71-09-38-41**).

SEEING THE SIGHTS

Puy is the historic center of the French lace industry; you'll find lace shops on every block. But to be assured of its handmade authenticity, look for the words DENTELLE DU PUY. As decreed by a 1931 local government ordinance, the display of this mark on lace is a privilege reserved for the real thing. The best selections of local lace can be found at **Spécialités du Velay,** 1 bd. St-Louis (☎ **04-71-09-09-34**); **Lucia Dentelles,** 28 place du plot (☎ **04-71-09-60-69**); and **Aux Souvenirs du Puy,** 60 rue Raphaël (☎ **04-71-05-76-71**).

Cathédrale Notre-Dame. Place du For. ☎ **04-71-05-45-52.** Admission to cathedral free; to cloisters and Chapel of Relics 25 F ($4) adults, 15 F ($2.40) ages 12–24, free for children 11 and under. Cathedral, daily 8:30am–7:30pm (Oct–Feb, until 6:30pm); cloisters and Chapel of Relics, Oct–Mar, daily 9:30am–noon and 2–4pm, Apr–June, daily 9:30am–12:30pm and 2–6pm, July–Sept, daily 9:30am–6:30pm.

The Romanesque Cathédrale Notre-Dame was conceived as a site for shelter and prayer for medieval pilgrims heading to the religious shrines of Santiago de Compostela in northwestern Spain. Marked by vivid Oriental and Byzantine influences, it's worth a visit. The cloisters contain carved capitals dating from the Carolingian era. The Chapelle des Reliques et Trésor d'Art Religieux contains fabrics and gold and silver objects from the church treasury, as well as an unusual enameled chalice from the 12th century.

Chapelle St-Michel-d'Aiguilhe. Atop the Rocher St-Michel. ☎ **04-71-09-50-03.** Admission 15 F ($2.40) adults, 8 F ($1.30) children 13 and under. Mid-June to mid-Sept, daily 9am–7pm; mid-Sept to early June, daily 9 or 10am–noon and 2–5 or 6pm, depending on the hours of sunrise and sunset; Dec 20–31, open 2–4pm only.

This 10th-century chapel, perched precariously atop a volcanic spur that rises abruptly from hilly terrain, is one of the city's most dramatic sights. It sits on the northwestern perimeter of Le Puy. Reaching its summit requires a very long climb up rocky stairs. When you get here you'll be struck by the Oriental influences in the floor plan, the arabesques, and the mosaics crafted from black stone. On view are some 12th-century murals and an 11th-century wooden depiction of Christ.

Musée Crozatier. In the Jardin Henri-Vinay. ☎ **04-71-09-38-90.** Fax 04-71-02-18-09. E-mail: m-crozat@mail.es-conseil.fr. Admission 20 F ($3.20) adults, 10 F ($1.60) children, free for children 5 and under. May–Sept, Wed–Mon 10am–noon and 2–6pm; Oct–Apr, Mon and Wed–Sat 10am–noon and 2–4pm, Sun 2–4pm.

If you appreciate handcrafts, you'll enjoy the displays of lace, some from the 16th century, at this museum, which also has a collection of carved architectural embellishments from the Romanesque era and paintings from the 14th to the 20th centuries.

ACCOMMODATIONS

Hôtel Brivas. Av. Charles-Massot, 43750 Vals-Près-Le-Puy. ☎ **04-71-05-68-66.** Fax 04-71-05-65-88. E-mail: brivas@aol.com.fr. 47 units. TV TEL. 294–310 F ($47.05–$49.60) double. AE, MC, V.

Set about a 2-minute drive southwest of the town center, adjacent to Le Dolaizon river, this hotel is the newest and most modern in town. The rooms are clean, streamlined, and simple with basic furnishings. The hotel and its restaurant cater to tour bus groups. The **restaurant** offers a fixed-price menu that ranges from 99 F to 195 F ($15.85 to $31.20).

Hôtel Régina. 34 bd. du Maréchal-Fayolle, 43000 Le Puy-en-Velay. ☎ **04-71-09-14-71.** Fax 04-71-09-18-57. 27 units. MINIBAR TV TEL. 335F–385F ($56.95–$65.45) double; 580–650 F ($92.80–$104) suite. AE, MC, V. Parking 25 F ($4).

In 1998, a radical renovation of this four-story hotel brought it up to the best three-star standards in town. Originally built late in the 19th century and operated by extended members of a local family (the Venosinos), it offers simple but thoughtfully decorated bedrooms. It's conveniently located close to the heart of town. The in-house **brasserie** offers affordable platters of food that begin at 78 F ($12.50) and fixed-price menus at 85 F to 230 F ($13.60 to $36.80). In the afternoon, it turns into a tea salon that attracts many local retirees and shopkeepers.

DINING

Le Bateau Ivre. 5 rue Portail-d'Avignon. ☎ **04-71-09-67-20.** Reservations recommended. Main courses 60–110 F ($9.60–$17.60); fixed-price menus 110–185 F ($17.60–$29.60). AE, MC, V. Tues–Sat noon–2:30pm and 7:30–10pm. Closed 1 week in June and Nov 1–15. FRENCH/AUVERGNAT.

Set in the heart of town and devoted to the traditions of the region, this restaurant occupies a pair of rustically old-fashioned dining rooms in a house whose interior is much older than its 19th-century facade. Monsieur Datessen, your host, prepares a variety of dishes utilizing the robust wines of the region, as well as lentils, which crop up in appealing and flavorful ways. Specialties include roasted versions of the Auvergne's black lambs, prepared with thyme and mashed potatoes studded with morels; beef of the Salers breed with local red wine and marrow sauce; and local whitefish (omble chevalier) served at least four different ways. Dedicated pilgrims to Le Puy always have this restaurant marked as the "serious" dining choice. Notice the lace that covers the windows and wooden tables: It was all handmade in Le Puy, mainly by elderly women in their living rooms.

Appendix A: France in Depth

France remains one of the world's most hyped, most talked about, and most written about destinations. It's packed with diversions and distractions of every sort: cultural, culinary, sensual, you name it. And perhaps that's why France has been called *le deuxième pays de tout le monde:* everyone's second country.

The French claim credit for developing the Gothic style of architecture and the cathedrals that stand as legacies of soaring stone for future generations. And ever since the Middle Ages, creators of everything from palaces to subway stations have drawn at least some inspiration from designs born in France. However, despite the thrilling monuments peppering the country, it would be wrong to assume that the culture's main contribution to the world is derived from stone, mortar, stained glass, and gilt. Its contributions to painting, literature, cuisine, fashion, and the art of fine living are staggering.

1 History 101

Dateline

- **121 B.C.** The Romans establish the province of Gallia Narbonensis to guard overland routes between Spain and Italy; its borders correspond roughly to today's Provence.
- **58–51 B.C.** Julius Caesar conquers Gaul (north-central France).
- **52 B.C.** The Roman city of Lutetia, later Paris, is built on a defensible island in the Seine.
- **2nd century A.D.** Christianity arrives in Gaul.
- **485–511** Under Clovis I, the Franks defeat the Roman armies and establish the Merovingian dynasty.
- **511 on** Confusion and disorder; feudalism and the power of the Catholic church grow.

continues

EARLY GAUL When the ancient Romans considered France part of their empire, their boundaries extended deep into the forests of the Paris basin and up to the edges of the Rhine. Part of Julius Caesar's early reputation came from his defeat of King Vercingetorix at Alésia in 52 B.C., a victory he was quick to publicize in one of the ancient world's literary masterpieces, *The Gallic Wars.* In that year the Roman colony of Lutetia (Paris) was established on an island in the Seine (Île de la Cité).

As the Roman Empire declined, its armies retreated to the flourishing colonies that had been established along a strip of the Mediterranean coast—among others, these included Orange, Montpellier, Nîmes, Narbonne, and Marseille, which retain some of the best Roman monuments in Europe.

As one of their legacies, the Roman armies left behind the Catholic church, which, for all its abuses, was the only real guardian of civilization during the anarchy following the Roman decline. A form of low Latin was the common language, and it slowly evolved into the archaic French that both delights and confuses today's medieval scholars.

The form of Christianity adopted by many of the chieftains was viewed as heretical by Rome. Consequently, when Clovis (king of northeastern Gaul's Franks and founder of the Merovingian dynasty) astutely converted to Catholicism, he won the approval of the pope, the political support of the powerful archbishop of Reims, and the loyalty of the many Gallic tribes who'd grown disenchanted with anarchy. (Clovis's baptism is viewed as the beginning of a collusion between the Catholic church and the French monarchy that flourished until the 1789 Revolution.) At the Battle of Soissons in 486, Clovis defeated the last vestiges of Roman power in Gaul. Other conquests that followed included expansions westward to the Seine, then to the Loire. After a battle in Dijon in 500, he became the nominal overlord of the king of Burgundy. Seven years later his armies drove the Visigoths into Spain, giving most of Aquitaine, in western France, to his newly founded Merovingian dynasty. Trying to make the best of an earlier humiliation, Anastasius, the Byzantium-based emperor of the Eastern Roman Empire, finally gave the kingdom of the Franks his legal sanction.

After Clovis's death in 511, his kingdom was split among his squabbling heirs. The Merovingian dynasty, however, managed to survive in fragmented form for another 250 years. During this period, the power of the bishops and the great lords grew, firmly entrenching the complex hierarchies and preoccupations of what we today know as feudalism. Although apologists for the Merovingians are quick to point out their achievements, the feudalistic quasi-anarchy of their tenuous reign has been (not altogether unfairly) identified by many historians as the Dark Ages.

THE CAROLINGIANS From the wreckage of the intrigue-ridden Merovingian court emerged a new dynasty: the Carolingians. One of their leaders, Charles Martel, halted a Muslim invasion of northern Europe at Tours in 743 and left a much-expanded kingdom to his son, Pepin. The Carolingian empire eventually

- **768** Charlemagne (768–814) becomes the Frankish king and establishes the Carolingian dynasty; from Aix-la-Chapelle (Aachen) he rules lands from northern Italy to Bavaria to Paris.
- **800** Charlemagne is crowned Holy Roman Emperor in Rome.
- **814** Charlemagne dies and his empire breaks up.
- **1066** William of Normandy (the Conqueror) invades England; his conquest is completed by 1087.
- **1140** St-Denis Cathedral, the first example of Gothic architecture, is completed.
- **1270** Louis IX (St. Louis), along with most of his army, dies in Tunis on the Eighth Crusade.
- **1309** The papal schism— Philip the Fair establishes the Avignon papacy, which lasts nearly 70 years; two popes struggle for domination.
- **1347–51** The bubonic plague (the Black Death) kills 33% of the population.
- **1431** The English burn Joan of Arc at the stake in Rouen for resisting their occupation of France.
- **1453** The French drive the English out of all of France except Calais; the Hundred Years' War ends.
- **1515–47** France captures Calais after centuries of English rule.
- **1562–98** The Wars of Religion: Catholics fight Protestants; Henri IV converts to Catholicism and issues the Edict of Nantes, granting limited rights to Protestants.
- **1643–1715** The reign of Louis XIV, the Sun King; France develops Europe's most powerful army, but wars in Flanders and court extravagance sow seeds of decline.

continues

- **1763** The Treaty of Paris effectively ends French power in North America.
- **1789–94** French Revolution: The Bastille is stormed on July 14, 1789; the Reign of Terror follows.
- **1793** Louis XVI and Marie Antoinette are guillotined.
- **1794** Robespierre and the leaders of the Reign of Terror are guillotined.
- **1799** Napoléon enters Paris and unites diverse factions; his military victories in northern Italy solidify his power in Paris.
- **1804** Napoléon crowns himself emperor in Notre-Dame de Paris.
- **1805–11** Napoléon and his armies successfully invade most of Europe.
- **1814–15** Napoléon abdicates after the failure of his Russian campaign; exiled to Elba, he returns; on June 18, 1815, finally defeated at Waterloo, he's exiled to St. Helena, where he dies in 1821.
- **1830–48** The reign of Louis-Philippe.
- **1848** A revolution topples Louis-Philippe; Napoléon III (nephew of Napoléon I) is elected president.
- **1851–71** President Napoléon declares himself Emperor Napoléon III.
- **1863** An exhibition of paintings marks the birth of Impressionism.
- **1870–71** The Franco-Prussian War: Paris falls; France cedes Alsace-Lorraine but aggressively colonizes North Africa and Southeast Asia.
- **1873** France loses Suez to the British; financial scandal wrecks an attempt to dredge the canal.
- **1889** The Eiffel Tower built for Paris's Universal Exhibition and the Revolution's centennial; architectural critics howl with contempt.

continues

stretched from the Pyrénées to a point deep in the German forests, encompassing much of modern France, Germany, and northern Italy. The heir to this vast land was Charlemagne. Crowned emperor in Rome on Christmas Day in 800, he returned to his capital at Aix-la-Chapelle (Aachen) and created the Holy Roman Empire. Charlemagne's rule saw a revived interest in scholarship, art, and classical texts, defined by scholars as the Carolingian Renaissance.

Despite Charlemagne's magnetism, cultural rifts formed in his sprawling empire, most of which was eventually divided between two of his three squabbling heirs. Charles of Aquitaine annexed the western region; Louis of Bavaria took the east. Historians credit this division with the development of modern France and Germany as separate nations. Shortly after Charlemagne's death, his fragmented empire was invaded by Vikings from the north, Muslim Saracens from the south, and Hungarians from the east.

THE MIDDLE AGES When the Carolingian dynasty died out in 987, Hugh Capet, comte de Paris and duc de France, officially began the Middle Ages with the establishment of the Capetian dynasty. In 1154, the annulment of Eleanor of Aquitaine's marriage to Louis VII of France and subsequent marriage to Henry II of England placed the western half of France under English control, and vestiges of their power remained for centuries. Meanwhile, vast forests and swamps were cleared for harvesting (often by the Middle Ages' hardest-working ascetics, Cistercian monks), the population grew, great Gothic cathedrals were begun, and monastic life contributed to every level of a rapidly developing social order. Politically driven marriages among the ruling families more than doubled the size of the territory controlled from Paris, a city that was increasingly recognized as the country's capital. Philippe II (reigned 1179 to 1223) infiltrated more prominent families with his genes than anyone else in France, successfully marrying members of his family into the Valois, Artois, and Vermandois. He also managed to win Normandy and Anjou back from the English.

Louis IX (St. Louis) emerged as the 13th century's most memorable king, though he ceded most of the hard-earned military conquests of his predecessors back to the English. Somewhat of a religious fanatic, he died of illness (along with most of his army) in 1270 in a boat anchored off Tunis. The vainglorious and not-very-wise pretext for his trip was the Eighth Crusade. At the time of his death, Notre-Dame and the Sainte-Chapelle in Paris had been completed, and the arts of tapestry making and stonecutting were flourishing.

During the 1300s, the struggle of French sovereignty against the claims of a rapacious Roman pope tempted Philip the Fair to encourage support for a pope based in Avignon. (The Roman pope, Boniface VIII, whom Philip publicly insulted and then assaulted in his home, is said to have died of the shock.) During one of medieval history's most bizarre episodes, two popes ruled simultaneously, one from Rome and one from Avignon. They competed fiercely for the spiritual and fiscal control of Christendom, until years of political intrigue turned the tables in favor of Rome and Avignon relinquished its claim in 1378.

The 14th century saw an increase in the wealth and power of the French kings, an increase in the general prosperity, and a decrease in the power of the feudal lords. The death of Louis X without an heir in 1316 prompted more than a decade of scheming and plotting before the eventual emergence of the Valois dynasty.

The Black Death began in the summer of 1348, killing an estimated 33% of Europe's population, decimating the population of Paris, and setting the stage for the exodus of the French monarchs to safer climes in such places as the Loire Valley. A financial crisis, coupled with a series of ruinous harvests, almost bankrupted the nation.

During the Hundred Years' War, the English made sweeping inroads into France in an attempt to grab the throne. At their most powerful, they controlled almost all the north (Picardy and Normandy), Champagne, parts of the Loire Valley, and the huge western region called Guyenne. The peasant-born charismatic visionary Joan of Arc rallied the dispirited French troops as well as the timid dauphin (crown prince), whom she managed to have crowned as Charles VII in the cathedral at Reims. As threatening to the Catholic church as she was to the English, she was declared a heretic and burned at the stake in Rouen in 1431. Led by the newly crowned king, a barely

- **1914–18** World War I; French casualties exceed five million.
- **1923** France occupies the Ruhr, Germany's industrial zone, demanding (and collecting) enormous war reparations.
- **1929** France retreats from the Ruhr and the Rhineland and constructs the Maginot Line, dubbed "impregnable."
- **1934** The Great Depression; a political crisis is spurred by clashes of left and right.
- **1936** Germans march into the demilitarized Rhineland; France takes no action.
- **1939** France and Britain guarantee to Poland, Romania, and Greece protection from aggressors; Germany invades Poland; France declares war.
- **1940** Paris falls to Germany on June 14; Marshal Pétain's Vichy government collaborates with the Nazis; General de Gaulle forms a government-in-exile in London to direct French resistance fighters.
- **1944** On June 6, the Allies invade the Normandy beaches; other Allied troops invade from the south; Paris is liberated in August.
- **1946–54** War in Indochina; the French withdraw from Southeast Asia; North and South Vietnam created.
- **1954–58** The Algerian revolution and subsequent independence from France; refugees flood France; the Fourth Republic collapses.
- **1958** De Gaulle initiates the Fifth Republic, calling for a France independent from the United States and Europe.
- **1960** France tests its first atomic bomb.
- **1968** Students riot in Paris; de Gaulle resigns.
- **1981** François Mitterrand becomes the first Socialist

continues

president since World War II.

- **1989** The bicentennial of the French Revolution and the centennial of the Eiffel Tower.
- **1993** Conservatives topple the Socialists, as Edouard Balladur becomes premier.
- **1994** The Channel Tunnel opens to link France with England.
- **1995** Jacques Chirac wins the French presidency on his third try and declares a war on unemployment; his popularity wanes and much unrest follows; terrorists bomb Paris several times.
- **1997** Strict immigration laws are enforced, causing strife for many African and Arab immigrants and dividing the country; French voters rebuff Chirac, electing Socialist Lionel Jospin as its new prime minister.
- **1998** France hosts and wins the World Cup.
- **2000** The euro is officially introduced. France gives legal status to unmarried couples.

cohesive France initiated reforms that strengthened its finances and vigor. After compromises among the quarreling factions, the French army drove the discontented English out, leaving them only the Norman port of Calais.

In the late 1400s, Charles VIII married Brittany's last duchess, Anne, for a unification of France with its Celtic-speaking western outpost. In the early 1500s, the endlessly fascinating François I, through war and diplomacy, strengthened the monarchy, rid it of its dependence on Italian bankers, coped with the intricate policies of the Renaissance, and husbanded the arts into a form of patronage that French monarchs continued to endorse for centuries.

Meanwhile, the growth of Protestantism and the unwillingness of the Catholic church to tolerate it led to civil strife. In 1572, Catherine de Médici reversed her policy of religious tolerance and ordered the St. Bartholomew's Day Massacre of hundreds of Protestants. Henri IV, tired of the bloodshed and fearful that a fanatically Catholic Spain would meddle in the religious conflicts, converted to Catholicism as a compromise in 1593. Just before being fatally stabbed by a half-crazed monk, he issued the Edict of Nantes in 1598, granting freedom of religion to Protestants in France.

THE PASSING OF FEUDALISM By now France was a modern state, rid of all but a few of the vestiges of feudalism. In 1624, Louis XIII appointed a Catholic cardinal, the duc de Richelieu, his chief minister. Amassing enormous power, Richelieu virtually ruled the country until his death in 1642. His sole objective was investing the monarchy with total power—he committed a series of truly horrible acts trying to attain this goal and paved the way for the eventual absolutism of Louis XIV.

Although he ascended the throne when he was only 9, with the help of his Sicilian-born chief minister, Cardinal Mazarin, Louis XIV was the most powerful monarch Europe had seen since the Roman emperors. Through first a brilliant military campaign against Spain and then a judicious marriage to one of its royal daughters, he expanded France to include the southern provinces of Artois and Roussillon. Later, a series of diplomatic and military victories along the Flemish border expanded the country toward the north and east. The estimated population of France at this time was 20 million, as opposed to eight million in England and six million in Spain. French colonies in Canada, the West Indies, and America (Louisiana) were stronger than ever. The mercantilism that Louis's brilliant finance minister, Colbert, implemented was one of the era's most important fiscal policies, hugely increasing France's power and wealth. The arts flourished, as did a sense of aristocratic style that's remembered with a bittersweet nostalgia today. Louis's palace of Versailles is the perfect monument to the most flamboyantly consumptive era in French history.

Louis's territorial ambitions so deeply threatened the other nations of Europe that, led by William of Orange, they united to hold him in check.

France entered a series of expensive and demoralizing wars that, coupled with high taxes and bad harvests, stirred up much civil discontent. England was viewed as a threat both within Europe and in the global rush for lucrative colonies. The great Atlantic ports, especially Bordeaux, grew and prospered because of France's success in the West Indian slave and sugar trades. Despite the country's power, the total number of French colonies diminished thanks to the naval power of the English. The rise of Prussia as a militaristic neighbor posed an additional problem.

THE REVOLUTION & THE RISE OF NAPOLEON Meanwhile, the Enlightenment was training a new generation of thinkers for the struggle against absolutism, religious fanaticism, and superstition. Europe was never the same after the Revolution of 1789, though the ideas that engendered it had been brewing for more than 50 years. On August 10, 1792, troops from Marseille, aided by a Parisian mob, threw the dim-witted Louis XVI and his tactless Austrian-born queen, Marie Antoinette, into prison. After months of bloodshed and bickering among violently competing factions, the two thoroughly humiliated monarchs were executed.

France's problems got worse before they got better. In the ensuing bloodbaths, both moderates and radicals were guillotined in full view of a bloodthirsty crowd that included voyeurs like Dickens's Mme Defarge, who brought her knitting every day to place de la Révolution (later renamed place de la Concorde) to watch the beheadings. The drama surrounding the collapse of the ancien régime and the beheadings of Robespierre's Reign of Terror provides the most heroic and horrible anecdotes in the history of France. From all this emerged the Declaration of the Rights of Man, an enlightened document published in 1789; its influence has been cited as a model of democratic ideals ever since. The implications of the collapse of the French aristocracy shook the foundations of every monarchy in Europe.

Only the militaristic fervor of Napoléon Bonaparte could reunite France and bring an end to the revolutionary chaos. A political and military genius who appeared on the landscape at a time when the French were thoroughly sickened by the anarchy following their Revolution, he restored a national pride that had been severely tarnished. He also established a bureaucracy and a code of law that has been emulated in other legal systems around the world. In 1799, at the age of 30, he entered Paris and was crowned First Consul and Master of France. Soon after, a decisive victory in his northern Italian campaign solidified his power at home. A brilliant politician, he made peace through a compromise with the Vatican, quelling the atheistic spirit of the earliest days of the Revolution.

Napoléon's victories made him the envy of Europe. Beethoven dedicated his Eroica symphony to Napoléon—but later retracted the dedication when Napoléon committed what Beethoven considered atrocities. Just as he was poised on the verge of conquering all Europe, Napoléon's famous retreat from Moscow during the winter of 1812 reduced his formerly invincible army to tatters, as 400,000 Frenchmen died in the Russian snows. Napoléon was then defeated at Waterloo by the combined armies of the English, Dutch, and Prussians. Exiled to the British-held island of St. Helena in the South Atlantic, he died in 1821, probably the victim of an unknown poisoner.

THE BOURBONS & THE SECOND EMPIRE In 1814, following the destruction of Napoléon and his dream, the Congress of Vienna redefined the map of Europe. The new geography was an approximation of the boundaries that had existed in 1792. The Bourbon monarchy was reestablished, with reduced powers for Louis XVIII, an archconservative, and a changing array of leaders who included the prince de Polignac and, later, Charles X. A renewal of the ancien régime's oppressions, however, didn't sit well in a France that had already spilled so much blood in favor of egalitarian causes.

In 1830, after censoring the press and dissolving Parliament, Louis XVIII was removed from power after yet more violent uprisings. Louis-Philippe, duc d'Orléans, was elected king under a liberalized constitution. His reign lasted for 18 years of calm prosperity during which England and France more or less collaborated on matters of foreign policy. The establishment of an independent Belgium and the French conquest of Algeria (1840–47) were to have resounding effects on French politics a century later. It was a time of wealth, grace, and expansion of the arts for most French people, though the industrialization of the north and east produced some of the 19th century's most horrific poverty.

A revolution in 1848, fueled by a financial crash and disgruntled workers in Paris, forced Louis-Philippe out of office. That year, Napoléon I's nephew, Napoléon III, was elected president. Appealing to the property-protecting instinct of a nation that hadn't forgotten the violent upheavals of less than a century before, he initiated a repressive right-wing government in which he was awarded the totalitarian status of emperor in 1851. Rebounding from the punishment they'd received during the Revolution and the minor role they'd played during the First Empire, the Second Empire's clergy enjoyed great power. Steel production was begun, and a railway system and Indochinese colonies were established. New technologies fostered new kinds of industry, and the bourgeoisie flourished. And the baron Georges-Eugène Haussmann radically altered Paris by laying out the grand boulevards the world knows today.

By 1866, an industrialized France began to see the Second Empire as more of a hindrance than an encouragement to its expansion. The dismal failure of colonizing Mexico and the increasing power of Austria and Prussia were setbacks to the empire's prestige. In 1870, the Prussians defeated Napoléon III at Sedan and held him prisoner with 100,000 of his soldiers. Paris was besieged by an enemy who only just failed to march its vastly superior armies through the capital.

After the Prussians withdrew, a violent revolt ushered in the Third Republic and its elected president, Marshal MacMahon, in 1873. Peace and prosperity slowly returned, France regained its glamour, a mania of building occurred, the Impressionists made their visual statements, and writers like Flaubert redefined the French novel into what today is regarded as the most evocative in the world. As if as a symbol of this period, the Eiffel Tower was built as part of the 1889 Universal Exposition.

By 1890, a new corps of satirists (including Zola) had exposed the country's wretched living conditions, the cruelty of the country's vested interests, and the underlying hypocrisy of late 19th–century French society. The 1894 Dreyfus Affair exposed the corruption of French army officers who had destroyed the career and reputation of a Jewish colleague (Albert Dreyfus), falsely and deliberately punished—as a scapegoat—for treason. The ethnic tensions identified by Zola led to further divisiveness in the rest of the 20th century.

THE WORLD WARS   International rivalries, thwarted colonial ambitions, and conflicting alliances led to World War I, which, after decisive German victories for 2 years, degenerated into the mud-slogged horror of trench warfare. Mourning between four and five million casualties, Europe was inflicted with psychological scars that never healed. In 1917, the United States broke the European deadlock by entering the war.

After the Allied victory, grave economic problems, plus the demoralization stemming from years of fighting, encouraged the growth of socialism and communism. The French government, led by a vindictive Georges Clemenceau, demanded every centime of reparations it could wring from a crushed Germany. The humiliation associated with this has often been cited as the origin of the German nation's almost obsessive determination to rise from the ashes of 1918 to a place in the sun.

The worldwide Great Depression had devastating repercussions in France. Poverty and widespread bankruptcies weakened the Third Republic to the point where successive coalition governments rose and fell with alarming regularity. The crises reached a crescendo on June 14, 1940, when Hitler's armies arrogantly marched down the Champs-Elysées, and newsreel cameras recorded French people openly weeping. Under the terms of the armistice, the north of France was occupied by the Nazis, and a puppet French government was established at Vichy under the authority of Marshal Pétain. The immediate collapse of the French army is viewed as one of the most significant humiliations in modern French history.

Pétain and his regime cooperated with the Nazis in unbearably shameful ways. Not the least of their errors included the deportation of more than 75,000 French Jews to German work camps. Pockets of resistance fighters (le maquis) waged small-scale guerrilla attacks against the Nazis throughout the course of the war and free-French forces continued to fight along with the Allies on battlegrounds like North Africa. Charles de Gaulle, the irascible giant whose personality is forever associated with the politics of his era, established himself as the head of the French government-in-exile, operating first from London and then from Algiers.

The scenario was radically altered on June 6, 1944, when the largest armada in history successfully established a bulkhead on the beaches of Normandy. Paris rose in rebellion even before the Allied armies arrived, and on August 26, 1944, Charles de Gaulle entered the capital as head of the government. The Fourth Republic was declared even as pockets of Nazi snipers continued to shoot from scattered rooftops throughout the city.

THE POSTWAR YEARS Plagued by the bitter residue of colonial policies that France had established during the 18th and 19th centuries, the Fourth Republic witnessed the rise and fall of 22 governments and 17 premiers. Many French soldiers died on foreign battlefields as once-profitable colonies in North Africa and Indochina rebelled. It took 80,000 French lives, for example, to put down a revolt in Madagascar. After suffering a bitter defeat in 1954, France ended the war in Indochina and freed its former colony. It also granted internal self-rule to Tunisia and (under slightly different circumstances) Morocco.

Algeria was to remain a greater problem. The advent of the 1958 Algerian revolution signaled the end of the much-maligned Fourth Republic. De Gaulle was called back from retirement to initiate a new constitution, the Fifth Republic, with a stronger set of executive controls. To nearly everyone's dissatisfaction, de Gaulle ended the Algerian war in 1962 by granting the country full independence. Screams of protest resounded long and loud, but the sun had set on most of France's far-flung empire. Internal disruption followed as vast numbers of *pieds-noirs* (French-born residents of Algeria recently stripped of their lands) flooded back into metropolitan France, often into makeshift refugee camps in Provence and Languedoc.

In 1968, major social unrest and a violent coalition hastily formed between the nation's students and blue-collar workers eventually led to the collapse of the government. De Gaulle resigned when his attempts to placate some of the marchers were defeated. The reins of power passed to his second-in-command, Georges Pompidou, and his successor, Valérie Giscard d'Estaing, both of whom continued de Gaulle's policies emphasizing economic development and protection of France as a cultural resource to the world.

THE 1980s & 1990s In 1981, François Mitterrand was elected the first Socialist president of France since World War II (with a close vote of 51%). In almost immediate response, many wealthy French decided to transfer their assets out of the country, much to the delight of banks in Geneva, Monaco, the Cayman Islands, and Vienna. Though reviled by the rich and ridiculed for personal mannerisms that often seemed inspired by Louis XIV, Mitterrand was reelected in 1988. During his two terms he spent billions of francs on his *grands projets* (like the Louvre pyramid, Opéra Bastille, Cité de la Musique, and Grande Arche de La Défense), some of which are now beginning to fall apart or reveal serious weaknesses.

In 1992, France played a leading role in the development of the European Union (EU), 15 countries that will ultimately abolish all trade barriers among themselves and share a single currency, the euro. More recent developments include France's interest in developing a central European bank for the regulation of a shared intra-European currency, a ruling that some politicians have interpreted as another block in the foundation of a united Europe.

In April 1993, voters dumped the Socialists and installed a new conservative government. Polls cited corruption scandals, rising unemployment, and urban insecurity as reasons for this. The Conservative premier Edouard Balladur had to "cohabit" the government with Mitterrand, whom he blamed for the country's growing economic problems. Diagnosed with terminal prostate cancer near the end of his second term, Mitterrand continued to represent France with dignity, despite his deterioration. The battle over who would succeed him was waged against Balladur with epic rancor by Jacques Chirac, tenacious survivor of many terms as mayor of Paris. Their public discord was among the most venomous since the days of Pétain.

On his third try, on May 7, 1995, Chirac won the presidency with 52% of the vote and immediately declared war on unemployment. Mitterrand turned over the reins of government on May 17 and died shortly thereafter. But Chirac's popularity soon faded in the wake of unrest caused by an 11.5% unemployment rate, a barrage of terrorist attacks by Algerian Muslims, and a stressed economy struggling to meet European Union entry requirements.

A wave of terrorist attacks from July to September 1995 brought an unfamiliar wariness to Paris. Six bombs were planted, killing seven people and injuring 115. In light of this, Parisians proved cautious if not fearful. Algerian Islamic militants, the suspected culprits, may have brought military guards to the Eiffel Tower, but they failed to throw France into panic.

Throughout 1995 and early 1996, France infuriated everyone from the members of Greenpeace to the governments of Australia and New Zealand by resuming its long-dormant policy of exploding nuclear bombs on isolated Pacific atolls for testing purposes. This policy continued until public outcry, both in France and outside its borders, exerted massive pressure to end the tests.

In May 1996, thousands of Parisian workers took to the streets, disrupting passenger train service to demand a work week shorter than the usual 39 hours. They felt that this move would help France's staggering unemployment figures. Employer organizations are resisting this idea, claiming that even if the work week were cut to 35 hours, businesses wouldn't be able to take on many new employees.

The drama of 1996 climaxed with the heat of the summer, when the police took axes to the doors of the Paris church of St-Bernard de la Chapelle. Nearly 300 African immigrants were removed by force from this place of refuge and deported. Strikes and protests continued to plague the country, and Chirac's political horizon became dimmer still—with a 12% unemployment rate and crime on an alarming increase. Terrorist scares continued to flood the borders of France throughout 1997, forcing a highly visible armed police force, as part of a nationwide program known as Vigipirate, to take to the streets of major cities. One of the unusual offshoots of the Vigipirate program involved the closing of the crypts of many of France's medieval churches to visitors, partly in fear of a terrorist bomb attack on national historic treasures.

In the latest power struggle between the Conservatives and the Socialists, in the spring of 1998, Conservatives were ousted in a majority of France's regional provinces, amounting to a powerful endorsement for Prime Minister Lionel Jospin's Socialist-led government.

In 1999, France joined with other European countries in adopting the euro as its standard of currency, although the French franc will still be in circulation during the lifetime of this edition. Only in 2002 will France abandon its familiar franc. The new currency will accelerate the creation of a single economy comprising nearly 300 million Europeans, with a combined gross national product approaching 9 trillion, larger than that of the United States.

France moved into the millennium by testing the practicality of new and progressive social legislation. On October 13, 1999, the French Parliament passed a new law giving legal status to unmarried couples, including homosexual unions. The law allow couples of same sex or not to enter into a union and be entitled to the same rights as married couples in such areas as housing, inheritance, income tax, and social welfare.

In 2000 France, it is estimated that some five-million couples live together without benefit of marriage. In 2000 the law faced extreme opposition including from conservative lawmakers who plan to appeal to the Constitutional Council to see if the law is indeed constitutional. The Catholic Church also denounced the new law, calling it "an assault on the family."

2 Art & Architecture from Pre-Roman to Postmodern

The art and architecture of France have contributed greatly to the nation's identity. In the last couple of years, vast sums of money have been earmarked for salvaging, cleaning, restoring, and documenting national treasures. Today many of the great buildings of France look as good as when they were first built.

The foundations of French art began with the Romans, who imported their monumental sense of symmetry and grandeur (and their engineering techniques) deep into the forests of northern France. But despite the strategic importance of Roman military bases like Lutetia (Paris), only the southernmost region was of any commercial or artistic merit. This region, through trade with the architecturally sophisticated Mediterranean, was quick to adopt the techniques common in the Roman world. Regarding architecture, it has been said that the Romans' triumphal arches, rhythmically massive aqueducts, and mausoleums fixed themselves in the French aesthetic for all time. Today some of the best-preserved ruins of the classical world are scattered though such Provençal towns as Nîmes, Orange, Saintes, and Arles.

ROMANESQUE   As Christianity made its way toward the Celtic tribes on the northern edges of Gaul, an abbreviated and naive kind of naturalism permeated the old Roman ideals, resulting in a crude, often-bulky aesthetic of geometric carvings and primitive masses. Some were influenced by Eastern motifs from Byzantium. Many purists consider Romanesque architecture a symbol of the growing power of the 11th- and 12th-century church, which in many areas was the only constant amid shifting feudal alliances. The earliest Romanesque buildings resembled thick-walled fortresses and often served as refuges during times of invasion. At first they were unembellished, relying on rounded arches and narrow windows for ornamentation.

Many critics think the echoing simplicity of the Cistercians—a reform-minded offshoot of the Benedictines—to be among the era's more spiritually alluring styles. The abbeys **Clairvaux** (in the Troyes area in the Champagne country) and **Fontenay** (in Burgundy) are the best remaining examples. By the 1100s, notably in Poitou, the facades and sections of the interiors of some Romanesque churches were almost completely covered with sculptures whose forms emphasized the architecture rather than served as separate works of art. Though many more visible Romanesque sculptures are unyielding and lifeless, the capitals topping massive columns are often charming, the most natural representations that can be found.

The first French Romanesque church was built around 1002 in Dijon (**St-Bénigne Monastery**). The flowering of the style appeared in the vast ecclesiastical complex of Cluny in Burgundy, which was begun in 1089 and then destroyed by zealous townspeople just after the Revolution.

The 10th and 11th centuries produced many churches, but also fortresses whose crenellations and thick walls often concealed dank, drafty, cramped quarters where cooped-up occupants barely managed to stay sane during times of war. Often, when a fortress was destroyed during a pillage, the survivors rebuilt it in a more fashionable form. In this way, some of the greatest châteaux of France were built, altered, upgraded, and transformed into elegant palaces preserved today as symbols of the Renaissance.

GOTHIC   About 400 years before the great châteaux of the Loire Valley reached their present form, the architects of the royal abbey of **St-Denis,** outside Paris, completed the first section of a radically new architectural style—Gothic. The cathedrals of **Noyon,** begun a year later in 1145, and **Laon,** launched in 1155, almost immediately exemplified the new principles, as did **Notre-Dame de Paris** when construction was undertaken in 1163. Gothic churches usually included a choir, a ring-around ambulatory, radiating chapels, pointed arches, clustered (rather than monolithic) columns, and ceilings held aloft by ribbed vaulting. Most important is the presence of wide, soaring windows occupying the space that in a Romanesque church would be devoted to thick stone walls. This new design usually required the addition of exterior flying buttresses to keep the weight of the heavy roof and ceiling from pushing the walls apart.

It was at **Chartres,** 60 miles southwest of Paris, that an adaptation of earlier Gothic principles developed for the first time into a Flamboyant High Gothic when a section of the existing cathedral was destroyed in a fire. The tendency toward increased elevation was more fully developed until the **cathedrals of Reims and Amiens** reached heights so dizzying that medieval worshipers couldn't help but be awed by the might and majesty of God.

The ecclesiastical sculpture that ornamented the portals and facades of the Gothic church progressed from a static kind of stern rigidity to a more fluid, more relaxed, often coquettish kind of naturalism. By the 14th century, ecclesiastical and especially secular carvings attained a kind of international refinement and courtliness that was copied in aristocratic circles throughout Europe.

THE RENAISSANCE It wasn't long, however, before the Renaissance helped the French realize that the glass-and-stone marvels erected to the glory of God were also fine examples of the skill and imagination of the humans who'd built them. When the 14th-century papal schism led to the recognition of Avignon, not Rome, as the legitimate seat of the papacy, a fortress that would also be a palace was required—hence the building of the **Palais des Papes.** No longer were aristocratic residences designed as gloomy, dank fortresses: Though defense was still a priority, the windows and doors were enlarged and interiors adorned with tapestries, paintings, elaborate religious artifacts (including triptychs), and music. Many of the new châteaux were inspired by Italian models—François I imported many designers, including Leonardo da Vinci, from Italy, whose influence changed French aesthetics forever; **Chambord,** the Renaissance king's hunting château, is a good example. Religious themes were abandoned as French painting modeled itself first after Flemish and then after northern Italian examples. To an increasing degree, artists began to distance themselves from church dictates.

BAROQUE The early 17th century witnessed the architectural burgeoning of Paris, whose skyline bristled with domes in the restrained baroque of the Italianate style. Louis XIV employed Le Vau, Perrault, both Mansarts, and Bruand for his buildings, with Le Nôtre in charge of the rigidly intelligent layouts of his gardens at Versailles. Meanwhile, court painters like **Boucher** depicted allegorical shepherdesses and cherubs at play, and **Georges de la Tour** used techniques of light and shadow (chiaroscuro) inspired by Caravaggio. The châteaux built during this era included the lavishly expensive **Vaux-le-Vicomte Clairvaux** (29 miles southeast of Paris), whose excesses led to the imprisonment of its owner, and the even more lavishly expensive royal residence of **Versailles,** whose excesses helped destroy the ancien régime.

NEOCLASSICISM Following the 1789 collapse of the monarchy, French architects returned to a dignified form of classicism that suited postrevolutionary ideals. Public parks in Metz, Bordeaux, Nancy, and Paris were laid out, sometimes requiring the demolition of acres of twisted medieval sections of cities. Styles inspired by the aesthetics of ancient Rome became the rage in painting, sculpture, and dress, though a brief fling with Egyptology followed the discovery of the Rosetta stone during Napoléon's campaign in Egypt. The revolutionary school of **David** came and went, and, within the new order, the artist **Ingres** strove for a kind of classical calm.

THE 19th CENTURY Around 1850, a new school of eclecticism combined elements from scattered eras of the past into new, sometimes inharmonious wholes. Between 1855 and 1869, Napoléon III and his chief architect, **Baron Haussmann,** demolished much of crumbling medieval Paris to lay out the wide avenues that today connect the various monuments in well-proportioned, broad vistas. New building techniques were developed, including the use of iron as the structural support of bridges, viaducts, and buildings such as the **National**

Library, completed in 1860. Naturally, this opened the way for Eiffel to design and erect the most frequently slurred building of its day, the **Eiffel Tower,** for the 1889 Universal Exposition in Paris.

Among sculptors, the only authentic giant to emerge from the 19th century was **Rodin.** His human figures were vital, passionate, and lifelike, and he became known for such works as *The Thinker* and *The Kiss.*

Delacroix became the greatest name in French Romantic painting, showing amazing skill as a colorist. When landscape painting rose in prominence in the mid-19th century, **Corot,** of the Barbizon school, was considered one of the best. To many critics the first modern painter in France was **Manet;** he painted portraits and scenes of everyday life but could also create a scandal (*Déjeuner sur l'herbe*) by depicting nudes among dressed figures. Manet isn't to be confused with **Monet,** a great innovator known for his series of paintings of water lilies and of Rouen cathedral. **Renoir** became celebrated for his sensuously rounded nudes in pearl white, and **Degas** turned to ballet dancers and scenes of racing and the theater for his inspiration.

Outside all movements, but equally important, was **Toulouse-Lautrec.** Satiric but amusing, his style was exemplified by the posters and sketches of the music-hall life he depicted.

THE 20th CENTURY   In the early 20th century the **Fauves** ("wild beasts") attracted the most attention, and the greatest of their lot was **Matisse,** who became known for his bright colors and flattened perspective.

Throughout the 20th century, exquisite **Beaux Arts** buildings continued to be erected throughout Paris, most at roughly the same height, giving it an evenly spaced skyline and rhythmically ornate facades that have caused it to be deemed the world's most beautiful city. The **Art Nouveau** movement added garlands of laurel and olive branches to the gray-white stone of elegant apartment buildings and hotels throughout France.

In the 1920s and 1930s, **Art Deco's** simplified elegance captivated sophisticated sensibilities. **Braque** defined cubism, and **Picasso** worked at his mission of turning the art world upside down. **Le Corbusier** developed his jutting, gently curved planes of concrete, opening the door for a new, but often less talented, school of modern French architects.

Critics haven't been kind to the rapidly rusting exposed structural elements of Paris's notorious **Centre Pompidou,** which is under renovation until 2000. In the 1980s, an obsolete rail station beside the Seine was transformed into the truly exciting **Musée d'Orsay,** and an expanse of dreary 19th-century slaughterhouses was transformed into a tourist site by the addition of a hypermodern science museum. In the 1990s, the **Opéra Bastille** brought new life to the decaying eastern edge of Le Marais but, predictably, sparked a controversy regarding its iconoclastic design. And the screams of outrage could be heard throughout France when **I. M. Pei's glass pyramid** was built as the postmodern centerpiece of one of the Louvre's most formal 17th-century courtyards.

Mitterrand inaugurated the **Grande Arche de La Défense** on France's bicentennial on July 14, 1989. This 35-story office complex shaped like a hollow cube is the endpoint of the *voie triomphale* (triumphal way) begun in 1664 at the Tuileries Gardens; its roof covers $2^{1}/_{2}$ acres (it's estimated that Notre-Dame could fit into its hollow core). One of the latest additions to the architectural scene (opened in 1995) is the **Cité de la Musique,** designed by the architect Christian de Portzamparc as a complex of interconnected post-cubist shapes.

Although the buildings of the Mitterrand presidency were "designed for eternity," critics are already finding flaws in the late president's "chance for immortality" $5.8-billion architectural spending spree. Many of the Mitterrand buildings are suffering defects and mishaps—stone slabs have fallen from the Opéra Bastille's facade, netting has had to be placed under the Grand Arche to prevent fragments of it from falling and hitting pedestrians below, and rain gushes into the orchestra pit at the Cité de la Musique.

The great French architect Paul Chametov has said, "At the end of a decade [the 1980s] that was tipsy from competitions, drunk from media hype, and driven mad by the expectations of a real-estate boom, we inherit an architecture that is only new on the day it is inaugurated."

President Jacques Chirac can hardly match the cultural monuments of his predecessor, falling slabs of marble or not. In 1996, he announced his building plans: the creation of a major new museum for African, Oceanic, and pre-Columbian art. Assigned to the Passy Wing of the Palais de Chaillot in Paris's Trocadéro section, it will open (we hope) in late 2001, just months before the end of Chirac's 7-year term.

3 A Taste of France

As any French person will tell you, French food is the best in the world. That's as true today as it was during the 19th-century heyday of the master chef Escoffier. A demanding patriarch who codified the rules of French cooking, he ruled the kitchens of the Ritz in Paris, standardizing the complicated preparation and presentation of haute cuisine. Thanks to Escoffier and his legendary flare-ups and his French-born colleagues, whose kitchen tantrums have been the bane of many a socialite's life, the French chef for years has been considered a temperamental egomaniac, bearing singlehandedly the burden of diffusing French civilization into the kitchens of the Anglo-Saxon world.

The demands of these chefs, however, aren't as far-fetched as they might seem, considering the intense scrutiny that has surrounded every aspect of France's culinary arts since the start of the Industrial Revolution.

Until the early 1800s, most French citizens didn't eat well. Many diets consisted of turnips, millet, fruits, berries, unpasteurized dairy products, and whatever fish or game could be had. Cooking techniques and equipment were unsanitary and crude, and starvation was a constant threat. Fear of famine was one of the rallying cries of the Revolution—everyone knows Marie Antoinette's "Let them eat cake" response to cries that the poor couldn't afford bread. (However, to be fair to Marie, this comment has been taken out of context. At the time, bread flour was much more expensive than cake flour, so her words weren't as callous as they might seem.)

At the foundation of virtually every culinary theory ever developed in France is a deep-seated respect for the *cuisine des provinces* (also known as *cuisine campagnarde*). Ingredients usually included only what was produced locally, and the rich and hearty result was gradually developed over several generations of *mères cuisinières*. Springing from an agrarian society with a vivid sense of nature's cycles, the cuisine provided appropriate nourishment for bodies that had toiled through a day in the open air. Specific dishes and cooking methods were as varied as the climates, terrains, and crops of France's many regions.

CUISINE BOURGEOISE & HAUTE CUISINE Cuisine bourgeoise and its pretentious cousin, haute cuisine, were refinements of country cooking that developed from the increased prosperity brought on by 19th-century industri-alization. As France grew more affluent, food and the rituals involved in its preparation and presentation became one of the hallmarks of culture. And as refrigerated trucks and railway cars carried meats, fish, and produce from one region to another, associations were formed and entire industries spawned, revolving around specific ingredients produced in specific districts. Like the country's wines (demarcated with "Appellation d'Origine Contrôlée"); lamb from the salt marshes of Pauillac; poultry from Bresse in Burgundy; and mel-ons, strawberries, apples, and truffles from specific districts command premi-ums over roughly equivalent ingredients produced in less legendary neighborhoods.

France often names a method of preparation (or a particular dish) after its region of origin. Dishes described as *à la normande* are likely to be prepared with milk, cream, or cheese or with Calvados, in honor of the dairy products and apple brandy produced in abundance within Norman borders. **Cassoulet** (a stewed combination of white beans, duck, pork, onions, and carrots) will forever be associated with Toulouse, where the dish originated. And something cooked *à la bordelaise* has probably been flavored with ample doses of red Bor-deaux (along with bone marrow, shallots, tarragon, and meat juices).

Other than caviar (which the French consume in abundance but don't pro-duce), the world's most elegant garnish is **truffles,** an underground fungus with a woodsy, oaky smell. Thousands of these are unearthed yearly from the Dor-dogne and Périgord forests, so if your menu proclaims a dish is *à la périgour-dine,* you'll almost certainly pay a premium for the truffles and foie gras.

And what's all the fuss about **foie gras?** It comes from either a goose or a duck (the rose-hued goose liver is the greater delicacy). The much-abused goose, however, has a rough life, being force-fed about a kilogram (2.2 pounds) of corn every day in a process the French call *gavage.* In about 22 days the ani-mal's liver is swollen to about 25 ounces (in many cases far more than that). When prepared by a Périgourdine housewife (some of whom sell the livers directly from their farmhouses to passing motorists), it's truly delicious. Foie gras is most often served with truffles; otherwise, it's called *au naturel.*

Bouillabaisse, a fish stew developed as a staple for fisherfolk along the Provence coast, has been elevated into one of the world's greatest dishes. Purists claim that key ingredients are *rascasse* (hogfish), a species found only in the Mediterranean; garlic-based aioli (a garlicky mayonnaise); and a medley of specific Provençal herbs—without these, the resulting stew simply isn't bouil-labaisse. A version of bouillabaisse prepared with a dollop of cream and lots of garlic may also be called **bourride Provençal.**

Diners will find that a rebirth of *cuisine du terroir* (country cuisine) has returned to France with a vengeance. Chefs (especially the younger ones) are making creative statements, many as cerebral as they are sensual. Never has there been such an emphasis on fresh and authentic ingredients derived local-ly or from specific regions and provinces. Some chefs (including one we know in Bordeaux) have been known to shut down their restaurants for the day if they cannot find exactly what they want in the marketplace that morning.

Impressions

The French will only be united under the threat of danger. Nobody can simply bring together a country that has 265 kinds of cheese.

—Charles de Gaulle

CUISINE MODERNE & CUISINE MINCEUR   The anti-Escoffier revolution has been raging for so long that many early rebels are returning to the old style, as exemplified by *boeuf à la bourguignonne, blanquette de veau,* and *pot-au-feu.* Yet the unfashionable expression nouvelle cuisine (even if it isn't all that "new") remains a viable part of the dining scene. Unlike another revolution, the battle between haute and nouvelle cuisine didn't begin in Paris. The romantic in us would like to think it started when Michel Guérard's beautiful wife, Christine, murmured in his ear, "Vous savez, Michel, mon cher—if you would lose some weight, you'd look vraiment fantastique."

For a man who loves food as much as Guérard, that was a formidable challenge. However, he set to work and ultimately invented *cuisine minceur,* a way to cook good French food without all the calories. You can sample it in Guérard's restaurant, Les Prés d'Eugénie, at Eugénie-les-Bains in the Landes, just east of the Basque country (see chapter 17). His *Cuisine Minceur* became a best-seller in North America (available now only in France), and the food critic Gael Greene hailed him as "the brilliant man who is France's most creative chef." Cuisine minceur is more of a diet cuisine than nouvelle or its later permutations. Yet the "new cuisine," like cuisine minceur, represents a major break with haute cuisine. Rich sauces are eliminated; cooking times that can destroy the best of fresh ingredients are considerably shortened. The aim is to release the natural flavor of food without covering it with layers of butter and cream. New flavor combinations in this widely expanding repertoire are often inspired.

Many chefs, including some of France's finest, dislike the word nouvelle when applied to cuisine. They call theirs *moderne,* which blends the finest dishes of the classic repertory with that of the nouvelle. Though widely defined, *cuisine moderne* basically means paying homage to the integrity of ingredients, certainly fresh ones, and working to bring out natural flavors and aromas.

4 By the Glass or Bottle: A Quick Lesson in French Wines

French cuisine achieves perfection when accompanied by wine, which is considered an integral part of every meal. Certain rules about wine drinking have been long established, but no one except traditionalists seems to follow them anymore. For example, if you're having a roast, a steak, or game, a good burgundy might be your choice. If it's chicken, lamb, or veal, perhaps you might choose a red from Bordeaux; a full-bodied red is perfect with a cheese like Camembert, as is a blanc de blanc with oysters. A light rosé (beaujolais) can go with almost anything.

Let your own good taste and your budget determine your wine choice. Most wine stewards, called *sommeliers,* are there to help you, and only in the most dishonest of restaurants will they push you toward the most expensive selections. Of course, if you prefer only bottled water or beer, then be firm and order them without embarrassment. Some restaurants include a beverage in their menu rates (*boisson compris*), but that's only in cheaper places. Some of the most satisfying wines we've drunk in France came from unlabeled house bottles or carafes, called *vin de la maison.* Unless you're a connoisseur, for the most part you needn't worry about labels and vintages.

You can rarely go wrong with a good burgundy or Bordeaux, but you may want to be more experimental. That's when the sommelier (who's likely to be a woman) can help, particularly if you tell him or her your taste in wine (semi-dry or very dry, for example). State frankly how much you're willing to pay and what you plan to order for your meal. If you're dining with others, you may want to order two or three bottles, selecting a wine to suit each course. However, even the French at most informal meals (especially if there are only two people dining) select only one wine to go with everything from hors d'oeuvres to cheese.

WINE LABELS   Since the late 19th century, French wine (at least French wine served in France) has been labeled. The general label is known as "Appellation d'Origine Contrôlée" (often abbreviated AC). The controls, for the most part, are designated by region. These simple, honest wines can be blended from grapes grown at any place in the region; some are composed of the vintages of different years.

The more specific the label, the better the wine is (in most cases). For example, instead of a Bordeaux, the wine might be labeled a Médoc, which is an intensely prestigious triangle of land extending some 50 miles north from Bordeaux. Wine labels can be narrowed down to a particular vine-growing property, such as a Château Haut-Brion, one of the greatest red wines of Bordeaux (this château produces only about 10,000 cases per year).

On some burgundies, you're likely to see the word *clos* (pronounced *clo*). Originally that meant a walled or otherwise enclosed vineyard, as in Clos de Beze, a celebrated Burgundian vineyard producing a superb red wine. *Cru* (pronounced *crew* and meaning "growth") suggests a wine of superior quality when it appears on a label as a vin de cru. Wines and vineyards are often divided into crus. A Grand Cru or Premier Cru should, by implication, be an even more superior wine.

Labels are only part of the story. It's the vintage that counts. Essentially, a vintage refers to a specific year's grape harvest and the wine made from those grapes. Therefore, any wine can be a vintage wine unless it was blended. Like people, there are good vintages and bad. The variation between wine produced in a "good year" and wine produced in a "bad year" can be major, even to the uninitiated palate.

Finally, **champagne** is the only wine that can be correctly served through all courses of a meal—but only to those who can afford its astronomical prices. (Did you know that only champagne made in France's Champagne region can by law be called champagne? True. A champagnelike wine made elsewhere in France cannot be called champagne and must be referred to as having been produced *à la méthode champenoise.* In America, each state has its own laws about this, so bubbly made in one state can be called champagne while bubbly made in another state cannot.) For more on bubbly, see the box "Champagne: The Fizz & the Fun" in chapter 9.

Appendix B:
Glossary of Useful Terms

A well-known character is the American or lapsed Canadian who returns from a trip to France and denounces the ever-so-rude French. But it is often amazing how a word or two of halting French will change their dispositions. At the very least, try to learn a few numbers, basic greetings, and—above all—the life raft, *Parlez-vous anglais?* (Do you speak English?). As it turns out, many people do speak a passable English and will use it liberally, if you demonstrate the basic courtesy of greeting them in their language. Go out, try our glossary, and don't be bashful. *Bonne chance!*

BASICS

English	French	Pronunciation
Yes/No	**Oui/Non**	wee/nohn
OK	**D'accord**	dah-*core*
Please	**S'il vous plaît**	seel voo *play*
Thank you	**Merci**	mair-*see*
You're welcome	**De rien**	duh ree-*ehn*
Hello (during daylight hours)	**Bonjour**	bohn-*jhoor*
Good evening	**Bonsoir**	bohn-*swahr*
Good-bye	**Au revoir**	o ruh-*vwahr*
What's your name?	**Comment vous appellez-vous?**	ko-mahn-voo-za-pell-ay-*voo?*
My name is	**Je m'appelle**	jhuh ma-*pell*
Happy to meet you	**Enchanté(e)**	ohn-shahn-*tay*
How are you?	**Comment allez-vous?**	kuh-mahn-tahl-ay-*voo?*
Fine, thank you, and you?	**Trés bien, merci, et vous?**	tray bee-ehn, mare-ci, ay *voo?*
So-so	**Comme ci, comme ça**	kum-*see,* kum-*sah*
I'm sorry/excuse me	**Pardon**	pahr-*dohn*
I'm so very sorry	**Désolé(e)**	day-zoh-*lay*
That's all right	**Il n'y a pas de quoi**	eel nee ah pah duh *kwah*

GETTING AROUND/STREET SMARTS

English	French	Pronunciation
Do you speak English?	**Parlez-vous anglais?**	par-lay-voo-ahn-*glay?*
I don't speak French	**Je ne parle pas français**	jhuh ne parl pah frahn-*say*

English	French	Pronunciation
I don't understand	**Je ne comprends pas**	jhuh ne kohm-*prahn* pas
Could you speak more loudly/ more slowly?	**Pouvez-vous parler plus fort/plus lentement?**	Poo-*vay*-voo par-lay ploo for/ploo lan-te-*ment*?
Could you repeat that?	**Répetez, s'il vous plaît**	ray-pay-*tay*, seel voo *play*
What is it?	**Qu'est-ce que c'est?**	kess-kuh-*say*?
What time is it?	**Qu'elle heure est-il?**	kel uhr eh-*teel*?
What?	**Quoi?**	kwah?
How? or What did you say?	**Comment?**	ko-*mahn*?
When?	**Quand?**	kahn?
Where is?	**Où est?**	ooh-eh?
Who?	**Qui?**	kee?
Why?	**Pourquoi?**	poor-*kwah*?
here/there	**ici/là**	ee-*see*/lah
left/right	**à gauche/à droite**	a goash/a drwaht
straight ahead	**tout droit**	too-drwah
I'm American/ Canadian/ British	**Je suis américain(e)/ canadien(e)/ anglais(e)**	jhe sweez a-may-ree-*kehn*/ can-ah-dee-*en*/ ahn-*glay* (*glaise*)
Fill the tank (of a car), please	**Le plein, s'il vous plaît**	luh plan, seel-voo-*play*
I'm going to	**Je vais à**	jhe vay ah
I want to get off at	**Je voudrais descendre à**	jhe voo-*dray* day-son drah-ah
airport	**l'aéroport**	lair-o-*por*
bank	**la banque**	lah bahnk
bridge	**pont**	pohn
bus station	**la gare routière**	lah gar roo-tee-*air*
bus stop	**l'arrêt de bus**	lah-*ray* duh boohss
by means of a bicycle	**en vélo/par bicyclette**	uh *vay*-low, par bee-see-*clet*
by means of a car	**en voiture**	ahn vwa-*toor*
cashier	**la caisse**	lah *kess*
cathedral	**cathédral**	ka-tay-*dral*
church	**église**	ay-*gleez*
dead end	**une impasse**	ewn am-*pass*
driver's license	**permis de conduire**	per-*mee* duh con-*dweer*
elevator	**l'ascenseur**	lah sahn *seuhr*
entrance (to a building or a city)	**une porte**	ewn port
exit (from a building or a freeway)	**une sortie**	ewn sor-*tee*
gasoline	**du pétrol/de l'essence**	duh pay-*troll*/de lay-*sahns*
ground floor	**rez-de-chausée**	ray-de-show-*say*
highway to	**la route pour**	la root por
hospital	**l'hôpital**	low-pee-*tahl*
insurance	**les assurances**	lez ah-sur-*ahns*
luggage storage	**consigne**	kohn-*seen*-yuh
museum	**le musée**	luh mew-*zay*
no entry	**sens interdit**	sehns ahn-ter-*dee*

English	French	Pronunciation
no smoking	défense de fumer	day-*fahns* de fu-may
on foot	à pied	ah pee-*ay*
one-day pass	ticket journalier	tee-kay jhoor-nall-ee-*ay*
one-way ticket	aller simple	ah-*lay sam*-pluh
police	la police	lah po-*lees*
rented car	voiture de location	vwa-*toor* de low-ka-see *on*
round-trip ticket	aller-retour	ah-*lay* re-*toor*
second floor	premier étage	prem-ee-*ehr* ay-*taj*
slow down	ralentir	rah-lahn-*teer*
store	le magazin	luh ma-ga-*zehn*
street	rue	roo
suburb	banlieu, environs	bahn-*lieu,* en-veer-*ohn*
subway	le métro	le may-tro
telephone	le téléphone	luh tay-lay-*phone*
ticket	un billet	uh *bee*-yay
ticket office	vente de billets	vahnt duh bee-*yay*
toilets	les toilettes/les WC	lay twa-*lets*/les vay-*say*
tower	tour	toor

NECESSITIES

English	French	Pronunciation
I'd like	Je voudrais	jhe voo-*dray*
a room	une chambre	ewn *shahm*-bruh
the key	la clé (la clef)	la clay
How much does it cost?	C'est combien?/ ça coûte combien?	say comb-bee-*ehn?*/ sah coot comb-bee-*ehn?*
That's expensive	C'est cher/chère	say share
Do you take credit cards?	Est-ce que vous acceptez les cartes de credit?	es-kuh voo zaksep-*tay* lay kart duh creh-*dee?*
I'd like to buy	Je voudrais acheter	jhe voo-dray ahsh-*tay*
aspirin	des aspirines/ des aspros	deyz ahs-peer-*een*/deyz ahs-*proh*
cigarettes	des cigarettes	day see-ga-*ret*
condoms	des préservatifs	day pray-ser-va-*teef*
dictionary	un dictionnaire	uh deek-see-oh-*nare*
dress	une robe	ewn robe
envelopes	des envelopes	days ahn-veh-*lope*
gift	un cadeau	uh kah-*doe*
handbag	un sac	uh sahk
hat	un chapeau	uh shah-*poh*
magazine	une revue	ewn reh-*vu*
map of the city	un plan de ville	unh plahn de *veel*
matches	des allumettes	dayz a-loo-*met*
necktie	une cravate	uh cra-*vaht*
newspaper	un journal	uh zhoor-*nahl*
phonecard	une carte téléphonique	uh cart tay-lay-fone-*eek*
postcard	une carte postale	ewn carte pos-*tahl*
road map	une carte routière	ewn cart roo-tee-*air*
shirt	une chemise	ewn che-*meez*
shoes	des chaussures	day show-*suhr*
skirt	une jupe	ewn jhoop

English	French	Pronunciation
soap	**du savon**	dew sah-*vohn*
socks	**des chaussettes**	day show-*set*
stamp	**un timbre**	uh *tam*-bruh
trousers	**un pantalon**	uh pan-tah-*lohn*
writing paper	**du papier à lettres**	dew pap-pee-*ay* a *let*-ruh

IN YOUR HOTEL

English	French	Pronunciation
Are taxes included?	**Est-ce que les taxes sont comprises?**	ess-keh lay taks son com-*preez*?
balcony	**un balcon**	uh bahl-cohn
bathtub	**une baignoire**	ewn bayn-*nwar*
for two occupants	**pour deux personnes**	poor duh pair-*sunn*
hot and cold water	**l'eau chaude et froide**	low showed ay fwad
Is breakfast included?	**Petit déjeuner inclus?**	peh-*tee* day-jheun-*ay* ehn-*klu*?
room	**une chambre**	ewn *shawm*-bruh
shower	**une douche**	ewn dooch
sink	**un lavabo**	uh la-va-*bow*
suite	**une suite**	ewn sweet
We're staying for . . . days	**On reste pour . . . jours**	ohn rest poor . . . jhoor
with air-conditioning	**avec climatization**	ah-*vek* clee-mah-tee-zah-ion
without	**sans**	sahn
youth hostel	**une auberge de jeunesse**	oon oh-bayrge-duh-jhe-*ness*

IN THE RESTAURANT

English	French	Pronunciation
I would like	**Je voudrais**	jhe voo-*dray*
to eat	**manger**	mahn-*jhay*
to order	**commander**	ko-mahn-*day*
Please give me	**Donnez-moi, s'il vous plaît**	doe-nay-*mwah*, seel voo play
an ashtray	**un cendrier**	uh sahn-dree-*ay*
a bottle of	**une bouteille de**	ewn boo-*tay* duh
a cup of	**une tasse de**	ewn tass duh
a glass of	**un verre de**	uh vair duh
a plate of breakfast	**une assiette de le petit-déjeuner**	ewn ass-ee-*et* duh luh puh-*tee* day-zhuh-*nay*
cocktail	**un apéritif**	uh ah-pay-ree-*teef*
check/bill	**l'addition/la note**	la-dee-see-*ohn*/la noat
dinner	**le dîner**	luh dee-*nay*
knife	**un couteau**	uh koo-*toe*
napkin	**une serviette**	ewn sair-vee-*et*
platter of the day	**un plat du jour**	uh plah dew jhoor
spoon	**une cuillère**	ewn kwee-*air*
Cheers!	**A votre santé!**	ah vo-truh sahn-*tay*!
Can I buy you a drink?	**Puis-je vous acheter un verre?**	*pwee*-jhe voo *zahsh*-tay uh *vaihr*?
fixed-price menu	**un menu**	uh may-*new*
fork	**une fourchette**	ewn four-*shet*

English	French	Pronunciation
Is the tip/ service included?	**Est-ce que le service est compris?**	ess-ke luh ser-*vees* eh com-*pree*?
Waiter!/Waitress!	**Monsieur!/ Mademoiselle!**	mun-*syuh*/mad-mwa-*zel*
wine list	**une carte des vins**	ewn cart day *van*
appetizer	**une entrée**	ewn en-*tray*
main course	**un plat principal**	uh plah pran-see-*pahl*
tip included	**service compris**	sehr-*vees* cohm-*pree*
wide-ranging sampling of the chef's best efforts	**menu dégustation**	may-*new* day-gus-ta-see-*on*
drinks not included	**boissons non comprises**	bwa-*sons* no com-*pree*

NUMBERS & ORDINALS

English	French	Pronunciation
zero	**zéro**	*zare*-oh
one	**un**	oon
two	**deux**	duh
three	**trois**	twah
four	**quatre**	*kaht*-ruh
five	**cinq**	sank
six	**six**	seess
seven	**sept**	set
eight	**huit**	wheat
nine	**neuf**	noof
ten	**dix**	deess
eleven	**onze**	ohnz
twelve	**douze**	dooz
thirteen	**treize**	trehz
fourteen	**quatorze**	kah-*torz*
fifteen	**quinze**	kanz
sixteen	**seize**	sez
seventeen	**dix-sept**	deez-*set*
eighteen	**dix-huit**	deez-*wheat*
nineteen	**dix-neuf**	deez-*noof*
twenty	**vingt**	vehn
twenty-one	**vingt-et-un**	vehnt-ay-*oon*
twenty-two	**vingt-deux**	vehnt-*duh*
thirty	**trente**	trahnt
forty	**quarante**	ka-*rahnt*
fifty	**cinquante**	sang-*kahnt*
sixty	**soixante**	swa-*sahnt*
sixty-one	**soixante-et-un**	swa-*sahnt*-et-*uh*
seventy	**soixante-dix**	swa-sahnt-*deess*
seventy-one	**soixante-et-onze**	swa-sahnt-et-*ohnze*
eighty	**quatre-vingts**	kaht-ruh-*vehn*
eighty-one	**quatre-vingt-un**	kaht-ruh-vehn-*oon*
ninety	**quatre-vingt-dix**	kaht-ruh-venh-*deess*
ninety-one	**quatre-vingt-onze**	kaht-ruh-venh-*ohnze*
one hundred	**cent**	sahn
one thousand	**mille**	meel

Glossary of Useful Terms

English	French	Pronunciation
one hundred thousand	**cent mille**	sahn meel
first	**premier**	*preh*-mee-ay
second	**deuxième**	*duhz*-zee-em
third	**troisième**	*twa*-zee-em
fourth	**quatrième**	*kaht*-ree-em
fifth	**cinquième**	*sank*-ee-em
sixth	**sixième**	*sees*-ee-em
seventh	**septième**	*set*-ee-em
eighth	**huitième**	*wheat*-ee-em
ninth	**neuvième**	*neuv*-ee-em
tenth	**dixième**	*dees*-ee-em

THE CALENDAR

English	French	Pronunciation
Sunday	**dimanche**	dee-*mahnsh*
Monday	**lundi**	luhn-*dee*
Tuesday	**mardi**	mahr-*dee*
Wednesday	**mercredi**	mair-kruh-*dee*
Thursday	**jeudi**	jheu-*dee*
Friday	**vendredi**	vawn-druh-*dee*
Saturday	**samedi**	sahm-*dee*
yesterday	**hier**	ee-*air*
today	**aujourd'hui**	o-jhord-*dwee*
this morning/ this afternoon	**ce matin/cet après-midi**	suh ma-*tan*/ set ah-preh mee-*dee*
tonight	**ce soir**	suh *swahr*
tomorrow	**demain**	de-*man*

Appendix C: Glossary of Basic Menu Terms

You're hungry, you don't want brains, but you don't understand a thing on the menu. What to do? Use the following list of menu terms (organized by food type) to help determine what exactly you're ordering.

Note: To order any of these items from a waiter, simply preface the French-language name with the phrase, "Je voudrais" (jhe voo-*dray*), which means, "I would like . . ." *Bon appétit!*

MEATS

French	English	Pronunciation
De l'agneau	Lamb	Duh l'ahn-*nyo*
Des ailes de poulet	Chicken wings	Dayz ehl duh poo-lay
De l'aloyau	Sirloin	Duh l'ahl-why-*yo*
Du bifteck	Steak	Dew beef-*tek*
De la blanquette	Stewed meat with white sauce, enriched with cream and eggs	Duh lah blon-*kette*
Du boeuf à la mode	Marinated beef braised with red wine and served with vegetables	Dew bewf ah lah *mhowd*
De la cervelle	Brains	Duh lah ser-*vel*
Du Chateaubriand	Double tenderloin, a long muscle from which filet steaks are cut	Dew sha-tow-bree-*ahn*
Du coq au vin	Chicken, stewed with mushrooms and wine	Dew cock o vhaihn
Des cuisses de grenouilles	Frogs' legs	*Day cweess duh gre-noo-yuh*
Du gigot	Haunch or leg of an animal, especially that of a lamb or sheep	*Dew jhi-goh*
Du jambon	Ham	*Dew jham-bohn*
Du lapin	Rabbit	*Dew lah-pan*
Du pot au feu	Beef stew	*Dew poht o fhe*
Du poulet	Chicken	*Dew poo-lay*

French	English	Pronunciation
Des quenelles	Rolls of pounded and baked chicken, veal, or fish, often pike, usually served warm	*Day ke-*nelle
Des ris de veau	Sweetbreads	*Day ree duh* voh
Des rognons	Kidneys	*Day row-*nyon
Un steak au poivre	Filet steak, embedded with fresh green or black peppercorns, flambéed and served with a cognac sauce	*Uh stake o pwah-*vruh
Du veau	Veal	*Dew voh*

FISH & SEAFOOD

French	English	Pronunciation
De l'anguille	Eel	Duh l'ahn-*ghwee-*uh
De la bouillabaisse	Mediterranean fish soup or stew made with tomatoes, garlic, saffron, and olive oil	Duh lah booh-ya-*besse*
Du brochet	Pike	Dew broh-*chay*
Des crevettes	Shrimp	Day kreh-*vette*
Du hareng	Herring	*Dew ahr-*rahn
Du homard	Lobster	*Dew oh-*mahr
Des huîtres	Oysters	*Dayz hoo-ee-truhs*
Du loup de mer	Wolf fish, a Mediterranean sea bass	*Dew loo-duh-*mehr
Des moules	Mussels	*Day moohl*
Des moules marinières	Mussels in herb-flavored white wine with shallots	*Day moohl mar-ee-nee-*air
Du poisson de rivière, or **poisson d'eau douce/du poisson de mer**	Fish (freshwater) and fish (saltwater)	*Dew pwah-sson duh ree-vee-*aire, *dew pwah-sson d'o* dooss/ *dew pwah-sson duh* mehr
Du saumon fumé	Smoked salmon	*Dew sow-mohn fu-*may
Du thon	Tuna	*Dew tohn*
De la truite	Trout	*Duh lah tru-*eet

SIDES/APPETIZERS

French	English	Pronunciation
Du beurre	Butter	Dew bhuhr
De la choucroute	Sauerkraut	Duh lah chew-*kroot*
Des escargots	Snails	Dayz ess-car-*goh*
Du foie	Liver	Dew fwoh
Du foie gras	Goose liver	Dew fwoh grah
Du pain	Bread	Dew pan
Des rillettes	Potted and minced pork and pork by-products, prepared as a roughly chopped pâté	*Day ree-*yett
Du riz	Rice	*Dew* ree

FRUITS/VEGETABLES

French	English	Pronunciation
De l'ananas	Pineapple	Duh l'ah-na-*nas*
De l'aubergine	Eggplant	Duh l'oh-ber-*jheen*
Du choux	Cabbage	Dew *shoe*
Du citron/ du citron vert	Lemon/lime	Dew cee-*tron*/ dew cee-*tron* vaire
Des épinards	Spinach	Dayz ay-pin-*ar*
Des fraises	Strawberries	Day frez
Des haricots verts	Green beans	*Day ahr-ee-coh* vaire
Une orange	Orange	*Ewn or-an*-jhe
Un pamplemousse	Grapefruit	*Uh pahm-pluh*-moose
Des petits pois	Green peas	*Day puh-tee* pwah
Des pommes frites	French fried potatoes	*Day puhm* freet
Des pommes de terre	Potatoes	*Day puhm duh* tehr
Du raisin	Grapes	*Dew ray*-zhan

BEVERAGES

French	English	Pronunciation
De la bière	Beer	Duh lah bee-*aire*
Boissons non compris	Drinks not included	*Bwa-son nohn com*-pree
Un café	Coffee	Uh ka-*fay*
Un café au lait	Coffee (with milk)	Uh ka-fay o *lay*
Un café crème	Coffee (with cream)	Uh ka-fay krem
Un café decaffeiné (un déca; slang)	Coffee (decaf)	Un ka-fay day-kah-fay-*e-nay* (uh day-kah)
Un café noir	Coffee (black)	Uh ka-fay nwahr
Un espresso (un express)	Coffee (espresso)	Un ka-fay ek-*sprehss-o* (uh ek-*sprehss*)
Du jus d'orange	Orange juice	*Dew joo d'or-an*-jhe
De l'eau	Water	Duh lo
Du lait	Milk	*Dew* lay
Du thé	Tea	*Dew* tay
Une tisane	Herbal tea	*Ewn tee*-zahn
Du vin blanc	White wine	*Dew vhin* blahn
Du vin rouge	Red wine	*Dew vhin* rooj

DESSERTS

French	English	Pronunciation
De la crème brûlée	Thick custard dessert with a caramelized topping	Duh lah krem bruh-*lay*
Du fromage	Cheese	*Dew fro*-mahjz
Du gâteau	Cake	*Dew gha*-tow
De la glace à la vanille	Vanilla ice cream	*Duh lah glass a lah vah*-ne-yuh
Une tarte	Tart	*Ewn tart*
Une tarte tatin	Caramelized upside-down apple pie	*Ewn tart tah*-tihn

SPICES/CONDIMENTS

French	English	Pronunciation
De la crème fraîche	Sour heavy cream	Duh lah krem *fresh*
De la moutarde	Mustard	*Duh lah moo*-tard-*uh*
Du poivre	Pepper	*Dew pwah*-vruh
Du sel	Salt	*Dew* sel
Du sucre	Sugar	*Dew suh*-kruh

COOKING METHODS

French	English	Pronunciation
À la Bourguignon	In the style of Burgundy, usually with red wine, mushrooms, bacon, and onions	Ah lah Boor-geehn-*nyon*
Un confit	Method of cooking whereby anything (including fish, meat, fruits, or vegetables) is simmered in a reduction of its own fat or juices	Uh khon-feeh
Cuit au feu de bois	Cooked over a wood fire	Kwee o fhe duh *bwoi*
à la Lyonnais	A method of food preparation native to Lyon and its region, that usually includes wine sauce accented with shredded and sautéed onions	*Ah lah lee-ohn*-nehz
En papillotte	Cooked in parchment paper	*Ehn pah-pee*-yott
Une terrine	Minced and potted meat, seasoned and molded into a crock	*Ewn tair*-ee
Vol-au-vent	Puff pastry shell	*Vhol-o*-vhen

Index

FROMMER'S® COMPLETE TRAVEL GUIDES

Alaska
Amsterdam
Arizona
Atlanta
Australia
Austria
Bahamas
Barcelona, Madrid &
  Seville
Beijing
Belgium, Holland &
  Luxembourg
Bermuda
Boston
British Columbia & the
  Canadian Rockies
Budapest & the Best of
  Hungary
California
Canada
Cancún, Cozumel &
  the Yucatán
Cape Cod, Nantucket &
  Martha's Vineyard
Caribbean
Caribbean Cruises & Ports
  of Call
Caribbean Ports of Call
Carolinas & Georgia
Chicago
China
Colorado
Costa Rica
Denmark
Denver, Boulder & Colorado
  Springs
England
Europe

European Cruises & Ports
  of Call
Florida
France
Germany
Greece
Greek Islands
Hawaii
Hong Kong
Honolulu, Waikiki &
  Oahu
Ireland
Israel
Italy
Jamaica
Japan
Las Vegas
London
Los Angeles
Maryland & Delaware
Maui
Mexico
Miami & the Keys
Montana & Wyoming
Montréal & Québec City
Munich & the Bavarian
  Alps
Nashville & Memphis
Nepal
New England
New Mexico
New Orleans
New York City
New Zealand
Nova Scotia, New Brunswick
  & Prince Edward Island
Oregon
Paris

Philadelphia & the
  Amish Country
Portugal
Prague & the Best of the
  Czech Republic
Provence & the Riviera
Puerto Rico
Rome
San Antonio & Austin
San Diego
San Francisco
Santa Fe, Taos & Albuquerque
Scandinavia
Scotland
Seattle & Portland
Singapore & Malaysia
South Africa
Southeast Asia
South Pacific
Spain
Sweden
Switzerland
Thailand
Tokyo
Toronto
Tuscany & Umbria
USA
Utah
Vancouver & Victoria
Vermont, New Hampshire
  & Maine
Vienna & the Danube Valley
Virgin Islands
Virginia
Walt Disney World &
  Orlando
Washington, D.C.
Washington State

FROMMER'S® DOLLAR-A-DAY GUIDES

Australia from $50 a Day
California from $60 a Day
Caribbean from $70 a Day
England from $70 a Day
Europe from $60 a Day

Florida from $60 a Day
Hawaii from $70 a Day
Ireland from $60 a Day
Italy from $70 a Day
London from $85 a Day

New York from $80 a Day
Paris from $85 a Day
San Francisco from $60 a Day
Washington, D.C.,
  from $60 a Day

FROMMER'S® PORTABLE GUIDES

Acapulco, Ixtapa &
  Zihuatanejo
Alaska Cruises & Ports of Call
Bahamas
Baja & Los Cabos
Berlin
California Wine Country
Charleston & Savannah
Chicago

Dublin
Hawaii: The Big Island
Las Vegas
London
Maine Coast
Maui
New Orleans
New York City
Paris

Puerto Vallarta, Manzanillo
  & Guadalajara
San Diego
San Francisco
Sydney
Tampa & St. Petersburg
Venice
Washington, D.C.

FROMMER'S® NATIONAL PARK GUIDES

Family Vacations in the
  National Parks
Grand Canyon

National Parks of the
  American West
Rocky Mountain

Yellowstone & Grand Teton
Yosemite & Sequoia/
  Kings Canyon
Zion & Bryce Canyon

FROMMER'S® MEMORABLE WALKS

Chicago
London

New York
Paris

San Francisco
Washington, D.C.

FROMMER'S® GREAT OUTDOOR GUIDES

New England
Northern California

Southern California & Baja
Southern New England

Washington & Oregon

FROMMER'S® BORN TO SHOP GUIDES

Born to Shop: China
Born to Shop: France

Born to Shop: Italy
Born to Shop: London

Born to Shop: New York
Born to Shop: Paris

FROMMER'S® IRREVERENT GUIDES

Amsterdam
Boston
Chicago
Las Vegas

London
Los Angeles
Manhattan
New Orleans

Paris
San Francisco
Seattle & Portland
Vancouver

Walt Disney World
Washington, D.C.

FROMMER'S® BEST-LOVED DRIVING TOURS

America
Britain
California

Florida
France
Germany

Ireland
Italy
New England

Scotland
Spain
Western Europe

THE UNOFFICIAL GUIDES®

Bed & Breakfasts in
  California
Bed & Breakfasts in
  New England
Bed & Breakfasts in
  the Northwest
Beyond Disney
Branson, Missouri
California with Kids
Chicago

Cruises
Disneyland
Florida with Kids
Golf Vacations in the
  Eastern U.S.
The Great Smoky &
  Blue Ridge
  Mountains
Inside Disney

Hawaii
Las Vegas
London
Miami & the Keys
Mini Las Vegas
Mini-Mickey
New Orleans
New York City
Paris

Safaris
San Francisco
Skiing in the West
Walt Disney World
Walt Disney World
  for Grown-ups
Walt Disney World
  for Kids
Washington, D.C.

SPECIAL-INTEREST TITLES

Frommer's Britain's Best Bed & Breakfasts and
  Country Inns
Frommer's Britain's Best Bike Rides
The Civil War Trust's Official Guide
  to the Civil War Discovery Trail
Frommer's Caribbean Hideaways
Frommer's Food Lover's Companion to France
Frommer's Food Lover's Companion to Italy
Frommer's Gay & Lesbian Europe
Frommer's Exploring America by RV
Hanging Out in Europe
Israel Past & Present

Mad Monks' Guide to California
Mad Monks' Guide to New York City
Frommer's The Moon
Frommer's New York City with Kids
The New York Times' Unforgettable
  Weekends
Places Rated Almanac
Retirement Places Rated
Frommer's Road Atlas Britain
Frommer's Road Atlas Europe
Frommer's Washington, D.C., with Kids
Frommer's What the Airlines Never Tell You